5/17/19

Chicago:

A Civic, Industrial, and Familial History

To Tom,

with Very Best Wishes,

Andrew Taylor Call

Old Chicago Crossing Press

Copyright, Notices, ISBN Numbers, and Other Information

Published by Old Chicago Crossing Press. Chicago, Illinois.
Author website: https://www.chicagoillinoisrediscovered.com/
The author's book website was designed by Anne Piedmont and Piedmont Research Associates of Roanoke, Virginia.
ISBN-13: 978-1541115743
ISBN-10: 1541115740

NOTICE: I have procured the rights for the publication, use, and reproduction of all images in this book. Images that belong to my own personal collection are cited accordingly. Image ID numbers for the Chicago History Museum images appear within their respective image captions in the respective chapters, except in the case of the front cover image, whose Image ID number is provided below on the present page.

Front Cover Image:
Blanchard's Map of Chicago and Environs (1888). (Image courtesy of the Chicago History Museum; CHM-Digital Object ID: ICHi-27745).

Back Cover Images (left to right from top row to bottom row):
- Michigan Southern Railroad Company Station in Chicago. (Image courtesy of Joseph Kirkland, *History of Chicago*, 1893).
- Nellie Kinzie. (Image courtesy of the Chicago History Museum).
- Dr. Alexander Wolcott, Jr. (Image courtesy of the Chicago History Museum).
- Fort Dearborn in later years. (Image courtesy of Joseph Kirkland, *History of Chicago*, 1893).
- Jacob Bunn. (Image courtesy of the Sangamon Valley Collection of The Lincoln Library of Springfield, Illinois).
- John Stryker. (Image courtesy of The Stryker Area Heritage Council of Ohio).
- John Whitfield Bunn. (Image courtesy of the family of the author).
- Col. Stephen Williamson Stryker. (Image courtesy of Rick Lawrence).
- Ada Willard Richardson as a young girl. (Author's personal collection).
- William Douglas Richardson. (Image courtesy of Ruth Solomon).
- Frank Hatch Jones, Esq. (Author's personal collection).
- Rev. Melancthon Woolsey Stryker. (Image courtesy of Hamilton College of Clinton, New York, and the Hamilton College Archives).
- Administration Building at the 1893 World's Columbian Exposition. (Image courtesy of Joseph Kirkland, *History of Chicago*, 1893).
- Loren Ralph Dodson. (Image courtesy of The Ohio State University).
- Florence (Ferguson) Lee. (Image courtesy of Susan Alland and her family).
- Bunn Capitol Grocery Company Coffee Tins. (Author's personal collection).

NOTICE: The front cover, spine/binding cover, and back cover of this book were designed and formatted by Matthew Musselman and Invoke Design, LLC, of Roanoke, Virginia. Janice A. Knox of Chicago also contributed to these designs. Matthew Musselman and Invoke Design, LLC, also prepared and inserted the images contained inside the book and provided counsel on book formatting issues.

Dedication

I dedicate this book to God the Father, God the Son, and God the Holy Spirit, Who made this entire work possible. I also dedicate this work to my family and friends whose love and support have helped me so tremendously in the composition of this work.

—Andrew Taylor Call of Chicago, Illinois

Table of Contents

NOTICE: The bibliography of this book is contained entirely within the footnotes. The footnotes and their contents constitute the bibliography for this book.

NOTICE: The genealogical segments of this book will often contain names that appear in **bold text** in order to aid the reader in following the specific lineages of the families that connect to Chicago and Cook County history.

Table of Acknowledgments

The author thanks the following people and organizations, in addition to others, for their friendship, support, memory, inspiration, and encouragement, without which this book would never have been possible.

NOTICE: The following lists are arranged in alphabetical order by first name or first word.

Family
- Ada Octavia Bunn Casper and Peter Casper
- Barbara Covey Thomas
- Bryan Henry
- Charles and Judy Taylor
- Charlotte Taylor Lyon and Stuart Lyon
- Dale Robertson and his family
- David McLean
- Debbie Covey Barbare
- Elizabeth "Ibby" Taylor Greer
- Jamie Overom Pyzik
- Jeannie Hemphill
- Kathleen Hogan Manuel
- Margaret Taylor
- Mark Peterson
- Matthew Baldwin Call
- Richard Lee Covey and Elvira Covey
- Robert H. Bunn and Sarah Bunn
- Roderic A. Covey
- Ruth Solomon and her family
- Susan Alland and Jim Bohannan
- Susan Covey
- The late Arthur G. Hailand, Jr.
- The late Benjamin Chandler Huselton
- The late Beverly Call Glover
- The late Edgar Chandler Huselton, Jr.
- The late F. John Taylor
- The late Henry Stryker Taylor and Elizabeth (Bunn) Taylor
- The late Sharon Dayton (Hogan family)
- The late Suzanne Huselton
- The late Thomas Keister Greer, Esq.
- The late William Frederic Call and Mary Elizabeth (Baldwin) Call
- W. Roderic Covey
- Wendy Overom Paymard
- Willard Bunn, III
- William Clyde Conner

Friends
- Adam P. Wood, CPA
- Andrew and Kathryn Cubria and their family
- Andrew K. Block
- Anna Marie Brucker
- Anne Piedmont and Piedmont Research Associates
- Anthony J. Leone, Jr., and Cathy Cragoe
- Arnie Anderson
- Barbara Schmidt and Twainquotes.com
- Barton and Heather Pembroke
- Becky Mushko
- Carol Orwig
- Charles Dennewitz
- Chuck Abraham, Esq.
- Clarence McGee and his family
- Claude Weil
- Cleveland Holden
- Connie Irwin
- Curtis Mann
- David Lane Foster and Joyce Meador Foster
- David Lewis Foster
- Deb and Alan Stranc
- Debbie McBride
- Diana Moore
- Doug Ferguson
- Ed Balakhanpour
- Elissa Ledvort

- Dr. Ervin Jordan
- Frances Vandervoort
- Frank Lipo
- Fredric J. Friedberg, Esq.
- Gary Boyd Roberts and New England Historic Genealogical Society
- Gary Ossewaarde
- Geoffrey Brown and Judith Moore Sherman
- George Ronald White
- George William Thomas, Esq.
- Georgianne Marcinkovich
- Greg Johnson
- Gwen, Tyrone, Allen, Megan, Rachel, Matthew, Trelinda, Carl, Stephan, and my other friends at The Quadrangle Club
- The Hon. Helen Marie Taylor
- Dr. J. Francis Amos, M.D.
- J. Shane Newcombe
- Jacob Lauser, Esq. and Wendy Lauser
- Janice Ann Knox
- Janie Christopher Chapman
- Jermaine P. Eccles-James, CNA
- Jhangir Esfandiari
- Joette Waddle
- John and Sue Major
- John K. Notz, Jr., Esq.
- John B. Weber
- John S. Hoff, Esq.
- John Wesley
- John W. Whitehead, Esq., and Nisha Whitehead
- Jonas Ryan Chin
- Joseph F. Vitu, Esq.
- Joseph Kett, Ph.D., Mark Thomas, Ph.D., Charles McCurdy, PhD., Kurt Hohenstein, Esq. and Ph.D., of the Corcoran Department of History at the University of Virginia
- Jennie Myers, Ph.D.
- Joshua Kesling, Esq.
- Joy M. Johnson, Esq.
- Katherine Benbow
- Kathleen Lemley Sponsler
- Katie Spindell
- Kellogg Fairbank
- Kenneth Lewis
- Kevin Collins
- Kevin Murdock
- Landon Metts
- Lynn Roundtree
- Marcia Ferguson Cox
- Marie Daraban
- Mark Hertzberg
- Matthew Musselman and Invoke Design, LLC
- Mercy Muendo, Esq.
- The late Michael P. Avramovich, Esq.
- Michal Safar
- Mike Meiners of the *St. Louis Post-Dispatch*
- Norma Jean McCoy and her family
- Pastors Ricky R. Malone and Marianna Malone; Pastor Ricky Malone's parents Rodney and Alberta; Pastor Ricky Malone's cousin Antiwan; Pastor Ricky Malone's grandmother Elouise, and their families.
- Peter Halliday
- Rada Burns
- Rebecca Belcher
- Rhonda L. Tipton
- Dr. Richard Hattwick
- Rick Lawrence
- Robert Iles McNeill and his family
- Roger and Vicky Whitaker
- Ruth Slottag
- Sandra Chiarlone, Esq.
- Sandra Keen McGlothlin, Esq.
- Sarah Yarrito, Angela Hoover, Josh, Michael, Lesley, Michael, Trenton, Ellen, and the other Chicago History Museum staff members

- Scott Berland, Esq. and Jamie Berland, Esq.
- Simplice Blahoua
- Stacey Petrek Butler, Esq. and Dr. Robert Butler, Ph.D. and their families
- Tricia Moyer Haskins, D.V.M.
- William Ferrell
- William W. Little, Esq. and Wendy Little

Organizations and Historical Resources

- Alderman Library of the University of Virginia and its staff
- Ancestry.com
- Appalachian School of Law
- Architects Club of Chicago
- Archive.org
- Cass County Historical Society
- Chicago Club
- Chicago History Museum, the Research Center, the Rights and Reproductions Department
- Evanston History Center
- Familysearch.org
- Findagrave.com
- Geneanet.org and its owner and manager, Tim Dowling
- Hamilton College of Clinton, New York
- Historical Society of Oak Park and River Forest, Illinois
- HistoryMiami (Miami History Museum) (Florida)
- Hyde Park Historical Society of Chicago
- Illinois State Historical Society
- Jackson Park Yacht Club
- The John G. Shedd Aquarium
- Knox College
- Library of Michigan
- Library of Virginia
- Main Library, Deering Library, and Schaffner Library at Northwestern University
- National Association of Watch and Clock Collectors

- New England Historic Genealogical Society
- New York Genealogical and Biographical Society
- Newspapers.com
- Northwestern University
- Ohio History Connection (Ohio Historical Society)
- Oriental Institute of the University of Chicago
- Pleasant Home Foundation
- The Quadrangle Club
- Ridge Historical Society
- Rogers Park/West Ridge Historical Society
- Rootsweb
- Sangamon County Historical Society
- Sangamon Valley Collection of the Lincoln Library of Springfield, Illinois
- *St. Louis Post Dispatch*, Mike Meiners, and the historical *St. Louis Star Times*
- The Art Institute of Chicago
- The Caxton Club
- The Field Museum of Natural History
- The Hagley Museum
- The John Marshall Law School of Chicago
- The Newberry Library
- The Ohio State University
- The Scoville Public Library of Salisbury, Connecticut
- University of Chicago
- University of Cincinnati and its Archives
- University of Virginia
- Washington University of St. Louis
- Western Reserve Historical Society
- Willard Family Association of America
- Wisconsin Historical Society

"A city that is set on a hill cannot be hidden."

Matthew 5:14.

Prologue:

At the Place of the Wild Onions

Perhaps it is an uncommon confession for one to say that one began one's work as a student of history with a box of maps, a multitude of Autumn afternoons, a tool chest, and a very large yard filled with colorful Appalachian leaves. Though this may fairly be judged unusual, the fact is that this is precisely how I began to develop into a student of history, culture, and geography. It was with these tools and resources that I began to develop a fascination with times, places, names, histories, and cultures. I was nine years old then.

I was born in Boynton Beach, Florida, and was raised in the Appalachian Mountains of Virginia. My maternal grandparents, who were natives of Illinois, had permanently relocated to Palm Beach County, Florida, after having spent many years as seasonal residents in Florida, Michigan, and Illinois. My mother and father eventually followed my grandparents to Florida, where I was born. After a few years of residence in Lake Worth, Florida, we moved to Virginia, where my mother had attended Hollins College in the 1970s, and where my aunt had attended boarding school. My grandmother and grandfather remained in Highland Beach, Florida, which is a southern suburb of Delray Beach, and a northern neighbor of Boca Raton. I subsequently grew up in Roanoke, Virginia, and in the neighboring suburban town of Rocky Mount, in Franklin County. Franklin County and Roanoke County, therefore, were where I spent most of my childhood years. We visited Florida often to see my grandparents and other relatives. Our home, an antebellum estate, built in 1854 and known as The Grove for its large forests, was located in the center of Rocky Mount.

Octobers and Novembers in Rocky Mount and Franklin County brought great amounts of fallen leaves. I would take the old rakes from the smokehouse tool shed and carve out whole systems of roads throughout the multi-acre yard of The Grove, our old home. The yard provided adequate space for an entire network of leaf-carved highways. All one needed to bring to the job was willingness to spend the time to create the roads from the fallen leaf beds that covered the large Appalachian Mountain estate. The leaf beds were sometimes several feet thick. Roads were always a point of fascination for me, and still are.

The road on which our house was located was the old Floyd-Franklin Turnpike. This was one of my favorite roads. The road began next to our house in the Town of Rocky Mount. In town the road was known as Floyd Avenue. From there the road traversed the entire western half of Franklin County before climbing the Blue Ridge Mountains of Franklin County and Floyd County. The Floyd-Franklin Turnpike ended in the Town of Floyd, located high in the Appalachian Mountains of southwest Virginia. I traveled this road many times with parents and friends when I was a young boy. I drove the road many times when I was grown. The road always inspired in me a desire to explore western horizons, geographies, and histories. This road remains one of my favorite roads, and always will. Wild onion grass was common in the large yard of our house in the Town of Rocky Mount. Wild onion grass was common along the Floyd-Franklin Turnpike, the old Carolina Highway (U.S. Rt. 220), the roads of nearby Roanoke, Virginia, and all roads in our part of the Appalachian Mountains.

The windows at The Grove provided the viewer with vistas of the Appalachian West. Sunsets were viewable from the windows of the Library Room at The Grove, and the evening light came through aged dogwoods and other old trees and shrubs that had been planted long before. It seemed for me that The Grove possessed a unique standing in time and space, a sort of link to other times and places from which one could instantly enter those other times and places. The Grove was for me a gateway to many places and experiences, and it was there and in Charlottesville, Virginia, where I began the historical research work that has culminated in the present book.

Though seemingly unrelated by context, the leaf roads of The Grove, the decommissioned mountain turnpikes of Franklin County and Floyd County, and the sunset-suffused western windows of the Library Room at The Grove all were starting points for me on the processes of interest, rediscovery, and research that have ended with the present book about Chicago. When I was a sophomore at the University of Virginia, in Charlottesville, I developed an interest in discovering more about our family history and genealogy in the Midwest and the Northeast. The present book represents more than seventeen years of historical search, research, documentation, rediscovery, discovery, assembly, and analysis. I was blessed to commence this journey of research with a profound head start, because I had been raised since birth around histories, pictures, cemeteries, and stories about our immense family.

I first became aware of the concept of Chicago when I was a young boy visiting my grandmother in Florida. A photograph of a middle-aged lady at a desk by a window was framed atop a living room table. I once asked who the lady was, and my grandmother told me it was Cousin Margot McKay from Chicago. From that point on, the names of Chicago and Margot McKay jointly symbolized a faraway and fascinating place of equally interesting history and experience, although I was by no means able to articulate this perspective in those terms at that time. I made my first visit to The Windy City at about the age of eleven. My mother, my now late stepfather, and I arrived by means of the Cardinal Train, an Amtrak service from Chicago to New York City whose route traversed much of the Appalachian Mountain region of Virginia, West Virginia, Kentucky, Ohio, and Indiana.

I first laid eyes on the immense railyards of Chicago as we approached Union Station from the south. I still remember the appearance of one of the railyard workers who stood near the train as we passed. The visit to the city encompassed a broad range of excellent experiences. Lincoln Park Zoo, The Drake Hotel, the Cape Cod Room, Trader Vic's at the Palmer House, the Newberry Library, Washington Square Park (where I saw my first Rolls-Royce), Robie House, the Art Institute of Chicago, and the Museum of Science and Industry were the highpoints for me of that visit. We then rented a car to go to Springfield to visit family. We proceeded to Galesburg, where we visited Knox College, the alma mater of my grandfather, great-grandfather, and granduncle from the Taylor family (who are discussed in Chapter 6, *Sprinters of the Steel Track*).

This book is about Chicago, about Cook County, about the State of Illinois, and about many places that interlocked with this city and county. It is a catalogue of the interlocking communities of the Great Lakes, Midwest, Ohio River Valley, Mississippi River Valley, New York, New Jersey, New England, and The South. Chicago is a geographical, social, and economic hub to which each of these places and histories connects powerfully. The purpose of this book is compound. It is the simultaneous celebration and completion of historical research, discovery, rediscovery, documentation, assembly, analysis, and commemoration of people, times, places, experiences, occurrences, cultures, organizations, memberships, leaderships, and the connections that exist among them. This book also celebrates civic leadership, vision for construction of cities, counties, regions, states, the United States of America, and even other countries of the world. Chicago and Cook County stand at the center of all of this. This book combines eclectic means of statement, explanation, analysis, and documentation. It is my hope as the author that this book will concurrently bring lost and forgotten histories of Chicago to the world and show how the world came to Chicago. Though this book does not constitute a traditional genealogy, it does use genealogy as a foundational means of explanation of the civic, industrial, and familial histories of Chicago that are the focus of this book.

The chapters that follow contain the largely unknown histories of people, companies, civic organizations, urban growth, opportunities identified, opportunities seized, honorable acts, and positive municipal developments both economic and political. All of these historical elements testify individually and uniquely of the greatness, uniqueness, and grandeur of Chicago and Cook County. This union of testimony and evidence will contribute further proof of the singular splendor of the Great Lakes Region, the general Midwest Region, and the United States of America. The people that appear in these pages are from every stratum of society. Homemakers, school teachers, railroad presidents, manufacturers, deaf hardware store workers, lawyers, and construction men all appear within the pages that follow. The organizations that appear herein include industrial corporations, small businesses, public schools, churches, coal mines, labor organizations, political machines, and many other entities. The foundational structure that associates all of these people and organizations is the combined family history of the Call, Taylor, Bunn, Stryker, Willard, Richardson, Regan, Hogan, Richards, Prentis, Wolcott, Kinzie, Peterson, Powers, McNeil, and other families from Illinois, Wisconsin, Ohio, Pennsylvania, New Jersey, New England, and New York. Every one of these families contributed to the civic and business life of Chicago and Cook County. I am a member of every one of these families through lineal and/or collateral kinship. Family history, therefore, forms the foundation, but not the entirety, of the narrative infrastructure of this book. I wish to take this opportunity to acknowledge the rhetorical inspiration that I have received from my late stepfather, attorney Thomas Keister Greer, Esquire (1921-2008), who titled his History Honors Thesis at the University of Virginia, *Genesis of a Virginia*

Frontier: Origins of Franklin County, Virginia, 1740-1785. The Thesis title that he chose inspired the title that I chose here for Chapter 1 of the present work: *Genesis of a Great Lakes Frontier.*

In 1804 my extended maternal family settled in what was to become Chicago.[1] The years that marked the arrival of my maternal forebears at the settlement of Fort Dearborn, Chicago, and the vicinity thereof, include 1804, approximately 1818-1820, 1834, and 1840, in addition to multiple subsequent years.[2] Our family surnames that are included among our lineal and collateral family that settled in, or contributed in some manner to, Chicago and Cook County, include Wolcott, Post, Whiting, Kinzie, Taylor, Cunningham, Stryker, Bunn, Willard, Richardson, Regan, Hogan, McKay, Ferguson, Brigham, Pettit, Brown, Jones, Cogan, and multiple others.[3]

I have intended the book to constitute a history of Chicago and the metropolitan region through the civic and industrial histories of our family and genealogy, and the many other histories that interlock with our family in Chicago. The book is not only about our family history in Chicago but is also about the many people with whom our various family branches were associated in different ways. The limits of the historical record have combined with the limits of space in the book to restrict the amounts of information included herein. Please know that while there are heavy focuses on people of prominence in civic affairs, business, industry, and the professions, those focuses are due to the simple fact that more information existed regarding those persons than did regarding our family who were laborers and farmers. I have attempted to collect and present the Chicago histories of as many of our family branches as possible that existed in this city and metropolitan region prior to about 1970.

The work by no means constitutes a comprehensive history of Chicago and Cook County, but does constitute an attempt to reconstruct, document, describe, and analyze combined experiences of our multiple interconnected families of Chicago, Cook County, and Illinois. The times, places, experiences, associations, and connections that form the foundation of this book would appear unconnected but for the fact that they are all connected to our families in some manner. To produce a history of Chicago is, by necessity, to produce a history of other places. A person can be, and very often is, from more than one place. I am one such person and claim Virginia and the Midwest as home. I claim the Appalachian Mountains and the Great Lakes as home. I claim Roanoke, Rocky Mount, and Chicago as home.

---

[1] Call, Andrew Taylor. (2016). Faded Bricks: Old Family Tales from the South Side of Chicago. Hyde Park History, Vol. 38, (No. 4), Pp. 1-7. Chicago, IL: Hyde Park Historical Society.

[2] Call, Andrew Taylor. (2016). Faded Bricks: Old Family Tales from the South Side of Chicago. Hyde Park History, Vol. 38, (No. 4), Pp. 1-7. Chicago, IL: Hyde Park Historical Society.

[3] Call, Andrew Taylor. (2016). Faded Bricks: Old Family Tales from the South Side of Chicago. Hyde Park History, Vol. 38, (No. 4), Pp. 1-7. Chicago, IL: Hyde Park Historical Society.

Many of the persons discussed herein were natives of places other than Chicago. Nevertheless, these persons contributed importantly, and in some cases centrally, to the growth, development, and prosperity of this city and region. The Illinois cities and counties of Springfield, Jacksonville, Morgan County, Cass County, and Winnebago County, in addition to many others, played vital and indispensable roles in the development of the civic and industrial character, wealth, and importance of Chicago and the metropolitan region. Our combined lineal and collateral families have resided and worked in Chicago and Cook County for more than two centuries and were among the founders of the City of Chicago, Cook County, and the State of Illinois. Many people in the history of the Midwest made a journey from the Appalachian Mountains, some from Virginia, as in the case of Cyrus Hall McCormick, some from Kentucky, as in the case of Abraham Lincoln and Shelby Moore Cullom, and some from New York, as in the case of John Villiers Farwell and the Willard family discussed herein. Many came to Illinois and to other parts of the Midwest from the Appalachian Mountains. I, too, have come to Illinois and the Midwest from the Appalachian Mountains of Virginia.

I have known well the wild onions of the Appalachian Mountains. These wild onions grew abundantly in the large yard of my childhood home in Rocky Mount. These wild onions grew along the Appalachian Mountains of Franklin County, Roanoke County, and Floyd County, where I spent so many happy years as a child and as a man. These same wild onions grew where Chicago and Cook County were established. The word, "Chicago," itself means, "Place of the Wild Onions." It would be right for me to say that I have come from one place of the wild onions to another place of the wild onions, and that I will always consider both places home.

Chapter 1

Genesis of a Great Lakes Frontier

"I shall certainly come and live with you that is if I ever leave this odd out of the way place to which, to tell the truth I am becoming daily more attached."[4]

—*Dr. Alexander Wolcott (1790-1830), a founder of Chicago and Cook County, in a letter to his sister informing her that he would gladly reside with her at Fishkill, New York, but that his ever-growing love for the minute frontier settlement called Chicago will not let him leave the land of the Wild Onions.*

Introduction

This chapter concerns the Chicago history of the Wolcott, Richards, Henshaw, Post, Whiting, Stryker, and Irwin branches of my mother's family. My great-grandmother, Charlotte Stryker, and my great-grandfather, Robert Cunningham Taylor, who were married in 1905, both descended from multiple founding families of Chicago and Cook County. These families also had been founders of Cass County, Morgan County, and Sangamon County, Illinois. One of our maternal cousins through the lineage of Charlotte (Stryker) Taylor, Dr. Alexander Wolcott (1790-1830), who was a Yale alumnus and native of East Windsor, Connecticut, arrived at the settlement of Chicago in approximately 1818-1820.[5]

The Richards, Prentice, Wolcott, and Henshaw Families of New England,

Illinois, and Chicago: The Richards Family

The Richards family were founders and prominent citizens of New London, Connecticut. John Richards of Eel River, Plymouth Colony, had the following children: **John Richards, who married Love Manwaring**; Israel Richards; Mary Richards, who married John Benmore; Penelope Richards; Lydia Richards, who married William Minar (or Maynard); Elizabeth Richards; Hannah Richards; and David Richards, who married Elizabeth Raymond.[6] The Eel River is a short river in Plymouth, Massachusetts, and was near the home of John Richards, who was the patriarch of our Richards family of New England and Chicago.

---

[4] Letter of Dr. Alexander Wolcott to Frances Wolcott Magill. (August 10, 1822). Dr. Alexander Wolcott Collection. Chicago History Museum Research Center and Archives.
[5] Kelly, Howard Atwood. (1920). A cyclopedia of American medical biography. Pp. 1252-1253. Baltimore, MD: The Norman, Remington Company. Google Books; Call, Andrew Taylor. (2016). Faded Bricks: Old Family Tales from the South Side of Chicago. Hyde Park History, Vol. 38, (No. 4), Pp. 1-7. Chicago, IL: Hyde Park Historical Society.
[6] Morse, Abner. (1861). A Genealogical Register of the Descendants of Several Ancient Puritans. Vol. III. P. 93. Boston, MASS: Press of H. W. Dutton & Son. Google Books.

John Richards married Love Manwaring. The following children were born to them: John Richards, who married Anna Prentice; **George Richards, who married Esther Hough**; Samuel Richards, who married Ann (Dennison) Hough; Love Richards; Oliver Richards; Lydia Richards, who married John Proctor; Mary Richards, who died young; Mary Richards; and Guy Richards.[7]

George Richards (1695-1750) married Hester Hough. George was High Sheriff of New London. They had the following children: John Richards, who married Hannah Greenleaf; George Richards, who married Catherine Fosdick; **Guy Richards, who married Elizabeth Harris; Mary Richards, who married Alexander Wolcott**; Love Richards, who married, first, Lemuel Rogers, and second, Nathaniel Coit; and Nathaniel Richards, who married Mary Leffingwell.[8]

Mary Richards was the daughter of George Richards and Hester (Hough) Richards of New London. **Mary Richards married Dr. Alexander Wolcott** of Windsor, Connecticut.[9] Dr. Wolcott was a Yale alumnus and a medical doctor. Dr. Alexander Wolcott and Mary (Richards) Wolcott had the following children: Simon Wolcott, who married, first, Lucy Rogers, and second, Charlotte (Woodbridge) Mumford; George Wolcott, who died in infancy; George Wolcott, who married a woman with the surname of Rowland; Christopher Wolcott, who married Lucy Parsons; **Alexander Wolcott, who married Frances Burbanks (these are the ancestors of the Wolcott-Magill-Balestier families of Chicago)**; **Guy Wolcott, who married Abigail Allyn**; Esther Wolcott, who died in infancy; Esther Wolcott, who married Samuel Treat; Mary Wolcott, who married Elihu Griswold; and Elizabeth Wolcott, who married Elizur Wolcott.[10] **Allyn Ellsworth Wolcott**, son of Guy Wolcott and Abigail Allyn, was a prominent Chicago attorney, historian, and author during the nineteenth century.

Guy Richards, son of George Richards and Hester (Hough) Richards, married Elizabeth Harris. The following children were born to them: Guy Richards, who married Hannah Dolbeare; **Esther Richards, who married John Prentiss (these are the ancestors of the Henshaw-McClure-Stryker-Taylor families of Chicago)**; Peter Richards, who married Catherine Mumford; Nathaniel Richards, who married Elizabeth Coit; Mary Richards, who married George

---

[7] Morse, Abner. (1861). A Genealogical Register of the Descendants of Several Ancient Puritans. Vol. III. Pp. 93-94. Boston, MASS: Press of H. W. Dutton & Son. Google Books.

[8] Morse, Abner. (1861). A Genealogical Register of the Descendants of Several Ancient Puritans. Vol. III. Pp. 94-95. Boston, MASS: Press of H. W. Dutton & Son. Google Books.

[9] Walforth, Reuben H. (1864). Hyde Genealogy; Or The Descendants, In The Female As Well As In The Male Lines, From William Hyde, Of Norwich. Vol. 1. Pp. 225-226. Albany, NY: J. Munsell. Google Books.

[10] Walforth, Reuben H. (1864). Hyde Genealogy; Or The Descendants, In The Female As Well As In The Male Lines, From William Hyde, Of Norwich. Vol. 1. Pp. 225-226. Albany, NY: J. Munsell. Google Books.

Avery; Elizabeth Richards, who died young; Elizabeth Richards, who married Timothy Green; Benjamin Richards, who married Mary Coit; Alexander Richards, who married Mary Colfax; and Hannah Richards, who married, first, Elijah Baccus, and second, Williams George.[11]

The Richards-Prentis Family

Valentine Prentice married Alice, whose surname was not documented by Charles James Fox Binney in his 1883 history and genealogy of the Prentice/Prentis/Prentiss Family of America. Valentine and Alice Prentice had a son named John Prentice, who married Hester.[12] The children born to John and Hester Prentice were the following persons: John Prentice; Joseph Prentice; **Jonathan Prentice, who married Elizabeth Latimer**; Hester Prentice, who married Benjamin Adam Gallop; Peter Prentice; Stephen Prentice; Mercy Prentice; Hannah Prentice, who married John Frink of Stonington; Thomas Prentice; Elizabeth Prentice; and Valentine Prentice.[13]

Jonathan Prentis, son of John and Hester Prentice, was a Justice of New London, member of the Governor's Council of New London, and was Deputy to the General Court.[14] **Jonathan Prentis married Elizabeth Latimer**, and the following children were born to them: Elizabeth Prentis, who married Samuel Edgecombe; Esther Prentis; Jonathan Prentis, who married Mary (Christophers) Gray; Hannah Prentis; Ann Prentis, who married, first, Thomas Coit, and second, Dr. Ebenezer Gray; Mary Prentis; and **John Prentis, who married Sarah Christophers (ancestors of the Prentis, Henshaw, McClure, Stryker, and Taylor families of Chicago, Morgan County, and Springfield).**[15]

John Prentis, son of Jonathan Prentis and Elizabeth (Latimer) Prentis, married Sarah Christophers, and the following children were born to them: Mary Prentis, who married, first, Peter Harris, and second, Richard Deshon; Elizabeth Prentis, who married Samuel Latimer, Jr.; John Prentis; Sarah Prentis, who married Capt. William Coit; Ann Prentis, who married Richard Law; Esther

---

[11] Morse, Abner. (1861). A Genealogical Register of the Descendants of Several Ancient Puritans. Vol. III. P. 96. Boston, MASS: Press of H. W. Dutton & Son. Google Books.

[12] Binney, Charles James Fox. (1883). The History and Genealogy of the Prentice, or Prentiss Family, in New England, Etc., from 1631 to 1883. Pp. 271-273. Boston, MASS: Charles James Fox Binney. Google Books.

[13] Binney, Charles James Fox. (1883). The History and Genealogy of the Prentice, or Prentiss Family, in New England, Etc., from 1631 to 1883. Pp. 271-273. Boston, MASS: Charles James Fox Binney. Google Books.

[14] Binney, Charles James Fox. (1883). The History and Genealogy of the Prentice, or Prentiss Family, in New England, Etc., from 1631 to 1883. Pp. 275-276. Boston, MASS: Charles James Fox Binney. Google Books.

[15] Binney, Charles James Fox. (1883). The History and Genealogy of the Prentice, or Prentiss Family, in New England, Etc., from 1631 to 1883. Pp. 275-276. Boston, MASS: Charles James Fox Binney. Google Books.

Prentis, who married Capt. Michael Mellaly; and **John Prentis, who married Esther Richards**.[16]

Capt. John Prentice, son of John Prentis and Sarah (Christophers) Prentis, married Esther Richards, and had the following children: **Sally Esther Prentiss, who married Daniel Henshaw (ancestors of the McClure, Stryker, Taylor families of Chicago, Morgan County, and Springfield)**; Elizabeth Prentice, who married, first, John Hallam, and second, George Chapman of New London; Mary Prentice, who married Samuel Allen and resided at Marietta, Ohio; John Prentis, who married Eunice Frink; **Nancy Prentis, who married Charles W. Goodrich of New Orleans (ancestors of the Prentice, Southmayd, and Holmes families of Chicago)**; Jonathan Prentis, who married Margaret Hartshorne and resided at Morgantown, West Virginia; Catherine M. Prentis, who married John Robertson of New York; and Henry Leonidas Prentis, who married Rebecca Mayberry of New London, and resided later at Belleville, West Virginia.[17] After the death of Capt. John Prentis, Esther (Richards) Prentis married, second, Samuel Hempstead, and third, William McLeary of Morgantown, West Virginia. Esther (Richards) Prentis McLeary moved to Belleville, West Virginia, and was interred in Morgantown.[18] West Virginia at that time was still Virginia.

<u>Three Branches of a Large Chicago Family:</u>

<u>The Richards-Prentis-Henshaw Family; the Richards-Wolcott Family;</u>

<u>and the Richards-Prentis-Southmayd Family</u>

Three branches of the Richards-Prentis family of Connecticut possessed extensive civic and industrial connections to Chicago over multiple generations: the Richards-Prentis-Henshaw family, the Richards-Wolcott family, and the Richards-Prentis-Southmayd family. Siblings Sally Esther Prentiss and Nancy Prentiss, who were the daughters of Capt. John Prentis and Esther (Richards) Prentis of Connecticut (see above), both were matriarchs of large families of Illinois that contributed immensely to the founding and development of Chicago and Cook County: Sally Esther Prentis married Daniel Henshaw, and these were the ancestors of the immense Richards-Prentis-Henshaw family of Illinois and Chicago; and Nancy Prentis married Charles Whiting Goodrich, and these were

---

[16] Binney, Charles James Fox. (1883). The History and Genealogy of the Prentice, or Prentiss Family, in New England, Etc., from 1631 to 1883. Pp. 282-288. Boston, MASS: Charles James Fox Binney. Google Books.

[17] Binney, Charles James Fox. (1883). The History and Genealogy of the Prentice, or Prentiss Family, in New England, Etc., from 1631 to 1883. Pp. 293-297. Boston, MASS: Charles James Fox Binney. Google Books.

[18] Binney, Charles James Fox. (1883). The History and Genealogy of the Prentice, or Prentiss Family, in New England, Etc., from 1631 to 1883. P. 288. Boston, MASS: Charles James Fox Binney. Google Books.

ancestors of the Richards-Prentis-Southmayd family of Chicago and New Orleans. For the Chicago history of the Richards-Prentis-Henshaw family, see the chapter, *Sprinters of the Steel Track*. For the Chicago history of the Richards-Prentis-Southmayd family, see the chapter, *The Horizons of Hyde Park*. Do not confuse the Richards-Wolcott family with the Richardson family, also of Chicago and Connecticut, which is discussed in the chapter, *The Foundations of Jackson Park*. We will now continue to the Chicago history of the Richards-Wolcott family. First, we must establish a basic historical foundation of the beginnings of Fort Dearborn.

Fort Dearborn

Alfred Theodore Andreas provided detailed chronology of the establishment and history of Fort Dearborn in his 1884 work, *History of Chicago*. After the conclusion of the Battle of Fallen Timbers and Gen. Anthony Wayne's decisive victory at that battle in 1794, the 1795 Treaty of Greenville, which ended the Northwest Indian War, established the foundation of expansionist jurisprudence upon which the permanent Chicago settlement was built.[19] The treaty contained, *inter alia*, the covenant for the cession and surrender of six square miles of land at the mouth of the Chicago River.[20] Vague reports existed of a prior fort at the place of the River Chicago, but the credibility of these reports has been largely impeached through multiple facts, not least of which was that the Native Americans of the River Chicagou region had no recollection of any prior fort.[21]

In about 1718 James Logan was commissioned by the Governor of Pennsylvania, who was the Scotsman Sir William Keith, to explore routes from the Atlantic Plain and Appalachian Mountains to the Mississippi River region.[22] Logan produced a route and navigation description at around the same time that described the route from Lake Huron, northward and west through the Straits of Michilimackina (Straits of Mackinac), and southward and west via the Lake Illinoise (Lake Michigan) to the River Chicagou.[23] Logan referred to a fort at the River Chicagou that had been garrisoned on only seldom occasions.[24] Andreas noted, however, that the oldest Native American residents of the Chicago River region possessed no

---

[19] Andreas, Alfred Theodore. (1884). History of Chicago. From The Earliest Period To The Present Time. P. 79. Chicago, IL: A. T. Andreas, Publisher. Archive.org.

[20] Andreas, Alfred Theodore. (1884). History of Chicago. From The Earliest Period To The Present Time. P. 79. Chicago, IL: A. T. Andreas, Publisher. Archive.org.

[21] Andreas, Alfred Theodore. (1884). History of Chicago. From The Earliest Period To The Present Time. P. 79. Chicago, IL: A. T. Andreas, Publisher. Archive.org.

[22] Andreas, Alfred Theodore. (1884). History of Chicago. From The Earliest Period To The Present Time. P. 79. Chicago, IL: A. T. Andreas, Publisher. Archive.org.

[23] Andreas, Alfred Theodore. (1884). History of Chicago. From The Earliest Period To The Present Time. P. 79. Chicago, IL: A. T. Andreas, Publisher. Archive.org.

[24] Andreas, Alfred Theodore. (1884). History of Chicago. From The Earliest Period To The Present Time. P. 79. Chicago, IL: A. T. Andreas, Publisher. Archive.org.

memory of any fort there.[25] In 1803, the United States sent Captain John Whistler to the place of the River Chicago to prepare a fort at the place to be known as Fort Dearborn, in honor of Henry Dearborn, who was President Thomas Jefferson's Secretary of War.[26] Whistler and the men he brought with him constructed Fort Dearborn over the course of the summer and fall of 1803.[27] Construction of Fort Dearborn was completed by the end of December, 1803, according to a report contained within the *American State Papers*, says Andreas.[28] Known since its construction as Fort Dearborn, the fort was garrisoned in 1803.[29] John Whistler was born in Ireland and served as the first Commandant of Fort Dearborn.[30] The architecture of the fort consisted of two block houses, an underground tunnel for emergency escape and supply purposes, a picket-form wall, a log house that contained the United States agency office, and cellars for storage.[31] The fort stood on the south side of the Chicago River, near the bend in the river that immediately preceded the debouchment point of the river at Lake Michigan.[32] Captain Whistler served under General John Burgoyne in the British Army during the Revolutionary War, and was taken prisoner at Saratoga when Burgoyne surrendered.

John Kinzie of Quebec and Chicago

John Kinzie (circa 1763-1828) was a native of Quebec and was the son of John McKenzie of Scotland. John Kinzie was educated in Williamsburgh, New York, apprenticed to a silversmith in Quebec, and relocated to Detroit to reside with his parents. Young John Kinzie became a silversmith and Indian trader at Detroit and traded with the Shawnees and Ottawas in the Old Northwest. Kinzie married, first, Margaret McKenzie, who was from Giles County, Virginia, and who had been captured by the Shawnee and carried to the Shawnee home of Chilicothe, in what

---

[25] Andreas, Alfred Theodore. (1884). History of Chicago. From The Earliest Period To The Present Time. P. 79. Chicago, IL: A. T. Andreas, Publisher. Archive.org.

[26] Andreas, Alfred Theodore. (1884). History of Chicago. From The Earliest Period To The Present Time. Pp. 79-80. Chicago, IL: A. T. Andreas, Publisher. Archive.org.

[27] Andreas, Alfred Theodore. (1884). History of Chicago. From The Earliest Period To The Present Time. P. 80. Chicago, IL: A. T. Andreas, Publisher. Archive.org.

[28] Andreas, Alfred Theodore. (1884). History of Chicago. From The Earliest Period To The Present Time. P. 80. Chicago, IL: A. T. Andreas, Publisher. Archive.org.

[29] Andreas, Alfred Theodore. (1884). History of Chicago. From The Earliest Period To The Present Time. P. 80. Chicago, IL: A. T. Andreas, Publisher. Archive.org.

[30] Andreas, Alfred Theodore. (1884). History of Chicago. From The Earliest Period To The Present Time. P. 80. Chicago, IL: A. T. Andreas, Publisher. Archive.org.

[31] Andreas, Alfred Theodore. (1884). History of Chicago. From The Earliest Period To The Present Time. P. 80. Chicago, IL: A. T. Andreas, Publisher. Archive.org.

[32] Andreas, Alfred Theodore. (1884). History of Chicago. From The Earliest Period To The Present Time. P. 80. Chicago, IL: A. T. Andreas, Publisher. Archive.org.

would become the State of Ohio.[33] The McKenzie girls were all kidnapped by the Shawnee and taken to Chilicothe, where the girls remained for about ten years. Alfred Theodore Andreas noted that the McKenzie girls either, "were taken, or found their way, to Detroit."[34] John Kinzie married Margaret McKenzie. Robert McKenzie of Giles County, Virginia, came to Detroit, and there discovered his lost daughters. Andreas stated, "[McKenzie] remained with them for a time; then returned to Virginia, accompanied by both his daughters, with their children, from whence Margaret [Margaret (McKenzie) Kinzie] never returned."[35] Andreas furthermore noted that, "Whatever might have been the cause of the separation, it was a final one. John Kinzie and his wife, Margaret, never met again."[36]

John Kinzie relocated to the St. Joseph River, in what would become the State of Michigan, and married Eleanor Lytle McKillip circa 1800.[37] Andreas stated that John and Eleanor moved to what would become Chicago in the spring of 1804, and that Kinzie was, "beloved by the Indians. . .[And that] He acquired the reputation of being, *par excellance*, 'the Indians' friend,' and through the most fearful scenes of danger, Shawnee-aw-kee, the Silverman, and his family, moved unscathed."[38] John Kinzie established a trading post at Fort Dearborn in 1804-1805, and later established branch trading posts at the Kankakee River, what would become Sangamon County, the Illinois River, and at Milwaukee.[39] The Kinzie family remained at Fort Dearborn for eight years. Kinzie owned the trading posts, was sutler to the soldiers of Fort Dearborn, and manufactured ornaments for the Native Americans of the region.[40] John and Eleanor (McKillip) Kinzie had the following children: **John Harris Kinzie (b. 1803), who married Juliette Magill**; **Ellen Marion Kinzie (b. 1805), who married Dr. Alexander Wolcott**; Maria Indiana Kinzie (b. 1807); and Robert Allen Kinzie (b. 1810).[41]

---

[33] Andreas, Alfred Theodore. (1884). History of Chicago. Vol. 1. P. 73. Chicago, IL: A. T. Andreas, Publisher. Google Books.
[34] Andreas, Alfred Theodore. (1884). History of Chicago. Vol. 1. P. 73. Chicago, IL: A. T. Andreas, Publisher. Google Books.
[35] Andreas, Alfred Theodore. (1884). History of Chicago. Vol. 1. P. 73. Chicago, IL: A. T. Andreas, Publisher. Google Books.
[36] Andreas, Alfred Theodore. (1884). History of Chicago. Vol. 1. P. 73. Chicago, IL: A. T. Andreas, Publisher. Google Books.
[37] Andreas, Alfred Theodore. (1884). History of Chicago. Vol. 1. P. 73. Chicago, IL: A. T. Andreas, Publisher. Google Books.
[38] Andreas, Alfred Theodore. (1884). History of Chicago. Vol. 1. P. 73. Chicago, IL: A. T. Andreas, Publisher. Google Books.
[39] Andreas, Alfred Theodore. (1884). History of Chicago. Vol. 1. P. 73. Chicago, IL: A. T. Andreas, Publisher. Google Books.
[40] Andreas, Alfred Theodore. (1884). History of Chicago. Vol. 1. P. 73. Chicago, IL: A. T. Andreas, Publisher. Google Books.
[41] Andreas, Alfred Theodore. (1884). History of Chicago. Vol. 1. P. 73. Chicago, IL: A. T. Andreas, Publisher. Google Books.

The War of 1812 was the framing context for the occurrence of the Fort Dearborn Massacre of August 15, 1812.[42] Benson J. Lossing kept a record of the War of 1812, and in this record Lossing chronicled the basic facts of the Battle of Fort Dearborn. The Battle of Fort Dearborn took place on August 15, 1812, when Captain Nathan Heald commanded the fort. Lt. Linai T. Helm and Ensign George Ronan assisted Heald, and Dr. Isaac Van Voorhis was the surgeon of Fort Dearborn.[43] Lossing recorded that, "'twelve children, all the masculine citizens except Mr. Kenzie [Kinzie] and his sons, Captain Wells, Ensign Ronan, Surgeon Van Voorhis, and twenty-six private soldiers, were murdered.'"[44] John Kinzie and his family survived the Massacre, even though John Kinzie had bravely accompanied the Fort Dearborn military in order to persuade the Potawatomies not to take any lives.[45]

Josiah Seymour Currey stated that Chief Topenebe of the Potawatomie Tribe was, "a firm friend of the whites and especially of the Kinzie family."[46] Chief Topenebe warned John Kinzie not to accompany the Fort Dearborn garrison in its departure from the fort by land, but to take a boat to St. Joseph, instead, where Kinzie could reunite with the surviving Fort Dearborn troops.[47] Chief Topenebe knew of the plan of the Potawatomie escorts to attack the Fort Dearborn garrison, but Kinzie ignored the warning and accompanied the troops.[48] Currey states, "Mr. Kinzie, however, decided to place his family in the boat, while he himself accompanied the troops, in the hope and belief that his presence would operate as a restraint upon the fury of the [Potawatomies] in case of an attack."[49] The boat party consisted of twelve people, including Eleanor (McKillip) Kinzie and her four children, John Harris Kinzie, Ellen Marion Kinzie, Maria Indiana Kinzie, and Robert Allen Kinzie. Other boat passengers included Josette La Framboise, who was a French-Ottawa nurse; Chandonaise, a clerk for John Kinzie; and two friendly

---

[42] Andreas, Alfred Theodore. (1884). History of Chicago. Vol. 1. P. 457. Chicago, IL: A. T. Andreas, Publisher. Google Books.

[43] Andreas, Alfred Theodore. (1884). History of Chicago. Vol. 1. P. 457. Chicago, IL: A. T. Andreas, Publisher. Google Books.

[44] Andreas, Alfred Theodore. (1884). History of Chicago. Vol. 1. P. 457. Chicago, IL: A. T. Andreas, Publisher. Google Books.

[45] Currey, Josiah Seymour. (1912). The Story of Old Fort Dearborn. P. 127. Chicago, IL: A. C. McClurg & Co. Google Books.

[46] Currey, Josiah Seymour. (1912). The Story of Old Fort Dearborn. P. 127. Chicago, IL: A. C. McClurg & Co. Google Books.

[47] Currey, Josiah Seymour. (1912). The Story of Old Fort Dearborn. P. 127. Chicago, IL: A. C. McClurg & Co. Google Books.

[48] Currey, Josiah Seymour. (1912). The Story of Old Fort Dearborn. P. 127. Chicago, IL: A. C. McClurg & Co. Google Books.

[49] Currey, Josiah Seymour. (1912). The Story of Old Fort Dearborn. P. 127. Chicago, IL: A. C. McClurg & Co. Google Books.

Potawatomies who delivered the warning message to the people of Fort Dearborn.[50]

The boat party departed from Fort Dearborn at the same time the garrison departed the fort, and, as Currey reported, "the boat was detained for a time while the party beheld the passage of the column just beginning its march."[51] Juliette Augusta (Magill) Kinzie, the daughter of Arthur Magill and Frances (Wolcott) Magill and the niece of Dr. Alexander Wolcott, wrote *Wau-Bun*, a memoir of pioneer settlement and experience in the Old Northwest. In *Wau-Bun*, Juliette Kinzie gave account of Eleanor (McKillip) Kinzie in the boat at Fort Dearborn: "Mrs. Kinzie 'was a woman of uncommon energy and strength of character,'" says the author of *Wau-Bun*, "'yet her heart died within her as she folded her arms around her helpless infants, and gazed upon the march of her husband and eldest child to certain destruction.'"[52] Currey noted that Antoine Ouilmette was considered to be part of the Potawatomie Tribe and could therefore remain at Fort Dearborn without fear of death. The Fort Dearborn garrison proceeded from the fort along the shore of Lake Michigan toward what would become the State of Indiana. As soon as the soldiers had left Fort Dearborn, the Potawatomies entered the fort, plundered it, and killed the loose Fort Dearborn livestock.[53]

The soldiers left the fort in peace and without any evidence of the massacre that was to occur right after. Mayor John Wentworth of Chicago lectured on the history of Fort Dearborn and Chicago and noted that the Native Americans who had resided near the fort were often friendly to the white settlers and tried to dissuade the Natives from more distant areas from hostilities toward the settlers. Along the route southeastward along Lake Michigan, the Potawatomie escort deviated from the course, acquired a large distance between himself and the soldiers, and disappeared over the long range of sandhills that existed there. Captain William Wells, who helped lead the garrison march, suddenly rode back to the men waving his hat in a circle, a gesture that meant that the men were surrounded by hostile Native Americans. Currey noted from the records that the, "Indians could now be seen in great numbers coming into view from behind the mounds of sand..."[54] Currey continued, "The troops were promptly formed and they had no sooner taken position than the Indians began firing upon them with deadly effect, the first victim

[50] Currey, Josiah Seymour. (1912). The Story of Old Fort Dearborn. Pp. 127-128. Chicago, IL: A. C. McClurg & Co. Google Books.
[51] Currey, Josiah Seymour. (1912). The Story of Old Fort Dearborn. P. 128. Chicago, IL: A. C. McClurg & Co. Google Books.
[52] Currey, Josiah Seymour. (1912). The Story of Old Fort Dearborn. Pp. 128-129. Chicago, IL: A. C. McClurg & Co. Google Books.
[53] Currey, Josiah Seymour. (1912). The Story of Old Fort Dearborn. Pp. 128-131. Chicago, IL: A. C. McClurg & Co. Google Books.
[54] Currey, Josiah Seymour. (1912). The Story of Old Fort Dearborn. Pp. 132-133. Chicago, IL: A. C. McClurg & Co. Google Books.

being a veteran of seventy years of age."[55] The Fort Dearborn soldiers, "fell rapidly under the withering fire of their. . .foes, who were now on all sides of them in overwhelming numbers."[56]

Throughout the course of the Battle of Fort Dearborn, the Natives and the soldiers switched positions, with the soldiers moving from the sandhills to an elevated place on the prairie, and the Natives moving from the prairie to the sandhills.[57] Much death and devasatation occurred. The bodies of the Fort Dearborn dead lay strewn about the prairie for four years, and, upon being discovered, were buried by the United States soldiers who came to rebuild Fort Dearborn.[58] Captain William Wells, "received a shot which passed through his lungs, and realizing that it was a mortal wound, he rode up to his niece, Mrs. Heald, still maintaining his position upon his horse. Seizing her hand, he exclaimed, 'farewell, my child.'"[59] After the battle was over, the Kinzie boat returned to the Kinzie House, "as it was impossible to continue their journey under the circumstances. . .trusting to the influence possessed by Mr. Kinzie to maintain their safety."[60]

John Kinzie joined the Kinzie boat passengers at the Kinzie House.[61] The Kinzies accompanied Chief Topenebe to St. Joseph River in Michigan, where the Kinzie family remained until November, 1812.[62] John Kinzie was captured and held as a prisoner of war by the British at Detroit, paroled, then later arrested on the grounds that the British suspected him of communicating with General William Henry Harrison. When the British officers in Detroit arranged for Kinzie to be sent to England, presumably to be tried as a war criminal, the British vessel on which Kinzie was held captive was, "chased by an American frigate and driven to Halifax [in what would become Canada]."[63] A. T. Andreas reported that a second attempt to transport John Kinzie to England failed when the vessel sprung a leak and was

---

[55] Currey, Josiah Seymour. (1912). The Story of Old Fort Dearborn. Pp. 132-133. Chicago, IL: A. C. McClurg & Co. Google Books.

[56] Currey, Josiah Seymour. (1912). The Story of Old Fort Dearborn. Pp. 138-139. Chicago, IL: A. C. McClurg & Co. Google Books.

[57] Currey, Josiah Seymour. (1912). The Story of Old Fort Dearborn. Pp. 138-140. Chicago, IL: A. C. McClurg & Co. Google Books.

[58] Currey, Josiah Seymour. (1912). The Story of Old Fort Dearborn. Pp. 138-141. Chicago, IL: A. C. McClurg & Co. Google Books.

[59] Currey, Josiah Seymour. (1912). The Story of Old Fort Dearborn. Pp. 138-141. Chicago, IL: A. C. McClurg & Co. Google Books.

[60] Currey, Josiah Seymour. (1912). The Story of Old Fort Dearborn. P. 150. Chicago, IL: A. C. McClurg & Co. Google Books.

[61] Currey, Josiah Seymour. (1912). The Story of Old Fort Dearborn. P. 150. Chicago, IL: A. C. McClurg & Co. Google Books.

[62] Currey, Josiah Seymour. (1912). The Story of Old Fort Dearborn. P. 170. Chicago, IL: A. C. McClurg & Co. Google Books.

[63] Andreas, Alfred Theodore. (1884). History of Chicago. Vol. 1. P. 74. Chicago, IL: A. T. Andreas, Publisher. Google Books.

forced to return to port.[64] Kinzie was thereafter imprisoned at Quebec, released, and allowed to return to his family in Detroit, where William Henry Harrison had his headquarters.[65] The Kinzies returned to Chicago in 1816, and the family returned to residence at the old Kinzie House.[66] Kinzie returned also to his work of silversmithing, trading with the Natives of the region, working closely with the American Fur Company, and through this work built a large business throughout the Great Lakes region extending from Chicago to Mackinac Island.[67]

Dr. Alexander Wolcott of Connecticut and Chicago

Dr. Alexander Wolcott (1790-1830) was the son of lawyer Alexander Wolcott, Sr. and Frances Burbank, and was the grandson of Dr. Alexander Wolcott and Mary (Richards) Wolcott.[68] Mary Richards was the sister of Guy Richards, who was the direct ancestor of the Taylor-Stryker-Henshaw-Prentiss-Richards family of Chicago, Springfield, Morgan County, and Cass County, Illinois. Dr. Alexander Wolcott of Chicago represented the United States government as Indian Agent at Chicago.[69] He succeeded Charles Jouett in that position in 1820 and remained in that position until his death in 1830.[70] Wolcott graduated from Yale in 1809 and was one of multiple Richards-Wolcott family members to relocate to the newly-formed communities of Chicago and Cook County.[71] Henry Wolcott, brother of Dr. Alexander, came to Chicago in 1836 and remained there until his death in 1846.[72] Prior to moving to Chicago, Henry Wolcott served as the Collector of the Port of Middletown, Connecticut, his home state, having been appointed to the

---

[64] Andreas, Alfred Theodore. (1884). History of Chicago. Vol. 1. P. 74. Chicago, IL: A. T. Andreas, Publisher. Google Books.

[65] Andreas, Alfred Theodore. (1884). History of Chicago. Vol. 1. P. 74. Chicago, IL: A. T. Andreas, Publisher. Google Books.

[66] Andreas, Alfred Theodore. (1884). History of Chicago. Vol. 1. P. 74. Chicago, IL: A. T. Andreas, Publisher. Google Books.

[67] Andreas, Alfred Theodore. (1884). History of Chicago. Vol. 1. P. 74. Chicago, IL: A. T. Andreas, Publisher. Google Books.

[68] Andreas, Alfred Theodore. (1884-1886). Reprint Edition, 1975. Vol. 1. Pp. 90-91. New York, NY: Arno Press. Google Books. Notice: Andreas erroneously identified Alexander Wolcott's mother as Lucy (Waldo) Wolcott. The mother was Frances (Burbanks) Wolcott.

[69] Andreas, Alfred Theodore. (1884-1886). Reprint Edition, 1975. Vol. 1. Pp. 90-91. New York, NY: Arno Press. Google Books.

[70] Andreas, Alfred Theodore. (1884-1886). Reprint Edition, 1975. Vol. 1. Pp. 90-91. New York, NY: Arno Press. Google Books.

[71] Andreas, Alfred Theodore. (1884-1886). Reprint Edition, 1975. Vol. 1. Pp. 90-91. New York, NY: Arno Press. Google Books.

[72] Andreas, Alfred Theodore. (1884-1886). Reprint Edition, 1975. Vol. 1. Pp. 90-91. New York, NY: Arno Press. Google Books.

office by President John Quincy Adams.[73] Henry Wolcott was the father of another Alexander Wolcott (not to be confused with Dr. Alexander Wolcott (1790-1830)), who served as the official Surveyor for Chicago and Cook County.[74]

The Marriage of Dr. Alexander Wolcott and Ellen Marion Kinzie of Chicago

Dr. Alexander Wolcott was a resident of the house known with formality as the Agency House, and with affectionate informality as "Cobweb Castle," located at the north side of the place where N. State Street intersects the Chicago River.[75] Chicago and Illinois historian Alfred Theodore Andreas noted that Wolcott's bachelor housekeeping merited the name of "Cobweb Castle" for the riverside residence.[76] The Wolcott and Kinzie families would intermarry twice: first, with the marriage of Dr. Alexander Wolcott and Ellen Marion Kinzie, who was the daughter of John Kinzie and Eleanor Kinzie; and second, with the marriage of John Harris Kinzie, who was the son of John Kinzie and Eleanor Kinzie, and Juliette Augusta Magill, who was the daughter of Arthur Magill and Frances (Wolcott) Magill, and the niece of Dr. Alexander Wolcott. John and Eleanor Kinzie sent their daughter, Ellen Marion, to school in Middletown, Connecticut, and it was in Connecticut that Ellen Marion met the Wolcott family.[77] The *Chicago Tribune* reported, "So when Dr. Wolcott came to Fort Dearborn the first person to greet him was Ellen Marion Kinzie, then about 15 years of age."[78] The *Chicago Tribune* centennial wedding memorial for the Wolcott-Kinzie wedding described the Wolcott-Kinzie courtship as follows: "[Ellen Marion] is described as 'a very comely lass' and no doubt it was her attractiveness that caused the young physician to tarry and become a permanent resident of the Fort Dearborn settlement."[79]

Dr. Alexander Wolcott married Ellen Marion Kinzie, the daughter of John Kinzie, on July 20, 1823.[80] The wedding took place at the Kinzie House and the ceremony was performed by Fulton County Justice of the Peace John Hamlin.[81]

---

[73] Andreas, Alfred Theodore. (1884-1886). Reprint Edition, 1975. Vol. 1. Pp. 90-91. New York, NY: Arno Press. Google Books.

[74] Andreas, Alfred Theodore. (1884-1886). Reprint Edition, 1975. Vol. 1. Pp. 90-91. New York, NY: Arno Press. Google Books.

[75] Andreas, Alfred Theodore. (1884-1886). Reprint Edition, 1975. Vol. 1. Pp. 90-91. New York, NY: Arno Press. Google Books.

[76] Andreas, Alfred Theodore. (1884-1886). Reprint Edition, 1975. Vol. 1. Pp. 90-91. New York, NY: Arno Press. Google Books.

[77] Chicago Tribune. (July 20, 1923). P. 3. Newspapers.com.

[78] Chicago Tribune. (July 20, 1923). P. 3. Newspapers.com.

[79] Chicago Tribune. (July 20, 1923). P. 3. Newspapers.com.

[80] Andreas, Alfred Theodore. (1884-1886). Reprint Edition, 1975. Vol. 1. Pp. 90-91. New York, NY: Arno Press. Google Books.

[81] Andreas, Alfred Theodore. (1884-1886). Reprint Edition, 1975. Vol. 1. Pp. 90-91. New York, NY: Arno Press. Google Books.

This wedding is often cited as the first wedding in the history of Chicago. At least two Native American Chiefs, who were friends of John Kinzie and Alexander Wolcott, attended the wedding and celebrated with the Wolcott and Kinzie families.[82] The Wolcott-Kinzie wedding was said to have been the first wedding in Chicago, but the marriage of Sarah Whistler to James Abbott of Detroit took place in 1804, preceding the Wolcott-Kinzie marriage by nineteen years.[83] Ellen Marion Kinzie has been identified by historical sources as the first white child born in Chicago.[84] Despite the occurrence of the Whistler-Abbott wedding of 1804, many Chicago historical sources nevertheless considered the Wolcott-Kinzie wedding to be the first wedding in Chicago history.[85]

The Wolcott-Kinzie wedding drew a large crowd of friends and family members, as was noted by the *Chicago Tribune* in its centennial memorial of the Wolcott-Kinzie wedding, July 20, 1923.[86] The family and friends of Alexander Wolcott and Ellen Marion Kinzie who attended the wedding were John Kinzie, Mrs. John Kinzie, John Harris Kinzie, Harris Kinzie, Robert Kinzie, Maria Indiana Kinzie, James Kinzie, Mr. and Mrs. Jean Baptiste Beaubien, Madore Beaubien, Mr. and Mrs. M. Du Pin, David McKee, Joseph Porthier, Victoire Mirandeau, Genevieve Mirandeau, Jean Baptiste Mirandeau, Mr. and Mrs. Antoine Ouilmette, Chief Che-Che-Pin-Quay (Alexander Robinson), and Chief Sauganash (Billy Caldwell).[87] The wedding guests described the Wolcott-Kinzie wedding as, "'the most scrumptious event of their lives.'"[88] The wedding feast consisted of wild game that was common around Fort Dearborn.[89] John Kinzie played several songs on his fiddle at the wedding party. "After the dinner the bride's father took his fiddle from a peg on the wall and played for the dance such airs as the 'Monie Musk,' 'Old Zip Coon,' 'Pop Goes the Weasel,' and 'Hell on the Wabash.'"[90] When Dr. Wolcott died in 1830, his widow, Ellen Marion, moved to Green Bay, in what would become the State of Wisconsin, to reside with her sister and brother-in-law, Maria Indiana Kinzie and Gen. David Hunter; David Hunter would become a Union Army General in the Civil War.[91] Alexander and Ellen Marion Wolcott had one child, a daughter, Mary, who died young.[92] David Hunter served at that time as the Commandant of Fort Howard, in what would become Wisconsin.[93]

---

[82] Chicago Tribune. (July 20, 1923). P. 3. Newspapers.com.
[83] The Evening Review. (East Liverpool, Ohio). (August 1, 1925). P. 4. Newspapers.com.
[84] Chicago Tribune. (October 15, 1899). P. 40. Newspapers.com.
[85] Chicago Tribune. (October 15, 1899). P. 40. Newspapers.com.
[86] Chicago Tribune. (July 20, 1923). P. 3. Newspapers.com.
[87] Chicago Tribune. (July 20, 1923). P. 3. Newspapers.com.
[88] Chicago Tribune. (July 20, 1923). P. 3. Newspapers.com.
[89] Chicago Tribune. (July 20, 1923). P. 3. Newspapers.com.
[90] Chicago Tribune. (July 20, 1923). P. 3. Newspapers.com.
[91] Chicago Tribune. (July 20, 1923). P. 3. Newspapers.com.
[92] Chicago Tribune. (July 20, 1923). P. 3. Newspapers.com.
[93] Chicago Tribune. (July 20, 1923). P. 3. Newspapers.com.

In 1820, Alexander Wolcott was a member of the exploration company whose purpose was the search and discovery of the source of the Mississippi River.[94] Governor Lewis Cass, Alexander Wolcott, Henry R. Schoolcraft, and Major Robert Forsyth constituted the exploration and discovery company and set out from Detroit on May 1, 1820.[95] The company returned to Lake Michigan in August, 1820, and at Green Bay the company divided into two companies: one company bound for the Mackinac Island and Straits of Mackinac, and the other company bound for Fort Dearborn and Chicago.[96] Wolcott, Forsyth, and Schoolcraft formed the company that journeyed from Green Bay to Chicago, which they reached on August 29, 1820.[97] Henry Schoolcraft described Wolcott favorably as one, "'commanding respect by his manners, judgment and intelligence.'"[98]

Alexander Wolcott, as United States Indian Agent, was an executor and signatory of the 1821 Treaty of Chicago, which ceded the land of the region to the United States.[99] John Kinzie, who held the position of Indian Sub-Agent, also signed the treaty, along with another Chicago founder, Jacob Butler Varnum.[100] In 1823, Wolcott moved into Fort Dearborn when the fortress was decommissioned by the United States government, and made Fort Dearborn, including the "post and property," a personal residence.[101] Wolcott occupied Fort Dearborn as a personal residence until the United States recommissioned the fort in 1828, at which time Wolcott and his family returned to the Agency House, "Cobweb Castle," and resumed residence there.[102] Alexander's will directed that his properties be transferred to his wife and child, but Ellen was his sole heir upon his death.[103] Ellen (Kinzie) Wolcott resided at the Agency House after the death of her husband until

---

[94] Andreas, Alfred Theodore. (1884-1886). Reprint Edition, 1975. Vol. 1. Pp. 90-91. New York, NY: Arno Press. Google Books.

[95] Andreas, Alfred Theodore. (1884-1886). Reprint Edition, 1975. Vol. 1. Pp. 90-91. New York, NY: Arno Press. Google Books.

[96] Andreas, Alfred Theodore. (1884-1886). Reprint Edition, 1975. Vol. 1. Pp. 90-91. New York, NY: Arno Press. Google Books.

[97] Andreas, Alfred Theodore. (1884-1886). Reprint Edition, 1975. Vol. 1. Pp. 90-91. New York, NY: Arno Press. Google Books.

[98] Andreas, Alfred Theodore. (1884-1886). Reprint Edition, 1975. Vol. 1. Pp. 90-91. New York, NY: Arno Press. Google Books.

[99] Andreas, Alfred Theodore. (1884-1886). Reprint Edition, 1975. Vol. 1. Pp. 90-91. New York, NY: Arno Press. Google Books.

[100] Andreas, Alfred Theodore. (1884-1886). Reprint Edition, 1975. Vol. 1. Pp. 90-91. New York, NY: Arno Press. Google Books.

[101] Andreas, Alfred Theodore. (1884-1886). Reprint Edition, 1975. Vol. 1. Pp. 90-91. New York, NY: Arno Press. Google Books.

[102] Andreas, Alfred Theodore. (1884-1886). Reprint Edition, 1975. Vol. 1. Pp. 90-91. New York, NY: Arno Press. Google Books.

[103] Andreas, Alfred Theodore. (1884-1886). Reprint Edition, 1975. Vol. 1. Pp. 90-91. New York, NY: Arno Press. Google Books.

1831.[104] A. T. Andreas included a lengthy letter from Alexander Wolcott to Governor Lewis Cass:

> "*Dear Governor:*— Thank God, I can at last in part disburthen my conscience of a crime that has long laid heavy upon it, the crime of neglecting to comply with your repeated requests respecting your queries. Many a time and oft, when I cast a rueful glance over the interminable string of 'Inquiries,' which could not be properly answered by a philosopher, till after at least ten years' study 'with all appliances and means to boot,' I have wished them at the bottom of the Red Sea, along with so many other wicked spirits, whose only object on earth was to disturb the repose of quiet, lazy people like myself. Could the necessary knowledge be acquired by the use of any kind of machinery, could it be accomplished by the use of steam it would be a matter of no difficulty. It is only to buy an engine, and the thing is done. But to find a person well acquainted with the Indian tongue who knows any thing about any other language on the face of the earth, or who can be made to comprehend its most simple principles, is a pretty impossible sort of an affair. Nevertheless, I have endeavored to do a little something to quiet certain stirrings and twitchings somewhere about the region of the pericardium, which have for a long time troubled me exceedingly; more especially whenever my eyes happened to rest upon a little ugly-looking book, full of notes of interrogation. That I have done so little, and that I have done that little so imperfectly, is only to be excused from the consideration that I have worked without tools. I have been in the situation, and met with the success, you will perhaps say, of a man who should attempt to polish a diamond with a wood rasp, or fashion a watch with a sledge hammer. That I have delayed it so long cannot be excused at all, unless you will accept of the true plea, that I was deterred by the hopelessness of the task, and you have full leave to laugh when I tell you that the confusion and want of arrangement in the papers arise from want of time. But it is literally true. Since I commenced my inquiries, some weeks ago, respecting the construction of the language, I have kept myself at it night and day: but I found such amazing difficulty at every step that my progress had been but slow, and it is now too late to make any attempt at arrangement, as Captain Whiting is ready to start. All, but what relates to language, has been written for a long time, and a meagre account it is. . ."[105]

---

[104] Andreas, Alfred Theodore. (1884-1886). Reprint Edition, 1975. Vol. 1. Pp. 90-91. New York, NY: Arno Press. Google Books.

[105] Andreas, Alfred Theodore. (1884-1886). Reprint Edition, 1975. Vol. 1. Pp. 90-91. New York, NY: Arno Press. Google Books.

Wolcott commented on the difficulty of translation and analysis that he personally encountered concerning the Native American languages of the Chicago region.[106]

Alexander Wolcott wrote many letters to his sister, Frances (Wolcott) Magill and many of these letters are extant. Wolcott wrote a letter on August 10, 1822, to Frances, who was then a resident of Glenhaven, Fishkill, New York.[107]

"My Dear Sister,

I am truly rejoiced to learn not only that you are [word not legible] settled down in your cottage at Glenhaven but that you are contented with the change. I visited Glenhaven repeatedly while in Fishkill and I can assure you I thought it one of the most romantic spots imaginable. I shall certainly come and live with you that is if I ever leave this odd out of the way place to which, to tell the truth I am becoming daily more attached."[108]

Alex Wolcott revealed in his late summer, 1822, letter to Frances that he was growing increasingly attached to Chicago, the minuscule frontier settlement of southwestern Lake Michigan.[109]

The inventory of annuities from July 15, 1826, identified each Potawatomie Chief to whom Dr. Wolcott paid an annuity when Wolcott served as United States Indian Agent.[110] Alexander Wolcott is counted among the most important of the founders of Chicago and Cook County, having served as the first permanent medical doctor in Chicago, in addition to having served in numerous other offices and capacities at Chicago and in Cook County.[111] Along with John Kinzie, J. B. Beaubien, and J. Crafts, Wolcott was one of the first and one of the founding settlers of Chicago and Cook County.[112] Wolcott House, Kinzie House, and Fort

---

[106] Andreas, Alfred Theodore. (1884-1886). Reprint Edition, 1975. Vol. 1. Pp. 90-91. New York, NY: Arno Press. Google Books.

[107] Letter of Dr. Alexander Wolcott to Frances Wolcott Magill. (August 10, 1822). Dr. Alexander Wolcott Collection. Chicago History Museum Research Center and Archives.

[108] Letter of Dr. Alexander Wolcott to Frances Wolcott Magill. (August 10, 1822). Dr. Alexander Wolcott Collection. Chicago History Museum Research Center and Archives.

[109] Letter of Dr. Alexander Wolcott to Frances Wolcott Magill. (August 10, 1822). Dr. Alexander Wolcott Collection. Chicago History Museum Research Center and Archives.

[110] A List of Chiefs of the Potawatomie Tribe of Indians to whom annuities were paid by Alex. Wolcott, Jr. Indian Agent. Chicago. (July 15, 1826). Dr. Alexander Wolcott Collection. Chicago History Museum Research Center and Archives.

[111] Kelly, Howard Atwood. (1920). A cyclopedia of American medical biography. P. 1252. Baltimore, MD: The Norman, Remington Company. Google Books; Call, Andrew Taylor. (2016). Faded Bricks: Old Family Tales from the South Side of Chicago. Hyde Park History, Vol. 38, (No. 4), Pp. 1-7. Chicago, IL: Hyde Park Historical Society.

[112] Currey, Josiah Seymour. (1918). Manufacturing and Wholesale Industries of Chicago. Vol. 1. P. 86. Chicago, IL: Thomas B. Poole Company. Google Books; Call, Andrew Taylor. (2016). Faded Bricks: Old Family Tales from the South Side of Chicago. Hyde Park History, Vol. 38, (No. 4), Pp. 1-7. Chicago, IL: Hyde Park Historical Society.

Dearborn constituted an architectural triad that signified and commemorated the birth of Chicago and Cook County.[113]

Wolcott was a real estate developer and owner, as proved by the fact that he Purchased Block 1 in Chicago, the place where Marina Towers is presently located.[114] The Wolcott Addition, along with the adjacent Kinzie Addition, constituted a central and principal quantity of the original real estate of Chicago. Alexander Wolcott and his father-in-law, John Kinzie, were two principal founders, early statesmen and officeholders, and founding urban developers and community builders of Chicago, as well as of Cook County.[115] Alexander Wolcott owned much of the land that would become State Street, and this street was, accordingly, originally known as Wolcott Street. The present Wolcott Avenue that runs from Rogers Park in the north to Englewood in the south was also named for Dr. Alexander Wolcott. Kinzie Street is named for John Kinzie. Other Chicago streets are named for Ellen Marion (Kinzie) Wolcott and Capt. William Wells.

John Harris Kinzie of Chicago

John Harris Kinzie was the son of John Kinzie and Eleanor (McKillip) Kinzie. John Harris Kinzie was the husband of Juliette Augusta Magill, who was the niece of Dr. Alexander Wolcott, and a cousin of the Strykers and Henshaws of Chicago and Central Illinois. Kinzie was a founder of the Chicago Board of Trade in April, 1848.[116] The publication known as *The Fifty-Fifth Annual Report of the Trade and Commerce of Chicago* (1912) contained a history of the leadership structures and staff of the Chicago Board of Trade. The founders of the Board of Trade included the following persons: Thomas Dyer, John P. Chapin, and Charles Walker served respectively as President and Vice-Presidents.[117] Gurdon Saltonstall Hubbard,

---

[113] Kelly, Howard Atwood. (1920). A cyclopedia of American medical biography. Pp. 1252-1253. Baltimore, MD: The Norman, Remington Company. Google Books; Call, Andrew Taylor. (2016). Faded Bricks: Old Family Tales from the South Side of Chicago. Hyde Park History, Vol. 38, (No. 4), Pp. 1-7. Chicago, IL: Hyde Park Historical Society.

[114] See: Marina City. Marinacity.org; Call, Andrew Taylor. (2016). Faded Bricks: Old Family Tales from the South Side of Chicago. Hyde Park History, Vol. 38, (No. 4), Pp. 1-7. Chicago, IL: Hyde Park Historical Society.

[115] The Rail-Roads, History and Commerce of Chicago: Three Articles Published in the Daily Democratic Press. (1854). Pp. 41-42. Chicago, IL: Democratic Press Job and Book Steam Printing Office; Call, Andrew Taylor. (2016). Faded Bricks: Old Family Tales from the South Side of Chicago. Hyde Park History, Vol. 38, (No. 4), Pp. 1-7. Chicago, IL: Hyde Park Historical Society.

[116] The Fifty-Fifth Annual Report of the Trade and Commerce of Chicago. (1913). P. VIII. Chicago, IL: Chicago Board of Trade. Hedstrom-Barry Co., Printers. Google Books.

[117] The Fifty-Fifth Annual Report of the Trade and Commerce of Chicago. (1913). P. VIII. Chicago, IL: Chicago Board of Trade. Hedstrom-Barry Co., Printers. Google Books.

Elisha S. Wadsworth, Thomas Richmond, John Rogers, Horatio G. Loomis, George F. Foster, Richard C. Bristol, John H. Dunham, Thomas Dyer, George A. Gibbs, John Harris Kinzie, Cyrenus Beers, Walter S. Gurney, Josiah H. Reed, Edward K. Rogers, Isaac H. Burch, Augustus H. Burley, John S. Read, William Butler Ogden, Orrington Lunt, Thomas Hale, Edward H. Hadduck, Isaac V. Jermain, and Laurin P. Hilliard constituted the founding board of directors of the Board of Trade.[118] William Loring Whiting served as the founding Secretary of the Board and Isaac Burch as its founding Treasurer.[119] William Loring Whiting was a third cousin of Charlotte (Stryker) Taylor, Henry Stryker Taylor, and the Stryker-Henshaw family of Chicago and Jacksonville, Illinois. The Whiting and Stryker-Henshaw consanguinity arose from the Prentis-Christophers-Leffingwell ancestry that the two branches of the larger family share in New England.

Founders of Rosehill Cemetery

John Harris Kinzie, William B. Ogden, John G. Hammond, Hiram A. Tucker, Levi D. Boone, Benjamin W. Raymond, Charles V. Dyer, James H. Reese, John Evans, Jonathan Burr, Levi B. Taft, E. K. Rogers, Robert H. Morford, Andrew T. Sherman, William Turner, George Schneider, C. H. Deihl, Andrew Nelson, James V. Z. Blaney, Henry Smith, Philo Judson, E. L. Jansen, and Francis H. Benson incorporated the Rosehill Cemetery Company.[120] The State of Illinois enacted the charter in February, 1859, according to Alfred Theodore Andreas.[121] The incorporators formed a Board of Consultation, with Kinzie, Ogden, Hammond, Tucker, Boone, Raymond, Dyer, Reese, Evans, Burr, Taft, Rogers, Morford, Sherman, Turner, Schneider, Deihl, and Nelson.[122] Benson, Jansen, Judson, Smith, and Blaney constituted the Board of Managers. The dedication of Rosehill Cemetery took place in July, 1859, in the presence of over 8,000 people.[123] Andrew Taylor Sherman, a co-founder and the first Treasurer of the Rosehill Cemetery Company, was a cousin both of Ada Willard (Richardson) Bunn and of the Willards of Chicago and Springfield (Chapter 5, *The Foundations of Jackson*

---

[118] The Fifty-Fifth Annual Report of the Trade and Commerce of Chicago. (1913). P. VIII. Chicago, IL: Chicago Board of Trade. Hedstrom-Barry Co., Printers. Google Books.

[119] The Fifty-Fifth Annual Report of the Trade and Commerce of Chicago. (1913). P. VIII. Chicago, IL: Chicago Board of Trade. Hedstrom-Barry Co., Printers. Google Books.

[120] Andreas, Alfred Theodore. (1884). History of Cook County, Illinois. P. 717. Chicago, IL: A. T. Andreas, Publisher. Google Books.

[121] Andreas, Alfred Theodore. (1884). History of Cook County, Illinois. P. 717. Chicago, IL: A. T. Andreas, Publisher. Google Books.

[122] Andreas, Alfred Theodore. (1884). History of Cook County, Illinois. P. 717. Chicago, IL: A. T. Andreas, Publisher. Google Books.

[123] Andreas, Alfred Theodore. (1884). History of Cook County, Illinois. P. 717. Chicago, IL: A. T. Andreas, Publisher. Google Books.

Park). The Rev. Josiah Brown family was the point of common Sherman and Willard ancestry. Roger Sherman (1721-1793), a founding father of the United States, was a first cousin of the Willards and Bunns through the Willard-Whiting-Brown family.

Stephen Williamson Stryker, the founder and President of Stryker & Barnes Company of Chicago, which was the largest fur garment manufacturer and dealer in both Chicago and the American West, was interred at Rosehill Cemetery. Morris Selz, founder and President of Selz, Schwab & Company, and a friend and business partner of John Whitfield Bunn, was also interred at Rosehill. For information on Stephen W. Stryker, Morris Selz, and John W. Bunn, please see Chapter 4, *Friends of the Leatherworkers*. Rosehill incorporators George Schneider and William B. Ogden were business associates of Jacob Bunn.

Truman Marcellus Post and the Posts of St. Louis

The Post family constitutes a branch of the Taylor-Stryker-Henshaw family of Chicago, St. Louis, Springfield, Morgan County, and Cass County, Illinois. The Posts resided in Jacksonville, Illinois, for a period, before relocating to St. Louis, Missouri, where they have remained for many generations. The Post family included lawyers and medical doctors, primarily, with the Illinois patriarch of the Post family having been an Illinois lawyer, a Christian minister, church leader, and Christian teacher. The Reverend Truman Marcellus Post (1810-1886) was the patriarch of the Posts of St. Louis and Illinois. Truman Marcellus Post was a pioneer real estate operator at Chicago, having been among the first landowners and land developers of the early settlement of Chicago.[124] Truman Post was a leader in the development of Congregational Christianity in Chicago and St. Louis, and this fact is proved by Post's service as a principal founder and long-time member of the Board of Directors of the Chicago Theological Seminary.[125] The Chicago Theological Seminary was located originally in the Lincoln Park community of Chicago, but relocated to the Hyde Park community many years

---

[124] Post, Truman Augustus. (1891). Truman Marcellus Post, D.D.: A Biography Personal and Literary. P. 112. Boston, MASS, and Chicago, IL: Congregational Sunday-School and Publishing Society. Google Books; Call, Andrew Taylor. (2016). Faded Bricks: Old Family Tales from the South Side of Chicago. Hyde Park History, Vol. 38, (No. 4), Pp. 1-7. Chicago, IL: Hyde Park Historical Society.

[125] Post, Truman Augustus. (1891). Truman Marcellus Post, D.D.: A Biography Personal and Literary. P. 218. Boston, MASS, and Chicago, IL: Congregational Sunday-School and Publishing Society. Google Books; Call, Andrew Taylor. (2016). Faded Bricks: Old Family Tales from the South Side of Chicago. Hyde Park History, Vol. 38, (No. 4), Pp. 1-7. Chicago, IL: Hyde Park Historical Society.

after its establishment.[126] Post was also a licensed Illinois lawyer.[127] As a Chicago city founder, and a church leader of St. Louis, Truman Post was recognized most prominently for his service as a minister of the Gospel of Jesus Christ.[128] While Post served and developed the Congregational Church primarily in St. Louis and in Jacksonville, Illinois, he also exerted tremendous impact on the development of the Congregational Church and Christian education at Chicago.[129] Dr. Post was Professor of Ecclesiastical History at the Chicago Theological Seminary and maintained a two-city ministry: a ministry to both St. Louis and Chicago.[130] Post remained a member of the board of directors of the Chicago Theological Seminary until his death in 1886.[131] Rev. Truman Marcellus Post was founder of both the Chicago Theological Seminary and the board of directors of the Seminary.[132]

Rev. Truman Post married Frances Alsop Henshaw in a double wedding. The other couple married at this wedding was that of Henry Brigham McClure and Harriet Hillhouse Henshaw. The wedding took place on October 5, 1835, in Middlebury, Vermont.[133] Both Truman Post and Henry Brigham McClure were

---

[126] Marlin-Warfield, Chris. Moving Forward. *Tower News*. Para. 5. Ctschicago.edu; Call, Andrew Taylor. (2016). Faded Bricks: Old Family Tales from the South Side of Chicago. Hyde Park History, Vol. 38, (No. 4), Pp. 1-7. Chicago, IL: Hyde Park Historical Society.

[127] See Generally: Post, Truman Augustus. (1891). Truman Marcellus Post, D.D.: A Biography Personal and Literary. P. 52. Boston, MASS, and Chicago, IL: Congregational Sunday-School and Publishing Society. Google Books; Call, Andrew Taylor. (2016). Faded Bricks: Old Family Tales from the South Side of Chicago. Hyde Park History, Vol. 38, (No. 4), Pp. 1-7. Chicago, IL: Hyde Park Historical Society.

[128] See generally: Post, Truman Augustus. (1891). Truman Marcellus Post, D.D.: A Biography Personal and Literary. Boston, MASS, and Chicago, IL: Congregational Sunday-School and Publishing Society. Google Books; Call, Andrew Taylor. (2016). Faded Bricks: Old Family Tales from the South Side of Chicago. Hyde Park History, Vol. 38, (No. 4), Pp. 1-7. Chicago, IL: Hyde Park Historical Society.

[129] See Generally: Post, Truman Augustus. (1891). Truman Marcellus Post, D.D.: A Biography Personal and Literary. Boston, MASS, and Chicago, IL: Congregational Sunday-School and Publishing Society. Google Books; Call, Andrew Taylor. (2016). Faded Bricks: Old Family Tales from the South Side of Chicago. Hyde Park History, Vol. 38, (No. 4), Pp. 1-7. Chicago, IL: Hyde Park Historical Society.

[130] Post, Truman Augustus. (1891). Truman Marcellus Post, D.D.: A Biography Personal and Literary. P. 218. Boston, MASS, and Chicago, IL: Congregational Sunday-School and Publishing Society. Google Books.

[131] Post, Truman Augustus. (1891). Truman Marcellus Post, D.D.: A Biography Personal and Literary. P. 218. Boston, MASS, and Chicago, IL: Congregational Sunday-School and Publishing Society. Google Books.

[132] Post, Truman Augustus. (1891). Truman Marcellus Post, D.D.: A Biography Personal and Literary. P. 218. Boston, MASS, and Chicago, IL: Congregational Sunday-School and Publishing Society. Google Books.

[133] Post, Truman Augustus. (1891). Truman Marcellus Post, D.D.: A Biography Personal and Literary. P. 74. Boston, MASS, and Chicago, IL: Congregational Sunday-School and Publishing Society. Google Books.

alumni of Middlebury College.[134] For information about the McClure family and Stryker family of Illinois and Michigan, and the Chicago histories of this branch of the family, see Chapter 6, *Sprinters of the Steel Track*. Truman M. Post and Frances (Henshaw) Post had the following children: Henry McClure Post, Martin Hayward Post, Catharine Harriet Post, Truman Augustus Post, Clara Harrison Post, and Frances Henshaw Post.[135] The family relocated to St. Louis and quickly became one of the most active families of civic leaders and professionals in St. Louis. Martin Hayward Post, son of Truman and Frances, became one of the most prominent ophthalmologists of St. Louis. Henry McClure Post and Truman Augustus Post were both famous St. Louis lawyers.[136] At approximately the same time when he married Frances Alsop Henshaw, Post had become a land speculator in Chicago, and owned multiple properties there.[137] The economic setbacks that confronted Post in 1837-1838, however, caused him to consider both a return to law practice and the sale of the Chicago lands that he owned.[138] Post related the following experiences regarding his time and business interests in Chicago:

> "'We entered Chicago by the trail of the Indians through the long grass of the prairie, for the most part of the year a marsh, but then dry. Fort Dearborn had a small garrison, and was the depot of government stores of various kinds for the Indians, of whom some 7,000, embracing extensively the tribes of the northwest, had rendezvoused here for a treaty. The place presented, besides the fort and its garrison, a small number of newly erected houses, principally cabins or shanties hurriedly put together, and wigwams or lodges of the Indians of the different tribes scattered about in the neighborhood. The germ of the town had already been laid off and platted on the south side of the river, and I felt so assured of its future

---

[134] Post, Truman Augustus. (1891). Truman Marcellus Post, D.D.: A Biography Personal and Literary. P. 16. Boston, MASS, and Chicago, IL: Congregational Sunday-School and Publishing Society. Google Books; McClure family history records.

[135] Post, Truman Augustus. (1891). Truman Marcellus Post, D.D.: A Biography Personal and Literary. P. 156. Boston, MASS, and Chicago, IL: Congregational Sunday-School and Publishing Society.

[136] McClure, Post, and Henshaw family historical records.

[137] Post, Truman Augustus. (1891). Truman Marcellus Post, D.D.: A Biography Personal and Literary. P. 112. Boston, MASS, and Chicago, IL: Congregational Sunday-School and Publishing Society. Google Books.

[138] Post, Truman Augustus. (1891). Truman Marcellus Post, D.D.: A Biography Personal and Literary. P. 112. Boston, MASS, and Chicago, IL: Congregational Sunday-School and Publishing Society. Google Books.

growth to considerable importance that I purchased a large part of one side of the public square, where now the courthouse stands, for $200. . ."" [139]

When Truman M. Post visited Chicago and purchased real estate interests there, Dr. Alexander Wolcott, a cousin of Post's wife, Frances Alsop (Henshaw) Post, had already been deceased for five years. Other Richards-Wolcott-Henshaw cousins remained in Chicago, however, as did the Whitings. [140] We will next briefly discuss the biographies of the children of Truman Marcellus Post and Frances Alsop (Henshaw) Post.

Truman Augustus Post (1837-1902) was one of the founders of the Bar Association of Saint Louis (St. Louis, Missouri), in April, 1874. [141] He served on the Committee on Admissions and the Committee on Grievances within the Bar Association of Saint Louis. He attended Illinois College and then Yale, and read law in the St. Louis law firm of Glover & Shepley. [142] He was admitted to the Missouri Bar in 1863. Post served as a soldier under Gen. Nathaniel Lyon when Lyon's troops seized Camp Jackson and helped preserve Missouri as a Union state. [143] Post served as private secretary to Illinois Governor Richard Yates, who was also a law partner of Henry McClure (McClure was the uncle of Truman A. Post). [144] In the Civil War Truman A. Post was a war correspondent, having reported on the events of the Battle of Shiloh in April, 1862. [145] Of significant interest and coincidence is the fact that Frederick Redfield Southmayd, Jr., a New Orleans cousin of the Posts of St. Louis, served in the Confederate Army and lost his right arm at the Battle of Shiloh. [146] Two cousins, therefore, Truman A. Post and Frederick R. Southmayd, Jr., experienced Shiloh in vastly diverse ways, and the Southmayd and Holmes families repatriated with subsequent fervent loyalty to the United States of America, and moved to Chicago. [147] Southmayd and his family later moved from Louisiana to Chicago, and partook of the civic and business

---

[139] Post, Truman Augustus. (1891). Truman Marcellus Post, D.D.: A Biography Personal and Literary. Pp. 59-60. Boston, MASS, and Chicago, IL: Congregational Sunday-School and Publishing Society. Google Books.

[140] Richards, Wolcott, Prentice, Henshaw, Whiting family historical records.

[141] Charter, Constitution and By-Laws of the Bar Association of the City of Saint Louis, And List of Officers And Members. (1885). St. Louis, MO: William J. Kesl, Printer and Stationer. Google Books.

[142] Thompson, Seymour D., and Jones, Leonard A. Editors. The American Law Review. (1902). Vol. 36. P. 250. St. Louis, MO: Review Publishing Company. Google Books.

[143] Thompson, Seymour D., and Jones, Leonard A. Editors. The American Law Review. (1902). Vol. 36. P. St. Louis, MO: Review Publishing Company. Google Books.

[144] Thompson, Seymour D., and Jones, Leonard A. Editors. The American Law Review. (1902). Vol. 36. P. 250. St. Louis, MO: Review Publishing Company. Google Books.

[145] Thompson, Seymour D., and Jones, Leonard A. Editors. The American Law Review. (1902). Vol. 36. P. 250. St. Louis, MO: Review Publishing Company. Google Books.

[146] Prentice, Southmayd, Henshaw family historical records.

[147] Prentice, Southmayd, Henshaw family historical records.

leadership of the city in the later nineteenth century.[148] For the Chicago history of the Southmayd and Holmes families, see Chapter 3, *The Horizons of Hyde Park*.

After the Civil War and after some years of law practice at St. Louis, Truman A. Post received appointment to the position of Supreme Court Reporter of Missouri.[149] Post reported and published twenty-three volumes of Supreme Court judgments and opinions for the State of Missouri (Volumes 42 through 64, inclusive both ends). Post was elected to the Missouri legislature, where he served two terms, 1872 and 1874.[150] Post was a member of the First Congregational Church of St. Louis, the church which his father, Truman Marcellus Post, founded and pastored. Truman Augustus Post earned the following eulogy from the St. Louis Bar Association, the law institution which he had co-founded: "'[Truman A. Post] was a well-endowed, well-cultured, brave, patient, laborious, strenuous, conscientious, unassuming, genial man, honored and beloved by all who knew him, who adorned his profession, and set a worthy example of intelligent and patriotic citizenship.'"[151] Truman A. Post never married.

Henry McClure Post (1840-1914) attended Yale and Illinois College, graduating from the latter.[152] He studied law and was admitted to the Missouri Bar in 1862. He practiced with his brother, Truman Augustus Post, in the Post Law Firm of St. Louis.[153] Henry McClure Post, M. S. Barnett, and Goldsmith Chandlee founded the Cuba Iron and Paint Mining Company in 1890. The company was a mining firm and paint manufacturer, was capitalized with $500,000, and possessed a corporate headquarters at East St. Louis, Illinois.[154] Henry married Emma Robb of Jacksonville, and at least three children were born to them: Harriet McClure Post, who married Dr. William Rawles, Ph.D.; Maud Henshaw Post; and Margaret Stanley Post, who married Henry Hunter Niemeyer of St. Louis. Rawles was the

[148] Prentice, Southmayd, Henshaw family historical records.
[149] Thompson, Seymour D., and Jones, Leonard A. Editors. The American Law Review. (1902). Vol. 36. P. 251. St. Louis, MO: Review Publishing Company. Google Books.
[150] Thompson, Seymour D., and Jones, Leonard A. Editors. The American Law Review. (1902). Vol. 36. P. 251. St. Louis, MO: Review Publishing Company. Google Books.
[151] Thompson, Seymour D., and Jones, Leonard A. Editors. The American Law Review. (1902). Vol. 36. P. 251. St. Louis, MO: Review Publishing Company. Google Books.
[152] Decennial Record of the Class of 1861, Yale College. (1872). P. 153. Cleveland, OH: Leader Printing Company. Google Books.
[153] Decennial Record of the Class of 1861, Yale College. (1872). P. 153. Cleveland, OH: Leader Printing Company. Google Books.
[154] The Age of Steel. (November 1, 1890). Vol. LXVIII. No. 18. P. 18. St. Louis, MO. Google Books; Chicago Journal of Commerce and Metal Industries. (1890). Vol. 57. Chicago, IL: Chicago Journal of Commerce Company. Google Books.

Dean of the School of Commerce and Finance at Indiana University in Bloomington.[155]

Martin Hayward Post (1851-1914) earned a Bachelor of Arts from Washington University in St. Louis and received a degree in medicine from St. Louis Medical College.[156] Post studied general surgery with Dr. John T. Hodgen, and afterward studied ophthalmology with Dr. John Green. Post continued the study of ophthalmology with Franciscus Cornelius Donders of Utrecht, and with Edward Nettleship of London.[157] Post returned to St. Louis and remained there as an ophthalmologist and civic leader. He was a member of the American College of Surgeons, the American Academy of Medicine, the St. Louis Academy of Science, the American Ophthalmological Society, and the Medical Society of City Hospital Alumni.[158] Post served as member of, and the Recording Secretary of, the St. Louis Medical Society and was President of the American Ophthalmological Society in 1914. He also held the Chairmanship of the Ophthalmological Section of the St. Louis Medical Society and was a gubernatorially-appointed member of the Board of Managers of the Missouri School for the Blind.[159] Post was, "an earnest Christian."[160] He was a member of the Congregational Church, and, "'never suffered to pass unheeded an opportunity to perform his duty as he saw it, or (in the words of Ian McLaren) 'to say a good word for Christ.'"[161] Dr. Martin H. Post

---

[155] Decennial Record of the Class of 1861, Yale College. (1872). P. 153. Cleveland, OH: Leader Printing Company. Google Books; St. Louis Post-Dispatch. (April 15, 1906). P. 6. Newspapers.com; The Indianapolis News. (August 11, 1947). P. 6. Newspapers.com.
[156] Kelly, Dr. Howard Atwood, and Burrage, Dr. Walter Lincoln. (1920). American Medical Biographies. P. 926. Baltimore, MD: The Norman, Remington Company. Google Books.
[157] Kelly, Dr. Howard Atwood, and Burrage, Dr. Walter Lincoln. (1920). American Medical Biographies. P. 926. Baltimore, MD: The Norman, Remington Company. Google Books.
[158] Kelly, Dr. Howard Atwood, and Burrage, Dr. Walter Lincoln. (1920). American Medical Biographies. P. 926. Baltimore, MD: The Norman, Remington Company. Google Books.
[159] Kelly, Dr. Howard Atwood, and Burrage, Dr. Walter Lincoln. (1920). American Medical Biographies. P. 926. Baltimore, MD: The Norman, Remington Company. Google Books.
[160] Kelly, Dr. Howard Atwood, and Burrage, Dr. Walter Lincoln. (1920). American Medical Biographies. P. 926. Baltimore, MD: The Norman, Remington Company. Google Books.
[161] Kelly, Dr. Howard Atwood, and Burrage, Dr. Walter Lincoln. (1920). American Medical Biographies. P. 926. Baltimore, MD: The Norman, Remington Company. Google Books.

married, first, Mary Laurence Tyler of Louisville, Kentucky, and second, Mary Brown Tanner of Jacksonville, Illinois.[162]

Clara Harrison Post (1846-1885), daughter of Rev. Truman Marcellus Post and Frances Alsop (Henshaw) Post, married Daniel Comstock Young of St. Louis.[163] Frances Henshaw Post (1836-1916), daughter of Rev. Truman Marcellus Post and Frances Alsop (Henshaw) Post, married Jacob Van Norstrand.[164] Lawyer Truman Post Young, son of Daniel Comstock Young and Clara Harrison (Post) Young, served as Assistant City Counselor to the City of St. Louis.[165] Daniel Comstock Young was the manager of the St. Louis branch of Browning, King & Company, a clothing company, and was a partner and owner of the company.[166] Browning, King & Company was formed in 1868 by William Browning and Edward Dewey of New York City, and Henry King of Chicago. The company possessed an immense presence in Chicago and was reported to have been the largest manufacturer of ready-made clothing in the world in 1890. The company generated annual revenue of $6,000,000 as of December 27, 1890, manufactured 1,367,000 garments that same year, and operated branches in St. Louis, Chicago, Cincinnati, Kansas City, Missouri, Milwaukee, St. Paul, Minneapolis, Brooklyn, and Omaha, also in 1890.[167]

The company opened the Chicago branch in 1873.[168] Daniel Comstock Young, who became a partner and owner of Browning, King & Company, was the founding manager of the St. Louis branch of Browning, King & Company, and prior to that time had been partner in the clothing firm of Young Brothers & Company of St. Louis.[169] Henry W. King (1828-1898) was President of the Chicago Relief and Aid Society.[170] King, William Browning, Edward Dewey, Daniel Comstock Young, and many others built the firm of Browning, King & Company into the largest wholesale clothing manufacturer in the United States.[171] King was active in church and civic work in Chicago and the historical record proves that King was a friend of Rev. Melancthon Woolsey Stryker of Fourth

[162] Kelly, Dr. Howard Atwood, and Burrage, Dr. Walter Lincoln. (1920). American Medical Biographies. P. 926. Baltimore, MD: The Norman, Remington Company. Google Books.
[163] St. Louis Post-Dispatch. (May 3, 1917). P. 7. Newspapers.com.
[164] Frances Henshaw (Post) Van Norstrand. Findagrave.com.
[165] St. Louis Post-Dispatch. (May 3, 1917). P. 7. Newspapers.com.
[166] St. Louis Post-Dispatch. (May 3, 1917). P. 7. Newspapers.com.
[167] Frank Leslie's Illustrated Newspaper. (December 27, 1890). Vol. LXXI. No. 1841. P. 397. Google Books.
[168] Frank Leslie's Illustrated Newspaper. (December 27, 1890). Vol. LXXI. No. 1841. P. 397. Google Books.
[169] St. Louis Post-Dispatch. (March 8, 1903). P. 16. Newspapers.com; St. Louis Post-Dispatch. (May 3, 1917). P. 7. Newspapers.com.
[170] New York Times. (April 14, 1898). P. 9. Newspapers.com.
[171] New York Times. (April 14, 1898). P. 9. Newspapers.com.

Presbyterian Church, Chicago.[172] *The New York Times* obituary for Henry W. King, appearing in the April 14, 1898, edition of the paper, stated, "President Stryker of Hamilton College will probably deliver the funeral oration."[173] King organized Barrett, King & Company in about 1854 in Chicago, and this firm subsequently became Browning, King & Company.[174] Stryker not only returned to Chicago, but returned to his former church pulpit at Fourth Presbyterian Church, to deliver the eulogy for Henry W. King on April 17, 1898.[175] King was a member and elder of Fourth Presbyterian Church and was a friend and colleague of Rev. Stryker in Chicago.[176] Stryker gave the following prayer at Henry King's funeral:

> "'We cannot forbear to entreat thee today for our land and for its rulers, and to ask thy blessing upon the President of these United States, and all who with him execute and maintain authority and law. Grant, Lord, that our flag may be washed in purity, and that in the name of the Lord we may lift up our banners. Chasten and purge us from all unholiness and all revengeful and bitter partisanship, that if thou dost call us as avengers to service that our sword may be made in heaven and that we may commit our souls to him that doeth right business.'"[177]

After this prayer, Rev. Stryker delivered the eulogy for Henry King. The eulogy emphasizes and exalts the absolute importance of bringing God, His commandments, His purposes, and His blessings to the world of civic and business affairs, so that the Father, Jesus Christ, and the Holy Spirit are exalted in business and civic work. Rev. Stryker's eulogy for Henry W. King included the following words:

"Eulogy of Henry W. King"

> "'No privilege could be greater to me than to be permitted in a few words to pay with you a tribute to the memory of a good man. I am not here to weave or to recite any mere fancies or eulogies, but it becomes a congregation and a church like this to recognize and to speak at such a time of what it has had and what it has. Those having acquaintance—and there are several here who knew him better than I, who only knew him in a general way—know what the life of our friend was as a citizen of a great city. It was lived here almost as boy and man and you knew him.

---

[172] New York Times. (April 14, 1898). P. 9. Newspapers.com.
[173] New York Times. (April 14, 1898). P. 9. Newspapers.com.
[174] New York Times. (April 14, 1898). P. 9. Newspapers.com.
[175] Chicago Tribune. (April 18, 1898). P. 7. Newspapers.com.
[176] Chicago Tribune. (April 18, 1898). P. 7. Newspapers.com.
[177] Chicago Tribune. (April 18, 1898). P. 7. Newspapers.com.

With whatever this city had of the highest, commercial, social, political, Henry W. King was identified, and I am confident and know that I do not dissent from the common judgment and estimation of this congregation and of that throng who knew and loved and appreciated him, to say that he lived well that difficult life, the life of a sincere and conscientious Christian merchant. If there were rebuke needed of the falsehood that the gospel of God is incompatible with business and that one cannot take the ten commandments and the beatitudes into the market and into the currents of this world's most active affairs our friend's life is the answer. He found room in a busy life to make a little space in every day for the life of the gospel. If you say to me that material things are so commanding and so preoccupying that you have not time to live the deepest and think the best I point you again to this life as the answer. Our friend found time for meditation; he found time for high thinking. He found time for many and always the best books and he found time for his Bible, and that no man can gainsay.'

Ever Ready to Aid the Needy

'It is a common enough phrase to say that if you wish to have work done in this world you must go to a busy man, and this man was busy. This busy man bore—and increasingly toward the latter years of his life—the burdens of others. Mr. King knew how to seek out the widow and the fatherless in their affliction and to keep himself unspotted from the world, and there are many others, too, who can raise their hands and say, 'I also loved him for what he was to me.' None would bow his head more quickly in acknowledgment of imperfection, but he tried and triumphantly followed his Lord and yours.

But it is not as a citizen, it is not merely as a counselor or a benefactor, that we speak of the man. Mr. King was a good church man—he was a member of the church of God. He gave to Christ in his early life an intelligent and a complete surrender. He went in and out before this congregation as an office bearer for nearly forty years. We shall never forget some of those prayers of his; we shall not forget his presence. We shall not hear again that strong and courageous and faithful voice, but the church he loved and served will live the longer and larger life for his life.'"[178]

Rev. Melancthon W. Stryker was a member of the Stryker family of Chicago, New York, and New Jersey, and his biography is contained in Chapter 2, *Builders of the Downtown*. The lives and work of the Posts of St. Louis and Chicago, Henry W.

---

[178] Chicago Tribune. (April 18, 1898). P. 7. Newspapers.com.

King of Chicago, and Daniel Comstock Young of St. Louis, show that great businesses are built upon honor and integrity. These people built what was once the largest clothing company in the world, and they placed Chicago and St. Louis at the center of this great company. We will next look at the work of Robert Irwin of St. Louis and Springfield, whose service in Illinois banking included the government and administration of the first bank in Chicago.

Robert Irwin, John Harris Kinzie, and the First Bank of Chicago

Robert Irwin (1808-1865) of St. Louis and Springfield gained an important leadership connection to the first bank in Chicago when he was elected to the board of directors of the State Bank of Illinois in 1840.[179] The State Bank of Illinois consisted of a parent corporation that comprised multiple subsidiaries, known as bank branches. Robert Irwin, John Irwin, Sarah Irwin, who married Benjamin Ferguson, and possibly other members of the Irwin family came from Monongahela City, Pennsylvania, to St. Louis and Springfield in the early nineteenth century.[180] For the genealogy of the Irwin family and how the Irwins connect to the Bunns and Fergusons of Springfield and Chicago, see Chapter 6, *Sprinters of the Steel Track*.

Alfred Theodore Andreas explained that the Chicago Branch of the State Bank of Illinois was established in June, 1835, and was the first bank to exist at Chicago.[181] Robert Irwin served on the board of directors of the parent State Bank of Illinois corporation at Springfield, which held leadership and jurisdiction over all of the branches, including the Chicago Branch. The founders of the Chicago Branch of the State Bank of Illinois were John Harris Kinzie, Gurdon S. Hubbard, Peter Pruyne, E. K. Hubbard, R. J. Hamilton, Walter Kimball, H. B. Clarke, G. W. Dole, and Edmund D. Taylor, who also collectively constituted the bank's first board of directors.[182] John H. Kinzie served as the first President of the Chicago Branch and W. H. Brown served as the first Cashier.[183] The office of the Chicago Branch was opened at the offices of Garrett, Brown, & Brother.[184] The branch opened in December, 1835, at LaSalle and S. Water Street.[185] Nathaniel Jennison

---

[179] Irwin family historical records.

[180] Irwin family historical records.

[181] Andreas, Alfred Theodore. (1884). History of Chicago. Vol. 1. Pp. 527-528. Chicago, IL: A. T. Andreas, Publisher. Google Books.

[182] Andreas, Alfred Theodore. (1884). History of Chicago. Vol. 1. Pp. 527-528. Chicago, IL: A. T. Andreas, Publisher. Google Books.

[183] Andreas, Alfred Theodore. (1884). History of Chicago. Vol. 1. Pp. 527-528. Chicago, IL: A. T. Andreas, Publisher. Google Books.

[184] Andreas, Alfred Theodore. (1884). History of Chicago. Vol. 1. Pp. 527-528. Chicago, IL: A. T. Andreas, Publisher. Google Books.

[185] Andreas, Alfred Theodore. (1884). History of Chicago. Vol. 1. Pp. 527-528. Chicago, IL: A. T. Andreas, Publisher. Google Books.

Brown and Augustus Garrett not only offered their company office as the opening space for the Chicago Branch, but they also held the distinction of being among the largest depositors, if not the largest depositors, of the bank.[186] Brown and Garrett deposited more than $34,000 in account at the Chicago Branch between December, 1835, and February, 1836.[187] Nathaniel J. Brown was a third cousin of Lucy (Willard) Richardson and of the Richardson family of Chicago and Springfield. The Brown genealogy and history are discussed in Chapter 5, *The Foundations of Jackson Park*. The common ancestors of the Willard-Richardson family and the Browns of Chicago, Lemont, and Cook County were Joseph Browne and Ruhamah (Wellington) Brown of Barnstable and Lexington, Massachusetts. In conclusion, Robert Irwin, the uncle of Elizabeth Jane (Ferguson) Bunn, helped govern and manage the first bank in Chicago history as a member of the board of directors of the State Bank of Illinois.

To Cross the Calumet with Iron Horses

The present section concerns the railroad histories of the Stryker and Bunn families of Chicago. For information concerning the James Monroe Stryker branch of the Richards-Wolcott-Henshaw-Stryker-Taylor macro-family, please consult the following chapter: *The Horizons of Hyde Park*. For access to the Stephen Williamson Stryker history element of the Richards-Wolcott-Henshaw-Stryker-Taylor macro-family, please consult the following chapter: *Friends of the Leatherworkers*. For the Stryker, Taylor, and Pierson branches of the Stryker macro-family of Chicago, please consult the more extensive history of those branches in the following chapter: *Sprinters of the Steel Track*.

John Stryker, Esq.:

The State of New York Helps to Build Chicago

There is a river that lies within the south side of Chicago, whose course and current constitute one of the foundations of American economic and geopolitical history. That river is the Calumet River and its geographical and geo-economic vicinities constitute the Calumet Corridor. John Stryker of Rome, New York, along with James Joy, Elisha Litchfield, John B. Jervis, and others, would change simultaneously the futures of Chicago, Cook County, the State of Illinois, and the United States when they brought the iron horse through the Calumet Corridor to the young city among the Wild Onions of Lake Michigan's western shores. John Stryker and his partners were arguably the most important fathers of the Chicago and Calumet Corridor railroad industry and the Great Lakes railroad industries.

---

[186] Andreas, Alfred Theodore. (1884). History of Chicago. Vol. 1. Pp. 527-528. Chicago, IL: A. T. Andreas, Publisher. Google Books.
[187] Andreas, Alfred Theodore. (1884). History of Chicago. Vol. 1. Pp. 527-528. Chicago, IL: A. T. Andreas, Publisher. Google Books.

Rome, located in Oneida County, New York, played one of the most important roles any place ever would in the creation and development of Chicago's railroad industries, infrastructures, and economies.

A company of visionary transportation developers from New York and Michigan would start, build, and develop what would become the most important Great Lakes railroad network. Their work began with the Michigan Southern Railroad Company and culminated in the New York Central Railroad Company, which was the largest corporation in the world at the time of its formation and would remain one of the world's largest corporations throughout its entire organizational existence. John Stryker was founder of the following companies that tremendously impacted the growth of Chicago and the Great Lakes: the Michigan Southern Railroad Company; the Lake Shore and Northern Indiana Railroad Company; the Northern Indiana and Chicago Railroad Company; the Lake Shore and Michigan Southern Railroad Company; the Chicago and Rock Island Railroad Company; and the New York Central Railroad Company. John Stryker and the Rome-Chicago Network of railroad financing and construction would lead to the creation of one of the largest and most significant transportational, geopolitical, economic, and industrial combinations in all recorded history.

This entire book represents a study of constitutions. Charters and articles of incorporation, the laws by which companies and other organizations are established, are constitutions. These laws are constitutions of companies and civic organizations. This book will, therefore, analyze multiple constitutions. The constitutions of the companies and civic organizations discussed herein have served not only as foundations of institutions, but also as the very grounds for the geographical, industrial, economic, and political development of Chicago and Cook County.

John Stryker and The Northern Indiana Railroad

John Stryker and his associates established a company pursuant to the law of February 11, 1848, a statute which created the regime under which railroad companies could be incorporated. The Northern Indiana Railroad Company was incorporated on March 3, 1851.[188] The purpose of the company was to construct continuous railroad routes from Toledo, Ohio, to Chicago, and from Toledo to Detroit.[189] The Toledo-Chicago route would be achieved by construction of a route from Toledo to the Ohio-Indiana state line at Williams County, at which point the

---

[188] The Charter And Laws Of The States Of Ohio, Indiana, Michigan and Illinois, Relating To The Michigan Southern and Northern Indiana Railroad Rail-Road Company. (1855). New York, NY: John Amerman, Printer. Google Books.
[189] The Charter And Laws Of The States Of Ohio, Indiana, Michigan and Illinois, Relating To The Michigan Southern and Northern Indiana Railroad Rail-Road Company. (1855). New York, NY: John Amerman, Printer. Google Books.

Buffalo & Mississippi Railroad Company would complete the route to Chicago. The Toledo-Detroit route would be achieved through construction of a route from Toledo to Monroe, Michigan, where the road would connect to, "any rail-road running from the direction of Detroit to the City of Toledo."[190] The law that incorporated the company identified the incorporators as John Stryker, John B. Jervis, Elisha C. Litchfield, Edwin C. Litchfield, Dennison Steele, John Fitch, John H. Whitaker, Edward Haskell, Thomas S. Stanfield, Charles Butler, and William C. Hannah.[191] The 1851 statute attached perpetuity of succession to the company, and attached by general reference the operational rights, powers, and duties relevant to the corporate purpose of railroad business.

The financing of the company consisted of the authorization of $500,000 in stock money, divisible by 5,000 shares of $100 values.[192] The charter set a limit of $1,000,000 on the company equity money, thereby allowing for progressive capitalization to continue for an additional amount of $500,000.[193] The financing contemplated by the law was simple and was not described further in the statute. John Stryker and the other men named in the Act were authorized to choose the time and place for the opening of subscription for the capital stock of the company. The law set a condition for the assembly of the original stockholder conference, and this condition required that $50,000 of the $500,000 stock money be subscribed before Stryker and the other incorporators could summon the stockholder conference.[194] The purpose of the stockholder meeting was to elect the board of directors. Section 4 of the law granted the company the powers of sale and negotiation of bonds and notes. The purpose of Section 4 was to enable corporate financing through debt moneys.[195] Section 5 of the law contained grants of connection rights to the company such that the company could connect to any other railroad company incorporated in either Michigan or Indiana. Section 5

---

[190] The Charter And Laws Of The States Of Ohio, Indiana, Michigan and Illinois, Relating To The Michigan Southern and Northern Indiana Railroad Rail-Road Company. (1855). New York, NY: John Amerman, Printer. Google Books.
[191] The Charter And Laws Of The States Of Ohio, Indiana, Michigan and Illinois, Relating To The Michigan Southern and Northern Indiana Railroad Rail-Road Company. (1855). New York, NY: John Amerman, Printer. Google Books.
[192] The Charter And Laws Of The States Of Ohio, Indiana, Michigan and Illinois, Relating To The Michigan Southern and Northern Indiana Railroad Rail-Road Company. (1855). New York, NY: John Amerman, Printer. Google Books.
[193] The Charter And Laws Of The States Of Ohio, Indiana, Michigan and Illinois, Relating To The Michigan Southern and Northern Indiana Railroad Rail-Road Company. (1855). New York, NY: John Amerman, Printer. Google Books.
[194] The Charter And Laws Of The States Of Ohio, Indiana, Michigan and Illinois, Relating To The Michigan Southern and Northern Indiana Railroad Rail-Road Company. (1855). New York, NY: John Amerman, Printer. Google Books.
[195] The Charter And Laws Of The States Of Ohio, Indiana, Michigan and Illinois, Relating To The Michigan Southern and Northern Indiana Railroad Rail-Road Company. (1855). New York, NY: John Amerman, Printer. Google Books.

granted the right to consolidate capital stock with the stock money of other railroad companies formed in Michigan or Indiana.[196] John Stryker also founded the Chicago, St. Charles, Mississippi & Air-Line Railroad Company, a company that contributed some of the earliest transportation development and route infrastructure for Chicago and Cook County, particularly the western part of the county.[197]

Alfred Theodore Andreas establishes the history of the Michigan Southern Railroad Company system in his work, *History of Chicago: Ending with the Year 1857*. The *Detroit Free Press* of August 8, 1849, reported that John Stryker, Elisha C. Litchfield, Edwin C. Litchfield, George Bliss, Joel Rathbone, Charles Noble, and Charles Butler were all members of the Finance Committee for the Michigan Southern Railroad Company.[198] These men had hired two teams of engineers to plan the construction of the railroad westward from the Detroit metropolitan region toward western Michigan, Indiana, and Chicago.[199] Coldwater and Hillsdale, Michigan, were two immediate route objectives for the Michigan Southern Railroad at the time of the *Detroit Free Press* report.[200]

The Northern Indiana Railroad Company began a financing plan in November, 1851, which was advertised in the November 5, 1851, edition of the *Hartford Courant*, a Connecticut newspaper.[201] The Connecticut article contained two reports: the first report was a generalized company financial report for the Northern Indiana; the second report described the development of the multilateral corporate construction and transportation network of Chicago and the Great Lakes that John Stryker and his colleagues were building.[202] The transportation development report, discussed farther below, described the Stryker plans for an integrated Great Lakes railroad system with Chicago at the center.[203] The financial report contained the following information: the advertised corporate financing plan was a debt financing plan, and consisted of the issuance of mortgage bonds that bore seven percent interest rates, and ten-year maturity times.[204] The company expected to sell $600,000 of the mortgage bonds.[205]

The report contained a notice that the mortgage associated with the debt financing plan was both the sole lien against the company and the first lien against

---

[196] The Charter And Laws Of The States Of Ohio, Indiana, Michigan and Illinois, Relating To The Michigan Southern and Northern Indiana Railroad Rail-Road Company. (1855). New York, NY: John Amerman, Printer. Google Books.
[197] Chicago Tribune. (April 7, 1853). P. 2. Newspapers.com.
[198] Detroit Free Press. (August 8, 1849). P. 2. Newspapers.com.
[199] Detroit Free Press. (August 8, 1849). P. 2. Newspapers.com.
[200] Detroit Free Press. (August 8, 1849). P. 2. Newspapers.com.
[201] Hartford Courant. (November 5, 1851). P. 3. Newspapers.com.
[202] Hartford Courant. (November 5, 1851). P. 3. Newspapers.com.
[203] Hartford Courant. (November 5, 1851). P. 3. Newspapers.com.
[204] Hartford Courant. (November 5, 1851). P. 3. Newspapers.com.
[205] Hartford Courant. (November 5, 1851). P. 3. Newspapers.com.

the company.[206] The report contained the "sole lien" notice to convey to the investor audience these three interlocking promises: the promise of capital adequacy, and that the company was not overburdened with debt moneys, the promise that the concomitant corporate insolvency risk was low, and the promise that safety and soundness defined the capital structure and financial risk allocation of the company at that time.[207] The statutory law of the State of Indiana granted the right to the company to issue the debt moneys and to undertake the financing plan in Indiana.[208] The Northern Indiana Railroad Company produced security interests for the prospective bondholders by means of a mortgage which permitted the issuance of $1,000,000 in mortgage bonds under the financing plan.[209]

The transportation development report for the Northern Indiana Railroad contained descriptions of the overall plan that John Stryker, Edwin C. Litchfield, George Bliss, Hugh White, Calvin Burr, and others had framed in order to build the railroad infrastructures of Chicago and the Great Lakes states.[210] The February 15, 1853, edition of *The New York Times* partially described the multilateral nature of the John Stryker railroad system of Chicago, Indiana, Ohio, Michigan, and New York.[211] The description occurred in a syndicated report from the *Galena Advertiser* of Illinois, and stated the following about the Michigan Southern and Northern Indiana Railroad Company:

> "The road was first projected by the State of Michigan; but, in 1849, it was found to be the property of E. C. LITCHFIELD of Detroit, his brother, and the following New York gentlemen: John Striker [sic], Charles Butler, Gov. Hunt, George Bliss, Gov. Marcy, Hugh White, and some others; and the Board of Directors now consists of the following gentlemen: Elisha C. Litchfield, John Striker [sic], George Bliss, Gov. Marcy, Charles Noble, Hugh White, John B. Jervis, Charles Butler, and Edwin C. Litchfield. In the completion of this road to Chicago, the Company in twelve months, 'laid down over two hundred miles of T rail, a task never before accomplished by any Railroad in the United States in the same length of time.'"[212]

The syndicated Galena report also indicated that John Stryker, Elisha C. Litchfield, Edwin C. Litchfield, Charles Butler, Charles Noble, Hugh White, John B. Jervis, George Bliss, and Governors Marcy and Hunt were the founders and

---

[206] Hartford Courant. (November 5, 1851). P. 3. Newspapers.com.
[207] Hartford Courant. (November 5, 1851). P. 3. Newspapers.com.
[208] Hartford Courant. (November 5, 1851). P. 3. Newspapers.com.
[209] Hartford Courant. (November 5, 1851). P. 3. Newspapers.com.
[210] Hartford Courant. (November 5, 1851). P. 3. Newspapers.com.
[211] The New York Times. (February 15, 1853). P. 8. Newspapers.com.
[212] The New York Times. (February 15, 1853). P. 8. Newspapers.com.

owners of the St. Charles and Mississippi Railroad Company of Chicago.[213] John Stryker, the Litchfield brothers of Detroit, and several other men retained membership on the board of directors of the Michigan Southern and Northern Indiana Railroad for many years, as was indicated by the notice of election of directors for the corporation that appeared in the August 20, 1857, edition of the *New York Tribune*.[214]

The September 5, 1853, edition of the *Buffalo Daily Courier* of New York carried a report from the *Cleveland Herald* of Ohio that John Stryker, E. C. Litchfield, E. B. Litchfield, Hon. Samuel F. Vinton, C. K. Buall, William Jarvis, and Hon. E. Lane, formed the Cleveland and Toledo Railroad Company.[215] The Cleveland & Toledo company resulted from the joinder of the Junction Railroad Company, and the Cleveland, Norwalk, and Toledo Railroad Company.[216] The road constituted another corporate element of the Chicago-Great Lakes railroad company network that Stryker, the Litchfields, and multiple others had planned.[217] Samuel Vinton of Gallipolis, Ohio, a town located on the Ohio River, and across from West Virginia, provided the key leadership of the Cleveland and Toledo Railroad Company.[218] The Cleveland journalist noted the high reputation that Vinton possessed for business abilities.[219]

The *Detroit Free Press* criticized "Judge Stryker," as it named him, and the Michigan Southern Railroad Company, for their attempts to secure a transportation monopoly over the Calumet River corridor of Indiana in January, 1851, thereby excluding from that market the Michigan Central Railroad Company.[220] Stryker, Charles Butler, and other Michigan Southern men were at Indianapolis and were accused of lobbying for the passage of an Indiana statute that would grant the Southern the exclusive rights over the Calumet Corridor that connects Chicago to the rest of Indiana.[221] The *Detroit Free Press* journalist worried that the Indiana legislature would enact a law that would create a regime in which the Michigan Southern would possess all railroad market power in the Lake Michigan region of Indiana, and that this Calumet monopoly would be injurious to the Michigan railroad market.[222] Stryker officially denied that he was party to the pleading for the legislative grant of the Calumet monopoly according to the Detroit report, and responded to the Michigan accusal with the statement that the Indiana bill of 1850

---

[213] The New York Times. (February 15, 1853). P. 8. Newspapers.com.
[214] New York Tribune. (August 20, 1857). P. 2. Newspapers.com.
[215] Buffalo Daily Courier. (September 5, 1853). Newspapers.com.
[216] Buffalo Daily Courier. (September 5, 1853). Newspapers.com.
[217] Buffalo Daily Courier. (September 5, 1853). Newspapers.com.
[218] Buffalo Daily Courier. (September 5, 1853). Newspapers.com.
[219] Buffalo Daily Courier. (September 5, 1853). Newspapers.com.
[220] Detroit Free Press. (January 20, 1851). P. 2. Newspapers.com.
[221] Detroit Free Press. (January 20, 1851). P. 2. Newspapers.com.
[222] Detroit Free Press. (January 20, 1851). P. 2. Newspapers.com.

that granted a Calumet monopoly to the Southern was "without company authority."[223]

The Detroit journalist rebutted Stryker's denial by noting that the Michigan Southern men had now twice attempted to obtain the Calumet monopoly.[224] The *Free Press* reported the fact that since Stryker, Butler, and the other Michigan Southern men were at Indianapolis for a second effort at securing the Calumet monopoly through legislative grant, the desire of the Southern men for the Calumet monopoly was proved to a high probability.[225] This chain of claims, allegations, denials, and rebuttals formed part of the great race to Chicago in which the Michigan Southern Railroad Company and the Michigan Central Railroad Company were competitors.[226] John Stryker, his partners, and the Michigan Southern would win the race to Chicago.

The Dixon Telegraph of Illinois, in its May 19, 1853, edition, reported that the St. Charles and Mississippi Railroad had elected a board of directors that included John Stryker of Rome, New York, Charles Butler of New York, Gurdon S. Hubbard and Amos Gager Throop of Chicago, Ira Minard and S. S. Jones of St. Charles, J. S. Waterman of Sycamore, S. M. Hitt and H. A. Mix of Ogle County, and S. Stahl and D. A. Barrows of Galena.[227] Amos G. Throop would later serve as the Mayor of Pasadena, California, and as the founder of Throop Polytechnic Institute, now known as the California Institute of Technology. Gurdon S. Hubbard was a business partner of the Wolcotts, Kinzies, Robert Irwin, Nathaniel Jennison Brown, and William Loring Whiting of Chicago. John Stryker, Elisha Litchfield, John B. Jervis, and the other Michigan Southern Railroad Company men completed the railroad to Chicago in February, 1852.

> "During the few months which followed, there were dozens of entanglements including clashes between the Stryker railroads and the Michigan Central people but the Michigan Southern drove its rails into Chicago in February 1852, beating the Central by three months."[228]

"John Stryker was also a key to the merging of the many separate railroads in New York into one New York Central Railroad."[229] The New York Central Railroad Company, the largest corporation that John Stryker co-founded and built

---

223 Detroit Free Press. (January 20, 1851). P. 2. Newspapers.com.
224 Detroit Free Press. (January 20, 1851). P. 2. Newspapers.com.
225 Detroit Free Press. (January 20, 1851). P. 2. Newspapers.com.
226 Detroit Free Press. (January 20, 1851). P. 2. Newspapers.com.
227 The Dixon Telegraph. (May 19, 1853). P. 4. Newspapers.com.
228 National Railway Bulletin. (1981). Vols. 46-47. Page number not identifiable at time of reference. National Railway Historical Society. Google Books.
229 National Railway Bulletin. (1981). Vols. 46-47. Page number not identifiable at time of reference. National Railway Historical Society. Google Books.

up, grew to $1.1 billion in assets by March, 1923.[230] Grosvenor M. Jones, who was Chief of the Finance and Investment Division of the United States Department of Commerce and Labor, reported the largest United States corporations by capital magnitudes in an interview with Theodore Knappen of the Washington, D.C., bureau of *The Magazine of Wall Street*, a New York City financial and industrial publication. Jones stated that the United States Steel Corporation was the largest corporation in the United States at this time, with a capital of $1.9 billion, and that the Pennsylvania Railroad Company was the second largest, with a capital of $1.2 billion.[231] The American Telephone and Telegraph Company and the New York Central Railroad Company tied for third largest United States company that year, each with a capital of $1.1 billion.[232] Standard Oil Company of New Jersey and the Southern Pacific Railroad Company tied for fourth place, each possessing a capital of $800,000,000.[233] The Baltimore & Ohio Railroad Company and the Union Pacific Railroad Company tied for fifth place with capital of $700,000,000 each, according to Jones and Knappen.[234]

Stryker and Bunn Railroad Companies of Chicago

The Half-Century's Progress of the City of Chicago: The City's Leading Manufacturers and Merchants, an 1887 encyclopedia of the city and region, contained the roster of railroad companies that operated at Chicago as of 1887 and stated the track mileage of each railroad in the city and region.[235] Of the fifty-two Chicago railroads existing in 1887, no fewer than eight of the companies had been founded or co-founded by Jacob Bunn, John Whitfield Bunn, John Stryker, and Thomas Blish Talcott.[236] The list of Bunn, Stryker, and Talcott-connected railroad companies included the following which were centered at Chicago, according to the 1887 compilers. The following list provides the name of the Chicago railroads, as of 1887, of which Jacob Bunn, John Bunn, and John Stryker were founders, owners, and/or members of the boards of directors. Thomas Talcott was a

---

[230] The Magazine of Wall Street. (March 31, 1923). Vol. 31. P. 29. New York, NY. Google Books.
[231] The Magazine of Wall Street. (March 31, 1923). Vol. 31. P. 29. New York, NY. Google Books.
[232] The Magazine of Wall Street. (March 31, 1923). Vol. 31. P. 29. New York, NY. Google Books.
[233] The Magazine of Wall Street. (March 31, 1923). Vol. 31. P. 29. New York, NY. Google Books.
[234] The Magazine of Wall Street. (March 31, 1923). Vol. 31. P. 29. New York, NY. Google Books.
[235] Half-Century's Progress of the City of Chicago: The City's Leading Manufacturers and Merchants. (1887). Part I. P. 354. Chicago, IL: International Publishing Company. Google Books.
[236] See corresponding references elsewhere herein.

legislative supporter and promoter of the Illinois Central, and was thus more indirectly associated with the founding of the Illinois Central Railroad Company. Mileage numbers for the railroads are stated, too.

1. Chicago & Alton Railroad — 280 miles; Jacob Bunn
2. Chicago, Rock Island & Pacific — 500 miles; John Stryker
3. Illinois Central Railroad — 308 miles; Thomas Talcott
4. Indianapolis, Decatur & Springfield — 85 miles; John Bunn
5. Lake Shore & Michigan Southern — 540 miles; John Stryker
6. Springfield & Northwestern — 47 miles; John Bunn
7. Toledo, Peoria & Warsaw — 227 miles; John Bunn
8. Wabash Railway — 473 miles; John Bunn[237]

1825 Tax Assessment Roll for Chicago

Historian Joseph Kirkland named the taxpayers and property holders who, in 1825, owned property at Chicago, and referred to the property owners as "early capitalists" in his 1892 work, *The Story of Chicago*.[238] Dr. Alexander Wolcott paid a tax of $5.72 on property that had been evaluated at $572.[239] Wolcott's father-in-law, John Kinzie, paid a tax of $5.00 on property evaluated at $500.[240] Alexander Robinson, known also as Chief Che-Che-Pin-Quay (Chief Blinking Eyes), owned property with a value of $200, and paid $2.00 in tax.[241] John Baptiste Beaubien held $1,000 in property, and was accordingly taxed $10.00.[242] John Crafts was the largest property owner at Chicago in 1825, and held $5,000 of assets there, paying a tax of $50.00.[243] The 1825 Assessment Roll that Kirkland produced showed a flat tax rate of one percent on properties held at Chicago.[244] The other people named on the Assessment Roll were Antoine Oiullemette (Wilmette), Peter Piche,

---

[237] Half-Century's Progress of the City of Chicago: The City's Leading Manufacturers and Merchants. (1887). Part I. P. 354. Chicago, IL: International Publishing Company. Google Books.

[238] Kirkland, Joseph. (1892). The Story of Chicago. P. 100. Chicago, IL: Dibble Publishing Company.

[239] Kirkland, Joseph. (1892). The Story of Chicago. P. 100. Chicago, IL: Dibble Publishing Company.

[240] Kirkland, Joseph. (1892). The Story of Chicago. P. 100. Chicago, IL: Dibble Publishing Company.

[241] Kirkland, Joseph. (1892). The Story of Chicago. P. 100. Chicago, IL: Dibble Publishing Company.

[242] Kirkland, Joseph. (1892). The Story of Chicago. P. 100. Chicago, IL: Dibble Publishing Company.

[243] Kirkland, Joseph. (1892). The Story of Chicago. P. 100. Chicago, IL: Dibble Publishing Company.

[244] Kirkland, Joseph. (1892). The Story of Chicago. P. 100. Chicago, IL: Dibble Publishing Company.

David McKee, Joseph Laframboise, Claude Laframboise, Louis Coutra, Jeremy Clermont, John K. Clark, and James Clybourne.[245]

---

[245] Kirkland, Joseph. (1892). The Story of Chicago. P. 100. Chicago, IL: Dibble Publishing Company.

Jean Baptiste Pointe DuSable. Founder of Chicago. First non-Native American settler of the place that would become Chicago. Pioneer businessman and explorer. (Image courtesy of the Chicago History Museum; Image ID ICHi-012166).

WM. WELLS.

Captain William Wells. Of the Northwest Territory, Fort Dearborn, and Chicago. Captured and adopted by the Miami Indians. Adopted as son by Chief Mechekaunahqua, whose name translates to "Little Turtle." Wells was given the name "Black Snake," by his adoptive Miami family. Wells married Waunangapeth, the daughter of Chief Mechekaunahqua. Wells served at Fort Dearborn and was killed in the massacre that occurred at the Battle of Fort Dearborn in 1812. Wells and Mechekaunahqua were connected collaterally and maritally to the Richards-Wolcott-Kinzie-Prentiss-Henshaw-Stryker family of Chicago, New York, New Jersey, and New England. (Image courtesy of Joseph Kirkland, *The Story of Chicago*, 1892).

LITTLE TURTLE ("ME-CHE-KAN-NAH-QUA").

Chief Mechekaunahqua ("Little Turtle"). Chief of the Miami Tribe. Adoptive father of William Wells. Extended marital relative of the Richards-Kinzie-Wolcott-Prentiss-Henshaw-Stryker family of Chicago. (Image courtesy of Joseph Kirkland, *The Story of Chicago*, 1892).

John Harris Kinzie. Of Chicago and Wisconsin. Husband of Juliette Augusta Magill, who was a member of the Richards-Prentiss-Henshaw family of Chicago, New England, and New York City. Co-founder of St. James Episcopal Church, the oldest Episcopal church in Chicago. Co-founder of the Chicago Board of Trade, the Chicago Branch of the State Bank of Illinois, and the Chicago Historical Society. First President of the Chicago Branch of the Illinois State Bank, which Robert Irwin served as a system-wide member of the Board of Directors. (Image courtesy of Joseph Kirkland, *The Story of Chicago*, 1892).

53

HON. D. P. COOK.

Daniel Pope Cook. Of Kentucky and Illinois. Cook County, Illinois, is named for Daniel Pope Cook. First Attorney General of Illinois. He was an Illinois lawyer, judge, and newspaper owner. Served as the second member of the United States Congress to be elected from Illinois. Daniel Pope Cook was the paternal great-grandfather of Susan Cook. Susan Cook was the wife of Henry Barrell House, who was a prominent federal bank overseer, bank executive, broker, and playwright of Chicago. Henry B. House was a member of the Irwin Family of Springfield and Chicago. (Image courtesy of Joseph Kirkland, *The Story of Chicago*, 1892).

Dr. Alexander Wolcott, Jr. Of Connecticut and Chicago. A founder of Chicago and Cook County. The first resident physician in Chicago history. De facto owner of Fort Dearborn. Husband of Ellen Marion Kinzie. Son-in-law of fellow Chicago founder John Kinzie. Wolcott was one of the first and most important land developers of Chicago. He was the uncle of Juliette Magill Kinzie and the brother of Henry Wolcott and Francis Wolcott Magill. (Image courtesy of the Chicago History Museum; Image ID ICHi-068727).

54

Nellie Kinzie, 1856. Daughter of John Harris Kinzie and Juliette Augusta (Magill) Kinzie, founders of Chicago. (Image courtesy of the Chicago History Museum; Image ID ICHi-168746; Juliette Gordon Low, photographer).

MRS. JULIETTE A KINZIE.
Author of Waubun.

Juliette (Magill) Kinzie. A founder of Chicago. Wife of John H. Kinzie. Niece of Dr. Alexander Wolcott. (Image courtesy of Joseph Kirkland, *The Story of Chicago*, 1892).

CHICAGO IN 1820.
FROM AN OLD VIEW.

Chicago in 1820. The DuSable-Kinzie Mansion at right. Fort Dearborn at left. Chicago River at center. This is about the time that Dr. Alexander Wolcott of Connecticut arrived as one of the founders of Chicago. (Image courtesy of the Chicago History Museum; Image ID ICHi-168748).

Alexander Wolcott. Of Chicago. Nephew of Dr. Alexander Wolcott. Son of Henry Wolcott. Nephew of Frances Wolcott Magill. Cousin of Juliette Magill Kinzie. Cook County Surveyor and Chicago land agent. Member of the company of Wolcott & Fox, which occupied the W. D. Kerfoot Block in the Burnt Out District of the city after the Great Fire of 1871. Wolcott was one of the first land surveyors in the Burnt Out District after the Great Fire. (Image courtesy of Joseph Kirkland, *The Story of Chicago*, 1892).

Interior view of old Fort Dearborn. Dr. Alexander Wolcott and his family resided at Fort Dearborn after the fort had been decommissioned as a military post. (Image courtesy of Joseph Kirkland, *The Story of Chicago*, 1892).

Alexander Robinson / Chief Che-Che-Pin-Quay. Chief of the Potawotamie Indian Tribe. Founder of Chicago. Close friend of Dr. Alexander Wolcott, John Kinzie, John Harris Kinzie, and Juliette Magill Kinzie. Land developer of the Northwest Side of Chicago. His name translated to "Blinking Eyes," a name given him because he possessed a neurological tic of the eyes. (Image courtesy of the Chicago History Museum; Image ID DN-0083967B).

Robert Irwin. Merchant of St. Louis and Springfield. Close friend of Abraham Lincoln. Banker to Abraham Lincoln. Member of the Board of Directors of the State Bank of Illinois, whose Chicago Branch was the first bank ever to exist at Chicago. Founder of Springfield Marine Bank. Uncle of Elizabeth Jane (Ferguson) Bunn and of Benjamin Hamilton Ferguson. Member of the Irwin-Ferguson-Bunn family of Chicago, Springfield, and the Pittsburgh metropolitan region of Pennsylvania. (Image courtesy of the Sangamon County Historical Society).

Money draft written on the Chicago Branch of the State Bank of Illinois. Robert Irwin served on the Board of Directors of the State Bank of Illinois, and thus shared governance powers and authority for the Chicago Branch of the State Bank. The State Bank of Illinois was the first bank to exist in Chicago. Robert Irwin, Nathaniel J. Brown, and John Harris Kinzie all were founders and/or governing members of this bank company. (Image courtesy of Joseph Kirkland, *The Story of Chicago*, 1892).

Andrew Cunningham. Member of the Cunningham family of Illinois. Native of Edinburgh, Scotland. Early Chicago settler in approximately 1834-1835. Subsequently relocated to Cass County, Illinois. Farmer, stockman, and founder of the large Cunningham Tannery Company of Cass County, Illinois, which supplied necessary leather goods to the Union Army during the Civil War. Thought to have attended business college at Chicago. Uncle of Jeanette (Cunningham) Taylor. Brother of Charles Cunningham, Esq., who served as British Imperial Consul to Turkey, in addition to having been a noted international merchant at Smyrna, Turkey. Charles Cunningham designed and established the multinational trade organization known as the Danube River Commission of Europe. (Image courtesy of Marcia Cox).

Robert Taylor. Native of Campbelltown, Mull of Kintyre, Argyle, Scotland. Early settler at Chicago in 1840. Subsequent settler at Cass County, Illinois. Husband of Jeanette Cunningham of Edinburgh. Father of thirteen. Farmer, stockman, and grain dealer. Vice-President and Director of the Farmers' National Bank of Virginia, Illinois. Supporter of the Presbyterian church of Cass County. Author's great-great-grandfather. (Image courtesy of author's personal collection).

William Butler Ogden. The first Mayor of Chicago. Ogden served with Jacob Bunn in establishing the Chicago Secure Depository Company and the Chicago and Alton Railroad Company, helping to lay the financial and transportation infrastructure of the city, Cook County, and the Midwest. (Image courtesy of Joseph Kirkland, *The Story of Chicago*, 1892).

GURDON S. HUBBARD (*Hurlbut*).

Gurdon Saltonstall Hubbard. One of the founders of Chicago and of the business and economy of the settlement, city, and county. Co-founder of the Chicago Branch of the Illinois State Bank. Served with John Stryker as co-founder of the Chicago, St. Charles and Mississippi Air Line Railroad Company. (Image courtesy of Joseph Kirkland, *The Story of Chicago*, 1892).

John Stryker, Esq. Of Rome, New York, and Chicago. Member of the Stryker Family of New Jersey, New York, and Illinois. Builder of New York, Ohio, Michigan, and Chicago industries. Co-founder, President, and member of Board of Directors of the Lake Shore & Michigan Southern Railroad Company of Cleveland and Chicago. Co-founder and Director of the Lake Shore & Northern Indiana Railroad Company of Chicago. Co-founder and Director of the Northern Indiana & Chicago Railroad Company. Co-founder and Director of the Chicago, Rock Island Railroad Company. Co-founder of the Detroit & State Line Railroad Company of Michigan and Ohio. Co-founder of the Chicago, St. Charles, and Mississippi Air Line Railroad Company. Contributed to the establishment and development of Greater Grand Crossing community and neighborhood of the South Side of Chicago through railroad development projects. Co-founder and a principal legal strategist of the New York Central Railroad Company, which became the largest corporation in the world in 1856, and which rapidly became a billion-dollar corporation by about 1900. The New York Central Railroad Company possessed an immense commercial, industrial, political, transportational, and infrastructural presence in Chicago and Cook County, in addition to all the Great Lakes states, including New York. President of the Rome Locomotive Works of Rome, New York. Stryker helped finance, construct, lead, and develop what would become more than $1 billion of railroad, manufacturing, maritime, and banking companies throughout Chicago, New York City, Rome, New York, Detroit, Cleveland, Indiana, and Iowa. (Image courtesy of the Stryker Area Heritage Council of Ohio).

Rev. Dr. Truman Marcellus Post, Esq. Of Jacksonville, St. Louis, and Chicago.
Lawyer. Middlebury College alumnus. Congregational minister. Pioneer Christian
teacher and scholar of Jacksonville, Morgan County, Illinois, Chicago, and St. Louis.
Early land owner, developer, and investor of Chicago. Founder of the Chicago
Theological Seminary. Board of Directors member of the Chicago Theological
Seminary. Husband of Frances Alsop Henshaw. Son-in-law of New England and
Atlantic trade merchant Daniel Henshaw and his wife Sarah Esther (Prentiss)
Henshaw. Patriarch of the Post Family of St. Louis. The Posts are all cousins of the
Taylors and Strykers of Chicago, Cass County, and Morgan County, Illinois. (Image
courtesy of *Truman Marcellus Post, D.D.: A Biography Personal and Literary*, by
Truman Augustus Post, Esq., 1891).

Joseph Medill. Mayor of Chicago. Builder of the Chicago Tribune Company into one of the foremost newspaper companies of the world. Served with Jacob Bunn as co-founder of the Chicago Secure Depository Company in 1869. (Image courtesy of Joseph Kirkland, *The Story of Chicago*, 1892).

Harriet Hillhouse (Henshaw) McClure. Of Jacksonville, Illinois. Illinois social and civic matron. Alumna of the Troy Female Seminary (Emma Willard School) in New York. Daughter of Daniel Henshaw and Sarah Esther (Prentiss) Henshaw of New England. Wife of Judge Henry Brigham McClure of Vermont, Michigan, and Jacksonville. Mother of Elizabeth Henshaw McClure, who married Judge Henry Stryker of Illinois. Harriet was the first cousin of Harriet Louise Richards, who married Daniel Huntington. Huntington and Richards were among the founders of the Metropolitan Museum of Art in New York City. (Image courtesy of author's personal collection).

63

St. James Episcopal Cathedral. John Harris Kinzie and Juliette Magill Kinzie were founders of this church, the first Episcopal church at Chicago. (Image courtesy of the Chicago History Museum; CHM-Digital Obj ID: ICHi-070167; Charles R. Clark, photographer).

Chapter 2

Builders of the Downtown

"For we know that if our earthly house of this tabernacle were dissolved, we have a building of God, an house not made with hands, eternal in the heavens."

2 Corinthians 5:1

Introduction

The present chapter concerns the Chicago history of the Bunn branch and the Ferguson branch of my mother's family. This chapter will include, among others, Jacob Bunn, Benjamin Hamilton Ferguson, John Whitfield Bunn, Rev. Melancthon Woolsey Stryker, and the Edwards in-laws of Springfield. Principal companies discussed herein include the Chicago Republican Company, the Chicago Secure Depository Company, the Chicago and Alton Railroad Company, A. C. McClurg Publishing Company, the Franklin Life Insurance Company, the LaSalle Life Insurance Company, and the Springfield Boiler Company. Principal civic organizations discussed here include Fourth Presbyterian Church and the Saints and Sinners Club, among many others. The present chapter also concerns the Bunn, Jones, Irwin, and House families of Chicago and Springfield. For the Union Stockyards history of the Bunn family, please consult Chapter 4, *Friends of the Leatherworkers*. For the Chicago histories of the Illinois Watch Company, Sangamo Electric Company, Central Illinois Public Service Company (and all Chicago subsidiaries), and the American Watch Trust Company, consult Chapter 8, *Ode to Pylons and Cannery Windows*.

The Springfield Beginnings

For the Springfield history of the Bunn family, the first businesses of the family in Illinois, and the earliest history of the Bunns in Illinois, see my first book, *Jacob Bunn: Legacy of an Illinois Industrial Pioneer* (2005) (Lawrenceville, VA: Brunswick Publishing Corporation). The Bunns were among the founders of the grocery, manufacturing, and railroad industries of Springfield and Sangamon County. They co-founded and developed a great number of companies and civic and social organizations in Springfield, but those are not the focus of the present book. The Bunns were every bit as active in the development and leadership of Chicago and Cook County businesses, industries, civic and social organizations as they were in the development of these things in Springfield. The Bunns, as with many people in this book, were from both Springfield and Chicago. The Bunns began with the J. Bunn Grocery Company of Springfield in 1840, which became a major grocery company in Illinois, and which was subsequently known as the J. & J. W. Bunn Grocery Company, the J. W. Bunn Grocery Company, and the Bunn

Capitol Grocery Company.[246] The Bunn Grocery Company merged with the Humphreys Company to form the Bunn & Humphreys Company, which operated seventeen grocery warehouses and food distribution centers throughout Illinois.[247]

The National Corporation Bureau was based at 108 S. LaSalle Street, in the Loop.[248] This organization published the reporter journal known as *The National Corporation Reporter* and announced the 1922 incorporation of John W. Bunn & Company of Springfield.[249] Jacob Bunn, Jr., George Wallace Bunn, Jr., and Willard Bunn, incorporated the company with $500,000 in capitalization money, but the 1922 report contained no specific description of the corporate financing.[250] John W. Bunn & Company traced back to 1840, with the establishment of the J. Bunn Grocery Company of Springfield by Jacob Bunn, older brother of John W. Bunn.[251] The reincorporated John W. Bunn & Company continued the commercial purpose of its organizational predecessors, and provided retail of groceries, merchandise, and confection products.[252] By 1871, J. & J. W. Bunn Grocery Company generated sales of $175,000 to $200,000 annually, according to John Carrol Power.[253] For more about the grocery company, see Chapter 5, *The Foundations of Jackson Park.*

The J. Bunn Bank Company: Honor and Integrity on the Prairie

Jacob Bunn was a strict Christian and practiced honor and integrity in business and civic work. When his bank, the J. Bunn Bank Company of Springfield, failed in the Panic of 1873, Bunn repaid all of his bank depositors as much as was possible even though he was excused from the burden of the total financial restoration of the bank depositors because of bankruptcy.[254] When told there was no need for him to work so hard in his old age, Bunn answered: "'For myself, no.

---

[246] Tea and Coffee Trade Journal. (1928). Vol. 54. Google Books.

[247] Sales Management. (1931). Vol. 27. Page number not visible at time of reference. Google Books.

[248] The National Corporation Reporter. (August 4, 1921-January 26, 1922). Vol. LXIII (63). Chicago, IL: The United States Corporation Bureau. Google Books.

[249] The National Corporation Reporter. (August 4, 1921-January 26, 1922). Vol. LXIII (63). P. 357. Chicago, IL: The United States Corporation Bureau. Google Books.

[250] The National Corporation Reporter. (August 4, 1921-January 26, 1922). Vol. LXIII (63). P. 357. Chicago, IL: The United States Corporation Bureau. Google Books.

[251] Power, John Carroll. (1871). History of Springfield, Illinois, Its Advantages As A Home And Advantages For Business, Manufacturing, Etc. P. 80. Springfield, IL: Springfield Board of Trade. Google Books.

[252] The National Corporation Reporter. (August 4, 1921-January 26, 1922). Vol. LXIII (63). P. 357. Chicago, IL: The United States Corporation Bureau. Google Books.

[253] Power, John Carroll. (1871). History of Springfield, Illinois, Its Advantages As A Home And Advantages For Business, Manufacturing, Etc. P. 80. Springfield, IL: Springfield Board of Trade. Google Books.

[254] St. Louis Post-Dispatch. (January 3, 1926). P. 55. Newspapers.com.

I need but little. . .But I must pay those bank debts before I die.'"[255] The Panic of 1873 caused the failures of many American banks and other companies. Bunn tried to save the J. Bunn Bank and the "farmers and tradesmen who depended upon [Bunn] to save them."[256] The *St. Louis Post-Dispatch* stated, "Himself he might have saved if he had been less intent upon saving others."[257] Bunn placed the bank in voluntary liquidation on January 1, 1878, after five years of attempting to restore the bank to solvency and wealth.[258] Bunn owed $800,000 in claims to the depositors.[259] Bunn initially had far more than enough money to repay every one of his bank depositors in full, and told his son, George Wallace Bunn: "'My gracious, son, I can pay everybody out.'"[260]

The liquidation of the Bunn property holdings caused the property prices to fall, however, which in turn caused their liquidation values to fall.[261] This occurrence meant that the moneys that were originally adequate for the full reimbursement of the Bunn Bank depositors were now severely deficient for that purpose.[262] The property values fell to $572,000, causing a $228,000 deficit to occur in the reimbursement process.[263] The court judged that the final liquidation of the Bunn assets, though deficient, acquitted Bunn of liability for the remaining sum of $228,000.[264] Though jurisprudentially absolved of liability for the remainder of the debt, Bunn believed he was morally liable for the remaining debt.[265] He worked to repay as much of the remaining debt as possible before his death in 1897.[266]

The Bunn Bank depositors held Bunn in high esteem and did not fault him for the bank failure.[267] Mary Todd Lincoln affirmed her faith in the financial management, honor, and skill of Jacob Bunn when she insisted that he remain her financial manager, despite the failure of the bank.[268] Jacob and John Whitfield Bunn acquired the watch factory at Springfield, which they would reorganize as the Illinois Watch Company, and Jacob planned to build the watch manufacturing business to such a point of corporate solvency and prosperity that Bunn could use the moneys made from it to repay the remaining balance of the bank debt.[269] For

---

[255] St. Louis Post-Dispatch. (January 3, 1926). P. 55. Newspapers.com.
[256] St. Louis Post-Dispatch. (January 3, 1926). P. 55. Newspapers.com.
[257] St. Louis Post-Dispatch. (January 3, 1926). P. 55. Newspapers.com.
[258] St. Louis Post-Dispatch. (January 3, 1926). P. 55. Newspapers.com.
[259] St. Louis Post-Dispatch. (January 3, 1926). P. 55. Newspapers.com.
[260] St. Louis Post-Dispatch. (January 3, 1926). P. 55. Newspapers.com.
[261] St. Louis Post-Dispatch. (January 3, 1926). P. 55. Newspapers.com.
[262] St. Louis Post-Dispatch. (January 3, 1926). P. 55. Newspapers.com.
[263] St. Louis Post-Dispatch. (January 3, 1926). P. 55. Newspapers.com.
[264] St. Louis Post-Dispatch. (January 3, 1926). P. 55. Newspapers.com.
[265] St. Louis Post-Dispatch. (January 3, 1926). P. 55. Newspapers.com.
[266] St. Louis Post-Dispatch. (January 3, 1926). P. 55. Newspapers.com.
[267] St. Louis Post-Dispatch. (January 3, 1926). P. 55. Newspapers.com.
[268] St. Louis Post-Dispatch. (January 3, 1926). P. 55. Newspapers.com.
[269] St. Louis Post-Dispatch. (January 3, 1926). P. 55. Newspapers.com.

the history of the Illinois Watch Company and its importance to Chicago, see Chapter 8, *Ode to Pylons and Cannery Windows*. Bunn devoted twenty years to building the Illinois Watch Company into an international company of technological significance. While he succeeded in developing the watch company into a global center of timekeeping technology and horological innovation, he was unable to repay the bank debt balance, which was ever-growing because of the cumulative interest money that attached to it.[270] While Bunn never achieved his purpose of the final and full repayment of the bank debt money, his children achieved that purpose for him.[271]

George Wallace Bunn, Sr., Henry Bunn, Jacob Bunn, Jr., and Alice Edwards Bunn chose to create the Bunn Memorial Fund in 1925.[272] The fund was a trust that was managed by J. H. Holbrook, Joseph Nixon Bunn, who was not related to the Bunns of Springfield and Chicago, and attorney B. L. Catron.[273] The purpose of the trust was the final and full repayment of the remaining bank debt.[274] The attorney for the trust, B. L. Catron, searched for the remaining J. Bunn Bank depositors who were living at the time, and searched for the heirs of the deceased bank depositors.[275] Catron accomplished the herculean job of locating the depositors and their heirs, but was only able to locate about six percent of the 1400 original depositors.[276] Most of the original depositors were dead by 1925.[277] Catron identified approximately 5,000 descendants, including children, grandchildren, and great-grandchildren, of the original depositors.[278]

The trust calculated the total debt money that was due to be $800,000, and this sum included the multiannual accrued interest moneys at the rate of five percent over a period of fifty years (1875-1925)—that is, with interest accrual calculated from the time prior to the bank's closure to the time of the memorial trust's distribution of the balance money.[279] The trust administration paid the $800,000 debt money to all 5,000 living depositors or the legal heirs thereof by January, 1926.[280] *The St. Louis Post-Dispatch* reported the following:

> "The children of Jacob Bunn will then go their ways, $800,000 poorer, but infinitely richer in the satisfaction of having created a worthy memorial to

---

[270] St. Louis Post-Dispatch. (January 3, 1926). P. 55. Newspapers.com.
[271] St. Louis Post-Dispatch. (January 3, 1926). P. 55. Newspapers.com.
[272] St. Louis Post-Dispatch. (January 3, 1926). P. 55. Newspapers.com.
[273] St. Louis Post-Dispatch. (January 3, 1926). P. 55. Newspapers.com.
[274] St. Louis Post-Dispatch. (January 3, 1926). P. 55. Newspapers.com.
[275] St. Louis Post-Dispatch. (January 3, 1926). P. 55. Newspapers.com.
[276] St. Louis Post-Dispatch. (January 3, 1926). P. 55. Newspapers.com.
[277] St. Louis Post-Dispatch. (January 3, 1926). P. 55. Newspapers.com.
[278] St. Louis Post-Dispatch. (January 3, 1926). P. 55. Newspapers.com.
[279] St. Louis Post-Dispatch. (January 3, 1926). P. 55. Newspapers.com.
[280] St. Louis Post-Dispatch. (January 3, 1926). P. 55. Newspapers.com.

J. Bunn, Banker, who gave his life that after all these years his debts might be paid to the uttermost, with interest at 5 per cent."[281]

The J. Bunn Bank was once the largest bank in Illinois outside of Chicago, and only a couple of Chicago banks were larger, but only by a small measure.[282] Elizabeth Bunn, the grandmother of author Andrew Taylor Call, grew up hearing about the honorable work of her Bunn family in repaying the J. Bunn Bank debt. The story remains a memorial to the business and civic ethics of the family and to Illinois business.

The Chicago Republican Company

Jacob Bunn served as one of the principal founders of the Chicago Republican Company.[283] Bunn also was the principal owner of the company.[284] The State of Illinois approved the organic statute for the Chicago Republican Company on February 13, 1865.[285] Analysis of the organic statute follows here.

Section 1 of the statute contained the incorporation clause for the company, and enumerated the individuals who participated in the organization of the corporation.[286] The organic statute of the corporation included the following names among the incorporation staff: Ira Y. Munn, John V. Farwell, Joseph K. C. Forrest, J. Young Scammon, Jesse Kilgore Dubois, Jacob Bunn, John Wood, J. Wilson Shaffer, Amos C. Babcock, Alonzo W. Mack, Francis A. Hoffman, and Henry C. Childs.[287] Section 1 established the body politic status of the company, as well as the corporate name, which was "Chicago Republican Company."[288] Perpetuity of succession was granted the company. Section 1 then attached a standard series of mutually respective powers and liabilities to the corporation. Section 1 attached the condition of suability and the power of litigation to the company. The statute

---

[281] St. Louis Post-Dispatch. (January 3, 1926). P. 55. Newspapers.com.

[282] The record for this fact has been lost. The author believes his recollection of the fact is correct.

[283] AN ACT to incorporate the Chicago Republican Company. Private Laws of the State of Illinois Passed by the Twenty-Fourth General Assembly, Convened January 2, 1865. Vol. 2. Pp. 117-119. Springfield, IL: Baker & Phillips, Printers. Google Books.

[284] Chicago Tribune. (October 19, 1897). P. 4. Newspapers.com.

[285] AN ACT to incorporate the Chicago Republican Company. Private Laws of the State of Illinois Passed by the Twenty-Fourth General Assembly, Convened January 2, 1865. Vol. 2. Pp. 117, 119. Springfield, IL: Baker & Phillips, Printers. Google Books.

[286] AN ACT to incorporate the Chicago Republican Company. Private Laws of the State of Illinois Passed by the Twenty-Fourth General Assembly, Convened January 2, 1865. Vol. 2. Pp. 117-118. Springfield, IL: Baker & Phillips, Printers. Google Books.

[287] AN ACT to incorporate the Chicago Republican Company. Private Laws of the State of Illinois Passed by the Twenty-Fourth General Assembly, Convened January 2, 1865. Vol. 2. P. 118. Springfield, IL: Baker & Phillips, Printers. Google Books.

[288] AN ACT to incorporate the Chicago Republican Company. Private Laws of the State of Illinois Passed by the Twenty-Fourth General Assembly, Convened January 2, 1865. Vol. 2. P. 118-119. Springfield, IL: Baker & Phillips, Printers. Google Books.

attached to the company the power of pleading, and the vulnerability to impleader. Power of defense and condition of defensibility were attached to the company in Section 1 of the organic statute. The power to create a corporate seal, and the powers of change and renewal of the common seal were then granted the company. Section 1 of the statute then supplied a general enablement and residual powers clause by which the Chicago Republican Company was vested with generic powers necessary for performance of the commercial purpose of the company.

Section 1 proceeded to the capitalization and financing clause. The financing of the corporation entailed an initial capitalization amount of $500,000.[289] The statute contained no further delineation of the financing of the company and omitted any further descriptions of debt financing and equity financing. The organic statute contained an evaluation clause that set the shares of stock at $100 per share.[290] The principal purpose of the equity financing was to create a fund of value to serve the corporate purpose.[291] Though substantively barren of any complex constitutive laws regarding the financing of the company, the organic statute installed a simple equity financing system. The statute furthermore attached a definitive scope and limit to the purpose of the capital fund of the company: specifically, the company was to use the capital fund value primarily for the operations of printing, publishing, binding, and newspaper manufacturing in Chicago and Cook County.[292]

Section 2 of the statute stated the corporate purpose. The corporate purpose of the Chicago Republican Company was the manufacture and publication of a newspaper in Chicago, as well as engagement in related manufacturing acts.[293]

Section 3 concerned certain corporate powers that were pertinent to company ownership of real property. The clause granted powers of purchase, tenure, sale, and disposal. The clause also contained a grant of power to the company to create collateralized security interests in the property held by the company. Mortgages, trust deeds, and other means of pledge were identified as relevant means of proper securitization.

---

[289] AN ACT to incorporate the Chicago Republican Company. Private Laws of the State of Illinois Passed by the Twenty-Fourth General Assembly, Convened January 2, 1865. Vol. 2. P. 118. Springfield, IL: Baker & Phillips, Printers. Google Books.

[290] AN ACT to incorporate the Chicago Republican Company. Private Laws of the State of Illinois Passed by the Twenty-Fourth General Assembly, Convened January 2, 1865. Vol. 2. P. 118. Springfield, IL: Baker & Phillips, Printers. Google Books.

[291] AN ACT to incorporate the Chicago Republican Company. Private Laws of the State of Illinois Passed by the Twenty-Fourth General Assembly, Convened January 2, 1865. Vol. 2. P. 118. Springfield, IL: Baker & Phillips, Printers. Google Books.

[292] AN ACT to incorporate the Chicago Republican Company. Private Laws of the State of Illinois Passed by the Twenty-Fourth General Assembly, Convened January 2, 1865. Vol. 2. P. 118. Springfield, IL: Baker & Phillips, Printers. Google Books.

[293] AN ACT to incorporate the Chicago Republican Company. Private Laws of the State of Illinois Passed by the Twenty-Fourth General Assembly, Convened January 2, 1865. Vol. 2. Pp. 117-119. Springfield, IL: Baker & Phillips, Printers. Google Books.

Section 4 of the statute added several more real property-relevant powers to the company. The clause contained grants of the powers of purchase, use, and tenure for the purpose of enabling the company to acquire real estate to establish a place of business in order to enable performance of the corporate purpose.[294] The clause set a limit of 200 feet of frontage space on any street in Chicago for the company's construction and land use. Clause 4 granted the company the power of construction of buildings necessary for performance of the corporate business purposes. Clause 4 required that conveyances and disposals of real property be supported by the votes of at least two-thirds of the shareholders of the company. Any sale, disposal, and alienation had to be supported by the testimony of the president and secretary of the company. Approval of such transactions was to be proved by affixation of the corporate seal.

Section 5 granted powers of lease. The law contained a grant of power of lease with respect to any space that the corporation should own but should not judge necessary for the performance of the purpose of the company.[295] Section 6 provided for the prospective administration of the company, allowing for adoption of bylaws for administration. Clause 6 included a grant of power to the company that enabled the design and adoption of corporate bylaws for aid in the performance of the corporate purpose.[296] Amendments to the bylaws were not allowable except when supported by votes representing two-thirds of the company shareholders. Clause 6 established a due process system in which notice was required to be given at least ten days prior to any conference at which proposals for amendments to company bylaws were to be filed.

Section 7, the final clause of the organic statute, included a regime in which a condition, a standard, and a necessity jointly constituted the grounds upon which the corporation would be vested with the right to begin business under the organic act.[297] The condition included the necessity of $100,000 of the statutorily authorized capital stock fund having been subscribed, as well as the further necessity of $50,000 of the $100,000 subscription amount of the capital stock fund having been received by the corporation by payment.[298] Only upon occurrence of

---

[294] AN ACT to incorporate the Chicago Republican Company. Private Laws of the State of Illinois Passed by the Twenty-Fourth General Assembly, Convened January 2, 1865. Vol. 2. Pp. 118-119. Springfield, IL: Baker & Phillips, Printers. Google Books.

[295] AN ACT to incorporate the Chicago Republican Company. Private Laws of the State of Illinois Passed by the Twenty-Fourth General Assembly, Convened January 2, 1865. Vol. 2. Pp. 118-119. Springfield, IL: Baker & Phillips, Printers. Google Books.

[296] AN ACT to incorporate the Chicago Republican Company. Private Laws of the State of Illinois Passed by the Twenty-Fourth General Assembly, Convened January 2, 1865. Vol. 2. P. 119. Springfield, IL: Baker & Phillips, Printers. Google Books.

[297] AN ACT to incorporate the Chicago Republican Company. Private Laws of the State of Illinois Passed by the Twenty-Fourth General Assembly, Convened January 2, 1865. Vol. 2. P. 119. Springfield, IL: Baker & Phillips, Printers. Google Books.

[298] AN ACT to incorporate the Chicago Republican Company. Private Laws of the State of Illinois Passed by the Twenty-Fourth General Assembly, Convened January 2, 1865. Vol. 2. P. 119. Springfield, IL: Baker & Phillips, Printers. Google Books.

these conditions could the corporation rightfully begin business in performance of the corporate purpose.[299] Clause 8 of the statute simply stated the date on which the statute was to take effect, which was February 13, 1865, the date of the approval of the Act.[300]

Let us now analyze the culture and political source from which the Chicago Republican Company derived its existence. Both the sociopolitical source and the civic culture of the Chicago Republican Company lay in the perception possessed by, as well as in the political commitment of, the company's organizers. Historian Richard Junger has noted that the incorporators of the Republican were opposed to what they alleged was the ideological weakness of the *Chicago Tribune*.[301] "But the *Republican*, [was] founded on an investment of $500,000 to counter a perceived wavering in the *Tribune* of Radical Republican ideology that included worker rights. . ."[302] The *Republican* advocated worker rights and sought to campaign against the labor exploitation that workers in Chicago had experienced.[303] Richard Junger quoted the following in his book about the Chicago Republican Company: "'on [the workers'] side a kind of capital is invested which employers ought not to seek to control, viz., the souls of men.'"[304]

As of October 12, 1865, the Chicago Republican Company was billed as the largest newspaper company in the West, and by implication, the largest in Chicago.[305] At this time, Charles Anderson Dana served as Editor of the newspaper.[306] *The Bryan Times* newspaper of Iowa contained an advertisement for the *Chicago Republican* in which the *Chicago Republican* was described politically and socially.[307] *The Bryan Times* stated: "A Thorough uncompromising Union Paper. In politics, devoted to the principles of Justice, Liberty and Equality.

---

[299] AN ACT to incorporate the Chicago Republican Company. Private Laws of the State of Illinois Passed by the Twenty-Fourth General Assembly, Convened January 2, 1865. Vol. 2. P. 119. Springfield, IL: Baker & Phillips, Printers. Google Books.

[300] AN ACT to incorporate the Chicago Republican Company. Private Laws of the State of Illinois Passed by the Twenty-Fourth General Assembly, Convened January 2, 1865. Vol. 2. P. 119. Springfield, IL: Baker & Phillips, Printers. Google Books.

[301] Junger, Richard. (2010). Becoming the Second City: Chicago's Mass News Media, 1833-1898. P. 98. Urbana, IL: University of Illinois Press. Google Books.

[302] Junger, Richard. (2010). Becoming the Second City: Chicago's Mass News Media, 1833-1898. P. 98. Urbana, IL: University of Illinois Press. Google Books.

[303] Junger, Richard. (2010). Becoming the Second City: Chicago's Mass News Media, 1833-1898. P. 98. Urbana, IL: University of Illinois Press. Google Books.

[304] Junger, Richard. (2010). Becoming the Second City: Chicago's Mass News Media, 1833-1898. P. 98. Urbana, IL: University of Illinois Press. Google Books.

[305] The Bryan Times. (October 12, 1865). The Largest Paper Published in the West: The Chicago Republican. Google Books.

[306] The Bryan Times. (October 12, 1865). The Largest Paper Published in the West: The Chicago Republican. Google Books.

[307] The Bryan Times. (October 12, 1865). The Largest Paper Published in the West: The Chicago Republican. Google Books.

The best men employed in the Commercial and Financial department."[308] The newspaper also advertised itself as a "foremost Family Paper of the West."[309] One remarkable fact about, and effect of, the journalism of the Chicago Republican Company possesses particular salience within the historical panorama of Cook County history: the Chicago Republican Company originated, through the journalism of Michael Ahern, the story of Mrs. O'Leary's cow having been the cause of the Great Chicago Fire of October 8, 1871.[310] Michael Ahern, who lived from 1850 to 1927, was the "*reporter for the* Chicago Republican *newspaper at the time of the Great Fire who later said he had invented the story about Mrs. O'Leary's cow starting the blaze.*"[311]

Historian Janet Steele described the culture and quality of the *Chicago Republican* as follows: "The *Chicago Republican* was pro-business, and pro-development. On city issues, it called for a free library, public health measures to stem a potential cholera epidemic, and equal pay for women's work."[312] Steele also described the staunch pro-railroad attitude that the Chicago Republican Company possessed: "A typical editorial argued the merits of railroad development, suggesting that private individuals should step aside in the interest of the public good—as defined by the needs of railroad corporations."[313] Steele illustrated vividly, through a quotation from the *Chicago Republican*, the culture and attitude that the *Republican* possessed with respect to issues of railroad development *vis a vis* the individual property owner:

> "'The city has a deep interest in every railroad making this point its centre of business, and. . .the general interests of the city should not be injured from mere motives of hostility to corporations. . . .Should a railroad be excluded because lotholders along a certain street object? Should the city stand still until John Smith can sell his lots at a profit?'"[314]

The supportive attitudes of the *Republican* for railroads and other heavy industries were unsurprising given the work and interests of the members of the company's leadership. The corporate and editorial leadership of the Chicago Republican

---

[308] The Bryan Times. (October 12, 1865). The Largest Paper Published in the West: The Chicago Republican. Google Books.
[309] The Bryan Times. (October 12, 1865). The Largest Paper Published in the West: The Chicago Republican. Google Books.
[310] Nobleman, Marc Tyler. (2006). The Great Chicago Fire. P. 45. Minneapolis, MN: Compass Point Books. Google Books.
[311] Nobleman, Marc Tyler. (2006). The Great Chicago Fire. P. 45. Minneapolis, MN: Compass Point Books. Google Books.
[312] Steele, Janet E. (1993). The Sun Shines for All: Journalism and Ideology in the Life of Charles A. Dana. P. 65. Syracuse, NY: Syracuse University Press. Google Books.
[313] Steele, Janet E. (1993). The Sun Shines for All: Journalism and Ideology in the Life of Charles A. Dana. P. 65. Syracuse, NY: Syracuse University Press. Google Books.
[314] Steele, Janet E. (1993). The Sun Shines for All: Journalism and Ideology in the Life of Charles A. Dana. P. 65. Syracuse, NY: Syracuse University Press. Google Books.

Company boasted many leading figures in industry and journalism.[315] Jacob Bunn and John Villiers Farwell were among the foremost industrialists and businessmen of both Chicago and the United States, and Charles Anderson Dana, Isaac Newton Higgins, Alonzo Mack, Van Buren Denslow, James F. Ballantyne, Henry M. Smith, and others were among the foremost journalists and editors in Chicago and in the United States.[316]

Charles Anderson Dana (1819-1897), a native of New Hampshire, attended Harvard for two years.[317] He joined the Brook Farm community of Roxbury, Massachusetts, for a time, and then took up a journalistic career by entering the employment of the *Harbinger*.[318] The *Harbinger* was a Boston company, and Dana later relocated to New York City to join the staff of the *New York Tribune*.[319] George Ripley, whom Dana had met at Brook Farm, cooperated with Dana to produce the *Appleton's New American Cyclopedia*.[320] Dana left the *New York Tribune* in 1862 for Washington, D.C., when he served President Abraham Lincoln as Assistant Secretary of War, serving under Secretary of War Edwin M. Stanton of Ohio.[321] Dana came to the Chicago Republican Company in 1865, when the company had only just been formed.[322] More facts concerning the Chicago career of Charles Anderson Dana can be read later on in this chapter.

---

[315] Andreas, Alfred Theodore. (1885). History of Chicago From the Earliest Period to the Present Time. Vol. II: From 1857 Until the Fire of 1871. Pp. 497-498. Chicago, IL: The A. T. Andreas Company, Publishers. Google Books.

[316] Andreas, Alfred Theodore. (1885). History of Chicago From the Earliest Period to the Present Time. Vol. II: From 1857 Until the Fire of 1871. Pp. 497-498. Chicago, IL: The A. T. Andreas Company, Publishers. Google Books.

[317] Andreas, Alfred Theodore. (1885). History of Chicago From the Earliest Period to the Present Time. Vol. II: From 1857 Until the Fire of 1871. P. 497. Chicago, IL: The A. T. Andreas Company, Publishers. Google Books.

[318] Andreas, Alfred Theodore. (1885). History of Chicago From the Earliest Period to the Present Time. Vol. II: From 1857 Until the Fire of 1871. P. 497. Chicago, IL: The A. T. Andreas Company, Publishers. Google Books.

[319] Andreas, Alfred Theodore. (1885). History of Chicago From the Earliest Period to the Present Time. Vol. II: From 1857 Until the Fire of 1871. P. 497. Chicago, IL: The A. T. Andreas Company, Publishers. Google Books.

[320] Andreas, Alfred Theodore. (1885). History of Chicago From the Earliest Period to the Present Time. Vol. II: From 1857 Until the Fire of 1871. P. 497. Chicago, IL: The A. T. Andreas Company, Publishers. Google Books.

[321] Andreas, Alfred Theodore. (1885). History of Chicago From the Earliest Period to the Present Time. Vol. II: From 1857 Until the Fire of 1871. P. 497. Chicago, IL: The A. T. Andreas Company, Publishers. Google Books.

[322] Andreas, Alfred Theodore. (1885). History of Chicago From the Earliest Period to the Present Time. Vol. II: From 1857 Until the Fire of 1871. P. 497. Chicago, IL: The A. T. Andreas Company, Publishers. Google Books.

Alonzo W. Mack (1822-1871) was a native of Vermont.[323] He worked in multiple professions, having been educated as a medical doctor and lawyer.[324] He also was a soldier and entrepreneur, and co-founded the Chicago Republican Company with Jacob Bunn, John Villiers Farwell, and the other men named earlier in this chapter.[325] Mack practiced medicine in Kalamazoo, Michigan, and later practiced law in Kankakee, Illinois.[326] Mack served in the Illinois Assembly, and in both houses, as a representative of Kankakee County, Will County, and Grundy County, all of which were outlier counties of Chicago and Cook County.[327] He served in the Civil War as founder and Colonel of the 76th Regiment of Illinois Volunteers.[328] He practiced law at Chicago until his death in January, 1871, about nine months prior to the Great Chicago Fire.[329] After Charles Dana resigned from the *Chicago Republican* in 1866, Jacob Bunn induced four men from the *Chicago Tribune* to work for the *Republican*: Van Buren Denslow, Henry M. Smith, James F. Ballantyne, and George D. Williston all were given jobs with Jacob Bunn's newspaper company.[330] Dr. Isaac Newton Higgins, M.D. (1834-1885), served both as an editor, and as General Manager of the Chicago Republican Company.[331] Higgins was a McKendree College alumnus and a medical doctor with a degree

---

[323] Andreas, Alfred Theodore. (1885). History of Chicago From the Earliest Period to the Present Time. Vol. II: From 1857 Until the Fire of 1871. P. 497. Chicago, IL: The A. T. Andreas Company, Publishers. Google Books.

[324] Andreas, Alfred Theodore. (1885). History of Chicago From the Earliest Period to the Present Time. Vol. II: From 1857 Until the Fire of 1871. P. 497. Chicago, IL: The A. T. Andreas Company, Publishers. Google Books.

[325] Andreas, Alfred Theodore. (1885). History of Chicago From the Earliest Period to the Present Time. Vol. II: From 1857 Until the Fire of 1871. P. 497. Chicago, IL: The A. T. Andreas Company, Publishers. Google Books.

[326] Andreas, Alfred Theodore. (1885). History of Chicago From the Earliest Period to the Present Time. Vol. II: From 1857 Until the Fire of 1871. P. 497. Chicago, IL: The A. T. Andreas Company, Publishers. Google Books.

[327] Andreas, Alfred Theodore. (1885). History of Chicago From the Earliest Period to the Present Time. Vol. II: From 1857 Until the Fire of 1871. P. 497. Chicago, IL: The A. T. Andreas Company, Publishers. Google Books.

[328] Andreas, Alfred Theodore. (1885). History of Chicago From the Earliest Period to the Present Time. Vol. II: From 1857 Until the Fire of 1871. P. 497. Chicago, IL: The A. T. Andreas Company, Publishers. Google Books.

[329] Andreas, Alfred Theodore. (1885). History of Chicago From the Earliest Period to the Present Time. Vol. II: From 1857 Until the Fire of 1871. P. 497. Chicago, IL: The A. T. Andreas Company, Publishers. Google Books.

[330] Andreas, Alfred Theodore. (1885). History of Chicago From the Earliest Period to the Present Time. Vol. II: From 1857 Until the Fire of 1871. P. 497. Chicago, IL: The A. T. Andreas Company, Publishers. Google Books.

[331] The Fifteenth Triennial and Forty-Ninth Annual Catalogue of M'Kendree College, Lebanon, Ills (Illinois). (1882-1883). P. 40. St. Louis, MO: R. P. Studley & Co., Printers. Google Books; Andreas, Alfred Theodore. (1885). History of Chicago From the Earliest Period to the Present Time. Vol. II: From 1857 Until the Fire of 1871. P. 497. Chicago, IL: The A. T. Andreas Company, Publishers. Google Books.

from Rush Medical College of Chicago.[332] He had edited the *Illinois State Register* prior to working for Jacob Bunn in Chicago, and later served fifteen years as an editor of the *San Francisco Morning Call*.[333] Dr. Higgins died in San Francisco.[334]

Van Buren Denslow served as Editor-In-Chief of the *Chicago Republican*, and was succeeded as chief editor by the Scottish-American journalist, James F. Ballantyne (1829-1870).[335] Born in Glasgow, Ballantyne learned the printing trade as an apprentice at age nine.[336] He studied at the Glasgow Mechanic's Institute, and at night schools as a young man.[337] He left Scotland for New York City in 1849, met his wife, a fellow Scottish immigrant named Joan Erie, at New York, and then they both relocated to Chicago in 1850.[338] Ballantyne worked for Chicago publisher Daniel O'Hara.[339] The Panic of 1857 caused the failure of the O'Hara Publishing Company, and Ballantyne then worked for the Chicago *Democratic Press*.[340] The *Chicago Tribune* acquired the *Democratic Press* and Ballantyne continued with the *Tribune*.[341] He had served as Commercial Editor of the *Press* prior to its acquisition by the *Tribune*, and then held the Commercial Editorship at

---

[332] The Fifteenth Triennial and Forty-Ninth Annual Catalogue of M'Kendree College, Lebanon, Ills (Illinois). (1882-1883). P. 40. St. Louis, MO: R. P. Studley & Co., Printers. Google Books

[333] The Fifteenth Triennial and Forty-Ninth Annual Catalogue of M'Kendree College, Lebanon, Ills (Illinois). (1882-1883). P. 40. St. Louis, MO: R. P. Studley & Co., Printers. Google Books; Andreas, Alfred Theodore. (1885). History of Chicago From the Earliest Period to the Present Time. Vol. II: From 1857 Until the Fire of 1871. P. 497. Chicago, IL: The A. T. Andreas Company, Publishers. Google Books.

[334] The Fifteenth Triennial and Forty-Ninth Annual Catalogue of M'Kendree College, Lebanon, Ills (Illinois). (1882-1883). P. 40. St. Louis, MO: R. P. Studley & Co., Printers. Google Books

[335] Andreas, Alfred Theodore. (1885). History of Chicago From the Earliest Period to the Present Time. Vol. II: From 1857 Until the Fire of 1871. P. 497. Chicago, IL: The A. T. Andreas Company, Publishers. Google Books.

[336] Andreas, Alfred Theodore. (1885). History of Chicago From the Earliest Period to the Present Time. Vol. II: From 1857 Until the Fire of 1871. P. 497. Chicago, IL: The A. T. Andreas Company, Publishers. Google Books.

[337] Andreas, Alfred Theodore. (1885). History of Chicago From the Earliest Period to the Present Time. Vol. II: From 1857 Until the Fire of 1871. P. 497. Chicago, IL: The A. T. Andreas Company, Publishers. Google Books.

[338] Andreas, Alfred Theodore. (1885). History of Chicago From the Earliest Period to the Present Time. Vol. II: From 1857 Until the Fire of 1871. P. 497. Chicago, IL: The A. T. Andreas Company, Publishers. Google Books.

[339] Andreas, Alfred Theodore. (1885). History of Chicago From the Earliest Period to the Present Time. Vol. II: From 1857 Until the Fire of 1871. P. 497. Chicago, IL: The A. T. Andreas Company, Publishers. Google Books.

[340] Andreas, Alfred Theodore. (1885). History of Chicago From the Earliest Period to the Present Time. Vol. II: From 1857 Until the Fire of 1871. P. 497. Chicago, IL: The A. T. Andreas Company, Publishers. Google Books.

[341] Andreas, Alfred Theodore. (1885). History of Chicago From the Earliest Period to the Present Time. Vol. II: From 1857 Until the Fire of 1871. P. 497. Chicago, IL: The A. T. Andreas Company, Publishers. Google Books.

the *Tribune*.[342] Ballantyne holds the distinctions, according to A. T. Andreas, of being both the first commercial editor at Chicago, and the first to produce and design the annual analyses and reviews of business and trade published by the *Chicago Tribune*.[343] Jacob Bunn recruited Ballantyne to serve as Commercial Editor of the Chicago Republican Company in August, 1866.[344] Ballantyne assumed the job of Editor-in-Chief of the *Republican* in 1867.[345] He retired from the *Republican* in May, 1869, because of disease, and died of consumption in 1870, at San Diego, California.[346]

The most renowned employee of the Chicago Republican Company was a man named Samuel Langhorne Clemens, better known as Mark Twain.[347] Jacob Bunn hired Mark Twain to work for the *Chicago Republican* as a journalist in 1868. Twain served as Western Correspondent for the *Republican* and turned in compelling and humorous journalism in that time. Mark Twain and fellow journalists and colleagues established the Jokers' Society while onboard a ship.[348] Twain wrote: "We established a Jokers' Society, and fined every member who furnished an unbearably bad joke."[349] Twain related several jokes from the new comedy club, including the following regarding the loss of a leg to a shark. The cost to members of offering a bad joke was a comedically ceremonial "public execution."

The St. Cloud Journal, a newspaper of St. Cloud, Minnesota, reported that the Chicago Republican Company added 30,000 new subscribers to its customer pool just in the month of May, 1868.[350] The report from *The St. Cloud Journal* noted that the growth in sales and subscription of the Chicago corporation was "unprecedented in the Northwest by any political paper."[351] In February, 1868, Mark Twain provided journalistic reportage of the women's clothing fashions that

[342] Andreas, Alfred Theodore. (1885). History of Chicago From the Earliest Period to the Present Time. Vol. II: From 1857 Until the Fire of 1871. Pp. 497-498. Chicago, IL: The A. T. Andreas Company, Publishers. Google Books.

[343] Andreas, Alfred Theodore. (1885). History of Chicago From the Earliest Period to the Present Time. Vol. II: From 1857 Until the Fire of 1871. P. 498. Chicago, IL: The A. T. Andreas Company, Publishers. Google Books.

[344] Andreas, Alfred Theodore. (1885). History of Chicago From the Earliest Period to the Present Time. Vol. II: From 1857 Until the Fire of 1871. P. 498. Chicago, IL: The A. T. Andreas Company, Publishers. Google Books.

[345] Andreas, Alfred Theodore. (1885). History of Chicago From the Earliest Period to the Present Time. Vol. II: From 1857 Until the Fire of 1871. P. 498. Chicago, IL: The A. T. Andreas Company, Publishers. Google Books.

[346] Andreas, Alfred Theodore. (1885). History of Chicago From the Earliest Period to the Present Time. Vol. II: From 1857 Until the Fire of 1871. P. 498. Chicago, IL: The A. T. Andreas Company, Publishers. Google Books.

[347] Daily Ohio Statesman (Columbus, Ohio). (May 29, 1868). P. 1. Newspapers.com.

[348] Daily Ohio Statesman (Columbus, Ohio). (May 29, 1868). P. 1. Newspapers.com.

[349] Daily Ohio Statesman (Columbus, Ohio). (May 29, 1868). P. 1. Newspapers.com.

[350] The St. Cloud Journal (St. Cloud, Minnesota). (June 11, 1868). P. 1. Newspapers.com.

[351] The St. Cloud Journal (St. Cloud, Minnesota). (June 11, 1868). P. 1. Newspapers.com.

he observed at a ceremony honoring Gen. Ulysses Grant.[352] The February 8, 1868, letter from Twain to the *Chicago Republican* contained the following report and comment.

"The fashions displayed by the ladies at the receptions of the great dignitaries of the Government may be regarded as orthodox and reliable, of course. I do not enjoy receptions, and yet I go to them, and inflict all manner of crowding, suffocation, and general discomfort upon myself, solely in order that I may be able to post the lady readers of newspapers concerning what they ought to wear when they wish to be utterly and exhaustively fashionable. Not being perfect in the technicalities of millinery, this duty is always tedious, and very laborious and fatiguing. I mention these things, because I wish to be credited with at least the good will to do well, even though I may chance, through ignorance, to fail of success. At Gen. Grant's reception, the other night, the most fashionably dressed lady was Mrs. G. C. She wore a pink satin dress, plain in front, but with a good deal of rake to it -- to the train, I mean; it was said to be two or three yards long. One could see it creeping along the floor some little time after the woman was gone. Mrs. C. wore also a white bodice, cut bias, with Pompadour sleeves, flounced with ruches; low neck, with the inside handkerchief not visible; white kid gloves. She had on a pearl necklace, which glinted lonely, high up in the midst of that barren waste of neck and shoulders. Her hair was grizzled into a tangled chapparal, forward of her ears; after it was drawn together, and compactly bound and plaited into a stump like a pony's tail, and furthermore was canted upward at a sharp angle, and ingeniously supported by a red velvet crupper, whose forward extremity was made fast with a half hitch around a hair pin on her poop-deck, which means, of course, the top of her head, if you do not understand fashion technicalities. Her whole top hamper was neat and becoming. She had a beautiful complexion when she first came, but it faded out by degrees in the most unaccountable way. However, it was not lost for good. I found the most of it on my shoulder afterwards. (I had been standing by the door when she had been squeezing in and out with the throng). There were other fashionably dressed ladies present, of course, but I only took notes of one, as a specimen. The subject is one of great interest to ladies, and I would gladly enlarge upon it if I were more competent to do it justice.

MARK TWAIN."[353]

The Chicago Republican Company was a vehicle for the political force and influence of Chicago and Illinois throughout the recently victorious Union, and throughout the recently reunited United States of America. A. T. Andreas noted

---

[352] Chicago Republican. (February 8, 1868). Page unknown. Twainquotes.com.
[353] Chicago Republican. (February 8, 1868). Page unknown. Twainquotes.com.

that the *Republican* was a staunch source of support for United States Protectionist policy.[354] It was within the wake of the Civil War, and within the infancy of the Reconstruction, that the Chicago Republican Company sought to promote and fortify the Republican Party—the party of reunification, the party of the victory of national union over secession, and the party of continental industrial power, expansion, and economy. The defense of national union meant the defense of political union and the *Chicago Republican* sought to enforce a post-war union of Republican Party values throughout the United States. Journalistic reactions to this new Chicago force would judge the *Republican*'s works to be tantamount to political colonization of the country.[355] Charles Anderson Dana, editor of the *Republican*, served as Assistant Secretary of War under Edwin M. Stanton. The cooperative interlock and alliance among federal political power, Republican Party power, and Chicago and Cook County power and influence, collectively culminated in the establishment of the Chicago Republican Company in January, 1865. Jacob Bunn, Charles Anderson Dana, John Villiers Farwell, Ira Y. Munn, Joseph K. C. Forrest, J. Young Scammon, Jesse Kilgore Dubois, John Wood, J. Wilson Shaffer, Amos C. Babcock, Alonzo W. Mack, Francis A. Hoffman, and Henry C. Childs constituted the leadership staff of the company, and thus formed a new caucus of national political leadership with headquarters at Chicago.[356]

The *White Cloud Kansas Chief*, a newspaper of White Cloud, Kansas, introduced the *Chicago Republican* as a new paper on July 6, 1865.[357] The *Republican* was a morning daily newspaper. The Kansas newspaper reported the following facts, which had been issued by Alonzo Mack, who was President of the Chicago Republican Company: "This paper will be under the editorial control of the Hon. Charles A. Dana, for many years the principal editor of the New York Tribune, and will be thoroughly Loyal Republican Administration Paper."[358] Alonzo Mack was from Kankakee, in Kankakee County, and served as a Republican Illinois senator.[359] Amos C. Babcock served as Chairman of the Illinois State Central Committee.[360] John Whitfield Bunn also served as Chairman of the Illinois Republican State Central Committee. Babcock led a politically influential whiskey pool organization at Washington, D.C.[361] Jacob Bunn owned the Riverton Alcohol Works Company of Riverton, in Sangamon County, which was a large

---

[354] Andreas, Alfred Theodore. (1885). History of Chicago From the Earliest Period to the Present Time. Vol. II: From 1857 Until the Fire of 1871. P. 497. Chicago, IL: The A. T. Andreas Company, Publishers. Google Books.
[355] The Detroit Free Press. (August 29, 1865). P. 2. Newspapers.com.
[356] White Cloud Kansas Chief. (July 6, 1865). P. 3. Newspapers.com.; AN ACT to incorporate the Chicago Republican Company. Private Laws of the State of Illinois Passed by the Twenty-Fourth General Assembly, Convened January 2, 1865. Vol. 2. P. 118. Springfield, IL: Baker & Phillips, Printers. Google Books.
[357] White Cloud Kansas Chief. (July 6, 1865). P. 3. Newspapers.com.
[358] White Cloud Kansas Chief. (July 6, 1865). P. 3. Newspapers.com.
[359] The Quad-City Times. (January 5, 1878). P. 2. Newspapers.com.
[360] The Quad-City Times. (January 5, 1878). P. 2. Newspapers.com.
[361] The Quad-City Times. (January 5, 1878). P. 2. Newspapers.com.

manufacturer of spirits.[362] Bunn also owned the Riverton Coal Company and much of the town of Riverton.[363] Jacob Bunn and Amos Babcock, therefore, shared interest in the liquor manufacturing industry.

Negative journalistic attitudes emerged as reactions to the political power and endeavors of the Chicago Republican Company and its leadership. The *Detroit Free Press* referred to the *Chicago Republican* as a "radical organ" in a report of September 2, 1865, in which the issues of federal political partisanship pertinent to tax policies were under analysis.[364] The *Detroit Free Press* edition of August 29, 1865, commented on the electioneering strategy that Republicans in Illinois undertook to seize control of the Ohio political atmosphere and the Ohio election process. Chicago, through the *Chicago Republican*, attempted a political colonization of Columbus, Ohio.[365] Possibly by evidence of these efforts, the Republican Party of Illinois, with Chicago as its center, may have undertaken to convert both Columbus, and Ohio, to Republican satellites of Chicago.[366] A tide of responsive journalism in Detroit defended Ohio and its Democratic Party, and condemned Chicago.[367]

Charles Anderson Dana and the *Chicago Republican* entered conversation and confrontation over political issues immediately after the newspaper company's establishment in January, 1865.[368] *The Chicago Republican* was a national newspaper and a national force and representation of the interests of the Republican Party.[369] One particular journalistic project in which the *Republican* attempted to impeach the character and credibility of Ohio Democrat George W. Morgan led to a multi-state newspaper war across the Great Lakes.[370] The *Urbana Union*, a newspaper of Urbana, Ohio, reported the facts. In October of 1865, Dana, editor of the *Republican*, and a former United States Secretary of War, publicly accused General George W. Morgan of cowardice during the process of the latter's Democratic Party candidacy for the Governorship of Ohio.[371] Public irony quickly produced public embarrassment for Dana and the *Chicago Republican* when *The Detroit Tribune*, a rival Republican newspaper, reported that Dana had inquired as to the identity of Gen. Morgan.[372] Dana's inquiry implied his ignorance of the identity of Morgan, despite the fact that Dana himself had edited the biographical encyclopedia in which Morgan was given an entry that exuded public praise and recognition of Morgan's military service and bravery.[373] Dana was the joint editor

---

[362] Decatur Weekly Republican. (January 10, 1878). P. 3. Newspapers.com.
[363] Decatur Weekly Republican. (January 10, 1878). P. 3. Newspapers.com.
[364] The Detroit Free Press. (September 2, 1865). P. 1. Newspapers.com.
[365] The Detroit Free Press. (August 29, 1865). P. 2. Newspapers.com.
[366] The Detroit Free Press. (August 29, 1865). P. 2. Newspapers.com.
[367] The Detroit Free Press. (August 29, 1865). P. 2. Newspapers.com.
[368] Urbana Union. (Urbana, Ohio). (October 4, 1865). P. 1. Newspapers.com.
[369] Urbana Union. (Urbana, Ohio). (October 4, 1865). P. 1. Newspapers.com.
[370] Urbana Union. (Urbana, Ohio). (October 4, 1865). P. 1. Newspapers.com.
[371] Urbana Union. (Urbana, Ohio). (October 4, 1865). P. 1. Newspapers.com.
[372] Urbana Union. (Urbana, Ohio). (October 4, 1865). P. 1. Newspapers.com.
[373] Urbana Union. (Urbana, Ohio). (October 4, 1865). P. 1. Newspapers.com.

of the *New American Encyclopedia*, Volume XVI of which contained the biography of George Morgan.[374] The journalism of *The Detroit Tribune* seized the opportunity for the national embarrassment of Dana and the *Chicago Republican*, and noted that if Dana would merely consult his own prior historical work, he would discover the answer to his question about the identity of Morgan.[375]

> "The Chicago Republican, edited by Charles A. Dana, late Assistant Secretary of War, wants to know who General George W. Morgan is—does it? Well, if Mr. Chas. A. Dana will turn to 'Vol. XVI, New American Encyclopedia, V-ZWI, edited by George Ripley and Charles A. Dana' he will find his life and character fully described by the biographical hand of Charles A. Dana aforesaid!"[376]

Editor Dana's charges against Morgan proved the national scope of political interests that the *Republican* possessed and exerted, and that Chicago was the central force for Republican politics. The *Urbana Union* continued:

> "If the late Assistant Secretary of War and the editor of the Cyclopedia, in the face of the public and what he has put forth over his own name in relation to General Morgan's career, can now eat his own words and insinuate what he dare not openly allege, cowardice against the Democratic nominee for Governor of Ohio—if he can do this he must be a greater liar and dirtier dog than—well—than ever the editor of the *Republican* is supposed to be."[377]

The Quad-City Times of Davenport, Iowa, provided an excellent overview of the history of the Chicago Republican Company. The January 5, 1878, edition of the *Quad-City Times* reported on the culture and history of the *Republican* and its leadership.[378] Referred to as "Jacob Bunn's Newspaper," the *Republican* was a company of immense financial magnitude and political force, though a company plagued with editorial turnover and instability.[379] Bunn was constantly preoccupied with the problems of creating stability among the *Republican* editorial department, and in doing so while the paper was losing money fast.[380] "He tried one man after another in the editorial room and in the business office. They were all styles of men, farmers, editors, broken-down preachers, society men, and men about town."[381] Charles Dana disliked the Chicago weather, and planned an escape from the Chicago editorial job when he asked President Andrew Johnson for appointment to the job of Collector of the Port of New York. Dana did not receive

---

[374] Urbana Union. (Urbana, Ohio). (October 4, 1865). P. 1. Newspapers.com.
[375] Urbana Union. (Urbana, Ohio). (October 4, 1865). P. 1. Newspapers.com.
[376] Urbana Union. (Urbana, Ohio). (October 4, 1865). P. 1. Newspapers.com.
[377] Urbana Union. (Urbana, Ohio). (October 4, 1865). P. 1. Newspapers.com.
[378] The Quad-City Times. (January 5, 1878). P. 2. Newspapers.com.
[379] The Quad-City Times. (January 5, 1878). P. 2. Newspapers.com.
[380] The Quad-City Times. (January 5, 1878). P. 2. Newspapers.com.
[381] The Quad-City Times. (January 5, 1878). P. 2. Newspapers.com.

the office from Johnson, according to the *Quad-City Times*.[382] "Dana was not adapted to the latitude of Chicago, and finally, in 1866, made an application to Andy Johnson to be made Collector of the port of New York."[383] The Great Chicago Fire burned the *Republican* down in October, 1871, and the Chicago Republican Company was subsequently reorganized as the *Chicago Inter Ocean* Company.[384] *The Inter-Ocean* billed itself as "The Only Republican Newspaper at Chicago."[385] Charles A. Dana died one day after Jacob Bunn, Bunn having died October 16, 1897, and Dana having died on October 17, 1897.[386] *The Inter Ocean* reported the following facts concerning the coincidence of deaths:

"It is somewhat of a coincidence that Mr. Bunn, who was the principal funder of the old Chicago Republican, should have departed from this life while Mr. Charles A. Dana, the first editor of that paper, was lying on his deathbed."[387]

The *Republican*, despite its size and capital, experienced constant economic failure.[388] *The Atlanta Constitution* stated that Jacob Bunn had invested $300,000 in the *Republican* in order to build and develop the company, and in order to perform its purpose of aggressively outcompeting the *Chicago Tribune*.[389] The occasion of the report on the *Republican* was the financial failure of Jacob Bunn in 1878, which was due to the economic fallout of the Panic of 1873.[390] Sympathy flavored the journalism contained in the *Atlanta Constitution* report on the economic failure of the Bunn companies of Illinois.[391] The report stated:

"Also, whenever an enterprise of [Bunn's] began to fall, he could not resist the temptation to bolster it up. So it was not long before Bunn was almost the sole proprietor of the paper [*Chicago Republican*], certainly the only moneyed man in the company. From 1866 to 1877 he made a gallant fight. How many managers and editors he consumed I don't known [sic] from the days of Ballantine and Nicolay down to those of McCullagh. There was a succession of experiments and cataclysms, and the paper was constant only in one thing—it didn't pay."[392]

The Chicago Republican Company developed an indelible reputation for financial loss and this reputation gave rise to a popular joke among newspaper and real estate men. The Chicago Republican Company stood at 93 Washington Street

---

[382] The Quad-City Times. (January 5, 1878). P. 2. Newspapers.com.
[383] The Quad-City Times. (January 5, 1878). P. 2. Newspapers.com.
[384] The Quad-City Times. (January 5, 1878). P. 2. Newspapers.com.
[385] The Inter Ocean. (August 22, 1903). P. 1. Newspapers.com.
[386] Chicago Tribune. (October 19, 1897). P. 4. Newspapers.com.
[387] The Inter Ocean. (October 18, 1897). P. 6. Newspapers.com.
[388] The Atlanta Constitution. (January 18, 1878). P. 1. Newspapers.com.
[389] The Atlanta Constitution. (January 18, 1878). P. 1. Newspapers.com.
[390] The Atlanta Constitution. (January 18, 1878). P. 1. Newspapers.com.
[391] The Atlanta Constitution. (January 18, 1878). P. 1. Newspapers.com.
[392] The Atlanta Constitution. (January 18, 1878). P. 1. Newspapers.com.

in the Chicago Loop. The building became known broadly as, "'Jake Bunn's Rat-Hole,' which he was represented as vainly endeavoring to fill with greenbacks."[393] The editorship of J. B. "Mack" McCullagh saw the lessening of the money losses within the company, but whatever late apparent fiscal convalescence may have been emergent under the editorial leadership of McCullagh was squarely quashed by the Great Chicago Fire of October 8, 1871, a catastrophe which reduced the colossal Loop community newspaper company to ruins.[394] *The Atlanta Constitution* reported that the insurance companies that had granted policies on the Chicago Republican Company paid around $27,000 to Bunn for the fire loss.[395] Jacob Bunn stated that the fire insurance policy moneys were "'the first money I ever got out of the Republican.'"[396] The financial curse of the Chicago Republican Company did not end with Bunn, but consumed the investments of Jonathan Young Scammon and Frank Palmer. Palmer, an Iowa Congressman, was said to have been "swallowed up as if he had been a very small thing" by the Chicago Republican Company "Rat-Hole" in the Loop.[397] The news article concluded with a thinly eulogistic, albeit patronizing and insulting, judgment of Bunn and the Chicago Republican Company:

> "Remembering how heroically 'Jake' Bunn stood by his hopeless enterprise, how he backed men he did not know and carried out plans he couldn't understand, I cannot help feeling genuine regret that his other ventures did not enable him to retrieve his losses in the Republican."[398]

Growth by corporate acquisition occurred at least once in the history of the Chicago Republican Company. The company purchased the *Chicago Morning Post* during the first fourteen months of the *Republican*'s corporate existence. The purchase contract involved consideration in which the sale of the *Morning Post* was given for $35,000. This contract was performed prior to the July 24, 1866, report that appeared in the *Cleveland Daily Leader*, a paper of Cleveland, Ohio.[399] The *Republican* had acquired multiple presses, including a six-cylinder Hoe press for the manufacturing process of the newspaper, and was confronted in its first two years of business operation with accumulating debts and liabilities.[400] Alfred Theodore Andreas, a preeminent historian of Chicago and the United States, wrote down key elements of the history of the *Chicago Morning Post* in his classic work, *History of Chicago: From 1857 Until the Fire of 1871*. The *Morning Post* was established in 1860 as a Democratic newspaper, and its political values, opinions, and judgments contrasted dramatically in some respects with those of the Chicago

---

[393] The Atlanta Constitution. (January 18, 1878). P. 1. Newspapers.com.
[394] The Atlanta Constitution. (January 18, 1878). P. 1. Newspapers.com.
[395] The Atlanta Constitution. (January 18, 1878). P. 1. Newspapers.com.
[396] The Atlanta Constitution. (January 18, 1878). P. 1. Newspapers.com.
[397] The Atlanta Constitution. (January 18, 1878). P. 1. Newspapers.com.
[398] The Atlanta Constitution. (January 18, 1878). P. 1. Newspapers.com.
[399] Cleveland Daily Leader. (July 24, 1866). P. 1. Newspapers.com.
[400] Cleveland Daily Leader. (July 24, 1866). P. 1. Newspapers.com.

Republican Company.[401] James W. Sheahan and Andre Matteson had both worked for the *Chicago Times*.[402] When Chicago agricultural machinery manufacturer Cyrus Hall McCormick purchased the *Chicago Times*, Sheahan and Matteson left the *Times* in order to start their own newspaper publishing company.[403] Sheahan and Matteson then established the *Post*.[404] Andreas indicated that the *Post* first appeared on December 25, 1860.[405] The December 13, 1860, edition of the *Chicago Tribune* contained a notice of the founding of the *Chicago Post*, and announced that the first edition of the *Post* would appear on December 22, 1860.[406]

The *Tribune* notice stated that the *Post* would be edited by James W. Sheahan, formerly Editor of the *Chicago Times*, and that the new paper would be "Daily, Commercial, Literary, and Local" in quality.[407] The *Tribune* notice described the purpose of the newly-formed *Post* as "devoted to the best interests of Chicago and the Northwest."[408] The Post was to be a non-political newspaper according to the *Tribune* notice, but the political neutrality of the paper changed markedly, because Andreas noted that "[t]he Post was a straightforward Democratic paper."[409] Managed by F. A. Eastman, and edited by Sheahan and Matteson, the *Chicago Post* supported the preservation of the Union, but failed to support either the policy of emancipation of slaves, or other the Radical Republican policies.[410] It would appear, therefore, that the sale to the Chicago Republican Company, a Radical Republican organization, was due to some financial emergency among the leadership of the *Post*, because the leadership chose to sell out to a company with dramatically different political values, judgments, and opinions than those held by

---

[401] Andreas, Alfred Theodore. (1885). History of Chicago From the Earliest Period to the Present Time. Vol. II: From 1857 Until the Fire of 1871. P. 497. Chicago, IL: The A. T. Andreas Company, Publishers. Google Books.

[402] Andreas, Alfred Theodore. (1885). History of Chicago From the Earliest Period to the Present Time. Vol. II: From 1857 Until the Fire of 1871. P. 497. Chicago, IL: The A. T. Andreas Company, Publishers. Google Books.

[403] Andreas, Alfred Theodore. (1885). History of Chicago From the Earliest Period to the Present Time. Vol. II: From 1857 Until the Fire of 1871. P. 497. Chicago, IL: The A. T. Andreas Company, Publishers. Google Books.

[404] Andreas, Alfred Theodore. (1885). History of Chicago From the Earliest Period to the Present Time. Vol. II: From 1857 Until the Fire of 1871. P. 497. Chicago, IL: The A. T. Andreas Company, Publishers. Google Books.

[405] Andreas, Alfred Theodore. (1885). History of Chicago From the Earliest Period to the Present Time. Vol. II: From 1857 Until the Fire of 1871. P. 497. Chicago, IL: The A. T. Andreas Company, Publishers. Google Books.

[406] Chicago Tribune. (December 13, 1860). P. 1. Newspapers.com.

[407] Chicago Tribune. (December 13, 1860). P. 1. Newspapers.com.

[408] Chicago Tribune. (December 13, 1860). P. 1. Newspapers.com.

[409] Andreas, Alfred Theodore. (1885). History of Chicago From the Earliest Period to the Present Time. Vol. II: From 1857 Until the Fire of 1871. P. 497. Chicago, IL: The A. T. Andreas Company, Publishers. Google Books.

[410] Andreas, Alfred Theodore. (1885). History of Chicago From the Earliest Period to the Present Time. Vol. II: From 1857 Until the Fire of 1871. P. 497. Chicago, IL: The A. T. Andreas Company, Publishers. Google Books.

the leadership of the *Post*.[411] Andreas noted that the *Chicago Post* did not succeed the way that Sheahan and Matteson had expected it to.[412] Sheahan, oddly for a publisher of a Democratic media organ, joined the staff of the Chicago Republican Company, and worked a time for Jacob Bunn.[413] It is a plausible theory, therefore, that Sheahan had become a Republican prior to working for Bunn.

The expanding financial risks and diminishing soundness of the large Chicago corporation became permanent elements of the company's reputation early in the company's history. The *Cleveland Daily Leader* report stated: "It costs money to start a new morning paper in Chicago, and keep it going to the point where it becomes self-supporting."[414] Joseph D. McCullagh, an Irishman by birth, worked for the *Cincinnati Enquirer* as its editor, and then assumed editorship of the *Chicago Republican*.[415] McCullagh later served as editor of the *St. Louis Globe*.[416] It is an interesting coincidence that Joseph "Mack" McCullagh, Jacob Bunn, and Charles Anderson Dana all died in 1897.

The Chicago Republican Company fervently espoused Radical Republican policies of Reconstruction, as well as constitutional reformation. *The Daily Ohio Statesman*, a newspaper of Columbus, Ohio, contained a *Chicago Republican* comment, judgment, and report on the issue of President Andrew Johnson's denial of pardon to a large class of persons in the former Confederacy.[417] The Chicago Republican Company, acknowledged expressly by the Columbus journalists as a central corporate power affiliate of the post-Civil War United States federal government, defended President Johnson's amendment to the Amnesty Proclamation policy.[418] The Republican journalist wrote: "'In his proclamation of a general amnesty, Mr. Johnson has, we think wisely, seen proper to withhold pardon from many who would have been embraced in Mr. Lincoln's offer.'"[419] The *Republican* thus advocated for an amended jurisprudence of reconstructive amnesty.[420] The altered regime that the Chicago men commended entailed the following policy elements: the United States deliver charge and accusal against the former prominent leaders of the Confederacy, and hold the accused persons under

---

[411] Andreas, Alfred Theodore. (1885). History of Chicago From the Earliest Period to the Present Time. Vol. II: From 1857 Until the Fire of 1871. P. 497. Chicago, IL: The A. T. Andreas Company, Publishers. Google Books; Wyandotte Commercial Gazette. (October 21, 1865). P. 2. Newspapers.com.

[412] Andreas, Alfred Theodore. (1885). History of Chicago From the Earliest Period to the Present Time. Vol. II: From 1857 Until the Fire of 1871. P. 497. Chicago, IL: The A. T. Andreas Company, Publishers. Google Books.

[413] Andreas, Alfred Theodore. (1885). History of Chicago From the Earliest Period to the Present Time. Vol. II: From 1857 Until the Fire of 1871. P. 497. Chicago, IL: The A. T. Andreas Company, Publishers. Google Books.

[414] Cleveland Daily Leader. (July 24, 1866). P. 1. Newspapers.com.

[415] The Florence Herald. (January 7, 1897). P. 3. Newspapers.com.

[416] The Florence Herald. (January 7, 1897). P. 3. Newspapers.com.

[417] Daily Ohio Statesman. (June 6, 1865). P. 1. Newspapers.com.

[418] Daily Ohio Statesman. (June 6, 1865). P. 1. Newspapers.com.

[419] Daily Ohio Statesman. (June 6, 1865). P. 1. Newspapers.com.

[420] Daily Ohio Statesman. (June 6, 1865). P. 1. Newspapers.com.

the burden of culpability, liability, jeopardy, and punishment.[421] The *Republican* wrote of the Southern men: "'They are the prominent men in the South, the men of wealth and influence, who have hitherto exercised a commanding power for evil over their less influential neighbors.'"[422] The punitive jurisprudential regime suggested by the *Republican* would have presented the former Confederates with two alternatives: conviction and punishment by death for their service to the Confederacy; and opportunity to prove loyalty to the United States of America through acts of good behavior.[423]

The Chicago-supported regime of Reconstruction policy and law placed the condition, burden, and standard of loyalty and good behavior upon the charged former Confederates, and attached to the accused class of persons the correlative duties of compliance with the condition of good behavior and loyalty, performance of the burden of good behavior and loyalty, and satisfaction of the standard of good behavior and loyalty to the reunited United States of America.[424] Accompanying the burden of proof of loyalty was the Damoclesian alternative that was one of judgment, conviction, condemnation, and punishment.[425] Thus, under the *Chicago Republican* amnesty regime both a right and a risk attached to the class of charged former Confederates: a right of redemption and repatriation on the one hand, and the risk of conviction and punishment on the other hand. The Chicago Republican Company supported Andrew Johnson's placement of the Southern men in a hostile, but not impossible, regime of repatriation jurisprudence. The Chicago men thus affirmed President Johnson's proposed regime, which made the Confederates into a sort of potentially condemned collectivized Theseus, a Theseus who was cast into the Minoan labyrinth in which the fierce and ghostly presence of jeopardy haunted the former prominent Confederates on their precarious and uncertain road to acquittal.[426] The men's only Ariadne's thread with which to chart their escape from the fearsome repatriation policy and law regime was through production of facts and proofs, through acts of good behavior, of the men's good citizenship and loyalty to the unified United States.[427] By that course only could the condemned navigate the dark stone walls of legal process to the distant labyrinth gates of acquittal. "'[President Johnson] has expressly declared that the cases of all who are excepted [from the amnesty] are held open for future consideration. He thus puts them upon their good behavior.'"[428] The Chicago Republican Company men described very simply the burden, condition, and standard upon the Southern men as follows: "'Whether they [the former Southern leaders] will be pardoned or hanged is made to depend greatly upon their future behavior as individuals.'"[429]

---

[421] Daily Ohio Statesman. (June 6, 1865). P. 1. Newspapers.com.
[422] Daily Ohio Statesman. (June 6, 1865). P. 1. Newspapers.com.
[423] Daily Ohio Statesman. (June 6, 1865). P. 1. Newspapers.com.
[424] Daily Ohio Statesman. (June 6, 1865). P. 1. Newspapers.com.
[425] Daily Ohio Statesman. (June 6, 1865). P. 1. Newspapers.com.
[426] Daily Ohio Statesman. (June 6, 1865). P. 1. Newspapers.com.
[427] Daily Ohio Statesman. (June 6, 1865). P. 1. Newspapers.com.
[428] Daily Ohio Statesman. (June 6, 1865). P. 1. Newspapers.com.
[429] Daily Ohio Statesman. (June 6, 1865). P. 1. Newspapers.com.

The *Republican* concluded its report with support and confirmation of President Johnson. "'In adopting this course, the President has, we believe, hit upon the most successful and speedy mode of restoring peace and good order in southern communities which could possibly have been devised.'"[430]

Twin detailed descriptions of the *Chicago Republican* and the *New York Tribune* that appeared in the New Orleans *Times-Picayune* edition of September 30, 1865, proved that the leaderships of both the *Tribune* and the *Republican* supported granting voting rights to African-Americans.[431] The New York Republican Convention of 1865 was a theater for the "ultra-Republican" policies of the Reconstruction Era in the United States.[432] Thurlow Weed administered the New York Republican Convention.[433] The Chicago Republican Company and the *New York Tribune* both promoted and advocated the grant of voting rights to African-American people.[434] The two newspapers, moreover, wished to make the grant of African-American voting rights conditions of the rehabilitation of the Southern states.[435] The New Orleans journalist reported as follows:

> "The resolutions of the New York Republican Convention show that the Conservatives, under the lead of Thurlow Weed, had at least a predominating influence in that body. The great question to be decided by it was the adoption of the Radical programme of, 1. Excluding the Southern States from representation in Congress, and holding them simply as conquered and subject provinces; and 2d. Insisting on negro suffrage as a condition precedent of any future political rehabilitation of the late seceded States. The organs of the Radical faction throughout the country demanded the adoption of this platform and its logical sequence, the condemnation of the policy adopted by Andrew Johnson. Among the most clamorous of these organs of Radical opinion were the New York Tribune and the Chicago Republican, both extremely able papers. But the Tribune, as well as the Evening Post, were opposed to the maintenance of the military regime. On the question of negro suffrage, however, they were all agreed [and in favor of it]."[436]

Jacob Bunn and the other Chicago industrialists and financiers who established and owned the *Chicago Republican* were active constitutional law reform agents who strongly supported granting voting rights and property rights to African-Americans, thus giving African-Americans the rights and powers of United States citizenship.[437] The *Republican* reported on an issue of the Reconstruction of

---

[430] Daily Ohio Statesman. (June 6, 1865). P. 1. Newspapers.com.

[431] Times-Picayune (New Orleans). (September 30, 1865). P. 4. Newspapers.com.

[432] Times-Picayune (New Orleans). (September 30, 1865). P. 4. Newspapers.com.

[433] Times-Picayune (New Orleans). (September 30, 1865). P. 4. Newspapers.com.

[434] Times-Picayune (New Orleans). (September 30, 1865). P. 4. Newspapers.com.

[435] Times-Picayune (New Orleans). (September 30, 1865). P. 4. Newspapers.com.

[436] Times-Picayune (New Orleans). (September 30, 1865). P. 4. Newspapers.com.

[437] Times-Picayune (New Orleans). (September 30, 1865). P. 4. Newspapers.com.

Mississippi in December, 1865. The legislative organization in Mississippi had enacted a law that banned African-Americans from renting land in Mississippi. President Andrew Johnson responded to the discriminatory law with an order that directed the Mississippi Freedmen's Bureau to strike down the law. The issue generated conflict in Mississippi. *The Wyandotte Commercial Gazette* of Kansas City, Kansas, included the *Chicago Republican* report in its December 30, 1865, edition.[438] The *Republican* stated the following on the Mississippi Reconstruction issue:

> "There is a natural dissatisfaction in Mississippi over the order of the President directing the Freedmen's Bureau to pay no attention to the recent law of the quasi Legislature of that State prohibiting people of color from renting land.—The late rebels there don't think this is that perfect freedom of self-government on which they have been counting. But at this distance, it is the prevailing opinion that President Johnson was perfectly right in the premises. It is his duty to protect the loyal freedmen from abuse and oppression on the part of the ex-rebels who lately claimed to be their owners; and there can be no oppression more extreme than the denial to a man of all opportunity to till the earth for himself. Only rebels and rebel sympathizers can object to this order of the President.—*Chicago Republican*."[439]

The *Chicago Republican* men were exerting influence over national policy, and were actively supporting the Radical Republican regimes, laws, and policies necessary to establish equal rights for minorities.

The Chicago Republican Company employed journalists who covered sports events, as well as political and economic events, and reported on the May, 1871, baseball match in which the Chicago White Stockings played the Fort Wayne Kekiongas.[440] Of special interest is the fact that James "Jim" Haynie, a Chicago sportswriter who served as the umpire for the White Stockings at the game against Fort Wayne, had less than one week prior, on May 11, umpired the game between the Chicago White Stockings and the Cleveland Forest Citys of Ohio.[441] Haynie's service as umpire at the Chicago-Cleveland match on May 11, 1871, garnered not only notable challenges and criticisms, but instigated a riot at the eighth inning of the game.[442] This was the case after Haynie had supposedly made six bad calls as

---

[438] The Wyandotte Commercial Gazette. (December 30, 1865). P. 2. Newspapers.com.

[439] The Wyandotte Commercial Gazette. (December 30, 1865). P. 2. Newspapers.com.

[440] The Brooklyn Daily Eagle. (May 16, 1871). P. 2. Newspapers.com.

[441] Schneider, Russell. (2004). The Cleveland Indians Encyclopedia. 3rd Edition. P. 8. Champaign, IL: Sports Publishing L.L.C. Google Books; The Brooklyn Daily Eagle. (May 16, 1871). P. 2. Newspapers.com.

[442] Schneider, Russell. (2004). The Cleveland Indians Encyclopedia. 3rd Edition. P. 8. Champaign, IL: Sports Publishing L.L.C. Google Books.

umpire at the Chicago-Cleveland game, all of which went in favor of Chicago.[443] Perhaps the reputation for biased judgment that Haynie earned at the Chicago-Cleveland match preceded him back to Cook County, because when he served as umpire for the White Stockings, he was humorously referred to as a good choice for the Chicago team in its match against the Fort Wayne Kekiongas.[444] The *Republican* commented: "'The game promises to be very close and exciting, and our boys will have to show better play than they have heretofore this season, or the Hoosiers will take them in. Jim Haynie will umpire the game.'"[445]

The *Brooklyn Daily Eagle* then framed the *Chicago Republican*'s comment with a comment flavored with no small dose of humor and irony: "So it seems that the White Stockings having found an umpire to decide in their favor, are going to push him forward on all occasions. If he umpired it is no wonder they won."[446] Though quite humorous, the case of Haynie's alleged bias of judgment, if genuine, fell within the class of corrupt behaviors that Henry Hanson Brigham, Kenesaw Mountain Landis, and the Cook County Grand Jury would aggressively seek to eradicate from the sport of baseball during the early twentieth century in response to the great Chicago Black Sox Scandal. Henry Brigham was a member of the Douglas-Brigham-McClure-Stryker-Taylor family of Chicago, Cook County, Springfield, Morgan County, and Michigan. The Fort Wayne Kekiongas took their name from the name of the settlement and village of Chief Misikinaahkwa ("Little Turtle") of the Miami Native American Tribe of Indiana.[447] Chief Little Turtle was connected to the Wolcott-Wells family of Chicago and Ohio in two ways: first, as the adoptive father of Capt. William Wells; second, through the marriage of his daughter to William Wells.[448] Wells was a casualty of the 1812 Battle of Fort Dearborn, also known as the Fort Dearborn Massacre.[449] The Wolcott-Kinzie-Wells Family of Chicago and Ohio was part of the Wolcott-Richards-Henshaw-Stryker-Taylor Family of Chicago.

The Cambridge City Tribune of Cambridge City, Indiana, reported that the *Chicago Republican* had coined the term "Woodhulling," a catchy and apparently

---

[443] Schneider, Russell. (2004). The Cleveland Indians Encyclopedia. 3rd Edition. P. 8. Champaign, IL: Sports Publishing L.L.C. Google Books.

[444] Schneider, Russell. (2004). The Cleveland Indians Encyclopedia. 3rd Edition. P. 8. Champaign, IL: Sports Publishing L.L.C. Google Books; The Brooklyn Daily Eagle. (May 16, 1871). P. 2. Newspapers.com.

[445] The Brooklyn Daily Eagle. (May 16, 1871). P. 2. Newspapers.com.

[446] The Brooklyn Daily Eagle. (May 16, 1871). P. 2. Newspapers.com.

[447] Gramling, Chad. (2007). Baseball in Fort Wayne. P. 7. Charleston, SC: Arcadia Publishing. Google Books.

[448] Brown, Henry. (1846). The Present and Future Prospects of Chicago: An Address Delivered Before The Chicago Lyceum. P. 45. Chicago, IL: Fergus Printing Company. Google Books.

[449] Brown, Henry. (1846). The Present and Future Prospects of Chicago: An Address Delivered Before The Chicago Lyceum. P. 15. Chicago, IL: Fergus Printing Company. Google Books.

condemnatory action verb whose meaning was "to violate one of the Ten Commandments."[450] The *Chicago Republican* provided warnings and preventative analysis of fraud markets that were emergent in the Reconstruction economies of the United States. New federal laws and policies inadvertently caused strange and illegal markets to begin to coalesce in the West. The *Marysville Locomotive*, a newspaper of Marysville, Kansas, syndicated a monitory report from the *Chicago Republican* in which the Chicago men warned of an impending tide of fraud in the transfers of soldiers' discharge papers.[451] "Western journals mention the fact that an active traffic in soldier's discharge papers has lately sprung up in various localities."[452] With the Civil War over, and Reconstruction processes underway, new laws and policies framed a changing national economy. The Southern Homestead Act of 1866, signed by President Andrew Johnson, claimed 46,000,000 acres of southern land for agricultural development through means of the homestead.[453]

The Homestead Act of May 20, 1862, a law which had been signed by President Abraham Lincoln, created a regime of rights and benefits accruable to United States servicemen and veterans (but not to servicemen of the Confederate States of America) of the Civil War.[454] The law permitted soldiers of the United States of America to count their military service time toward their required homestead residency time under the terms of the 1862 statute.[455] The Homestead Act built a regime of laws, policies, standards, limits, duties, and benefits, as well as the servicemen's privilege of application of military time served against the time standard for residence.[456] The soldiers, who could claim the military service time privilege, could thereby claim a benefit under the regime of the Homestead Act.[457] People without United States military service could not lawfully claim the applicable military service privilege or benefit, but could possibly, through operation of fraud, acquire the benefit and privilege that was due exclusively to soldiers.[458] The particular value of the rights and benefits created by the Homestead Act of 1862, through the grant of the servicemen's privilege, catalyzed the illegal

---

[450] The Cambridge City Tribune. (August 31, 1871). P. 1. Newspapers.com.

[451] The Marysville Locomotive (Kansas). (March 4, 1871). P. 1. Newspapers.com.

[452] The Marysville Locomotive (Kansas). (March 4, 1871). P. 1. Newspapers.com.

[453] Zuczek, Richard. (2006). Encyclopedia of the Reconstruction Era. Vol. 1 (A-L). P. 54. Westport, CT: Greenwood Press. Google Books.

[454] Homestead Act of 1862. Background. National Archives. Archives.gov

[455] Homestead Act of 1862. Background. National Archives. Archives.gov

[456] Homestead Act of 1862. Background. National Archives. Archives.gov

[457] Homestead Act of 1862. Background. National Archives. Archives.gov

[458] The Marysville Locomotive (Kansas). (March 4, 1871). P. 1. Newspapers.com.; Homestead Act of 1862. Background. National Archives. Archives.gov; The Homestead Act of 1862. Homestead National Monument of America. National Park Service. Nps.gov

market for soldiers' discharge papers.[459] The Homestead Act also created for United States soldiers an immunity from the age requirement that applicants be 21 years old at the time of filing of their pleading for property rights under the Act.[460] This limited immunity to the age standard extended the benefits of the Act to a class of applicants whose age was under 21 years at the time of land property application.[461] The soldiers' immunity to the Homestead Act age standard also communicated to the soldiers that the United States valued their time of service.

The *Chicago Republican* journalists discerned with acuity the risks, as well as the opportunities, attendant upon the fast-changing economies of the United States, particularly the West.[462] The newspaper warned all soldiers and veterans of a nascent and impending fraudulent market that was robbing soldiers and veterans of their rights and benefits under the laws of the United States.[463] Frontier fraud was growing along with frontier opportunity, and the Western economies were conducive to it. The *Republican* reported that Western newspapers had begun to report the occurrences of fraudulent transfers of soldiers' discharge papers.[464] It was a western fraud market that grew and became a risk to the integrity of soldiers' benefits.[465] The fact that multiple reports and warnings had sprung up among the Western newspapers proves that the fraud market for military discharge papers had matured far beyond the inchoate, and had achieved a most rapid and economically infectious dispersion along the frontier places of the West.[466] Due to the sheer robustness of its journalistic power, Chicago served as a beacon of report, warning, observation, and information to all subjects of westward immigration. The *Chicago Republican* noted that the soldiers' discharge documents could not transfer rights, benefits, or interests but to the soldiers to whom they were granted.

> "Inasmuch as such papers are of no use or value, and can not be made honestly valuable to any one but the soldiers themselves—for no right or interest can be conveyed with them—it is not a violent presumption that the basis of whatever speculation may be involved in the business, is to use the papers dishonestly. The peculiar form of swindling contemplated

---

[459] The Marysville Locomotive (Kansas). (March 4, 1871). P. 1. Newspapers.com.; Homestead Act of 1862. Background. National Archives. Archives.gov; The Homestead Act of 1862. Homestead National Monument of America. National Park Service. Nps.gov

[460] The Homestead Act of 1862. Homestead National Monument of America. National Park Service. Nps.gov

[461] The Homestead Act of 1862. Homestead National Monument of America. National Park Service. Nps.gov

[462] The Marysville Locomotive (Kansas). (March 4, 1871). P. 1. Newspapers.com.

[463] The Marysville Locomotive (Kansas). (March 4, 1871). P. 1. Newspapers.com.

[464] The Marysville Locomotive (Kansas). (March 4, 1871). P. 1. Newspapers.com.

[465] The Marysville Locomotive (Kansas). (March 4, 1871). P. 1. Newspapers.com.

[466] The Marysville Locomotive (Kansas). (March 4, 1871). P. 1. Newspapers.com.

by the speculators, has not yet been developed; but the probabilities are that attempts will be made to adopt an extensive system of personating soldiers entitled to homesteads under the law recently passed."[467]

The federal laws and legal regimes that were discussed above constituted the foundation for the inference that the fraudulent market for soldiers' discharge papers stemmed in part from the desire to steal Homestead-based property rights.[468] The *Chicago Republican* implied the definite depth of sophistication of the western fraud market when it noted the intermodal quality of the western frauds that were operative relevant to military benefits. Both military benefits and land rights constituted mutually operational elements of the new western land frauds. For just as the heat mirages of the North American Desert integrate elements of both land and space into their optical trickeries, the frontier frauds incorporated the mutual operations of both military benefits and realty rights into the instrumentations of their rugged defalcations. The *Republican* report followed the fraud theory and analysis with the warning that soldiers never lose or intentionally part with their discharge papers.[469] "In any case, no soldier should ever permit the official record of his honorable service to pass out of his own hands."[470] The *Republican* article concluded the report with a final analysis intended to ensure the welfare of the soldiers, and the prevention of fraud against the federal government.

> "When [the soldier] presents his claims for benefits accruing under any of the acts of Congress, that record [the discharge paper] will be found valuable; and the man into whose hands it may have been permitted to pass for a trifling consideration, will doubtless be able to exact a heavy profit on his investment, as the price of producing his paper when it is wanted. The traffic alluded to has all the surface indications of fraud, of which the Government or the soldiers, or both, are to be the victims; and effectual measures should be taken to discourage or suppress it at once."[471]

The journalism from the Homestead fraud article above showed that the federal opportunities for property development and land settlement associated with Manifest Destiny and its concomitant expansions were accompanied by the spectres of fraud, abuse, and the challenges to law enforcement on the American

---

[467] The Marysville Locomotive (Kansas). (March 4, 1871). P. 1. Newspapers.com.
[468] The Marysville Locomotive (Kansas). (March 4, 1871). P. 1. Newspapers.com.; Homestead Act of 1862. Background. National Archives. Archives.gov; The Homestead Act of 1862. Homestead National Monument of America. National Park Service. Nps.gov
[469] The Marysville Locomotive (Kansas). (March 4, 1871). P. 1. Newspapers.com.
[470] The Marysville Locomotive (Kansas). (March 4, 1871). P. 1. Newspapers.com.
[471] The Marysville Locomotive (Kansas). (March 4, 1871). P. 1. Newspapers.com.

frontiers. The contents of the report were reproduced in the March 9, 1871, edition of the *Freeborn County Standard*, a newspaper of Albert Lea, Minnesota.[472]

The Chicago Republican Company directed political influence toward Columbus, Ohio, and toward Washington, D.C., in April, 1871, when it not only supported Benjamin Wade for the Governorship of Ohio, but also expressed its desire for Wade to receive the Presidential nomination in 1872.[473] The *Chicago Republican* comment that was syndicated in the *Emporia Weekly News* of Kansas, stated that: "The Chicago *Republican* thinks it wouldn't be a bad plan to nominate 'old Ben' for the Presidency in 1872."[474] Wade (1800-1878) had served as a judge in the courts of Ashtabula County, Ohio.[475] He served as Vice-President of the United States during the Civil War and as United States Senator from Ohio for eighteen years.[476] The Ashtabula County Bar Association of Ohio convened to produce a eulogistic resolution for Wade after Wade's death. Present at Wade's funeral were several newspaper companies.[477] The Chicago Republican Company, then known as the *Chicago Inter Ocean*, was represented at Benjamin Wade's funeral by W. F. Swift.[478] The *Cleveland Herald*, represented by William Lloyd, the *Cleveland Leader*, represented by Robert S. Pierce, and the *Ashtabula Telegraph*, represented by James Reed, all attended the funeral held at Wade's residence.[479] It was almost certain that Wade had befriended Jacob Bunn and John Whitfield Bunn through Civil War leadership, through the Republican Party, through association with Abraham Lincoln, and through Midwest political and professional leadership. Therefore, the support that the *Chicago Republican* gave to Wade flowed from a strong network of friendship and respect among the men involved. By supporting Wade for the Ohio Governorship, as well as recommending him for the 1872 Presidency, the Chicago Republican Company also supported and promoted the Cleveland metropolitan region, as well as the State of Ohio.[480]

When efforts emerged to make Pennsylvanian James Gillespie Blaine a Republican Presidential candidate, the *Chicago Republican* responded that "'he

---

[472] Freeborn County Standard. (March 9, 1871). P. 4. Newspapers.com.

[473] Emporia Weekly News. (April 7, 1871). P. 2. Newspapers.com.

[474] Emporia Weekly News. (April 7, 1871). P. 2. Newspapers.com.

[475] Riddle, Albert Gallatin. (1888). The Life of Benjamin F. Wade. P. 368-369. Cleveland, OH: The Williams Publishing Company. Google Books.

[476] Riddle, Albert Gallatin. (1888). The Life of Benjamin F. Wade. P. 368-369. Cleveland, OH: The Williams Publishing Company. Google Books.

[477] Riddle, Albert Gallatin. (1888). The Life of Benjamin F. Wade. P. 368-370. Cleveland, OH: The Williams Publishing Company. Google Books.

[478] Riddle, Albert Gallatin. (1888). The Life of Benjamin F. Wade. P. 370. Cleveland, OH: The Williams Publishing Company. Google Books.

[479] Riddle, Albert Gallatin. (1888). The Life of Benjamin F. Wade. P. 370. Cleveland, OH: The Williams Publishing Company. Google Books.

[480] Emporia Weekly News. (April 7, 1871). P. 2. Newspapers.com.

would run well without a tin-kettle tied to his tail.'"[481] The ambiguous comment probably alluded to the tin-kettle, or "growler," a container for alcoholic drink known and used both then and today in beverage commerce and parlance.[482] The October 5, 1871, edition of the *Chicago Republican* condemned with satire the organization known as the National Commercial Convention. Stating that neither acts, nor efficiency, was the output of the organization, but rather that "the staple product of these assemblages was resolutions," the *Republican* classified the organization as being nothing more than a "society for mutual admiration."[483] The report declared the Convention to be at best a futile, and at worst a fraudulent, organization, and expressed this charge through the medium of mordent satire. "And the venerable and distinguished fogies who constitute the Conventions seem really to believe that they are managing the affairs of the country, and, which is stranger, a great many people are of the same opinion."[484] The report suffixed its overt criticism of the Baltimore conference with a comedic and dismissive judgment: "What an unhappy, fidgety concern it would be, if it could be moved to activity by resolutions."[485]

Joseph "Mack" McCullagh of Cincinnati left the *Chicago Republican* as Editor-in-Chief on November 16, 1871, and accepted an editorial post with the *St. Louis Democrat*.[486] The *Republican* appears to have often incorporated a hint of humor into diverse classes of comment and report. The *Detroit Free Press* incorporated the *Republican's* notice of the grant of marriage licenses as follows:

> "The Chicago Republican adopts this method of introducing its list of marriage licenses: 'The Clerk of the County Court wore a diamond pin in his shirt front and a sardonyx smile on his brow as he slung out dispensations to throw teakettles at each other to the following couples yesterday.'"[487]

Mack McCullagh of Cincinnati joined the *Chicago Republican* in January of 1871. Announcement of the change in the paper's editorial leadership came with many facts about the prices and quality of the paper. *The McArthur Enquirer* of McArthur, Ohio, contained the report in its edition of January 11, 1871.[488] W. H. Schuyler, who had previously worked as Business Manager of the *Chicago*

---

[481] The Tennessean (Nashville, Tennessee). (September 8, 1871). P. 2. Newspapers.com.

[482] The Reason: A Journal of Prohibition. (May, 1887). Vol. 2, Number 5. P. 60. Geneva, IL: J. N. Wheeler, Publisher. Google Books.

[483] The Waterloo Press (Waterloo, Iowa). (October 5, 1871). P. 2. Newspapers.com.

[484] The Waterloo Press (Waterloo, Iowa). (October 5, 1871). P. 2. Newspapers.com.

[485] The Waterloo Press (Waterloo, Iowa). (October 5, 1871). P. 2. Newspapers.com.

[486] Memphis Daily Appeal. (November 17, 1871). P. 1. Newspapers.com.

[487] Detroit Free Press. (August 6, 1871). P. 5. Newspapers.com.

[488] The McArthur Enquirer. (January 11, 1871). P. 1. Newspapers.com.

Evening Post, took on the role of publisher of the *Chicago Republican* at the same time.[489] The Republican Company advertised the publication of both daily (*The Daily Republican*) and weekly (*The Weekly Republican*) media editions.[490] The scope of collection, comment, report, and analysis included global markets, among a broad class of other subjects.[491] The notice and advertisement came with a description and a promotion: "THE CHICAGO REPUBLICAN UNDER New Management and Ownership, Will be fresh and spicy in its news; bold, honest, and independent in its opinions; full and reliable in its markets, and The Cheapest Newspaper Published."[492]

The Chicago Republican Company recovered from the physical destruction caused by the Great Chicago Fire, and rebuilt at least as early as November, 1871. The November 21, 1871, edition of the *Pittsburgh Weekly Gazette* of Pittsburgh, Pennsylvania, reported that the company had fully rebuilt, and had resumed manufacture and publication of the newspaper. The Pittsburgh report said that the resurrected Chicago company operated with a new technical improvement in the presentational quality of the type of printing used in the news manufacture: "The Chicago *Republican* appeared this morning in its old form and size, with new type throughout."[493]

The *Minneapolis Star Tribune* noted a rumor that Jonathan Young Scammon purchased the *Chicago Republican* from Jacob Bunn in December, 1871.[494] The Minneapolis report was not delivered as fact, but as rumor.[495] Although other historical records indicate that Jacob Bunn retained some ownership and governance powers over the company until approximately 1877. Sidney Howard Gay was said to have assumed the editorship of the paper also in December, 1871.[496] Gay was an editor of the *New York Tribune* prior to coming to Chicago, and had helped edit the *Chicago Tribune* before coming to the *Republican*.[497]

The Chicago Republican Company resumed publication and manufacture of the newspaper in a single-sheet form shortly after the Great Chicago Fire. *The Indianapolis News* noted that: "The Chicago Republican, which has been printing a small sheet since the fire, appeared yesterday morning in its old shape, and will hereafter be published regularly."[498] A February 3, 1871, report from the *Knoxville Daily Chronicle* showed that the Chicago Republican Company did not always

---

[489] The McArthur Enquirer. (January 11, 1871). P. 1. Newspapers.com.
[490] The McArthur Enquirer. (January 11, 1871). P. 1. Newspapers.com.
[491] The McArthur Enquirer. (January 11, 1871). P. 1. Newspapers.com.
[492] The McArthur Enquirer. (January 11, 1871). P. 1. Newspapers.com.
[493] Pittsburgh Weekly Gazette. (November 21, 1871). P. 1. Newspapers.com.
[494] Star Tribune (Minneapolis, Minnesota). (December 29, 1871). P. 1. Newspapers.com.
[495] Star Tribune (Minneapolis, Minnesota). (December 29, 1871). P. 1. Newspapers.com.
[496] Star Tribune (Minneapolis, Minnesota). (December 29, 1871). P. 1. Newspapers.com.
[497] Star Tribune (Minneapolis, Minnesota). (December 29, 1871). P. 1. Newspapers.com.
[498] The Indianapolis News. (November 20, 1871). P. 1. Newspapers.com.

approve of politicians merely because of their membership in the Republican Party. Congressman Roderick Random Butler, a Republican of Tennessee, announced his intention to sue the *Chicago Republican*.[499] Congressman Butler stated slander as the theory and grounds of the intended case against the Chicago men. The prayer for recovery in the case was said to be for a sum of $15,000.[500] The report contained no additional facts.

The Chicago-made building materials that were sent to Colorado for the construction of houses came before the satirical crosshairs of the *Republican*. The *Washington Telegraph* of Washington, Arkansas, contained the comment: "The Chicago Republican says of the two hundred ready made houses shipped from that city to Colorado, that 'they can be put up in a minute and blown down in two.'"[501] *The Burlington Free Press* of Burlington, Vermont, announced that Bavarian-born John George Nicolay, a personal secretary of Abraham Lincoln, and a colleague and close friend of brothers Jacob and John Whitfield Bunn, entered the role of Managing Editor of the *Chicago Republican* in July, 1870.[502] Nicolay served prior to the job with the *Chicago Republican* as United States Consul at Paris.[503] John G. Nicolay (1832-1901) worked with John Milton Hay to produce, assemble, and write the *Life of Abraham Lincoln*, a biography that was originally published *seriatim* in *Century Magazine*.[504] Nicolay entered the publishing business at Pittsfield, Illinois, and became the publisher, owner, and editor of the *Pittsfield County Press* prior to reaching majority. He later served as personal assistant to Ozias M. Hatch, who was the Illinois Secretary of State.[505] The Bunn Brothers obviously thought highly of Nicolay for them to have chosen him to be Editor of the largest newspaper in Chicago.

The *Norfolk Post* of Norfolk, Virginia, denied the validity of the explanation given by the *Chicago Republican* of the success of the *New York Herald*. Chicago said that the success of the *Herald* was, "'owing to circumstances which are unfortunately inseparable from the wild-oats' era of a young country.'"[506] The *Norfolk Post* bluntly disagreed with the Chicago journalism and denied the *Chicago Republican's* characterization of the *Herald*. The *Norfolk Post* argued that the success of the *Herald* was due to that company's high caliber of leadership and its commitment to the business of news media production, and not to some fog of political and civic immaturity that prevalently, though amorphously, hovered

---

[499] Knoxville Daily Chronicle. (February 3, 1871). P. 1. Newspapers.com.
[500] Knoxville Daily Chronicle. (February 3, 1871). P. 1. Newspapers.com.
[501] Washington Telegraph. (December 6, 1871). P. 1. Newspapers.com.
[502] The Burlington Free Press. (July 23, 1870). P. 1. Newspapers.com.
[503] The Burlington Free Press. (July 23, 1870). P. 1. Newspapers.com.
[504] Fort Wayne Weekly Sentinel. (October 2, 1901). P. 2. Newspapers.com.
[505] Fort Wayne Weekly Sentinel. (October 2, 1901). P. 2. Newspapers.com.
[506] The Norfolk Post. (September 19, 1865). P. 2. Newspapers.com.

across the spaces of the young American republic.[507] Norfolk praised the business and governance practices demonstrated by James Gordon Bennett, Sr., who was publisher and owner of the *Herald*.[508] The *Norfolk Post*, moreover, struck three blows at once when it charged the *Chicago Republican* with being a mere partisan counterforce to the *Chicago Tribune*, described the *New York Tribune* as a preeminent failure, and implied that the *Chicago Tribune* represented an immoral and tyrannical force.

> "No journal in America ever had so grand an opportunity open to it, to become the leading guide of morals, virtue, and all that is commendable, as the [New York] *Tribune*, and 'what is it' now? A mere partizan [sic]. And the papers of Chicago are no better; for the [Chicago] *Republican* itself was established in the hope of counteracting the demoralizing influence and tyrannical spirit of the *Tribune* of that city."[509]

Consequently, through its extolment of James Gordon Bennett, the *Norfolk Post* arguably implicitly derogated Jacob Bunn, Alonzo Mack, Charles Anderson Dana, John Farwell, and the others who founded and built the *Chicago Republican* into a national organ of policy and law. There was no mystery concerning the fact that the Chicago Republican Company had been established to produce a newspaper that was fully meant to serve as the principal Republican Party organ of Chicago, of Illinois, and of the United States.[510] Appurtenant to such a role came the ardent supports and promotions for Abraham Lincoln, his regiments of statesmen, the Republican Party, and the growth and development of continental industrial power and economy, with Chicago and railroads at the center of it all.[511] As Alonzo Mack, Jacob Bunn, Charles Anderson Dana, John Farwell, and many other parties intended: "This paper will be. . . thoroughly [a] Loyal Republican Administration Paper."[512]

The Chicago Republican Company, its leadership, and its journalistic staff, sought to protect the rights and safety of African-Americans during the Reconstruction Era.[513] The company also sought to safeguard, through a powerful journalistic and political influence, federal governmental powers, authority, and

---

[507] The Norfolk Post. (September 19, 1865). P. 2. Newspapers.com.

[508] The Norfolk Post. (September 19, 1865). P. 2. Newspapers.com.

[509] The Norfolk Post. (September 19, 1865). P. 2. Newspapers.com.

[510] White Cloud Kansas Chief. (July 6, 1865). P. 3. Newspapers.com.

[511] Steele, Janet E. (1993). The Sun Shines for All: Journalism and Ideology in the Life of Charles A. Dana. P. 65. Syracuse, NY: Syracuse University Press. Google Books; White Cloud Kansas Chief. (July 6, 1865). P. 3. Newspapers.com.

[512] White Cloud Kansas Chief. (July 6, 1865). P. 3. Newspapers.com.

[513] Wyandotte Commercial Gazette. (October 21, 1865). P. 2. Newspapers.com.

jurisdiction during the Reconstruction Era.[514] The *Wyandotte Commercial Gazette* of Kansas City, Kansas, included in its October 21, 1865, edition, the September 13, 1865, report of the *Chicago Republican* that dealt with the issues and exigencies of the policies and laws of nascent Reconstruction Era Mississippi.[515] The *Republican* correspondent who was stationed at Post-Civil War Jackson, Mississippi, to cover the federal administration, and the residual post-Civil War military and social conflicts there, delivered an account framed with the rhetorical quality of a political manifesto.[516] Unfortunately, neither the Kansas City report, nor the Chicago report, identified the *Republican* journalist at Jackson by name.[517] The article focused on a multitiered case of challenges and conflicts of public interest, policy, law, civil liberty, and federal supremacy.[518] Due to the fact that the very fiber of federalism was central to this issue, the Supremacy Clause, expressed in Article VI, Clause 2, of the Constitution of the United States of America, possessed paramount relevance to the case.[519]

Mutual challenges and conflicts between the United States government and the recently defeated Confederacy were multiple, and included diverse federal-state conflicts of policy and law.[520] Principal parties to the case of policy and law conflict in Mississippi were President Andrew Johnson, U.S. Secretary of State William Henry Seward, Provisional Governor of Mississippi William Lewis Sharkey, Union Army General Henry Warner Slocum, and Judge Merwin, a

---

[514] Wyandotte Commercial Gazette. (October 21, 1865). P. 2. Newspapers.com.; Garner, James Wilford. (1902). Reconstruction in Mississippi. Pp. 100-104. New York, NY: The MacMillan Company. Google Books; Impeachment Investigation: Testimony Taken Before the Judiciary Committee of the House of Representatives in the Investigation of the Charges Against Andrew Johnson. (1867). Second Session of 39th Congress; First Session of 40th Congress. Pp. 1094-1097. Washington, D.C.: Government Printing Office. Google Books.

[515] Wyandotte Commercial Gazette. (October 21, 1865). P. 2. Newspapers.com.

[516] Wyandotte Commercial Gazette. (October 21, 1865). P. 2. Newspapers.com.

[517] Wyandotte Commercial Gazette. (October 21, 1865). P. 2. Newspapers.com.

[518] Wyandotte Commercial Gazette. (October 21, 1865). P. 2. Newspapers.com; Impeachment Investigation: Testimony Taken Before the Judiciary Committee of the House of Representatives in the Investigation of the Charges Against Andrew Johnson. (1867). Second Session of 39th Congress; First Session of 40th Congress. Pp. 1094-1097. Washington, D.C.: Government Printing Office. Google Books.

[519] Wyandotte Commercial Gazette. (October 21, 1865). P. 2. Newspapers.com; Impeachment Investigation: Testimony Taken Before the Judiciary Committee of the House of Representatives in the Investigation of the Charges Against Andrew Johnson. (1867). Second Session of 39th Congress; First Session of 40th Congress. Pp. 1094-1097. Washington, D.C.: Government Printing Office. Google Books.

[520] Wyandotte Commercial Gazette. (October 21, 1865). P. 2. Newspapers.com.; Impeachment Investigation: Testimony Taken Before the Judiciary Committee of the House of Representatives in the Investigation of the Charges Against Andrew Johnson. (1867). Second Session of 39th Congress; First Session of 40th Congress. Pp. 1094-1097. Washington, D.C.: Government Printing Office. Google Books.

Mississippi judge and judicial appointee of Governor Sharkey.[521] Historian James Wilford Garner of Columbia University, who was a member of the Mississippi Historical Society, provided invaluable comments, reports, and analysis of the facts and case in his 1902 work, *Reconstruction in Mississippi*.[522] The elements of the Mississippi policy conflict in immediately-post-Civil War 1865 included the fact that Gen. Henry Warner Slocum issued Order No. 22. This order set up a martial jurisprudential regime in which the law specifically created a bar to the creation and assembly of state-originated militia organizations in Mississippi.[523] The Order stated the grounds, theory, and reasons for the bar to state-level militarization to be the fact of the "'herculean efforts' of Mississippi for four years to overthrow the government of the United States. . ."[524] The theory held that a State charged with treason could not be entrusted with defense, even if that State were within the processes of repatriation.[525] Slocum articulated additionally as a foundational reason for Order No. 22 the fact that Mississippi surrendered to United States authority not because of civic repentance, but because of the necessity and force of "sheer exhaustion."[526] Slocum corroborated his policy argument both with the fact that Gov. Sharkey had failed to confer with the United States War Department when he commenced the assembly of state military

---

[521] Wyandotte Commercial Gazette. (October 21, 1865). P. 2. Newspapers.com.; Garner, James Wilford. (1902). Reconstruction in Mississippi. Pp. 100-104. New York, NY: The MacMillan Company. Google Books; Impeachment Investigation: Testimony Taken Before the Judiciary Committee of the House of Representatives in the Investigation of the Charges Against Andrew Johnson. (1867). Second Session of 39th Congress; First Session of 40th Congress. Pp. 1094-1097. Washington, D.C.: Government Printing Office. Google Books.

[522] Garner, James Wilford. (1902). Reconstruction in Mississippi. Pp. 100-104. New York, NY: The MacMillan Company. Google Books.

[523] Wyandotte Commercial Gazette. (October 21, 1865). P. 2. Newspapers.com.; Garner, James Wilford. (1902). Reconstruction in Mississippi. Pp. 100-104. New York, NY: The MacMillan Company. Google Books; Impeachment Investigation: Testimony Taken Before the Judiciary Committee of the House of Representatives in the Investigation of the Charges Against Andrew Johnson. (1867). Second Session of 39th Congress; First Session of 40th Congress. Pp. 1094-1097. Washington, D.C.: Government Printing Office. Google Books.

[524] Garner, James Wilford. (1902). Reconstruction in Mississippi. Pp. 100-104. New York, NY: The MacMillan Company. Google Books.

[525] Wyandotte Commercial Gazette. (October 21, 1865). P. 2. Newspapers.com.; Garner, James Wilford. (1902). Reconstruction in Mississippi. Pp. 100-104. New York, NY: The MacMillan Company. Google Books; Impeachment Investigation: Testimony Taken Before the Judiciary Committee of the House of Representatives in the Investigation of the Charges Against Andrew Johnson. (1867). Second Session of 39th Congress; First Session of 40th Congress. Pp. 1094-1097. Washington, D.C.: Government Printing Office. Google Books.

[526] Garner, James Wilford. (1902). Reconstruction in Mississippi. P. 101. New York, NY: The MacMillan Company. Google Books.

organizations, and with the fact that the Mississippi military organizations would invariably cause chaos for the peace and enforcement of Reconstruction law and policy.[527] Enforcement of Order No. 22 flowed quickly throughout Mississippi, and the bar to the creation of military organizations other than those with approval and administration from the United States War Department was quickly set up.[528] The jurisprudential regime of Order No. 22 contained not only the bar discussed immediately prior, but also the concomitant standards and duties of loyalty (to the United States) and conduct that served to enforce the bar. Order No. 22 created a system of charge, culpability, seizure, arrest, conviction, and punishment for persons who breached the bar.[529]

The Supremacy Clause manifested clearly in Order No. 22, thus illustrating the ever-relevant comment of the late legal philosopher and historian, Edward S. Corwin, which described the Supremacy Clause as "the linchpin of the constitution."[530] A linchpin though the Supremacy Clause certainly is, the Slocum-Sharkey case caused a dangerous resistance to the jurisprudential operational torque and durability of that linchpin of federalism that had been revived and re-enforced only months before in April, 1865, at Appomattox Courthouse, Virginia.[531] Garner stated that the Slocum-Sharkey incident was a case for which solution would robustly materialize in 1867, in the form of the Reconstruction Act, a law which would terminate Sharkey's Mississippi Militia, and would enact a bar to the creation of any militia organizations in former Confederate States.[532] The Reconstruction Act created a law and policy regime in which there was ratification of the policy merits of Slocum's Order No. 22.[533] The difference, however, was that the new bar would emanate from the regime of a federal statutory law, and not from the more procedurally vulnerable and contestable order of a Reconstruction

[527] Garner, James Wilford. (1902). Reconstruction in Mississippi. P. 101. New York, NY: The MacMillan Company. Google Books.

[528] Garner, James Wilford. (1902). Reconstruction in Mississippi. Pp. 101-102. New York, NY: The MacMillan Company. Google Books.

[529] Garner, James Wilford. (1902). Reconstruction in Mississippi. Pp. 101-102. New York, NY: The MacMillan Company. Google Books.

[530] Princeton Alumni Weekly. (October 22, 1963). Vol. LXIV, Number 5. A Memorial to Edward S. Corwin. P. 11. Google Books.

[531] Garner, James Wilford. (1902). Reconstruction in Mississippi. Pp. 100-104. New York, NY: The MacMillan Company. Google Books.

[532] Garner, James Wilford. (1902). Reconstruction in Mississippi. P. 103. New York, NY: The MacMillan Company. Google Books.

[533] Wyandotte Commercial Gazette. (October 21, 1865). P. 2. Newspapers.com.; Garner, James Wilford. (1902). Reconstruction in Mississippi. Pp. 100-104. New York, NY: The MacMillan Company. Google Books; Impeachment Investigation: Testimony Taken Before the Judiciary Committee of the House of Representatives in the Investigation of the Charges Against Andrew Johnson. (1867). Second Session of 39th Congress; First Session of 40th Congress. Pp. 1094-1097. Washington, D.C.: Government Printing Office. Google Books.

Era administrator and military officer.[534] Summarily, the Slocum policy arguments would receive dramatic ratification from the Reconstruction Act, while the Sharkey arguments would receive equally dramatic rebuttal from it.[535]

One of several central elements of this case of policy conflict was the safety and welfare of African-Americans.[536] A letter from Secretary of State Seward to Governor Sharkey, dated August 28, 1865, contained the relevant facts. An African-American man had been killed by a white man named Jackson in Warren County, Mississippi.[537] The murder took place on August 12, 1865. The place of the crime was "about fifty miles above Vicksburg."[538] The military searched for Jackson, found him, arrested him, and imprisoned him at Vicksburg.[539] Governor Sharkey conferred with Judge Merwin regarding the criminal case.[540] The conference produced a judgment from Merwin that issued a writ of habeas corpus for defendant Jackson.[541] Gen. Slocum, openly suspicious of both what he judged

---

[534] Wyandotte Commercial Gazette. (October 21, 1865). P. 2. Newspapers.com.; Garner, James Wilford. (1902). Reconstruction in Mississippi. Pp. 100-104. New York, NY: The MacMillan Company. Google Books; Impeachment Investigation: Testimony Taken Before the Judiciary Committee of the House of Representatives in the Investigation of the Charges Against Andrew Johnson. (1867). Second Session of 39th Congress; First Session of 40th Congress. Pp. 1094-1097. Washington, D.C.: Government Printing Office. Google Books.

[535] Wyandotte Commercial Gazette. (October 21, 1865). P. 2. Newspapers.com.; Garner, James Wilford. (1902). Reconstruction in Mississippi. Pp. 100-104. New York, NY: The MacMillan Company. Google Books; Impeachment Investigation: Testimony Taken Before the Judiciary Committee of the House of Representatives in the Investigation of the Charges Against Andrew Johnson. (1867). Second Session of 39th Congress; First Session of 40th Congress. Pp. 1094-1097. Washington, D.C.: Government Printing Office. Google Books.

[536] Wyandotte Commercial Gazette. (October 21, 1865). P. 2. Newspapers.com.

[537] Impeachment Investigation: Testimony Taken Before the Judiciary Committee of the House of Representatives in the Investigation of the Charges Against Andrew Johnson. (1867). Second Session of 39th Congress; First Session of 40th Congress. P. 1097. Washington, D.C.: Government Printing Office. Google Books.

[538] Impeachment Investigation: Testimony Taken Before the Judiciary Committee of the House of Representatives in the Investigation of the Charges Against Andrew Johnson. (1867). Second Session of 39th Congress; First Session of 40th Congress. P. 1097. Washington, D.C.: Government Printing Office. Google Books.

[539] Impeachment Investigation: Testimony Taken Before the Judiciary Committee of the House of Representatives in the Investigation of the Charges Against Andrew Johnson. (1867). Second Session of 39th Congress; First Session of 40th Congress. P. 1097. Washington, D.C.: Government Printing Office. Google Books.

[540] Impeachment Investigation: Testimony Taken Before the Judiciary Committee of the House of Representatives in the Investigation of the Charges Against Andrew Johnson. (1867). Second Session of 39th Congress; First Session of 40th Congress. P. 1097. Washington, D.C.: Government Printing Office. Google Books.

[541] Impeachment Investigation: Testimony Taken Before the Judiciary Committee of the House of Representatives in the Investigation of the Charges Against Andrew Johnson.

to be the anarchical tendencies of former Confederates, and the ramifications of permitting local law to prevail over federal law, directly challenged the validity of the writ of habeas corpus, and relied on a public interest and welfare theory based upon a foundation of Supremacy Clause law.[542] The case of the conflict of laws led to the conference of Sec. William Henry Seward with President Andrew Johnson.[543] The policy and law that constituted the output of the Johnson-Seward conference quashed the writ of habeas corpus that Judge Merwin had issued and ratified the refusal of Gen. Henry Slocum to comply with Merwin's court order.[544] The resultant ratification of Slocum's refusal, and the operationally concurrent quashal of Mississippi jurisdiction and the judicial and procedural powers of Sharkey and Merwin, corroborated the law of the Supremacy Clause as a foundation of Reconstruction.[545] With respect to the criminal charge and legal process against defendant Jackson, the effect of the judgment and law of the Johnson-Seward conference appears to have ratified his subjectability to the criminal process without freedom from captivity.[546] Secretary of State Seward remitted a letter, dated August 28, 1865, to Governor Sharkey, that contained the following words, all of which constituted a jural regime of judgment, opinion, law

(1867). Second Session of 39th Congress; First Session of 40th Congress. P. 1097. Washington, D.C.: Government Printing Office. Google Books.

[542] Wyandotte Commercial Gazette. (October 21, 1865). P. 2. Newspapers.com.; Garner, James Wilford. (1902). Reconstruction in Mississippi. Pp. 100-104. New York, NY: The MacMillan Company. Google Books; Impeachment Investigation: Testimony Taken Before the Judiciary Committee of the House of Representatives in the Investigation of the Charges Against Andrew Johnson. (1867). Second Session of 39th Congress; First Session of 40th Congress. Pp. 1094-1097. Washington, D.C.: Government Printing Office. Google Books.

[543] Impeachment Investigation: Testimony Taken Before the Judiciary Committee of the House of Representatives in the Investigation of the Charges Against Andrew Johnson. (1867). Second Session of 39th Congress; First Session of 40th Congress. P. 1097. Washington, D.C.: Government Printing Office. Google Books.

[544] Impeachment Investigation: Testimony Taken Before the Judiciary Committee of the House of Representatives in the Investigation of the Charges Against Andrew Johnson. (1867). Second Session of 39th Congress; First Session of 40th Congress. P. 1097. Washington, D.C.: Government Printing Office. Google Books.

[545] Wyandotte Commercial Gazette. (October 21, 1865). P. 2. Newspapers.com.; Garner, James Wilford. (1902). Reconstruction in Mississippi. Pp. 100-104. New York, NY: The MacMillan Company. Google Books; Impeachment Investigation: Testimony Taken Before the Judiciary Committee of the House of Representatives in the Investigation of the Charges Against Andrew Johnson. (1867). Second Session of 39th Congress; First Session of 40th Congress. Pp. 1094-1097. Washington, D.C.: Government Printing Office. Google Books.

[546] Impeachment Investigation: Testimony Taken Before the Judiciary Committee of the House of Representatives in the Investigation of the Charges Against Andrew Johnson. (1867). Second Session of 39th Congress; First Session of 40th Congress. P. 1097. Washington, D.C.: Government Printing Office. Google Books.

and policy pertinent not only to the Jackson criminal case, but to the case of Mississippi courts and jurisdiction in the Reconstruction Era. Both the criminal defendant named Jackson, and the City of Jackson, therefore, were on trial, and in a manner of analysis, both lost.[547] Seward's letter to Sharkey read as follows:

> "Upon due consideration of the state of affairs in Mississippi, as well as in several of the other states which have been afflicted by the evils of insurrection, the President [Andrew Johnson] is of the opinion that it is inexpedient to rescind the suspension of the writ of *habeas corpus* in the case which, in the papers named, you have submitted to him. Anarchy must in any case be prevented, as the process of reorganization, though seemingly begun very well, nevertheless is yet only begun. I have the honor to be your excellency's obedient servant, WILLIAM H. SEWARD."[548]

Turmoil intervened further in the Reconstruction process in Mississippi when President Johnson nullified Gen. Slocum's Order No. 22 on August 30, 1865.[549] The revocation of the order came from the War Department to Gen. Slocum. The effect of the revocation was the strike and removal of the regime of anti-militia law and policy that Order No. 22 had established. The intervention of the vacuum of jurisprudential stability led to serious constitutional issues, and incited vehement condemnation of both the Johnson Administration, and of the Mississippi government, by the *Chicago Republican*.[550]

The *Republican* writer accused the former Confederates at Mississippi of being "jubilant."[551] The writer also warned that Mississippi militias, as well as further violence to African-Americans, would be guaranteed if federal power were not

---

[547] Impeachment Investigation: Testimony Taken Before the Judiciary Committee of the House of Representatives in the Investigation of the Charges Against Andrew Johnson. (1867). Second Session of 39th Congress; First Session of 40th Congress. P. 1097. Washington, D.C.: Government Printing Office. Google Books.

[548] Impeachment Investigation: Testimony Taken Before the Judiciary Committee of the House of Representatives in the Investigation of the Charges Against Andrew Johnson. (1867). Second Session of 39th Congress; First Session of 40th Congress. P. 1097. Washington, D.C.: Government Printing Office. Google Books.

[549] Garner, James Wilford. (1902). Reconstruction in Mississippi. P. 103. New York, NY: The MacMillan Company. Google Books.

[550] Wyandotte Commercial Gazette. (October 21, 1865). P. 2. Newspapers.com.; Garner, James Wilford. (1902). Reconstruction in Mississippi. Pp. 100-104. New York, NY: The MacMillan Company. Google Books; Impeachment Investigation: Testimony Taken Before the Judiciary Committee of the House of Representatives in the Investigation of the Charges Against Andrew Johnson. (1867). Second Session of 39th Congress; First Session of 40th Congress. Pp. 1094-1097. Washington, D.C.: Government Printing Office. Google Books.

[551] Wyandotte Commercial Gazette. (October 21, 1865). P. 2. Newspapers.com.

more strictly established and enforced as components of Reconstruction policy.[552] Arguing that there was a perilously salient misperception in the North that the South could be administered and repatriated without the necessity of large-scale federal intervention and power, the *Republican* stated that not only was federal power necessary to reconstruct the South, but that the withdrawal of Northern military forces would cause potentially irreparable disorder.[553] The *Republican* argued that withdrawing Union military forces from the South would cause the South to reestablish slavery.[554] One key argument of the *Republican* journalism contained in the 1865 report was that African-Americans would be vulnerable to attack, oppression, and death, due both to the withdrawal of Union forces, and to the formation of state militia organizations administered by former Confederates.[555] The Chicago men zealously argued for the continuation of Union military presence in the South, not only to ensure the processes of reunification and Reconstruction, but also to protect the rights of African-Americans.[556] The purpose, words, judgment, and opinion of the *Chicago Republican* mirrored the purpose, words, judgment and opinion that Sec. of State Seward set forth in his letter to Governor Sharkey (quoted above).[557]

Condemnation of "Northern sympathizers with Southern traitors"[558] was communicated in a September, 1866, edition of the *Chicago Republican*, which was syndicated in the *Harrisburg Telegraph* of September 19, 1866.[559] The political report and comment came with the argument that Northerners who showed sympathy for Southern traitors should be judged unfit for public office.[560] Gen. Ulysses S. Grant had recently impeached the suitability for public office of Hiester Clymer of Pennsylvania, a man judged to be a sympathizer with Confederate causes.[561] Clymer had received the nomination for the Governorship of Pennsylvania, and Grant made a public announcement in opposition both to

---

[552] Wyandotte Commercial Gazette. (October 21, 1865). P. 2. Newspapers.com.

[553] Wyandotte Commercial Gazette. (October 21, 1865). P. 2. Newspapers.com.

[554] Wyandotte Commercial Gazette. (October 21, 1865). P. 2. Newspapers.com.

[555] Wyandotte Commercial Gazette. (October 21, 1865). P. 2. Newspapers.com.

[556] Wyandotte Commercial Gazette. (October 21, 1865). P. 2. Newspapers.com.

[557] Impeachment Investigation: Testimony Taken Before the Judiciary Committee of the House of Representatives in the Investigation of the Charges Against Andrew Johnson. (1867). Second Session of 39th Congress; First Session of 40th Congress. P. 1097. Washington, D.C.: Government Printing Office. Google Books; Wyandotte Commercial Gazette. (October 21, 1865). P. 2. Newspapers.com.

[558] Harrisburg Telegraph (Harrisburg, Pennsylvania). (September 19, 1866). P. 2. Newspapers.com.

[559] Harrisburg Telegraph (Harrisburg, Pennsylvania). (September 19, 1866). P. 2. Newspapers.com.

[560] Harrisburg Telegraph (Harrisburg, Pennsylvania). (September 19, 1866). P. 2. Newspapers.com.

[561] Harrisburg Telegraph (Harrisburg, Pennsylvania). (September 19, 1866). P. 2. Newspapers.com.

Clymer's candidacy, and to the attitudes of those who had nominated Clymer.[562] The summary of Grant's positions on the subjects of Northern sympathy and the suitability of Copperheads for public offices was reported as follows by the *Harrisburg Telegraph*, a newspaper of Harrisburg, Pennsylvania:

> "The article we copy from the *Chicago Republican* is [remarkable] in all respects, as showing Grant's abhorrence for Northern sympathizers with Southern traitors. He has no hesitation in asserting that he is opposed to Northern Copperheads being elected to responsible offices, while he especially refers to the insult offered to loyal men, by the nomination of Hiester Clymer as a candidate for Governor of Pennsylvania. *Gen. Grant is openly of the opinion, that no soldier, who has any respect for himself as a man, can vote for Hiester Clymer.* Soldiers of the Keystone State, have you confidence in the judgment of your great leader?"[563]

Once again, one can see the media influence of the Chicago Republican Company in the United States, in the North, and in the South. Jacob Bunn, the Chicago Republican Company, and Bunn's friends and colleagues affected national policy and law, and helped to make Chicago a center of political power and, specifically, a center of Republican Party political power.

The Chicago & Alton Railroad Company

The current section concerns part of the Chicago history of the Bunn branch of my mother's family. The State of Illinois approved an organic statute to create the Chicago & Alton Railroad Company on February 18, 1861.[564] The statutory law created a preliminary administrative company whose purpose included, among other things, the acquisition and reconstitution of the Alton and Sangamon Railroad Company, the Chicago and Mississippi Railroad Company, and the Chicago, Alton and St. Louis Railroad Company.[565] The statute contained a roster of incorporators. The names of the incorporators were as follows: James Robb, Charles Moran, Adrian Iselin, Nathan Peck, Louis Von Hoffman, Lewis H. Meyer,

---

[562] Harrisburg Telegraph (Harrisburg, Pennsylvania). (September 19, 1866). P. 2. Newspapers.com.

[563] Harrisburg Telegraph (Harrisburg, Pennsylvania). (September 19, 1866). P. 2. Newspapers.com.

[564] AN ACT to incorporate the Chicago and Alton Railroad Company. Private Laws of the State of Illinois Passed By The Twenty-Second General Assembly, Convened January 7, 1861. (1861). Pp. 489-492. Springfield: Bailhache & Baker, Printers. Google Books.

[565] AN ACT to incorporate the Chicago and Alton Railroad Company. Private Laws of the State of Illinois Passed By The Twenty-Second General Assembly, Convened January 7, 1861. (1861). Pp. 489-492. Springfield: Bailhache & Baker, Printers. Google Books.

Septimus Crookes, William B. Ogden, Jacob Bunn, J. J. Mitchell, Joseph B. White, and E. M. Gilbert.[566]

The statute possessed the notable quality of establishing two different companies for a shared purpose: the railroad company was the main company and an auxiliary company was established to help start the railroad company.[567] That is, the statute created the Chicago and Alton Railroad Company and the nameless preliminary administrative company that formed the auxiliary commission for the establishment of the railroad company.[568] The incorporators were appointed by the statute as a body of commissioners.[569] The purpose of the commission was the formation of a railroad corporation that would possess the name, "Chicago and Alton Railroad Company." Multiple rights, liabilities, obligations, powers, privileges, and franchises would attach to the company.[570] The new company established by the organic statute would derive assets in part from the old Alton and Sangamon Railroad Company, which held the previous name Chicago and Mississippi Railroad Company, and also from the Chicago, Alton and St. Louis Railroad Company.[571] The new Chicago and Alton Railroad Company constituted, therefore, a reconstruction of prior companies.[572]

The statute attached property acquisition powers to the preliminary administrative company for the purposes of purchase, transfer, and conveyance of property derivative from the Alton and Sangamon Railroad Company and the Alton and St. Louis Railroad Company.[573] The statute attached the power of purchase and the power of transfer to the new corporate commission as powers

---

[566] AN ACT to incorporate the Chicago and Alton Railroad Company. Private Laws of the State of Illinois Passed By The Twenty-Second General Assembly, Convened January 7, 1861. (1861). P. 489. Springfield: Bailhache & Baker, Printers. Google Books.
[567] AN ACT to incorporate the Chicago and Alton Railroad Company. Private Laws of the State of Illinois Passed By The Twenty-Second General Assembly, Convened January 7, 1861. (1861). Pp. 489-492. Springfield: Bailhache & Baker, Printers. Google Books.
[568] AN ACT to incorporate the Chicago and Alton Railroad Company. Private Laws of the State of Illinois Passed By The Twenty-Second General Assembly, Convened January 7, 1861. (1861). Pp. 489-492. Springfield: Bailhache & Baker, Printers. Google Books.
[569] AN ACT to incorporate the Chicago and Alton Railroad Company. Private Laws of the State of Illinois Passed By The Twenty-Second General Assembly, Convened January 7, 1861. (1861). Pp. 489-492. Springfield: Bailhache & Baker, Printers. Google Books.
[570] AN ACT to incorporate the Chicago and Alton Railroad Company. Private Laws of the State of Illinois Passed By The Twenty-Second General Assembly, Convened January 7, 1861. (1861). Pp. 489-492. Springfield: Bailhache & Baker, Printers. Google Books.
[571] AN ACT to incorporate the Chicago and Alton Railroad Company. Private Laws of the State of Illinois Passed By The Twenty-Second General Assembly, Convened January 7, 1861. (1861). Pp. 489-492. Springfield: Bailhache & Baker, Printers. Google Books.
[572] AN ACT to incorporate the Chicago and Alton Railroad Company. Private Laws of the State of Illinois Passed By The Twenty-Second General Assembly, Convened January 7, 1861. (1861). Pp. 489-492. Springfield: Bailhache & Baker, Printers. Google Books.
[573] AN ACT to incorporate the Chicago and Alton Railroad Company. Private Laws of the State of Illinois Passed By The Twenty-Second General Assembly, Convened January 7, 1861. (1861). Pp. 489-492. Springfield: Bailhache & Baker, Printers. Google Books.

ancillary to the more general power of acquisition of the assets of the prior companies, the Alton and Sangamon Railroad Company and the Chicago, Alton and St. Louis Railroad Company.[574] The enablement clause of the statute constructed an architecture of purpose. The power of property transfer and power of purchase served the general power of property acquisition that the statute attached to the company and the statutory commissioners.[575] The purpose of the organic statute was compound, including the powers, rights, privileges, obligations, franchises, and properties of the Alton and Sangamon Railroad, and the Chicago, Alton and St. Louis Railroad Company.[576]

The statute described the standards, acts, and process that would govern the acts of the preliminary administrative company in the bringing about of the new railroad company.[577] The statute attached the following duties to the commission company for the purpose of structuring the railroad company incorporation process. The preliminary administrative company was obligated to tender, through the filing with the Secretary of State of Illinois, the testimony, evidence, and proof of possession of the liens and payments regarding the property of the two prior railroad companies from which the new company was to be formed. The administrative company also had to produce evidence, certified by the United States District Court for the Northern District of Illinois, of the performance of the liens, obligations, and payments relevant to the acquisition of the assets, properties, rights, privileges, powers, and franchises of the prior two railroad company organization.[578] The collection and filing of the information described above would then cause the incorporation of the Chicago and Alton Railroad Company.[579]

The jurisprudential structure of the new company system also consisted of the following. The statute attached to the Chicago and Alton Railroad Company suability, liability, perpetuity (of corporate existence), the power of litigation, the power of pleading, subjectability to impleader, and the general powers and rights

---

[574] AN ACT to incorporate the Chicago and Alton Railroad Company. Private Laws of the State of Illinois Passed By The Twenty-Second General Assembly, Convened January 7, 1861. (1861). Pp. 489-492. Springfield: Bailhache & Baker, Printers. Google Books.
[575] AN ACT to incorporate the Chicago and Alton Railroad Company. Private Laws of the State of Illinois Passed By The Twenty-Second General Assembly, Convened January 7, 1861. (1861). Pp. 489-492. Springfield: Bailhache & Baker, Printers. Google Books.
[576] AN ACT to incorporate the Chicago and Alton Railroad Company. Private Laws of the State of Illinois Passed By The Twenty-Second General Assembly, Convened January 7, 1861. (1861). Pp. 489-492. Springfield: Bailhache & Baker, Printers. Google Books.
[577] AN ACT to incorporate the Chicago and Alton Railroad Company. Private Laws of the State of Illinois Passed By The Twenty-Second General Assembly, Convened January 7, 1861. (1861). Pp. 489-492. Springfield: Bailhache & Baker, Printers. Google Books.
[578] AN ACT to incorporate the Chicago and Alton Railroad Company. Private Laws of the State of Illinois Passed By The Twenty-Second General Assembly, Convened January 7, 1861. (1861). Pp. 489-492. Springfield: Bailhache & Baker, Printers. Google Books.
[579] AN ACT to incorporate the Chicago and Alton Railroad Company. Private Laws of the State of Illinois Passed By The Twenty-Second General Assembly, Convened January 7, 1861. (1861). Pp. 489-492. Springfield: Bailhache & Baker, Printers. Google Books.

to perform the corporate purpose of the Chicago and Alton Railroad Company.[580] The names stated in the statute composed the initial board of directors of the Chicago and Alton Railroad Company. The initial term of service of these individuals on the board of directors was to last until the first Monday in April, 1862.[581] The place of the headquarters of the Chicago and Alton Railroad Company was Chicago. The statute prescribed the time, place, and manner of the election of the successors of the initial board of directors named herein.[582] The Chicago and Alton Railroad Company was to serve notice to the public of the election conference for thirty days prior to the occurrence of the election of the succeeding board of directors, and was obligated to serve notice to the public by means of publication in one or more newspapers that circulated at Chicago and at New York City.[583] Failure to elect the succeeding board of directors (succeeding the initial statutory board of directors) would not constitute dissolution of the railroad corporation, but would constitute, instead, continuity of the initial board of directors, which would continue until the occurrence of the election of a succeeding directorate.[584] A majority of directors were required to hold Illinois citizenship.[585] All directors were required to own at least one hundred shares of stock in the railroad corporation.[586] The directorial duty of stock ownership ensured that the directors possessed a property interest in the company, and therefore, a general interest in the prosperity and development of the company.

The organic statute contained and outlined a system of financing for the corporation. Stock money and debt money formed the dual nature of the corporate financing for the company. The statute enabled financing of the corporation through means of creation, issuance, and sale of first mortgage bonds, income

[580] AN ACT to incorporate the Chicago and Alton Railroad Company. Private Laws of the State of Illinois Passed By The Twenty-Second General Assembly, Convened January 7, 1861. (1861). Pp. 489-492. Springfield: Bailhache & Baker, Printers. Google Books.
[581] AN ACT to incorporate the Chicago and Alton Railroad Company. Private Laws of the State of Illinois Passed By The Twenty-Second General Assembly, Convened January 7, 1861. (1861). Pp. 489-492. Springfield: Bailhache & Baker, Printers. Google Books.
[582] AN ACT to incorporate the Chicago and Alton Railroad Company. Private Laws of the State of Illinois Passed By The Twenty-Second General Assembly, Convened January 7, 1861. (1861). Pp. 489-492. Springfield: Bailhache & Baker, Printers. Google Books.
[583] AN ACT to incorporate the Chicago and Alton Railroad Company. Private Laws of the State of Illinois Passed By The Twenty-Second General Assembly, Convened January 7, 1861. (1861). Pp. 489-492. Springfield: Bailhache & Baker, Printers. Google Books.
[584] AN ACT to incorporate the Chicago and Alton Railroad Company. Private Laws of the State of Illinois Passed By The Twenty-Second General Assembly, Convened January 7, 1861. (1861). Pp. 489-492. Springfield: Bailhache & Baker, Printers. Google Books.
[585] AN ACT to incorporate the Chicago and Alton Railroad Company. Private Laws of the State of Illinois Passed By The Twenty-Second General Assembly, Convened January 7, 1861. (1861). Pp. 489-492. Springfield: Bailhache & Baker, Printers. Google Books.
[586] AN ACT to incorporate the Chicago and Alton Railroad Company. Private Laws of the State of Illinois Passed By The Twenty-Second General Assembly, Convened January 7, 1861. (1861). Pp. 489-492. Springfield: Bailhache & Baker, Printers. Google Books.

bonds, common stock, and preferred stock.[587] The financing of the corporation was to occur, therefore, through the means of debt and equity ownership.[588] Jacob Bunn not only served the Chicago and Alton Railroad Company as a founder, but also served the preliminary administrative company for the railroad corporation as a commissioner.[589] Jacob Bunn additionally was one of the principal owners of the Chicago and Alton Railroad Company by the year 1862.[590] Timothy Beach Blackstone would also play a central role in building the Chicago and Alton Railroad Company of Chicago.

Ida Hinman, a historian and biographer of Timothy Beach Blackstone, related how Blackstone became involved with the Chicago & Alton Railroad Company. In her 1917 work, *Biography of Timothy B. Blackstone*, Hinman discussed the Civil War years evolution of the Chicago & Alton company.[591] Hinman noted the 1861 Illinois statute that constituted the Chicago and Alton Railroad Company, explaining how the preliminary administrative company created by the Illinois law reorganized the bankrupt railroad company.[592] The Chicago and Alton Railroad entered a contract for lease of the Chicago and Joliet Railroad Company in 1864. Blackstone entered the corporate leadership of the Chicago and Alton in 1864, and assumed the presidency of the railroad.[593] Timothy Blackstone advocated and executed a plan of corporate growth for the Chicago and Alton Railroad Company that included construction and acquisition.[594] Hinman stated that Blackstone took on leadership of a company in possession of 250 miles of railroad and forwarded the plan of perfecting a route to connect Chicago to St. Louis.[595] President Blackstone undertook the construction of the route from East St. Louis, Illinois, to

---

[587] AN ACT to incorporate the Chicago and Alton Railroad Company. Private Laws of the State of Illinois Passed By The Twenty-Second General Assembly, Convened January 7, 1861. (1861). Pp. 489-492. Springfield: Bailhache & Baker, Printers. Google Books.
[588] AN ACT to incorporate the Chicago and Alton Railroad Company. Private Laws of the State of Illinois Passed By The Twenty-Second General Assembly, Convened January 7, 1861. (1861). Pp. 489-492. Springfield: Bailhache & Baker, Printers. Google Books.
[589] AN ACT to incorporate the Chicago and Alton Railroad Company. Private Laws of the State of Illinois Passed By The Twenty-Second General Assembly, Convened January 7, 1861. (1861). Pp. 489-492. Springfield: Bailhache & Baker, Printers. Google Books.
[590] Snodgrass, Mary Ellen. (2015). The Civil War Era and Reconstruction: An Encyclopedia of Social, Political, Cultural, and Economic History. Vols. 1-2. P. 515. New York City, NY: Routledge. Google Books.
[591] Hinman, Ida. (1917). Biography of Timothy B. Blackstone. New York, NY: Methodist Book Concern Press. Google Books.
[592] Hinman, Ida. (1917). Biography of Timothy B. Blackstone. P. 21. New York, NY: Methodist Book Concern Press. Google Books.
[593] Hinman, Ida. (1917). Biography of Timothy B. Blackstone. P. 21. New York, NY: Methodist Book Concern Press. Google Books.
[594] Hinman, Ida. (1917). Biography of Timothy B. Blackstone. P. 21. New York, NY: Methodist Book Concern Press. Google Books.
[595] Hinman, Ida. (1917). Biography of Timothy B. Blackstone. P. 21. New York, NY: Methodist Book Concern Press. Google Books.

Alton, Illinois, and thus added to the robustness of Chicago—Mississippi River Valley commercial and industrial connectivity.[596]

The Blackstone administration was responsible for the addition of 600 miles of railroad to the company's route portfolio.[597] Chicago and Alton Railroad Company road infrastructure totaled 850 miles by 1890.[598] Blackstone's reputation was characterized by honesty, integrity, and loyalty to community and public trust.[599] Chicago and Alton earnings totaled $2,000,000 annually by 1868. Financial safety and soundness characterized the reputation of the stock moneys and debt moneys offered and issued by the company, and the strong market desire for the investment opportunities that attached to the Chicago and Alton securities was nigh uniform.[600] Hinman pointed to the fact that the Chicago and Alton Railroad Company was popular among civic organizations that were seeking investment opportunities. "Its securities were eagerly sought after by the most conservative financiers and were recommended as one of the safest of endowment investments for charitable, educational or other public institutions."[601] Hinman described the quality of Blackstone's leadership as one driven by Christian moral principles, and cited as a case in point Blackstone's refusal to accept a certain offer for his large investment holdings in the Chicago and Alton for fear of exerting a negative economic impact on the smaller shareholders of the company.[602] Blackstone enforced, therefore, as company policy and law a policy of safety and soundness with respect to the manner of exchanges and investments of Chicago and Alton Railroad Company securities moneys. He held the status of majority shareholder in the Chicago and Alton by the late nineteenth century, and his ownership status in the company ensured the continuity of the culture and manner of investment described immediately above. Hinman stated, "One reason for the success of the road was that Mr. Blackstone would not allow any speculating with the stock, and as he owned the majority of the stock he was able to prevent this."[603]

By reasonable inference from Hinman's analysis, historians could judge that Blackstone wished to stem the emergence of a trader speculation culture and thus

---

[596] Hinman, Ida. (1917). Biography of Timothy B. Blackstone. P. 21. New York, NY: Methodist Book Concern Press. Google Books.

[597] Hinman, Ida. (1917). Biography of Timothy B. Blackstone. P. 21. New York, NY: Methodist Book Concern Press. Google Books.

[598] Hinman, Ida. (1917). Biography of Timothy B. Blackstone. P. 21. New York, NY: Methodist Book Concern Press. Google Books.

[599] Hinman, Ida. (1917). Biography of Timothy B. Blackstone. P. 21. New York, NY: Methodist Book Concern Press. Google Books.

[600] Hinman, Ida. (1917). Biography of Timothy B. Blackstone. P. 21. New York, NY: Methodist Book Concern Press. Google Books.

[601] Hinman, Ida. (1917). Biography of Timothy B. Blackstone. P. 21. New York, NY: Methodist Book Concern Press. Google Books.

[602] Hinman, Ida. (1917). Biography of Timothy B. Blackstone. P. 21. New York, NY: Methodist Book Concern Press. Google Books.

[603] Hinman, Ida. (1917). Biography of Timothy B. Blackstone. P. 21. New York, NY: Methodist Book Concern Press. Google Books.

preserve the long-term investment culture of the company.[604] Blackstone not only helped to build and lead the Chicago and Alton Railroad Company into preeminence among Chicago and Midwestern railroads, but used the company as a moral instrument for the promotion of a culture and policy that preserved and protected long-term investment loyalty, long-term interest in development of a great company, and a culture in which the civic and public benefits of transportation were deemed to be objects of a sacred public trust and stewardship.[605] From this remarkable good faith, Blackstone helped to build Chicago and the Midwest.[606] Blackstone perpetuated the business culture that was espoused by Jacob Bunn: a business culture defined by Judeo-Christian values of property, stewardship, and good faith, and not a business culture defined by selfish speculation and reckless stock manipulation.[607]

In 1887, the *Annual Report of the Railroad and Warehouse Commission of the State of Illinois* provided a comprehensive body of information about the Chicago and Alton Railroad Company.[608] The corporation was organized by the preliminary company and initial board of directors on October 16, 1862.[609] The authority for this process of formation derived from the organic statute of February 18, 1861.[610] The Chicago and Alton Railroad Company possessed a common stock fund valued at $14,110,800.[611] The company possessed a preferred stock fund valued at $3,479,500.[612] The total equity capital fund of the corporation stood, in 1887, at a value of $17,590,300.[613] The entire number of stockholders in the corporation stood at 1,529.[614] Seventy-two of these stockholders held Illinois citizenship. The

---

[604] Hinman, Ida. (1917). Biography of Timothy B. Blackstone. P. 21. New York, NY: Methodist Book Concern Press. Google Books.

[605] Hinman, Ida. (1917). Biography of Timothy B. Blackstone. P. 21. New York, NY: Methodist Book Concern Press. Google Books.

[606] Hinman, Ida. (1917). Biography of Timothy B. Blackstone. P. 21. New York, NY: Methodist Book Concern Press. Google Books.

[607] Hinman, Ida. (1917). Biography of Timothy B. Blackstone. P. 21. New York, NY: Methodist Book Concern Press. Google Books.

[608] Sixteenth Annual Report of the Railroad And Warehouse Commission of Illinois. (1887). Pp. 46-50. Springfield, IL: H. W. Rokker, Printer and Binder. Google Books.

[609] Sixteenth Annual Report of the Railroad And Warehouse Commission of Illinois. (1887). P. 46. Springfield, IL: H. W. Rokker, Printer and Binder. Google Books.

[610] Sixteenth Annual Report of the Railroad And Warehouse Commission of Illinois. (1887). P. 46. Springfield, IL: H. W. Rokker, Printer and Binder. Google Books.

[611] Sixteenth Annual Report of the Railroad And Warehouse Commission of Illinois. (1887). P. 47. Springfield, IL: H. W. Rokker, Printer and Binder. Google Books.

[612] Sixteenth Annual Report of the Railroad And Warehouse Commission of Illinois. (1887). P. 47. Springfield, IL: H. W. Rokker, Printer and Binder. Google Books.

[613] Sixteenth Annual Report of the Railroad And Warehouse Commission of Illinois. (1887). P. 47. Springfield, IL: H. W. Rokker, Printer and Binder. Google Books.

[614] Sixteenth Annual Report of the Railroad And Warehouse Commission of Illinois. (1887). P. 47. Springfield, IL: H. W. Rokker, Printer and Binder. Google Books.

amount of shares of capital stock held in Illinois stood at 28,300.[615] The amount of stock held in Illinois stood at $2,830,000.[616] The workforce of the corporation included 4,322 people.[617] The amount of Chicago and Alton Railroad Company railroad track stood at 1,100.02 miles.[618] This track amount included the main line from Chicago to East St. Louis, Illinois, as well as multiple branch lines.[619] The executive leadership staff of the company in 1887 was as follows:

Name of Officer	**Job**
1. Timothy B. Blackstone	President
2. James C. McMullin	Vice-President
3. Corydon Beckwith	General Solicitor
4. Chauncey Kelsey	Auditor
5. Charles H. Chappell	General Manager
6. Joseph H. Wood	General Manager's Assistant
7. T. M. Bates	Superintendent of Transportation
8. A. M. Richards	Division Superintendent
9. S. D. Reeve	Division Superintendent
10. K. F. Booth	Chief Engineer
11. Henry H. Courtright	General Freight Agent
12. James Charlton	General Passenger and Ticket Agent
13. A. V. Hartwell	Purchasing Agent
14. W. K. Morley	Superintendent of Telegraph
15. C. Huntington	General Baggage Agent
16. William Wilson	Master Mechanic (Superintendent of Machinery)
17. William Riley	General Road

[615] Sixteenth Annual Report of the Railroad And Warehouse Commission of Illinois. (1887). P. 47. Springfield, IL: H. W. Rokker, Printer and Binder. Google Books.
[616] Sixteenth Annual Report of the Railroad And Warehouse Commission of Illinois. (1887). P. 47. Springfield, IL: H. W. Rokker, Printer and Binder. Google Books.
[617] Sixteenth Annual Report of the Railroad And Warehouse Commission of Illinois. (1887). P. 50. Springfield, IL: H. W. Rokker, Printer and Binder. Google Books.
[618] Sixteenth Annual Report of the Railroad And Warehouse Commission of Illinois. (1887). P. 48. Springfield, IL: H. W. Rokker, Printer and Binder. Google Books.
[619] Sixteenth Annual Report of the Railroad And Warehouse Commission of Illinois. (1887). Pp. 47-48. Springfield, IL: H. W. Rokker, Printer and Binder. Google Books.

The Board of Directors of the Chicago and Alton Railroad Company consisted of the following individuals:

Name of Director	Residence
1. George Straut	Chicago, Illinois
2. James C. McMullin	Chicago, Illinois
3. John Crerar	Chicago, Illinois
4. Lorenzo Blackstone	Norwich, Connecticut
5. John J. Mitchell	St. Louis, Missouri
6. Timothy B. Blackstone	Chicago, Illinois
7. John B. Drake	Chicago, Illinois
8. Morris K. Jesup	New York City, New York
9. William Slater	Norwich, Connecticut[621]

The corporation equipment included diverse classes of vehicle. The company owned 226 locomotives, 119 passenger cars of various classes and purposes, and 6,511 freight cars of various classes and purposes.[622]

The Chicago Secure Depository Company

We now turn our attention to an important financial organization: the Chicago Secure Depository Company. Given the generally scant fossil record of information concerning the corporation, we must concentrate and double our analysis of the organic statute that brought forth the corporation.[623] We can extract detailed information concerning the statutorily-attached qualities of a corporation whose organizational history remains largely obscure.

---

[620] Sixteenth Annual Report of the Railroad And Warehouse Commission of Illinois. (1887). Pp. 47-48. Springfield, IL: H. W. Rokker, Printer and Binder. Google Books.
[621] Sixteenth Annual Report of the Railroad And Warehouse Commission of Illinois. (1887). P. 48. Springfield, IL: H. W. Rokker, Printer and Binder. Google Books.
[622] Sixteenth Annual Report of the Railroad And Warehouse Commission of Illinois. (1887). P. 49. Springfield, IL: H. W. Rokker, Printer and Binder. Google Books.
[623] Private Laws Of The State of Illinois Passed by the Twenty-Sixth General Assembly, Convened January 4, 1869. Vol. 3. Pp. 395-397. Springfield, IL: Illinois Journal Printing Office. Google Books.

Jacob Bunn served as an incorporator of the Chicago Secure Depository Company in 1869.[624] On March 31, 1869, the State of Illinois approved the statute entitled, "AN ACT incorporating the Chicago Secure Depository Company."[625] The Illinois organic statute contained a long roster of incorporators.[626] There were 106 people, to be precise.[627] Among this collection of people were multiple leading figures in Chicago industry and Great Lakes regional industry.[628] Several of the incorporators included:

1. John Wentworth
2. Joseph M. Medill
3. J. Young Scammon
4. John Villiers Farwell
5. John B. Drake
6. Ezra Butler McCagg
7. George Mortimer Pullman
8. William B. Ogden
9. James F. Joy
10. Jacob Bunn
11. Potter Palmer[629]

The corporate purpose of the Chicago Secure Depository Company was compound.[630] The corporate purpose of the large financial company comprised the creation and offer of the services of deposit, receipt, safe storage of items of value,

---

[624] Private Laws Of The State of Illinois Passed by the Twenty-Sixth General Assembly, Convened January 4, 1869. Vol. 3. P. 395. Springfield, IL: Illinois Journal Printing Office. Google Books.

[625] Private Laws Of The State of Illinois Passed by the Twenty-Sixth General Assembly, Convened January 4, 1869. Vol. 3. P. 395. Springfield, IL: Illinois Journal Printing Office. Google Books.

[626] Private Laws Of The State of Illinois Passed by the Twenty-Sixth General Assembly, Convened January 4, 1869. Vol. 3. P. 395. Springfield, IL: Illinois Journal Printing Office. Google Books.

[627] Private Laws Of The State of Illinois Passed by the Twenty-Sixth General Assembly, Convened January 4, 1869. Vol. 3. P. 395. Springfield, IL: Illinois Journal Printing Office. Google Books.

[628] Private Laws Of The State of Illinois Passed by the Twenty-Sixth General Assembly, Convened January 4, 1869. Vol. 3. P. 395. Springfield, IL: Illinois Journal Printing Office. Google Books.

[629] Private Laws Of The State of Illinois Passed by the Twenty-Sixth General Assembly, Convened January 4, 1869. Vol. 3. P. 395. Springfield, IL: Illinois Journal Printing Office. Google Books.

[630] Private Laws Of The State of Illinois Passed by the Twenty-Sixth General Assembly, Convened January 4, 1869. Vol. 3. Pp. 396-397. Springfield, IL: Illinois Journal Printing Office. Google Books.

and insurance upon the items of value accepted for trust, safety, and stewardship.[631] The general corporate purpose and culture of the company were, therefore, defined by trust, stewardship, safety, and soundness.[632]

The means by which goods were to be placed on deposit with the Chicago Secure Depository Company included trust, contract, and bailment.[633] The jural architecture of the organization was designed such that suability and liability attached to the company.[634]

The organic statute created and attached to the company a specific power by which the corporation could choose the rates of charge and cost for the custodial services that the company would supply, as well as the rates of charge and cost for the insurance products that the company was chartered to supply.[635] The statute additionally attached a limit to the powers of the company by means of creation of a ban on the creation and issuance of loans upon the values of goods received in trust.[636] The corporation was not incorporated and designed to offer loans, but was incorporated and designed to supply services and products of trust, safety, soundness, and insurance relevant to goods deposited.[637]

The organic statute authorized an initial capital stock money of $100,000. The statute additionally contained the grant of power to the company to increase the capital stock money to $500,000. The individual shares of ownership in the company were to be divided with values of $100.[638] The statute also attached a

---

[631] Private Laws Of The State of Illinois Passed by the Twenty-Sixth General Assembly, Convened January 4, 1869. Vol. 3. Pp. 396-397. Springfield, IL: Illinois Journal Printing Office. Google Books.

[632] Private Laws Of The State of Illinois Passed by the Twenty-Sixth General Assembly, Convened January 4, 1869. Vol. 3. Pp. 396-397. Springfield, IL: Illinois Journal Printing Office. Google Books.

[633] Private Laws Of The State of Illinois Passed by the Twenty-Sixth General Assembly, Convened January 4, 1869. Vol. 3. Pp. 396-397. Springfield, IL: Illinois Journal Printing Office. Google Books.

[634] Private Laws Of The State of Illinois Passed by the Twenty-Sixth General Assembly, Convened January 4, 1869. Vol. 3. P. 396. Springfield, IL: Illinois Journal Printing Office. Google Books.

[635] Private Laws Of The State of Illinois Passed by the Twenty-Sixth General Assembly, Convened January 4, 1869. Vol. 3. P. 396-397. Springfield, IL: Illinois Journal Printing Office. Google Books.

[636] Private Laws Of The State of Illinois Passed by the Twenty-Sixth General Assembly, Convened January 4, 1869. Vol. 3. P. 397. Springfield, IL: Illinois Journal Printing Office. Google Books.

[637] Private Laws Of The State of Illinois Passed by the Twenty-Sixth General Assembly, Convened January 4, 1869. Vol. 3. P. 396-397. Springfield, IL: Illinois Journal Printing Office. Google Books.

[638] Private Laws Of The State of Illinois Passed by the Twenty-Sixth General Assembly, Convened January 4, 1869. Vol. 3. P. 396. Springfield, IL: Illinois Journal Printing Office. Google Books.

budget to the corporation.[639] The budget stated that the value contained within the capital stock money of the company was to be used first for the acquisition of physical space to be the place of the company.[640] The budget stated that the money was to be used secondly for the investment in United States registered bonds.[641]

The statute created the following plan and process for the initial administration of the corporation.[642] Upon the subscription and payment of the capital stock of $100,000, the summons for a meeting of stockholders would necessarily occur.[643] The statute provided for notice of time and place for the initial stockholders meeting.[644] The notice of time and place for the stockholders meeting was to be served to the public through publication of the information for ten days within one of the daily newspapers of Chicago.[645] The purposes of the meeting were the identification, choice, and election of the board of directors of the corporation.[646] No further information about this company has been discovered as of the time of the writing of this book. We will next discuss the Ferguson family of Springfield and Chicago, who also worked with banking and insurance.

The Fergusons of Pennsylvania, Springfield, and Chicago

The genealogy of the Ferguson family of Pennsylvania, Ohio, Springfield, and Chicago follows here. James Ferguson married Rachel Walker. James and Rachel (Walker) Ferguson had the following children: Margaret Ferguson; **William Ferguson**; **Matthew Ferguson**; and James Ferguson. The Ferguson family

---

[639] Private Laws Of The State of Illinois Passed by the Twenty-Sixth General Assembly, Convened January 4, 1869. Vol. 3. P. 396. Springfield, IL: Illinois Journal Printing Office. Google Books.

[640] Private Laws Of The State of Illinois Passed by the Twenty-Sixth General Assembly, Convened January 4, 1869. Vol. 3. P. 396. Springfield, IL: Illinois Journal Printing Office. Google Books.

[641] Private Laws Of The State of Illinois Passed by the Twenty-Sixth General Assembly, Convened January 4, 1869. Vol. 3. P. 396. Springfield, IL: Illinois Journal Printing Office. Google Books.

[642] Private Laws Of The State of Illinois Passed by the Twenty-Sixth General Assembly, Convened January 4, 1869. Vol. 3. P. 396. Springfield, IL: Illinois Journal Printing Office. Google Books.

[643] Private Laws Of The State of Illinois Passed by the Twenty-Sixth General Assembly, Convened January 4, 1869. Vol. 3. P. 396. Springfield, IL: Illinois Journal Printing Office. Google Books.

[644] Private Laws Of The State of Illinois Passed by the Twenty-Sixth General Assembly, Convened January 4, 1869. Vol. 3. P. 396. Springfield, IL: Illinois Journal Printing Office. Google Books.

[645] Private Laws Of The State of Illinois Passed by the Twenty-Sixth General Assembly, Convened January 4, 1869. Vol. 3. P. 396. Springfield, IL: Illinois Journal Printing Office. Google Books.

[646] Private Laws Of The State of Illinois Passed by the Twenty-Sixth General Assembly, Convened January 4, 1869. Vol. 3. P. 396. Springfield, IL: Illinois Journal Printing Office. Google Books.

emigrated from County Antrim, Ireland, to Cumberland County, Pennsylvania, locating near Chambersburg in about 1750. James Ferguson held the rank of Ensign in Captain Joseph Armstrong's Rangers of the Frontier for Cumberland County. James and Rachel were members of the Rocky Spring Presbyterian Church in Cumberland County. James established a plantation and a tannery company in Cumberland County, which is located in the Appalachian Mountains.[647] The family was Scots-Irish.

William Ferguson, son of James and Rachel (Walker) Ferguson, married Sarah Liggett, who was the daughter of Samuel Liggett of Franklin County, Pennsylvania.[648] James Ferguson married Margery Denney; Margaret Ferguson married William Dixon; Matthew Ferguson married Ann Chestnut; William Ferguson, son of James and Rachel (Walker) Ferguson, was a Revolutionary War veteran, and served in Captain James Fisher's Company within the Cumberland County Militia. William Ferguson and Sarah (Liggett) Ferguson relocated to Washington County, Pennsylvania, in metropolitan Pittsburgh, in 1796.[649] William's brother James Ferguson, and other Ferguson family members, were founders of Chilicothe, Ohio, in 1798, and helped establish Chilicothe as the Capital of the Northwest Territory prior to Ohio statehood.[650] The Fergusons were also founders of the State of Ohio and Ross County, Ohio, and James Ferguson served as a judge on the first Court of Common Pleas for Chilicothe and Ross County.[651]

William Ferguson and Sarah (Liggett) Ferguson had the following children: Rachel Ferguson, who married Rev. Samuel Ralston; Martha Ferguson; Samuel Ferguson; James Ferguson; William Ferguson; Margaret Ferguson; Isabella Ferguson; **Matthew Ferguson, who married Ann Ferguson (daughter of Matthew Ferguson and Ann (Chesnut) Ferguson)**; **Benjamin Ferguson, who married Sarah Irwin of Washington County**; Sarah Ferguson; and Florence Ferguson, among possibly others.[652]

Benjamin Ferguson (1798-1842), the son of William Ferguson and Sarah (Liggett) Ferguson, married Sarah Irwin of Monongahela City, Pennsylvania, and relocated to Springfield, Sangamon County, Illinois. Their children were William

---

[647] Bennett, Henry Holcomb. (1902). The County of Ross. Pp. 470-473. Madison, WI: Selwyn A. Brant. Google Books.

[648] Bennett, Henry Holcomb. (1902). The County of Ross. Pp. 470-473. Madison, WI: Selwyn A. Brant. Google Books; Ferguson and Liggett family history records.

[649] Bennett, Henry Holcomb. (1902). The County of Ross. Pp. 470-473. Madison, WI: Selwyn A. Brant. Google Books.

[650] Bennett, Henry Holcomb. (1902). The County of Ross. Pp. 470-473. Madison, WI: Selwyn A. Brant. Google Books.

[651] Bennett, Henry Holcomb. (1902). The County of Ross. Pp. 470-473. Madison, WI: Selwyn A. Brant. Google Books.

[652] Delaware County, Ohio, History. Ferguson Family. Delawareohiohistory.com.

Irwin Ferguson, Elizabeth Jane Ferguson, Robert Ferguson, and Benjamin Hamilton Ferguson. Benjamin Ferguson started the Ferguson Construction Company of Springfield and helped build the original Illinois State Capitol there in 1839.[653] Abraham Lincoln and Benjamin Ferguson were close friends. Lincoln gave the eulogy at Ferguson's funeral in 1842. Lincoln stated:

> "In his intercourse with his fellow men, he possessed that rare uprightness of character, which was evidenced by his having no disputes or bickerings of his own, while he was ever the chosen arbiter to settle those of his neighbors. In very truth he was, the noblest work of God—an honest man."[654]

William Ferguson married Sarah Liggett. Their son, Matthew Ferguson, married Ann Ferguson, who was the daughter of Matthew Ferguson and Ann (Chesnut) Ferguson. Matthew Ferguson and Ann (Ferguson) Ferguson had a son, William Ferguson, who married Phoebe Ward.[655] William Ferguson and Phoebe (Ward) Ferguson had the following children: **Matthew Ferguson; Florence Ferguson, who married William Lee; Helen Edith Ferguson; and Clara Ferguson.**[656] It was this branch of the Ferguson family whose members were among the founders of the Pullman community and neighborhood of Chicago. Matthew, Florence, Helen, and Clara Ferguson were all second cousins of Elizabeth Jane Ferguson, who married Jacob Bunn of Springfield and Chicago.[657] William Ferguson, who married Phoebe Ward, was a first cousin of the Springfield Fergusons and the later generations of Bunns from Springfield and Chicago.[658]

Benjamin Hamilton Ferguson of Springfield

Benjamin Hamilton Ferguson (1835-1903) was a native of Springfield, Illinois. He was the son of Benjamin Ferguson and Sarah (Irwin) Ferguson, both natives of the Pittsburgh region of Pennsylvania. The Fergusons and Irwins were among the

---

[653] Ferguson, Bunn, Irwin family history records.
[654] Herald and Review. (Decatur, Illinois). (February 8, 2009). P. 14. Newspapers.com.
[655] Bennett, Henry Holcomb. (1902). The County of Ross. Pp. 470-473. Madison, WI: Selwyn A. Brant. Google Books; Ferguson family history from Susan Alland and Jim Bohannan. Ancestry.com.
[656] McLean, John. (1919). One-Hundred Years In Illinois: 1818-1918. P. 243. Chicago, IL: Peterson Linotyping Co. Google Books.
[657] McLean, John. (1919). One-Hundred Years In Illinois: 1818-1918. Chicago, IL: Peterson Linotyping Co. Google Books.
[658] Ferguson family history from Susan Alland and Jim Bohannan. Ancestry.com; McLean, John. (1919). One-Hundred Years In Illinois: 1818-1918. Chicago, IL: Peterson Linotyping Co. Google Books; Bennett, Henry Holcomb. (1902). The County of Ross. Pp. 470-473. Madison, WI: Selwyn A. Brant. Google Books.

founding families of Western Pennsylvania. Benjamin Ferguson served as president of the Springfield Marine Bank. He also was a founder of the Springfield Gas & Electric Company. He married Alice Edwards, who was the daughter of Judge Benjamin S. Edwards of Illinois and the granddaughter of Ninian Edwards, who had served as Governor of Illinois. Alice (Edwards) Ferguson also was the niece of Albert Gallatin Edwards (A. G. Edwards), the founder of the St. Louis investment brokerage house bearing the same name. Benjamin and Alice (Edwards) Ferguson never had children.

On June 6, 1890, the Illinois Secretary of State granted approval of articles of incorporation for the Springfield Boiler and Manufacturing Company.[659] The initial capitalization of the corporation was $188,000.[660] The incorporators of the Springfield Boiler and Manufacturing Company included Benjamin Hamilton Ferguson, A. L. Ide, John McCreery, and other persons.[661] The purpose of the new corporation was the manufacture of boilers.[662] In approximately January of 1903, Owsley Brown, a 1900 graduate of Princeton University, had been elected treasurer of the Springfield Boiler and Manufacturing Company.[663] At least as early as May of 1917, the Springfield Boiler and Manufacturing Company included air pressure tanks among its product lines.[664] A 1921 advertisement for the firm appeared in a publication of the American Society of Mechanical Engineers, and enumerated company products for high pressure usage, marine usage, and portable usage.[665]

As of 1921, Springfield Boiler owned offices in Chicago, Pittsburgh, San Francisco, and many other American cities.[666] The 1921 advertisement featured the "SPRINGFIELD SECTIONAL ALL STEEL WATER TUBE boiler," as well as a detailed artistic industrial depiction of these products.[667] In 1922, the company advertised that it manufactured steel stacks.[668] Springfield Boiler Company, as it was known by at least as early as 1925, operated multiple offices around the United

---

[659] Chicago Daily Tribune. (June 7, 1890). P. 8. ProQuest Historical Newspapers: Chicago Tribune. Database at Northwestern University.
[660] Chicago Daily Tribune. (June 7, 1890). P. 8. ProQuest Historical Newspapers: Chicago Tribune. Database at Northwestern University.
[661] The Iron Age (June 12, 1890). Vol. 45. P. 1000. Google Books.
[662] The Iron Age (June 12, 1890). Vol. 45. P. 1000. Google Books.
[663] The Princeton Alumni Weekly. (January 31, 1903). Vol. III, Number 17. P. 283. Princeton, NJ: The Princeton Publishing Company Incorporated. Google Books.
[664] Refrigerating World. (May, 1917). Vol. 52, Number 5. P. 70. New York, NY. Google Books.
[665] Condensed Catalogues of Mechanical Equipment. (October, 1921). Vol. 11. Pp. 85-87, 682-683, 686. New York, NY: American Society of Mechanical Engineers. Google Books.
[666] Condensed Catalogues of Mechanical Equipment. (October, 1921). Vol. 11. Pp. 86-87. New York, NY: American Society of Mechanical Engineers. Google Books.
[667] Condensed Catalogues of Mechanical Equipment. (October, 1921). Vol. 11. Pp. 86-87. New York, NY: American Society of Mechanical Engineers. Google Books.
[668] Refrigerating World. (November, 1922). Vol. 57, Number 11. P. 72. New York, NY: The Ice Trade Journal Company. Google Books.

States during the early twentieth century.[669] The corporation owned a branch office in Chicago, as well as in the following places, by the beginning of 1925: Cincinnati, New York City, Cleveland, Pittsburgh, Boston, Philadelphia, Richmond, Atlanta, Buffalo, Detroit, Duluth, Minneapolis, Kansas City, Denver, and San Francisco.[670] The company contributed much to the plumbing and heating technologies of the United States and Chicago.

Benjamin H. Ferguson served as a co-founder of the Franklin Life Insurance Company on April 20, 1898.[671] The company was created by law pursuant to the organic statute of May 26, 1869, which contained the grant of power to create life insurance companies within the State of Illinois.[672] The purpose of the 1869 statute was described as follows: "An act to organize and regulate the business of life insurance."[673] The Franklin Life Insurance Company was incorporated in Sangamon County, Illinois.[674] James R. B. Van Cleave held the office of Superintendent of Insurance in Illinois at the time of incorporation of Franklin Life Insurance.[675] The company purpose comprised the creation of insurance upon the lives of persons, as well as the creation of all classes of insurance related to the principal purpose of life insurance.[676] The company also planned to "grant and dispose of annuities."[677] The chartered corporate name was "Franklin Life Insurance Company."[678] The place of the company was Springfield.[679] The original leadership structure of the company consisted of a nine-member board of directors, with the majority of the nine members required to possess Illinois citizenship.[680] The original capital structure of the company consisted of equity stock money of

---

[669] Advertisement for the Springfield Boiler Company. January 6, 1925. Sangamoncountyhuistory.org.

[670] Advertisement for the Springfield Boiler Company. January 6, 1925. Sangamoncountyyhistory.org.

[671] Charters of American Life Insurance Companies. Pp. 25-26. New York, NY: The Spectator Company. Google Books.

[672] Charters of American Life Insurance Companies. P. 25. New York, NY: The Spectator Company. Google Books.

[673] Charters of American Life Insurance Companies. P. 25. New York, NY: The Spectator Company. Google Books.

[674] Charters of American Life Insurance Companies. P. 25. New York, NY: The Spectator Company. Google Books.

[675] Charters of American Life Insurance Companies. P. 25. New York, NY: The Spectator Company. Google Books.

[676] Charters of American Life Insurance Companies. P. 25. New York, NY: The Spectator Company. Google Books.

[677] Charters of American Life Insurance Companies. P. 25. New York, NY: The Spectator Company. Google Books.

[678] Charters of American Life Insurance Companies. P. 25. New York, NY: The Spectator Company. Google Books.

[679] Charters of American Life Insurance Companies. Pp. 25-26. New York, NY: The Spectator Company. Google Books.

[680] Charters of American Life Insurance Companies. P. 25. New York, NY: The Spectator Company. Google Books.

$100,000, divisible into 4,000 shares of $25 each.[681] The corporation was transformed into a mutual company later and the original capital stock fund was retired.[682] The Franklin Life Insurance Company included the following incorporators:

1. Howard K. Weber
2. B. H. Ferguson
3. George N. Black
4. James H. Barkley
5. J. P. Lindley
6. R. F. Herndon
7. Edgar S. Barnes
8. Joseph M. Grout
9. George B. Stadden[683]

Edward C. Akin, the Attorney General of Illinois at the time of the filing of the pleading for the grant of articles of incorporation for Franklin Life Insurance Company, reviewed the pleading document, granted approval of the pleading, and approved the charter.[684] The company bore a logo with the image of Benjamin Franklin contained in a circle, with the external rim of the circle containing the name, "The Franklin Life Insurance Company—Springfield Illinois."[685] As of 1910, Edgar S. Scott served as President of Franklin Life.[686] G. B. Stadden served as Vice President of the company in 1910.[687] The July 29, 1910, edition of *The Insurance Field—(Life Edition)* stated that Franklin Life Insurance Company had gained a major commercial presence in Chicago and Cook County through the purchase of the La Salle Life Insurance Company of Chicago.[688] The Franklin Life Insurance Company's purchase of La Salle Life Insurance Company not only solidified Franklin Life as one of the principal insurance companies of Chicago,

---

[681] Charters of American Life Insurance Companies. P. 25. New York, NY: The Spectator Company. Google Books.

[682] Charters of American Life Insurance Companies. P. 25. New York, NY: The Spectator Company. Google Books.

[683] Charters of American Life Insurance Companies. P. 25. New York, NY: The Spectator Company. Google Books.

[684] Charters of American Life Insurance Companies. P. 26. New York, NY: The Spectator Company. Google Books.

[685] The Insurance Field. (October 3, 1907). Vol. 16, Number 14. P. 23. Louisville, Kentucky: The Insurance Field Company, Inc. Google Books.

[686] The Weekly Underwriter. (December 17, 1910). Vol. 83, Number 25. P. 505. New York, NY: Underwriter Printing and Publishing Company. Google Books.

[687] The Weekly Underwriter. (December 17, 1910). Vol. 83, Number 25. P. 505. New York, NY: Underwriter Printing and Publishing Company. Google Books.

[688] The Insurance Field. (July 29, 1910). Vol. 22, Number 4B. P. 5. Louisville, Kentucky: The Insurance Field Company, Inc. Google Books.

but also increased Franklin Life Insurance Company assets by $100,000.[689] Franklin Life furthermore increased the quantity of its insurance in force through the purchase of the La Salle Life Insurance Company, because La Salle's insurance in force quantity existent at the time of its purchase by Franklin Life equaled $1,000,000.[690]

As of 1910, Franklin Life possessed insurance in force of more than $40,000,000.[691] Also in 1910, Franklin Life Insurance Company assets exceeded $5,000,000.[692] The Franklin Life Insurance Company surplus was reported at $775,000 at the time of the company's acquisition of La Salle Life Insurance Company of Chicago.[693] George T. Abbott was president of La Salle Life Insurance Company and W. T. Church, who was an attorney, was the secretary of La Salle Life Insurance Company.[694] The board of directors of the newly consolidated Franklin Life Insurance Company included J. O. Humphrey, George B. Stadden, and Will Taylor, possibly among other unnamed directors.[695] La Salle Life Insurance Company created a policy of reinsurance for the Bankers National of Chicago.[696] La Salle also created a plan of reinsurance for Corn Belt Life of Danville, Illinois.[697] Further La Salle insurance product output included policies of direct insurance.[698]

Franklin B. Macomber worked for Franklin Life Insurance Company in 1916.[699] During that same year Macomber served as a member of the Illinois Committee of the 1916 Ways and Means Committee of the Chicago Association of Commerce.[700] As of the year 1917, Franklin Life Insurance Company owned an office in

---

[689] The Insurance Field. (July 29, 1910). Vol. 22, Number 4B. P. 5. Louisville, Kentucky: The Insurance Field Company, Inc. Google Books.

[690] The Insurance Field. (July 29, 1910). Vol. 22, Number 4B. P. 5. Louisville, Kentucky: The Insurance Field Company, Inc. Google Books.

[691] The Insurance Field. (July 29, 1910). Vol. 22, Number 4B. P. 5. Louisville, Kentucky: The Insurance Field Company, Inc. Google Books.

[692] The Insurance Field. (July 29, 1910). Vol. 22, Number 4B. P. 5. Louisville, Kentucky: The Insurance Field Company, Inc. Google Books.

[693] The Insurance Field. (July 29, 1910). Vol. 22, Number 4B. P. 5. Louisville, Kentucky: The Insurance Field Company, Inc. Google Books.

[694] The Insurance Field. (July 29, 1910). Vol. 22, Number 4B. P. 5. Louisville, Kentucky: The Insurance Field Company, Inc. Google Books.

[695] The Insurance Field. (July 29, 1910). Vol. 22, Number 4B. P. 5. Louisville, Kentucky: The Insurance Field Company, Inc. Google Books.

[696] The Insurance Field. (July 29, 1910). Vol. 22, Number 4B. P. 5. Louisville, Kentucky: The Insurance Field Company, Inc. Google Books.

[697] The Insurance Field. (July 29, 1910). Vol. 22, Number 4B. P. 5. Louisville, Kentucky: The Insurance Field Company, Inc. Google Books.

[698] The Insurance Field. (July 29, 1910). Vol. 22, Number 4B. P. 5. Louisville, Kentucky: The Insurance Field Company, Inc. Google Books.

[699] Chicago Commerce. (January 21, 1916). Vol. 11, Number 38. Pp. 1, 6-7. Chicago, IL: The Chicago Association of Commerce. Google Books.

[700] Chicago Commerce. (January 21, 1916). Vol. 11, Number 38. Pp. 1, 6-7. Chicago, IL: The Chicago Association of Commerce. Google Books.

Chicago.[701] The office was located at 175 W. Jackson Street, within The Loop community.[702] F. B. Macomber served as the Manager of the Chicago office in 1917.[703] Charles Becker, in cooperation with multiple business colleagues, acquired control of the Franklin Life Insurance Company in 1939.[704] At the time of its 1939 transfer of ownership to Becker and his associates, Franklin Life Insurance Company held $177,000,000 of life insurance in force.[705] Growth remained a constant and principal quality of the development of the corporation. As of 1951, the Franklin Life Insurance Company possessed in excess of $1,000,000,000 of life insurance in force.[706] The achievement of surpassing the $1 Billion mark in insurance in force was due largely to the leadership of Charles Becker and the Becker administration of Franklin Life.[707] As of 1968, the Franklin Life Insurance Company held $7,000,000,000 of life insurance in force.[708] The multibillion insurance company had begun in Springfield, grown to include Chicago and Cook County, and long possessed a prominent commercial presence in Chicago as one of the largest insurance companies ever located in Chicago and Cook County.[709]

Another Ferguson cousin, John C. McKeever of Joliet, was President of the Gerlach-Barklow Company of Joliet, the largest calendar manufacturer in the United States. John C. McKeever was also President of the Illinois Manufacturers' Association, a Chicago-based organization with thousands of members.[710] Another Ferguson cousin, John Archibald Simeral of Pittsburgh, founded and owned the Famous Biscuit Company of Pittsburgh, one of the largest cracker, biscuit, cake, and bread manufacturers of Pennsylvania and Ohio.[711] Simeral was co-founder and director of the National Cracker and Biscuit Manufacturers' Company, which had

---

[701] Blue Book of Chicago Commerce. (1917). Vol. 2. P. 263. Chicago, IL: The Chicago Association of Commerce. Google Books.

[702] Blue Book of Chicago Commerce. (1917). Vol. 2. P. 263. Chicago, IL: The Chicago Association of Commerce. Google Books.

[703] Blue Book of Chicago Commerce. (1917). Vol. 2. P. 263. Chicago, IL: The Chicago Association of Commerce. Google Books.

[704] Chicago Daily Tribune. (March 31, 1951). P. B7. ProQuest Historical Newspapers: Chicago Tribune. Database at Northwestern University.

[705] Chicago Daily Tribune. (June 26, 1968) P. A4. ProQuest Historical Newspapers: Chicago Tribune. Database at Northwestern University.

[706] Chicago Daily Tribune. (March 31, 1951). P. B7. ProQuest Historical Newspapers: Chicago Tribune. Database at Northwestern University.

[707] Chicago Daily Tribune. (March 31, 1951). P. B7. ProQuest Historical Newspapers: Chicago Tribune. Database at Northwestern University; see also: Chicago Daily Tribune. (June 26, 1968) P. A4. ProQuest Historical Newspapers: Chicago Tribune. Database at Northwestern University.

[708] Chicago Daily Tribune. (June 26, 1968) P. A4. ProQuest Historical Newspapers: Chicago Tribune. Database at Northwestern University.

[709] See sources and references herein.

[710] Ferguson family history records.

[711] Ferguson family history records.

offices in Pittsburgh, Chicago, and elsewhere.[712] These companies all distributed broadly throughout the Great Lakes and the Appalachian Mountains.

The Irwin Family of Washington County, Pennsylvania, and Illinois

Elizabeth Jane Ferguson (1832-1886), who was the wife of Jacob Bunn, was the daughter of Benjamin Ferguson and Sarah (Irwin) Ferguson of Washington County, Pennsylvania. The Irwin family had been among the founders of Washington County, Pennsylvania, which lies in the western portion of metropolitan Pittsburgh. William Irwin was a Justice of the Peace in Washington County. Sarah Irwin was the sister of John Irwin (1804-1859), Robert Irwin (1808-1865) and Jane Irwin.[713] There may also have been other siblings. Multiple members of the Irwin family were subsequently connected to Chicago.

Robert Irwin and the State Bank of Illinois and Chicago

Robert Irwin, John Carr, and Augustus Carr started the Carr & Irwin Company of St. Louis, which was a mercantile company.[714] Robert married Clara Doyle, a Philadelphia native, in St. Louis, and the couple moved to Springfield after Irwin dissolved the Carr & Irwin Company in 1834.[715] At Springfield Irwin started the Williams and Irwin Company, a dry goods firm, with his brother, John Irwin, and John Williams. Robert Irwin and Clara (Doyle) Irwin had the following children: Eliza J. Irwin, who married William Marston of New York City; Sarah Ella Irwin, who married Charles D. Chase of Deerfield, New Hampshire; and Robert T. Irwin of Springfield.[716] John Carroll Power and his wife, S. A. Power, noted in their 1876 history of Sangamon County that Robert and Clara (Doyle) Irwin had two other children who died young. William Marston was a multimillionaire railroad capitalist of New York, Wisconsin, and Illinois during the time of the Civil War.[717] Robert Irwin served on the board of directors of the State Bank of Illinois, which was a multi-branch bank company whose Chicago branch was the first bank in Chicago history. For more information about this history, see Chapter 1, *Genesis of a Great Lakes Frontier.*

---

[712] Ferguson family history records.

[713] Irwin family historical records.

[714] Lawpracticeofabrahamlincoln.org; see History of Sangamon County, Illinois (Chicago: Inter-state Publishing Company, 1881). P. 681; see Power, John Carroll. (1876). History of the Early Settlers of Sangamon County, Illinois. P. 405. Springfield, IL: E. A. Wilson and Company.

[715] Lawpracticeofabrahamlincoln.org; see History of Sangamon County, Illinois (Chicago: Inter-state Publishing Company, 1881), 681; see Power, John Carroll. (1876). History of the Early Settlers of Sangamon County, Illinois. P. 405. Springfield, IL: E. A. Wilson and Company.

[716] Findagrave.com. Clara (Doyle) Irwin. Oak Ridge Cemetery, Springfield, Illinois.

[717] Irwin family historical records.

Charles D. Chase and Sarah Ella (Irwin) Chase had a daughter, Elinor Irwin Chase, who married Guerdon Stearns Holden of Cleveland, Ohio. Guerdon S. Holden owned the *Cleveland Plain Dealer* newspaper and Forest City Publishing Company of Cleveland.[718] Albert Fairchild Holden, brother of Guerdon S. Holden, owned Island Creek Coal Company of Cleveland and Pond Creek Coal Company of Cleveland.[719] These coal companies were among the largest in the world, controlled much of the coal development of West Virginia, Virginia, and Kentucky, and heavily impacted the coal towns of Grundy, Pikeville, Logan, Island Creek, and many others. Guerdon and Elinor (Chase) Holden were among the founders and leading philanthropists of the Cleveland Museum of Art.[720] The Holdens attended the 1938 Springfield wedding of Elizabeth Bunn and Henry Stryker Taylor. The Holdens of Cleveland were cousins of Elizabeth Bunn through the Irwin family.[721] The Guerdon and Elinor (Chase) Holden Art Collection at the Cleveland Museum of Art remains one of the most significant European art collections at the museum.[722]

John Irwin, brother of Sarah (Irwin) Ferguson, Jane (Irwin) Stockdale, and Robert Irwin, married Margaret Jack Guthrie. John Irwin and Margaret (Guthrie) Irwin had three children: William Irwin of Colorado; Hetty Irwin, who married Judge A. N. J. Crook, who was a lawyer, Mayor of Springfield, member of the Illinois legislature, and Receiver in the Land Office of Oklahoma; and Margaret Irwin, who married Cleveland J. Salter of Springfield.[723]

The Irwin and Stockdale Family of Springfield and Chicago

Jane Irwin married William Stockdale. They had the following children, possibly in addition to others: Sarah Irwin Stockdale, who married Elon Pratt House; Elizabeth "Jennie" Stockdale, who married James Madison Brittin; and Margaret Stockdale, who married lawyer Samuel D. Scholes of Springfield.[724] All three of these children would have descendants who resided in Chicago, and these three children were the parents of the Irwin-Stockdale-Scholes branch; the Irwin-

---

[718] Irwin, Ferguson, and Bunn family history records.

[719] Irwin, Ferguson, and Bunn family history records.

[720] Irwin, Ferguson, and Bunn family history records.

[721] Irwin, Ferguson, and Bunn family history records.

[722] Irwin, Ferguson, and Bunn family history records.

[723] Power, John Carroll. (1876). History Of The Early Settlers Of Sangamon County, Illinois. Pp. 405-406. Springfield, IL: Edwin A. Wilson & Co. Google Books; Findagrave.com. Judge A. N. J. Crook. Oak Ridge Cemetery, Springfield, Illinois.

[724] Wallace, Joseph. (1904). Past And Present Of The City Of Springfield And Sangamon County, Illinois. Pp. 126-129. Chicago, IL: S. J. Clarke Publishing Company. Google Books.

Stockdale-Brittin-Kane-Zelle branch; and the Irwin-Stockdale-House branch. We discuss the Chicago history of these three branches next.

The Irwin-Scholes Branch of Springfield and Chicago

Samuel D. Scholes and Margaret (Stockdale) Scholes had the following children: James B. Scholes; Alice Scholes; Samuel D. Scholes, a Springfield lawyer with the firm of Scholes & Barber; and Jessie Scholes, who married planing mill owner Robert Vredenburgh. James B. Scholes, son of Samuel and Margaret (Stockdale) Scholes worked for General Electric in Chicago.[725] No additional information about James B. Scholes has been discovered at the time of the writing of this book.

The Irwin-Stockdale-Brittin-Kane-Zelle Branch of Springfield and Chicago

Elizabeth Irwin (Stockdale) Brittin and James Madison Brittin had the following children: William Brittin, who moved to North Dakota; and Flora Brittin, who married Judge Charles Philo Kane of Springfield. Flora (Brittin) Kane (1856-1939) married Charles P. Kane (1850-1918).[726] The following children were born to them: Caroline Kane, who married Carl Hubert Streiff; Elizabeth Kane, who married Dr. Oscar Zelle; Philo Beers Kane; and Eugene S. Kane. Elizabeth Kane (1886-1955) married Oscar L. Zelle (1885-1967).[727] Oscar Zelle was a prominent medical doctor in Springfield, a fellow of the American College of Surgeons, and a fifty-year member of the American Medical Association.[728] Elizabeth and Oscar had a son, Dr. Charles Kane Zelle, whom we will discuss next.

Dr. Charles Kane Zelle of Chicago and Springfield

Dr. Charles Kane Zelle (1916-1997), the son of Dr. Oscar L. Zelle and Elizabeth (Kane) Zelle, was a cousin of Henry Barrell House, a cousin of many of the descendants of Jacob Bunn and of the Fergusons of Springfield, through the Zelle-Kane-Britton-Stockdale-Irwin families of Illinois.[729] Dr. Zelle and Henry House were both descendants of the Irwin family.[730] Zelle attended Lake Forest Academy in the north shore Chicago suburb of Lake Forest, located in Lake County.[731] He

---

[725] Wallace, Joseph. (1904). Past And Present Of The City Of Springfield And Sangamon County, Illinois. Pp. 126-129. Chicago, IL: S. J. Clarke Publishing Company. Google Books.

[726] Irwin family historical records; see Findagrave.com. Dr. Oscar L. Zelle, Elizabeth (Kane) Zelle, Philo Kane, James Madison Brittin, Elizabeth Irwin (Stockdale) Brittin.

[727] Irwin family historical records; see Findagrave.com. Dr. Oscar L. Zelle, Elizabeth (Kane) Zelle, Philo Kane, James Madison Brittin, Elizabeth Irwin (Stockdale) Brittin.

[728] Irwin family historical records; see Findagrave.com. Dr. Oscar L. Zelle, Elizabeth (Kane) Zelle, Philo Kane, James Madison Brittin, Elizabeth Irwin (Stockdale) Brittin.

[729] Bunn, Ferguson, Irwin, Stockdale family history records.

[730] The Palm Beach Post. (September 16, 1997). P. 20. Newspapers.com.

[731] The Palm Beach Post. (September 16, 1997). P. 20. Newspapers.com.

was an alumnus of Dartmouth College, and received the degree of Doctor of Medicine from Northwestern University.[732] He later taught medicine as a member of the medical faculty of Northwestern.[733] A renowned Illinois obstetrician and gynecologist, he delivered many of the children of Springfield, Illinois, including the mother of author Andrew Taylor Call.[734] He was Medical Director for Arnar Stone Laboratories, Inc., a company located in Mt. Prospect, which is a Chicago suburb.[735] Dr. Zelle served also as Vice-President of Medical Affairs for Arnar Stone Laboratories, Inc., in the 1970s.[736] Arnar Stone Laboratories was a subsidiary of American Hospital Supply Corporation at the time when Kane Zelle was Vice-President of Medical Affairs for the company.[737] American Hospital Supply Corporation was an Evanston company at the time when Dr. Zelle worked for Arnar Stone Laboratories, Inc.[738] In addition to having engaged in medical practice and corporate leadership within the Chicago medical sciences industry, he was a prominent real estate owner in Chicago.[739] Zelle co-wrote the book, *The Fight Against Germs*, with Robert Weisman, in 1941. Zelle was a close friend of Henry Stryker Taylor and Elizabeth (Bunn) Taylor and was a cousin of Elizabeth (Bunn) Taylor through the Irwin family.[740]

The Irwin-Stockdale-House Branch of Chicago and Springfield

Sarah Irwin Stockdale, daughter of William Stockdale and Jane (Irwin) Stockdale, married Judge Elon Pratt House of Springfield.[741] Sarah Stockdale resided with Jacob Bunn and Elizabeth (Ferguson) Bunn in Springfield when she was a teenager, and was a cousin and close friend of Alice Edwards Bunn, the youngest child of Jacob and Elizabeth (Ferguson) Bunn.[742] Alice Bunn and Sarah Irwin Stockdale remained close friends through adulthood.[743] Sarah Irwin

---

[732] The Palm Beach Post. (September 16, 1997). P. 20. Newspapers.com.
[733] The Palm Beach Post. (September 16, 1997). P. 20. Newspapers.com.
[734] Memoirs of Elizabeth Taylor Greer and Jenny Zelle, Esq.
[735] The Palm Beach Post. (September 16, 1997). P. 20. Newspapers.com.
[736] Kern, Kenneth R. (1972). Executive Directory of the U.S. Pharmaceutical Industry. Page number not apparent. Chemical Economic Services. Google Books.
[737] Kern, Kenneth R. (1972). Executive Directory of the U.S. Pharmaceutical Industry. Page number not apparent. Chemical Economic Services. Google Books.
[738] Chicago, Cook County, Industrial Directory. (1973). Page number not apparent. Chicago, IL: Chicago Cook County Industrial Directory, Inc. Google Books.
[739] Memoir of Jenny Zelle, Esq.
[740] Bunn family history records.
[741] Irwin family historical records; see Findagrave.com. Dr. Oscar L. Zelle, Elizabeth (Kane) Zelle, Philo Kane, James Madison Brittin, Elizabeth Irwin (Stockdale) Brittin.
[742] Banton, Albert W., Balm, Ellen Carol, O'Bright, Jill York. (September, 1987). Historic Resource Study and Historic Structures Report: Blocks 7 and 10, Elijah Iles' Addition, Springfield, Illinois.
[743] Alice Edwards Bunn memoir about the Jacob Bunn house in Springfield; Bunn, Irwin historical records.

(Stockdale) House and Elon Pratt House had a son, Henry Barrell House, who is discussed next.

Henry Barrell House of Chicago and Springfield:

Banker and Vaudevillian Playwright

Henry Barrell House was the son of Judge Elon Pratt House and Sarah Irwin (Stockdale) House, both natives of Springfield.[744] Through the Stockdale family of his mother, Henry B. House was descended from the Irwins and was kin to the Fergusons and Bunns of Springfield and Chicago.[745] Henry B. House worked in Chicago as a banker, broker, Vaudevillian playwright, theater director, and performer.[746] House was a prominent member of the Chicago Chapter of the American Institute of Banking. A locally noted Vaudevillian writer, House wrote *Sophie Should Worry*, which was a musical play that featured male performers as women from various strata of contemporary society.[747] *The Bank Man*, the monthly journal of the Chicago Chapter of the American Institute of Banking, contained a report of the Vaudeville play, and described the performance as a remarkable success. *Sophie Should Worry* consisted of a plot in which certain social issues of the Gilded Age were dramatized, and a story reflective of the complex and diverse sociology of Chicago at the time.[748]

> "The transition of bank men into rampant suffragettes, sunbonnet girls, waitresses and ballet dancers was the big feature of this show, the most successful [the] Chicago Chapter has ever given and shows that the bank men of this city can produce a play that ranks among the foremost musical theatrical productions given to date."[749]

While House wrote the script for the play, George F. Bainbridge composed the music for the work, which was performed on December 5 and 6, 1913, at Chicago's

---

[744] Sons of the American Revolution. (1928). Vol. 23. Page number not apparent. National Society of the Sons of the American Revolution. Google Books.

[745] Bunn, Irwin, Stockdale, and House family history records.

[746] The Bank Man. (January, 1914). Vol. IX. Number 1. P. 1. Chicago, IL: Chicago Chapter of the American Institute of Banking. Google Books.

[747] The Bank Man. (January, 1914). Vol. IX. Number 1. P. 1. Chicago, IL: Chicago Chapter of the American Institute of Banking. Google Books.

[748] The Bank Man. (January, 1914). Vol. IX. Number 1. P. 1. Chicago, IL: Chicago Chapter of the American Institute of Banking. Google Books.

[749] The Bank Man. (January, 1914). Vol. IX. Number 1. P. 1. Chicago, IL: Chicago Chapter of the American Institute of Banking. Google Books.

Globe Theater.[750] Henry House also served as the director of the play.[751] The Globe Theater was located at Wabash Avenue and Seventh Street.[752] The play featured joint protagonists, a husband and wife named Esau M. Cumming and Mary Uppan Cumming.[753] The plot consisted of comedically dramatized themes of competitive political aspirations, and the story consisted of Esau and Mary running against each other for the office of mayor of Cummingtown.[754] The story specifically consisted of Esau campaigning on the promotion of cabaret, and Mary campaigning against the cabaret, with Esau winning the mayoral race.[755] Henry House played Esau Cumming and Arthur A. Briggs played Mary Uppan Cumming.[756] Norton Swift, Franklin Le Pelley, Milton Wilkening, Julius Scheffner, Carl E. Schiffner, F. J. Morris, Ray A. Blomgren, Ralph Huntington, Frelling C. Foster, Leigh Sargent, William K. Armitage, Harry Royle, and Jay W. Hays were the other actors from the cast of the play.[757]

In 1911, House wrote *Yapp from Home*, a play featuring a protagonist by the name of Lord Hardscrabble, whom House played onstage.[758] The 1910-1911 executive leadership of *The Bank Man* included Thomas J. Nugent as Editor; A. F. Moeller, Business Manager; Malcolm McDowell, Advisory Member; Thad S. Kerr, Advertising Manager; F. H. Thiese, Circulation Manager.[759] *The Bank Man* Executive Board consisted of C. W. Alison, John M. Drummond, Everett B. Mann, David Johnstone, F. E. Musgrove, Charles Peterson, W. F. Rowe, J. W. Rubecamp, R. I. Simons, H. S. Smale, and R. D. Spaulding.[760] The Chicago Chapter of the American Institute of Banking was headquartered at Room 226 of the

---

[750] The Bank Man. (January, 1914). Vol. IX. Number 1. P. 1. Chicago, IL: Chicago Chapter of the American Institute of Banking. Google Books.

[751] The Bank Man. (January, 1914). Vol. IX. Number 1. P. 1. Chicago, IL: Chicago Chapter of the American Institute of Banking. Google Books.

[752] Chicago Tribune. (December 5, 1913). P. 9. Newspapers.com.

[753] Chicago Tribune. (December 5, 1913). P. 9. Newspapers.com.

[754] Chicago Tribune. (December 5, 1913). P. 9. Newspapers.com.

[755] Chicago Tribune. (December 5, 1913). P. 9. Newspapers.com.

[756] Chicago Tribune. (December 5, 1913). P. 9. Newspapers.com.

[757] Chicago Tribune. (December 5, 1913). P. 9. Newspapers.com.

[758] The Bank Man. (January, 1911). Vol. VI. Number 1. P. 8. Chicago, IL: Chicago Chapter of the American Institute of Banking. Mount Morris, IL: Kable Brothers. Google Books.

[759] The Bank Man. (January, 1911). Vol. VI. Number 1. P. 8. Chicago, IL: Chicago Chapter of the American Institute of Banking. Mount Morris, IL: Kable Brothers. Google Books.

[760] The Bank Man. (January, 1911). Vol. VI. Number 1. P. 8. Chicago, IL: Chicago Chapter of the American Institute of Banking. Mount Morris, IL: Kable Brothers. Google Books.

Northwestern University Building in Chicago.[761] The 1910-1911 executive leadership of the Chicago Chapter consisted of Leigh Sargent, President; Charles W. Alison, Vice-President; Herman E. Ellefson, Financial Secretary; David Johnstone, Corresponding Secretary; and Louis J. Meahl, Treasurer.[762] The Board of Directors consisted of Smale, Rowe, Simons, Musgrove, and Rubecamp.[763]

Henry House also wrote the Vaudeville musical play, *Janitress Janet*, and earned a notable reputation in Chicago Vaudevillian circles in 1908, when he created the character of the Earl of Hardcastle.[764] As of May, 1912, Henry House was employed by the Chicago brokerage company of Allerton, Green & King, and was elected to serve as a Chicago Chapter Delegate to the Salt Lake City Convention of the American Institute of Banking and American Bankers' Association.[765] House worked for the National Bank Examiners' Chicago office in 1911.[766] House left Chicago in 1914 to take a job as an Assistant Cashier with the First National Bank of St. Paul in Minnesota.[767] This bank was advertised as the oldest bank in Minnesota at the time, in 1914.[768] Henry House served for at least five years as Assistant to the National Bank Examiner in the Chicago office of the National Bank Examiner.[769] House then became Auditor of the Continental & Commercial National Bank of Chicago.[770] He started in banking at the Springfield Marine Bank, which had been founded by his ancestor Robert Irwin, and by Jacob Bunn and

[761] The Bank Man. (January, 1911). Vol. VI. Number 1. P. 8. Chicago, IL: Chicago Chapter of the American Institute of Banking. Mount Morris, IL: Kable Brothers. Google Books.

[762] The Bank Man. (January, 1911). Vol. VI. Number 1. P. 8. Chicago, IL: Chicago Chapter of the American Institute of Banking. Mount Morris, IL: Kable Brothers. Google Books.

[763] The Bank Man. (January, 1911). Vol. VI. Number 1. P. 8. Chicago, IL: Chicago Chapter of the American Institute of Banking. Mount Morris, IL: Kable Brothers. Google Books.

[764] Journal of the American Bankers' Association Including Bulletin of the American Institute of Banking. (June, 1913-June, 1914). Vol. 6. P. 601. New York, NY: American Bankers' Association. Google Books.

[765] Journal of the American Bankers' Association Including Bulletin of the American Institute of Banking. (June, 1912-June, 1913). Vol. 5. P. 53. New York, NY: American Bankers' Association. Google Books.

[766] The Inter Ocean. (October 8, 1911). P. 5. Newspapers.com.

[767] Minneapolis Star Tribune. (November 16, 1914). P. 6. Newspapers.com.

[768] Minneapolis Star Tribune. (November 16, 1914). P. 6. Newspapers.com.

[769] The Banking Law Journal. (January-December, 1916). Vol. XXXIII. P. 88c. New York, NY: Alfred F. White, Publisher. Google Books.

[770] The Banking Law Journal. (January-December, 1916). Vol. XXXIII. P. 88c. New York, NY: Alfred F. White, Publisher. Google Books.

others.[771] For the Chicago history of Robert Irwin, see Chapter 1, *Genesis of a Great Lakes Frontier*.

Janitress Janet debuted at the Ziegfeld Theater of Chicago from November 8 to November 11, 1911.[772] *The United States Investor*, a financial trade journal, commented that *Janitress Janet* drew large crowds, nearly selling out all the seats, despite the heavy storms and rains that took place on those nights.[773] Henry House wrote the play and George Bainbridge composed the music.[774] John H. Grior composed the lyrics to the songs.[775] Of additional interest, Ruth Regan, wife of Willard Bunn, Sr., who was himself a cousin of Henry B. House, was an alumna of the Ziegfeld Chicago Musical College, and graduated with a Piano Degree not many years prior to the production of Henry House's Vaudeville musical play.[776] Ruth Regan debuted as a soloist pianist with the Ziegfeld organization at the age of sixteen in Chicago.[777]

Henry B. House worked for the Allerton, Green & King Company, which is a firm that warrants further description at this point. The Allerton, Green & King Company comprised Samuel Waters Allerton, Frank R. Green, Calvin P. King, Mason B. Starring, Newton C. King, and William K. Hoagland.[778] When the new company opened its office at The Rookery in January, 1910, the *Electric Traction Weekly* reported the grand opening, and noted the professional experiences of the firm's organizers.[779] Calvin and Newton King both came from Havana, in Mason County, Illinois, northwest of Springfield.[780] Walter Scott Allerton and Horace True Currier provide a detailed biography of Samuel W. Allerton in their 1900 history of the Allerton family. Samuel Allerton came to Chicago in 1860, and

[771] The Banking Law Journal. (January-December, 1916). Vol. XXXIII. P. 88b. New York, NY: Alfred F. White, Publisher. Google Books.

[772] The United States Investor. (November 18, 1911). P. 1909. New York, NY. Google Books.

[773] The United States Investor. (November 18, 1911). P. 1909. New York, NY. Google Books.

[774] The United States Investor. (November 18, 1911). P. 1909. New York, NY. Google Books.

[775] The United States Investor. (November 18, 1911). P. 1909. New York, NY. Google Books.

[776] Regan family history records.

[777] Regan family history records.

[778] Electric Traction Weekly. (January 8, 1910). Vol. 6. P. 45. Chicago, IL. Google Books.

[779] Electric Traction Weekly. (January 8, 1910). Vol. 6. P. 45. Chicago, IL. Google Books.

[780] Electric Traction Weekly. (January 8, 1910). Vol. 6. P. 45. Chicago, IL. Google Books.

praised the city as the place, "where the world turned around every twenty-four hours."[781]

Allerton discerned the disorganized and amorphous livestock market that existed at the city then and sought to enter that market but possessed no business connection with which to gain a position.[782] Allerton then began to put together proposals for new business ideas. Allerton met a Mr. Tobey, who introduced Allerton to a Mr. Willard at the George Smith Company bank.[783] Allerton failed to convince Willard of the viability of Allerton's underwriting proposal, was consequently denied the contemplated underwriting offer, and was subsequently directed and introduced by a helpful stranger from Syracuse, possibly John D. Norton, to the Chicago firm of Aiken & Norton.[784] The Tobey-Willard connection failed to produce the loan that Allerton sought, and this disappointment caused Allerton to seek a different audience of bankers. Edmund Aiken and John D. Norton became that new audience, and were the principals with whom Allerton would work.[785] Allerton convinced Aiken and Norton of the viability of his proposal, but the Civil War started at about the same time, drawing the issue of national currency to the forefront of public policy and commercial policy analysis.[786] The United States confronted a currency crisis and needed national banks to aid the effort of standardizing national circulable moneys.[787] Allerton noted an opportunity that was concurrently patriotic and profitable when he offered to co-organize a new national bank in Chicago with Aiken and several other men

---

[781] Allerton, Walter Scott, and Currier, Horace True. (1900). A History Of The Allerton Family In The United States. Pp. 85-86 Chicago, IL: Samuel Waters Allerton. Google Books.

[782] Allerton, Walter Scott, and Currier, Horace True. (1900). A History Of The Allerton Family In The United States. Pp. 85-86 Chicago, IL: Samuel Waters Allerton. Google Books.

[783] Allerton, Walter Scott, and Currier, Horace True. (1900). A History Of The Allerton Family In The United States. Pp. 85-86 Chicago, IL: Samuel Waters Allerton. Google Books.

[784] Allerton, Walter Scott, and Currier, Horace True. (1900). A History Of The Allerton Family In The United States. Pp. 85-86 Chicago, IL: Samuel Waters Allerton. Google Books; Morris, Henry Crittenden. (1902). Pp. 133-135. The History of the First National Bank of Chicago. Chicago, IL: R. R. Donnellly & Sons Company. Google Books.

[785] Morris, Henry Crittenden. (1902). Pp. 133-135. The History of the First National Bank of Chicago. Chicago, IL: R. R. Donnellly & Sons Company. Google Books.

[786] Allerton, Walter Scott, and Currier, Horace True. (1900). A History Of The Allerton Family In The United States. Pp. 85-86 Chicago, IL: Samuel Waters Allerton. Google Books.

[787] Allerton, Walter Scott, and Currier, Horace True. (1900). A History Of The Allerton Family In The United States. Pp. 85-86 Chicago, IL: Samuel Waters Allerton. Google Books.

who would each subscribe $10,000 to the concern.[788] Aiken apparently accepted Allerton's national bank concept proposal and this alliance led to the creation of the First National Bank of Chicago.[789] Samuel Waters Allerton of Chicago (1828-1914) was a cousin of Ada Willard (Richardson) Bunn through the Atherton family of Worcester, Massachusetts, from which both Allerton and Richardson descended.

Frank Hatch Jones, Esq.

Frank Hatch Jones (1854-1931) was born on March 6, 1854, in Griggsville, Pike County, Illinois.[790] He was the son of George Whitfield Jones and Cecelia (Bennett) Jones, and a descendant of Mayflower passenger and Mayflower Compact signer George Soule, as well as of Colonel John Jones, the developer of Mt. Desert, Maine.[791] Frank Jones attended Griggsville High School.[792] He attended Yale, graduating in 1875.[793] At Yale he was a member of Skull and Bones and Delta Kappa Epsilon.[794] Jones studied law under two different lawyers, one in Pittsfield, Illinois, and a Professor Dwight of New York, before matriculating at the Chicago Law School.[795] This law school was an institutional component of Northwestern University and a predecessor of the current law school of Northwestern. Jones graduated from law school in 1878.[796] He was admitted to the Illinois Bar in 1879, and entered law practice at Springfield, where he became

---

[788] Allerton, Walter Scott, and Currier, Horace True. (1900). A History Of The Allerton Family In The United States. Pp. 85-86 Chicago, IL: Samuel Waters Allerton. Google Books.

[789] Allerton, Walter Scott, and Currier, Horace True. (1900). A History Of The Allerton Family In The United States. Pp. 85-86 Chicago, IL: Samuel Waters Allerton. Google Books; Morris, Henry Crittenden. (1902). Pp. 133-135. The History of the First National Bank of Chicago. Chicago, IL: R. R. Donnellly & Sons Company. Google Books.

[790] Chamberlain, Joshua Lawrence. Editor. (1899). Universities And Their Sons. Vol. III. P. 352. Boston, MASS: R. Herndon Company. Google Books.

[791] Chamberlain, Joshua Lawrence. Editor. (1899). Universities And Their Sons. Vol. III. P. 352. Boston, MASS: R. Herndon Company. Google Books.

[792] Chamberlain, Joshua Lawrence. Editor. (1899). Universities And Their Sons. Vol. III. P. 352. Boston, MASS: R. Herndon Company. Google Books; Interview with Mark Hertzberg, a historian and author of Wisconsin.

[793] Chamberlain, Joshua Lawrence. Editor. (1899). Universities And Their Sons. Vol. III. P. 352. Boston, MASS: R. Herndon Company. Google Books.

[794] Chamberlain, Joshua Lawrence. Editor. (1899). Universities And Their Sons. Vol. III. P. 352. Boston, MASS: R. Herndon Company. Google Books.

[795] Chamberlain, Joshua Lawrence. Editor. (1899). Universities And Their Sons. Vol. III. P. 352. Boston, MASS: R. Herndon Company. Google Books.

[796] Chamberlain, Joshua Lawrence. Editor. (1899). Universities And Their Sons. Vol. III. P. 352. Boston, MASS: R. Herndon Company. Google Books.

acquainted with the Bunn family.[797] Jones married Sarah Irwin Bunn, daughter of Jacob Bunn and Elizabeth Jane (Ferguson) Bunn, on November 22, 1882.[798] Sarah (Bunn) Jones died in 1892.[799]

Jones, a Democrat, was elected to the Illinois House of Representatives for the 1891-1892 legislative term.[800] He relocated to Chicago in 1893, after the death of his wife, Sarah Irwin (Bunn), and the same year of the World's Columbian Exposition.[801] Jones owned the Jones Law Firm at the Monadnock Building in the Loop, and served as Postmaster of Chicago.[802] He received appointment from President Grover Cleveland to the office of First Assistant Postmaster General of the United States and occupied the office from 1893-1897.[803] He returned to Chicago in September, 1897, after a four-year residency in Washington, D.C., during the years of service as First Assistant Postmaster General of the United States.[804] Jones was a member of the Union League Club and the University Club of Chicago, as well as of the Alibi Club of Washington, D.C. He also served as Secretary of the Illinois State Bar Association, an organization of which he was an active member.[805]

Frank H. Jones worked with Bluford Wilson, Samuel T. Dresser, Timothy McGrath, and Henry A. Stevens as an incorporator of the Wisconsin corporation called the Portage & Southwestern Railroad Company.[806] The State of Wisconsin granted corporate status to the company on November 7, 1887.[807] The 1889 Wisconsin report stated the capitalization money of the company to be $3,375,000,

[797] Chamberlain, Joshua Lawrence. Editor. (1899). Universities And Their Sons. Vol. III. P. 352. Boston, MASS: R. Herndon Company. Google Books.

[798] Chamberlain, Joshua Lawrence. Editor. (1899). Universities And Their Sons. Vol. III. P. 352. Boston, MASS: R. Herndon Company. Google Books.

[799] Chamberlain, Joshua Lawrence. Editor. (1899). Universities And Their Sons. Vol. III. P. 352. Boston, MASS: R. Herndon Company. Google Books.

[800] Chamberlain, Joshua Lawrence. Editor. (1899). Universities And Their Sons. Vol. III. P. 352. Boston, MASS: R. Herndon Company. Google Books.

[801] Chamberlain, Joshua Lawrence. Editor. (1899). Universities And Their Sons. Vol. III. P. 352. Boston, MASS: R. Herndon Company. Google Books.

[802] Bunn and Jones family historical records.

[803] Chamberlain, Joshua Lawrence. Editor. (1899). Universities And Their Sons. Vol. III. P. 352. Boston, MASS: R. Herndon Company. Google Books.

[804] Chamberlain, Joshua Lawrence. Editor. (1899). Universities And Their Sons. Vol. III. P. 352. Boston, MASS: R. Herndon Company. Google Books.

[805] Chamberlain, Joshua Lawrence. Editor. (1899). Universities And Their Sons. Vol. III. P. 352. Boston, MASS: R. Herndon Company. Google Books.

[806] Governor's Message And Accompanying Documents Of The State Of Wisconsin. (1889). Vol. II. P. 398. Madison, WI: Democrat Printing Company, State Printers. Google Books.

[807] Governor's Message And Accompanying Documents Of The State Of Wisconsin. (1889). Vol. II. P. 398. Madison, WI: Democrat Printing Company, State Printers. Google Books.

and implicitly described the plan and manner of financing as one consisting only of stock money.[808] The report made no reference to debt money as an element of the corporate financing.[809] The robust route description identified in detail the places located along the anticipatory railroad route, naming Portage, Columbia County, Wisconsin, as the northern terminus and the Wisconsin-Illinois border as the southern terminus.[810] The intervening places included Columbia County, Iowa County, Dane County, LaFayette County, and Grant County.[811] The southern terminus would be located at a place one mile from the Mississippi River and the route system would gain further geographical significance and centrality by building a branch to Madison, the capital city.[812] Jones also was a founder of the Chicago Southern Railroad Company, which operated a route from Chicago to Paris, Illinois. Jones was a co-founding junior executive of the Continental Illinois National Bank and Trust Company in 1910 and was a trustee of many gold mining claims and lands in the Pacific West.[813] Jones also served on the board of directors of the Chicago Opera House Company.[814]

Frank Jones helped reform the pawnbroker, loan, and interest economy of Chicago in the early twentieth century when he became a builder and executive officer of the First State Pawners' Society of Illinois, at least as early as 1916.[815] Loan administrator Samuel Wolfort delivered a loan market policy and law reform report in 1916, which was published in Volume 1, *Department Serial Number 3*, of the *Bulletin Of The Department of Public Welfare of the City of Chicago*. The Wolfort report outlined the purpose, history, market, and policy reformation victories of the First State Pawners' Society of Illinois, which was one of the most significant companies to reinstitute policies and practices of honesty, justice, and

---

[808] Governor's Message And Accompanying Documents Of The State Of Wisconsin. (1889). Vol. II. P. 398. Madison, WI: Democrat Printing Company, State Printers. Google Books.

[809] Governor's Message And Accompanying Documents Of The State Of Wisconsin. (1889). Vol. II. P. 398. Madison, WI: Democrat Printing Company, State Printers. Google Books.

[810] Governor's Message And Accompanying Documents Of The State Of Wisconsin. (1889). Vol. II. P. 398. Madison, WI: Democrat Printing Company, State Printers. Google Books.

[811] Governor's Message And Accompanying Documents Of The State Of Wisconsin. (1889). Vol. II. P. 398. Madison, WI: Democrat Printing Company, State Printers. Google Books.

[812] Governor's Message And Accompanying Documents Of The State Of Wisconsin. (1889). Vol. II. P. 398. Madison, WI: Democrat Printing Company, State Printers. Google Books.

[813] Bunn and Jones family historical records.

[814] Bunn and Jones family historical records.

[815] McDermott, Valeria D. Editor. Bulletin Of The Department Of Public Welfare: City Of Chicago. (October, 1916). Vol. 1, Number 3. P. 39. Chicago, IL. Google Books.

honor in the Chicago loan market.[816] Frank Jones played a key role in the reformative company.[817] The company was formed in 1899 under the State of Illinois statute whose purpose was the creation of loan companies that would strike and remove the usurious lending economy that had developed in Illinois prior to 1899.[818] The State of Illinois set a limit on the interest rates chargeable on Illinois loans at three percent.[819] Failure to enforce the anti-usury law and policy reduced the Illinois loan law to a futility, and reduced the statewide interest rate limit to scarcely more than a nominal limit with no legal force.[820] The statutory law evidently, according to the Wolfort report, created both recourse and remedy for borrowers who were victims of usury in Illinois, but, for the already burdened borrowers, the costs of claiming the recourse and remedy superseded the benefits derivative of the recourse and remedy.[821] The statutory law enforcement failure caused the practical nullification of the anti-usury law and policy, and created an illegal capital market defined by loansharking practices.[822]

The Merchants Club of Chicago challenged the established usurious Illinois loan economy when it aided the establishment of the First State Pawners' Society, a Chicago organization which would publicly administer and enforce fair loans, fair rates of interest, fair plans of amortization, and fair practices of pignoration (the action of pledging property).[823] In doing so the Merchants Club would produce, through the First State Pawners' Society, a renewed economy of exemplary growth, revenues, and profits according to policies of honor and integrity.[824] Samuel Wolfort stated the following history and policy analysis:

> "For a number of years Chicago Pawnbrokers had no competition and were reaping a harvest by charging a rate of interest from 5 [per] cent. a month to 10 per cent. a month, and even higher rates on small loans. The

---

[816] McDermott, Valeria D. Editor. Bulletin Of The Department Of Public Welfare: City Of Chicago. (October, 1916). Vol. 1, Number 3. P. 39. Chicago, IL. Google Books.
[817] McDermott, Valeria D. Editor. Bulletin Of The Department Of Public Welfare: City Of Chicago. (October, 1916). Vol. 1, Number 3. P. 39. Chicago, IL. Google Books.
[818] McDermott, Valeria D. Editor. Bulletin Of The Department Of Public Welfare: City Of Chicago. (October, 1916). Vol. 1, Number 3. P. 39. Chicago, IL. Google Books.
[819] McDermott, Valeria D. Editor. Bulletin Of The Department Of Public Welfare: City Of Chicago. (October, 1916). Vol. 1, Number 3. P. 39. Chicago, IL. Google Books.
[820] McDermott, Valeria D. Editor. Bulletin Of The Department Of Public Welfare: City Of Chicago. (October, 1916). Vol. 1, Number 3. P. 39. Chicago, IL. Google Books.
[821] McDermott, Valeria D. Editor. Bulletin Of The Department Of Public Welfare: City Of Chicago. (October, 1916). Vol. 1, Number 3. P. 39. Chicago, IL. Google Books.
[822] McDermott, Valeria D. Editor. Bulletin Of The Department Of Public Welfare: City Of Chicago. (October, 1916). Vol. 1, Number 3. P. 39. Chicago, IL. Google Books.
[823] McDermott, Valeria D. Editor. Bulletin Of The Department Of Public Welfare: City Of Chicago. (October, 1916). Vol. 1, Number 3. P. 39. Chicago, IL. Google Books.
[824] McDermott, Valeria D. Editor. Bulletin Of The Department Of Public Welfare: City Of Chicago. (October, 1916). Vol. 1, Number 3. P. 39. Chicago, IL. Google Books.

legal rate at all times was only 3 per cent. Very little attention was paid to the law, as it cost the borrower too much to invoke its aid. The Merchants Club, an organization of Chicago's foremost citizens, some years ago realized the injustice to the poor and needy in demanding such high interest, and seeking a way to remedy this evil, had a bill drawn up and passed by the Legislature at Springfield allowing the incorporation, under the control of the State Bank Examiner, of corporations having a paid up capital of $50,000.00, to organize and loan money at a rate not to exceed 1 per cent. for interest and ½ per cent. for insurance and storage."[825]

Merchants Club members formed The First State Pawners' Society of Illinois as an organizational force through which to bring justice, fair governance, and enforcement to the loan market of Illinois.[826] Merchants Club members built an equity financing plan pursuant to which they subscribed $50,000 in stock money, and in so doing satisfied the stock money base limit for Illinois pawnbroker companies.[827] The company office was located at 27 West Washington Street.[828] The Society concurrently acted as market regulator, justice factor, and reformatory party in the Illinois loan market, and experienced so much success that the Society was able profitably to reduce the standard contractual interest rate to 1 percent per month on all loan contracts.[829]

The company capitalized on the loan market with honor and integrity and drew so much revenue and profit from the capital market that the company instituted growth-purposed financing that increased the stock money to $800,000 through subscription plans.[830] Growth supported the opening of a second company office in 1916, which was located at 39 S. Halsted.[831] As of the time of the 1916 Wolfort report, the First State Pawners' Society had executed 617,346 loan contracts.[832] The total collective loan value stemming from these contracts was $14,172,416.00

---

[825] McDermott, Valeria D. Editor. Bulletin Of The Department Of Public Welfare: City Of Chicago. (October, 1916). Vol. 1, Number 3. P. 39. Chicago, IL. Google Books.
[826] McDermott, Valeria D. Editor. Bulletin Of The Department Of Public Welfare: City Of Chicago. (October, 1916). Vol. 1, Number 3. P. 39. Chicago, IL. Google Books.
[827] McDermott, Valeria D. Editor. Bulletin Of The Department Of Public Welfare: City Of Chicago. (October, 1916). Vol. 1, Number 3. P. 39. Chicago, IL. Google Books.
[828] McDermott, Valeria D. Editor. Bulletin Of The Department Of Public Welfare: City Of Chicago. (October, 1916). Vol. 1, Number 3. P. 39. Chicago, IL. Google Books.
[829] McDermott, Valeria D. Editor. Bulletin Of The Department Of Public Welfare: City Of Chicago. (October, 1916). Vol. 1, Number 3. P. 39. Chicago, IL. Google Books.
[830] McDermott, Valeria D. Editor. Bulletin Of The Department Of Public Welfare: City Of Chicago. (October, 1916). Vol. 1, Number 3. P. 39. Chicago, IL. Google Books.
[831] McDermott, Valeria D. Editor. Bulletin Of The Department Of Public Welfare: City Of Chicago. (October, 1916). Vol. 1, Number 3. P. 39. Chicago, IL. Google Books.
[832] McDermott, Valeria D. Editor. Bulletin Of The Department Of Public Welfare: City Of Chicago. (October, 1916). Vol. 1, Number 3. P. 39. Chicago, IL. Google Books.

at the time of the Wolfort report.[833] The leadership structure and staff consisted of many leading people of the city. John Villiers Farwell served as President of the First State Pawners' Society and John Graves Shedd served as Vice-President.[834] David R. Forgan was Treasurer; Thomas E. Donnelly was Secretary.[835] The board of directors serving concurrently with the named executives included Rollin A. Keyes, Edward B. Butler, and Edward A. Bancroft.[836] Frank Jones served among the executive leadership staff of the Society and was appointed to the Society leadership by the Mayor of Chicago.[837] John W. Scott had been appointed to the company leadership by the Illinois Governor and Samuel Wolfort served as Manager for the company.[838]

The Wolfort report showed how an honorable and justice-driven Chicago company revolutionized and reformed the corrupted capital market of Illinois.[839] The First State Pawners' Society formulated a theory for the honorable commercial operation of the Chicago loan market.[840] The theory produced manifold benefits for the city, for Cook County, and for Illinois.[841] The company and theory simultaneously reformed the Chicago loan market, produced growth-sustaining revenue and profit, and created affordable loan moneys and credit with fair and affordable interest rates for the poor borrowers of Chicago.[842] The First State Pawners' Society also shattered, deposed, and dispossessed much of the stronghold of the corrupt and usurious market operators of the city and county.[843]

[833] McDermott, Valeria D. Editor. Bulletin Of The Department Of Public Welfare: City Of Chicago. (October, 1916). Vol. 1, Number 3. P. 39. Chicago, IL. Google Books.
[834] McDermott, Valeria D. Editor. Bulletin Of The Department Of Public Welfare: City Of Chicago. (October, 1916). Vol. 1, Number 3. P. 39. Chicago, IL. Google Books.
[835] McDermott, Valeria D. Editor. Bulletin Of The Department Of Public Welfare: City Of Chicago. (October, 1916). Vol. 1, Number 3. P. 39. Chicago, IL. Google Books.
[836] McDermott, Valeria D. Editor. Bulletin Of The Department Of Public Welfare: City Of Chicago. (October, 1916). Vol. 1, Number 3. P. 39. Chicago, IL. Google Books.
[837] McDermott, Valeria D. Editor. Bulletin Of The Department Of Public Welfare: City Of Chicago. (October, 1916). Vol. 1, Number 3. P. 39. Chicago, IL. Google Books.
[838] McDermott, Valeria D. Editor. Bulletin Of The Department Of Public Welfare: City Of Chicago. (October, 1916). Vol. 1, Number 3. P. 39. Chicago, IL. Google Books.
[839] McDermott, Valeria D. Editor. Bulletin Of The Department Of Public Welfare: City Of Chicago. (October, 1916). Vol. 1, Number 3. P. 39. Chicago, IL. Google Books.
[840] McDermott, Valeria D. Editor. Bulletin Of The Department Of Public Welfare: City Of Chicago. (October, 1916). Vol. 1, Number 3. P. 39. Chicago, IL. Google Books.
[841] McDermott, Valeria D. Editor. Bulletin Of The Department Of Public Welfare: City Of Chicago. (October, 1916). Vol. 1, Number 3. P. 39. Chicago, IL. Google Books.
[842] McDermott, Valeria D. Editor. Bulletin Of The Department Of Public Welfare: City Of Chicago. (October, 1916). Vol. 1, Number 3. P. 39. Chicago, IL. Google Books.
[843] McDermott, Valeria D. Editor. Bulletin Of The Department Of Public Welfare: City Of Chicago. (October, 1916). Vol. 1, Number 3. P. 39. Chicago, IL. Google Books.

Frank Hatch Jones and Nellie Grant Sartoris

Ellen Wrenshall "Nellie" Grant (1855-1922) was the daughter of Gen. Ulysses S. Grant and Julia (Dent) Grant.[844] Nellie first married Algernon Sartoris, an Englishman, and the two children who were born to this marriage were Algernon Sartoris and Vivian Sartoris.[845] After her divorce from Sartoris, Nellie returned to the United States in 1894 and regained United States citizenship by federal statute.[846] She married Frank Hatch Jones in 1912.[847] The Jones-Sartoris wedding generated much newspaper publicity.[848] Nellie tragically suffered from a stroke shortly after her marriage to Jones, however, and became largely incapacitated.[849] She died on August 30, 1922, at 1130 Lake Shore Drive, which was the Jones residence in the Gold Coast neighborhood of Chicago.[850] Both Frank Jones and Nellie (Grant) Jones were interred at Oak Ridge Cemetery in Springfield, where Abraham Lincoln and the Bunns were also interred. Frank and Nellie Jones were buried in the Bunn Family Plot at the cemetery. Poet Eugene Field, who was a friend of Rev. Melancthon W. Stryker of Chicago (see Stryker history, *infra*), wrote a poem for Nellie Grant Sartoris called *Nellie*, upon the death of President Ulysses S. Grant in 1885, and in honor of both the late President and his daughter.[851] Field's poem follows here:

> "His listening soul hears no echo of battle,
>   No paean of triumph nor welcome of fame;
> But down through the years comes a little one's prattle,
>   And softly he murmurs her idolized name.
> And it seems as if now at his heart she were clinging
>   As she clung in those dear, distant years to his knee;
> He sees her fair face, and he hears her faint singing—
>   And Nellie is coming from over the sea.
> While each patriot's hope stays the fulness of sorrow,

---

[844] Chicago Historical Society Bulletin. (November, 1922). Vol. 1. No. 4. P. 28. Chicago, IL: Chicago Historical Society. Google Books.

[845] Chicago Historical Society Bulletin. (November, 1922). Vol. 1. No. 4. P. 28. Chicago, IL: Chicago Historical Society. Google Books.

[846] Chicago Historical Society Bulletin. (November, 1922). Vol. 1. No. 4. P. 28. Chicago, IL: Chicago Historical Society. Google Books.

[847] Chicago Historical Society Bulletin. (November, 1922). Vol. 1. No. 4. P. 28. Google Books.

[848] Interview with historian Mark Hertzberg.

[849] Interview with historian Mark Hertzberg; Mrs. Frank Hatch Jones (Nellie Grant). Journal of the Illinois State Historical Society. (1908-1984). Vol. 15. Jstor and archive.org.

[850] Chicago Historical Society Bulletin. (November, 1922). Vol. 1. No. 4. P. 28. Google Books.

[851] Strock, Ian Randal. (2016). Ranking the First Ladies: True Tales and Trivia, from Martha to Michele. New York, NY: Carrel Books. Google Books.

While our eyes are bedimmed and our voices are low,
He dreams of the daughter who comes with the morrow
  Like an angel come back from the dear long ago.
Ah, what to him now is a nation's emotion,
  And what for our love or our grief careth he?
A swift-speeding ship is a-sail on the ocean,
  And Nellie is coming from over the sea!
O daughter—my daughter! when Death stands before me
  And beckons me off to that far misty shore,
Let me see your loved form bending tenderly o'oer me,
  And feel your dear kiss on my lips as of yore.
In the grace of your love all my anguish abating,
  I'll bear myself bravely and proudly as he,
And know the sweet peace that hallowed his waiting
  When Nellie was coming from over the sea."[852]

Frank H. Jones and Chicago Civic Work

Both Frank Jones and John Whitfield Bunn were Governing Members of the Chicago Historical Society.[853] Other Governing Members included Charles Richard Crane, Richard Teller Crane, Philip Danforth Armour, Edward Tyler Blair, Isabelle Farnsworth Blackstone (Mrs. Timothy B. Blackstone), Hobart C. Chatfield-Taylor, Frederick D. Countiss, Joseph M. Cudahy, Edward A. Cudahy, Charles Gates Dawes, Rufus Dawes, Charles Deering, Albert Blake Dick, Kellogg Fairbank, Stanley Field (of the Field Museum of Natural History), John Jacob Glessner, Harold Fowler McCormick, Robert Todd Lincoln, Samuel Insull, William V. Kelley, Victor Fremont Lawson, George Alexander McKinlock, Julius Rosenwald, Charles Henry Wacker, Edward Larned Ryerson, and Joseph Turner Ryerson.[854] Many of these people were business associates of Jacob and John Whitfield Bunn in multiple companies, civic groups, and social organizations.

The incorporators of the Chicago Historical Society were William Barry, James Van Zandt Blaney, Mason Brayman, William Hubbard Brown, Nathan Smith Davis, Van Hollis Higgins, John Harris Kinzie, George Manierre, Ezra Butler McCagg, Mahlon Dickerson Ogden, William Butler Ogden, Charles Henry Ray, Franklin Scammon, Jonathan Young Scammon, Mark Skinner, William A. Smallwood, Edward Islay Tinkham, Samuel Dexter Ward, and Joseph Dana

---

[852] Field, Eugene. (1916). The Poems of Eugene Field. Nellie. P. 229. New York, NY: Charles Scribner's Sons. Google Books.

[853] Charter, Constitution, By-Laws, Membership List, Annual Report for the Year Ending October 31, 1917. (1918). Pp. 12, 13. Chicago, IL: Chicago Historical Society. Google Books.

[854] Charter, Constitution, By-Laws, Membership List, Annual Report for the Year Ending October 31, 1917. (1918). Pp. 11-14. Chicago, IL: Chicago Historical Society. Google Books.

Webster.[855] Mason Brayman, Ezra McCagg, William Ogden, and Jonathan Scammon all were corporate partners of Jacob Bunn in other Chicago companies.[856] John Harris Kinzie was associated with Robert Irwin, who was an uncle-in-law to Jacob Bunn, in the leadership and administration of the State Bank of Illinois and its Chicago Branch, the first bank established in Chicago.[857] John H. Kinzie was also the husband of Juliette Augusta Magill, who was the niece of Dr. Alexander Wolcott, and who was, through the Wolcott family, a cousin of Henry Stryker Taylor and Robert Cunningham Taylor, Jr. (who were, respectively, the maternal grandfather and granduncle of author Andrew Taylor Call).

Frank Jones was a member of the Commercial Club of Chicago and held diverse leadership positions within the club.[858] For the 1907-1908 business year, Jones served on the Reception Committee with Committee Chairman Charles H. Wacker, Benjamin Carpenter, Leslie Carter, and Charles L. Strobel.[859] Jones was a member of the executive committee of the club in 1908-1909, having served with John Graves Shedd, Rollin A. Keyes, Albert J. Earling, John W. Scott, Edwin G. Foreman, John Villiers Farwell, Jr., Theodore W. Robinson, John Jacob Glessner, and Frederick Greeley.[860] John J. Glessner was the principal founder of the Chicago Symphony Orchestra. Also in 1908-1909, Jones was Chairman of the Reception Committee, a board whose other members at the same time as Jones were Stanley Field, Adolphus C. Bartlett, John W. G. Cofran, and Emerson B. Tuttle.[861] Jones was the Club Vice-President for the 1910-1911 business year, and a member of the executive committee during that same time along with Francis C. Farwell, Edward F. Carry, David R. Forgan, Theodore W. Robinson, Arthur T. Aldis, James B. Forgan, William J. Chalmers, Charles H. Conover, and Clayton Mark.[862] During the 1911-1912 club year, Jones served on the Lake Bluff Naval Training Station Committee within the Commercial Club.[863] The other members

---

[855] Charter, Constitution, By-Laws, Membership List, Annual Report for the Year Ending October 31, 1917. (1918). P. 10. Chicago, IL: Chicago Historical Society. Google Books.

[856] See references supplied elsewhere herein.

[857] Andreas, Alfred Theodore. (1884). History of Chicago. Vol. 1. Pp. 527-528. Chicago, IL: A. T. Andreas, Publisher. Google Books.

[858] The Commercial Club of Chicago: Year-Book for 1912-1913. (1913). Pp. 19, 20, 25, 28. Chicago, IL: The Executive Committee of the Commercial Club. Google Books.

[859] The Commercial Club of Chicago: Year-Book for 1912-1913. (1913). Pp. 19, 20, 25, 28. Chicago, IL: The Executive Committee of the Commercial Club. Google Books.

[860] The Commercial Club of Chicago: Year-Book for 1912-1913. (1913). Pp. 19, 20, 25, 28. Chicago, IL: The Executive Committee of the Commercial Club. Google Books.

[861] The Commercial Club of Chicago: Year-Book for 1912-1913. (1913). Pp. 19, 20, 25, 28. Chicago, IL: The Executive Committee of the Commercial Club. Google Books.

[862] The Commercial Club of Chicago: Year-Book for 1912-1913. (1913). Pp. 19, 20, 25, 28. Chicago, IL: The Executive Committee of the Commercial Club. Google Books.

[863] The Commercial Club of Chicago: Year-Book for 1912-1913. (1913). Pp. 19, 20, 25, 28. Chicago, IL: The Executive Committee of the Commercial Club. Google Books.

of the Lake Bluff Naval Station Committee were committee chairman Walter H. Wilson, Benjamin Carpenter, Alexander A. McCormick, and Allen B. Pond.[864] Jones and his fellow committeemen helped establish the Great Lakes Naval Station that remains to this day.

Frank Jones resided in Gold Coast neighborhood at 10 Tower Court in 1909.[865] He founded the City Club of Chicago in the autumn of 1903. The City Club of Chicago founders were Frank H. Jones, Frank H. Scott, Albert L. Baker, George E. Hooker, Charles H. Hulbird, Allen B. Pond, George E. Cole, Julius S. Stern, Walter L. Fisher, Graham Taylor, and T. K. Webster.[866] The City Club was and remains the most important public policy discussion club for Chicago. A description of the club's origins follows here:

> "'People thought we would die out in a year or so, but we persisted, and we certainly have shown our right to live. In 1904 we invented a new word, 'Piperized.' We asked Captain Alexander R. Piper to come here and go into the police situation, and certainly we raised a lot of dust. . .They did not like it at all, but we came out of it with a more efficient police force. Then we did another thing which really should become history. We found a certain professor of political science at the University of Chicago and we got him to go into the question of the resources and revenues of the City of Chicago, and that thing, you know, flowered out into what afterwards was the Merriam Commission, and was a great surprise to all the politicians of Chicago.'"[867]

Jones continued service as Secretary of the Continental and Commercial Trust & Savings Bank in 1915, according to the June, 1915, edition of *The Investors' Manual*.[868] Robert Todd Lincoln was a member of the Continental and Commercial board of directors at this time and George M. Reynolds was the company President.[869] John Jay Abbott and Arthur Reynolds were both Vice-Presidents; Charles C. Willson was Cashier; William P. Kopf was Assistant Secretary; Henry C. Olcott was Manager of the Bond Department; Robert J. Hercock and Albert S. Martin were both Assistant Cashiers.[870] The capital, surplus, and profits were listed

---

[864] The Commercial Club of Chicago: Year-Book for 1912-1913. (1913). Pp. 19, 20, 25, 28. Chicago, IL: The Executive Committee of the Commercial Club. Google Books.
[865] Lakeside Directory of Chicago. (1909). Vol. 2.
[866] The City Club Bulletin. (January 1, 1912-December 31, 1912). Vol. 5. P. 185. Chicago, IL: City Club of Chicago. Google Books.
[867] The City Club Bulletin. (January 1, 1912-December 31, 1912). Vol. 5. P. 185. Chicago, IL: City Club of Chicago. Google Books.
[868] The Investors' Manual. (June, 1915). P. 3. Google Books.
[869] The Investors' Manual. (June, 1915). P. 3. Google Books.
[870] The Investors' Manual. (June, 1915). P. 3. Google Books.

at $5,000,000 in 1915, which, in conjunction with the assets of the Hibernian Banking Association of Chicago, formed the assets of the holding company known as the Continental and Commercial National Bank of Chicago.[871] Jones was a co-founder of this banking company network, which would become the largest bank in Chicago.

Frank Jones served as a member of the Board of Directors of the Union League Club in 1902, along with George Birkhoff, Jr., I. S. Blackwelder, William A. Gardner, Reuben H. Donnelly, James H. Hiland, Leroy A. Goddard, John M'Laren, and Jerome G. Steever. Robert Mather was President of the Union League Club in 1902.[872] Jones served on the Union League Club Board of Directors in 1903, under the Club Presidency of Edgar A. Bancroft, and continued Board of Directors service to the Club in 1904, in conjunction with the Presidency of Wallace Heckman.[873] John Whitfield Bunn was also a member of the Union League Club, and received a memorial notice from the Club upon his death on June 7, 1920.[874] Jones and John Whitfield Bunn were both members of the Chicago Club.[875] Jones was a member of the Iroquois Club, Chicago Golf Club, Onwentsia Country Club, Commercial Club, and Bankers' Club.[876] Frank Jones helped develop the Chicago summer resort community of Edgewater when he served as an executive leader of the Saddle And Cycle Club in 1911.[877] Serving along with Jones on the Saddle And Cycle Club board of directors in 1911 were John T. McCutcheon, William McCormick Blair, and John S. Runnells, all of whom were members of the Chicago Club along with Jones and John W. Bunn.[878] Arthur Jerome Eddy, Esq., Charles Deering, James Deering, Richard Teller Crane, Charles R. Corwith, Hobart C. Chatfield-Taylor, and Philip Danforth Armour all were members of the Saddle & Cycle Club along with Frank Jones.[879] Jones was a

[871] The Investors' Manual. (June, 1915). P. 3. Google Books.

[872] Year-Book Of The Union League Club Of Chicago. (1921). P. 17. Chicago, IL: Union League Club. Google Books.

[873] Year-Book Of The Union League Club Of Chicago. (1921). Pp. 17-18. Chicago, IL: Union League Club. Google Books.

[874] Year-Book Of The Union League Club Of Chicago. (1921). P. 117. Chicago, IL: Union League Club. Google Books.

[875] Bunn, Jones family history records.

[876] Marquis, Albert Nelson. Editor. The Book of Chicagoans: A Biographical Dictionary Of Leading Living Men Of The City Of Chicago. (1911). Vol. 2. P. 371. Chicago, IL: A. N. Marquis & Company. Google Books.

[877] Year-Book of the Saddle And Cycle Club. (1915). P. 25. Chicago, IL: Saddle And Cycle Club. Google Books.

[878] Year-Book of the Saddle And Cycle Club. (1915). P. 25. Chicago, IL: Saddle And Cycle Club. Google Books; Personal history records of author Andrew Taylor Call.

[879] Year-Book of the Saddle And Cycle Club. (1915). Pp. 37-41. Chicago, IL: Saddle And Cycle Club. Google Books.

resident of 820 Tower Court in Gold Coast neighborhood in 1911, and owned an office at 129 S. Clark Street the same year.[880]

Frank Jones contributed to the urban railroad development of Chicago through multiple years of service as Vice-President of the Calumet Electric Street Railway Company. John Farson of Chicago and Oak Park served as President of the Calumet Electric, and Jones served as his Vice-President.[881] *The McGraw American Street Railway Investments Manual* of 1905 described the company and its transportation routes and services. The Calumet Electric dated from 1890 and operated an extensive system of routes through the South Side of Chicago.[882] The company provided a complex network of services and routes that extended from Hammond, Indiana, to downtown Chicago via various connections to other transit companies.[883] The Calumet Electric routes included Hammond, Indiana, South Chicago, Parkside, Cheltenham Beach, Manhattan Beach, Robey, Roseland, Auburn Park, Burnside, Kensington, Pullman, West Pullman, Fernwood, South Shore, Woodlawn, and Grand Crossing.[884] The Calumet Electric connected to the South Side Elevated Railroad Company at Stony Island Avenue and 63rd Street in Woodlawn.[885] The Calumet connected to the Illinois Central Railroad Company at Grand Crossing and 67th Street and to the Chicago City Railway Company.[886] The company route portfolio contained ninety miles of railroad in Chicago and Indiana, much of which traversed the different communities and neighborhoods of the former Hyde Park Township, which had been annexed to Chicago in 1889.[887] The Calumet Electric system main routes totaled forty-eight miles of railroad, and the system secondary routes consisted of forty-two miles of railroad.[888] The company

---

[880] Marquis, Albert Nelson. Editor. The Book of Chicagoans: A Biographical Dictionary Of Leading Living Men Of The City Of Chicago. (1911). Vol. 2. P. 371. Chicago, IL: A. N. Marquis & Company. Google Books.

[881] Chicago Securities. (1905). Vol. 15. P. 96. Chicago, IL: The Chicago Directory Company. Google Books.

[882] American Street Railway Investments. (1905). P. 50. Street Railway Journal (publisher). New York, NY: McGraw Publishing Company. Google Books.

[883] American Street Railway Investments. (1905). P. 50. Street Railway Journal (publisher). New York, NY: McGraw Publishing Company. Google Books.

[884] American Street Railway Investments. (1905). P. 50. Street Railway Journal (publisher). New York, NY: McGraw Publishing Company. Google Books.

[885] American Street Railway Investments. (1905). P. 50. Street Railway Journal (publisher). New York, NY: McGraw Publishing Company. Google Books.

[886] American Street Railway Investments. (1905). P. 50. Street Railway Journal (publisher). New York, NY: McGraw Publishing Company. Google Books.

[887] American Street Railway Investments. (1905). P. 50. Street Railway Journal (publisher). New York, NY: McGraw Publishing Company. Google Books.

[888] American Street Railway Investments. (1905). P. 50. Street Railway Journal (publisher). New York, NY: McGraw Publishing Company. Google Books.

operated 227 train cars, including 115 motor cars, and 112 trailer cars.[889] The manufacturing companies that supplied the motor and trailer cars to the company included Pullman, St. Louis, Lamokin, and American. Motor elements were supplied by General Electric, Walker, and Detroit, among other vendor manufacturers.[890] The route system of the Calumet caused the company to overlay the territory of John Stryker's Michigan Southern Railroad Company, which, in the middle nineteenth century, was one of the commercial belligerent parties to the Great Chicago Frog War, along with the Illinois Central Railroad Company.[891]

The 1905 report indicated that the Calumet Electric Street Railway Company consisted of a compound financing plan in which both debt money and stock money constituted elements of the total capitalization money.[892] The equity element consisted of an authorized $5,000,000 in stock money, with $500,000 outstanding as of the time of the 1905 report. The stock share par value stood at $100 at the time of the 1905 report. The debt money element was two-part and consisted of first mortgage gold bonds with an interest rate of six percent, a maturity time of twenty years (1892-1912), and a semiannual (March and September) payment plan for the interest money. $3,000,000 had been authorized, and $2,949,000 had been issued, in the form of consolidated mortgage on gold bonds at five percent interest.[893] The consolidated mortgage due date was 1909.[894]

The leadership staff and structure of the company consisted of John Farson, President; E. E. Simmons, Secretary and Treasurer; H. M. Sloan as General Manager; C. M. Peterson as Chief Engineer; and Fred W. Murphy as Master Mechanic.[895] Edwin A. Potter was Receiver for the company in 1905, as stated in the report.[896] The board of directors consisted of John Farson, Frank H. Jones,

---

[889] American Street Railway Investments. (1905). P. 50. Street Railway Journal (publisher). New York, NY: McGraw Publishing Company. Google Books.
[890] American Street Railway Investments. (1905). P. 50. Street Railway Journal (publisher). New York, NY: McGraw Publishing Company. Google Books.
[891] American Street Railway Investments. (1905). P. 50. Street Railway Journal (publisher). New York, NY: McGraw Publishing Company. Google Books; See John Stryker information and references elsewhere in this book.
[892] American Street Railway Investments. (1905). P. 50. Street Railway Journal (publisher). New York, NY: McGraw Publishing Company. Google Books.
[893] American Street Railway Investments. (1905). P. 50. Street Railway Journal (publisher). New York, NY: McGraw Publishing Company. Google Books.
[894] American Street Railway Investments. (1905). P. 50. Street Railway Journal (publisher). New York, NY: McGraw Publishing Company. Google Books.
[895] American Street Railway Investments. (1905). P. 50. Street Railway Journal (publisher). New York, NY: McGraw Publishing Company. Google Books.
[896] American Street Railway Investments. (1905). P. 50. Street Railway Journal (publisher). New York, NY: McGraw Publishing Company. Google Books.

Edwin A. Potter, G. E. Adams, and Charles R. Corwith.[897] The company office was located at the New York Life Insurance Building of Chicago.[898]

John Farson, Esq. of Oak Park

John Farson (1855-1910) was a close friend of Frank Jones. Farson was a native of Indiana, and an alumnus of the Illinois Industrial University, later known as the University of Illinois.[899] Of significant note is the fact that John Whitfield Bunn was a founder, the founding Treasurer, and a thirty-seven-year member of the board of trustees of the University of Illinois. Farson arrived in Chicago after the Great Fire of 1871 and had only $25 in his pocket upon arrival.[900] He first worked for a tailor, then for Preston, Kiean & Company, which was a banking company.[901] Farson became a lawyer, worked with the S. A. Kean Law Firm, and then organized the law firm of Farson, Leach & Company.[902] Farson ended the firm of Farson, Leach & Company, and formed a law firm with his sons John Farson, Jr., and William Farson.[903]

John Farson married Mamie Ashworth and the two built a mansion in Oak Park at the corner of Pleasant Street and Home Avenue.[904] Chicago architect George Washington Maher, a native of Mill Creek, Randolph County, West Virginia, was the architect for Pleasant Home.[905] The name of the Farson estate was, and remains,

---

[897] American Street Railway Investments. (1905). P. 50. Street Railway Journal (publisher). New York, NY: McGraw Publishing Company. Google Books.

[898] American Street Railway Investments. (1905). P. 50. Street Railway Journal (publisher). New York, NY: McGraw Publishing Company. Google Books.

[899] Cummings, Kathleen Ann. (2002). Pleasant Home 1897: A History of the John Farson House, George Washington Maher, Architect. (Reproduced by Pleasant Home Foundation at Pleasanthome.org).

[900] Cummings, Kathleen Ann. (2002). Pleasant Home 1897: A History of the John Farson House, George Washington Maher, Architect. (Reproduced by Pleasant Home Foundation at Pleasanthome.org).

[901] Cummings, Kathleen Ann. (2002). Pleasant Home 1897: A History of the John Farson House, George Washington Maher, Architect. (Reproduced by Pleasant Home Foundation at Pleasanthome.org).

[902] Cummings, Kathleen Ann. (2002). Pleasant Home 1897: A History of the John Farson House, George Washington Maher, Architect. (Reproduced by Pleasant Home Foundation at Pleasanthome.org).

[903] Cummings, Kathleen Ann. (2002). Pleasant Home 1897: A History of the John Farson House, George Washington Maher, Architect. (Reproduced by Pleasant Home Foundation at Pleasanthome.org).

[904] Cummings, Kathleen Ann. (2002). Pleasant Home 1897: A History of the John Farson House, George Washington Maher, Architect. (Reproduced by Pleasant Home Foundation at Pleasanthome.org).

[905] Cummings, Kathleen Ann. (2002). Pleasant Home 1897: A History of the John Farson House, George Washington Maher, Architect. (Reproduced by Pleasant Home Foundation at Pleasanthome.org).

Pleasant Home.[906] John and Mamie (Ashworth) Farson were members of the First Methodist Church of Oak Park, and John was President of both the Chicago Automobile Club and the American Automobile Association.[907] William Henry Burtner, Jr., of Cincinnati, was a member of the board of directors of the American Automobile Association, and possibly knew Farson through that shared association.[908] It is probable that Frank Jones was a regular guest at the Farson home in Oak Park. The Mills family owned Pleasant Home after the Farsons did, and Mills Park, the backyard of Pleasant Home, is named for that family. The Pleasant Home estate continues today as a museum and history center in Oak Park under the management of the Pleasant Home Foundation.

William Henry Burtner, Jr., of Cincinnati

William Henry Burtner, Jr. (1873-1932), was a native of Cincinnati, and the son of William Henry Burtner, Sr., and Teresa Elizabeth (Deagle) Burtner, both of Cincinnati.[909] William Henry Burtner, Jr., was grandson of early Cincinnati building contractor and land developer, Peter Burtner.[910] William H. Burtner, Jr., graduated from the University of Michigan with a Bachelor of Laws in 1894, and continued legal studies at Yale University, where he received the degree of Master of Laws in 1895.[911] Burtner practiced law at Cincinnati and took an active role in Ohio civic work.[912] Burtner was counselor to the Ohio State Historical Site Marking Commission.[913] He served the 13th Ward of Cincinnati as Republican

---

[906] Cummings, Kathleen Ann. (2002). Pleasant Home 1897: A History of the John Farson House, George Washington Maher, Architect. (Reproduced by Pleasant Home Foundation at Pleasanthome.org).

[907] Cummings, Kathleen Ann. (2002). Pleasant Home 1897: A History of the John Farson House, George Washington Maher, Architect. (Reproduced by Pleasant Home Foundation at Pleasanthome.org).

[908] Cummings, Kathleen Ann. (2002). Pleasant Home 1897: A History of the John Farson House, George Washington Maher, Architect. (Reproduced by Pleasant Home Foundation at Pleasanthome.org); Goss, Charles Frederic. (1912). Cincinnati, The Queen City: 1788-1912. Pp. 780-781 (as reproduced by University of Michigan Law School in its Student Profile for William Henry Burtner, Jr.).

[909] Bulletin of Yale University: New Haven 15 October 1932. (1932). P. 252. New Haven, CT: Yale University. Yale University Library online.

[910] Bulletin of Yale University: New Haven 15 October 1932. (1932). P. 252. New Haven, CT: Yale University. Yale University Library online.

[911] Bulletin of Yale University: New Haven 15 October 1932. (1932). P. 252. New Haven, CT: Yale University. Yale University Library online.

[912] Bulletin of Yale University: New Haven 15 October 1932. (1932). P. 252. New Haven, CT: Yale University. Yale University Library online.

[913] Bulletin of Yale University: New Haven 15 October 1932. (1932). P. 252. New Haven, CT: Yale University. Yale University Library online.

precinct committeeman and as Secretary of the Republican Central Committee.[914] He was a director of the Avondale Republican Club and Vice-President of the Southwestern (Ohio) Fish and Game Commission. Burtner was an Episcopalian, and married Alice Elizabeth Miller of Cincinnati in a ceremony at Mackinac Island, Michigan, in 1915.[915] Alice's father was Postmaster of Cincinnati. Burtner was a member of the Cincinnati Automobile Club and a member of the board of directors of the American Automobile Association.[916] He was admitted to law practice not only in Ohio, but before the Supreme Court of Michigan, and in multiple United States District and Circuit Courts.[917] Burtner continued the tradition of family involvement in the machine tool manufacturing industry and served as President of the American Heel Machine Company of Cincinnati, Special Counsel and Secretary of the Cincinnati Metal Products Company, and as Secretary and Treasurer of Barker & Company of Cincinnati.[918] He also was a member of the boards of directors of the University of Michigan Club of Cincinnati and the Yale Club of Cincinnati.[919] Burtner's grandfather, Peter Burtner, was a native of metropolitan Pittsburgh, and was the brother of Pittsburgh and Butler businessmen Capt. Philip Burtner and William Burtner. The Burtner family is part of the Call-Baldwin-Burtner family of Ohio and Pennsylvania, and was one of the founding families of Pittsburgh, Allegheny County, and Butler County, in Pennsylvania. For more about the Burtner family, see Chapter 6, *Sprinters of the Steel Track*.

Fred Bennett Jones

Fred Bennett Jones was the brother of Frank Hatch Jones. Born in January, 1858, Fred Jones graduated from the Jerseyville High School in Pike County, Illinois.[920]

---

[914] Bulletin of Yale University: New Haven 15 October 1932. (1932). P. 252. New Haven, CT: Yale University. Yale University Library online.

[915] Bulletin of Yale University: New Haven 15 October 1932. (1932). P. 252. New Haven, CT: Yale University. Yale University Library online.

[916] Goss, Charles Frederic. (1912). Cincinnati, The Queen City: 1788-1912. Pp. 780-781 (as reproduced by University of Michigan Law School in its Student Profile for William Henry Burtner, Jr.).

[917] Goss, Charles Frederic. (1912). Cincinnati, The Queen City: 1788-1912. Pp. 780-781 (as reproduced by University of Michigan Law School in its Student Profile for William Henry Burtner, Jr.).

[918] Goss, Charles Frederic. (1912). Cincinnati, The Queen City: 1788-1912. Pp. 780-781 (as reproduced by University of Michigan Law School in its Student Profile for William Henry Burtner, Jr.).

[919] Goss, Charles Frederic. (1912). Cincinnati, The Queen City: 1788-1912. Pp. 780-781 (as reproduced by University of Michigan Law School in its Student Profile for William Henry Burtner, Jr.).

[920] Marquis, Albert Nelson. Editor. The Book of Chicagoans: A Biographical Dictionary Of Leading Living Men Of The City Of Chicago. (1911). Vol. 2. P. 371. Chicago, IL: A.

He went to work for the Adams & Westlake Company of Chicago in 1877 and remained at this company until retirement in 1908, at the age of 50.[921] He was hired originally as a stock clerk for Adams & Westlake, and later worked as a commercial traveler (this was another name for a traveling salesman).[922] Jones then served as Managing Director before being elected Secretary of the company.[923] He served both as Secretary, and subsequently as Vice-President, of the Adams & Westlake Company, and was a member of the board of directors of the company.[924] Fred held membership in the Chicago Athletic Association, where he also served on the board of directors, and was a founding member of the Mid-Day Club.[925] Fred was a member of the Chicago Club, the Exmoor Country Club of Highland Park, the Old Elm Club of Highland Park, and the Washington Park Club of the South Side of Chicago.[926] William Lee, a part of the Ferguson family of the Pullman community, was one of the chief engineers in charge of construction of the Washington Park Club, working under Major Benyouard.[927] In Wisconsin Jones was a member of the Delavan Lake Golf Club and the Delavan Lake Yacht Club.[928] Jones was a founding member of the Delavan Lake Improvement Association, an organization that was formed at The Rookery building of Chicago on February 8, 1907.[929] Frank Lloyd Wright operated an architectural office at The

N. Marquis & Company. Google Books; Interviews and historical records provided by historian Mark Hertzberg about Fred Bennett Jones.

[921] Marquis, Albert Nelson. Editor. The Book of Chicagoans: A Biographical Dictionary Of Leading Living Men Of The City Of Chicago. (1911). Vol. 2. P. 371. Chicago, IL: A. N. Marquis & Company. Google Books; Interviews and historical records provided by historian Mark Hertzberg about Fred Bennett Jones; Interview with historian Mark Hertzberg.

[922] Interviews and historical records provided by historian Mark Hertzberg about Fred Bennett Jones; Interview with historian Mark Hertzberg.

[923] Interviews and historical records provided by historian Mark Hertzberg about Fred Bennett Jones; Interview with historian Mark Hertzberg.

[924] Marquis, Albert Nelson. Editor. The Book of Chicagoans: A Biographical Dictionary Of Leading Living Men Of The City Of Chicago. (1911). Vol. 2. P. 371. Chicago, IL: A. N. Marquis & Company. Google Books; Interviews and historical records provided by historian Mark Hertzberg about Fred Bennett Jones.

[925] Marquis, Albert Nelson. Editor. The Book of Chicagoans: A Biographical Dictionary Of Leading Living Men Of The City Of Chicago. (1911). Vol. 2. P. 371. Chicago, IL: A. N. Marquis & Company. Google Books; Interviews and historical records provided by historian Mark Hertzberg about Fred Bennett Jones.

[926] Interviews and historical records provided by historian Mark Hertzberg about Fred Bennett Jones.

[927] Chicago Tribune. (July 15, 1883). P. 18. Newspapers.com.

[928] Interviews and historical records provided by historian Mark Hertzberg about Fred Bennett Jones.

[929] Interviews and historical records provided by historian Mark Hertzberg about Fred Bennett Jones.

Rookery in 1898-1899, and in 1905 was commissioned to redesign the lobby at The Rookery.[930]

Fred Jones was a resident of 804 Tower Court in Gold Coast neighborhood, where he was a neighbor of his brother, Frank.[931] Fred was President of the Great Western Manufacturing Company, and also was a director of the Curtain Supply Company.[932] He was also a member of the Art Institute of Chicago.[933] Fred died April 9, 1933.[934] He was a global traveler.[935] Fred never married, but was often in the company of Dora Mortimer of Chicago, as is seen from the photograph of Jones and Mortimer at the Giza Plateau of Egypt.[936] Dora Mortimer's specific relationship to Jones has not been ascertained.[937] Nevertheless, the two were friends, and traveled together.[938] Fred commissioned architect Frank Lloyd Wright to design an estate, including a summer cottage, at Delavan Lake in Walworth County, Wisconsin.[939] The estate, known as Penwern, was the Fred Jones estate until the time of his death.[940] Dora Mortimer was said to have looked after the main house on the estate grounds for Jones.[941]

---

[930] Interviews and historical records provided by historian Mark Hertzberg about Fred Bennett Jones.

[931] Marquis, Albert Nelson. Editor. The Book of Chicagoans: A Biographical Dictionary Of Leading Living Men Of The City Of Chicago. (1911). Vol. 2. P. 371. Chicago, IL: A. N. Marquis & Company. Google Books; Interviews and historical records provided by historian Mark Hertzberg about Fred Bennett Jones.

[932] Wallace, Joseph. (1904). Past And Present Of The City Of Springfield And Sangamon County Illinois. Vol. II. P. 1573. Chicago, IL: S. J. Clarke Publishing Company. Google Books.

[933] Annual Report of the Trustees of the Art Institute of Chicago. (1923). Vols. 45-48. Page number not clear. Chicago, IL: Art Institute of Chicago. Google Books.

[934] Railway Age. (April 22, 1933). Vol. 94. P. 610. Philadelphia, PA: Simmons-Boardman Publishing Company. Google Books.

[935] Interviews and historical records provided by historian Mark Hertzberg about Fred Bennett Jones.

[936] Interviews and historical records provided by historian Mark Hertzberg about Fred Bennett Jones.

[937] Interviews and historical records provided by historian Mark Hertzberg about Fred Bennett Jones.

[938] Interviews and historical records provided by historian Mark Hertzberg about Fred Bennett Jones.

[939] Interviews and historical records provided by historian Mark Hertzberg about Fred Bennett Jones.

[940] Interviews and historical records provided by historian Mark Hertzberg about Fred Bennett Jones.

[941] Interviews and historical records provided by historian Mark Hertzberg about Fred Bennett Jones.

George Whitfield Jones

George Whitfield Jones, the father of Frank and Fred Jones, was born March 18, 1826, in Boston, Massachusetts.[942] He relocated to Pike County, Illinois, with his parents.[943] George later formed a wheat drill manufacturing company with a partner at Peoria.[944] Historian Joseph Wallace, Esq., of Springfield, commented that the Jones wheat drill company was the first of its kind in the American West.[945] Jones sold his interest in the company and moved to Pike County, where he ran successfully for the office of Pike County Circuit Court Clerk.[946] Jones later held the post of Clerk of the Appellate Court of the Central Grand Division of Illinois, having won election to that office in 1878.[947] George Jones oversaw thirty-five Illinois counties as Clerk of the Central Grand Division.[948] George married Cecelia Bennett, who was born in 1832 in New York.[949] Their three children were William Jones, who died in infancy, Frank Hatch Jones, and Fred Bennett Jones, discussed above.[950]

---

[942] Wallace, Joseph. (1904). Past And Present Of The City Of Springfield And Sangamon County Illinois. Vol. II. P. 1570. Chicago, IL: S. J. Clarke Publishing Company. Google Books.

[943] Wallace, Joseph. (1904). Past And Present Of The City Of Springfield And Sangamon County Illinois. Vol. II. P. 1570. Chicago, IL: S. J. Clarke Publishing Company. Google Books.

[944] Wallace, Joseph. (1904). Past And Present Of The City Of Springfield And Sangamon County Illinois. Vol. II. P. 1573. Chicago, IL: S. J. Clarke Publishing Company. Google Books.

[945] Wallace, Joseph. (1904). Past And Present Of The City Of Springfield And Sangamon County Illinois. Vol. II. P. 1573. Chicago, IL: S. J. Clarke Publishing Company. Google Books.

[946] Wallace, Joseph. (1904). Past And Present Of The City Of Springfield And Sangamon County Illinois. Vol. II. P. 1573. Chicago, IL: S. J. Clarke Publishing Company. Google Books.

[947] Wallace, Joseph. (1904). Past And Present Of The City Of Springfield And Sangamon County Illinois. Vol. II. P. 1573. Chicago, IL: S. J. Clarke Publishing Company. Google Books.

[948] Wallace, Joseph. (1904). Past And Present Of The City Of Springfield And Sangamon County Illinois. Vol. II. P. 1573. Chicago, IL: S. J. Clarke Publishing Company. Google Books.

[949] Wallace, Joseph. (1904). Past And Present Of The City Of Springfield And Sangamon County Illinois. Vol. II. P. 1573. Chicago, IL: S. J. Clarke Publishing Company. Google Books.

[950] Wallace, Joseph. (1904). Past And Present Of The City Of Springfield And Sangamon County Illinois. Vol. II. P. 1573. Chicago, IL: S. J. Clarke Publishing Company. Google Books.

Rev. Melancthon Woolsey Stryker of Chicago and New York

The Chicago and Morgan County Strykers also gave much to Christian leadership and ecclesiastical development in Illinois and elsewhere. Reverend Melancthon Woolsey Stryker was another cousin of Charlotte (Stryker) Taylor, and the Taylors of Chicago, Springfield, Morgan County, and Cass County, Illinois. Rev. Stryker was involved in service to multiple Christian organizations in Chicago and the State of New York. Melancthon Stryker was a member of the Chicago Historical Society, as were John Whitfield Bunn, Juliette Magill Kinzie, and John Harris Kinzie, who was a founding member of the Chicago Historical Society.[951] Melancthon Woolsey Stryker served on the Board of Honorary Directors of the McCormick Theological Seminary at Chicago.[952] In this capacity Stryker worked directly with Cyrus Hall McCormick in the leadership of the Seminary.[953]

Moreover, Stryker served on the Board of Directors of the Board of Aid for Colleges and Academies of the Presbyterian Church in the United States of America, a Chicago-based charitable Christian organization.[954] Rev. Stryker and Rev. Thomas C. Hall of Chicago, along with Rev. J. G. K. McClure of Evanston, and Rev. M. L. Haines of Indianapolis, constituted part of the 1891 board of directors of The Presbyterian Board of Aid for Colleges and Academies, which had an office at 23 Montauk Block of 115 Monroe Street, Chicago, in addition to a post office box, P.O. Box 294, Chicago.[955] When Stryker was on the Board,

---

[951] Chicago Historical Society: Charter, Constitution, By-Laws, Roll of Membership (1901). Pp. V, 7, 17, 25, 29, 42, 47. Chicago, IL: Chicago Historical Society. Google Books; Call, Andrew Taylor. (2016). Faded Bricks: Old Family Tales from the South Side of Chicago. Hyde Park History, Vol. 38, (No. 4), Pp. 1-7. Chicago, IL: Hyde Park Historical Society.

[952] Minutes of the General Assembly of the Presbyterian Church in the United States of America. (1888). Vol. 11. P. 194. Philadelphia, PA: MacCalla & Company, Printers. Google Books; Call, Andrew Taylor. (2016). Faded Bricks: Old Family Tales from the South Side of Chicago. Hyde Park History, Vol. 38, (No. 4), Pp. 1-7. Chicago, IL: Hyde Park Historical Society.

[953] Minutes of the General Assembly of the Presbyterian Church in the United States of America. (1888). Vol. 11. P. 194. Philadelphia, PA: MacCalla & Company, Printers. Google Books; Call, Andrew Taylor. (2016). Faded Bricks: Old Family Tales from the South Side of Chicago. Hyde Park History, Vol. 38, (No. 4), Pp. 1-7. Chicago, IL: Hyde Park Historical Society.

[954] Minutes of the General Assembly of the Presbyterian Church in the United States of America. (1888). Vol. 11. P. 258. Philadelphia, PA: MacCalla & Company, Printers. Google Books; Call, Andrew Taylor. (2016). Faded Bricks: Old Family Tales from the South Side of Chicago. Hyde Park History, Vol. 38, (No. 4), Pp. 1-7. Chicago, IL: Hyde Park Historical Society.

[955] Eighth Annual Report of the Board of Aid for Colleges and Academies of the Presbyterian Church in the United States of America. (1891). Page number not specified. Chicago, IL: Knight, Leonard & Company, Printers. Google Books.

Charles M. Charnley was Treasurer of the Board, and Rev. Hervey D. Ganse was Secretary of the Board.[956] Charnley's brother built the architecturally significant Gold Coast neighborhood estate known as the Charnley-Persky House, which was designed by Louis Sullivan and a young Frank Lloyd Wright. The other members of the Board of Aid in 1891 were Cyrus Hall McCormick, The Hon. Dan P. Eells of Cleveland, Thomas Lord of Evanston, The Hon. James McMillan of Detroit, Rev. J. H. Worcester, W. H. Swift, Rev. S. J. McPherson, who was Vice-President of the Board, and Rev. Herrick Johnson, who was President of the Board.[957]

One of the foremost ministers and church leaders of Chicago, Rev. Stryker also served as the fourth Pastor of Fourth Presbyterian Church in Chicago, having served from 1885 until 1892.[958] Fourth Presbyterian was located at Rush Street and Superior Street at the time of Stryker's pastoral leadership there.[959] This building predated the present building of Fourth Presbyterian Church located at N. Michigan Avenue and E. Delaware Place. Rev. Melancthon W. Stryker was an *ex officio* member of the Board of Managers of The Presbyterian Hospital of Chicago, along with Rev. S. J. McPherson, Rev. Herrick Johnson, D.D., Rev. John H. Barrows, D.D., and Rev. A. E. Kittredge, D.D.[960] Cyrus Hall McCormick, Jr., also served on the Board of Managers at about the same time as Stryker and the other named men.[961]

Rev. Stryker officiated the funeral for Henry Field (1841-1890) of Chicago.[962] Henry was the brother of Marshall Field (1835-1906) and was born in Conway, Massachusetts.[963] He relocated to Chicago in 1861, found a job with Cooley, Farwell & Company, and was later a founding member of Field, Leiter & Company

[956] Eighth Annual Report of the Board of Aid for Colleges and Academies of the Presbyterian Church in the United States of America. (1891). Page number not specified. Chicago, IL: Knight, Leonard & Company, Printers. Google Books.

[957] Eighth Annual Report of the Board of Aid for Colleges and Academies of the Presbyterian Church in the United States of America. (1891). Page number not specified. Chicago, IL: Knight, Leonard & Company, Printers. Google Books.

[958] Wind, James P., & Lewis, James W. (Eds.). (1994). American Congregations: Portraits of Twelve Religious Communities. Vol. 1. P. 515. Chicago, IL: The University of Chicago Press. Google Books; Call, Andrew Taylor. (2016). Faded Bricks: Old Family Tales from the South Side of Chicago. Hyde Park History, Vol. 38, (No. 4), Pp. 1-7. Chicago, IL: Hyde Park Historical Society.

[959] The Artistic Guide To Chicago And The World's Columbian Exposition. (1892). P. 143. Columbian Art Company. Google Books.

[960] Andreas, Alfred Theodore. (1886). History Of Chicago: From The Earliest Period To The Present Time. P. 522. Chicago, IL: The A. T. Andreas Company. Google Books.

[961] Andreas, Alfred Theodore. (1886). History Of Chicago: From The Earliest Period To The Present Time. P. 522. Chicago, IL: The A. T. Andreas Company. Google Books.

[962] Pierce, Frederick Clifton. (1901). Vol. II. Pp. 706-707. Chicago, IL: Hammond Press and W. B. Conkey Company. Google Books.

[963] Pierce, Frederick Clifton. (1901). Vol. II. Pp. 706-707. Chicago, IL: Hammond Press and W. B. Conkey Company. Google Books.

of Chicago, until retiring from partnership in 1878.[964] He rejoined the company, which had become Marshall Field & Company, in 1881, and remained with the firm until 1882.[965] Henry Field married Florence Lathrop, who was the daughter of Jedediah Hyde Lathrop (1806-1889) of Chicago and Elmhurst, the latter place being a western suburb of the city.[966] Field was a member of the Board of Trustees of the Art Institute of Chicago and was a founding director of the first Chicago Opera Festival, which took place in 1885.[967] In addition to being a director of the Chicago Relief and Aid Society, and President of the Chicago Home for the Friendless, Field was a member of Fourth Presbyterian Church.[968] Jedediah Hyde Lathrop was a land developer of Chicago and Cook County, and was a third cousin of Charlotte (Stryker) Taylor and the Strykers and Taylors of Chicago, Springfield, and Morgan County. Lathrop Avenue in the western Chicago suburb of River Forest is named for him.

Rev. Melancthon Stryker possessed an excellent reputation as a hymnologist. The February 9, 1882, issue of *The Independent*, a Christian faith journal of New York City, reported that Stryker collaborated with Hubert P. Main to produce and arrange *The Church Praise Book*, a hymnal that contained over 700 hymns and more than 400 tunes.[969] The hymnal was published by Biglow & Main of 31 Randolph Street in Chicago and 76 East Ninth Street in New York City.[970] Stryker also wrote *Christian Chorals, for the Chapel and Fireside*, at some point prior to the March, 1886, issue of Vol. 82 of *The Missionary Herald*, a Boston journal, and the journal which announced the hymnal.[971] The 1886 choral hymn book was marketed and available for sale for fifty cents in 1886, and had also been published by Biglow & Main.[972]

Rev. Stryker served as Moderator of the Chicago Presbytery.[973] He built Fourth Presbyterian Church into a large congregation and community in the city. Volume

---

[964] Pierce, Frederick Clifton. (1901). Vol. II. Pp. 706-707. Chicago, IL: Hammond Press and W. B. Conkey Company. Google Books.

[965] Pierce, Frederick Clifton. (1901). Vol. II. Pp. 706-707. Chicago, IL: Hammond Press and W. B. Conkey Company. Google Books.

[966] Pierce, Frederick Clifton. (1901). Vol. II. Pp. 706-707. Chicago, IL: Hammond Press and W. B. Conkey Company. Google Books.

[967] Pierce, Frederick Clifton. (1901). Vol. II. Pp. 706-707. Chicago, IL: Hammond Press and W. B. Conkey Company. Google Books.

[968] Pierce, Frederick Clifton. (1901). Vol. II. Pp. 706-707. Chicago, IL: Hammond Press and W. B. Conkey Company. Google Books.

[969] The Independent. (February 9, 1882). P. 18. New York, NY. Google Books.

[970] The Independent. (February 9, 1882). P. 18. New York, NY. Google Books.

[971] The Missionary Herald. (March, 1886). Vol. LXXXII. P. 112. Boston, MASS: Press of Stanley & Usher. Google Books.

[972] The Missionary Herald. (March, 1886). Vol. LXXXII. P. 112. Boston, MASS: Press of Stanley & Usher. Google Books.

[973] Stryker family history records.

XIX of the 1891 *Minutes of the General Assembly of the Presbyterian Church in the United States of America* reported the organizational statistics of Presbyterian congregations across the United States. The General Assembly report for the Synod of Illinois stated that Fourth Presbyterian Church possessed a membership of 590, a leadership structure of ten elders, and comparatively immense numbers associated with Christian missions and missionary works.[974] The September 24, 1892, issue of *The Christian Union*, a journal based at Clinton Hall, New York City, announced that Rev. Stryker would leave the chief pastorate of Fourth Presbyterian Church and accept the Presidency of his alma mater, Hamilton College, in Clinton, New York.[975] Rev. Isaac Pierson Stryker and Pierson Tivins Stryker, who were respectively the father and brother of Rev. Melancthon Woolsey Stryker, were also Chicago residents in the nineteenth century.

Rev. Stryker married Clara Elizabeth Goss. The following children were born to them: Lloyd Paul Stryker, Esq., Assistant District Attorney for New York County; Evelyn Stryker, who married Winthrop T. Scarritt of Kansas City, Missouri; and Alida Stryker, who married Elihu Root, Jr., who was the son of United States Senator Elihu Root of New York.[976] Winthrop Scarritt worked for the White Motor Car Company of Kansas City.[977] Elihu Root, Jr., and Alida (Stryker) Root had a son named Elihu Root, III.[978]

Women's Presbyterian Board of Missions of the Northwest

Clara (Goss) Stryker, the wife of Rev. Melancthon Stryker, served in multiple leadership capacities as a member of the Women's Presbyterian Board of Missions of the Northwest, an organization headquartered in Room 48 of the McCormick Block of Chicago.[979] She was a member of the Board of Managers of the Board of Missions and served in that capacity with the following fellow Managers in 1892: Mrs. C. N. Hartwell, Mrs. J. H. Barrows, Mrs. S. J. McPherson, Miss E. Skinner, Mrs. E. H. Whitney, Mrs. L. R. Hall, Mrs. W. C. Goudy, Mrs. D. C. Marquis, Ms. E. Blaikie, Mrs. J. L. Withrow, Mrs. Thomas Kane, Mrs. Thomas C. Hall, Mrs. William H. Swift, Mrs. J. D. Webster, Mrs. T. D. Wallace, Mrs. T. W. Harvey, Mrs. W. L. Moss, Mrs. Edward Ely, Mrs. A. W. Green, Mrs. H. M. Merriman,

---

[974] Minutes of the 103rd General Assembly of the Presbyterian Church in the United States of America. (1891). Vol. XIX. P. 332. Google Books.

[975] The Christian Union. (September 24, 1892). P. 528. Google Books.

[976] The Cornell Alumni News. (September 1, 1914-August 31, 1915). Vol. 17. P. 288. Ithaca, NY: Cornell University. Google Books.

[977] The Cornell Alumni News. (September 1, 1914-August 31, 1915). Vol. 17. P. 288. Ithaca, NY: Cornell University. Google Books.

[978] Stryker family history records.

[979] Twenty-First Annual Report Of The Women's Presbyterian Board Of Missions Of The Northwest. (April, 1892). Chicago, IL: C. H. Blakely & Company, Printers. Google Books.

Mrs. A. L. Ashley, Ms. Mary Erwin Paul, Mrs. Frederick Campbell, Mrs. J. Frothingham, Mrs. Robert M. Wells, Ms. Isabel Parker, Mrs. Elisha P. Whitehead, and Mrs. S. D. Ward, all of Chicago.[980] Many women from other Midwestern cities and towns served on the Board of Managers, as well. The women from the Chicago suburbs who served on the Managers Board at the same time as Mrs. Stryker were Mrs. J. G. K. McClure of Lake Forest, Mrs. N. D. Hillis of Evanston, Mrs. E. C. Linsley of Hinsdale, Mrs. W. C. Gray of Oak Park, and Mrs. William Douglass of Oak Park.[981] Mrs. Stryker served on the Standing Committee on Prayer Meetings, along with Mrs. Campbell, Mrs. Frothingham, Mrs. McPherson, Mrs. Wallace, and Mrs. Hillis.[982]

The twenty-seventh annual conference of the Women's Presbyterian Board of Missions of the Northwest took place at the Central Presbyterian Church of St. Paul, Minnesota.[983] Rev. Stryker delivered the opening address, and spoke about the importance of mission work, and about the importance of seeing all missionary work, both home and foreign, as united.[984] Mrs. H. D. Penfield of 2455 Prairie Avenue, Chicago, served as President of the Board of Missions at this time.[985] The Board of Missions had been chartered in 1875.[986]

The Saints and Sinners Club of Chicago

Rev. Melancthon Stryker was a well-known party to what journalist Cleveland Moffett referred to as the bibliomania of Chicago during the nineteenth century.[987]

---

[980] Twenty-First Annual Report Of The Women's Presbyterian Board Of Missions Of The Northwest. (April, 1892). Chicago, IL: C. H. Blakely & Company, Printers. Google Books.

[981] Twenty-First Annual Report Of The Women's Presbyterian Board Of Missions Of The Northwest. (April, 1892). Chicago, IL: C. H. Blakely & Company, Printers. Google Books.

[982] Twenty-First Annual Report Of The Women's Presbyterian Board Of Missions Of The Northwest. (April, 1892). Chicago, IL: C. H. Blakely & Company, Printers. Google Books.

[983] Twenty-First Annual Report Of The Women's Presbyterian Board Of Missions Of The Northwest. (April, 1892). Chicago, IL: C. H. Blakely & Company, Printers. Google Books.

[984] Twenty-First Annual Report Of The Women's Presbyterian Board Of Missions Of The Northwest. (April, 1892). Chicago, IL: C. H. Blakely & Company, Printers. Google Books.

[985] Twenty-First Annual Report Of The Women's Presbyterian Board Of Missions Of The Northwest. (April, 1892). Chicago, IL: C. H. Blakely & Company, Printers. Google Books.

[986] Twenty-First Annual Report Of The Women's Presbyterian Board Of Missions Of The Northwest. (April, 1892). Chicago, IL: C. H. Blakely & Company, Printers. Google Books.

[987] Moffett, Cleveland. Godey's Magazine. (January, 1896). O Rare 'Gene Field. Vol. 132, No. 787. Pp. 155-156. Google Books.

Moffett, in his work, *O Rare 'Gene Field*, inventoried the Chicago experiences of Eugene Field in Vol. 132 of *Godey's Magazine*, and discussed Stryker's friendship with Field. Moffett chronicled the Saints and Sinners Club in his memoir piece for *Godey's*.[988] Eugene Field, a central light of Chicago literary society, founded the Saints and Sinners Club with Rev. Melancthon Stryker of Chicago's Fourth Presbyterian Church, W. F. Poole, who was Librarian of the Newberry Library, T. A. Van Laun, Rev. Frank M. Bristol, Rev. F. W. Gunsaulus, Slason Thompson of the *Chicago Daily News*, Frank M. Larned, W. Irving Way, George Millard, and Francis Wilson.[989] Eugene Field was himself employed by the *Chicago Daily News*, and thus combined interlocking careers in journalism and literature.[990] The Saints and Sinners Club derived from the specific tradition that these named men had of assembling for comradery, bibliophilic discussion, and philosophical dialogue, at a particular corner of A. C. McClurg's Publishing Company.[991] George Millard became acquainted with Field, who was a *Daily News* journalist, early in Field's time at Chicago.[992] The original name of the literary salon meetings organization was the Saints and Sinners Corner.[993] This habitual company evolved organizationally into the formalized Saints and Sinners Club, with the same named people as the founders and members of the Club.[994] Millard was in charge of a rare book department at Chicago, and thus possessed the requisite fervor for membership in a club whose organizational purpose was rooted principally within the rich culture of bibliomania, rare book collection, and all things literary.[995] Therefore, the loose but loyal confederation of literary men that assembled regularly at McClurg's Publishing House was known originally as the Saints and Sinners Corner, and now as the Saints and Sinners Club.[996] Cleveland Moffett described the social power and mystique that the Saints and Sinners Club

---

[988] Moffett, Cleveland. Godey's Magazine. (January, 1896). O Rare 'Gene Field. Vol. 132, No. 787. Pp. 155-156. Google Books.

[989] Moffett, Cleveland. Godey's Magazine. (January, 1896). O Rare 'Gene Field. Vol. 132, No. 787. Pp. 155-156. Google Books.

[990] Moffett, Cleveland. Godey's Magazine. (January, 1896). O Rare 'Gene Field. Vol. 132, No. 787. Pp. 155-156. Google Books.

[991] Moffett, Cleveland. Godey's Magazine. (January, 1896). O Rare 'Gene Field. Vol. 132, No. 787. Pp. 155-156. Google Books.

[992] Moffett, Cleveland. Godey's Magazine. (January, 1896). O Rare 'Gene Field. Vol. 132, No. 787. Pp. 155-156. Google Books.

[993] Moffett, Cleveland. Godey's Magazine. (January, 1896). O Rare 'Gene Field. Vol. 132, No. 787. Pp. 155-156. Google Books.

[994] Moffett, Cleveland. Godey's Magazine. (January, 1896). O Rare 'Gene Field. Vol. 132, No. 787. Pp. 155-156. Google Books.

[995] Moffett, Cleveland. Godey's Magazine. (January, 1896). O Rare 'Gene Field. Vol. 132, No. 787. Pp. 155-156. Google Books.

[996] Moffett, Cleveland. Godey's Magazine. (January, 1896). O Rare 'Gene Field. Vol. 132, No. 787. Pp. 155-156. Google Books.

possessed in Chicago, specifically noting that Field's personality was the core of the club's personality.[997]

> "[The acquaintanceship of Field and Millard] ripened into friendship, and it was not long before Field was on intimate terms not only with Mr. Millard, but with half a dozen others, mostly clergymen, who were also ardent patrons of the Corner. . .So often did these friends meet in their favorite corner, and so often frequent and delightful were the talks they had about books and things, and (most of all) so strong was the binding power of Field's magnetism and personality, that the Corner at McClurg's came to be a recognized institution, destined to work as a leaven in the community with far-reaching influence. The name was given by Field, always happy at fitting epithets, and so in the city of Chicago, reputed to be humdrum and commonplace, there came into being the Saints and Sinners' Club, a little oasis in the desert of hustling and money-getting, a delightful coterie, enveloped in an atmosphere of genial philosophy and ancient lore that seemed to carry one back to similar gatherings in Fleet Street a century or so ago. These men loved books first, and so came to love each other."[998]

The Saints and Sinners Club was born in a corner of the publishing house building of Alexander C. McClurg, a Pittsburgh native and early vanguard of the Chicago publishing industry.[999] McClurg originally joined the S. C. Griggs Company of Chicago in 1859.[1000] The company began in 1848, with S. C. Griggs as the founder.[1001] McClurg served in the Union Army during the Civil War, began with the rank of Captain, served in all battles at which the Army of the Cumberland participated, and eventually earned the rank of Brigadier-General.[1002] General

---

[997] Moffett, Cleveland. Godey's Magazine. (January, 1896). O Rare 'Gene Field. Vol. 132, No. 787. Pp. 155-156. Google Books.

[998] Moffett, Cleveland. Godey's Magazine. (January, 1896). O Rare 'Gene Field. Vol. 132, No. 787. Pp. 155-156. Google Books.

[999] Moffett, Cleveland. Godey's Magazine. (January, 1896). O Rare 'Gene Field. Vol. 132, No. 787. Pp. 155-156. Google Books; Half-Century's Progress of the City of Chicago: The City's Leading Manufacturers and Merchants. Part I. P. 354. Chicago, IL: International Publishing Company. Google Books.

[1000] Half-Century's Progress of the City of Chicago: The City's Leading Manufacturers and Merchants. (1887). Part I. P. 354. Chicago, IL: International Publishing Company. Google Books.

[1001] Half-Century's Progress of the City of Chicago: The City's Leading Manufacturers and Merchants. (1887). Part I. P. 354. Chicago, IL: International Publishing Company. Google Books.

[1002] Half-Century's Progress of the City of Chicago: The City's Leading Manufacturers and Merchants. (1887). Part I. P. 354. Chicago, IL: International Publishing Company. Google Books.

McClurg returned to Chicago, and in approximately 1865, he achieved partnership in the S. C. Griggs Company.[1003] Frederick Smith of Maine joined the Griggs Company in 1862 as a clerk and became a partner in 1866.[1004] The company name changed to Jansen, McClurg & Company in 1872, reflecting the additional partnership of E. L. Jansen.[1005] When Jansen retired from the company in 1886, the company name became A. C. McClurg & Company.[1006] The publishing house stood at 117, 119, and 121 Wabash Avenue, located at the junction of Wabash and Madison Street in the Loop community.[1007] Thus, the Saints and Sinners Club, formed prior to 1896, was established in the Loop community. The McClurg Publishing House employed more than 150 people as of 1887, and was reputed to be equal to or greater than any publishing house of the East Coast.[1008] Inferable from Cleveland Moffett's history of the Saints and Sinners Club was the fact that George Millard was employed in the Rare Book Department of the McClurg Publishing House when he, Eugene Field, Melancthon Stryker, and the other men named above, formed the Saints and Sinners Club.[1009] Of further interest and relevance is the fact that Ogden Trevor McClurg, son of Alexander McClurg and Eleanor (Wheeler) McClurg, was a prominent Chicago businessman, publisher, bibliophile, and developer of the Gold Coast neighborhood.[1010] Rev. Melancthon Stryker, in addition to having been a founder and member of the Saints and Sinners

---

[1003] Half-Century's Progress of the City of Chicago: The City's Leading Manufacturers and Merchants. (1887). Part I. P. 354. Chicago, IL: International Publishing Company. Google Books.

[1004] Half-Century's Progress of the City of Chicago: The City's Leading Manufacturers and Merchants. (1887). Part I. P. 354. Chicago, IL: International Publishing Company. Google Books.

[1005] Half-Century's Progress of the City of Chicago: The City's Leading Manufacturers and Merchants. (1887). Part I. P. 354. Chicago, IL: International Publishing Company. Google Books.

[1006] Half-Century's Progress of the City of Chicago: The City's Leading Manufacturers and Merchants. (1887). Part I. P. 354. Chicago, IL: International Publishing Company. Google Books.

[1007] Half-Century's Progress of the City of Chicago: The City's Leading Manufacturers and Merchants. (1887). Part I. P. 354. Chicago, IL: International Publishing Company. Google Books.

[1008] Half-Century's Progress of the City of Chicago: The City's Leading Manufacturers and Merchants. (1887). Part I. P. 354. Chicago, IL: International Publishing Company. Google Books.

[1009] Moffett, Cleveland. Godey's Magazine. (January, 1896). O Rare 'Gene Field. Vol. 132, No. 787. Pp. 155-156. Google Books; Half-Century's Progress of the City of Chicago: The City's Leading Manufacturers and Merchants. Part I. P. 354. Chicago, IL: International Publishing Company. Google Books.

[1010] Chicago Tribune. (January 26, 2012). Graydon Megan. "Barbara McClurg Potter, 1925-2012: Chicago civic figure with ties to city's history." articles.chicagotribune.com; ancestry.com

Club, was also a member of both the Chicago Literary Club and the Chicago Historical Society.[1011]

While President of Hamilton College, Rev. Stryker wrote *The Well By The Gate*, a 1903 work intended to revive Christian faith and remind people of the simple truths of God, Jesus Christ, Holy Spirit, salvation, and simple faith.[1012] In the book, Stryker warned against the risk of people forgetting the pure and simple truth of the Gospel of Jesus Christ and becoming complacent with lifeless religious process.

> "Audit is one thing, credit quite another. Better five words with the understanding than ten thousand words in an unknown tongue. Do we *know it*? Do we *mean it*? Formulas which have been vital to others may be barren to us. We profane Scripture when we turn phrases that once breathed and burned and bled into common shibboleths. Mme. de Stael once said, 'Better a smaller vocabulary and a fuller heart!' True religion is not a self-monologue, but a dialogue with the Father of our spirits. It means reciprocity. The thing needful is not that we recite the great creeds of the fourth century, or match with music the lyric fervors of Charles Wesley and Henry Lyte—great as these are—but that we 'speak that we do know.' First *test*, then *testimony*. It is the tones of experience that command attention."[1013]

Rev. Stryker left $20,000 to the Presbyterian Theological Seminary of Chicago when he died, in addition to a sum to Hamilton College, from which he had graduated.[1014] Rev. Stryker has to be remembered as one of the pillars and key builders of Christian ministry and missionary work in Chicago, as well as one of the fathers of the Chicago historical and literary communities.

Jedediah Hyde Lathrop of Chicago

Jedediah Hyde Lathrop was a third cousin of Elizabeth Henshaw (McClure) Stryker, and a third cousin of many of the Strykers and Taylors of Chicago and Morgan County. The shared Lathrop-Stryker ancestors were the Richards, Hough, Hyde, and Post families of Connecticut. Thomas Barbour Bryan, William B. Ogden, Edwin S. Sheldon, Sidney Sawyer, George P. A. Healy, and others

---

[1011] Stryker family history records.

[1012] Stryker, Melancthon Woolsey. The Well By The Gate. (1903). Pp. 67-68. Philadelphia, PA: Presbyterian Board of Publication and Sabbath-School Work. Google Books.

[1013] Stryker, Melancthon Woolsey. The Well By The Gate. (1903). Pp. 67-68. Philadelphia, PA: Presbyterian Board of Publication and Sabbath-School Work. Google Books.

[1014] School And Society. (1931). Page number not apparent. New York, NY: Educational Review. Google Books.

organized Graceland Cemetery Company, and obtained corporate status on February 22, 1861.[1015] Thomas Bryan was the first President of the company.[1016] Jedediah Hyde Lathrop was a member of the Board of Managers with his son, Bryan Lathrop, Thomas Patterson, C. W. Litchfield, and Owen F. Aldis.[1017] John Harris Kinzie and Dr. Alexander Wolcott were both interred at Graceland Cemetery.[1018] Jedediah Hyde Lathrop was a founder of the western Chicago suburb of Elmhurst, and a land developer of Chicago and Cook County. His son, Bryan Lathrop, was also a Chicago business and civic leader, and built the house in Gold Coast neighborhood which now houses the Fortnightly Club.[1019] Lathrop Avenue in River Forest is named for Jedidiah Lathrop, who was a developer in that area.

The Wabash Railroad Company:

A Principal Chicago Railroad System

John Whitfield Bunn was co-founder of the Wabash Railroad Company system.[1020] On May 23, 1889, an article appeared in the *Chicago Daily Tribune* of May 23, 1889, entitled, *WABASH CONSOLIDATION: THE FIRST STEPS TAKEN BY THE PURCHASING COMMITTEE.*[1021] The new Wabash system corporation comprised multiple companies that were incorporated throughout the Midwest and Great Lakes.[1022] Other than Illinois, the relevant places of incorporation of the constituent companies included Ohio, Indiana, and Michigan.[1023] The construction of the new corporation occurred through the aid of a Purchasing Committee the purpose of which was purchase and ownership of prior Wabash system assets.[1024] The Purchasing Committee acted as a preliminary administrative company for the

---

[1015] Andreas, Alfred Theodore. (1884). History of Cook County, Illinois. P. 720. Chicago, IL: A. T. Andreas, Publisher. Google Books.

[1016] Andreas, Alfred Theodore. (1884). History of Cook County, Illinois. P. 720. Chicago, IL: A. T. Andreas, Publisher. Google Books.

[1017] Andreas, Alfred Theodore. (1884). History of Cook County, Illinois. P. 720. Chicago, IL: A. T. Andreas, Publisher. Google Books.

[1018] Andreas, Alfred Theodore. (1884). History of Cook County, Illinois. P. 721. Chicago, IL: A. T. Andreas, Publisher. Google Books; Graceland Cemetery Records for Dr. Alexander Wolcott (1790-1820).

[1019] Richards, Hough, Hyde, Post, Lathrop, Stryker family history records; Fortnightly Club website and history.

[1020] Chicago Daily Tribune. (May 23, 1889). P. 10. ProQuest Newspapers: Chicago Tribune. Database at Northwestern University.

[1021] Chicago Daily Tribune. (May 23, 1889). P. 10. ProQuest Newspapers: Chicago Tribune. Database at Northwestern University.

[1022] Chicago Daily Tribune. (May 23, 1889). P. 10. ProQuest Newspapers: Chicago Tribune. Database at Northwestern University.

[1023] Chicago Daily Tribune. (May 23, 1889). P. 10. ProQuest Newspapers: Chicago Tribune. Database at Northwestern University.

[1024] Chicago Daily Tribune. (May 23, 1889). P. 10. ProQuest Newspapers: Chicago Tribune. Database at Northwestern University.

construction and establishment of the newly consolidated Wabash Railroad Company.[1025] This organizational dynamic closely resembled the case of the Chicago and Alton Railroad Company in 1861, in which a preliminary administrative company acted as an aid to the construction and establishment of a reorganized Chicago and Alton Railroad Company.[1026] Jacob Bunn co-founded the Chicago and Alton Railroad Company and served as a member of the auxiliary company through which the reconstituted Chicago and Alton Railroad Company came to corporate and operational fruition.[1027] In the case of the Wabash Railroad Company, John W. Bunn was co-founder, and also a member of the preliminary administrative company through which the Wabash Railroad Company would enter reconstituted existence.[1028] John and Jacob Bunn both were founders and builders of the companies that led to the consolidated Wabash Railroad Company, such as the Toledo, Peoria & Warsaw Railway Company, and the Toledo, Peoria & Western Railway Company. The Toledo, Peoria & Warsaw owned a locomotive named the "Jacob Bunn," in addition to locomotives named "John V. Ayer" and "Portland."[1029]

The reorganization of the Wabash system took place upon the foundation of a court order that a Judge Gresham entered.[1030] Attached to the court order was a grant of authority to the Purchasing Committee for the purposes of the purchase and the business administration of the newly consolidated Wabash system.[1031] "Judge Gresham has entered an order confirming the recent sale of the Wabash lines and instructing that a transfer of the property be made to the purchasers upon their application."[1032] The court order came with a grant of power to the Purchasing Committee for the purposes of aid, authority, purchase, and administration of assets of the existing contributory companies in order to reconstruct a new

---

[1025] Chicago Daily Tribune. (May 23, 1889). P. 10. ProQuest Newspapers: Chicago Tribune. Database at Northwestern University.

[1026] Chicago Daily Tribune. (May 23, 1889). P. 10. ProQuest Newspapers: Chicago Tribune. Database at Northwestern University; see also: AN ACT to incorporate the Chicago and Alton Railroad Company. Private Laws of the State of Illinois Passed By The Twenty-Second General Assembly, Convened January 7, 1861. (1861). Pp. 489-492. Springfield: Bailhache & Baker, Printers. Google Books.

[1027] AN ACT to incorporate the Chicago and Alton Railroad Company. Private Laws of the State of Illinois Passed By The Twenty-Second General Assembly, Convened January 7, 1861. (1861). Pp. 489-492. Springfield: Bailhache & Baker, Printers. Google Books.

[1028] Chicago Daily Tribune. (May 23, 1889). P. 10. ProQuest Newspapers: Chicago Tribune. Database at Northwestern University.

[1029] Stringham, Paul. (1993). Toledo, Peoria & Western: Tried, Proven & Willing. Peoria, IL: Deller Archive; thanks also to historian Charles Dennewitz of Ohio.

[1030] Chicago Daily Tribune. (May 23, 1889). P. 10. ProQuest Newspapers: Chicago Tribune. Database at Northwestern University.

[1031] Chicago Daily Tribune. (May 23, 1889). P. 10. ProQuest Newspapers: Chicago Tribune. Database at Northwestern University.

[1032] Chicago Daily Tribune. (May 23, 1889). P. 10. ProQuest Newspapers: Chicago Tribune. Database at Northwestern University.

corporation that would exist as a union of the prior companies and assets.[1033] Among the companies constitutive of the new and nascent Wabash Railroad Company was the Wabash Eastern of Illinois, a corporation that had been established on May 13, 1889.[1034] The incorporators of the Wabash Eastern of Illinois included John W. Bunn, General George W. Smith, John M. Harlan, Abram M. Pence, and Charles Henrotin.[1035] The same men collectively constituted the initial Board of Directors of the Wabash Eastern of Illinois.[1036]

The capitalization money of the Wabash Eastern of Illinois was $12,000,000.[1037] The Purchasing Committee held title to the capitalization money, with each director holding title to one share.[1038] The Indiana organizational element of the new consolidated Wabash Railroad Company was incorporated on May 17, 1889.[1039] The Indiana corporation was capitalized with an initial stock money of $9,000,000.[1040] The Purchasing Committee held title to the $9,000,000 stock money of the Indiana organization.[1041] The Toledo Western Railroad Company constituted the Ohio organizational element of the consolidated Wabash Railroad Company and represented an initial capitalization money of $700,000.[1042] The Detroit & State Line Wabash Railroad Company constituted the Michigan organizational element of the consolidated Wabash Railroad Company.[1043] The Chicago Daily Tribune report did not specify the stock money or the debt money associated with the Detroit & State Line Railroad Company.[1044]

[1033] Chicago Daily Tribune. (May 23, 1889). P. 10. ProQuest Newspapers: Chicago Tribune. Database at Northwestern University.

[1034] Chicago Daily Tribune. (May 23, 1889). P. 10. ProQuest Newspapers: Chicago Tribune. Database at Northwestern University.

[1035] Chicago Daily Tribune. (May 23, 1889). P. 10. ProQuest Newspapers: Chicago Tribune. Database at Northwestern University.

[1036] Chicago Daily Tribune. (May 23, 1889). P. 10. ProQuest Newspapers: Chicago Tribune. Database at Northwestern University.

[1037] Chicago Daily Tribune. (May 23, 1889). P. 10. ProQuest Newspapers: Chicago Tribune. Database at Northwestern University.

[1038] Chicago Daily Tribune. (May 23, 1889). P. 10. ProQuest Newspapers: Chicago Tribune. Database at Northwestern University.

[1039] Chicago Daily Tribune. (May 23, 1889). P. 10. ProQuest Newspapers: Chicago Tribune. Database at Northwestern University.

[1040] Chicago Daily Tribune. (May 23, 1889). P. 10. ProQuest Newspapers: Chicago Tribune. Database at Northwestern University.

[1041] Chicago Daily Tribune. (May 23, 1889). P. 10. ProQuest Newspapers: Chicago Tribune. Database at Northwestern University.

[1042] Chicago Daily Tribune. (May 23, 1889). P. 10. ProQuest Newspapers: Chicago Tribune. Database at Northwestern University.

[1043] Chicago Daily Tribune. (May 23, 1889). P. 10. ProQuest Newspapers: Chicago Tribune. Database at Northwestern University.

[1044] Chicago Daily Tribune. (May 23, 1889). P. 10. ProQuest Newspapers: Chicago Tribune. Database at Northwestern University.

The article indicated the jurisprudential elements of the consolidation process relevant to the new 1889 Wabash Railroad Company.[1045] Subsequent to the incorporation of the constituent railroad companies in Illinois, Ohio, Michigan, and Indiana, the Purchasing Committee would transfer its organizational property in the railroad assets within each of these states to the individual constituent Wabash Railroad Company constituent companies.[1046] After the respective transfers of property in the railroad assets to the companies located in Illinois, Ohio, Michigan, and Indiana, the companies all would be joined in a corporate union under the name of Wabash Railroad Company.[1047] The consolidated Wabash Railroad Company represented a union of organizations, properties, and moneys.[1048] Additionally included among the constituent companies within the new Wabash Railroad Company system was the Wabash Western, which had already acquired the relevant property and assets west of the Mississippi River.[1049] The new Wabash Railroad Company, therefore, contained a route portfolio that included Ohio, Michigan, Indiana, Illinois, and Trans-Mississippi western regions, as well. Of significant note is that Jacob Bunn was an original supporter of the Northern Cross Railroad Company, which was the oldest element of the Wabash Railroad Company system. John Whitfield Bunn was a founder and member of the board of directors of the Toledo, Peoria and Warsaw Railroad Company, which also was one of the element companies of the Wabash Railroad Company. Both of the Bunn brothers were, consequently, founders and builders of the Wabash Railroad Company system from its earliest origins to its greatest extent.[1050]

The statutory law of Illinois supplied additional obligatory process that required a form of due process to be served to the stockholders of the constituent railroad companies of the new Wabash Railroad Company. The Illinois law provided the following elements of due process relevant to the corporate consolidation process and performance: a conference must take place at which stockholders either deliver approval or objection to the proposed plan of corporate consolidation; notice must be given for a time of sixty days prior to the occurrence of the stockholders'

[1045] Chicago Daily Tribune. (May 23, 1889). P. 10. ProQuest Newspapers: Chicago Tribune. Database at Northwestern University.

[1046] Chicago Daily Tribune. (May 23, 1889). P. 10. ProQuest Newspapers: Chicago Tribune. Database at Northwestern University.

[1047] Chicago Daily Tribune. (May 23, 1889). P. 10. ProQuest Newspapers: Chicago Tribune. Database at Northwestern University.

[1048] Chicago Daily Tribune. (May 23, 1889). P. 10. ProQuest Newspapers: Chicago Tribune. Database at Northwestern University.

[1049] Chicago Daily Tribune. (May 23, 1889). P. 10. ProQuest Newspapers: Chicago Tribune. Database at Northwestern University.

[1050] Bunn family history records.

conference.[1051] The concepts that were integral to the consolidation plan and process included due process, conference, time, notice, approval, and objection.[1052]

As of May 23, 1889, the date of publication of the *Chicago Daily Tribune* article reporting the Wabash consolidation plan, the Illinois stockholders had already received the due process of the sixty days' notice, but the stockholders of the remaining constituent railroad companies had not yet received their sixty days' notice.[1053] The article indicated that the Illinois stockholders intended to hold a conference on the consolidation on July 27, 1889, and would deliver approval of the consolidation plan at that time and conference.[1054] General George W. Smith administered the jurisprudential aspects of the consolidation, and General McNulta apparently, from the context of the article report, administered the Illinois assets to be consolidated into the new Wabash Railroad Company.[1055]

The article stated that the plan for executive leadership and staffing of the consolidated Wabash Railroad Company remained largely indefinite, but that O. D. Ashley would probably serve as President of the corporation and Charles Henrotin would probably serve as Treasurer of the corporation.[1056] The multilateral agreement among the constituent Wabash Railroad Company sysyem companies called for a board of directors that would consist of nine persons.[1057] Jay Gould participated as a principal party to the consolidation of the Wabash System.[1058] The consolidation agreement identified the nine persons who would serve as the initial Board of Directors of the consolidated Wabash Railroad Company.[1059] The board of directors included the following persons.

1. James F. Joy
    a. James Joy was a business partner of John Stryker. Joy and Stryker co-founded the Michigan Southern Railroad Company, which was the first railroad company system to connect Chicago to the East

[1051] Chicago Daily Tribune. (May 23, 1889). P. 10. ProQuest Newspapers: Chicago Tribune. Database at Northwestern University.

[1052] Chicago Daily Tribune. (May 23, 1889). P. 10. ProQuest Newspapers: Chicago Tribune. Database at Northwestern University.

[1053] Chicago Daily Tribune. (May 23, 1889). P. 10. ProQuest Newspapers: Chicago Tribune. Database at Northwestern University.

[1054] Chicago Daily Tribune. (May 23, 1889). P. 10. ProQuest Newspapers: Chicago Tribune. Database at Northwestern University.

[1055] Chicago Daily Tribune. (May 23, 1889). P. 10. ProQuest Newspapers: Chicago Tribune. Database at Northwestern University.

[1056] Chicago Daily Tribune. (May 23, 1889). P. 10. ProQuest Newspapers: Chicago Tribune. Database at Northwestern University.

[1057] Chicago Daily Tribune. (May 23, 1889). P. 10. ProQuest Newspapers: Chicago Tribune. Database at Northwestern University.

[1058] Chicago Daily Tribune. (May 23, 1889). P. 10. ProQuest Newspapers: Chicago Tribune. Database at Northwestern University.

[1059] Chicago Daily Tribune. (May 23, 1889). P. 10. ProQuest Newspapers: Chicago Tribune. Database at Northwestern University.

Coast. Joy and Stryker founded multiple other railroad companies of Chicago, Detroit, and Cleveland, as well.

2. O. D. Ashley
3. Thomas H. Hubbard
4. Edgar T. Welles
5. General George W. Smith
6. John Whitfield Bunn
7. John Harlan
8. Abram M. Pence
9. Charles Henrotin
    a. Charles Henrotin founded the Chicago Stock Exchange.[1060]

The capital structure of the consolidated Wabash Railroad Company contained multiple financial elements. First, we will address the equity element of the capital structure. The article indicated that the organization plan contemplated a bifurcated system of equity financing.[1061] The consolidated Wabash Railroad Company possessed an initial capitalization amount of $52,000,000. The capital amount comprised two classes of equity moneys: common stock and preferred stock.[1062] The preferred stock amount was to be $24,000,000 and the common stock amount was to be $28,000,000.[1063] The agreement attached yield (dividend) priority to the rights that accompanied the preferred stock money, with a rate of seven percent.[1064] After the satisfaction of the yield revenue rights of the preferred stockholders the company would distribute yield revenue to the common stockholders in satisfaction of the equity rights that attached to that class of stockholder.[1065]

Let us now address the debt money element of the capital structure. The organization plan contemplated a trifurcated debt financing system in which $35,000,000 would be issued in the asset class of first mortgage bonds.[1066] The plan further provided for the issuance of $14,000,000 in the asset class of second mortgage bonds.[1067] Finally, the plan called for the issuance of $30,000,000 in the

---

[1060] Chicago Daily Tribune. (May 23, 1889). P. 10. ProQuest Newspapers: Chicago Tribune. Database at Northwestern University.

[1061] Chicago Daily Tribune. (May 23, 1889). P. 10. ProQuest Newspapers: Chicago Tribune. Database at Northwestern University.

[1062] Chicago Daily Tribune. (May 23, 1889). P. 10. ProQuest Newspapers: Chicago Tribune. Database at Northwestern University.

[1063] Chicago Daily Tribune. (May 23, 1889). P. 10. ProQuest Newspapers: Chicago Tribune. Database at Northwestern University.

[1064] Chicago Daily Tribune. (May 23, 1889). P. 10. ProQuest Newspapers: Chicago Tribune. Database at Northwestern University.

[1065] Chicago Daily Tribune. (May 23, 1889). P. 10. ProQuest Newspapers: Chicago Tribune. Database at Northwestern University.

[1066] Chicago Daily Tribune. (May 23, 1889). P. 10. ProQuest Newspapers: Chicago Tribune. Database at Northwestern University.

[1067] Chicago Daily Tribune. (May 23, 1889). P. 10. ProQuest Newspapers: Chicago Tribune. Database at Northwestern University.

asset class of debenture bonds.[1068] The plan attached a limit to the right of foreclosure on the second mortgage bonds.[1069] The plan called for the limit on the foreclosure rights of the second mortgage bondholder creditors to apply until the occurrence of corporate payment default, for a time of six months, on two of the second mortgage bond debt coupons.[1070] The limit would attach to the powers of the second mortgage bondholders through means of a waiver of the rights of foreclosure that would normally attach to these debt moneys.[1071]

The stipulated default occurrence would constitute simultaneous grounds for three consequent and distinct jurisprudential occurrences: the quashal of the limit on the bondholders' foreclosure rights; the quashal of the bondholders' waiver of the second mortgage bondholder foreclosure rights; and the attachment of the relevant foreclosure rights to the second mortgage debt bondholders.[1072] The plan contemplated the capital revenue operation of the debenture bond instruments to entail the yield of revenue in the amount of six percent, based on the precedent condition that earnings would be adequate to enable the payment of yield revenue in this amount.[1073] By attaching voting rights to the statuses of the debenture bondholders, the Wabash Railroad Company debt financing plan did not distinguish markedly between the debenture bond class of ownership and the preferred stock class of ownership. In reality, the plan created a strong similarity between the equity financing class on the one hand, and the debt financing class on the other hand.[1074] The Chicago journalist reported, "[t]he debentures have voting power and are practically nothing more than a preferred stock."[1075] The entire capital fund of the consolidated Wabash Railroad Company and system encompassed $131,000,000 in the year 1889.[1076]

The article entitled, *Wabash Eastern Incorporated*, which also appeared on page 10 of the May 23, 1889, edition of the *Chicago Daily Tribune* reported the facts

---

[1068] Chicago Daily Tribune. (May 23, 1889). P. 10. ProQuest Newspapers: Chicago Tribune. Database at Northwestern University.

[1069] Chicago Daily Tribune. (May 23, 1889). P. 10. ProQuest Newspapers: Chicago Tribune. Database at Northwestern University.

[1070] Chicago Daily Tribune. (May 23, 1889). P. 10. ProQuest Newspapers: Chicago Tribune. Database at Northwestern University.

[1071] Chicago Daily Tribune. (May 23, 1889). P. 10. ProQuest Newspapers: Chicago Tribune. Database at Northwestern University.

[1072] Chicago Daily Tribune. (May 23, 1889). P. 10. ProQuest Newspapers: Chicago Tribune. Database at Northwestern University.

[1073] Chicago Daily Tribune. (May 23, 1889). P. 10. ProQuest Newspapers: Chicago Tribune. Database at Northwestern University.

[1074] Chicago Daily Tribune. (May 23, 1889). P. 10. ProQuest Newspapers: Chicago Tribune. Database at Northwestern University.

[1075] Chicago Daily Tribune. (May 23, 1889). P. 10. ProQuest Newspapers: Chicago Tribune. Database at Northwestern University.

[1076] Chicago Daily Tribune. (May 23, 1889). P. 10. ProQuest Newspapers: Chicago Tribune. Database at Northwestern University.

concerning the recent incorporation of the Wabash Eastern Railway Company.[1077] The articles of incorporation were filed at Decatur, in Macon County, Illinois.[1078] The headquarters of the corporation was at Chicago.[1079] The incorporators included John W. Bunn, John M. Harlan, Abram M. Pence, George W. Smith, and Charles Henrotin.[1080] As stated in the prior article on the same page of the *Chicago Daily Tribune*, the initial corporate capitalization money for the Wabash Eastern Railway Company stood at $12,000,000.[1081] The article specified only equity financing as the means of capitalization, contained no reference to any form of debt financing, and indicated that the equity shares possessed the price of $1,000 each.[1082]

In January of 1890, John W. Bunn acted as co-founder of the North & South Railroad Company of Illinois.[1083] The purpose of the corporation was to extend the route of the St. Louis and Illinois Central Railroad Company, formerly known as the St. Louis and Chicago Railroad Company.[1084] The corporate capitalization money for the company was $800,000, but the report stated no further facts regarding the financing of the company.[1085] The company connected to Chicago, although apparently only indirectly.[1086] The incorporators included the following persons, with residences of these persons indicated as follows:

1. John Whitfield Bunn
   a. Springfield, Illinois
2. C. H. Basworth
   a. Springfield, Illinois
3. J. M. Stark
   a. Pawnee, Illinois
4. David T. Withers
   a. New York

[1077] Chicago Daily Tribune. (May 23, 1889). P. 10. ProQuest Newspapers: Chicago Tribune. Database at Northwestern University.

[1078] Chicago Daily Tribune. (May 23, 1889). P. 10. ProQuest Newspapers: Chicago Tribune. Database at Northwestern University.

[1079] Chicago Daily Tribune. (May 23, 1889). P. 10. ProQuest Newspapers: Chicago Tribune. Database at Northwestern University.

[1080] Chicago Daily Tribune. (May 23, 1889). P. 10. ProQuest Newspapers: Chicago Tribune. Database at Northwestern University.

[1081] Chicago Daily Tribune. (May 23, 1889). P. 10. ProQuest Newspapers: Chicago Tribune. Database at Northwestern University.

[1082] Chicago Daily Tribune. (May 23, 1889). P. 10. ProQuest Newspapers: Chicago Tribune. Database at Northwestern University.

[1083] Chicago Daily Tribune. (January 24, 1890). P. 18. ProQuest Newspapers: Chicago Tribune. Database at Northwestern University.

[1084] Chicago Daily Tribune. (January 24, 1890). P. 18. ProQuest Newspapers: Chicago Tribune. Database at Northwestern University.

[1085] Chicago Daily Tribune. (January 24, 1890). P. 18. ProQuest Newspapers: Chicago Tribune. Database at Northwestern University.

[1086] Chicago Daily Tribune. (January 24, 1890). P. 18. ProQuest Newspapers: Chicago Tribune. Database at Northwestern University.

5. Gerald L. Hoyt
   a. New York[1087]

The space limits of this book prevent any further discussion of these railroad companies, but John W. Bunn and the other men named above developed much of the Chicago railroad industry, helped develop the Calumet Corridor of Chicago, Cook County, and Northern Indiana, and helped develop principal railroad connections between Chicago and Pittsburgh, Pennsylvania.

John Whitfield Bunn and South Chicago Real Estate

John W. Bunn owned real estate in Chicago, as was evidenced by the 1916 report of a real estate sale and transfer of land located in the Calumet River district of Chicago.[1088] The article entitled, *Calumet District Sale*, which appeared in the January 30, 1916, edition of the *Chicago Daily Tribune*, indicated that the sale was a "noteworthy transaction."[1089] The purchaser of the land was the By-Products Coke corporation of New York.[1090] The sellers were John W. Bunn, Adeline Lemark, and Ethel L. Farmer, who apparently held the real estate as tenants in common.[1091] The contract for the sale of land encompassed the sale of a tract of thirteen acres that was located at One Hundred and Eighth Street and the Calumet River.[1092] The real estate contained approximately seven hundred feet of frontage space on the Calumet River.[1093] The real estate brokerage firm of Mead & Coe handled the sale of the land and the purchase price paid in consideration for the land was reported at $70,000.[1094] The corporate buyer owned a factory near the place of the land sold and apparently planned for additional expansion at the site.[1095]

John Stryker also helped develop the Calumet River region of Chicago and Northern Indiana. In addition to having been founder of the Michigan Southern

---

[1087] Chicago Daily Tribune. (January 24, 1890). P. 18. ProQuest Newspapers: Chicago Tribune. Database at Northwestern University.

[1088] Chicago Daily Tribune. (January 30, 1916). P. 18. ProQuest Newspapers: Chicago Tribune. Database at Northwestern University.

[1089] Chicago Daily Tribune. (January 30, 1916). P. 18. ProQuest Newspapers: Chicago Tribune. Database at Northwestern University.

[1090] Chicago Daily Tribune. (January 30, 1916). P. 18. ProQuest Newspapers: Chicago Tribune. Database at Northwestern University.

[1091] Chicago Daily Tribune. (January 30, 1916). P. 18. ProQuest Newspapers: Chicago Tribune. Database at Northwestern University.

[1092] Chicago Daily Tribune. (January 30, 1916). P. 18. ProQuest Newspapers: Chicago Tribune. Database at Northwestern University.

[1093] Chicago Daily Tribune. (January 30, 1916). P. 18. ProQuest Newspapers: Chicago Tribune. Database at Northwestern University.

[1094] Chicago Daily Tribune. (January 30, 1916). P. 18. Retrieved from ProQuest Newspapers: Chicago Tribune. Database at Northwestern University.

[1095] Chicago Daily Tribune. (January 30, 1916). P. 18. ProQuest Newspapers: Chicago Tribune. Database at Northwestern University.

Railroad Company, the Northern Indiana and Chicago Railroad Company, the Lake Shore and Northern Indiana Railroad Company, the Lake Shore and Michigan Southern Railroad Company, the Detroit, Monroe and Toledo Railroad Company, the Chicago and Rock Island Railroad Company, and the St. Charles and Mississippi Airline Railroad Company, all of which were Chicago companies, John Stryker was a founder of the New York Central Railroad Company, which was also one of the most important companies of Chicago and New York City.[1096] The 1981 issue of the *National Railway Bulletin*, the publication of The National Railway Historical Society, discussed the prime significance of John Stryker to the inception of the New York Central Railroad Company. The author stated, "John Stryker was also a key to the merging of the many separate railroads in New York into one New York Central Railroad."[1097] John Stryker and John Whitfield Bunn both were founders of the Calumet River industrial district and Calumet Corridor.

Memories of the Bessemer Road

The present section of this chapter concerns the Chicago history of both the Richardson branch and the Bunn branch of my mother's family. One of the most important manufacturing companies to exist in Springfield and Chicago was a corporation that was formed and originally rooted in Springfield: the Springfield Iron Company.[1098] This corporation individually achieved scientific and technological supremacies that affected global markets, intellectual property, and chemical and metal technologies.[1099] Moreover, the Springfield Iron Company, jointly with multiple other companies both larger and smaller than it, co-founded the following compound companies: the $100 million Bessemer Steel Trust; the $55 million Republic Iron and Steel Company; and the large Springfield Coal Trust.[1100] Springfield Iron Company was both a Springfield corporation and a Chicago corporation at the time of its contributions to the establishment of all three of these corporate trusts.[1101] The company, therefore, was prolific both in the

---

[1096] Stryker family history records.

[1097] National Railway Bulletin. (1981). Vols. 46-47. Pp. 26, et. Seq. National Railway Historical Society. Google Books.

[1098] Call, Andrew Taylor. (2005). Jacob Bunn: Legacy of an Illinois Industrial Pioneer. Pp. 110-112. Lawrenceville, VA: Brunswick Publishing Corporation. Retrieved from Google Books. See: Articles of Incorporation for the Springfield Iron Company, August 18, 1871.

[1099] Chicago Tribune. (June 4, 1891). P. 3. Newspapers.com.

[1100] New York Tribune. (April 4, 1896). P. 1. Newspapers.com; The Saint Paul Globe. (January 16, 1898). P. 1. Newspapers.com; A History of the City of Chicago: Its Men and Institutions. (1900). P. 242. Chicago, IL: The Inter Ocean. Google Books.

[1101] New York Tribune. (April 4, 1896). P. 1. Newspapers.com; The Saint Paul Globe. (January 16, 1898). P. 1. Newspapers.com; A History of the City of Chicago: Its Men and Institutions. (1900). P. 242. Chicago, IL: The Inter Ocean. Google Books; Andreas, Alfred Theodore. (1886). History of Chicago. Vol. 3. P. 478. Chicago, Illinois: The A. T. Andreas Company, Publishers. Google Books.

manufacture of iron products and technologies, and in the promotion and development of commercially and technologically related industrial trusts.[1102] The Springfield Iron Company not only developed an immense economic presence at Chicago, but also contributed to the Cook County economy through participation in the formation and leadership of the Bessemer Steel Trust and the Republic Iron and Steel Company, both of which possessed partial political and economic heritage in Chicago.[1103] For the more exhaustive histories of the Richardsons, consult Chapter 5, *The Foundations of Jackson Park*.

Springfield Iron Company of Springfield and Chicago

The summer of the year 1871 witnessed the incorporation of the Springfield Iron Company, at Springfield, Sangamon County, Illinois. The State of Illinois granted incorporation to the Springfield Iron Company on August 18, 1871.[1104] The incorporators were the following persons:

1. Charles Ridgely
2. John Whitfield Bunn
3. George M. Brinkerhoff
4. William Douglas Richardson
5. La Fayette Smith
6. Charles E. Hay
7. John Williams
8. Alexander Starne
9. H. B. Hayes
10. Orlin H. Miner
11. George Pasfield[1105]

Pursuant to the relevant Illinois company enablement Act of February 18, 1857, a statute whose grant of authority encompassed the creation and incorporation of chemical companies, manufacturing companies, mining companies, and

---

[1102] New York Tribune. (April 4, 1896). P. 1. Newspapers.com; The Saint Paul Globe. (January 16, 1898). P. 1. Newspapers.com; A History of the City of Chicago: Its Men and Institutions. (1900). P. 242. Chicago, IL: The Inter Ocean. Google Books; Andreas, Alfred Theodore. (1886). History of Chicago. Vol. 3. P. 478. Chicago, Illinois: The A. T. Andreas Company, Publishers. Google Books.

[1103] New York Tribune. (April 4, 1896). P. 1. Newspapers.com; The Saint Paul Globe. (January 16, 1898). P. 1. Newspapers.com; A History of the City of Chicago: Its Men and Institutions. (1900). P. 242. Chicago, IL: The Inter Ocean. Google Books.

[1104] Call, Andrew Taylor. (2005). Jacob Bunn: Legacy of an Illinois Industrial Pioneer. Pp. 110-112. Lawrenceville, VA: Brunswick Publishing Corporation. Retrieved from Google Books. See: Articles of Incorporation for the Springfield Iron Company, August 18, 1871.

[1105] Call, Andrew Taylor. (2005). Jacob Bunn: Legacy of an Illinois Industrial Pioneer. P. 112. Lawrenceville, VA: Brunswick Publishing Corporation. Retrieved from Google Books. See: Articles of Incorporation for the Springfield Iron Company, August 18, 1871.

mechanical companies, the Secretary of State of Illinois granted approval and issuance of the Articles of Incorporation of the Springfield Iron Company.[1106]

Allow us now to analyze the jurisprudential architecture of the organic statute. Section One of the Articles of Incorporation established the name of the company, stating that the name of the new corporation would be, "The Springfield Iron Company."[1107] The second clause of the Articles of Incorporation established, and attached the following business purposes to the corporation: mining of coal, mining of iron, manufacturing of iron, and manufacturing of steel.[1108] The third clause of the Articles was the financing clause, and established an original equity money of $300,000.[1109] The fourth clause established a time in which the company was to exist, and that specific company lifetime was fifty years.[1110] The Articles established, through the fifth clause, the division of the capital stock of $300,000 into three thousand shares of one-hundred dollars each.[1111] The sixth clause attached a limit to the number of persons who could serve on the board of directors of the corporation, restricting the directorial staff to five persons.[1112] The sixth clause also identified by name the five persons to serve on the original board of directors of the corporation, who were identified as follows:

1. Charles Ridgely
2. George M. Brinkerhoff
3. Orlin H. Miner
4. William Douglas Richardson

[1106] Call, Andrew Taylor. (2005). Jacob Bunn: Legacy of an Illinois Industrial Pioneer. Pp. 111. Lawrenceville, VA: Brunswick Publishing Corporation. Retrieved from Google Books. See: Articles of Incorporation for the Springfield Iron Company, August 18, 1871.

[1107] Call, Andrew Taylor. (2005). Jacob Bunn: Legacy of an Illinois Industrial Pioneer. P. 111. Lawrenceville, VA: Brunswick Publishing Corporation. Retrieved from Google Books.

[1108] Call, Andrew Taylor. (2005). Jacob Bunn: Legacy of an Illinois Industrial Pioneer. P. 111. Lawrenceville, VA: Brunswick Publishing Corporation. Retrieved from Google Books.

[1109] Call, Andrew Taylor. (2005). Jacob Bunn: Legacy of an Illinois Industrial Pioneer. P. 111. Lawrenceville, VA: Brunswick Publishing Corporation. Retrieved from Google Books.

[1110] Call, Andrew Taylor. (2005). Jacob Bunn: Legacy of an Illinois Industrial Pioneer. P. 111. Lawrenceville, VA: Brunswick Publishing Corporation. Retrieved from Google Books.

[1111] Call, Andrew Taylor. (2005). Jacob Bunn: Legacy of an Illinois Industrial Pioneer. P. 111. Lawrenceville, VA: Brunswick Publishing Corporation. Retrieved from Google Books.

[1112] Call, Andrew Taylor. (2005). Jacob Bunn: Legacy of an Illinois Industrial Pioneer. P. 111. Lawrenceville, VA: Brunswick Publishing Corporation. Retrieved from Google Books.

5. John Whitfield Bunn[1113]

The seventh clause of the Articles of Incorporation established the place of business and operation of the Springfield Iron Company at Springfield, Sangamon County, Illinois.[1114] The final clause, which was not identified by number, constituted the testimonium clause, and contained the testimony, evidence, and proof of the fact that the named company incorporators had genuinely and knowingly acted as parties to the process of incorporation of the Springfield Iron Company. The final clause thus confirmed the genuineness of the relevant incorporative will of the named persons.[1115]

The Springfield Iron Company developed a prominent position among the commercial organizations of Chicago when, in 1881, the company established an agency office there.[1116] The original manager of the Chicago office of the Springfield Iron Company was W. E. Mack. Mack retired in 1882, one year after establishment of the office.[1117] C. I. Wickersham succeeded W. E. Mack as Manager of the Chicago office. C. I. Wickersham occupied this position until 1884.[1118] B. L. Keen succeeded Wickersham as Manager of the Chicago office in 1884. Under the administrations of Mack, Wickersham, and Keen in Cook County, the Springfield Iron Company possessed a strategically ideal place among the railroad components manufacturers of the United States. This was so because of the location of Springfield Iron Company at Chicago, which was the center of the nation's railroad industry markets.[1119] B. L. Keen was a native of Philadelphia, and had been employed by the Springfield Iron Company at the Springfield factory for one year, according to Alfred Theodore Andreas.[1120] Keen, through his work at Springfield Iron, helped connect Chicago and Springfield, as did Jacob Bunn, John Whitfield Bunn, William Douglas Richardson, and others through Springfield Iron

[1113] Call, Andrew Taylor. (2005). Jacob Bunn: Legacy of an Illinois Industrial Pioneer. P. 111. Lawrenceville, VA: Brunswick Publishing Corporation. Retrieved from Google Books.

[1114] Call, Andrew Taylor. (2005). Jacob Bunn: Legacy of an Illinois Industrial Pioneer. P. 111. Lawrenceville, VA: Brunswick Publishing Corporation. Retrieved from Google Books.

[1115] Call, Andrew Taylor. (2005). Jacob Bunn: Legacy of an Illinois Industrial Pioneer. Pp. 111-112. Lawrenceville, VA: Brunswick Publishing Corporation. Retrieved from Google Books.

[1116] Andreas, Alfred Theodore. (1886). History of Chicago. Vol. 3. P. 478. Chicago, Illinois: The A. T. Andreas Company, Publishers. Google Books.

[1117] Andreas, Alfred Theodore. (1886). History of Chicago. Vol. 3. P. 478. Chicago, Illinois: The A. T. Andreas Company, Publishers. Google Books.

[1118] Andreas, Alfred Theodore. (1886). History of Chicago. Vol. 3. P. 478. Chicago, Illinois: The A. T. Andreas Company, Publishers. Google Books.

[1119] Andreas, Alfred Theodore. (1886). History of Chicago. Vol. 3. P. 478. Chicago, Illinois: The A. T. Andreas Company, Publishers. Google Books.

[1120] Andreas, Alfred Theodore. (1886). History of Chicago. Vol. 3. P. 478. Chicago, Illinois: The A. T. Andreas Company, Publishers. Google Books.

and other companies.[1121] Springfield Iron Company was the largest maker of railroad angle-splice bars in the United States at one time, and supplied much of the American market for these railroad construction materials.[1122]

Dr. Alphonse Hennin and the Novel Ammonia Process

Not least among the technological innovations of the Springfield Iron Company was a chemical discovery made by the Belgian-American chemist, Dr. Alphonse Hennin, who served as the chief chemist of the company.[1123] The *Chicago Tribune* of June 4, 1891, reported that Dr. Hennin discovered and derived a new chemical process from the regular industrial operations of the company.[1124] Dr. Hennin discovered processes and practices that could efficiently produce ammonia and tar through the use of coal.[1125] Hennin had spent more than two years using tests and trials to produce an improvement in, "the manufacture of fuel gas for metallurgical and other purposes. . ."[1126] The Hennin process involved the production of a fuel gas of which sixty percent was combustible matter.[1127] The means central and efficacious to the process included the following elements:

> "The apparatus consists of cylindrical producers, ten feet in diameter and fifteen feet high, made of wrought iron and lined with fire brick. The fuel is fed into a hopper at the top of the producer and the bed of fire is supported on a grate near the bottom. The combustion which generates the heat for distillation is maintained by blasts of steam and air which are introduced radially through tuyeres just above the grate. The novelty of the invention consists in so regulating the relative proportions of steam and air as to maintain in this lower portion of the producer an incandescent zone, or bed of fuel, at a sufficient temperature to decompose practically all of the steam admitted and at the same time so regulating the supply of fresh fuel that the upper portion of the producer is kept at a temperature sufficiently low to allow the formation of ammonia, and prevent its decomposition."[1128]

[1121] Andreas, Alfred Theodore. (1886). History of Chicago. Vol. 3. P. 478. Chicago, Illinois: The A. T. Andreas Company, Publishers. Google Books; see: Call, Andrew Taylor. (2005). Jacob Bunn: Legacy of an Illinois Industrial Pioneer. P. 111. Lawrenceville, VA: Brunswick Publishing Corporation. Retrieved from Google Books.
[1122] Jacob Bunn: Legacy of an Illinois Industrial Pioneer. Pp. 111-112. Lawrenceville, VA: Brunswick Publishing Corporation. Retrieved from Google Books.
[1123] Chicago Tribune. (June 4, 1891). P. 3. Newspapers.com.
[1124] Chicago Tribune. (June 4, 1891). P. 3. Newspapers.com.
[1125] Chicago Tribune. (June 4, 1891). P. 3. Newspapers.com.
[1126] Chicago Tribune. (June 4, 1891). P. 3. Newspapers.com.
[1127] Chicago Tribune. (June 4, 1891). P. 3. Newspapers.com.
[1128] Chicago Tribune. (June 4, 1891). P. 3. Newspapers.com.

The article that appeared in the *Chicago Tribune* indicated that the Hennin Method possessed a degree of novelty adequate to deserve the grant of a United States patent.[1129] The novel Hennin process motivated pleadings for grants of patents in every major country of Europe, additionally.[1130] The technological novelty and creativity of the Springfield Iron Company were rewarded, therefore, not only by the official attachment of the rights and benefits of intellectual property, but also by the promotion of the name and culture of the Springfield Iron Company overseas.[1131] The company had possessed a presence in Chicago for approximately ten years at the time when Dr. Hennin discovered the novel chemical and fuel processes.[1132] Chicago and Springfield had again contributed to the development of global technology and science, this time through the effort and ingenuity of Dr. Alphonse Hennin.[1133] The company implemented the technology for the Hennin Method when it constructed the machinery necessary for performance of the integral processes. Using the Hennin Method, the company was, as of 1891, able to produce a quantitative range of 5,000,000 to 6,000,000 cubic feet of gas per day, through consumption of forty to fifty tons of coal per day.[1134] The Hennin Method was praised by Secretary Knapp of the Chicago Gas Company as a specialized and efficient scientific improvement. Knapp believed the Hennin Method would produce particularly significant value for iron and glass factories.[1135]

Granville Taylor Woods of Ohio

Granville Taylor Woods was an African-American inventor, electrician, and industrial entrepreneur. He was born in Columbus, Ohio, on April 23, 1856.[1136] He attended school until the age of ten years, and continued education at the workshop and through night coursework.[1137] Woods worked for the Springfield Iron Company in 1874.[1138] He received two years of mechanical and electrical engineering instruction in college and participated in an apprenticeship at a

---

[1129] Chicago Tribune. (June 4, 1891). P. 3. Newspapers.com.
[1130] Chicago Tribune. (June 4, 1891). P. 3. Newspapers.com.
[1131] Chicago Tribune. (June 4, 1891). P. 3. Newspapers.com.
[1132] Chicago Tribune. (June 4, 1891). P. 3. Newspapers.com.
[1133] Chicago Tribune. (June 4, 1891). P. 3. Newspapers.com.
[1134] Chicago Tribune. (June 4, 1891). P. 3. Newspapers.com.
[1135] Chicago Tribune. (June 4, 1891). P. 3. Newspapers.com.
[1136] Simmons, William J., Turner, Henry McNeal. (1887). Men of Mark: Eminent, Progressive and Rising. P. 107. Cleveland, OH: George M. Rewell & Co. Google Books.
[1137] Simmons, William J., Turner, Henry McNeal. (1887). Men of Mark: Eminent, Progressive and Rising. P. 107. Cleveland, OH: George M. Rewell & Co. Google Books.
[1138] Simmons, William J., Turner, Henry McNeal. (1887). Men of Mark: Eminent, Progressive and Rising. P. 107. Cleveland, OH: George M. Rewell & Co. Google Books.

machine shop.[1139] He was said to have visited nearly every country of the world as a sailor aboard the British steamer ship *Ironsides*, on which he worked as an engineer.[1140] After returning to Ohio, Woods established an engineering company at Cincinnati, and became a world-renowned inventor of electrical technologies.[1141] Woods' inventions included the "Synchronous Multiplex Railway Telegraph."[1142] *The American Catholic Tribune*, a Cincinnati newspaper, referred to Woods as "the greatest electrician in the world," in its April 1, 1887, edition.[1143] Woods invented railroad signaling and communication systems whose purposes were the transfer of train traffic information and the prevention of railroad accidents.[1144] Rev. William J. Simmons stated that:

> "Mr. Woods claims that his invention is for the purpose of averting accidents by keeping each train informed of the whereabouts of the one immediately ahead or following it; in communicating with stations from moving trains; and in promoting general, social and commercial intercourse."[1145]

Jacob Bunn, John Whitfield Bunn, and William Douglas Richardson were founders, executive officers, and owners of the Springfield Iron Company. These men and the other others who controlled and administered the company hired Granville Taylor Woods when he was a young man, and this was a socially progressive act on the part of the company leadership. The Bunn brothers and William D. Richardson were all founders and owners of railroad companies of all sizes and were among the chief manufacturers of railroad parts in North America. Woods encountered at Springfield Iron Company an environment conducive to innovations in railroad technologies, and the experience, though constitutive of

---

[1139] Simmons, William J., Turner, Henry McNeal. (1887). Men of Mark: Eminent, Progressive and Rising. Pp. 107-108. Cleveland, OH: George M. Rewell & Co. Google Books.
[1140] Simmons, William J., Turner, Henry McNeal. (1887). Men of Mark: Eminent, Progressive and Rising. P. 108. Cleveland, OH: George M. Rewell & Co. Google Books.
[1141] Simmons, William J., Turner, Henry McNeal. (1887). Men of Mark: Eminent, Progressive and Rising. Pp. 108, et seq. Cleveland, OH: George M. Rewell & Co. Google Books.
[1142] Simmons, William J., Turner, Henry McNeal. (1887). Men of Mark: Eminent, Progressive and Rising. Pp. 111, et seq. Cleveland, OH: George M. Rewell & Co. Google Books.
[1143] Simmons, William J., Turner, Henry McNeal. (1887). Men of Mark: Eminent, Progressive and Rising. Pp. 111, et seq. Cleveland, OH: George M. Rewell & Co. Google Books.
[1144] Simmons, William J., Turner, Henry McNeal. (1887). Men of Mark: Eminent, Progressive and Rising. P. 110. Cleveland, OH: George M. Rewell & Co. Google Books.
[1145] Simmons, William J., Turner, Henry McNeal. (1887). Men of Mark: Eminent, Progressive and Rising. P. 110. Cleveland, OH: George M. Rewell & Co. Google Books.

only a comparatively brief time in his career, must have contributed partly to his lifetime devotion to railroad invention and technological revolution for the industry. Granville T. Woods was indisputably the most famous, and one of the most significant, people to have ever been associated with the Springfield Iron Company of Springfield and Chicago.[1146]

Joining the Trusts

The Springfield Iron Company cooperated with numerous other companies to establish the Springfield Coal Trust.[1147] Multiple newspapers reported the facts relevant to this new trust. *The Saint Paul Globe*, a newspaper of Saint Paul, Minnesota, provided detailed facts regarding the Trust in January of 1898.[1148] The Springfield Coal Trust was, like all corporate trusts, a company made of companies.[1149] The companies that collaborated to establish the Trust included the Springfield Iron Company, the Black Diamond Coal & Tile Company, the Citizens' Coal Mining Company, Springfield Coal Mining & Tile Company, Springfield Co-operative Coal Mining Company, Capital Coal Company, Woodside Coal Company, Sangamon Coal Company, Junction Mining Company, and the Westend Coal Mining Company.[1150] The Springfield Coal Trust also was known as the Springfield Coal Association.[1151]

One of the first acts of the Springfield Coal Trust was the increase of coal prices by 50 cents per ton.[1152] The price increase drew the attention of Sangamon County and the State of Illinois.[1153] The Springfield Coal Trust members stated that the reason why they raised the price of coal was that the member companies had recently advanced the wages of the company employees by the rate of seven and a half cents per ton.[1154] *The Saint Paul Globe* indicated that the coal trust drew the investigatory attention of Sangamon County.[1155] Apparently some legal processes had occurred prior to the facts that were provided in the Saint Paul news report.[1156] Inference of this fact is possible because the report stated that the grand jury had indicted the coal trust and its member coal companies of Springfield.[1157] With the indictments and charges having been delivered, the Sangamon County grand jury

---

[1146] Simmons, William J., Turner, Henry McNeal. (1887). Men of Mark: Eminent, Progressive and Rising. Pp. 107, et seq. Cleveland, OH: George M. Rewell & Co. Google Books.
[1147] The Saint Paul Globe. (January 16, 1898). P. 1. Newspapers.com.
[1148] The Saint Paul Globe. (January 16, 1898). P. 1. Newspapers.com.
[1149] The Saint Paul Globe. (January 16, 1898). P. 1. Newspapers.com.
[1150] The Saint Paul Globe. (January 16, 1898). P. 1. Newspapers.com.
[1151] The Saint Paul Globe. (January 16, 1898). P. 1. Newspapers.com.
[1152] The Saint Paul Globe. (January 16, 1898). P. 1. Newspapers.com.
[1153] The Saint Paul Globe. (January 16, 1898). P. 1. Newspapers.com.
[1154] The Saint Paul Globe. (January 16, 1898). P. 1. Newspapers.com.
[1155] The Saint Paul Globe. (January 16, 1898). P. 1. Newspapers.com.
[1156] The Saint Paul Globe. (January 16, 1898). P. 1. Newspapers.com.
[1157] The Saint Paul Globe. (January 16, 1898). P. 1. Newspapers.com.

had apparently collected facts, evidences, and proofs regarding the coal trust.[1158] The Sangamon County Circuit Court grand jury delivered a verdict of indictment and issued charges against several of the member companies of the coal trust.[1159] *The Islander*, a newspaper of Friday Harbor, Washington, reported that the Sangamon County grand jury had issued indictments against ten of the member companies of the coal trust.[1160] The *Kansas City Journal* of Kansas City, Missouri, reported that the ground for the charges against the Springfield Coal Trust was conspiracy to defraud.[1161] The Springfield Coal Trust, because of its connection to the Springfield Iron Company, would probably have possessed some degree of connection to the Chicago coal markets.

The *Decatur Daily Review*, a newspaper of Decatur, Illinois, reported on May 2, 1899, the facts of the first trial of the Springfield Coal Trust, as well as the fact that a second trial had begun recently prior to the Decatur report.[1162] The original legal processes instituted against the Springfield Coal Trust included the production, collection, and filing of claims, facts, and pleadings before the Sangamon County Circuit Court grand jury, which produced the verdict that supported charge and indictment of the company.[1163] The verdict supported charges against ten of the coal trust member companies.[1164] The purpose of the State of Illinois' litigation was the recovery for breach of the state's right to freedom from conspiracies.[1165] The theory of recovery in the case included the claim by the State of Illinois of the right to recovery for corporate conspiracy to defraud.[1166] The foundation of the charge, indictment, and complaint was conspiracy to defraud consumers.[1167] The case processes led to trial of the relevant facts and laws on the merits.[1168] The first trial resulted in a non-unanimous verdict in which nine jurors voted for conviction, and three jurors voted for acquittal, of the company.[1169] The mutually conflictive verdicts returned by the jury in the first trial necessitated a second trial.[1170] The diversity of verdicts in the first trial suggested the diversity of attitude regarding industrial monopolies at the time.

The Springfield Iron Company was one of the multiple companies that co-founded the Bessemer Steel Pool.[1171] Established in 1896, the Bessemer Steel Pool was an immense combination company whose purpose was the regulation of the

---

[1158] The Saint Paul Globe. (January 16, 1898). P. 1. Newspapers.com.

[1159] The Saint Paul Globe. (January 16, 1898). P. 1. Newspapers.com.

[1160] The Islander. (January 27, 1898). P. 1. Newspapers.com.

[1161] The Kansas City Journal. (January 16, 1898). P. 6. Newspapers.com.

[1162] The Decatur Daily Review. (May 2, 1899). P. 1. Newspapers.com.

[1163] The Decatur Daily Review. (May 2, 1899). P. 1. Newspapers.com.

[1164] The Decatur Daily Review. (May 2, 1899). P. 1. Newspapers.com.

[1165] The Decatur Daily Review. (May 2, 1899). P. 1. Newspapers.com.

[1166] The Decatur Daily Review. (May 2, 1899). P. 1. Newspapers.com.

[1167] The Decatur Daily Review. (May 2, 1899). P. 1. Newspapers.com.

[1168] The Decatur Daily Review. (May 2, 1899). P. 1. Newspapers.com.

[1169] The Decatur Daily Review. (May 2, 1899). P. 1. Newspapers.com.

[1170] The Decatur Daily Review. (May 2, 1899). P. 1. Newspapers.com.

[1171] The Philadelphia Times. (March 31, 1896). P. 4. Newspapers.com.

prices of Bessemer steel products.[1172] *The Philadelphia Times*, a newspaper of Pennsylvania, reported a large quantity of facts regarding the Bessemer Steel Pool.[1173] The Philadelphia report was based on a Pittsburgh report received on March 30, 1896, and was published on March 31, 1896.[1174] The Bessemer Steel Pool was created with a comprehensive scope of membership.[1175] The Trust was coupled *ab initio* with the purpose that every United States steel producer join the new monopoly.[1176] The formative Trust conference took place in New York City at some time very shortly prior to the Pittsburgh and Philadelphia news reports in 1896.[1177]

The Bessemer Steel Pool was established by multiple companies from throughout the United States. The companies represented a heavy concentration of Midwestern states and cities.[1178] The member companies had collectively produced more than 3,000,000 tons of Bessemer steel in 1895, the year prior to the establishment of the Bessemer Steel Pool.[1179] The list that follows contains the following information about the Bessemer Pool companies: name of the co-founding member company; place of the co-founding member company.

	Company Name	Company Place
1.	Carnegie Steel Company	Pittsburgh, Pennsylvania
2.	Jones & Laughlin Company	Pittsburgh, Pennsylvania
3.	National Tube Works Company	McKeesport, Pennsylvania
4.	Hainsworth Steel Company	Pittsburgh, Pennsylvania
5.	Shoenberg & Company	Pittsburgh, Pennsylvania
6.	Spang Steel & Iron Company	South Pittsburg, Pennsylvania
7.	Cambria Iron Company	Johnstown, Pennsylvania
8.	Bethlehem Iron Company	South Bethlehem, Pennsylvania
9.	Illinois Steel Company	Chicago
10.	Johns Company	Cleveland, Ohio
11.	Lackawanna Iron & Steel Company	Scranton, Pennsylvania
12.	Lickdale Iron Company	Lebanon, Pennsylvania
13.	Wellman Steel Company	Thurlow, Pennsylvania
14.	Shenango Valley Steel Company	New Castle, Pennsylvania
15.	Maryland Steel Company	Sparrows' Point, Maryland
16.	Riverside Iron Works	Wheeling, West Virginia
17.	Wheeling Steel Works	Benwood, West Virginia
18.	Ashland Steel Company	Ashland, Kentucky

[1172] The Philadelphia Times. (March 31, 1896). P. 4. Newspapers.com.
[1173] The Philadelphia Times. (March 31, 1896). P. 4. Newspapers.com.
[1174] The Philadelphia Times. (March 31, 1896). P. 4. Newspapers.com.
[1175] The Philadelphia Times. (March 31, 1896). P. 4. Newspapers.com.
[1176] The Philadelphia Times. (March 31, 1896). P. 4. Newspapers.com.
[1177] The Philadelphia Times. (March 31, 1896). P. 4. Newspapers.com.
[1178] The Philadelphia Times. (March 31, 1896). P. 4. Newspapers.com.
[1179] The Philadelphia Times. (March 31, 1896). P. 4. Newspapers.com.

19. Ohio Steel Company	Youngstown, Ohio
20. Bellaire Nail Works	Bellaire, Ohio
21. Cleveland Rolling Mill	Cleveland, Ohio
22. Junction Iron & Steel Company	Mingo Junction, Ohio
23. Gilbert, King & Warner Company	Columbus, Ohio
24. Otis Steel Company	Cleveland, Ohio
25. Springfield Iron Company	Chicago
26. Union Steel Company	Alexandria, Indiana
27. West Superior Iron & Steel Company	West Superior, Wisconsin
28. Colorado Fuel & Iron Company	Pueblo, Colorado[1180]

Two Chicago companies, three Cleveland companies, one Columbus company, and six companies of Pittsburgh and the Pittsburgh metropolitan region were founders of the Bessemer Steel Trust company.[1181] One of the two Chicago companies was the Springfield Iron Company.[1182] The significant existence and reputation of the Springfield Iron Company as a Chicago company in 1896 was highlighted by the *Philadelphia Times* report, because the news article listed Chicago, and not Springfield, as the principal place associated with the Springfield Iron Company.[1183] It is important to remember, however, that the Springfield Iron Company was of great importance at both Springfield and Chicago, and represented both cities significantly within the national coal, iron, and steel markets.[1184] Both Sangamon County and Cook County were, therefore, represented by the Springfield Iron Company.[1185] At the time when the Springfield Iron Company participated in the creation of the Bessemer Steel Pool company, the Springfield Iron Company had been present in Chicago for approximately fifteen years.[1186] The Springfield Iron Company had existed for twenty-five years at the time when it became a party to the formation of the Bessemer Steel Pool company.[1187] The Springfield Iron Company first manufactured Bessemer steel in

---

[1180] The Philadelphia Times. (March 31, 1896). P. 4. Newspapers.com.

[1181] The Philadelphia Times. (March 31, 1896). P. 4. Newspapers.com.

[1182] The Philadelphia Times. (March 31, 1896). P. 4. Newspapers.com.

[1183] The Philadelphia Times. (March 31, 1896). P. 4. Newspapers.com.

[1184] Call, Andrew Taylor. (2005). Jacob Bunn: Legacy of an Illinois Industrial Pioneer. P. 111. Lawrenceville, VA: Brunswick Publishing Corporation. Retrieved from Google Books.

[1185] Andreas, Alfred Theodore. (1886). History of Chicago. Vol. 3. P. 478. Chicago, Illinois: The A. T. Andreas Company, Publishers. Google Books.

[1186] Andreas, Alfred Theodore. (1886). History of Chicago. Vol. 3. P. 478. Chicago, Illinois: The A. T. Andreas Company, Publishers. Google Books.

[1187] Call, Andrew Taylor. (2005). Jacob Bunn: Legacy of an Illinois Industrial Pioneer. P. 111. Lawrenceville, VA: Brunswick Publishing Corporation. Retrieved from Google Books.

1887.[1188] The *Chicago Tribune* issue of September 9, 1887, reported the facts as follows.

> "The first lot of Bessemer steel was made today at the works of the Springfield Iron Company. It was a complete success in every particular. Regular work in the steel-rail department will begin tomorrow. This new department is equal to the production of 500 tons of steel daily."[1189]

Mathematical extrapolation from the facts reported would lead to the calculation that the reported Bessemer steel product manufacturing capacity of the Springfield Iron Company would have stood at 182,500 tons in September, 1887.[1190] The *New York Tribune*, a newspaper of New York City, also identified the Springfield Iron Company principally with the City of Chicago in its 1896 enumeration of the companies that were co-founders and members of the new Bessemer Steel Trust.[1191]

The meeting at which the Bessemer Steel Pool company was formed took place at the Astor Room of the Waldorf Hotel in New York City.[1192] The *New York Tribune* described the conference as one of secrecy.[1193] The meeting produced not only the creation of the Bessemer Steel Pool, but also the issuance of policies, laws, and practices that regulated the sales and prices of steel and tin products.[1194] The Pool company acted as maker of law and policy for the steel industry and the tin industry.[1195] The inaugural legislative acts taken by the Bessemer Steel Pool included the pegging of the price of steel billets for the Eastern market at $22.75 per ton; the pegging of the price for steel billets for the Western market at $20.25 per ton; the pegging of the price of tin bars for the Western market at $22 per ton; and the pegging of the price of tin sheet bars for the Western market at $23 per ton.[1196] The ratifications of the price pegs caused changes in product costs.[1197] The ratification of the new price peg for the steel billet product of the Western market increased the cost of steel billets in the Western market by 25 cents over the prior price peg that had been agreed upon at the first day of the Waldorf meeting.[1198] The ratification of the price peg for steel billets in the Eastern market caused the price to increase by $3.25 over the price of $19.50, the product price that the *New*

[1188] Chicago Tribune. (September 9, 1887). P. 3. Newspapers.com.
[1189] Chicago Tribune. (September 9, 1887). P. 3. Newspapers.com.
[1190] Chicago Tribune. (September 9, 1887). P. 3. Newspapers.com.
[1191] New York Tribune. (April 4, 1896). P. 1. Newspapers.com.
[1192] New York Tribune. (April 4, 1896). P. 1. Newspapers.com.
[1193] New York Tribune. (April 4, 1896). P. 1. Newspapers.com.
[1194] New York Tribune. (April 4, 1896). P. 1. Newspapers.com.
[1195] New York Tribune. (April 4, 1896). P. 1. Newspapers.com.
[1196] New York Tribune. (April 4, 1896). P. 1. Newspapers.com.
[1197] New York Tribune. (April 4, 1896). P. 1. Newspapers.com.
[1198] New York Tribune. (April 4, 1896). P. 1. Newspapers.com.

York Tribune reported was prevalent in the Eastern market at the time of the Waldorf conference.[1199]

The market power and economic influence of the Bessemer Pool were, as the facts and proofs demonstrate, quite immediately manifest.[1200] Output, price, and sale were, therefore, key subject matters of the Waldorf meeting.[1201] Of additional cultural interest is the fact that the Waldorf Hotel, named for the renowned New York City capitalist William Waldorf Astor, had opened a mere three years prior to its hosting of the convention for the creation of the $100,000,000 Bessemer Steel Pool company. William Waldorf Astor had opened the hotel for business in March of 1893.[1202] The Bessemer Steel Trust meeting took place around the Easter holiday of 1896.[1203] Once the meeting had been concluded, those in attendance expressed their urgencies in returning to their homes to spend the Easter holiday.[1204]

In addition to having participated as one of the smaller founding members of the Bessemer Steel Pool in 1896, the Springfield Iron Company was one of the member companies of the consolidation plan that established the Republic Iron and Steel Company in 1899.[1205] The jurisprudential environment of the United States at this time was supportive of the creation of monopolies and trust organizations. The judgment and opinion from the case of *United States v. E. C. Knight Company*, a United States Supreme Court case in which Chief Justice Melville Weston Fuller delivered the majority opinion, provided approval for trusts and similar organizations comprised of manufacturing companies. The case interpreted the Commerce Clause of the Constitution of the United States of America (Art. I, Sec. 8., Clause 3) in a manner that allowed manufacturing monopolies to enjoy immunity from the Sherman Antitrust Act.[1206] Within the majority opinion in *E. C. Knight*, Justice Fuller stated, *inter alia*, the following with respect to the interpretation of the congressional powers derivative of the Commerce Clause.

> "The argument is that the power to control the manufacture of refined sugar is a monopoly over a necessary of life, to the enjoyment of which by a large part of the population of the United States interstate commerce is indispensable, and that therefore the general government, in the exercise of the power to regulate commerce, may repress such monopoly directly and set aside the instruments which have created it. But this argument cannot be confined to necessaries of life merely, and must include all

---

[1199] New York Tribune. (April 4, 1896). P. 1. Newspapers.com.

[1200] New York Tribune. (April 4, 1896). P. 1. Newspapers.com.

[1201] New York Tribune. (April 4, 1896). P. 1. Newspapers.com.

[1202] Turkel, Stanley. (2009). Great American Hoteliers: Pioneers of the Hotel Industry. P. 136. Bloomington, IN: AuthorHouse. Google Books.

[1203] New York Tribune. (April 4, 1896). P. 1. Newspapers.com.

[1204] New York Tribune. (April 4, 1896). P. 1. Newspapers.com.

[1205] The Brooklyn Daily Eagle. (September 1, 1901). P. 17. Newspapers.com.

[1206] U.S. v. E. C. Knight Company. 156 U.S. 12. (1895). Justia.com.

articles of general consumption. Doubtless the power to control the manufacture of a given thing involves, in a certain sense, the control of its disposition, but this is a secondary, and not the primary, sense, and although the exercise of that power may result in bringing the operation of commerce into play, it does not control it, and affects it only incidentally and indirectly. Commerce succeeds to manufacture, and is not a part of it. The power to regulate commerce is the power to prescribe the rule by which commerce shall be governed, and is a power independent of the power to suppress monopoly. But it may operate in repression of monopoly whenever that comes within the rules by which commerce is governed, or whenever the transaction is itself a monopoly of commerce."[1207]

The law of *E. C. Knight* thus gave rise to policies and practices that profoundly affected commercial organizations.[1208] The Springfield Iron Company contributed to the creation of no fewer than three corporate monopolies: the Springfield Coal Trust company in 1887; the Bessemer Steel Pool company in 1896; and the Republic Steel Company in 1899.

The historical record proves that John Whitfield Bunn, a founder, vice-president, and director of the Springfield Iron Company, remained a member of the company leadership from the time of the company's incorporation in August, 1871, until the time of the company's contributory merger into the Republic Steel Company, in 1899.[1209] The March 13, 1897, issue of Volume 70 of *The Chicago Journal Of Commerce And Metal Industries* contained a leadership report from the Springfield Iron Company.[1210] "The stockholders of the Springfield Iron Company, Springfield, Ill., at their recent annual meeting elected the old directors as follows: Charles Ridgely, William Ridgely, John C. Lamb, John W. Bunn, George N. Black and Edward Ridgely."[1211] Every direct and circumstantial fact pertinent to the continuity of the leadership personnel of the Springfield Iron Company indicates that John Whitfield Bunn would have participated in some manner in the decision

---

[1207] U.S. v. E. C. Knight Company. 156 U.S. 12. (1895). Justia.com.

[1208] U.S. v. E. C. Knight Company. 156 U.S. 12. (1895). Justia.com; See also Rohr, John Anthony. Ethics for Bureaucrats: An Essay On Law And Values. (1978). Pp. 49-86. New York, NY: MARCEL DEKKER, INC. John Anthony Rohr developed the concept of regime values, which are the core values that fuel the legal systems within cultures.

[1209] Call, Andrew Taylor. (2005). Jacob Bunn: Legacy of an Illinois Industrial Pioneer. P. 112. Lawrenceville, VA: Brunswick Publishing Corporation. Google Books; See: Articles of Incorporation for the Springfield Iron Company, August 18, 1871; Chicago Journal Of Commerce And Metal Industries. (March 13, 1897). Vol. 70. Number 13. P. 16. Google Books.

[1210] Chicago Journal Of Commerce And Metal Industries. (March 13, 1897). Vol. 70. Number 13. P. 16. Google Books.

[1211] Chicago Journal Of Commerce And Metal Industries. (March 13, 1897). Vol. 70. Number 13. P. 16. Google Books.

to merge the Springfield Iron Company into the new Republic Steel Company.[1212] Additionally, the fact that William Barrett Ridgely, a close friend of the Bunn brothers, rose so rapidly and prominently within the leadership structure of the new Republic Iron and Steel Company strongly suggests that Bunn, who, like Ridgely, was also from Chicago and Springfield, would have participated in some manner in the formation of the Republic Iron and Steel Company.[1213]

The necessary legal process that joined the Springfield Iron Company to the other companies that were establishing the Republic Iron and Steel Company entailed the 1899 grant of a warranty deed to the property held by the Springfield Iron Company.[1214] *The Republic*, a newspaper of Columbus, Indiana, contained the relevant report. "A warranty deed conveying to the Republic Iron and Steel Company the plant of the Springfield Iron company, for a consideration of $200,000, has been filed."[1215] The incorporation of Springfield Iron Company into the new Republic Iron and Steel Company caused development to occur in the form of operational revitalization.[1216] The Republic Iron and Steel Company reactivated the dormant Springfield Iron Company mills in July, 1899.[1217] *The St. Joseph Herald*, a newspaper of St. Joseph, Missouri, reported the facts. "The 22-inch mill at the Springfield Iron Company's works, now owned by the Republican [sic] Iron and Steel Company, started today after an idleness of several years. Two hundred additional men will be given employment."[1218]

The financial structure of the Republic Iron and Steel Company, as reported by *The Brooklyn Daily Eagle*, consisted of an equity financing that produced $55,000,000 in stock money.[1219] The financing plan set the par value of the stock at $100 per share.[1220] The financing plan contemplated a bifurcation of the equity money into two classes of moneys: common stock, and preferred stock.[1221] The common stock money consisted of $30,000,000.[1222] The preferred stock money

---

[1212] Call, Andrew Taylor. (2005). Jacob Bunn: Legacy of an Illinois Industrial Pioneer. Pp. 111-112. Lawrenceville, VA: Brunswick Publishing Corporation. Google Books; See: Articles of Incorporation for the Springfield Iron Company, August 18, 1871; Chicago Journal Of Commerce And Metal Industries. (March 13, 1897). Vol. 70. Number 13. P. 16. Google Books.

[1213] Call, Andrew Taylor. (2005). Jacob Bunn: Legacy of an Illinois Industrial Pioneer. P. 112. Lawrenceville, VA: Brunswick Publishing Corporation. Retrieved from Google Books. See: Articles of Incorporation for the Springfield Iron Company, August 18, 1871; Chicago Journal Of Commerce And Metal Industries. (March 13, 1897). Vol. 70. Number 13. P. 16. Google Books.

[1214] The Republic. (May 16, 1899). P. 1. Newspapers.com.

[1215] The Republic. (May 16, 1899). P. 1. Newspapers.com.

[1216] The St. Joseph Herald. (July 19, 1899). P. 6. Newspapers.com.

[1217] The St. Joseph Herald. (July 19, 1899). P. 6. Newspapers.com.

[1218] The St. Joseph Herald. (July 19, 1899). P. 6. Newspapers.com.

[1219] The Brooklyn Daily Eagle. (April 22, 1899). P. 15. Newspapers.com.

[1220] The Brooklyn Daily Eagle. (April 22, 1899). P. 15. Newspapers.com.

[1221] The Brooklyn Daily Eagle. (April 22, 1899). P. 15. Newspapers.com.

[1222] The Brooklyn Daily Eagle. (April 22, 1899). P. 15. Newspapers.com.

consisted of $25,000,000.[1223] The financing plan attached priority of rights as to distribution of corporate assets to the preferred stock money.[1224] The Chicago Inter-Ocean Company, which had been co-founded and owned by Jacob Bunn (as the Chicago Republican Company), published an encyclopedia of Chicago history in which the history of the Republic Iron and Steel Company was provided.[1225] The Republic Iron and Steel Company resulted from the consolidation of the following steel and iron companies.

Name of Company	Place of Company
1. Andrews Brothers Company	Youngstown, Ohio
2. Brown-Bonnell Iron Company	Youngstown, Ohio
3. Mahoning Valley Iron Company	Youngstown, Ohio
4. Cherry Valley Iron Works	Leetonia, Ohio
5. Atlantic Company	
6. Union Rolling Mill Company	
7. Corns Iron and Steel Company	Massillon, Ohio
8. Toledo Rolling Mill Company	Toledo, Ohio
9. Lake Erie Iron Company	Cleveland, Ohio
10. Mitchell Tranter Company	Cincinnati, Ohio
11. Eagle Iron and Steel Company	Ironton, Ohio
12. Indiana Iron Company	Muncie, Indiana
13. Muncie Iron and Steel Company	Muncie, Indiana
14. White River Mills	Muncie, Indiana
15. Union Steel Company	Alexandria, Indiana
16. Marion Steel and Iron Company	Marion, Indiana
17. Westerman Stewart Iron Company	Marion, Indiana
18. Wetherald Rolling Mill Company	Frankton, Indiana
19. Indiana Forge and Rolling Mill Co.	New Albany, Indiana
20. Central Iron and Steel Company	Brazil, Indiana
21. Wabash Iron Company	Terre Haute, Indiana
22. Terre Haute Iron and Steel Company	Terre Haute, Indiana
23. Tudor Iron Works	East St. Louis, Missouri
24. Springfield Iron Company	Springfield, Illinois (and Chicago)
25. Inland Iron and Forge Company	East Chicago, Indiana
26. Sylvan Steel Company	Moline, Illinois
27. Alabama Rolling Mill Company	Birmingham, Alabama[1226]

[1223] The Brooklyn Daily Eagle. (April 22, 1899). P. 15. Newspapers.com.

[1224] The Brooklyn Daily Eagle. (April 22, 1899). P. 15. Newspapers.com.

[1225] A History of the City of Chicago: Its Men and Institutions. (1900). P. 242. Chicago, IL: The Inter Ocean. Google Books.

[1226] A History of the City of Chicago: Its Men and Institutions. (1900). P. 242. Chicago, IL: The Inter Ocean. Google Books.

The original leadership structure of the new company consisted of the following persons and jobs.

	Person	Job
1.	R. S. Warner	President
2.	George D. Wick	First Vice-President
3.	Samuel Thomas	Second Vice-President
4.	James C. Corns	Third Vice-President
5.	George M. Bard	Fourth Vice-President
6.	Silas J. Llewellyn	Secretary
7.	John F. Taylor	Treasurer
8.	A. P. Bartlett	Assistant Treasurer
9.	Harry Rubens	General Counsel[1227]

Executive Committee Leadership[1228]

10. Myron C. Wick
11. Alexis W. Thompson
12. John F. Taylor
13. T. A. Meysenburg
14. G. Watson French
15. George D. Wick[1229]

Board of Directors[1230]
16. August Belmont
17. Myron C. Wick
18. Grant B. Schley
19. Randolph S. Warner
20. George R. Sheldon
21. J. D. Caldwell
22. G. Watson French
23. Alexis W. Thompson
24. George D. Wick
25. John F. Taylor
26. Harry Rubens
27. T. A. Meysenburg
28. L. E. Cochran

[1227] A History of the City of Chicago: Its Men and Institutions. (1900). P. 242. Chicago, IL: The Inter Ocean. Google Books.
[1228] A History of the City of Chicago: Its Men and Institutions. (1900). P. 242. Chicago, IL: The Inter Ocean. Google Books.
[1229] A History of the City of Chicago: Its Men and Institutions. (1900). P. 242. Chicago, IL: The Inter Ocean. Google Books.
[1230] A History of the City of Chicago: Its Men and Institutions. (1900). P. 242. Chicago, IL: The Inter Ocean. Google Books.

29. James C. Corns
30. H. W. Hassinger
31. P. I. Kimberly
32. George M. Bard
33. George M. Clark
34. Samuel Thomas
35. S. J. Llewellyn[1231]

William Barrett Ridgely was among the early builders and developers of the Republic Iron and Steel Company.[1232] William Barrett Ridgely of Chicago and Springfield was originally employed by the Springfield Iron Company.[1233] Ridgely was soon promoted to the offices of General Manager and Vice President after beginning with Republic.[1234] The Republic Iron and Steel Company was headquartered at the Chicago Stock Exchange building in 1901.[1235] The United States Steel Corporation had been established in 1901, having been incorporated in February, 1901. William B. Ridgely was a 1879 alumnus of the Rensselaer Polytechnic Institute of Troy, New York.[1236] He received a degree in Civil Engineering.[1237] Ridgely found a job at the Springfield Iron Company, where he remained until the establishment of the Republic Steel Company.[1238] At Republic Steel, Ridgely held the offices of Chicago District Manager and Secretary of the company.[1239] William Barrett Ridgely was a grandson of prominent banker and capitalist Nicholas H. Ridgely, who had relocated from Baltimore to St. Louis, and then to Springfield.[1240] As of 1901, William Barrett Ridgely was a member of the Technical Club of Chicago, the Exmoor Golf Club, the Marquette Club, and the University Club, all of Chicago and the metropolitan region.[1241] Ridgely was also a member of the Sangamo Club of Springfield, the Iron and Steel Institute of Great Britain, the American Society of Mechanical Engineers, and the American Institute of Mining Engineers.[1242] William Douglas Richardson, the founder and president of Richardson Construction Company of Chicago, was a co-founder and owner of Springfield Iron Company, and also had been a member of the Technical Club of Chicago.

[1231] A History of the City of Chicago: Its Men and Institutions. (1900). P. 242. Chicago, IL: The Inter Ocean. Google Books.
[1232] The Brooklyn Daily Eagle. (September 1, 1901). P. 17. Newspapers.com.
[1233] The Brooklyn Daily Eagle. (September 1, 1901). P. 17. Newspapers.com.
[1234] The Brooklyn Daily Eagle. (September 1, 1901). P. 17. Newspapers.com.
[1235] The Brooklyn Daily Eagle. (September 1, 1901). P. 17. Newspapers.com.
[1236] The Brooklyn Daily Eagle. (September 1, 1901). P. 17. Newspapers.com.
[1237] The Brooklyn Daily Eagle. (September 1, 1901). P. 17. Newspapers.com.
[1238] The Brooklyn Daily Eagle. (September 1, 1901). P. 17. Newspapers.com.
[1239] The Brooklyn Daily Eagle. (September 1, 1901). P. 17. Newspapers.com.
[1240] The Brooklyn Daily Eagle. (September 1, 1901). P. 17. Newspapers.com.
[1241] The Brooklyn Daily Eagle. (September 1, 1901). P. 17. Newspapers.com.
[1242] The Brooklyn Daily Eagle. (September 1, 1901). P. 17. Newspapers.com.

Chapter 3

The Horizons of Hyde Park

"Zebulun will dwell at the seashore; And he shall be a haven for ships. . ."

Genesis 49:13[1243]

Introduction

The current chapter concerns the histories of the Stryker, Ingraham, Downs, Ferguson, Lee, and Henshaw families of Chicago. For the railroad histories of the Strykers, consult the following chapters: (1) Chapter 1, *Genesis of a Great Lakes Frontier*, for the John Stryker railroad history of Chicago; (2) Chapter 6, *Sprinters of the Steel Track* for the Stryker, Taylor, and Brigham histories relevant to the Chicago railroad industry. Although a portion of the Regan history occurs within Hyde Park Township, that history can be located within Chapter 7, *Chicago Irish and Old Brickwork*.

The southeast quarter of the City of Chicago contains what was once known as Hyde Park Township. Paul Cornell founded and developed Hyde Park Township as a settlement along Lake Michigan. The old township boundaries run from 39th Street in the north to 138th Street in the south, and from State Street in the west to Lake Michigan on the east. Chicago incorporated Hyde Park Township in 1889, and thereby laid the foundation for the development of a multitude of distinct, unique, and remarkable urban communities and neighborhoods.[1244] Today the old Hyde Park Township region of Chicago contains the well-known communities of Hyde Park, Kenwood, Oakland, Woodlawn, South Shore, South Chicago, East Side, Hegewisch, Chatham, Pullman, Roseland, Washington Park, Grand Boulevard, Greater Grand Crossing, Calumet Heights, Burnside, part of Douglas, and other communities.[1245] Within these communities are many distinct and unique neighborhoods. Lake Michigan forms the eastern boundary of old Hyde Park Township, and the Calumet River traverses the old township. Commercial and industrial waters, therefore, have defined the horizons of Hyde Park Township since its inception. The Calumet and Lake Michigan have framed much of the geography and development of old Hyde Park Township. This southeastern quarter of the city has been a grand foundation of Chicago history and urban development since the nineteenth century. Many parks, including several of international historical and architectural renown, also exist in the Hyde Park Township region of Chicago. These parks include the Midway Plaisance, Jackson Park, Burnham Park, Washington Park, Harold Washington Park, Nichols Park, and others.

This chapter concerns the Stryker, Pettit, Southmayd, Holmes, and Henshaw lineages and branches of my mother's family. Henry Parsons' 1920 genealogical

---

[1243] Bible.knowingjesus.com
[1244] Hyde Park Historical Society.
[1245] Hyde Park Historical Society.

record of the Parsons family and allied families contains detailed records of the Stryker family of Wisconsin, Chicago, and Cook County. The Chicago communities of Kenwood, Hyde Park, Woodlawn, and Douglas are all represented in the present chapter, as are the Cook County municipalities of Oak Park and Riverside. Members of the Stryker family have resided in all of these Chicago communities for a long time.

Let us first identify relevant persons. James Monroe Stryker was born February 14, 1819, in Owasco, Cayuga County, New York.[1246] James married Ella Maria Brooks, on September 25, 1845.[1247] The wedding took place at Kenosha, Wisconsin. James and Ella Stryker had eight children, many of whom resided in Chicago and Cook County and contributed to the civic and industrial organizations there.[1248] The children of James and Ella Maria (Brooks) Stryker were Ellen Amelia Stryker (born August 22, 1846), who married James Edward Pettit on October 16, 1866, at Kenosha, Wisconsin; James Monroe Stryker (born September 6, 1849); Eva Stryker (born July 29, 1851, and died October, 1852); Carrie Warburton Stryker (born August 15, 1853); Ida Stryker (born September 9, 1855); John Brooks Stryker (born October 16, 1858); Louis (sometimes Lewis) Harvey Stryker (born June 10, 1861); and May Isabella Stryker (born September 3, 1863).[1249] The Henry Parsons list of the James Monroe Stryker children is an essential resource on the Chicago Strykers. Cordelia Lydia Stryker, a cousin of the Chicago Strykers, married Henry Edward Ankeny of West Virginia.[1250]

Multiple members of our Stryker family contributed importantly to the establishment, planning, coordination, financing, physical construction, and executive management of the 1893 World's Columbian Exposition. The ancestors who contributed to the 1893 World's Columbian Exposition included no fewer than three members of my mother's family, and one relative from my father's Ohio family. John Whitfield Bunn, William Douglas Richardson, and Milo Barnum Richardson were the three ancestors from my mother's family who participated in the 1893 World's Columbian Exposition. William Henry Burtner of Cincinnati,

[1246] Parsons, Henry. (1920). Parsons Family: Descendants of Cornet Joseph Parsons, Springfield 1636—Northampton 1655. Vol. 2. Pp. 290-291. New Haven, CT: The Tuttle, Morehouse and Taylor Co. Google Books.
[1247] Parsons, Henry. (1920). Parsons Family: Descendants of Cornet Joseph Parsons, Springfield 1636—Northampton 1655. Vol. 2. Pp. 290-291. New Haven, CT: The Tuttle, Morehouse and Taylor Co. Google Books.
[1248] Parsons, Henry. (1920). Parsons Family: Descendants of Cornet Joseph Parsons, Springfield 1636—Northampton 1655. Vol. 2. Pp. 290-291. New Haven, CT: The Tuttle, Morehouse and Taylor Co. Google Books.
[1249] Parsons, Henry. (1920). Parsons Family: Descendants of Cornet Joseph Parsons, Springfield 1636—Northampton 1655. Vol. 2. P. 291. New Haven, CT: The Tuttle, Morehouse and Taylor Co. Google Books.
[1250] Cordelia Lydia (Stryker) Ankeny interment record at Masonic Cemetery in Eugene, Oregon. Findagrave.com.

Ohio, was the relative from my father's family who contributed to the 1893 Chicago World's Fair. For these histories, see Chapters 5 and 6. Before we discuss the Stryker histories of Kenwood, Hyde Park, Woodlawn, and Douglas, let us briefly discuss William Douglas Richardson.

William Douglas Richardson, my great-great-great-grandfather, was actively engaged in the Hyde Park community and the Woodlawn community of Chicago through his leadership at the 1893 World's Columbian Exposition. Richardson's contributions were to the construction and design of the buildings and other structural elements of the Chicago World's Fair. He also built many churches and hotels at Chicago. After a period of time of engagement in the insurance and real estate businesses at Springfield, with the company of Richardson & Latham, Richardson entered the building construction business.[1251] The Richardson Construction Company had been awarded construction contracts for principal elements of the Illinois State Capitol building and the Abraham Lincoln Monument located in Oak Ridge Cemetery in Springfield.[1252] For the 1893 Chicago World's Fair, Richardson held the office of Superintendent of Exterior Covering.[1253] He also held the office of Superintendent of Buildings and Grounds for the 1893 Chicago World's Fair.[1254] Richardson furthermore contributed to the development of Chicago cultural organizations when he served as one of the multiple founding donors of the Columbian Museum in 1893, having contributed $50 towards the creation and support of the Columbian Museum at Hyde Park.[1255] The Columbian Museum initially existed at Hyde Park and occupied the Palace of Fine Arts

---

[1251] Call, Andrew Taylor. (2005). Jacob Bunn: Legacy of an Illinois Industrial Pioneer. Pp. 109-117. Lawrenceville, VA: Brunswick Publishing Corporation. Google Books; Call, Andrew Taylor. (2016). Faded Bricks: Old Family Tales from the South Side of Chicago. Hyde Park History, Vol. 38, (No. 4), Pp. 1-7. Chicago, IL: Hyde Park Historical Society.

[1252] Call, Andrew Taylor. (2005). Jacob Bunn: Legacy of an Illinois Industrial Pioneer. P. 110. Lawrenceville, VA: Brunswick Publishing Corporation; Call, Andrew Taylor. (2016). Faded Bricks: Old Family Tales from the South Side of Chicago. Hyde Park History, Vol. 38, (No. 4), Pp. 1-7. Chicago, IL: Hyde Park Historical Society.

[1253] Engineering News and American Railway Journal. (January-June, 1892). Vol. XXVII. P. 50. New York, NY: Engineering News Publishing Co. Google Books; Call, Andrew Taylor. (2016). Faded Bricks: Old Family Tales from the South Side of Chicago. Hyde Park History, Vol. 38, (No. 4), Pp. 1-7. Chicago, IL: Hyde Park Historical Society.

[1254] Call, Andrew Taylor. (2005). Jacob Bunn: Legacy of an Illinois Industrial Pioneer. P. 110. Lawrenceville, VA: Brunswick Publishing Corporation; Call, Andrew Taylor. (2016). Faded Bricks: Old Family Tales from the South Side of Chicago. Hyde Park History, Vol. 38, (No. 4), Pp. 1-7. Chicago, IL: Hyde Park Historical Society.

[1255] Gifts for Museum. Chicago Tribune. (Nov. 5, 1893). P. 12. Chicago Tribune Archives; Call, Andrew Taylor. (2016). Faded Bricks: Old Family Tales from the South Side of Chicago. Hyde Park History, Vol. 38, (No. 4), Pp. 1-7. Chicago, IL: Hyde Park Historical Society.

building.[1256] The Columbian Museum of Chicago would become known subsequently as the Field Museum.[1257] The Field Museum remains one of the largest and greatest museums of natural history and anthropology in the world and possesses a diverse and immense collection comprising some 30 million specimens.[1258]

John Whitfield Bunn, my great-great-great-granduncle, and a principal industrialist of Chicago and Springfield,[1259] contributed to the executive leadership of the Fair through service as a member of the Illinois Board of World's Fair Commissioners for the 1893 World's Columbian Exposition.[1260] As a member of the Illinois State Board of World's Fair Commissioners, Bunn held the office of Treasurer of the Illinois State Board for the 1893 Chicago World's Fair.[1261] Both Richardson and Bunn contributed to the development of Hyde Park, Woodlawn, and Jackson Park. For more about these histories, see Chapter 5.

The Stryker Genealogy of New Jersey, New York, and Illinois

Jan Stryker married Lambertje Seubering. Their children were as follows: Altje Stryker, who married Abraham Jorise Brinckerhoff; Jannetje Stryker, who married, first, Cornelius Jansen Berrien, and second, Samuel Edsall; Garrit Janse Stryker, who married Styntie Gerritse Dorland; Angenietje Stryker, who married, first, Claes Tyson, and second, Jan Cornelise Boomgaert; Hendrick Stryker, who married Catherine Huys; Eytie Stryker, who married Stoffel Probasco; **Pieter**

[1256] Ford, Liam T. A. (2009). Soldier Field: A Stadium and Its City. P. 7. Chicago, IL: The University of Chicago Press. Google Books; Call, Andrew Taylor. (2016). Faded Bricks: Old Family Tales from the South Side of Chicago. Hyde Park History, Vol. 38, (No. 4), Pp. 1-7. Chicago, IL: Hyde Park Historical Society.

[1257] Field Museum History. (2016). Para. 5. Fieldmuseum,.org; Call, Andrew Taylor. (2016). Faded Bricks: Old Family Tales from the South Side of Chicago. Hyde Park History, Vol. 38, (No. 4), Pp. 1-7. Chicago, IL: Hyde Park Historical Society.

[1258] Field Museum (2016). Para. 1. Fieldmuseum.org; Call, Andrew Taylor. (2016). Faded Bricks: Old Family Tales from the South Side of Chicago. Hyde Park History, Vol. 38, (No. 4), Pp. 1-7. Chicago, IL: Hyde Park Historical Society.

[1259] See generally: Call, Andrew Taylor. (2005). Jacob Bunn: Legacy of an Illinois Industrial Pioneer. Lawrenceville, VA: Brunswick Publishing Corp. Call, Andrew Taylor. (2016). Faded Bricks: Old Family Tales from the South Side of Chicago. Hyde Park History, Vol. 38, (No. 4), Pp. 1-7. Chicago, IL: Hyde Park Historical Society.

[1260] Plumbe, George A. (Compiler). The Daily News Almanac and Political Register for 1893. (1893). Chicago, IL: Chicago Daily News Company. P. 227. Google Books; Call, Andrew Taylor. (2016). Faded Bricks: Old Family Tales from the South Side of Chicago. Hyde Park History, Vol. 38, (No. 4), Pp. 1-7. Chicago, IL: Hyde Park Historical Society.

[1261] Plumbe, George E. (Compiler). The Daily News Almanac and Political Register for 1893. (1893). Chicago, IL: The Chicago Daily News Company. P. 227. Google Books; Call, Andrew Taylor. (2016). Faded Bricks: Old Family Tales from the South Side of Chicago. Hyde Park History, Vol. 38, (No. 4), Pp. 1-7. Chicago, IL: Hyde Park Historical Society.

Stryker, who married Annetje Barends; and Sara Stryker, who married Joris Hansen Bergen.[1262]

Peter Stryker married Annetje Barends. The following children were born to them: Lammatje Stryker, who died in infancy; Lammetje Stryker, who died of smallpox at age seven; **Jan Stryker, who married, first, Margarita Schenk**, and second, Sara Bergen; Barent Stryker, who died of smallpox at age three; Jacob Stryker, who probably married Annetje Vanderbeek; Barent Stryker, who married Libertje Hegeman; Hendrick Stryker; Syntje Stryker, who married Aert Vanderbilt; Pieter Stryker, who married Jannetje Martense; Hendrick Stryker, who married Marretje (surname unknown); and Lammetje Stryker, who married, first, Johannes Lott, and second, Christiaens Lupardus.[1263]

Jan Stryker married Margarita Schenk. The children born to them were the following: **Pieter Stryker, who married Antje Deremer**; Johannes Stryker, who married Cornelia Duryea; Annetje Stryker, who married Roelof Cowenhoven; Magdalena Stryker, who married Aert Middagh; Margarita Stryker died in infancy; Abraham Stryker, who married, first, Ida Ryder, second, Katriena Cornell, and third, Katriena Hogeland; Lammetje Stryker, who married, first, Garret Stoothoff, and second, Jan Amerman; Jacobus Stryker, who married Geertje Duryea; and Margarita Stryker, who married Jacobus Cornell.[1264]

<u>Two Large Stryker Families of Chicago:</u>

<u>The Stryker-Williamson Family and the Stryker-Cornell Family</u>

Pieter Stryker married Antje Deremer. The following children were born to them: Jacobus Stryker, who married Sarah Metselaer; Sarah Stryker, who married Rev. Johannes Van Harlengen; **Annie Stryker, who married Court Williamson**; Elizabeth Stryker, who married Aaron Auten; Gretie Stryker, who married Jones Brokaw; Maria Stryker, who married Hendrick Banta; Maregrite (spelling unclear) Stryker; **John Stryker, who married Lydia Cornell**; Lydia Stryker; and Magdalena Stryker, who married John Brokaw.[1265]

<u>The Stryker-Williamson Family of New York and Chicago</u>

Annie Stryker married Court Williamson. They are the ancestors of Stephen Williamson Stryker. For his biography see Chapter 4, *Friends of the*

[1262] Stryker, William Scudder. (1887). Genealogy of the Stryker Family. Pages not marked. Camden, NJ: Sinnickson Chew, Printer.
[1263] Stryker, William Scudder. (1887). Genealogy of the Stryker Family. Pages not marked. Camden, NJ: Sinnickson Chew, Printer.
[1264] Stryker, William Scudder. (1887). Genealogy of the Stryker Family. Pages not marked. Camden, NJ: Sinnickson Chew, Printer.
[1265] Stryker, William Scudder. (1887). Genealogy of the Stryker Family. Pages not marked. Camden, NJ: Sinnickson Chew, Printer.

Leatherworkers. Court Williamson and Ann (Stryker) Williamson had a daughter, Lucretia Williamson, who married Jeremiah Williamson.[1266] Jeremiah and Lucretia (Williamson) Williamson had a daughter, Elizabeth Williamson, who married Benjamin S. Stryker, who was the son of Stephen D. Stryker and Mary (Bogart) Stryker.[1267] Benjamin S. Stryker and Elizabeth (Williamson) Stryker had the following children: Lucretia Stryker, who died young; Harriet Stryker, who married Garret Hageman; Stephen Stryker, who died young; **Stephen Williamson Stryker**, who married, first, Mary Fisher, and second, Annie Smith.[1268] Stephen Williamson Stryker was a cousin of all of the other Strykers of Chicago and Morgan County in this book, who were descended from the **John Stryker and Lydia Cornell branch** of the family.

The Stryker-Cornell Family of New Jersey, Morgan County, and Chicago

The **John Stryker and Lydia (Cornell) Stryker family** produced three distinct, but closely related, familial branches which became extremely prominent in the histories of Chicago and Morgan County, Illinois: the **Stryker-Harrison-Addy-Dart-McClure-Taylor branch**; the **Stryker-Friese-Brooks-Downs-Ingraham-Pettit branch**; and the **Stryker-Pierson-Livingston-Goss-Root branch**. The Stryker-Harrison-Addy-Dart-McClure-Taylor branch included both the Stryker-McClure-Taylor family and the Stryker-Pierson family, both of which achieved prominence in Chicago business and industry, in Jacksonville, Morgan County, Illinois, and in Carrolton, Greene County, Illinois.

The **Stryker-Friese-Brooks-Downs-Ingraham-Pettit branch** included these families in both Chicago and Kenosha, Wisconsin. The **Stryker-Pierson branch** included the Stryker, Woolsey, Livingston, Goss, and Root families of Chicago and New York. There are two Stryker-Pierson families that are closely related, but are nevertheless separate branches: first, the **Ornan Pierson and Maria (Stryker) Pierson family** of Carrollton, Illinois, and Chicago, which was a familial subset of the **Stryker-Harrison-Addy-Dart-McClure-Taylor branch**; and second, the **Daniel Perrine Stryker and Harriet (Pierson) Stryker family** of New Jersey, New York, and Chicago, which included Chicago and New York railroad founder John Stryker, Rev. Melancthon Woolsey Stryker, and many others.

John Stryker (1740-1786) married Lydia Cornell (1746-1795). John Stryker served in the Revolutionary War, was Captain of a Light Horse Troop in Somerset County, New Jersey, and was connected to the State Troops of New Jersey. John

[1266] Hutchinson, Elmer T. (1949 and 2008). Documents Relating To The Colonial History Of The State Of New Jersey, Calendar Of New Jersey Wills, Vol. XII. (1810-1813). P. 425. Westminster, MD: Heritage Books. Google Books.
[1267] Stryker, William Scudder. (1887). Genealogy of the Stryker Family. Pages not marked. Camden, NJ: Sinnickson Chew, Printer.
[1268] Stryker, William Scudder. (1887). Genealogy of the Stryker Family. Pages not marked. Camden, NJ: Sinnickson Chew, Printer.

served as Aide-de-Camp to Gen. George Washington, and once ambushed and captured Gen. Cornwallis and his British troops in New Jersey, sent them running, captured the goods left behind, and gave them to General Washington and his men.[1269] John Stryker was a prominent businessman and farmer, and a member of the Dutch Church. The epitaph upon Stryker's gravestone reads as follows: "In memory of John Stryker, who died March 25, 1786, aged 46 years and 23 days. God my Redeemer lives, And often from the skies Looks down and watches all my dust. Till he shall bid it rise."[1270]

John Stryker and Lydia (Cornell) Stryker had the following children: Mary Stryker, who married Jacobus Quick; Peter I. Stryker, who married, first, Magdalena Schenk, and second, Maria Mercer; John I. Stryker, who married Maria Van Cleef; **Henry Stryker, who married Esther Harrison**; Abraham Stryker, who married Margaret Waterhouse; Anna Stryker, who married Daniel S. Gurnee; Lydia Stryker, who married John Tomby; Jacobus Stryker, who died young; **James I. Stryker, who married Margaret Friese**; and **Daniel Perrine Stryker, who married Harriet Pierson**.[1271]

Dr. Peter I. Stryker (1766-1859), son of Capt. John Stryker and Lydia (Cornell) Stryker, was a medical doctor of Millstone and Somerville, New Jersey. He was Sheriff of Somerset County and a member of the New Jersey Senate. Dr. Stryker served as Governor of New Jersey for an interim period.[1272] Active in military service, Dr. Stryker was promoted to the rank of Major General in New Jersey.[1273] Dr. Peter Stryker was a brother of Henry Stryker, whose descendants include the Strykers and Taylors of Morgan County and Chicago, and the Strykers and Piersons of Carrollton and Chicago. Peter was also the brother of James I. Stryker and Daniel Perrine Stryker, both of whom had descendants who were prominent in Chicago history, as is discussed herein.[1274] Dr. Peter Stryker helped start the copper mining industry of New Jersey.[1275] Stryker co-founded and co-owned the

---

[1269] Stryker family historical records.

[1270] Stryker, William Scudder. (1887). Genealogy of the Stryker Family. Pages not marked. Camden, NJ: Sinnickson Chew, Printer.

[1271] Stryker, William Scudder. (1887). Genealogy of the Stryker Family. Pages not marked. Camden, NJ: Sinnickson Chew, Printer.

[1272] Snell, James P. (1881). History of Hunterdon and Somerset Counties, New Jersey, With Illustrations and Biographical Sketches of Its Prominent Men and Pioneers. P. 637. Philadelphia, PA: Everts & Peck. Google Books.

[1273] Snell, James P. (1881). History of Hunterdon and Somerset Counties, New Jersey, With Illustrations and Biographical Sketches of Its Prominent Men and Pioneers. P. 637. Philadelphia, PA: Everts & Peck. Google Books.

[1274] Stryker, William Scudder. (1887). Genealogy of the Stryker Family. Pages not marked. Camden, NJ: Sinnickson Chew, Printer.

[1275] Snell, James P. (1881). History of Hunterdon and Somerset Counties, New Jersey. P. 680. Philadelphia, PA: Everts & Peck. Google Books.

Washington Mining Company and the Somerville Mining Company.[1276] These New Jersey copper mining companies developed the copper mining economy of New Jersey and shipped copper ore in barrels to markets as far as Boston.[1277] Stryker and his partner, Albert Cammann, constructed a drift mine in the Appalachian foothills of Somerville, and mined copper from the Kearney-Stryker-Cammann Tract.[1278] Dr. Peter Stryker and Albert Cammann also founded the Flemington Mining Company of Hunterdon County in 1834. The Flemington Mining Company was another copper mining company and was chartered to operate with an original stock money of up to, but not more than, $500,000.[1279] Interestingly, the Bunns of Springfield and Chicago came from Hunterdon County to Illinois. Dr. Peter Stryker's brother, Henry Stryker, became the patriarch of two Stryker families of Chicago: the Stryker-Addy-McClure-Taylor family, and the Stryker-Pierson family, which are discussed in Chapter 6.

The Stryker-Harrison Branch of Morgan County and Chicago

Henry Stryker, son of Capt. John Stryker and Lydia (Cornell) Stryker, married Esther Harrison. The following children were born to them: Hannah Stryker; John Stryker; Maria Stryker, who married William Corbit; Charlotte Stryker, who married Dr. Daniel Babbitt; Henry Stryker, who died young; Lucetta Stryker; **Henry Stryker, who married, first, Anna Addy, second, Elizabeth Addy, and third, Sophia Amelia Dart**; and Abram Stryker.[1280] For the Chicago history of the Henry Stryker branch of the family, see Chapter 6, *Sprinters of the Steel Track*.

The Stryker-Pierson Branch of Chicago

Daniel Perrine Stryker, son of Capt. John Stryker and Lydia (Cornell) Stryker, was a graduate of the College of New Jersey (Princeton). He married Harriet Pierson. The children born to Daniel and Harriet (Pierson) Stryker were the following: Mary Stryker; **John Stryker, who married Frances Hubbard**; Phebe Nutman Stryker; Daniel Perrine Stryker; and **Isaac Pierson Stryker, who married Alida Livingston Woolsey**.[1281] For the history of John Stryker (1808-

---

[1276] Snell, James P. (1881). History of Hunterdon and Somerset Counties, New Jersey. P. 680. Philadelphia, PA: Everts & Peck. Google Books.

[1277] Snell, James P. (1881). History of Hunterdon and Somerset Counties, New Jersey. P. 680. Philadelphia, PA: Everts & Peck. Google Books.

[1278] Snell, James P. (1881). History of Hunterdon and Somerset Counties, New Jersey. P. 680. Philadelphia, PA: Everts & Peck. Google Books.

[1279] Acts of the Fifty-Seventh General Assembly of the State of New Jersey. (1832). Pp. 133-135. Trenton, NJ. Google Books.

[1280] Stryker, William Scudder. (1887). Genealogy of the Stryker Family. Pages not marked. Camden, NJ: Sinnickson Chew, Printer.

[1281] Stryker, William Scudder. (1887). Genealogy of the Stryker Family. Pages not marked. Camden, NJ: Sinnickson Chew, Printer.

1885), who was one of the founders of the Chicago railroad industry, see Chapter 1, *Genesis of a Great Lakes Frontier*. For the history of the Rev. Isaac Pierson Stryker and Alida (Woolsey) Stryker branch, see Chapter 2, *Builders of the Downtown*. The next section will discuss the history of the Stryker-Friese-Brooks-Downs-Ingraham-Pettit family of Chicago.

<u>The Stryker-Friese-Brooks-Downs-Ingraham-Pettit Branch of Chicago</u>

James I. Stryker, son of Capt. John Stryker and Lydia (Cornell) Stryker, married Ann Margaret Friese. The following children were born to them: Daniel Perrine Stryker, who married Mary Yates; Adam F. Stryker; John Stryker; Charlotte Stryker, who married L. D. Harrison; Lydia Cornell Stryker, who married Nathan Lawton; **James Monroe Stryker, who married Ellen Maria Brooks**; Henry F. Stryker, who married Mary A. Hart; and Abram J. Stryker.[1282] The Chicago history of James Monroe Stryker, Ellen Maria Brooks, and their many descendants is discussed in this chapter (infra).

The Strykers of Hyde Park, Kenwood, Woodlawn, and Douglas

James Monroe Stryker (1819-1887) was the son of James I. Stryker and Ann Margaret (Friese) Stryker and became a father of early Chicago industry and infrastructure. James Monroe Stryker co-founded the Illinois Pneumatic Gas Company of Chicago in 1869.[1283] The purpose of the early Chicago fuel and power corporation was the manufacture and sale of gas from petroleum products, as well as the manufacture and sale of gas and gas distribution machinery.[1284] In addition to having been an early settler of Chicago, James Monroe Stryker also was one of the pioneers of Kenosha, Wisconsin.[1285] In 1845, Stryker married Ellen Maria

---

[1282] Stryker, William Scudder. (1887). Genealogy of the Stryker Family. Pages not marked. Camden, NJ: Sinnickson Chew, Printer.

[1283] Private Laws of the State of Illinois, Passed by the Twenty-Sixth General Assembly, Convened January 4, 1869. (1869). Vol. II. Springfield, IL: Illinois Journal Printing Office. Pp. 391-392. Google Books; Call, Andrew Taylor. (2016). Faded Bricks: Old Family Tales from the South Side of Chicago. Hyde Park History, Vol. 38, (No. 4), Pp. 1-7. Chicago, IL: Hyde Park Historical Society.

[1284] Private Laws of the State of Illinois, Passed by the Twenty-Sixth General Assembly, Convened January 4, 1869. (1869). Vol. II. Springfield, IL: Illinois Journal Printing Office. Pp. 391-392. Google Books; Call, Andrew Taylor. (2016). Faded Bricks: Old Family Tales from the South Side of Chicago. Hyde Park History, Vol. 38, (No. 4), Pp. 1-7. Chicago, IL: Hyde Park Historical Society.

[1285] Lyman, Francis H. (1916). The City of Kenosha and Kenosha County, Wisconsin. Vol. II. P. 444. Chicago, IL: The S. J. Clarke Publishing Company. Google Books; Call, Andrew Taylor. (2016). Faded Bricks: Old Family Tales from the South Side of Chicago. Hyde Park History, Vol. 38, (No. 4), Pp. 1-7. Chicago, IL: Hyde Park Historical Society.

Brooks at Kenosha.[1286] In the year 1865, Stryker contributed to the fossil fuel industry of Wisconsin when he co-founded the Kenosha Oil-Mining and Manufacturing Company.[1287] This corporation was established for the purpose of drilling and exploration for petroleum in Wisconsin, and was chartered with an original stock money of $500,000.[1288]

The Stryker family long maintained close and active association with both Kenosha and Chicago, as can be seen from the fact that multiple children of James Monroe Stryker and Ellen Brooks Stryker resided in Kenwood and Woodlawn close to the turn of the Twentieth Century.[1289] The children of James Monroe Stryker and Ellen Maria (Brooks) Stryker included James Monroe Stryker, Jr., Louis Harvey Stryker, Ellen Amelia Stryker, May Isabella Stryker, Carrie Warburton Stryker, Eva Stryker, Ida Eugenie Stryker, John Brooks Stryker, and others.[1290] John Brooks Stryker (1858-1882), a resident of both Chicago and Kenosha, died at the age of 23.[1291] James Monroe Stryker, Sr., founded and owned Stryker & Company, which was a large garment retail company that was located in the Chicago downtown at the time of the Civil War.[1292] James also served as a Delegate to the Chicago River and Harbor Convention in July of 1847.[1293]

[1286] Parsons, Henry. (1920). Parsons Family: Descendants of Cornet Joseph Parsons. Vol. 2. Pp. 290-291. New Haven, CT: The Tuttle, Morehouse & Taylor Co. Google Books; Call, Andrew Taylor. (2016). Faded Bricks: Old Family Tales from the South Side of Chicago. Hyde Park History, Vol. 38, (No. 4), Pp. 1-7. Chicago, IL: Hyde Park Historical Society.

[1287] Acts of a General Nature Passed by the Legislature of Wisconsin, In the Year 1865, Together with Joint Resolutions and Memorials. (1865). Madison, WI: William J. Park, State Printer—Capitol Office. Pp. 173-175. Google Books; Call, Andrew Taylor. (2016). Faded Bricks: Old Family Tales from the South Side of Chicago. Hyde Park History, Vol. 38, (No. 4), Pp. 1-7. Chicago, IL: Hyde Park Historical Society.

[1288] Acts of a General Nature Passed by the Legislature of Wisconsin, In the Year 1865, Together with Joint Resolutions and Memorials. (1865). Madison, WI: William J. Park, State Printer—Capitol Office. Pp. 173-175. Google Books; Call, Andrew Taylor. (2016). Faded Bricks: Old Family Tales from the South Side of Chicago. Hyde Park History, Vol. 38, (No. 4), Pp. 1-7. Chicago, IL: Hyde Park Historical Society.

[1289] The Chicago Blue Book of Selected Names of Chicago and Suburban Towns. (1899). Chicago, IL: The Chicago Directory Company. Pp. 234, 677. Google Books; Call, Andrew Taylor. (2016). Faded Bricks: Old Family Tales from the South Side of Chicago. Hyde Park History, Vol. 38, (No. 4), Pp. 1-7. Chicago, IL: Hyde Park Historical Society.

[1290] Parsons, Henry. (1920). Parsons Family: Descendants of Cornet Joseph Parsons. Vol. 2. P. 291. New Haven, CT: The Tuttle, Morehouse & Taylor Co. Google Books; Call, Andrew Taylor. (2016). Faded Bricks: Old Family Tales from the South Side of Chicago. Hyde Park History, Vol. 38, (No. 4), Pp. 1-7. Chicago, IL: Hyde Park Historical Society.

[1291] Findagrave.com. John Brooks Stryker. Green Ridge Cemetery, Kenosha, Wisconsin.

[1292] Stryker family history records and historic Chicago City directories.

[1293] Hall, William Mosley, et al. (1882). Chicago River-And-Harbor-Convention: An Account Of Its Origin And Proceedings. P. 67. Chicago, IL: Fergus Printing Company. Google Books.

James Monroe Stryker, Jr., of Woodlawn and Hyde Park

James Monroe Stryker, Jr. worked in the life insurance industry while residing in Chicago, having served as General Agent for John Hancock Mutual Life Insurance Company for Chicago and Northern Illinois.[1294] In 1895, Stryker resided at 4627 Lake Avenue and worked at an office located at 79 Dearborn.[1295] Stryker additionally owned a mechanical invention company in Chicago and was a patented inventor and entrepreneur, having acquired patents for diverse classes of machinery. Stryker received a patent for a bag closing and fastening mechanism known as "The Bag-Tie," in approximately the year 1909. For this fastening innovation he received United States Patent Number 915,503.[1296] In 1885, Stryker received a patent for a "Combined Wash-Stand and Bureau," a species of multipurpose furniture whose purposes included both sanitation and storage.[1297] For this innovative and multipurpose form of furniture, Stryker was granted Patent 323,970 A.[1298] In 1900, Stryker received United States Patent Number 683,867 A for an improved class of butler's knife.[1299] At the time when James Monroe Stryker, Jr., received the patent for the improved form of butler's knife in the year 1900, he most probably resided at 6030 Woodlawn Avenue in the Woodlawn community and on the edge of the Midway Plaisance. The probability of this place of residence for Stryker at that time is corroborated by the fact that Stryker resided at this same place as of the end of 1899, along with several of the other Stryker family relatives.[1300]

[1294] Hayden, H. R. (Ed.). The Annual Cyclopedia of Insurance in the United States: 1895-1896. (1896). Hartford, CT: H. R. Hayden. P. 20. Google Books; Call, Andrew Taylor. (2016). Faded Bricks: Old Family Tales from the South Side of Chicago. Hyde Park History, Vol. 38, (No. 4), Pp. 1-7. Chicago, IL: Hyde Park Historical Society.

[1295] 1895 Chicago Directory.

[1296] Official Gazette of the United States Patent Office. Vol. CXL. (March, 1909). P. 660. Washington, D.C.: Government Printing Office. Google Books; Call, Andrew Taylor. (2016). Faded Bricks: Old Family Tales from the South Side of Chicago. Hyde Park History, Vol. 38, (No. 4), Pp. 1-7. Chicago, IL: Hyde Park Historical Society.

[1297] See: United States Patent 323,970 A. Google Patents; Call, Andrew Taylor. (2016). Faded Bricks: Old Family Tales from the South Side of Chicago. Hyde Park History, Vol. 38, (No. 4), Pp. 1-7. Chicago, IL: Hyde Park Historical Society.

[1298] See: United States Patent 323,970 A. Google Patents; Call, Andrew Taylor. (2016). Faded Bricks: Old Family Tales from the South Side of Chicago. Hyde Park History, Vol. 38, (No. 4), Pp. 1-7. Chicago, IL: Hyde Park Historical Society.

[1299] See: United States Patent 683,867 A. Google Patents; Call, Andrew Taylor. (2016). Faded Bricks: Old Family Tales from the South Side of Chicago. Hyde Park History, Vol. 38, (No. 4), Pp. 1-7. Chicago, IL: Hyde Park Historical Society.

[1300] The Chicago Blue Book of Selected Names of Chicago and Suburban Towns. (1899). P. 677. Chicago, IL: The Chicago Directory Company, Publishers. Babel and Hathitrust; Call, Andrew Taylor. (2016). Faded Bricks: Old Family Tales from the South Side of Chicago. Hyde Park History, Vol. 38, (No. 4), Pp. 1-7. Chicago, IL: Hyde Park Historical Society.

In 1901, Stryker was the Chicago Representative of the Mutual Life Insurance Company of New York and worked from an office at the Tacoma Building.[1301] He continued to work as an insurance agent in 1909, and resided that year at 3907 Vincennes Avenue, near the border of the Douglas community and the Oakland community, and near the Bronzeville neighborhood.[1302]

Ida Eugenie Stryker and Myron Day Downs, Jr. of Kenwood

Ida Eugenie Stryker (1855-1930) of Chicago married Myron Day Downs, Jr. (1845-1936). Myron was the son of Myron Day Downs, Sr., and Lydia Elizabeth Downs. The Downs-Stryker marriage ceremony was performed by our other Stryker cousin, the Reverend Melancthon Woolsey Stryker of Chicago.[1303] Those who attended the Stryker-Downs wedding at Fourth Presbyterian Church were James Monroe Stryker, Charles Downs, Frank Runnels, and Walter Downs.[1304] 210 guests attended the reception party, and a caterer named Eckhardt provided the menu for the party.[1305] Ida wore a trousseau which, "consisted of a white faille francaise, cut a la princess, and trimmed with thread lace and pears."[1306] A collar of white velour fig leaves outlined the corsage bodice.[1307] "She wore a demiveil and carried lilies of the valley."[1308] Myron and Ida spent a lengthy honeymoon in Europe before returning home to Chicago.[1309]

Multiple society parties took place in February, 1890, including events hosted by Mrs. John Villiers Farwell, Mrs. Lyman Gage, and Mrs. W. H. Salisbury, the last of which was attended by Ida Downs, Mrs. S. H. Crane, Mrs. A. Judson Cole, Mrs. Robert Owens, Mrs. Alfred Daniels, Miss Eagle, Miss Irma Smith, Mrs. Theodore E. Elmer, and many others.[1310]

Ida Eugenie (Stryker) Downs and her husband Myron Day Downs, Jr., resided at 4722 Kenwood Avenue in the year 1898,[1311] and maintained this place of

---

[1301] City of Chicago Directory. (1901).

[1302] 1909 Lakeside Directory of Chicago. (1909). Vol. 2.

[1303] Stryker, William Scudder. (1887). Genealogical Record of the Strycker Family. P. 88. Camden, NJ: Sinnickson, Chew, Printer. Google Books; Call, Andrew Taylor. (2016). Faded Bricks: Old Family Tales from the South Side of Chicago. Hyde Park History, Vol. 38, (No. 4), Pp. 1-7. Chicago, IL: Hyde Park Historical Society.

[1304] The Inter Ocean. (April 21, 1886). P. 7. Newspapers.com.

[1305] The Inter Ocean. (April 21, 1886). P. 7. Newspapers.com.

[1306] The Inter Ocean. (April 21, 1886). P. 7. Newspapers.com.

[1307] The Inter Ocean. (April 21, 1886). P. 7. Newspapers.com.

[1308] The Inter Ocean. (April 21, 1886). P. 7. Newspapers.com.

[1309] The Inter Ocean. (April 21, 1886). P. 7. Newspapers.com.

[1310] Chicago Tribune. (February 15, 1890). P. 2. Newspapers.com.

[1311] Brockett, Hattie Nourse, & Hatcher, Georgia Stockton. (1898). Directory of the National Society of the Daughters of the American Revolution. P. 126. Google Books; Call, Andrew Taylor. (2016). Faded Bricks: Old Family Tales from the South Side of

residence probably continuously at least through the year 1918. Ida (Stryker) Downs engaged actively in civic life in Chicago, having been a member of the Chicago Woman's Club.[1312] The Chicago Woman's Club was an organization whose purposes included societal reform and social improvement.[1313] The Chicago Woman's Club, whose membership included the Chicago social reformer, Jane Addams, contributed importantly and influentially to the creation of, "the first juvenile court in the United States."[1314] Ida also held a life membership in the Chicago Chapter of the National Society of the Daughters of the American Revolution.[1315] When Ida was a life member of the Chicago Chapter, the Chapter officers included Mrs. Robert Hall Wiles as Regent, Mrs. J. A. Coleman as Vice-Regent, Miss Helen R. Gilbert as Recording Secretary, Mrs. Charles F. Millspaugh as Corresponding Secretary, Miss Eliza Hosmer as Registrar, Mrs. Frederick W. Lee as Treasurer, and Mrs. John R. Wilson as Historian.[1316] Myron and Ida visited the Low Mansion resort in Bradford, Vermont, in the late summer of 1902.[1317]

Ida Stryker Downs also was a member of the Chicago South Side Club, an organization which was located in the Kenwood community at the, "southwest corner of Woodlawn Avenue and Forty-Sixth Street."[1318] The Chicago South Side Club was an organization whose purpose included the confrontation and analysis of social issues affecting women in Chicago, as was proven by the Club's efforts in the year 1914 to survey and understand sources of, "conditions demoralizing to

Chicago. Hyde Park History, Vol. 38, (No. 4), Pp. 1-7. Chicago, IL: Hyde Park Historical Society.

[1312] Thirty-ninth Annual Announcement of the Chicago Woman's Club. (1915-1916). P. 98. Google Books; Call, Andrew Taylor. (2016). Faded Bricks: Old Family Tales from the South Side of Chicago. Hyde Park History, Vol. 38, (No. 4), Pp. 1-7. Chicago, IL: Hyde Park Historical Society.

[1313] Knupfer, Anne Meis. (2005). Clubs, Women's. The Electronic Encyclopedia of Chicago. Encyclopedia of Chicago History online; Call, Andrew Taylor. (2016). Faded Bricks: Old Family Tales from the South Side of Chicago. Hyde Park History, Vol. 38, (No. 4), Pp. 1-7. Chicago, IL: Hyde Park Historical Society.

[1314] Knupfer, Anne Meis. (2005). Clubs, Women's. Para. 2. The Electronic Encyclopedia of Chicago. Encyclopedia of Chicago History online; Call, Andrew Taylor. (2016). Faded Bricks: Old Family Tales from the South Side of Chicago. Hyde Park History, Vol. 38, (No. 4), Pp. 1-7. Chicago, IL: Hyde Park Historical Society.

[1315] The American Monthly Magazine. (January-June, 1901). Vol. XVIII. P. 973. Washington, D.C.: National Society of the Daughters of the American Revolution. Google Books.

[1316] Officers, Directors, and Programs of the Chicago Chapter of the National Society of Daughters of the American Revolution. (1900-1901). P. 7. Google Books.

[1317] The United Opinion. (September 5, 1902). P. 1. Newspapers.com.

[1318] Directory and Register of Women's Clubs: City of Chicago and Vicinity. (1915). Pp. 149-152. Chicago, IL: Linden Brothers & Harry H. De Clerque. Google Books; Call, Andrew Taylor. (2016). Faded Bricks: Old Family Tales from the South Side of Chicago. Hyde Park History, Vol. 38, (No. 4), Pp. 1-7. Chicago, IL: Hyde Park Historical Society.

women and girls in the saloons of Chicago."[1319] Ida Downs died November 15, 1930, nine days prior to her sister, Mary (Stryker) Ingraham.[1320] Ida was still a resident of 4722 Kenwood Avenue in the Kenwood community at her death. Ida's funeral services were provided by the chapel at 4227 Cottage Grove Avenue, on Tuesday, November 18, 1930, at 3:00 P.M.[1321] Ida was interred at Green Ridge Cemetery in Kenosha.[1322]

Myron survived Ida and lived another six years, dying in November, 1936.[1323] Myron worked for 57 years for the John V. Farwell Company, and was a member of the Kenwood Church and the Mayflower Society.[1324] Myron and Ida were members of the South Shore Country Club, located in the South Shore community along Lake Michigan, at the southern end of Jackson Park.[1325] The South Shore Country Club was organized in 1906 and closed in 1974. The club buildings and grounds now serve as the South Shore Cultural Center. The old club hosted, among many other events, card games and knitting parties, called knitting bees, according to the Chicago publication known as the *Paint, Oil And Drug Review*, which had been established in 1883.[1326] The funeral services for Myron Day Downs, Jr., were provided by the funeral home at 5708 Madison Street, and Downs was taken to Kenosha to be buried with Ida at Green Ridge Cemetery.[1327]

Louis Harvey Stryker of Woodlawn and The Loop

Louis Harvey Stryker (1861-1922) resided in the Woodlawn community at 6030 Woodlawn in the year 1898, along with his brother, James Monroe Stryker, Jr., and their mother, Ellen M. (Brooks) Stryker.[1328] In 1901, Louis Stryker resided at the Wyoming Hotel of Chicago, and worked as a clerk at 215/201 Dearborn.[1329]

[1319] Chicago Public Library Book Bulletin. (1913). Vols. 3-4. P. 60. Chicago, IL: Chicago Public Library. Google Books; Call, Andrew Taylor. (2016). Faded Bricks: Old Family Tales from the South Side of Chicago. Hyde Park History, Vol. 38, (No. 4), Pp. 1-7. Chicago, IL: Hyde Park Historical Society.
[1320] Chicago Tribune. (November 17, 1930). P. 20. Newspapers.com.
[1321] Chicago Tribune. (November 17, 1930). P. 20. Newspapers.com.
[1322] Chicago Tribune. (November 17, 1930). P. 20. Newspapers.com; Findagrave.com. Ida Eugenie (Stryker) Downs.
[1323] Chicago Tribune. (November 15, 1936). P. 20. Newspapers.com.
[1324] Chicago Tribune. (November 15, 1936). P. 20. Newspapers.com.
[1325] Chicago Tribune. (November 15, 1936). P. 20. Newspapers.com.
[1326] Paint, Oil And Drug Review. (1917). P. 96. Chicago, IL. Google Books.
[1327] Chicago Tribune. (November 15, 1936). P. 20. Newspapers.com; Findagrave.com. Myron Day Downs, Jr.
[1328] The Chicago Blue Book of Selected Names of Chicago and Suburban Towns. (1899). Chicago, IL: Chicago Directory Company. Pp. 234, 677. Google Books; Call, Andrew Taylor. (2016). Faded Bricks: Old Family Tales from the South Side of Chicago. Hyde Park History, Vol. 38, (No. 4), Pp. 1-7. Chicago, IL: Hyde Park Historical Society.
[1329] 1901 City of Chicago Directory. (1901).

Louis worked as a stenographer at the Kaiserhof Hotel in 1906 and in 1909, presumably having held the same position through the intervening years.[1330] The Kaiserhof was another downtown hotel, and was located at 262 to 274 Clark Street.[1331] Unfortunately, very little biographical record remains of Louis Stryker as of the time of the writing of this book.

<u>Mary Isabelle Stryker and Robert F. Ingraham</u>

<u>of the Douglas and Oakland Communities of Chicago</u>

Mary Isabelle Stryker (1863-1930) married Robert F. Ingraham, who was a New York native who had moved to Chicago in the nineteenth century. Robert worked as the Northern Illinois Sales Representative of the Chicago Stove Works Company in 1897.[1332] John F. Cady served as the Chicago Sales Representative at the same time.[1333] As of December 23, 1899, Robert was Illinois Sales Representative for Bergstrom Brothers & Company.[1334] In 1900 Mary Isabelle (Stryker) Ingraham and her husband, Robert F. Ingraham, resided with many other people at a boarding house on Wabash Avenue in the South Town district of Chicago, in the 2nd Ward, and in Census Enumeration District 44.[1335] Robert worked as a salesman in 1900.[1336] Mary and Robert resided at 3907 Vincennes Avenue in 1906.[1337] This is located within the Douglas community on the south side of the city, and near the Bronzeville neighborhood. The Ingrahams continued to reside at 3907 Vincennes Avenue in 1910.[1338] Robert owned some source of business income in 1910, as indicated by the occupation description provided in the 1910 *United States Census* report, although the relevant handwriting of the census enumerator was not entirely clear at the time of reference.[1339]

Robert and Mary were dog enthusiasts and registered their Airedale Terrier stud, Briar Bramble, with the American Kennel Club.[1340] Briar Bramble held American

[1330] 1909 Lakeside Directory of Chicago. (1909). Vol. 2; City of Chicago Directory. (1906).

[1331] 1909 Lakeside Directory of Chicago. (1909). Vol. 2; City of Chicago Directory. (1906).

[1332] The Metal Worker. (January-June, 1897). Vol. 47. P. 38. New York, NY: David Williams Company. Google Books.

[1333] The Metal Worker. (January-June, 1897). Vol. 47. P. 38. New York, NY: David Williams Company. Google Books.

[1334] The Metal Worker. (December 23, 1899). P. 29. Google Books.

[1335] 1900 United States Census. Ancestry.com.

[1336] 1900 United States Census. Ancestry.com.

[1337] City of Chicago Directory. (1906).

[1338] 1910 United States Census. Ancestry.com.

[1339] 1910 United States Census. Ancestry.com.

[1340] American Kennel Club Stud Book. (January 1-December 31, 1910). Vol. 27. P. 8. New York, NY: The American Kennel Club, Inc. Google Books.

Kennel Club registration number 136,367, and was black with tan and grizzle colors.[1341] The dog was whelped April 10, 1909, and was by Strathearn Barkerend Monitor (American Kennel Club 110,719) out of Gamecock's Lassie (American Kennel Club 111,515).[1342] The breeder was Leroy J. Loker of Batavia, Illinois.[1343] Robert died March 4, 1919, and the family held a private funeral.[1344] Mary continued to reside at 3907 Vincennes Avenue in 1920, where her brother James Monroe Stryker shared the rented apartment with her.[1345] The 1920 *United States Census* listed no jobs for either Mary or James.[1346] The Vincennes Avenue address was located in Ward 3 of the city in 1920, and within Census Enumeration District 132.[1347] Mary died in 1930 and was interred at Green Ridge Cemetery in Kenosha, Wisconsin. Her father, James Monroe Stryker, had been a founding industrialist, businessman, and civic leader of Kenosha, in addition to having been an important and early Chicago businessman, industrialist, and inventor.[1348]

John Stryker and the Great Chicago Frog War

The crossing of the Lake Shore and Michigan Southern Railroad Company and the Illinois Central Railroad Company was located in what was then Hyde Park Township, and what is presently known as the community of Greater Grand Crossing.[1349] The Chicago community of Greater Grand Crossing takes its name from this crossroads, which was the place of a terrible and fatal occurrence in 1853.[1350] A collision that involved a Michigan Southern train and an Illinois Central train took place in 1853, causing the death of 18 people and the injury of 40 other people.[1351] Historian Wallace Best described the history of the crossing, and stated that Roswell Mason constructed railroads for the Illinois Central across the Lake Shore and Michigan Southern line at a place now located at 75th Street and South Chicago Avenue.[1352]

Chicago lawyer and land developer Paul Cornell developed the area around the railroad crossing, and named the community "Grand Crossing," because of the two

[1341] American Kennel Club Stud Book. (January 1-December 31, 1910). Vol. 27. P. 8. New York, NY: The American Kennel Club, Inc. Google Books.

[1342] American Kennel Club Stud Book. (January 1-December 31, 1910). Vol. 27. P. 8. New York, NY: The American Kennel Club, Inc. Google Books.

[1343] American Kennel Club Stud Book. (January 1-December 31, 1910). Vol. 27. P. 8. New York, NY: The American Kennel Club, Inc. Google Books.

[1344] Chicago Tribune. (March 8, 1919). P. 15. Newspapers.com.

[1345] 1920 United States Census. Ancestry.com.

[1346] 1920 United States Census. Ancestry.com.

[1347] 1920 United States Census. Ancestry.com.

[1348] Findagrave.com. Mary Isabelle (Stryker) Ingraham. Green Ridge Cemetery.

[1349] Best, Wallace. (2004). Greater Grand Crossing. Encyclopedia of Chicago (online).

[1350] Best, Wallace. (2004). Greater Grand Crossing. Encyclopedia of Chicago (online).

[1351] Best, Wallace. (2004). Greater Grand Crossing. Encyclopedia of Chicago (online).

[1352] Best, Wallace. (2004). Greater Grand Crossing. Encyclopedia of Chicago (online).

named railroad company routes that intersected at the place.[1353] Therefore, despite the catastrophe that took place at the grand crossing of the two early Chicago railroads, a community would spring forth from the place, and remains today the large Chicago community of Greater Grand Crossing.[1354] Paul Cornell built a community on the industrial infrastructure laid by John Stryker, Elisha Litchfield, John B. Jervis, James F. Joy, and the other early Chicago-Michigan-Ohio-New York railroad fathers.[1355] The Chicago frog war was due to the disputes over the rights of way of the old Stryker and Illinois Central crossing in this part of Hyde Park Township, and this crossroads involved the piece of railroad infrastructure known as a frog. The frog is a railroad element that is used in the construction of rail crossings. Since the railroad war was fought between two companies over the rights of way associated with the railroad crossing, the war necessarily pertained to railroad frogs. In summary, the old Stryker crossroads would later lead to the foundation of the community of Greater Grand Crossing by Paul Cornell.[1356]

The Stryker Empire of Chicago, Ohio, Michigan, Indiana, and New York

John Stryker, grandson of Capt. John Stryker and Lydia (Cornell) Stryker, served as one of the preeminent industrialists whose railroad development projects enabled Chicago to become the greatest and most important railroad center of the world.[1357] Stryker co-founded and built the Michigan Southern Railroad Company, served as a member of the board of directors of the Michigan Southern Railroad Company, and thereby spearheaded the construction and development of the first railroad company to connect Chicago to the east coast.[1358] Stryker also served as President of the Michigan Southern Railroad Company.[1359] He and many other business partners founded the Northern Indiana & Chicago Railroad Company, the

---

[1353] Best, Wallace. (2004). Greater Grand Crossing. Encyclopedia of Chicago (online).
[1354] Best, Wallace. (2004). Greater Grand Crossing. Encyclopedia of Chicago (online).
[1355] Best, Wallace. (2004). Greater Grand Crossing. Encyclopedia of Chicago (online).
[1356] Best, Wallace. (2004). Greater Grand Crossing. Encyclopedia of Chicago (online).
[1357] See: Stryker, William Norman. (1979). The Stryker Family in America. Vol. 1. Pp. 141-143. W. N. Stryker, Publisher. Google Books; Call, Andrew Taylor. (2016). Faded Bricks: Old Family Tales from the South Side of Chicago. Hyde Park History, Vol. 38, (No. 4), Pp. 1-7. Chicago, IL: Hyde Park Historical Society.
[1358] Andreas, Alfred Theodore. (1975). History of Chicago. Vol. 1. Pp. 259-260. New York, NY: Arno Press. Google Books; Call, Andrew Taylor. (2016). Faded Bricks: Old Family Tales from the South Side of Chicago. Hyde Park History, Vol. 38, (No. 4), Pp. 1-7. Chicago, IL: Hyde Park Historical Society.
[1359] First Annual Report of the President and Directors of the Lake Shore & Michigan Southern Railway Company to the Stockholders, For the Fiscal Year Ending December 31st, 1870. (1871). P. 57. Cleveland, OH: Fairbanks, Benedict & Company. Google Books; Call, Andrew Taylor. (2016). Faded Bricks: Old Family Tales from the South Side of Chicago. Hyde Park History, Vol. 38, (No. 4), Pp. 1-7. Chicago, IL: Hyde Park Historical Society.

overall infrastructural, transportational, and commercial plan of the entire Stryker railroad network having been to make Chicago a foremost center of railroad industry and railroad cartography.[1360] John Stryker co-founded the Northern Indiana Railroad Company,[1361] and additionally co-founded the consolidated Michigan Southern & Northern Indiana Railroad Company, a company which he served and led also as a member of the board of directors.[1362] Furthermore, John Stryker co-founded the Chicago and Rock Island Railroad Company, which laid the foundations for much of the Beverly, Morgan Park, and Mt. Greenwood communities of the southwest side of Chicago.[1363] Stryker led the company also through service as a member of the board of directors of the Chicago and Rock Island Railroad Company.[1364]

Finally, John Stryker was one of the principal founders of the great New York Central Railroad Company,[1365] a corporation with which Cornelius Vanderbilt was prominently associated. All of these railroad corporations supported the industrial and residential growth of Chicago and Cook County, as well as of the entire Great Lakes region of North America.[1366] The union of Chicago, New York, Michigan, Indiana, and Ohio railroad companies that has been rightly referred to as the

---

[1360] Stryker, William Norman. (1979). The Stryker Family in America. Vol. 1. Pp. 141-143, 550. W. N. Stryker, Publisher. Google Books; Call, Andrew Taylor. (2016). Faded Bricks: Old Family Tales from the South Side of Chicago. Hyde Park History, Vol. 38, (No. 4), Pp. 1-7. Chicago, IL: Hyde Park Historical Society.

[1361] Daniels, E. D. (1904). A Twentieth Century History and Biographical Record of LaPorte County, Indiana. Pp. 69-70. Chicago, IL: The Lewis Publishing Company. Google Books; Call, Andrew Taylor. (2016). Faded Bricks: Old Family Tales from the South Side of Chicago. Hyde Park History, Vol. 38, (No. 4), Pp. 1-7. Chicago, IL: Hyde Park Historical Society.

[1362] Poor, Henry V. (Ed.). (1857). American Railroad Journal: Steam, Navigation, Commerce, Mining, Manufactures. P. 309. New York, NY: J. H. Schultz & Company. Google Books; Call, Andrew Taylor. (2016). Faded Bricks: Old Family Tales from the South Side of Chicago. Hyde Park History, Vol. 38, (No. 4), Pp. 1-7. Chicago, IL: Hyde Park Historical Society.

[1363] Historical information from the Ridge Historical Society of Chicago.

[1364] The Chicago, Rock Island & Pacific Railway System and Representative Employees. (1900). Pp. 70-74. Chicago, IL: Biographical Publishing Company. Google Books; Call, Andrew Taylor. (2016). Faded Bricks: Old Family Tales from the South Side of Chicago. Hyde Park History, Vol. 38, (No. 4), Pp. 1-7. Chicago, IL: Hyde Park Historical Society.

[1365] Stryker, William Norman. (1979). The Stryker Family in America. Vol. 1. Pp. 141-143. W. N. Stryker, Publisher. Google Books; Call, Andrew Taylor. (2016). Faded Bricks: Old Family Tales from the South Side of Chicago. Hyde Park History, Vol. 38, (No. 4), Pp. 1-7. Chicago, IL: Hyde Park Historical Society.

[1366] See: Stryker, William Norman. (1979). The Stryker Family in America. Vol. 1. Pp. 141-143. W. N. Stryker, Publisher. Google Books; Call, Andrew Taylor. (2016). Faded Bricks: Old Family Tales from the South Side of Chicago. Hyde Park History, Vol. 38, (No. 4), Pp. 1-7. Chicago, IL: Hyde Park Historical Society.

"Stryker Empire,"[1367] by historian and relation William Norman Stryker, contributed foundationally and essentially to the commercial and industrial identities of Chicago, Cook County, and the entire Great Lakes railroad corridor from Illinois to the State of New York.[1368] The New York Central Railroad Company, of which Stryker was a major founder and corporate leader,[1369] was the largest corporation in the United States in 1856.[1370] The New York Central Railroad Company also was said to have been the largest corporation in the world at the time of its formation in the year 1853.[1371] Chicago and the Great Lakes both constituted essential elements of the transportational routes and service markets that the Stryker Empire railroad companies collectively possessed and developed.[1372]

John Stryker, Elisha Litchfield, James Joy, and others, as the founders and leaders of the Michigan Southern Railroad Company, led the railroad developments that would enable Paul Cornell to create the Chicago community known as Greater Grand Crossing. The Michigan Southern and the Illinois Central Railroad Company would experience a fatal accident in the infancy of Chicago and Cook County railroading that would lead to the formation of a new community.

[1367] Stryker, William Norman. (1979). The Stryker Family in America. Vol. 1. P. 550. W. N. Stryker, Publisher. Google Books; Call, Andrew Taylor. (2016). Faded Bricks: Old Family Tales from the South Side of Chicago. Hyde Park History, Vol. 38, (No. 4), Pp. 1-7. Chicago, IL: Hyde Park Historical Society.

[1368] See: Stryker, William Norman. (1979). The Stryker Family in America. Vol. 1. Pp. 141-143, 550. W. N. Stryker, Publisher. Google Books; Call, Andrew Taylor. (2016). Faded Bricks: Old Family Tales from the South Side of Chicago. Hyde Park History, Vol. 38, (No. 4), Pp. 1-7. Chicago, IL: Hyde Park Historical Society.

[1369] See: Stryker, William Norman. (1979). The Stryker Family in America. Vol. 1. Pp. 141-143, 550. W. N. Stryker, Publisher. Google Books; Call, Andrew Taylor. (2016). Faded Bricks: Old Family Tales from the South Side of Chicago. Hyde Park History, Vol. 38, (No. 4), Pp. 1-7. Chicago, IL: Hyde Park Historical Society.

[1370] Seavoy, Ronald E. (2006). An Economic History of the United States From 1607 to the Present. P. 148. New York, NY: Routledge. Google Books; Call, Andrew Taylor. (2016). Faded Bricks: Old Family Tales from the South Side of Chicago. Hyde Park History, Vol. 38, (No. 4), Pp. 1-7. Chicago, IL: Hyde Park Historical Society.

[1371] Starr, Timothy. (2012). Railroad Wars of New York State. P. 81. Charleston, SC: The History Press. Google Books; Call, Andrew Taylor. (2016). Faded Bricks: Old Family Tales from the South Side of Chicago. Hyde Park History, Vol. 38, (No. 4), Pp. 1-7. Chicago, IL: Hyde Park Historical Society.

[1372] Moody, John. (1919). Moody's Analyses of Investments: Part 1—Steam Railroads. Pp. 287, 391, 1198. New York, NY: Moody's Investors Service. Google Books; Stryker, William Norman. (1979). The Stryker Family in America. Vol. 1. P. 550. W. N. Stryker, Publisher. Google Books; Call, Andrew Taylor. (2016). Faded Bricks: Old Family Tales from the South Side of Chicago. Hyde Park History, Vol. 38, (No. 4), Pp. 1-7. Chicago, IL: Hyde Park Historical Society.

James Monroe Stryker, Sr.,

and the Illinois Pneumatic Gas Company of Chicago

James Monroe Stryker (1819-1887), grandson of Capt. John Stryker and Lydia (Cornell) Stryker, was a member of my great-grandmother's Stryker family from Chicago and Morgan County, Illinois. The early part of the latter half of the nineteenth century in Chicago proffered evidence of the feverish excitement derivative of progress made in patented power utilities technology. Structured organizational, economic, technological, and industrial development, entrepreneurship, financing, and incorporation indelibly defined and influenced the qualities and modes of Chicago utilities commerce and industry at this time. One corporate organization whose existence constituted testimony of these socioeconomic phenomena in Chicago was the Illinois Pneumatic Gas Company.[1373] Much of the information that concerns this large Chicago industrial corporation derives from the United States Supreme Court opinion in the case of *Illinois Pneumatic Gas Company v. Joseph A. Berry, et al.*[1374] Associate Justice Stephen Johnson Field delivered the judgment and opinion in the case. The opinion narrated an important chapter in the economic history of Chicago and Cook County.[1375]

The Illinois organic statute that contained the act of incorporation for the Illinois Pneumatic Gas Company additionally supplies significant, relevant, and diverse corporate data.[1376] Let us first analyze the law that established the company. The company was incorporated legislatively by the State of Illinois with the name, Illinois Pneumatic Gas Company, on March 24, 1869. The incorporators included James Monroe Stryker, James J. Pettit, Timothy Wright, and Charles W. Drew.[1377]

[1373] AN ACT to incorporate the Illinois Pneumatic Gas Company. (1869). Private Laws of the State of Illinois Passed By The Twenty-Sixth General Assembly, Convened January 4, 1869. Vol. II. Springfield, IL: Illinois Journal Printing Office. Pp. 391-392. Google Books.

[1374] Illinois Pneumatic Gas Company v. Berry. (1885). 113 U.S. 1003-1005. United States Supreme Court Reports. Cases Argued and Decided Before the Supreme Court of the United States. (1886). Rochester, NY: The Lawyers' Co-Operative Publishing Company. Google Books.

[1375] Illinois Pneumatic Gas Company v. Berry. (1885). 113 U.S. 1003-1005. United States Supreme Court Reports. Cases Argued and Decided Before the Supreme Court of the United States. (1886). Rochester, NY: The Lawyers' Co-Operative Publishing Company. Google Books.

[1376] AN ACT to incorporate the Illinois Pneumatic Gas Company. (1869). Private Laws of the State of Illinois Passed By The Twenty-Sixth General Assembly, Convened January 4, 1869. Vol. II. Springfield, IL: Illinois Journal Printing Office. Pp. 391-392. Google Books.

[1377] AN ACT to incorporate the Illinois Pneumatic Gas Company. (1869). Private Laws of the State of Illinois Passed By The Twenty-Sixth General Assembly, Convened January 4, 1869. Vol. II. Springfield, IL: Illinois Journal Printing Office. Pp. 391-392. Google Books.

The first paragraph of the incorporation statute attached to the company multiple statuses, powers, and liabilities. The statute attached to the company the status of body politic with power of succession, in addition to contractual powers. The law gave the company suit and litigation powers, as well as the property-relevant powers by which to effect acquisition, tenure, use and enjoyment, sale, encumbrance, grant, and transfer of interests in real property and personal property.[1378] The law also attached suability to the company.

The commercial purpose of the company defined the scope of the corporate powers enumerated previously and comprised the production and sale of gas for lighting machinery. The A. C. Rand patent in petroleum technology constituted the central value from which the commercial purpose of the company stemmed. The A. C. Rand patent was jointly owned by James M. Stryker, James J. Pettit, Charles W. Drew, and Timothy Wright. The patent granted a monopoly whose scope included the intellectual property rights in multiple related technologies that enabled the extraction of gas from petroleum and petroleum byproducts, and the manufacture of gas production and distribution machinery.[1379] As can be discerned from the historical context from which the company emanated, a joint estate in a petroleum technology patent thus effectuated the commercial purpose of the new Chicago corporation.[1380]

The financial structure of the Illinois Pneumatic Gas Company consisted of a simple equity financing.[1381] Absent from the capitalization clause of the incorporation statute was any reference to debt financing. The organic statute stipulated an initial equity money of $500,000, which was to be divided into five thousand shares, each share valued at $100 par. The process and manner of subscription of the equity capital were to be defined in policies contained in the jurisprudence of anticipatory corporate bylaws.[1382] The statute did not contain a

---

[1378] AN ACT to incorporate the Illinois Pneumatic Gas Company. (1869). Private Laws of the State of Illinois Passed By The Twenty-Sixth General Assembly, Convened January 4, 1869. Vol. II. Springfield, IL: Illinois Journal Printing Office. Pp. 391-392. Google Books.

[1379] AN ACT to incorporate the Illinois Pneumatic Gas Company. (1869). Private Laws of the State of Illinois Passed By The Twenty-Sixth General Assembly, Convened January 4, 1869. Vol. II. Springfield, IL: Illinois Journal Printing Office. Pp. 391-392. Google Books.

[1380] Illinois Pneumatic Gas Company v. Berry. (1885). 113 U.S. 1003-1005. United States Supreme Court Reports. Cases Argued and Decided Before the Supreme Court of the United States. (1886). Rochester, NY: The Lawyers' Co-Operative Publishing Company. Google Books.

[1381] AN ACT to incorporate the Illinois Pneumatic Gas Company. (1869). Private Laws of the State of Illinois Passed By The Twenty-Sixth General Assembly, Convened January 4, 1869. Vol. II. Springfield, IL: Illinois Journal Printing Office. Pp. 391-392. Google Books.

[1382] AN ACT to incorporate the Illinois Pneumatic Gas Company. (1869). Private Laws of the State of Illinois Passed By The Twenty-Sixth General Assembly, Convened

grant of authority for construction of pipes in any public thoroughfares in Chicago. The law contained an express ban on participation in banking activities and established an express limit on the amount of real estate that the corporation could own at any point in time; the limit was $50,000.[1383] The limit served to ensure that the company leadership personnel remained loyal to the chartered commercial purpose. The statute contained a grant of authority for design and adoption of bylaws necessary for performance of the business purpose of the company. The company possessed the authority to design and use a corporate seal.[1384]

The geographical scope of the A. C. Rand patent included Wisconsin, Illinois, Michigan, and Iowa. The incorporators adopted bylaws in September of 1869. Pursuant to the bylaws, the company elected nine persons to the board of directors. Mahlon S. Frost served as the first Treasurer and General Manager of the company. Joseph A. Berry served as a member of the board of directors. The company successfully manufactured gas production and distribution machinery, but rapidly experienced economic failure.[1385] After multiple court judgments attached liabilities to the company, the corporate Treasurer and General Manager, Mahlon S. Frost, entered into agreement with the directorate of the company to continue the business of the firm under his management and upon the condition that the members of the corporate leadership structure supply the capital necessary for payment and dissolution of the corporate debts.[1386]

The Lakeside Annual Directory of the City of Chicago for the years 1875 and 1876 listed the address of the Illinois Pneumatic Gas Company as 242 Madison.[1387]

January 4, 1869. Vol. II. Springfield, IL: Illinois Journal Printing Office. Pp. 391-392. Google Books.

[1383] AN ACT to incorporate the Illinois Pneumatic Gas Company. (1869). Private Laws of the State of Illinois Passed By The Twenty-Sixth General Assembly, Convened January 4, 1869. Vol. II. Springfield, IL: Illinois Journal Printing Office. Pp. 391-392. Google Books.

[1384] AN ACT to incorporate the Illinois Pneumatic Gas Company. (1869). Private Laws of the State of Illinois Passed By The Twenty-Sixth General Assembly, Convened January 4, 1869. Vol. II. Springfield, IL: Illinois Journal Printing Office. Pp. 391-392. Google Books.

[1385] Illinois Pneumatic Gas Company v. Berry. (1885). 113 U.S. 1003-1005. United States Supreme Court Reports. Cases Argued and Decided Before the Supreme Court of the United States. (1886). Rochester, NY: The Lawyers' Co-Operative Publishing Company. Google Books.

[1386] Illinois Pneumatic Gas Company v. Berry. (1885). 113 U.S. 1003-1005. United States Supreme Court Reports. Cases Argued and Decided Before the Supreme Court of the United States. (1886). Rochester, NY: The Lawyers' Co-Operative Publishing Company. Google Books.

[1387] The Lakeside Annual Directory of the City of Chicago. (1875-1876). P. 523. Chicago, IL: Donnelley, Loyd And Company. Google Books.

Parker Grace served as the General Agent of the company at this time.[1388] The Illinois Pneumatic Gas Company physically survived the Great Chicago Fire of October 8, 1871, but the physical and economic devastation caused by the Great Chicago Fire had so violently transformed the previously positive commercial situation of the firm that the leadership of the company decided to relocate the company to Detroit, Michigan.[1389] The Illinois Pneumatic Gas Company was subsequently organizationally transformed into the Detroit Heating and Lighting Company.[1390] By the year 1890, the corporation had developed a robust multistate presence in the Great Lakes region of the Midwest, and operated corporate offices in both Detroit and Chicago.[1391] While the company headquarters, though originally located in Chicago, were subsequently transferred to Detroit by the Berry brothers, the company retained a prominent commercial presence in Chicago.[1392] The Chicago office of the company was now located at 88 Lake Street.[1393]

The *Chicago Tribune* contained a report in October of 1869, nearly seven months subsequent to the incorporation of the Illinois Pneumatic Gas Company, in which the original technology manufactured and sold by the company was described.[1394] The Illinois Pneumatic Gas Company contributed an industrial exhibit to the Illinois State Agricultural Fair in 1869. The company exhibit was located in the Mechanics' Hall and consisted of the display of the "combination gas machine."[1395] The corporate office was headquartered at Room 1 of the First National Bank Building in Chicago. Timothy Wright, who served as an incorporator of the firm, served as the company president at this time in 1869.[1396]

[1388] The Lakeside Annual Directory of the City of Chicago. (1875-1876). P. 523. Chicago, IL: Donnelley, Loyd And Company. Google Books.

[1389] Mills, John H. Heat. (1890). Vol. I. Page not specified. Boston, MASS: Press of American Printing and Engraving Co. Google Books.

[1390] Mills, John H. Heat. (1890). Vol. I. Page not specified. Boston, MASS: Press of American Printing and Engraving Co. Google Books.

[1391] Mills, John H. Heat. (1890). Vol. I. Page not specified. Boston, MASS: Press of American Printing and Engraving Co. Google Books.

[1392] Mills, John H. Heat. (1890). Vol. I. Page not specified. Boston, MASS: Press of American Printing and Engraving Co. Google Books.

[1393] Mills, John H. Heat. (1890). Vol. I. Page not specified. Boston, MASS: Press of American Printing and Engraving Co. Google Books.

[1394] Chicago Tribune. (Oct. 4, 1869). Agricultural Fairs. P. 0_1. ProQuest Historical Newspapers.

[1395] Chicago Tribune. (Oct. 4, 1869). Agricultural Fairs. P. 0_1. ProQuest Historical Newspapers.

[1396] Chicago Tribune. (Oct. 4, 1869). Agricultural Fairs. P. 0_1. ProQuest Historical Newspapers. See also: AN ACT to incorporate the Illinois Pneumatic Gas Company. (1869). Private Laws of the State of Illinois Passed By The Twenty-Sixth General Assembly, Convened January 4, 1869. Vol. II. Springfield, IL: Illinois Journal Printing Office. Pp. 391-392. Google Books.

The novel Chicago gas machine functioned by compulsion of air through gasoline vapors in order to effect carburetion of the air, and to render the air adequately combustible for purposes of fuel consumption.[1397] The report distinguished between the Illinois Pneumatic Gas Company process based on the A. C. Rand patent, and the contemporaneous technology and process of coal-gas production. Whereas the latter technology involved the process of decomposition, the process derivative of the Rand patent technology involved the process of compulsion of air through gasoline in order to infuse the air with the necessary combustible element.[1398]

One report in 1877 indicated that the Illinois Pneumatic Gas Company technology could derive 1,000 cubic feet of consumable fuel gas from one gallon of gasoline.[1399] The context and tone of the report indicated that this production ratio was competitive, marketable, and excellent. The report stated that the gas produced by the Illinois Pneumatic Gas Company process possessed a candle-power of 20.5.[1400] Candle-power was a metric of energy power. The technological installation process for the novel company gas production and distribution machinery involved the digging of a pit six feet in depth, and the deposit of a gas tank within the space dug from the ground.[1401] The dugout space would then contain, first, an encapsulative water tank whose purpose was the defensive insulation against potential explosions of the encapsulated gas tank. The gas tank was then deposited within the insulative water tank. A pump and pipe system supplied the compulsion of air through the gasoline tank for the purpose of carburetion of the air for use as consumable fuel.[1402] The dugout contained, therefore, a two-part concentric tank system in which the outer tank was for insulation against explosions, and the inner tank was for storage of the necessary gas resource. The plumbing system transferred the air to, through, and from the tank system and to the house, creating an individualized carbureted gas main for every household that purchased the company's machinery.

[1397] Chicago Tribune. (Oct. 4, 1869). Agricultural Fairs. P. 0_1. ProQuest Historical Newspapers.

[1398] Chicago Tribune. (Oct. 4, 1869). Agricultural Fairs. P. 0_1. ProQuest Historical Newspapers.

[1399] Hunt, Robert. (1878). Ure's Dictionary of Arts, Manufactures, And Mines. Vol. IV. Pp. 569-570. London: Longmans, Green, And Co. Google Books.

[1400] Hunt, Robert. (1878). Ure's Dictionary of Arts, Manufactures, And Mines. Vol. IV. Pp. 569-570. London: Longmans, Green, And Co. Google Books.

[1401] Hunt, Robert. (1878). Ure's Dictionary of Arts, Manufactures, And Mines. Vol. IV. Pp. 569-570. London: Longmans, Green, And Co. Google Books.

[1402] Hunt, Robert. (1878). Ure's Dictionary of Arts, Manufactures, And Mines. Vol. IV. Pp. 569-570. London: Longmans, Green, And Co. Google Books.

Of significance was the fact that the Illinois Pneumatic Gas Company machinery had been purchased by important persons in Chicago.[1403] The company's fuel machinery had been installed at the residence of Paul Cornell, who was the principal founder and developer of Hyde Park Township, which was later incorporated into the City of Chicago as a major geographical addition to the city.[1404] The Illinois Pneumatic Gas Company machinery had also been installed at the residences of N. H. Judd, O. W. Potter, W. N. Brainard, and H. B. Lewis.[1405] The article reported that these purchasers had indicated satisfaction with the company's machinery.[1406] Of additional commercial and historical significance was the fact that the safety of the A. C. Rand patent technology was recognized by contemporaneous insurance companies.[1407] The insurance company deliberations, risk-assessments, and judgments regarding the safety of the Rand technology constituted testimonies of the commercial safety and viability of the technology at the time.[1408] It is tragic that only a relatively sparse quantity of information remains regarding the Illinois Pneumatic Gas Company. This company nonetheless contributed to the development and progress of utility technology in Chicago, Cook County, Detroit, and the Midwest.

The Pettits of Oak Park and Riverside

The significance of grain-relevant commerce defines the present section. The conceptual and economic elements of grain brokerage and grain contract constituted much of the grain commerce of Chicago. As is proved from historical information supplied herein, *infra*, entire careers were built upon the grain commerce of Chicago. The information provided here shows that people were regularly commuting into the downtown from Cook County suburbs as early as the earliest part of the twentieth century.

Ella (Stryker) Pettit (1846-1899), daughter of James Monroe Stryker, Sr., and Ellen (Brooks) Stryker of Chicago and Wisconsin, died on September 21, 1899, at her residence at 145 Campbell Avenue, in Chicago.[1409] She was taken to Kenosha

---

[1403] Chicago Tribune. (Oct. 4, 1869). Agricultural Fairs. P. 0_1. ProQuest Historical Newspapers.

[1404] Chicago Tribune. (Oct. 4, 1869). Agricultural Fairs. P. 0_1. ProQuest Historical Newspapers.

[1405] Chicago Tribune. (Oct. 4, 1869). Agricultural Fairs. P. 0_1. ProQuest Historical Newspapers.

[1406] Chicago Tribune. (Oct. 4, 1869). Agricultural Fairs. P. 0_1. ProQuest Historical Newspapers.

[1407] Hunt, Robert. (1878). Ure's Dictionary of Arts , Manufactures, And Mines. Vol. IV. Pp. 569-570. London: Longmans, Green, And Co. Google Books.

[1408] Hunt, Robert. (1878). Ure's Dictionary of Arts , Manufactures, And Mines. Vol. IV. Pp. 569-570. London: Longmans, Green, And Co. Google Books.

[1409] Chicago Tribune. (September 22, 1899). P. 5. Newspapers.com.

for burial at Green Ridge Cemetery.[1410] Her husband, James E. Pettit (1842-1909), survived her by a decade. James and Ella had three children: James Stryker Pettit (1868-1889) of Chicago; Harry Eber Pettit (1875-1944) of Chicago, Oak Park, and Riverside; and Alice Stryker Pettit (1869-1942) of Chicago and Oak Park.[1411]

Harry Eber Pettit was a son of James Edward Pettit and Ellen Amelia Stryker. Harry spent decades in Chicago as a grain commission merchant and in independent grain brokerage. Harry was a member of the Chicago Board of Trade in 1904. He served as a commission merchant with the company known by the name Logan & Ryan. This company was located at Number 2, Board of Trade Building.[1412] In 1906, Pettit continued as a member of the Chicago Board of Trade. He remained in 1906 with the company of Logan & Ryan, and worked from the office located at Number 2, Board of Trade Building.[1413] In approximately 1911 or 1912, Pettit resigned from Logan & Ryan to accept a position with the Chicago grain firm of Clement, Curtis & Company.[1414] Harry and Annie Pettit were residents of at least two different houses in Oak Park prior to relocating to the Village of Riverside in western Cook County. One of the Pettit houses in Oak Park was on Home Avenue, located slightly south of the Pleasant Home mansion that was built by John Farson, Esq.

Harry E. Pettit was a member of the Chicago Board of Trade in 1913, holding the position of commission merchant with the company known as Thomson & McKinnon. He then worked at the company office located at Number 3, Rookery Building.[1415] In 1930 Harry Pettit and wife Annie resided in the Village of Riverside, a western suburb of Chicago located in Cook County.[1416] The Pettit house was located on Herrick Road.[1417] At this time Pettit worked as a grain broker with the Chicago Board of Trade.[1418] Laura Moody, a Louisiana native, was listed in the *1930 United States Census* as a servant at the Pettit residence.[1419] At some

---

[1410] Chicago Tribune. (September 22, 1899). P. 5. Newspapers.com; Findagrave.com. Ella (Stryker) Pettit. Green ridge Cemetery, Kenosha, Wisconsin.

[1411] Findagrave.com. Family of James E. Pettit and Ella (Stryker) Pettit. Green Ridge Cemetery, Kenosha, Wisconsin.

[1412] Chicago Board of Trade. The Forty-Sixth Annual Report of the Trade and Commerce of Chicago For The Year Ended December 31, 1903. (1904). P. 254. Chicago, IL: The J. M. W. Jones Stationery and Printing Company. Google Books.

[1413] Chicago Board of Trade. The Forty-Eighth Annual Report of the Trade and Commerce of Chicago For The Year Ended December 31, 1905. (1906). P. 254. Chicago, IL: The J. M. W. Jones Stationery and Printing Company. Google Books.

[1414] The Grain Dealers Journal. (1912). Vol. XVIII. P. 782. Google Books.

[1415] Chicago Board of Trade. (1914). The Fifty-Sixth Annual Report of the Trade and Commerce of Chicago For The Year Ended December 31, 1913. P. 185. Chicago, IL: Hedstrom-Barry Co., Printers. Google Books.

[1416] 1930 United States Census. Cook County, Illinois. Ancestry.com.

[1417] 1930 United States Census. Cook County, Illinois. Ancestry.com.

[1418] 1930 United States Census. Cook County, Illinois. Ancestry.com.

[1419] 1930 United States Census. Cook County, Illinois. Ancestry.com.

time between 1930 and 1940, Harry Pettit resigned from the Chicago Board of Trade to form an independent grain brokerage company.[1420] In 1940, Harry and Annie resided at Cowley-Herrick Road, again in Riverside, Cook County, Illinois.[1421] Dorthey Carey, a native of Texas, resided with the Pettits, and served as a maid at the Pettit residence.[1422] The fact of the residency of Harry and Annie Pettit in the Cook County villages of Oak Park and Riverside demonstrates Chicago was heavily connected to the multiple Cook County suburbs. Many people commuted among the city and suburbs.

Alice Stryker Pettit was the only sister of Harry Eber Pettit.[1423] Alice resided on Marion Street in Oak Park, a western Cook County suburb of Chicago, in 1940.[1424] At one point, Alice resided at the Carleton Hotel in Oak Park.[1425] The Carleton Hotel is one of the most historically significant hotels in Oak Park and in all of metropolitan Chicago, and is located one block away from the Pleasant Home estate of John Farson, Esq. (see Chapter 2, *Builders of the Downtown*). The Carleton Hotel is also near the boundaries of the Cook County villages of Forest Park and River Forest. It is possible that Harry Eber Pettit, his wife Annie, and his sister, Alice Stryker Pettit, knew Dr. Clarence Edmonds Hemingway (1871-1928) and Grace (Hall) Hemingway (1872-1951), who resided on Oak Park Avenue. These were the parents of author Ernest Miller Hemingway (1899-1961). The Hemingway family was long-established and prominent in Oak Park and Chicago. The Pettits were the same age as the Hemingways and may have known them socially in Chicago and Oak Park.

Both Alice Pettit and Harry Pettit were interred at Forest Home Cemetery in Forest Park, also a western Cook County suburb.[1426] Harry and Alice had a brother named James S. Pettit (1868-1889), also a Chicago resident, who died at the age of twenty-one years.[1427]

Civil War Memoirs of Ella Stryker and James E. Pettit of Chicago

Allow us now to turn back two generations to present some letters that show the culture, pressures, and circumstances that defined the Civil War Era in Chicago. James E. Pettit, a Civil War soldier, requested to marry Ella Stryker, who was a

---

[1420] 1940 United States Census. Cook County, Illinois. Ancestry.com.
[1421] 1940 United States Census. Cook County, Illinois. Ancestry.com.
[1422] 1940 United States Census. Cook County, Illinois. Ancestry.com.
[1423] Alice Stryker Pettit. Interment record at Findagrave.com.
[1424] 1940 United States Census. Cook County, Illinois. Ancestry.com.
[1425] Oak Park City Directory.
[1426] Forest Home Cemetery interment records for Harry Eber Pettit and Alice Stryker Pettit, located at Alice Stryker Pettit. Findagrave.com.
[1427] James Pettit interment record at Green Ridge Cemetery in Kenosha, Wisconsin. Findagrave.com.

daughter of James Monroe Stryker, Sr. James Pettit had asked James Stryker for Stryker's daughter's hand in marriage, and Stryker's recorded answer bears witness concurrently to a deep Christian faith, and to the poignant circumstances of the time when this marriage proposal and grant of permission occurred. James Stryker's grant of permission to James Pettit to marry Ella Stryker is suffused with Christian faith, hope, and blessing. The text of James M. Stryker's letter to James E. Pettit follows below.

> "Chicago.
> May 8th 1866.
>
> Letter to Mr. J. E. Pettit.
>   Dear Sir. Your letter of March, was duly rec'd & ought to have been answered at an earlier date, but the request you make is one of such importance that I could not write at once. - It is a hard thing to give away a beloved child & I had hoped to be spared the trial for sometime yet, but as I find her heart is already yours, I cannot withhold my consent to your union - Ella has been a Dear good Daughter to me, & I trust she will be a true & faithful wife to you - Her happiness is in your keeping. Oh cherish and protect her always. May neither of you ever have cause to regret your choice and that the blessing of God may rest upon you both is the prayer of Yours Sincerely. J.M. Stryker."[1428]

Let us now examine a letter written to James E. Pettit by his dying mother. The Pettit letter, much like the Stryker letter, *supra*, contains evidence not only of the turbulence of the time of the Civil War in the Chicago metropolitan region, but also of the Christian faith of the family. The document that follows may have been James E. Pettit's last letter from his mother. Please note that some of the words are difficult to read in the original record. Therefore, this transcription may contain an occasional minor error in meaning. The first letter below was written to James Pettit by his brother. The second letter below was written by the mother to her son, James E. Pettit.

> "Kenosha, Wisconsin.
> March 25th, 1863.
>
>   Dear Bro. Your [letter] of 22nd inst received to day I was much interested by the account you gave of your .....I suppose when you get this you will probably have armied in the vicinity of Frederikstown. As regards things I am..........Last night a grand mass meeting was held at Chammous

---

[1428] Letter of James Monroe Stryker, Sr., to James E. Pettit. Chicago, May 8, 1866. The letter was contributed by Debbie Ann McBride.

Hall for the purpose of framing ....The copperheads represented by Genl .....attempted to break up the meeting but ingloriously failed. A pledge was reported & adapted to which all who support the efforts of the government in suppressing the Rebellion are requesting to sign their names.

Mother requests me to leave space for a line or two if she feels able. She will try & write a little. For the past two or three weeks Mother has appeared to be growing weaker & weaker in spite of all the efforts we can make & for the past two or three days she has had spells of what appeared to be sinking & growing cold & numb. I hardly know whether our Dear mother will be spared us for any great length of time. Her [constitution] has been so weakened by her sickness & that it is almost impossible to get up the lest favorable reaction. We are expecting some medicine tomorrow from Chicago that I hope may have a favorable effect. Mother is so weak that she cannot sit up but a few minutes at a time but 'while there is life their is hope'. Lank Parker leaves for his future home to night, instead of going to ....he goes on a farm to work about 70 miles down in Ill. He is to work for Jones the Mason. Carl Stetson has just got home from Memphis. He is in .....33 Reg. walks like a ghost, he's been sick for eight weeks with Tifoid Fever. Have been making ink to day. This has been written with it. Made three galls, I will send papers from time to time whenever there is anything worth sending. It is just telegraphed through that gold had gone down to 1.35 a fall of 10 since yesterday. It is thought that Visbrg [Vicksburg] has been taken, if it was not, it soon will be & then Peace will soon come & our distanced country may be whole again. Has Hank arrived at Hdq yet. Write us after as possible. & I will try to respond. All send love. From your Affect. bro. Eg.

(Continued On the same letter.) March 26th 1863."

Letter to James Pettit from his mother:

"My Darling 'Baby Jim' I feel a little more comfortable this morning & I will try to write a few lines as it may be the last I shall be able to write you my dear child. Life is fast receding from my view and unless there is a change soon for the better I shall pass away to the world of Rest. I suffer very much - feel faint most of the time - vomit two or three times a day - no appetite - my breast is quite painful & has a cancerous appearance - right arm nearly helpless. I am nothing but a skeleton - cannot weight over 70 lbs, perhaps not that. Expect a new medicine to day - the same that cured Jim Lark. It is my last hope. You must keep cheerful & not fret about me - I am cheerful & keep up good courage as usual - dressed every day & sit up a little as much as I am able to & if you were here I should talk & laugh with you as usual. Dr. Heborn says I will recover but I doubt it. If I never see you in this world, we shall meet again. Darling shall we not, in a brighter more beautiful world? May our God preserve & keep you unspoiled from the world. We will keep you advised as often as possible.

William is very unhappy in Columbus. He is anxious to have you write to him. Goodbye beloved. If I can I will write again soon. Your loving mother L. H. Pettit.

I have not heard from Henry - has he left Dubuque yet - They have a fine daughter & are much pleased with it. Charles Mathers little boy is to be buried to day - died of Dyptheria. Duncan Seymour is very feeble. * cannot live long. I think Neighbours all well as usual."[1429]

The Henshaws

Joshua Henshaw of Boston married Mary Webster of Boston. Their children included Daniel Henshaw and Joshua Henshaw.[1430] Daniel Henshaw married Elizabeth Bass, who was the great-granddaughter of John Alden and Priscilla (Mullins) Alden of The Mayflower and Plymouth Colony. The children born to Daniel Henshaw and Elizabeth (Bass) Henshaw included the following: **Benjamin Henshaw, who married Huldah (Stillman) Sumner Green**; **William Henshaw, who married Phebe Swan**; and many others.[1431] Benjamin Henshaw and Huldah (Stillman) Henshaw had the following children: **Daniel Henshaw, who married Sarah "Sally" Esther Prentis**; Joseph Henshaw; **Joshua Henshaw, who married Esther Burnham**; Sarah Henshaw, who died in infancy; Sarah Henshaw; and John Henshaw.[1432]

Three Henshaw Family Branches of Chicago:

The Henshaw-Swan-Goulding-Livermore Branch; the

Henshaw-Burnham Branch; and the Henshaw-Prentis Branch

The Henshaw-Swan-Goulding-Livermore Branch of Galesburg and Chicago

Daniel Henshaw and Elizabeth (Bass) Henshaw had a son named William Henshaw, who married Phebe Swan. William and Phebe (Swan) Henshaw had a son named Joseph Henshaw, who married Relief Goulding.[1433] Joseph and Relief (Goulding) Henshaw had a son, Daniel Henshaw, who married Diantha Livermore.[1434] Daniel and Diantha resided in Galesburg, Knox County, Illinois.[1435] Their son, Frederick Eugene Henshaw, became a prominent real estate developer

---

[1429] Letter from L. H. Pettit to her son, James E. Pettit. March 25, 1863. Kenosha, Wisconsin. Letter contributed by Debbie Ann McBride.

[1430] Cutter, William Richard. (1914). New England Families: Genealogical and Memorial. Vol. II. P. 931. New York, NY: Lewis Historical Publishing Company. Google Books.

[1431] Henshaw family historical records; rawbw.com.

[1432] Henshaw family historical records; rawbw.com.

[1433] Henshaw family historical records; rawbw.com.

[1434] Henshaw family historical records; rawbw.com.

[1435] Henshaw family historical records; rawbw.com.

of the Hyde Park community of Chicago.[1436] Frederick Eugene Henshaw and wife Ella (Stevens) Henshaw resided at 6115 Kimbark Avenue in 1901, at the time of the marriage of their daughter, Bertha Winifred Henshaw, to J. Harwood Springer.[1437] Frederick Henshaw and wife continued to reside at 6115 Kimbark Avenue in 1905.[1438] Their daughter, Elsie Carolyn Henshaw, married Harry Loveland Kinne, who resided at Lake Geneva, Wisconsin.[1439] The wedding occurred at the Sixth Presbyterian Church. Reverend William P. Merrill performed the marriage ceremony.[1440] Irma Henshaw, another daughter of Frederick Eugene Henshaw, and a sister of Elsie Carolyn Henshaw, attended the wedding as Maid of Honor.[1441] Eldridge Golden Henshaw, brother of Frederick Eugene Henshaw, resided in Chicago at about the time of his service in the Civil War.[1442] Adelaide Lunette Henshaw, sister of Frederick Eugene Henshaw and Eldridge Golden Henshaw, also resided in Chicago.[1443]

The Henshaw-Burnham Branch of Chicago and California

Joshua Henshaw married Esther Burnham, and their son, John Leavitt Henshaw (1792-1832), married Ann Maria Corey. Their children were John Cory Henshaw; Anne Henshaw; Frederick William Henshaw; Caroline Henrietta Cox Henshaw; Edward Carrington Henshaw, who married Sarah Edwards Tyler; and George Holt Henshaw.[1444] Edward Carrington Henshaw married Sarah Edwards Tyler. Edward served as a soldier in the Union Army during the Civil War. Sarah Edwards (Tyler) Henshaw was instrumental in the establishment of the Chicago Sanitary Fair in 1863, which provided aid and support for the Union soldiers during the Civil War.[1445] She worked with Mrs. A. H. Hoge, Mrs. J. A. Rice of Adrian, Michigan, Miss V. Campbell of Detroit, Mrs. D. P. Livermore, E. W. Blatchford, Miss M. Louise Urlson, and Miss Jennie E. McLaren of Chicago, and Mrs. S. M.

[1436] Henshaw family historical records; rawbw.com.

[1437] Chicago Daily Tribune. (November 18, 1901). P. 7. ProQuest Newspapers at Northwestern University.

[1438] Chicago Daily Tribune. (June 28, 1905). P. 9. ProQuest Newspapers at Northwestern University.

[1439] Chicago Daily Tribune. (June 28, 1905). P. 9. ProQuest Newspapers at Northwestern University.

[1440] Chicago Daily Tribune. (June 28, 1905). P. 9. ProQuest Newspapers at Northwestern University.

[1441] Chicago Daily Tribune. (June 28, 1905). P. 9. ProQuest Newspapers at Northwestern University.

[1442] Henshaw family historical records; rawbw.com.

[1443] Henshaw family historical records; rawbw.com.

[1444] Henshaw family historical records; rawbw.com.

[1445] Andreas, Alfred Theodore. (1885). History of Chicago. From the Earliest Period to the Present Time. Vol. II. Pp. 320-321. Chicago, IL: The A. T. Andreas Company. Google Books.

Langworthy of Dubuque, Iowa.[1446] Sarah Henshaw was Associate Manager and official historian of the Chicago Branch of the Northwest Sanitary Commission.[1447] Edward Carrington Henshaw and Sarah Edwards (Tyler) Henshaw had the following children: Edward Tyler Henshaw; Charles Edwards Henshaw; Charlotte Henshaw; Stanley Henshaw; Frederick William Henshaw; William Griffith Henshaw; and Tyler T. Henshaw.[1448]

One of the cousins from the Henshaw-Burnham branch of our family, Tyler Tubbs Henshaw, who was the son of Frederick William Henshaw and Grace Susan (Tubbs) Henshaw of Oakland, California, graduated from the University of Chicago in 1911.[1449] Tyler Henshaw graduated from the University of Chicago in the same class as did the adventurer, anthropologist, illustrator, and author, Cyrus Leroy Baldridge.[1450] Upon graduation from the University of Chicago, Tyler Henshaw attended Harvard Law School. He died at a tragically premature age in the year 1913.[1451] The Henshaws were also prominent in California business, industry, and law.[1452]

The Henshaw-Prentis Family of Morgan County, St. Louis, and Chicago

Daniel Henshaw (1762-1825) married Sarah "Sally" Esther Prentis, who was the daughter of Capt. John Prentis and Esther (Richards) Prentis.[1453] The Richards and Prentis genealogies and histories are contained in Chapter 1, *Genesis of a Great Lakes Frontier*. Daniel Henshaw and Sarah Esther (Prentis) Henshaw had many children, including Rev. John Prentis Kewley Henshaw, who served as the

---

[1446] Andreas, Alfred Theodore. (1885). History of Chicago. From the Earliest Period to the Present Time. Vol. II. Pp. 320-321. Chicago, IL: The A. T. Andreas Company. Google Books.

[1447] Henshaw family historical records; rawbw.com; Henshaw, Sarah Edwards. (1894). Our Family: A Little Account of it for my Descendants. Oakland, CA: Sarah Edwards Tyler Henshaw.

[1448] Henshaw family historical records; rawbw.com.

[1449] The University of Chicago Magazine. (November, 1913-July, 1914). Vol. VI. P. 164. Chicago, IL: The University of Chicago Press. Google Books; Call, Andrew Taylor. (2016). Faded Bricks: Old Family Tales from the South Side of Chicago. Hyde Park History, Vol. 38, (No. 4), Pp. 1-7. Chicago, IL: Hyde Park Historical Society; Henshaw family historical records; rawbw.com.

[1450] Alumni Directory of the University of Chicago. (1919). Pp. 512-513. Chicago, IL: The University of Chicago Press. Google Books.

[1451] The University of Chicago Magazine. (November, 1913-July, 1914). Vol. VI. P. 164. Chicago, IL: The University of Chicago Press. Google Books; Call, Andrew Taylor. (2016). Faded Bricks: Old Family Tales from the South Side of Chicago. Hyde Park History, Vol. 38, (No. 4), Pp. 1-7. Chicago, IL: Hyde Park Historical Society.

[1452] Henshaw family historical records; rawbw.com.

[1453] Cutter, William Richard. (1914). New England Families: Genealogical and Memorial. Vol. II. P. 931. New York, NY: Lewis Historical Publishing Company. Google Books.

Episcopal Bishop of Rhode Island, as the Provisional Bishop of Maine, and who was a founder of the American Bible Society.[1454] Daniel Henshaw and Sarah Esther (Prentis) Henshaw had a daughter named Harriet Hillhouse Henshaw, who married Henry Brigham McClure.[1455] For the histories of Harriet Hillhouse (Henshaw) McClure and the McClure family, see Chapter 6, *Sprinters of the Steel Track*.

The children of Daniel Henshaw and Sarah Esther (Prentis) Henshaw were the following: **Sarah Hayward Henshaw, who married Charles Richards**; a daughter whose name was not recorded; Rev. John Prentiss Kewley Henshaw; Elizabeth Hallum Henshaw; Julia Ann Henshaw; Mary Catherine Henshaw; Evan Houghton Henshaw; **Emmeline Stillman Henshaw, who married Daniel Whitney**; Margaret Stanley Henshaw; Charles Henry Henshaw; **Frances Alsop Henshaw, who married Rev. Truman Marcellus Post, Esq.**; and **Harriet Hillhouse Henshaw, who married Henry Brigham McClure, Esq.**[1456] The Henshaw-Post family and the Henshaw-McClure family both included civic and business leaders of Chicago, St. Louis, and Jacksonville, Illinois, as is discussed throughout this book in Chapter 6, *Sprinters of the Steel Track*, and Chapter 1, *Genesis of a Great Lakes Frontier*.

Sarah Hayward Henshaw and Charles Richards

Sarah Hayward Henshaw, daughter of Daniel Henshaw and Sarah Esther (Prentis) Henshaw, married Charles Richards, who was the son of Guy Richards and Hannah (Dolbeare) Richards of New London. Charles Richards was the first cousin of Sarah Esther Prentis, who married Daniel Henshaw. Charles Richards also was the first cousin of the Wolcotts of Chicago, through the Richards family of New London.[1457] Charles Richards and Sarah (Henshaw) Richards' daughter, Harriet Sophia Richards (1822-1893), married Daniel Huntington.[1458] Daniel and Harriet were founders of the Metropolitan Museum of Art in New York City, and Daniel served as the founding Vice-President of the Museum.[1459] Harriet Hillhouse Henshaw was the aunt of Harriet Sophia Richards through the Henshaw family. Moreover, the two women were cousins through the Richards family.[1460]

[1454] Thirty-Second Annual Report of the American Bible Society, Presented May 11, 1848. P. 157. New York, NY: American Bible Society. Google Books; Journal of the Twenty-Third Annual Convention of the Protestant Episcopal Church in Maine. (1842). P. 3. Augusta, Maine: Gardiner. Google Books.

[1455] Binney, C. J. F. (1883). The History and Genealogy of the Prentice, or Prentiss Family, of New England, Etc. from 1631 to 1883. 2nd Ed. Pp. 293-294. Boston, MASS: C. J. F. Binney.

[1456] Henshaw family historical records; rawbw.com.

[1457] Richards, Wolcott, Henshaw family historical records.

[1458] Biography of Harriet Sophia Richards and her husband Daniel Huntington. Philadelphia Museum of Art. Philamuseum.org.

[1459] Spassky, Natalie. (1985). American Paintings In The Metropolitan Museum of Art. Vol. II. Pp. 57-58. New York, NY: The Metropolitan Museum of Art. Google Books.

[1460] Henshaw and Richards family historical records; rawbw.com.

Daniel Huntington was a renowned portrait artist, and was President of the National Academy of Design, a Trustee of the National Museum of Art, a life member of the New York Historical Society, a life member of the New York Geographical Society, a founding trustee of the Lenox Library, and a trustee of the New York Public Library.[1461] He was a graduate of Hamilton College in Clinton, New York, and was a founder and long-time President of the Century Club of New York City.[1462] His works include portraits of Abraham Lincoln, Martin Van Buren, Louis Agassiz, Albert Gallatin, Ulysses S. Grant, Philip Sheridan, William Tecumseh Sherman, Admiral DuPont, Mrs. Rutherford Birchard Hayes, Mrs. Benjamin Harrison, William Cullen Bryant, and others.[1463] Artist Samuel Fanshaw painted a miniature portrait of Harriet Sophia (Richards) Huntington which exists within the collection of the Philadelphia Museum of Art.[1464] Harriet Sophia (Richards) Huntington of New York City bore a striking resemblance to her aunt, Harriet Hillhouse (Henshaw) McClure of Illinois.

Emmeline Stillman Henshaw and Daniel Whitney of Green Bay, Wisconsin

Emmeline Stillman Henshaw, daughter of Daniel Henshaw and Sarah Esther (Prentis) Henshaw, married Daniel Whitney.[1465] They were the principal founders of Green Bay, Wisconsin.[1466] Daniel and Emmeline (Henshaw) Whitney had the following children: Henry Clay Whitney; Harriet Hayward Whitney; Charles Richards Whitney; John Prentis Kane Whitney; Daniel Henshaw Whitney, who married Eva Rosina Baeder; Joshua Whitney, who married Elizabeth Frances Irwin; **William Beaumont Whitney**, who married, first, Laura Margaret Clewell of Cincinnati, and second, Emma Varian.[1467] William Beaumont Whitney, who was a first cousin of Elizabeth Henshaw (McClure) Stryker of Jacksonville, Illinois, entered the coal industry of Pennsylvania, and became one of the most important builders of the coal industry of Philadelphia, Pittsburgh, and the Appalachian Mountains of Virginia and eastern Kentucky.[1468] William B. Whitney

---

[1461] Leonard, John W. (1907). Who's Who In New York City And State. Vol. 3. P. 717. New York, NY: L. R. Hamersly and Company. Google Books.

[1462] Leonard, John W. (1907). Who's Who In New York City And State. Vol. 3. P. 717. New York, NY: L. R. Hamersly and Company. Google Books.

[1463] Leonard, John W. (1907). Who's Who In New York City And State. Vol. 3. P. 717. New York, NY: L. R. Hamersly and Company. Google Books.

[1464] Philadelphia Museum of Art. Philamuseum.org.

[1465] Henshaw family historical records; rawbw.com.

[1466] Martin, Deborah Beaumont. (1913). History of Brown County, Wisconsin: Past and Present. Vol. II. Pp. 48-55. Chicago, IL: S. J. Clarke Publishing Company. Google Books.

[1467] Martin, Deborah Beaumont. (1913). History of Brown County, Wisconsin: Past and Present. Vol. II. Pp. 48-55. Chicago, IL: S. J. Clarke Publishing Company. Google Books.

[1468] Martin, Deborah Beaumont. (1913). History of Brown County, Wisconsin: Past and Present. Vol. II. Pp. 48-55. Chicago, IL: S. J. Clarke Publishing Company. Google

was Assistant to James S. Cox, who was President of the Lehigh Coal and Navigation Company of Pennsylvania.[1469] Whitney was promoted to Coal Manager for the Lehigh Coal and Navigation Company, and combined the coal work with the operationally interlocking work of railroad management when he became Treasurer of both the Delaware Water Gap Railroad Company and the Nesquehoning Valley Railroad Company.[1470] Whitney joined with Otto Kemmerer and George D. McCreary to establish the Whitney, McCreary & Kemmerer Company, which provided brokerage and agency for the Upper Lehigh coal deposits that were owned by John Leisenring and his associates.[1471]

William B. Whitney was a Sunday School teacher and a Bible Class Teacher, having held teaching posts at St. Andrew's Sunday School, St. Luke's Sunday School, Christ Church, and St. Michael's Church, in addition to his work as Deputy to the Convention of the Episcopal Diocese of Pennsylvania.[1472] He served on the boards of directors of the Whitney & Kemmerer Coal Company of Philadelphia, the Alden Coal Company of Alden Station, Pennsylvania, and the Stonega Coke and Coal Company of Philadelphia and Virginia.[1473] Whitney co-founded the Theodore Starr Savings Bank of Philadelphia, and served on the board of directors of the Girard National Bank of Philadelphia.[1474] Frederick Moon, who was Secretary of the Alden Coal Company, reported the following eulogistic resolution in honor of William B. Whitney from the board of directors of Alden:

> "'By his kindly and generous nature, great business energy, industry and ability, he had achieved success in the battle of life, and his work was well and faithfully done. His sterling honesty, sound judgment, fair dealings, and candid open business methods, made him as respected and esteemed by those with whom he was brought into business relations, as his charitableness, warmth of affection, and amiable disposition endeared him to those with whom he was more closely associated by the ties of friendship.'"[1475]

Books; In Memoriam: W. Beaumont Whitney (1832-1906). (1910). Philadelphia, PA: J. B. Lippincott Company. Google Books.

[1469] In Memoriam: W. Beaumont Whitney (1832-1906). (1910). P. 9. Philadelphia, PA: J. B. Lippincott Company. Google Books.

[1470] In Memoriam: W. Beaumont Whitney (1832-1906). (1910). P. 9. Philadelphia, PA: J. B. Lippincott Company. Google Books.

[1471] In Memoriam: W. Beaumont Whitney (1832-1906). (1910). P. 10. Philadelphia, PA: J. B. Lippincott Company. Google Books.

[1472] In Memoriam: W. Beaumont Whitney (1832-1906). (1910). P. 10. Philadelphia, PA: J. B. Lippincott Company. Google Books.

[1473] In Memoriam: W. Beaumont Whitney (1832-1906). (1910). Pp. 36-38. Philadelphia, PA: J. B. Lippincott Company. Google Books.

[1474] In Memoriam: W. Beaumont Whitney (1832-1906). (1910). Pp. 32-35. Philadelphia, PA: J. B. Lippincott Company. Google Books.

[1475] In Memoriam: W. Beaumont Whitney (1832-1906). (1910). P. 37. Philadelphia, PA: J. B. Lippincott Company. Google Books.

William B. Whitney was a founder and director of the Stonega Coke and Coal Company, which became one of the largest coal companies, and possibly the largest, in the Virginia coalfields.[1476] The Stonega Coke & Coal Company of Philadelphia operated a branch at Chicago. Stonega was headquartered in Philadelphia and owned the company towns of Stonega, Andover, Arno, Derby, Dunbar, Exeter, Imboden, Keokee, Osaka (pronounced O-say-kee), Pine Branch, and Roda, all in Southwest Virginia.[1477] In 1908, Stonega Coke and Coal Company owned a Chicago office that was located at 204 N. Dearborn Street, C6621, with a telephone number apparently listed as 1218.[1478] The Stonega Coke and Coal Company owned and operated 966 coke ovens in Wise County, Virginia.[1479] This company employed a very large workforce, and historian Crandall A. Shifflett noted that the Stonega Coke and Coal Company was the largest employer of coal miners in the Commonwealth of Virginia.[1480] The economic power and scope of the company would have positively impacted the neighboring communities of Grundy, Pound, Abingdon, Haysi, Hurley, Clintwood, Cumberland Gap, Pennington Gap, Big Stone Gap, the two Bristols of Virginia and Tennessee, Gate City, Dungannon, Dante, Sun, and many other communities of southwest Virginia during the early twentieth century.[1481]

The Richards-Prentiss-Henshaw-Southmayd Family

of Connecticut, Louisiana, and Illinois

Capt. John Prentis and Esther (Richards) Prentis are the ancestors of two major families in Chicago history: the **Richards-Prentis-Henshaw family**, and the **Richards-Prentis-Southmayd** family. For discussion of the Richards-Prentis-Henshaw family of Chicago, see Chapter 6, *Sprinters of the Steel Track*. For the

---

[1476] In Memoriam: W. Beaumont Whitney (1832-1906). (1910). P. 38. Philadelphia, PA: J. B. Lippincott Company. Google Books; Shifflett, Crandall A. (2000). Coal Towns: Life, Work, and Culture in Company Towns of Southern Appalachia, 1880-1960. P. XVII. Knoxville, TN: The University of Tennessee Press. Google Books.

[1477] Shifflett, Crandall A. (2000). Coal Towns: Life, Work, and Culture in Company Towns of Southern Appalachia, 1880-1960. P. XVII. Knoxville, TN: The University of Tennessee Press. Google Books; In Memoriam: W. Beaumont Whitney (1832-1906). (1910). P. 38. Philadelphia, PA: J. B. Lippincott Company. Google Books.

[1478] Chicago Central Business and Office Building Directory. (1908). P. 279. Chicago, IL: The Winters Publishing Company. Google Books.

[1479] A Hand Book On The Minerals And Mineral Resources of Virginia: Prepared for the Virginia Commission to the St. Louis Exposition. (1904). P. 28. Salem, VA: Salem Printing and Publishing Company. Google Books.

[1480] Shifflett, Crandall A. (2000). Coal Towns: Life, Work, and Culture in Company Towns of Southern Appalachia, 1880-1960. P. XVII. Knoxville, TN: The University of Tennessee Press. Google Books.

[1481] Shifflett, Crandall A. (2000). Coal Towns: Life, Work, and Culture in Company Towns of Southern Appalachia, 1880-1960. P. XVII, et. al. Knoxville, TN: The University of Tennessee Press. Google Books.

discussion of the Richards-Wolcott family of Chicago, see Chapter 1, *Genesis of a Great Lakes Frontier*. We will now proceed to the Chicago history of the Richards-Prentis-Southmayd family.

Three branches of the Richards-Prentis family of Connecticut possessed extensive civic and industrial connections to Chicago over multiple generations: the Richards-Prentis-Henshaw family; the Richards-Wolcott family; and the Richards-Prentis-Southmayd family. Capt. John Prentiss and Esther (Richards) Prentiss, who are my great-great-great-great-great-grandparents, founded an immense family with many Chicago branches. Siblings Sally Esther Prentiss and Nancy Prentiss, who were the daughters of Capt. John Prentis and Esther (Richards) Prentis of Connecticut (see above), both were matriarchs of large families of Illinois that contributed to the founding and development of Chicago and Cook County. Sally Esther Prentis married Daniel Henshaw, and these were the ancestors of the large Richards-Prentis-Henshaw family of Illinois and Chicago; and Nancy Prentis married Charles Whiting Goodrich, and these were ancestors of the Richards-Prentis-Southmayd family of Chicago and New Orleans. For the Chicago history of the Richards-Prentis-Henshaw family, see Chapter 6, *Sprinters of the Steel Track*. Do not confuse the Richards family with the Richardson family, also of Chicago and Connecticut, which is discussed thoroughly in Chapter 5, *The Foundations of Jackson Park*. We will now continue to the Chicago history of the Richards-Prentis-Southmayd family.

Col. Frederick R. Southmayd, Jr., of New Orleans and Chicago:

The One-Armed Hero of the South and the North

Frederick Redfield Southmayd, Jr. (1839-1893), was the son of Frederick Redfield Southmayd, Sr., and Catherine Prentis (Goodrich) Southmayd.[1482] Through his mother, Catherine Prentis (Goodrich) Southmayd, Frederick R. Southmayd was the grandson of Charles Whiting Goodrich and Nancy (Prentis) Goodrich.[1483] Through this lineage, Frederick was the great-grandson of Captain John Prentis and Esther (Richards) Prentiss.[1484] Col. Frederick R. Southmayd, Jr., the principal subject of this section of the present chapter, was a second cousin of Elizabeth Henshaw (McClure) Stryker of Jacksonville, Illinois, and was a cousin of the McClure-Stryker-Taylor family of Chicago, Springfield, Morgan County, and Cass County, Illinois.

[1482] Cornish, Louis H. (1902). A National Register of the Society, Sons of the American Revolution. P. 335. New York, NY: Louis H. Cornish. Google Books.

[1483] Cornish, Louis H. (1902). A National Register of the Society, Sons of the American Revolution. P. 335. New York, NY: Louis H. Cornish. Google Books.

[1484] Cornish, Louis H. (1902). A National Register of the Society, Sons of the American Revolution. P. 335. New York, NY: Louis H. Cornish. Google Books.

Captain John Prentis was the Captain of the sloop, "Oliver Cromwell," a sloop-of-war in the Revolutionary War.[1485] Charles Whiting Goodrich, a New Orleans merchant, married Nancy Prentis, who was the daughter of Capt. John Prentis and Esther (Richards) Prentis.[1486] The children born to Charles Whiting Goodrich and Nancy (Prentis) Goodrich were the following: William M. Goodrich, who married Cornelia Griswold; Harriet Goodrich, who married Edward McGee; Charlotte Goodrich; **Catherine Prentis Goodrich, who married Frederick Redfield Southmayd** (1803-1859), a merchant of New Orleans; Mary Goodrich; and Rev. Charles Goodrich.[1487] Frederick Redfield Southmayd and Catherine Prentis (Goodrich) Southmayd had the following children: Charles Gooodrich Southmayd, who was a Yale alumnus; **Frederick Redfield Southmayd, Jr.; Rebecca Bull Southmayd, who married Enoch Turner Holmes, Sr.**; Catherine Southmayd; and Julia Maria Southmayd.[1488] Rev. Charles Goodrich, the son of Charles Whiting Goodrich and Nancy (Prentis) Goodrich, was Rector Emeritus of New Orleans, and founded the original St. Paul's Episcopal Church of New Orleans.[1489] The Prentis-Goodrich-Southmayd family of Connecticut moved to New Orleans before the Civil War.

Frederick R. Southmayd, Jr. enlisted as a private in the Army of the Confederate States of America, rose to the rank of Colonel, and lost his right arm at the Battle of Shiloh in 1862.[1490] After the Civil War ended in April, 1865, Southmayd returned home to New Orleans. The *Monroe Morning World*, a newspaper of Monroe, Louisiana, noted that Southmayd, "established the only Red Cross branch in the south; [and] for five years he directed it, as it was called upon almost annually to handle disasters that piled on the lowered resistance of the defeated states."[1491] He was a member and leader of the Howard Association of New

[1485] Cornish, Louis H. (1902). A National Register of the Society, Sons of the American Revolution. P. 335. New York, NY: Louis H. Cornish. Google Books.
[1486] Dwight, Benjamin W. (1874). The History of the Descendants of John Dwight of Dedham, Massachusetts. Vol. I. P. 529. New York, NY: John F. Trow & Son. Google Books.
[1487] Binney, C. J. F. (1883). The History and Genealogy of the Prentice, or Prentiss Family, of New England, Etc. from 1631 to 1883. 2nd Ed. P. 296. Boston, MASS: C. J. F. Binney; Dwight, Benjamin W. (1874). The History of the Descendants of John Dwight of Dedham, Massachusetts. Vol. I. P. 529. New York, NY: John F. Trow & Son. Google Books.
[1488] Binney, C. J. F. (1883). The History and Genealogy of the Prentice, or Prentiss Family, of New England, Etc. from 1631 to 1883. 2nd Ed. P. 296. Boston, MASS: C. J. F. Binney; Dwight, Benjamin W. (1874). The History of the Descendants of John Dwight of Dedham, Massachusetts. Vol. I. P. 529. New York, NY: John F. Trow & Son. Google Books.
[1489] Cutter, William Richard. (1930). American Biography: A New Encyclopedia. Vol. 41. P. New York, NY: American Historical Society. Google Books.
[1490] Monroe Morning World. (December 11, 1949). P. 33. Newspapers.com.
[1491] Monroe Morning World. (December 11, 1949). P. 33. Newspapers.com.

Orleans. The Louisiana paper stated: "The one-armed colonel shared the accomplishments of the old Howard Association, that organization of generous-spirited New Orleanians who had nursed the sick in the hideous yellow fever epidemics."[1492] Southmayd was the key founder of the Red Cross of New Orleans in 1882.[1493] He helped Clara Barton develop the Red Cross nationally, and helped Barton bring nursing services to New Orleans and the people afflicted by the yellow fever epidemics in Florida.[1494]

Clara Barton honored Southmayd and his dedicated service to people and communities in the following recollection: "the Red Cross was hailed as a benediction wherever he [Southmayd] passed."[1495] When a yellow fever epidemic struck Florida in 1888, Clara Barton and Fred Southmayd organized a Red Cross expedition to bring nursing and medical aid to the suffering population there. He and the nurses that he recruited had already been exposed to yellow fever and possessed immunity to the disease. "The colonel recruited 30 nurses. Ever a thorough man, he took men and women, white and Negro—the only criterion was experience. They left that night for Jacksonville."[1496]

While traveling to Jacksonville, Florida, the New Orleans Red Cross discovered that the northern Florida town of MacClenny had fallen to an epidemic of yellow fever.[1497] The town was heavily quarantined, sealed off with military force, and isolated. Orders were given to the guard to kill anyone who tried to escape the town.[1498] When Southmayd received word of the situation at MacClenny, he was told that the emergency quarantine law ordered trains to continue past the town, and neither to stop nor to slow down near the town.[1499] The quarantine law cut off all supplies to MacClenny, which amounted to a forced starvation of the town.[1500] Southmayd refused to tolerate the evils of the draconian quarantine policy, and summoned nurses to help him bring the Red Cross nursing services to the dying town.[1501]

As the train that was carrying the New Orleans Red Cross through Florida neared MacClenny, Southmayd and his nurses planned an excuse for slowing the train down. When the train slowed, the nurses left the train and walked to MacClenny.[1502] The ten nurses that Southmayd gathered together for the

[1492] Monroe Morning World. (December 11, 1949). P. 33. Newspapers.com.
[1493] Monroe Morning World. (December 11, 1949). P. 33. Newspapers.com.
[1494] Monroe Morning World. (December 11, 1949). P. 33. Newspapers.com.
[1495] Monroe Morning World. (December 11, 1949). P. 33. Newspapers.com.
[1496] Monroe Morning World. (December 11, 1949). P. 33. Newspapers.com.
[1497] Monroe Morning World. (December 11, 1949). P. 33. Newspapers.com.
[1498] Monroe Morning World. (December 11, 1949). P. 33. Newspapers.com.
[1499] Monroe Morning World. (December 11, 1949). P. 33. Newspapers.com.
[1500] Monroe Morning World. (December 11, 1949). P. 33. Newspapers.com.
[1501] Monroe Morning World. (December 11, 1949). P. 33. Newspapers.com.
[1502] Monroe Morning World. (December 11, 1949). P. 33. Newspapers.com.

MacClenny nursing mission gained access to MacClenny, brought the Red Cross medical services with them, and remained at the plagued community for two months. The New Orleans Red Cross, Fred Southmayd, and his nurses managed to eradicate the yellow fever epidemic at MacClenny and restore the town to health.[1503]

After the MacClenny mission Fred Southmayd and the nurses returned to New Orleans.[1504] The work at MacClenny had caused Southmayd to make enemies.[1505] Southmayd and his nurses were criticized for their work at MacClenny, and the nurses, who were women, were publicly criticized for being too daring in their medical work.[1506] Southmayd was summoned to Washington, D.C., "to keep peace" amidst what was becoming a public relations crisis for the New Orleans Red Cross.[1507] After the Washington meetings, Southmayd decided not to return home to New Orleans, but to move to Chicago.[1508] The New Orleans Red Cross languished when Southmayd left the city permanently for Chicago, but the citizens of New Orleans revived their Red Cross branch in 1916 and memorialized with great admiration and respect the work and life of Fred Southmayd, Jr., the one-armed colonel.[1509]

Col. Frederick R. Southmayd, Jr.

and The Illinois Society of the Sons of the American Revolution

At Chicago, Frederick R. Southmayd, Jr., took an active interest in the promotion, organization, and development of multiple civic organizations, including United States heritage groups. He co-founded the Illinois Society of the Sons of the American Revolution at Chicago with multiple other Revolutionary War soldier descendants.[1510] He led the group also as a member of the organization's Board of Managers.[1511] The Illinois Society of the S.A.R. was

---

[1503] Monroe Morning World. (December 11, 1949). P. 33. Newspapers.com.
[1504] Monroe Morning World. (December 11, 1949). P. 33. Newspapers.com.
[1505] Monroe Morning World. (December 11, 1949). P. 33. Newspapers.com.
[1506] Monroe Morning World. (December 11, 1949). P. 33. Newspapers.com.
[1507] Monroe Morning World. (December 11, 1949). P. 33. Newspapers.com.
[1508] Monroe Morning World. (December 11, 1949). P. 33. Newspapers.com.
[1509] Monroe Morning World. (December 11, 1949). P. 33. Newspapers.com.
[1510] Year Book of the Illinois Society of the Sons of the American Revolution Incorporated. (1896). Pp. 3-5. Chicago, Illinois: Wm. Johnston Printing Co. Google Books.
[1511] Year Book of the Illinois Society Of The Sons of the American Revolution Incorporated. (1896). Pp. 3-5. Chicago, Illinois: Wm. Johnston Printing Co. Google Books.

founded on January 14, 1890, at Chicago.[1512] The preliminary processes that culminated in the creation of the Illinois Society entailed multiple parties and conferences.[1513] John Carroll Power and Richmond Wolcott cooperated as a steering committee for the purpose of establishing the Illinois Society of the S.A.R., in April, 1889, at Springfield, and Wolcott, A. A. North, and C. A. Pease drafted the constitution for the Illinois Society.[1514] The Illinois founders imported the pattern of the constitution of the New Jersey Society of the Sons of the American Revolution as a model for the Illinois Society constitution.[1515] William McDowell, who served as a Vice-President of the National Society, visited Illinois to collect data upon, deliberate upon, and judge the plan to create an Illinois Society.[1516] Chicago replaced Springfield as the place of headquarters for the Society, because Springfield was not deemed to be an efficient location for such organizational work.[1517] The organizational conference of the Illinois Society took place at the Iroquois Club and the Union League Club, in early January, 1890.[1518] The Iroquois Club and Union League Club conferences consecutively resulted in the creation of the Illinois Society on January 14, 1890, at the Club Room of the Grand Pacific Hotel of Chicago.[1519]

The Illinois Society headquarters were located at Chicago.[1520] The founders of the Illinois Society of the S.A.R., and the founders' respective leadership functions

---

[1512] Year Book of the Illinois Society Of The Sons of the American Revolution Incorporated. (1896). Pp. 3-5. Chicago, Illinois: Wm. Johnston Printing Co. Google Books.
[1513] Year Book of the Illinois Society Of The Sons of the American Revolution Incorporated. (1896). Chicago, Illinois: Wm. Johnston Printing Co. Google Books.
[1514] Year Book of the Illinois Society Of The Sons of the American Revolution Incorporated. (1896). Pp. 20-21. Chicago, Illinois: Wm. Johnston Printing Co. Google Books.
[1515] Year Book of the Illinois Society Of The Sons of the American Revolution Incorporated. (1896). Pp. 20-21. Chicago, Illinois: Wm. Johnston Printing Co. Google Books.
[1516] Year Book of the Illinois Society Of The Sons of the American Revolution Incorporated. (1896). Pp. 20-21. Chicago, Illinois: Wm. Johnston Printing Co. Google Books.
[1517] Year Book of the Illinois Society Of The Sons of the American Revolution Incorporated. (1896). Pp. 20-21. Chicago, Illinois: Wm. Johnston Printing Co. Google Books.
[1518] Year Book of the Illinois Society Of The Sons of the American Revolution Incorporated. (1896). Pp. 20-21. Chicago, Illinois: Wm. Johnston Printing Co. Google Books.
[1519] Year Book of the Illinois Society Of The Sons of the American Revolution Incorporated. (1896). Pp. 20-21. Chicago, Illinois: Wm. Johnston Printing Co. Google Books.
[1520] Year Book of the Illinois Society Of The Sons of the American Revolution Incorporated. (1896). Pp. 20-21. Chicago, Illinois: Wm. Johnston Printing Co. Google Books.

within the organization, included the following persons and jobs: General George Crook served as the first President; Reverend Charles E. Cheney served as the First Vice-President; Hobart C. Chatfield-Taylor served as the Second Vice-President; Richard Robins served as Secretary; Horatio L. Wait served as Treasurer; John D. Vandercook served as Registrar; George E. Plumbe served as Historian; and C. R. Vandercook served as Sergeant-At-Arms.[1521] Additional founders included the following persons who served as the founding Board of Managers of the Illinois Society of the S.A.R.: Frederick Redfield Southmayd, Jr., of Chicago; John W. Vance of Springfield; Edward A. Hill of Chicago; John C. Long of Chicago; Daniel H. Paddock of Kankakee; John Carroll Power of Springfield; T. B. Witherspoon of Chicago; John A. Jameson of Chicago; Wheeler Bartram of Chicago; James Nevins Hyde of Chicago; Benjamin A. Fessenden of Chicago; Frederic C. Hale of Chicago; Anson B. Cook of Libertyville; Philip G. Monroe of Chicago; and Rockwood W. Hosmer of Chicago.[1522] George B. Abbott served as Delegate at Large in 1890 and Horatio L. Wait served as Delegate in 1890.[1523] Southmayd was Registrar of the Society for the business year ending December 3, 1891, and returned to membership within the Board of Managers for the business year ending December 3, 1892.[1524] Illinois Society founder John Carroll Power, mentioned above, was one of the most significant historians of Illinois, and produced a history of Sangamon County which remains a classic to the present day.[1525] The Constitution of the Illinois Society of the Sons of the American Revolution contained the following preamble:

> "The objects of this Society shall be to perpetuate the memory of the men who, by their services or sacrifices during the war of the American Revolution, achieved the independence of the American people; to unite and promote fellowship among their descendants; to inspire them and the community at large with a more profound

---

[1521] Year Book of the Illinois Society Of The Sons of the American Revolution Incorporated. (1896). Pp. 3-5. Chicago, Illinois: Wm. Johnston Printing Co. Google Books.

[1522] Year Book of the Illinois Society Of The Sons of the American Revolution Incorporated. (1896). Pp. 3-5. Chicago, Illinois: Wm. Johnston Printing Co. Google Books.

[1523] Year Book of the Illinois Society Of The Sons of the American Revolution Incorporated. (1896). Pp. 3-5. Chicago, Illinois: Wm. Johnston Printing Co. Google Books.

[1524] Year Book of the Illinois Society Of The Sons of the American Revolution Incorporated. (1896). Pp. 3-5. Chicago, Illinois: Wm. Johnston Printing Co. Google Books.

[1525] Year Book of the Illinois Society Of The Sons of the American Revolution Incorporated. (1896). Pp. 3-5. Chicago, Illinois: Wm. Johnston Printing Co. Google Books.

reverence for the principles of the government founded by our forefathers; to encourage historical research in relation to the American Revolution; to acquire and preserve the records of the individual services of the patriots of the war, as well as documents, relics, and landmarks; to mark the scenes of the Revolution by appropriate memorials; to celebrate the anniversaries of the prominent events of the war; to foster true patriotism; to maintain and extend the institutions of American freedom; and to carry out the purposes expressed in the preamble to the constitution of our country and the injunctions of Washington in his farewell address to the American people."[1526]

Section Fifth of the Bylaws of the Society established Chicago as the place of headquarters for the Society.[1527] Section Fifth permitted meetings to be held at other places in the State of Illinois, so long as the alternate places were chosen through votes of the Board of Managers of the Society, or by Society membership, held at a General Meeting.[1528] The establishment of the Illinois Society of the S.A.R. increased the standing of Chicago as a national center of historical stewardship, preservation, and education.[1529] Frederick Southmayd brought to the Illinois Society, both as a founder and as a member of the Board of Managers, a complex historical sensitivity, knowledge, and experience. He was a former Confederate soldier in the Civil War, a repatriated member of the restored American Union, and a man of deep colonial ancestry in the North American colonies that joined to create the United States of America in 1776.

The complete list of founding members of the Illinois Society of the S.A.R. named the following men: Frederick R. Southmayd, Jr., Gen. George Crook, Capt. Richard Robins, T. B. Witherspoon, Jerome T. Buck, J. W. Hosmer, W. E. Reed, M.D., George G. Minor, E. W. Haskins, Albert N. Percy, Benjamin A. Fessenden, Herbert C. French, Edwin L. Sherman, Frederick J. Shaler, William Sabin, Charles Francis Keeler, Edward A. Hill, George B. Abbott, M.D., The Reverend Samuel Fallows, John George Ryan, Isaac Blackwelder, Judge John A. Jamison, Albert T. Anderson, George W. Culver, Edwin F. Abbott, Hiram A. Hawkins, James H. Shields, Josiah Gray, Frank M. Alley, Stephen M. Slade, Wheeler Bartram,

---

[1526] Year Book of the Illinois Society Of The Sons of the American Revolution Incorporated. (1896). Pp. 3-5, 10. Chicago, Illinois: Wm. Johnston Printing Co. Google Books.
[1527] Year Book of the Illinois Society Of The Sons of the American Revolution Incorporated. (1896). P. 14. Chicago, Illinois: Wm. Johnston Printing Co. Google Books.
[1528] Year Book of the Illinois Society Of The Sons of the American Revolution Incorporated. (1896). P. 14. Chicago, Illinois: Wm. Johnston Printing Co. Google Books.
[1529] Year Book of the Illinois Society Of The Sons of the American Revolution Incorporated. (1896). Chicago, Illinois: Wm. Johnston Printing Co. Google Books.

Frederick C. Hale, Joseph P. Condo, Theron R. Woodard, John Carroll Power, A. T. Dusenberry, Rev. Charles E. Cheney, and Dr. James Nevins Hyde.[1530]

Col. Frederick R. Southmayd, Jr.:

Founding Ambassador of the 1893 World's Fair

Frederick Southmayd was a tireless promoter and agent for Chicago, and for the 1893 World's Columbian Exposition.[1531] Southmayd cooperated with a formidable cabinet of Cook County leaders to represent to the world that Chicago had arrived as a city of global significance.[1532] One could in all fairness say that Southmayd was one of the very men whose efforts earned for Chicago the name of "Windy City."[1533] Historians John Moses and Joseph Kirkland noted that the "booming"[1534] promotions and representations that Southmayd and his fellow workers gave on behalf of Chicago and Cook County, in order to bring the World's Columbian Exposition to the city, were as probative as they were efficient, for these expressions of municipal advocacy led to Chicago being chosen as the place of the Exposition by the United States Congress.[1535] Moses and Kirkland stated the following:

> "Among those who distinguished themselves by indefatigable and successful exertions at this time in the way of visiting and canvassing may be mentioned: Carter H. Harrison, Robert A. Walker, J. W. Ela, George M. Pullman, Patrick Kelley, E. J. Martin, F. R. Southmayd, J. F. Woodruff, Richard Waterman, John B. Payne, Gov. Joseph W. Fifer, Lt.-Gov. L. B. Ray, W. A. S. Graham, Gen. John C. Black, J. B. Carron, J. M. Clark, C. T. Yerkes, W. C. Goudy, and F. W. Peck."[1536]

[1530] Hall, Henry. (1890). Year Book of the Societies Composed of Descendants of the Men of the Revolution. P. 155. New York, NY: The Republic Press. Google Books.

[1531] Moses, John, and Kirkland, Joseph. (1895). History of Chicago, Illinois. Vol. II. P. 468. Chicago, Illinois: Munsell & Co., Publishers. Google Books.

[1532] Moses, John, and Kirkland, Joseph. (1895). History of Chicago, Illinois. Vol. II. P. 468. Chicago, Illinois: Munsell & Co., Publishers. Google Books.

[1533] Moses, John, and Kirkland, Joseph. (1895). History of Chicago, Illinois. Vol. II. P. 468. Chicago, Illinois: Munsell & Co., Publishers. Google Books.

[1534] Moses, John, and Kirkland, Joseph. (1895). History of Chicago, Illinois. Vol. II. P. 468. Chicago, Illinois: Munsell & Co., Publishers. Google Books.

[1535] Moses, John, and Kirkland, Joseph. (1895). History of Chicago, Illinois. Vol. II. P. 468. Chicago, Illinois: Munsell & Co., Publishers. Google Books.

[1536] Moses, John, and Kirkland, Joseph. (1895). History of Chicago, Illinois. Vol. II. P. 468. Chicago, Illinois: Munsell & Co., Publishers. Google Books.

Col. Frederick R. Southmayd, Jr.:

Visionary of the Chicago Confederate Memorial

Frederick Southmayd repatriated absolutely as a member of the United States of America after the defeat of the Confederacy, whose secession he had served as a Confederate soldier from New Orleans. He chose Chicago as a new home, and thus migrated northward along the Mississippi River Valley to the Great Lakes. Southmayd wished to provide a proper memorial for the estimated 7,000 Confederate soldiers who had died at Camp Douglas, the United States prison for the Confederate soldiers located at Chicago.[1537] The desire for a memorial for the thousands of unmarked dead at Camp Douglas led Southmayd and several friends to establish a new memorial organization by which to give proper burial and memorial to the Confederates.[1538] Frederick Southmayd, Col. John George Ryan, Gen. Isaac Newton Stiles, and others founded the Ex-Confederate Association of Chicago.[1539]

The September 10, 1889, edition of *The Independence Daily Reporter*, a newspaper of Independence, Kansas, contained a report that supplied proofs and evidences of the civic and patriotic sentiments held by Southmayd and his colleagues. These civic and patriotic sentiments demonstrated the ex-Confederate men's total repatriation as citizens of the United States.[1540] Volume 1 of the January, 1893, edition of the monthly journal known as *The Confederate Veteran Magazine*, a publication based in Nashville, Tennessee, contained a history of the Ex-Confederate Association of Chicago, the organization's memorial purpose, and Southmayd's participation as a founder of that organization.[1541] The Ex-Confederate Association of Chicago was established with the aim of creating a memorial for the Confederate soldiers of Camp Douglas, the Union prison of Cook County. A conference of the Ex-Confederate Association of Chicago that preceded the January, 1893, edition of *Confederate Veteran*, contained the following report:

> "This Association has appointed a committee for the purpose of raising funds with which to erect a monument over 7,000 American soldiers who died while prisoners of war at Camp Douglass, and who now lie in unmarked and neglected graves at Oakwoods Cemetery, near this city, where several acres have been assigned us through the medium of the War Department, on which we purpose to erect this monument as a fitting

---

[1537] The Confederate Veteran Magazine. (January, 1893). Vol. 1. No. 1. P. 13. Google Books.

[1538] The Confederate Veteran Magazine. (January, 1893). Vol. 1. No. 1. P. 13. Google Books.

[1539] The Confederate Veteran Magazine. (January, 1893). Vol. 1. No. 1. P. 13. Google Books.

[1540] The Independence Daily Reporter. (September 10, 1889). P. 4. Newspapers.com.

[1541] The Confederate Veteran Magazine. (January, 1893). Vol. 1. No. 1. P. 13. Google Books.

memorial to our former companions in arms. And we trust that as it is lifted toward the peaceful skies it may be symbolical of that sweet and enduring peace with which a great nation emphasizes its unstinted, brotherly reunion. On our committee are the names of three honorary members of our Association who were gallant soldiers of the Union Army, viz., Gen. I. N. Stiles, Gen. Joseph Stockton and Charles P. Packer, President of the Park National Bank of Chicago, which is the depository of the fund. We request our friends to send contributions to the above-named bank. Any information in regard to the matter can be obtained by addressing either Col. John George Ryan, chairman, or F. R. Southmayd, secretary, Room 615, No. 225 Dearborn street, Chicago."[1542]

The efforts of the Ex-Confederate Association of Chicago produced an immense memorial at Oakwoods Cemetery, which is located in the Woodlawn community of Chicago, and in what was once part of old Hyde Park Township. After many years as a Chicago civic leader, Frederick Southmayd died in 1893. He was interred at Oakwoods Cemetery, and his grave lies only a few feet from the great Confederate Mound and soldiers' memorial which he helped to create only shortly before his own death. Southmayd, Ryan, Stiles, and others helped to make Chicago a point of healing after the Civil War, a place of fusion of companionship, memorial, and sympathy. Chicago became one of the fountains of reconciliatory diplomacy and national restoration, a place that helped heal the remnant social and political fissures of the American Civil War, and a place where former Confederates could demonstrate their repatriation as United States citizens with the same vivid commitment, civic leadership, and municipal patriotism that were demonstrated by Southmayd and his Ex-Confederate brethren.[1543]

Frederick Southmayd resided at 2458 S. Wabash Avenue. This place is located within the Douglas community of the Chicago South Side.[1544] Frederick, his wife, Matilda Southmayd, and their daughters Emily and Catherine Southmayd, were all members of the Second Presbyterian Church of Chicago, where they all were admitted to membership within the church by letter on December 7, 1890.[1545] The September 4, 1889, edition of the *Fort Worth Daily Gazette* contained a detailed report of the work of several former Confederates of Chicago to give a proper and honorable burial to the Confederate soldiers who died at the Camp Douglas prison

---

[1542] The Confederate Veteran Magazine. (January, 1893). Vol. 1. No. 1. P. 13. Google Books.
[1543] The Confederate Veteran Magazine. (January, 1893). Vol. 1. No. 1. P. 13. Google Books.
[1544] The Chicago Blue Book of Selected Names of Chicago and Suburban Towns. (1890). P. 145. Chicago, Illinois: The Chicago Directory Company. Livinghistoryofillinois.com
[1545] The Second Presbyterian Church of Chicago: June 1st, 1842, to June 1st, 1892. (1892). P. 172. Published by Second Presbyterian Church. Printed at Chicago, IL, by Knight, Leonard & Co., Printers. Google Books.

at Chicago.[1546] The article was titled, "HONORING THE DEAD. Monument to the Soldiers who Died Prisoners of War at Camp Douglas. Money Wanted for the Cause—Address of the Ex-Confederate Association of Chicago to Their Countrymen."[1547] The article reads as follows:

"This association, which virtually had its incention [sic] and sprang into existence at the grave of the nation's illustrious general, U. S. Grant, has appointed the committee whose names are attached to this address for the purpose of raising funds with which to erect a monument over the 7000 American soldiers who died while prisoners of war at Camp Douglas, and who now lie in unmarked and neglected graves at Oakwoods cemetery, near this city, where several acres have been assigned us through the medium of the war department, on which we purpose to erect this monument as a fitting memorial to our former companions in arms. And we trust as it is lifted toward the peaceful skies it may be symbolical of that sweet and enduring peace with which a great nation emphasizes its unstinted, brotherly reunion. These men, during our terrible civil conflict, wore the gray, fought beneath a flag that went down in disaster and defeat, in a cause that is buried in the deep grave of oblivion and can never be resurrected. Whether that cause was right or wrong is of little avail now, for we are again a united, happy and prosperous people. As we have said, these men wore the gray, but the fact still remains that they were American citizens and American soldiers, and it is the common sentiment of the noble and liberal people of this great land of ours that no American soldier's grave should be neglected, whether he sleeps beneath the ice and snows of the North, or reposes beneath the flowers and forests of the South. And now, our countrymen, while yet the echoes of our rejoicing over the successful estalishment [sic] of constitutional republican government in this fair land by the wisdom and devotion of our common ancestry are sounding in our ears, we ask you to aid us in erecting over these men a monument that is to commemorate only American valor, which is the common inheritance of us all. On our committee are the names of three honorary members of our association, who were gallant soldiers in the Union army, viz: Gen. I. N. Stiles, Gen. Joseph Stockton and Charles P. Packer, president of the Park national bank of Chicago, which is the depository of the fund. We request our friends to send contributions to the above-named bank. Sums in any amount will be gladly received, and they will be duly acknowledged by the secretary of the committee. Any information in regard to the matter can be obtained by

---

[1546] Fort Worth Daily Gazette. (September 4, 1889). P. 4. Newspapers.com.
[1547] Fort Worth Daily Gazette. (September 4, 1889). P. 4. Newspapers.com.

addressing either Col. John George Ryan, chairman, or F. R. Southmayd, secretary, room 615, No. 225 Dearborn street, Chicago."[1548]

John White was President of the Ex-Confederate Association of Chicago.[1549] Other members of the organizational board were John G. Ryan, who served as Chairman of the Association, Frederick R. Southmayd, who was Secretary of the Association, Charles P. Packer, H. T. Coffee, R. Lee France, Joseph Stockton, I. N. Stiles, George Forrester, and R. H. Stewart.[1550] Manifest throughout the Fort Worth report were the tones and meanings of unequivocal political reconciliation, repatriation, and reunion among the Association's board members.[1551] The very fact that three Union Army officers cooperated with Frederick Southmayd and the other former Confederates to create and administer the Ex-Confederate Association of Chicago proved the strength of restored union and alliance.[1552] Chicago possessed the distinction of hosting this organization, and thereby also possessed the dignity of being a central and symbolic place of postbellum reconciliation, union, and alliance.[1553] The political hemorrhage of secession and war, rooted in the worsening divisions and alienations that flowed through earlier United States history, manifested violently at Fort Sumter, terminated finally at Appomattox Courthouse, and healed civically, in part, at Chicago in 1889 with the construction of this monument at Oakwoods Cemetery.[1554] The Confederate Monument at Oakwoods Cemetery, in the Woodlawn community of Chicago, signified a resurrected American national union.[1555]

Frederick Southmayd admired particularly the 1858 poem, *The Loved and Lost*, which was a poem that had been written by an author identified only by the name, "Dorcas." Wishing to promote the meaning and ethics of the poem, Southmayd shared the poem with the *Chicago Tribune*, in 1888. The December 6, 1888, edition of the *Tribune* carried the final stanza of the poem, which read as follows:

> "It bid us do the work that they laid down—Take up the song where they broke off the strain; So journeying till we reach the heavenly town, Where are laid up our treasures and our crown, And our lost loved ones will be found again."[1556]

[1548] Fort Worth Daily Gazette. (September 4, 1889). P. 4. Newspapers.com.
[1549] Fort Worth Daily Gazette. (September 4, 1889). P. 4. Newspapers.com.
[1550] Fort Worth Daily Gazette. (September 4, 1889). P. 4. Newspapers.com.
[1551] Fort Worth Daily Gazette. (September 4, 1889). P. 4. Newspapers.com.
[1552] Fort Worth Daily Gazette. (September 4, 1889). P. 4. Newspapers.com.
[1553] Fort Worth Daily Gazette. (September 4, 1889). P. 4. Newspapers.com.
[1554] Fort Worth Daily Gazette. (September 4, 1889). P. 4. Newspapers.com.
[1555] Fort Worth Daily Gazette. (September 4, 1889). P. 4. Newspapers.com.
[1556] Chicago Tribune. (December 6, 1888). P. 10. Newspapers.com.

Southmayd apparently submitted the poem, *The Loved and Lost*, to the *Chicago Tribune* with the purpose and hope that some reader would know the name of the poem's author.[1557] It is unknown whether Southmayd discovered the identity of the poem's author, who bore only the cryptic *nom- de-plume*, "Dorcas." It could not have been mere coincidence that Southmayd appreciated this poem so much, whose verse poignantly celebrated loved ones who had been lost to death, because Southmayd had experienced and witnessed the terrible losses of the Civil War and the yellow fever plagues of the postbellum South.[1558] *The Loved and Lost* originally appeared as a published poem within the September, 1858, edition of *Church of England Magazine*.[1559]

Rebecca Bull (Southmayd) Holmes, sister of Frederick Southmayd and Charles Goodrich Southmayd, died in 1890, at New Orleans. Rebecca married Enoch Turner Holmes, Sr., of New Orelans. That same year, Frederick Southmayd penned an opinion in the *Chicago Tribune*. The opinion served the purpose of severe reform and charged another newspaper with misapprehension of the meaning of statesmanship. Southmayd argued for the genuine and honorable meaning of politics.[1560]

> "Politics, in its highest meaning (which is the true one) 'is the science of government—that part of ethics which consists in the regulation and government of a nation or State, for the preservation of its safety, peace, and prosperity, the argumentation of its strength and resources, and the protection of its citizens in their rights, with the preservation and improvement of their morals.'"[1561]

Frederick Southmayd worked with Postmaster General Adlai Ewing Stevenson in convincing Alabama congressmen and other prominent Alabamians in 1889 that Chicago would be the optimal place for the 1893 World's Columbian Exposition.[1562] Stevenson and Southmayd visited several civic leaders of Birmingham, Alabama, around September 26, 1889, in order to represent Chicago as the best city to receive the Columbian Exposition.[1563] Southmayd personally

---

[1557] Chicago Tribune. (December 6, 1888). P. 10. Newspapers.com.
[1558] Chicago Tribune. (December 6, 1888). P. 10. Newspapers.com.
[1559] *The Loved and Lost*. Scholarly Editing: The Annual Of The Association For Documentary Editing. (2013). Vol. 34. Scholarlyediting.org.
[1560] Chicago Tribune. (July 14, 1890). P. 8. Newspapers.com.
[1561] Chicago Tribune. (July 14, 1890). P. 8. Newspapers.com.
[1562] The Daily City News (Newcastle, Pennsylvania). (September 27, 1889). P. 4. Newspapers.com.
[1563] The Montgomery Advertiser (Alabama). (September 26, 1889). P. 2. Newspapers.com.

visited the houses of congressmen at Birmingham.[1564] Since the United States Congress possessed the power of choice with respect to the place for the Exposition, people from the various cities under consideration to be awarded the Fair were all tasked with the job of providing arguments, proofs, facts, and evidences for why their respective home cities would be the ideal places for the Fair. Southmayd's work with Adlai Stevenson in promoting Chicago in the South demonstrated again the reconciliation and repatriation of former Confederates who once again viewed the United States as a union, not a nation of division.[1565]

The 1893 World's Fair created a plethora of issues relevant to government and public administration. One such issue was whether the Fair should operate on Sundays.[1566] A related issue that emerged was whether Chicago should permit the Fair personnel to sell alcoholic beverages on Sundays.[1567] The Hyde Park Auxiliary of the Columbian Sabbath Observance Society advocated both for the closing of the Fair on Sundays, and for the revocation of the order that granted the privilege to sell alcoholic beverages on Sundays.[1568] The Observance Society met at the Hyde Park Methodist Church on Tuesday, February 2, 1892, to discuss and decide how to prosecute the case for the Sunday closure and Sunday alcoholic beverage ban.[1569] John M. Locke, an Episcopalian, submitted the following statement: "Episcopalians are in favor of petitioning the World's Fair Directory to close the Exposition on Sunday, as well as revoking the order permitting the sale of liquors upon the grounds."[1570]

Multiple Episcopal congregations supported the Sunday closure policy and the resultant closure pleading, according to Locke.[1571] Judge Hibbard presided over the meeting of the Hyde Park Auxiliary of the Sabbath Observance Society and appointed a resolutions committee to produce, design, and formalize opinions and resolutions for the Society regarding the Sunday closure policies and issues.[1572] The Sunday Closure Policy Committee consisted of Frederick Southmayd, Paul Cornell, and John M. Locke.[1573] E. F. Cragin was Chairman of the Columbian Sabbath Observance Society.[1574] Cragin urged employers to grant half-holidays to employees during the Exposition, and the Sunday Closure Policy Committee

---

[1564] The Montgomery Advertiser (Alabama). (September 26, 1889). P. 2. Newspapers.com.
[1565] Fort Worth Daily Gazette. (September 4, 1889). P. 4. Newspapers.com.
[1566] Chicago Tribune. (February 3, 1892). P. 2. Newspapers.com.
[1567] Chicago Tribune. (February 3, 1892). P. 2. Newspapers.com.
[1568] Chicago Tribune. (February 3, 1892). P. 2. Newspapers.com.
[1569] Chicago Tribune. (February 3, 1892). P. 2. Newspapers.com.
[1570] Chicago Tribune. (February 3, 1892). P. 2. Newspapers.com.
[1571] Chicago Tribune. (February 3, 1892). P. 2. Newspapers.com.
[1572] Chicago Tribune. (February 3, 1892). P. 2. Newspapers.com.
[1573] Chicago Tribune. (February 3, 1892). P. 2. Newspapers.com.
[1574] Chicago Tribune. (February 3, 1892). P. 2. Newspapers.com.

appears from the report to have drawn upon a precedented diplomacy in formulating the arguments for the Sunday closure policy at the Fair.

Frederick Southmayd, Paul Cornell, and John M. Locke compared the Sunday closure policy at the Paris Exposition to the one under consideration at the 1893 Exposition. The three committeemen cited the public policy precedent that had been established at the Paris Exposition, a fair at which European and American exhibitioners closed their exhibits in observance of the Sabbath Day. Southmayd, Cornell, and Locke thus built an argument for the Sunday closure policy based on the precedent and policy of a prior exposition, and in so doing blended diplomatic policy with precedential policy in formulating the policy argument for the observance of the Sabbath at Chicago.[1575] The *Tribune* report summarized the policy resolution as follows:

> "The resolutions submitted by the committee were adopted. They said that desecration of the Sabbath in America would be an injustice to European countries where efforts are now in progress to reinstate Sunday observance, and that we should not go back from the example given Europe at the Paris Exposition by English and Americans who closed their exhibits Sunday."[1576]

J. Sidney Villere and Frederick Southmayd were promoters and founders of the Louisiana Exhibit at the World's Columbian Exposition.[1577] The January 31, 1891, edition of the *Opelousas Courier* of Louisiana, reported that Southmayd and Villere were members of the Sons of Louisiana, a history and heritage organization, and were exhorting Louisianans to help build and finance an excellent Louisiana exhibit for the Chicago World's Fair.[1578] At the January 6, 1891, meeting of the Society of Sons of Louisiana, Southmayd and Villere were appointed to constitute a promotion committee for the representation of Louisiana at the forthcoming Columbian Exposition.[1579] As members of the Society of the Sons of Louisiana at Chicago, both men were well-situated to represent both Chicago and Louisiana to the world, and to represent the two places to each other.[1580] This mutual representation reiterated the reconciliatory diplomacy between the reunited North and South that existed in Chicago, and again fostered the renewal of civic union of post-Reconstruction America.[1581] The 1891 Chicago

---

[1575] Chicago Tribune. (February 3, 1892). P. 2. Newspapers.com.
[1576] Chicago Tribune. (February 3, 1892). P. 2. Newspapers.com.
[1577] The Opelousas Courier. (January 31, 1891). P. 4. Newspapers.com.
[1578] The Opelousas Courier. (January 31, 1891). P. 4. Newspapers.com.
[1579] The Opelousas Courier. (January 31, 1891). P. 4. Newspapers.com.
[1580] The Opelousas Courier. (January 31, 1891). P. 4. Newspapers.com.
[1581] The Opelousas Courier. (January 31, 1891). P. 4. Newspapers.com.

report, which was carried by *The Opelousas Courier*, stated the following in the concluding language of its appeal to Louisiana to represent itself at Chicago:

> "Louisiana has never been one whit behind any other State, in doing her whole duty, nor has she ever lacked sons of broad minds and public spirit to maintain her honor and show her glory; and certainly at a juncture so fraught with the country's honor and her own proud name, she will through her sons be equal to this grand occasion. Our Society will most gladly aid in this, to any extent within its individual and collective power.
>
> Very Respectfully,
> —J. Sidney Villere,
> —F. R. Southmayd."[1582]

We will next discuss the Chicago history of Enoch Turner Holmes, Jr., who was the nephew of Col. Frederick R. Southmayd, Jr.

Enoch Turner Holmes, Jr. of Chicago

Enoch Turner Holmes, Jr., was the son of Enoch Turner Holmes and Rebecca Bull (Southmayd) Holmes, of New Orleans.[1583] Enoch T. Holmes, Jr., was also the nephew of Col. Frederick Redfield Southmayd, Jr., of New Orleans and Chicago, and the nephew of Charles Goodrich Southmayd of New Orleans. Enoch T. Holmes, Jr., married Annie Hepburn of New Orleans.[1584] The children born to Enoch and Annie (Hepburn) Holmes included Margaret Holmes, who married Ambrose Riley Trumbo of Chicago; Anne Holmes, who married Charles Shepard Reed, Jr., also of Chicago; and Enoch Turner Holmes, III, who died at the age of eight.[1585]

Mrs. Enoch Turner Holmes was associated with the Chicago-based Illinois Wilson and Marshall Women's League at least as early as 1912, according to the October 8, 1912, edition of *The Inter Ocean*.[1586] Mrs. Holmes was a member of Les Matinées Francaises, a Chicago-based French culture salon club whose members discussed French culture and performed French works at Francophile salon gatherings.[1587] Mrs. Dorr E. Felt of 432 Wellington Avenue hosted Les Matinées Francaises and its members on November 7, 1915, at the Felt home on Wellington Avenue. Mrs. Dorr E. Felt was the wife of Dorr Eugene Felt of Chicago

---

[1582] The Opelousas Courier. (January 31, 1891). P. 4. Newspapers.com.

[1583] Cutter, William Richard. (1930). American Biography: A New Encyclopedia. Vol. 41. New York, NY: American Historical Society. Google Books.

[1584] Cutter, William Richard. (1930). American Biography: A New Encyclopedia. Vol. 41. New York, NY: American Historical Society. Google Books.

[1585] Cutter, William Richard. (1930). American Biography: A New Encyclopedia. Vol. 41. New York, NY: American Historical Society. Google Books.

[1586] The Inter Ocean. (October 8, 1912). P. 6. Newspapers.com.

[1587] Chicago Tribune. (November 17, 1915). P. 13. Newspapers.com.

and Michigan. Dorr Felt was the inventor of the comptometer, the co-founder of the Felt & Tarrant Manufacturing Company of Chicago, and the holder of forty-six patents.[1588] The members of Les Matinées Francaises at the time included Mrs. Enoch Turner Holmes, Jr., Mrs. Jefferson Jackson, Mrs. Charles B. Bowers, Ms. Emma L. Walton, Ms. Gertrude Spoor, Mrs. Elwin A. Roser, Ms. Josephine Van Meenen, Ms. Marjorie Westerlund, Ms. Leonore Ray, and Mrs. Harvey D. Welsh.[1589]

Marie Lydia Standish was the Director of Les Matinées Francaises, and was reputed to be one of the foremost students and presenters of French language and culture in Chicago.[1590] She had studied at the Auteuril convent.[1591] Standish oversaw the productions and performances of the Chicago Francophile club, and in January, 1915, she managed the production of a performance of a play by Henri Bordeaux, which was to be held at the 6255 N. Kenmore residence of Lightner Henderson, in what would become the Edgewater community of the Chicago North Side.[1592] At the club's event at the Henderson home Standish performed a reading. Mrs. Luella Chilson-Ohrman sang, Mrs. Harry Wilder Osborne played an unspecified instrument, and a play by Henri Bourdeax was performed by members Mrs. Jefferson Jackson, Mrs. Elwin A. Roser, Mrs. William Bates Price, and Mrs. Harold Grosvenor Sperling.[1593] Mrs. Enoch Turner Holmes, Jr., helped manage the salon event, working with Mrs. Lightner Henderson, Mrs. Charles B. Bowers, Mrs. Walter Gerhardt Deemer, Mrs. Arthur E. George, Mrs. Benjamin Levering, Mrs. Walter Dwight Moody, Mrs. George Bateman Beatty, Mrs. Henry Noble Foster, Mrs. John E. Kehoe, Mrs. William A. Tubbs, Ms. Maude Berry, Ms. Gertrude Spoor, Ms. Lydia Earle Whitted, Ms. Leonore Ray, and Ms. Marjorie Westerlund.[1594] The tea tables at the event were managed by Mrs. J. Roland Kay and Mrs. Frederic D. Ansley.[1595]

Enoch Turner Holmes, Jr., and his wife resided at 735 Waveland Avenue in the Lake View community, near Lincoln Park.[1596] In 1920, their daughter, Margaret Holmes, married Ambrose Riley Trumbo of 430 Diversey Parkway, a place located on the border of Lake View community and Lincoln Park community.[1597] Ambrose and Margaret were said to have spent a yearlong honeymoon in California before

[1588] Dorr Eugene Felt biographical sketch. Findagrave.com.
[1589] Chicago Tribune. (November 17, 1915). P. 13. Newspapers.com.
[1590] Chicago Tribune. (January 8, 1915). P. 11. Newspapers.com.
[1591] Chicago Tribune. (January 8, 1915). P. 11. Newspapers.com.
[1592] Chicago Tribune. (January 8, 1915). P. 11. Newspapers.com.
[1593] Chicago Tribune. (January 8, 1915). P. 11. Newspapers.com.
[1594] Chicago Tribune. (January 8, 1915). P. 11. Newspapers.com.
[1595] Chicago Tribune. (January 8, 1915). P. 11. Newspapers.com.
[1596] Chicago Tribune. (September 9, 1920). P. 21. Newspapers.com.
[1597] Chicago Tribune. (September 9, 1920). P. 21. Newspapers.com.

returning to Chicago.[1598] Another daughter, Ann Holmes, married Charles Shepherd Reed, Jr., and was later a resident of Ottawa, Illinois.[1599] Ann Holmes Reed was interred at Rosehill Cemetery on the North Side of Chicago.[1600] Rosehill Cemetery was co-founded by Jedediah Hyde Lathrop, a cousin of Enoch Turner Holmes, Jr., and Frederick Southmayd, Jr.

Mrs. Enoch Turner Holmes was one of many Chicagoans who contributed to the civic and social development of Miami, as can be seen from the fact that both Holmes and Mrs. Walter Deemer, who both were members of the Chicago Francophile club, were two of the founders of the Miami League of Women Voters.[1601]

Enoch Turner Holmes, Jr., served on the Cook County Grand Jury in February, 1899, with John Jacob Glessner, John Graves Shedd, Patrick Brennan, Harry J. Cassady, David Chapman, Henry Cork, William R. Donley, Patrick J. Fay, Lyman D. Hammond, Lewis P. Hammond, Thomas E. Healy, William J. Hinrichs, William C. Hollister, William A. Hutchinson, Joseph T. Kendall, R. J. Kittredge, Nicholas J. Neary, Thomas C. S. Nolan, Edwin S. Sibley, Alistair I. Valentine, Charles B. Van Kirk, and H. L. Wendt.[1602] This Cook County grand jury cooperated with Judge Elbert Henry Gary, Illinois State's Attorney Charles Samuel Deneen, and Assistant Illinois State's Attorney Howard O. Sprogle.[1603] The purpose for which the grand jury had been summoned and assembled was the search, detection, and investigation of gambling in Chicago. Judge Gary complimented the grand jurors by saying they all appeared to be honest citizens, and accordingly charged the grand jurors with the powers of search, deliberation, judgment, charge, and ignoramus (ignoramus is a concept from jurisprudence that means "refusal to charge," "refusal to create liability").[1604] John J. Glessner, industrialist of Chicago and Ohio, and the principal founder of the Chicago Symphony Orchestra, served as Foreman of this particular Cook County Grand Jury.[1605] During that same court day, the grand jury produced judgment and charge against John Leonard for having committed robbery of wine merchant Henry Hachmeister at 242 Orleans Street.[1606] Albert Eddy, Bernard Timmerman, and six others had been excused from grand jury duty for personal reasons.[1607] At the time

---

[1598] Chicago Tribune. (September 9, 1920). P. 21. Newspapers.com.
[1599] Chicago Tribune. (August 2, 1933). P. 20. Newspapers.com.
[1600] Chicago Tribune. (August 2, 1933). P. 20. Newspapers.com.
[1601] The Miami News. (October 26, 1940). P. 7. Newspapers.com.
[1602] Chicago Tribune. (February 21, 1899). P. 2. Newspapers.com.
[1603] Chicago Tribune. (February 21, 1899). P. 2. Newspapers.com.
[1604] Chicago Tribune. (February 21, 1899). P. 2. Newspapers.com.
[1605] Chicago Tribune. (February 21, 1899). P. 2. Newspapers.com.
[1606] Chicago Tribune. (February 21, 1899). P. 2. Newspapers.com.
[1607] Chicago Tribune. (February 21, 1899). P. 2. Newspapers.com.

of the convention of the winter, 1899, Cook County Grand Jury, Holmes resided at 1643 Briar Place, in the Lake View community.[1608]

Enoch Holmes helped to promote the 1893 World's Columbian Exposition when he served as a founder and committee member of the State of Louisiana organization at the 1893 World's Fair.[1609] The Louisiana delegation possessed responsibility for producing and representing the State of Louisiana at the World's Fair.[1610] The State of Louisiana established its World's Fair headquarters at the Grand Pacific Hotel in Chicago under the supervision of Louisiana Lieutenant Governor Charles Parlange, and decorated the office, "with cane, cotton and other Louisiana products."[1611] Archer Brown, who was a son-in-law of United States Supreme Court Chief Justice Melville Weston Fuller, possessed the responsibility for looking after the Louisiana Delegation for the World's Fair. Brown would have worked with both Holmes and Frederick Southmayd, Jr., in developing the Louisiana exhibit at Chicago for the Fair, in addition to his work with Lt. Governor Parlange.[1612] Melville Weston Fuller worked with John Whitfield Bunn and many others to establish the Abraham Lincoln Association. The Louisiana Exhibit at the World's Columbian Exposition showed the aesthetic care and precision that defined the production of state buildings and exhibits at the Fair.

Enoch Holmes was elected a Delegate to the 1900 Illinois Democratic Convention, and represented the Twenty-Fifth Ward of Chicago.[1613] Holmes's fellow Delegates from the Twenty-Sixth were Donald L. Morrill, Thomas Whalen, George Bayle, A. J. Ford, Edward Madden, John A. Mahoney, Charles A. McDonald, and Peter Phillip.[1614] A Southerner who had relocated to the North, Holmes, like his uncle, Frederick R. Southmayd, Jr., would have retained possession of sympathies for the Democratic Party.[1615] Enoch Turner Holmes died December 27, 1927, in Miami, and was returned to Chicago for interment six months after his death.[1616]

Enoch T. Holmes worked as an inventor in Chicago and discovered a process for "treating fibrous substances."[1617] On the basis of this discovery, Holmes successfully obtained United States Patent 704,259.[1618] The novel process included

---

[1608] The Inter Ocean. (February 21, 1899). P. 3. Newspapers.com.

[1609] The New Orleans Times-Democrat. (October 21, 1892). P. 1. Newspapers.com.

[1610] The New Orleans Times Democrat. (October 21, 1892). P. 1. Newspapers.com.

[1611] The New Orleans Times Democrat. (October 21, 1892). P. 1. Newspapers.com.

[1612] The New Orleans Times Democrat. (October 21, 1892). P. 1. Newspapers.com.

[1613] Chicago Tribune. (June 23, 1900). P. 4. Newspapers.com.

[1614] Chicago Tribune. (June 23, 1900). P. 4. Newspapers.com.

[1615] Chicago Tribune. (June 23, 1900). P. 4. Newspapers.com.

[1616] The Miami News. (June 16, 1928). P. 7. Newspapers.com.

[1617] Noyes, William A. Editor. Review of American Chemical Research. (July 8, 1902). Vol. 8-9. P. 98. Easton, PA: The Chemical Publishing Company. Google Books.

[1618] Noyes, William A. Editor. Review of American Chemical Research. (July 8, 1902). Vol. 8-9. P. 98. Easton, PA: The Chemical Publishing Company. Google Books.

the boiling of flax straw in an alkaline solution at temperatures of six or seven degrees (the specific temperature metric was not clear from the report).[1619] The metrics and elements that constituted the treatment process included the following: 100 pounds of fibrous substance per 50 gallons of alkaline solution; pressure of 80 to 100 pounds; boiling time of four to six hours.[1620] Holmes assigned one-third of the patent on the chemical process to John C. Brocklebank of Chicago.[1621] The chemical patent report did not specify the purpose of the Holmes-Brocklebank patent assignment, but supports the theory that Holmes and Brocklebank intended to form an industrial partnership to capitalize on the patented chemical process.[1622]

Holmes served as Ward Superintendent for the Thirty-Fifth Ward of Chicago.[1623] The City Council approved payment of a claim filed by Holmes for payment for his service as Ward Superintendent for the Thirty-Fifth Ward, in 1900.[1624] Assistant Chicago Superintendent of Streets F. W. Solon apparently provided statement, affidavit, and support for the right of Holmes to collect payment for the administrative service that Holmes had given.[1625] In 1900 the boundaries of the Thirty-Fifth Ward were Austin on the west (6,000 west); Laramie on the east (5,200 west); North Avenue on the north (1,600 north); and 12th Street on the south (1,200 south).[1626] This ward was located at the western end of Chicago, and near Cicero and Oak Park. The Green Line of the Chicago Transit Authority traverses the center of this area now, before entering Oak Park.

The Fergusons of Pullman:

<u>Founders of the Pullman Community, Cousins of the Fergusons of Springfield</u>

Dr. John McLean, M.D., a historian of Illinois, and a relative of the Fergusons and Lees of Chicago, wrote a 1919 history of the Ferguson and allied families in

---

[1619] Noyes, William A. Editor. Review of American Chemical Research. (July 8, 1902). Vol. 8-9. P. 98. Easton, PA: The Chemical Publishing Company. Google Books.
[1620] Noyes, William A. Editor. Review of American Chemical Research. (July 8, 1902). Vol. 8-9. P. 98. Easton, PA: The Chemical Publishing Company. Google Books.
[1621] Noyes, William A. Editor. Review of American Chemical Research. (July 8, 1902). Vol. 8-9. P. 98. Easton, PA: The Chemical Publishing Company. Google Books.
[1622] Noyes, William A. Editor. Review of American Chemical Research. (July 8, 1902). Vol. 8-9. P. 98. Easton, PA: The Chemical Publishing Company. Google Books.
[1623] Proceedings of the City Council of Chicago. (1900). Page number not clear at time of obtainment of record. Chicago, IL: The City Council. Google Books.
[1624] City Of Chicago. Sixth Annual Report Of The Civil Service Commission To His Honor, The Mayor. (January 16, 1901). Vol. 6. P. 349. Chicago, IL: Printed for the Civil Service Commission. Google Books.
[1625] City Of Chicago. Sixth Annual Report Of The Civil Service Commission To His Honor, The Mayor. (January 16, 1901). Vol. 6. P. 349. Chicago, IL: Printed for the Civil Service Commission. Google Books.
[1626] 1900 Census Ward Boundaries for the City of Chicago. alookatcook.com.

Illinois. McLean discussed the Fergusons of Chicago with considerable detail. William Ferguson died in DuQuoin, Illinois. The widowed Anna Ferguson relocated with her family to Hyde Park Township, in the southern Chicago metropolitan region, prior to the time when Chicago annexed Hyde Park Township.[1627] The four children born to William and Anna Ferguson were Matthew Ferguson; Florence Ferguson, who married William Lee; Helen Edith Ferguson; and Clara Ferguson.[1628] The family were among the founding settlers of the Pullman community and neighborhood of Chicago.[1629] Matthew Ferguson worked for the Pullman Company and was killed in a train accident in Indiana while he was delivering a shipment of train cars to Louisville, Kentucky.[1630]

When George Pullman started developing the industrial community and neighborhood in Hyde Park Township that would bear his name, he originally operated through a purchasing agent named Col. James H. Bowen.[1631] The reason for the Bowen purchasing agency was that it concealed Pullman's identity and Pullman wanted to keep his property acquisition plan secret.[1632] The reason for the transactional secrecy, according to McLean, was that Pullman knew that if the information were publicized that he was buying up large quantities of space in the Calumet Corridor, the property market would respond to the market information disclosure with a land grab and consequentially soaring prices.[1633] That is, if the public had noticed George Pullman buying multiple properties in a specific place, the public, not least of whom were the Calumet property sellers, would probably have assumed that the values of properties in that place would soon increase in value, perhaps tremendously.[1634]

The theorized and fearfully anticipated Calumet land grab would have resulted in a localized Calumet land boom. The land grab could have caused a real estate bubble that could have both hindered Pullman's land plan and nullified his prospective accounting for costs, benefits, and developments in the Calumet

[1627] McLean, John. (1919). One-Hundred Years In Illinois: 1818-1918. P. 229. Chicago, IL: Peterson Linotyping Co. Google Books.

[1628] McLean, John. (1919). One-Hundred Years In Illinois: 1818-1918. P. 243. Chicago, IL: Peterson Linotyping Co. Google Books.

[1629] McLean, John. (1919). One-Hundred Years In Illinois: 1818-1918. Pp. 229, 243. Chicago, IL: Peterson Linotyping Co. Google Books.

[1630] McLean, John. (1919). One-Hundred Years In Illinois: 1818-1918. P. 243. Chicago, IL: Peterson Linotyping Co. Google Books.

[1631] McLean, John. (1919). One-Hundred Years In Illinois: 1818-1918. P. 229. Chicago, IL: Peterson Linotyping Co. Google Books.

[1632] McLean, John. (1919). One-Hundred Years In Illinois: 1818-1918. P. 229. Chicago, IL: Peterson Linotyping Co. Google Books.

[1633] McLean, John. (1919). One-Hundred Years In Illinois: 1818-1918. P. 229. Chicago, IL: Peterson Linotyping Co. Google Books.

[1634] McLean, John. (1919). One-Hundred Years In Illinois: 1818-1918. P. 229. Chicago, IL: Peterson Linotyping Co. Google Books.

Corridor.[1635] The probable price increase might have immobilized, or at least delayed, the Pullman development plan by making the plan untenable, or at the very least, impractical, as McLean has stated.[1636] Mr. Pullman's sterling reputation and personal financial resource, therefore, posed a peculiar market risk to himself, in that his reputation would have preceded him and caused a potentially insurmountable land grab. This fact led to the Pullman organization's choice of a policy of secrecy regarding the property acquisitions undertaken for the establishment of the Pullman community and neighborhood.[1637] McLean reported that the secrecy policy remained intact until Pullman had acquired, through Col. Bowen, some 3,000 acres for the future community, at which time the public discovered that George Pullman was the force and operator behind the entire process and organization.[1638] Presumably, the lion's share of the reputation-derivative market risk that Pullman had sought to avoid had in fact been avoided by the time the disclosure of Pullman's identity and standing as a party to the development plan occurred.[1639]

Of additional interest is the fact that John Whitfield Bunn, an early land owner and investor in the Calumet Corridor of southern Cook County and Indiana, transferred ownership of his Calumet property to Col. James H. Bowen after 1870, and no later than 1889.[1640] John Bunn had acquired the property in the Calumet Corridor in 1870, and appears from the relevant 1889 Illinois General Assembly real estate report to have been the second owner of that portion of the Calumet region, second in time and title only to William B. Egan, who had entered the land in 1853 with original rights that stemmed from a military land warrant.[1641] The Egan-Bunn property contained forty-six and a half acres located within Hyde Park Township and South Chicago, and was more specifically situated within Section 7 of Township 37 North, Range 15.[1642] This land was located north of the Indiana

[1635] McLean, John. (1919). One-Hundred Years In Illinois: 1818-1918. P. 229. Chicago, IL: Peterson Linotyping Co. Google Books.

[1636] McLean, John. (1919). One-Hundred Years In Illinois: 1818-1918. P. 229. Chicago, IL: Peterson Linotyping Co. Google Books.

[1637] McLean, John. (1919). One-Hundred Years In Illinois: 1818-1918. P. 229. Chicago, IL: Peterson Linotyping Co. Google Books.

[1638] McLean, John. (1919). One-Hundred Years In Illinois: 1818-1918. P. 229. Chicago, IL: Peterson Linotyping Co. Google Books.

[1639] McLean, John. (1919). One-Hundred Years In Illinois: 1818-1918. P. 229. Chicago, IL: Peterson Linotyping Co. Google Books.

[1640] Reports Made to the General Assembly of Illinois. (1889). Vol. IV. P. 26. Springfield, IL: Springfield Printing Co., State Printers. Google Books.

[1641] Reports Made to the General Assembly of Illinois. (1889). Vol. IV. P. 26. Springfield, IL: Springfield Printing Co., State Printers. Google Books; McLean, John. (1919). One-Hundred Years In Illinois: 1818-1918. P. 229. Chicago, IL: Peterson Linotyping Co. Google Books.

[1642] Reports Made to the General Assembly of Illinois. (1889). Vol. IV. P. 26. Springfield, IL: Springfield Printing Co., State Printers. Google Books.

boundary line, and stood adjacent to Hyde Lake and Wolf Lake.[1643] Wolf lake remains to this day and occupies space in both Illinois and Indiana. Hyde Lake, however, is presently nothing more than a phantom lake. There is nothing left of Hyde Lake but a residual marsh. The Chicago community of Hegewisch, which, along with Riverdale, is the southernmost community of Chicago, occupies this space presently.

The Illinois General Assembly report proves that Bunn was one of the earliest real estate developers and investors in the Calumet region, in Hyde Park Township, and in south Chicago. Bunn would, also in 1889, be a key mover in the construction and development of the Calumet Corridor and south Chicago when he became a founder, director, and owner of the $131,000,000 Wabash Railroad Company in May, 1889.[1644] In the twin capacities of railroad founder and real estate developer, therefore, John W. Bunn served as one of the earliest industrial developers and owners of the Calumet region of Chicago, Cook County, southern Hyde Park Township and south Chicago.[1645] Given the time range of the Bunn-Bowen realty transfer and grant, it is possible that Bunn sold the land to Bowen for the Pullman community development plan, because, as Dr. McLean has explained, Bowen was agent for George Pullman in the corporate development purchases of southern Hyde Park Township.[1646] While the Pullman development theory of the Bunn-Bowen transfer and grant possesses credibility, it is impeached somewhat by facts that support an alternative theory based on the reported chain of title for the Egan-Bunn-Bowen space.[1647]

[1643] Reports Made to the General Assembly of Illinois. (1889). Vol. IV. P. 26. Springfield, IL: Springfield Printing Co., State Printers. Google Books; McLean, John. (1919). One-Hundred Years In Illinois: 1818-1918. P. 229. Chicago, IL: Peterson Linotyping Co. Google Books.

[1644] Reports Made to the General Assembly of Illinois. (1889). Vol. IV. P. 26. Springfield, IL: Springfield Printing Co., State Printers. Google Books; McLean, John. (1919). One-Hundred Years In Illinois: 1818-1918. P. 229. Chicago, IL: Peterson Linotyping Co. Google Books.

[1645] Reports Made to the General Assembly of Illinois. (1889). Vol. IV. P. 26. Springfield, IL: Springfield Printing Co., State Printers. Google Books; McLean, John. (1919). One-Hundred Years In Illinois: 1818-1918. P. 229. Chicago, IL: Peterson Linotyping Co. Google Books.

[1646] Reports Made to the General Assembly of Illinois. (1889). Vol. IV. P. 26. Springfield, IL: Springfield Printing Co., State Printers. Google Books; McLean, John. (1919). One-Hundred Years In Illinois: 1818-1918. P. 229. Chicago, IL: Peterson Linotyping Co. Google Books.

[1647] Reports Made to the General Assembly of Illinois. (1889). Vol. IV. P. 26. Springfield, IL: Springfield Printing Co., State Printers. Google Books; McLean, John. (1919). One-Hundred Years In Illinois: 1818-1918. P. 229. Chicago, IL: Peterson Linotyping Co. Google Books.

The Chicago & Calumet Canal & Dock Company appears from the 1889 Illinois legislative report to have acquired title to the Calumet space after Bowen.[1648] The reported chain of title contains, therefore, no references to transfer and grant from James Bowen to George Pullman, from John Bunn to George Pullman, or from either Bunn or Bowen to the Pullman Company.[1649] The absences of these alternative realty transfers severely attenuate, but do not nullify, the Pullman development theory for the purpose of the Bunn-Bowen realty transfer and grant.[1650] This is so because Bowen may have, as special purchasing agent for Pullman, retained a trusteeship title over the Calumet space for the benefit of Pullman, whilst the Pullman secrecy policy remained intact to keep Mr. Pullman's identity secret during the land development process of the Pullman community development plan.[1651] Perhaps Bowen, with direction from Mr. Pullman, alienated the old Bunn property when Pullman decided the land was no longer needed for the Pullman development project, which could explain the transfer to the Chicago & Calumet Canal & Dock Company.[1652]

A supplementary and concomitant theory of the Bunn-Bowen transfer and grant stems from the foundation of the trust relationship created by the Pullman-Bowen secrecy policy.[1653] Bowen could have purchased the space from Bunn with the purpose of holding the property in trusteeship for Pullman until the time of dissolution of the Pullman-Bowen agency-based land development trust. If Bowen

---

[1648] Reports Made to the General Assembly of Illinois. (1889). Vol. IV. P. 26. Springfield, IL: Springfield Printing Co., State Printers. Google Books; McLean, John. (1919). One-Hundred Years In Illinois: 1818-1918. P. 229. Chicago, IL: Peterson Linotyping Co. Google Books.

[1649] Reports Made to the General Assembly of Illinois. (1889). Vol. IV. P. 26. Springfield, IL: Springfield Printing Co., State Printers. Google Books; McLean, John. (1919). One-Hundred Years In Illinois: 1818-1918. P. 229. Chicago, IL: Peterson Linotyping Co. Google Books.

[1650] Reports Made to the General Assembly of Illinois. (1889). Vol. IV. P. 26. Springfield, IL: Springfield Printing Co., State Printers. Google Books; McLean, John. (1919). One-Hundred Years In Illinois: 1818-1918. P. 229. Chicago, IL: Peterson Linotyping Co. Google Books.

[1651] Reports Made to the General Assembly of Illinois. (1889). Vol. IV. P. 26. Springfield, IL: Springfield Printing Co., State Printers. Google Books; McLean, John. (1919). One-Hundred Years In Illinois: 1818-1918. P. 229. Chicago, IL: Peterson Linotyping Co. Google Books.

[1652] Reports Made to the General Assembly of Illinois. (1889). Vol. IV. P. 26. Springfield, IL: Springfield Printing Co., State Printers. Google Books; McLean, John. (1919). One-Hundred Years In Illinois: 1818-1918. P. 229. Chicago, IL: Peterson Linotyping Co. Google Books.

[1653] Reports Made to the General Assembly of Illinois. (1889). Vol. IV. P. 26. Springfield, IL: Springfield Printing Co., State Printers. Google Books; McLean, John. (1919). One-Hundred Years In Illinois: 1818-1918. P. 229. Chicago, IL: Peterson Linotyping Co. Google Books.

subsequently transferred the property to Pullman, this act would have dissolved the Pullman-Bowen land development trust, re-vested Pullman with legal title and equitable title to the Calumet space, and safely added the realty to the Pullman project portfolio without causing the theorized Calumet land grab.[1654] Irrespective of the technical purpose of the Bunn-Bowen transfer and grant, the Pullmans, Bunns, Fergusons, Lees, and Col. Bowen all were civic and industrial founders of the Calumet region of Chicago and Indiana.[1655]

Dr. McLean also mentioned that Pullman acquired 1,300 additional acres after the public discovery of his identity as the leader of the industrial construction and development plan.[1656] Once acquisition of the Calumet space had been secured by Pullman, design plans and civil engineering plans became immediately necessary for the preparation, development, and use of the space for the intended Pullman Company community, factory complex, and neighborhood.[1657] The survey that prepared and inventoried the newly acquired Calumet space was undertaken by Welland F. Sargent, who was aided by William Lee.[1658] Sargent and Lee, therefore, were two key providers of the civil engineering services that studied, prepared, and provided the planning foundation for the Calumet space for George Pullman and the Pullman Company development program.[1659] We must view Sargent and Lee, who were in the service of George M. Pullman, to be engineering founders of the Pullman community and neighborhood of Chicago.[1660]

[1654] Reports Made to the General Assembly of Illinois. (1889). Vol. IV. P. 26. Springfield, IL: Springfield Printing Co., State Printers. Google Books; McLean, John. (1919). One-Hundred Years In Illinois: 1818-1918. P. 229. Chicago, IL: Peterson Linotyping Co. Google Books.

[1655] Reports Made to the General Assembly of Illinois. (1889). Vol. IV. P. 26. Springfield, IL: Springfield Printing Co., State Printers. Google Books; McLean, John. (1919). One-Hundred Years In Illinois: 1818-1918. P. 229. Chicago, IL: Peterson Linotyping Co. Google Books.

[1656] McLean, John. (1919). One-Hundred Years In Illinois: 1818-1918. P. 229. Chicago, IL: Peterson Linotyping Co. Google Books.

[1657] McLean, John. (1919). One-Hundred Years In Illinois: 1818-1918. P. 229. Chicago, IL: Peterson Linotyping Co. Google Books.

[1658] McLean, John. (1919). One-Hundred Years In Illinois: 1818-1918. P. 229. Chicago, IL: Peterson Linotyping Co. Google Books.

[1659] McLean, John. (1919). One-Hundred Years In Illinois: 1818-1918. P. 229. Chicago, IL: Peterson Linotyping Co. Google Books.

[1660] McLean, John. (1919). One-Hundred Years In Illinois: 1818-1918. P. 229. Chicago, IL: Peterson Linotyping Co. Google Books.

Henry Washington Lee:

A Father of the Calumet Corridor and the South Side of Chicago

Henry Washington Lee was the son of William Lee by a prior marriage. He was known as the "Father of the Calumet," a title which possessed multiple simultaneous meanings. Lee was a founder and father of Calumet River development, the Calumet Canal/Calumet-Saugashkee Canal System, the development of Lake Calumet, the development of the engineering plans for sanitation and harbor development at Chicago and Lake Michigan, and the Calumet Corridor industrial community. Henry Lee owned the *Calumet Record*, a newspaper of the Calumet Corridor, south side, and southeast side of Chicago.[1661] The *Calumet Record* was published on a weekly basis.[1662] Lee was considered a father of Calumet River industrial and infrastructural development. He was an official of the Sanitary District of Chicago and combined the methods of public policy advocacy with the sciences of civil engineering in order to create a new, improved economy of significance for the Calumet Corridor and the South Side of Chicago.[1663] His son, William Lee, continued his committed development of Chicago and the Calumer Corridor.

The Ferguson Sisters and the Pullman High School

Michael Loftus Ahern compiled a Chicago Public School staff directory in his 1886 political history of Chicago. Ahern listed both Florence and Helen Ferguson of the Pullman community as teachers at the Pullman High School in Public School District Number 11, as of 1886/1887.[1664] D. R. Martin, a Pullman resident, was the Superintendent of the Pullman High School when the Ferguson sisters were teachers there.[1665] The other Pullman High School teachers at this time included Lucy Silke of 1434 Michigan Avenue, Louise Vasburg of Pullman, Margaret McCartney of Hyde Park, Mrs. Q. M. Biden of Pullman, Laura White of Pullman, Anna Vasburg of Pullman, Max Merrifield of Pullman, Louise Frainor of 4326 Chapel Road, Fannie Callaway of Pullman, Carrie Lassaman of Normal Park, Nellie Leckie of South Englewood, Louise Rennick of Brookline, Lenore Goodwin

---

[1661] McLean, John. (1919). One-Hundred Years In Illinois: 1818-1918. P. 243. Chicago, IL: Peterson Linotyping Co. Google Books.
[1662] McLean, John. (1919). One-Hundred Years In Illinois: 1818-1918. P. 243. Chicago, IL: Peterson Linotyping Co. Google Books.
[1663] The Times (Munster, Indiana). (February 24, 1913). P. 1. Newspapers.com.
[1664] Ahern, Michael Loftus (1886). The Political History of Chicago. First Ed. P. 357. Chicago, IL: Michael Loftus Ahern. Google Books.
[1665] Ahern, Michael Loftus (1886). The Political History of Chicago. First Ed. P. 357. Chicago, IL: Michael Loftus Ahern. Google Books.

of E. 40th Street, Mary Smith of Pullman, and Jane Beach of Pullman.[1666] The 1921 Chicago Board of Education directory of public schools listed Helen Edith Ferguson as the Head Assistant to Principal Daniel R. Martin at the George M. Pullman High School for 1921-1922 school year.[1667]

Lydia Morton Lee, daughter of William Lee and Florence (Ferguson) Lee, graduated from the University of Chicago with the degree of Bachelor of Philosophy in 1914.[1668] Lydia married James Pearce.[1669] Multiple members of this branch of the Ferguson family attended the University of Chicago and received degrees from a variety of departments.

Memories of The Hotel Florence in Pullman

That the Hotel Florence was central to the social life of the Pullman community and neighborhood was evident from its standing as a premier community social venue. Clara Ferguson, daughter of William and Anna Ferguson, attended a dance party at the Hotel Florence in early January, 1888, along with a large number of people.[1670] A large dance reception took place at the hotel in February, 1888, with Clara in attendance.[1671] The wedding announcement for William Lee and Florence Ferguson appeared in the November 11, 1888, edition of the *Tribune*, and said that the couple would make their home in the "city of brick," referring to Pullman, after the wedding ceremony at the Ferguson home in Pullman.[1672] The Ferguson-Lee wedding took place on the evening of Thursday, November 15, 1888, at Florence Ferguson's home, and Rev. E. C. Oggel, who was the Pastor of the renowned Green Stone Church of Pullman, performed the marriage ceremony.[1673] After a honeymoon in St. Louis, the Lees made their home at the Hotel Florence in Pullman.[1674] William Lee was employed as a civil engineer with the Village Department of Public Works in Pullman at the time of the wedding.[1675] The residence of the Ferguson sisters and their mother was Number 6 Arcade Row, in

---

[1666] Ahern, Michael Loftus (1886). The Political History of Chicago. First Ed. P. 357. Chicago, IL: Michael Loftus Ahern. Google Books.
[1667] Directory of the Public Schools of the City of Chicago: 1921-1922. (1921). P. 25. Chicago, IL: Board of Education, City of Chicago. Google Books.
[1668] Alumni Directory of the University of Chicago. (1919). P. 266. Chicago, IL: The University of Chicago Press. Google Books.
[1669] Alumni Directory of the University of Chicago. (1919). P. 266. Chicago, IL: The University of Chicago Press. Google Books.
[1670] The Inter Ocean. (January 8, 1888). P. 16. Newspapers.com.
[1671] The Inter Ocean. (February 19, 1888). P. 15. Newspapers.com.
[1672] Chicago Tribune. (November 11, 1888). P. 16. Newspapers.com.
[1673] Chicago Tribune. (November 18, 1888). P. 14. Newspapers.com.
[1674] Chicago Tribune. (November 18, 1888). P. 14. Newspapers.com.
[1675] Chicago Tribune. (November 18, 1888). P. 14. Newspapers.com.

Pullman.[1676] By March, 1890, William Lee was employed as the Engineer of the Village of Harvey, a suburb located in Cook County, and adjacent to the southern boundary of Chicago.[1677] As early as September, 1882, William Lee served as a civil engineer for the Pullman community, but accepted a job as an engineer with the Hennepin Canal at that time.[1678]

William Lee co-engineered the Washington Park Club and track ground in 1883 within the Washington Park community of Chicago. Many people joined to establish the Washington Park Club in 1883.[1679] Potter Palmer, Marshall Field, Seneca D. Kimbark, Anson B. Jenks (who was a cousin of Ada Willard (Richardson) Bunn), Wirt Dexter, Lyman Blair, Nathaniel K. Fairbank, Samuel W. Allerton, Watson F. Blair, Joseph Sears, W. W. Kimball, Charles Hutchinson, Levi Z. Leiter, Gen. Philip Henry Sheridan, J. T. Chumasero, George M. Pullman, and many others, formed the club in 1883.[1680] Cottage Grove Avenue, South Park Avenue, 61st Street, and 63rd Street framed the Washington Park Club grounds.[1681] Anson Brown Jenks, Esq., founded the Chicago law firm of Walker & Jenks with The Hon. Gilbert Carlton Walker, who later served as the thirty-sixth Governor of Virginia.[1682] As noted above, Jenks was a founder of the Washington Park Club and a cousin of Ada Willard (Richardson) Bunn.

The space consisted of a clubhouse and a richly designed and engineered grounds.[1683] The original leadership of the club included Gen. Philip Sheridan as President, and Samuel Waters Allerton, Nathaniel Kellogg Fairbank, J. W. Doane, and A. S. Gage as Vice-Presidents. John R. Walshe served as Treasurer.[1684] J. E. Brewster served as Secretary, and the initial Executive Committee consisted of H. J. MacFarland, C. D. Hamill, James Van Inwagen, Martin A. Ryerson, and M. B. Hull.[1685] The purpose of the Washington Park Club was the promotion of fellowship, citizenship, and sport.[1686] The *Tribune* journalist who reported on the formation of the club noted that the club was an organizational imitation of the Jerome Club and the Coney Island Club of New York City, and of the Pimlico Club of Baltimore, and that, like all of those clubs, the Washington Park Club would serve to provide private club facilities in conjunction with public sporting exhibitions and events with the aim of blessing and fostering community in the

---

[1676] The Inter Ocean. (November 18, 1888). P. 15. Newspapers.com.

[1677] The Inter Ocean. (March 15, 1891). P. 23. Newspapers.com.

[1678] Chicago Tribune. (September 10, 1882). P. 7. Newspapers.com.

[1679] Chicago Tribune. (July 15, 1883). P. 18. Newspapers.com.

[1680] Chicago Tribune. (July 15, 1883). P. 18. Newspapers.com.

[1681] Chicago Tribune. (July 15, 1883). P. 18. Newspapers.com.

[1682] A History of the City of Chicago: Its Men and Institutions. (1900). P. 392. Chicago, IL: Chicago Inter Ocean Company. Google Books.

[1683] Chicago Tribune. (July 15, 1883). P. 18. Newspapers.com.

[1684] Chicago Tribune. (July 15, 1883). P. 18. Newspapers.com.

[1685] Chicago Tribune. (July 15, 1883). P. 18. Newspapers.com.

[1686] Chicago Tribune. (July 15, 1883). P. 18. Newspapers.com.

city.[1687] Solon Spencer Beman led the architectural conception of the club and grounds, while N. F. Barrett produced the necessary landscape engineering.[1688] William Lee provided the civil engineering under the supervision of a senior engineer named Major Benyouard.[1689] The *Tribune* report stated that: "These gentlemen have worked together with a view of making the buildings and landscape harmonize, and the entire plat as picturesque as possible."[1690] The club and grounds were situated between the Woodlawn community and the Englewood community, west and southwest of the Hyde Park community and the Kenwood community, and were accessible by the Lake Shore & Michigan Southern Railroad Company, the Illinois Central Railroad Company, the Chicago & Rock Island Railroad Company, and the Pittsburg & Fort Wayne Railroad Company.[1691] Two of these railroad companies, the Rock Island Railroad and the Michigan Southern Railroad, were founded, developed, and controlled by John Stryker and his partners and friends.[1692]

The club grounds were intended to contain both elements of privacy and publicness, with an exclusive club institutionally cooperating in civic companionship with a public sports space.[1693] The club was exclusive and patterned its membership standards on other local clubs.[1694] The clubhouse was designed with basement, attic, and a sloping entrance element that declined to the adjacent racetrack grounds.[1695] Lumber storage and servants' quarters were housed in the upper spaces of the clubhouse, and the kitchen, cellar, heating machinery room, and storage rooms occupied the foundational space.[1696] The ladies' waiting room, billiards room, parlor, entrance hall, and multiple private dining rooms, among other spaces and uses, occupied the main floor of the clubhouse.[1697] The sports grounds consisted of a main track, a practice track, a judge's stand, a timer's stand, a steeple-chase track, clubhouse, grandstand, gate lodge, stables and sheds, public terrace, club members' terrace, and various entrances.[1698]

William Lee and Florence Ferguson were two of a long list of Pullman community residents who attended a St. Valentine's Day social at the Hotel Florence on February 14, 1888.[1699] The party was one at which young men

---

[1687] Chicago Tribune. (July 15, 1883). P. 18. Newspapers.com.
[1688] Chicago Tribune. (July 15, 1883). P. 18. Newspapers.com.
[1689] Chicago Tribune. (July 15, 1883). P. 18. Newspapers.com.
[1690] Chicago Tribune. (July 15, 1883). P. 18. Newspapers.com.
[1691] Chicago Tribune. (July 15, 1883). P. 18. Newspapers.com.
[1692] Chicago Tribune. (July 15, 1883). P. 18. Newspapers.com.
[1693] Chicago Tribune. (July 15, 1883). P. 18. Newspapers.com.
[1694] Chicago Tribune. (July 15, 1883). P. 18. Newspapers.com.
[1695] Chicago Tribune. (July 15, 1883). P. 18. Newspapers.com.
[1696] Chicago Tribune. (July 15, 1883). P. 18. Newspapers.com.
[1697] Chicago Tribune. (July 15, 1883). P. 18. Newspapers.com.
[1698] Chicago Tribune. (July 15, 1883). P. 18. Newspapers.com.
[1699] The Inter Ocean. (February 15, 1888). P. 3. Newspapers.com.

presented Valentine's Day souvenirs to young ladies of the Pullman community.[1700] Both William Lee and Florence Ferguson, who were both single people at the time, attended the event.[1701] The journalist described the Pullman community streets that night as snow covered and slick with the residues of snow and ice so common to Februaries in the Great Lakes.[1702] It is of high probability that the snow-laden Valentine's Day social at the Florence Hotel was a key experience in the courtship of the young William Lee and Florence Ferguson— who were one of so many young couples of Mr. Pullman's City of Brick on the far South Side of Gilded Age Chicago.[1703] The party that evening ended quietly against the dark winter night which began the Lenten Season.[1704]

The October 7, 1888, edition of *The Inter Ocean* noted that Anna Ferguson was receiving several family members and friends at her home at Number 6 Arcade Row, which was located near the Hotel Florence.[1705] William Lee held the position of Representative of the Department of Works for Hyde Park District of Chicago at the time of Hyde Park Township's annexation by the City of Chicago in 1889.[1706] Soon after the annexation, William Lee was replaced as Hyde Park District Public Works Department Representative by William C. Walsh.[1707] Dewitt Clinton Cregier was Mayor of Chicago at the time of the city's annexation of Hyde Park Township, and he was searching for a Chief Engineer for the recently acquired Hyde Park District of Chicago.[1708] The *Inter Ocean* journalist referenced an official by the name of Commissioner Purdy who was the one to whom the occupant of the office of Chief Engineer would answer.[1709]

Clara Ferguson worked in an accounting office in Pullman in 1890, according to a November 23, 1890, report of the *Inter Ocean*.[1710] The Pullman community held a leap year cotillion party at the Hotel Florence in November or December of 1888. Helen Edith Ferguson, Clara Ferguson, and Florence (Ferguson) Lee all were in attendance.[1711] The reporter said of the event, "The leap year party at Hotel Florence is acknowledged by gentlemen favored with invitations [to] have been a grand success."[1712] In September of 1889, Pullman residents hosted a hayride

[1700] The Inter Ocean. (February 15, 1888). P. 3. Newspapers.com.
[1701] The Inter Ocean. (February 15, 1888). P. 3. Newspapers.com.
[1702] The Inter Ocean. (February 15, 1888). P. 3. Newspapers.com.
[1703] The Inter Ocean. (February 15, 1888). P. 3. Newspapers.com.
[1704] The Inter Ocean. (February 15, 1888). P. 3. Newspapers.com.
[1705] The Inter Ocean. (October 7, 1888). P. 10. Newspapers.com.
[1706] The Inter Ocean. (August 6, 1889). P. 7. Newspapers.com.
[1707] The Inter Ocean. (August 6, 1889). P. 7. Newspapers.com.
[1708] The Inter Ocean. (August 6, 1889). P. 7. Newspapers.com.
[1709] The Inter Ocean. (August 6, 1889). P. 7. Newspapers.com.
[1710] The Inter Ocean. (November 23, 1890). P. 22. Newspapers.com.
[1711] The Inter Ocean. (December 2, 1888). P. 9. Newspapers.com.
[1712] The Inter Ocean. (December 2, 1888). P. 9. Newspapers.com.

party.[1713] The party was heavily attended, and both Helen and Clara Ferguson attended, along with their friend Minnie Pogue.[1714]

As of 1891, Clara Ferguson was a member of the Idylwylde Tennis Club of Pullman, a social and recreational organization which she also served as Secretary and Treasurer.[1715] The April 26, 1891, edition of the Chicago *Inter Ocean* reported that the Idylwylde Tennis Club held a meeting at which Minnie Pogue was elected club president and Clara Ferguson was elected club secretary and treasurer.[1716] The club meeting appears from the record to have taken place on Monday, April 20, 1891. At the meeting the club members welcomed new members, planned for the approaching spring, 1891, sports season, and projected the improvement of the sports grounds of the club.[1717] Clara's sisters, Helen Ferguson and Florence (Ferguson) Lee, were probably also members of the club. The article announced that the tennis season would open in May of that same year.[1718]

William Lee left the position of Assistant City Engineer of Hyde Park in April, 1890, in order to assume the position of engineer for the T. W. Harvey Lumber Company.[1719] The lumber company planned to construct a new village in Cook County that was to be established around the economic and civic foundation of the Harvey Company, a manufacturing corporation.[1720] The new company-developed place and settlement would become Harvey, in southern Cook County.[1721] In such capacity, Lee acted as a founding engineer of Harvey, as he had been a founding civil engineer of the Pullman community and neighborhood several years prior.[1722]

Major Henry Washington Lee served as Secretary of the Calumet Manufacturers' Association, which was an organization whose purpose was the promotion and protection of industrial interests in the Calumet corridor of Illinois and Indiana.[1723] Lee was a committed promoter of the Calumet District and the two-state industrial link, and tirelessly sought the development of the region.[1724] The May 3, 1919, edition of *The Economist*, a Chicago journal, showed that Major Lee envisioned the Calumet District as the foremost industrial center of the world in terms of economic magnitude and concentration.[1725] On or around May 3, 1919, Lee issued a promotion pamphlet that essentially conducted a commercial census of the

---

[1713] The Inter Ocean. (September 15, 1889). P. 22. Newspapers.com.
[1714] The Inter Ocean. (September 15, 1889). P. 22. Newspapers.com.
[1715] The Inter Ocean. (April 26, 1891). P. 22. Newspapers.com.
[1716] The Inter Ocean. (April 26, 1891). P. 22. Newspapers.com.
[1717] The Inter Ocean. (April 26, 1891). P. 22. Newspapers.com.
[1718] The Inter Ocean. (April 26, 1891). P. 22. Newspapers.com.
[1719] Chicago Tribune. (April 13, 1890). P. 28. Newspapers.com.
[1720] Chicago Tribune. (April 13, 1890). P. 28. Newspapers.com.
[1721] Chicago Tribune. (April 13, 1890). P. 28. Newspapers.com.
[1722] Chicago Tribune. (April 13, 1890). P. 28. Newspapers.com.
[1723] The Economist. (May 3, 1919). P. 818. Chicago, IL. Google Books.
[1724] The Economist. (May 3, 1919). P. 818. Chicago, IL. Google Books.
[1725] The Economist. (May 3, 1919). P. 818. Chicago, IL. Google Books.

Calumet District, and announced that the District contained 413 industrial organizations at the time when Lee completed the business census.[1726] Lee and William M. Ryan, who was President of the Ryan Car Company, sought to organize the commercial and organizational power of the Calumet District.[1727] The Calumet Manufacturers' Association contained 75 members as of May 3, 1919, according to *The Economist* edition of the same date.[1728] The development of the Calumet River, and the consequent creation of navigability of the river and its connection to the neighboring waterways and Lake Michigan, were two purposes of the Manufacturers' Association, and were two goals of Henry Lee, William Ryan, and many other interested persons.[1729] *The Economist* report stated the following: "The association is working for the completion of the navigability of the Calumet River, various new 'good roads' routes, better street car facilities, improved sanitation, factory welfare work and better housing conditions."[1730]

John Whitfield Bunn owned extensive real estate in the Calumet District during both the nineteenth and the twentieth centuries.[1731] Selz, Schwab & Company located one of their factories in the Calumet District at Gary, and John Abel Peterson helped develop a large life insurance company within the Calumet Corridor at East Chicago, Indiana. Continental Can Company owned a factory in Gary. John Whitfield Bunn helped build the Calumet District into one of the largest industrial spaces of the world through his founding of the Wabash Railroad Company, whose transportation routes formed some of the most significant arteries of the Calumet Corridor. This transportation network helped develop the great Chicago-Pittsburgh transportation and industrial connection. For the history of the Wabash Railroad Company and John W. Bunn, see Chapter 2, *Builders of the Downtown*; for the history of the Stryker railroad companies, see Chapter 1, *Genesis of a Great Lakes Frontier*.

John Stryker was a founder of the Lake Shore & Michigan Southern Railway Company, the Northern Indiana & Chicago Railroad Company, the Lake Shore & Northern Indiana Railroad Company, and the New York Central Railroad Company, all of whose routes and rights of way collectively charted and plumbed the Calumet Corridor with a vital system and infrastructure of railroad transportation to the other Midwestern cities and to New York City. Later, in the twentieth century, Henry Stryker Taylor, who was one of the two largest individual stockholders of the Pennsylvania Railroad Company, also exerted administrative influence over the Calumet Corridor by dint of a majority ownership interest in one of the largest corporations to exist in Chicago and the metropolitan region. The

---

[1726] The Economist. (May 3, 1919). P. 818. Chicago, IL. Google Books.
[1727] The Economist. (May 3, 1919). P. 818. Chicago, IL. Google Books.
[1728] The Economist. (May 3, 1919). P. 818. Chicago, IL. Google Books.
[1729] The Economist. (May 3, 1919). P. 818. Chicago, IL. Google Books.
[1730] The Economist. (May 3, 1919). P. 818. Chicago, IL. Google Books.
[1731] See references elsewhere herein.

Bunns, Strykers, Taylors, and other interconnected families gave a great deal to the creation and development of the Calumet Corridor of Chicago, Cook County, and northwestern Indiana.

William Lee of Hyde Park and the Calumet River

William Lee participated in the United States Engineer Office survey of the Calumet River in 1885. Receiving orders from Assistant United States Engineer G. A. M. Liljencrantz, Lee engineered the verification of the geographical and topographical reckonings for the plan and design of, "one complete [Calumet River] system."[1732] U.S. Engineer Liljencrantz received an order from Major Thomas H. Hanbury of the United States Army Corps of Engineers to perform a survey of the Calumet River from, "a point half a mile east of Hammond [Indiana] to the forks of the river. . ."[1733] The Calumet River system consisted of the Grand Calumet River, the Little Calumet River, and Lake Calumet.[1734] A prior survey of the river system took place in 1881, and the recognized significance of the river was solidified by legislative will when the River and Harbor Act of July 5, 1884, became law.[1735]

William Lee resigned from the office of Assistant City Engineer of Hyde Park, Chicago, in approximately early April, 1890, in order to join the T. W. Harvey Lumber Company.[1736] The Harvey lumber and land company was designing and building a village and manufacturing facility at South Lawn at the time when Lee joined their personnel.[1737] Turlington W. Harvey targeted real estate at South Lawn, located in the Thornton Township of southern Cook County, for the development of an industrial town similar to that which had been founded by

---

[1732] Letter of Asst. Engineer G. A. M. Liljencrantz. (February 27, 1885). United States Engineer Office. Chicago, IL. Contained in Annual Report of the Chief of Engineers, United States Army, to the Secretary of War for the Year 1885. Part III. Pp. 2061-2064. Washington, D.C.: Government Printing Office. Google Books.

[1733] Letter of Asst. Engineer G. A. M. Liljencrantz. (February 27, 1885). United States Engineer Office. Chicago, IL. Contained in Annual Report of the Chief of Engineers, United States Army, to the Secretary of War for the Year 1885. Part III. P. 2061. Washington, D.C.: Government Printing Office. Google Books.

[1734] Letter of Asst. Engineer G. A. M. Liljencrantz. (February 27, 1885). United States Engineer Office. Chicago, IL. Contained in Annual Report of the Chief of Engineers, United States Army, to the Secretary of War for the Year 1885. Part III. Pp. 2061-2064. Washington, D.C.: Government Printing Office. Google Books.

[1735] Letter of Asst. Engineer G. A. M. Liljencrantz. (February 27, 1885). United States Engineer Office. Chicago, IL. Contained in Annual Report of the Chief of Engineers, United States Army, to the Secretary of War for the Year 1885. Part III. P. 2062. Washington, D.C.: Government Printing Office. Google Books.

[1736] Chicago Tribune. (April 13, 1890). P. 28. Archives.chicagotribune.com

[1737] Chicago Tribune. (April 13, 1890). P. 28. Archives.chicagotribune.com

George Mortimer Pullman, as discussed above.[1738] William Lee was a common party, therefore, to the founding leadership of both the Pullman community, and Harvey, Illinois, which would be named in honor of Turlington W. Harvey, the lumber industrialist and the principal developer of the Cook County town of Harvey.[1739] Historian Joseph C. Biggott set forth a comparison between Pullman and Harvey in which he noted several similarities and one major difference:

> "The founders envisioned Harvey as a model town, a blend of capitalism and Christianity. The investors provided residents with a high quality of city services, similar to nearby Pullman. But unlike Pullman, Harvey encouraged home ownership by offering potential residents a variety of house plans."[1740]

Harvey, Illinois, grew as a community to include a population of 5,395 persons by 1900, approximately one decade after establishment of the town.[1741] Protestant Christianity was the prevalent religious form in Harvey, with Roman Catholicism gaining a church there in 1899, due to the influence of Irish residents.[1742]

William Lee attended the nineteenth annual meeting and dinner of the Western Society of Engineers, an organization of which he was a member, on January 4, 1898.[1743] The meeting was held at the Technical Club of Chicago, a club in which William Douglas Richardson held membership at around the same time as the occurrence of the annual meeting of the Western Society.[1744] The William and Florence (Ferguson) Lee family relocated to Hyde Park community, and resided at 5637 S. Dorchester Avenue, a place located only a few blocks from the University of Chicago and three blocks from the Midway Plaisance.[1745]

[1738] Bigott, Joseph C. (2005). Harvey, Illinois. Encyclopedia of Chicago. encyclopedia.chicagohistory.org

[1739] Bigott, Joseph C. (2005). Harvey, Illinois. Encyclopedia of Chicago. encyclopedia.chicagohistory.org

[1740] Bigott, Joseph C. (2005). Harvey, Illinois. Encyclopedia of Chicago. encyclopedia.chicagohistory.org

[1741] Bigott, Joseph C. (2005). Harvey, Illinois. Encyclopedia of Chicago. encyclopedia.chicagohistory.org

[1742] Bigott, Joseph C. (2005). Harvey, Illinois. Encyclopedia of Chicago. encyclopedia.chicagohistory.org

[1743] Chicago Tribune. (January 5, 1898). P. 5. Newspapers.com.

[1744] Chicago Tribune. (January 5, 1898). P. 5. Newspapers.com.

[1745] Photograph of William Lee, Florence (Ferguson) Lee, and other family members.

Jacob Bunn. Of Springfield and Chicago. Co-founder, owner, and publisher of the Chicago Republican Newspaper Company (later the *Inter-Ocean Newspaper*), the largest newspaper in Chicago and in the American West. Co-founder and owner of the Chicago & Alton Railroad Company. Co-founder of the Chicago Secure Depository Company. Banker and financier to Abraham Lincoln. Manager of Abraham Lincoln's presidential campaign and campaign fund in 1860. Illinois coal and real estate developer. Promoter of the Union Stockyards through railroad development. President of the Illinois Watch Company. Founder of the Watch and Jewelers' Trust Company of Chicago. Close friend and advisor of Abraham Lincoln and the Lincoln Family. Banker to the Lincoln family. Central figure in Republican Party development and management at Chicago and Springfield. (Image courtesy of the Sangamon Valley Collection of the Lincoln Library, Springfield, Illinois).

John Whitfield Bunn. Of Springfield and Chicago. Younger brother of Jacob Bunn. Co-founder, co-owner, and Director of the Wabash Railroad Company system of Chicago and the Midwest. President of the Wabash Railroad Company of Chicago. Co-founder, Vice-President, and Director of Selz, Schwab & Company of Chicago, the largest shoe and boot manufacturer in the world. Major promoter and developer of the Chicago Union Stockyards. Founding Treasurer of the Chicago Fat Stock Show. Co-founder and member of the Saddle & Sirloin Club of Chicago. Co-founder, Vice-President, and Director of the Springfield Iron Company of Chicago and Springfield. Treasurer of the Illinois Board of World's Fair Commissioners for the 1893 World's Columbian Exposition at Chicago. Co-founding executive of the 1893 Chicago World's Fair. Co-founder of the Watch and Jewelers' Trust Company of Chicago. Land investor at Chicago. Treasurer of the Illinois State Board of Agriculture, which positively impacted the Cook County economy with immense force and development. Co-manager of Abraham Lincoln's campaign and campaign fund in 1860. Illinois Commissioner of Pensions for Civil War. Close friend and advisor of Abraham Lincoln and the Lincoln Family. Co-founder and Director of the Abraham Lincoln Association. One of the fathers of the South Chicago and Calumet River industrial corridor and the Chicago-Pittsburgh industrial nexus. Co-founder and founding Treasurer of the University of Illinois. Member of the Chicago Club, the Union League Club of Chicago, and the Chicago Historical Society, as well as of the Illini Country Club, Sangamo Club, and Springfield Fishing Club of Springfield. (Image courtesy of the Sangamon Valley Collection of the Lincoln Library of Springfield, Illinois).

John Whitfield Bunn of Chicago and Springfield. This portrait was painted by Cecilia Beaux, the renowned American society portraitist (1855-1942). (Image courtesy of author's family).

John Whitfield Bunn in one of his many corporate offices. (Image courtesy of the Sangamon Valley Collection of the Lincoln Library of Springfield, Illinois).

Benjamin Hamilton Ferguson. Of Springfield. President of Springfield Marine Bank. Co-founder of Springfield Boiler Company of Springfield and Chicago. Co-founder of Franklin Life Insurance Company of Springfield and Chicago. Friend of Abraham Lincoln. Co-founder of Springfield Gas & Electric Company, which became the City Water Light & Power Company of Springfield. Cousin of the Fergusons of Chicago, who were founders of the Pullman community and neighborhood of the far South Side of the city. Brother of Elizabeth Jane (Ferguson) Bunn. Brother-in-law of Jacob Bunn. (Image courtesy of *Jacob Bunn: Legacy of an Illinois Industrial Pioneer*, Andrew Taylor Call, 2005; image originally from Springfield Marine Bank, Springfield, Illinois, 2005).

Elizabeth Jane (Ferguson) Bunn. Of Springfield. A leading Illinois philanthropist and social matron. Co-founder of the Springfield Home for the Friendless. Wife of Jacob Bunn. Mother of seven children. Sister of Benjamin H. Ferguson and California lawyer and State Senator William Irwin Ferguson. Close friend of Abraham Lincoln and the Lincoln family. Cousin of the Fergusons of Chicago, who were founders of the Pullman community and neighborhood of the far South Side of the city. (Image courtesy of author's personal collection).

Leonard Richardson. Of Chicago and Litchfield County, Connecticut. Co-founder and co-owner of the Barnum & Richardson Company of Chicago and Connecticut. The Barnum & Richardson Company became the largest railroad components manufacturer at Chicago and in the world. Founder of the Chicago railroad components manufacturing industry. Iron mining capitalist of Connecticut. Founded the Chicago branch and factory of the Barnum & Richardson Company. A father of the industries of Litchfield County, Connecticut, and Cook County, Illinois. Business partner of William Henry "Iron Man" Barnum, the Democratic United States Senator from Connecticut. Father of Milo Barnum Richardson. Uncle of William Douglas Richardson of Chicago. (Image courtesy of Geoffrey Brown and Judith Moore Sherman).

Stephen Williamson Stryker. Of Chicago and New York. Member of the Stryker family of Illinois, New Jersey, and New York. Co-founder and co-owner of Stryker & Barnes Company of Chicago. Stryker & Barnes, subsequently known as Stryker & Company, was the largest fur and fur garment dealer both in Chicago and in the entire American West. Co-founder and leader of the Chicago Zouaves, a military organization that served during the Civil War. Key developer of the Chicago garment and fur production and distribution industries. Cousin of the other Strykers of Jacksonville and Chicago. (Image courtesy of Rick Lawrence).

Michigan Southern Railroad Company station before the Great Chicago Fire of 1871. John Stryker was the principal founder, owner, and builder of the Lake Shore & Michigan Southern Railroad Company. He served also as President of the company. Stryker was founder of multiple major elements of the railroad economy, railroad infrastructures, and route systems of Chicago, Cook County, and the entire Midwest. (Image courtesy of Joseph Kirkland, *The Story of Chicago*, 1892).

Potter Palmer. Of New York and Chicago. Served with Jacob Bunn as a founder of the Chicago Secure Depository Company. Founder of the Palmer House Hotel of Chicago. Dry goods merchant. Land developer and a founder of the Gold Coast neighborhood of the North Side of Chicago. Primary developer of State Street, which had once been owned by Dr. Alexander Wolcott. State Street was once known as Wolcott Street in honor of the city founder and land developer, Dr. Alexander Wolcott. (Image courtesy of Joseph Kirkland, *The Story of Chicago*, 1892).

John Wentworth. Of Chicago. Known as "Long John" Wentworth. Stood six feet six inches tall. Mayor of Chicago. Served with Jacob Bunn as co-founder of the Chicago Secure Depository Company. Member of Chicago Historical Society, along with John Whitfield Bunn and John Harris Kinzie. Co-founder of the Union League Club, an organization in which John Whitfield Bunn, Frank Hatch Jones, and Willard Bunn, Jr., also held membership. Wentworth also co-founded the Chicago Board of Education. (Image courtesy of Joseph Kirkland, *The Story of Chicago*, 1892).

Illinois Central Railroad Company station at Chicago in 1855. Thomas Blish Talcott of the Willard family of Winnebago County, Sangamon County, Kane County, and Chicago, served as an important advocate and promoter of the Illinois Central Railroad Company. (Image courtesy of Joseph Kirkland, *The Story of Chicago*, 1892).

Abraham Lincoln. Of Kentucky, Indiana, and Illinois. Sixteenth President of the United States. Served as the lawyer for the **Bunn** brothers of Springfield and Chicago. Jacob Bunn and John Whitfield Bunn managed the Lincoln Presidential Campaign and the financing associated with the 1860 presidential campaign. The Bunns were also bankers for Lincoln and Mary Todd Lincoln, and were among the closest friends and advisors of Lincoln, both before and during his political career. (Image courtesy of Joseph Kirkland, *The Story of Chicago*, 1892).

George Mortimer Pullman. Of New York and Chicago. Founder of the Pullman Company, which manufactured railroad passenger and sleeper cars. Founder of the Pullman community and neighborhood of the far South Side of Chicago. Pullman co-founded the Chicago Secure Depository Company with Jacob Bunn. Member of the Chicago Club, along with John Whitfield Bunn and Frank Hatch Jones. (Image courtesy of Joseph Kirkland, *The Story of Chicago*, 1892).

William Ferguson of DuQuoin, Illinois. Father of Matthew, Helen, Clara, and Florence Ferguson, all of the Pullman community of Chicago. Member of the Ferguson Family of Pennsylvania, Ohio, Springfield, and Chicago. Cousin of Elizabeth Jane (Ferguson) Bunn and Benjamin Hamilton Ferguson of Springfield. (Image courtesy of Susan Alland and her family).

Judge Henry Stryker of Jacksonville, Morgan County, Illinois. Stryker was a member of the law firm of McClure & Stryker in Jacksonville. He founded the Stryker Bank Company of Jacksonville. Founder and executive officer of the Episcopal Diocese of Springfield and the Episcopal Church polity of Morgan County. Founder of the Morgan County Bar Association. Pictured here with his grandchildren. Grandchildren: Henry Stryker Taylor (far right); Robert Cunningham Taylor (second from right); Elizabeth Stryker Capps (girl at center); John Babinger Hart (third from left) and Joseph Hall Hart, Jr. (second from left); Henry McClure Capps; and William Thomas Capps, Jr. at far left and not within picture. The Hart brothers of Cincinnati would go on to serve in important functions with Pan American World Airways. John Babinger Hart established a construction company in Fort Lauderdale, Florida, and built multiple buildings there. McClure Capps was a Yale University alumnus who married Ruth Goldwyn, the daughter of film producer Samuel Goldwyn. He became an art director in Hollywood. William T. Capps, Jr. became President of the J. Capps & Son Company, a leading clothing manufacturer and bulletproof textile maker. Elizabeth Stryker Capps became a teacher of the deaf in Jacksonville after graduating from MacMurray College and Columbia University. Many of these people were connected to Chicago and Cook County. (Image courtesy of author's personal collection).

Portrait of Elizabeth Henshaw (McClure) Stryker. Daughter of Judge Henry Brigham McClure and Harriet Hillhouse (Henshaw) McClure of Michigan and Jacksonville, Morgan County, Illinois. Wife of Judge Henry Stryker. Mother of Charlotte, Louise, Elizabeth, Harriet, and Henry Stryker. Graduate of the Jacksonville Female Seminary. Member of Trinity Episcopal Church. Member of the Illinois Federation of Women's Clubs. Member and officer of the Jacksonville Chapter of the National Society of Daughters of the American Revolution. Member of the Jacksonville Country Club. Member of the Douglass-Brigham-Prentiss-Henshaw-Stryker Family of New England, New York, Chicago, St. Louis, and Morgan County. (Image and portrait courtesy of author's personal collection).

Charles Benjamin Farwell. United States Senator from Illinois. Brother of industrialist John Villiers Farwell. Friend of Jacob Bunn and John Whitfield Bunn. (Image courtesy of *Men of Illinois*, by Halliday Witherspoon, 1902).

John Farwell. Founder of John V. Farwell Company of Chicago. Mentor to Marshall Field. Friend and business partner of Jacob Bunn and John W. Bunn. Church leader. Developer of Rogers Park and Lake Forest. (Image courtesy of *Men of Illinois*, by Halliday Witherspoon, 1902).

ANDREW J. HAWS.

Andrew Jackson Haws. Of Pittsburgh, Butler County, and Johnstown, Pennsylvania. Member of the Call-Baldwin-Burtner-Haws family of Pennsylvania, Ohio, and Illinois. Inventor. Founder and President of the A. J. Haws Firebrick Company of Johnstown, Pennsylvania, Pittsburgh, Chicago, Philadelphia, and other places. This company possessed a major presence in Chicago both through operation of an office there, and through having been a principal supplier of bricks for the construction of myriad Chicago factories. Haws was a member of the Burtner family of Pittsburgh and the Pittsburgh metropolitan region. He was a first cousin of William Henry Burtner, Sr. of Cincinnati. (Image courtesy of a Cambria County, Pennsylvania, historical reference work).

Edwin Stapleton Conway. Chicago industrialist. President of the Kimball Piano Company. Father of Carle Cotter Conway of Oak Park, Illinois, and later New York City. (Image courtesy of Heather and Barton Pembroke).

Morris Selz and his son Jacob Harry Selz. Of Germany and Chicago. Morris Selz founded the firm of M. Selz & Company at Chicago with John Whitfield Bunn, Max Meyer, and Joseph Rutter. The company, known subsequently as Selz, Schwab & Company, would become the largest and most important shoe and boot manufacturer and distributor in Chicago, and in the world. Morris Selz served as President of Selz, Schwab & Company. Morris co-founded the Standard Club of Chicago in 1869 and served as its President for a time. J. Harry Selz helped lead Selz, Schwab & Company, and worked with Jacob Bunn, Jr., and John Whitfield Bunn. Harry and Morris were both members of the Union League Club, along with John Whitfield Bunn and Frank Hatch Jones. (Image courtesy of *Men of Illinois*, by Halliday Witherspoon, 1902).

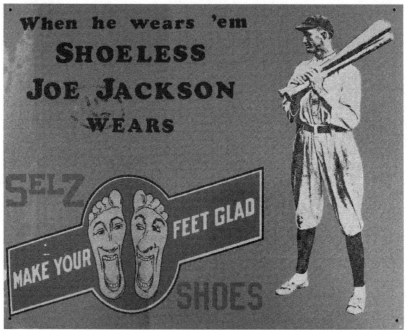

Selz, Schwab & Company Metal Advertisements. This metal plate advertisement featured an artistic interpretation of Joseph Jefferson "Shoeless Joe" Jackson of the Chicago White Sox. A star baseball player of Chicago, Jackson was a commercial spokesman for Selz, Schwab & Company. (Images and ads courtesy of author's personal collection).

Selz, Schwab & Co. wall ad near Maxwell Street, Chicago. Pritikin Brothers tobacco store and merchant's stand in the Maxwell Street area. (Image courtesy of the Chicago History Museum; CHM-Digital Obj ID: ICHi-36094; Charles R. Clark, photographer).

George Whitfield Bunn, Sr. Of New Jersey, Texas, and California. Brother of Jacob Bunn and John Whitfield Bunn of Springfield and Chicago. Founder and Director of the Bank of Tomales, California. Rancher in California and Texas. Owner of the Bunn Ranch Company of Crockett County, Texas. Community leader in Marin County, California. Husband of Mahala Ann (Bloom) Bunn. Father of George Whitfield Bunn, Jr., of Texas and Minnesota. (Image courtesy of Jamie Overom Pyzik and Wendy Overom Paymard).

Chicago and Alton Railroad Company tourist tickets from 1882. The advertisement promotes the travel and transportation service from Chicago to St. Louis, and to the Rocky Mountains. Jacob Bunn was a principal founder, reorganizer, and owner of the Chicago and Alton Railroad Company. (Image courtesy of the Chicago History Museum; CHM-Digital Obj ID: ICHi-038187).

Jacob Bunn Spindle Crib. This antique spindle crib belonged to Jacob Bunn and Elizabeth Jane (Ferguson) Bunn. The crib was later moved to the front hall of the Bunn residence, where Lincoln and other visitors would enter the house. Abraham Lincoln, a close friend of the Bunn and Ferguson families, often visited the Bunn residence in Springfield. Lincoln would drape his coats over the Bunn Spindle Crib when he visited the Jacob Bunn house. The Bunn Spindle Crib has remained in the Bunn and Taylor families for six generations. (Jacob Bunn Spindle Crib from author's personal collection).

Chapter 4

Friends of the Leatherworkers

"The garment, whether the warp or the woof, or any article of leather from which the mark has departed when you washed it, it shall then be washed a second time and will be clean."

Leviticus 13:58

Introduction

The present chapter concerns the Chicago history of the Bunn branch and the Stryker branch of my mother's family. The following key family members, among others, appear in this book chapter: Jacob Bunn, John Whitfield Bunn, Elizabeth Jane (Ferguson) Bunn, Jacob Bunn, Jr., George Whitfield Bunn, Sr., George Whitfield Bunn, Jr., Chester Selden Bunn, Emily Mae Bunn, John Stryker, and Stephen Williamson Stryker. This chapter contains the Chicago histories of the Bunn and Stryker families and the Chicago leather products and related manufacturing industries. For the Bunn and Stryker railroad histories, consult Chapter 1, *Genesis of a Great Lakes* Frontier, and Chapter 2, *Builders of the Downtown*. For the Bunn electrical, public utilities, and timepiece manufacturing industries, consult Chapter 8, *Ode to Pylons and Cannery Windows*.

Genealogy of the Bunn Family

Cook County has since its inception encompassed tremendous commercial diversity, industrial possibility, and entrepreneurial opportunity. The Bunn family has embodied commitment to preservation and development of these landscapes of potential and these fields of commerce and industry that were abundantly present in Cook County.[1746] The ethics of vision, honor, and commitment, jointly encapsulated within the moral structure of Judeo-Christian history and faith, have been possessed by multiple generations, and vast numbers of family members. These people participated in, helped discover, and helped develop, social, civic, commercial, and industrial welfare and opportunity within Chicago and Cook County, and the broader surrounding regions, as well. From the time of the first generation of the Bunn family in Illinois, until the present time, six generations of the Bunn family have been connected to Chicago and Cook County in some manner, whether through full-time residency, part-time residency, significant commercial and industrial engagements and contributions, civic engagements, or some combination of these factors.

The historical research efforts of scholar, author, and historian James Alfred Ellis have been invaluable. Ellis succeeded in the project of assembly of genealogical and historical information concerning the early generations of the Bunn family in

---

[1746] See generally: Call, Andrew Taylor. (2005). Jacob Bunn: Legacy of an Illinois Industrial Pioneer. Lawrenceville, Virginia: Brunswick Publishing Corporation.

New Jersey, as well as in Illinois.[1747] United States historians will remain indebted to Ellis for his monumental contributions to the histories of New Jersey and Illinois, and the United States generally. The book, *History of the Bunn Family in America*,[1748] by James Alfred Ellis, will herein supply an excellent thematic overture of times, places, histories, and occurrences. We proceed here from this broad historical context of information to undertake specific discussion and analysis of the Chicago and Cook County histories of the Bunn family.

The Bunn family, originally of German and Dutch heritage,[1749] and for centuries adherents of Protestant Christian faith, had long resided in Hunterdon County, situated in western New Jersey.[1750] This geographical region falls within the larger geographical and social contexts of the eastern piedmont of the Appalachian Mountains. Subsequent research has concluded that this Bunn family was of German and Dutch heritage, not of English heritage. Though Ellis's theory that the Bunn family was of English origin has been proven incorrect, everything else in the Ellis book is correct. Let us first summarize the generations of the Bunn family, so as to construct a convenient chronological framework in which to continue within our desired trajectories of historical description and analysis. The work of historian James Alfred Ellis has proved invaluable, and it is largely from his monumental work of research that the following information has been collected and assembled herein.[1751]

Jacob Bunn was born in 1736.[1752] He died on March 15, 1808.[1753] Jacob Bunn married Maria Elizabetha, whose surname remains undetermined.[1754] Maria Elizabetha was born in 1744. She died in 1817.[1755] The Bunn family was devoutly Christian.[1756] The family members attended the Presbyterian Church that was located in Alexandria, Hunterdon County, New Jersey.[1757] Jacob Bunn and Maria

---

[1747] See generally: Ellis, James Alfred. (Ed.). (1928). History of the Bunn Family of America. Chicago, Illinois: Romanzo Norton Bunn, Publisher. Babel and Hathitrust.org.

[1748] Ellis, James Alfred. (Ed.). (1928). History of the Bunn Family of America. Chicago, Illinois: Romanzo Norton Bunn, Publisher. Babel and Hathitrust.org.

[1749] This fact of ethnicity has been established through genetic trials and tests.

[1750] Ellis, James Alfred. (Ed.). (1928). History of the Bunn Family of America. Chicago, Illinois: Romanzo Norton Bunn, Publisher. Pp. 200, *et seq*. Babel and Hathitrust.org.

[1751] Ellis, James Alfred. (Ed.). (1928). History of the Bunn Family of America. Chicago, Illinois: Romanzo Norton Bunn, Publisher. Pp. 200, *et seq*. Babel and Hathitrust.org.

[1752] Ellis, James Alfred. (Ed.). (1928). History of the Bunn Family of America. Chicago, Illinois: Romanzo Norton Bunn, Publisher. P. 200. Babel and Hathitrust.org.

[1753] Ellis, James Alfred. (Ed.). (1928). History of the Bunn Family of America. Chicago, Illinois: Romanzo Norton Bunn, Publisher. P. 200. Babel and Hathitrust.org.

[1754] Ellis, James Alfred. (Ed.). (1928). History of the Bunn Family of America. Chicago, Illinois: Romanzo Norton Bunn, Publisher. P. 200. Babel and Hathitrust.org.

[1755] Ellis, James Alfred. (Ed.). (1928). History of the Bunn Family of America. Chicago, Illinois: Romanzo Norton Bunn, Publisher. P. 200. Babel and Hathitrust.org.

[1756] Bunn Family notes, memoirs, and records.

[1757] Ellis, James Alfred. (Ed.). (1928). History of the Bunn Family of America. Chicago, Illinois: Romanzo Norton Bunn, Publisher. Pp. 200-201, et seq. 202. Babel and Hathitrust.org.; Bunn Family history, memoirs, and notes.

Elizabetha Bunn married and had the following children:[1758] John Peter Bunn was born on October 26, 1770.[1759] John Peter Bunn married Elizabeth Rockefeller.[1760] Descendants of the John Peter Bunn—Elizabeth Rockefeller line ultimately resided in Chicago and the Chicago suburbs for multiple generations.[1761] Henry Bunn, who was the father of Jacob Bunn and John Whitfield Bunn, both of Springfield and Chicago, was born October 19, 1772.[1762] Henry Bunn married Mary Sigler.[1763] Rosanna Bunn was born on June 9, 1774.[1764] Rosanna married John Raub.[1765] Jacob Bunn was born March 7, 1776.[1766] This Jacob Bunn was an uncle of the Jacob Bunn who relocated to Illinois. Jacob Bunn, born 1776, married Lydia Carhart.[1767] Mary Elizabeth Bunn was born on March 11, 1778.[1768] Mary Elizabeth Bunn married Nathaniel Rittenhouse.[1769] Matthias Bunn was born in February, 1780.[1770] Matthias Bunn appears to have never married, having died at the age of 18 years, in 1799.[1771] Philip Bunn was born May 5, 1783.[1772] Philip Bunn never married.[1773] Elizabeth Bunn married a member of the Siegler family.[1774] John

---

[1758] Ellis, James Alfred. (Ed.). (1928). History of the Bunn Family of America. Chicago, Illinois: Romanzo Norton Bunn, Publisher. P. 202. Babel and Hathitrust.org.

[1759] Ellis, James Alfred. (Ed.). (1928). History of the Bunn Family of America. Chicago, Illinois: Romanzo Norton Bunn, Publisher. P. 202. Babel and Hathitrust.org.

[1760] Ellis, James Alfred. (Ed.). (1928). History of the Bunn Family of America. Chicago, Illinois: Romanzo Norton Bunn, Publisher. P. 202. Babel and Hathitrust.org.

[1761] Bunn Family records, notes, and memoirs.

[1762] Ellis, James Alfred. (Ed.). (1928). History of the Bunn Family of America. Chicago, Illinois: Romanzo Norton Bunn, Publisher. Pp. 202-203. Babel and Hathitrust.org.

[1763] Ellis, James Alfred. (Ed.). (1928). History of the Bunn Family of America. Chicago, Illinois: Romanzo Norton Bunn, Publisher. P. 203. Babel and Hathitrust.org.

[1764] Ellis, James Alfred. (Ed.). (1928). History of the Bunn Family of America. Chicago, Illinois: Romanzo Norton Bunn, Publisher. P. 204. Babel and Hathitrust.org.'

[1765] Ellis, James Alfred. (Ed.). (1928). History of the Bunn Family of America. Chicago, Illinois: Romanzo Norton Bunn, Publisher. P. 204. Babel and Hathitrust.org.

[1766] Ellis, James Alfred. (Ed.). (1928). History of the Bunn Family of America. Chicago, Illinois: Romanzo Norton Bunn, Publisher. P. 202. Babel and Hathitrust.org.

[1767] Ellis, James Alfred. (Ed.). (1928). History of the Bunn Family of America. Chicago, Illinois: Romanzo Norton Bunn, Publisher. P. 202. Babel and Hathitrust.org.

[1768] Ellis, James Alfred. (Ed.). (1928). History of the Bunn Family of America. Chicago, Illinois: Romanzo Norton Bunn, Publisher. P. 204. Babel and Hathitrust.org.

[1769] Ellis, James Alfred. (Ed.). (1928). History of the Bunn Family of America. Chicago, Illinois: Romanzo Norton Bunn, Publisher. P. 204. Babel and Hathitrust.org.

[1770] Ellis, James Alfred. (Ed.). (1928). History of the Bunn Family of America. Chicago, Illinois: Romanzo Norton Bunn, Publisher. P. 202, 205. Babel and Hathitrust.org.

[1771] Ellis, James Alfred. (Ed.). (1928). History of the Bunn Family of America. Chicago, Illinois: Romanzo Norton Bunn, Publisher. P. 202. Babel and Hathitrust.org.

[1772] Ellis, James Alfred. (Ed.). (1928). History of the Bunn Family of America. Chicago, Illinois: Romanzo Norton Bunn, Publisher. P. 202. Babel and Hathitrust.org.

[1773] Ellis, James Alfred. (Ed.). (1928). History of the Bunn Family of America. Chicago, Illinois: Romanzo Norton Bunn, Publisher. P. 202. Babel and Hathitrust.org.

[1774] Ellis, James Alfred. (Ed.). (1928). History of the Bunn Family of America. Chicago, Illinois: Romanzo Norton Bunn, Publisher. P. 202. Babel and Hathitrust.org.

William Bunn was born on May 29, 1787.[1775] John William Bunn married Prudence Foster.[1776] This concludes the summary of the children of Jacob Bunn and Maria Elizabetha Bunn.

Henry Bunn was born October 19, 1772, in Hunterdon County, New Jersey.[1777] He was the son of Jacob Bunn and Maria Elizabetha (surname undetermined) Bunn.[1778] Henry Bunn married Mary Sigler.[1779] Mary Sigler was born on April 7, 1788, in Mifflin County, Pennsylvania.[1780] The children born to Henry Bunn and Mary Sigler Bunn included the following persons: Sarah Ann Bunn was born November 26, 1809.[1781] Elizabeth Bunn was born January 18, 1812.[1782] Elizabeth Bunn married John Harple Eckel.[1783] Jacob Bunn, who later relocated to Illinois, was born March 18, 1814.[1784] Jacob Bunn married Elizabeth Jane Ferguson.[1785] Jacob Bunn was one of the most important industrialists of Chicago and Springfield, Illinois, as is discussed herein. Descendants of the Jacob Bunn— Elizabeth Jane Ferguson line have been prominently connected to Chicago, Cook County, and the neighboring villages and counties for multiple generations. William Bunn was born on February 14, 1817.[1786] William Bunn married Ellen Alpaugh.[1787] George Whitfield Bunn, who later relocated to Marin County, California,[1788] was born January 28, 1820.[1789] Descendants of the George Whitfield

[1775] Ellis, James Alfred. (Ed.). (1928). History of the Bunn Family of America. Chicago, Illinois: Romanzo Norton Bunn, Publisher. P. 202, et seq. Babel and Hathitrust.org.
[1776] Ellis, James Alfred. (Ed.). (1928). History of the Bunn Family of America. Chicago, Illinois: Romanzo Norton Bunn, Publisher. P. 202, et seq. Babel and Hathitrust.org.
[1777] Ellis, James Alfred. (Ed.). (1928). History of the Bunn Family of America. Chicago, Illinois: Romanzo Norton Bunn, Publisher. P. 203, et seq. Babel and Hathitrust.org.
[1778] Ellis, James Alfred. (Ed.). (1928). History of the Bunn Family of America. Chicago, Illinois: Romanzo Norton Bunn, Publisher. P. 202, et seq. Babel and Hathitrust.org.
[1779] Ellis, James Alfred. (Ed.). (1928). History of the Bunn Family of America. Chicago, Illinois: Romanzo Norton Bunn, Publisher. P. 203, et seq. Babel and Hathitrust.org.
[1780] Ellis, James Alfred. (Ed.). (1928). History of the Bunn Family of America. Chicago, Illinois: Romanzo Norton Bunn, Publisher. P. 203, et seq. Babel and Hathitrust.org.
[1781] Ellis, James Alfred. (Ed.). (1928). History of the Bunn Family of America. Chicago, Illinois: Romanzo Norton Bunn, Publisher. P. 203, et seq. Babel and Hathitrust.org.
[1782] Ellis, James Alfred. (Ed.). (1928). History of the Bunn Family of America. Chicago, Illinois: Romanzo Norton Bunn, Publisher. P. 203, et seq. Babel and Hathitrust.org.
[1783] Ellis, James Alfred. (Ed.). (1928). History of the Bunn Family of America. Chicago, Illinois: Romanzo Norton Bunn, Publisher. P. 207, et seq. Babel and Hathitrust.org.
[1784] Ellis, James Alfred. (Ed.). (1928). History of the Bunn Family of America. Chicago, Illinois: Romanzo Norton Bunn, Publisher. P. 208, et seq. Babel and Hathitrust.org.
[1785] Ellis, James Alfred. (Ed.). (1928). History of the Bunn Family of America. Chicago, Illinois: Romanzo Norton Bunn, Publisher. P. 209, et seq. Babel and Hathitrust.org.
[1786] Ellis, James Alfred. (Ed.). (1928). History of the Bunn Family of America. Chicago, Illinois: Romanzo Norton Bunn, Publisher. P. 210, et seq. Babel and Hathitrust.org.
[1787] Ellis, James Alfred. (Ed.). (1928). History of the Bunn Family of America. Chicago, Illinois: Romanzo Norton Bunn, Publisher. P. 210, et seq. Babel and Hathitrust.org.
[1788] Bunn Family records, notes, and memoirs.
[1789] Ellis, James Alfred. (Ed.). (1928). History of the Bunn Family of America. Chicago, Illinois: Romanzo Norton Bunn, Publisher. P. 203, et seq. Babel and Hathitrust.org.

Bunn line ultimately resided in Chicago and the Chicago suburbs for multiple generations.[1790] Lucinda Bunn was born in 1822.[1791] Lucinda married Henry Johnson.[1792] Mary Eleanor Bunn was born on December 3, 1824.[1793] Mary Eleanor married Louis Van Syckle.[1794] Henry Bunn was born on January 13, 1827.[1795] Henry Bunn married Sarah Gardner.[1796] John Whitfield Bunn, who relocated to Illinois, was born on June 21, 1831.[1797] John Whitfield Bunn never married. John became one of the foremost industrialists of Chicago, Cook County, and the neighboring counties of Illinois and northwestern Indiana.[1798] The details of this element of the Chicago history are discussed elsewhere herein. Finally, Augustus Bunn was the last child of Henry Bunn and Mary Sigler Bunn.[1799] Augustus died at the age of 16 days.[1800] Henry Bunn established a farming company in rural western New Jersey, and engaged also in banking there.[1801] It is notable that the name "Whitfield" occurred no fewer than five times as a middle name within the Bunn family; the relevant cases being those of John Whitfield Bunn, George Whitfield Bunn, George Whitfield Bunn, Jr., Aaron Whitfield Eckel, and another George Whitfield Bunn who was the son of William Bunn (William Bunn was a brother of Jacob Bunn of Illinois, and John Whitfield Bunn of Illinois).[1802] The Henry Bunn farming business was prosperous, and the Bunns had built up a large agricultural business by 1859, the time of Henry's death.[1803] Henry owned a small banking company in Hunterdon County, according to his last will and testament. This concludes the summary of the children of Henry Bunn and Mary Sigler Bunn.

[1790] Bunn Family records, notes, and memoirs.

[1791] Ellis, James Alfred. (Ed.). (1928). History of the Bunn Family of America. Chicago, Illinois: Romanzo Norton Bunn, Publisher. P. 203, et seq. Babel and Hathitrust.org.

[1792] Ellis, James Alfred. (Ed.). (1928). History of the Bunn Family of America. Chicago, Illinois: Romanzo Norton Bunn, Publisher. P. 203, et seq. Babel and Hathitrust.org.

[1793] Ellis, James Alfred. (Ed.). (1928). History of the Bunn Family of America. Chicago, Illinois: Romanzo Norton Bunn, Publisher. P. 210. Babel and Hathitrust.org.

[1794] Ellis, James Alfred. (Ed.). (1928). History of the Bunn Family of America. Chicago, Illinois: Romanzo Norton Bunn, Publisher. P. 210. Babel and Hathitrust.org.

[1795] Ellis, James Alfred. (Ed.). (1928). History of the Bunn Family of America. Chicago, Illinois: Romanzo Norton Bunn, Publisher. P. 203. Babel and Hathitrust.org.

[1796] Ellis, James Alfred. (Ed.). (1928). History of the Bunn Family of America. Chicago, Illinois: Romanzo Norton Bunn, Publisher. Pp. 203-204. Babel and Hathitrust.org.

[1797] Ellis, James Alfred. (Ed.). (1928). History of the Bunn Family of America. Chicago, Illinois: Romanzo Norton Bunn, Publisher. P. 210. Babel and Hathitrust.org.

[1798] See sources contained herein generally.

[1799] Ellis, James Alfred. (Ed.). (1928). History of the Bunn Family of America. Chicago, Illinois: Romanzo Norton Bunn, Publisher. P. 204. Babel and Hathitrust.org.

[1800] Ellis, James Alfred. (Ed.). (1928). History of the Bunn Family of America. Chicago, Illinois: Romanzo Norton Bunn, Publisher. P. 204. Babel and Hathitrust.org.

[1801] Bunn Family records, notes, and memoirs.

[1802] Ellis, James Alfred. (Ed.). (1928). History of the Bunn Family of America. Chicago, Illinois: Romanzo Norton Bunn, Publisher. Pp. 207, 210. Babel and Hathitrust.org.; Bunn Family records, notes, and memoirs.

[1803] Bunn Family records, notes, and memoirs.

Let us now enumerate the immediate family members of the Jacob Bunn family of Springfield and Chicago. Jacob Bunn married Elizabeth Jane Ferguson on April 17, 1851, at Springfield, Sangamon County, Illinois.[1804] Elizabeth Ferguson of Pennsylvania was born May 12, 1832,[1805] and was a daughter of Benjamin Ferguson and Sarah (Irwin) Ferguson.[1806] Both the Ferguson and the Irwin families were natives of the Pittsburgh vicinity of western Pennsylvania.[1807] Seven children were born to Jacob Bunn and Elizabeth Ferguson Bunn. William Ferguson Bunn was born March 18, 1852.[1808] Mary Bunn was born April 29, 1854, and died at about the age of two.[1809] Sarah Irwin Bunn was born January 19, 1856.[1810] Sarah married statesman, lawyer, and industrialist Frank Hatch Jones of Chicago and Springfield.[1811] Frank Jones' biography is supplied and analyzed in Chapter 2. Sarah (Bunn) Jones died in November, 1892.[1812] Sarah and Frank Jones had no children.[1813] Henry Bunn was born August 9, 1858.[1814] George Wallace Bunn was born January 13, 1861.[1815] Jacob Bunn, Jr. was born October 21, 1864.[1816] Alice Edwards Bunn was the youngest child of Jacob and Elizabeth (Ferguson) Bunn and was born November 13, 1867.[1817] This concludes the summary of the children of Jacob Bunn and Elizabeth Jane (Ferguson) Bunn. The relevant genealogical map having been plotted here, we will focus on the first four generations of the Bunn family which possessed significant connections to Chicago and Cook County.

[1804] Ellis, James Alfred. (Ed.). (1928). History of the Bunn Family of America. Chicago, Illinois: Romanzo Norton Bunn, Publisher. P. 209. Babel and Hathitrust.org.

[1805] Ellis, James Alfred. (Ed.). (1928). History of the Bunn Family of America. Chicago, Illinois: Romanzo Norton Bunn, Publisher. P. 209. Babel and Hathitrust.org.

[1806] Temple, Wayne C. (Fall-Winter, 2008). Senator William Irwin Ferguson, Esq. Journal of the Illinois State Historical Society. Vol. 101, Number 3/4. P. 348. Jstor.

[1807] Temple, Wayne C. (Fall-Winter, 2008). Senator William Irwin Ferguson, Esq. Journal of the Illinois State Historical Society. Vol. 101, Number 3/4. P. 348. Jstor.

[1808] Ellis, James Alfred. (Ed.). (1928). History of the Bunn Family of America. Chicago, Illinois: Romanzo Norton Bunn, Publisher. P. 218. Babel and Hathitrust.org.

[1809] Ellis, James Alfred. (Ed.). (1928). History of the Bunn Family of America. Chicago, Illinois: Romanzo Norton Bunn, Publisher. P. 209. Babel and Hathitrust.org.

[1810] Ellis, James Alfred. (Ed.). (1928). History of the Bunn Family of America. Chicago, Illinois: Romanzo Norton Bunn, Publisher. P. 209. Babel and Hathitrust.org.

[1811] Ellis, James Alfred. (Ed.). (1928). History of the Bunn Family of America. Chicago, Illinois: Romanzo Norton Bunn, Publisher. P. 209. Babel and Hathitrust.org.

[1812] Ellis, James Alfred. (Ed.). (1928). History of the Bunn Family of America. Chicago, Illinois: Romanzo Norton Bunn, Publisher. P. 209. Babel and Hathitrust.org.

[1813] Ellis, James Alfred. (Ed.). (1928). History of the Bunn Family of America. Chicago, Illinois: Romanzo Norton Bunn, Publisher. P. 209. Babel and Hathitrust.org.

[1814] Ellis, James Alfred. (Ed.). (1928). History of the Bunn Family of America. Chicago, Illinois: Romanzo Norton Bunn, Publisher. P. 219. Babel and Hathitrust.org.

[1815] Ellis, James Alfred. (Ed.). (1928). History of the Bunn Family of America. Chicago, Illinois: Romanzo Norton Bunn, Publisher. P. 219. Babel and Hathitrust.org.

[1816] Ellis, James Alfred. (Ed.). (1928). History of the Bunn Family of America. Chicago, Illinois: Romanzo Norton Bunn, Publisher. P. 220. Babel and Hathitrust.org.

[1817] Ellis, James Alfred. (Ed.). (1928). History of the Bunn Family of America. Chicago, Illinois: Romanzo Norton Bunn, Publisher. P. 209. Babel and Hathitrust.org.

The Bunn Brothers and Abraham Lincoln

Jacob Bunn and John W. Bunn were two of the closest friends of Abraham Lincoln and the Lincoln family. Benjamin Ferguson and Robert Irwin, who were in-laws of the Bunns, were also close friends and supporters of Lincoln. Historian and lawyer Jesse William Weik commented, regarding John W. Bunn, that, "He and Lincoln were the closest of friends."[1818] Jacob Bunn was a regular and important legal client of Lincoln.[1819] John Bunn was a political protégé of Lincoln.[1820] Jesse William Wcik collected and assembled into a recollective volume original memoirs from men who had known Lincoln personally. The recollection and memoir that John Bunn provided to Weik showed the close friendship and working relationship that Lincoln and the Bunn brothers shared. Jacob Bunn, John W. Bunn, Robert Irwin, and others formed the Abraham Lincoln 1860 Presidential Campaign Committee. The John Bunn memoir in Jesse Weik's book stated the following about the creation of this political campaign organization:

"Shortly after Mr. Lincoln's nomination for President in May, 1860, Judge Stephen T. Logan, a warm friend and former law partner of Mr. Lincoln and one who had been active in his political interest, came to me at my brother Jacob Bunn's store, where I was then employed, and reminded me that Mr. Lincoln would necessarily receive a large amount of correspondence which should be attended to promptly and which would require clerical assistance; that prominent Republicans all over the country would be coming to Springfield to visit him; that the entertainment of these gentlemen would be an item of some consequence and that there would be various other expenses incident to the Springfield end of the campaign, all of which Mr. Lincoln, being a man of limited means, could ill afford to bear. Judge Logan then suggested that a fund for that purpose should be provided by Mr. Lincoln's personal friends in Springfield, at the same time handing me his check for five hundred dollars accompanied by a list of nine other friends of Mr. Lincoln including such men as Colonel John Williams, my brother Jacob Bunn, O. M. Hatch, Thomas Condell, and Robert Irwin, each one of whom, he was sure, would be glad to contribute five hundred dollars for a fund for this general purpose. He directed me to act as treasurer of the fund and I at once called on the gentlemen named,

---

[1818] Weik, Jesse William. (1922). The Real Lincoln: A Portrait. P. 285. Boston, MASS: Houghton Mifflin Company. Google Books.
[1819] Weik, Jesse William. (1922). The Real Lincoln: A Portrait. P. 285. Boston, MASS: Houghton Mifflin Company. Google Books.
[1820] Weik, Jesse William. (1922). The Real Lincoln: A Portrait. P. 285. Boston, MASS: Houghton Mifflin Company. Google Books.

obtaining, as predicted, five hundred dollars from each one, thus accumulating the fund of five thousand dollars for the purposes indicated by Judge Logan.

Shortly after this John G. Nicolay, then a clerk in the office of O. M. Hatch, agreed, without compensation, to give such time as he could to attend to Mr. Lincoln's political correspondence. Mr. Hatch was then Secretary of State, and he and the clerks in his office arranged their duties so that Mr. Nicolay might have considerable time at his disposal in connection with Mr. Lincoln's correspondence. In the early part of August a great Republican rally, said to have been attended by seventy-five thousand people, was held at the State Fair Grounds in Springfield. The expenses attendant upon that mammoth gathering of the people consumed the unexpended portion of the five thousand dollars that had been raised. After the rally a meeting of the committee of gentlemen who had contributed the fund was held and each of the original subscribers put in an additional five hundred dollars. Meanwhile Mr. Lincoln's correspondence had so materially increased that Mr. Nicolay found it practically impossible for him to take care of it without assistance. At the meeting of the committee, referred to, the question of procuring an assistant for Nicolay was canvassed. The names of various persons were suggested, but none seemed to possess the peculiar qualifications deemed requisite for one who would necessarily have the responsible duties attending the disposal of Mr. Lincoln's weighty and oftentimes delicate correspondence. Finally Milton Hay suggested that his nephew John Hay, who was studying law in his office, had marked literary talent, decided tact, and was otherwise well equipped to fill the position and that, too, without expense to the committee. Moreover, he contended, it would be an excellent thing for a young Hay in the way of practical experience. After due consideration the committee decided to make requisition on John Hay for his services and he immediately took his place beside Mr. Nicolay. The two worked together throughout the remainder of the campaign, disposing of Mr. Lincoln's correspondence which, especially after the election, and until the departure of Mr. Lincoln for Washington, in February, 1861, was very large and important."[1821]

Judge Jesse Weik reported that, "[Mr. Lincoln] relied on Mr. Bunn and repeatedly called on him and certain other discreet friends asking for reports of

---

[1821] Weik, Jesse William. (1922). The Real Lincoln: A Portrait. Pp. 280-284. Boston, MASS: Houghton Mifflin Company. Google Books.

developments. [Lincoln] insisted that he should be told everything."[1822] John Bunn continued to work with Lincoln after Lincoln was elected to the Presidency. Bunn expressed to Lincoln his concern over the personal character of Salmon Portland Chase of Ohio. Jesse Weik reported the memoir as follows:

"One day after the election had resulted successfully I went over to Mr. Lincoln's room in the State House, and as I passed up the stairway I met Salmon P. Chase, of Ohio, coming away. When I entered the room I said to Mr. Lincoln, rather abruptly, 'You don't want to put that man in your cabinet, I hope?' It was an impertinent remark on my part, but Mr. Lincoln received it kindly, and replied to me in a characteristic way, by saying, 'Why do you say that?' 'Because,' I answered, 'he thinks he is a great deal bigger than you are.' 'Well,' inquired Lincoln, 'do you know of any other men who think they are bigger than I am?' I replied, 'I cannot say that I do, but why do you ask me that?' 'Because,' said Mr. Lincoln, 'I want to put them all in my cabinet.'"[1823]

President Lincoln and the Bunn brothers remained close friends through the time of Lincoln's presidency. Once, when Lincoln expressed concern to John Bunn that John had spent too much money, $1,000 in personal money, on the political canvassing effort for Lincoln, Lincoln warned that Bunn could not afford this cost. Bunn answered as follows:

"'Yes, Mr. Lincoln, I am able to lose it because when you have reached Washington you are going to give me an office.' The statement seemed to startle him and the look in his face grew very serious. He promptly denied that he had promised me any office whatever. 'No, Mr. Lincoln,' I replied, 'you have not promised me anything, but you are going to give me an office just the same.' 'What office do you think I am going to give you?' he asked. 'The office of Pension Agent here in Illinois,' I exclaimed. 'During Isaac B. Curran's term as Pension Agent under [President James] Buchanan I have done all the work in the office in order to get the deposits in my brother's bank. The salary amounts to one thousand dollars, and when you go to Washington you are going to give me that office.' To this he made no word of reply, and there was therefore no way of determining what effect my prediction made upon him. All I know is that three days after his inauguration as President, Caleb B. Smith, his Secretary of the

[1822] Weik, Jesse William. (1922). The Real Lincoln: A Portrait. P. 284. Boston, MASS: Houghton Mifflin Company. Google Books.
[1823] Weik, Jesse William. (1922). The Real Lincoln: A Portrait. P. 287. Boston, MASS: Houghton Mifflin Company. Google Books.

Interior in Washington, sent to Springfield my commission as Pension Agent."[1824]

John Bunn discussed the time when Lincoln encouraged him to run for the office of Treasurer for the City of Springfield. Lincoln told Bunn how to go about campaigning for the position.

"'In the year of 1857 [he related] Mr. Lincoln asked me one day if I did not wish to run for city treasurer of Springfield. The city was then almost hopelessly Democratic and the proposition rather startled me. He, however, gave me encouragement to believe that I could be elected if I would go about the matter in the right way. My brother, Jacob Bunn, who was present, said to him, 'John will run if you want him to.' The candidate of the Democrats was Charles Ridgely. I confess I was pleased with the idea, and when the Republican city convention met I was an interested auditor of the proceedings. I expected to hear my own virtues extolled in the lofty way common in such conventions. Lincoln told me nothing of his plans as to how the announcement of my candidacy would be made or in what manner I would be brought out. The convention was nearly over and I began to think the matter of my nomination had been forgotten. In a city so Democratic as Springfield Republican nominations were regarded at best as rather formal and perfunctory affairs. Near the close of the convention a young man—a lawyer who was an inmate of Lincoln's office— addressed the chairman and said he would like to make a nomination for the office of city treasurer, but that, if the suggestion he should make did not meet with the favor of every delegate present, he would withdraw the name. He then put my name in nomination, but again said: 'If there is any delegate on this floor opposed to the candidacy of Mr. Bunn I do not wish his name to be voted upon or to go on the ticket.' No one objected and I was nominated by acclamation.

When I saw who was nominating me and knew that he was an inmate of Mr. Lincoln's office, I, of course, knew very well that he was acting under Mr. Lincoln's orders. The result of the election was that I was chosen for treasurer, and I may say I was again chosen in 1858, 1859, and in 1860. In all these campaigns I was, so to speak, under the political wing of Mr. Lincoln.

A day or two after the first nomination for city treasurer I was going uptown and saw Mr. Lincoln ahead of me. He waited until I caught up and said to me, 'How are you running?' I told him I didn't know how I was running. Then he said, 'Have you asked anybody to vote for you?' I said

---
[1824] Weik, Jesse William. (1922). The Real Lincoln: A Portrait. P. 287-288. Boston, MASS: Houghton Mifflin Company. Google Books.

that I had not. 'Well,' said he, 'if you don't think enough of your success to ask anybody to vote for you, it is probable they will not do it, and that you will not be elected.' I said to him, 'Shall I ask Democrats to vote for me?' He said, 'Yes, ask everybody to vote for you.' Just then a well-known Democrat, named Ragsdale, was coming up the sidewalk. Lincoln said, 'Now, you drop back there and ask Mr. Ragsdale to vote for you.' I turned and fell in with Mr. Ragsdale, told him of my candidacy, and said I hoped he would support me. To my astonishment he promised me that he would. Mr. Lincoln walked slowly along and fell in with me again and inquired, 'Well, what did Ragsdale say? Will he vote for you?' I answered, 'Yes, he told me he would.' 'Well then,' said Lincoln, 'you are sure of two votes at the election, mine and Ragsdale's.' This was my first lesson in politics and I received it from a welcome source.'"[1825]

Lincoln had counseled John Bunn on politics and was Bunn's original political promoter. Bunn helped promote Lincoln, as well, as has been discussed above. John Bunn would become one of the most important, perhaps the most important, figure in Illinois Republican politics around the turn of the twentieth century. Bunn was a key developer of the Illinois State Fair.[1826] He founded the Lincoln Library of Springfield, served as the president of the Lincoln Library board of directors, and was a promoter of public libraries generally.[1827] Bunn was Treasurer of the Illinois State Board of Agriculture from 1859-1898, and in this position helped build the Board into a dynamic and powerful organ of agriculture and industry.[1828] Bunn was one of the founders of the University of Illinois (at Urbana-Champaign) in 1867. He served as the founding Treasurer of the University and held the office of Treasurer of the university from 1867 until 1893.[1829] Bunn served more than three decades on the board of trustees of the University of Illinois.

John W. Bunn founded the Abraham Lincoln Centennial Association with United States Supreme Court Chief Justice Melville Weston Fuller of Chicago,

---

[1825] Weik, Jesse William. (1922). The Real Lincoln: A Portrait. Pp. 285-287. Boston, MASS: Houghton Mifflin Company. Google Books.
[1826] Journal of the Illinois State Historical Society (1908-1984).
Vol. 13, No. 1 (April, 1920). P. 279. Springfield, IL: Illinois State Historical Society. Google Books.
[1827] Journal of the Illinois State Historical Society (1908-1984).
Vol. 13, No. 1 (April, 1920). P. 278. Springfield, IL: Illinois State Historical Society. Google Books.
[1828] Journal of the Illinois State Historical Society (1908-1984).
Vol. 13, No. 1 (April, 1920). P. 277. Springfield, IL: Illinois State Historical Society. Google Books.
[1829] Journal of the Illinois State Historical Society (1908-1984).
Vol. 13, No. 1 (April, 1920). P. 277. Springfield, IL: Illinois State Historical Society. Google Books.

U.S. Senator Shelby Moore Cullom, U.S. Senator Albert J. Hopkins, Joseph G. Gannon, Adlai E. Stevenson, Illinois Governor Charles S. Deneen, Illinois Supreme Court Chief Justice John P. Hand, Judge J. Otis Humphrey, Illinois Secretary of State James A. Rose, Benjamin F. Caldwell, Illinois Governor Richard Yates, Melville E. Stone, Esq., and Dr. William Jayne.[1830] Melville Weston Fuller served as the eighth Chief Justice of the Supreme Court of the United States. John W. Bunn was president of the Lincoln Centennial Association from 1918 until 1920.[1831] The Lincoln Centennial Association became the Abraham Lincoln Association.[1832] John's grandnephew, George Wallace Bunn, Jr., would serve as president of the Abraham Lincoln Association later. For the biographies of brothers Willard Bunn and George Wallace Bunn, Jr., see Chapter 8, *Ode to Pylons and Cannery Windows*. The purposes of the Lincoln Centennial Association and the Abraham Lincoln Association include the celebration, commemoration, and preservation of the history, legacy, and memory of Abraham Lincoln, and the research, collection, and interpretation of biographical information about Lincoln.[1833] John and Jacob Bunn built and operated one of the most powerful political machines in Illinois history, and controlled much of Chicago, Springfield, and the State of Illinois, through the power they possessed in the Republican Party.[1834] Chicago Mayor Long John Wentworth, a friend and business partner of Jacob Bunn, attested this fact.

John Whitfield Bunn of Chicago and Springfield

John Whitfield Bunn was born June 21, 1831, in Hunterdon County, New Jersey. The son of Henry Bunn and Mary (Sigler) Bunn, John grew up with his siblings on the Bunn farmstead in Bunn Valley. Like his older brother Jacob Bunn, John would assume major and central leadership functions in both Chicago and Springfield. John and Jacob Bunn would both serve as principal industrial developers of both Chicago and Springfield. In multiple ways, the brothers were from both cities, and contributed much to the growth and development of the industrial economies of Illinois and the entire Great Lakes region of the United States. The two brothers and their friends helped to link Sangamon County and Cook County in one of the most powerful and economically concentrated political and industrial networks in American history.

The occurrences that culminated in John Bunn choosing to relocate to Illinois from the farm in western New Jersey stemmed principally from advocacy of his

---

[1830] Lincoln Centennial: Addresses Delivered at the Memorial Exercises Held at Springfield, Illinois, February 12, 1909. P. Springfield, IL: The Illinois Centennial Commission. Google Books.
[1831] The Abraham Lincoln Association. Abrahamlincolnassociation.org.
[1832] The Abraham Lincoln Association. Abrahamlincolnassociation.org.
[1833] The Abraham Lincoln Association. Abrahamlincolnassociation.org.
[1834] Bunn family history records.

older brother Jacob.[1835] What the author of this book has referred to previously as the "Wheelbarrow Dialogue" was a conversation between the two brothers in a farm field in New Jersey.[1836] The conversation contained an older brother's invitation to a younger brother to journey westward to Illinois and commence a new livelihood along the western frontier.[1837] John Bunn decided to make the journey to Illinois, arriving in 1847, eleven years after Jacob Bunn had arrived in Illinois. For John Bunn, the year 1847 would mark the beginning of a life of commitment to civic development and industrial development, and a career that would connect to multiple organizations that would be among the most historically important, economically significant, and industrially colossal elements of Chicago industry, culture, economy, and civic society. Beginning as a clerk in the wholesale house known as the J. Bunn Grocery Company of Springfield, John Bunn quickly learned the practices of the grocery business in a city that was of emerging importance as the Illinois state capital.

When the Civil War started, John W. Bunn served Illinois when Governor Richard Yates appointed Bunn as a special agent for the Union Army, the United States government, and the State of Illinois.[1838] With this commission Bunn moved the very first United States troops from Chicago to Cairo, Illinois.[1839] This strategic military movement was vital to the protection of the Ohio River border region, and the strategically significant riverport of Cairo.[1840] For his Civil War service as an intelligence and espionage agent for Illinois and for the United States, Bunn was awarded, on April 20, 1911, a large memorial trophy cup that honored by name Bunn and multiple other Illinois men who had given significant service to Illinois.[1841]

John W. Bunn occupied leadership positions within the Illinois Republican State Central Committee for a long time, and served as Treasurer of the Committee.[1842] The State Central Committee was one of the most powerful Illinois political organizations, and possessed key and strategic presences at both Chicago and Springfield.[1843] The Committee maintained a practical operating Chicago headquarters at the Grand Pacific Hotel in the Loop.[1844] The 1876 convention of the Illinois Republican State Central Committee took place at the Grand Pacific

[1835] Call, Andrew Taylor. (2005). Jacob Bunn: Legacy of an Illinois Industrial Pioneer. Pp. 30, 243. Lawrenceville, VA: Brunswick Publishing Corporation.
[1836] Call, Andrew Taylor. (2005). Jacob Bunn: Legacy of an Illinois Industrial Pioneer. Pp. 30, 243. Lawrenceville, VA: Brunswick Publishing Corporation.
[1837] Call, Andrew Taylor. (2005). Jacob Bunn: Legacy of an Illinois Industrial Pioneer. Pp. 30, 243. Lawrenceville, VA: Brunswick Publishing Corporation.
[1838] Marengo Republican-News. (June 24, 1920). P. 6. Newspapers.com.
[1839] Marengo Republican-News. (June 24, 1920). P. 6. Newspapers.com.
[1840] Marengo Republican-News. (June 24, 1920). P. 6. Newspapers.com.
[1841] John Whitfield Bunn Memorial Civil War Trophy. Author's personal collection.
[1842] Marengo Republican-News. (June 24, 1920). P. 6. Newspapers.com.
[1843] The Stark Daily Democrat. (September 28, 1876). P. 1 Newspapers.com.
[1844] The Stark Daily Democrat. (September 28, 1876). P. 1 Newspapers.com.

Hotel on September 14.[1845] A. C. Babcock, a business partner of Jacob Bunn, was Committee President at the time of the convention.[1846] Daniel Shepherd was Committee Secretary, and G. Schneider was Committee Treasurer.[1847] The Executive Board of the State Central Committee included A. C. Babcock, John W. Bunn, Charles B. Farwell, James P. Root, Gill J. Burr, E. W. Marsh, E. W. Wider, Julius White, J. B. Colton, and W. H. Barlow.[1848] Farwell and Root represented Chicago, and Bunn officially represented Springfield.[1849] Bunn also unofficially represented Chicago in a broader political and civic sense, due to possessing such a broad range of work there.[1850] The 1876 State Central Committee District Representatives were George T. Williams of Chicago, Philip A. Hogue of Chicago, Julius White of Chicago, C. W. Marsh of Sycamore, James Shaw of Mt. Carroll, Norman H. Ryan of Amboy, James Goodspeed of Joliet, H. A. Kenyon of Dwight, John B. Colton of Galesburg, H. F. McAlister of Oquawka, M. D. Maosic of New Canton, J. C. Salter of Jacksonville, Jacob Wheeler of Havanna, M. F. Kanan of Decatur, W. H. Barlow of Effingham, J. R. Tanner of Louisville, E. W. Wider of East St. Louis, R. B. Stinson of Anna, and J. N. Wasson of Shawneetown.[1851]

Jacob Bunn powerfully influenced Illinois Republican politics and was described by Chicago Mayor Long John Wentworth, who had been a business associate of Bunn, as the head of the most powerful political machine that ever existed in Illinois.[1852] Wentworth stated that, "it was impossible for many years to get any measure through the Legislature if Bunn opposed it."[1853] Jacob Bunn was a business associate of Joseph Rutter, and worked with Rutter's bank in Chicago, while John W. Bunn co-founded Selz, Schwab & Company with Morris Selz, Joseph Rutter, and Max Meyer, also in Chicago.[1854] Mayor Wentworth, who respected Bunn, nevertheless stated that Bunn, "controlled one legislature after another" in Illinois.[1855] The Bunn Republican machine, particularly through its immensely capitalized Chicago Republican Company, essentially controlled the politics of the State of Illinois and much of Chicago, in addition to its exertion of tremendous influence over national law and policy in Reconstruction Era

[1845] The Stark Daily Democrat. (September 28, 1876). P. 1 Newspapers.com.
[1846] The Stark Daily Democrat. (September 28, 1876). P. 1 Newspapers.com.
[1847] The Stark Daily Democrat. (September 28, 1876). P. 1 Newspapers.com.
[1848] The Stark Daily Democrat. (September 28, 1876). P. 1 Newspapers.com.
[1849] The Stark Daily Democrat. (September 28, 1876). P. 1 Newspapers.com.
[1850] The Stark Daily Democrat. (September 28, 1876). P. 1 Newspapers.com.
[1851] The Stark Daily Democrat. (September 28, 1876). P. 1 Newspapers.com.
[1852] Weekly Davenport Democrat. (January 10, 1878). P. 1. Newspapers.com.
[1853] Weekly Davenport Democrat. (January 10, 1878). P. 1. Newspapers.com.
[1854] Weekly Davenport Democrat. (January 10, 1878). P. 1. Newspapers.com; see also references elsewhere in this chapter.
[1855] Weekly Davenport Democrat. (January 10, 1878). P. 1. Newspapers.com.

America.[1856] The failure of the J. Bunn Bank in 1878 caused Jacob Bunn to lose much control over Illinois politics, according to Mayor Wentworth.[1857] While there is no doubt that the Bunn brothers possessed great power over the politics of Chicago, Springfield, and the State of Illinois as a whole, one must remember that these men were a part of their time—a time when machine politics were often prominently visible and operative elements in politics. The brothers used this power for much good in Illinois, too, and should be remembered for their honor and integrity in business, industry, and civic affairs both in Illinois and nationally.

John W. Bunn continued to remain active in Republican politics into the twentieth century. Bunn, Charles Farwell, Richard Rowett, W. F. L. Hadley, A. C. Babcock, Robert Bell, George T. Williams, Herman Benze, E. A. Filkins, A. J. Hopkins, A. M. Jones, John T. Browning, C. D. Trimble, C. G. Culver, John B. Colton, H. F. McAllister, E. J. Pearce, John Gordon, M. D. Beecher, R. B. McPherson, Henry Von Sellors, John R. Tanner, W. McAdams, and Thomas W. Scott established the Illinois Republican State Central Committee at the Grand Pacific Hotel of Chicago in July, 1878.[1858] The Grand Pacific Hotel of Chicago was, because of its popularity with the Republican Party men, in many ways the center of power in Illinois.

John W. Bunn supported William McKinley of Ohio in the United States presidential race of 1896, and was a member of the McKinley Commercial Club of Chicago.[1859] Bunn attended the Chicago conference of the Commercial McKinley Club No. 1 as a speaker and supporter.[1860] Many prominent people were seated on the McKinley Commercial Club conference platform, and among them were John W. Bunn, Morris Selz, John Villiers Farwell, Charles Benjamin Farwell, John V. Farwell, Jr., Charles H. Schwab, Jacob Harry Selz, Alexander C. McClurg, Simon Florsheim, Marshall Field, John Graves Shedd, Harlowe Niles Higinbotham, Lyman Gage, Harry Gordon Selfridge, W. W. Kimball, Abraham Hart, Henry Hart, Joseph Schaffner, Max Leopold, Dr. A. H. Green, W. H. Hooper, and John A. Colby, among many others.[1861] John Bunn, Morris Selz, J. Harry Selz, and Charles H. Schwab, were founders and owners of Selz, Schwab & Company, the largest shoe and boot manufacturer of Chicago, and the largest in the world.[1862] Bunn worked with Schwab, Lyman Gage, and Harlow N. Higinbotham as a founder, public administrator, and executive leader of the 1893 World's

[1856] Weekly Davenport Democrat. (January 10, 1878). P. 1. Newspapers.com; see Chapter 2, Builders of the Downtown, herein, for discussion of the Chicago Republican Company and its political influence.
[1857] Weekly Davenport Democrat. (January 10, 1878). P. 1. Newspapers.com.
[1858] Chicago Tribune. (July 25, 1878). P. 1. Newspapers.com.
[1859] The Inter Ocean. (November 13, 1896). P. 2. Newspapers.com.
[1860] The Inter Ocean. (November 13, 1896). P. 2. Newspapers.com.
[1861] The Inter Ocean. (November 13, 1896). P. 2. Newspapers.com.
[1862] Bunn family history records. See references elsewhere in book.

Columbian Exposition.[1863] Jacob Bunn worked closely with John V. Farwell in founding and owning the Chicago Republican Company, which was the largest newspaper company of Chicago, and the largest in the American West.[1864] Jacob Bunn, Jr. worked with Jacob Harry Selz in Chicago, and both were among the top executives at Selz, Schwab & Company.[1865] John Farwell was Marshall Field's business mentor. Marshall Field was John Graves Shedd's business mentor. W. W. Kimball was mentor to Edwin Stapleton Conway, whose son, Carle Cotter Conway, was business mentor to Loren Ralph Dodson of the Call-Ramsey-Peterson family of Ohio, Indiana, and Chicago (see Chapter 8, *Ode to Pylons and Cannery Windows*).

Morris Selz was a founder of the Union League Club.[1866] The Morris Selz family resided near 8th Street and Wabash Avenue at the time of the Great Fire in 1871.[1867] Emanuel F. Selz died in 1940 while on the golf course at the Lake Shore Country Club, and was a resident of 179 Lake Shore Drive at the time of his death.[1868] Emanuel was a member of the Cliff Dwellers' Club, the Mid-Day Club, and the Lake Shore Country Club.[1869] He also was a member of the Chicago Symphony Orchestra Association.[1870] The many Selz family members were friends with the many Bunn family members, and both families collaborated in business, civic work, and politics.

Morris Selz, Seneca D. Kimbark, J. Q. Grant, John Hoffman, W. C. Phillips, Ed Walker, William Busby, M. A. Farwell, Isaac Barefield, Lyman Blair, and John H. Howard were elected Second Ward delegates to the 1882 Chicago Republican Convention.[1871] Selz and multiple others of this political company continued participation in Second Ward Republican politics through subsequent years.[1872] Selz promoted the political work of John Logan and Richard Oglesby in Chicago, and was an active member of the Second Ward Logan Club, which was an organizational agent for John Logan and Richard Oglesby there.[1873] The Second Ward Logan Club counted many African-Americans among its membership, and also counted Col. Huntington Wolcott Jackson, a distant cousin of the Strykers, Taylors, and Henshaws of Chicago and Morgan County, as a member.[1874] Lyman Blair was a business partner of Jacob Bunn in the Chicago Secure Depository

---

[1863] Bunn family history records. See references elsewhere in book.
[1864] Bunn family history records. See references elsewhere in book.
[1865] Bunn family history records. See references elsewhere in book.
[1866] Chicago Tribune. (May 16, 1904). P. 10. Newspapers.com.
[1867] Chicago Tribune. (April 29, 1940). P. 12. Newspapers.com.
[1868] Chicago Tribune. (April 29, 1940). P. 12. Newspapers.com.
[1869] Chicago Tribune. (April 29, 1940). P. 12. Newspapers.com.
[1870] Chicago Tribune. (April 29, 1940). P. 12. Newspapers.com.
[1871] Chicago Tribune. (March 28, 1882). P. 7. Newspapers.com.
[1872] Chicago Tribune. (April 9, 1884). P. 2. Newspapers.com.
[1873] Chicago Tribune. (April 9, 1884). P. 2. Newspapers.com.
[1874] Chicago Tribune. (April 9, 1884). P. 2. Newspapers.com.

Company, and Morris Selz was closely connected to John W. Bunn and Jacob Bunn in Chicago industry and Republican politics at the Illinois and national levels. Morris Selz was a member of the Citizens' Association in 1885, and served on the Association's 1885 board of directors along with Marshall Field, Richard Teller Crane, John Jacob Glessner, C. L. Hutchinson, Martin A. Ryerson, and multiple other civic leaders.[1875] The Citizens' Association was a public policy and reform organization, and one of great political power and controversy, as was proved by the fact that the Democratic Chicago Mayor, Carter Henry Harrison, Sr. (1825-1893), filed a $400,000 libel suit against Edwin Lee Brown, who then was President of the Association.[1876] Brown and the other Association members opposed Mayor Harrison on public policy grounds, and charged him with corruption.[1877] Brown publicly opined in the October 14, 1885, edition of the *Chicago Tribune* that Harrison brought the defamation suit against Brown not because Harrison cared what Brown thought of Harrison, but because Brown was the speaker of the entire Citizens' Association, a Republican Party organization that Carter Harrison feared politically.[1878] Harrison was no friend of the Republican Party political powers of Chicago and Springfield.

Carter Harrison's mayoral tenure ended in death and destruction when Harrison attracted the obsession and rancor of a young Irish-American, Patrick Eugene Joseph Prendergast (1868-1894).[1879] Prendergast burglarized the Harrison home at Ashland and Jackson Boulevard on October 28, 1893, and murdered Harrison with pistol shots.[1880] Prendergast, who worked as a distributor for the *Chicago Inter-Ocean* and for the *Evening Post*, irrationally imagined that Mayor Harrison would appoint him to the job of Corporation Counsel for Chicago. Prendergast regarded Harrison's failure to appoint him to the said job as a personal betrayal.[1881] Prendergast's brother, John Prendergast, worked at the post office at the time of the murder.[1882] Multiple litigatory processes finally concluded with trial, conviction, and judgment, and Patrick Prendergast, having been judged sane, was hanged at the Cook County Jail at 11:47 A.M., on July 14, 1894.[1883] There was no connection between Prendergast and the Bunn brothers, and Jacob Bunn had long-since disposed of the Chicago Republican Newspaper (Chicago *Inter Ocean*) by the time of Prendergast's murderous act.

[1875] Chicago Tribune. (October 14, 1885). P. 8. Newspapers.com.
[1876] Chicago Tribune. (October 14, 1885). P. 8. Newspapers.com.
[1877] Chicago Tribune. (October 14, 1885). P. 8. Newspapers.com.
[1878] Chicago Tribune. (October 14, 1885). P. 8. Newspapers.com.
[1879] Chicago Tribune. (December 30, 1893). P. 2. Newspapers.com.
[1880] Chicago Tribune. (December 30, 1893). P. 2. Newspapers.com.
[1881] Chicago Tribune. (December 30, 1893). P. 2. Newspapers.com.
[1882] Chicago Tribune. (December 30, 1893). P. 2. Newspapers.com.
[1883] The Argos Reflector (Indiana). July 19, 1894. P. 2. Newspapers.com.

John W. Bunn promoted his close friends Richard Oglesby and John Logan from Springfield and from Chicago, as was evidenced by the Grand Pacific Hotel conference of the Republican State Central Committee of August 22, 1884.[1884] Bunn was joined at the Grand Pacific Hotel by United States Senator Shelby Moore Cullom (of Illinois), who would become the principal founder of the United States Commerce Commission in 1887, D. T. Littler, U.S. Congressman Reuben Ellwood (of Illinois), and Governor Oglesby himself.[1885] Bunn, Oglesby, Cullom, and Ellwood held Carter Harrison, who was a Democrat, in low regard, and believed that he was an overconfident and poor political representative of the State of Illinois.[1886]

Shelby Cullom (1829-1914) was a close friend of Jacob Bunn and John W. Bunn.[1887] Cullom studied law at Springfield, was admitted to the Illinois Bar, elected to the office of City Attorney for Springfield in 1855, and became friends with the Bunns in Springfield.[1888] He was elected to the Illinois State House of Representatives in 1856, and again in 1860, serving until 1861.[1889] Afterwards Cullom ran successful congressional campaigns, and won election as United States Congressman from Illinois from 1865 until 1871.[1890] He chaired the Committee on Territories during the Forty-First Congress, and returned to the Illinois legislature after service as congressman.[1891] Cullom served as Governor of Illinois for a term from 1877 to 1883, but resigned prior to the expiration of the gubernatorial term, and returned to federal politics.[1892] He was elected United States Senator from Illinois in 1882, and served in that office from 1883 until 1913.[1893] Cullom chaired the Committee on Interstate Commerce from 1887 until 1893, from 1895 to 1901,

[1884] Chicago Tribune. (August 23, 1884). P. 2. Newspapers.com.
[1885] Chicago Tribune. (August 23, 1884). P. 2. Newspapers.com.
[1886] Chicago Tribune. (August 23, 1884). P. 2. Newspapers.com.
[1887] Call, Andrew Taylor. (2005). Jacob Bunn: Legacy of an Illinois Industrial Pioneer. Pp. 103-104. Lawrenceville, VA: Brunswick Publishing Corporation.
[1888] Biographical Directory of the United States Congress: 1774-Present. Cullom, Shelby Moore (1829-1914). Bioguide.congress.gov; Call, Andrew Taylor. (2005). Jacob Bunn: Legacy of an Illinois Industrial Pioneer. Pp. 103-104. Lawrenceville, VA: Brunswick Publishing Corporation.
[1889] Biographical Directory of the United States Congress: 1774-Present. Cullom, Shelby Moore (1829-1914). Bioguide.congress.gov.
[1890] Biographical Directory of the United States Congress: 1774-Present. Cullom, Shelby Moore (1829-1914). Bioguide.congress.gov.
[1891] Biographical Directory of the United States Congress: 1774-Present. Cullom, Shelby Moore (1829-1914). Bioguide.congress.gov.
[1892] Biographical Directory of the United States Congress: 1774-Present. Cullom, Shelby Moore (1829-1914). Bioguide.congress.gov.
[1893] Biographical Directory of the United States Congress: 1774-Present. Cullom, Shelby Moore (1829-1914). Bioguide.congress.gov.

and again from 1909 to 1911.[1894] Cullom additionally chaired the Committee on Expenditures of Public Money from 1885 until 1887, and chaired the Committee on Foreign Relations from 1901 to 1911.[1895] He was Republican Conference Chairman from 1911 to 1913.[1896]

Always committed to both Illinois and national civic organizations, Cullom was a Regent of the Smithsonian Institution from 1885 until 1913, and was Chairman and Resident Commissioner of the Lincoln Memorial Commission in 1913 and 1914. He was a member of the commission that designed and planned a legal system of the Hawaiian Islands.[1897] Cullom collaborated with Jacob Bunn, Gen. John Anderson McClernand, John Williams, Alexander Starne, Charles W. Matheny, Asa Eastman, Charles Ridgely, James Wilson, Munson Carter, Preston Breckinridge, Joseph G. McCoy, John Bone, Peyton Harrison, and Andrew B. McConnell, all of Sangamon County, and Horatio M. Vandever, D. D. Shumway, William A. Goodrich, William S. Frink, Calvin Goudy, Lewis E. Thompson, William B. Hall, and Charles A. Manners, all of Christian County, in the formation and incorporation of the Pana, Springfield and Northwestern Railroad Company in 1865.[1898] Cullom sponsored and promoted the Cullom Act of February 4, 1887, which created the Interstate Commerce Commission. Cullom was the principal founder of the Interstate Commerce Commission.[1899]

United States Senator Thomas Henry Carter of Montana, who sponsored the Carter Act of June 6, 1900, which framed the first civil government of Alaska, asked Shelby Cullom and John W. Bunn about Abraham Lincoln's complexion and hair color around the centennial anniversary of Lincoln's birth.[1900] Bunn responded with a short letter whose words were as follows:

"'Dear Senator: Your favor of the 13th inst., received and contents noted.

[1894] Biographical Directory of the United States Congress: 1774-Present. Cullom, Shelby Moore (1829-1914). Bioguide.congress.gov.

[1895] Biographical Directory of the United States Congress: 1774-Present. Cullom, Shelby Moore (1829-1914). Bioguide.congress.gov.

[1896] Biographical Directory of the United States Congress: 1774-Present. Cullom, Shelby Moore (1829-1914). Bioguide.congress.gov.

[1897] Biographical Directory of the United States Congress: 1774-Present. Cullom, Shelby Moore (1829-1914). Bioguide.congress.gov.

[1898] Call, Andrew Taylor. (2005). Jacob Bunn: Legacy of an Illinois Industrial Pioneer. P. 103. Lawrenceville, VA: Brunswick Publishing Corporation; An Act to Incorporate the Pana, Springfield and Northwestern Railroad Company. 24th General Assembly, State of Illinois (1865).

[1899] Biographical Directory of the United States Congress: 1774-Present. Cullom, Shelby Moore (1829-1914). Bioguide.congress.gov.

[1900] Belvidere, Illinois, Republican-Northwestern. (February 12, 1909). P. 1. Newspapers.com.

Dr. Jayne and I think Lincoln's hair was dark brown and that his complexion was dark but not swarthy. You must remember that Mr. Lincoln had just started his whiskers when he left for Washington."[1901]

The Bunn letter was incorporated into a letter to Senator Carter from Shelby Cullom, a letter in which Cullom endorsed Bunn and Dr. William Jayne as men that, "know more about Lincoln and his history than any two men living."[1902] Abraham Lincoln had appointed Dr. William Jayne to the Governorship of the Dakota Territory.[1903] Dr. Jayne was a close friend of Jacob and John W. Bunn.

The political competition between Illinois Governor John Riley Tanner and Shelby Cullom ran at high water in 1900, when Tanner predicted that Senator Cullom would lose the 1900 United States Senate race to a Democrat. John W. Bunn brought tremendous support again to his friend Cullom, and Cullom won reelection to the Senate on January 22, 1901, having defeated Democratic challenger Samuel Alschuler.[1904] The May 13, 1900, edition of *The St. Louis Republic*, noted that Bunn, "was too rich to work," but that he would run the Cullom committee in name, and that, "Cullom has no stancher friend than Bunn."[1905] Tanner withdrew from the race, according to the *Tribune Almanac and Political Register* of New York City.[1906] When Cullom died in 1914, John Bunn, Charles Ridgely, William Ridgely, Dr. George Pasfield, and Dr. William Jayne attended the visitation for Cullom at the home of Mrs. Charles Ridgely in Springfield.[1907] Cullom was said to have been a distant cousin of the Ridgelys.[1908]

John W. Bunn, The Illinois Centennial Commission,

and the Richard Oglesby Monument

John Whitfield Bunn was a member of the Illinois Centennial Commission, which was an organization whose purpose was the creation of a memorial of the first century of Illinois statehood (1818-1918).[1909] The Commission possessed

---

[1901] Belvidere, Illinois, Republican-Northwestern. (February 12, 1909). P. 1. Newspapers.com.

[1902] Belvidere, Illinois, Republican-Northwestern. (February 12, 1909). P. 1. Newspapers.com.

[1903] Belvidere Daily Republican. (January 31, 1914). P. 1.

[1904] The Tribune Almanac and Political Register. (1902). P. 297. New York, NY: The Tribune Association. Google Books. See also Wikipedia article and reference sources: United States Senate Elections: 1900, 1901.

[1905] The St. Louis Republic. (May 13, 1900). P. 4. Newspapers.com.

[1906] The Tribune Almanac and Political Register. (1902). P. 297. New York, NY: The Tribune Association. Google Books.

[1907] Belvidere Daily Republican. (January 31, 1914). P. 1. Newspapers.com.

[1908] Belvidere Daily Republican. (January 31, 1914). P. 1. Newspapers.com.

[1909] Langland, James. Editor. (1918-1919). The Chicago Daily News Almanac and Year-Book for 1919. P. 832. Chicago, IL: The Chicago Daily News Company. Google Books.

statewide administrative power and jurisdiction, and had notable organizational presence at Chicago.[1910] James Langland, the Editor of *The Chicago Daily News and Almanac and Year-Book For 1919*, compiled the leadership information for the Centennial Commission in the 1919 *Almanac*. The Commission leadership included the following persons of Chicago: Chairman Dr. Otto L. Schmidt of 38 Dearborn, William Pelouze of 12 W. Delaware Place, Judge Thomas F. Scully of the Cook County Building, Rev. Frederic Siedenburg, S. J., of 617 Ashland Block, Wallace Rice of 2701 Best Avenue, and Frederick Bruegger of 5420 Cornell Avenue.[1911] Other Commission members included Dr. Edward Bowe of Jacksonville, John J. Brown of Vandalia, Mrs. Jessie Palmer Weber of Springfield, George Pasfield, Jr., of Springfield, The Hon. William Butterworth of Moline, The Hon. Leon Colp of Marion, Rev. R. W. Ennis of Mason City, Professor E. B. Greene of the University of Illinois, and Edmund J. James of Urbana, who was President of the University of Illinois.[1912] The Hon. A. J. Poorman of Fairfield, Hugh S. Magill, Jr., of Springfield, Horace Bancroft of Springfield, Halbert O. Crews of Springfield, and Professor Clarence Walworth Alvord of the University of Illinois were the other Commission members.[1913] The Illinois Centennial Commission produced the Illinois Centennial Monument of Chicago, which remains to this day in the Logan Square community at Logan Square Park, where W. Logan Boulevard crosses N. Kedzie Boulevard. John W. Bunn, as a member of the Illinois Centennial Commission, helped to plan and arrange for this monument.

John W. Bunn, John S. Runnells, John Barton Payne, Charles L. LeForgee, and Martin B. Bailey constituted the Oglesby Monument Commission, an organization of gubernatorial appointees that constructed the Richard Oglesby Memorial.[1914] Bunn and Runnells both were Chicago Club members.[1915] LeForgee was from Decatur and Bailey was from Danville.[1916] The Oglesby Memorial remains to this day atop a prominent hill in Lincoln Park, located adjacent to the North Pond, immediately west of Cannon Drive, and a short distance north of Lincoln Park Zoo.[1917] The Commission retained the French-American artist, Leonard Crunelle,

---

[1910] Langland, James. Editor. (1918-1919). The Chicago Daily News Almanac and Year-Book for 1919. P. 832. Chicago, IL: The Chicago Daily News Company. Google Books.
[1911] Langland, James. Editor. (1918-1919). The Chicago Daily News Almanac and Year-Book for 1919. P. 832. Chicago, IL: The Chicago Daily News Company. Google Books.
[1912] Langland, James. Editor. (1918-1919). The Chicago Daily News Almanac and Year-Book for 1919. P. 832. Chicago, IL: The Chicago Daily News Company. Google Books.
[1913] Langland, James. Editor. (1918-1919). The Chicago Daily News Almanac and Year-Book for 1919. P. 832. Chicago, IL: The Chicago Daily News Company. Google Books.
[1914] The Chicago Daily News Almanac And Year Book For 1919. (1918). P. 867. Chicago, IL: The Chicago Daily News Company. Google Books.
[1915] Bunn family historical records.
[1916] The Chicago Daily News Almanac And Year Book For 1919. (1918). P. 867. Chicago, IL: The Chicago Daily News Company. Google Books.
[1917] Richard Oglesby Monument. Chicagoparkdistrict.com.

as the sculptor of the monument.[1918] Crunelle studied sculpture under the world-renowned Chicago sculptor, Lorado Taft, who established the Midway Studios in Woodlawn, on the south side of the Midway Plaisance.[1919] Crunelle worked as a coal miner in Illinois prior to studying sculpture, and his artistic legacy in Chicago is significant.[1920] He completed the Oglesby Memorial statue in 1919, one year prior to the death of John W. Bunn.[1921]

Richard James Oglesby (1824-1899) was a United Stated Senator from Illinois.[1922] A native of Oldham County, Kentucky, Oglesby was orphaned in youth, raised in Decatur, Macon County, Illinois, and learned the trades of rope maker, carpenter, and farmer.[1923] He studied law, and was admitted to the Illinois Bar in 1845, developed a strong friendship with the Bunn brothers of Springfield and Chicago, and received their support throughout his career.[1924]

Selz, Schwab & Company of Chicago:

The Largest Manufacturer of Shoes and Boots in the World

John Whitfield Bunn served as one of the founders of the Chicago shoe and boot manufacturing company known as Selz, Schwab & Company.[1925] The company was organized in 1871 under the commercial name of M. Selz & Company.[1926] It is important to notice that the company was organized in September of 1871, approximately one month prior to the Great Chicago Fire of October 8, 1871.[1927] Four men served as the founders of the new shoe and boot manufacturer.[1928] Those four were John Whitfield Bunn, Morris Selz, Joseph Rutter, and Max Meyer.[1929]

[1918] Richard Oglesby Monument. Chicagoparkdistrict.com.

[1919] Richard Oglesby Monument. Chicagoparkdistrict.com.

[1920] Richard Oglesby Monument. Chicagoparkdistrict.com.

[1921] Richard Oglesby Monument. Chicagoparkdistrict.com; Bunn family historical records.

[1922] Biographical Directory of the United States Congress. Richard James Oglesby. Bioguide.congress.gov.

[1923] Biographical Directory of the United States Congress. Richard James Oglesby. Bioguide.congress.gov.

[1924] Biographical Directory of the United States Congress. Richard James Oglesby. Bioguide.congress.gov.

[1925] Journal of the Illinois State Historical Society (1908-1984). Vol. 13, No. 2. Pp. 273-280. Jstor.

[1926] Journal of the Illinois State Historical Society (1908-1984) Vol. 13, No. 2 (Jul., 1920). P. 277. Jstor.

[1927] Andreas, Alfred Theodore. (1886). History of Chicago. Vol. 3. P. 730. Chicago, Illinois: The A. T. Andreas Company, Publishers. Google Books.

[1928] Andreas, Alfred Theodore. (1886). History of Chicago. Vol. 3. P. 730. Chicago, Illinois: The A. T. Andreas Company, Publishers. Google Books.

[1929] Andreas, Alfred Theodore. (1886). History of Chicago. Vol. 3. P. 730. Chicago, Illinois: The A. T. Andreas Company, Publishers. Google Books.

Morris Selz was a native of Wurtemberg, Germany.[1930] He was born October 2, 1826.[1931] According to one historical account, Selz arrived in the United States at the age of sixteen, "with one Prussian dollar as his entire capital. . ."[1932] The 1913 *Shoe and Leather Reporter* obituary for Morris Selz indicated that one Prussian dollar was worth, presumably at the time of his arrival in the United States in approximately 1842, seventy-seven cents in United States currency.[1933] United States historian Alfred Theodore Andreas indicated that Selz arrived in the United States in the year 1844.[1934] In 1845, Selz first chose Talbotton, Georgia, as the place to begin in the United States.[1935] There was a Jewish community in Talbotton during the nineteenth century, and the family of Isidor Straus, who was later the owner of the Macey's Department Store company, also resided there for a time.[1936] Remaining in Georgia until 1851, Selz engaged in business as a merchant.[1937] In 1851, Selz relocated to California, and engaged in business as a miner and clothing merchant.[1938] He later relocated to Chicago in 1854.[1939] In approximately 1854, Selz formed the firm of Selz & Cohn, a company whose business purpose was clothing sales.[1940] Selz was a founder and member of both the Standard Club of Chicago and the Union League Club of Chicago.[1941] On May 10, 1863, Morris Selz married Rosa Frank, who was also a native of Wurtemberg.[1942] Rosa (Frank) Selz died in 1869.[1943] The two sons born to Morris and Rosa Selz were Jacob Harry Selz

---

[1930] Shoe and Leather Reporter. (June 5, 1913). Vol. 110, Number 10. P. 15. Google Books.

[1931] Andreas, Alfred Theodore. (1886). History of Chicago. Vol. 3. P. 730. Chicago, Illinois: The A. T. Andreas Company, Publishers. Google Books.

[1932] Shoe and Leather Reporter. (June 5, 1913). Vol. 110, Number 10. P. 15. Google Books.

[1933] Shoe and Leather Reporter. (June 5, 1913). Vol. 110, Number 10. P. 15. Google Books.

[1934] Andreas, Alfred Theodore. (1886). History of Chicago. Vol. 3. P. 730. Chicago, Illinois: The A. T. Andreas Company, Publishers. Google Books.

[1935] Andreas, Alfred Theodore. (1886). History of Chicago. Vol. 3. P. 730. Chicago, Illinois: The A. T. Andreas Company, Publishers. Google Books.

[1936] Hieke, Anton. (2013). Jewish Identity in the Reconstruction South. P. 144. Berlin: Walter de Gruyter. Google Books.

[1937] Andreas, Alfred Theodore. (1886). History of Chicago. Vol. 3. P. 730. Chicago, Illinois: The A. T. Andreas Company, Publishers. Google Books.

[1938] Andreas, Alfred Theodore. (1886). History of Chicago. Vol. 3. Pp. 730-731. Chicago, Illinois: The A. T. Andreas Company, Publishers. Google Books.

[1939] Andreas, Alfred Theodore. (1886). History of Chicago. Vol. 3. P. 730. Chicago, Illinois: The A. T. Andreas Company, Publishers. Google Books.

[1940] Andreas, Alfred Theodore. (1886). History of Chicago. Vol. 3. P. 731. Chicago, Illinois: The A. T. Andreas Company, Publishers. Google Books.

[1941] Shoe and Leather Reporter. (June 5, 1913). Vol. 110, Number 10. P. 15. Google Books.

[1942] Andreas, Alfred Theodore. (1886). History of Chicago. Vol. 3. P. 731. Chicago, Illinois: The A. T. Andreas Company, Publishers. Google Books.

[1943] Andreas, Alfred Theodore. (1886). History of Chicago. Vol. 3. P. 731. Chicago, Illinois: The A. T. Andreas Company, Publishers. Google Books.

and Manuel F. Selz.[1944] Morris Selz subsequently married Hannah Kohn of Chicago.[1945] One son and one daughter were born to Morris and Hannah (Kohn) Selz, and their names were Abraham Kohn Selz and Lillie G. Selz.[1946]

The M. Selz & Company was constructed upon sound and well-conceived market principles. The company factory was constructed near the intersection of Wabash Avenue and Randolph Street, in the Loop.[1947] The company subsequently relocated to the northeast corner of Madison Street and Franklin Street, in January of 1873.[1948] Morris Selz, John Bunn, Max Meyer, and Joseph Rutter perceived and identified the opportunity to make shoes and boots from the abundant leftover Chicago Union Stockyards leather byproduct.[1949] The Chicago Union Stockyards, therefore, constituted an economic and industrial foundation from which have been derived myriad additional Chicago organizations: railroad companies, meat-packing companies, shoe and boot companies, canning companies, and many more.[1950] M. Selz & Company, later incorporated as Selz, Schwab &Company, was one such industrial and organizational derivative of the Chicago Union Stockyards— and indeed one of the most important industrial companies to ever exist in Chicago history, Cook County history, Pittsburgh, Pennsylvania, history, and United States economic history as a whole.

M. Selz & Company experienced a superlatively auspicious inaugural year among the population of Chicago industries, having generated sales of $1,000,000 by approximately the time of its second year of operation, in 1872.[1951] Selz, Schwab & Company employed approximately 1,500 people by the beginning of the twentieth century. Selz factories at that time were located in Chicago, Joliet, Genoa, and Elgin.[1952] The company manufactured 12,000 pairs of shoes and boots

[1944] Andreas, Alfred Theodore. (1886). History of Chicago. Vol. 3. P. 731. Chicago, Illinois: The A. T. Andreas Company, Publishers. Google Books.
[1945] Andreas, Alfred Theodore. (1886). History of Chicago. Vol. 3. P. 731. Chicago, Illinois: The A. T. Andreas Company, Publishers. Google Books.
[1946] Andreas, Alfred Theodore. (1886). History of Chicago. Vol. 3. P. 731. Chicago, Illinois: The A. T. Andreas Company, Publishers. Google Books.
[1947] Andreas, Alfred Theodore. (1886). History of Chicago. Vol. 3. P. 730. Chicago, Illinois: The A. T. Andreas Company, Publishers. Google Books.
[1948] Andreas, Alfred Theodore. (1886). History of Chicago. Vol. 3. P. 730. Chicago, Illinois: The A. T. Andreas Company, Publishers. Google Books.
[1949] Bunn and Selz family historical records.
[1950] Bunn, Selz, and Call family historical records.
[1951] Wilson, Mark R., Porter, Stephen R., Reiff, Janice. (2005). "Selz, Schwab & Co." in The Electronic Encyclopedia of Chicago. Chicago, IL: Chicago Historical Society. Encyclopedia.chicagohistory.org.
[1952] Wilson, Mark R., Porter, Stephen R., Reiff, Janice. (2005). "Selz, Schwab & Co." in The Electronic Encyclopedia of Chicago. Chicago, IL: Chicago Historical Society. Encyclopedia.chicagohistory.org.

per day at this time.[1953] The approximate extrapolated annual output for the company would have hovered around 4,380,000 shoes and boots at this time.[1954]

The Inter-Ocean newspaper contained an excellent eulogistic biography of Max Meyer (1834-1889) in the obituary that appeared for him in 1889.[1955] Meyer was a native of Sommerau, Bavaria.[1956] As a teenager, Meyer worked for a dry goods company in Baden-Baden, eventually working in the management of the dry goods company.[1957] Meyer emigrated to Chicago in 1854.[1958] He worked as a clerk for Rosenfeld & Rosenberg, a Chicago dry goods company. In approximately 1860, after several years of work with Rosenfeld & Rosenberg, Meyer started a partnership company with two partners.[1959] The new firm, known as Weineman, Frank & Meyer, was a dry goods business. The company ended in 1871. Meyer then became partner of Meyer, Strauss, Goodman & Company, which was a wholesale clothing dealer.[1960] It was at this time that Meyer co-founded M. Selz & Company with Morris Selz, John Whitfield Bunn, and Joseph Rutter. Meyer, Strauss, Goodman & Company was destroyed in the Great Chicago Fire, but rebuilt fast.[1961] The owners used the barn at the residence of one of the members of the company as the temporary and emergency place of business for the company in the destructive wake of the Great Fire. Meyer and his partners in the firm of Weineman, Frank & Meyer repaid 100 percent of the debt they owed to creditors.[1962]

The financial panic associated with the paper money crisis of the Civil War years affected Weineman, Frank & Meyer. The company contracted for payment of the debt at the rate of 60 cents per dollar.[1963] *The Inter Ocean* reported that Meyer, two years after the 60 percent payment of the original company debt, invited all of the company creditors to a banquet in New York City.[1964] Meyer gave checks for the remaining debt moneys to each creditor, plus the interest moneys, and thus performed 100 percent repayment of the original debts.[1965] For Max Meyer, as for Jacob Bunn and the other Bunn family members, commerce and performance of

---

[1953] Wilson, Mark R., Porter, Stephen R., Reiff, Janice. (2005). "Selz, Schwab & Co." in The Electronic Encyclopedia of Chicago. Chicago, IL: Chicago Historical Society. Encyclopedia.chicagohistory.org.

[1954] Wilson, Mark R., Porter, Stephen R., Reiff, Janice. (2005). "Selz, Schwab & Co." in The Electronic Encyclopedia of Chicago. Chicago, IL: Chicago Historical Society. Encyclopedia.chicagohistory.org.

[1955] The Inter Ocean. (March 3, 1889). P. 2. Newspapers.com.

[1956] The Inter Ocean. (March 3, 1889). P. 2. Newspapers.com.

[1957] The Inter Ocean. (March 3, 1889). P. 2. Newspapers.com.

[1958] The Inter Ocean. (March 3, 1889). P. 2. Newspapers.com.

[1959] The Inter Ocean. (March 3, 1889). P. 2. Newspapers.com.

[1960] The Inter Ocean. (March 3, 1889). P. 2. Newspapers.com.

[1961] The Inter Ocean. (March 3, 1889). P. 2. Newspapers.com.

[1962] The Inter Ocean. (March 3, 1889). P. 2. Newspapers.com.

[1963] The Inter Ocean. (March 3, 1889). P. 2. Newspapers.com.

[1964] The Inter Ocean. (March 3, 1889). P. 2. Newspapers.com.

[1965] The Inter Ocean. (March 3, 1889). P. 2. Newspapers.com.

duties were matters of honesty and honor.[1966] The ethics of honesty and honor pervaded the Bunn companies, as well as the companies of those associated with the Bunns. Meyer, Morris Selz, and John W. Bunn all were members of the Union League Club.[1967] Meyer belonged to the Citizens' Association, and was a member of the Board of Directors of the Union League Club. John and Charles Farwell were friends with Meyer and with the Bunn brothers.[1968] Meyer resided at 2621 Michigan Avenue at the time of his death in 1889.[1969] Meyer was the father of eight children.[1970]

The Great Chicago Fire of October 8, 1871, brought destruction to the physical property of M. Selz & Company, jeopardizing the future of the young enterprise. The builders of the company, however, were committed not only to the reconstruction and salvation of the physically ruined shoe company, but also the salvation of the City of Chicago from the ruination caused by the Great Chicago Fire. Morris Selz, John Bunn, Max Meyer, and Joseph Rutter rebuilt the physical infrastructure of the company, establishing the means for a future of rapid growth and corporate globalization for the Chicago shoe industry.[1971] Charles Schwab, who would later serve as Comptroller of the City of Chicago, would become a partner of M. Selz & Company, and the name of the firm reflected that fact.[1972] Other important people who were connected to the company were Jacob Harry Selz and Manuel Frank Selz, both of whom were sons of Morris Selz and Rosa (Frank) Selz. Joseph Rutter also served with the company as an executive officer. Charles Schwab served as a member of the Board of Directors of the 1893 World's Columbian Exposition, was a member of the Standard Club and the Union League Club, and helped administer the Chicago Home for Jewish Orphans, in addition possibly to having served as a founder of the Home.[1973]

J. F. O'Brien of Selz, Schwab & Company served on the Ways and Means Committee of the Chicago Association of Commerce, in which he served the Railway and Steamboat Warehouse Committee.[1974] *The Advertiser*, a paper of Lawrence, Kansas, contained an advertisement for Selz, Schwab & Company, and noted that the firm employed 200 traveling salesmen and owned at least ten

---

[1966] The Inter Ocean. (March 3, 1889). P. 2. Newspapers.com.

[1967] The Inter Ocean. (March 3, 1889). P. 2. Newspapers.com; Chicago Tribune. (April 4, 1886). P. 10. Newspapers.com.

[1968] The Inter Ocean. (March 3, 1889). P. 2. Newspapers.com.

[1969] The Inter Ocean. (March 3, 1889). P. 2. Newspapers.com.

[1970] The Inter Ocean. (March 3, 1889). P. 2. Newspapers.com.

[1971] Selz, Bunn family history records.

[1972] Call, Andrew Taylor. (2005). Jacob Bunn: Legacy of an Illinois Industrial Pioneer. Pp. 137, 148. Lawrenceville, VA: Brunswick Publishing Corporation; Notable Men of Chicago and Their City. (1910). Chicago, IL: Chicago Daily Journal.

[1973] Call, Andrew Taylor. (2005). Jacob Bunn: Legacy of an Illinois Industrial Pioneer. Pp. 137, 148. Lawrenceville, VA: Brunswick Publishing Corporation; Notable Men of Chicago and Their City. (1910). Chicago, IL: Chicago Daily Journal.

[1974] Hide and Leather. (January 25, 1919). Vol. 57, No. 4. P. 33. Chicago, IL: Hide and Leather. Google Books.

factories in 1914.[1975] Six Selz factories were then located in Chicago, and four were located in Pittsburgh, Pennsylvania.[1976] John W. Bunn had built a large commercial and industrial connection between Chicago and Pittsburgh both through the Wabash Railroad Company and through Selz, Schwab & Company. Morris Selz was a co-founder of the Standard Club of Chicago in 1869. The other founders of the club were B. Loewenthal, B. Mergentheim, G. Snydacker, M. Einstein, Sigmund Floersheim, and E. Frankenthal.[1977] The Standard Club was formed on April 4, 1869, only days after the Chicago Club was formed on March 25, 1869.

Many pallbearers served at Morris Selz' funeral in 1913.[1978] The honorary pallbearers were John Whitfield Bunn, Simon Yondorf, Isaac Meyer, J. L. Gatzert, Max Ederheimer, J. Edmund Strong, F. F. Baldwin, Max Frank, Bernard Rosenberg, Simon H. Kohn, Joseph Rosenbaum, Eli M. Strauss, Carl Meyer, John A. Reichelt, Sr., Joseph Horner, Leopold Bloom, Alfred L. Austrian, Mark Kahn, Levy Mayer, and M. S. Florsheim. The active pallbearers were J. F. O'Brien, H. M. Slaymaker, H. A. Rose, H. A. Bollman, S. L. Levi, S. H. Axman, F. W. Yocky, and A. J. Gillette.[1979] Morris was survived by his three sons, Jacob Harry Selz, Abraham Kohn Selz, and Emanuel Frank Selz.[1980] The Selz home was at 1717 Michigan Avenue at the time of Morris' death in 1913.[1981] Morris was buried at Rosehill Cemetery in the North Side of Chicago.[1982] Many hundreds of Selz' business associates attended his funeral and at least 100 automobiles followed the hearse to Rosehill Cemetery for the interment.[1983] *The Kentucky Advocate*, a newspaper of Danville, Kentucky, reported Selz' death. *The Kentucky Advocate* stated that A. B. Norrod, who represented Selz, Schwab & Company in central Kentucky, and John Magee who owned a large Selz, Schwab & Company dealership in Danville, were prominent agents and promoters of the Chicago company.[1984] The obituary paid tribute to the two Kentucky businessmen and to their excellent and loyal service to the company.[1985] This type of memorial journalism is excellent in that it includes and honors people, other than only the close business associates of the deceased, who were associated with the deceased and who worked for the deceased. This class of journalism, exhibited brilliantly by the Kentucky reporter, creates and fosters civic and commercial community across many places and regions.[1986]

[1975] The Advertiser. (March 5, 1914). P. 4. Newspapers.com.

[1976] The Advertiser. (March 5, 1914). P. 4. Newspapers.com.

[1977] Chicago Tribune. (April 4, 1886). P. 10. Newspapers.com.

[1978] The Inter Ocean. (May 5, 1913). P. 5. Newspapers.com.

[1979] The Inter Ocean. (June 5, 1913). P. 5. Newspapers.com.

[1980] The Inter Ocean. (May 5, 1913). P. 5. Newspapers.com.

[1981] The Inter Ocean. (May 5, 1913). P. 5. Newspapers.com.

[1982] The Inter Ocean. (May 5, 1913). P. 5. Newspapers.com.

[1983] The Inter Ocean. (June 6, 1913). P. 5. Newspapers.com.

[1984] Kentucky Advocate. (June 26, 1913). P. 1. Newspapers.com.

[1985] Kentucky Advocate. (June 26, 1913). P. 1. Newspapers.com.

[1986] Kentucky Advocate. (June 26, 1913). P. 1. Newspapers.com.

The Chicago Association of Commerce appointed Jacob Harry Selz, President of Selz, Schwab & Company, to membership on a policy committee. The purpose of the committee was to meet with members of the Illinois Congressional Delegation at Washington, D.C., and encourage the legislative approval of financing for railroad construction at Chicago. The report of Selz' appointment to the policy committee appeared in the February 8, 1919, edition of *Hide and Leather*, a leather products manufacturing and sales journal.[1987]

J. Harry Selz made it known that Selz, Schwab & Company would not export its products to any foreign country until all of its American markets had been fully supplied.[1988] Harry Selz put the policy of national economic loyalty into practice when he rejected an offer for 200,000 pairs of shoes from a European country, because he believed that the American markets should receive preference from American companies.[1989] The Chicago company held dear the values of national loyalty among companies, and the priority of United States national economic interests among American companies.[1990]

Selz, Schwab & Company sought to reform policies of the footwear manufacturing industry that prevailed at the time of company's existence. The firm joined the Florsheim Shoe Company of Chicago to support the dissolution of the United Shoe Machinery Trust, an immense company associated with Thomas Plant.[1991] The Shoe Machinery Trust had acquired a monopoly within the footwear machinery manufacturing and supply industry.[1992] Within the assumed statuses of industrial reformation promoter and economic policy advocate, Selz, Schwab & Company donned the ancillary status of federal antitrust policy advocate.[1993] These organizational acts aligned with Theodore Roosevelt's social reform plan to dissolve certain industrial trusts.[1994] Viewed from these perspectives, Selz, Schwab & Company, and by derivation, Chicago industrial leadership, acted not only as one of the principal operators within the shoe and boot manufacturing industry of the world, but also as a federal public policy advocate.[1995]

Evidence of the global magnitude and the international reputation of the Selz, Schwab & Company can be derived from the following economic testimony. The government of France contracted with Selz, Schwab & Company to manufacture

---

[1987] Hide and Leather. (February 8, 1919). Vol. 57, No. 6. P. 25. Chicago, IL: Hide and Leather. Google Books.
[1988] Chicago History. (1966). Vol. VII. Page number not clearly discoverable at time of reference. Chicago, IL: Chicago Historical Society. Google Books.
[1989] Chicago History. (1966). Vol. VII. Page number not clearly discoverable at time of reference. Chicago, IL: Chicago Historical Society. Google Books.
[1990] Chicago History. (1966). Vol. VII. Page number not clearly discoverable at time of reference. Chicago, IL: Chicago Historical Society. Google Books.
[1991] The Louisville Courier-Journal. (June 4, 1913). P. 10. Newspapers.com.
[1992] The Louisville Courier-Journal. (June 4, 1913). P. 10. Newspapers.com.
[1993] The Louisville Courier-Journal. (June 4, 1913). P. 10. Newspapers.com.
[1994] The Philadelphia Enquirer. (April 26, 1912). P. 8. Newspapers.com.
[1995] Chicago History. (1966). Vol. VII. Page number not clearly discoverable at time of reference. Chicago, IL: Chicago Historical Society. Google Books.

and supply the footwear for much of the French Army. What is more, the company received a comparably significant contract from the United Kingdom, in order to supply the British Army with footwear. The contracts were made during World War I.[1996]

In the year 1907, Selz, Schwab & Company had registered no fewer than ten trademarks for commercial use.[1997] The trademarks covered the names of multiple rubber footwear products and leather footwear products.[1998] Seven of the Selz, Schwab & Company registered trademarks granted intellectual property relevant to leather footwear products and marketing.[1999] The remaining three registered trademarks related to rubber footwear products and associated marketing.[2000] The trademarks were granted over the time period lasting from October 22, 1907, until December 17, 1907.[2001] The ten trademarks referred to footwear products of the following classes, and were assigned the following trademark numbers (see table below). The corresponding trademark reference volumes and page numbers were recorded in the United States Patent Office volume cited herein. The only place associated with each trademark registration was Chicago.[2002]

Trademark, Time, Product Class	Number
Trademark of October 22, 1907 (Rubber):	65,813
Trademark of October 22, 1907 (Rubber):	65,814
Trademark of October 22, 1907 (Rubber):	65,815
Trademark of October 29, 1907 (Leather):	65,863
Trademark of October 29, 1907 (Leather):	65,864
Trademark of October 29, 1907 (Leather):	65,865
Trademark of October 29, 1907 (Leather):	65,866
Trademark of November 5, 1907 (Leather):	66,009
Trademark of November 5, 1907 (Leather):	66,010
Trademark of December 17, 1907 (Leather):	66,674[2003]

[1996] Harness. (January, 1915). Vol. XXVIII, No. 11. P. 20. New York, NY: The Trade News Publishing Company. Google Books.

[1997] Annual Report For The Commissioner Of Patents For The Year 1907. (1908). P. 703. Washington, D.C.: Government Printing Office. Google Books.

[1998] Annual Report For The Commissioner Of Patents For The Year 1907. (1908). P. 703. Washington, D.C.: Government Printing Office. Google Books.

[1999] Annual Report For The Commissioner Of Patents For The Year 1907. (1908). P. 703. Washington, D.C.: Government Printing Office. Google Books.

[2000] Annual Report For The Commissioner Of Patents For The Year 1907. (1908). P. 703. Washington, D.C.: Government Printing Office. Google Books.

[2001] Annual Report For The Commissioner Of Patents For The Year 1907. (1908). P. 703. Washington, D.C.: Government Printing Office. Google Books.

[2002] Annual Report For The Commissioner Of Patents For The Year 1907. (1908). P. 703. Washington, D.C.: Government Printing Office. Google Books.

[2003] Annual Report For The Commissioner Of Patents For The Year 1907. (1908). P. 703. Washington, D.C.: Government Printing Office. Google Books.

In 1908, Selz, Schwab & Company undertook a factory expansion project.[2004] The place of the factory and expansion project was located on Superior Street, between Kingsbury Street and Roberts.[2005] The expansion project improved the manufacturing capacity of the corporation, increasing daily production to 6,000 shoes.[2006] The expansion project also accommodated a workforce of 2,000 persons.[2007] Hailed as the largest welt shoe manufacturing plant in the world at the time of the expansion project, the factory sales revenue was expected to approximate $5,000,000 annually under circumstances of full capacity manufacture.[2008] The factory expansion notice that appeared within the March 14, 1908, edition of *The Shoe Retailer And Boots And Shoes Weekly* contained an artistic representation of the new Selz, Schwab & Company factory.[2009] The richly illustrated advertisement contained the factory as the principal element, and showed a Selz, Schwab & Company freight train, with freight cars marked with the "Selz" brand name.[2010] The picture also included cargo trucks that bore the "Selz" name.[2011] The ad showed that the company owned a Chicago railroad route and service, as well as a fleet of trucks at least as early as 1908, and probably much earlier.

The market demands for shoes and boots, caused by the necessities of World War I, brought opportunity for American manufacturers. The January, 1915, edition of the New York City-based leather trade journal known as *Harness* reported that Selz, Schwab & Company, as well as Sinsheimer Brothers Company of Chicago, contracted to manufacture and supply 500,000 pairs of army shoes for Great Britain for $1,500,000.[2012]

In December of 1893, the Committee on Finance, a committee within the United States Senate, formulated and delivered a complex battery of questions regarding

---

[2004] The Shoe Retailer And Boots And Shoes Weekly. (March 14, 1908). Handsome New Factory. Pp. 67-68. Google Books.

[2005] The Shoe Retailer And Boots And Shoes Weekly. (March 14, 1908). Handsome New Factory. Pp. 67-68. Google Books.

[2006] The Shoe Retailer And Boots And Shoes Weekly. (March 14, 1908). Handsome New Factory. Pp. 67-68. Google Books.

[2007] The Shoe Retailer And Boots And Shoes Weekly. (March 14, 1908). Handsome New Factory. Pp. 67-68. Google Books.

[2008] The Shoe Retailer And Boots And Shoes Weekly. (March 14, 1908). Handsome New Factory. Pp. 67-68. Google Books.

[2009] The Shoe Retailer And Boots And Shoes Weekly. (March 14, 1908). Handsome New Factory. Pp. 67-68. Google Books.

[2010] The Shoe Retailer And Boots And Shoes Weekly. (March 14, 1908). Handsome New Factory. Pp. 67-68. Google Books.

[2011] The Shoe Retailer And Boots And Shoes Weekly. (March 14, 1908). Handsome New Factory. Pp. 67-68. Google Books.

[2012] Harness. (January, 1915). Vol. XXVIII, No. 11. P. 20. New York, NY: The Trade News Publishing Company. Google Books.

tariff information to multiple organizations throughout the United States.[2013] Selz, Schwab & Company answered the multiple questions, thus providing ample information about the firm at that point in time, and giving a broad description of the specific data that concerned the company.[2014] In approximately 1893-1894, the Selz, Schwab Company represented an invested capital amount of $1,475,000.[2015] The corporate sales revenue for the firm remained relatively constant at about $2,000,000 annually, with only minor fluctuation alluded to in the answer to the tariff inquiry.[2016] The business administration of Selz, Schwab & Company both articulated a policy, and expressed an attitude, regarding the issues, costs, and benefits relevant to an industrial tariff on "sundries" products.[2017] Selz, Schwab & Company specifically stated that due both to the company's overwhelming superiority to its foreign competitors in magnitude and production, and to the company's superlative administration practices, the company would derive no benefit from the attachment of tariffs to imports from foreign competitors.[2018] The corporate answer to the Senatorial inquiry partially elucidated the sociology of European and American industrial relations during the Gilded Age.[2019] The Selz, Schwab & Company answer to the tariff issue questions stated that at the time of the answer, one of the company employees was the son of a German footwear manufacturer, and that the reason why the employee wished to work for Selz, Schwab & Company was to gain knowledge of the firm's administration practices, equipment, and operations, so that the son could return to Germany to aid in improvement of his father's footwear manufacturing concern there.[2020] The answer

---

[2013] Replies To Tariff Inquiries. (1895). Bulletin Number 55, Part 4. Committee On Finance, United States Senate. Schedule 1—Sundries. P. 80. Washington, D.C.: Government Printing Office. Google Books.

[2014] Replies To Tariff Inquiries. (1895). Bulletin Number 55, Part 4. Committee On Finance, United States Senate. Schedule 1—Sundries. P. 80. Washington, D.C.: Government Printing Office. Google Books.

[2015] Replies To Tariff Inquiries. (1895). Bulletin Number 55, Part 4. Committee On Finance, United States Senate. Schedule 1—Sundries. P. 80. Washington, D.C.: Government Printing Office. Google Books.

[2016] Replies To Tariff Inquiries. (1895). Bulletin Number 55, Part 4. Committee On Finance, United States Senate. Schedule 1—Sundries. P. 80. Washington, D.C.: Government Printing Office. Google Books.

[2017] Replies To Tariff Inquiries. (1895). Bulletin Number 55, Part 4. Committee On Finance, United States Senate. Schedule 1—Sundries. P. 80. Washington, D.C.: Government Printing Office. Google Books.

[2018] Replies To Tariff Inquiries. (1895). Bulletin Number 55, Part 4. Committee On Finance, United States Senate. Schedule 1—Sundries. P. 80. Washington, D.C.: Government Printing Office. Google Books.

[2019] Replies To Tariff Inquiries. (1895). Bulletin Number 55, Part 4. Committee On Finance, United States Senate. Schedule 1—Sundries. P. 80. Washington, D.C.: Government Printing Office. Google Books.

[2020] Replies To Tariff Inquiries. (1895). Bulletin Number 55, Part 4. Committee On Finance, United States Senate. Schedule 1—Sundries. P. 80. Washington, D.C.: Government Printing Office. Google Books.

letter stated the following: "We have at present the son of a German shoe manufacturer in our employ, who is here for the sole purpose of learning our methods with a view to their introduction into his father's factory."[2021] The willingness of Selz, Schwab & Company to hire the German immigrant, knowing his purpose and its potential to increase commercial competition for Selz, Schwab, was testimony of a definite sense of Euro-American cultural, industrial, and economic fellowship and sisterhood.[2022]

Selz, Schwab & Company became embroiled in labor disputes in 1887.[2023] The issue centered on whether thirteen young female employees would join the labor union known as the Shoemakers' Assembly (the newspaper article supplies this name as the apparent name of the relevant labor union in the dispute, but the context of the language is not entirely clear).[2024] The labor issue was filed with District 24 of the Shoemakers' Assembly with pleadings, testimonies, productions of evidence, proofs, and arguments, to obtain deliberation and judgment on the merits of the labor case.[2025] The Selz, Schwab & Company employee who acted as chief communication agent on behalf of the company was one named Superintendent Tilt.[2026] This Selz, Schwab & Company labor issue had developed to the point of a policy impasse, with Tilt on the one side, and the union representatives on the other side.[2027] Superintendent Tilt refused to acknowledge and authorize the union among thirteen girls who were employees of the company.[2028] The denial of the right to form the union at the company among the young women who worked for Selz, Schwab & Company was reported by the Exectuvie Council of the Shoemakers' Assembly.[2029] The Executuvie Council issued the following statement regarding the dispute:

[2021] Replies To Tariff Inquiries. (1895). Bulletin Number 55, Part 4. Committee On Finance, United States Senate. Schedule 1—Sundries. P. 80. Washington, D.C.: Government Printing Office. Google Books.

[2022] Replies To Tariff Inquiries. (1895). Bulletin Number 55, Part 4. Committee On Finance, United States Senate. Schedule 1—Sundries. P. 80. Washington, D.C.: Government Printing Office. Google Books.

[2023] Selz, Schwab & Co.'s Trouble. (January 30, 1887). The Chicago Tribune. P. 9. Chicago Tribune Archives.

[2024] Selz, Schwab & Co.'s Trouble. (January 30, 1887). The Chicago Tribune. P. 9. Chicago Tribune Archives.

[2025] Selz, Schwab & Co.'s Trouble. (January 30, 1887). The Chicago Tribune. P. 9. Chicago Tribune Archives.

[2026] Selz, Schwab & Co.'s Trouble. (January 30, 1887). The Chicago Tribune. P. 9. Chicago Tribune Archives.

[2027] Selz, Schwab & Co.'s Trouble. (January 30, 1887). The Chicago Tribune. P. 9. Chicago Tribune Archives.

[2028] Selz, Schwab & Co.'s Trouble. (January 30, 1887). The Chicago Tribune. P. 9. Chicago Tribune Archives.

[2029] Selz, Schwab & Co.'s Trouble. (January 30, 1887). The Chicago Tribune. P. 9. Chicago Tribune Archives.

"These thirteen girls would join our union, but Tilt has impressed them with the idea that they could get along better by not joining, and so they keep aloof. The Executive Board called at the shop today and interviewed the girls, and they said they would join if Tilt told them to do so. I notice a statement that prison labor has something to do with the strike. I wish to say emphatically that it has no connection whatever with the strike, it being simply one of principle entirely."[2030]

Superintendent Tilt also offered a public statement on the issue, demonstrating preference for the employees who had not struck, and bias against the ones who had.[2031]

"'We have got in about fifty new hands, both men and girls, and won't displace any of them to make room for the ones who have struck. A committee of three called here today and talked with the girls, asking if I used any influence in keeping them from joining the union. Of course I haven't. I have been the best friend the Knights of Labor had in the shop, and have been in favor of unions, but not of a lot of blatherskites running them. A number of foreigners asked my advice yesterday when they were ordered out. I told them the best thing they could do was to obey orders. I told them the strike was ill-advised, and as we are paying out in wages $2,500 a week, if they staid out a week they would lose so much to find out that we were running our own business.'"[2032]

The District 24 Executive Council contacted one "Mr. Selz," presumably Morris Selz, who referred the union to Superintendent Tilt for discussion of the labor issues.[2033] The article reported that Tilt offered "no encouragement" to the union regarding the union's pleadings.[2034]

The *Chicago Daily Tribune* featured an article from February 20, 1890, in which Selz, Schwab & Company was identified as a major party to expansive development of the wholesale district in downtown Chicago.[2035] The real estate at issue in the physical growth of the business district was located near Van Buren

---

[2030] Selz, Schwab & Co.'s Trouble. (January 30, 1887). The Chicago Tribune. P. 9. Chicago Tribune Archives.

[2031] Selz, Schwab & Co.'s Trouble. (January 30, 1887). The Chicago Tribune. P. 9. Chicago Tribune Archives.

[2032] Selz, Schwab & Co.'s Trouble. (January 30, 1887). The Chicago Tribune. P. 9. Chicago Tribune Archives.

[2033] Selz, Schwab & Co.'s Trouble. (January 30, 1887). The Chicago Tribune. P. 9. Chicago Tribune Archives.

[2034] Selz, Schwab & Co.'s Trouble. (January 30, 1887). The Chicago Tribune. P. 9. Chicago Tribune Archives.

[2035] Chicago Daily Tribune. (February 20, 1890). P. 3. Retrieved from ProQuest Newspapers: Chicago Tribune. Database at Northwestern University.

Street and Harrison Street.[2036] The other parties who owned real estate at or near this place included the following people:

1. John Villiers Farwell
2. Charles Benjamin Farwell
3. E. Nelson Blake
4. Herman H. Kohlsaat
5. Alderman Arthur Dixon
6. J. W. Paxton
7. I. N. W. Sherman
8. Adams estate heirs who were unnamed in the article[2037]

The article stated that Selz, Schwab & Company planned to construct some physical presence at the place near Van Buren Street and Harrison Street.[2038] The article stated that if Selz, Schwab & Company moved to this location, then other wholesale commercial organizations would certainly follow, and construct presences near the same place.[2039] Growth of industry and commerce, and the impacts of these elements of urban growth in the Gilded Age, are manifest in this article.[2040]

Selz, Schwab & Company expanded to Elgin, Illinois, in 1897.[2041] Elgin is a large and important northwest suburb of Chicago and is one of the cities located on the Fox River. The firm acquired the Ludlow Shoe Company of Elgin in approximately the winter of 1897.[2042] The $100,000 purchase added another factory to the Selz, Schwab & Company system.[2043] The *Chicago Daily Tribune* article in which the company purchase was announced indicated that the Selz, Schwab & Company had, "controlled the output of the Elgin factory since last September. . ."[2044] The Elgin shoe plant manufactured 1,000 pairs of shoes every

[2036] Chicago Daily Tribune. (February 20, 1890). P. 3. Retrieved from ProQuest Newspapers: Chicago Tribune. Database at Northwestern University.

[2037] Chicago Daily Tribune. (February 20, 1890). P. 3. Retrieved from ProQuest Newspapers: Chicago Tribune. Database at Northwestern University.

[2038] Chicago Daily Tribune. (February 20, 1890). P. 3. Retrieved from ProQuest Newspapers: Chicago Tribune. Database at Northwestern University.

[2039] Chicago Daily Tribune. (February 20, 1890). P. 3. Retrieved from ProQuest Newspapers: Chicago Tribune. Database at Northwestern University.

[2040] Chicago Daily Tribune. (February 20, 1890). P. 3. Retrieved from ProQuest Newspapers: Chicago Tribune. Database at Northwestern University.

[2041] Chicago Daily Tribune. (February 4, 1897). P. 7. Retrieved from ProQuest Newspapers: Chicago Tribune. Databased at Northwestern University.

[2042] Chicago Daily Tribune. (February 4, 1897). P. 7. Retrieved from ProQuest Newspapers: Chicago Tribune. Databased at Northwestern University.

[2043] Chicago Daily Tribune. (February 4, 1897). P. 7. Retrieved from ProQuest Newspapers: Chicago Tribune. Databased at Northwestern University.

[2044] Chicago Daily Tribune. (February 4, 1897). P. 7. Retrieved from ProQuest Newspapers: Chicago Tribune. Databased at Northwestern University.

day at the time of the factory's acquisition by Selz, Schwab & Company.[2045] The article stated that Selz, Schwab & Company planned to increase the plant manufacturing capacity to 4,000 shoes (presumably at a production rate of 4,000 per day, but the article did not specify the production rate).[2046]

The Leatherworkers Support the Chicago Telephone Tunnel System

Selz, Schwab & Company acted as organizational co-founder of, and commercial supporter of, the Chicago Tunnel System.[2047] The article entitled, "FREIGHT WHIRLED BENEATH STREETS: Subway Under Chicago Ownership Becomes Potent Factor in Commerce," described the rapid emergence of the Chicago Subway Company tunnel system beneath the city streets.[2048] Jonathan Ogden Armour (J. Ogden Armour) and others gained dominion over the Chicago Subway Company in June of 1907.[2049] The operating company for the tunnel system was the Illinois Tunnel Company.[2050] Samuel McRoberts, who served as Treasurer of Armour & Company, assumed the office of President of the Chicago Subway Company.[2051] The Illinois Tunnel Company, through the leadership of J. Ogden Armour and Samuel McRoberts, cooperated with multiple industrial and mercantile organizations to build and establish the Chicago subway tunnel system.[2052] The January 9, 1908, edition of the *Chicago Tribune* reported, "Many Connections Are Made. The following list indicates the status of the company's affairs with reference to its patrons. . ."[2053]

Contracts for freight transportation defined the promotion and support that the multiple Chicago commercial organizations gave the Illinois Tunnel Company and Chicago subway system.[2054] The list of the co-founding and commercially supportive organizations, cited from the *Chicago Tribune* article, included the

---

[2045] Chicago Daily Tribune. (February 4, 1897). P. 7. Retrieved from ProQuest Newspapers: Chicago Tribune. Databased at Northwestern University.

[2046] Chicago Daily Tribune. (February 4, 1897). P. 7. Retrieved from ProQuest Newspapers: Chicago Tribune. Databased at Northwestern University.

[2047] Chicago Daily Tribune. (January 9, 1908). P. 11. Retrieved from ProQuest Newspapers: Chicago Tribune. Database at Northwestern University.

[2048] Chicago Daily Tribune. (January 9, 1908). P. 11. Retrieved from ProQuest Newspapers: Chicago Tribune. Database at Northwestern University.

[2049] Chicago Daily Tribune. (January 9, 1908). P. 11. Retrieved from ProQuest Newspapers: Chicago Tribune. Database at Northwestern University.

[2050] Chicago Daily Tribune. (January 9, 1908). P. 11. Retrieved from ProQuest Newspapers: Chicago Tribune. Database at Northwestern University.

[2051] Chicago Daily Tribune. (January 9, 1908). P. 11. Retrieved from ProQuest Newspapers: Chicago Tribune. Database at Northwestern University.

[2052] Chicago Daily Tribune. (January 9, 1908). P. 11. Retrieved from ProQuest Newspapers: Chicago Tribune. Database at Northwestern University.

[2053] Chicago Daily Tribune. (January 9, 1908). P. 11. Retrieved from ProQuest Newspapers: Chicago Tribune. Database at Northwestern University.

[2054] Chicago Daily Tribune. (January 9, 1908). P. 11. Retrieved from ProQuest Newspapers: Chicago Tribune. Database at Northwestern University.

following railroad, manufacturing, and mercantile organizations, among which were several that Jacob Bunn, John Whitfield Bunn, and John Stryker co-founded, co-owned, and helped to build. The table follows here:

The Co-Founding Mercantile Patron Organizations

1. Selz, Schwab & Company
   a. John Whitfield Bunn was co-founder, co-owner, and Vice President of Selz, Schwab & Company.
   b. Jacob Bunn, Jr. served as Vice President of Selz, Schwab & Company.
2. Marshall Field & Company
3. Carson Pirie Scott & Company
4. J. V. Farwell Company
5. Boston Store
6. The Fair
7. Mandel Brothers
8. Steele-Wedeles Company
9. Sprague, Warner & Company
10. McNeil & Higgins
11. Durand & Kasper
12. Reid, Murdoch & Company
13. James B. Clow & Sons
14. James S. Kirk & Company
15. Thomson-Taylor Spice Company
16. Chase & Sanborn
17. George B. Carpenter & Company
18. M. D. Wells Company
19. D. B. Scully & Company
20. Butler Brothers
21. J. W. Butler Paper Company
22. Franklin MacVeagh & Company
23. W. M. Hoyt & Company
24. Spaulding & Merrick
25. Western Electric Company
26. N. K. Fairbank Company[2055]

The Co-Founding Railroad Patron Organizations

1. Chicago, Rock Island and Pacific Railroad Company
   a. John Stryker was a founder and builder of this corporation.
2. Wabash Railway Company

[2055] Chicago Daily Tribune. (January 9, 1908). P. 11. Retrieved from ProQuest Newspapers: Chicago Tribune. Database at Northwestern University.

     a. John Whitfield Bunn was a founder, builder, and President of this corporation and railroad system.
3. Chicago and Alton Railroad Company
     a. Jacob Bunn was a founder and owner of this railroad corporation.
4. Lake Shore & Michigan Southern Railroad Company
     a. John Stryker was a founder and owner of this railroad corporation and system.
5. New York, Chicago and St. Louis
6. Atcheson, Topeka and Santa Fe Railroad Company
7. Chicago, Milwaukee & St. Paul (The Milwaukee Road)
8. Great Western
9. Erie Railroad
10. Monon Railroad
11. Pittsburgh, Cincinnati, Chicago and St. Louis
12. Baltimore & Ohio
13. Chicago and Northwestern
14. Illinois Central
15. Pittsburgh, Fort Wayne and Chicago
16. Chicago, Burlington and Quincy
17. Chicago and Eastern Illinois
18. Cleveland, Cincinnati, Chicago and St. Louis
19. New York, Chicago and St. Louis (The Nickel Plate Road)[2056]

The Leatherworkers Develop Chicago Industrial Baseball

The corporate culture of Selz, Schwab & Company was one of community, fraternity, and recreational activities.[2057] The January-to-July issue of the 1891 edition of *The Shoe and Leather Reporter* contained a news report that showed the strength of community at Selz, Schwab & Company.[2058] In approximately April of 1891, the following companies cooperated to create a, "boot and shoe baseball league."[2059] The Firms that constituted the charter members of the industrial baseball league included Selz, Schwab & Company, C. M. Henderson & Company, Phelps, Dodge & Palmer, and the C. H. Fargo Company.[2060] The report indicated that the new baseball league welcomed interest and membership from any other wholesale house that wanted to create an industrial baseball team, and

---

[2056] Chicago Daily Tribune. (January 9, 1908). P. 11. Retrieved from ProQuest Newspapers: Chicago Tribune. Database at Northwestern University.

[2057] The Shoe and Leather Reporter. (January-July, 1891). Vol. LI. P. 1098. Boston, Massachusetts: The Shoe and Leather Reporter. Google Books.

[2058] The Shoe and Leather Reporter. (January-July, 1891). Vol. LI. P. 1098. Boston, Massachusetts: The Shoe and Leather Reporter. Google Books.

[2059] The Shoe and Leather Reporter. (January-July, 1891). Vol. LI. P. 1098. Boston, Massachusetts: The Shoe and Leather Reporter. Google Books.

[2060] The Shoe and Leather Reporter. (January-July, 1891). Vol. LI. P. 1098. Boston, Massachusetts: The Shoe and Leather Reporter. Google Books.

join the new Chicago shoe and boot manufacturers' baseball league.[2061] The executive leadership staff of the baseball league organization included the following persons and jobs:

Persons and Jobs

1. A. C. Schwab
   a. President
2. W. Rea Colcord
   a. Vice President
3. P. S. Keating
   a. Secretary and Treasurer[2062]

The January-to-July issue of the 1887 edition of the industry journal known as *The Shoe and Leather Reporter* showed the growing popularity of baseball among shoe and boot manufacturing company employees. The article consequently testified of the emerging popularity of industrial baseball and industrial baseball club organizations in the United States.[2063] Chicago was a central place for this cultural development in which industrial activity and sports were joined with community and organizational patriotism.[2064] *The Shoe and Leather Reporter* news article contained reportage of several Chicago baseball club exhibitions.[2065] Scores and outcomes were reported, as well.[2066] The summer of 1887 was busy with Chicago industrial baseball club activity.[2067] The baseball team of Selz, Schwab & Company faced the baseball team of the Storm & Hill Company. Storm & Hill's team was victorious, with a score of 10 to 5.[2068] Greensfelder, Florsheim & Company also competed, winning a victory of 22 to 16 over the baseball team of the Felix & Marston Company.[2069] G. W. Ludlow & Company won a victory over

---

[2061] The Shoe and Leather Reporter. (January-July, 1891). Vol. LI. P. 1098. Boston, Massachusetts: The Shoe and Leather Reporter. Google Books.

[2062] The Shoe and Leather Reporter. (January-July, 1891). Vol. LI. P. 1098. Boston, Massachusetts: The Shoe and Leather Reporter. Google Books.

[2063] The Shoe and Leather Reporter. (January-July, 1887). Vol. XLIII. P. 1164. Google Books.

[2064] The Shoe and Leather Reporter. (January-July, 1887). Vol. XLIII. P. 1164. Google Books.

[2065] The Shoe and Leather Reporter. (January-July, 1887). Vol. XLIII. P. 1164. Google Books.

[2066] The Shoe and Leather Reporter. (January-July, 1887). Vol. XLIII. P. 1164. Google Books.

[2067] The Shoe and Leather Reporter. (January-July, 1887). Vol. XLIII. P. 1164. Google Books.

[2068] The Shoe and Leather Reporter. (January-July, 1887). Vol. XLIII. P. 1164. Google Books.

[2069] The Shoe and Leather Reporter. (January-July, 1887). Vol. XLIII. P. 1164. Google Books.

the team of J. W. Jones, earning a score of 21 to W. J. Jones' score of 13.[2070] In 1904, the industry journal known as *The Shoe Retailer And Boots And Shoes Weekly*, reported that the Selz, Schwab & Company baseball team had defeated a baseball team known as the Montclares, with a score of 13 to 3.[2071]

Selz, Schwab & Company remained an active party to the development of Chicago industrial baseball in the twentieth century.[2072] As of May, 1914, Selz, Schwab & Company was a member of the Chicago Manufacturers' Baseball League.[2073] This league also consisted of Quaker Oats Company, R. R. Donnelly & Sons, the Western Shade Cloth Company, and the Chicago Pneumatic Tool Company.[2074] The Chicago Manufacturers' Baseball League was reorganized in 1914, with the previously named companies as charter members of the league.[2075] The League constitution was drafted and adopted in 1914.[2076] Planning for game schedules and procurement of playing grounds also occurred.[2077] The executive leadership staff of the League consisted of the following persons and jobs:

Persons and Jobs

1. Henry M. Tufo
    a. President
    b. Henry M. Tufo served as Manager of the Little Giants baseball team of the Chicago Pneumatic Tool Company.
2. R. G. Dennis
    a. Vice President
3. George Bures
    a. Secretary and Treasurer[2078]

[2070] The Shoe and Leather Reporter. (January-July, 1887). Vol. XLIII. P. 1164. Google Books.

[2071] The Shoe Retailer And Boots And Shoes Weekly. (July 20, 1904). Vol. 51, Number 1. P. 76. Boston, Massachusetts: The Shoe Retailer And Boots And Shoes Weekly. Google Books.

[2072] Ideal Power. (May, 1914). Vol. 11, Number 1. P. 17. Chicago, Illinois: Chicago Pneumatic Tool Company. Google Books.

[2073] Ideal Power. (May, 1914). Vol. 11, Number 1. P. 17. Chicago, Illinois: Chicago Pneumatic Tool Company. Google Books.

[2074] Ideal Power. (May, 1914). Vol. 11, Number 1. P. 17. Chicago, Illinois: Chicago Pneumatic Tool Company. Google Books.

[2075] Ideal Power. (May, 1914). Vol. 11, Number 1. P. 17. Chicago, Illinois: Chicago Pneumatic Tool Company. Google Books.

[2076] Ideal Power. (May, 1914). Vol. 11, Number 1. P. 17. Chicago, Illinois: Chicago Pneumatic Tool Company. Google Books.

[2077] Ideal Power. (May, 1914). Vol. 11, Number 1. P. 17. Chicago, Illinois: Chicago Pneumatic Tool Company. Google Books.

[2078] Ideal Power. (May, 1914). Vol. 11, Number 1. P. 17. Chicago, Illinois: Chicago Pneumatic Tool Company. Google Books.

The Leatherworkers Promote Production Quality

Morris Selz once stated the following with regard to the purpose and quality of Selz, Schwab & Company operations: "IT IS *the aim of every manufacturer to supply a better grade of goods at a lower price than the other fellow.*"[2079] J. Harry Selz served as President of the Chicago Shoe Trades Association.[2080] In 1914, J. Harry Selz solicited the United Shoe Machinery Trust to establish an exhibit demonstrating the range of processes that occur from slaughter of the animal to the final production stages of the shoe product. Selz stated, "In addition to the exhibits of individual firms and companies we hope to induce the United Shoe Machinery corporation to put in a working exhibit showing all the processes that take place between the live calf and the finished shoe."[2081] Selz noted the advertisement and marketing opportunities that would come with the manufacturing exhibit for which he advocated.[2082] "This is a wonderful opportunity for advertising by all lines."[2083] The December 5, 1914, report from the industry journal known as *Hide And Leather* indicated that Emanuel Frank Selz had returned to Chicago from a visit to Boston.[2084] Boston, like Chicago and St. Louis, was a leader of the shoe and boot manufacturing industry, and it is probable that Selz had visited companies and executives of the Boston shoe industry while there.

Selz, Schwab & Company was the plaintiff party to a case concerning the interlocking issues of negligence, liability, duty, and grounds for liability, and this case led to judgments, opinions, law, and policy that significantly affected corporate liability jurisprudence.[2085] In 1902, the City of Chicago operated a water pipe that burst, causing the injurious flooding of the basement of a Selz, Schwab & Company building.[2086] The company successfully sued the city for damages, based on a tort theory of negligence. The trial court delivered judgment for the plaintiff company, awarding the plaintiff damages in the amount of $27,100.[2087] The City of Chicago sued to appeal the Superior Court judgment and obtain reversal of the judgment, but the appellate court affirmed the lower court

---

[2079] Costs And Statistics. (1914). P. 169. Chicago, Illinois: A. W. Shaw Company. Google Books.

[2080] Chicago Commerce. (March 26, 1921). Pp. 13, 14. Chicago, Illinois: Chicago Association of Commerce. Google Books.

[2081] Chicago Commerce. (March 26, 1921). Pp. 13, 14. Chicago, Illinois: Chicago Association of Commerce. Google Books.

[2082] Chicago Commerce. (March 26, 1921). Pp. 13, 14. Chicago, Illinois: Chicago Association of Commerce. Google Books.

[2083] Chicago Commerce. (March 26, 1921). Pp. 13, 14. Chicago, Illinois: Chicago Association of Commerce. Google Books.

[2084] Hide And Leather. (December 5, 1914). P. 9. Google Books.

[2085] Chicago Daily Tribune. (December 18, 1902). P. 12. Retrieved from ProQuest newspapers: Chicago Tribune. Database at Northwestern University.

[2086] Chicago Daily Tribune. (December 18, 1902). P. 12. Retrieved from ProQuest newspapers: Chicago Tribune. Database at Northwestern University.

[2087] Chicago Daily Tribune. (December 18, 1902). P. 12. Retrieved from ProQuest newspapers: Chicago Tribune. Database at Northwestern University.

judgment.[2088] The Appellate court's affirmance of the Superior Court judgment and remedy of $27,100 was based on a foundation and principle of law in which liability attaches to cities when cities engage in activities that involve some amount of private benefit.[2089] The purpose, attachment, and accrual of private benefits to the City of Chicago, therefore, caused for the City the assumptions of risks and tort liabilities, where apparent immunities would otherwise have attached.[2090]

> "The principle on which this decision is based is that 'when a business is conducted by a municipality in part for profit, even if principally for public purposes, the municipality is liable for damages caused by negligence in its management.'"[2091]

Selz, Schwab & Company supplied multiple opportunities for employees to continue on to successful careers within the American shoe and boot industry.[2092] One example was that of Herman Siegrist, who began as a Selz employee within the twelve hour service department of the company.[2093] Siegrist subsequently worked for Hannahsons Shoe Company of Haverhill, Massachusetts, where he helped with the design, implementation, and administration of the operational practice known as the twelve hour plan.[2094] This operations plan entailed the processing, fulfilment, and shipment of product orders within twelve hours of the receipt of the product orders.[2095]

Herman Siegrist, gaining experience at Selz, Schwab & Company in Chicago, was indisputably qualified to administer the design and implementation of the twelve hour plan at Hannahsons Shoe Company.[2096] The September 2, 1922, issue of the industry journal known as the *Boot and Shoe Recorder* indicated the following with regard to Herman Siegrist and the administrative experience he contributed to Hannahsons Shoe Company after having gained earlier and formative knowledge and experience at Selz, Schwab & Company: "It is through

---

[2088] Chicago Daily Tribune. (December 18, 1902). P. 12. Retrieved from ProQuest newspapers: Chicago Tribune. Database at Northwestern University.

[2089] Chicago Daily Tribune. (December 18, 1902). P. 12. Retrieved from ProQuest newspapers: Chicago Tribune. Database at Northwestern University.

[2090] Chicago Daily Tribune. (December 18, 1902). P. 12. Retrieved from ProQuest newspapers: Chicago Tribune. Database at Northwestern University.

[2091] Chicago Daily Tribune. (December 18, 1902). P. 12. Retrieved from ProQuest newspapers: Chicago Tribune. Database at Northwestern University.

[2092] Boot and Shoe Recorder. (September 2, 1922). Vol. 81, Number 20. P. 165. Google Books.

[2093] Boot and Shoe Recorder. (September 2, 1922). Vol. 81, Number 20. P. 165. Google Books.

[2094] Boot and Shoe Recorder. (September 2, 1922). Vol. 81, Number 20. P. 165. Google Books.

[2095] Boot and Shoe Recorder. (September 2, 1922). Vol. 81, Number 20. P. 165. Google Books.

[2096] Boot and Shoe Recorder. (September 2, 1922). Vol. 81, Number 20. P. 165. Google Books.

his efforts that such rapid strides in that department of the Hannahsons Shoe Company has [sic] been made. In his new position he has charge of all stock and shipping."[2097]

One particular 1920 advertisement for Selz, Schwab & Company contained abundant information concerning the corporation's magnitude and prosperity.[2098] The company had taken out a full-page advertisement.[2099] The advertisement stated that one, "Selz standard learned in 50 years of shoe-making,"[2100] contained the following simple sales and value proposition: "Good shoes—all leather, fine workmanship, fair prices."[2101] The advertisement contained history and testimony as to quality of product.[2102] The advertisement demonstrated the tradition of Selz, Schwab & Company loyalty to the consumer and the corporation's loyalty to exclusively high standards of production.[2103] "[The company's] founder, Morris Selz, set standards that often have been difficult to maintain when, in the trade, compromise was general. But never has the name Selz been associated with any but good shoes."[2104]

The 1920 advertisement also produced evidence of historical acts of the company that proved the standards, values, and practices of the company. "If ever a shoe that is faulty gets out into distribution, we recall it."[2105] The company gave the example of a case in which the firm applied this standard of strict product excellence and the concomitant practice of quality enforcement. "Once, a long time ago, some shoes went to our dealers that after a while showed faulty thread—thread that rotted easily. We recalled them all."[2106] Selz, Schwab & Company adhered to these standards, values, and practices even when the obligatory burden of a product quality guarantee did not encumber them. "Another time some shoes which cracked prematurely, went into distribution. As they were patent leather, no guarantee held us—but we asked our dealers to send them all back."[2107] The advertisement demonstrated the company values of safety, loyalty, and care, and the company selected and used standards and practices that served those values.[2108] "Thus we have kept ever before us the principles of the founder of the House of Selz. Thus we have kept faith with the public."[2109]

[2097] Boot and Shoe Recorder. (September 2, 1922). Vol. 81, Number 20. P. 165. Google Books.
[2098] The Saturday Evening Post. (July 3, 1920). P. 91. Google Books.
[2099] The Saturday Evening Post. (July 3, 1920). P. 91. Google Books.
[2100] The Saturday Evening Post. (July 3, 1920). P. 91. Google Books.
[2101] The Saturday Evening Post. (July 3, 1920). P. 91. Google Books.
[2102] The Saturday Evening Post. (July 3, 1920). P. 91. Google Books.
[2103] The Saturday Evening Post. (July 3, 1920). P. 91. Google Books.
[2104] The Saturday Evening Post. (July 3, 1920). P. 91. Google Books.
[2105] The Saturday Evening Post. (July 3, 1920). P. 91. Google Books.
[2106] The Saturday Evening Post. (July 3, 1920). P. 91. Google Books.
[2107] The Saturday Evening Post. (July 3, 1920). P. 91. Google Books.
[2108] The Saturday Evening Post. (July 3, 1920). P. 91. Google Books.
[2109] The Saturday Evening Post. (July 3, 1920). P. 91. Google Books.

This remarkable and informative advertisement appeared only weeks after the death of John Whitfield Bunn, who had not only served as co-founder and Vice President of Selz, Schwab & Company, but who had also served as one of the absolutely principal builders of the firm throughout the firm's history.[2110] John W. Bunn was one of the founders, owners, and longstanding executives who was responsible for the rapid and global growth of the corporation.[2111] The advertisement indicated the commercial scope of the company by indicating that the company manufactured and maintained 1,000 different forms of footwear. "For men, women and children—1000 styles— a range of prices. At dealers' everywhere."[2112] The advertisement stated explicitly that Selz, Schwab & Company operated 30,000 different distributorships as of the year 1920. "And here—'midst our Fiftieth Anniversary—let us give credit to the 30,000 Selz dealers and their part in Selz success. Many have been with us for 10, 15, 25, 40 years."[2113] The advertisement paid esteem to the Selz dealers who helped integrally to build the corporation's market and growth.[2114] "We have grown and profited together. Our ideals have been the same."[2115] The advertisement also indicated that Selz, Schwab & Company possessed offices in Chicago and in Pittsburgh, Pennsylvania.[2116] Royal Blue brand for men and women and Liberty Bell brand for children were the two Selz brands specifically named in the 1920 advertisement.[2117] Artistic depictions of these Selz shoe brands appeared at the top of the advertisement.[2118]

The Great Depression would signal the collapse and organizational termination of Selz, Schwab & Company. The corporation, however, would in one sense continue through the entrepreneurial efforts of several of its former employees.[2119] The company liquidation marked the end of an almost sixty-year corporate career in which this Chicago company became the largest and greatest shoe and boot manufacturer in the world.[2120] In 1930, of the twelve factories that existed within the company at the time of liquidation, the largest factory singularly generated

---

[2110] Journal of the Illinois State Historical Society (1908-1984)
Vol. 13, No. 2 (Jul., 1920). P. 277. Google Books.
[2111] Journal of the Illinois State Historical Society (1908-1984).
Vol. 13, No. 2 (Jul., 1920). P. 277. Google Books; The Saturday Evening Post. (July 3, 1920). P. 91. Google Books.
[2112] The Saturday Evening Post. (July 3, 1920). P. 91. Google Books.
[2113] The Saturday Evening Post. (July 3, 1920). P. 91. Google Books.
[2114] The Saturday Evening Post. (July 3, 1920). P. 91. Google Books.
[2115] The Saturday Evening Post. (July 3, 1920). P. 91. Google Books.
[2116] The Saturday Evening Post. (July 3, 1920). P. 91. Google Books.
[2117] The Saturday Evening Post. (July 3, 1920). P. 91. Google Books.
[2118] The Saturday Evening Post. (July 3, 1920). P. 91. Google Books.
[2119] Chicago Daily Tribune. (March 20, 1930). P. 25. ProQuest Newspapers: Chicago Tribune. Database at Northwestern University.
[2120] Chicago Daily Tribune. (March 20, 1930). P. 25. Retrieved from ProQuest Newspapers: Chicago Tribune. Database at Northwestern University.

revenue of more than $6,000,000 annually.[2121] *The Chicago Daily Tribune* article, "Old Employes Get Factory as Shoe Firm Liquidates," indicated that the other factories, located in Illinois, Wisconsin, Indiana, and Connecticut, would be, "sold or dismantled."[2122] The announcement was given by Edward F. Selz, who had succeeded J. Harry Selz as President of the corporation after Harry's death.[2123] Edward F. Selz served as Vice President and acting President of the corporation at the time of the news article concerning the corporation's liquidation.[2124] The company that would start from one of the post-closure Selz factories would perpetuate Chicago's reputation as the world's center of shoe and boot manufacturing, develop to international prominence, and become one of the most recognized contemporary brands of footwear. The name was Cole-Haan.

The Cole, Haan & Rood Company of Chicago:

An Organizational Legacy of Selz, Schwab & Company

Five employees of Selz, Schwab & Company, who had been officers of the company, planned to acquire the largest factory (the factory that individually generated annual revenue of over $6,000,000 by 1930) for the purpose of establishing a new shoe manufacturing company.[2125] The *Chicago Tribune* article of March 20, 1930, identified the former Selz, Schwab & Company employees as C. Trafton Cole, William B. Rood, Edward Haan, Murdoch McGregor, and Charles A. Simpson.[2126] The new company established by these men was known by the name of Cole, Rood, Haan & McGregor.[2127] The prior Selz, Schwab & Company factory that would constitute the factory of Cole, Rood, Haan & McGregor was located at 514 West Superior Street.[2128] The new company acquired the old Selz factory by means of a contract of lease with a low rate of rent, and additionally acquired the Selz, Schwab & Company trademarks at no additional cost.[2129] The operational aspect and the intellectual property aspect of the new

---

[2121] Chicago Daily Tribune. (March 20, 1930). P. 25. Retrieved from ProQuest Newspapers: Chicago Tribune. Database at Northwestern University.

[2122] Chicago Daily Tribune. (March 20, 1930). P. 25. Retrieved from ProQuest Newspapers: Chicago Tribune. Database at Northwestern University.

[2123] Chicago Daily Tribune. (March 20, 1930). P. 25. Retrieved from ProQuest Newspapers: Chicago Tribune. Database at Northwestern University.

[2124] Chicago Daily Tribune. (March 20, 1930). P. 25. Retrieved from ProQuest Newspapers: Chicago Tribune. Database at Northwestern University.

[2125] Chicago Daily Tribune. (March 20, 1930). P. 25. Retrieved from ProQuest Newspapers: Chicago Tribune. Database at Northwestern University.

[2126] Chicago Daily Tribune. (March 20, 1930). P. 25. Retrieved from ProQuest Newspapers: Chicago Tribune. Database at Northwestern University.

[2127] Chicago Daily Tribune. (March 20, 1930). P. 25. Retrieved from ProQuest Newspapers: Chicago Tribune. Database at Northwestern University.

[2128] Chicago Daily Tribune. (March 20, 1930). P. 25. Retrieved from ProQuest Newspapers: Chicago Tribune. Database at Northwestern University.

[2129] Chicago Daily Tribune. (March 20, 1930). P. 25. Retrieved from ProQuest Newspapers: Chicago Tribune. Database at Northwestern University.

company were, therefore, conveniently imported from the remaining assets of the dissolved Selz, Schwab & Company. The article indicated that C. Trafton Cole, William B. Rood, Murdoch McGregor, and Charles A. Simpson all had served as executive officers of Selz, Schwab & Company.[2130] The collective administrative experience brought by these people to the new company from Selz, Schwab & Company would have constituted invaluable experiential and managerial assets for the new organization.[2131] This collective experience translated to longstanding market success.

Cole, Rood, Haan & McGregor Company began during the season of economic woe and uncertainty known as the Great Depression. The company survived the Great Depression and prospered. The firm observed that the shoe manufacturing business had improved, according to a report from July, 1932, published by the *Journal Gazette* of Mattoon, Illinois. The leadership of the firm forecasted a sudden upturn in footwear purchases and gave as the reason for this market improvement the fact that so many shoe merchants possessed deficient quantities of footwear merchandise in the face of the major demand and necessity for footwear.[2132]

The Cole, Rood, Haan & McGregor Company men diagnosed an economy in which the increasingly robust shoe and boot market was underserved by what was a weak product supply, and sought to remedy the identified deficit through large-scale manufacturing.[2133] The economic forecast was syndicated in the *Belvidere Daily Republican* of Belvidere, Illinois.[2134] By 1942, the new company was known as Cole-Rood & Haan Company. They owned a factory located at 18 E. 24th Street, in the Near South Side community of Chicago.[2135] The May 16, 1943, edition of the *Chicago Tribune* contained a Cole-Rood & Haan Company advertisement for a comptometer operator.[2136] The words of the ad read as follows: "Small office of old estab. Shoe mf. Pleasant working conditions and congenial associates. Opportunity for advancement even after the war is over. Within 2 blocks of elevated, surface cars and buses."[2137] The ad targeted the labor market of the World War II production economy.[2138]

Shortly before Christmas, 1944, Cole, Rood & Haan placed an advertisement in the *Chicago Tribune* seeking new workers.[2139] New clerks were sought for general office work within the company. The benefits offered to the potential employees

---

[2130] Chicago Daily Tribune. (March 20, 1930). P. 25. Retrieved from ProQuest Newspapers: Chicago Tribune. Database at Northwestern University.
[2131] Chicago Daily Tribune. (March 20, 1930). P. 25. Retrieved from ProQuest Newspapers: Chicago Tribune. Database at Northwestern University.
[2132] Journal Gazette. (July 29, 1932). P. 8. Newspapers.com.
[2133] Journal Gazette. (July 29, 1932). P. 8. Newspapers.com.
[2134] Belvidere Daily Republican. (July 29, 1932). P. 2. Newspapers.com.
[2135] Chicago Tribune. (November 21, 1942). P. 27. Newspapers.com.
[2136] Chicago Tribune. (May 16, 1943). P. 62. Newspapers.com.
[2137] Chicago Tribune. (May 16, 1943). P. 62. Newspapers.com.
[2138] Chicago Tribune. (May 16, 1943). P. 62. Newspapers.com.
[2139] Chicago Tribune. (December 14, 1944). P. 33. Newspapers.com.

included hospital insurance, flexible hours, good working conditions, rights attachable to a profit sharing plan, and rights to a retirement trust.[2140] The advertisement emphasized the excellent quality of the work environment, as well as the excellent quality of the opportunity for post-war employment.[2141] The words of the advertisement implied a desire to cater to, and capitalize on, the production labor market of World War II.[2142] At least as early as August, 1946, the firm phone number was Cal. 3540.[2143] Cole, Haan & Rood supplied the United States Army with many snow boots, ski boots, and mountain boots during World War II, according to historian Charles Lemons.[2144] Once again, Chicago industry served national defense and national service.[2145]

A 1950 advertisement for L. Strauss & Company promoted its Cole-Haan line of products.[2146] The company took the name, "Cole-Haan," at least as early as 1950, and promoted its reputation as the world's finest shoemaker.[2147] The L. Strauss & Company ad appeared in the December 4, 1950, edition of *The Indianapolis Star* of Indiana, and advertised Cole-Haan shoes made from the skins of baby alligators, golden horned lizards, and blue suede with alligator trim.[2148] Cole-Haan self-identified as, "the same company of cobblers—the same ideal—'the finest footwear on earth.'"[2149]

Nike Inc. purchased the Cole-Haan Company in 1988 for approximately $95,000,000.[2150] In 2012, Nike sold the Cole-Haan business for $570,000,000 to a private equity firm.[2151] The report from the *Northwest Herald*, a paper of Woodstock, Illinois, mentioned that Cole-Haan had been famous for its "flapper-friendly" leather shoes in the Jazz Age.[2152] From 1930 until 1988, the Cole-Haan Company had produced the highest quality of shoes and boots for civilian and military comsumption, and carried forward the reputation of its old company heritage as a spinoff of Selz, Schwab & Company. These two Chicago companies changed the world of shoe and boot manufacturing, distribution, and technology.

[2140] Chicago Tribune. (December 14, 1944). P. 33. Newspapers.com.

[2141] Chicago Tribune. (December 14, 1944). P. 33. Newspapers.com.

[2142] Chicago Tribune. (December 14, 1944). P. 33. Newspapers.com.

[2143] Chicago Tribune. (August 14, 1946). P. 37. Newspapers.com.

[2144] Lemons, Charles R. (2011). Uniforms of the US Army Ground Forces 1939—1945: Addendum. P. 121. Additional bibliographical information not apparent at time of reference. Google Books.

[2145] Lemons, Charles R. (2011). Uniforms of the US Army Ground Forces 1939—1945: Addendum. P. 121. Additional bibliographical information not apparent at time of reference. Google Books.

[2146] The Indianapolis Star. (December 4, 1950). P. 3. Newspapers.com.

[2147] The Indianapolis Star. (December 4, 1950). P. 3. Newspapers.com.

[2148] The Indianapolis Star. (December 4, 1950). P. 3. Newspapers.com.

[2149] The Indianapolis Star. (December 4, 1950). P. 3. Newspapers.com.

[2150] The San Bernardino County Sun. (April 26, 1988). P. 18. Newspapers.com.

[2151] Northwest Herald. (November 17, 2012). P. 30. Newspapers.com.

[2152] Northwest Herald. (November 17, 2012). P. 30. Newspapers.com.

The Leatherworkers Develop the Chicago Meatpacking Industry

The Selz, Schwab & Company founders remained always close friends, and shared many civic and social activities in Chicago.[2153] Morris Selz contributed a large amount of money to the University of Chicago in order to establish a scholarship for women. Emanuel Frank Selz was a member of the Standard Club, and J. Harry Selz was a member of the Standard Club and the Union League Club.[2154] Morris Selz co-founded the Standard Club and the Union League Club, and was President of the Standard Club. John Whitfield Bunn was a member of the Chicago Club, the Union League Club of Chicago, and the Saddle & Sirloin Club of Chicago.[2155] John W. Bunn co-founded the Saddle & Sirloin Club in 1903, and was one of its most important members.[2156] John Bunn represented the commercial link and economic interface that connected the Chicago Union Stockyards to the shoe and boot industry, agricultural sectors, and the Illinois legislature.[2157]

John W. Bunn worked with his close friends, The Hon. La Fayette Funk and James W. Judy, and the three men helped start the Illinois Farmers Institute System, the National Farmers Institute System, the Illinois Stallion Registry Office, and the Chicago Fat Cattle Show (also called the Chicago Fat Stock Show and the American Fat Stock Show).[2158] Bunn was the founding Treasurer of the Chicago and American Fat Cattle Show, which began in 1878, was administered by the Illinois State Board of Agriculture, and was located at the Exposition Building on the Chicago lakefront.[2159] American agricultural and industrial historian Edward Wentworth stated that Bunn recognized the immeasurable value

---

[2153] Bunn, Selz, Call family historical records.

[2154] The Elite Directory and Club List of Chicago. (1890-1891). P. 304. Chicago, IL: The Elite Directory Company. Google Books; Call, Andrew Taylor. (2005). Jacob Bunn: Legacy of an Illinois Industrial Pioneer. P. 147. Lawrenceville, VA: Brunswick Publishing Corporation.

[2155] Journal of the Illinois State Historical Society (1908-1984). Vol. 13, No. 1 (April, 1920). P. 277. Springfield, IL: Illinois State Historical Society. Google Books.

[2156] Wentworth, Edward N. (1920). A Biographical Catalogue Of The Portrait Gallery Of The Saddle And Sirloin Club. Pp. 264-265. Chicago, IL: Union Stock Yards. Archive.org; Runnion, Dale F. (2009). The Saddle and Sirloin Portrait Collection: A Biographical Catalogue. P. 37. Livestockexpo.org.

[2157] Wentworth, Edward N. (1920). A Biographical Catalogue Of The Portrait Gallery Of The Saddle And Sirloin Club. Pp. 264-265. Chicago, IL: Union Stock Yards. Archive.org.

[2158] Wentworth, Edward N. (1920). A Biographical Catalogue Of The Portrait Gallery Of The Saddle And Sirloin Club. Pp. 264-265. Chicago, IL: Union Stock Yards. Archive.org; Runnion, Dale F. (2009). The Saddle and Sirloin Portrait Collection: A Biographical Catalogue. P. 37. Livestockexpo.org.

[2159] Wentworth, Edward N. (1920). A Biographical Catalogue Of The Portrait Gallery Of The Saddle And Sirloin Club. Pp. 264-265. Chicago, IL: Union Stock Yards. Archive.org.

of the Chicago Fat Stock Show, remained a staunch support of the organization, and, "always paid the premiums regardless of the financial outcome of the show."[2160] Wentworth commented that Bunn, La Fayette Funk, and James Judy all promoted much Illinois legislation that improved the policies and laws for farmers and stockmen.[2161] Bunn served as Treasurer of the Illinois State Board of Agriculture for thirty-nine years, from 1859-1898, and was also a major landowner in Illinois.[2162] The State Board of Agriculture was based in Springfield, but possessed a heavy presence in Chicago, as well, and was a major force for development at the Union Stockyards.

In about 1934, The Saddle & Sirloin Club of Chicago, of which John W. Bunn was a founder in 1903, and the Union Stockyards, then headed by Fredrick H. Prince, commissioned portraitist, Robert F. Grafton, to repaint the portraits of the several hundred Saddle & Sirloin Club members.[2163] The original portraits had been lost in the Stockyards Fire of 1934.[2164] Grafton succeeded in repainting 164 of the portraits before his death, and Othmar Hoffler, Joseph Allworthy, Arvid Nyholm, Benjamin Kanne, and Ernest Klempner painted the remaining portraits.[2165] The entire Saddle & Sirloin Club portrait collection contains over 300 portraits of leaders from the meatpacking and agricultural industry of North America, and constitutes, "the largest collection of quality portraits by noted artists in the world devoted to a single industry," according to historian Dale F. Runnion.[2166] The Saddle & Sirloin Club Portrait Collection is maintained and curated in Louisville, Kentucky, at the headquarters of the North American International Livestock Exposition. The triptych portrait of John Whitfield Bunn, La Fayette Funk, and James W. Judy remains there to this day as a part of the Saddle & Sirloin Club Portrait Collection.

Jacob and John Bunn both owned Chicago real estate, with John owning particularly extensive property in the Calumet River Corridor of Chicago, a region which he had helped develop tremendously as a founder of the Wabash Railroad Company in 1889, and as a founder of Selz, Schwab & Company in 1871 (see

---

[2160] Wentworth, Edward N. (1920). A Biographical Catalogue Of The Portrait Gallery Of The Saddle And Sirloin Club. Pp. 264-265. Chicago, IL: Union Stock Yards. Archive.org.

[2161] Wentworth, Edward N. (1920). A Biographical Catalogue Of The Portrait Gallery Of The Saddle And Sirloin Club. Pp. 264-265. Chicago, IL: Union Stock Yards. Archive.org.

[2162] Wentworth, Edward N. (1920). A Biographical Catalogue Of The Portrait Gallery Of The Saddle And Sirloin Club. Pp. 264-265. Chicago, IL: Union Stock Yards. Archive.org.

[2163] Runnion, Dale F. (2009). The Saddle and Sirloin Portrait Collection: A Biographical Catalogue. P. 37. Livestockexpo.org.

[2164] Runnion, Dale F. (2009). The Saddle and Sirloin Portrait Collection: A Biographical Catalogue. P. 37. Livestockexpo.org.

[2165] Runnion, Dale F. (2009). The Saddle and Sirloin Portrait Collection: A Biographical Catalogue. P. 37. Livestockexpo.org.

[2166] Runnion, Dale F. (2009). The Saddle and Sirloin Portrait Collection: A Biographical Catalogue. P. 37. Livestockexpo.org.

Chapter 3, *The Horizons of Hyde Park*, and Chapter 2, *Builders of the Downtown*).[2167]

<u>The Leatherworkers are Founders of the Saddle & Sirloin Club of Chicago</u>

John W. Bunn, James W. Judy, and La Fayette Funk were members of the Saddle & Sirloin Club at the Union Stockyards.[2168] As a major organizational builder and developer of the Chicago Union Stockyards, and as the founding Treasurer of the Chicago Fat Stock Show, which evolved institutionally into what is presently the North American International Livestock Exposition located in Louisville, Kentucky, John Bunn contributed to the meatpacking industry in a most central and productive manner.[2169] To compound the economic and civic synchronicity represented by his work as developer of the Union Stockyards, as Illinois farm manager, as Treasurer of the Illinois State Board of Agriculture, as a founder of the University of Illinois, and as founder and Vice-President of Selz, Schwab & Company, John W. Bunn was a founding member of the Saddle & Sirloin Club of Chicago.[2170] Bunn was a member of the Saddle & Sirloin Club until his death in 1920.[2171] The Saddle & Sirloin Club, organized in 1903, served as the undisputed social and political headquarters of the Chicago meatpacking industry, and resultantly, as the center of power of the meatpacking industry of the entire world.[2172] Decisions made by the members of this club, held in meetings at the

---

[2167] Bunn family historical records.

[2168] Wentworth, Edward N. (1920). A Biographical Catalogue Of The Portrait Gallery Of The Saddle And Sirloin Club. Pp. 264-265. Chicago, IL: Union Stock Yards. Archive.org.

[2169] Wentworth, Edward N. (1920). A Biographical Catalogue Of The Portrait Gallery Of The Saddle And Sirloin Club. Pp. 264-265. Chicago, IL: Union Stock Yards. Archive.org; Saddle & Sirloin Club Portrait Collection. North American International Livestock Exposition. Alphabetical Listing of Members of the Saddle & Sirloin Club. P. 50. Livestockexpo.org.

[2170] Wentworth, Edward N. (1920). A Biographical Catalogue Of The Portrait Gallery Of The Saddle And Sirloin Club. Pp. 264-265. Chicago, IL: Union Stock Yards. Archive.org; Saddle & Sirloin Club Portrait Collection. North American International Livestock Exposition. Alphabetical Listing of Members of the Saddle & Sirloin Club. P. 50. Livestockexpo.org.

[2171] Wentworth, Edward N. (1920). A Biographical Catalogue Of The Portrait Gallery Of The Saddle And Sirloin Club. Pp. 264-265. Chicago, IL: Union Stock Yards. Archive.org; Saddle & Sirloin Club Portrait Collection. North American International Livestock Exposition. Alphabetical Listing of Members of the Saddle & Sirloin Club. P. 50. Livestockexpo.org.

[2172] Wentworth, Edward N. (1920). A Biographical Catalogue Of The Portrait Gallery Of The Saddle And Sirloin Club. Pp. 264-265. Chicago, IL: Union Stock Yards. Archive.org; Saddle & Sirloin Club Portrait Collection. North American International Livestock Exposition. Alphabetical Listing of Members of the Saddle & Sirloin Club. P. 50. Livestockexpo.org.

clubhouse at the Union Stockyards, affected the entire meatpacking and farming economies of North America and the world.

The Chicago Union Stockyards and the Saddle & Sirloin Club, which derived its name from the two cuts of meat that bear the same names, would be organizationally reflected in the Butchers' Board of Trade of San Francisco.[2173] The Butchers' Board of Trade was co-organized by Henry Miller (born in Germany as Heinrich Kreiser) and Charles Lux, two founders of the Miller & Lux Company of San Francisco.[2174] The Miller & Lux Company was once one of the largest meatpacking companies in the world, and was among the worthiest economic rivals to the Chicago Union Stockyards and the Saddle & Sirloin Club.[2175] Even Miller & Lux, however, found it difficult to compete with the Chicago Union Stockyards, the Saddle & Sirloin Club, and the American Cattle Trust of Chicago, which consisted of Swift & Company, Armour & Company, Morris Company, Cudahy Company, and the Wilson Company, all of which were Chicago companies.[2176]

Lawyer Thomas Keister Greer, Esq. (1921-2008), of Virginia and California, who was the stepfather of author Andrew Taylor Call, became one of the foremost corporate lawyer representatives for the California meatpacking and cash crop industries, and represented companies that were in direct competition with the Chicago companies that were established by John W. Bunn, Jacob Bunn, N. K. Fairbank, John Stryker, Stephen Williamson Stryker, Philip Danforth Armour, Gustavus Franklin Swift, Nelson Morris, Thomas E. Wilson, Patrick Cudahy, Michael Cudahy, and so many others. Greer was Junior General Counsel to the Miller & Lux Company of San Francisco, in the 1950s, and thus represented one of the greatest and most powerful agribusiness corporations in world history.[2177]

The Leatherworkers and the Chicago Union Stockyards

Jacob Bunn, John Whitfield Bunn, and John Stryker all promoted and developed the Chicago Union Stockyards, and worked with many other people in doing so. Each helped in a different way. Some forms of participation involved direct executive leadership within the Union Stockyards organizational structures, and

---

[2173] Wentworth, Edward N. (1920). A Biographical Catalogue Of The Portrait Gallery Of The Saddle And Sirloin Club. Pp. 264-265. Chicago, IL: Union Stock Yards.
Archive.org; Saddle & Sirloin Club Portrait Collection. North American International Livestock Exposition. Alphabetical Listing of Members of the Saddle & Sirloin Club. P. 50. Livestockexpo.org; *See generally* Igler, David. (2001). Industrial Cowboys: Miller & Lux and the Transformation of the Far West, 1850-1920. Berkeley, CA: University of California Press. Google Books.
[2174] Igler, David. (2001). Industrial Cowboys: Miller & Lux and the Transformation of the Far West, 1850-1920. Berkeley, CA: University of California Press. Google Books.
[2175] Igler, David. (2001). Industrial Cowboys: Miller & Lux and the Transformation of the Far West, 1850-1920. Berkeley, CA: University of California Press. Google Books.
[2176] Igler, David. (2001). Industrial Cowboys: Miller & Lux and the Transformation of the Far West, 1850-1920. Berkeley, CA: University of California Press. Google Books.
[2177] Greer, Call family history records.

other forms of participation entailed indirect, but still significant, leadership relevant to the establishment and development of the Union Stockyards.

John Bunn helped develop the agricultural and industrial scope of the Chicago Union Stockyards through having been a co-founder and the founding Treasurer of the Chicago Fat Stock Show.[2178] The Chicago Fat Stock Show was an organization which derived from both the Illinois State Board of Agriculture and the Chicago Union Stockyards,[2179] and was the precursor to the North American International Livestock Exposition.[2180] The North American International Livestock Exposition is based in Louisville, Kentucky, and began there after the Chicago Union Stockyards closed permanently.

Of additional and key relevance to the genesis of the Chicago Union Stockyards is the fact that the Chicago & Alton Railroad Company, of which Jacob Bunn was a principal founder and owner, was one of the nine railroad companies that joined in cooperative effort to establish the "union" of railroad interests that created the Chicago Union Stockyards.[2181] The organizational union of railroad interests and efforts also included the Michigan Southern Railroad Company and the Chicago, Rock Island & Pacific Railroad Company, both of which had been founded, co-owned, and developed by John Stryker.[2182] Jacob Bunn and John Stryker, therefore, founded three of the nine railroads that were responsible for the creation of the Chicago Union Stockyards. Jacob Bunn founded the Chicago and Alton Railroad

---

[2178] Runnion, Dale F. The Saddle & Sirloin Portrait Collection: A Biographical Catalogue. (2009). P. 48. Livestockexpo.org; Call, Andrew Taylor. (2016). Faded Bricks: Old Family Tales from the South Side of Chicago. Hyde Park History, Vol. 38, (No. 4), Pp. 1-7. Chicago, IL: Hyde Park Historical Society.

[2179] Pacyga, Dominic A. (2015). Slaughterhouse: Chicago's Union Stock Yard and the World It Made. Pp. 100-106. Chicago, IL: The University of Chicago Press. Google Books; Call, Andrew Taylor. (2016). Faded Bricks: Old Family Tales from the South Side of Chicago. Hyde Park History, Vol. 38, (No. 4), Pp. 1-7. Chicago, IL: Hyde Park Historical Society.

[2180] Runnion, Dale F. The Saddle & Sirloin Portrait Collection: A Biographical Catalogue. (2009). Pp. 37, 48. Livestockexpo.org; See also: John Whitfield Bunn biography at P. 50 of the document contained at the following website: Livestockexpo.org; Call, Andrew Taylor. (2016). Faded Bricks: Old Family Tales from the South Side of Chicago. Hyde Park History, Vol. 38, (No. 4), Pp. 1-7. Chicago, IL: Hyde Park Historical Society.

[2181] Pacyga, Dominic A. (2015). Slaughterhouse: Chicago's Union Stock Yard and the World It Made. P. 206. Chicago, IL: The University of Chicago Press. Google Books; Call, Andrew Taylor. (2016). Faded Bricks: Old Family Tales from the South Side of Chicago. Hyde Park History, Vol. 38, (No. 4), Pp. 1-7. Chicago, IL: Hyde Park Historical Society.

[2182] Pacyga, Dominic A. (2015). Slaughterhouse: Chicago's Union Stock Yard and the World It Made. P. 206. Chicago, IL: The University of Chicago Press. Google Books; Call, Andrew Taylor. (2016). Faded Bricks: Old Family Tales from the South Side of Chicago. Hyde Park History, Vol. 38, (No. 4), Pp. 1-7. Chicago, IL: Hyde Park Historical Society.

Company. John Stryker founded both the Chicago and Rock Island Railroad Company and the Michigan Southern Railroad Company.[2183] Historian Louise Carroll Wade noted that the nine railroads that organized the Chicago Union Stockyards were the following: The Burlington; the Chicago and North Western; the Chicago and Milwaukee; the Rock Island; the Chicago and Alton; the Michigan Southern; the Michigan Central; the Illinois Central; and the Pittsburgh, Fort Wayne and Chicago.[2184]

Jacob Bunn also owned the Bunn Pork Packing Company of Springfield, and was long interested in meatpacking and agribusiness development.[2185] Jacob Bunn co-founded and co-owned the Germania Sugar Company of Livingston County, Illinois, and the Freeport Sugar Beet Company of Stephenson County, Illinois, which both represented a tremendous capital investment.[2186] Jacob Bunn was in business with brothers Ernst and Gottlieb Gennert in the former company, and with Jerome Increase Case and Charles Henry Rosenstiel in the latter company.[2187] The Freeport Sugar Beet Company was an immense complex, employed about 400 people in 1871, contained twenty-two miles of industrial plumbing pipe, and generated sales revenue of $500,000 annually by about 1873.[2188] Jacob Bunn, Charles Henry Rosenstiel, and Jerome Increase Case all were heavily engaged in farming and farm management.[2189] Bunn was Treasurer and Superintendent of the Germania Sugar Company, and raised grain and cattle in addition to the work of sugar manufacturing at the Livingston County company.[2190] Jerome Increase Case founded J. I. Case Machinery Company of Racine, Wisconsin.[2191]

John W. Bunn held membership within the commercially and industrially renowned Saddle & Sirloin Club of Chicago from 1903 until his death in 1920.[2192]

[2183] Stryker and Bunn family history records.

[2184] Wade, Louise Carroll. (1987). Chicago's Pride: The Stockyards, Packingtown, and Environs in the Nineteenth Century. Pp. 48-49. Urbana, IL: University of Illinois Press. Google Books.

[2185] The reference source for this fact was a Doctoral Dissertation from the University of Illinois. The name of the author/doctoral candidate and the publication date are no longer available to the author of this book.

[2186] Inter Ocean. (October 22, 1874). P. 3. Newspapers.com; Freeport Journal-Standard. (January 26, 1926). P. 7. Newspapers.com.

[2187] Inter Ocean. (October 22, 1874). P. 3. Newspapers.com; Freeport Journal-Standard. (January 26, 1926). P. 7. Newspapers.com.

[2188] Freeport Journal-Standard. (January 26, 1926). P. 7. Newspapers.com; Call, Andrew Taylor. (2005). Jacob Bunn: Legacy of an Illinois Industrial Pioneer. Pp. 122, 125. Lawreneville, VA: Brunswick Publishing Corporation. Google Books.

[2189] Freeport Journal-Standard. (January 26, 1926). P. 7. Newspapers.com.

[2190] Inter Ocean. (October 22, 1874). P. 3. Newspapers.com.

[2191] Freeport Journal-Standard. (January 26, 1926). P. 7. Newspapers.com.

[2192] Wentworth, Edward N. (1920). A Biographical Catalogue Of The Portrait Gallery Of The Saddle And Sirloin Club. Pp. 264-265. Chicago, IL: Union Stock Yards. Archive.org; Saddle & Sirloin Club Portrait Collection. North American International

The fact that John W. Bunn co-founded the Saddle & Sirloin Club comported fully with the fact of his decades-long involvement as an industrial developer of the Chicago Union Stockyards. The Saddle & Sirloin Club constituted the social and political headquarters of the meatpacking industry, and was located at the Chicago Union Stockyards.[2193] The Saddle & Sirloin Club was not only central to the meatpacking industry, but also was essentially a great United States industrial and agricultural history museum.[2194] As was discussed above, The Saddle & Sirloin Club commissioned the painting of portraits of multiple persons whose individual contributions to agriculture and the meatpacking industry impacted both agriculture and industry.[2195]

The commercial, industrial, and economic magnitudes and importance of the Chicago Union Stockyards cannot be overstated. When the Union Stockyards closed and ceased to exist as an organization, it had processed over one billion animals.[2196] We have produced evidence from which we can derive proof of the longstanding commitment and support that Jacob Bunn, John Whitfield Bunn, and John Stryker gave to the Chicago Union Stockyards. The Bunn brothers and John Stryker contributed centrally to the formation and development of the Chicago Union Stockyards through railroad organizations and their development, agricultural organizations and their development, and social organizations and their development.[2197]

Livestock Exposition. Alphabetical Listing of Members of the Saddle & Sirloin Club. P. 50. Livestockexpo.org.

[2193] Saddle & Sirloin Club Portrait Collection Biographies. P. 50. Livestockexpo.org; Call, Andrew Taylor. (2016). Faded Bricks: Old Family Tales from the South Side of Chicago. Hyde Park History, Vol. 38, (No. 4), Pp. 1-7. Chicago, IL: Hyde Park Historical Society.

[2194] Wentworth, Edward N. (1920). A Biographical Catalogue Of The Portrait Gallery Of The Saddle And Sirloin Club. Pp. 264-265. Chicago, IL: Union Stock Yards. Archive.org; Saddle & Sirloin Club Portrait Collection. North American International Livestock Exposition. Alphabetical Listing of Members of the Saddle & Sirloin Club. P. 50. Livestockexpo.org.

[2195] Wentworth, Edward N. (1920). A Biographical Catalogue Of The Portrait Gallery Of The Saddle And Sirloin Club. Pp. 264-265. Chicago, IL: Union Stock Yards. Archive.org; Saddle & Sirloin Club Portrait Collection. North American International Livestock Exposition. Alphabetical Listing of Members of the Saddle & Sirloin Club. P. 50. Livestockexpo.org.

[2196] Pacyga, Dominic A. (2005). Union Stock Yard. The Electronic Encyclopedia of Chicago. Encyclopedia of Chicago History website; Call, Andrew Taylor. (2016). Faded Bricks: Old Family Tales from the South Side of Chicago. Hyde Park History, Vol. 38, (No. 4), Pp. 1-7. Chicago, IL: Hyde Park Historical Society.

[2197] Wentworth, Edward N. (1920). A Biographical Catalogue Of The Portrait Gallery Of The Saddle And Sirloin Club. Pp. 264-265. Chicago, IL: Union Stock Yards. Archive.org; Saddle & Sirloin Club Portrait Collection. North American International Livestock Exposition. Alphabetical Listing of Members of the Saddle & Sirloin Club. P. 50. Livestockexpo.org; Call, Andrew Taylor. (2016). Faded Bricks: Old Family Tales

The State of Illinois enacted a statute on February 13, 1865, which incorporated the company known as The Union Stock Yard and Transit Company of Chicago.[2198] Section 1 of the statute, which contained the incorporation clause, demonstrated the powerful Bunn-Stryker connection to the Union Stock Yard and Transit Company and the formation of the company.[2199] James F. Joy, who was a close friend and business associate of John Stryker, was one of the founders and incorporators of the new company.[2200] The company incorporators included James F. Joy, Virginius A. Turpin, John L. Hancock, Roselle M. Hough, Sidney A. Kent, Charles M. Culbertson, Lyman Blair, David Kreigh, Joseph Sherwin, Martin L. Sykes, Jr., George W. Cass, John F. Tracy, Timothy B. Blackstone, Joseph H. Moore, John S. Barry, Homer E. Sargent, Burton C. Cook, John Drake, and William D. Judson.[2201]

While James F. Joy worked with John Stryker to finance, develop, and construct many of the largest Chicago railroad companies from the 1840s and onward, Lyman Blair worked with Jacob Bunn in the formation of the Chicago Secure Depository Company in 1869. Jacob Bunn also was associated, at least indirectly, with Timothy B. Blackstone in the Chicago and Alton Railroad Company, a company of which Bunn was the principal founder and an owner. Section 1 of the Union Stock Yard and Transit Company statute attached to the corporation the perpetuity of corporate succession, the power to execute contracts, the power to sue, suability, the power to create and change a corporate seal, and a general class of un-enumerated powers, rights, and immunities necessary for the performance of the defined corporate purpose.[2202] The purpose of the company was the

---

from the South Side of Chicago. Hyde Park History, Vol. 38, (No. 4), Pp. 1-7. Chicago, IL: Hyde Park Historical Society.

[2198] AN ACT to Incorporate the Union Stock Yard and Transit Company of Chicago. Private Laws Of The State Of Illinois, Passed By The Twenty-Fourth General Assembly, Convened January 2, 1865. (1865). Vol. II. Pp. 678-683. Springfield, IL: Baker & Phillips, Printers. Google Books.

[2199] AN ACT to Incorporate the Union Stock Yard and Transit Company of Chicago. Private Laws Of The State Of Illinois, Passed By The Twenty-Fourth General Assembly, Convened January 2, 1865. (1865). Vol. II. Pp. 678-683. Springfield, IL: Baker & Phillips, Printers. Google Books.

[2200] AN ACT to Incorporate the Union Stock Yard and Transit Company of Chicago. Private Laws Of The State Of Illinois, Passed By The Twenty-Fourth General Assembly, Convened January 2, 1865. (1865). Vol. II. Pp. 678-683. Springfield, IL: Baker & Phillips, Printers. Google Books.

[2201] AN ACT to Incorporate the Union Stock Yard and Transit Company of Chicago. Private Laws Of The State Of Illinois, Passed By The Twenty-Fourth General Assembly, Convened January 2, 1865. (1865). Vol. II. Pp. 678-683. Springfield, IL: Baker & Phillips, Printers. Google Books.

[2202] AN ACT to Incorporate the Union Stock Yard and Transit Company of Chicago. Private Laws Of The State Of Illinois, Passed By The Twenty-Fourth General Assembly,

construction of manufacturing and transportational infrastructures for animal processing, slaughter, meatpacking, food transfer, and distribution.[2203] The 1865 law specified the place of the Stock Yards to be at the south limit of the City of Chicago, and west of Wallace Street.[2204]

Section 2 of the statute identified the multiple anticipatory structural elements of the inchoate Chicago Union Stockyards. "Yards, inclosures, buildings, structures, and railway lines, tracks, switches and turnouts, aqueducts," would constitute the infrastructures of the new stock yard center and would enable the intake, housing, slaughter, feeding, management, irrigation, and transfer processes that would collectively form the operations of the Stockyards.[2205] The statute contemplated a broad economy of agricultural and industrial operations, and granted the power to the company to construct and develop one or more hotels for the purpose of providing accommodations for the expected high volume of market actors, which would include, "drovers, dealers and the public doing business at the said yards."[2206]

Section 3 of the statute provided the power to connect the Union Stock Yard Company railroad system to the routes of the existing Chicago railroad companies.[2207] This auxiliary connection would link Union Stock Yard service with the transportation services of all of the Chicago railroad companies which possessed termini at Chicago.[2208] The statute placed the Union Stock Yard

Convened January 2, 1865. (1865). Vol. II. Pp. 678-683. Springfield, IL: Baker & Phillips, Printers. Google Books.

[2203] AN ACT to Incorporate the Union Stock Yard and Transit Company of Chicago. Private Laws Of The State Of Illinois, Passed By The Twenty-Fourth General Assembly, Convened January 2, 1865. (1865). Vol. II. Pp. 678-683. Springfield, IL: Baker & Phillips, Printers. Google Books.

[2204] AN ACT to Incorporate the Union Stock Yard and Transit Company of Chicago. Private Laws Of The State Of Illinois, Passed By The Twenty-Fourth General Assembly, Convened January 2, 1865. (1865). Vol. II. Pp. 678-683. Springfield, IL: Baker & Phillips, Printers. Google Books.

[2205] AN ACT to Incorporate the Union Stock Yard and Transit Company of Chicago. Private Laws Of The State Of Illinois, Passed By The Twenty-Fourth General Assembly, Convened January 2, 1865. (1865). Vol. II. Pp. 678-683. Springfield, IL: Baker & Phillips, Printers. Google Books.

[2206] AN ACT to Incorporate the Union Stock Yard and Transit Company of Chicago. Private Laws Of The State Of Illinois, Passed By The Twenty-Fourth General Assembly, Convened January 2, 1865. (1865). Vol. II. Pp. 678-683. Springfield, IL: Baker & Phillips, Printers. Google Books.

[2207] AN ACT to Incorporate the Union Stock Yard and Transit Company of Chicago. Private Laws Of The State Of Illinois, Passed By The Twenty-Fourth General Assembly, Convened January 2, 1865. (1865). Vol. II. Pp. 678-683. Springfield, IL: Baker & Phillips, Printers. Google Books.

[2208] AN ACT to Incorporate the Union Stock Yard and Transit Company of Chicago. Private Laws Of The State Of Illinois, Passed By The Twenty-Fourth General Assembly,

Company at the front of urban development in the expanding metropolitan region.[2209] Section 3 authorized the new company to construct railroad connections not only to every Chicago railroad, but also to the ancillary and auxiliary routes of each railroad at the city for the purpose of framing a metropolitan network of transfer and access centered on the growth and economy of the Stock Yard.[2210] The statute's series of permissions thus presented a diorama of public policy in which the role of the Stock Yard would be central to Cook County and Chicago industrial development. Railroads entered Chicago from a line drawn between Lake Michigan and the southwest corner of the city limit, and between the southwest corner of the city limit and the point marked by section 19, township 39 north, range 14, east of the third principal meridian.[2211] Under the regime of the 1865 Act, the Union Stock Yard and Transit Company held the express power to contract with the Chicago railroad companies to create a metropolitan industrial network of transfers, approaches, accesses, and facilities.[2212] Section 3 of the Act, therefore, centrally laid the physical roadbeds of agro-industrial Chicago and Cook County with the metaphysical timbers, cables, and asphalts of contract, offer, negotiation, acceptance, and consideration. Section 4 of the Act granted realty property powers to the company, and authorized the company to receive, possess, and administer all lands transferred or donated to the company for the purpose of the performance of the stated corporate purpose.[2213]

The Act provided a specific policy and law that were authoritative in cases in which the company could accept and receive transfers of land from parties who

Convened January 2, 1865. (1865). Vol. II. Pp. 678-683. Springfield, IL: Baker & Phillips, Printers. Google Books.

[2209] AN ACT to Incorporate the Union Stock Yard and Transit Company of Chicago. Private Laws Of The State Of Illinois, Passed By The Twenty-Fourth General Assembly, Convened January 2, 1865. (1865). Vol. II. Pp. 678-683. Springfield, IL: Baker & Phillips, Printers. Google Books.

[2210] AN ACT to Incorporate the Union Stock Yard and Transit Company of Chicago. Private Laws Of The State Of Illinois, Passed By The Twenty-Fourth General Assembly, Convened January 2, 1865. (1865). Vol. II. Pp. 678-683. Springfield, IL: Baker & Phillips, Printers. Google Books.

[2211] AN ACT to Incorporate the Union Stock Yard and Transit Company of Chicago. Private Laws Of The State Of Illinois, Passed By The Twenty-Fourth General Assembly, Convened January 2, 1865. (1865). Vol. II. Pp. 678-683. Springfield, IL: Baker & Phillips, Printers. Google Books.

[2212] AN ACT to Incorporate the Union Stock Yard and Transit Company of Chicago. Private Laws Of The State Of Illinois, Passed By The Twenty-Fourth General Assembly, Convened January 2, 1865. (1865). Vol. II. Pp. 678-683. Springfield, IL: Baker & Phillips, Printers. Google Books.

[2213] AN ACT to Incorporate the Union Stock Yard and Transit Company of Chicago. Private Laws Of The State Of Illinois, Passed By The Twenty-Fourth General Assembly, Convened January 2, 1865. (1865). Vol. II. Pp. 678-683. Springfield, IL: Baker & Phillips, Printers. Google Books.

were infants, *femme coverts* (covered women), or mental incompetents, all of which were parties who possessed no valid power to transfer land.[2214] To counteract the possibility of such transfers, whose infant, *femme covert*, or *non compos mentis* counterparties would be deficient in their contractual or donative capacities, Section 4 contained a running prospective ratification of all real estate transfers to the company that might emanate from contractual transfers or donative transfers from such classes of incapacitated counterparties.[2215] The Section 4 ratification policy permitted the company to accept such deficiently-transferred properties, but permitted the company to use the lands so transferred only for the purpose of railroad construction. The Act further stipulated the duty of company payment of any remedies awarded to the incapacitated parties for the company's acceptance of the parties' incapacitated transfers, according to the law and policy established by the State of Illinois in the Act of June 22, 1852, which governed the condemnation of rights of way for purposes of internal improvements.[2216]

Section 5 of the statute provided for the financing of the Union Stock Yard and Transit Company and authorized an original capitalization of $1,000,000.[2217] The capitalization was effected through equity financing, and the $1,000,000 was to be divided into 10,000 shares of $100 each.[2218] No debt financing accompanied the equity financing in the statutory financing provisions, and the initial company capital, therefore, appears to have been composed entirely of stock money.[2219]

[2214] AN ACT to Incorporate the Union Stock Yard and Transit Company of Chicago. Private Laws Of The State Of Illinois, Passed By The Twenty-Fourth General Assembly, Convened January 2, 1865. (1865). Vol. II. Pp. 678-683. Springfield, IL: Baker & Phillips, Printers. Google Books.

[2215] AN ACT to Incorporate the Union Stock Yard and Transit Company of Chicago. Private Laws Of The State Of Illinois, Passed By The Twenty-Fourth General Assembly, Convened January 2, 1865. (1865). Vol. II. Pp. 678-683. Springfield, IL: Baker & Phillips, Printers. Google Books.

[2216] AN ACT to Incorporate the Union Stock Yard and Transit Company of Chicago. Private Laws Of The State Of Illinois, Passed By The Twenty-Fourth General Assembly, Convened January 2, 1865. (1865). Vol. II. Pp. 678-683. Springfield, IL: Baker & Phillips, Printers. Google Books.

[2217] AN ACT to Incorporate the Union Stock Yard and Transit Company of Chicago. Private Laws Of The State Of Illinois, Passed By The Twenty-Fourth General Assembly, Convened January 2, 1865. (1865). Vol. II. Pp. 678-683. Springfield, IL: Baker & Phillips, Printers. Google Books.

[2218] AN ACT to Incorporate the Union Stock Yard and Transit Company of Chicago. Private Laws Of The State Of Illinois, Passed By The Twenty-Fourth General Assembly, Convened January 2, 1865. (1865). Vol. II. Pp. 678-683. Springfield, IL: Baker & Phillips, Printers. Google Books.

[2219] AN ACT to Incorporate the Union Stock Yard and Transit Company of Chicago. Private Laws Of The State Of Illinois, Passed By The Twenty-Fourth General Assembly, Convened January 2, 1865. (1865). Vol. II. Pp. 678-683. Springfield, IL: Baker & Phillips, Printers. Google Books.

Section 6 contained the terms of corporate governance, established the corporate board of directors, and named the following persons to the directorate: James F. Joy, Timothy B. Blackstone, John B. McCullough, Virginius A. Turpin, Martin L. Sykes, John F. Tracy, John L. Hancock, Roselle M. Hough, and Charles M. Culbertson. Section 6 placed limits on the number of directors, and mandated that there be no fewer than five directors, and no more than nine.[2220] Section 7 governed proxy votes, and Section 8 created the jobs of President, Treasurer, and Secretary within the company.[2221] Section 9 permitted the company to construct railroads along, upon, and across roads and watercourses, but placed upon the company the duty never to unnecessarily impede any watercourse or any road.[2222] Section 10 created and vested in the company the power of debt financing, and defined the debt financing parameters by preventing the creation and distribution of debt instruments of less than $500 values, by limiting the total allowable debt financing money to $500,000, and by banning debt interest rates of more than ten percent.[2223]

Section 10 contained a collateral property and security interest creation permission and authorized the company to create security interests to induce potential debtholders to purchase debt instruments from the company, giving these investors the promise of collateralized security.[2224] The company was empowered to create security interests through both mortgages and deeds of trust executable on company property, and the scope of company property that could be pledged for security interests was liberal, embracing all company property both current and anticipatory at the time of the executions of the security interest mortgages or

---

[2220] AN ACT to Incorporate the Union Stock Yard and Transit Company of Chicago. Private Laws Of The State Of Illinois, Passed By The Twenty-Fourth General Assembly, Convened January 2, 1865. (1865). Vol. II. Pp. 678-683. Springfield, IL: Baker & Phillips, Printers. Google Books.
[2221] AN ACT to Incorporate the Union Stock Yard and Transit Company of Chicago. Private Laws Of The State Of Illinois, Passed By The Twenty-Fourth General Assembly, Convened January 2, 1865. (1865). Vol. II. Pp. 678-683. Springfield, IL: Baker & Phillips, Printers. Google Books.
[2222] AN ACT to Incorporate the Union Stock Yard and Transit Company of Chicago. Private Laws Of The State Of Illinois, Passed By The Twenty-Fourth General Assembly, Convened January 2, 1865. (1865). Vol. II. Pp. 678-683. Springfield, IL: Baker & Phillips, Printers. Google Books.
[2223] AN ACT to Incorporate the Union Stock Yard and Transit Company of Chicago. Private Laws Of The State Of Illinois, Passed By The Twenty-Fourth General Assembly, Convened January 2, 1865. (1865). Vol. II. Pp. 678-683. Springfield, IL: Baker & Phillips, Printers. Google Books.
[2224] AN ACT to Incorporate the Union Stock Yard and Transit Company of Chicago. Private Laws Of The State Of Illinois, Passed By The Twenty-Fourth General Assembly, Convened January 2, 1865. (1865). Vol. II. Pp. 678-683. Springfield, IL: Baker & Phillips, Printers. Google Books.

security interest deeds of trust.[2225] Section 11 placed a broad limit on the company, and forbade the firm to engage in either the business of passenger transportation, or freight transportation in Chicago.[2226] The Union Stockyards constitution, as contained in the 1865 organic Act, contemplated the commercial, industrial, and infrastructural centrality of the Union Stockyards to the City of Chicago and Cook County.

<u>Colonel Stephen Williamson Stryker of Chicago:</u>

<u>The Leatherworkers Dominate the Fur Garment Trade of the American West</u>

This section concerns Stephen Williamson Stryker (1836-1897) and the Chicago fur and leather garment industry. A cousin of the McClure, Stryker, and Taylor families of Chicago, Morgan County, and Springfield, Illinois, Stephen Williamson Stryker served in the United States Army during the Civil War, holding the office of Colonel of the Forty-Fourth New York Infantry.[2227] According to historian William Osgood Stoddard, John Hay described the quality of the Forty-Fourth New York Infantry, which was also referred to as Ellsworth's Avengers, as follows.[2228] John Hay characterized the military organization in a comment dated October 26, 1861, which appeared in the *Missouri Republican*, a newspaper of St. Louis.[2229]

> "'It is the People's Ellsworth Regiment of New York, selected from every town in the State with the exception of the cities of New York and Troy. Magnificent in physique and morale, well dressed, well equipped, well armed, officered by the perfectly trained Chicago boys and commanded

---

[2225] AN ACT to Incorporate the Union Stock Yard and Transit Company of Chicago. Private Laws Of The State Of Illinois, Passed By The Twenty-Fourth General Assembly, Convened January 2, 1865. (1865). Vol. II. Pp. 678-683. Springfield, IL: Baker & Phillips, Printers. Google Books.

[2226] AN ACT to Incorporate the Union Stock Yard and Transit Company of Chicago. Private Laws Of The State Of Illinois, Passed By The Twenty-Fourth General Assembly, Convened January 2, 1865. (1865). Vol. II. Pp. 678-683. Springfield, IL: Baker & Phillips, Printers. Google Books.

[2227] Stoddard, William Osgood. (2002). Dispatches From Lincoln's White House: The Anonymous Civil War Journalism of Presidential Secretary William O. Stoddard. Burlingame, Michael, Ed. P. 262. Lincoln, NE: University of Nebraska Press. Google Books.

[2228] Stoddard, William Osgood. (2002). Dispatches From Lincoln's White House: The Anonymous Civil War Journalism of Presidential Secretary William O. Stoddard. Burlingame, Michael, Ed. P. 262. Lincoln, NE: University of Nebraska Press. Google Books.

[2229] Stoddard, William Osgood. (2002). Dispatches From Lincoln's White House: The Anonymous Civil War Journalism of Presidential Secretary William O. Stoddard. Burlingame, Michael, Ed. P. 262. Lincoln, NE: University of Nebraska Press. Google Books.

by Ellsworth's friend and companion, Col. Stryker, lacing the effeminacy of the Seventh and the brutality of the Fire Boys, it unites the refinement of the one with the muscle of the other, and goes into the field animated by the loftiest motives of patriotism and the highest incentives to daring.'"[2230]

Stephen Williamson Stryker appears to have entered the Chicago garment industry at some time after the Civil War. Stryker established the Chicago garment manufacturing company of Stryker & Barnes. This company manufactured, retailed, and adjusted myriad varieties of fur garments and headwear.[2231] Stephen W. Stryker filed a pleading for grant of patent for a novel form of fur collar to be used in the fur garment industry.[2232] The filing of the patent pleading occurred on July 15, 1873.[2233] The United States Patent Office granted United States patent 148,389 to Stryker for the novel invention on March 10, 1874.[2234] George B. Cornell and N. H. Sherburne served as witnesses to the Stryker patent pleading.[2235] The pleading contained, *inter alia*, the following words of purpose and description:

> "Be it known that I, STEPHEN W. STRYKER, of Chicago, in the county of Cook and State of Illinois, have invented a new and useful Improvement in Fur Collars; and I do hereby declare the following to be a full, clear, and exact description thereof, which will enable others skilled in the art to which my invention appertains to make and use the same, reference being had to the accompanying drawing forming part of this specification, in which- Figure 1 is a general plan, showing the form before being sewed, and Fig. 2 is a general plan of the same when completed. . . My invention relates to that class of fur collars which are worn by ladies, and has for its object to provide the front of the same with lapels and to that end it consists, in connection with the said lapels, of the novel shape of the front portion of the collar, whereby the lapels are made to lie smooth upon the

---

[2230] Stoddard, William Osgood. (2002). Dispatches From Lincoln's White House: The Anonymous Civil War Journalism of Presidential Secretary William O. Stoddard. Burlingame, Michael, Ed. P. 262. Lincoln, NE: University of Nebraska Press. Google Books.

[2231] See references included herein.

[2232] Specifications And Drawings of Patents Issued From The United States Patent Office for March, 1874. P. 330. Washington, D.C.: Government Printing Office. Google Books.

[2233] Specifications And Drawings of Patents Issued From The United States Patent Office for March, 1874. P. 330. Washington, D.C.: Government Printing Office. Google Books.

[2234] Specifications And Drawings of Patents Issued From The United States Patent Office for March, 1874. P. 330. Washington, D.C.: Government Printing Office. Google Books.

[2235] Specifications And Drawings of Patents Issued From The United States Patent Office for March, 1874. P. 330. Washington, D.C.: Government Printing Office. Google Books.

front of the same when turned back, and to adapt the collar to the form of the wearer when buttoned."[2236]

Stryker & Barnes paid for a two-part advertisement that appeared in the September 26, 1868, issue of the *Chicago Tribune*, which put customers on notice that the company had recently received, "A NEW **STYLE HAT**,"[2237] called the "C. B. T."[2238] The advertisement contained no description of the advertised C. B. T. hat.[2239] One could safely infer from the fact of omission of product description in the case of this ad that the "C. B. T." hat was obviously a widely known product in that time and among the target market audiences of the place.[2240] The advertisement that accompanied the hat advertisement was for both hats and furs, and stated the following: "**HATS. FURS. STRYKER & BARNES,** Fashionable Hatters and Furriers, Have the LARGEST and best selected stock of Hats, Caps, and LADIES' FINE FURS ever offered in the West."[2241] The company address was 112 and 114 Washington Street, at the corner of Clark Street.[2242] McKenzie of 103 Madison Street advertised silk hats, and its supremacy in the provision of silk hats in Chicago.[2243] The G. H. Amidon Company of New York City operated a branch at Chicago, located at the corner of Wabash Avenue and Washington Street, in the Loop.[2244] The Chicago office of the G. H. Amidon Company would apparently dissolve at some point within eight months of the 1868 advertisement, a fact that is supported by proof from the frontpage hats and garments column from the *Chicago Tribune* issue of May 29, 1869.[2245]

The Stryker & Barnes Company advertised Chicago market supremacy and Western market supremacy both in the hat trade, and in the fur trade, in an advertisement that appeared in the November 4, 1868 issue of the *Chicago Tribune*.[2246] The other garment companies that advertised that day included the Brewster Company of the Sherman House, which manufactured and sold mink cloaks, as well as bordered mantillas, both of which were ladies' garments.[2247] The Stryker & Barnes Company, located at 112 and 114 Washington Street at the corner of Clark Street, claimed the status of possessing the, "Largest and Most

---

[2236] Specifications And Drawings of Patents Issued From The United States Patent Office for March, 1874. P. 330. Washington, D.C.: Government Printing Office. Google Books.

[2237] Chicago Tribune. (September 26, 1868). P. 1. Newspapers.com.

[2238] Chicago Tribune. (September 26, 1868). P. 1. Newspapers.com.

[2239] Chicago Tribune. (September 26, 1868). P. 1. Newspapers.com.

[2240] Chicago Tribune. (September 26, 1868). P. 1. Newspapers.com.

[2241] Chicago Tribune. (September 26, 1868). P. 1. Newspapers.com.

[2242] Chicago Tribune. (September 26, 1868). P. 1. Newspapers.com.

[2243] Chicago Tribune. (September 26, 1868). P. 1. Newspapers.com.

[2244] Chicago Tribune. (September 26, 1868). P. 1. Newspapers.com.

[2245] Chicago Tribune. (May 29, 1869). P. 1. Newspapers.com.

[2246] Chicago Tribune. (November 4, 1868). P. 1. Newspapers.com.

[2247] Chicago Tribune. (November 4, 1868). P. 1. Newspapers.com.

Elegant Stock OF **LADIES' FURS EVER OFFERED IN THE CITY.**"[2248] The A. Herzog Company of 70 Lake Street manufactured fur garments and provided fur garment inspection services.[2249] The Hoffman Company of 88 N. Clark Street advertised that it was, **"THE OLDEST GERMAN JEWELRY BUSINESS."**[2250] The intended meaning of the Hoffman Company was probably that the firm was the oldest German jewelry organization in Chicago.[2251] Hoffman sold gold ware, silver ware, American watches, French watches, diamonds, and other jewels.[2252]

The November 16, 1868 issue of the *Chicago Tribune* proved the fact that the Stryker & Barnes Company was a large-scale manufacturer of fur garments, in addition to the company being a large retailer of fur garments.[2253] The advertisement focused on the manufacturing aspect of the company, rather than exclusively upon the retailing aspect of the company.[2254] The advertisement contained the following words: **"STRYKER & BARNES   FUR MANUFACTURERS** Astrachan Sacques of Superior Quality. **Sea Coast Maine Mink Furs of all Fashionable Shapes. Furs Altered and Repaired.**"[2255]

The December 18, 1868, issue of the *Chicago Tribune* contained a Stryker & Barnes Company advertisement in which the firm promoted its stock of, "Royal Ermine, Russian and Hudson's Bay Sable, Siberian Squirrel, and all other Furs now worn by Ladies."[2256] J. A. Smith & Company, located at 98 State Street, joined the Stryker & Barnes Company on the front page of the same edition of the *Chicago Tribune*, and advertised its merchandise of **"RICH FURS."**[2257]

The December 19, 1868 issue of the *Chicago Tribune* contained a Stryker & Barnes Company advertisement replete with mercantile detail.[2258] The company advertised hats, caps, and furs, with emphasis on the holiday classes of hat that the company had received the day of the advertisement.[2259] Stryker & Barnes reiterated their status as the largest hat company in Chicago, and in the West, and promoted six styles of Astrachan caps, in addition to London caps, skating caps, driving caps, and winter caps.[2260] The company allotted special space for the promotion of its "Sea Coast Maine Mink" garments.[2261] Stryker & Barnes added the following words of promotion: "An inspection of our stock, we think, will convince any one

---

[2248] Chicago Tribune. (November 4, 1868). P. 1. Newspapers.com.
[2249] Chicago Tribune. (November 4, 1868). P. 1. Newspapers.com.
[2250] Chicago Tribune. (November 4, 1868). P. 1. Newspapers.com.
[2251] Chicago Tribune. (November 4, 1868). P. 1. Newspapers.com.
[2252] Chicago Tribune. (November 4, 1868). P. 1. Newspapers.com.
[2253] Chicago Tribune. (November 16, 1868). P. 1. Newspapers.com.
[2254] Chicago Tribune. (November 16, 1868). P. 1. Newspapers.com.
[2255] Chicago Tribune. (November 16, 1868). P. 1. Newspapers.com.
[2256] Chicago Tribune. (December 18, 1868). P. 1. Newspapers.com.
[2257] Chicago Tribune. (December 18, 1868). P. 1. Newspapers.com.
[2258] Chicago Tribune. (December 19, 1868). P. 1. Newspapers.com.
[2259] Chicago Tribune. (December 19, 1868). P. 1. Newspapers.com.
[2260] Chicago Tribune. (December 19, 1868). P. 1. Newspapers.com.
[2261] Chicago Tribune. (December 19, 1868). P. 1. Newspapers.com.

wishing to purchase good and perfect goods, that our prices are low, and our FUR ROOM the best lighted apartment in the country."[2262]

The February 4, 1869 issue of the *Chicago Tribune* advertised that Stryker & Barnes carried, "A Fresh Supply of White Fox, Bear and Wolf Robes."[2263] The April 8, 1869 issue of the *Chicago Tribune* contained information regarding the regularity of inventory turnover and renewal that Stryker & Barnes experienced on a daily basis.[2264] "STRYKER & BARNES, The Leading Hatters of the West, Are daily receiving all the New Styles of Gents', Young Men's and Boy's FASHIONABLE HEAD DRESS for Spring Wear."[2265] The advertisement showed the diversity of clothing offered by the Stryker & Barnes Company.

Multiple companies appeared within the garment advertisement column that appeared on Page 1 of the May 29, 1869, edition of the *Chicago Tribune*.[2266] Brewster of the Sherman House, Barstow's at 104 Randolph, Bishop & Barnes at 115 Lake Street, Stryker & Barnes at the corner of Washington Street and Clark Street, and Loomis at 95 Clark Street all populated the hat advertisement column that day.[2267] Stryker & Barnes reiterated their superlative scope of merchandise with the words, "KEEP THE BEST STOCK OF **HATS** IN THE WEST."[2268] Dunlap advertised summer dress hats, while Brewster at the Sherman House advertised multiple varieties of Panama hats and straw hats.[2269] Bishop & Barnes of 115 Lake Street advertised the fact that they were the company that preferentially and exclusively received the merchandise stock of Mr. G. H. Amidon of Broadway, New York City, when Mr. Amidon dissolved the Chicago branch of his business.[2270] The Loomis Company asserted that it possessed the broadest diversity of hats in the West.[2271] While the Loomis Company alleged supremacy of diversity in hat stock at that time, Stryker & Barnes asserted supremacy of commercial size, and possibly also of product quality: "**STRYKER & BARNES. THE LEADING HATTERS OF THE WEST.**"[2272] The commercial language of the advertisements was tightly suffused with subtle allegations of multiple classes of commercial supremacy.[2273] The diverse commercial supremacies could coexist truthfully, for while one company might possess the greatest scope of product, another company might at the same time possess the greatest volume of product.[2274] The firms advertised these diverse commercial

---

[2262] Chicago Tribune. (December 19, 1868). P. 1. Newspapers.com.

[2263] Chicago Tribune. (February 4, 1869). P. 1. Newspapers.com.

[2264] Chicago Tribune. (April 8, 1869). P. 1. Newspapers.com.

[2265] Chicago Tribune. (April 8, 1869). P. 1. Newspapers.com.

[2266] Chicago Tribune. (May 29, 1869). P. 1. Newspapers.com.

[2267] Chicago Tribune. (May 29, 1869). P. 1. Newspapers.com.

[2268] Chicago Tribune. (May 29, 1869). P. 1. Newspapers.com.

[2269] Chicago Tribune. (May 29, 1869). P. 1. Newspapers.com.

[2270] Chicago Tribune. (May 29, 1869). P. 1. Newspapers.com.

[2271] Chicago Tribune. (May 29, 1869). P. 1. Newspapers.com.

[2272] Chicago Tribune. (May 29, 1869). P. 1. Newspapers.com.

[2273] Chicago Tribune. (May 29, 1869). P. 1. Newspapers.com.

[2274] Chicago Tribune. (May 29, 1869). P. 1. Newspapers.com.

supremacies to the market audiences of the times and places of Post-Civil War and Reconstruction Era Chicago.[2275] The June 5, 1869 advertisement for Stryker & Barnes in the *Chicago Tribune* listed several forms of hat that they carried in stock: "**Stryker & Barnes**, The Leading Hatters of the West. **Dress Silk Hats, Drab Beaver Hats. Pearl Cassimere Hats, Panama Hats, New and Nobby Straw Hats.** Washington and Clark-sts."[2276]

The company of Barnes, Stryker & Barnes, consistently claimed to be the largest dealer in hats in Chicago, and the largest in the American West.[2277] The company, which had changed its commercial name to the Barnes, Stryker & Barnes Company as of 1870, advertised its broad class of children's hats in the April 2, 1870, edition of the *Chicago Tribune*.[2278] The *Chicago Tribune* of June 17, 1870 contained a detailed advertisement for the company.[2279] The company advertisement stated multiple facts concerning the business. The advertisement contained the following words: "BARNES, STRYKER & BARNES, The Leading Hatters of the West, HAVE THE LARGEST AND BEST **STOCK OF NOBBY HATS** IN THIS CITY OR ANY OTHER. Corner Washington & Clark-sts."[2280] On December 3, 1870, the Barnes, Stryker & Barnes Company advertised its new, "**HOLIDAY DRESS SILK HAT—Now Ready.**"[2281] The company continued to claim the status of the preeminent furriers and hatters of Chicago and of the American West.[2282]

The Farwell Brothers of Chicago

John Villiers Farwell (1825-1908) and Charles Benjamin Farwell (1823-1903), who were both close friends and business associates of Jacob Bunn and John Bunn in Chicago, contributed significantly to the agricultural and architectural development Texas.[2283] The Farwell brothers were the sons of Henry Farwell and Nancy (Jackson) Farwell of Painted Post, New York.[2284] The family moved from the Appalachian Mountains of New York to Illinois, in 1838.[2285] John graduated

---

[2275] Chicago Tribune. (May 29, 1869). P. 1. Newspapers.com.

[2276] Chicago Tribune. (June 5, 1869). P. 1. Newspapers.com.

[2277] Chicago Tribune. (June 17, 1870). P. 1. Newspapers.com.

[2278] Chicago Tribune. (April 2, 1870). P. 1. Newspapers.com.

[2279] Chicago Tribune. (June 17, 1870). P. 1. Newspapers.com.

[2280] Chicago Tribune. (June 17, 1870). P. 1. Newspapers.com.

[2281] Chicago Tribune. (December 3, 1870). P. 1. Newspapers.com.

[2282] Chicago Tribune. (December 3, 1870). P. 1. Newspapers.com.

[2283] Call, Andrew Taylor. (2005). Jacob Bunn: Legacy of an Illinois Industrial Pioneer. Pp. 129-131; The National Cyclopaedia of American Biography. (1910). Vo. XIV. P. 228. New York, NY: James T. White & Company; Handbook of Texas Online. (2010). Gracy, David B. Farwell, John Villiers. Texas State Historical Association. Tshaonline.org.

[2284] Handbook of Texas Online. (2010). Gracy, David B. Farwell, John Villiers. Texas State Historical Association. Tshaonline.org.

[2285] Handbook of Texas Online. (2010). Gracy, David B. Farwell, John Villiers. Texas State Historical Association. Tshaonline.org.

from Mount Morris Seminary in 1845, came to Chicago, and found employment with the city.[2286] John then found employment first with the Hamilton & White Company, and later with the Hamlin & Day Company.[2287] John married Abigail Gates Taylor, and one daughter was born to the couple prior to Abigail's death in 1851.[2288] John Farwell became a member of the Wadsworth & Phelps Company of Chicago and married Emeret Cooley.[2289] The company became Cooley, Farwell & Company in 1862.[2290] Farwell had served as General Manager of Wadsworth & Phelps, and eventually assumed ownership of Cooley, Farwell & Company, at which time the company became John V. Farwell and Company.[2291]

John V. Farwell served as an elector for Abraham Lincoln in 1860, and worked closely with Jacob Bunn and John W. Bunn as part of the Abraham Lincoln Presidential Campaign of 1860.[2292] Both the Bunns and Farwell served the United States during the Civil War. John W. Bunn was Special Agent for Illinois Governor Richard Yates and President Abraham Lincoln, helped organize the Cairo Expedition, and led the first Union Army troops from Chicago to Cairo, Illinois. John V. Farwell organized the Chicago Board of Trade Regiment for the Union Army.[2293] President Ulysses S. Grant appointed Farwell Commissioner of Indian Affairs in 1869, in which federal office Farwell traveled, "'some 10,000 miles in

---

[2286] Handbook of Texas Online. (2010). Gracy, David B. Farwell, John Villiers. Texas State Historical Association. Tshaonline.org.

[2287] Call, Andrew Taylor. (2005). Jacob Bunn: Legacy of an Illinois Industrial Pioneer. Pp. 129-131; The National Cyclopaedia of American Biography. (1910). Vo. XIV. P. 228. New York, NY: James T. White & Company.

[2288] Handbook of Texas Online. (2010). Gracy, David B. Farwell, John Villiers. Texas State Historical Association. Tshaonline.org.

[2289] Handbook of Texas Online. (2010). Gracy, David B. Farwell, John Villiers. Texas State Historical Association. Tshaonline.org.

[2290] Handbook of Texas Online. (2010). Gracy, David B. Farwell, John Villiers. Texas State Historical Association. Tshaonline.org.

[2291] Handbook of Texas Online. (2010). Gracy, David B. Farwell, John Villiers. Texas State Historical Association. Tshaonline.org.

[2292] Call, Andrew Taylor. (2005). Jacob Bunn: Legacy of an Illinois Industrial Pioneer. Pp. 129-131. Lawrenceville, VA: Brunswick Publishing Corporation; The National Cyclopaedia of American Biography. (1910). Vo. XIV. P. 228. New York, NY: James T. White & Company; Handbook of Texas Online. (2010). Gracy, David B. Farwell, John Villiers. Texas State Historical Association. Tshaonline.org.

[2293] Call, Andrew Taylor. (2005). Jacob Bunn: Legacy of an Illinois Industrial Pioneer. Pp. 90-91, 129-131. Lawrenceville, VA: Brunswick Publishing Corporation; The National Cyclopaedia of American Biography. (1910). Vo. XIV. P. 228. New York, NY: James T. White & Company; Marengo Republican-News. (June 24, 1920). P. 6. Newspapers.com; Report Of The Adjutant General Of The State of Illinois. (1900). Vol. I. (covering the years 1861-1866). P. 243. Springfield, IL: Phillips Bros., State Printers. Google Books.

the discharge of his duties.'"[2294] Like the Bunn brothers, John Farwell was a leading Christian industrialist, and served as the chief of the Chicago Branch of the United States Christian Commission during the Civil War years.[2295] Farwell befriended Dwight Lyman Moody, the renowned Christian minister and church builder of Chicago, and worked with Moody to establish the Moody Church and the Moody Bible Institute.[2296] Farwell founded the North Market Mission of Chicago with Dwight L. Moody, and this charitable organization provided homes for homeless children.[2297]

The John V. Farwell Company grew to become one of the largest dry goods firms in the United States and achieved gross sales revenue of $9,000,000 in 1869. The July 3, 1870, edition of the *Lawrence Daily Journal* of Kansas, reported that John V. Farwell & Company employed 150 people and possessed a practically comprehensive scope of merchandise.[2298] The Kansas newspaper described the geographical scope of the company's sales distribution as continental and international, ranging from the Pacific to the Atlantic, and noted that the company was represented in Europe by a purchasing agent.[2299] The Kansas journalist noted that both Chicago and the American West were indebted to John V. Farwell & Company for centering the dry goods business sector in Chicago and for creating an efficient continental network of product distribution.[2300] Farwell began with Hamilton & White Company at about the age of fifteen years, and received a wage of $8 per month. He then found a job with the Hamlin & Day Company when he was about sixteen. Hamlin & Day paid him a wage of $250 a year, or $20.83 per

[2294] Call, Andrew Taylor. (2005). Jacob Bunn: Legacy of an Illinois Industrial Pioneer. P. 130. Lawrenceville, VA: Brunswick Publishing Corporation; The National Cyclopaedia of American Biography. (1910). Vo. XIV. P. 228. New York, NY: James T. White & Company; Handbook of Texas Online. (2010). Gracy, David B. Farwell, John Villiers. Texas State Historical Association. Tshaonline.org.

[2295] Handbook of Texas Online. (2010). Gracy, David B. Farwell, John Villiers. Texas State Historical Association. Tshaonline.org; Call, Andrew Taylor. (2005). Jacob Bunn: Legacy of an Illinois Industrial Pioneer. P. 130. Lawrenceville, VA: Brunswick Publishing Corporation; The National Cyclopaedia of American Biography. (1910). Vo. XIV. P. 228. New York, NY: James T. White & Company.

[2296] Call, Andrew Taylor. (2005). Jacob Bunn: Legacy of an Illinois Industrial Pioneer. P. 130. Lawrenceville, VA: Brunswick Publishing Corporation; The National Cyclopaedia of American Biography. (1910). Vo. XIV. P. 228. New York, NY: James T. White & Company; Handbook of Texas Online. (2010). Gracy, David B. Farwell, John Villiers. Texas State Historical Association. Tshaonline.org.

[2297] Farwell, John Villiers. (1911). Some Recollections of John V. Farwell: A Brief Description of his Early Life and Business Reminiscences. Pp. 101-115. Chicago, IL: R. R. Donnelley & Sons Company. Google Books.

[2298] Lawrence Daily Journal. (July 3, 1870). P. 2. Newspapers.com.

[2299] Lawrence Daily Journal. (July 3, 1870). P. 2. Newspapers.com.

[2300] Lawrence Daily Journal. (July 3, 1870). P. 2. Newspapers.com.

month.[2301] Next, he worked for the Wadsworth & Phelps Company, where he earned a wage of $50 per month at the age of about eighteen years.[2302] John Farwell was the business mentor for the young Marshall Field (1835-1906), who was a farmboy from Conway, Masachusetts, and gave Field his beginning in business at Chicago.[2303]

This company became Cooley, Wadsworth & Company, and Farwell became a partner in that company, which was described as the most important dry goods company of the city.[2304] The Wadsworth & Phelps Company became the Elisha Wadsworth Company, which in turn became Cooley, Farwell & Company. John V. Farwell and Marshall Field assumed the key ownership of Cooley, Farwell & Company, and Cooley retired in 1864 from the company. The company became Farwell, Field & Company, and Levi Leiter joined the company.[2305] Marshall Field and Levi Leiter left the company, and joined with Potter Palmer to form the Field, Leiter & Palmer Company.[2306] The two chains of companies became, respectively, John V. Farwell & Company, and Field, Leiter & Company. These two firms became the J. V. Farwell Company and Marshall Field & Company.[2307]

Beginning as a fifteen year old dry goods worker with an annual wage of $96, Farwell rose to become the greatest merchant of the American West, and led a company to annual revenue of $9,000,000 by 1869.[2308] The Kansas obituary finished with a brief, but powerful, eulogy for Farwell: "He typified in many ways the character of the city which he helped to make. He deserves to be remembered, and he will be remembered, as one of the strongest of Chicago's pioneer citizens."[2309]

Jacob Bunn, Elizabeth Jane (Ferguson) Bunn, and John W. Bunn worked with multiple other people in Springfield to form the Springfield Home for the Friendless, which provided homes, food, jobs, and opportunities for women and children whose families had been ruined by the Civil War, as was reported by Illinois historians John Carroll Power and J. A. Chesnut.[2310] The founders of the

[2301] The Inter Ocean. (August 22, 1908). P. 6. Newspapers.com.

[2302] The Inter Ocean. (August 22, 1908). P. 6. Newspapers.com.

[2303] Madsen, Axel. (2002). The Marshall Fields: The Evolution of an American Business Dynasty. Pp. 21-22. Hoboken, NJ: John Wiley & Sons, Inc; Call, Andrew Taylor. (2005). Jacob Bunn: Legacy of an Illinois Industrial Pioneer. P. 130. Lawrenceville, VA: Brunswick Publishing Corporation.

[2304] The Inter Ocean. (August 22, 1908). P. 6. Newspapers.com.

[2305] The Inter Ocean. (August 22, 1908). P. 6. Newspapers.com.

[2306] The Inter Ocean. (August 22, 1908). P. 6. Newspapers.com.

[2307] The Inter Ocean. (August 22, 1908). P. 6. Newspapers.com.

[2308] The Inter Ocean. (August 22, 1908). P. 6. Newspapers.com.

[2309] The Inter Ocean. (August 22, 1908). P. 6. Newspapers.com.

[2310] Power, John Carroll. (1871). History Of Springfield, Illinois. P. 59. Springfield, IL: Springfield Board of Trade, J. C. Power, and Illinois State Journal Print; Google Books;

Springfield Home for the Friendless included Mrs. Elizabeth (Ferguson) Bunn, Antrim Campbell, Dr. Lathrop, Mrs. Eliza Pope, Mrs. Mercy Conkling, Mrs. Louisa Draper, Mrs. Susan Cook, Mrs. Lydia Williams, Mrs. Harriet Campbell, Ms. Ann Eastman, Mrs. Maria Lathrop, Mrs. Mary Hay, Mrs. Catharine Hickox, Mrs. Mary Ann Dennis, and Mrs. Elizabeth Matheny, in addition to Jacob Bunn, George Pasfield, Samuel H. Treat, George P. Bowen, S. H. Melvin, J. C. Conkling, and James Campbell.[2311] Jacob Bunn served as the first Treasurer of the Springfield Home for the Friendless, and S. H. Melvin served as the first President of the Home, Judge Treat having declined to serve as President.[2312]

John Farwell was Superintendent of the North Market Mission, built the Chicago Tabernacle for Dwight Moody, and co-founded the Chicago Y.M.C.A. in 1857.[2313] The Bunn and Farwell business relationship was most prominently seen in the fact that Jacob Bunn and John Farwell co-founded the Chicago Republican Company in 1865 for the purposes of creating the most powerful Republican Party voice in Chicago and in the country, creating a heavily financed foundation for Abraham Lincoln and his policies, and challenging the media power of the *Chicago Tribune*.[2314] For the detailed history of the Chicago Republican Company and the Bunn-Farwell business connection, refer to Chapter 2, *Builders of the Downtown*.

John Farwell had entered the Texas land and cattle business in 1882, as a member of the Capitol Freehold Land and Investment Company, thus entering the Texas land and cattle markets at almost the same time when George Whitfield Bunn, Sr., entered the Texas land and cattle markets.[2315] The Farwell brothers were members of the Texas Capitol Syndicate, and helped with the financing and construction of the Texas State Capitol in Austin, Travis County.[2316] For their services and work,

Call, Andrew Taylor. (2005). Jacob Bunn: Legacy of an Illinois Industrial Pioneer. P. 52. Lawrenceville, VA: Brunswick Publishing Corporation.

[2311] Power, John Carroll. (1871). History Of Springfield, Illinois. P. 59. Springfield, IL: Springfield Board of Trade, J. C. Power, and Illinois State Journal Print. Google Books; Call, Andrew Taylor. (2005). Jacob Bunn: Legacy of an Illinois Industrial Pioneer. P. 52. Lawrenceville, VA: Brunswick Publishing Corporation.

[2312] Power, John Carroll. (1871). History Of Springfield, Illinois. P. 59. Springfield, IL: Springfield Board of Trade, J. C. Power, and Illinois State Journal Print. Google Books.

[2313] Call, Andrew Taylor. (2005). Jacob Bunn: Legacy of an Illinois Industrial Pioneer. Pp. 130-131. Lawrenceville, VA: Brunswick Publishing Corporation; The National Cyclopaedia of American Biography. (1910). Vo. XIV. P. 228. New York, NY: James T. White & Company; Farwell, John Villiers. (1911). Some Recollections of John V. Farwell. P. Chicago, IL: R. R. Donnelley & Sons Company. Google Books.

[2314] Call, Andrew Taylor. (2005). Jacob Bunn: Legacy of an Illinois Industrial Pioneer. P. 131. Lawrenceville, VA: Brunswick Publishing Corporation.

[2315] Handbook of Texas Online. (2010). Gracy, David B. *Farwell, John Villiers*. Texas State Historical Association. Tshaonline.org; Bunn family history records; Multiple historical memoirs related by Wendy Overom Paymard to Andrew Taylor Call.

[2316] Handbook of Texas Online. (2010). Gracy, David B. Farwell, John Villiers. Texas State Historical Association. Tshaonline.org.

the State of Texas, through Governor Oran Roberts, granted the Farwells three-million acres of Texas farmland: three million acres of Texas ranchland for construction of the $3,000,000 state capitol at Austin.[2317] The Farwell brothers' ranch was the XIT Ranch, and was reported to be the largest cattle ranch in the world at the time.[2318] The XIT Ranch contained 3,000,000 acres in ten Texas counties, located in the panhandle.[2319] While many Texans thought the XIT Ranch was essentially worthless space, the Farwell brothers proved them wrong when they developed the ranch into a modern agricultural and industrial company that operated with efficiency and productivity. The Farwells controlled much of north Texas politics through the XIT employees, and the XIT power extended from Lubbock to the Oklahoma panhandle border, according to the *Odessa American*, a newspaper of Odessa, Texas.[2320] The XIT Ranch contained multiple production and administration districts and owned 150,000 head of cattle at one time.[2321]

John V. Farwell composed memoirs prior to his death which were published posthumously by his son, John Villiers Farwell Jr., in 1911. Farwell, Sr., stated in the chapter titled, *Early Business Reminiscences*, the crucial importance of perseverance.

> "As I look back over my business life, a flood of memories comes over me, to verify the fact that 'if one's foresight was only as good as his hindsight,' how many pages, black with disappointment and regrets, might be luminous with success in every respect of the enchanting word. Yet the mistakes a man makes are often the corner-stones of that success. It is only the man who loses confidence in himself, because of them, that is obliged to make an assignment for the benefit of his creditors; but the man who trains his guns of grit, grace, and gumption upon apparently insurmountable difficulties will carry their strongholds in due time; and to begin with nothing but a sound mind in a sound body, instead of one million dollars, is the best capital a young man can have for his gun-carriages and ammunition."[2322]

John V. Farwell related the experiences of a Christian Commission meeting of some six-hundred persons at Point of Rocks, Illinois, at which testimonies of

---

[2317] The Odessa American. (November 18, 1962). P. 39. Newspapers.com.
[2318] The Odessa American. (November 18, 1962). P. 39. Newspapers.com.
[2319] The Odessa American. (November 18, 1962). P. 39. Newspapers.com.
[2320] The Odessa American. (November 18, 1962). P. 39. Newspapers.com.
[2321] The Odessa American. (November 18, 1962). P. 39. Newspapers.com.
[2322] Farwell, John Villiers. (1911). Some Recollections of John V. Farwell: A Brief Description of his Early Life and Business Reminiscences. P. 65. Chicago, IL: R. R. Donnelley & Sons Company. Google Books.

salvation in Jesus Christ were shared by various men.[2323] One African-American solider of the Union Army, who had lost both eyes in the Civil War, proclaimed his faith in Jesus Christ.[2324] The blinded soldier proclaimed that though he had lost his earthly sight, his eyes of Christian faith were as strong as ever, and he eagerly awaited grasping his eternal reward in Christ according to the promises of the Heavenly Father God.[2325] Another soldier, a Caucasian man, shared the testimony of his recent acceptance of Jesus Christ as Lord and Savior, and told the people present how Satan severely attacked his faith in God. The man was completely overcome with fear, but he turned to God as the great Captain of the Universe, prayed for deliverance, and received from God the marching order: "Get thee behind me, Satan."[2326] The man said that the command was immediately obeyed, and that God restored his peace and faith. The man's testimony follows here:

> "In the midst of the conflict, apparently overcome, [the soldier] thought of the great Captain— went to Him, and returned with the marching order, 'Get thee behind me, Satan,' which was instantly obeyed, and then with the pathos of the new 'creature' in Christ Jesus, and a mind quickened with energy of this new birth, he called on his fellow-soldiers to enlist under the blood-stained and victorious banner of King Jesus, whose kingdom is not of this world, but is set up within us."[2327]

John V. Farwell built a strong friendship with Dwight Lyman Moody in Chicago and through the process of Christian ministry work.[2328] Farwell earned $96 in his first year in Chicago, and he donated $50 of that money to help start the first

---

[2323] Farwell, John Villiers. (1911). Some Recollections of John V. Farwell: A Brief Description of his Early Life and Business Reminiscences. Pp. 76-77. Chicago, IL: R. R. Donnelley & Sons Company. Google Books.

[2324] Farwell, John Villiers. (1911). Some Recollections of John V. Farwell: A Brief Description of his Early Life and Business Reminiscences. P. 76. Chicago, IL: R. R. Donnelley & Sons Company. Google Books.

[2325] Farwell, John Villiers. (1911). Some Recollections of John V. Farwell: A Brief Description of his Early Life and Business Reminiscences. P. 76. Chicago, IL: R. R. Donnelley & Sons Company. Google Books.

[2326] Farwell, John Villiers. (1911). Some Recollections of John V. Farwell: A Brief Description of his Early Life and Business Reminiscences. Pp. 76-77. Chicago, IL: R. R. Donnelley & Sons Company. Google Books.

[2327] Farwell, John Villiers. (1911). Some Recollections of John V. Farwell: A Brief Description of his Early Life and Business Reminiscences. Pp. 76-77. Chicago, IL: R. R. Donnelley & Sons Company. Google Books.

[2328] Farwell, John Villiers. (1911). Some Recollections of John V. Farwell: A Brief Description of his Early Life and Business Reminiscences. Pp. 101-115. Chicago, IL: R. R. Donnelley & Sons Company. Google Books.

Methodist Episcopal brick church of Chicago.[2329] Farwell worked with his Sunday School teacher, "who was a converted drunkard from Galena," to build the Methodist church.[2330] In the process of developing this congregation, Farwell noticed a young man at the Sunday School that Farwell attended. That man was Dwight Moody.[2331] Moody dedicated much time to recruiting pupils for the Sunday School, and inspired Farwell to do the same.[2332] The activities of these men and the multiple others with whom they worked led to a Chicago Christian Revival in 1857-1858. Farwell founded the North Market Hall Mission Sunday School with Dwight Moody, and developed an immense ministry for the city.[2333] The North Market Hall Mission Sunday School became both the largest Sunday School in Chicago and one of the centers of Christian revival in Chicago.[2334] In 1860, Farwell accepted the Superintendent office of the North Market Hall Mission Sunday School.[2335] After attending the prayer meeting at the D. R. Holt parlor on Michigan Avenue, Farwell saw yet another opportunity for confession of faith in Christ.[2336] Farwell publicly confessed his faith in Jesus Christ as God and Savior at the noonday prayer meeting at Metropolitan Hall, where the following experience took place:

> "Of course I went, and while there made up a programme in my own mind, which was to attend the noon prayer meeting in Metropolitan Hall, which was crowded every day, and let every one know where I stood. I took my

[2329] Farwell, John Villiers. (1911). Some Recollections of John V. Farwell: A Brief Description of his Early Life and Business Reminiscences. P. 101. Chicago, IL: R. R. Donnelley & Sons Company. Google Books.

[2330] Farwell, John Villiers. (1911). Some Recollections of John V. Farwell: A Brief Description of his Early Life and Business Reminiscences. P. 101. Chicago, IL: R. R. Donnelley & Sons Company. Google Books.

[2331] Farwell, John Villiers. (1911). Some Recollections of John V. Farwell: A Brief Description of his Early Life and Business Reminiscences. Pp. 101-115. Chicago, IL: R. R. Donnelley & Sons Company. Google Books.

[2332] Farwell, John Villiers. (1911). Some Recollections of John V. Farwell: A Brief Description of his Early Life and Business Reminiscences. Pp. 101-115. Chicago, IL: R. R. Donnelley & Sons Company. Google Books.

[2333] Farwell, John Villiers. (1911). Some Recollections of John V. Farwell: A Brief Description of his Early Life and Business Reminiscences. Pp. 101-115. Chicago, IL: R. R. Donnelley & Sons Company. Google Books.

[2334] Farwell, John Villiers. (1911). Some Recollections of John V. Farwell: A Brief Description of his Early Life and Business Reminiscences. Pp. 101-115. Chicago, IL: R. R. Donnelley & Sons Company. Google Books.

[2335] Farwell, John Villiers. (1911). Some Recollections of John V. Farwell: A Brief Description of his Early Life and Business Reminiscences. P. 102. Chicago, IL: R. R. Donnelley & Sons Company. Google Books.

[2336] Farwell, John Villiers. (1911). Some Recollections of John V. Farwell: A Brief Description of his Early Life and Business Reminiscences. P. 102. Chicago, IL: R. R. Donnelley & Sons Company. Google Books.

seat in the center of the hall, where every one could see me plainly. There were several on their feet at the same time, and, waiting for an opportunity, I did not rise until the leader of the meeting rose, but every one saw my intention, and my speechless confession of Christ before men helped me to sing 'Praise God from whom all blessings flow' as never before. The next day, on my way to New York and Hartford, the trees and even the crooked rail fences seemed to be singing it with me, without interruption or intermission. Everywhere everything was vocal with its spiritual melody."[2337]

John Farwell recorded a remarkable experience in which Abraham Lincoln visited the Moody Sunday School of Chicago. Lincoln's words to the children of the Moody Sunday School exerted a powerful effect, according to Farwell, who recounted that one of the boys who heard President Lincoln speak served in the Civil War as a captain, and later became Postmaster of Chicago.[2338]

"After Mr. Lincoln was elected President, but before he was inaugurated, he visited Mr. Moody's Sunday school on the condition that he would not be asked for a speech. He left the dinner table of one of Chicago's prominent citizens and the assembled guests to keep this appointment. When the opening exercises were concluded, Mr. Moody remarked that the President had visited them on condition that he was not to be asked to speak, but if he wished to say anything after seeing and hearing fifteen hundred poor children sing the Gospel of Christ, of course they would keep their ears open, as they would probably never have another President of the United States there. As Lincoln moved down the center of such an audience, he stopped and said in substance: 'I was once as poor as any child here, and I want to say to you that if you learn and obey the teachings of the Bible in your lives, some one of you may become a President of the United States some day.' When the war broke out and Lincoln called for troops, seventy-five young men from this school enlisted. One eighteen year old boy was chosen captain of a Board of Trade regiment company

---

[2337] Farwell, John Villiers. (1911). Some Recollections of John V. Farwell: A Brief Description of his Early Life and Business Reminiscences. P. 102. Chicago, IL: R. R. Donnelley & Sons Company. Google Books.
[2338] Farwell, John Villiers. (1911). Some Recollections of John V. Farwell: A Brief Description of his Early Life and Business Reminiscences. Pp. 103-104. Chicago, IL: R. R. Donnelley & Sons Company. Google Books.

and distinguished himself. After the war he became the postmaster of Chicago."[2339]

The Winnipeg Tribune of Canada identified the young man from the Moody Sunday School who went on to municipal and national public service. That young man who became Postmaster of Chicago was James Andrew Sexton, who also held the chief command of the Grand Army of the Republic.[2340] The principle of visionary succession was described by Andrew Taylor Call in that author's 2005 book, *Jacob Bunn: Legacy of an Illinois Industrial Pioneer*. Call defined the principle of visionary succession as follows:

> "Inheriting the fundamental and essential ethics of vision, integrity and legacy from business mentors, and then in turn 'bequeathing' these same principles to the next generation of leaders. . .The concepts of legator, the one who bestows, and legatee, the one who receives, are appropriate in this instance, as they accurately describe the nature of the relationship between the parties in the context of Visionary Succession."[2341]

Abraham Lincoln mentored John W. Bunn in politics.[2342] Jacob Bunn mentored John W. Bunn in business.[2343] Jacob Bunn, Jr., John W. Bunn, and Henry Bunn mentored Robert Carr Lanphier in business.[2344] The principle of visionary succession runs throughout the course of this book and the author's 2005 history referenced immediately above. Abraham Lincoln mentored the young men of Mr. Moody's Chicago Sunday school.[2345] Jacob Bunn mentored Watson Bradley Dickerman at the J. Bunn Bank of Springfield. The young Dickerman went on to New York City, established the Dominick and Dickerman Company, the oldest brokerage firm of New York City, and served as President of the New York Stock

---

[2339] Farwell, John Villiers. (1911). Some Recollections of John V. Farwell: A Brief Description of his Early Life and Business Reminiscences. Pp. 103-104. Chicago, IL: R. R. Donnelley & Sons Company. Google Books.

[2340] The Winnipeg Tribune. (February 1, 1919). P. 32. Newspapers.com.

[2341] Call, Andrew Taylor. (2005). Jacob Bunn: Legacy of an Illinois Industrial Pioneer. P. 243. Lawrenceville, VA: Brunswick Publishing Corporation.

[2342] See chapter sections and references provided in this chapter, *supra*.

[2343] Call, Andrew Taylor. (2005). Jacob Bunn: Legacy of an Illinois Industrial Pioneer. Lawrenceville, VA: Brunswick Publishing Corporation.

[2344] Lanphier, Robert Carr, and Thomas , Benjamin. (1949). Sangamo: A History of Fifty Years. Springfield, IL: Sangamo Electric Company; Call, Andrew Taylor. (2005). Jacob Bunn: Legacy of an Illinois Industrial Pioneer. P. 243. Lawrenceville, VA: Brunswick Publishing Corporation.

[2345] Farwell, John Villiers. (1911). Some Recollections of John V. Farwell: A Brief Description of his Early Life and Business Reminiscences. Pp. 101-115. Chicago, IL: R. R. Donnelley & Sons Company. Google Books.

Exchange in 1890-1891.[2346] Dickerman also served as President of the Norfolk & Southern Railroad Company, and as a member of the board of directors of the Long Island Loan & Trust Company.[2347] Jacob Bunn also mentored Floyd K. Whittemore, who worked for Bunn as Cashier at the J. Bunn Bank of Springfield. Whittemore relocated to Chicago, served as the Acting Assistant United States Treasurer at Chicago in the Benjamin Harrison administration, and served as the State Treasurer of Illinois.[2348] Abraham Lincoln mentored John W. Bunn. John V. Farwell mentored Marshall Field. Marshall Field mentored Aaron Montgomery Ward. These relationships all demonstrate the principle of visionary succession.

Charles Benjamin Farwell (1823-1903) attended Elmira Academy in New York.[2349] He conducted farming and surveying work in Illinois, and relocated to Chicago, where he served as Clerk of Cook County from 1853 until 1861.[2350] He was Chairman of the Cook County Board of Supervisors in 1868, and was National Bank Examiner in 1869.[2351] Farwell ran successfully as a Republican for the United States Congress, and served in the Forty-Second and Forty-Third Congresses (1871-1875).[2352] When Gen. John A. Logan, United States Senator from Illinois, died in 1893, Farwell was elected to fill Logan's Senate seat from Illinois.[2353] Senator Farwell held that office from 1887 until 1891, died in Lake Forest, Illinois, and was interred at Rosehill Cemetery in Chicago.[2354] Charles Farwell was a friend of Jacob Bunn and John Whitfield Bunn, and formed part of the Illinois Republican industrial network that influenced so much of Chicago, the State of Illinois, and

---

[2346] Call, Andrew Taylor. (2005). Jacob Bunn: Legacy of an Illinois Industrial Pioneer. Pp. 169-170. Lawrenceville, VA: Brunswick Publishing Corporation; Hall, Henry. (1895-1896). America's Successful Men of Affairs: An Encyclopedia of Contemporaneous Biography. Vol. 1. P. 192. New York, NY: The New York Tribune.

[2347] Call, Andrew Taylor. (2005). Jacob Bunn: Legacy of an Illinois Industrial Pioneer. Pp. 169-170. Lawrenceville, VA: Brunswick Publishing Corporation; Hall, Henry. (1895-1896). America's Successful Men of Affairs: An Encyclopedia of Contemporaneous Biography. Vol. 1. P. 192. New York, NY: The New York Tribune.

[2348] Call, Andrew Taylor. (2005). Jacob Bunn: Legacy of an Illinois Industrial Pioneer. Pp. 169-170. Lawrenceville, VA: Brunswick Publishing Corporation; Witherspoon, Halliday. (1902). Men of Illinois. P. 425. Chicago, IL: Halliday Witherspoon.

[2349] Biographical Directory of the United States Congress: 1774-Present. Charles Benjamin Farwell. Bioguide.congress.gov.

[2350] Biographical Directory of the United States Congress: 1774-Present. Charles Benjamin Farwell. Bioguide.congress.gov.

[2351] Biographical Directory of the United States Congress: 1774-Present. Charles Benjamin Farwell. Bioguide.congress.gov.

[2352] Biographical Directory of the United States Congress: 1774-Present. Charles Benjamin Farwell. Bioguide.congress.gov.

[2353] Biographical Directory of the United States Congress: 1774-Present. Charles Benjamin Farwell. Bioguide.congress.gov.

[2354] Biographical Directory of the United States Congress: 1774-Present. Charles Benjamin Farwell. Bioguide.congress.gov.

the United States during the Civil War, the Reconstruction Era, and the Gilded Age.

John V. Farwell was a principal developer of the Rogers Park community and founded the Rogers Park Building and Land Company in cooperation with Paul Pratt, George Pratt, Luther L. Greenleaf, Stephen P. Lunt, George Estes, and Charles H. Morse.[2355] The company developed the settlement that had been established by Philip McGregor Rogers, Catherine Rogers, and Patrick Touhy, who married Catherine Rogers.[2356]

Thomas Keister Greer, Esq.:

Lawyer of Virginia and San Francisco whose Corporate Clients Competed with

the Chicago Meatpacking Industry

It is important at this point for me to give a biography of my late stepfather, Thomas Keister Greer, Esq. (1921-2008), whose legal career connected overwhelmingly to California companies that were in direct competition with the Chicago meatpacking industry. Thomas Keister Greer's California corporate client, the Miller & Lux Company of San Francisco, competed directly with the Chicago meatpacking and agribusiness industries that John Whitfield Bunn, Jacob Bunn, John Stryker, Stephen Williamson Stryker, Morris Selz, Charles Schwab, Joseph Rutter, Max Meyer, Gustavus Franklin Swift, Philip Danforth Armour, Nelson Morris, Patrick Cudahy, Michael Cudahy, and Thomas E. Wilson, among many others, created, built, and developed.

Thomas Keister Greer, Esq. of Rocky Mount, Virginia, and San Francisco, was Junior General Counsel to the Miller & Lux Company of San Francisco by the age of thirty-three. The Miller & Lux Company was one of the greatest and most significant cattle, land, and meatpacking companies in American history, and was one of the most important competitors of the Chicago meatpacking industry.[2357] Thomas Keister Greer was born in Premier, McDowell County, West Virginia, and was the son of Moses Theodrick Greer and Goldie Lillian (Shaw) Greer. The Greers were a founding family of Virginia, and resided in Franklin County, Virginia, for many generations before a fire caused them to lose their home. The Greer family then moved to the coalfields of McDowell County, West Virginia, after the fire in 1900.[2358] The Shaw family, originally of Carroll County, Virginia, relocated to Roanoke, Virginia, where William Fernoy Shaw, the father of Goldie

[2355] Archer, Jacque Day, and Santoro, Jamie Wirsbinski. (2007). Images of America: Rogers Park. P. 20. Charleston, SC: Arcadia Publishing. Google Books.

[2356] Archer, Jacque Day, and Santoro, Jamie Wirsbinski. (2007). Images of America: Rogers Park. Pp. 7, 20. Charleston, SC: Arcadia Publishing. Google Books.

[2357] Igler, David. (2001). Industrial Cowboys: Miller & Lux and the Transformation of the Far West, 1850-1920. Berkeley, CA: University of California Press. Google Books.

[2358] Greer family history records.

Lillian Shaw, co-founded and co-owned a soda pop manufacturing company.[2359] After a time of residence in Roanoke, the Shaw family moved to Welch, in McDowell County, West Virginia, where William Fernoy Shaw owned a contracting company. Moses Theodrick Greer and Goldie Lillian (Shaw) Greer were the step-grandparents of author Andrew Taylor Call.[2360]

Moses Theodrick Greer trained as a butcher in Cincinnati, Ohio, and returned to Welch to work as a butcher for the Premier-Pocahontas Coal Company.[2361] Moses T. Greer also managed coal company grocery stores all over McDowell County for the rest of his life. Thomas Keister Greer moved to Roanoke, Virginia, in about 1936, with his mother and siblings. His father, Moses, remained in West Virginia and visited when he was able.[2362] The old Route 460, which connects Roanoke, Virginia, to the coalfields of Virginia and West Virginia, ran through Salem, Shawsville, Elliston, Christiansburg, Blacksburg, Pembroke, Pearisburg, Narrows, and Glen Lyn, all in Virginia. The road connected Roanoke County, Montgomery County, Giles County, Bland County, Tazewell County, and Buchanan County, all in Virginia. Moses T. Greer referred to one section of the old road near Shawsville as the, "long straight stretch," because of its very long and straight section in the Shawsville vicinity, an unusual case for a road in the Appalachian Mountains.[2363] Author Andrew Taylor Call drove this same road for three years between Rocky Mount, Virginia, Roanoke, and Grundy, Virginia, while a law student at the Appalachian School of Law. The long straight stretch of Route 460 in the Appalachian Mountains of southwest Virginia has been an important road of memories for the Call and Greer families for several generations.[2364] The long straight stretch paralleled the old Norfolk and Western Railway Company routes that connected Roanoke to southwest Virginia, West Virginia, Kentucky, and Ohio. These routes were among the most significant coal hauling routes in the country.[2365]

Thomas Keister Greer was an alumnus of Andrew Lewis High School in Salem, Virginia. He was also an alumnus both of the University of Virginia and the University of Virginia School of Law. He was the foremost riparian rights lawyer in the United States. He won the Virginia Debating Championship with three fellow Andrew Lewis High School classmates, won a Du Pont Scholarship to the University of Virginia, and served as an officer in the United States Marine Corps during World War II. He survived the Battle of Okinawa. Greer returned from the war and finished his studies as a History Major (with Honors) at the University of Virginia.[2366] He then entered the law school of the University of Virginia and graduated in 1948. Greer entered law practice in Virginia and California. He was

---

[2359] Greer and Shaw family history records.
[2360] Greer and Shaw family history records.
[2361] Greer family history records.
[2362] Greer family history records.
[2363] Greer family history records.
[2364] Greer and Call family history records.
[2365] Greer and Call family history records.
[2366] Greer and Call family history records.

a member of the Jefferson Literary and Debating Society while at the University of Virginia and was a member of the University of Virginia Cross Country Team.[2367]

Greer was a member of the California Bar, the Virginia Bar, and the San Francisco Bar Association. Greer was the General Counsel for, and a member of the board of directors of, the Salyer Land Company of California. He also served as counsel to the Crockett & Gamboge Company of California. Both of these companies were leading American agribusiness companies. The California companies named here were all immense land, cattle, cash crop, and water companies. Greer rose to the top of the corporate law and riparian rights law practice sectors of California, and argued cases before the California Supreme Court, the United States Supreme Court, and the United States Courts of Appeal for the Fourth, Seventh, and Ninth Circuits.[2368] He played a key role in the litigation victory for the Miller & Lux Company in the 1950s, solved the largest corporate fraud case in California legal history up to that time, and helped save the Miller & Lux Company. This case established Greer permanently and was the basis for his becoming one of the leading corporate litigators in the United States.[2369]

Greer served on the board of directors of First Virginia Bank of Rocky Mount, Virginia, and served on the boards of directors of the Bank of Boone's Mill, the Bank of Ferrum, the People's National Bank of Rocky Mount, and the large parent First Virginia Banks Company of Falls Church, all in Virginia. Greer owned the *Franklin County Times*, a newspaper of Rocky Mount, and was an owner of multiple land interests. He served eight years on the Board of Visitors (board of directors) of the University of Virginia, having been appointed by Virginia Governors to two consecutive four-year terms. He founded the Franklin County Historical Society and was a recognized legal historian, historian of Virginia, historian of the Civil War, and historian of American politics. His book, *The Great Moonshine Conspiracy Trial of 1935*, remains a classic of Virginia legal history. Greer's University of Virginia Senior Honors Thesis, *Genesis of a Virginia Frontier: The Origins of Franklin County, Virginia, 1740-1785*, remains a classic account of the creation and early history of Franklin County, Virginia. It was the title of this work by Thomas Greer that inspired author Andrew Taylor Call to name the first chapter of the present book, *Genesis of a Great Lakes Frontier*.[2370]

[2367] Call, Taylor, and Greer family historical records.
[2368] Call, Taylor, and Greer family historical records.
[2369] Call, Taylor, and Greer family historical records.
[2370] Call, Taylor, and Greer family historical records.

Chapter 5

The Foundations of Jackson Park

"For which of you, intending to build a tower, sitteth not down first, and counteth
the cost, whether he have *sufficient* to finish *it*?"

Luke 14:28

<u>Introduction</u>

This chapter concerns the Willard, Richardson, Bunn, Comstock, and Talcott
families of Chicago and the Cook County metropolitan region. This chapter is a
narrative of how Chicago and Cook County changed the faces of construction
methodologies, construction materials, the manufacture of standardized railroad
wheels, the engineering and construction of continental railroad systems and
harbor infrastructure in North America, Asia, and South America, inventions of
food and beverage machinery, and the development of aviation technology in the
service of national defense, patriotic civilian participation, and continental safety.
Chicago laid the foundations of Jackson Park, and upon these grounds helped
establish the future of North America and the Midwest as places of global vision,
economic power, innovation, and legacy.

The Richardson family of Chicago and Springfield possessed multiple
connections to the establishment, development, leadership, and ownership of
diverse United States and international industries and works, many of which were
based in Chicago and Cook County, and many of which affected the surrounding
region. The chapter encompasses the 1893 World's Columbian Exposition, the
building construction industry, inventions, aviation, airborne security and
surveillance, the United States Civil Air Patrol, and other fields of work in and
around Chicago and Cook County. For the Springfield Iron Company history
relevant to William Douglas Richardson and others, consult Chapter 2, *Builders of
the Downtown*.

Multiple members of the Richardson family contributed importantly to the
establishment, planning, coordination, financing, physical construction, and
executive management of the 1893 World's Columbian Exposition. Throughout
this book multiple names are used for the World's Columbian Exposition. These
names include: World's Columbian Exposition, 1893 World's Fair, 1893 Chicago
World's Fair, the Fair, Columbian Exposition, and possibly others. They all refer
to the 1893 World's Columbian Exposition of Chicago. Our family ancestors who
contributed to the 1893 World's Columbian Exposition included no fewer than
three members of my mother's family and one relative from my father's Ohio
family. John Whitfield Bunn, William Douglas Richardson, and Milo Barnum
Richardson were the three ancestors from my mother's family who participated in
the 1893 World's Columbian Exposition. William Henry Burtner of Cincinnati,

Ohio, was the relative from my father's family who contributed to the 1893 Chicago World's Fair. William Douglas Richardson was actively engaged in the Hyde Park community and the Woodlawn community of Chicago through his leadership at the 1893 World's Columbian Exposition. Richardson's contributions were to the construction and manufacture of the buildings and other structural elements of the Chicago World's Fair. He also built many churches and hotels at Chicago. After a period of time of engagement in the insurance and real estate businesses at Springfield, with the company of Richardson & Latham, Richardson entered the building construction business.[2371] He started the Richardson Construction Company.

The Richardson Construction Company had been awarded construction contracts for principal elements of the Illinois State Capitol building and the Abraham Lincoln Monument located in Oak Ridge Cemetery in Springfield.[2372] For the 1893 Chicago World's Fair, Richardson held the office of Superintendent of Exterior Covering.[2373] He also held the office of Superintendent of Buildings and Grounds for the 1893 Chicago World's Fair.[2374] He served the Union in the Civil War and served in subsequent Illinois military service, having served as a colonel in the Illinois National Guard (5th Regiment), to which office he was commissioned on June 20, 1876.[2375] He was frequently known as "Colonel Richardson" among both military and civilian company. Richardson furthermore contributed to the development of Chicago cultural organizations when he served as one of the multiple founding donors of the Columbian Museum in 1893, having contributed $50 towards the creation and support of the Columbian Museum at Hyde Park.[2376]

[2371] Call, Andrew Taylor. (2005). Jacob Bunn: Legacy of an Illinois Industrial Pioneer. Pp. 109-117. Lawrenceville, VA: Brunswick Publishing Corporation. Google Books; Call, Andrew Taylor. (2016). Faded Bricks: Old Family Tales from the South Side of Chicago. Hyde Park History, Vol. 38, (No. 4), Pp. 1-7. Chicago, IL: Hyde Park Historical Society.

[2372] Call, Andrew Taylor. (2005). Jacob Bunn: Legacy of an Illinois Industrial Pioneer. P. 110. Lawrenceville, VA: Brunswick Publishing Corporation. Google Books; Call, Andrew Taylor. (2016). Faded Bricks: Old Family Tales from the South Side of Chicago. Hyde Park History, Vol. 38, (No. 4), Pp. 1-7. Chicago, IL: Hyde Park Historical Society.

[2373] Engineering News and American Railway Journal. (January-June, 1892). Vol. XXVII. P. 50. New York, NY: Engineering News Publishing Co. Google Books; Call, Andrew Taylor. (2016). Faded Bricks: Old Family Tales from the South Side of Chicago. Hyde Park History, Vol. 38, (No. 4), Pp. 1-7. Chicago, IL: Hyde Park Historical Society.

[2374] Call, Andrew Taylor. (2005). Jacob Bunn: Legacy of an Illinois Industrial Pioneer. P. 110. Lawrenceville, VA: Brunswick Publishing Corporation. Google Books; Call, Andrew Taylor. (2016). Faded Bricks: Old Family Tales from the South Side of Chicago. Hyde Park History, Vol. 38, (No. 4), Pp. 1-7. Chicago, IL: Hyde Park Historical Society.

[2375] Biennial Report of the Adjutant-General of Illinois, appearing within Reports Made to the General Assembly of Illinois at Its Thirtieth Regular Session. Vol. I, Part I. (1875-1876). P. 341. Springfield, IL: D. W. Lusk & Company, State Printer. Google Books.

[2376] Gifts for Museum. *Chicago Tribune*. (Nov. 5, 1893). P. 12. Chicago Tribune Archives. Archives.chicagotribune.com; Call, Andrew Taylor. (2016). Faded Bricks: Old

The Columbian Museum initially existed at Hyde Park, and occupied the Palace of Fine Arts building.[2377] The Columbian Museum of Chicago would become known subsequently as the Field Museum.[2378] The Field Museum remains one of the largest and greatest museums of natural history and anthropology in the world, and possesses a diverse and immense collection comprising some 30 million specimens.[2379] While it was possible that the William D. Richardson who was the chemist and executive at Swift & Company of Chicago was the William D. Richardson who contributed the $50 to the Columbian Museum in 1893, it is more probable that the donor was William Douglas Richardson, who oversaw construction of the World's Fair and the very place of the Columbian Museum. There were two, and possibly three, men named William D. Richardson in Chicago at this time.

Milo Barnum Richardson, a first cousin of William Douglas Richardson, held membership within the Connecticut Board of World's Fair Commissioners for the 1893 World's Columbian Exposition of Chicago.[2380] Milo B. Richardson served also as President of the Barnum & Richardson Company, a major manufacturing company with offices and factories in Chicago and in Lime Rock, Connecticut (discussed in detail below).[2381] The Barnum & Richardson Company manufactured railroad wheels, as well as other railroad industry components. The company possessed the distinction of having been the largest railroad parts manufacturer in the United States.[2382] The Chicago office of the Barnum & Richardson Company

Family Tales from the South Side of Chicago. Hyde Park History, Vol. 38, (No. 4), Pp. 1-7. Chicago, IL: Hyde Park Historical Society.

[2377] Ford, Liam T. A. (2009). Soldier Field: A Stadium and Its City. P. 7. Chicago, IL: The University of Chicago Press. Google Books; Call, Andrew Taylor. (2016). Faded Bricks: Old Family Tales from the South Side of Chicago. Hyde Park History, Vol. 38, (No. 4), Pp. 1-7. Chicago, IL: Hyde Park Historical Society.

[2378] Field Museum History. (2016). Para. 5. Fieldmuseum.org. History Section; Call, Andrew Taylor. (2016). Faded Bricks: Old Family Tales from the South Side of Chicago. Hyde Park History, Vol. 38, (No. 4), Pp. 1-7. Chicago, IL: Hyde Park Historical Society.

[2379] Field Museum (2016). Para. 1. Fieldmuseum.org; Call, Andrew Taylor. (2016). Faded Bricks: Old Family Tales from the South Side of Chicago. Hyde Park History, Vol. 38, (No. 4), Pp. 1-7. Chicago, IL: Hyde Park Historical Society.

[2380] Connecticut At The World's Fair: Report Of The Commissioners From Connecticut Of The Columbian Exposition of 1893 At Chicago. (1898). Hartford, CT: Press of the Case, Lockwood & Brainard Company. Pp. 28, 146, 148. Retrieved from Google Books; Call, Andrew Taylor. (2016). Faded Bricks: Old Family Tales from the South Side of Chicago. Hyde Park History, Vol. 38, (No. 4), Pp. 1-7. Chicago, IL: Hyde Park Historical Society.

[2381] Certified List of Illinois Corporations. (1905). Danville, IL: Illinois Printing Company. P. 283. Retrieved from Google Books; Call, Andrew Taylor. (2016). Faded Bricks: Old Family Tales from the South Side of Chicago. Hyde Park History, Vol. 38, (No. 4), Pp. 1-7. Chicago, IL: Hyde Park Historical Society.

[2382] William Henry Barnum Passes Away. Masonrytoday.com; Call, Andrew Taylor. (2016). Faded Bricks: Old Family Tales from the South Side of Chicago. Hyde Park History, Vol. 38, (No. 4), Pp. 1-7. Chicago, IL: Hyde Park Historical Society.

was located at 64 S. Jefferson, located in the Near West community of Chicago.[2383] Milo Barnum Richardson was a first cousin of my great-great-great-grandfather, William Douglas Richardson, and was a part of the family of my grandmother Elizabeth (Bunn) Taylor.[2384] The present chapter will concentrate on the following persons who were directly connected to Chicago and Cook County through residence, work, business, or some combination of these factors: William Douglas Richardson, Leonard Richardson, Milo Barnum Richardson, Charles Richardson, Jr., Willard Richardson, Dr. Frank Richardson, Myron Hutchinson Richardson, Charles Richardson, Esq., James Henry Richardson, Hiram Adsit Richardson, and the wives of these people. As with most people in this book, many of these individuals connected in various manners to places other than Chicago, as well.

To summarize, this chapter will include histories of the Willard, Richardson, Barnum, Talcott, Comstock, Lewis, Whiting, and other branches from my maternal grandmother's family from Illinois, New York, and New England. Let us first provide the genealogical history of the four Chicago-connected Willard families discussed herein.

<u>The Willard Family Genealogy of New England and Illinois</u>

Henry Willard (1655-1701), son of Maj. Simon Willard, married Mary Lakin.[2385] The children of Henry and Mary (Lakin) Willard were as follows: Henry Willard; Simon Willard; John Willard; **Hezekiah Willard**; Mary Willard; Sarah Willard; Joseph Willard; Samuel Willard; James Willard; Josiah Willard; Abigail Willard; Jonathan Willard; Susanna Willard; and Tabitha Willard.[2386] **Hezekiah Willard married Anna Wilder**. Anna was the daughter of Thomas Wilder. The children born to Hezekiah and Anna (Wilder) Willard were as follows: Thomas Willard; Phineas Willard; Hezekiah Willard; Anna Willard; Mary Willard; **Ephraim Willard**; and Elizabeth Willard.[2387]

[2383] The Lakeside Annual Directory of the City of Chicago. (1876). Chicago, IL: Donnelly, Loyd & Company. P. 149. Retrieved from Google Books; Call, Andrew Taylor. (2016). Faded Bricks: Old Family Tales from the South Side of Chicago. Hyde Park History, Vol. 38, (No. 4), Pp. 1-7. Chicago, IL: Hyde Park Historical Society.

[2384] Call Family, Bunn Family, and Richardson Family genealogical records. Call, Andrew Taylor. (2016). Faded Bricks: Old Family Tales from the South Side of Chicago. Hyde Park History, Vol. 38, (No. 4), Pp. 1-7. Chicago, IL: Hyde Park Historical Society.

[2385] Willard, Joseph, Walker, Charles Wilkes, Pope, Henry Charles. (1915). Willard Genealogy, Sequel to Willard Memoir. P. 18. Boston, MASS: The Willard Family Association. Archive.org.

[2386] Willard, Joseph, Walker, Charles Wilkes, Pope, Henry Charles. (1915). Willard Genealogy, Sequel to Willard Memoir. Pp. 18-20. Boston, MASS: The Willard Family Association. Archive.org.

[2387] Willard, Joseph, Walker, Charles Wilkes, Pope, Henry Charles. (1915). Willard Genealogy, Sequel to Willard Memoir. P. 32. Boston, MASS: The Willard Family Association. Archive.org.

Ephraim Willard (1726-1803) married Azubah Atherton.[2388] Azubah was the daughter of Peter Atherton and Experience (Wright) Atherton. The children of Ephraim Willard and Azubah (Atherton) Willard were as follows: Ephraim Willard, Jr.; Israel Willard; Azubah Willard; Lois Willard; Joshua Willard; Experience Willard; Mercy Willard; Anna Willard; Lucy Willard; Katy Willard; and Peter Willard.[2389] **Ephraim Willard, Jr. (1748-1821) married Lois Geary (also spelled Gary) (1754-1834).**[2390] Ephraim served under Captain Thomas Gates on the march to Cambridge, Massachusetts, when the company was answering the call to the Lexington Alarm of April 19, 1775.[2391] Ephraim also served on a Bennington Alarm in 1777, having served as a sergeant under Captain Stuart in Col. Josiah Willard's regiment.[2392] The following children were born to Ephraim and Lois (Geary) Willard: Dorothy Willard; Abel Willard; Elizabeth Willard; Israel Willard; Joseph Willard; Lois Willard; Ephraim Willard; Manasseh Willard; Clarissa Willard; **Asa Willard**; Catherine Willard; Orissa Willard; and Joshua Willard.[2393]

Asa Willard (1789-1847) married Lucy Whiting, and moved to Illinois. The Willard-Whiting lineages include the following families and ancestors: Maj. Simon Willard; Massachusetts Governor and Harvard University co-founder Thomas Dudley; Massachusetts Governor Simon Bradstreet; the poet Anne (Dudley) Bradstreet; Judge Thomas Danforth; Capt. Thomas Lake; Rev. Samuel Whiting; Rev. Joseph Whiting; Rev. John Whiting; Rev. Josiah Brown; and many others. Lucy (Whiting) Willard descended from many of the founding families of New England, including the Whiting family itself.

[2388] Willard, Joseph, Walker, Charles Wilkes, Pope, Henry Charles. (1915). Willard Genealogy, Sequel to Willard Memoir. Pp. 54-55. Boston, MASS: The Willard Family Association. Archive.org

[2389] Willard, Joseph, Walker, Charles Wilkes, Pope, Henry Charles. (1915). Willard Genealogy, Sequel to Willard Memoir. Pp. 54-55. Boston, MASS: The Willard Family Association. Archive.org

[2390] Willard, Joseph, Walker, Charles Wilkes, Pope, Henry Charles. (1915). Willard Genealogy, Sequel to Willard Memoir. P. 116. Boston, MASS: The Willard Family Association. Archive.org

[2391] Willard, Joseph, Walker, Charles Wilkes, Pope, Henry Charles. (1915). Willard Genealogy, Sequel to Willard Memoir. P. 116. Boston, MASS: The Willard Family Association. Archive.org

[2392] Willard, Joseph, Walker, Charles Wilkes, Pope, Henry Charles. (1915). Willard Genealogy, Sequel to Willard Memoir. P. 116. Boston, MASS: The Willard Family Association. Archive.org

[2393] Willard, Joseph, Walker, Charles Wilkes, Pope, Henry Charles. (1915). Willard Genealogy, Sequel to Willard Memoir. P. 116. Boston, MASS: The Willard Family Association. Archive.org

The Whiting-Cotton-Danforth-Bradstreet-Dudley Lineage

Historian Charles Henry Browning recorded the Whiting history and traced the Whiting lineage back to William the Conqueror.[2394] Browning was a member of the American Historical Association, and his work remains an important resource for research to this day.[2395] The Willard-Whiting lineage of descent proceeds as follows from Rev. Samuel Whiting, the immigrant ancestor of the family. Rev. Samuel Whiting (1597-1679) married Elizabeth St. John (1605-1677).[2396] Samuel and Elizabeth (St. John) Whiting immigrated to America in 1636, and settled at Lynn, Massachusetts.[2397] One of the children born to Samuel and Elizabeth was **Rev. Joseph Whiting (1641-1723), who married Sarah Danforth.**[2398] Sarah was the daughter of Judge Thomas Danforth, who served as Deputy Governor of Massachusetts and as President/Governor of Maine.[2399] Thomas Danforth also served as the founding Treasurer of Harvard College, and as a judge at the Salem Witch Trials of Salem, Massachusetts.[2400] **Rev. John Whiting (1681-1752) was a son of Rev. Joseph Whiting and Sarah (Danforth) Whiting, and married Mary Cotton (1689-1731), who was the daughter of Rev. John Cotton.**[2401] By paternal lineage, Mary Cotton was the granddaughter of Rev. Seaborn Cotton and the great-granddaughter of Rev. John Cotton of Boston, England, who later was a founder of Boston, Massachusetts.[2402] Mary (Cotton) Whiting's mother was Anne (Lake) Cotton, who was the daughter of Thomas Lake,[2403] co-founder and owner of the Clark & Lake Company that developed the Kennebec, Maine, colony, Arrowsic Island, and much industry in colonial coastal Maine.[2404] Mary (Cotton) Whiting's grandmother, Dorothy (Bradstreet) Cotton, was the daughter of

---

[2394] Browning, Charles Henry. (1891). Americans of Royal Descent. 2nd Edition. Philadelphia, PA: Porter & Coates. Google Books.

[2395] Browning, Charles Henry. (1891). Americans of Royal Descent. 2nd Edition. Philadelphia, PA: Porter & Coates. Google Books.

[2396] Browning, Charles Henry. (1891). Americans of Royal Descent. 2nd Edition. P. 72 Philadelphia, PA: Porter & Coates. Google Books.

[2397] Browning, Charles Henry. (1891). Americans of Royal Descent. 2nd Edition. P. 72 Philadelphia, PA: Porter & Coates. Google Books.

[2398] Browning, Charles Henry. (1891). Americans of Royal Descent. 2nd Edition. P. 72 Philadelphia, PA: Porter & Coates. Google Books.

[2399] Browning, Charles Henry. (1891). Americans of Royal Descent. 2nd Edition. P. 72 Philadelphia, PA: Porter & Coates. Google Books.

[2400] Danforth, Cotton, Dudley, Bradstreet, Whiting, Willard family history records.

[2401] Browning, Charles Henry. (1891). Americans of Royal Descent. 2nd Edition. P. 72 Philadelphia, PA: Porter & Coates. Google Books.

[2402] Browning, Charles Henry. (1891). Americans of Royal Descent. 2nd Edition. P. 72 Philadelphia, PA: Porter & Coates. Google Books.

[2403] Browning, Charles Henry. (1891). Americans of Royal Descent. 2nd Edition. P. 72 Philadelphia, PA: Porter & Coates. Google Books.

[2404] Danforth, Cotton, Dudley, Bradstreet, Whiting, Willard family history records.

Massachusetts Governor Simon Bradstreet and the granddaughter of Massachusetts Governor Thomas Dudley.[2405]

Thomas Dudley's daughter, the poet Anne Dudley, married Simon Bradstreet (becoming known to history as the poet, Anne Bradstreet).[2406] Simon and Anne (Dudley) Bradstreet's daughter, Dorothy Bradstreet, married Rev. Seaborn Cotton.[2407] Rev. John Cotton, son of Rev. Seaborn and Dorothy (Bradstreet) Cotton, married Anne Lake.[2408] Mary Cotton, daughter of Rev. John Cotton and Anne (Lake) Cotton, married Rev. John Whiting.[2409] The children born to Rev. John Whiting and Mary (Cotton) Whiting included the following persons: Judge Thomas Whiting (1717-1776); and Mary Whiting (b. 1713).[2410] **Judge Thomas Whiting married Mary Lake**, who was probably kin to Captain Thomas Lake, the aforementioned colonial business and industrial pioneer of Kennebec, Maine.[2411] Thomas Whiting and Mary (Lake) Whiting had the following children: **William Whiting (1760-1832), who married Rebecca Brown**; Mary Whiting, who married first, Capt. Barron, and second, Judge Simon Strong; Lucy Whiting, who married Dr. Joseph Hunt; and Lydia Whiting, who married John Mullekin.[2412]

William Whiting (1760-1832) married Rebecca Brown (1762-1848).[2413] Rebecca was the daughter of Rev. Josiah Brown and Mary (Prentiss) Brown.[2414] Mary (Prentiss) Brown was the daughter of Rev. John Prentiss of Lancaster.[2415] The children born to William and Rebecca (Brown) Whiting included the

[2405] Browning, Charles Henry. (1891). Americans of Royal Descent. 2nd Edition. Pp. 72-73 Philadelphia, PA: Porter & Coates. Google Books; Drake, Samuel G. (1855). The New England Historical and Genealogical Register. Vol. IX. P. 113. Boston, MASS: New England Historic Genealogical Society. Samuel G. Drake, Publisher. Google Books.
[2406] Drake, Samuel G. (1855). The New England Historical and Genealogical Register. Vol. IX. P. 113. Boston, MASS: New England Historic Genealogical Society. Samuel G. Drake, Publisher. Google Books.
[2407] Drake, Samuel G. (1855). The New England Historical and Genealogical Register. Vol. IX. P. 113. Boston, MASS: New England Historic Genealogical Society. Samuel G. Drake, Publisher. Google Books.
[2408] Browning, Charles Henry. (1891). Americans of Royal Descent. 2nd Edition. P. 72 Philadelphia, PA: Porter & Coates. Google Books.
[2409] Browning, Charles Henry. (1891). Americans of Royal Descent. 2nd Edition. P. 72 Philadelphia, PA: Porter & Coates. Google Books.
[2410] Browning, Charles Henry. (1891). Americans of Royal Descent. 2nd Edition. Pp. 72-73 Philadelphia, PA: Porter & Coates. Google Books.
[2411] Browning, Charles Henry. (1891). Americans of Royal Descent. 2nd Edition. P. 72 Philadelphia, PA: Porter & Coates. Google Books.
[2412] Browning, Charles Henry. (1891). Americans of Royal Descent. 2nd Edition. Pp. 72-73 Philadelphia, PA: Porter & Coates. Google Books.
[2413] Browning, Charles Henry. (1891). Americans of Royal Descent. 2nd Edition. P. 72 Philadelphia, PA: Porter & Coates. Google Books.
[2414] Browning, Charles Henry. (1891). Americans of Royal Descent. 2nd Edition. P. 72 Philadelphia, PA: Porter & Coates. Google Books.
[2415] Browning, Charles Henry. (1891). Americans of Royal Descent. 2nd Edition. P. 72 Philadelphia, PA: Porter & Coates. Google Books.

following persons: William Whiting, who married Hannah Conant; Harriet Whiting, who married Jonas Haven; Henry Whiting; Prentiss Whiting, who married Harriet Willard; Mary Whiting, who married Frederick White; **Lucy Whiting, who married Asa Willard**; and George Whiting, who married Julia Ann Weelock.[2416]

In summary, the lineage of Lucy (Whiting) Willard is thus, given by generation from Rev. Samuel Whiting to Lucy (Whiting) Willard, herself: Rev. Samuel Whiting married Elizabeth St. John; Rev. Joseph Whiting married Sarah Danforth; Rev. John Whiting married Mary Cotton; Thomas Whiting married Mary Lake; William Whiting married Rebecca Brown; Lucy Whiting married Asa Willard. Asa Willard and Lucy (Whiting) Willard came to Illinois as early settlers, and their descendants have served as builders of Chicago and Cook County, as well as of Rockford, Rockton, Winnebago County, Springfield and Sangamon County.[2417]

Asa Willard and Lucy (Whiting) Willard of Illinois: The Parents of Four Willard Branches of Illinois that Helped Build Chicago, Cook County, Springfield, Sangamon County, Winnebago County, and Multiple Other Illinois Cities and Counties

Asa Willard married Lucy Whiting.[2418] The children born to this marriage included the following persons: Aurelia Willard; Alexander Perry Willard, who married Louise Higgie of Chemung County, New York; Orissa Willard; Mary Willard; and Sophia Willard. The second wife of Asa Willard was Martha Moore, the daughter of James Moore.[2419] The child born to Asa's second marriage was James Moore Willard (b. 1840).[2420] Asa Willard worked as a cabinetmaker at Lisbon, Kendall County, Illinois. He helped promote the Gospel of Jesus Christ along a fast-growing Illinois frontier.[2421] Asa co-founded the Auxiliary Chapter of the American Bible Society for Grundy County, Illinois, and for Kendall County, Illinois.[2422] The Grundy-Kendall Chapter of the American Bible Society was

---

[2416] Browning, Charles Henry. (1891). Americans of Royal Descent. 2nd Edition. Pp. 72-73 Philadelphia, PA: Porter & Coates. Google Books.

[2417] Danforth, Cotton, Dudley, Bradstreet, Whiting, Willard family history records.

[2418] Willard, Joseph, Walker, Charles Wilkes, Pope, Henry Charles. (1915). Willard Genealogy, Sequel to Willard Memoir. P. 227. Boston, MASS: The Willard Family Association. Archive.org.

[2419] Willard, Joseph, Walker, Charles Wilkes, Pope, Henry Charles. (1915). Willard Genealogy, Sequel to Willard Memoir. P. 227. Boston, MASS: The Willard Family Association. Archive.org.

[2420] Willard, Joseph, Walker, Charles Wilkes, Pope, Henry Charles. (1915). Willard Genealogy, Sequel to Willard Memoir. P. 227. Boston, MASS: The Willard Family Association. Archive.org.

[2421] Thirty-Second Annual Report of the American Bible Society, Presented May 11, 1848. P. 142. New York, NY: American Bible Society. Google Books.

[2422] Thirty-Second Annual Report of the American Bible Society, Presented May 11, 1848. P. 142. New York, NY: American Bible Society. Google Books.

organized in 1847.[2423] Asa Willard held the office of President of the Grundy-Kendall Chapter.[2424] Willard worked with C. C. Wright and Dr. G. Kendall in founding the Grundy-Kendall Chapter of the American Bible Society.[2425] C. C. Wright served as Corresponding Secretary of the Chapter and Dr. G. Kendall was the Treasurer of the Chapter.[2426]

The purpose of the American Bible Society was to promote, share, and publicize the Word of God and the Christian faith, and to fulfill the work of the Great Commission, which is the commandment of Christ Jesus to bring His word to all the nations of the world (the Great Commission is found within the synoptic Gospels of Matthew (Chapter 28), and Mark (Chapter 16)). The Great Commission formed the central purpose, policy, and value of the Constitution of the American Bible Society.[2427] Article I of the Constitution of the American Bible Society stated the purpose of the organization as follows:

> "THIS Society shall be known by the name of the AMERICAN BIBLE SOCIETY, of which the sole object shall be to encourage a wider circulation of the Holy Scriptures without note or comment. The only copies in the English language, to be circulated by the Society, shall be of the version now in common use."[2428]

One of the founders of the American Bible Society, which was a New York City-based organization, was John Prentice Kewley Henshaw, the Episcopal Bishop of Rhode Island.[2429] Rev. John P. K. Henshaw was a member of the Richards-Wolcott-Prentice-Henshaw-McClure-Stryker-Taylor family of New England, New York City, and Illinois. Rev. John P. K. Henshaw was the granduncle of Charlotte (Stryker) Taylor of Illinois (See Chapter 6, *Sprinters of the Steel Track*). A large number of branches of this macro-family would contribute heavily and powerfully to the founding and development of Chicago, Cook County, and the entire civic, political, and economic existence of the surrounding Great Lakes region. Please refer to the following chapters in this book for the Chicago history of the Richards-Wolcott-Prentice-Henshaw-McClure-Stryker-Taylor families:

[2423] Thirty-Second Annual Report of the American Bible Society, Presented May 11, 1848. P. 142. New York, NY: American Bible Society. Google Books.

[2424] Thirty-Second Annual Report of the American Bible Society, Presented May 11, 1848. P. 142. New York, NY: American Bible Society. Google Books.

[2425] Thirty-Second Annual Report of the American Bible Society, Presented May 11, 1848. P. 142. New York, NY: American Bible Society. Google Books.

[2426] Thirty-Second Annual Report of the American Bible Society, Presented May 11, 1848. P. 142. New York, NY: American Bible Society. Google Books.

[2427] Thirty-Second Annual Report of the American Bible Society, Presented May 11, 1848. P. 8. New York, NY: American Bible Society. Google Books.

[2428] Thirty-Second Annual Report of the American Bible Society, Presented May 11, 1848. P. 8. New York, NY: American Bible Society. Google Books.

[2429] Thirty-Second Annual Report of the American Bible Society, Presented May 11, 1848. P. 157. New York, NY: American Bible Society. Google Books.

Genesis of a Great Lakes Frontier; *The Horizons of Hyde Park*; and *Sprinters of the Steel Track*.

Asa Willard and Lucy (Whiting) Willard parented children that would begin several different family branches that would contribute to Chicago and the Chicago metropolitan region in positive and diverse ways. The four Willard branches that would connect directly with the development of Chicago were the Willard-Talcott branch of Rockton and Winnebago County; the Willard-Comstock branch of Winnebago County and Elgin, Kane County, Illinois (Elgin is a northwestern Chicago suburb); the Willard-Lewis branch of the Chicago South Side communities of Woodlawn and Englewood; and the Willard-Richardson-Bunn branch of Chicago and Springfield. Each branch of the family contained people with broadly different experiences. The myriad individuals from the different Willard family branches connected in many ways to a tremendous amount of the urban geography of Chicago and the Great Lakes region.

The Chicago-relevant Willard family branches will be discussed in this chapter, and in the following sequence: the Willard-Talcott line; the Willard-Comstock line; the Willard-Lewis line; and the Willard-Richardson-Bunn line. Each branch of the Willard-Whiting family gave to Illinois in a different way, and descendants of these families settled throughout the entire State, residing in Kendall County, Chicago, Elgin, Winnebago County, Springfield, Sangamon County, Galesburg, Cobden, Union County, and Irvington.

The Willard-Talcott Line

The Willard-Talcott line began with Asa Willard and Lucy (Whiting) Willard's daughter, Sophia E. Willard, who married Thomas Blish Talcott (1806-1888).[2430] Thomas Blish Talcott married Sophia Willard on June 5, 1843, at Rockton, Winnebago County.[2431] Thomas B. Talcott and Sophia (Willard) Talcott were among the developers and promoters of Winnebago County, Illinois.[2432] Thomas was born in Hebron, Connecticut, and was the son of William Talcott and Dorothy (Blish) Talcott.[2433] He grew up partly in Rome, Oneida County, New York. Thomas served as a Major within the 157th New York Militia. He later worked in business at Chemung County, New York, with his brothers Sylvester Talcott and Wait Talcott.[2434] Thomas Blish Talcott was a founder of Rockton, Illinois, and helped to establish Winnebago County, Illinois, with his father, and many other

---

[2430] Portrait And Biographical Record of Winnebago and Boone Counties, Illinois. (1892). P. 681. Chicago, IL: Biographical Publishing Company. Google Books.
[2431] Portrait And Biographical Record of Winnebago and Boone Counties, Illinois. (1892). P. 681. Chicago, IL: Biographical Publishing Company. Google Books.
[2432] Portrait And Biographical Record of Winnebago and Boone Counties, Illinois. (1892). Pp. 681, 682. Chicago, IL: Biographical Publishing Company. Google Books.
[2433] Portrait And Biographical Record of Winnebago and Boone Counties, Illinois. (1892). P. 681. Chicago, IL: Biographical Publishing Company. Google Books.
[2434] Portrait And Biographical Record of Winnebago and Boone Counties, Illinois. (1892). P. 681. Chicago, IL: Biographical Publishing Company. Google Books.

settlers, including William Dunbar, Simon Doty, and Stephen Mack, who was a fur trader from Boston, Massachusetts.[2435] Thomas B. Talcott worked to help develop the governments of Winnebago County in different ways, such as through co-establishing the original Winnebago Board of County Commissioners.[2436] Talcott served as a founding member of the Winnebago County Board of Commissioners.[2437] The space of Winnebago County included at the time of its creation the spaces that would subsequently become Boone County to the east, and a portion of Stephenson County to the west.[2438] The easternmost part of Winnebago County, therefore, would have extended close to what would become the northwestern suburbs of Chicago. Talcott was elected to the Illinois Senate in 1849, and, in this capacity, Talcott represented Winnebago County as a member of the Whig Party. The 1892 biography of Talcott states that he was the first Whig to have been elected to the Illinois Senate from that electoral district of Illinois.[2439]

It was through his service in the Illinois Senate that Talcott was prominently connected, as a promotive legislator, with the creation of the Illinois Central Railroad Company. The biographical report stated the following: "During his term in the Senate, the Illinois Central Railroad was chartered, with the condition of paying the State seven per cent. of its gross earnings."[2440] The Illinois Central Railroad Company came into existence as a corporation on February 10, 1851. The Illinois statutory law that created the company named Robert Schuyler, George Griswold, Gouverneur Morris, Franklin Haven, David A. Neal, Robert Rantoul, Jr., Jonathan Sturgis, George W. Ludlow, John F. A. Sanford, Henry Grinnell, William H. Aspinwall, Leroy Wiley, and Joseph W. Alsop as the incorporators of the new company.[2441] The statutory charter of the railroad company contained a broad geographical plan for the railroad routes to be built: the company was to survey and construct a system of railroad routes that would establish mutual transportation links to the City of Chicago, the Illinois & Michigan Canal, the City of Cairo, the City of Galena, and to a point opposite the Town of Dubuque, Iowa,

---

[2435] Portrait And Biographical Record of Winnebago and Boone Counties, Illinois. (1892). P. 681. Chicago, IL: Biographical Publishing Company. Google Books.
[2436] Portrait And Biographical Record of Winnebago and Boone Counties, Illinois. (1892). P. 681. Chicago, IL: Biographical Publishing Company. Google Books.
[2437] Portrait And Biographical Record of Winnebago and Boone Counties, Illinois. (1892). P. 681. Chicago, IL: Biographical Publishing Company. Google Books.
[2438] Portrait And Biographical Record of Winnebago and Boone Counties, Illinois. (1892). P. 681. Chicago, IL: Biographical Publishing Company. Google Books.
[2439] Portrait And Biographical Record of Winnebago and Boone Counties, Illinois. (1892). P. 681. Chicago, IL: Biographical Publishing Company. Google Books.
[2440] Portrait And Biographical Record of Winnebago and Boone Counties, Illinois. (1892). P. 681. Chicago, IL: Biographical Publishing Company. Google Books.
[2441] AN ACT to incorporate the Illinois Central Railroad company. (February 10, 1851). Private Laws of the State of Illinois Passed at the First Session of the Seventeenth General Assembly, Begun and Held at the City of Springfield, January 6, 1851. P. 61 Springfield, IL: Lanphier & Walker, Printers. Google Books.

located along the Mississippi River.[2442] The Illinois Central Railroad system plan contemplated, therefore, a Lake Michigan—Mississippi River—Ohio River transportation network.

Derivable from the words of the 1851 Act was the fact that the Illinois Central Railroad route and system plan reflected robust expectations regarding the multiple civic and economic benefits that would accrue due to a Great Lakes—Mississippi River—Ohio River transportation network.[2443] The 1851 Act installed a single form of financing by which to capitalize the new company: the statutory financing system provided for a capitalization process using only stock money, and no debt money.[2444] Equity, and not bonded debt, therefore, constituted the means of financing. Section 4 of the Act contained the financing plan and specifically attached to the company the power to raise $1,000,000 in stock money, with the equity stock sum to be divided into shares of $100 each.[2445] The Act also permitted the increase of the stock money sum, and attached the following limit to the financing: the financing could not produce a sum of stock money greater than the total sum of the money consumed in the costs and expenditures undertaken on account of the new company.[2446] Stated alternatively, the Illinois Central Railroad Company financing could produce, through subscriptions, stock money up to the limit that was determined by the metric of the sum of the costs that were accrued on account of the company.[2447]

The first Board of Directors of the Illinois Central Railroad Company consisted of all of the men who served as the incorporators of the Illinois Central (all of

---

[2442] AN ACT to incorporate the Illinois Central Railroad company. (February 10, 1851). Private Laws of the State of Illinois Passed at the First Session of the Seventeenth General Assembly, Begun and Held at the City of Springfield, January 6, 1851. P. 61 Springfield, IL: Lanphier & Walker, Printers. Google Books.

[2443] AN ACT to incorporate the Illinois Central Railroad company. (February 10, 1851). Private Laws of the State of Illinois Passed at the First Session of the Seventeenth General Assembly, Begun and Held at the City of Springfield, January 6, 1851. P. 61 Springfield, IL: Lanphier & Walker, Printers. Google Books.

[2444] AN ACT to incorporate the Illinois Central Railroad company. (February 10, 1851). Private Laws of the State of Illinois Passed at the First Session of the Seventeenth General Assembly, Begun and Held at the City of Springfield, January 6, 1851. P. 62 Springfield, IL: Lanphier & Walker, Printers. Google Books.

[2445] AN ACT to incorporate the Illinois Central Railroad company. (February 10, 1851). Private Laws of the State of Illinois Passed at the First Session of the Seventeenth General Assembly, Begun and Held at the City of Springfield, January 6, 1851. P. 62 Springfield, IL: Lanphier & Walker, Printers. Google Books.

[2446] AN ACT to incorporate the Illinois Central Railroad company. (February 10, 1851). Private Laws of the State of Illinois Passed at the First Session of the Seventeenth General Assembly, Begun and Held at the City of Springfield, January 6, 1851. P. 62 Springfield, IL: Lanphier & Walker, Printers. Google Books.

[2447] AN ACT to incorporate the Illinois Central Railroad company. (February 10, 1851). Private Laws of the State of Illinois Passed at the First Session of the Seventeenth General Assembly, Begun and Held at the City of Springfield, January 6, 1851. P. 62 Springfield, IL: Lanphier & Walker, Printers. Google Books.

whom are named above), except for William H. Aspinwall.[2448] Section 27 of the Act, which is the final clause of the 1851 charter of the Illinois Central, declared the law to be a public act: a law that created an organization (the Illinois Central Railroad Company) in which joinder of public interests and private interests created a union of broad civic interests for the State of Illinois.[2449] The final clause of the Act essentially joined public interests and private interests into a union of holistically-interpreted societal interests, thus promoting a policy and law of cooperation, alliance, and union among public and private interests.[2450] Such policies and laws are commendable at all times, as they recognize that private interests and public interests must operate collectively, constructively, and mutually within a general societal framework for the common good of Mankind.

Thomas Blish Talcott also served as a co-founder and active promoter of the Galena and Chicago Union Railroad Company.[2451] This railroad company was the first railroad to exist in Chicago.[2452] Charles A. Church and H. H. Waldo provided a history of the Galena and Chicago Union Railroad Company in their 1905 work, *Past and Present of the City of Rockford And Winnebago County, Illinois.*[2453] The creation process for the Galena and Chicago Union Railroad Company was slow and prolonged by numerous factors.[2454] The actual incorporation of the company took place on January 16, 1836, with the passage of the Illinois statute entitled, "AN ACT to incorporate the Galena and Chicago Union Railroad Company."[2455]

[2448] AN ACT to incorporate the Illinois Central Railroad company. (February 10, 1851). Private Laws of the State of Illinois Passed at the First Session of the Seventeenth General Assembly, Begun and Held at the City of Springfield, January 6, 1851. P. 63 Springfield, IL: Lanphier & Walker, Printers. Google Books.

[2449] AN ACT to incorporate the Illinois Central Railroad company. (February 10, 1851). Private Laws of the State of Illinois Passed at the First Session of the Seventeenth General Assembly, Begun and Held at the City of Springfield, January 6, 1851. P. 74 Springfield, IL: Lanphier & Walker, Printers. Google Books.

[2450] AN ACT to incorporate the Illinois Central Railroad company. (February 10, 1851). Private Laws of the State of Illinois Passed at the First Session of the Seventeenth General Assembly, Begun and Held at the City of Springfield, January 6, 1851. P. 74 Springfield, IL: Lanphier & Walker, Printers. Google Books.

[2451] Church, Charles A., & Waldo, H. H. (1905). Past and Present of the City of Rockford And Winnebago County, Illinois. Pp. 59-62. Chicago, IL: S. J. Clarke Publishing Company. Google Books.

[2452] Church, Charles A., & Waldo, H. H. (1905). Past and Present of the City of Rockford And Winnebago County, Illinois. P. 59. Chicago, IL: S. J. Clarke Publishing Company. Google Books.

[2453] Church, Charles A., & Waldo, H. H. (1905). Past and Present of the City of Rockford And Winnebago County, Illinois. Pp. 59-62. Chicago, IL: S. J. Clarke Publishing Company. Google Books.

[2454] Church, Charles A., & Waldo, H. H. (1905). Past and Present of the City of Rockford And Winnebago County, Illinois. Pp. 59-62. Chicago, IL: S. J. Clarke Publishing Company. Google Books.

[2455] AN ACT to incorporate the Galena and Chicago Union Railroad Company. (January 16, 1836). Laws of the State of Illinois, Passed By The Ninth General Assembly, At

The purpose of the corporation was to construct a railroad from Chicago to Galena, in Jo Daviess County, Illinois.[2456] The statute empowered the following corporation commissioners to establish the company: William Bennett, Thomas Drummond, J. C. Goodhue, Peter Semple, J. M. Turner, E. D. Taylor, and J. B. Thomas, Jr.[2457] Section 3 of the chartering Act of the railroad company set forth the financing system for the organization. The law established a single form of financing: the capitalization of the corporation would be accomplished through the subscription and payment of $100,000 in stock money. The legislature did not grant the railroad company the power to use debt money in the corporate financing system.[2458] The financing system, therefore, consisted of equity, but not debt. The $100,000 stock money was to be divided into shares of $100 each.[2459] The law granted the company the power to increase the stock money up to a sum of $1,000,000 provided that conditions of economic necessity mandated the increase. The law attached the limit of $1,000,000 to the financing for the company, so that the financing could not produce more than $1,000,000 in total stock money.[2460]

Ebenezer Peck and T. W. Smith were two of the most significant promoters of the Galena and Chicago Union Railroad Company, and their work helped induce the legislation of the Act that chartered the company.[2461] As Church and Waldo stated: "The road became an important factor in the great transportation system of

---

Their Second Session, Commencing December 7, 1835, and Ending January 18, 1836. Pp. 24-30. Vandalia, IL: J. Y. Sawyer, Public Printer. Google Books.

[2456] AN ACT to incorporate the Galena and Chicago Union Railroad Company. (January 16, 1836). Laws of the State of Illinois, Passed By The Ninth General Assembly, At Their Second Session, Commencing December 7, 1835, and Ending January 18, 1836. Pp. 24-25. Vandalia, IL: J. Y. Sawyer, Public Printer. Google Books.

[2457] AN ACT to incorporate the Galena and Chicago Union Railroad Company. (January 16, 1836). Laws of the State of Illinois, Passed By The Ninth General Assembly, At Their Second Session, Commencing December 7, 1835, and Ending January 18, 1836. P. 25. Vandalia, IL: J. Y. Sawyer, Public Printer. Google Books.

[2458] AN ACT to incorporate the Galena and Chicago Union Railroad Company. (January 16, 1836). Laws of the State of Illinois, Passed By The Ninth General Assembly, At Their Second Session, Commencing December 7, 1835, and Ending January 18, 1836. P. 25. Vandalia, IL: J. Y. Sawyer, Public Printer. Google Books.

[2459] AN ACT to incorporate the Galena and Chicago Union Railroad Company. (January 16, 1836). Laws of the State of Illinois, Passed By The Ninth General Assembly, At Their Second Session, Commencing December 7, 1835, and Ending January 18, 1836. P. 25. Vandalia, IL: J. Y. Sawyer, Public Printer. Google Books.

[2460] AN ACT to incorporate the Galena and Chicago Union Railroad Company. (January 16, 1836). Laws of the State of Illinois, Passed By The Ninth General Assembly, At Their Second Session, Commencing December 7, 1835, and Ending January 18, 1836. P. 25. Vandalia, IL: J. Y. Sawyer, Public Printer. Google Books.

[2461] Church, Charles A., & Waldo, H. H. (1905). Past and Present of the City of Rockford And Winnebago County, Illinois. P. 59. Chicago, IL: S. J. Clarke Publishing Company. Google Books.

Chicago, as well as towns along the line."[2462] James Seymour was hired in 1837 as the Chief Engineer for the survey, planning, and construction of the railroad.[2463] Seymour surveyed and plotted the company route from N. Dearborn Street in Chicago to the Des Plaines River.[2464] A moratorium befell the construction process in 1838 and did not lift until 1839.[2465] Construction of necessary railroad infrastructure resumed in 1839, and foundations were laid along Madison Street in Chicago.[2466] Another moratorium set in when the City of Chicago, which had been incorporated only recently prior, on March 4, 1837, failed to produce adequate money for the construction.[2467] The moratorium halted railroad construction and caused fear among the people of Winnebago County and other counties located along the planned route from Chicago to Galena, in Jo Daviess County.[2468] The financial crisis issue, therefore, galvanized the people of Winnebago County, and others, to cooperate to bring the chartered railroad to physical fruition, and to build the first railroad of Chicago.[2469] Church and Waldo stated: "The suspension of operations was a source of profound regret to the citizens of the Rock River Valley, who had made several attempts to obtain better connection with Chicago. . ."[2470]

[2462] Church, Charles A., & Waldo, H. H. (1905). Past and Present of the City of Rockford And Winnebago County, Illinois. P. 59. Chicago, IL: S. J. Clarke Publishing Company. Google Books.
[2463] Church, Charles A., & Waldo, H. H. (1905). Past and Present of the City of Rockford And Winnebago County, Illinois. P. 59. Chicago, IL: S. J. Clarke Publishing Company. Google Books.
[2464] Church, Charles A., & Waldo, H. H. (1905). Past and Present of the City of Rockford And Winnebago County, Illinois. P. 59. Chicago, IL: S. J. Clarke Publishing Company. Google Books.
[2465] Church, Charles A., & Waldo, H. H. (1905). Past and Present of the City of Rockford And Winnebago County, Illinois. P. 59. Chicago, IL: S. J. Clarke Publishing Company. Google Books.
[2466] Church, Charles A., & Waldo, H. H. (1905). Past and Present of the City of Rockford And Winnebago County, Illinois. P. 59. Chicago, IL: S. J. Clarke Publishing Company. Google Books.
[2467] Church, Charles A., & Waldo, H. H. (1905). Past and Present of the City of Rockford And Winnebago County, Illinois. P. 59. Chicago, IL: S. J. Clarke Publishing Company. Google Books.
[2468] Church, Charles A., & Waldo, H. H. (1905). Past and Present of the City of Rockford And Winnebago County, Illinois. P. 59. Chicago, IL: S. J. Clarke Publishing Company. Google Books.
[2469] Church, Charles A., & Waldo, H. H. (1905). Past and Present of the City of Rockford And Winnebago County, Illinois. P. 59. Chicago, IL: S. J. Clarke Publishing Company. Google Books.
[2470] Church, Charles A., & Waldo, H. H. (1905). Past and Present of the City of Rockford And Winnebago County, Illinois. P. 59. Chicago, IL: S. J. Clarke Publishing Company. Google Books.

The historical record contains proofs of the fact that Winnebago County helped to build the first railroad infrastructure of Chicago.[2471] One proof of the central significance of Winnebago County and its people to the completion of the Galena and Chicago Union Railroad Company was that Thomas Blish Talcott, a founder and developer of Winnebago County, served as a Delegate from Winnebago County to the Rockford Convention, the purpose of which was to guarantee the completion of the Galena and Chicago Union Railroad Company.[2472] Sequential conferences took place at which representatives of the places affected by the railroad project contributed support, aid, and promotion to the project: "The agitation was continued in Winnebago County for several years. The first railroad meeting in Rockford was held November 28, 1845."[2473]

Anson Miller served as Chairman of the first Rockford conference, and Seldon M. Church served as Secretary of that conference.[2474] The first Rockford conference contained specific deliberations and judgments that produced a resolution to appoint and dispatch Winnebago County citizens as Delegates to an anticipatory second Rockford conference at which the plans and means for finishing the construction of the Galena and Chicago Union Railroad Company would be formulated.[2475] The second Rockford conference took place on January 7, 1846. A state of emergency defined the two Rockford conferences, because the concerned persons, counties, towns, and cities, all judged the extreme necessity and urgency of building the railroad to Chicago, collectively for the benefit of all of the Rock River communities, for Chicago, and for the State of Illinois.[2476]

The two Rockford conferences must be recognized as essential to the original building of Chicago and Cook County railroad transportation infrastructures and economies. Jason Marsh, T. D. Robertson, and William Hulin constituted an executive board that assisted the process of organizing the conference. The appointments of Delegates to the second Rockford conference then took place, and the following Winnebago County persons were chosen as Delegates to the

---

[2471] Church, Charles A., & Waldo, H. H. (1905). Past and Present of the City of Rockford And Winnebago County, Illinois. Pp. 59-60. Chicago, IL: S. J. Clarke Publishing Company. Google Books.

[2472] Church, Charles A., & Waldo, H. H. (1905). Past and Present of the City of Rockford And Winnebago County, Illinois. P. 59. Chicago, IL: S. J. Clarke Publishing Company. Google Books.

[2473] Church, Charles A., & Waldo, H. H. (1905). Past and Present of the City of Rockford And Winnebago County, Illinois. P. 59. Chicago, IL: S. J. Clarke Publishing Company. Google Books.

[2474] Church, Charles A., & Waldo, H. H. (1905). Past and Present of the City of Rockford And Winnebago County, Illinois. P. 59. Chicago, IL: S. J. Clarke Publishing Company. Google Books.

[2475] Church, Charles A., & Waldo, H. H. (1905). Past and Present of the City of Rockford And Winnebago County, Illinois. P. 59. Chicago, IL: S. J. Clarke Publishing Company. Google Books.

[2476] Church, Charles A., & Waldo, H. H. (1905). Past and Present of the City of Rockford And Winnebago County, Illinois. P. 59. Chicago, IL: S. J. Clarke Publishing Company. Google Books.

Rockford conference for the purpose of helping to complete the railroad to Chicago: Thomas Blish Talcott, Horace Miller, A. C. Gleason, Robert Barrett, Harvey Gregory, Robert J. Cross, Asa Farnsworth, Stephen Mack, Leman Pettibone, Guy Hulett, Snyder J. Fletcher, Alonzo Hall, Daniel B. Baker, E. S. Cable, Harvey Woodruff, Joseph Manchester, George Haskell, Willard Wheeler, E. H. Potter, Newton Crawford, J. C. Goodhue, S. M. Church, Anson Miller, Jason Marsh, and T. D. Robertson.[2477]

A Chicago conference occurred on December 5, 1845, for the purpose of appointing Delegates to the Rockford conference of January 7, 1846. Mayor Augustus Garrett served as Chairman of the Chicago conference, and Isaac N. Arnold served as Secretary of the conference.[2478] The Chicago residents who were chosen to represent the city at the Rockford conference were Jonathan Young Scammon, Isaac N. Arnold, J. B. F. Russell, Mark Skinner, Thomas Dyer, E. W. Tracy, John Daulin, Stephen F. Gail, William H. Brown, Walter Loomis Newberry, William E. Jones, Bryan W. Raymond, Francis C. Sherman, William Jones, and Mayor Augustus Garrett.[2479] Jonathan Young Scammon was later an industrial colleague and associate of Jacob Bunn in Chicago, and both Scammon and Bunn were founders and owners of the Chicago Republican Company, publisher of the largest newspaper in Chicago and in the American West.

The Winnebago delegation and the Chicago delegation joined delegations from Stephenson County, Boone County, Ogle County, McHenry County, Jo Daviess County, Rock County, Lee County, and Kane County.[2480] The Rockford conference contained collections of information, deliberations upon the information, and judgments of information that produced multiple resolutions. The resolutions set forth policies and laws to effect the completion of the Galena and Chicago Union Railroad Company and to create a Northern Illinois industrial and agricultural corridor.[2481] William Butler Ogden, Charles Walker, John Locke Scripps, Isaac Arnold, John B. Turner, and B. W. Raymond spearheaded efforts to get subscriptions of stock money for the railroad. John Van Nortwick was the company's first civil engineer. George W. Waite, "drove the first grading peg, at

---

[2477] Church, Charles A., & Waldo, H. H. (1905). Past and Present of the City of Rockford And Winnebago County, Illinois. P. 59. Chicago, IL: S. J. Clarke Publishing Company. Google Books.

[2478] Church, Charles A., & Waldo, H. H. (1905). Past and Present of the City of Rockford And Winnebago County, Illinois. Pp. 59-60. Chicago, IL: S. J. Clarke Publishing Company. Google Books.

[2479] Church, Charles A., & Waldo, H. H. (1905). Past and Present of the City of Rockford And Winnebago County, Illinois. Pp. 59-60. Chicago, IL: S. J. Clarke Publishing Company. Google Books.

[2480] Church, Charles A., & Waldo, H. H. (1905). Past and Present of the City of Rockford And Winnebago County, Illinois. P. 60. Chicago, IL: S. J. Clarke Publishing Company. Google Books.

[2481] Church, Charles A., & Waldo, H. H. (1905). Past and Present of the City of Rockford And Winnebago County, Illinois. P. 60. Chicago, IL: S. J. Clarke Publishing Company. Google Books.

the corner of Kinsie [Kinzie] and Halstead Streets."[2482] The first Galena and Chicago Union locomotive engine came to Chicago in October, 1848, having been shipped from the eastern United States. John Ebbert and I. D. Johnson worked as the original engineers and drivers for the railroad.[2483] To summarize, the Willard-Talcott family helped establish Winnebago County and contributed centrally to the original railroad industry of Chicago, Cook County, Winnebago County, and the intervening and neighboring counties mentioned above. The Willard-Talcott family helped establish both the Illinois Central Railroad Company and the Galena and Chicago Union Railroad Company through support and leadership contributions to the creation and development of the Illinois Central Railroad Company and the Galena and Chicago Union Railroad Company.[2484]

The Willard-Comstock Line

Asa and Lucy (Whiting) Willard's daughter, Mary Lois Willard, married Ansel Comstock.[2485] Charles Bird Comstock (1853-1921),[2486] a son of Ansel and Mary (Willard) Comstock, was a resident of Elgin, Illinois.[2487] Charles B. Comstock married Mary Munsill Jenkins of Honesdale, Pennsylvania.[2488] *The Commemorative Biography of Northeastern Pennsylvania* (1900) stated that Charles Comstock served as Secretary of the Condensed Milk Company in Elgin.[2489] The condensed milk company that employed Charles Bird Comstock was the Borden's Condensed Milk Company of Elgin and Chicago.[2490] Historical sources indicate that Charles served both as a bookkeeper and as Secretary at

---

[2482] Church, Charles A., & Waldo, H. H. (1905). Past and Present of the City of Rockford And Winnebago County, Illinois. P. 61. Chicago, IL: S. J. Clarke Publishing Company. Google Books.

[2483] Church, Charles A., & Waldo, H. H. (1905). Past and Present of the City of Rockford And Winnebago County, Illinois. P. 61. Chicago, IL: S. J. Clarke Publishing Company. Google Books.

[2484] Church, Charles A., & Waldo, H. H. (1905). Past and Present of the City of Rockford And Winnebago County, Illinois. Chicago, IL: S. J. Clarke Publishing Company. Google Books; Portrait And Biographical Record of Winnebago and Boone Counties, Illinois. (1892). P. 681. Chicago, IL: Biographical Publishing Company. Google Books.

[2485] Comstock, John Adams. (1949). A History and Genealogy of the Comstock Family in America. Page not clear. Privately printed by Commonwealth Press. Google Books.

[2486] Death Records in Elgin, Illinois. Vol. 1, Part 1: With burials at Bluff City Cemetery and elsewhere as recorded in the cemetery sextons' ledgers/ coordinated by the City of Elgin Heritage Commission.

[2487] Commemorative Biography of Northeastern Pennsylvania. (1900). P. 460. Chicago, IL: J. H. Beers Company. Google Books.

[2488] Commemorative Biography of Northeastern Pennsylvania. (1900). P. 460. Chicago, IL: J. H. Beers Company. Google Books.

[2489] Commemorative Biography of Northeastern Pennsylvania. (1900). P. 460. Chicago, IL: J. H. Beers Company. Google Books.

[2490] Twelfth Annual Report of the State Food Commissioner of Illinois for Year, 1911. (1912). P. 44. Springfield, IL: Illinois State Journal Co., State Printers. Google Books.

Borden's Condensed Milk Company in Elgin.[2491] This firm was a large and significant food manufacturing company of Chicago and the metropolitan region.[2492] Elgin is a large and industrially important northwestern suburb of Chicago, and is located in Cook and Kane counties. Mary (Jenkins) Comstock held the office of Regent of the Elgin Chapter of the Daughters of the American Revolution.[2493] She was noted as having been, "active many years in church and literary circles of Elgin."[2494] Charles B. Comstock and Mary (Jenkins) Comstock resided for many years at 121 College Street in Elgin.[2495] There have been no further discoveries as of the time of authorship of the present book regarding Charles' work at the Borden Condensed Milk Company.

The Willard-Lewis Line

Asa Willard and Martha (Moore) Willard's son, James Moore Willard, married Helen F. Lewis.[2496] Helen was the daughter of David Lewis and Lucy (Hall) Lewis of Verona, New York.[2497] The family moved to Chicago almost certainly prior to 1900. James worked in the mercantile business in Chicago.[2498] The Willards were residents of the Woodlawn community of Chicago in 1900.[2499] The *1900 United States Census* listed James Willard, his wife Helen F. (Lewis) Willard, and their daughter, Elouise Willard, as residents of the Hyde Park Township district of Chicago, which included Woodlawn, Hyde Park, Kenwood, Douglas, South Shore, and many other communities and neighborhoods.[2500] The Willard residence stood at 6352 Jackson Avenue.[2501] Jackson Avenue is known today as Maryland

---

[2491] Elgin City Directory. (1909-1910); 1900 United States Census; Twelfth Annual Report of the State Food Commissioner of Illinois for Year, 1911. (1912). P. 44. Springfield, IL: Illinois State Journal Co., State Printers. Google Books.

[2492] Twelfth Annual Report of the State Food Commissioner of Illinois for Year, 1911. (1912). P. 44. Springfield, IL: Illinois State Journal Co., State Printers. Google Books.

[2493] Chicago Tribune. (September 12, 1943). P. 26. Newspapers.com.

[2494] Chicago Tribune. (September 12, 1943). P. 26. Newspapers.com.

[2495] Elgin City Directory. (1909-1910); Elgin City Directory. (1920). P. 170.

[2496] Willard, Joseph, Walker, Charles Wilkes, Pope, Henry Charles. (1915). Willard Genealogy, Sequel to Willard Memoir. P. 392. Boston, MASS: The Willard Family Association. Archive.org

[2497] Willard, Joseph, Walker, Charles Wilkes, Pope, Henry Charles. (1915). Willard Genealogy, Sequel to Willard Memoir. P. 392. Boston, MASS: The Willard Family Association. Archive.org

[2498] Willard, Joseph, Walker, Charles Wilkes, Pope, Henry Charles. (1915). Willard Genealogy, Sequel to Willard Memoir. P. 392. Boston, MASS: The Willard Family Association. Archive.org

[2499] 1900 United States Census. Ancestry.com.

[2500] 1900 United States Census. Ancestry.com.

[2501] 1900 United States Census. Ancestry.com.

Avenue.[2502] The Willard residence was within Census Enumeration District 1091, which was located in Ward 34.[2503] James Moore Willard worked in commercial traveler provisions.[2504] Helen (Lewis) Willard was a homemaker and their daughter, Elouise, worked as a stenographer in 1900.[2505] The Willard family relocated from Woodlawn to the Englewood community, also on the south side of Chicago, in approximately 1901, and resided at 7140 Normal Avenue that year.[2506] James worked as a salesman in 1901, as indicated by the *City of Chicago Directory* of that year.[2507] In 1906, James, Helen, and Elouise all resided at 515 W. 70th Street in the Englewood community on the south side of Chicago.[2508] At the same time, James owned a grocery store company located at 510 W. 70th Street, located several blocks from the Willard house.[2509] In 1909, James continued to own and operate the grocery store at 515 W. 70th Street.[2510] Willard's Store would have been one of the oldest grocery businesses of Englewood.

In 1910, James, Helen, and Elouise resided at 415 70th Street, in a rented apartment.[2511] Tirza Avery was then a boarder at the Willard residence.[2512] James continud to own the grocery store in Englewood.[2513] The 1910 location of the Willard residence was within Census Enumeration District 1388 of Ward 32.[2514] The north-south streets that defined Census Enumeration District 1388 were Wallace to the west and Stewart to the east.[2515] These geographically definitive facts clearly located the Willard residence within the Englewood community. In 1920, James, Helen, and Elouise, along with Tirza Avery, who continued to board with the Willards, and another lodger (Fannie Scott), all resided at 315 W. 67th Street.[2516] This address was located within the eastern part of the Englewood community and was close to both Stewart Avenue and Yale Avenue. These were the two north-south roads that marked the east and west boundaries of Census Enumeration District 1971, the district in which the Willard residence stood in

---

[2502] Chicago Streets. chsmedia.org; Thank you to Michael Safar, President of the Hyde Park Historical Society of Chicago, for researching the name history of the Hyde Park and Woodlawn streets of Jackson Avenue and Maryland Avenue.
[2503] 1900 United States Census. Ancestry.com; 1900 Census Ward 34 Enumeration Districts, Chicago, Illinois. Alookatcook.com.
[2504] 1900 United States Census. Ancestry.com.
[2505] 1900 United States Census. Ancestry.com.
[2506] City of Chicago Directory. (1901).
[2507] City of Chicago Directory. (1901).
[2508] City of Chicago Directory. (1906).
[2509] City of Chicago Directory. (1906).
[2510] Lakeside Directory of Chicago. (1909).
[2511] 1910 United States Census. Ancestry.com.
[2512] 1910 United States Census. Ancestry.com.
[2513] 1910 United States Census. Ancestry.com.
[2514] 1910 United States Census. Ancestry.com; 1910 Census Ward 32 Enumeration Districts, Chicago, Illinois. Alookatcook.com.
[2515] 1910 Census Ward 32 Enumeration Districts, Chicago, Illinois. Alookatcook.com.
[2516] 1920 United States Census. Ancestry.com.

1920.[2517] James Moore Willard died in 1923.[2518] He was buried in West Aurora Cemetery in Aurora, Illinois.[2519] Aurora is a large western Chicago suburb that is located in DuPage County and in Kane County. James Moore Willard (1840-1923), Helen (Lewis) Willard (1836/1837-1938), Mabel Willard (1880-1890), and Elouise Willard (1869-1958), were all successively interred at the same grave at West Aurora Cemetery.[2520]

As a widow, Helen (Lewis) Willard resided at Stewart Avenue and at 6717 Perry Avenue, both addresses being located within the Englewood community.[2521] In 1930, Helen and Eloise Willard resided at 6937 Stewart Avenue, which was in the Englewood community, in Ward 17, and in Census Enumeration District 636.[2522] Eloise worked as a stenographer at a wholesale book company in 1930.[2523] No discovery has been made of the name of the book company. Helen died on February 18, 1937. She was a resident of 6717 Perry Avenue at the time of her death.[2524] The memorial services were provided by the chapel at 63rd Street and Harvard Avenue.[2525] The *Chicago Tribune* obituary for Helen Willard did not name the chapel where her funeral services were provided, but external historical sources and evidences almost certainly prove that the chapel was that of Lain & Son, located at W. 63rd Street and Harvard.[2526] Eloise M. Willard survived her father, mother, and her sister.[2527] The *1940 United States Census* listed Eloise Willard at 6433 Stewart Avenue.[2528] This residence was in Ward 17 and in the Englewood community.[2529] Eloise worked as an accountant in 1940.[2530] The historical records show no evidence that Eloise Willard ever married. No further discoveries of biographical facts concerning the Englewood Willards have occurred as of the time of the authorship of the present book.

Joseph Wellington Willard and Lammot du Pont

Manasseh Willard (1785-1836) was a son of Ephraim Willard (1748-1821) and Lois (Geary) Willard (1754-1834), and an elder brother of Asa Willard (1789-

[2517] 1920 Census Ward 32 Enumeration Districts, Chicago, Illinois. Alookatcook.com; 1920 United States Census. Ancestry.com.

[2518] West Aurora Cemetery Record for James M. Willard. findagrave.com.

[2519] West Aurora Cemetery Record for James M. Willard. findagrave.com.

[2520] West Aurora Cemetery Record for James M. Willard. findagrave.com

[2521] 1930 United States Census. Ancestry.com; Chicago Tribune. (February 20, 1937). P. 12. Newspapers.com.

[2522] 1930 United States Census. Ancestry.com; 1930 Census Ward 17 Enumeration Districts, Chicago, Illinois. Alookatcook.com.

[2523] 1930 United States Census. Ancestry.com.

[2524] Chicago Tribune. (February 20, 1937). P. 12. Newspapers.com.

[2525] Chicago Tribune. (February 20, 1937). P. 12. Newspapers.com.

[2526] Chicago Tribune. (November 10, 1948). P. 34. Newspapers.com.

[2527] Chicago Tribune. (February 20, 1937). P. 12. Newspapers.com.

[2528] 1940 United States Census. Ancestry.com.

[2529] 1940 United States Census. Ancestry.com.

[2530] 1940 United States Census. Ancestry.com.

1847), who married Lucy Whiting (Asa Willard is discussed above).[2531] Manasseh Willard married Sarah McDuffie, a daughter of Daniel McDuffie and Mary McDuffie.[2532] The children born to Manasseh and Sarah (McDuffie) Willard included the following people: Mary Anne Sarah Willard; George Wilson Willard; Caroline Amanda Willard; **Joseph Wellington Willard**; Manasseh Darwin Willard; Orissa Azina Willard; Amelia Anne Willard; and Fanny Williston Willard.[2533]

Joseph Wellington Willard entered the American explosives industry and contributed much to the corporate and technological development of the explosives industry of the United States.[2534] Joseph Wellington Willard was a first cousin of the Willards, Richardsons, Comstocks, and Talcotts of Chicago, Springfield, and Winnebago County, Illinois. Historian Henry Howe of Columbus, Ohio, declared Joseph W. Willard as the inventor of Hercules Powder, which was an explosive chemical and technology.[2535] Howe outlined the extensive and innovative work that Willard had undertaken at Santa Cruz and San Francisco in the explosives manufacturing industry in the middle and later nineteenth century.[2536] After serving as Superintendent of the California Powder Company of Santa Cruz, where he invented Hercules Powder, Willard helped manage the San Francisco branch of the California Powder Works.[2537]

Joseph W. Willard founded the Cleveland, Ohio, branch of the California Powder Works in 1877.[2538] The Ohio branch represented the California company efficiently in markets that were too far from California for the San Francisco and Santa Cruz company to serve efficiently.[2539] The California Powder Works decided

---

[2531] Willard, Joseph, Walker, Charles Wilkes, Pope, Henry Charles. (1915). Willard Genealogy, Sequel to Willard Memoir. P. 226. Boston, MASS: The Willard Family Association. Archive.org

[2532] Willard, Joseph, Walker, Charles Wilkes, Pope, Henry Charles. (1915). Willard Genealogy, Sequel to Willard Memoir. P. 226. Boston, MASS: The Willard Family Association. Archive.org

[2533] Willard, Joseph, Walker, Charles Wilkes, Pope, Henry Charles. (1915). Willard Genealogy, Sequel to Willard Memoir. P. 226. Boston, MASS: The Willard Family Association. Archive.org

[2534] The News Journal (Wilmington, Delaware). (June 18, 2000). P. 111. Newspapers.com

[2535] Howe, Henry. (1891). Historical Collections of Ohio. Vol. III. P. XIX. Columbus, OH: Henry Howe & Son. Google Books.

[2536] Howe, Henry. (1891). Historical Collections of Ohio. Vol. III. P. XIX. Columbus, OH: Henry Howe & Son. Google Books.

[2537] Howe, Henry. (1891). Historical Collections of Ohio. Vol. III. P. XIX. Columbus, OH: Henry Howe & Son. Google Books.

[2538] The Biographical Cyclopedia And Portrait Gallery With An Historical Sketch Of The State Of Ohio. (1891). Vol. V. P. 1154. Cincinnati, OH: Western Biographical Publishing Company, Publishers. Google Books; Howe, Henry. (1891). Historical Collections of Ohio. Vol. III. P. XIX. Columbus, OH: Henry Howe & Son. Google Books.

[2539] The Biographical Cyclopedia And Portrait Gallery With An Historical Sketch Of The State Of Ohio. (1891). Vol. V. P. 1154. Cincinnati, OH: Western Biographical Publishing

to convert the Cleveland branch into an independent company in 1881, which was to be called the Hercules Powder Company, named after Willard's Hercules Powder invention.[2540] Consequently, Joseph W. Willard co-founded the Hercules Powder Company of Cleveland, Ohio, working with the California management in the founding process.[2541] Willard became an important party to the Cleveland industrial economy and was civically active at Cleveland.[2542] He was a member of the Western Reserve Historical Society.[2543] He remained in charge of the Cleveland factory for many years, and served as its General Manager.[2544] It was at Willard's Cleveland office that Lammot du Pont (1831-1884) of Delaware would contact him to help establish a new Du Pont explosives company in New Jersey.[2545]

Joseph W. Willard became a friend, fellow technologist, and business partner of Lammot du Pont of Wilmington, Delaware, and Philadelphia.[2546] Historian George H. Kerr commented in his 1938 work, *Du Pont Romance: a reminiscent narrative of E. I. Du Pont De Nemours and Company*, that Swedish industrialist Alfred Nobel had discovered the chemical known as nitroglycerin, and that Lammot du Pont took special interest in the possibilities for this chemical discovery.[2547] Lammot du Pont failed to convince his uncle, Henry du Pont, that the merits of nitroglycerin superseded the merits of "Black Powder," but succeeded in

Company, Publishers. Google Books; Howe, Henry. (1891). Historical Collections of Ohio. Vol. III. P. XIX. Columbus, OH: Henry Howe & Son. Google Books.

[2540] The Biographical Cyclopedia And Portrait Gallery With An Historical Sketch Of The State Of Ohio. (1891). Vol. V. P. 1154. Cincinnati, OH: Western Biographical Publishing Company, Publishers. Google Books; Howe, Henry. (1891). Historical Collections of Ohio. Vol. III. P. XIX. Columbus, OH: Henry Howe & Son. Google Books.

[2541] Howe, Henry. (1891). Historical Collections of Ohio. Vol. III. P. XIX. Columbus, OH: Henry Howe & Son. Google Books; The Biographical Cyclopedia And Portrait Gallery With An Historical Sketch Of The State Of Ohio. (1891). Vol. V. P. 1154. Cincinnati, OH: Western Biographical Publishing Company, Publishers. Google Books.

[2542] The Biographical Cyclopedia And Portrait Gallery With An Historical Sketch Of The State Of Ohio. (1891). Vol. V. P. 1154. Cincinnati, OH: Western Biographical Publishing Company, Publishers. Google Books; Howe, Henry. (1891). Historical Collections of Ohio. Vol. III. P. XIX. Columbus, OH: Henry Howe & Son. Google Books.

[2543] The Biographical Cyclopedia And Portrait Gallery With An Historical Sketch Of The State Of Ohio. (1891). Vol. V. P. 1154. Cincinnati, OH: Western Biographical Publishing Company, Publishers. Google Books.

[2544] Howe, Henry. (1891). Historical Collections of Ohio. Vol. III. P. XIX. Columbus, OH: Henry Howe & Son. Google Books.

[2545] Howe, Henry. (1891). Historical Collections of Ohio. Vol. III. P. XIX. Columbus, OH: Henry Howe & Son. Google Books; Kerr, George H. (1938). Du Pont Romance: a reminiscent narrative of E. I. Du Pont de Nemours and company. PP. 95-96. Du Pont Printing Division: 1938; Wilkinson, Norman B. (1984). Lammot du Pont and the American Explosives Industry. University Press of Virginia. Google Books.

[2546] The News Journal (Wilmington, Delaware). (June 18, 2000). P. 111. Newspapers.com.

[2547] Kerr, George H. (1938). Du Pont Romance: a reminiscent narrative of E. I. Du Pont de Nemours and company. PP. 95-96. United States: Du Pont Printing Division. Ancestry.com.

organizing a new company for the manufacture of nitroglycerin product in 1880.[2548] Kerr noted that Lammot du Pont did receive the support of Henry du Pont in the nitroglycerin company venture, but also received support from Laflin & Rand and from a person or organization named Hazard.[2549] Lammot du Pont invited Joseph W. Willard of Cleveland to help him with the planning for the new factory and company.[2550] Joseph Willard examined and surveyed the place at Repaupo, New Jersey, in 1880, for the nitroglycerine factory that Lammot du Pont envisioned at the time.[2551] Lammot du Pont expressed to Willard his vision and enthusiasm for the explosives factory and company plans when he stated to Willard: "Here, Joe, will someday be the largest dynamite plant in America."[2552]

Lammot du Pont included his friend, Joseph Willard of Cleveland, in the founding of the Repauno Chemical Company. Du Pont preferred the altered name, Repauno, to the actual New Jersey river name, Repaupo, and thus changed the one letter "p" to an "n." Charles A. Morse, nephew of Joseph W. Willard, and another cousin of the Willards, Richardsons, Comstocks, and Talcotts of Chicago, Springfield, and Winnebago County, Illinois, also assisted Lammot du Pont with the founding of the Repauno Chemical Company, after Joseph W. Willard recommended that du Pont hire Morse to help him manage the human resources and hiring for the new explosives factory.[2553] Historians George H. Kerr and Norman B. Wilkinson both discussed, in separate works, the important contributions of Joseph W. Willard to the creation of the Repauno Chemical Company.[2554] Kerr and Wilkinson both stated that Lammot du Pont consulted with Joseph W. Willard in order to obtain guidance in establishing a new explosives company.[2555] Clear from the histories is the fact that Joseph Willard provided logistical support in the founding of the Repauno Chemical Company and advised

[2548] Kerr, George H. (1938). Du Pont Romance: a reminiscent narrative of E. I. Du Pont de Nemours and company. PP. 95-96. United States: Du Pont Printing Division. Ancestry.com.

[2549] Kerr, George H. (1938). Du Pont Romance: a reminiscent narrative of E. I. Du Pont de Nemours and company. PP. 95-96. United States: Du Pont Printing Division. Ancestry.com.

[2550] Kerr, George H. (1938). Du Pont Romance: a reminiscent narrative of E. I. Du Pont de Nemours and company. PP. 95-96. United States: Du Pont Printing Division. Ancestry.com.

[2551] The News Journal (Wilmington, Delaware). (June 18, 2000). P. 111. Newspapers.com.

[2552] The News Journal (Wilmington, Delaware). (June 18, 2000). P. 111. Newspapers.com.

[2553] Wilkinson, Norman B. (1984). Lammot du Pont and the American Explosives Industry. University Press of Virginia. Google Books.

[2554] Kerr, George H. (1938). Du Pont Romance: a reminiscent narrative of E. I. Du Pont de Nemours and company. PP. 95-96. Du Pont Printing Division: 1938; Wilkinson, Norman B. (1984). Lammot du Pont and the American Explosives Industry. University Press of Virginia. Google Books.

[2555] Wilkinson, Norman B. (1984). Lammot du Pont and the American Explosives Industry. University Press of Virginia. Google Books.

du Pont as to the optimal geography and topography for the new company.[2556] Willard, moreover, recommended his nephew, Charles A. Morse, to aid Lammot du Pont further in the new company.[2557] Joseph W. Willard at this time managed the Hercules Powder Company factory at Newburgh, Cuyahoga County, Ohio, located in suburban Cleveland.[2558]

Both as the General Manager of the Cleveland Branch of the California Powder Works, and as the founder of the Hercules Powder Company of Cleveland, Joseph W. Willard was well-qualified to be a co-founder of the Repauno Chemical Company. Lammot du Pont recognized this fact, eagerly chose Willard to be a co-founder of Repauno Chemical Company with him, and the two friends started what would become the largest dynamite company in the world: the Repauno Chemical Company.[2559] *The Tammany Times*, a newspaper of New York City, reported that the Repauno Chemical Company manufactured and sold millions of pounds of explosives every year at least as early as 1898.[2560] *The Tammany Times* furthermore reported that the Repauno Chemical Company produced almost all of the explosives that were used in the construction of the Chicago Drainage Canal.[2561]

The 1878 *Industries of Cleveland: Trade, Commerce and Manufactures*, assembled and published by the Cleveland Chamber of Commerce, allotted a large space for the Hercules Powder Company and the work of Joseph W. Willard.[2562] The Cleveland report named Willard as the inventor of Hercules Powder and described his work as managing executive of the Hercules Powder Company.[2563] The explosives industry dealt in multiple chemicals, all of which were judged to possess flammability and explosiveness risks that made the chemicals too

---

[2556] Kerr, George H. (1938). Du Pont Romance: a reminiscent narrative of E. I. Du Pont de Nemours and company. PP. 95-96. Du Pont Printing Division: 1938; Wilkinson, Norman B. (1984). Lammot du Pont and the American Explosives Industry. University Press of Virginia. Google Books; The News Journal (Wilmington, Delaware). (June 18, 2000). P. 111. Newspapers.com.

[2557] Wilkinson, Norman B. (1984). Lammot du Pont and the American Explosives Industry. University Press of Virginia. Google Books.

[2558] Kerr, George H. (1938). Du Pont Romance: a reminiscent narrative of E. I. Du Pont de Nemours and company. PP. 95-96. Du Pont Printing Division: 1938; Wilkinson, Norman B. (1984). Lammot du Pont and the American Explosives Industry. University Press of Virginia. Google Books.

[2559] Innovations Start Here. History. Dupont.com.

[2560] The Tammany Times. (November 7, 1898). Vol. 11. No. 26. P. 16. New York, NY. Google Books.

[2561] The Tammany Times. (November 7, 1898). Vol. 11. No. 26. P. 5. New York, NY. Google Books.

[2562] Industries of Cleveland: Trade, Commerce and Manufactures. (1879). P. 147. Cleveland, OH: Cleveland Chamber of Commerce. Richard Edwards, Publisher. Google Books.

[2563] Industries of Cleveland: Trade, Commerce and Manufactures. (1879). P. 147. Cleveland, OH: Cleveland Chamber of Commerce. Richard Edwards, Publisher. Google Books.

inconvenient to use at times.[2564] Joseph W. Willard invented the Hercules Powder chemical to satisfy the market for more reliable, safe, and manageable explosive agents.[2565] The Cleveland report contained the following history:

> "In this year (1874), however, J. W. Willard came to the rescue and supplied a want long felt in blasting operations, and on November 4 of that year, secured letters patent for the Hercules Powder, which is composed of the nitro-glycerine, carbonate of magnesia and other chemicals, therefore coming under the generic term 'dynamite,' with twenty times the power of the best blasting powder, to the pound, yet perfectly safe in its transportation and handling, as it can be thrown from any height or sustain any shock and will not explode."[2566]

Joseph W. Willard not only founded the Hercules Powder Company of Cleveland, but also managed the affairs of the company.[2567] Working for Willard was William Willson, who was the Superintendent of the workforce of twenty men at the Cuyahoga factory.[2568] The Cleveland report did not mention the financing of the Hercules Powder Company, but did specify that annual sales revenues totaled $150,000 as of 1878.[2569] The company's address was 184 Superior Street, located on Public Square, in downtown Cleveland.[2570] J. A. Wesener was the representative

---

[2564] Industries of Cleveland: Trade, Commerce and Manufactures. (1879). P. 147. Cleveland, OH: Cleveland Chamber of Commerce. Richard Edwards, Publisher. Google Books.
[2565] Industries of Cleveland: Trade, Commerce and Manufactures. (1879). P. 147. Cleveland, OH: Cleveland Chamber of Commerce. Richard Edwards, Publisher. Google Books.
[2566] Industries of Cleveland: Trade, Commerce and Manufactures. (1879). P. 147. Cleveland, OH: Cleveland Chamber of Commerce. Richard Edwards, Publisher. Google Books.
[2567] Industries of Cleveland: Trade, Commerce and Manufactures. (1879). P. 147. Cleveland, OH: Cleveland Chamber of Commerce. Richard Edwards, Publisher. Google Books; The Biographical Cyclopedia And Portrait Gallery With An Historical Sketch Of The State Of Ohio. (1891). Vol. V. P. 1154. Cincinnati, OH: Western Biographical Publishing Company, Publishers. Google Books; Howe, Henry. (1891). Historical Collections of Ohio. Vol. III. P. XIX. Columbus, OH: Henry Howe & Son. Google Books.
[2568] Industries of Cleveland: Trade, Commerce and Manufactures. (1879). P. 147. Cleveland, OH: Cleveland Chamber of Commerce. Richard Edwards, Publisher. Google Books.
[2569] Industries of Cleveland: Trade, Commerce and Manufactures. (1879). P. 147. Cleveland, OH: Cleveland Chamber of Commerce. Richard Edwards, Publisher. Google Books.
[2570] Industries of Cleveland: Trade, Commerce and Manufactures. (1879). P. 147. Cleveland, OH: Cleveland Chamber of Commerce. Richard Edwards, Publisher. Google Books.

of the Hercules Powder Company at Akron, Ohio, in 1889.[2571] The Chicago branch of Hercules Powder Company was located at 1321 Monadnock Building in 1896.[2572] The company also owned branches in the following cities and towns as of 1896: St. Louis, Indianapolis, Clifton Forge, Virginia, Wilmington, Delaware, Lima, Ohio, Joplin, Missouri, Houghton, Michigan, Bradford, Pennsylvania, Atlanta, Georgia, and Mexico City.[2573]

The Hercules Powder Company of Cleveland impacted the construction and development of the United States and the world and would have exerted positive impact on both major cities and small towns. The Hercules Powder Company presence in Clifton Forge, Alleghany County, Virginia, would almost certainly have provided the explosives technologies necessary for the coal mining and railroad construction projects of neighboring Greenbrier County, Monroe County, and Pocahontas County, West Virginia, and for the same projects in neighboring Botetourt County, Roanoke County, and Montgomery County, Virginia. Consequently, the Hercules Powder Company of Cleveland would have positively impacted construction and development in the nearby Virginia communities of Roanoke, Salem, Blacksburg, Christiansburg, Iron Gate, Eagle Rock, Gala, Oriskany, Buchanan, Low Moor, Fincastle, New Castle, Sweet Chalybeate Springs, and Crows. The Hercules Powder Company would also have positively impacted the nearby West Virginia communities of White Sulphur Springs, Lewisburg, Marlinton, Ronceverte, Blue Sulphur Springs, Red Sulphur Springs, Green Sulphur Springs, Sweet Springs, Salt Springs, Hinton, Mullins, Beckley, Rainelle, Talcott, Alderson, Prince, Thurmond, Charleston, Huntington, Montgomery, Welch, Shaft Hollow, Coalwood, War, Cucumber, Matewan, Williamson, Princeton, Bluefield, Bramwell, Jolo, Logan, Island Creek, and many others. Hercules Powder Company would have brought useful technology to the cities and towns of the entire Great Lakes area and to the communities of the Ohio River valley, the Greenbrier River valley, the Tygart River valley, the Kanawha River valley, the Jackson River valley, the James River valley, the New River valley, the Roanoke River valley, and many other places.

The Repauno Chemical Company possessed a Chicago office located at 84 Van Buren Street, according to the *Ninth Annual Report Of The Factory Inspectors Of Illinois*, from December 15, 1901.[2574] Louis Arrington, who was the Inspector of Factories and Workshops for the State of Illinois at the time of the Illinois industrial inspection and industrial census, signed and submitted the official 1901 industrial report to Illinois Governor Richard Yates, Jr., whose father, Richard Yates, had also been Illinois Governor and a close friend and political collaborator

[2571] The Summit County Beacon. (June 5, 1889). P. 4. Newspapers.com.

[2572] Stone. (December, 1895-May, 1896). Vol. XII. P. 87. Chicago, IL: The D. H. Ranck Publishing Company. Google Books.

[2573] Stone. (December, 1895-May, 1896). Vol. XII. P. 87. Chicago, IL: The D. H. Ranck Publishing Company. Google Books.

[2574] Ninth Annual Report of the Factory Inspectors of Illinois: December 15, 1901. (1902). P. 170. Springfield, IL: Phillips Bros., State Printers. Google Books.

with Jacob Bunn, John W. Bunn, and others.[2575] The 1901 industrial census report stated that the Chicago branch of Repauno Chemical Company employed seven persons.[2576] The factory inspection report enumerated the workforce by sex and age, and stated that one girl over the age of sixteen, and six boys over the age of sixteen, constituted the workforce of the Chicago office at that time.[2577] Louis Arrington worked from an office that was located at the New Era Building in Chicago, where the Illinois Office of Inspector of Factories And Workshops was headquartered.[2578] Louis Arrington was one of the most important stewards of Illinois economic data. To be the Inspector of Factories and Workshops for the State of Illinois in the industrial age would make one a key executive in the public administration of the industrial economies of Chicago, Cook County, Illinois, and the Midwest.

The Willard-Richardson-Bunn Line

Asa Willard and Lucy (Whiting) Willard had a son named Alexander Perry Willard (1815-1865).[2579] Alexander Willard, a native of Vernon, Oneida County, New York, relocated to Springfield, and established two companies at Springfield: the Willard & Johns Company of Springfield, with partner E. G. Johns; and the Willard & Zimmerman Company, which provided paint contracting services and building materials.[2580] E. G. Johns was a native of Buckingham County, Virginia, and was a pioneer Illinois businessman. New York native Robert Zimmerman was Willard's partner in the latter company and was also a pioneer Illinois businessman.[2581]

Alexander Perry Willard married Louise Higgie of Chemung County, New York. Two children were born to this marriage: Lucy Willard, and a child who died young.[2582] Lucy Willard married William Douglas Richardson, a Connecticut native who relocated to Chicago and Springfield, and who remained active in both

---

[2575] Ninth Annual Report of the Factory Inspectors of Illinois: December 15, 1901. (1902). P. 170. Springfield, IL: Phillips Bros., State Printers. Google Books.
[2576] Ninth Annual Report of the Factory Inspectors of Illinois: December 15, 1901. (1902). P. 170. Springfield, IL: Phillips Bros., State Printers. Google Books.
[2577] Ninth Annual Report of the Factory Inspectors of Illinois: December 15, 1901. (1902). P. 170. Springfield, IL: Phillips Bros., State Printers. Google Books.
[2578] Ninth Annual Report of the Factory Inspectors of Illinois: December 15, 1901. (1902). Springfield, IL: Phillips Bros., State Printers. Google Books.
[2579] Wallace, Joseph. (1904). Past and Present of the City of Springfield and Sangamon County, Illinois. P. 203. Chicago, IL: S. J. Clarke Publishing Company. Google Books.
[2580] Power, John Carroll. (1876). History of the Early Settlers of Sangamon County. P. 769. Springfield, IL: Edwin A. Wilson & Co. Google Books; Wallace, Joseph. (1904). Past and Present of the City of Springfield and Sangamon County, Illinois. P. 203. Chicago, IL: S. J. Clarke Publishing Company. Google Books.
[2581] Wallace, Joseph. (1904). Past and Present of the City of Springfield and Sangamon County, Illinois. P. 203. Chicago, IL: S. J. Clarke Publishing Company. Google Books.
[2582] Wallace, Joseph. (1904). Past and Present of the City of Springfield and Sangamon County, Illinois. P. 203. Chicago, IL: S. J. Clarke Publishing Company. Google Books.

cities, as will be discussed below.[2583] The children born to William Douglas Richardson and Lucy (Willard) Richardson were Ada Willard Richardson (1861-1945) and Emma Louise Richardson (1860-1946).[2584] Emma Louise Richardson married civil engineer and electrician Charles Henry Lanphier (1854-1920) of Springfield, Illinois.[2585] The four children born to Charles Henry Lanphier and Emma Louise (Richardson) Lanphier of Springfield were William Richardson Lanphier (died young); Douglas Crenshaw Lanphier (died young); Francine Ada Lanphier; and Annie Richardson Lanphier, who married Scott Lynn.[2586]

Ada Willard Richardson married George Wallace Bunn (1861-1938), who was a son of Jacob Bunn (1814-1897) and Elizabeth Jane (Ferguson) Bunn (1832-1886). For a far more complete account of the Bunn family of Chicago and Springfield, please see the chapters in this book that treat those matters. This concludes the Willard history element of the Willard-Richardson-Bunn history of Chicago. Next, we will proceed to the Richardson history element of the Willard-Richardson-Bunn history of Chicago.

The Foundations of Jackson Park

The Richardsons migrated from Connecticut to Illinois during the nineteenth century. The family remained equally a part of Chicago and Springfield throughout multiple generations. The Chicago and Cook County companies and civic organizations that constitute the central elements of the present section include the following: the Richardson Construction Company; the Barnum & Richardson Company; the Springfield Iron Company; the Richardson investment company; the United States Civil Air Patrol; the Illinois Wing of the Civil Air Patrol; the Chicago Civil Air Patrol; and the 1893 World's Columbian Exposition (1893 Chicago World's Fair). Other organizations from Chicago and from other places additionally will emerge subsequently within this chapter as the historical narrative continues.

The history of the Richardson family in the United States includes the following persons and events. Thomas Richardson (1742-1806) of London, England, was the son of William Richardson and Prudence (Heath) Richardson. Thomas Richardson married Abigail Lloyd in Scotland in 1771.[2587] Abigail Lloyd (1750-1803), daughter of John Lloyd and Abigail (McAdam) Lloyd, was a native of Colmonell,

---

[2583] Wallace, Joseph. (1904). Past and Present of the City of Springfield and Sangamon County, Illinois. P. 203. Chicago, IL: S. J. Clarke Publishing Company. Google Books.
[2584] Wallace, Joseph. (1904). Past and Present of the City of Springfield and Sangamon County, Illinois. P. 203. Chicago, IL: S. J. Clarke Publishing Company. Google Books.
[2585] Wallace, Joseph. (1904). Past and Present of the City of Springfield and Sangamon County, Illinois. P. 203. Chicago, IL: S. J. Clarke Publishing Company. Google Books.
[2586] Wallace, Joseph. (1904). Past and Present of the City of Springfield and Sangamon County, Illinois. P. 203. Chicago, IL: S. J. Clarke Publishing Company. Google Books.
[2587] Richardson family genealogical records.

Ayrshire, Scotland.[2588] Thomas and Abigail immigrated to Connecticut at some time near 1776.[2589] The first three children born to Thomas and Abigail were born in Colmonell, Ayrshire, Scotland.[2590] The latter two children were born in New York and in St. Ours, Ontario, Canada.[2591] The children born to Thomas Richardson and Abigail (Lloyd) Richardson include the following persons: Thomas Richardson (1772-1825), who married Hannah Smith (born 1775); William Richardson (born 1774); Abigail Richardson, the twin of William Richardson (born 1774), who married Daniel Lyman (born 1770); **John Richardson (1777-1834), who married Dorothy Cobb (1774-1859)**; and Betsy Richardson (born 1776), who married Avery Atkins (born 1774).[2592]

John Richardson (1777-1834) married Dorothy Cobb (1774-1859) at the Church of Christ located in Norfolk, Litchfield County, Connecticut, on May 15, 1798.[2593] Dorothy was a native of Attleborough, Taunton County, Massachusetts, and was the daughter of Nathan Cobb, Jr. (1737-1823) and Abigail (Shores) Cobb (1744/1745-1832).[2594] The children born to John Richardson and Dorothy (Cobb) Richardson include the following persons: Charlotte Richardson (1801-1876), who married William Dean; **Henry Earle Richardson (1803-1869), who married Betsey Elizabeth Johns (1809-1901)**; James Richardson (1805-1846); and **Leonard Richardson (1808-1864), who married Lucy Ann Barnum**.[2595]

Henry Earle Richardson (1803-1869) married Betsey Elizabeth Johns (1809-1901).[2596] Henry and Betsey resided at Lime Rock, Litchfield County, Connecticut.[2597] As a widow, Betsy resided at Springfield, Sangamon County, Illinois.[2598] The children born to Henry and Betsey (Johns) Richardson include the following persons: Mary Lucretia Richardson (1827-1897), who married Hosea

---

[2588] Solomon, Ruth. (2012). Richardson family genealogical records: Family Group Record for Thomas Richardson.

[2589] Solomon, Ruth. (2012). Richardson family genealogical records: Family Group Record for Thomas Richardson.

[2590] Solomon, Ruth. (2012). Richardson family genealogical records: Family Group Record for Thomas Richardson.

[2591] Solomon, Ruth. (2012). Richardson family genealogical records: Family Group Record for Thomas Richardson.

[2592] Solomon, Ruth. (2012). Richardson family genealogical records: Family Group Record for Thomas Richardson.

[2593] Solomon, Ruth. (2015). Richardson family genealogical records: Family Group Record for John Richardson.

[2594] Solomon, Ruth. (2015). Richardson family genealogical records: Family Group Record for John Richardson.

[2595] Solomon, Ruth. (2015). Richardson family genealogical records: Family Group Record for John Richardson.

[2596] Solomon, Ruth. (2017). Richardson family genealogical records: Family Group Record for Henry Earle Richardson.

[2597] Solomon, Ruth. (2017). Richardson family genealogical records: Family Group Record for Henry Earle Richardson.

[2598] Solomon, Ruth. (2017). Richardson family genealogical records: Family Group Record for Henry Earle Richardson.

Beebe Pratt (1804-1888) at Canaan, Connecticut; Betsey Elizabeth Richardson (1829-1830); Ellen E. Richardson (1831-1909), who married William H. Dauchy (1826-1901) at Salisbury, Connecticut; Lucy Maria Richardson (1833-1922), who married Edward Sands Cross (1831-1916), and died at Elyria, Lorain County, Ohio; **James Henry Richardson (1835-1917), who married, first, Elizabeth Gray of Salisbury, Connecticut (born 1839), and second, Deborah Adsit (1840-1926) of Chicago; William Douglas Richardson (1837-1923), who married, first, Lucy Willard (1839/1841-1917) of Springfield, and second, Clara Trim (born about 1858) of Madison, Wisconsin**; Martha Douglas Richardson (1840-1908), who married Lyman B. Judd (1842-1916); **Dr. Frank Richardson (1845-1921), who married Mary Hutchinson (1846-1922)**; Ada Richardson (1849-1923); and **Charles Richardson (1853-1932), who married Nettie Morgan Smith (1866-1930) of Springfield**.[2599] Lucy Maria (Richardson) Cross of Cleveland and Elyria was not only a civic leader in Cleveland and metropolitan Cuyahoga and Lorain Counties in Ohio, but was also a civic leader in Miami during the Great Florida Land Boom. Lucy co-founded the Miami League of Women Voters in about 1920.[2600] Like Jean (Criswell) Wilson Littlewood of Pittsburgh (see Chapter 6), Lucy (Richardson) Cross was part of the community of Midwesterners who powerfully and positively influenced the business and civic life of South Florida.

James Henry Richardson (1835-1917) first married Elizabeth Gray (born 1839).[2601] James Henry Richardson married, second, Deborah Adsit of Chicago, and both resided at Chicago during the time of the Civil War.[2602] Their son, Hiram Adsit Richardson (1865-1926), was born in Chicago.[2603] Hiram A. Richardson married Jean Boyle Crawford (1869-1953).[2604] James Henry Richardson and Elizabeth (Gray) Richardson had the following children: Anna Pratt Richardson, who married Arthur Fuller; James Richardson; and Ellen Elizabeth Richardson, who married Irving Edgar Prior.

Leonard Richardson (1808-1864) married Lucy Ann Barnum (1814-1889).[2605] Lucy was a daughter of Milo Barnum and Laura (Tibbals) Barnum of

---

[2599] Solomon, Ruth. (2017). Richardson family genealogical records: Family Group Record for Henry Earle Richardson.

[2600] Though the relevant original reference source has been lost, the author believes he has recalled the facts correctly.

[2601] Solomon, Ruth. (2014). Richardson family genealogical records: Family Group Record for James Henry Richardson.

[2602] Solomon, Ruth. (2014). Richardson family genealogical records: Family Group Record for James Henry Richardson.

[2603] Solomon, Ruth. (2014). Richardson family genealogical records: Family Group Record for James Henry Richardson.

[2604] Solomon, Ruth. (2014). Richardson family genealogical records: Family Group Record for James Henry Richardson.

[2605] Solomon, Ruth. (2017). Richardson family genealogical records: Family Group Record for Leonard Richardson. Author's personal collection.

Connecticut.[2606] The circus entrepreneur, Phineas Taylor Barnum (1810-1891), also of Connecticut, was a cousin of Milo Barnum. The children born to Leonard Richardson and Lucy (Barnum) Richardson include the following persons: Milo Barnum Richardson (1849-1912); James Leonard Richardson (1852-1911); and Caroline Barnum Richardson (1857-1924). Milo Barnum Richardson married Ellen Caroline Miner (1848-1925).[2607] The children born to Milo Barnum Richardson and Ellen Caroline (Miner) Richardson include the following persons: Lucy Caroline Richardson (1874-1903), who married Robert Winch Harwood (1869-1939) of Lime Rock, Connecticut, and Natick, Massachusetts; Bessie Richardson (1876-1877); Milo Barnum Richardson, Jr. (1879-1936), who married Edith Cuyler Vanderlip (born 1883); and Edward Miner Richardson (1883-1941).[2608] Robert Winch Harwood and Lucy Caroline (Richardson) Harwood had a son, Richardson Harwood (1903-1980), who owned the Harwood Baseball Company of Natick, Massachusetts.[2609] This company, founded by Harrison Harwood, invented and manufactured the standard form and design baseball for Major League Baseball.[2610]

William Douglas Richardson married Lucy Willard, who was a daughter of Alexander Perry Willard and Louise (Higgie) Willard.[2611] Charles Richardson, brother of William Douglas Richardson, married Nettie Morgan Smith (1866-1930), a daughter of William Fuller Smith and Electa Jane Loomis.[2612] The children born to Charles Richardson and Nettie (Smith) Richardson were: Betsey Elizabeth Richardson (1888-1888); Charles Richardson, Jr. (1889-1968), who married Hazel Howard (1893-1957); Harry Earl Richardson (1892-1953); Betsy Elizabeth Richardson (1892-1981), who married Charles Washington Keyes (1903-1988); and Horace Wiggins Richardson (1900-1980), who married, first, Betty Waugh (b. 1904), and second, Marion Thackston (1906-1972) of Atlanta, Georgia.[2613]

William Douglas Richardson and the Richardson Construction Company of Chicago and Springfield gained a worldwide reputation through construction work

---

[2606] Cutter, William Richard. (1913). New England Families: Genealogical and Memorial. Vol. III. P. 1189. New York, NY: Lewis Historical Publishing Company. Google Books.

[2607] Solomon, Ruth. (2017). Richardson family genealogical records: Family Group Record for Leonard Richardson. Author's personal collection.

[2608] Solomon, Ruth. (2017). Richardson family genealogical records: Family Group Record for Milo Barnum Richardson. Author's personal collection.

[2609] Cutter, William Richard. (1913). New England Families, Genealogical and Memorial. Vol. III. P. 1189. New York, NY: Lewis Historical Publishing Company. Google Books.

[2610] Harwood Baseball Factory. Natick Center Cultural District. Natickcenter.org.

[2611] Wallace, Joseph. (1904). Past and Present of the City of Springfield and Sangamon County, Illinois. P. 203. Chicago, IL: S. J. Clarke Publishing Company. Google Books.

[2612] Solomon, Ruth. (2016). Richardson family genealogical records: Family Group Record for Charles Richardson.

[2613] Solomon, Ruth. (2016). Richardson family genealogical records: Family Group Record for Charles Richardson.

in Russia, Argentina, Mexico, Chicago, Springfield, and in connection to the 1893 World's Columbian Exposition.[2614] The broad and diverse class of construction projects undertaken by the company created unprecedented civil engineering works and inventions that contributed to the globalization of Chicago construction, engineering, and design.[2615]

Historical records appear so far to be unanimous in their report of the fact that Richardson Construction Company invented the construction material known as "staff."[2616] The development of this unusual building material stemmed from a peculiar class of structural and engineering necessities that arose during the planning processes for the Fair.[2617] The 1893 Chicago World's Fair, therefore, drove not only a tide of architectural creativity, but also a current of construction engineering creativity and development.[2618] Architect Daniel Hudson Burnham (1846-1912) evidently approved of the product and reputation of Richardson Construction Company, because he hired William D. Richardson and the Richardson Construction Company to serve in several top executive offices that supervised the design, development, and construction of the buildings of the Fair.[2619]

The Richardson Construction Company undertook multiple significant construction projects throughout a long and varied organizational life.[2620] The company contracted for the construction of the Imperial Waterworks at St. Petersburg, Russia.[2621] *The Buffalo Commercial* newspaper of Buffalo, New York, contained a report of the multiple projects that Richardson had completed as of the year 1900.[2622] *The Buffalo Commercial* report contains one of the relatively rare lists of major construction projects undertaken by Col. William D. Richardson. The report proved that Col. Richardson had gained an international reputation for a broad scope of construction and engineering projects.[2623] The projects elicited admiration from contemporary scientific and engineering communities. *The Buffalo Commercial* stated that, "The works have been written of extensively in

[2614] The Buffalo Commercial. (Mar. 6, 1900). P.11. Newspapers.com.
[2615] Shankland, Edward C. The Designers and Organizers of the Fair. The Engineering News. Vol. VI. (October, 1893-March, 1894). Pp. 509-518. New York, NY: The Engineering Magazine Company. Google Books.
[2616] The Buffalo Commercial. (Mar. 6, 1900). P.11. Newspapers.com.
[2617] Shankland, Edward C. The Designers and Organizers of the Fair. The Engineering News. Vol. VI. (October, 1893-March, 1894). Pp. 509-518. New York, NY: The Engineering Magazine Company. Google Books.
[2618] Shankland, Edward C. The Designers and Organizers of the Fair. The Engineering News. Vol. VI. (October, 1893-March, 1894). Pp. 509-518. New York, NY: The Engineering Magazine Company. Google Books.
[2619] Shankland, Edward C. The Designers and Organizers of the Fair. The Engineering News. Vol. VI. (October, 1893-March, 1894). Pp. 509-518. New York, NY: The Engineering Magazine Company. Google Books.
[2620] The Buffalo Commercial. (Mar. 6, 1900). P.11. Newspapers.com.
[2621] The Buffalo Commercial. (Mar. 6, 1900). P.11. Newspapers.com.
[2622] The Buffalo Commercial. (Mar. 6, 1900). P.11. Newspapers.com.
[2623] The Buffalo Commercial. (Mar. 6, 1900). P.11. Newspapers.com.

scientific and construction journals."[2624] Col. Richardson also served as the contractor for much of the second Illinois State Capitol building.[2625]

William D. Richardson attended a preliminary Fair banquet at the Richelieu in February, 1893, at which a large number of members of the administrative and artisanal leadership of the Chicago World's Fair presented their respective reports regarding their preparatory work for the Fair.[2626] The Chicago *Inter-Ocean* report of the affair stated the following:

> "Over a wealth of snowy linen and dazzling wine glasses reflecting the lights from the ceiling in endless miniature Director General Davies with the chiefs of his departments and Director of Works Burnham with his staff exchanged declarations of fellowship and renewed old vows of fraternity last night."[2627]

The banquet drew a large attendant company of contributors to the development and planning of the Fair.[2628] The banquet table structurally consisted of a central table element, joined by two long branch tables.[2629] Many parties to the logistical projecting of the Fair were seated at the tables.[2630] Director of Works Daniel Burnham, Assistant Director of Works Graham, Secretary of Works M. P. Pickett, and Director General Davis (which was also spelled "Davies" within the same article) all were seated at the central table, along with Moses P. Handy, and F. J. V. Skiff, who served as Chief of the Mining Department.[2631] At the adjoining branch tables were seated William Douglas Richardson, E. G. Nourse, R. H. Pierce, E. W. Murphy, Rudolph Ulrich, John W. Alvord, F. Sargent, Philip Codman, F. J. Mulcahy, F. O. Cloyes, Alexander Sandier, and C. Y. Turner, who served as Assistant Director of Decoration.[2632] Others seated at the tables included W. H. Holcomb, who served as the General Manager of Transportation, and Colonel Edmund Rice, the Commander of the Columbian Guard, John E. Owens, Assistant Auditor C. V. Barrington, W. S. MacHarg, Chief Engineer E. C. Shankland, Chief of Design C. B. Atwood, and Assistant Chief Hornsby of Electricity.[2633] Major Frederick Brackett, Colonel Dawson, Willard A. Smith, who was Chief of Transportation Exhibits, Chief Peabody of Liberal Arts, Chief Clerk Brewer, Secretary of Installation Hirst, Chief Buchanan of Agriculture, and H. C. Ives, who served as Chief of Fine Arts, all were seated at the tables.[2634]

[2624] The Buffalo Commercial. (Mar. 6, 1900). P.11. Newspapers.com.
[2625] The Buffalo Commercial. (Mar. 6, 1900). P.11. Newspapers.com.
[2626] The Inter-Ocean. (February 10, 1893). P. 4. Newspapers.com.
[2627] The Inter-Ocean. (February 10, 1893). P. 4. Newspapers.com.
[2628] The Inter-Ocean. (February 10, 1893). P. 4. Newspapers.com.
[2629] The Inter-Ocean. (February 10, 1893). P. 4. Newspapers.com.
[2630] The Inter-Ocean. (February 10, 1893). P. 4. Newspapers.com.
[2631] The Inter-Ocean. (February 10, 1893). P. 4. Newspapers.com.
[2632] The Inter-Ocean. (February 10, 1893). P. 4. Newspapers.com.
[2633] The Inter-Ocean. (February 10, 1893). P. 4. Newspapers.com.
[2634] The Inter-Ocean. (February 10, 1893). P. 4. Newspapers.com.

The banquet played host and audience to numerous memorial toasts and dedications, as well as to comments and warnings relevant to diverse public interests.[2635] W. S. MacHarg offered a toast comment in which he exhorted the United States government to prevent the importation of disease-bearing materials.[2636] The comment proved that the public interests of health and sanitation attached firmly to the root purpose of the 1893 Chicago World's Fair.[2637] MacHarg answered the toast comment entitled, "Health as It Regards the World's Fair," with the warning that the import of disease-bearing materials violated United States health interests.[2638] From the foundation of the complaint against the import of contaminated rags entering Atlantic ports, MacHarg encouraged the United States Congress to legislate against the commercial transportation and import practices that had rendered maritime commerce a vector of disease.[2639] The voices of the public-minded company in attendance at the banquet that day constituted only one of many modes in which Chicago assumed the role of policy reformer, with the city donning the statuses of both source and agent of United States public health preservation and reformation.[2640]

The *Inter-Ocean* newspaper reported another case of the passionate narratology of public interest that characterized the banquet.[2641] The banquet included a discourse rife with consideration of the public interests of history, culture, and physical output as a legacy for posterity.[2642] Willard A. Smith, who served as the Chief of Transportation Exhibits, offered an answer to a specific class of questions and comments aimed at the issue of the injustice and unfitness of allowing the World's Fair buildings and other structures to be removed at the closure of the Fair.[2643] The buildings of the World's Fair were constructed to be temporary and to be entirely susceptible to removal.[2644] In consequence of this fact, multiple parties had evidently expressed fear that the predestined deconstruction and removal of the architectural wonders of the World's Fair would necessarily lead to cultural oblivion with respect to the Fair, its values, achievements, and memory.[2645] "[Willard A. Smith] referred to the frequent remarks that it was a pity that such magnificent structures should pass away."[2646] The answer that Willard Smith gave to allay the collective fear of this anticipatory cultural oblivion was that the dramatically brief temporal existence and duration of the architectural grandeurs of the World's Fair would not plunge the monuments into oblivion, but would,

---

[2635] The Inter-Ocean. (February 10, 1893). P. 4. Newspapers.com.
[2636] The Inter-Ocean. (February 10, 1893). P. 4. Newspapers.com.
[2637] The Inter-Ocean. (February 10, 1893). P. 4. Newspapers.com.
[2638] The Inter-Ocean. (February 10, 1893). P. 4. Newspapers.com.
[2639] The Inter-Ocean. (February 10, 1893). P. 4. Newspapers.com.
[2640] The Inter-Ocean. (February 10, 1893). P. 4. Newspapers.com.
[2641] The Inter-Ocean. (February 10, 1893). P. 4. Newspapers.com.
[2642] The Inter-Ocean. (February 10, 1893). P. 4. Newspapers.com.
[2643] The Inter-Ocean. (February 10, 1893). P. 4. Newspapers.com.
[2644] The Inter-Ocean. (February 10, 1893). P. 4. Newspapers.com.
[2645] The Inter-Ocean. (February 10, 1893). P. 4. Newspapers.com.
[2646] The Inter-Ocean. (February 10, 1893). P. 4. Newspapers.com.

quite contrastively, propel them to everlasting memorial.[2647] When confronted with the public fear that the loss of the Fair buildings and other structures would erase the memory of the Fair, Smith answered the fear with the following words:

> "I don't consider it so. It is right that they should pass away. The impression the buildings make will remain on the hearts and minds of the people forever. Although the temples of Rome and Greece fell before the hands of vandals their effect was never lost on humanity."[2648]

Smith's words were intended as a promise of cultural memorial, a promise of community memory, a warranty against cultural oblivion, and a confirmation of the durability of the achievement of Chicago in producing the 1893 World's Columbian Exposition.[2649] Willard A. Smith, William Douglas Richardson, and Edward Clapp Shankland all were members of the Technical Club, which was located at 228-230 S. Clark Street in approximately 1900.[2650] Shankland, who was both colleague and friend to Richardson, was Vice-President of the Technical Club in 1896.[2651] Willard Smith's public promise warranted that the Fair, its works and wonders of cultural ambassadorship, architecture, and expression, though apportioned only a brief temporariness of time, nevertheless would bear an innate and seminal perpetuity of cultural memory and spirit.[2652] *The Inter-Ocean* newspaper report concluded with the following comment: "Mr. Ives followed with a toast on 'Fine Arts.' All the toasts were extempore and every gentleman responded before the party dispersed."[2653]

Through the Fair, Chicago would reach and connect to the whole world, and the city's powerful hand would never fade from its potent grip upon the world's history.[2654] The civil engineering and architectural work at the 1893 World's Fair broadcast the reputation of many people. The *Arizona Sentinel*, a newspaper of Yuma, commented that Colonel W. D. Richardson of Chicago had built the buildings for the World's Fair without incurring any litigation.[2655] "W. D. Richardson, who visited Yuma last week in Company with Judge E. M. Sanford,

---

[2647] The Inter-Ocean. (February 10, 1893). P. 4. Newspapers.com.

[2648] The Inter-Ocean. (February 10, 1893). P. 4. Newspapers.com.

[2649] The Inter-Ocean. (February 10, 1893). P. 4. Newspapers.com.

[2650] Articles of Association, By-Laws, Officers and Members of the Technical Club. (August, 1900). Chicago, IL: The technical Club. Research Center of the Chicago History Museum.

[2651] Articles of Association, By-Laws, Officers and Members of the Technical Club. (August, 1900). Chicago, IL: The technical Club. Research Center of the Chicago History Museum.

[2652] The Inter-Ocean. (February 10, 1893). P. 4. Newspapers.com.

[2653] The Inter-Ocean. (February 10, 1893). P. 4. Newspapers.com.

[2654] The Inter-Ocean. (February 10, 1893). P. 4. Newspapers.com.

[2655] The Arizona Sentinel. (March 24, 1894). P. 1. Newspapers.com.

spent $13,000,000 in putting up the Columbian Fair buildings at Chicago, and never had a suit of any kind for or against him."[2656]

William D. Richardson was also the contractor for the White City at the 1893 World's Columbian Exposition. Colonel Richardson invented the building material known as staff.[2657] "As the inventor of staff, Col. Richardson is widely known."[2658] The Buffalo newspaper commented upon the positive engineering effects that the staff building material caused. "It was his invention that made possible the marvelous beauty of the white city, and the buildings were at once the delight and admiration of all who saw them."[2659]

The Fall-Winter issue of Volume VI of the construction industry journal known as *The Engineering Magazine* (October, 1893-March, 1894) contained detailed facts relevant to the invention of the staff construction material by Colonel Richardson, as well as multiple facts regarding the executive leadership turnover that occurred during the preparation times leading up to the Chicago Fair.[2660] Edward Clapp Shankland, Chief Engineer of the Chicago World's Fair, authored the article titled, *DESIGNERS AND ORGANIZERS OF THE FAIR*, which was published in *The Engineering Magazine*, referenced immediately above.[2661] Shankland wrote about the achievements of the leadership at the Chicago Fair and included multiple significant facts relevant to the inventive work of Colonel Richardson.[2662] In addition to having served as Superintendent of Grounds and Buildings for the Chicago Fair, Richardson had previously held the office of Superintendent of Exterior Covering for the Fair.[2663] Edward Shankland provided a history of certain key facts and elements relevant to the appointments and turnovers in the technological leadership of the Fair, which follow farther below.[2664]

[2656] The Arizona Sentinel. (March 24, 1894). P. 1. Newspapers.com.

[2657] The Buffalo Commercial. (March 6, 1900). P. 11. Newspapers.com.

[2658] The Buffalo Commercial. (March 6, 1900). P. 11. Newspapers.com.

[2659] The Buffalo Commercial. (March 6, 1900). P. 11. Newspapers.com.

[2660] Shankland, Edward C. The Designers and Organizers of the Fair. The Engineering News. Vol. VI. (October, 1893-March, 1894). Pp. 512-514. New York, NY: The Engineering Magazine Company. Google Books.

[2661] Shankland, Edward C. The Designers and Organizers of the Fair. The Engineering News. Vol. VI. (October, 1893-March, 1894). Pp. 512-514. New York, NY: The Engineering Magazine Company. Google Books.

[2662] Shankland, Edward C. The Designers and Organizers of the Fair. The Engineering News. Vol. VI. (October, 1893-March, 1894). Pp. 509-518. New York, NY: The Engineering Magazine Company. Google Books.

[2663] Shankland, Edward C. The Designers and Organizers of the Fair. The Engineering News. Vol. VI. (October, 1893-March, 1894). P. 512. New York, NY: The Engineering Magazine Company. Google Books.

[2664] Shankland, Edward C. The Designers and Organizers of the Fair. The Engineering News. Vol. VI. (October, 1893-March, 1894). Pp. 512-513. New York, NY: The Engineering Magazine Company. Google Books.

Multiple American cities were parties to the competition to receive the Columbian Exposition.[2665] The Chicago City Council, and the Mayor of Chicago, who at that time was DeWitt C. Cregier, decided to appoint a, "'committee of 100 citizens to take preliminary steps towards securing the location of the World's Fair in Chicago.'"[2666] Mayor Cregier, believing subsequently that a larger membership within the Chicago promotion committee would exert greater influence in favor of Chicago as the place of the Columbian Exposition, called for the appointment of 256 persons for the promotion committee.[2667] Resultantly, the organization known as the World's Exposition of 1892 was established as a company from a committee of 35 persons who, in August of 1889, had been elected from Mayor Cregier's Chicago promotion committee of 256 persons.[2668] The persons who signed the State of Illinois articles of incorporation for the World's Exposition of 1892 company included the following: Ferdinand W. Peck, DeWitt C. Cregier, George Schneider, Anthony F. Seeberger, W. C. Seipp, John R. Waller, and E. Nelson Blake.[2669] Octave Chanute and E. T. Jeffery represented the World's Exposition Company in Paris shortly after the establishment of the World's Exposition Company.[2670] Jeffery and Chanute acted as collectors of information when they were sent to Paris to examine and report concerning the exposition taking place at Paris at that time.[2671] The Finance Committee, chaired by Lyman J. Gage, effected the financing of $500,000, which was merely one-tenth of the $5,000,000 capitalization money that the World's Exposition Company was incorporated to generate.[2672] Chicago entrepreneur Otto Young established an emergency finance

---

[2665] Shankland, Edward C. The Designers and Organizers of the Fair. The Engineering News. Vol. VI. (October, 1893-March, 1894). P. 509. New York, NY: The Engineering Magazine Company. Google Books.
[2666] Shankland, Edward C. The Designers and Organizers of the Fair. The Engineering News. Vol. VI. (October, 1893-March, 1894). P. 509. New York, NY: The Engineering Magazine Company. Google Books.
[2667] Shankland, Edward C. The Designers and Organizers of the Fair. The Engineering News. Vol. VI. (October, 1893-March, 1894). P. 509. New York, NY: The Engineering Magazine Company. Google Books.
[2668] Shankland, Edward C. The Designers and Organizers of the Fair. The Engineering News. Vol. VI. (October, 1893-March, 1894). P. 509. New York, NY: The Engineering Magazine Company. Google Books.
[2669] Shankland, Edward C. The Designers and Organizers of the Fair. The Engineering News. Vol. VI. (October, 1893-March, 1894). P. 509. New York, NY: The Engineering Magazine Company. Google Books.
[2670] Shankland, Edward C. The Designers and Organizers of the Fair. The Engineering News. Vol. VI. (October, 1893-March, 1894). P. 509. New York, NY: The Engineering Magazine Company. Google Books.
[2671] Shankland, Edward C. The Designers and Organizers of the Fair. The Engineering News. Vol. VI. (October, 1893-March, 1894). P. 509. New York, NY: The Engineering Magazine Company. Google Books.
[2672] Shankland, Edward C. The Designers and Organizers of the Fair. The Engineering News. Vol. VI. (October, 1893-March, 1894). P. 509. New York, NY: The Engineering Magazine Company. Google Books.

committee the purpose of which was to effect the financing of the remaining amount of approximately $4,500,000 for the company.[2673] Young served on this emergency finance board with B. R. De Young and D. K. Hill, and the emergency committee succeeded in generating the remainder of the money.[2674]

Much in the manner of a court case, the City of Chicago stood as a party to a national competition of interests, and one in which multiple municipal parties competed fervently for the approval from the United States Congress as the place for the Columbian Exposition.[2675] The case involved the matter and issue of the place of the Columbian Exposition. The various contestant cities were the several litigant parties to the case. The United States Congress was the court and jury. The issue was the pending uncertainty of place for the Exposition. The municipal parties filed pleadings, facts, proofs, and arguments before the Congress. As Edward C. Shankland stated, Chicago won her cause before the court of the United States Congress, and the Congress enacted a law that chose Chicago as the place for the Columbian Exposition.[2676] After granting approval to Chicago as the host place of the Columbian Exposition, the Congress ordered that more money be raised for the Exposition and urged the financing of an additional $5,000,000, which would, when performed, raise total supportive capital money for the Exposition to the amount of $10,000,000.[2677]

Shankland reported that one of the first issues to be examined by the leadership of the World's Columbian Exposition was the specific place in Chicago to be chosen for the World's Fair.[2678] The members of the leadership chose Jackson Park from among multiple place options in Chicago.[2679] The Buildings and Grounds Committee consisted of Chairman E. T. Jeffery, Lyman J. Gage, H. B. Stone,

[2673] Shankland, Edward C. The Designers and Organizers of the Fair. The Engineering News. Vol. VI. (October, 1893-March, 1894). P. 509. New York, NY: The Engineering Magazine Company. Google Books.

[2674] Shankland, Edward C. The Designers and Organizers of the Fair. The Engineering News. Vol. VI. (October, 1893-March, 1894). P. 509. New York, NY: The Engineering Magazine Company. Google Books.

[2675] Shankland, Edward C. The Designers and Organizers of the Fair. The Engineering News. Vol. VI. (October, 1893-March, 1894). Pp. 509-510. New York, NY: The Engineering Magazine Company. Google Books.

[2676] Shankland, Edward C. The Designers and Organizers of the Fair. The Engineering News. Vol. VI. (October, 1893-March, 1894). P. 510. New York, NY: The Engineering Magazine Company. Google Books.

[2677] Shankland, Edward C. The Designers and Organizers of the Fair. The Engineering News. Vol. VI. (October, 1893-March, 1894). P. 510. New York, NY: The Engineering Magazine Company. Google Books.

[2678] Shankland, Edward C. The Designers and Organizers of the Fair. The Engineering News. Vol. VI. (October, 1893-March, 1894). P. 510. New York, NY: The Engineering Magazine Company. Google Books.

[2679] Shankland, Edward C. The Designers and Organizers of the Fair. The Engineering News. Vol. VI. (October, 1893-March, 1894). P. 510. New York, NY: The Engineering Magazine Company. Google Books.

Charles H. Schwab, J. P. Ketchum, R. A. Waller, and Secretary A. W. Sawyer.[2680] Charles Henry Schwab of the Buildings and Grounds Committee was a business partner and close friend of John Whitfield Bunn. Both Schwab and Bunn were among the chief leadership and ownership of Selz, Schwab & Company. For extensive information concerning Selz, Schwab & Company, see Chapter 4, *Friends of the Leatherworkers*.

The Buildings and Grounds Committee chose Burnham & Root to serve as the consulting architects for the Fair.[2681] The Buildings and Grounds Committee also appointed Frederick Law Olmsted and his firm, F. L. Olmsted & Co., to serve as consulting landscape architects for the Fair.[2682] The Committee additionally appointed A. Gottlieb as the consulting engineer for the Fair.[2683] These three mutually relevant appointments took place on August 20, 1890.[2684] Daniel Hudson Burnham assumed the office of Chief of Construction for the Fair in October, 1890.[2685] Burnham, Gottlieb, and F. L. Olmsted & Company then established an advisory board for the purpose of creation and development of the design plans and architectural plans for the entire World's Fair.[2686] Burnham served as Chairman of the Advisory Board.[2687] Frederick Law Olmsted's partner, H. S. Codman, produced and submitted general plans for the entire Fair, and these plans were accepted and ratified by the World's Fair leadership structure on December

---

[2680] Shankland, Edward C. The Designers and Organizers of the Fair. The Engineering News. Vol. VI. (October, 1893-March, 1894). P. 510. New York, NY: The Engineering Magazine Company. Google Books.

[2681] Shankland, Edward C. The Designers and Organizers of the Fair. The Engineering News. Vol. VI. (October, 1893-March, 1894). P. 511. New York, NY: The Engineering Magazine Company. Google Books.

[2682] Shankland, Edward C. The Designers and Organizers of the Fair. The Engineering News. Vol. VI. (October, 1893-March, 1894). P. 511. New York, NY: The Engineering Magazine Company. Google Books.

[2683] Shankland, Edward C. The Designers and Organizers of the Fair. The Engineering News. Vol. VI. (October, 1893-March, 1894). P. 511. New York, NY: The Engineering Magazine Company. Google Books.

[2684] Shankland, Edward C. The Designers and Organizers of the Fair. The Engineering News. Vol. VI. (October, 1893-March, 1894). P. 511. New York, NY: The Engineering Magazine Company. Google Books.

[2685] Shankland, Edward C. The Designers and Organizers of the Fair. The Engineering News. Vol. VI. (October, 1893-March, 1894). P. 511. New York, NY: The Engineering Magazine Company. Google Books.

[2686] Shankland, Edward C. The Designers and Organizers of the Fair. The Engineering News. Vol. VI. (October, 1893-March, 1894). P. 511. New York, NY: The Engineering Magazine Company. Google Books.

[2687] Shankland, Edward C. The Designers and Organizers of the Fair. The Engineering News. Vol. VI. (October, 1893-March, 1894). P. 511. New York, NY: The Engineering Magazine Company. Google Books.

1, 1890.[2688] The ratification established the foundation of policy and law relevant to the design, architecture, and construction for the Chicago World's Fair.[2689]

Executive turnover within the Fair leadership was rampant. Dion Geraldine, who had served as General Superintendent of the Fair, resigned from that general management office in the fall of 1892.[2690] Soon after the time of Mr. Geraldine's resignation, William Douglas Richardson completed performance of the job and duties of the office of Superintendent of Exterior Covering.[2691] The two leadership transitions coincided harmoniously. Richardson, therefore, assumed the job and office of General Superintendent of Buildings, because Dion Geraldine had already resigned from the office of General Manager for the Fair, and the office of General Manager thus remained vacant.[2692] William Pretyman had served as Director of Color.[2693] Ernest R. Graham served as Assistant Chief of Construction.[2694] Rudolph Ulrich held the office of Landscape Superintendent.[2695] Edward C. Shankland assumed the office of Chief Engineer upon the resignation of Chief A. Gottlieb.[2696] Frank D. Millet became Director of Decoration after William Pretyman resigned the office of Director of Color in May of 1892.[2697] Colonel Edmund Rice assumed

[2688] Shankland, Edward C. The Designers and Organizers of the Fair. The Engineering News. Vol. VI. (October, 1893-March, 1894). P. 511. New York, NY: The Engineering Magazine Company. Google Books.

[2689] Shankland, Edward C. The Designers and Organizers of the Fair. The Engineering News. Vol. VI. (October, 1893-March, 1894). P. 511. New York, NY: The Engineering Magazine Company. Google Books.

[2690] Shankland, Edward C. The Designers and Organizers of the Fair. The Engineering News. Vol. VI. (October, 1893-March, 1894). P. 513. New York, NY: The Engineering Magazine Company. Google Books.

[2691] Shankland, Edward C. The Designers and Organizers of the Fair. The Engineering News. Vol. VI. (October, 1893-March, 1894). P. 513. New York, NY: The Engineering Magazine Company. Google Books.

[2692] Shankland, Edward C. The Designers and Organizers of the Fair. The Engineering News. Vol. VI. (October, 1893-March, 1894). P. 513. New York, NY: The Engineering Magazine Company. Google Books.

[2693] Shankland, Edward C. The Designers and Organizers of the Fair. The Engineering News. Vol. VI. (October, 1893-March, 1894). P. 512. New York, NY: The Engineering Magazine Company. Google Books.

[2694] Shankland, Edward C. The Designers and Organizers of the Fair. The Engineering News. Vol. VI. (October, 1893-March, 1894). P. 512. New York, NY: The Engineering Magazine Company. Google Books.

[2695] Shankland, Edward C. The Designers and Organizers of the Fair. The Engineering News. Vol. VI. (October, 1893-March, 1894). P. 512. New York, NY: The Engineering Magazine Company. Google Books.

[2696] Shankland, Edward C. The Designers and Organizers of the Fair. The Engineering News. Vol. VI. (October, 1893-March, 1894). Pp. 512-514. New York, NY: The Engineering Magazine Company. Google Books.

[2697] Shankland, Edward C. The Designers and Organizers of the Fair. The Engineering News. Vol. VI. (October, 1893-March, 1894). P. 512. New York, NY: The Engineering Magazine Company. Google Books.

the office of chief executive of the Guard for the World's Fair in May of 1892.[2698] Marshal Edward Murphy assumed control of the fire service for the World's Fair in December of 1892.[2699] R. H. Pierce succeeded Frederick Sargent as Electrical Engineer when Sargent resigned the office.[2700] Charles F. Foster assumed the office of Mechanical Engineer upon the resignation from that office by J. C. Slocum.[2701] Augustus St. Gaudens served as the executive Sculptor for the Fair.[2702]

Daniel Burnham selected the following architectural firms to serve as parties to the design of the multiple building elements of the Chicago Fair. The list contains the architect and the design element of the World's Fair for which the architect was responsible. Edward C. Shankland's list contained the following facts.

Architect	Fair Architectural Design Element
1. Richard M. Hunt	Fair Administration Building
2. Peabody & Stearns	Machinery Hall
3. McKim, Meade & White	Agricultural Building
4. George B. Post	Manufacturers and Liberal Arts Building
5. Van Brunt & Howe	Electricity Building
6. Solon Spencer Beman	Mines and Mining Building
7. Adler & Sullivan	Transportation Building
8. Henry Ives Cobb	Fisheries Building
9. Burling & Whitehouse	Festival Hall
10. Jenney & Mundie	Horticultural Building[2703]

Major Benjamin Cummings Truman, who represented the Department of Floriculture of the 1893 Chicago World's Fair, wrote a history of the Fair that was titled, *HISTORY OF THE WORLD'S FAIR: BEING A COMPLETE*

[2698] Shankland, Edward C. The Designers and Organizers of the Fair. The Engineering News. Vol. VI. (October, 1893-March, 1894). Pp. 512-513. New York, NY: The Engineering Magazine Company. Google Books.

[2699] Shankland, Edward C. The Designers and Organizers of the Fair. The Engineering News. Vol. VI. (October, 1893-March, 1894). P. 513. New York, NY: The Engineering Magazine Company. Google Books.

[2700] Shankland, Edward C. The Designers and Organizers of the Fair. The Engineering News. Vol. VI. (October, 1893-March, 1894). P. 513. New York, NY: The Engineering Magazine Company. Google Books.

[2701] Shankland, Edward C. The Designers and Organizers of the Fair. The Engineering News. Vol. VI. (October, 1893-March, 1894). P. 513. New York, NY: The Engineering Magazine Company. Google Books.

[2702] Shankland, Edward C. The Designers and Organizers of the Fair. The Engineering News. Vol. VI. (October, 1893-March, 1894). P. 511. New York, NY: The Engineering Magazine Company. Google Books.

[2703] Shankland, Edward C. The Designers and Organizers of the Fair. The Engineering News. Vol. VI. (October, 1893-March, 1894). P. 511. New York, NY: The Engineering Magazine Company. Google Books.

DESCRIPTION OF THE WORLD'S COLUMBIAN EXPOSITION FROM ITS INCEPTION.[2704] Major Truman provided in this history the roster of the persons and offices that composed the Director of Works leadership structure of the 1893 Chicago World's Fair. Major Truman enumerated the persons and jobs as follows:

Person	Job
1. Daniel Burnham	Director of Works
2. William D. Richardson	General Superintendent of Buildings
3. E. R. Graham	Assistant Director of Works
4. M. B. Pickett	Secretary of Works
5. Frederick L. Olmsted & Co.	Landscape Architects
6. R. Ulrich	Superintendent of Landscape
7. Charles B. Atwood	Designer-In-Chief
8. F. D. Millet	Director of Decoration
9. C. Y. Turner	Assistant Director of Decoration
10. E. D. Allen	Superintendent of Painting
11. W. H. Holcomb	General Manager of Transportation
12. E. G. Nourse	Assistant General Manager of Transportation
13. E. C. Shankland	Chief Engineer
14. William S. McHarg	Engineer of Water Supply and Sewerage
15. C. M. Wilkes	Assistant Engineer of Water Department
16. Dr. John E. Owens, M.D.	Medical Director
17. R. H. Pierce	Electrical Engineer
18. W. E. Brown	Building Superintendent
19. B. B. Cheeseman	Building Superintendent
20. J. K. Freitag	Building Superintendent
21. H. S. Hibbard	Building Superintendent
22. C. A. Jordan	Building Superintendent
23. J. H. Murphy	Building Superintendent
24. A. C. Speed	Building Superintendent
25. F. W. Watts	Building Superintendent
26. M. Young	Building Superintendent
27. C. D. Arnold	Chief of Photography Department
28. C. F. Foster	Mechanical Engineer
29. J. W. Alvord	Engineer of Grades and Surveys
30. G. H. Binkley	Assistant Engineer of Grades and Surveys
31. F. J. Mulcahy	Purchasing Agent

[2704] Truman, Benjamin Cummings. (1893). History of the World's Fair: Being a Complete Description of the World's Columbian Exposition From Its Inception P. 67. Chicago, IL: Mammoth Publishing Company. Google Books.

32. Edward W. Murphy	Fire Marshal, 14th Battalion of the Chicago Fire Department
33. F. O. Cloyes	Chief Draftsman
34. D. A. Collins	Superintendent of Interior Docking
35. E. R. Loring	Superintendent of Plumbing
36. A. A. Clark	Superintendent of Midway Plaisance
37. J. Worcester	Superintendent of Elevated Railway[2705]

The sculpture personnel of the 1893 World's Fair consisted of many artists.[2706] Chief Engineer Edward C. Shankland provided the list of sculptors and the works that they contributed to the Fair.[2707] The architects that had been hired were authorized to choose the sculptors whom they wished to perform the necessary sculpture work that flowed from the architects' respective designs and plans.[2708] Permission to choose the sculptors was granted subject to the advice of Augustus St. Gaudens.[2709] Shankland provided the list of the sculptors and their sculpture contributions to the Fair as follows.[2710]

Sculptor	Sculpture Work
1. Philip Martiny	Fine Arts and Agricultural Buildings
2. L. G. Mead	Main Pediment of Agricultural Building
3. J. J. Boyle	Transportation Building
4. Karl Bitter	Administration Building
5. M. A. Waagen	Machinery Hall and Colonnade
6. E. C. Potter	Peristyle
7. D. C. French	Peristyle
8. Lorado Taft	Horticultural Building
9. Miss Alice Rideout	Woman's Building
10. A. P. Proctor	Lions of the Art Building

[2705] Truman, Benjamin Cummings. (1893). P. 67. Chicago, IL: Mammoth Publishing Company. Google Books.

[2706] Shankland, Edward C. The Designers and Organizers of the Fair. The Engineering News. Vol. VI. (October, 1893-March, 1894). P. 515. New York, NY: The Engineering Magazine Company. Google Books.

[2707] Shankland, Edward C. The Designers and Organizers of the Fair. The Engineering News. Vol. VI. (October, 1893-March, 1894). P. 515. New York, NY: The Engineering Magazine Company. Google Books.

[2708] Shankland, Edward C. The Designers and Organizers of the Fair. The Engineering News. Vol. VI. (October, 1893-March, 1894). P. 515. New York, NY: The Engineering Magazine Company. Google Books.

[2709] Shankland, Edward C. The Designers and Organizers of the Fair. The Engineering News. Vol. VI. (October, 1893-March, 1894). P. 515. New York, NY: The Engineering Magazine Company. Google Books.

[2710] Shankland, Edward C. The Designers and Organizers of the Fair. The Engineering News. Vol. VI. (October, 1893-March, 1894). P. 515. New York, NY: The Engineering Magazine Company. Google Books.

11. T. Baur	Lions of the Art Building
12. A. P. Proctor	Animals of the bridges
13. E. Kemys	Animals of the bridges
14. D. C. French	Statue of the Republic
15. Carl Rohl-Smith	Statue of Franklin
16. J. Gelert	Figure of Neptune on rostral columns
17. Frederick MacMonnies	MacMonnies Fountain
18. Augustus St. Gaudens	Statues of Goddess Diana and Columbus[2711]

Daniel Burnham charged William D. Richardson with responsibility for the design and plan for construction of the exterior coverings of the structures of the Fair. The job bore the necessity, and the resultant opportunity, for technological development and innovation. Richardson performed the job duties and this performance resulted in the invention of a most suitable building material: staff. "When it was determined to make the exterior of all the buildings of staff, the construction department entered an entirely new field."[2712] Chief Engineer Shankland reported that experts from Boston and New York were unable to develop a plan for the construction of the structural exteriors with the staff material.[2713] They were also unable to advise on the issue in any way.[2714] A Chicagoan, however, rose to the necessity of the job when Richardson executed a plan for the application of staff to the exterior surfaces of the World's Fair structures.[2715] "Mr. Burnham made a happy choice when he put W. D. Richardson, who had formerly been a contractor of large experience, in charge of this work."[2716]

The historical record brings proofs of the facts relevant to the success of the Richardson method. "That [Richardson] succeeded will be questioned by no one who saw the buildings, with their statues, and the animal figures on the bridges

---

[2711] Shankland, Edward C. The Designers and Organizers of the Fair. The Engineering News. Vol. VI. (October, 1893-March, 1894). P. 515. New York, NY: The Engineering Magazine Company. Google Books.

[2712] Shankland, Edward C. The Designers and Organizers of the Fair. The Engineering News. Vol. VI. (October, 1893-March, 1894). P. 514. New York, NY: The Engineering Magazine Company. Google Books.

[2713] Shankland, Edward C. The Designers and Organizers of the Fair. The Engineering News. Vol. VI. (October, 1893-March, 1894). P. 514. New York, NY: The Engineering Magazine Company. Google Books.

[2714] Shankland, Edward C. The Designers and Organizers of the Fair. The Engineering News. Vol. VI. (October, 1893-March, 1894). P. 514. New York, NY: The Engineering Magazine Company. Google Books.

[2715] Shankland, Edward C. The Designers and Organizers of the Fair. The Engineering News. Vol. VI. (October, 1893-March, 1894). P. 514. New York, NY: The Engineering Magazine Company. Google Books.

[2716] Shankland, Edward C. The Designers and Organizers of the Fair. The Engineering News. Vol. VI. (October, 1893-March, 1894). P. 514. New York, NY: The Engineering Magazine Company. Google Books.

and terraces, all constructed under Mr. Richardson's supervision."[2717] The April 26, 1891, edition of the *Chicago Tribune* contained the following news item: "Mr. Burnham appointed with the consent of the committee W. D. Richardson to be superintendent of foundations, bridges, and piers in Jackson Park. He also appointed Max Young inspector of grading and filing."[2718]

The *St. Louis Post-Dispatch* reported a possible etymology for the word "staff," referring to the famed building material at the 1893 World's Fair.[2719] The St. Louis newspaper indicated that Col. William D. Richardson, the inventor of staff, told Daniel Burnham that the material was a, "good staff to lean on."[2720] Burnham, impressed with the metaphor, is reported to have answered, "'Why not call it staff?'"[2721] Historian Walter L. Bradley challenged the genuineness of this etymology, however, and alleged that the Burnham-Richardson dialogue that reportedly produced the name "staff" for the novel building material was merely a "pleasant fiction."[2722] Richardson himself stated, according to S. T. Jacobs, the following regarding the etymology of the word "staff":

> "'In the American language, words creep in rather peculiarly. We give a sort of 'nickname' to places and things, and why we do so is hard to explain. The word 'staff' was applied to this material when we first commenced to make it and I presume it will always retain that name.'"[2723]

The historical record produces multiple proofs that establish with certainty that Richardson was the one to invent both the physical material known as staff and the attendant construction methods of staff. Even if, by chance, Richardson did not invent the name, "staff," he certainly invented the material itself.[2724] Let the reader, therefore, judge the merits of the tangential etymological issue of the word's lexical source. Let us next turn attention to the technological and operational elements of the Richardson construction method.

S. T. Jacobs composed an 1894 history memorandum in which he accounted for the principal and circumstantial facts relevant to the Richardson Method of

---

[2717] Shankland, Edward C. The Designers and Organizers of the Fair. The Engineering News. Vol. VI. (October, 1893-March, 1894). P. 514. New York, NY: The Engineering Magazine Company. Google Books.

[2718] The Chicago Tribune. (April 26, 1891). P. 4. Newspapers.com.

[2719] The St. Louis Post-Dispatch. (February 22, 1903). P. 52. Newspapers.com.

[2720] The St. Louis Post-Dispatch. (February 22, 1903). P. 52. Newspapers.com.

[2721] The St. Louis Post-Dispatch. (February 22, 1903). P. 52. Newspapers.com.

[2722] Bradley, Walter L. (December 5, 1903). Picturesque Chinese Kites. Scientific American: An Illustrated Journal of Art, Science & Mechanics. Vol. 89. P. 410. New York, NY: Munn & Co. Google Books.

[2723] Jacobs, S. T. (February, 1894). The Inland Architect and News Record. Vol. 23, Issue 1. P. 5. Chicago, IL: The Inland Publishing Company. Google Books.

[2724] Jacobs, S. T. (February, 1894). The Inland Architect and News Record. Vol. 23, Issue 1. Pp. 5-6. Chicago, IL: The Inland Publishing Company. Google Books.

construction for the Fair.[2725] Fortunately for posterity, Mr. Jacobs' personal memorandum was subsequently published in the monthly architectural and construction journal known as *The Inland Architect and News Record*.[2726] In 1894, *The Inland Architect and News Record* journal leadership structure and staff consisted of L. Muller, Jr., who served as Manager; C. E. Illsley, who served as Associate Editor; and Robert Craik McLean, who served as Editor.[2727] Contributors to Volume 23 of the journal included Daniel Hudson Burnham, Louis Henry Sullivan, William Le Baron Jenney, Irving K. Pond, Allen B. Pond, Dankmar Adler, Henry Van Brunt, William Paul Gerhard, and P. B. Wight.[2728] Dankmar Adler was, interestingly, the brother-in-law of Morris Selz, who is discussed in Chapter 4, *Friends of the Leatherworkers*. Volume 23, Issue Number 1, of *The Inland Architect and News Record* contained a detailed and extensive history of the development of the "staff" building material for the 1893 Chicago World's Fair.[2729] S. T. Jacobs' memorandum was published as a history article that was titled, *Staff And Sculpture Work of the World's Fair*.[2730] Jacobs introduced the subject matter with prefatory words that reflected the professional relationship that existed between Jacobs and Richardson.[2731] Jacobs and Richardson became acquainted on September 24, 1891, in connection with the developmental stages of the construction of the Fair.[2732]

> "IN 'writing up' a history of any important work or event, especially to one unaccustomed to it, even though familiar with all the facts, there are many obstacles to overcome. Thoughts crowd in upon you in jumbled confusion, and need to be presented to the reader in order. However, as this article is intended only for a correct history of that part of the work accomplished for the World's Columbian Exposition coming directly under the supervision of Mr. W. D. Richardson, as superintendent of exterior covering, and is an abstract from a memorandum written more for

---

[2725] Jacobs, S. T. (February, 1894). The Inland Architect and News Record. Vol. 23, Issue 1. Pp. 5-6. Chicago, IL: The Inland Publishing Company. Google Books.

[2726] Jacobs, S. T. (February, 1894). The Inland Architect and News Record. Vol. 23, Issue 1. Pp. 5-6. Chicago, IL: The Inland Publishing Company. Google Books.

[2727] The Inland Architect and News Record. (February, 1894). Vol. 23, Issue 1. P. 1. Chicago, IL: The Inland Publishing Company. Google Books.

[2728] The Inland Architect and News Record. (February, 1894). Vol. 23, Issue 1. P. 1. Chicago, IL: The Inland Publishing Company. Google Books.

[2729] Jacobs, S. T. (February, 1894). The Inland Architect and News Record. Vol. 23, Issue 1. Pp. 5-6. Chicago, IL: The Inland Publishing Company. Google Books.

[2730] Jacobs, S. T. (February, 1894). The Inland Architect and News Record. Vol. 23, Issue 1. Pp. 5-6. Chicago, IL: The Inland Publishing Company. Google Books.

[2731] Jacobs, S. T. (February, 1894). The Inland Architect and News Record. Vol. 23, Issue 1. P. 5. Chicago, IL: The Inland Publishing Company. Google Books.

[2732] Jacobs, S. T. (February, 1894). The Inland Architect and News Record. Vol. 23, Issue 1. P. 5. Chicago, IL: The Inland Publishing Company. Google Books.

my own use than for any other purpose, it will probably not make much difference, so long as the main facts are presented."[2733]

According to Jacobs, when he and Richardson met in the fall of 1891, "nothing of any importance had been done so far as construction of the buildings was concerned."[2734] The Grading and Landscape Department exercised jurisdiction over the grounds of Jackson Park at that time. The Fair was in the nascent stages of development, and only the initial construction of the Woman's Building had begun.[2735] The Richardson Construction Company of Chicago would serve as a valuable organizational resource, both because the company served as a collector of international construction information, and because the company functioned as a practical and extensive database and library for construction concepts, processes, material uses, and construction theories.[2736] The architectural genealogy of the Fair was, therefore, complex, international, and multiethnic, and consisted of construction processes and histories collected by the Richardson Construction Company from no fewer than four continents: North America, Europe, Africa, and South America.[2737]

For an extended time, Richardson visited multiple countries of the world to examine construction processes and construction materials used in the diverse places and cultural traditions that he studied.[2738] Upon returning to Chicago in early 1891, Richardson met with the members of the executive leadership of the Fair.[2739] This conference produced abundant information that had been collected from observation and examination of multiple places.[2740] Having visited Lisbon, Buenos Aires, Algiers, Brazil, Paraguay, and Uruguay, probably in addition to other countries and foreign cities, Richardson observed diverse construction methods.[2741] Jacobs reported that: "Mr. Richardson had traveled extensively and had taken careful note of the way buildings were constructed in different

---

[2733] Jacobs, S. T. (February, 1894). The Inland Architect and News Record. Vol. 23, Issue 1. P. 5. Chicago, IL: The Inland Publishing Company. Google Books.

[2734] Jacobs, S. T. (February, 1894). The Inland Architect and News Record. Vol. 23, Issue 1. P. 5. Chicago, IL: The Inland Publishing Company. Google Books.

[2735] Jacobs, S. T. (February, 1894). The Inland Architect and News Record. Vol. 23, Issue 1. P. 5. Chicago, IL: The Inland Publishing Company. Google Books.

[2736] Jacobs, S. T. (February, 1894). The Inland Architect and News Record. Vol. 23, Issue 1. Pp. 5-6. Chicago, IL: The Inland Publishing Company. Google Books.

[2737] Jacobs, S. T. (February, 1894). The Inland Architect and News Record. Vol. 23, Issue 1. Pp. 5-6. Chicago, IL: The Inland Publishing Company. Google Books.

[2738] Jacobs, S. T. (February, 1894). The Inland Architect and News Record. Vol. 23, Issue 1. P. 5. Chicago, IL: The Inland Publishing Company. Google Books.

[2739] Jacobs, S. T. (February, 1894). The Inland Architect and News Record. Vol. 23, Issue 1. P. 5. Chicago, IL: The Inland Publishing Company. Google Books.

[2740] Jacobs, S. T. (February, 1894). The Inland Architect and News Record. Vol. 23, Issue 1. P. 5. Chicago, IL: The Inland Publishing Company. Google Books.

[2741] Jacobs, S. T. (February, 1894). The Inland Architect and News Record. Vol. 23, Issue 1. P. 5. Chicago, IL: The Inland Publishing Company. Google Books.

countries."[2742] Richardson reported that the construction process and materials popular at Lisbon involved the molding and laying of clay forms, followed by the exterior molding and laying of plaster forms upon the foundational clay forms.[2743] In Brazil, the construction process consisted of the molding and establishment of canvas forms, and the subsequent deposition of plaster forms upon the foundational canvas forms.[2744] The relevant construction process at Algiers, a city that was then part of the French Empire, consisted of the molding of adobe forms, followed by the laying of stucco forms upon the adobe forms.[2745] The construction process that prevailed in Montivideo, Uruguay, entailed the molding and laying of forms made overwhelmingly of stucco.[2746] Paraguayan construction process consisted of the creation of forms made from sun-dried brick, and the subsequent molding and laying of stucco forms upon the dried brick forms.[2747]

William D. Richardson proposed an architectural synthesis for the construction materials of the Chicago Fair, a synthesis of the multiple construction data that he had collected internationally for Chicago.[2748] Jacobs stated: "Mr. Richardson observed all the uses of stucco, or plaster of paris [sic], and told the exposition people that, strengthened with fiber, such as sisal or hemp, it would make a splendid material to use for the covering of the buildings."[2749] The new material proposed by Richardson was "staff."[2750] After the proposal for the use of staff, trials were undertaken to judge the safety, soundness, and efficiency of the new building material.[2751] The members of the leadership of the Fair adopted staff as the official construction material for the Fair after the trials produced favorable results.[2752] Staff thus emerged as a central building material for the World's Fair,

[2742] Jacobs, S. T. (February, 1894). The Inland Architect and News Record. Vol. 23, Issue 1. P. 5. Chicago, IL: The Inland Publishing Company. Google Books.

[2743] Jacobs, S. T. (February, 1894). The Inland Architect and News Record. Vol. 23, Issue 1. P. 5. Chicago, IL: The Inland Publishing Company. Google Books.

[2744] Jacobs, S. T. (February, 1894). The Inland Architect and News Record. Vol. 23, Issue 1. P. 5. Chicago, IL: The Inland Publishing Company. Google Books.

[2745] Jacobs, S. T. (February, 1894). The Inland Architect and News Record. Vol. 23, Issue 1. P. 5. Chicago, IL: The Inland Publishing Company. Google Books.

[2746] Jacobs, S. T. (February, 1894). The Inland Architect and News Record. Vol. 23, Issue 1. P. 5. Chicago, IL: The Inland Publishing Company. Google Books.

[2747] Jacobs, S. T. (February, 1894). The Inland Architect and News Record. Vol. 23, Issue 1. P. 5. Chicago, IL: The Inland Publishing Company. Google Books.

[2748] Jacobs, S. T. (February, 1894). The Inland Architect and News Record. Vol. 23, Issue 1. P. 5. Chicago, IL: The Inland Publishing Company. Google Books.

[2749] Jacobs, S. T. (February, 1894). The Inland Architect and News Record. Vol. 23, Issue 1. P. 5. Chicago, IL: The Inland Publishing Company. Google Books.

[2750] Jacobs, S. T. (February, 1894). The Inland Architect and News Record. Vol. 23, Issue 1. P. 5. Chicago, IL: The Inland Publishing Company. Google Books.

[2751] Jacobs, S. T. (February, 1894). The Inland Architect and News Record. Vol. 23, Issue 1. P. 5. Chicago, IL: The Inland Publishing Company. Google Books.

[2752] Jacobs, S. T. (February, 1894). The Inland Architect and News Record. Vol. 23, Issue 1. P. 5. Chicago, IL: The Inland Publishing Company. Google Books.

and Chicago was the place of its initial trial and successful use.[2753] The staff building material possessed, therefore, an innate complexity both of material constitution and historical culture.[2754] An international catalogue of construction data and architectural history cohabited, in a manner, the contents of the new staff material along with the fibers, cements, and plasters that constituted its physical substance.[2755] Staff consisted of a mixture of stucco and fiber. The fiber additive served to strengthen the stucco as an exterior covering material.[2756] The construction process that produced staff involved the collection of fiber from either sisal or hemp sources, and the subsequent beating of the fiber into a soft "feathery" consistency.[2757] Jacobs stated the following: "Anyone familiar with ordinary stucco work will easily understand it [staff]. It really is stucco, with the exception of the addition of the fiber."[2758] Liquid plaster is joined with the pulverized fiber to form a union that produces a form of fortified stucco.[2759]

Jacobs then described the construction processes that produced the sculptures and architectural design forms for the buildings of the Chicago Fair.[2760] The gelatine mold process consisted of the production of an original model, a standard form from which all other identical forms were to be derived.[2761] The designer or sculptor would first make the standard model of whatever architectural form, or art form, was desired.[2762] A case would then be constructed for the standard form, and the case would enclose the standard form with a margin of approximately one inch of space between the interior of the case, and the exterior of the standard form.[2763] The case would follow the form of the model encased within it, creating concentric

[2753] Jacobs, S. T. (February, 1894). The Inland Architect and News Record. Vol. 23, Issue 1. P. 5. Chicago, IL: The Inland Publishing Company. Google Books.

[2754] Jacobs, S. T. (February, 1894). The Inland Architect and News Record. Vol. 23, Issue 1. P. 5. Chicago, IL: The Inland Publishing Company. Google Books.

[2755] Jacobs, S. T. (February, 1894). The Inland Architect and News Record. Vol. 23, Issue 1. P. 5. Chicago, IL: The Inland Publishing Company. Google Books.

[2756] Jacobs, S. T. (February, 1894). The Inland Architect and News Record. Vol. 23, Issue 1. Pp. 5-6. Chicago, IL: The Inland Publishing Company. Google Books.

[2757] Jacobs, S. T. (February, 1894). The Inland Architect and News Record. Vol. 23, Issue 1. Pp. 5-6. Chicago, IL: The Inland Publishing Company. Google Books.

[2758] Jacobs, S. T. (February, 1894). The Inland Architect and News Record. Vol. 23, Issue 1. P. 5. Chicago, IL: The Inland Publishing Company. Google Books.

[2759] Jacobs, S. T. (February, 1894). The Inland Architect and News Record. Vol. 23, Issue 1. P. 5. Chicago, IL: The Inland Publishing Company. Google Books.

[2760] Jacobs, S. T. (February, 1894). The Inland Architect and News Record. Vol. 23, Issue 1. Pp. 5-6. Chicago, IL: The Inland Publishing Company. Google Books.

[2761] Jacobs, S. T. (February, 1894). The Inland Architect and News Record. Vol. 23, Issue 1. Pp. 5-6. Chicago, IL: The Inland Publishing Company. Google Books.

[2762] Jacobs, S. T. (February, 1894). The Inland Architect and News Record. Vol. 23, Issue 1. Pp. 5-6. Chicago, IL: The Inland Publishing Company. Google Books.

[2763] Jacobs, S. T. (February, 1894). The Inland Architect and News Record. Vol. 23, Issue 1. P. 6. Chicago, IL: The Inland Publishing Company. Google Books.

forms: the model form and the case form.[2764] The space that separated the case and the standard form would then be filled with gelatine or hot glue.[2765] The poured gelatine or glue filling would then engulf the standard form within the case, and harden around the standard form.[2766] The result would be the mold from which all the derivative identical sculpture forms could be made.[2767] The hardened gelatine or glue mold would permit, "an almost unlimited number of casts, as for instance on the large buildings, thousands of casts were necessary of the same pattern to finish the cornices, etc., around the entire building."[2768] The workers would paint the gelatine mold with a thin coating of plaster of paris in order to maximize the smoothness of the forms of the casts derived from the molds.[2769] The staff material was mixed together and poured into the standard form mold.[2770] The cast that resulted from this process would then be allowed to dry out and harden.[2771] The dry cast was, in its final form, ready to be used in the construction of the buildings. Jacobs stated: "The cast is then removed from the mold and allowed to harden, after which it can be nailed up the same as a board."[2772] The staff would be further strengthened by the addition of Portland cement when the form made from the staff was to be attached to buildings or structures near Lake Michigan or the Jackson Park water bodies, such as the lagoon.[2773] The cement additive produced a reinforced staff material capable of enduring the deterioration risks associated with the proximity to the water.[2774] These were the principal processes that formed the construction of staff and the making of the staff design and sculptures of the 1893 Chicago World's Fair.[2775]

[2764] Jacobs, S. T. (February, 1894). The Inland Architect and News Record. Vol. 23, Issue 1. P. 6. Chicago, IL: The Inland Publishing Company. Google Books.

[2765] Jacobs, S. T. (February, 1894). The Inland Architect and News Record. Vol. 23, Issue 1. P. 6. Chicago, IL: The Inland Publishing Company. Google Books.

[2766] Jacobs, S. T. (February, 1894). The Inland Architect and News Record. Vol. 23, Issue 1. P. 6. Chicago, IL: The Inland Publishing Company. Google Books.

[2767] Jacobs, S. T. (February, 1894). The Inland Architect and News Record. Vol. 23, Issue 1. P. 6. Chicago, IL: The Inland Publishing Company. Google Books.

[2768] Jacobs, S. T. (February, 1894). The Inland Architect and News Record. Vol. 23, Issue 1. P. 6. Chicago, IL: The Inland Publishing Company. Google Books.

[2769] Jacobs, S. T. (February, 1894). The Inland Architect and News Record. Vol. 23, Issue 1. P. 6. Chicago, IL: The Inland Publishing Company. Google Books.

[2770] Jacobs, S. T. (February, 1894). The Inland Architect and News Record. Vol. 23, Issue 1. P. 6. Chicago, IL: The Inland Publishing Company. Google Books.

[2771] Jacobs, S. T. (February, 1894). The Inland Architect and News Record. Vol. 23, Issue 1. P. 6. Chicago, IL: The Inland Publishing Company. Google Books.

[2772] Jacobs, S. T. (February, 1894). The Inland Architect and News Record. Vol. 23, Issue 1. P. 6. Chicago, IL: The Inland Publishing Company. Google Books.

[2773] Jacobs, S. T. (February, 1894). The Inland Architect and News Record. Vol. 23, Issue 1. P. 6. Chicago, IL: The Inland Publishing Company. Google Books.

[2774] Jacobs, S. T. (February, 1894). The Inland Architect and News Record. Vol. 23, Issue 1. P. 6. Chicago, IL: The Inland Publishing Company. Google Books.

[2775] Jacobs, S. T. (February, 1894). The Inland Architect and News Record. Vol. 23, Issue 1. P. 6. Chicago, IL: The Inland Publishing Company. Google Books.

The Richardson Construction Company pioneered the development and the application of staff, and oversaw the manufacture of approximately 500,000 separate ornamental staff casts for the central and principal buildings of the Fair.[2776] The company made far more staff casts for the other Fair buildings, including the state and foreign buildings at the Fair.[2777] The Richardson Construction Company used a tremendous volume of material resource and made approximately 1,000,000 barrels of plaster for the Fair.[2778] The volume of the staff production for the World's Fair exhausted the plaster production resources of the United States, making it necessary to use the fiber resources of Mexico, according to S. T. Jacobs.[2779] Chicago was consequently forced to import hemp from Australia and New Zealand in order to supply the necessary amounts of fiber for staff production at the Fair.[2780] As Jacobs said, the magnitudes of the Fair buildings and grounds were reflected by the magnitudes of the consumption, use, and importation of raw materials both domestically and internationally. Jacobs stated: "It is such details as this which assist one to a conception of the immensity of the buildings."[2781] The 1893 Chicago World's Columbian Exposition stimulated an entire economy of international building materials trade.[2782] Jackson Park, and the Chicago communities of Hyde Park and Woodlawn, joined to become the center and foundation for a complex and high-volume international, multi-continental, and multi-hemispheric commerce in raw construction materials.[2783] The workforce associated with the construction of the World's Fair grounds and buildings grew to a significant size, as did the great piles of gelatine molds, shaped wooden cases, and the myriad staff casts of human and animal heads, limbs, and other forms:

> "From this small beginning the work grew until we were carrying some six hundred men on the pay-rolls, men earning salaries from $5 to $25 per day. Mr. Richardson was obliged to scour the country to get enough sculptors to hurry the work to completion in time, and such a conglomeration of nationalities as was brought together I do not believe

---

[2776] Jacobs, S. T. (February, 1894). The Inland Architect and News Record. Vol. 23, Issue 1. P. 6. Chicago, IL: The Inland Publishing Company. Google Books.

[2777] Jacobs, S. T. (February, 1894). The Inland Architect and News Record. Vol. 23, Issue 1. P. 6. Chicago, IL: The Inland Publishing Company. Google Books.

[2778] Jacobs, S. T. (February, 1894). The Inland Architect and News Record. Vol. 23, Issue 1. P. 6. Chicago, IL: The Inland Publishing Company. Google Books.

[2779] Jacobs, S. T. (February, 1894). The Inland Architect and News Record. Vol. 23, Issue 1. P. 6. Chicago, IL: The Inland Publishing Company. Google Books.

[2780] Jacobs, S. T. (February, 1894). The Inland Architect and News Record. Vol. 23, Issue 1. P. 6. Chicago, IL: The Inland Publishing Company. Google Books.

[2781] Jacobs, S. T. (February, 1894). The Inland Architect and News Record. Vol. 23, Issue 1. P. 6. Chicago, IL: The Inland Publishing Company. Google Books.

[2782] Jacobs, S. T. (February, 1894). The Inland Architect and News Record. Vol. 23, Issue 1. Pp. 5-6. Chicago, IL: The Inland Publishing Company. Google Books.

[2783] Jacobs, S. T. (February, 1894). The Inland Architect and News Record. Vol. 23, Issue 1. Pp. 5-6. Chicago, IL: The Inland Publishing Company. Google Books.

has ever been equaled—no, not even by the now famous Midway Plaisance! It was a veritable 'Babel.' We were fortunate in getting a few among them who seemed able to speak all known languages, and these were often pressed into service as interpreters, to straighten our questions pertaining to the work, etc. However, all matters were amicably arranged, and by hard work and continual crowding the great task was completed in time, May 1, 1893. Many of the privileged visitors who were admitted to the studios expressed doubts that such a vast confusion of arms, bodies, heads, legs, etc., which seemed to be scattered everywhere, could be gotten together and put in shape upon the buildings; but, as stated, the task was accomplished and everything entirely completed in time for the opening, with the exception of some minor pieces of sculpture work, which were contracted far too late to finish on time."[2784]

William Douglas Richardson and the Richardson Construction Company of Chicago contributed much construction data, technological innovation, and advice on construction processes. Both also contributed to the development of the unique qualities, places, and international reputations of the Chicago communities of Hyde Park and Woodlawn, and the reputation of the great park known as Jackson Park.[2785]

The World's Fair works caused the Richardson Construction Company to expand what was an already worldwide reputation for excellence in massive construction projects.[2786] Col. Richardson, founder and President of the construction company, was sought out internationally by heads of state to provide the engineering and construction services for whole cities and countries.[2787] The work contracts that Richardson accepted impacted infrastructure, urban planning, industrial development, sanitation, national economic development, and continental development throughout the world.[2788] Due to his work in Chicago, as well as his prior work in Buffalo, Richardson was asked to help organize the Buffalo Pan-American Exposition of New York.[2789]

Richardson Construction Company built the Guarantee Company of Buffalo in 1895.[2790] The carpenters and plasterers employed in the Guaranty Building construction jobs organized a strike in 1895, when Lee Gorton and John Donsen, both non-union carpenters working on the Guaranty job, refused to join the

---

[2784] Jacobs, S. T. (February, 1894). The Inland Architect and News Record. Vol. 23, Issue 1. P. 6. Chicago, IL: The Inland Publishing Company. Google Books.
[2785] Jacobs, S. T. (February, 1894). The Inland Architect and News Record. Vol. 23, Issue 1. Pp. 5-6. Chicago, IL: The Inland Publishing Company. Google Books.
[2786] The Buffalo Enquirer. (August 1, 1899). P. 7. Newspapers.com.
[2787] The Buffalo Enquirer. (August 1, 1899). P. 7. Newspapers.com.
[2788] The Buffalo Enquirer. (August 1, 1899). P. 7. Newspapers.com.
[2789] The Buffalo Enquirer. (August 1, 1899). P. 7. Newspapers.com; Buffalo Evening News. (October 7, 1895). P. 1. Newspapers.com.
[2790] Buffalo Evening News. (October 7, 1895). P. 1. Newspapers.com.

carpenters and plasterers union.[2791] The union members gave an order to Richardson to terminate the employment of Gorton and Donsen, because of their refusal to join the labor union, but Richardson refused to comply.[2792]

> "Col. W. D. Richardson, who is supervising the construction of the edifice, says he will not discharge the men and that he will bring an army of out of town workmen here before he will submit to the demands of the strikers."[2793]

Richardson apparently did not support labor organizations, at least not under the circumstances of the Guaranty Company construction job at Buffalo.[2794] The August 1, 1899, edition of the *Buffalo Enquirer*, a newspaper of Buffalo, New York, listed multiple construction projects that Richardson had completed and designed. Richardson designed and constructed the sewer system of St. Petersburg, Russia.[2795] Richardson contracted with either Tsar Alexander III or Tsar Nicholas II for the construction of the St. Petersburg sewer system: "He designed and supervised the construction of the great sewer system of St. Petersburg, Russia."[2796]

The Republic of Argentina gave the Richardson Construction Company the contract for the construction of the great Buenos Aires Government Docks and maritime port infrastructure.[2797] For this work, the Argentine government paid the Richardson Construction Company $21,000,000.[2798] The construction work contemplated by the $21 million contract was undertaken at some point prior to 1894, with payment for the work also received prior to that time.[2799] "In Buenos Ayres [sic], Argentine Republic, he laid out the series of government docks. This contract cost the South American Republic $21,000,000."[2800] The Buenos Aires port and dock construction job would have involved building the port infrastructure on the Rio De La Plata River (River Plate), which receives tributary waters from the Paraguay River, the Uruguay River, and the Parana River, and which debouches at the Atlantic Ocean as an immensely broad river estuary.

The Buffalo Enquirer reiterated that Richardson invented staff: "Col. Richardson is also the inventor of staff. Were it not for him Chicago's Exposition would not have been the grand affair it was. He made possible the White City."[2801] The

---

[2791] Buffalo Evening News. (October 7, 1895). P. 1. Newspapers.com.

[2792] Buffalo Evening News. (October 7, 1895). P. 1. Newspapers.com.

[2793] Buffalo Evening News. (October 7, 1895). P. 1. Newspapers.com.

[2794] Buffalo Evening News. (October 7, 1895). P. 1. Newspapers.com.

[2795] The Buffalo Enquirer. (August 1, 1899). P. 7. Newspapers.com.

[2796] The Buffalo Enquirer. (August 1, 1899). P. 7. Newspapers.com.

[2797] The Buffalo Enquirer. (August 1, 1899). P. 7. Newspapers.com.

[2798] The Buffalo Enquirer. (August 1, 1899). P. 7. Newspapers.com.

[2799] The Seattle Post-Intelligencer. (March 10, 1894). P. 4. Newspapers.com; The Buffalo Enquirer. (August 1, 1899). P. 7. Newspapers.com.

[2800] The Buffalo Enquirer. (August 1, 1899). P. 7. Newspapers.com.

[2801] The Buffalo Enquirer. (August 1, 1899). P. 7. Newspapers.com.

architectural and construction challenges posed by the World's Fair proved impossible to those who were considered the greatest engineering minds of the day.[2802] The construction and design issues, therefore, presented ideal opportunities for invention and a revolution in building materials.[2803] It was the Richardson Construction Company of Chicago that emerged as the successful builder and as the physical force behind the World's Fair.[2804] "He made possible the White City. All the brightest engineers in the country were studying how to cover the gigantic skeletons of the big buildings on the fair grounds with a cheap material."[2805] Invention of a new building material enabled the Fair. "Brick and plaster compositions were talked of, but all were too expensive and would require too long a time to carry out. Col. Richardson came forward with an invention which settled the great problem. It was staff."[2806] Richardson built the Manufactures and Liberal Arts Building of the 1893 World's Fair, a building that enclosed and covered 35 acres of land.[2807] "Col. Richardson also built the huge arches upholding the roof of the Manufactures' and Liberal Arts' Building at Chicago. The roof of this building covered thirty-five acres."[2808] Each supporting arch was 370 feet long.[2809] The entire arch-supported roof was one-third of a mile long.[2810]

In conference with Director of Works Carleton of the Buffalo Pan-American Exposition, Richardson gave advice about emergency services, sewerage, and other necessary services and infrastructures.[2811] The Carleton-Richardson conference of 1899 involved Director Carleton asking hundreds of questions of Richardson regarding issues of construction and administration.[2812] The conference and consultation interview included the following comments, opinions, and analyses.

> "'Above all, the sanitary arrangements of the Exposition must be ample,' said Col. Richardson. 'Unless every means is adopted to carry off waste matter the greatest inconvenience and embarrassment will ensue, as it did at Chicago. The sanitary conditions there were imperfect and insufficient. Almost every day gangs of men had to be put at work tearing and ripping up sewers which had proved inadequate to carry of the refuse. There was a twelve-inch sewer leading from the Liberal Arts' Building, and one day when it rained heavily the pipes were unable to carry off the immense

---

[2802] The Buffalo Enquirer. (August 1, 1899). P. 7. Newspapers.com.

[2803] The Buffalo Enquirer. (August 1, 1899). P. 7. Newspapers.com.

[2804] The Buffalo Enquirer. (August 1, 1899). P. 7. Newspapers.com.

[2805] The Buffalo Enquirer. (August 1, 1899). P. 7. Newspapers.com.

[2806] The Buffalo Enquirer. (August 1, 1899). P. 7. Newspapers.com.

[2807] The Buffalo Enquirer. (August 1, 1899). P. 7. Newspapers.com.

[2808] The Buffalo Enquirer. (August 1, 1899). P. 7. Newspapers.com.

[2809] Buffalo Evening News. (August 2, 1899). P. 8. Newspapers.com.

[2810] Buffalo Evening News. (August 2, 1899). P. 8. Newspapers.com.

[2811] The Buffalo Enquirer. (August 1, 1899). P. 7. Newspapers.com.

[2812] The Buffalo Enquirer. (August 1, 1899). P. 7. Newspapers.com.

quantities of water collected by the thirty-five acre roof, and necessarily had to burst. Of course, it caused no end of trouble. That is what the engineers of the Pan-American want to see to. Have the sanitary arrangements perfect and an immense deal of time, trouble and money will be saved. Another thing. The fire department on the Exposition grounds and the fire apparatus in the various buildings ought to be more than ample. Exposition managers dislike spending their subscribed money on anything that doesn't appeal to the eye. But a thoroughly equipped fire department is an absolute necessity for the protection of the thousands who will daily entrust their lives to the Exposition managers.'"[2813]

The *Buffalo Evening News* of Buffalo, New York, reiterated the points and facts of the August 1, 1899, report from *The Buffalo Enquirer*, giving further emphasis to the significance of the Richardson Construction Company works.[2814] The City of Buffalo, New York, was planning an exposition in 1899.[2815] Newcomb Carlton, Director of Works for the Pan-American Exposition at Buffalo, consulted with Richardson about the issues of design, construction, and management of an immense fair and exposition.[2816] The *Buffalo Evening News* journalist reported the story as follows:

"Col. William D. Richardson, the man who put the roof on the Manufactures and Liberal Arts building at Chicago after the men who were considered the best engineers in the world had failed and had said it was impossible to roof the building, is in the city today, consulting with Newcomb Carlton, the Pan-American director of works. Col. Richardson has performed so many difficult feats in engineering that a rehearsal of them is something like a statistical work. He is probably better known on account of his work on the Manufactures and Liberal Arts building than anything else, although he has done many things more difficult. The building covered 35 acres. It was the largest building ever covered with a single roof. The arches were 370 feet long and there was a third of a mile of them. He is the man who invented staff. When it was found at Chicago that any attempt to create buildings of stone would cost hundreds of millions, Col. Richardson came forward with staff, which made the White City possible."[2817]

The *Buffalo Evening News* reiterated Col. Richardson's construction of the Imperial Waterworks of St. Petersburg, Russia, as well as his construction of the Buenos Aires docks and port infrastructure of Argentina.[2818] In the interview with

---

[2813] The Buffalo Enquirer. (August 1, 1899). P. 7. Newspapers.com.
[2814] Buffalo Evening News. (August 2, 1899). P. 8. Newspapers.com.
[2815] Buffalo Evening News. (August 2, 1899). P. 8. Newspapers.com.
[2816] Buffalo Evening News. (August 2, 1899). P. 8. Newspapers.com.
[2817] Buffalo Evening News. (August 2, 1899). P. 8. Newspapers.com.
[2818] Buffalo Evening News. (August 2, 1899). P. 8. Newspapers.com.

the *Buffalo Evening News*, Richardson offered the following advice to the reporter. In addition to advising the construction of, "lost and found departments," and "cosy places," he said that nursing stations, rest stations for naps and sit-downs, and a carefully-designed sewer system were all necessary for an exposition.[2819] Richardson stated the following:

> "'The trouble with all expositions is that the management has never had experience in expositions. . .The men building an exposition fail to appreciate the importance of what appears in the beginning to be a matter of small importance. For instance, every exposition should have a lost and found department, to be used not only for lost articles, but for lost people. Nobody thought in the beginning that such a thing could be possible. It could not be figured that a man woud [sic] lose his 12-year-old boy or that a mother would lose her 6-months'-old baby. I have known cases of women losing their husbands and husbands losing their wives—not people from the country, but intelligent, educated people who have made trips to Europe. You would be surprised to see how many things a woman can lose. Why, we found 57 sets of false teeth in the public comfort departments at Chicago. A woman would wash her face and hands and comb her hair, and for some reason or other take out her teeth, place them on the washstand and walk away without them. And false hair! We found enough switches to start a dozen hair stores. We found 5000 umbrellas— ' 'one of those was mine,' interrupted Director of Concessions Taylor. 'There you are,' continued Col. Richardson." [Col. Richardson continues]: 'We found more than a thousand bonnets. Women would sit down on a bench, take off their hats and walk away, leaving the hat on the bench. They would leave their bonnets in the washrooms after combing their hair. They left rings enough to fill 20 pawn-shops, watches, and even skirts. Now, there is another thing that strikes me just now, and that is the nursery. There should be in the beginning an immense nursery, with a corps of competent nurses, where mothers can leave their children for half a day or a whole day, or for an hour, paying a small sum. Think of the relief to women who are compelled to bring their children to Buffalo, if they want to make the trip themselves. They know the baby will have plenty to eat and good care, toys to play with, and all that. Suppose a woman wants to feed her baby. She must have a place where the child can nurse. We are not so far advanced as France, and women here are too timid to allow their babies to nurse in public, as in Paris. There must be enough lavatories, places where people can sit down, places where they can lie down if they wish; there must be, in a word, some place where they can get all the comforts of home in addition to the pleasures of an exposition. Speaking of little things that people forget, we had one 12-inch sewer to carry away waste water from the manufactures and liberal arts building. One morning

---

Buffalo Evening News. (August 2, 1899). P. 8. Newspapers.com.

it began to rain. 'How much rain will this roof catch?' somebody asked. All of us started to figure, but before we could figure it up the sewer blew up, so great was the amount of water running into it. It took four 12-inch sewers after that to take care of the rain on the roof.'"[2820]

Richardson shared with Carlton the lessons learned from the logistical challenges and failures of the Chicago World's Fair. Improvements to security, nursing support, lost and found services, child care, and sewer systems were central to the conference with Director Carlton.[2821]

The Richardson Construction Company of Chicago

and the Industrial Development of Russia and Argentina

The City of Chicago contributed to the establishment and development of the transportation industry and infrastructures of Russia and the Pacific Ocean in no small part through the works of the Richardson Construction Company.[2822] W. D. Richardson received the contract, most probably directly from Tsar Alexander III of Russia, to provide the engineering and contracting services for the construction of the North American terminals of the Amur Steamship Company.[2823] Russia contracted with Col. W. D. Richardson for the survey, examination, and choice of the place for the American port for the new Russo-American company. While the Russian, Pacific, and North American routes constituted the principal geographical elements of the new company and system, a route on the Amur River of Russia, in addition to a route on the Baltic Sea were included among the whole transportation service plan of the new company.[2824] The *New York Sun* reported that five Brazilian vessels had been purchased for the Amur Steamship Company, and that new vessels would be built for the contemplated oceanic service.[2825] Richardson served as a co-founder and the founding engineer of the Amur Steamship Company.[2826]

The Prattville Progress, a newspaper of Prattville, Alabama, provided additional report in February of 1894, following quickly the January report of the *New York Sun* concerning the Russo-American transportation development project.[2827] *The Prattville Progress* omitted the information concerning the capitalization money of the new company, but largely repeated the facts from the *New York Sun* report of the prior month.[2828] The Alabama paper stated the following: "William D. Richardson, a Chicago capitalist, contractor and engineer, who has been at

---

[2820] Buffalo Evening News. (August 2, 1899). P. 8. Newspapers.com.
[2821] Buffalo Evening News. (August 2, 1899). P. 8. Newspapers.com.
[2822] New York Sun. (January 24, 1894). P. 1. Newspapers.com.
[2823] New York Sun. (January 24, 1894). P. 1. Newspapers.com.
[2824] New York Sun. (January 24, 1894). P. 1. Newspapers.com.
[2825] New York Sun. (January 24, 1894). P. 1. Newspapers.com.
[2826] New York Sun. (January 24, 1894). P. 1. Newspapers.com.
[2827] The Prattville Progress. (February 2, 1894). P. 1. Newspapers.com.
[2828] The Prattville Progress. (February 2, 1894). P. 1. Newspapers.com.

Tacoma, Wash., in the interest of the Amur Steamship Company, has made a report on the Pacific coast ports."[2829]

Multiple newspapers reported the facts regarding the establishment of a Russo-American steamship company and transportation system, a company and system that were supported by United States and Russian political and industrial interests.[2830] The *Chicago Tribune* of January 24, 1894, provided the following report and facts with the title, *FOR THE BIG RUSSIAN-AMERICAN LINE: William D. Richardson Makes Investigations for a Western Terminus*: "William D. Richardson, Chicago capitalist, contractor, and engineer, who has been here six weeks in the interest of the Amoor [sic] Steamship company, left Saturday night for New York to make report on Pacific coast ports."[2831] The *New York Sun* also reported that W. D. Richardson had spent six weeks in Tacoma, Washington, for the purpose of examination and choice of a place proper for the erection of the terminal for the new Russian-American Direct Transportation Company.[2832] Different newspaper reports stated the original capitalization money of the new Russo-American company variously at quantities of $50,000,000,[2833] and $37,000,000.[2834]

The new company encompassed a plan of intermodal transportation, a plan specifically containing both continental and maritime elements, and, therefore, both railroad and steamship means of transfer.[2835] The new Pacific Ocean company would connect from the terminal of the Trans-Siberian Railroad at Vladivostok, located on the Pacific coast of Russia, to a port located at some place along the Pacific coast of the United States.[2836] "[Richardson's] object was to ascertain the port best situated for the Amoor [sic] Steamship company's line, to ply between Vladivostock [sic], Siberia, the terminus of Vladivostock [sic]-St. Petersburg Transcontinental railroad, now building."[2837] The *Chicago Tribune* report indicated that Colonel William D. Richardson was the founding General Manager of the new company, in addition to being the founding American contractor and engineer for the company.[2838] The *Chicago Tribune* report was echoed by a report that appeared in the *Estherville Daily News* of Estherville, Iowa, on February 1, 1894.[2839] Moreover, the *Oshkosh Northwestern*, a newspaper of Oshkosh, Wisconsin, contained a similar report that added the fact that Richardson was, "much interested in the timber resources of Puget sound [sic] and examined the

---

[2829] The Prattville Progress. (February 2, 1894). P. 1. Newspapers.com.

[2830] New York Sun. (January 24, 1894). P. 1. Newspapers.com.

[2831] Chicago Tribune. (January 24, 1894). P. 10. Newspapers.com.

[2832] New York Sun. (January 24, 1894). P. 1. Newspapers.com.

[2833] New York Sun. (January 24, 1894). P. 1. Newspapers.com.

[2834] The Saint Paul Globe. (April 2, 1894). P. 2. Newspapers.com.

[2835] New York Sun. (January 24, 1894). P. 1. Newspapers.com.

[2836] New York Sun. (January 24, 1894). P. 1. Newspapers.com.

[2837] Chicago Tribune. (January 24, 1894). P. 10. Newspapers.com.

[2838] Chicago Tribune. (January 24, 1894). P. 10. Newspapers.com.

[2839] Estherville Daily News. (February 1, 1894). P. 10. Newspapers.com.

sound harbors closely."[2840] The words "much interested," as used by the journalist in the *Oshkosh Northwestern*, express an ambiguity by not clarifying whether the fact intended was that Colonel Richardson was personally interested as an investor in the timber resources of Puget Sound, or that he was interested in the resources exclusively as agent and officer of the Amur Steamship Company.[2841] While the first fact was possible under the circumstances, the second fact was definite under the circumstances.[2842] In either case, it was the latter fact that was almost certainly the one intended as the object of expression by the words of the *Oshkosh Northwestern* article.[2843]

Russian imperial regime change occurred in the autumn of 1894 when Tsar Alexander III (Aleksandr III Aleksandrovich) died, and was succeeded by his eldest son, Nicholas II (Nikolai Aleksandrovich), on November 1, 1894. The Russo-American transportation company continued to exist through the regime change, though certain plans for the company were changing at that time. *The Dalles Times-Mountaineer*, a newspaper of Dalles, Oregon, reported that the place of the North American port and terminal of the company had been relocated to Everett, Washington.[2844] Colonel William Douglas Richardson of Chicago had chosen Tacoma, Washington, to be the North American port of the company, but John Davison Rockefeller of Cleveland, Ohio, subsequently persuaded Russia and other interested investors to choose Everett, Washington, to be the North American port and terminal for the new Russo-American company.[2845] *The Dalles Times-Mountaineer* reported that John D. Rockefeller held considerable property at Everett, Washington.[2846] Whatever comments or concerns that Colonel Richardson may have expressed regarding the issue of the relocation of the Russo-American terminal have yet to be discovered.

A *Los Angeles Times* report of February 6, 1894, stated that five steamships which had lain at New York Harbor for approximately one year were to be brought to San Francisco from New York City, around Cape Horn of South America.[2847] The report mentioned two possible purposes for the vessels: that of use in the operation of the Russo-American company on the one hand, and that of use in the operation of the Asian Route and the Panama Route of the Pacific Mail service on the other hand.[2848] The five vessels at New York Harbor were the Seguranca, the Vigilancia, the Alliance, the Finance, and the Advance.[2849] The *Los Angeles Times* report stated that the United States and Brazilian Steamship company had held

[2840] The Oshkosh Northwestern. (January 24, 1894). P. 4. Newspapers.com.
[2841] The Oshkosh Northwestern. (January 24, 1894). P. 4. Newspapers.com.
[2842] The Oshkosh Northwestern. (January 24, 1894). P. 4. Newspapers.com.
[2843] The Oshkosh Northwestern. (January 24, 1894). P. 4. Newspapers.com.
[2844] The Dalles Times-Mountaineer. (November 10, 1894). P. 1. Newspapers.com.
[2845] Chicago Tribune. (January 24, 1894). P. 10. Newspapers.com;
The Dalles Times-Mountaineer. (November 10, 1894). P. 1. Newspapers.com.
[2846] The Dalles Times-Mountaineer. (November 10, 1894). P. 1. Newspapers.com.
[2847] The Los Angeles Times. (February 6, 1894). P. 2. Newspapers.com.
[2848] The Los Angeles Times. (February 6, 1894). P. 2. Newspapers.com.
[2849] The Los Angeles Times. (February 6, 1894). P. 2. Newspapers.com.

primary property to the five vessels, but that the Standard Oil Company had held security interest property in the five vessels; and, pursuant to the security interest property, the Standard Oil Company had attached the vessels as collateral for the payment of debt at some time prior to one year before the February 6, 1894 report in the *Los Angeles Times*.[2850]

The Anaconda Standard, a newspaper of Anaconda, Montana, reported on November 12, 1894, that the Great Northern Railroad Company was, "a factor in the combination,"[2851] the combination referred to being the Russo-American company.[2852] The formal name of the new Russo-American company was the Russian-American Direct Transportation Company.[2853] *The Saint Paul Globe* of Saint Paul, Minnesota, reported the following on April 2, 1894, regarding the company:

> "A local paper makes the statement that a company has organized to operate a large fleet of steamships between Vladivostock [sic], the eastern terminus of the great trans-Siberian railway, and some point on the Pacific coast, probably San Diego. The organization is known as the Russian-American Direct Transportation company, with a capital of $37,000,000."[2854]

The *Buffalo Commercial*, a newspaper of Buffalo, New York, reported concerning the Pan-American Exposition of 1900, a fair at Buffalo.[2855] Under the article title, "RESIGNED. Col. Richardson Severs His Connection With The Pan-American," the Buffalo paper reported that Richardson had resigned from service with the Pan-American Exposition Company of Buffalo due to a disagreement with Newcomb Carlton, who served as Director General of the Pan-American Exposition.[2856] The most significant facts contained in the *Buffalo Commercial* report were those that constituted the enumeration of the construction projects undertaken by Richardson.[2857] The newspaper commented that Richardson had served as the building contractor for the Imperial Waterworks of St. Petersburg, Russia.[2858] The article also stated that Richardson had refused a particularly high-profile construction contract offer from the Emperor of Japan, who was, in 1900, Emperor Meiji-tenno, also known as Meiji-taitei, or Meiji The Great.[2859] The Japanese Emperor had offered Col. Richardson the contract for the construction of

---

[2850] The Los Angeles Times. (February 6, 1894). P. 2. Newspapers.com.
[2851] The Anaconda Standard. (November 12, 1894). P. 1. Newspapers.com.
[2852] The Anaconda Standard. (November 12, 1894). P. 1. Newspapers.com.
[2853] The Saint Paul Globe. (April 2, 1894). P. 2. Newspapers.com.
[2854] The Saint Paul Globe. (April 2, 1894). P. 2. Newspapers.com.
[2855] The Buffalo Commercial. (March 6, 1900). P. 11. Newspapers.com.
[2856] The Buffalo Commercial. (March 6, 1900). P. 11. Newspapers.com.
[2857] The Buffalo Commercial. (March 6, 1900). P. 11. Newspapers.com.
[2858] The Buffalo Commercial. (March 6, 1900). P. 11. Newspapers.com.
[2859] The Buffalo Commercial. (March 6, 1900). P. 11. Newspapers.com.

a palace for the Emperor's son at Tokyo.[2860] Richardson refused the Emperor of Japan's offer only because Richardson was committed to duties with the Pan-American Exposition, and wished to remain loyal to the job, duties, and professional relationships with the Pan-American Exposition Company.[2861] In consideration for the construction services, Emperor Meiji-tenno offered Richardson an annual salary of $10,000 for a time of five years.[2862] Additionally, the Emperor offered Richardson and his family free housing, and payment of all additional expenses.[2863] The *Buffalo Commercial* commented on this fact as follows: "The Colonel refused the offer because he was engaged on the work for the Pan-American Exposition and did not feel justified in giving that up for the more advantageous offer of the Emperor of Japan."[2864] The reputation that Colonel Richardson and the Richardson Construction Company possessed was global in scope and exalted in honor.[2865]

The *Japan Weekly Mail* reported on February 3, 1894, additional facts relevant to William D. Richardson's relationship with Russia, and with Russian continental and maritime industries.[2866] The report indicated that Richardson served as Special Agent simultaneously for the government of Russia, the Russian Transcontinental Railroad, and the Amur Steamship Company.[2867] In this office and capacity, Richardson served as co-founder of the Russian-American Direct Steamship Company.[2868] One purpose of the Russian Transcontinental Railroad was to promote and facilitate commerce with the Pacific coast of the United States. The Russo-American commercial alliance represented a global intermodal system of trade and transportation.[2869] The Richardson Construction Company of Chicago provided both technological wherewithal and promotive agency for the Russo-American Pacific trade alliance and contributed to the commercial growth of Russo-American trade and diplomacy.[2870]

Chicago, therefore, through William D. Richardson, helped develop trans-Pacific and trans-Atlantic commerce, Russo-American commercial diplomacy, and Russo-American industrial diplomacy.[2871] The journalism of the *Japan Weekly*

[2860] The Buffalo Commercial. (March 6, 1900). P. 11. Newspapers.com.
[2861] The Buffalo Commercial. (March 6, 1900). P. 11. Newspapers.com.
[2862] The Buffalo Commercial. (March 6, 1900). P. 11. Newspapers.com.
[2863] The Buffalo Commercial. (March 6, 1900). P. 11. Newspapers.com.
[2864] The Buffalo Commercial. (March 6, 1900). P. 11. Newspapers.com.
[2865] The Buffalo Commercial. (March 6, 1900). P. 11. Newspapers.com.
[2866] The Japan Weekly Mail. (February 3, 1894). P. 154. Google Books.
[2867] The Japan Weekly Mail. (February 3, 1894). P. 154. Google Books.
[2868] The Saint Paul Globe. (April 2, 1894). P. 2. Newspapers.com; The Japan Weekly Mail. (February 3, 1894). P. 154. Google Books.
[2869] The Saint Paul Globe. (April 2, 1894). P. 2. Newspapers.com; The Japan Weekly Mail. (February 3, 1894). P. 154. Google Books.
[2870] The Saint Paul Globe. (April 2, 1894). P. 2. Newspapers.com; The Japan Weekly Mail. (February 3, 1894). P. 154. Google Books.
[2871] The Saint Paul Globe. (April 2, 1894). P. 2. Newspapers.com; The Japan Weekly Mail. (February 3, 1894). P. 154. Google Books.

Mail article of 1894 was optimistic about the roles played by William D. Richardson and the Richardson Construction Company; both the City of Chicago and Cook County, through the Richardson Construction Company, helped lay the groundwork for developments of future cities and commercial centers.[2872] The journalistic language of the 1894 article was replete with hope for Russo-American friendship, commercial alliance, mutually-fostered economic growth, and industrial diplomacy.[2873] The following relevant words from the 1894 *Japan Weekly Mail* article, which were expressive of hopeful and friendly attitudes, bear out this fact.

> "The portion of Siberia traversed by the trans-Siberian Railway is a great plain similar to that west of the Mississippi River, only larger. It is said to be capable of agricultural settlement, but destitute of timber. For this reason it is thought that close trade relations with the United States will be fostered by the Russian Government, not only for the building of the railway but for the construction of the cities and stations which will naturally spring up along the line of the road."[2874]

The Seattle Post-Intelligencer of March 10, 1894, included a report of tremendous value regarding William D. Richardson and his work in Russia and Argentina.[2875] The article noted the central role that Richardson played as contractor and engineer for the Russian Transcontinental Railway (Trans-Siberian Railway), and that he was the United States Agent for the Tsars.[2876] Richardson apparently managed the United States raw materials contributions for the construction of the Russian transcontinental railroad in addition to being a business colleague of the Tsar in forming the Amur Steamship Company.[2877] Richardson was searching for a suitable United States Pacific coast port for the mutual terminal and connection points for the Amur Steamship Company and the United States railroads.[2878] One of his sisters, possibly Lucy Maria (Richardson) Cross of Elyria and Cleveland, Ohio, accompanied him on the Pacific port examination expeditions.[2879]

Tsar Alexander III, Tsar Nicholas II, and W. D. Richardson planned to build approximately fifteen oceanic vessels on the Pacific coast of America for the purpose of creating the Russo-American corporate fleet.[2880] The estimated fifteen

[2872] The Japan Weekly Mail. (February 3, 1894). P. 154. Google Books.
[2873] The Japan Weekly Mail. (February 3, 1894). P. 154. Google Books.
[2874] The Japan Weekly Mail. (February 3, 1894). P. 154. Google Books.
[2875] The Seattle Post-Intelligencer. (March 10, 1894). P. 4. Newspapers.com.
[2876] The Seattle Post-Intelligencer. (March 10, 1894). P. 4. Newspapers.com.
[2877] The Seattle Post-Intelligencer. (March 10, 1894). P. 4. Newspapers.com.
[2878] The Seattle Post-Intelligencer. (March 10, 1894). P. 4. Newspapers.com.
[2879] The Seattle Post-Intelligencer. (March 10, 1894). P. 4. Newspapers.com.
[2880] The Seattle Post-Intelligencer. (March 10, 1894). P. 4. Newspapers.com.

vessels to be built would combine with the five vessels purchased from the Brazilian route— vessels which were encumbered with the Standard Oil Company security interests; this combination would make an anticipatory Russo-American Direct Steamship Company and Amur Steamship Company fleet of about twenty Pacific vessels.[2881] Richardson co-founded the Amur Steamship Company and the Russo-American Direct Steamship Company, having co-founded the companies with Tsar Alexander III and Tsar Nicholas II.[2882] Richardson also co-established, with the Tsars, the Russian Trans-Siberian Railway system.

The Argentine work undertaken by Richardson Construction Company included a $6,000,000 contract for the Argentine capitol, according to *The Seattle Post-Intelligencer*.[2883] Politics complicated the Argentine capitol construction contract, however, because of a political revolution that took place then.[2884] The original contract between the Argentine Republic and Richardson Construction Company of Chicago stipulated that Argentina would pay Richardson with 6,000,000 acres of Argentine real estate.[2885] The real estate possessed an estimated value of between $8,000,000 and $9,000,000 (United States Dollars) at the time of the contract.[2886] Additional terms of the contract appeared to create an insurmountable impracticability, which resulted in impossibility.[2887] The Bank of England agreed to accept Richardson's six-million-acre land interest in Argentina, and pay him $6,000,000, minus the commission cost of $1,000,000. Richardson would then receive $5,000,000, spend $1,600,000 for the construction of the Argentine government building, and reserve a fund of $400,000 for the purposes of bribing the Argentine government officials of the Argentine Cabinet.[2888] Richardson would then divide the remaining $3,000,000 with the Argentine President.[2889] Political revolution intervened, canceled the contract, and removed the Argentine President and the "kid cabinet" from their political offices.[2890] Richardson left for London on the next available ship.[2891] He returned to complete other work under different terms.

[2881] The Seattle Post-Intelligencer. (March 10, 1894). P. 4. Newspapers.com.

[2882] The Seattle Post-Intelligencer. (March 10, 1894). P. 4. Newspapers.com; New York Sun. (January 24, 1894). P. 1. Newspapers.com; Chicago Tribune. (January 24, 1894). P. 10; The Los Angeles Times. (February 6, 1894). P. 2. Newspapers.com; The Prattville Progress. (February 2, 1894). P. 1. Newspapers.com.

[2883] The Seattle Post-Intelligencer. (March 10, 1894). P. 4. Newspapers.com.

[2884] The Seattle Post-Intelligencer. (March 10, 1894). P. 4. Newspapers.com.

[2885] The Seattle Post-Intelligencer. (March 10, 1894). P. 4. Newspapers.com.

[2886] The Seattle Post-Intelligencer. (March 10, 1894). P. 4. Newspapers.com.

[2887] The Seattle Post-Intelligencer. (March 10, 1894). P. 4. Newspapers.com.

[2888] The Seattle Post-Intelligencer. (March 10, 1894). P. 4. Newspapers.com.

[2889] The Seattle Post-Intelligencer. (March 10, 1894). P. 4. Newspapers.com.

[2890] The Seattle Post-Intelligencer. (March 10, 1894). P. 4. Newspapers.com.

[2891] The Seattle Post-Intelligencer. (March 10, 1894). P. 4. Newspapers.com.

It is unclear from the Seattle report how much performance of the Richardson Construction Company contract with the Argentine Republic had taken place, but scrutiny of the reported facts supports the theory that the Richardson contract with the Argentine Republic had been executed and that Richardson had received title to the six million acres of the Argentine Republic.[2892] This is not a certainty of fact, but a probability of fact given the words of the 1894 report.[2893] It is possible, therefore, that at one time, William D. Richardson of Chicago owned six million acres of Argentina, even if only for a brief time, and only to be deprived of its value soon after by the nullifying effects of political insurrection.[2894] The relationship between Richardson and the Argentine Republic apparently was excellent, however, and was characterized by good diplomacy, because the Argentine Republic paid Richardson $21,000,000 for the construction of the Port of Buenos Aires in 1890-1891.[2895] He also appears to have constructed at least one major government building at Buenos Aires, for the sum of $6,000,000, during the 1890s.[2896] The historical record appears to confirm that Richardson Construction Company received at least $27,000,000 in gross contract revenue from the government of Argentina alone in about 1891-1892.[2897]

The *Seattle Post-Intelligencer* report contained a long-quoted memoir from a Seattle man who knew Richardson. The memoir stated the following:

> "He is a native of Connecticut and a nephew of Richardson, partner of the late Seven-Mule Barnum [United States Senator William Henry Barnum of Connecticut (Dem.)], the Democratic leader. Richardson is a good mechanical engineer, and got his training in the shop instead of the college. He was at one time president of the Springfield, Ill., Rolling Mill Company. He gained notoriety in connection with contracts on the Illinois capitol at Springfield. I met him at the Palmer house, Chicago, in 1890, when he had just returned from the Argentine Republic. He was well acquainted with a number of prominent politicians, including Farwell, Gresham and Carter Harrison, and seemed to have good financial standing."[2898]

Richardson learned construction from apprenticing in the workshop, not from attending a formal engineering curriculum at a college or university. This difference from the formally educated engineers at the 1893 Fair would take a

---

[2892] The Seattle Post-Intelligencer. (March 10, 1894). P. 4. Newspapers.com.

[2893] The Seattle Post-Intelligencer. (March 10, 1894). P. 4. Newspapers.com.

[2894] The Seattle Post-Intelligencer. (March 10, 1894). P. 4. Newspapers.com.

[2895] The Buffalo Enquirer. (August 1, 1899). P. 7. Newspapers.com.

[2896] The Seattle Post-Intelligencer. (March 10, 1894). P. 4. Newspapers.com.

[2897] The Buffalo Enquirer. (August 1, 1899). P. 7. Newspapers.com; The Seattle Post-Intelligencer. (March 10, 1894). P. 4. Newspapers.com.

[2898] The Seattle Post-Intelligencer. (March 10, 1894). P. 4. Newspapers.com.

dramatic turn.[2899] The value of the workshop education cannot be overstated. It was a workshop-educated construction contractor from the Appalachian Mountains of Litchfield County, Connecticut, who solved the construction problems that faced the architects of the 1893 World's Columbian Exposition.[2900] The formally educated engineers who were recruited to solve certain key construction problems of the Fair failed to produce solutions to the problems that blocked the physical progress of the Exposition.[2901] These were problems which would have terminated the plan for the Exposition only soon after its beginning but for the solutions discovered by Richardson.[2902] Therefore, at the World's Fair, workshop-trained men supervised the college-educated men. Richardson Construction Company invented a novel building material—staff— and in so doing advanced construction science to a new point.[2903] Col. Richardson and his men would have counseled and managed the college-educated engineers in the construction of the Fair buildings.

The Chicago—California Connection:

From the Great Lakes to the North American Desert

Chicago and Cook County helped develop southern California technology, agriculture, and industry. William Douglas Richardson of Chicago developed large agricultural and riparian infrastructures in California. He engineered aqueducts through the North American Desert and worked with capitalists of New York City and Great Britain to originate an agricultural and industrial town in San Bernardino County. Richardson joined several other businessmen in establishing the Chicala Water Company of California in approximately the winter of 1897.[2904] The *Los Angeles Herald* and *The Los Angeles Times* provided key information about these Chicago-California companies. The "Chicala" company name was a combination of the words, "Chicago," "California," and "Los Angeles," thus representing the three places associated with the company, the company's origins, and the commercial work of the company.[2905]

[2899] Buffalo Evening News. (August 2, 1899). P. 8. Newspapers.com; The Seattle Post-Intelligencer. (March 10, 1894). P. 4. Newspapers.com.

[2900] Buffalo Evening News. (August 2, 1899). P. 8. Newspapers.com; The Seattle Post-Intelligencer. (March 10, 1894). P. 4. Newspapers.com.

[2901] Buffalo Evening News. (August 2, 1899). P. 8. Newspapers.com; The Seattle Post-Intelligencer. (March 10, 1894). P. 4. Newspapers.com.

[2902] Buffalo Evening News. (August 2, 1899). P. 8. Newspapers.com; The Seattle Post-Intelligencer. (March 10, 1894). P. 4. Newspapers.com.

[2903] Buffalo Evening News. (August 2, 1899). P. 8. Newspapers.com; The Seattle Post-Intelligencer. (March 10, 1894). P. 4. Newspapers.com.

[2904] Los Angeles Herald. (March 25, 1897). P. 7. Newspapers.com.

[2905] Los Angeles Times. (August 7, 1897). P. 9. Newspapers.com.

The Chicala Water Company purchased land in Rialto, San Bernardino County, in 1897, for agricultural development purposes.[2906] The company also sought to develop Rialto as a settlement.[2907] John H. Carruthers was the General Manager of the company at this time.[2908] Chicala Water Company acquired the land rights and water rights of the prior Semi-Tropic Land Company.[2909] The place of the Chicala development and operation, and the place of the Semi-Tropic development and operation, was Lytle Creek, in the Rialto area of San Bernardino County.[2910] The Anglo-American Canaigre Company retained property in 8,000 acres of land at the Lytle Creek area at the time of the formation of the Chicala Water Company and its entry into the Rialto region.[2911] The Anglo-American Canaigre Company owned 5,000 acres in Merced County, California, and 5,000 acres of land in Arizona, near Phoenix.[2912] The Chicala Water Company appears to have represented a capital investment of at least $1,000,000 as of May, 1898.[2913] In connection with the Chicala Water Company, the Anglo-American Canaigre Company also appears from the report to have represented assets of at least $1,000,000.[2914]

W. D. Richardson filed proofs and facts at San Bernardino with the San Bernardino County Recorder in support of the capital strength and soundness of the Chicala Water Company.[2915] The purpose of the documentary and evidentiary bolster was to secure the interests of the bondholder investors of the Chicala Water Company.[2916] The filing of the records by Richardson appears to have been done to create security interests for the bondholders and to give promise and comfort as to the security of the debt moneys being invested in Chicala and Rialto.[2917] Richardson filed the following records at Rialto, San Bernardino County: the deed of transfer of all Rialto property interests of the San Francisco Savings Union to both the Chicala Water Company and the organizationally affiliated Anglo-American Canaigre Company; one trust deed from the Chicala Water Company with a value of $1,000,000; and one trust deed from the United States Mortgage and Trust Company with a value of $1,000,000.[2918] The United States Mortgage and Trust Company acted as trustee in the case of the transfer noted above. Apparently, Richardson and the additional settlors of the trust mentioned above sought to create security interests for the bondholders through the creation of the

---

[2906] Los Angeles Herald. (March 25, 1897). P. 7. Newspapers.com.

[2907] Los Angeles Herald. (May 5, 1898). P. 9. Newspapers.com.

[2908] Los Angeles Herald. (March 25, 1897). P. 7. Newspapers.com.

[2909] Los Angeles Herald. (March 25, 1897). P. 7. Newspapers.com.

[2910] Los Angeles Herald. (March 25, 1897). P. 7. Newspapers.com.

[2911] Los Angeles Herald. (March 25, 1897). P. 7. Newspapers.com.

[2912] Los Angeles Herald. (March 25, 1897). P. 7. Newspapers.com.

[2913] Los Angeles Herald. (May 5, 1898). P. 9. Newspapers.com.

[2914] Los Angeles Herald. (May 5, 1898). P. 9. Newspapers.com.

[2915] Los Angeles Herald. (May 5, 1898). P. 9. Newspapers.com.

[2916] Los Angeles Herald. (May 5, 1898). P. 9. Newspapers.com.

[2917] Los Angeles Herald. (May 5, 1898). P. 9. Newspapers.com.

[2918] Los Angeles Herald. (May 5, 1898). P. 9. Newspapers.com.

trust.[2919] The *Los Angeles Herald* reporter noted that at the time of the filing of the three documents at Rialto, both the Chicala Water Company and the Anglo-American Canaigre Company had generated adequate capital to continue development and settlement work at Rialto.[2920]

On August 5, 1897, Chicala Water Company filed a claim at San Bernardino for 98,000 inches of the water resource of Lytle Creek and its tributaries.[2921] The Chicala water rights claim included multiple geographically connected places and water resources, and included both the surface flow waters and the underflow waters of Lytle Creek, as follows:

Place of Water Resource	Quantity of Water Resource
1. Lytle Creek	50,000 inches
2. Lytle Creek lower narrows	30,000 inches
3. Lytle Creek middle fork	5,000 inches
4. Lytle Creek north fork	5,000 inches
5. Lytle Creek south fork	5,000 inches
6. Myers Canyon	3,000 inches[2922]

The Chicala Water Company planned to use the claimed water resources for "irrigation and domestic use."[2923] The company would distribute the benefits of the water resources to places in San Bernardino County, Los Angeles County, and Riverside County.[2924] The places intended as recipients of the benefits of the company water resources lay south of the San Gabriel timberland reservation, and south of the San Bernardino Forest preserve.[2925] The Chicala Water Company business plan called for construction of multiple canals throughout the three-county region.[2926] The Chicala construction plan intended separate canals to serve the separate water resources stated in each of the Chicala claims specified above.[2927] The construction plan called for one canal with a depth of ten feet, and a width of 25 feet, to serve the Lytle Creek 50,000 inch claim and water resource.[2928] The plan called for one canal with ten-foot depth, and 20-foot width, for the lower narrows claim and water resource.[2929] Four additional and separate canals, each possessing a three-foot depth, and a 12-foot width, would be built to

[2919] Los Angeles Herald. (May 5, 1898). P. 9. Newspapers.com.
[2920] Los Angeles Herald. (May 5, 1898). P. 9. Newspapers.com.
[2921] The Los Angeles Times. (August 7, 1897). P. 9. Newspapers.com.
[2922] The Los Angeles Times. (August 7, 1897). P. 9. Newspapers.com.
[2923] The Los Angeles Times. (August 7, 1897). P. 9. Newspapers.com.
[2924] The Los Angeles Times. (August 7, 1897). P. 9. Newspapers.com.
[2925] The Los Angeles Times. (August 7, 1897). P. 9. Newspapers.com.
[2926] The Los Angeles Times. (August 7, 1897). P. 9. Newspapers.com.
[2927] The Los Angeles Times. (August 7, 1897). P. 9. Newspapers.com.
[2928] The Los Angeles Times. (August 7, 1897). P. 9. Newspapers.com.
[2929] The Los Angeles Times. (August 7, 1897). P. 9. Newspapers.com.

serve the claims and water resources of the middle fork, north fork, south fork, and Myers Canyon.[2930]

Col. William D. Richardson of Chicago served as Chief Engineer for the Chicala Water Company, and for the construction and development projects undertaken by the company.[2931] The *Los Angeles Times* report of August 7, 1897, predicted legal conflicts for Chicala Water Company, because the Chicala claims were filed in the wake of a recent Los Angeles County trial and judgment that established an exhaustive law and policy for the use of the Lytle Creek water resource.[2932] The geographical and topographical descriptions of the Chicala and Rialto settlement placed the community west of Lytle Creek, east of the Los Angeles County—San Bernardino County line, south of the Sierra Madre Mountains, and north of the Jurupa Mountains.[2933]

The Chicala Water Company worked with the Anglo-American Canaigre Company to develop the agriculture of the industrial plant known as canaigre. Canaigre is a plant from whose root one could extract tannin, a chemical necessary to the tanning process.[2934] The *Los Angeles Herald* reported on April 12, 1897, that the Anglo-American Canaigre Company, aided by the Chicala Water Company, employed a large workforce engaged in the collection and cultivation of the canaigre root.[2935] *The Pacific Rural Press*, a California newspaper, provided a detailed report on the Chicala and Anglo-American Canaigre Company projects in California.[2936] The canaigre plant, known in scientific nomenclature as *Rumex hymenosepalus*, is a plant from the dock family, is native to the North American Desert, and has historically been cultivated in California, Arizona, New Mexico, and Texas, possibly in addition to Mexico and other places.[2937] The canaigre root was described as having been, "very rich with tannin."[2938]

The Anglo-American Canaigre Company provided 200 men with cultivation jobs at the Rialto Canaigre groves as of April, 1897.[2939] The cultivation prospectus that the company reported to the *San Bernardino Sun* in April, 1897, predicted that the company would have 8,000 acres of canaigre under cultivation in

[2930] The Los Angeles Times. (August 7, 1897). P. 9. Newspapers.com.

[2931] The Los Angeles Times. (August 7, 1897). P. 9. Newspapers.com.

[2932] The Los Angeles Times. (August 7, 1897). P. 9. Newspapers.com.

[2933] The San Bernardino County Sun. (September 18, 1897). P. 4. Newspapers.com.

[2934] The Los Angeles Times. (February 13, 1897). P. 9. Newspapers.com.

[2935] Los Angeles Herald. (April 12, 1897). P. 4. Newspapers.com.

[2936] The Pacific Rural Press. (April 10, 1897). P. 230. California Digital Newspaper Collection.

[2937] The Pacific Rural Press. (April 10, 1897). P. 230. California Digital Newspaper Collection.

[2938] The Pacific Rural Press. (April 10, 1897). P. 230. California Digital Newspaper Collection.

[2939] The Pacific Rural Press. (April 10, 1897). P. 230. California Digital Newspaper Collection.

California.[2940] Andrew McLean of New York City served as President of the company.[2941] Henry B. Wall of Rialto, California, served as company Vice-President and Western Manager.[2942] George H. Tousey of New York City served as Secretary and Auditor of the company.[2943] Wolston R. Brown of New York City served as Treasurer.[2944] John H. Carruthers of New York City was the General Manager.[2945] William D. Richardson of Chicago was the Chief Engineer for the Anglo-American company.[2946] Superintendent Segars worked with Richardson, Carruthers, and Judge J. H. Henderson in multiple corporate affairs with the canaigre company.[2947] By April, 1897, the Anglo-American Canaigre Company held property to 22,000 acres of California land, buildings, and infrastructure, including the Semi-Tropic Hotel, all Rialto realty lots that had not been sold at the time, and the extensive plumbing systems existing in the Rialto region.[2948] The Anglo-American Canaigre Company acquired title to essentially all realty and infrastructures that once were owned by the Semi-Tropic Company.[2949] Through purchases and acquisitions the Anglo-American Canaigre Company assumed nearly all the assets of the Semi-Tropic Company, and thereby stood as the organizational, economic, commercial, and industrial heir to Semi-Tropic.[2950]

The Anglo-American Canaigre Company advertised technological innovations in the tanning process, publishing reports of the improved speed of the new tanning technologies involving the canaigre root.[2951] Plant production, however, would not go unchallenged by issues of resource availability. The May 1, 1897, edition of *The Pacific Rural Press* related the issue of the deficit of canaigre seeds that compelled the Anglo-American Canaigre Company leadership to adopt a novel

---

[2940] The Pacific Rural Press. (April 10, 1897). P. 230. California Digital Newspaper Collection.

[2941] The Pacific Rural Press. (April 10, 1897). P. 230. California Digital Newspaper Collection.

[2942] The Pacific Rural Press. (April 10, 1897). P. 230. California Digital Newspaper Collection.

[2943] The Pacific Rural Press. (April 10, 1897). P. 230. California Digital Newspaper Collection.

[2944] The Pacific Rural Press. (April 10, 1897). P. 230. California Digital Newspaper Collection.

[2945] The Pacific Rural Press. (April 10, 1897). P. 230. California Digital Newspaper Collection.

[2946] The San Bernardino County Sun. (July 27, 1917). P. 4. Newspapers.com.

[2947] The San Bernardino County Sun. (July 27, 1917). P. 4. Newspapers.com.

[2948] The Pacific Rural Press. (April 10, 1897). P. 230. California Digital Newspaper Collection.

[2949] The Pacific Rural Press. (April 10, 1897). P. 230. California Digital Newspaper Collection.

[2950] The Pacific Rural Press. (April 10, 1897). P. 230. California Digital Newspaper Collection.

[2951] The Pacific Rural Press. (April 10, 1897). P. 230. California Digital Newspaper Collection.

policy of materials conservation and use.[2952] During approximately the spring season of 1897, a deficit of canaigre seeds emerged which would challenge the growth and viability of the company.[2953] To overcome the serious deficit of canaigre seeds, the company adopted an improved plan and policy of conservation and operation that would literally create material adequacy from an apparent material deficit.[2954] Thus, an economic puzzle had been solved. Pursuant to the new policy and operation, the company would chop off the crowns of the canaigre plant and replant the crowns on the company plantations, so as to engineer the adequacy of the raw botanic resource necessary for crop production.[2955] The Anglo-American Canaigre Company leadership thereby extracted simultaneously a new practice, an operational improvement, and a formula for surplus and adequacy from the raw issue of deficit that had lain before the company in April, 1897.[2956] In summary, through the work of William D. Richardson and the Richardson Construction Company, Chicago participated centrally in the development and engineering of southern California construction, agriculture, hydrological technologies, chemical industry, and investment. Richardson was co-founder and the founding engineer of the Chicala Water Company, and probably co-founded the Anglo-American Canaigre Company, as well. He was an executive of both companies.

<u>The Guaranty Construction Company of Chicago:</u>

<u>Builder of Chicago, New York City, Cleveland, Buffalo, and Cincinnati</u>

Col. William Douglas Richardson possibly co-founded the Guaranty Construction Company of Chicago, in collaboration with George M. Moulton, in the middle of the 1890s.[2957] It is certain that George Moulton was the principal founder of the company, and it was probable that Richardson was a co-founder of the firm with Moulton, assumption of the latter fact having been corroborated by facts and circumstances presented in multiple contemporary journalistic reports.[2958] What was documentarily certain, however, was that Richardson was the General Manager of the company, and as such, was one of the key executive

---

[2952] The Pacific Rural Press. (May 1, 1897). P.276. California Digital Newspaper Collection.
[2953] The Pacific Rural Press. (May 1, 1897). P.276. California Digital Newspaper Collection.
[2954] The Pacific Rural Press. (May 1, 1897). P.276. California Digital Newspaper Collection.
[2955] The Pacific Rural Press. (May 1, 1897). P.276. California Digital Newspaper Collection.
[2956] The Pacific Rural Press. (May 1, 1897). P.276. California Digital Newspaper Collection.
[2957] The Buffalo Commercial. (January 19, 1895). P. 11. Newspapers.com.
[2958] The Inter Ocean. (January 1, 1896). P. 20. Newspapers.com; The Inter Ocean. (September 1, 1896). P. 5. Newspapers.com.

officers of the firm.[2959] The Guaranty Construction Company was not the same firm as the Richardson Construction Company, which has been discussed above in detail. Richardson was the founder and president of the Richardson Construction Company but was also an executive and owner of the Guaranty Construction Company. Both of these organizations were Chicago companies.

Col. Richardson was a venture capitalist, as well as a construction man, and invested in multiple corporations throughout the United States and the world. One of the most important buildings that the Guaranty Construction Company built at Chicago was the Fisher Building, located in the Loop, on Van Buren Street.[2960] At this time, Guaranty Construction Company headquarters were located at 713-715 Monadnock Building, located in the Loop, on Jackson Boulevard.[2961]

Lucius Fisher was both the owner and the namesake of the Fisher Building.[2962] D. H. Burnham & Company was the architect for the building.[2963] The Northwestern Terra Cotta Company provided the terra cotta building materials for the structure.[2964] Northwestern Terra Cotta Company offices were located at Wrightwood Avenue and Clybourn Avenue.[2965] The total construction cost for the Fisher Building was reported at $1,250,000, as of January 1, 1896.[2966] The Fisher Building was eighteen stories in height and possessed a French Gothic style of design.[2967] Pioneer Fire Proof Construction Company, of which William Moulton was President, provided the fireproof material construction of the building.[2968] The faces of the building fronted Dearborn Street, Van Buren Street, and Third Avenue.[2969] The Fisher Building held two records, as reported by the Chicago *Inter Ocean* newspaper: "Lucius Fisher's building is a world-beater in two particulars, first as the highest structure ever erected in Chicago under one contract, because the Masonic Temple had many builders, and second in the lightning speed of it."[2970] *The Inter Ocean* proved the speed with the following comment: "Oct. 12 it was level with the street; Nov. 12 a flag was flying from the topmost post of steel, nineteen stories up; Dec. 12, the great steel skeleton was practically inclosed."[2971]

The plumbing infrastructure for the Fisher Building was provided by the D. M. Quay Company, which was headquartered at the Monadnock Building, along with the Guaranty Construction Company. Derivable from the *Inter Ocean* report of

---

[2959] The Inter Ocean. (January 1, 1896). P. 20. Newspapers.com.
[2960] The Inter Ocean. (January 1, 1896). P. 20. Newspapers.com.
[2961] The Inter Ocean. (January 1, 1896). P. 20. Newspapers.com.
[2962] The Inter Ocean. (January 1, 1896). P. 20. Newspapers.com.
[2963] The Inter Ocean. (January 1, 1896). P. 20. Newspapers.com.
[2964] The Inter Ocean. (January 1, 1896). P. 20. Newspapers.com.
[2965] The Inter Ocean. (January 1, 1896). P. 20. Newspapers.com.
[2966] The Inter Ocean. (January 1, 1896). P. 20. Newspapers.com.
[2967] The Inter Ocean. (January 1, 1896). P. 20. Newspapers.com.
[2968] The Inter Ocean. (January 1, 1896). P. 20. Newspapers.com; The Inter Ocean. (September 1, 1896). P. 5. Newspapers.com.
[2969] The Inter Ocean. (January 1, 1896). P. 20. Newspapers.com.
[2970] The Inter Ocean. (January 1, 1896). P. 20. Newspapers.com.
[2971] The Inter Ocean. (January 1, 1896). P. 20. Newspapers.com.

January 1, 1896, are the obvious community, cooperation, and alliance that defined the relationship of the Monadnock Building construction companies.[2972] The D. M. Quay Company was a powerful developer of infrastructure in the Midwest.[2973] Historian William Melancthon Glasgow, who was a member of the Pennsylvania State Historical Society, provided detailed biographical facts for Ohio-born David Milroy Quay.[2974] David Milroy Quay, a native of the Rushsylvania region of Logan County, Ohio, began professional work as a carpenter at Northwood, Ohio.[2975] He removed to Kansas City, Missouri, in 1884, where he engaged in plumbing, ventilation, and heating work.[2976] Quay moved to Chicago in 1891, where he remained for about ten years, and where he remained in the plumbing and engineering contracting business.[2977] Quay married Mary M. Speer of Northwood, Ohio.[2978] The June 15, 1895, issue of the New York City and Chicago-headquartered plumbing, heating, and ventilation technologies journal known as *Heating and Ventilation*, complimented David Quay on his work at Chicago, and pinpointed him as an emerging leader of plumbing and ventilation construction.[2979] The industry journalist stated the following compliment:

> "One of the rising engineers in this country is D. M. Quay, of the Wells-Newton-Quay Company, Chicago. Mr. Quay is already well in the front rank, and if he doesn't rise to be a leader, then a practical certainty will have gone wrong."[2980]

Of interest is the fact that the Heating and Ventilation Publishing Company maintained its Chicago office at Number 825, Monadnock Block, which was the same building shared by the D. M. Quay Company and the Guaranty Construction

---

[2972] The Inter Ocean. (January 1, 1896). P. 20. Newspapers.com.

[2973] The Inter Ocean. (January 1, 1896). P. 20. Newspapers.com.

[2974] Glasgow, William Melancthon. (1908). The Geneva Book: Comprising a History of Geneva College And a Biographical Catalogue of the Alumni and Many Students. P. 305. Philadelphia, PA: Press of the Westbrook Publishing Company. Google Books.

[2975] Glasgow, William Melancthon. (1908). The Geneva Book: Comprising a History of Geneva College And a Biographical Catalogue of the Alumni and Many Students. P. 305. Philadelphia, PA: Press of the Westbrook Publishing Company. Google Books.

[2976] Glasgow, William Melancthon. (1908). The Geneva Book: Comprising a History of Geneva College And a Biographical Catalogue of the Alumni and Many Students. P. 305. Philadelphia, PA: Press of the Westbrook Publishing Company. Google Books.

[2977] Glasgow, William Melancthon. (1908). The Geneva Book: Comprising a History of Geneva College And a Biographical Catalogue of the Alumni and Many Students. P. 305. Philadelphia, PA: Press of the Westbrook Publishing Company. Google Books.

[2978] Glasgow, William Melancthon. (1908). The Geneva Book: Comprising a History of Geneva College And a Biographical Catalogue of the Alumni and Many Students. P. 305. Philadelphia, PA: Press of the Westbrook Publishing Company. Google Books.

[2979] Heating and Ventilation. (June 15, 1895). P. 31. New York, NY: The H. & V. Publishing Company. Google Books.

[2980] Heating and Ventilation. (June 15, 1895). P. 31. New York, NY: The H. & V. Publishing Company. Google Books.

Company.[2981] The Monadnock Building was a place replete with community and commercial alliance, a veritable temple of industrial friendship and cooperation.[2982] The Monadnock Block was a center of Chicago industry, a hub of Cook County growth, and an epicenter of American technological innovation.[2983] S. W. Hume was the managing executive of the Chicago office of the Heating & Ventilation Publishing Company at the time of the May, 1895, *Heating and Ventilation* monthly report.[2984] The Fisher Building plumbing system, provided by D. M. Quay, consisted of steam-source heated water resources, as well as the most recent drainage technologies.[2985] Every sink and basin was furnished with piped connection to hot water sources.[2986] Additionally, all Fisher Building offices were supplied with a potable water resource via a system of drinking water pipe connections.[2987] The building material used for the manufacture of the pipes, valves, joints, and fittings comprised a brass-nickel alloy.[2988]

The other construction inputs to the Fisher Building that the *Inter Ocean* enumerated included the Edward Baggot Company, a design and decoration firm that was located at 169 and 171 Adams Street, in the Loop.[2989] Baggot designed the forms for the plumbing and electrical fixtures, and thus amalgamated the elements of decoration and infrastructure, bringing a renowned skill to the aesthetic element of the Fisher Building architecture.[2990] With a stated reputation as, "the West's headquarters for artistic and beautiful workmanship," the Baggot Company produced results which the *Inter Ocean* writer described as follows: "the electric and gas fixtures of the Fisher Building are simply out of sight."[2991] Other metal craftsmanship elements of the Fisher Building included the metalwork that was produced by the Winslow Brothers Company of Chicago, a firm whose office was located at Carroll Avenue, Ada Street, and Fulton Street.[2992] The Fitz Simons & Connell Company manufactured the foundation for the Fisher Building, and

[2981] Heating and Ventilation. (June 15, 1895). P. 16. New York, NY: The H. & V. Publishing Company. Google Books; The Inter Ocean. (January 1, 1896). P. 20. Newspapers.com.

[2982] Heating and Ventilation. (June 15, 1895). P. 16. New York, NY: The H. & V. Publishing Company. Google Books; The Inter Ocean. (January 1, 1896). P. 20. Newspapers.com.

[2983] Heating and Ventilation. (June 15, 1895). P. 16. New York, NY: The H. & V. Publishing Company. Google Books; The Inter Ocean. (January 1, 1896). P. 20. Newspapers.com.

[2984] Heating and Ventilation. (June 15, 1895). P. 16. New York, NY: The H. & V. Publishing Company. Google Books.

[2985] The Inter Ocean. (January 1, 1896). P. 20. Newspapers.com.

[2986] The Inter Ocean. (January 1, 1896). P. 20. Newspapers.com.

[2987] The Inter Ocean. (January 1, 1896). P. 20. Newspapers.com.

[2988] The Inter Ocean. (January 1, 1896). P. 20. Newspapers.com.

[2989] The Inter Ocean. (January 1, 1896). P. 20. Newspapers.com.

[2990] The Inter Ocean. (January 1, 1896). P. 20. Newspapers.com.

[2991] The Inter Ocean. (January 1, 1896). P. 20. Newspapers.com.

[2992] The Inter Ocean. (January 1, 1896). P. 20. Newspapers.com.

drove the pilings into the ground at the site.[2993] The Fitz Simons & Connell Company had offices at the Tacoma Building in Chicago.[2994] The George F. Kimball Company of 450 Wabash Avenue manufactured the plate glass for the building.[2995] Brokerage services for leases of the occupancy spaces within the Fisher Building were provided by the firm of William A. Merigold & Company of 204 Dearborn Street.[2996]

The *Inter Ocean* journalist celebrated the Guaranty Construction Company's Fisher Building completion, and added to the celebratory announcement two additional laudatory notices: first, that the Guaranty Construction Company had recently completed construction of the tallest building of Buffalo, New York, which was the Guaranty Building; and second, that Guaranty Construction Company had contracted to build the Gibson Building of Cincinnati, Ohio, which was to be the tallest building at Cincinnati.[2997]

The Guaranty Construction Company was a maker of skyscrapers for a growing country, with a construction portfolio including the Fisher Building of Chicago, the Guaranty Building of Buffalo, and the Gibson Building of Cincinnati.[2998] The Richardson Construction Company was a maker of megaliths, with a construction portfolio ranging from the Illinois State Capitol and the Lincoln Monument at Springfield, to the Trans-Siberian Railway system of Russia, the Port of Buenos Aires in Argentina, and the 1893 Chicago World's Fair buildings.

The *Inter Ocean* report named the members of the executive leadership of the Guaranty Construction Company as follows: George M. Moulton served as President; William D. Richardson served as General Manager; Theodore Starrett served as Vice-President; and C. F. Eicker served as Treasurer.[2999] Col. George M. Moulton and Col. William D. Richardson both represented and embodied the acute interests that the City of Chicago took in the development and building of other cities in the United States.[3000] George Moulton had worked with his father, Joseph T. Moulton, in the company known as Joseph T. Moulton & Son. The Chicago company was reputed to be the preeminent builder of elevators in the West as of 1895. George Moulton was a son of Joseph Tilton Moulton. Joseph T. Moulton (1826-1896) was a builder of grain elevators.[3001] He was a native of Gelford, New Hampshire.[3002] After serving as an apprentice in carpentry in New England, Moulton relocated to Chicago, in approximately 1851.[3003] He established the company of J. T. Moulton & Son at Chicago, and commenced contracting for the

[2993] The Inter Ocean. (January 1, 1896). P. 20. Newspapers.com.
[2994] The Inter Ocean. (January 1, 1896). P. 20. Newspapers.com.
[2995] The Inter Ocean. (January 1, 1896). P. 20. Newspapers.com.
[2996] The Inter Ocean. (January 1, 1896). P. 20. Newspapers.com.
[2997] The Inter Ocean. (January 1, 1896). P. 20. Newspapers.com.
[2998] The Inter Ocean. (January 1, 1896). P. 20. Newspapers.com.
[2999] The Inter Ocean. (January 1, 1896). P. 20. Newspapers.com.
[3000] The Buffalo Enquirer. (January 19, 1895). P. 1. Newspapers.com.
[3001] The Inter Ocean. (September 1, 1896). P. 5. Newspapers.com.
[3002] The Inter Ocean. (September 1, 1896). P. 5. Newspapers.com.
[3003] The Inter Ocean. (September 1, 1896). P. 5. Newspapers.com.

construction of grain elevators.[3004] The company work expanded throughout the United States and it was reported that nearly every large grain elevator in the United States had been built by J. T. Moulton & Son of Chicago.[3005] Three children were born to Joseph Moulton and his wife, whom he had married before moving to Chicago.[3006] The two sons were Col. George M. Moulton and William A. Moulton.[3007] George Moulton assumed the leadership of J. T. Moulton & Son upon the death of his father.[3008] William served as President of the Pioneer Fire Proofing Company of Chicago.[3009] The daughter was Mrs. L. D. Kneeland. Joseph Moulton's funeral services were expected to be officiated by Rev. W. W. Fenn of the Church of the Messiah.[3010] Moulton was an active member of Chicago Masonic organizations.[3011] At the time of his death, Joseph T. Moulton was a resident of Groveland Park, a South Side neighborhood located in the Douglas community, near the Lake Michigan lakefront.[3012]

George M. Moulton became a friend and colleague of William D. Richardson at some point prior to January, 1895.[3013] The January 19, 1895, edition of *The Buffalo Commercial* of Buffalo, New York, contained a report of the, "CHICAGO MEN IN TOWN."[3014] The report bore several headlines, including: "GOOD NEWS. Thirteen-Story Building to be Started in 12 Days. CHICAGO MEN IN TOWN. Col. Moulton Described the Great Structure to be Built at Pearl and Court Streets. ITS COST WILL BE $600,000."[3015]

> "In twelve days the great 13-story building at the corner of Church and Pearl streets will be started. Such is the statement made by two good-looking and handsomely dressed Chicago gentlemen who went to the city hall this morning to look up the building laws and make preparations for the big undertaking. Both are colonels. One is Col. George E. Moulton, who is the promoter and financial man of the enterprise, and the other is Col. W. D. Richardson, a practical builder and the man who will look after the detail."[3016]

Moulton and Richardson conferred with several Buffalo public officials that day, including City Clerk Hubbell, Commissioner Gatchell, Commissioner Mooney,

---

[3004] The Inter Ocean. (September 1, 1896). P. 5. Newspapers.com.
[3005] The Inter Ocean. (September 1, 1896). P. 5. Newspapers.com.
[3006] The Inter Ocean. (September 1, 1896). P. 5. Newspapers.com.
[3007] The Inter Ocean. (September 1, 1896). P. 5. Newspapers.com.
[3008] The Inter Ocean. (September 1, 1896). P. 5. Newspapers.com.
[3009] The Inter Ocean. (September 1, 1896). P. 5. Newspapers.com.
[3010] The Inter Ocean. (September 1, 1896). P. 5. Newspapers.com.
[3011] The Inter Ocean. (September 1, 1896). P. 5. Newspapers.com.
[3012] The Inter Ocean. (September 1, 1896). P. 5. Newspapers.com.
[3013] The Buffalo Commercial. (January 19, 1895). P. 11. Newspapers.com.
[3014] The Buffalo Commercial. (January 19, 1895). P. 11. Newspapers.com.
[3015] The Buffalo Commercial. (January 19, 1895). P. 11. Newspapers.com.
[3016] The Buffalo Commercial. (January 19, 1895). P. 11. Newspapers.com.

and Commissioner Pankow.[3017] The three Commissioners represented the Board of Public Works of Buffalo.[3018] A subsequent conference took place among the colonels, the Buffalo Bureau of Buildings, and the Buffalo Bureau of Streets.[3019] George Moulton issued a statement about the construction and development plan for the new 13-story building. Moulton said: "'We expect to put up a building that will be an ornament to this city. The men who are back of the project have not gone into the scheme with their eyes shut.'"[3020] Moulton declared the faith of Chicago businessmen in the future of Buffalo as a great American city, and communicated his wish to include primarily Buffalo residents in the construction process:

> "'We believe that Buffalo has a great future before her. We figure that out because as near as we can calculate the erection of new and expensive buildings has not been overdone as it has in some cities. We think that Buffalo is the coming city of this country and for that very reason we are putting up this building. It will be a 13-story concern and the exterior will be the handsomest in town. It will be terra cotta and unlike anything that there is in Buffalo at present. We shall build it the way the Morgan Building at Pearl and Niagara streets has been constructed. The building will be of brick and steel. The steel frames will be placed in position first and we shall build the walls afterwards. That is the modern way of constructing a new building and it has been a great success. The new structurne [sic] is to cost $600,000. I don't care to say where the money is coming from. The building will be put up by the Guaranty Building Company of Buffalo. Who are in that company I do not care to make known just now. Our lawyer is engaged in drawing up the articles of incorporation. The Guaranty Building Company bought the Hascal L. Taylor estate, the face price being $200,000. The contract for the erection of the structure has been let to the Guaranty Construction Company of Chicago for $600,000. The structure will be built under the management of Mr. Richardson. The building will be modern in every sense of the word. It will be well lighted and the offices will be the finest in this city. We expect to heat it with electricity. Four high-grade electric elevators will carry passengers in the building, and, as I have said, modern ideas will prevail in the erection. We expect to get the electric power from the Niagara Falls Power Company if it succeeds in transmitting Niagara power to this city by the time the building is completed. If the power is not here then we shall have our own independent electric plant in the building. We expect to begin work on the first day of February and the building will be completed by the first day of next year. We shall probably have between

---

[3017] The Buffalo Commercial. (January 19, 1895). P. 11. Newspapers.com.
[3018] The Buffalo Commercial. (January 19, 1895). P. 11. Newspapers.com.
[3019] The Buffalo Commercial. (January 19, 1895). P. 11. Newspapers.com.
[3020] The Buffalo Commercial. (January 19, 1895). P. 11. Newspapers.com.

500 and 600 men at work putting it up. All the work will be done by Buffalo workmen as far as it lies in our power. We expect to spend every dollar on the building in this city except, of course, when it is detrimental to our interests."[3021]

The work of Moulton and Richardson amounted to an invitation to municipal and economic stewardship in that it enabled a large number of Buffalo residents to participate in the project.[3022] This inclusion manifested not only as the hire of hundreds of Buffalo construction workers, but also as the hire of a Buffalo excavation company. The Guaranty Building Company of Buffalo, and the Guaranty Construction Company of Chicago, hired the Brown & Stabell Company of Buffalo for the work of excavation of the site for the planned Guaranty Building.[3023]

The Guaranty Construction Company continued multi-state construction work throughout the Great Lakes region in 1897 when the firm built the Onondaga County Bank building at Syracuse, New York. Richardson oversaw the construction project.[3024] Buffalo, New York, became one of the places of interest for Richardson and Moulton after the 1893 World's Fair.[3025] The January 19, 1895, edition of *The Buffalo Enquirer* explained the particulars of a plan of Chicago developers and construction men to build a skyscraper at Buffalo.[3026] George M. Moulton and William D. Richardson co-founded the Guaranty Building Company in January, 1895.[3027] The articles of incorporation were prepared at that time for the establishment of the company as the real estate development corporation that would hold title to the new building that Moulton and Richardson planned to build at Buffalo.[3028] It appears that the new building would contain thirteen stories and was designed to be a paragon of architectural and engineering innovation.[3029] The building's operational infrastructure would consist of electricity-driven heating systems, and four electric elevator systems.[3030]

In addition to founding the Richardson Construction Company of Chicago and Springfield, William Douglas Richardson co-founded the Richardson investment company of Chicago, the Springfield Iron Company of Springfield and Chicago, the Amur Steamship Company, the Russo-American Direct Transportation Company, the Russian Trans-Siberian Railway system, the Chicala Water Company, the Richardson & Latham Company of Springfield, the Guaranty Building Company, the 1893 World's Columbian Exposition, the Springfield &

[3021] The Buffalo Commercial. (January 19, 1895). P. 11. Newspapers.com.
[3022] The Buffalo Commercial. (January 19, 1895). P. 11. Newspapers.com.
[3023] The Buffalo Enquirer. (February 2, 1895). P. 5. Newspapers.com.
[3024] The Buffalo Commercial. (January 16, 1897). P. 10. Newspapers.com.
[3025] The Buffalo Enquirer. (January 19, 1895). P. 1. Newspapers.com.
[3026] The Buffalo Enquirer. (January 19, 1895). P. 1. Newspapers.com.
[3027] The Buffalo Enquirer. (January 19, 1895). P. 1. Newspapers.com.
[3028] The Buffalo Enquirer. (January 19, 1895). P. 1. Newspapers.com.
[3029] The Buffalo Enquirer. (January 19, 1895). P. 1. Newspapers.com.
[3030] The Buffalo Enquirer. (January 19, 1895). P. 1. Newspapers.com.

St. Louis Narrow Gauge Railroad Company, and the Guaranty Construction Company of Chicago, in addition to the original industrial economy of Argentina.[3031] He also possibly co-founded the Anglo-American Canaigre Company and the Springfield Coal Trust Company.

Richardson Construction Company:

The New Illinois State Capitol and the Joliet Workers

William Douglas Richardson brought construction jobs to prison inmates at the Joliet Penitentiary in Joliet, Will County, Illinois. The general timeframe of the work contracts between the Richardson Construction Company and State of Illinois, in which the Joliet inmates were the workers, was the 1870s. The contracts consisted of consideration in which industrial jobs and wages were exchanged for labor. The contract of August 1, 1872, contained consideration in which stone-cutting jobs and wages were exchanged for the work of the inmates.[3032] M. Selz & Company, later known as Selz, Schwab & Company, also entered a contract with the Joliet Penitentiary on September 1, 1872, providing shoe and boot manufacturing jobs to the inmates.[3033]

The approximate concurrence of the Selz and the Richardson work contracts meant that both John Whitfield Bunn and William D. Richardson provided jobs and industrial work to the Joliet inmates either near, or at, the same time.[3034] The Joliet work contracts can be described as follows. The State of Illinois, through its governmental subsidiary known as the Commission of the Illinois State Penitentiary, entered into contracts with various commercial and industrial organizations.[3035] The contractual parties, therefore, consisted of both public and private organizations.[3036] The form of consideration that existed with apparent uniformity within the contracts essentially consisted of the mutual exchange of

---

[3031] Richardson family history records. Notice: It is probable that William D. Richardson was a co-founder of the Guaranty Construction Company of Chicago, and that fact, though not proved directly, is assumed here with relative circumstantial safety.

[3032] Report of the Commissioners of the Illinois State Penitentiary for the Two Years Ending September 30, 1876. (1876). Page number not clearly ascertainable. Google Books.

[3033] Report of the Commissioners of the Illinois State Penitentiary for the Two Years Ending September 30, 1876. (1876). Page number not clearly ascertainable. Google Books.

[3034] Report of the Commissioners of the Illinois State Penitentiary for the Two Years Ending September 30, 1876. (1876). Page number and additional bibliographical data were not clearly ascertainable at the time of reference. Google Books.

[3035] Report of the Commissioners of the Illinois State Penitentiary for the Two Years Ending September 30, 1876. (1876). Page number and additional bibliographical data were not clearly ascertainable at the time of reference. Google Books.

[3036] Report of the Commissioners of the Illinois State Penitentiary for the Two Years Ending September 30, 1876. (1876). Page number and additional bibliographical data were not clearly ascertainable at the time of reference. Google Books.

industrial jobs, wages, and opportunities on the one hand, for the labor of the inmates, on the other hand.[3037] The mutual inducement element of the contracts, therefore, innately blended public and private interests.[3038] *Exhibit Q* of the 1876 *Report of the Commissioners of the Illinois State Penitentiary* contained the list of employment contracts with the Joliet inmates.[3039] The August 1, 1872, Joliet inmate labor contract to which the Richardson Construction Company was the commercial party, stipulated the hire of 225 men.[3040] The Richardson contract stipulated a daily wage of 81 cents per man.[3041] The time stipulated for the length of the contract was five years.[3042] The full performance contemplated by the contract would not be given, however, due to a nullification in 1876. After nullification of the contract occurred on June 15, 1876, when nearly four years of the contractual time had transpired, the resultant contractual voidness led to the creation and performance of at least one, and possibly multiple, subsequent short-time work contracts.[3043] These short-time contracts were executed in order to fill the economic void caused by the June 15, 1876 termination of the August 1, 1872 contract.[3044] The subsequent contract, or contracts, stipulated a daily wage of 50 cents per man. The new contract ended on January 1, 1877, and the number of men employed under the new contract did not appear to change as a result of the

---

[3037] Report of the Commissioners of the Illinois State Penitentiary for the Two Years Ending September 30, 1876. (1876). Page number and additional bibliographical data were not clearly ascertainable at the time of reference. Google Books.

[3038] Report of the Commissioners of the Illinois State Penitentiary for the Two Years Ending September 30, 1876. (1876). Page number and additional bibliographical data were not clearly ascertainable at the time of reference. Google Books.

[3039] Report of the Commissioners of the Illinois State Penitentiary for the Two Years Ending September 30, 1876. (1876). Page number and additional bibliographical data were not clearly ascertainable at the time of reference. Google Books.

[3040] Report of the Commissioners of the Illinois State Penitentiary for the Two Years Ending September 30, 1876. (1876). Page number and additional bibliographical data were not clearly ascertainable at the time of reference. Google Books.

[3041] Report of the Commissioners of the Illinois State Penitentiary for the Two Years Ending September 30, 1876. (1876). Page number and additional bibliographical data were not clearly ascertainable at the time of reference. Google Books.

[3042] Report of the Commissioners of the Illinois State Penitentiary for the Two Years Ending September 30, 1876. (1876). Page number and additional bibliographical data were not clearly ascertainable at the time of reference. Google Books.

[3043] Report of the Commissioners of the Illinois State Penitentiary for the Two Years Ending September 30, 1876. (1876). Page number and additional bibliographical data were not clearly ascertainable at the time of reference. Google Books.

[3044] Report of the Commissioners of the Illinois State Penitentiary for the Two Years Ending September 30, 1876. (1876). Page number and additional bibliographical data were not clearly ascertainable at the time of reference. Google Books.

termination of the original contract.[3045] The number of men employed probably remained 225.

Richardson made a bid as a Democrat for the office of Treasurer of the State of Illinois, as was reported in the March 30, 1878, issue of the *Chicago Tribune*.[3046] The Chicago *Inter-Ocean* reported on May 11, 1875, that the Springfield & St. Louis Narrow Gauge Railroad Company was incorporated with a capital fund of $200,000 in the spring of 1875, with William D. Richardson, Charles Henry Lanphier, C. H. Buchar, A. L. Ide, Charles Ridgely, and R. D. Lawrence all serving as the incorporators.[3047] Alexander Starne served as President of the company and Richardson served as Vice-President.[3048] The report did not specify the elements of the financial structure of the company, but mentioned that the purpose of the railroad was to connect stone quarries with Springfield and St. Louis.[3049] St. Louis was a major railroad center and one of the largest and most important cities of North America.

Colonel Richardson died on December 7, 1923, at Loxley, Alabama.[3050] The obituary contained a great deal of information concerning the international construction work undertaken by Richardson. *The Onlooker*, a newspaper of Foley, Baldwin County, Alabama, contained the detailed obituary for Richardson. The funeral service was provided by a local Episcopal church, and the service consisted of "the simple Episcopal ceremony."[3051] The article stated that Richardson had relocated from his home of Connecticut to Chicago during the rapid development years of the city. The obituary mentioned his work in planning the construction and design of the Illinois State Capitol buildings and grounds, as well as his work in constructing the Abraham Lincoln Memorial at Oak Ridge Cemetery in Springfield.[3052] The article's description of his work in Chicago, though tragically barren of specific facts, said: "He was pioneer in some almost unbelievable engineering feats in Chicago."[3053] The article contained the only references that have been rediscovered thus far about his friendship with Cornelius Vanderbilt (1794-1877). Abraham Lincoln had appointed Richardson to a position of authority during the Civil War, and it was in this post that Richardson was ordered by President Lincoln to seize several maritime vessels to which Cornelius Vanderbilt held property at the time. When Richardson delivered the orders to Vanderbilt, Commodore Vanderbilt answered with refusal and profanity. The article reported the following specific facts:

[3045] Report of the Commissioners of the Illinois State Penitentiary for the Two Years Ending September 30, 1876. (1876). Page number and additional bibliographical data were not clearly ascertainable at the time of reference. Google Books.

[3046] The Chicago Tribune. (March 30, 1878). Newspapers.com.

[3047] Chicago Inter-Ocean. (May 11, 1875). P. 2. Newspapers.com.

[3048] Chicago Inter-Ocean. (May 11, 1875). P. 2. Newspapers.com.

[3049] Chicago Inter-Ocean. (May 11, 1875). P. 2. Newspapers.com.

[3050] The Onlooker. (December 13, 1923). P. 1. Newspapers.com.

[3051] The Onlooker. (December 13, 1923). P. 1. Newspapers.com.

[3052] The Onlooker. (December 13, 1923). P. 1. Newspapers.com.

[3053] The Onlooker. (December 13, 1923). P. 1. Newspapers.com.

"Aristocracy meant nothing to Col. Richardson, so he politely arrested Vanderbilt and hailed him before the executive chief, Abraham Lincoln, at Washington. The ensuing investigation rendered the situation clear, and the predicament arising from Vanderbilt's misapprehension was at a happy end when he made out a bill of sale and gave the boats to the government."[3054]

The relationship between Colonel Richardson and Commodore Vanderbilt turned quickly into a strong friendship. Thereafter, whenever Richardson was in New York City, he always stayed with the Vanderbilts at their home.[3055]

The Onlooker stated that Richardson had visited every country in the world, and had built the $1,000,000 mansion at Joliet for the President of the 1893 World's Columbian Exposition.[3056] The Russian construction work that Richardson undertook included the planning and engineering of the Trans-Siberian Railway, the Eurasian railroad system that connected St. Petersburg to Vladivostok, the Pacific Ocean port located south of the debouchment of the Amur River, and near to Manchuria and China.[3057] The Richardson Construction Company also built large-scale irrigation infrastructure in Mexico and in California.[3058] The journalist said of Richardson, "He engineered the railroad from what is now Petrograd to Vladivostok; he was engaged in irrigation projects in Mexico and California."[3059]

The Onlooker additionally alluded to Richardson's commercial relationship with the Studebaker family of Indiana, and Richardson's cooperative efforts with the Studebakers in introducing large-scale industry to Argentina. The journalist reported: "[Richardson] was intimate with Lincoln, Commodore Vanderbilt and the elder Studebakers, with the last named of whom he was associated in the inchoation of the industrial development of Argentina."[3060] Richardson's obituary from *The Onlooker*, therefore, contains vital and essential biographical information about what he did in America and abroad. The Alabama newspaper proved to be a key and invaluable resource of biographical information.[3061]

Brothers Myron Hutchinson Richardson

and Charles Richardson, Esq. of Chicago

Myron Hutchinson Richardson (1871-1951) was a son of Dr. Frank Richardson and Mary (Hutchinson) Richardson of Wichita, Kansas, and a nephew of William

---

[3054] The Onlooker. (December 13, 1923). P. 1. Newspapers.com.
[3055] The Onlooker. (December 13, 1923). P. 1. Newspapers.com.
[3056] The Onlooker. (December 13, 1923). P. 1. Newspapers.com.
[3057] The Onlooker. (December 13, 1923). P. 1. Newspapers.com.
[3058] The Onlooker. (December 13, 1923). P. 1. Newspapers.com.
[3059] The Onlooker. (December 13, 1923). P. 1. Newspapers.com.
[3060] The Onlooker. (December 13, 1923). P. 1. Newspapers.com.
[3061] The Onlooker. (December 13, 1923). P. 1. Newspapers.com.

Douglas Richardson of Chicago and Springfield.[3062] Myron demonstrated an aptitude for technological development, a skill that resulted in his receiving several patents for diverse inventions throughout multiple years. *The Topeka State Journal* in 1894 reported that Richardson, then a resident of Wichita, had received a patent for a new form of windmill.[3063] The report contained news regarding several Kansas patents that had been awarded during the week of March 20, 1894.[3064] At some point after 1894 Richardson relocated to Chicago.[3065] At Chicago, Richardson was an inventor and a real estate broker.[3066]

A patent grant notice for Myron H. Richardson of Chicago appeared in Volume 35 of the *Western Electrician*, an industry journal for American electrical technology, science, and industry.[3067] The notice was coupled with a report that stated that the United States Patent Office had awarded patent 774,481 jointly to Myron Richardson and to Oscar J. Lee, both of Chicago, for the invention of a novel form of railroad signal technology.[3068] The patentees had filed the pleading for the grant of patent on June 2, 1902.[3069] The United States Patent Office granted the patent on or around November 19, 1902.[3070] The following words conveyed the purpose and description of the novel railroad signal.[3071]

> "In a railway signaling system are a pair of line conductors normally maintained at a difference of electric potential, a third conductor and a number of signal devices interposed in multiple between the conductor and one of the first-named conductors. Contacts are arranged in multiple between the third conductor and the remaining one of the first-named conductors, and located at points corresponding to the signal devices."[3072]

The April 24, 1904, issue of *The Wichita Daily Eagle* indicated that Myron Richardson had established a real estate brokerage company in Chicago.[3073] The

---

[3062] Solomon, Ruth. Family Group Sheet for Dr. Frank Richardson.
[3063] The Topeka State Journal. (March 22, 1894). P. 1. Newspapers.com.
[3064] The Topeka State Journal. (March 22, 1894). P. 1. Newspapers.com.
[3065] The Wichita Daily Eagle. (April 24, 1904). P. 13. Newspapers.com.
[3066] The Wichita Daily Eagle. (April 24, 1904). P. 13. Newspapers.com; United States Patent 731,129 A. Door-sign. Myron H. Richardson, patentee. Google Patents.
[3067] Western Electrician. (July 2-December 31, 1904). Vol. 35. P. 422. Chicago, IL: Electrician Publishing Company. Google Books.
[3068] Western Electrician. (July 2-December 31, 1904). Vol. 35. P. 422. Chicago, IL: Electrician Publishing Company. Google Books.
[3069] Western Electrician. (July 2-December 31, 1904). Vol. 35. P. 422. Chicago, IL: Electrician Publishing Company. Google Books.
[3070] Western Electrician. (July 2-December 31, 1904). Vol. 35. P. 422. Chicago, IL: Electrician Publishing Company. Google Books.
[3071] Western Electrician. (July 2-December 31, 1904). Vol. 35. P. 422. Chicago, IL: Electrician Publishing Company. Google Books.
[3072] Western Electrician. (July 2-December 31, 1904). Vol. 35. P. 422. Chicago, IL: Electrician Publishing Company. Google Books.
[3073] The Wichita Daily Eagle. (April 24, 1904). P. 13. Newspapers.com.

real estate office was located in the Title and Trust Building.[3074] "Myron H. Richardson, a son of Dr. Frank Richardson of Wichita, is in the real estate business with offices in the Title and Trust Building."[3075] The historical record contains proofs of the fact that Richardson engaged in a diverse array of work, having conducted regular technological trials and experiments, in addition to having engaged in the real estate sector.[3076] He was based in Chicago for both lines of work.[3077]

Richardson was awarded a patent for a novel automatic door sign, which was a mechanism designed to carry advertisements.[3078] For this he received United States Patent 731,129.[3079] The patent was awarded on June 16, 1903, nearly three months after Richardson had filed the pleading for the grant of the patent on March 23, 1903.[3080] The patent record contained the following introduction: "Be it known that I, MYRON H. RICHARDSON, a citizen of the United States, residing at Chicago, in the county of Cook and State of Illinois, have invented a new and useful Automatic Door-Sign. . ."[3081] The excerpt that follows here is from the description provided by Richardson in support of the pleading for the grant of the patent:

"The operation of the device will be readily understood and may be described as follows: When the door is closed, the sign 0 hangs vertically downward, as indicated in dotted lines in Fig. 1, being hidden from the view of the person opening the door from the rear side. When, however, the door is opened, the movement thereof toward open position causes the upper edge of the door to engage bail D and rock or swing the same upwardly, thereby drawing on the connection F, and hence swinging the sign 0 about its point of pivotal connection B to the door, and hence raising the free end of such sign so that said sign will project or extend transversely across the door, as indicated in full lines in Fig. 1, and hence displaying the sign on the back side thereof through the transparent or glass panel J of the door. In order to prevent the sign from swinging too

---

[3074] The Wichita Daily Eagle. (April 24, 1904). P. 13. Newspapers.com.

[3075] The Wichita Daily Eagle. (April 24, 1904). P. 13. Newspapers.com.

[3076] The Wichita Daily Eagle. (April 24, 1904). P. 13. Newspapers.com; Western Electrician. (July 2-December 31, 1904). Vol. 35. P. 422. Chicago, IL: Electrician Publishing Company. Google Books.

[3077] The Wichita Daily Eagle. (April 24, 1904). P. 13. Newspapers.com; Western Electrician. (July 2-December 31, 1904). Vol. 35. P. 422. Chicago, IL: Electrician Publishing Company. Google Books.

[3078] United States Patent 731,129 A. Door-sign. Myron H. Richardson, patentee. Google Patents. (June 16, 1903).

[3079] United States Patent 731,129 A. Door-sign. Myron H. Richardson, patentee. Google Patents. (June 16, 1903).

[3080] United States Patent 731,129 A. Door-sign. Myron H. Richardson, patentee. Google Patents. (June 16, 1903).

[3081] United States Patent 731,129 A. Door-sign. Myron H. Richardson, patentee. Google Patents. (June 16, 1903).

far upwardly, a stop K may be suit-ably connected to the sign and arranged to engage a stop-pin L, fixed in a convenient part of the door adjacent to the edge thereof, as clearly shown."[3082]

Volume 38 of the trade journal *Fabrics, Fancy-Goods & Notions*, accounting for the year 1904, reported that Myron Richardson and C. E. Wright, both of Chicago, cooperated to produce a novel form of comb for which they jointly were awarded United States Patent 748,420.[3083] Volume 38, Issue Number 2, of the industry journal known as *Fabrics, Fancy-Goods & Notions*, reported the grant of this patent for the novel form of comb.[3084] The report was one of a long list of similar patent grant reports that appeared on the same page of the referenced publication, and contained only the names and the cities of residence of the inventors, the forms of invention patented, and the patent numbers.[3085]

On September 15, 1919, Myron Richardson filed a pleading for a patent for a novel form of "gas engine."[3086] The United States Patent Office granted the patent at some time around November 30, 1920.[3087] The patent number was 1,360,316.[3088] The words of purpose and description for the novel gas engine were as follows:

> "An engine comprising a cylinder having two alining [sic] bores of different sizes in open communication; a piston in and fitting each of said bores; and a connection connecting the pistons together causing the pistons to move toward each other for compressing a charge to effect maximum compression of such charge in the smaller bore."[3089]

[3082] United States Patent 731,129 A. Door-sign. Myron H. Richardson, patentee. Google Patents. (June 16, 1903).

[3083] Fabrics, Fancy-Goods & Notions: A Journal of Information for Jobbers & Retailers of Dry Goods, Fancy Goods & Notions. Vol. 38, Issue Number 2. (February, 1904). P. 42. New York, NY: The Henry C. Nathan Company, Publishers. Google Books.

[3084] Fabrics, Fancy-Goods & Notions: A Journal of Information for Jobbers & Retailers of Dry Goods, Fancy Goods & Notions. Vol. 38, Issue Number 2. (February, 1904). P. 42. New York, NY: The Henry C. Nathan Company, Publishers. Google Books.

[3085] Fabrics, Fancy-Goods & Notions: A Journal of Information for Jobbers & Retailers of Dry Goods, Fancy Goods & Notions. Vol. 38, Issue Number 2. (February, 1904). P. 42. New York, NY: The Henry C. Nathan Company, Publishers. Google Books.

[3086] Official Gazette of the United States Patent Office. (November, 1920). Vol. 280. P. 829. Washington, D.C.: Government Printing Office. Google Books.

[3087] Official Gazette of the United States Patent Office. (November, 1920). Vol. 280. P. 829. Washington, D.C.: Government Printing Office. Google Books.

[3088] Official Gazette of the United States Patent Office. (November, 1920). Vol. 280. P. 829. Washington, D.C.: Government Printing Office. Google Books.

[3089] Official Gazette of the United States Patent Office. (November, 1920). Vol. 280. P. 829. Washington, D.C.: Government Printing Office. Google Books.

Additionally, Myron Richardson was awarded Patent 1,925,676 for the invention of a novel improvement to vending machines.[3090] Advance Machine Company of Chicago held the status of assignee of this patent.[3091] Myron H. Richardson continued to work with technological improvements to vending machines, a fact supported by the grant of a subsequent patent for vending machinery technology.[3092] This novel vending machinery improvement patent received by Richardson contained, *inter alia*, the following words of purpose and description:

> "This invention relates to improvements in vending machines in which the articles are vended from the original package and is particularly adapted, though not necessarily limited in its use, for vending cigars, and one of the objects of the invention is to provide improved means whereby the article to be delivered will be clearly visible while in the machine and the revenue stamp upon the original package will also be clearly visible. . .To the attainment of these ends and the accomplishment of other new and useful objects as will appear, the invention consists in the features of novelty in substantially the construction, combination and arrangement of the several parts hereinafter more fully described and claimed and shown in the accompanying drawings illustrating this invention, and in which Figure 1 is a front elevation of a machine of this character constructed in accordance with the principles of this invention. . ."[3093]

On May 22, 1934, the United States granted Myron Richardson an additional patent for a novel technological improvement to vending machines.[3094] In the case of this vending technology improvement, Myron H. Richardson of Chicago served as co-inventor with Albert E. Gebert of Wilmette, Illinois, a Cook County suburb of Chicago.[3095]

The *1900 United States Census* indicated that Myron Richardson resided at 1147 Washington Boulevard, located in Ward 13.[3096] The *1910 United States Census* listed Richardson as a resident of the 4500 block of Oakenwald Avenue, in the 6th Ward of Chicago.[3097] This residence was located in the Kenwood community. At

---

[3090] United States Patent 1,925,676. Vending Machine. Myron H. Richardson, inventor. Google Patents. (September 5, 1933).

[3091] United States Patent 1,925,676. Vending Machine. Myron H. Richardson, inventor. Google Patents. (September 5, 1933).

[3092] United States Patent 1,927,502. (September 19, 1933). Vending Machine. Myron H. Richardson, inventor. Google Patents.

[3093] United States Patent 1,927,502. (September 19, 1933). Vending Machine. Myron H. Richardson, inventor. Google Patents.

[3094] United States Patent 1,960,065. (May 22, 1934). Vending Machine. Albert E. Gebert, Myron H. Richardson, inventors. Google Patents.

[3095] United States Patent 1,960,065. (May 22, 1934). Vending Machine. Albert E. Gebert, Myron H. Richardson, inventors. Google Patents.

[3096] 1900 United States Census. Ancestry.com.

[3097] 1910 United States Census. Ancestry.com.

this time he worked as an independent real estate salesman.[3098] The *1920 United States Census* listed Myron and wife Judith Richardson as residents of Monticello Avenue, located in the 27th Ward of Chicago.[3099] In 1920, their daughter, also named Judith Richardson, was listed as being six years old.[3100] The search for Myron Richardson in the *1930 U.S. Census* did not produce any results. The *1940 United States Census* listed Myron H. and Judith Richardson as residents of 4901 Monticello Avenue.[3101] In 1940, Myron worked as a mechanical engineer at a machinery factory.[3102] Myron and his wife, Judith (Cornell) Richardson, resided in the Albany Park community at this time. Their daughter was Judith Cornell Richardson of Chicago (1913-2000), and later of Wilmington, North Carolina.

Charles Richardson, Esq., was a brother of Myron H. Richardson, and a son of Dr. Frank Richardson and Mary (Hutchinson) Richardson of Kansas.[3103] Charles relocated from Kansas to Springfield, Illinois, as a teenager.[3104] At Springfield he worked as a manager of the cigar stand at the Leland Hotel. The Richardson family maintained connections not only to Springfield, but also to the hotel industry.[3105] Charles' uncle, also named Charles Richardson (a son of Henry Earle Richardson and Betsy (Johns) Richardson), served as the General Manager of the Leland Hotel.[3106] The family association was almost certainly a factor in Charles' decision to relocate from Kansas to Springfield to work at the Leland.[3107] While working as the cigar stand manager, Charles Richardson (the son of Dr. Frank Richardson of Kansas) attended high school in Springfield.[3108] He graduated from high school at

---

[3098] 1910 United States Census. Ancestry.com.

[3099] 1920 United States Census. Ancestry.com.

[3100] 1920 United States Census. Ancestry.com.

[3101] 1940 United States Census. Ancestry.com.

[3102] 1940 United States Census. Ancestry.com.

[3103] Biographical Record: This Volume Contains Biographical Sketches Of Leading Citizens of Sedgwick County, Kansas. (1901). p. 440. Chicago, IL: Biographical Publishing Company. Archive.org.

[3104] Biographical Record: This Volume Contains Biographical Sketches Of Leading Citizens of Sedgwick County, Kansas. (1901). p. 440. Chicago, IL: Biographical Publishing Company. Archive.org.

[3105] Biographical Record: This Volume Contains Biographical Sketches Of Leading Citizens of Sedgwick County, Kansas. (1901). p. 440. Chicago, IL: Biographical Publishing Company. Archive.org

[3106] Call, Andrew Taylor. (2005). Jacob Bunn: Legacy of an Illinois Industrial Pioneer. P. 144. Lawrenceville, VA: Brunswick Publishing Corporation.

[3107] Biographical Record: This Volume Contains Biographical Sketches Of Leading Citizens of Sedgwick County, Kansas. (1901). p. 440. Chicago, IL: Biographical Publishing Company. Archive.org; Call, Andrew Taylor. (2005). Jacob Bunn: Legacy of an Illinois Industrial Pioneer. P. 144. Lawrenceville, VA: Brunswick Publishing Corporation.

[3108] Biographical Record: This Volume Contains Biographical Sketches Of Leading Citizens of Sedgwick County, Kansas. (1901). p. 440. Chicago, IL: Biographical Publishing Company. Archive.org.

the age of twenty years, and was class valedictorian in a class of 44 people.[3109] Charles was about fourteen years old when he began work as manager of the cigar stand at the Leland Hotel.[3110] After graduation from high school in Springfield, Charles relocated to Chicago, where he began the study of law.[3111] He read law under the supervision of the law firm of Shope, Barrett & Rogers.[3112] Charles also practiced law with Shope, Barrett & Rogers until he enlisted in the United States Army during the Spanish-American War.[3113] He was killed on August 20, 1898, at Santiago, Cuba, and was reported to have been killed in battle soon after leaving the trenches.[3114]

Judith Cornell Richardson of Chicago

and the Commercialization of Black Light Technology

Myron H. Richardson married Judith Cornell. They had one child, a daughter named Judith Cornell Richardson, who was born in 1913. Judith was a trained dancer in Chicago and then became a scientist and industrial entrepreneur. She started the Richardson Advertising Company of Chicago, which employed seventeen people in about the 1930s.[3115] Judith Cornell Richardson was inspired by her father's many patented vending machine inventions and conducted experiments with machines and the scientific and forensic applications of ultraviolet light. Judith started Black Light Products Company of Chicago, which was headquartered at 67 East Lake Street in the Loop. The company designed, patented, and manufactured black light technologies, including black light lamps, bulbs, black light forensic tools, chalks, coloring tools, and paints.[3116] It was

---

[3109] Biographical Record: This Volume Contains Biographical Sketches Of Leading Citizens of Sedgwick County, Kansas. (1901). p. 440. Chicago, IL: Biographical Publishing Company. Archive.org.

[3110] Biographical Record: This Volume Contains Biographical Sketches Of Leading Citizens of Sedgwick County, Kansas. (1901). p. 440. Chicago, IL: Biographical Publishing Company. Archive.org.

[3111] Biographical Record: This Volume Contains Biographical Sketches Of Leading Citizens of Sedgwick County, Kansas. (1901). p. 440. Chicago, IL: Biographical Publishing Company. Archive.org.

[3112] Biographical Record: This Volume Contains Biographical Sketches Of Leading Citizens of Sedgwick County, Kansas. (1901). p. 440. Chicago, IL: Biographical Publishing Company. Archive.org.

[3113] Biographical Record: This Volume Contains Biographical Sketches Of Leading Citizens of Sedgwick County, Kansas. (1901). p. 440. Chicago, IL: Biographical Publishing Company. Archive.org.

[3114] Biographical Record: This Volume Contains Biographical Sketches Of Leading Citizens of Sedgwick County, Kansas. (1901). p. 440. Chicago, IL: Biographical Publishing Company. Archive.org.

[3115] Chicago Tribune. (September 19, 1946). P. 25. Newspapers.com.

[3116] Black Light in Evangelism. (July, 1955). Ministry: International Journal For Pastors. Ministrymagazine.org.

unusual for a woman to be the president of a corporation at this time, and Judith often used the name "J. Cornell Richardson" for business communications, business contacts, and business dealing. Judith grew up in Albany Park.

Judith Cornell Richardson was founder and President of Black Light Products Company; and her husband, Richard Knight Cornell, was Vice-President of the company.[3117] The company employed one chemist, one engineer, one technical personnel staff member, and three additional staff members by approximately 1956, according to James F. Mauk and his *Industrial Research Laboratories of the United States* (1956).[3118] Black Light Products Company also manufactured and developed fluorescent lighting technologies, invisible-marking and examination fluids, paints, lacquers, and printing inks, among other lighting machines, tools, pigments, and processes.[3119] Black light refers essentially to ultraviolet light, the species of light that occurs beyond the visible light spectrum of the electromagnetic scale, and whose frequency places it adjacent to the blue and violet lights of the visible light spectrum. Black light is, therefore, the invisible higher-frequency neighbor of violet light. Black light can reveal and illuminate marks, structures, evidences, and forms that visible light cannot reveal. Judith Richardson commercially developed black light machines for searching and discovering spoilage in food before evidence of spoilage would become apparent to the naked eye and developed black light machines that aided United States national defense through the detection of subtle counterfeits of documents used by spies during World War II and the Cold War.[3120]

Richard Knight Cornell (1904-1980), husband of Judith Cornell Richardson, graduated from Brown University in 1926, where he was a member of Alpha Tau Omega Fraternity. Cornell founded and owned the Nelco Industries Company of Chicago.[3121] The firm developed and manufactured plastics, and was headquartered at 53 W. Jackson Boulevard in the Chicago Loop.[3122]

[3117] Mauk, James F. (1956). Industrial Research Laboratories of the United States. P. 69. Washington, D.C.: National Academy of Sciences and National Research Council. Google Books.

[3118] Mauk, James F. (1956). Industrial Research Laboratories of the United States. P. 69. Washington, D.C.: National Academy of Sciences and National Research Council. Google Books.

[3119] Mauk, James F. (1956). Industrial Research Laboratories of the United States. P. 69. Washington, D.C.: National Academy of Sciences and National Research Council. Google Books.

[3120] Detroit Free Press. (September 12, 1946). P. 7. Newspapers.com.

[3121] Brown Alumni Monthly (Brown University). (May, 1981). P. 46. Archive.org.

[3122] Kline, Gordon Mabey. (1953). Modern Plastics Worldwide World Encyclopedia With Buyer's Guide. Page number not apparent. Plastics Catalogue Corporation. Google Books.

The Barnum & Richardson Company of Connecticut and Chicago:

An Early Connection for Appalachian New England and the Great Lakes

Leonard Richardson and Milo Barnum Richardson of Lime Rock, Connecticut, both contributed immensely to the development of the Chicago railroad components manufacturing industry.[3123] New England historian William Richard Cutter provided several key facts concerning the development of this industry. Just as John Stryker connected Chicago to Indiana, Ohio, Michigan, and New York through development of the Michigan Southern Railroad Company and the New York Central Railroad Company system, and just as John Whitfield Bunn connected Chicago to Indiana, Ohio, and Pittsburgh through the Wabash Railroad Company, Leonard Richardson, William Henry Barnum, and Milo Barnum Richardson, along with multiple others, led the industrial links between the Appalachian Mountains of New England and the railroad industry of Chicago and Cook County.

Leonard Richardson engaged in the manufacture of iron products at Lime Rock, Connecticut, with his father-in-law, Milo Barnum.[3124] Lime Rock was located within the Town of Salisbury, Connecticut.[3125] Milo Barnum, Leonard Richardson, William Henry Barnum, and Milo Barnum Richardson, therefore, helped to build industry in the following Connecticut communities: Lime Rock, Norfolk, Canaan, North Canaan, East Canaan, Falls Village, Salisbury, Torrington, Litchfield, and many others. The American painter, Walter Elmer Schofield (1867-1944), painted *The Powerhouse, Falls Village, Connecticut* (circa 1914), which depicts the power generation building of Falls Village against a landscape of heavy winter snowfall. The painting shows the powerful industrial character of Litchfield County, Connecticut. The painting forms part of the American collection at the Art Institute of Chicago.[3126]

The iron ore resources of the Appalachian Mountains of northwestern Connecticut were tremendous, and Salisbury and Lime Rock both proved to be major sources of the American iron industry, both in terms of the extraction

---

[3123] Cutter, William Richard. (1913). New England Families: Genealogical and Memorial. Vol. III. P. 1189. New York, NY: Lewis Historical Publishing Company. Google Books.

[3124] Cutter, William Richard. (1913). New England Families: Genealogical and Memorial. Vol. III. P. 1189. New York, NY: Lewis Historical Publishing Company. Google Books.

[3125] Cutter, William Richard. (1913). New England Families: Genealogical and Memorial. Vol. III. P. 1189. New York, NY: Lewis Historical Publishing Company. Google Books.

[3126] Schofield, Walter Elmer. The Powerhouse: Falls Village, Connecticut. (Circa 1914). Oil on canvas. Art Institute of Chicago. Artic.edu.

processes and the manufacturing processes.[3127] The commercial richness of these places in Connecticut possessed, therefore, many benefits for economic development.[3128] The Appalachian iron range of Connecticut would provide primary foundations not only for New England industry, but also for Chicago and Cook County industry.[3129] Northwestern Connecticut would contribute mightily to the growth of American railroad technology and infrastructure, and would be a central part of Chicago's development.[3130]

Milo Barnum (1790-1860), father-in-law of Leonard Richardson, and co-founder of the Barnum & Richardson Company, retired from the Barnum & Richardson Company in 1852, leaving Leonard the remaining principal owner of the firm.[3131] The name of the company changed, consequently, to Richardson, Barnum & Company.[3132] The company increased its output power in Connecticut in 1858 and in 1862, when the company acquired, respectively, the Beckley Furnace of East Canaan, and the Forbes Furnace of East Canaan.[3133] The company expansion, led by Leonard Richardson, included not only the augmentation of the iron mining and production assets available to the company, but also the establishment of a major factory for railroad parts manufacturing at Chicago. Richardson established the Chicago branch of the Barnum and Richardson Company in approximately 1862, when he acquired a foundry that was located at 64 S. Jefferson Street, in what would later become the Near West Side community of Chicago.[3134] With the creation of of the Chicago presence of the company came the incorporation of the company under the name, "Barnum & Richardson Manufacturing Company."

[3127] Cutter, William Richard. (1913). New England Families: Genealogical and Memorial. Vol. III. P. 1189. New York, NY: Lewis Historical Publishing Company. Google Books.

[3128] Cutter, William Richard. (1913). New England Families: Genealogical and Memorial. Vol. III. P. 1189. New York, NY: Lewis Historical Publishing Company. Google Books.

[3129] Cutter, William Richard. (1913). New England Families: Genealogical and Memorial. Vol. III. P. 1189. New York, NY: Lewis Historical Publishing Company. Google Books.

[3130] Cutter, William Richard. (1913). New England Families: Genealogical and Memorial. Vol. III. P. 1189. New York, NY: Lewis Historical Publishing Company. Google Books.

[3131] Cutter, William Richard. (1913). New England Families: Genealogical and Memorial. Vol. III. P. 1189. New York, NY: Lewis Historical Publishing Company. Google Books.

[3132] Cutter, William Richard. (1913). New England Families: Genealogical and Memorial. Vol. III. P. 1189. New York, NY: Lewis Historical Publishing Company. Google Books.

[3133] Cutter, William Richard. (1913). New England Families: Genealogical and Memorial. Vol. III. P. 1189. New York, NY: Lewis Historical Publishing Company. Google Books.

[3134] Cutter, William Richard. (1913). New England Families: Genealogical and Memorial. Vol. III. P. 1189. New York, NY: Lewis Historical Publishing Company. Google Books.

Leonard died in January of 1864, but he had guided the company as one of the two principal members of the company leadership. He brought the company to Chicago.[3135] Leonard laid the foundation for both the Barnum & Richardson Manufacturing Company and the City of Chicago to become, together, the world center of railroad wheel and railroad castings production. Richardson and William Henry Barnum co-founded the Rocky Dell Institute, a school at Lime Rock, Connecticut, in 1860.[3136] William Henry Barnum, known alternatively as "Iron Man Barnum" and as "Seven-Mule Barnum," was a major force in the United States Democratic Party in the nineteenth century, having served as Chairman of the Democratic National Committee, and as a United States Congressman from Connecticut.[3137] Barnum was one of the most prominent railroad company developers in America, and one of New England's most powerful politicians.

Leonard Richardson saw the great opportunities for the development of the railroad parts manufacturing market in Chicago, and he carried out the plan to connect the iron ores of Appalachian Connecticut to the foundry floors of Great Lakes Illinois.[3138] The Barnum & Richardson Company was reorganized in May, 1864, after the death of Leonard Richardson, by the Richardson family heirs; the new company name that was chosen was the Barnum-Richardson Company, with a hyphen replacing the ampersand from the prior corporate name.[3139] Company expansion plans continued to manifest, and the company built new Connecticut furnaces and foundries in 1870, and in 1872, at Lime Rock, and at East Canaan, respectively.[3140] The Chicago development of the Barnum-Richardson Company included the building of a new railroad car wheel factory there in 1873.[3141] The physical growth of the company at Chicago itself proved that the company survived the Great Chicago Fire of October 8, 1871.[3142] According to William Richard Cutter, the Chicago factory possessed a manufacturing output power of

---

[3135] Cutter, William Richard. (1913). New England Families: Genealogical and Memorial. Vol. III. P. 1189. New York, NY: Lewis Historical Publishing Company. Google Books.

[3136] The Hartford Courant. (July 28, 1930). P. 13. Newspapers.com.

[3137] The Hartford Courant. (July 28, 1930). P. 13. Newspapers.com.

[3138] Cutter, William Richard. (1913). New England Families: Genealogical and Memorial. Vol. III. P. 1189. New York, NY: Lewis Historical Publishing Company. Google Books.

[3139] Cutter, William Richard. (1913). New England Families: Genealogical and Memorial. Vol. III. P. 1189. New York, NY: Lewis Historical Publishing Company. Google Books.

[3140] Cutter, William Richard. (1913). New England Families: Genealogical and Memorial. Vol. III. P. 1189. New York, NY: Lewis Historical Publishing Company. Google Books.

[3141] Cutter, William Richard. (1913). New England Families: Genealogical and Memorial. Vol. III. P. 1189. New York, NY: Lewis Historical Publishing Company. Google Books.

[3142] Cutter, William Richard. (1913). New England Families: Genealogical and Memorial. Vol. III. P. 1189. New York, NY: Lewis Historical Publishing Company. Google Books.

300 railroad wheels per day. As extrapolated from Cutter's history report, the absolute annualized rate of company output at Chicago would have stood, therefore, at 109,500 wheels; the actual annualized manufacturing output at Chicago would have probably fallen close to this absolute annualized amount.[3143] The daily railroad wheel output of the Lime Rock factories of the Barnum-Richardson Company stood at 100 wheels; the theoretical absolute annualized quantity of wheel output for the Lime Rock factories would, by extrapolation, have amounted to 36,500 wheels.[3144] The consolidated absolute hypothetical annualized output of the Barnum & Richardson Company, inclusive of the Chicago and the Connecticut factories, would have stood at 146,000 railroad wheels.[3145] The actual consolidated annualized output for the company probably would have closely followed this hypothetical maximum degree of output.[3146] The company would have manufactured probably millions of railroad car wheels over the course of its existence in Chicago and Connecticut.

The 1887 *Poor's Directory of Railway Officials*, a key directory of railroad leadership structures and personnel, provided the official personnel of the Barnum & Richardson Company.[3147] The 1887 leadership staff included the following persons: William Henry Barnum served as President; John Van Nortwick served as Vice-President; Albert Alling served as Treasurer and General Manager; and William E. Best served as Secretary. The Board of Directors consisted of William Henry Barnum, John Van Nortwick, Charles W. Barnum, Milo Barnum Richardson, Albert Alling, John Crerar, and Volney C. Turner.[3148] Turner, Alling, and Crerar were full-time residents of Chicago.[3149] John Van Nortwick was a resident of Batavia, Illinois.[3150] Batavia is located now in both Kane County and DuPage County, which are both western suburban counties of Chicago. Milo Barnum Richardson, William Henry Barnum, and Charles W. Barnum were

---

[3143] Cutter, William Richard. (1913). New England Families: Genealogical and Memorial. Vol. III. P. 1189. New York, NY: Lewis Historical Publishing Company. Google Books.

[3144] Cutter, William Richard. (1913). New England Families: Genealogical and Memorial. Vol. III. P. 1189. New York, NY: Lewis Historical Publishing Company. Google Books.

[3145] Cutter, William Richard. (1913). New England Families: Genealogical and Memorial. Vol. III. P. 1189. New York, NY: Lewis Historical Publishing Company. Google Books.

[3146] Cutter, William Richard. (1913). New England Families: Genealogical and Memorial. Vol. III. P. 1189. New York, NY: Lewis Historical Publishing Company. Google Books.

[3147] Poor's Railroad Manual. (1887). P. 223. New York, NY: Poor's Railroad Manual. Google Books.

[3148] Poor's Railroad Manual. (1887). P. 223. New York, NY: Poor's Railroad Manual. Google Books.

[3149] Poor's Railroad Manual. (1887). P. 223. New York, NY: Poor's Railroad Manual. Google Books.

[3150] Poor's Railroad Manual. (1887). P. 223. New York, NY: Poor's Railroad Manual. Google Books.

residents of Lime Rock, Connecticut, but participated heavily in Chicago through this company, and possibly others.[3151] Walter Joseph Dubia (born 1868) helped to build and administer the Chicago branch of Barnum & Richardson.[3152] Dubia left the auditing office of the Chicago & Alton Railway Company to enter the service of Barnum & Richardson in 1890.[3153] Dubia brought extensive accountancy experience to Barnum & Richardson, having served five years in accounting services at the Chicago & Alton Railway Company.[3154] He began as a bookkeeper with Barnum & Richardson.[3155] In 1899, Dubia was promoted to multiple simultaneous offices in the firm: those of Secretary, Treasurer, Chicago General Manager, and member of the Board of Directors.[3156] Walter Dubia married Mary V. McCaffrey.[3157] The children born to them were Harry C. Dubia and Marie A. Dubia.[3158] A brother of Walter Dubia, Harry Amos Dubia, served as President of the Industrial Savings Bank of Chicago.[3159] The Dubia brothers were sons of Henry Franklin Dubia and Harriet (Kennedy) Dubia.[3160] Walter Dubia resided at 4449 Ellis Avenue, located in the Kenwood community of Chicago, and held membership in the Sheridan Club and in the Knights of Columbus.[3161] Walter Dubia began as a young man working for the Chicago & Alton Railroad Company, a corporation that had been founded and co-owned by Jacob Bunn. It is probable that the Dubia brothers knew the Bunn brothers and William Douglas Richardson in Chicago.

The 1892 issue of *The Official Railway List*, a railroad industry journal, contained a detailed advertisement for the Barnum & Richardson Company.[3162] By

[3151] Poor's Railroad Manual. (1887). P. 223. New York, NY: Poor's Railroad Manual. Google Books.

[3152] Leonard, John W. (1905). Vol. I. P. 173. The Book of Chicagoans. Chicago, IL: A. N. Marquis & Company. Google Books.

[3153] Leonard, John W. (1905). Vol. I. P. 173. The Book of Chicagoans. Chicago, IL: A. N. Marquis & Company. Google Books.

[3154] Leonard, John W. (1905). Vol. I. P. 173. The Book of Chicagoans. Chicago, IL: A. N. Marquis & Company. Google Books.

[3155] Leonard, John W. (1905). Vol. I. P. 173. The Book of Chicagoans. Chicago, IL: A. N. Marquis & Company. Google Books.

[3156] Leonard, John W. (1905). Vol. I. P. 173. The Book of Chicagoans. Chicago, IL: A. N. Marquis & Company. Google Books.

[3157] Leonard, John W. (1905). Vol. I. P. 173. The Book of Chicagoans. Chicago, IL: A. N. Marquis & Company. Google Books.

[3158] Leonard, John W. (1905). Vol. I. P. 173. The Book of Chicagoans. Chicago, IL: A. N. Marquis & Company. Google Books.

[3159] Leonard, John W. (1905). Vol. I. P. 173. The Book of Chicagoans. Chicago, IL: A. N. Marquis & Company. Google Books.

[3160] Leonard, John W. (1905). Vol. I. P. 173. The Book of Chicagoans. Chicago, IL: A. N. Marquis & Company. Google Books.

[3161] Leonard, John W. (1905). Vol. I. P. 173. The Book of Chicagoans. Chicago, IL: A. N. Marquis & Company. Google Books.

[3162] The Official Railway List. (1892). P. 106. Chicago, IL: The Railway Purchasing Agent Company. Google Books.

this time, Barnum & Richardson had returned the conjunctional symbol within its corporate name from hyphen to ampersand.[3163] The advertisement contained multiple facts pertinent to the specific railroad products made by the firm.[3164] The diverse scope of product output included locomotive wheels, freight car wheels, passenger car wheels, street car wheels, railroad crossings, railroad frogs, rail switches, street railway curves, and a broadly defined class of iron castings and machinery of practically all forms.[3165] In 1892, at the time of the advertisement in *The Official Railway List*, the company remained at 64 S. Jefferson Street in Chicago.[3166] The company ambitiously drew attention to the special infrastructural benefits that attached to its products.[3167] The three advertised structural product benefits that the firm promoted were as follows: "Wheels are made perfectly cylindrical, uniform in chill, and with treads ground."[3168] Scientific and precision circularity, uniformity in chilling process, and innovative tread designs, therefore, all constituted benefits attachable to these railroad consumer products, and put Barnum & Richardson Company at the forefront of the whole railroad parts industry.[3169]

Additional companies that were parties to the railroad components manufacturing industry, and which were present in Chicago, Cook County, or Lake County, included the following firms: Springfield Iron Company, Washburn & Moen Manufacturing Company, Graham Twist Drill and Chuck Company, H. Channon Company, Indianapolis Frog & Switch Company, Morden Frog & Crossing Works Company, Adams & Westlake Company, American Bridge Works Company, Brown Bonnell Iron Company, Buda Foundry and Manufacturing Company, Chicago Shafting & Pulley Company, Chicago Forge & Bolt Company, Car Truck Supply Company, Chicago Tire & Spring Company, Congdon Brake Shoe Company, Drexel Railway Supply Company, Fairbanks Morse & Company, Fowler Rolling Mill Company, Gates Iron Works Company, Graham & Morton Transportation Company, Grant Locomotive Works Company, Kane Company, Bakeman & Company, Harden Hand Grenade Fire Extinguisher Company, Harrington & King Perforating Company, Harvey Steel Car Company, Heath & Milligan Company, R. W. Hunt Company, Illinois Alloy Company,

---

[3163] The Official Railway List. (1892). P. 106. Chicago, IL: The Railway Purchasing Agent Company. Google Books.
[3164] The Official Railway List. (1892). P. 106. Chicago, IL: The Railway Purchasing Agent Company. Google Books.
[3165] The Official Railway List. (1892). P. 106. Chicago, IL: The Railway Purchasing Agent Company. Google Books.
[3166] The Official Railway List. (1892). P. 106. Chicago, IL: The Railway Purchasing Agent Company. Google Books.
[3167] The Official Railway List. (1892). P. 106. Chicago, IL: The Railway Purchasing Agent Company. Google Books.
[3168] The Official Railway List. (1892). P. 106. Chicago, IL: The Railway Purchasing Agent Company. Google Books.
[3169] The Official Railway List. (1892). P. 106. Chicago, IL: The Railway Purchasing Agent Company. Google Books.

Illinois Steel Company, Jenney-Hein Company, C. C. Jerome Company, P. McEntee Company, McGill Brothers Company, McGuire Manufacturing Company, L. Manase Company, Marsh & Bingham Company, Murray & Company, National Car Heating Company, National Surface Guard Company, Pettibone, Mulliken & Company, Pneumatic Gate Company, Q. & C. Company, Railway Improvement Company, Railway Master Mechanic Company, Fred A. Rich Company, Morris Sellers & Company, Frank B. Stone Company, B. E. Tilden Company, Vulcan Iron Works Company, and the Western Fence Company.[3170]

In November, 1887, Barnum & Richardson Company commissioned the construction of a four-story building located at 61 S. Jefferson Street. The new building was to contain 3,926 square feet.[3171] In 1890, Chicago witnessed a series of strikes within different labor sectors ranging from door manufacturing work and planing mill work, to railroad parts molding work.[3172] *The Davenport Morning Star*, a newspaper of Davenport, Iowa, reported the occurrences of strikes at Chicago, listing the companies that were affected.[3173] One of the strikes occurred at the Barnum & Richardson Company factory located at Robey Avenue and Blue Island Avenue.[3174] This location would presently be at the intersection of Damen Avenue and Blue Island Avenue in the Lower West Side community, near the Pilsen neighborhood and the Heart of Italy neighborhood.[3175] The *Morning Star* stated that 150 workers went on strike at Barnum & Richardson, and that as many as 30,000 were about to strike in the planing mills throughout the city.[3176] Central to the strikes was the issue of the eight-hour workday, according to the *Morning Star* reporter.[3177] 400 men went on strike at C. J. L. Meyer & Sons Company, a manufacturer of cabinets, doors, blinds, and sashes.[3178] The strike at the Palmer & Fuller Company involved 500 men.[3179] 300 men struck at the Hinsey & Weiss Company. A quantity of 800 to 1,600 men carried the strike to the Malleable Iron Works Company, which was located at 26th Street and Rockwell Street.[3180] The McCormick Harvester Company strike included the iron molders, and was expected to include all 2,500 men on the McCormick job rolls if grants were not made of the rights claimed by the McCormick workers.[3181] The *Morning Star* reported that the Illinois Steel Company had granted the eight-hour workday to its

---

[3170] The Official Railway List. (1892). Pp. XV-XXI. Chicago, IL: The Railway Purchasing Agent Company. Google Books.
[3171] The Chicago Tribune. (November 20, 1887). P. 6. Newspapers.com.
[3172] The Davenport Morning Star. (May 3, 1890). P. 2. Newspapers.com.
[3173] The Davenport Morning Star. (May 3, 1890). P. 2. Newspapers.com.
[3174] The Davenport Morning Star. (May 3, 1890). P. 2. Newspapers.com.
[3175] Arsenty, Neil. The Old Streets of Chicago. (June 27, 2013). Chicagonow.com.
[3176] The Davenport Morning Star. (May 3, 1890). P. 2. Newspapers.com.
[3177] The Davenport Morning Star. (May 3, 1890). P. 2. Newspapers.com.
[3178] The Davenport Morning Star. (May 3, 1890). P. 2. Newspapers.com.
[3179] The Davenport Morning Star. (May 3, 1890). P. 2. Newspapers.com.
[3180] The Davenport Morning Star. (May 3, 1890). P. 2. Newspapers.com.
[3181] The Davenport Morning Star. (May 3, 1890). P. 2. Newspapers.com.

200 molders.[3182] This grant constituted an effective act of diplomacy, because the grant prevented the strike of the Illinois Steel molders.[3183] The opposite form of corporate diplomacy occurred at the Fairbank Canning Company, where the General Manager, referred to in the report only by the surname of Lewis, issued denials of the claims made by the 500 workers of their rights to an eight-hour workday.[3184] The report indicated that a strike of the 500 men at Fairbank Canning Company would follow immediately, because of General Manager Lewis' denial of the workers' demands.[3185] In 1902, Barnum & Richardson purchased six lots of land that had been derived from the Grant Locomotive Company subdivision space.[3186] The Illinois Steel Company, additionally, had purchased eight lots from the Grant Locomotive Company subdivision space.[3187]

During the late nineteenth century, industrial companies began to run afoul of a new regime of Chicago sanitation laws.[3188] The Democratic mayoral regime and administration of Carter Henry Harrison, Sr., promoted the development of Chicago safety and sanitation jurisprudence.[3189] The initial and triannual *Report of the Department of Smoke Inspection of the City of Chicago* (1907-1910) contained a history of the Chicago Department of Smoke Inspection, as well as a history of the smoke regulation jurisprudence that had developed in Chicago since the first Chicago smoke ordinance was enacted on April 18, 1881.[3190] While the Chicago Department of Smoke Inspection was itself created in 1907, a smoke policy, a smoke law, and a smoke administration had existed under the jurisdiction of the Chicago Department of Health.[3191] Mayor Carter Harrison, Sr., appointed Fred U. Adams as the first Chicago Smoke Inspector in 1881.[3192] Charles George succeeded Fred Adams as Chicago Smoke Inspector in 1887, when John A. Roche won election as Mayor of Chicago.[3193] Politics influenced the job of Chicago Smoke Inspector to some degree, because when Mayor Carter H. Harrison, Sr., Mayor John A. Roche, Mayor George Bell Swift, and Mayor Hopkins were variously elected to the office of Mayor of Chicago, each man appointed a different Chicago Smoke Inspector. Prior to the creation of the Department of Smoke

[3182] The Davenport Morning Star. (May 3, 1890). P. 2. Newspapers.com.
[3183] The Davenport Morning Star. (May 3, 1890). P. 2. Newspapers.com.
[3184] The Davenport Morning Star. (May 3, 1890). P. 2. Newspapers.com.
[3185] The Davenport Morning Star. (May 3, 1890). P. 2. Newspapers.com.
[3186] The Inter-Ocean. (September 7, 1902). P. 22. Newspapers.com.
[3187] The Inter-Ocean. (September 7, 1902). P. 22. Newspapers.com.
[3188] The Chicago Tribune. (November 26, 1892). P. 3. Newspapers.com.
[3189] Report of the Department of Smoke Inspection the City of Chicago. (1911). Pp. 12-16. Chicago, IL: Department of Smoke Inspection of the City of Chicago. Google Books.
[3190] Report of the Department of Smoke Inspection the City of Chicago. (1911). Pp. 12-16. Chicago, IL: Department of Smoke Inspection of the City of Chicago. Google Books.
[3191] Report of the Department of Smoke Inspection the City of Chicago. (1911). Pp. 12-16. Chicago, IL: Department of Smoke Inspection of the City of Chicago. Google Books.
[3192] Report of the Department of Smoke Inspection the City of Chicago. (1911). Pp. 12-16. Chicago, IL: Department of Smoke Inspection of the City of Chicago. Google Books.
[3193] Report of the Department of Smoke Inspection the City of Chicago. (1911). Pp. 12-16. Chicago, IL: Department of Smoke Inspection of the City of Chicago. Google Books.

Inspection, the job, office, and duties of the Smoke Inspector operated as administrative subsidiaries of the Sanitary Bureau of the Department of Health.[3194] Andrew Young served as the Chief Sanitary Inspector when Charles George held the office of Smoke Inspector.[3195] Consequently, Smoke Inspector George was answerable to Chief Sanitary Inspector Young.[3196]

The Society for the Prevention of Smoke was established in 1891 as an organizational answer to the inconceivably rapid growth of major industries in Chicago and Cook County.[3197] The Society for the Prevention of Smoke was a private organization, unconnected to the municipal government, which possessed the purpose of preparing the city and its appearance for the 1893 World's Fair.[3198] Headquartered at the Monadnock Building, the Society leadership structure consisted of Bryan Lathrop, who served as President of the Society; E. J. Phelps, who served as Secretary of the Society; and C. F. White, who served as Chief Engineer of the Society.[3199] Bryan Lathrop, son of Jedediah Hyde Lathrop of Chicago and Elmhurst, was a cousin of the Stryker-Taylor family of Chicago, Springfield, Jacksonville, and Cass County, Illinois. Jedidiah Hyde Lathrop was a third cousin of Harriet Hillhouse (Henshaw) McClure, Elizabeth Henshaw (McClure) Stryker, and Charlotte (Stryker) Taylor. The Bryan Lathrop Mansion exists today as the Fortnightly Club in Gold Coast neighborhood.

After the 1893 reelection of Carter Henry Harrison, Sr., as Mayor of Chicago, Harrison appointed Fred U. Adams to succeed Charles George as Smoke Inspector.[3200] Mayor Carter Harrison was assassinated in 1893 by Patrick Joseph Prendergast and this event caused John Patrick Hopkins to succeed Harrison as Mayor.[3201] Mayor George Bell Swift appointed Daniel May to serve as Smoke Inspector in 1895, as successor to Fred Adams.[3202] The administration of Mayor George Swift reorganized the Chicago Department of Health so that the Office of

---

[3194] Report of the Department of Smoke Inspection the City of Chicago. (1911). Pp. 12-16. Chicago, IL: Department of Smoke Inspection of the City of Chicago. Google Books.
[3195] Report of the Department of Smoke Inspection the City of Chicago. (1911). Pp. 12-16. Chicago, IL: Department of Smoke Inspection of the City of Chicago. Google Books.
[3196] Report of the Department of Smoke Inspection the City of Chicago. (1911). Pp. 12-16. Chicago, IL: Department of Smoke Inspection of the City of Chicago. Google Books.
[3197] Report of the Department of Smoke Inspection the City of Chicago. (1911). Pp. 12-16. Chicago, IL: Department of Smoke Inspection of the City of Chicago. Google Books.
[3198] Report of the Department of Smoke Inspection the City of Chicago. (1911). Pp. 12-16. Chicago, IL: Department of Smoke Inspection of the City of Chicago. Google Books.
[3199] Report of the Department of Smoke Inspection the City of Chicago. (1911). Pp. 12-16. Chicago, IL: Department of Smoke Inspection of the City of Chicago. Google Books.
[3200] Report of the Department of Smoke Inspection the City of Chicago. (1911). Pp. 12-16. Chicago, IL: Department of Smoke Inspection of the City of Chicago. Google Books.
[3201] Report of the Department of Smoke Inspection the City of Chicago. (1911). Pp. 12-16. Chicago, IL: Department of Smoke Inspection of the City of Chicago. Google Books.
[3202] Report of the Department of Smoke Inspection the City of Chicago. (1911). Pp. 12-16. Chicago, IL: Department of Smoke Inspection of the City of Chicago. Google Books.

Smoke Inspector was answerable directly to the Commissioner of Health, and not to the Sanitary Bureau within the Department of Health.[3203]

In the fall of 1892, Charles George, the Smoke Inspector of the City of Chicago, prosecuted several smoke cases against several companies, among which was Barnum & Richardson.[3204] Smoke Inspector George, who had succeeded Smoke Inspector Adams as Chief of the Chicago Department of Smoke Inspection in 1887, carried out the prosecutions on the grounds that the defendant firms had breached the Chicago smoke laws.[3205] Therefore, the grounds of the prosecutions comprised the fact of the defendant firms' alleged violations of the municipal smoke laws.[3206] The prosecutorial theory that drove the smoke prosecutions was the city's right to recovery for infractions of the smoke laws. The remedy available to the City of Chicago in the smoke cases entailed, presumably from the words of the report, payment of punitive costs for violation of the municipal smoke laws.[3207] The relevant judicial process was probably provided by the Circuit Court of Cook County. When the smoke case defendants paid the costs for violations of the Chicago smoke laws, Justice Glennon granted dismissals of the multiple smoke suits, including the suit against the Barnum & Richardson Company.[3208] The news report did not specify whether the dismissals were granted due to a plea bargain plan in which the defendant parties agreed to pay contracted-for costs for their culpability, or were granted due to a simple payment of costs upon confession of culpability. In either case, however, the defendant parties' payments of the costs appear from the news report to have prevented further judicial processes that could have led to more severe convictions and punishments.[3209] The multiple dismissals, in turn, appear to have caused the quashal of an apparently residual jeopardy and the avoidance of further convictions for the defendant parties.[3210]

Evidences of the decline of the Barnum & Richardson Company emerged in the early twentieth century. At least as early as 1901, Barnum & Richardson was selling off Chicago properties.[3211] Reuben Miller of Pittsburgh, Pennsylvania (at that time the city name was spelled "Pittsburg," with the "h" being added later), bought from the Crescent Steel Company the former Barnum & Richardson Company land and buildings of 64-66 Clinton Street, for a purchase price of $35,000.[3212] In 1909, Barnum & Richardson Company sold another manufacturing

---

[3203] Report of the Department of Smoke Inspection the City of Chicago. (1911). Pp. 12-16. Chicago, IL: Department of Smoke Inspection of the City of Chicago. Google Books.
[3204] The Chicago Tribune. (November 26, 1892). P. 3. Newspapers.com.
[3205] Report of the Department of Smoke Inspection the City of Chicago. (1911). Pp. 12-16. Chicago, IL: Department of Smoke Inspection of the City of Chicago. Google Books.
[3206] Report of the Department of Smoke Inspection the City of Chicago. (1911). Pp. 12-16. Chicago, IL: Department of Smoke Inspection of the City of Chicago. Google Books.
[3207] The Chicago Tribune. (November 26, 1892). P. 3. Newspapers.com.
[3208] The Chicago Tribune. (November 26, 1892). P. 3. Newspapers.com.
[3209] The Chicago Tribune. (November 26, 1892). P. 3. Newspapers.com.
[3210] The Chicago Tribune. (November 26, 1892). P. 3. Newspapers.com.
[3211] The Chicago Tribune. (July 21, 1901). P. 31. Newspapers.com.
[3212] The Chicago Tribune. (July 21, 1901). P. 31. Newspapers.com.

property at Chicago, as was recorded in the Chicago *Inter-Ocean Newspaper*.[3213] Anthony Biggio and Frank Biggio purchased 7,550 square feet of manufacturing space from Barnum & Richardson in November, 1909.[3214] Alex Friend & Company provided brokerage for the land sale contract between the Biggios and Barnum & Richardson.[3215] Prior to the Biggio purchase, Barnum & Richardson had sold other Chicago property to Louis B. Shaw and the Machinists Supply Company, a firm whose leadership Shaw apparently served.[3216] The purchase price for one of the Barnum & Richardson Company properties located on Jefferson Street was reported to be $33,000.[3217] Multiple factors contributed to the fall of the company. These factors included the fact that mining technologies were transforming the iron extraction industry and these changes affected the company.[3218]

The Hartford Courant, a newspaper of Hartford, Connecticut, reported that the Barnum & Richardson factories and furnaces at Lime Rock had closed in 1918.[3219] It was reported that a workforce of 1,500 persons had been employed at Barnum & Richardson in and around Lime Rock.[3220] The fall of Barnum & Richardson, therefore, introduced severe economic decline for Lime Rock at the end of World War I.[3221] Vacant Lime Rock drew the attention and interest of multiple artists, and their relocation there after the closure of the Barnum & Richardson Company transformed the former industrial community into an arts community.[3222] A 1954 article that appeared in *The Hartford Courant* stated that the Barnum & Richardson Company began to fail in 1900, and that the company closed in 1925.[3223] The same report confirmed that Barnum & Richardson was known to be the largest manufacturer of, "railroad car [wheels] and big castings" in the world.[3224] The September 11, 1875, issue of *The Chicago Tribune* contained a report that praised the size and importance of the Barnum & Richardson Company. The report began with the following words: "It is conceded that this house [Barnum & Richardson Company] has an eminence second to none in the manufacture of car wheels and castings of every description."[3225] William Henry Barnum, the son of Milo Barnum, and the uncle of Milo Barnum Richardson, possessed the sobriquet of "Iron Man," according to the *Tribune*, because of his expertise and influence in the

---

[3213] The Inter-Ocean. (November 17, 1909). P. 18. Newspapers.com.

[3214] The Inter-Ocean. (November 17, 1909). P. 18. Newspapers.com.

[3215] The Inter-Ocean. (November 17, 1909). P. 18. Newspapers.com.

[3216] The Inter-Ocean. (November 17, 1909). P. 18. Newspapers.com.

[3217] The Inter-Ocean. (November 17, 1909). P. 18. Newspapers.com.

[3218] The Hartford Courant. (July 28, 1930). P. 13. Newspapers.com.

[3219] The Hartford Courant. (July 28, 1930). P. 13. Newspapers.com.

[3220] The Hartford Courant. (July 28, 1930). P. 13. Newspapers.com.

[3221] The Hartford Courant. (July 28, 1930). P. 13. Newspapers.com.

[3222] The Hartford Courant. (July 28, 1930). P. 13. Newspapers.com.

[3223] The Hartford Courant. (August 22, 1954). P. 54. Newspapers.com.

[3224] The Hartford Courant. (August 22, 1954). P. 54. Newspapers.com.

[3225] The Chicago Tribune. (September 11, 1875). P. 4. Newspapers.com.

iron and railroad parts manufacturing industries.[3226] Due largely to the chemical and technological expertise of "Iron Man" Barnum, the Barnum & Richardson Company railroad car wheels were considered to be the standard for the world:

> "For nearly thirty years [William Henry Barnum] had made a continuous practical study of car-wheel manufacture, and iron suitable for making same. The results are the superior wheels, cast at the firm's shops in Chicago; wheels which, in all essentials, are admitted to be the standard."[3227]

Since the time when Leonard Richardson established the Barnum & Richardson Company at Chicago, and through to the end of the nineteenth century, the company impacted Chicago, Cook County, the Great Lakes, the entire country, and much of the world through the creation and manufacture of novel and diverse machineries for the railroad industries and sectors of the world.

Charles Richardson, Jr.:

A Father of Chicago Aviation, Illinois Aviation, and National Defense

Charles Richardson, Jr. (1889-1968) was a son of Charles Richardson (1853-1932) and Nettie Morgan (Smith) Richardson (1866-1930), and a nephew of William Douglas Richardson (1837-1923).[3228] Charles Richardson, Jr., married Hazel Howard (1893-1957).[3229] Twin sons were born to this union: Willard Harding Richardson (1918-2008); and Howard Chandler Richardson (1918-1931).[3230] The sons were born in New York City.[3231] According to the *1910 United States Census*, Charles Richardson, Jr., was employed in railroad surveying work, and was a resident of Springfield, Illinois, along with his parents and siblings.[3232] Charles worked for the Patent Button Company at least as early as 1920.[3233] The 1920 residence of the Richardson family was West 190th Street in Manhattan, New York City.[3234] In 1930 the family continued to reside in New York City.[3235] The 1930 Census only specified Manhattan as the place of residence.[3236] After relocating to Illinois at some time after 1930, the Richardson family came to Chicago. In 1940, Charles Richardson was a resident of 7639 Eastlake Terrace,

---

[3226] The Chicago Tribune. (September 11, 1875). P. 4. Newspapers.com.
[3227] The Chicago Tribune. (September 11, 1875). P. 4. Newspapers.com.
[3228] Solomon, Ruth. (2017). Family Group Record for Charles Richardson, Jr.
[3229] Solomon, Ruth. (2017). Family Group Record for Charles Richardson, Jr.
[3230] Solomon, Ruth. (2017). Family Group Record for Charles Richardson, Jr.
[3231] Solomon, Ruth. (2017). Family Group Record for Charles Richardson, Jr.
[3232] 1910 United States Census. Ancestry.com.
[3233] 1920 United States Census. Ancestry.com.
[3234] 1920 United States Census. Ancestry.com.
[3235] 1930 United States Census. Ancestry.com.
[3236] 1930 United States Census. Ancestry.com.

located in the Rogers Park community of Chicago.[3237] This place of residence was located within Ward 49.[3238] The *1940 United States Census* stated that Charles worked as a business manager for a button manufacturer.[3239] Charles' brother, Harry Earl Richardson, worked for the Patent Button Company and served in management jobs for the company in Knoxville, Tennessee, and in Atlanta, Georgia. Harry Earl Richardson was an alumnus of the University of Illinois. He later attended Harvard University.[3240]

Charles Richardson transitioned from the button business to the heating business in Chicago.[3241] Of special interest are his military and auxiliary civilian defense service at Chicago, and his service as a co-founder, leader, and builder of the United States Civil Air Patrol, its Illinois Wing (state branch), and its Chicago headquarters. Richardson served as Deputy Wing Commander of the Illinois Wing of the United States Civil Air Patrol at least as early as 1948.[3242] The United States Civil Air Patrol was, and remains, the civilian auxiliary organization that is connected to the United States Air Force.[3243]

Lieutenant Colonel Richardson, as Illinois Wing Commander of the United States Civil Air Patrol, served to build the organization locally and nationally.[3244] The Civil Air Patrol was incorporated as the, "permanent civilian auxiliary"[3245] of the United States Air Force in 1948.[3246] Lt. Col. Charles Richardson served as an active and promotive executive within the United States Civil Air Patrol (in its organizational status as civilian auxiliary to the United States Air Force), and its Illinois Wing, since the inception of both organizations, as was proved by a report from the *Journal Gazette* of Mattoon, Illinois.[3247] He was prominently associated with the Civil Air Patrol, and with its Illinois Wing, as early as 1943.[3248] In September of 1943, Richardson, then serving as an intelligence officer, spoke to the Civil Air Patrol conference at Ridge Park at which the Beverly Hills (Illinois) Squadron was holding a rally.[3249] He was joined by speakers Captain Jack Christenson of the courier service and Captain Jay Leason of the transportation service. Lieutenant William A. Denehie, the Beverly Hills squadron leader, introduced Richardson, Leason, and Christenson.[3250] Richardson, who held the rank of Major in 1945, was connected to the Civil Air Patrol as a co-founder and

---

[3237] 1910 United States Census. Ancestry.com.

[3238] 1910 United States Census. Ancestry.com.

[3239] 1940 United States Census. Ancestry.com.

[3240] Richardson family historical records.

[3241] The Mt. Vernon Register-News. (August 2, 1951). P. 8. Newspapers.com.

[3242] The Decatur Daily Review. (October 18, 1948). P. 17. Newspapers.com.

[3243] The Mt. Vernon Register-News. (August 2, 1951). P. 8. Newspapers.com.

[3244] The Pantagraph. (June 24, 1950). P. 5. Newspapers.com.

[3245] Chicago Tribune. (October 1, 1949). P. 25. Newspapers.com.

[3246] Chicago Tribune. (October 1, 1949). P. 25. Newspapers.com.

[3247] Journal Gazette. (October 18, 1948). P. 1. Newspapers.com.

[3248] Chicago Tribune. (September 8, 1943). P.27. Newspapers.com.

[3249] Chicago Tribune. (September 8, 1943). P.27. Newspapers.com.

[3250] Chicago Tribune. (September 8, 1943). P.27. Newspapers.com.

builder.[3251] Lieutenant General Ira C. Eaker and Brigadier General F. P. Lahm presented Major Richardson with a Civil Air Patrol Citation of Merit in August, 1945.[3252] The award ceremony took place at State Street and Madison Street in Chicago. The *Chicago Tribune* contained the report and accompanying photograph of the award ceremony.[3253]

Charles Richardson, who held the rank of Lieutenant Colonel by 1949, assumed the office of Wing Commander (the chief executive officer) of the Illinois Civil Air Patrol.[3254] He succeeded Gordon A. DaCosta as Illinois Wing Commander.[3255] Lt. Colonel Charles Richardson participated as the principal force in the accomplishment of two especially significant organizational and administrative projects for the Civil Air Patrol in the autumn of 1949: the founding of the Chicago headquarters of the Illinois Wing of the Civil Air Patrol; and the consequent reorganization of the Illinois Wing of the Civil Air Patrol.[3256] The *Chicago Tribune* reported that Richardson summoned the founding conference for the new Chicago headquarters. The entire Illinois Wing was to convene at this conference on October 1, 1949.[3257] Richardson transferred the Illinois Wing headquarters from Springfield to Chicago.[3258] The new O'Hare International Airport had just opened in Chicago at this time. While not stated expressly in the October 1, 1949, article from the *Chicago Tribune*, the fact appears circumstantially evident that Richardson perceived in the founding of the O'Hare International Airport of Chicago a perfect opportunity for the development, growth, and revitalization of the Illinois Wing of the Civil Air Patrol.[3259] The new Chicago headquarters possessed joint offices in two places: the administrative office was located in downtown Chicago, probably on Jackson Boulevard; and the field office of the Illinois Wing was located at O'Hare International Airport.[3260] The founding conference of the Chicago headquarters took place at a newly-dedicated O'Hare International Airport.[3261] The *Chicago Tribune* report stated the following:

> "The first meeting of the entire Illinois wing of the civil air patrol, under leadership of a newly formed state headquarters here, is scheduled for this morning at the recently dedicated O'Hare international airport. Mannheim and Higgins rds [roads]. More than 60 CAP airplanes and about 350 senior and junior members of both sexes, are expected to attend the meeting to begin at 10 a.m. Members of the 42 Illinois CAP units have been invited

[3251] Chicago Tribune. (August 2, 1945). P. 5. Newspapers.com.
[3252] Chicago Tribune. (August 2, 1945). P. 5. Newspapers.com.
[3253] Chicago Tribune. (August 2, 1945). P. 5. Newspapers.com.
[3254] The Times of Munster, Indiana. (June 10, 1949). P. 11. Newspapers.com.
[3255] The Times of Munster, Indiana. (June 10, 1949). P. 11. Newspapers.com.
[3256] Chicago Tribune. (October 1, 1949). P. 25. Newspapers.com.
[3257] Chicago Tribune. (October 1, 1949). P. 25. Newspapers.com.
[3258] Chicago Tribune. (October 1, 1949). P. 25. Newspapers.com.
[3259] Chicago Tribune. (October 1, 1949). P. 25. Newspapers.com.
[3260] Chicago Tribune. (October 1, 1949). P. 25. Newspapers.com.
[3261] Chicago Tribune. (October 1, 1949). P. 25. Newspapers.com.

to the meeting to discuss a plans and training program for the CAP and to meet new CAP staff members appointed during the summer by Maj. Gen. Lucas V. Beau, air force regular who heads the national CAP setup. The meeting was called by Col. Charles Richardson Jr., Illinois CAP commander."[3262]

The program for the founding conference of the new Chicago headquarters of the Illinois Wing included a breakfast provided by the Skymotive Aviation Management Corporation.[3263] The breakfast took place at the Skymotive restaurant at the company's hangar located at the southern end of O'Hare International Airport.[3264] The business meeting took place after breakfast at the United States Air Force office located at the northeast corner of O'Hare.[3265] Col. Richardson should be regarded as one of the early promoters and supporters of O'Hare International Airport.

The *Chicago Tribune* report stated that the CAP planes were mostly unequipped with the technologies for high frequency radio communications with the O'Hare International Airport Air Traffic Control tower.[3266] Due to the technological issue, the Air Traffic Control implemented a light-signal-based communication system for the control and direction of the Civil Air Patrol aircraft.[3267] The Air Traffic Control tower was administered by the Civil Aeronautics Administration (CAA).[3268] To permit the navigational guidance of the Civil Air Patrol aircraft, the CAA provided a specialized legal process in order to accommodate the radio frequency limits of the Civil Air Patrol aircraft.[3269] The special legal process consisted of a waiver and a grant: the waiver of the federal law that required that the aircraft possess the 278 kilocycle (or comparable) radio frequency-functional radio technologies; and the grant of the light-signal communication system of air traffic control.[3270] The founding of the Chicago headquarters of the Illinois Wing of the Civil Air Patrol, therefore, led to a special jurisprudential regime that accommodated the needs and specifications of the Civil Air Patrol and its aircraft.[3271] This occasion represented an excellent cooperation, alliance, and harmony between federal bureaucracy and state bureaucracy.[3272] Col. Richardson led the implementation of a novel radio communication plan for the Illinois Wing of the Civil Air Patrol. "Richardson is expected to tell the wing organization of a CAP radio voice and key communications network thru [sic] Illinois in conjunction

---

[3262] Chicago Tribune. (October 1, 1949). P. 25. Newspapers.com.
[3263] Chicago Tribune. (October 1, 1949). P. 25. Newspapers.com.
[3264] Chicago Tribune. (October 1, 1949). P. 25. Newspapers.com.
[3265] Chicago Tribune. (October 1, 1949). P. 25. Newspapers.com.
[3266] Chicago Tribune. (October 1, 1949). P. 25. Newspapers.com.
[3267] Chicago Tribune. (October 1, 1949). P. 25. Newspapers.com.
[3268] Chicago Tribune. (October 1, 1949). P. 25. Newspapers.com.
[3269] Chicago Tribune. (October 1, 1949). P. 25. Newspapers.com.
[3270] Chicago Tribune. (October 1, 1949). P. 25. Newspapers.com.
[3271] Chicago Tribune. (October 1, 1949). P. 25. Newspapers.com.
[3272] Chicago Tribune. (October 1, 1949). P. 25. Newspapers.com.

with amateur radio operators."[3273] He also led the effort in reactivating the Illinois Civil Air Patrol units at Springfield, Belleville, Danville, Decatur, Vandalia, East St. Louis, and Peoria.[3274] Richardson developed the Pontiac branch of the Illinois Wing, having inducted a 50-member squadron at Pontiac, Illinois, on September 29, 1949.[3275]

The Pantagraph, a newspaper of Bloomington, Illinois, reported on June 24, 1950, that Richardson co-founded and activated the Logan County, Illinois, branch of the Illinois Civil Air Patrol.[3276] Serving with Richardson were Lieutenant Colonel Lloyd Rechner and Al W. Ahrens.[3277] Rechner served as Deputy Illinois Wing Commander under Illinois Wing Commander Richardson.[3278] Ahrens served as the temporary Commander of the Logan County Unit of the Illinois Civil Air Patrol.[3279] The opening of the Logan County unit was celebrated with prayer and blessing, which were administered by Rev. Joseph A. O'Dea of St. Patrick's Church.[3280] After the prayer, blessing, and formal dedication of the new organization, multiple celebratory and technologically significant aviation exhibits took place.[3281] Vere "Speed" Wikoff delivered an acrobatic air show. Jack Tillman, who was from Pekin, Illinois, exhibited a parachute jump. The Malerich Brothers exhibited crop dusting, and the Decatur Plane Club exhibited remote control powers of model aircraft.[3282] Charles Richardson continued to develop the Illinois Wing and worked with Fred J. Avery to reorganize the Sterling, Illinois, squadron of the Illinois Wing.[3283] The *Sterling Daily Gazette*, a newspaper of Sterling, Illinois, located in Whiteside County, reported that Richardson and Avery, both of Chicago, had landed at the Sterling Airport on Sunday, May 20, 1951, for the conference on the reorganization of the Sterling Squadron of the Illinois Wing.[3284]

In April of 1951, Charles Richardson led the effort to reactivate multiple Chicago search, rescue, surveillance, and defense systems and programs of the Illinois Wing of the Civil Air Patrol.[3285] *The Daily Herald*, a newspaper of Chicago, reported that the Illinois Wing was, "busily engaged in reactivating and organizing flying groups in order to keep up with the general defense and mobilization trends now in evidence throughout the nation."[3286] Illinois Group One administered nine separate flight routes, services, and surveillance plans. The Group One flight plans

---

[3273] Chicago Tribune. (October 1, 1949). P. 25. Newspapers.com.

[3274] Chicago Tribune. (October 1, 1949). P. 25. Newspapers.com.

[3275] Chicago Tribune. (October 1, 1949). P. 25. Newspapers.com.

[3276] The Pantagraph. (June 24, 1950). P. 5. Newspapers.com.

[3277] The Pantagraph. (June 24, 1950). P. 5. Newspapers.com.

[3278] The Pantagraph. (June 24, 1950). P. 5. Newspapers.com.

[3279] The Pantagraph. (June 24, 1950). P. 5. Newspapers.com.

[3280] The Pantagraph. (June 24, 1950). P. 5. Newspapers.com.

[3281] The Pantagraph. (June 24, 1950). P. 5. Newspapers.com.

[3282] The Pantagraph. (June 24, 1950). P. 5. Newspapers.com.

[3283] Sterling Daily Gazette. (May 22, 1951). P. 10. Newspapers.com.

[3284] Sterling Daily Gazette. (May 22, 1951). P. 10. Newspapers.com.

[3285] The Daily Herald. (April 6, 1951). P. 39. Newspapers.com.

[3286] The Daily Herald. (April 6, 1951). P. 39. Newspapers.com.

covered the following places: DuPage County, Aurora, Wheatland Field, York Township, the Lombard area, and Elmhurst.[3287] These places represent Cook County, DuPage County, and Kane County.[3288] Multiple Chicago area pilots served these search, surveillance, defense, and rescue flights.[3289] The Illinois Group One plan also included search, surveillance, and rescue services for the following places, among others: Jefferson Park, Addison, Maywood, Melrose Park, O'Hare Airport, Bensenville, St. Charles, Sky Haven Airport, and Mitchell Airport.[3290] The nine flight plans that composed the Illinois Group One plan were as follows: Aurora Flight, DuPage Flight, Elmhurst Flight, Jefferson Park Flight, Lombard Flight, Maywood Flight, O'Hare Squadron, St. Charles Flight, and Sky Haven Flight.[3291]

The Suburbanite Economist, a Chicago newspaper, reported the eager recruitment programs and efforts of the Illinois Wing. In May of 1951, the Oak Lawn-Harlem branch of the Illinois Wing led an aviation education campaign for people interested in learning more about the Civil Air Patrol, the United States Air Force, and aviation generally.[3292] The Oak Lawn-Harlem branch cooperated with the Englewood Evening School, a school located at 6201 Stewart Avenue in Chicago, to prepare and serve the multiple interrelated curricula necessary for aviation education and training.[3293] The Englewood Evening School provided courses in, "navigation meteorology, pre-flight subjects and military organization. . ."[3294] Charles Richardson oversaw all of the educational programs for the Illinois Wing.

Charles Richardson retired from the office of Illinois Wing Commander of the United States Civil Air Patrol on or about August 2, 1951.[3295] *The Mt. Vernon Register-News*, a newspaper of Mt. Vernon, Illinois, reported the relevant facts. Colonel Herman E. Lacy succeeded Richardson as Illinois Wing Commander.[3296] "He succeeds Col. Charles Richardson, Jr., a Chicago Heating Company executive who asked to be relieved of his command because of the press of other business."[3297] Both Richardson and Lacy served as Chicago corporate executives at the time of their mutual Civil Air Patrol administrative transitions in 1951. Lacy was Chairman of the Board of Directors of Helmco, Inc., a Chicago company that dealt in soda fountain machinery.[3298] At the time of Richardson's retirement, the Illinois Civil Air Patrol consisted of 3,000 members, all of whom served on

---

[3287] The Daily Herald. (April 6, 1951). P. 39. Newspapers.com.

[3288] The Daily Herald. (April 6, 1951). P. 39. Newspapers.com.

[3289] The Daily Herald. (April 6, 1951). P. 39. Newspapers.com.

[3290] The Daily Herald. (April 6, 1951). P. 39. Newspapers.com.

[3291] The Daily Herald. (April 6, 1951). P. 39. Newspapers.com.

[3292] Suburbanite Economist. (May 9, 1951). P. 83. Newspapers.com.

[3293] Suburbanite Economist. (May 9, 1951). P. 83. Newspapers.com.

[3294] Suburbanite Economist. (May 9, 1951). P. 83. Newspapers.com.

[3295] The Mt. Vernon Register-News. (August 2, 1951). P. 8. Newspapers.com.

[3296] The Mt. Vernon Register-News. (August 2, 1951). P. 8. Newspapers.com.

[3297] The Mt. Vernon Register-News. (August 2, 1951). P. 8. Newspapers.com.

[3298] The Mt. Vernon Register-News. (August 2, 1951). P. 8. Newspapers.com.

volunteer status without compensation. The news report stated that Illinois Wing Commander Lacy wished to build the Illinois Wing to a membership of 20,000 persons.[3299]

The wording of the *Mt. Vernon Register-News* article does not appear to be identifying the name of the Chicago heating company of which Richardson was an executive.[3300] This fact is discernible from the fact that while the article used capital letters to refer to the heating company, thereby creating the appearance of a proper noun, the article used the same capitalization practice within the same article, and in a manner where it was clear that a common noun, not a proper noun, was the object of expression of the words.[3301] A company by the name of "Chicago Heating Company," which was located at 40 N. Clark Street, existed during the nineteenth century, but it remains uncertain whether this firm was the same firm that was referenced in the *Mt. Vernon Register-News* report.[3302] Therefore, a possible discovery, but not a definite discovery, of the identity of the Chicago heating company with which Richardson was employed as an executive has occurred.[3303] In any case, Charles Richardson was an executive at a Chicago heating company. In addition to having been longtime residents of Rogers Park, the Richardsons were also residents of the northern Chicago suburb known as Glenview.

Willard Harding Richardson, son of Col. Charles Richardson and Hazel (Howard) Richardson, grew up in Rogers Park, and graduated from Sullivan High School in 1938.[3304] Sullivan High School is a historic public school in the Rogers Park community.[3305] Herbert C. Hansen was the Principal of Sullivan at the time when Richardson was a student there. John F. Erzinger was the Assistant Principal then.[3306]

In conclusion of this segment of the history, Charles Richardson, Jr., was one of the fathers of civil aviation, airborne surveillance, airborne search and rescue, and civil air defense for Chicago, for Cook County, and for the State of Illinois. Richardson helped establish both Chicago and the State of Illinois as national centers of airborne defense through his reorganization of the Illinois Civil Air Patrol and his founding of the Chicago headquarters of the Illinois Civil Air Patrol.

[3299] The Mt. Vernon Register-News. (August 2, 1951). P. 8. Newspapers.com.

[3300] The Mt. Vernon Register-News. (August 2, 1951). P. 8. Newspapers.com.

[3301] The Mt. Vernon Register-News. (August 2, 1951). P. 8. Newspapers.com.

[3302] The Metal Worker. (July-December, 1894). Vol. 42. P. 73. New York, NY: David Williams, Publisher. Google Books.

[3303] The Mt. Vernon Register-News. (August 2, 1951). P. 8. Newspapers.com.

[3304] The Navillus. (1938). Yearbook of Sullivan High School of Rogers Park, Chicago. P. 38. Ancestry.com.

[3305] The Navillus. (1938). Yearbook of Sullivan High School of Rogers Park, Chicago. Ancestry.com.

[3306] The Navillus. (1938). Yearbook of Sullivan High School of Rogers Park, Chicago. P. 38. Ancestry.com.

George Wallace Bunn, Sr. and Ada Willard (Richardson) Bunn

Ada Willard Richardson (1861-1945), daughter of William Douglas Richardson, married George Wallace Bunn, Sr. (1861-1938), of Springfield. Two sons were born to them: Willard Bunn (1888-1959) and George Wallace Bunn, Jr. (1890-1973). Ada was a social matron of Springfield and a championship golfer. George and Ada were members of the Springfield Golf Club, where Ada captured the Ladies' Championship Cup in 1904, having outscored Miss Mary Hudson.[3307] Ada shared second prize with Robert Loose in a mixed foursome golf match played in Springfield in late April, 1901, at the opening of the golf season there.[3308] Ms. Helen Matheny and Hughs Diller won the match, and shared first prize.[3309] George Wallace Bunn was also an accomplished golfer in Springfield.

George Wallace Bunn served as president of Bunn Capitol Company of Springfield, which had been founded by his father, Jacob Bunn. George also co-founded the insurance firm known as the Lincoln Casualty Company and served on the boards of directors of the Illinois Watch Company, Sangamo Electric Company, and Springfield Marine Bank. George was chairman of Springfield Marine Bank and was a founder of the Bunn Memorial Trust which repaid the debts from the J. Bunn Bank failure (see Chapter 2, *Builders of the Downtown*). As a member of the boards of directors of Illinois Watch Company and Sangamo Electric Company, George Wallace Bunn was closely connected to many aspects of Chicago business and industry (see Chapter 8, *Ode to Pylons and Cannery Windows*).[3310]

George W. Bunn also owned the Wishbone Brand of food products and helped to develop the brand nationally through production and distribution of the once-famous Wishbone Coffee.[3311] Bunn Capitol Grocery Company later sold the Wishbone brand to the Manhattan Coffee Company, which in turn sold the brand to Lipton Tea, who marketed Wishbone Salad Dressing products.[3312] The Wishbone Salad Dressing label remains a prominent food brand to this day. George was famous for offering gifts of cornmeal mush to people he met in Springfield.[3313] George Wallace Bunn, Sr., Willard Bunn, Howard Humphreys, Rogers Humphreys, John E. Hall, A. C. Flood, and O. W. Johnson founded the Bunn &

[3307] The McHenry Plaindealer. (September 22, 1904). P. 7. Newspapers.com.

[3308] The St. Louis Republic. (April 21, 1901). P. 36. Newspapers.com.

[3309] The St. Louis Republic. (April 21, 1901). P. 36. Newspapers.com.

[3310] Bunn family historical records.

[3311] Bunn family historical records; The Decatur Herald. (April 9, 1948). P. 26. Newspapers.com.

[3312] Fitzell, Philip B. (1982). Private Labels, Store Brands, and Generic Products. Page number not discernible at time of reference. AVI Publishing Company. Google Books; The Decatur Herald. (April 9, 1948). P. 26. Newspapers.com.

[3313] Memoir shared with Andrew Taylor Call by Robert Hatcher Bunn. (Undated).

Humphreys Company in 1928.[3314] The Bunn & Humphreys Company owned the Capitol Grocery Company and owned the following brands: 1840 Coffee, Old Timer Coffee, Old Timer, Jr. Coffee, Capitol Coffee, Lincoln Coffee, Mary Todd Coffee, and Wishbone Coffee, among possibly other coffee brands.[3315] The Bunn & Humphreys Company was a multimillion-dollar company in the early twentieth century, and, in 1931, advertised that it was the only company in the world to possess a coffee humidor technology and process for coffee production and manufacture.[3316] The Bunn & Humphreys Company promoted the, "new-crop tang—plantation freshness" of its coffee brands, and attributed these qualities to its self-proclaimedly unique humidor process.[3317] George Regan Bunn (1915-2002), the grandson of George Wallace Bunn, and the son of Willard Bunn, would continue the Bunn family tradition of technological innovation in the food and beverage industry by inventing new coffee technologies that would bring revolutionary improvements to the coffee industry. George Regan Bunn founded the Bunn-O-Matic Corporation, which remains today an industry leader in coffee technologies and other beverage technologies.[3318]

The Browns of Michigan and Chicago:

Cousins of the Willards of Chicago, Springfield, and Winnebago County

Lucy (Willard) Richardson, wife of William Douglas Richardson, was the granddaughter of Asa Willard and Lucy (Whiting) Willard. Lucy (Whiting) Willard was the daughter of William Whiting and Rebecca (Brown) Whiting of Lancaster, Massachusetts. Rebecca (Brown) Whiting was the daughter of Rev. Josiah Brown and Prudence (Prentiss) Brown. Rev. Josiah Brown was a Harvard graduate and was the son of Joseph Brown and Ruhamah (Wellington) Brown.[3319] Ruhamah Wellington was the daughter of Benjamin Wellington and Elizabeth (Sweetman) Wellington.[3320]

Joseph Brown and Ruhamah (Wellington) Brown had the following children: Ruhamah Brown; **Daniel Brown, who married Ann Bright** (direct ancestors of

---

[3314] Articles of Incorporation of Bunn And Humphreys, Inc. (October 22, 1928). State of Illinois; Call, Andrew Taylor. (2005). Jacob Bunn: Legacy of an Illinois Industrial Pioneer. Pp. 24-26, 262. Lawrenceville, VA: Brunswick Publishing Corporation.

[3315] The Decatur Herald. (August 1, 1931). Newspapers.com.

[3316] The Decatur Herald. (August 1, 1931). Newspapers.com.

[3317] The Decatur Herald. (August 1, 1931). Newspapers.com.

[3318] Memorial to George Regan Bunn. (Princeton, Class of 1938). Princeton University. Paw.princeton.edu.

[3319] Binney, C. J. F. (1883). The History and Genealogy of the Prentice, or Prentiss Family, of New England, Etc. from 1631 to 1883. 2nd Ed. P. 169. Boston, MASS: C. J. F. Binney. Google Books.

[3320] Cutter, William Richard. (1914). New England Families: Genealogical and Memorial. Vol. III. P. 1366. New York, NY: Lewis Historical Publishing Company. Google Books.

the Browns of Michigan, Chicago, Lemont, and Cook County, Illinois); John Brown; Joseph Brown; James Brown; **Rev. Josiah Brown, who married Prudence Prentiss** (direct ancestors of the Willards of Illinois); Benjamin Brown; and William Brown.[3321] Daniel Brown and Ann (Bright) Brown had a son, Nathaniel Bowman Brown, who married Abigail Page.[3322] Nathaniel Bowman Brown and Abigail (Page) Brown had a son, Daniel Liberty Brown (1775-1857), who married Polly Jennison.[3323] Daniel Liberty Brown and Polly (Jennison) Brown had many children, including the following: **Nathaniel Jennison Brown**; Lemuel Brown; Joseph Brown; Anson Brown; Annis Brown; Rebecca Brown, and others.[3324] The Brown family were among the founders of Ann Arbor, Washtenaw County, Michigan.[3325]

Several of the Brown children were also founders of Chicago and Cook County.[3326] Nathaniel Jennison Brown (1812-1900) was a merchant at Chicago as early as 1835, shipping lumber to Chicago from the Michigan forests.[3327] Brown was one of the founders of the Chicago lumber industry.[3328] At Chicago Nathaniel J. Brown befriended merchant and land developer Augustus Garrett and the two men formed the limited partnership known as the Garrett & Brown Company.[3329] The early Chicago law firm of Spring & Goodrich provided the legal services necessary for the formation of the Garrett & Brown Company.[3330] The company became profitable and led Brown and Garrett to organize a general partnership for

---

[3321] Cutter, William Richard. (1914). New England Families: Genealogical and Memorial. Vol. III. P. 1366. New York, NY: Lewis Historical Publishing Company. Google Books.

[3322] Cutter, William Richard. (1914). New England Families: Genealogical and Memorial. Vol. III. P. 1366. New York, NY: Lewis Historical Publishing Company. Google Books.

[3323] Lockwood, Mary. (1895). Lineage Book Of The Charter Members Of The Daughters Of The American Revolution. P. 40. Harrisburg, PA: Harrisburg Publishing Company. Google Books.

[3324] Brown Family Cemetery. Findagrave.com.

[3325] Conard, Howard Louis. (1892). Chicago. Nathaniel J. Brown: Biographical Sketch And Reminiscences Of A Noted Pioneer. Google Books.

[3326] Conard, Howard Louis. (1892). Chicago. Nathaniel J. Brown: Biographical Sketch And Reminiscences Of A Noted Pioneer. Google Books.

[3327] Conard, Howard Louis. (1892). Chicago. Nathaniel J. Brown: Biographical Sketch And Reminiscences Of A Noted Pioneer. P. 5. Google Books.

[3328] Conard, Howard Louis. (1892). Chicago. Nathaniel J. Brown: Biographical Sketch And Reminiscences Of A Noted Pioneer. P. 5. Google Books.

[3329] Conard, Howard Louis. (1892). Chicago. Nathaniel J. Brown: Biographical Sketch And Reminiscences Of A Noted Pioneer. Pp. 5-6. Google Books.

[3330] Conard, Howard Louis. (1892). Chicago. Nathaniel J. Brown: Biographical Sketch And Reminiscences Of A Noted Pioneer. Pp. 5-6. Google Books.

the purpose of land acquisition and development in Chicago and Cook County.[3331] The new general partnership of Garrett & Brown bought the lot owned by Chicago Postmaster John Bates on Dearborn and built an auction house there.[3332] The Garrett & Brown Company auction house became the largest and most significant auction house in the American West.[3333] The Garrett & Brown Company employed an African-American man named Colonel George as the official crier and announcer for the company auctions. Colonel George was not only a very prominent figure in the early days of Chicago commerce, but also a public relations leader and ambassador for the most important auction company in Chicago and in the American West.[3334]

The Garrett & Brown Company once owned 9,000 acres of Chicago and Cook County real estate and handled sales of Chicago land to settlers and speculators alike.[3335] As the Chicago land boom of the 1830s cooled down, Garrett & Brown exited the market, dissolved, and left a tremendous legacy as the most important broker and dealer of Chicago land in the time of the founding of the village and city of Chicago.[3336] Nathaniel J. Brown was also one of the founding land speculators and developers of Madison, Wisconsin, and Milwaukee. He once owned approximately 4,480 acres of Madison and much of downtown Milwaukee.[3337] From Chicago, Nathaniel J. Brown helped to establish and develop Madison and Milwaukee, and additionally operated a large office in New York City. Brown also was prominently associated with the founding of the State Bank of Illinois and its Chicago Branch, which was the first bank in Chicago history (See Chapter 1, *Genesis of a Great Lakes Frontier*).

Nathaniel J. Brown would have known, either directly or indirectly, Robert Irwin of St. Louis and Springfield. Irwin served on the board of directors of the State Bank of Illinois and, therefore, held governing powers over the entire State Bank of Illinois and its Chicago Branch. Robert Irwin was the brother of Sarah Irwin, who married Benjamin Ferguson. Robert Irwin was an uncle of Elizabeth Jane (Ferguson) Bunn and an uncle-in-law of Jacob Bunn (See Chapter 1, *Genesis of a*

[3331] Conard, Howard Louis. (1892). Chicago. Nathaniel J. Brown: Biographical Sketch And Reminiscences Of A Noted Pioneer. Pp. 5-6. Google Books.

[3332] Conard, Howard Louis. (1892). Chicago. Nathaniel J. Brown: Biographical Sketch And Reminiscences Of A Noted Pioneer. Pp. 5-6. Google Books.

[3333] Conard, Howard Louis. (1892). Chicago. Nathaniel J. Brown: Biographical Sketch And Reminiscences Of A Noted Pioneer. Pp. 5-6. Google Books.

[3334] Conard, Howard Louis. (1892). Chicago. Nathaniel J. Brown: Biographical Sketch And Reminiscences Of A Noted Pioneer. P. 7. Google Books.

[3335] Conard, Howard Louis. (1892). Chicago. Nathaniel J. Brown: Biographical Sketch And Reminiscences Of A Noted Pioneer. P. 7. Google Books.

[3336] Conard, Howard Louis. (1892). Chicago. Nathaniel J. Brown: Biographical Sketch And Reminiscences Of A Noted Pioneer. Pp. 5-7. Google Books.

[3337] Conard, Howard Louis. (1892). Chicago. Nathaniel J. Brown: Biographical Sketch And Reminiscences Of A Noted Pioneer. P. 7-8. Google Books.

Great Lakes Frontier). Nathaniel J. Brown was one of the principal building contractors of the Illinois and Michigan Canal system, having been hired by William F. Thornton to build two sections of the Canal through southwestern Cook County at what is presently Lemont.[3338] Thornton was President of the Board of Canal Commissioners.[3339] Nathaniel Brown and other members of the Brown family were founders of Lemont, a Chicago suburb in southwestern Cook County.[3340] The Brown family are interred at the Brown Family Cemetery in Lemont.[3341]

When Stephen A. Douglas was campaigning for United States Congress from Illinois, he visited the Brown house. When Brown opened the door, Douglas said, "I am Stephen A. Douglas, and I am a candidate for Congress in this district. I want to get my dinner and have my horse fed, and then I want to make a speech to your men."[3342] Historian Howard Louis Conard stated that, "Mr. Brown had never seen Douglas before, and he looked the young man over with surprise."[3343] Brown noticed that Douglas was short, wore unseemly clothes, and rode a, "very lean and hungry-looking horse."[3344] Having judged that Douglas would fail to make a vote-worthy impression on Brown's laboring men, Brown told Douglas the following: "'Mr. Douglas, my men are all [Andrew] Jackson men, and if you will just quietly go along to Naperville, where you have told me you intend going, and not let the men see you, they won't know what a diminutive little cuss you are, and I will guarantee that you will get every one of these votes.'"[3345] Conard reported that Douglas followed Brown's counsel, made no public announcement of any kind whatsoever, and passed through Athens District unnoticed.[3346] On election day, Douglas received every vote from the men in the Athens District.[3347]

[3338] Conard, Howard Louis. (1892). Chicago. Nathaniel J. Brown: Biographical Sketch And Reminiscences Of A Noted Pioneer. P. 10. Google Books.

[3339] Conard, Howard Louis. (1892). Chicago. Nathaniel J. Brown: Biographical Sketch And Reminiscences Of A Noted Pioneer. P. 10. Google Books.

[3340] Conard, Howard Louis. (1892). Chicago. Nathaniel J. Brown: Biographical Sketch And Reminiscences Of A Noted Pioneer. Google Books.

[3341] Brown Family Cemetery. Findagrave.com.

[3342] Conard, Howard Louis. (1892). Chicago. Nathaniel J. Brown: Biographical Sketch And Reminiscences Of A Noted Pioneer. P. 15. Google Books.

[3343] Conard, Howard Louis. (1892). Chicago. Nathaniel J. Brown: Biographical Sketch And Reminiscences Of A Noted Pioneer. P. 15. Google Books.

[3344] Conard, Howard Louis. (1892). Chicago. Nathaniel J. Brown: Biographical Sketch And Reminiscences Of A Noted Pioneer. P. 15. Google Books.

[3345] Conard, Howard Louis. (1892). Chicago. Nathaniel J. Brown: Biographical Sketch And Reminiscences Of A Noted Pioneer. P. 15. Google Books.

[3346] Conard, Howard Louis. (1892). Chicago. Nathaniel J. Brown: Biographical Sketch And Reminiscences Of A Noted Pioneer. P. 15. Google Books.

[3347] Conard, Howard Louis. (1892). Chicago. Nathaniel J. Brown: Biographical Sketch And Reminiscences Of A Noted Pioneer. P. 15. Google Books.

Col. William Douglas Richardson. Of Chicago and Springfield. Construction and development contractor. Founder and President of the Richardson Construction Company of Chicago and Springfield. Co-founder and Director of the Springfield Iron Company of Chicago and Springfield. Major employer of prison inmates at Joliet Penitentiary, providing stone-cutting and related work opportunities to the inmates. Co-founder, manager, and Superintendent of Buildings and Grounds for the 1893 Chicago World's Columbian Exposition. Superintendent of Exterior Covering for the 1893 Chicago World's Fair. Builder of the White City, and most of the remainder of the 1893 World's Fair grounds. Founder of Richardson Investment Company of Chicago. Served as co-founder and developer, along with Tsar Alexander III, Tsar Nicholas II, Collis Potter Huntington, and John Davison Rockefeller, of the Russian-American Direct Transportation Company. Co-founder, consulting engineer, and contractor of the Amur Steamship Company and the Russian-American Direct Transportation Company. Founding General Manager of the Russian-American Direct Transportation Company. American agent of the Amur Steamship Company of Russia. Building contractor and engineer for the Russian Trans-Siberian Railway system of Russia and Asia, the Imperial Waterworks and sewer system of St. Petersburg, Russia, the Port of Buenos Aires, Argentine Republic, the Lincoln Memorial of Springfield, the second Illinois State Capitol building of Springfield, and many churches and hotels of Chicago. Member of the Technical Club of Chicago. Through construction business and industrial entrepreneurship, Richardson helped to expand the technological, architectural, and infrastructural influence and reputation of Chicago, Cook County, and Springfield, throughout the entire world. Husband of Lucy Willard. Father of Ada Willard Richardson and Emma Louise Richardson. (Image courtesy of Ruth Solomon).

William Douglas Richardson at approximately 29 years of age. (Image courtesy of Ruth Solomon).

Lucy (Willard) Richardson. Of Springfield. Daughter of Alexander Willard and Louise Higgie. Illinois social matron. Wife of William Douglas Richardson. Mother of Ada Willard Richardson and Emma Louise Richardson. Niece of James Moore Willard of Chicago, who was a resident of the Woodlawn community and subsequently of the Englewood community, both located on the South Side of the city. (Image courtesy of Ruth Solomon).

Milo Barnum Richardson. Of Litchfield County, Connecticut, and Chicago. President of the Barnum & Richardson Company of Chicago and Connecticut. Co-founding manager of the 1893 Chicago World's Columbian Exposition. Member of the Connecticut Board of World's Fair Commissioners for the 1893 Chicago World's Fair. Co-founder of Brownell Car Company of St. Louis, a worldwide railway car maker that supplied much of the Chicago market. One of the industrial founders of Huntington, West Virginia. Co-founder of the Ensign Manufacturing Company of Huntington, West Virginia. Served with Collis P. Huntington as one of the industrial founders and fathers of Huntington, West Virginia. Co-founder of the Caledonia-American Life Insurance Company of America (New York City), the Rochester Car Wheel Works Company of Rochester, New York, and multiple other companies. President of the Iron Bank of Falls Village, Connecticut. Director of the Hartford & Connecticut Western Railroad Company, the Housatonic Railroad Company, and many other corporations. Industrial developer of Chicago, Cook County, New York City, Connecticut, and Huntington, West Virginia. (Image courtesy of The Scoville Public Library of Salisbury, Connecticut).

Charles Timothy Regan. Of Wisconsin. Founder and partner of a large land company at Chippewa Falls, Wisconsin. Traveling salesman for the Chippewa Valley Mercantile Company of Wisconsin. Vice-President of the Crooked River Mining Company, a gold mining company of Wisconsin, Idaho, and Washington. Husband of Margaret Hanrahan. Father of seven. Son of Timothy Regan and Margaret (Dacey) Regan of Ireland and Wisconsin. Great-great-grandfather of author Andrew Taylor Call. (Image courtesy of author's personal collection).

Margaret (Hanrahan) Regan. Of Wisconsin and Chicago. Wife of Charles Timothy Regan of Wisconsin. Mother of seven. Resident of Chicago and Evanston after death of husband. Member of the Wisconsin Federation of Women's Clubs. Member of the Auxiliary Council to help clean up Chippewa Falls. Board of Directors of Associated Charities organization of Chippewa Falls. Member of Faber Reading Circle of Chippewa Falls. Great-great-grandmother of author Andrew Taylor Call. (Image courtesy of author's personal collection).

Robert Cunningham Taylor, Sr. Of Virginia, Cass County, Illinois. Thirteenth child of Robert Taylor and Jeanette (Cunningham) Taylor. Husband of Charlotte Stryker, whose family had many generations of Chicago residents and connections. Father of two. President of Taylor Land Company, which controlled thousands of acres of Illinois farmland. Co-founder and President of the People's Bank of Virginia, Illinois. Founder of Cass County Title and Trust Company of Illinois. Director of Farmers' National Bank of Virginia, Illinois. (Image courtesy of author's personal collection).

Henry Barrell House. Of Chicago and Springfield. Member of the Irwin-House Family. Chicago bank examiner, banker, broker, and playwright. Assistant to the Chief Examiner of the Chicago District of the National Bank Examiner's Office, United States Department of the Treasury. Auditor of Commercial National Bank of Chicago. Member of the Chicago Chapter of the American Institute of Banking. Member of the Chicago brokerage company of Allerton, Greene & King. Playwright of local prominence in Cook County and Springfield. Resident of the River North neighborhood. (Image courtesy of *The Banking Law Journal*, Vol. 33, 1916).

Oswell Laurie McNeil, Esq. Of Chicago and Blue Island. Member of the Taylor Family. Lawyer. Graduate of Northwestern University School of Law. Founder of McNeil Law Firm of Chicago. Co-founder of Railway Supplymens' and Mutual Catalogue Company of Chicago. Co-founder of the National Sunday School Publishing Company of Chicago. Co-founder of Delmar's Candy & Ice Cream Company of the Edgewater and Uptown communities of Chicago. Resident of the area shared by the East Garfield Park community, the Near West Side community, and the Tri-Taylor neighborhood. (Image courtesy of Diana Moore).

Robert Lincoln McNeil, Esq. Of Chicago and Seattle, Washington. Lawyer. Member of the Taylor family of Illinois. Graduate of Northwestern University Law School. (Image courtesy of Diana Moore).

John Abel Peterson (at left). Of Swayzee, Indiana. Member of the Van Duyn-Peterson-Ramsey-Call Family of Ohio, Indiana, and Illinois. Co-founder and member of Board of Directors of the Farmers National Life Insurance Company of America (Chicago). Co-founder and member of Board of Directors of the Farmers National Life Insurance of America, Inc., of East Chicago, Indiana. Co-founder and member of the Board of Directors of the Indiana Farmers' Grain Dealers Association, which consolidated cooperatively the grain and elevator industry of Indiana, and which possessed commercial presence in Chicago through ownership of a major agricultural publishing company. Co-founder of the Indiana Farmers' Institute. Capitalist. Industrialist. Philanthropist. Large-scale farmer and land entrepreneur of Indiana and Illinois. Donor of the Bloomington Bible Chair, a program in Bible studies at Indiana University, Bloomington. **Dr. Mahlon Bluford Peterson (at right).** Graduate of Chicago College of Medicine and Surgery (now Loyola University). Established a medical practice at Chicago. Later practiced medicine at Houston, Texas. (Image courtesy of Mark Peterson).

470

William Henry Burtner, Sr. Of Cincinnati. Member of the Burtner-Baldwin-Call Family of Ohio and Pennsylvania. Co-founder, Vice-President, and Board of Directors member of the Lodge & Davis Machine Tool Company of Cincinnati and Chicago. Co-founder, Vice-President, and member of the Board of Directors of the Davis & Egan Machine Tool Company of Cincinnati and Chicago, the largest machine tool manufacturer of Chicago and Cincinnati, and one of the largest in the world (manufacturer of locomotive engines, lathes, rifles, and many other forms of machine). Co-founder, President, and Director of the Cincinnati Planer Company. Contributed to the industrial exhibits of the 1893 World's Columbian Exposition as executive of the Lodge & Davis Machine Tool Company of Cincinnati, a company that constructed and contributed an immense industrial exhibit for the 1893 World's Fair. Helped build Cincinnati and Chicago, respectively, into the largest, and one of the largest, machine tool manufacturing centers of the world. (Image courtesy of *The Iron Trade Review*, Vol. 39, Issue 21, 1906).

Frank Hatch Jones, Esq. Of Chicago and Pike County, Illinois. Member of the Jones Family of Chicago and Pike County, Illinois, and, through marriage, of the Bunn family of Chicago and Springfield. Chicago lawyer, capitalist, statesman, and industrialist. Postmaster of Chicago. Assistant Postmaster General of the United States. Founder of the Jones Law firm of Chicago. Co-founder of the First State Pawners' Society of Chicago. Co-founder of the Chicago & Southern Railway Company. Co-founder of the City Club of Chicago. Contributed to the creation, location, and establishment of the Great Lakes Naval Station of Lake County, Illinois. Director of the Chicago Opera House Company. Co-founder of the Portage & Southwestern Railroad Company of Wisconsin. Member of the Chicago Club, Union League Club, Saddle & Cycle Club, Commercial Club, Chicago Golf Club, Onwentsia Country Club, Chicago Historical Society, City Club of Chicago, and Mid-Day Club. Married Sarah Irwin Bunn first. After Sarah's death, Frank married Ellen Wrenshall (Grant) Sartoris. Son-in-law first of Jacob Bunn, and second of President Ulysses S. Grant. Resident of Gold Coast neighborhood. Brother of Fred Bennett Jones of Chicago and Wisconsin. (Image courtesy of author's personal collection).

Ada Willard Richardson. Of Springfield. Illinois social matron. Wife of George Wallace Bunn, Sr. Daughter of William Douglas Richardson and Lucy (Willard) Richardson of Chicago and Springfield. Mother of Willard Bunn and George W. Bunn, Jr. Grand-niece of Chicago and Connecticut railroad industry leader Leonard Richardson. First cousin of Chicago and Connecticut railroad industry leader and civic leader Milo Barnum Richardson. First cousin of Charles Richardson, Jr., of Chicago and Springfield, Illinois. Grand-niece of James Moore Willard of Chicago. Championship golfer in Illinois. Member of the Springfield Golf Club. Member of the Willard-Richardson Family of Chicago, Springfield, and Connecticut. Member of the Dudley-Bradstreet-Danforth-Whiting-Brown-Wellington-Prentice-Stanton Family of New England, Chicago, and Springfield. (Image courtesy of author's personal collection).

Ada Willard Richardson. Pictured here as a young girl, circa 1871. (Image courtesy of author's personal collection).

473

Joseph Wellington Willard. Of Cleveland, Ohio. Founder of the Cleveland Branch of the California Powder Works Company. Founder of the Hercules Powder Company of Cleveland. Co-founder of the Repauno Chemical Company of New Jersey. Business partner of Lammot DuPont, Sr. Member of the Western Reserve Historical Society of Cleveland. Inventor of Hercules Powder, a form of explosive. Member of the Willard Family of Massachusetts, Illinois, and Ohio. First cousin of the Willards and some of the Richardsons of Chicago, Springfield, and Winnebago County, Illinois. Member of the Civil Engineers Club of Cleveland. (Image courtesy of *The Biographical Cyclopaedia And Portrait Gallery With An Historical Sketch Of The State of Ohio*. Vol 5, 1891).

Clara Ferguson. Of Chicago. Co-founder of the Pullman community and neighborhood. Teacher at the Pullman High School of Chicago. Secretary and Treasurer of the Idylwylde Tennis Club of Pullman community. Member of the Idylwylde Tennis Club. Resident of the Pullman community. Member of the Ferguson Family of Chicago, Springfield, and Pennsylvania. (Image courtesy of Susan Alland and her family).

474

Florence (Ferguson) Lee. Of Chicago. Wife of William Lee. Co-founder of the Pullman community and neighborhood of Chicago. School teacher at the Pullman High School, Chicago. Cousin of Benjamin Hamilton Ferguson and of Elizabeth Jane (Ferguson) Bunn. Resident of Pullman and Hyde Park. Member of the Ferguson Family of Chicago, Springfield, and Pennsylvania. (Image courtesy of Susan Alland and her family).

The Hotel Florence of the Pullman community and neighborhood of the far South Side of Chicago. Civil engineer William Lee and wife, Florence (Ferguson) Lee, were among the founders of the Pullman community and neighborhood. The Lees resided at the Hotel Florence after their marriage, prior to relocating to the Hyde Park community. The Hotel Florence was named for Florence Pullman, daughter of George Mortimer Pullman, the Chicago railroad industrialist and railroad car manufacturer after whom the community and neighborhood were named. George M. Pullman was the principal founder of the Pullman community and neighborhood, as well as the Pullman Company. (Image courtesy of Joseph Kirkland, *The Story of Chicago*, 1892).

The William Lee and Ferguson family at their home located at 5637 S. Dorchester Avenue in the Hyde Park community of Chicago. Of Chicago. William Lee, Florence (Ferguson) Lee, Anna Clara Ferguson (right), and baby Morton Lee Pearce. William Lee was a civil engineer. Served as Assistant Surveyor of the Pullman community and industrial neighborhood. Co-founder of Pullman neighborhood and community of Chicago. Chief Engineer for the Hyde Park District of the City of Chicago. Husband of Florence Ferguson. Founding civil engineer for the Harvey settlement of southern Cook County, near Blue Island and South Holland. The Fergusons were cousins of the Springfield Fergusons. (Image courtesy of Susan Alland and her family).

Helen Edith Ferguson in 1900. Of Chicago. A founder of Pullman community and neighborhood of Chicago. Teacher at the Pullman High School. Member of the Ferguson Family of Pennsylvania, Ohio, Springfield, and Chicago. Cousin of the Fergusons of Springfield. (Image courtesy of Susan Alland and her family).

476

Charles Timothy Regan and Margaret (Hanrahan) Regan of Chippewa Falls, Wisconsin. Great-great-grandparents of author Andrew Taylor Call. (Image courtesy of author's personal collection).

John Farson, Esq. Chicago railroad industrialist. President of the Calumet Electric Street Railway Company of Chicago. Frank Hatch Jones, Esq., served as Vice-President of this company when Farson served as the company's President. (Image courtesy of the Historical Society of Oak Park and River Forest and the Pleasant Home Foundation of Oak Park).

Pleasant Home Mansion of Oak Park, Illinois. The residence of John Farson, Esq., who was a close friend and business associate of Frank Hatch Jones, Esq., also of Chicago. The home was designed by architect George Washington Maher, a West Virginia native who relocated to Chicago and became one of the city's most famous and influential architects. (Image courtesy of the Historical Society of Oak Park and River Forest and the Pleasant Home Foundation of Oak Park).

Pleasant Home. Summer season with palm trees and fountain in yard. (Image courtesy of the Historical Society of Oak Park and River Forest and the Pleasant Home Foundation of Oak Park).

Jacob Bunn, Jr. Of Springfield and Chicago. Vice-President of Selz, Schwab & Company of Chicago. Co-founder, President, co-owner of Sangamo Electric Company of Springfield and Chicago. President of Illinois Watch Company of Springfield and Chicago. Co-founder of Economy Electric Devices Company of Chicago. Principal executive, through instrumentality of parent corporate ownership of Sangamo Electric Company, of the Allied Tool and Machine Company of Chicago. Member of National Advisory Council of the National Business League of Chicago, along with Dr. William R. Harper, President of the University of Chicago, Dr. Andrew S. Draper, President of the University of Illinois, and Dr. Edmund J. James, President of Northwestern University. Exerted powerful influence over Cook County industrial economy. Member of the Chicago Athletic Association. (Image courtesy of *Sangamo: A History of Fifty Years*, by Robert C. Lanphier and Benjamin P. Thomas, 1949).

George Wallace Bunn, Sr. Of Springfield. Director of Illinois Watch Company of Springfield and Chicago. President of Springfield Marine Bank. President of Bunn Capitol Grocery Company of Springfield. Founder of Bunn & Humphreys Company. Owner of Wishbone and other food brands. Director of Sangamo Electric Company of Springfield and Chicago. Founder and Director of Lincoln Mutual Casualty Company. Illinois philanthropist. Member of clubs in Springfield. Owned summer home at Salter's Point on Buzzards Bay, in Massachusetts. Devoted fan of the Chicago Cubs. (Image courtesy of author's personal collection).

Monadnock Building in the Chicago Loop. The Bunn, Richardson, and Jones families owned many companies headquartered in this building. (Image courtesy of Janice A. Knox).

Fisher Building in the Chicago Loop. William Douglas Richardson, George Moulton, and the Guaranty Construction Company of Chicago built this building. (Image courtesy of Janice A. Knox).

Melancthon Woolsey Stryker as a student at Hamilton College in New York. Member of the Stryker Family of New Jersey, New York, and Illinois. (Image courtesy of Hamilton College Archives of Hamilton College in Clinton, New York).

Dr. Melancthon Woolsey Stryker, D.D. Of Chicago and New York. Head Pastor of Fourth Presbyterian Church of Chicago, from 1886-1892. Built Fourth Presbyterian Church into one of the largest church congregations of Chicago. Hymnologist, Christian scholar, and author. Served on the Committee of the McCormick Theological Seminary of Chicago. Member of Advisory Board of the Presbyterian Hospital of Chicago. Subsequently President of Hamilton College in New York. Founder and member of the Saints and Sinners Club of Chicago. Member of the Chicago Literary Club. (Image courtesy of Hamilton College Archives of Hamilton College in Clinton, New York).

Dr. Melancthon Woolsey Stryker. (Image courtesy of Hamilton College Archives).

Dr. Melancthon Woolsey Stryker, D.D. (on right). Stryker was the President of Hamilton College in Clinton, New York. He is standing here with Andrew Carnegie of Pittsburgh (center), and United States Senator Elihu Root of New York (left), who served as United States Secretary of State under President Theodore Roosevelt, and as United States Secretary of War under President William McKinley. Stryker is conferring the Honorary Doctor of Laws Degree upon Andrew Carnegie in this picture. This picture is from 1914, when Stryker was serving as the 9th President of Hamilton College. Elihu Root, Jr., married Alida Stryker, who was the daughter of Dr. Melancthon Woolsey Stryker. (Image courtesy of Hamilton College Archives).

Henry Hanson Brigham. Of Wisconsin, Chicago, and Glencoe. Member of the Douglass-Brigham family of Vermont, Massachusetts, Illinois, and Wisconsin. Cousin of Henry Stryker Taylor, Robert Cunningham Taylor, Jr., and others of Chicago and central Illinois. Telegrapher with Chicago & North Western Railway Company. Refrigeration technology and petroleum industrialist. Founder and President of the North American Car Company of Chicago (this company owned and operated about 9,000 refrigerator, oil, and poultry railcars by approximately 1930). President of National Tank Car Company of Chicago. Board of Directors of Commerce Petroleum Company of Chicago and Tulsa, Oklahoma. Founder and President of the Atlantic Seaboard Despatch Company of Chicago. Executive with Booth Fisheries, Inc., of Chicago, a major American fish production company. Co-founder of the Traffic Club of Chicago. Reformer of baseball. Foreman of the 1920 Cook County Grand Jury that investigated the 1919 Chicago Black Sox Scandal, and which indicted Joseph Jefferson "Shoeless Joe" Jackson, and multiple other White Sox team members for their alleged participation in the conspiracy to throw the 1919 World Series (Chicago White Sox versus Cincinnati Reds). Member of the Ravenswood Club, Traffic Club, Skokie Golf Club. (Image courtesy of the Chicago History Museum; Image ID DN-0072606).

John A. Roche. The thirtieth Mayor of Chicago. Roche appointed Charles George to the office of Smoke Inspector of Chicago. The famous smoke cases involved prosecutions against company party defendants including the Barnum & Richardson Company, which was founded and owned by the Richardsons and Barnums of Chicago and Connecticut. (Image courtesy of Joseph Kirkland, *The Story of Chicago*, 1892).

George French Brigham, Jr. Of Wisconsin, Chicago, and Tulsa. President of the Commerce Petroleum Company of Chicago and Tulsa, Oklahoma. Southwestern representative of the North American Car Company of Chicago. Member of the Traffic Club, Petroleum Club, Independent Oil Men's Association, and the American Petroleum League, all of Chicago. Brother of Henry Hanson Brigham and Edmund Douglass Brigham of Wisconsin and Chicago. Cousin of Henry Stryker Taylor and Robert Cunningham Taylor, Jr. of Chicago and Springfield. Member of the Douglass-Brigham Family of New England, Wisconsin, and Illinois. (Image courtesy of Roy Hoffman, et al., *Oklahomans and their State: A Newspaper Reference Work*, 1919).

485

Charlotte Stryker as a young woman. Of Jacksonville, Morgan County, Illinois, and Virginia, Cass County, Illinois. Graduate of Mary Burnham Institute of Massachusetts. Student of European culture and history. Singer of German art songs (Lieder). Wife of Robert Cunningham Taylor, Sr. Mother of two. Daughter of Judge Henry Stryker and Elizabeth Henshaw (McClure) Stryker of Jacksonville. Member of Trinity Episcopal Church, Jacksonville. Member of Jacksonville Country Club, where she was a championship golfer. Member of the Douglass-Brigham-Prentiss-Henshaw-McClure-Stryker Family of New England, New York, St. Louis, and Illinois. Great-grandmother of author Andrew Taylor Call. (Image courtesy of author's personal collection).

Louise McClure (Stryker) Capps. Of Jacksonville, Illinois, and Wequetonsing, Michigan. Louise was the daughter of Judge Henry Stryker of Jacksonville, Illinois. Member of Trinity Episcopal Church. Wife of William Thomas Capps. Mother of three. Louise inherited the J. Capps & Son Company from her late husband, William Thomas Capps, Sr., who was the President of the company. J. Capps & Son Company was one of the largest clothing manufacturers in the United States, manufactured bulletproof clothing, and possessed an immense presence in Chicago and Texas. Louise was also an accomplished golfer in Illinois, and a member of Jacksonville Country Club. Sister of Charlotte (Stryker) Taylor, Elizabeth (Stryker) Hart, Henry McClure Stryker, and Harriet Stryker. (Image courtesy of author's personal collection).

Elizabeth Henshaw (Stryker) Hart. Of Jacksonville and Cincinnati. Elizabeth was the daughter of Judge Henry Stryker of Jacksonville, Illinois. Elizabeth married Dr. Joseph Hall Hart, Sr. of Cincinnati, who was a professor at the University of Chicago and later at Illinois College. Their two sons, Joseph Hall Hart, Jr. and John Babinger Hart founded the Cincinnati Builders Credit Company with Joseph Hart, Sr. The company was a bank for Cincinnati building contractors. Elizabeth was a member of Trinity Episcopal Church, a championship golfer in Illinois, a member of the Jacksonville Country Club, and probably held membership in other clubs in Cincinnati and Ft. Lauderdale. Joseph Hall Hart, Sr. was a part of the Hall family of Cincinnati, which founded and owned the Hall's Safe and Lock Company of Cincinnati and Chicago. This was the largest safe and lock manufacturer in the world. Elizabeth was the sister of Charlotte (Stryker) Taylor, Louise (Stryker) Capps, Henry McClure Stryker, and Harriet Stryker. Elizabeth was an alumna of Smith College. (Image courtesy of author's personal collection).

WILLIAM T. CAPPS

William Thomas Capps, Sr. Of Jacksonville and Chicago. William was the husband of Louise McClure Stryker, and the President of the J. Capps & Son Company. He founded the Midland Casualty Company of Chicago and was on the board of directors of the Southern Gypsum Company of North Holston, Virginia, a mining and plaster manufacturing company which had an office in Chicago. Yale alumnus. (Image courtesy of *25-Year Record, Class of Ninety-Three, Yale College*, 1918).

J. Capps & Son Company Factory in Jacksonville, Illinois. This company became one of the largest clothing manufacturers in the United States, and possessed a large presence not only in Jacksonville, but in Chicago, Texas, and in many other places in the United States. The company was owned by William Thomas Capps, Sr., and Louise McClure (Stryker) Capps of Illinois and Michigan. (Image courtesy of author's personal collection).

George Whitfield Bunn, Jr. Of Dallas, Texas, and Duluth, Minnesota. Son of George Whitfield Bunn, Sr., and Mahala Ann (Bloom) Bunn. Nephew of Jacob Bunn and John Whitfield Bunn of Springfield and Chicago. President of the Dallas Storage and Warehouse Company of Texas. This company engaged in a transfer and storage business across the United States and had much business in Chicago and the metropolitan area. Vice-President of the H. Miscampbell Body Corporation of Duluth, Minnesota. This company was advertised as the largest bus and truck manufacturer in the northwestern United States. Husband of Alice (Fishbough) Bunn. Father of Chester Selden Bunn and Emily May Bunn. Notice map of Texas and Texas counties in background. (Image courtesy of Jamie Overom Pyzik and Wendy Overom Paymard).

George Whitfield Bunn, Jr. Pictured as a young man. (Image courtesy of Jamie Overom Pyzik and Wendy Overom Paymard).

Chester S. Bunn (at left), Alice (Fishbough) Bunn (front left), Emily May (Bunn) Palmer (back right), George Whitfield Bunn, Jr. (front right), and baby Dorothy Palmer. (Image courtesy of Jamie Overom Pyzik and Wendy Overom Paymard).

Henry Hanson Brigham (back left). Of Wisconsin and Chicago. Pictured here with the Cook County Grand Jury that investigated the 1919 Black Sox Scandal. Brigham served as Foreman of the Cook County Grand Jury in the Black Sox Scandal case. Member of the Douglass-Brigham Family of New England, Wisconsin, and Chicago. (Image courtesy of the Chicago History Museum; Image ID DN-0072424).

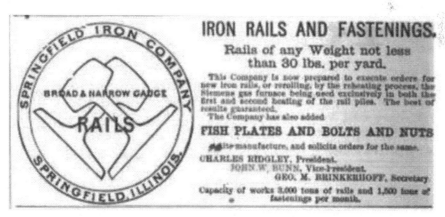

Springfield Iron Company advertisement. John Whitfield Bunn and William Douglas Richardson co-founded the Springfield Iron Company with Charles Ridgely, George M. Brinkerhoff, and others. The company quickly became one of the largest iron rail manufacturers of Chicago and the United States, was a pacesetter in chemical technologies, and a leading Chicago corporation. (Image courtesy of *The Railway Age*, Vol. 3, 1878).

Chicago Union Stockyards. Jacob Bunn, John Whitfield Bunn, and John Stryker all contributed to the development and leadership of the Union Stockyards. John Whitfield Bunn co-founded the Saddle & Sirloin Club, which was a social, commercial, and industrial club that was located at the Stockyards, and was arguably the social and economic headquarters of the meatpacking industry of the world. John W. Bunn's portrait, and multiple other portraits of meatpacking industry leaders and agricultural leaders, hung in the Saddle & Sirloin Club until a fire destroyed the club building and all the portraits. John W. Bunn served as co-founding Treasurer of the Chicago Fat Stock Show, which was commercially connected to the Stockyards. The Continental Can Company, one of the largest industrial companies of Chicago and Cook County, operated no fewer than two factories at the Union Stockyards. Jacob Bunn and John Stryker founded three of the nine railroads that created the Chicago Union Stockyards. (Image courtesy of the Chicago History Museum; CHM-Digital Obj ID: ICHi-51198).

Chicago Union Stockyards Gate. (Image courtesy of the Chicago History Museum; CHM-Digital Obj ID: DN-0006740; *Chicago Daily News* negatives collection).

Union Stockyards cattle corral with Hereford cattle. Year 1929. Notice the Pennsylvania Railroad Company sign located in the background. Prize-winning Hereford cattle in pen at Union Stockyards. Henry Stryker Taylor served as one of the two largest individual (non-institutional) shareholders of the Pennsylvania Railroad Company. The Continental Can Company, one of the largest industrial companies of Chicago, Cook County, and vicinity, operated no fewer than two factories at the Union Stockyards. (Image courtesy of the Chicago History Museum; CHM-Digital Obj ID: DN-0090236; *Chicago Daily News* negatives collection).

Chicago Union Stockyards corral with Angus cattle, 1929. Notice the New York Central Railroad Company sign in the background. Prize stock at the stockyards purchased for railroad dining car service. John Stryker co-founded the New York Central Railroad Company. (Image courtesy of the Chicago History Museum; CHM-Digital Obj ID: DN-0090238; *Chicago Daily News* negatives collection).

Rock Island Railroad freight house (in Chicago) –perspective view. John Stryker co-founded the Chicago and Rock Island Railroad Company and served as a member of the company board of directors. (Image courtesy of the Chicago History Museum; CHM-Digital Obj ID: HB-22505; Hedrich-Blessing Collection; William S. Engdahl, photographer).

Interior of the Lake Shore and Michigan Southern Railroad Company depot in Chicago. John Stryker co-founded the Lake Shore and Michigan Railroad Company, which was the first railroad company to complete a railroad route to Chicago from the East. Stryker served also as President of the railroad and developed the company into one of the most important railroad systems of Chicago and the entire Midwest. The photograph was produced by Lovejoy and Foster, located at 88 State Street. (Image courtesy of the Chicago History Museum; CHM-Digital Obj ID: ICHi-05326).

Fourth Presbyterian Church building located at 866 N. Michigan Avenue. Rev. Melancthon Woolsey Stryker, D.D., served as the fourth Pastor of Fourth Presbyterian Church prior to the construction of the Michigan Avenue church pictured here. Stryker was a member of the Stryker Family of New Jersey, New York, and Illinois. (Image courtesy of the Chicago History Museum; CHM-Digital Obj ID: ICHi-25832).

Fourth Presbyterian Church. Crowds standing outside the Fourth Presbyterian Church for an Easter parade. Rev. Melancthon Stryker was Pastor of Fourth Presbyterian from 1886-1892. Stryker developed the church into one of the largest congregations in Chicago. (Image courtesy of the Chicago History Museum; CHM-Digital Obj ID: DN-0083812; *Chicago Daily News* negatives collection).

Fred Bennett Jones and Dora Mortimer at the Giza Plateau of Egypt. Jones was a Chicago railroad industry executive. Vice-President of the Adams & Westlake Company of Chicago, manufacturer of railroad lights and other railroad fixture technologies. The lady with Jones is Dora Mortimer of Chicago. Fred Jones was the brother of Frank Hatch Jones, Esq., and was thus connected to the Bunn family of Chicago and Springfield by marriage. (Image courtesy of John and Sue Major, and Mark Hertzberg).

John Davison Rockefeller in 1885. Of Cleveland, Ohio. Co-founder of Standard Oil Company of Ohio. Founder of the University of Chicago. Associated with Tsars Alexander III and Nicholas II of Russia, as well as with William Douglas Richardson and Collis Potter Huntington, in the establishment and planning of the Russian-American Direct Transportation Company and the Russo-American pan-hemispheric intermodal transportation network from St. Petersburg and Moscow to Pacific North America, Chicago, and New York City. (Image courtesy of Schmoop (The Gilded Age section)).

Collis Potter Huntington. Of Connecticut. Served as co-founder of Ensign Manufacturing Company of Huntington, West Virginia, with Milo Barnum Richardson of Connecticut and Chicago. Associated with William Douglas Richardson of Chicago, John Davison Rockefeller of Cleveland, and Tsars Alexander III and Nicholas II of Russia in the construction, planning, and establishment of the Russo-American Direct Transportation Company and the Russo-American pan-hemispheric intermodal transportation network from St. Petersburg and Moscow to Pacific North America, Chicago and New York City. (Image courtesy of Schmoop (Transcontinental Railroad section)).

497

Tsar Nicholas II, Nikolay II Aleksandrovich, Emperor of Russia. Tsar Nicholas and William Douglas Richardson of Chicago developed a strong friendship at some point in the late nineteenth century. Richardson served as one of the Emperor's closest advisors on subjects of Russian industrialization, transportation, and infrastructure. The Richardson Construction Company of Chicago provided some of the most significant participation in Russian imperial technological and infrastructural development and expansion. Richardson, John Davison Rockefeller, and Collis Potter Huntington, among others, collaborated and partnered with the Russian Empire to develop and create a Russo-American pan-hemispheric intermodal transportation system and network that extended from St. Petersburg and Moscow to Pacific North America, Chicago, and New York City. (Image courtesy of Wikipedia).

Tsar Alexander III, Aleksandr III Aleksandrovich, Emperor of Russia. Father of Tsar Nicholas II of Russia. Tsar Alexander formed a strong friendship with William Douglas Richardson of Chicago. The Richardson Construction Company of Chicago provided some of the most significant contributions to Russian imperial technological and infrastructural development and expansion. Richardson, John Davison Rockefeller, and Collis Potter Huntington, among others, collaborated and partnered with the Russian Empire to develop and create a Russo-American pan-hemispheric intermodal transportation system and network that extended from St. Petersburg and Moscow to Pacific North America, Chicago, and New York City. (Image courtesy of Wikipedia).

Myron Hutchinson Richardson. Of Kansas and Chicago. Founder of Richardson Realty Company of Chicago. Son of Dr. Frank Richardson. Nephew of William Douglas Richardson. First cousin of Ada Willard (Richardson) Bunn. Patented inventor of novel windmill technology, vending machines, combustion engine, and advertisement technologies. Real estate broker at Chicago. Resident of the Near West Side community, Kenwood community, and the Albany Park community. (Image courtesy of Ruth Solomon).

Charles Richardson, Esq. Of Springfield and Chicago. Chicago lawyer. Son of Dr. Frank Richardson. Nephew of William Douglas Richardson. First cousin of Ada Willard (Richardson) Bunn. Killed in Spanish-American War. (Image courtesy of Ruth Solomon).

Dr. Frank Richardson. Medical doctor of Springfield, Illinois, and Wichita, Kansas. Druggist, farmer and stockman. Brother of William Douglas Richardson of Chicago, James Henry Richardson of Chicago, Charles Richardson of Springfield, Lucy Maria (Richardson) Cross of Cleveland and Elyria, Ohio, and many other siblings. Father of Charles Richardson, Esq., of Springfield and Chicago, and Myron Hutchinson Richardson of Chicago. Uncle of Ada Willard (Richardson) Bunn. Retired to Denver, Colorado. (Image courtesy of Ruth Solomon).

James Henry Richardson. Resident of Chicago during the Civil War era. Brother of William Douglas Richardson, Dr. Frank Richardson, Charles Richardson Sr., and others of Chicago, Springfield, and Kansas. Father of Hiram Adsit Richardson of Chicago. Uncle of Ada Willard (Richardson) Bunn. (Image courtesy of Ruth Solomon).

Class officers of St. Luke's Hospital nurses' training school. (Image courtesy of the Chicago History Museum; CHM-Digital Obj ID: ICHi-61544).

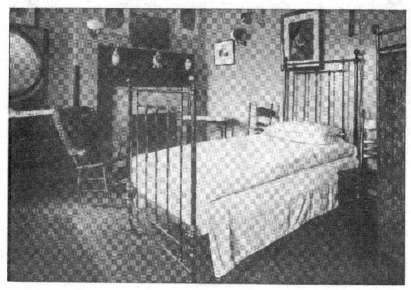

ST. LUKE'S HOSPITAL, CHICAGO (PRIVATE ROOM).

Private room in St. Luke's Hospital. Location was 1435 S. Michigan Avenue, and Indiana Avenue. Dr. Mahlon Bluford Peterson completed medical residency at St. Luke's Hospital. Juliette Magill Kinzie, a cousin of the Strykers, Henshaws, and McClures, co-founded the hospital. (Image courtesy of the Chicago History Museum; CHM-Digital Obj ID: ICHi-024758).

Exterior view of St. Luke's Hospital in Chicago, Illinois, 1908. Dr. Mahlon Peterson finished medical residency here. Juliette Kinzie founded the hospital. (Image courtesy of the Chicago History Museum; CHM-Digital Obj ID: DN-0006666).

Dr. Mahlon Bluford Peterson. Of Grant County, Indiana, and Chicago. Medical doctor and chiropractor of Chicago. Pictured here holding a skeletal element. Resident of the East Garfield Park community of the West Side of Chicago. Graduate of the Chicago College of Medicine and Surgery (now Loyola University). Holder of medical license in Illinois. Interned at St. Luke's Hospital of Chicago, a hospital which had been established partly by Juliette Magill Kinzie. Member of the Van Duyn-Peterson-Ramsey-Call Family of Ohio, Indiana, and Illinois. (Image courtesy of Mark Peterson).

The Hogans and Regans of Chippewa County, Wisconsin. Of Ireland, Wisconsin, Illinois, Texas, and Montana. Woman at center top is Ruth Regan. Man center left holding little girl is Thomas Stephen Hogan, a lawyer and one of the fathers of the Texas oil industry. Many Hogans and Regans would settle in Chicago and the metropolitan region. This is the O'Keefe-Hogan-Hanrahan-Regan Family. (Image courtesy of author's personal collection).

Thomas Stephen Hogan, Esq., and wife Kitty Donovan. Hogan and Donovan were natives of Chippewa Falls, Wisconsin. Hogan was a multimillionaire petroleum industrialist and mineral mine developer of Texas, Montana, Colorado, Illinois, Indiana, and Mexico. School teacher at Chippewa Falls. Copper miner at Butte, Montana. Lawyer. Labor organizer. Christian counselor to law and industry. Secretary of State of Montana. Deputy Secretary of the United States Department of the Interior. Founder of the National Farm Loan Bank system, a New Deal banking organization with headquarters at St. Louis, Missouri. Builder and owner of the Petroleum Tower of Midland, Texas. Founder of Hogan Oil Company. Developer of oilfields and coalfields of Texas, Montana, Colorado, and other places. Developer of gold mining companies in Mexico and other places. Named "Mr. Midland" for his work as the primary father of Midland, Texas, as a petroleum center. Hogan was one of the fathers of the Permian Oil Basin of Texas and served to locate Texas at the forefront of petroleum development and technology. Hogan was the first cousin of Ruth (Regan) Bunn of Wisconsin, Chicago, and Springfield, and was part of the immense O'Keefe-Hogan-Hanrahan-Regan Family of Wisconsin and Chicago. (Images courtesy of Kathleen Hogan Manuel and the late Sharon Dayton).

Old Wishbone Coffee tins from the Bunn Capitol Grocery Company of Springfield. George Wallace Bunn, Sr., who was the son of Jacob and Elizabeth (Ferguson) Bunn, was the President of this company. Bunn Capitol Grocery Company owned many different famous food brands, including Wishbone, Lincoln, Old Timer, Bunny, Capitol, JWB, and many others. (Tins and picture from author's personal collection).

John W. Bunn Civil War Memorial Trophy. John Whitfield Bunn served as a spy for the United States of America and the Union Army during the Civil War. He led the first group of Union Army soldiers from Chicago to Cairo, Illinois, and served as an intelligence agent for U.S. Army Gen. R. K. Swift and for Governor Richard Yates. This memorial cup was given to Bunn for his Civil War service. The front inscription on the cup states: "Presented to John W. Bunn. April 20, 1911. In commemoration of a patriotic service rendered to his country. April 20, 1861." The rear inscription names the men who presented the cup to Bunn as follows: "J. Otis Humphrey, Logan Hay, Edgar S. Scott, Owsley Brown, George B. Stadden, Henry M. Merriam, Henry A. Converse, James L. Cook, Walter McC. Allen, Philip Barton Warren, John C. Cook, Edward A. Hall, Stuart Brown, Nicholas R. Roberts, Latham T. Souther, James A. Easley, Henry Abels, George Pasfield, Jr., W. F. Workman." The Bunn Memorial Cup has remained in the Bunn family for six generations and belongs to author Andrew Taylor Call. (Civil War Memorial Cup from author's personal collection).

Chapter 6

Sprinters of the Steel Track

A Railroad Man's Prayer

"O, Lord, now that I have flagged Thee, lift up my feet from the rough road of life and plant them safely on the deck of the train of salvation. Let me use the safety lamp known as prudence and all the couplings in the train with the strong arm of love; and let my hand lamp be the Bible. And, Heavenly Father, keep all switches closed that lead off on the sidings, especially those with a blind end. Oh, Lord, if it by Thy pleasure, have every semaphore block along the line show white light of hope that I may make the run of life without stopping. And, Lord, give us the Ten Commandments for the schedule; and when I have finished on schedule time and pulled into the dark station of death, may the Superintendent of the Universe say: 'Well done, thou good and faithful servant, come and sign the pay roll and receive your check for eternal happiness.'"[3348]

—An Anonymous Christian Railroad Worker

Introduction

This chapter concerns the Chicago and Cook County histories of the Douglas, Brigham, McClure, Stryker, Taylor, Pierson, Holt, Cogan, and McNeil families. The Brigham-Holt family; the Brigham-Cogan family; the Douglas-Brigham family; and the Taylor-McNeil family are the four main family branches covered herein. All four of these branches are connected and are among the lineal and collateral ancestors of my grandfather, Henry Stryker Taylor (1908-1994). Charlotte Stryker, mother of Henry Stryker Taylor, and my great-grandmother, was a daughter of Elizabeth Henshaw (McClure) Stryker, who was the daughter of Judge Henry Brigham McClure (1809-1881) and Harriet Hillhouse Henshaw.[3349] No fewer than four branches of the American Brigham family settled in Chicago. No fewer than four branches of the Brigham family contributed to the development of Cook County in some form, either through settlement and residence, through business engagement, or through some joinder of these civic relationships.[3350] The

---

[3348] A Railroad Man's Prayer. The source document was photographically reproduced on Pinterest. Additional bibliographical facts unavailable at the time of reference.

[3349] Binney, C. J. F. (1883). The History and Genealogy of the Prentice, or Prentiss Family, of New England, Etc. from 1631 to 1883. 2nd Ed. P. 294. Boston, MASS: C. J. F. Binney.

[3350] Brigham, W. I. Tyler. (1907). The History of the Brigham Family; a record of several thousand descendants of Thomas Brigham the emigrant, 1603-1653. Emma E. Brigham, Ed. New York, NY: The Grafton Press, Genealogical Publishers. Google Books; see reference sources supplied elsewhere in this book concerning the Pennsylvania Railroad Company, Henry Stryker Taylor, and Robert Cunningham Taylor, Jr.

four relevant branches of the American Brigham family include the Draper-Douglas-Brigham-McClure branch; the Draper-Brigham-Holt branch; the Draper-Brigham-Cogan branch; and the Douglas-Brigham branch.[3351] The Draper-Douglas-Brigham-McClure branch additionally includes multiple individuals from the Stryker and the Taylor families, which both receive treatment and explanation elsewhere in this book. For the other histories of the Stryker family in this book, consult the following chapters: *Genesis of a Great Lakes Frontier* and *Friends of the Leatherworkers*.

Narrative efficiency and utility necessitate that the several branches of these combined families be discussed separately within this chapter. Therefore, each branch receives treatment in a subsection of the present chapter. The compartmentalized scheme of historical analysis will proceed as follows. First, we will discuss the Chicago history of the Douglas-Brigham-McClure-Stryker-Taylor family, its contributions to the founding of Michigan, and its history in Morgan County, Illinois. More recent generations of this branch of the family were connected to Chicago and Cook County in multiple ways. Second, we will discuss the Brigham-Cogan branch of the extended family and its connections to Chicago. Third we will discuss the Brigham-Holt family of Chicago. Fourth and finally, we will discuss the Douglas-Brigham family of Chicago, St. Louis, and Oklahoma, and its contributions to the growth of Cook County industry. The McNeils, a branch of the Taylor family, are discussd separately herein. These branches all connect prominently to Chicago and Northern Illinois in multiple ways.

The Douglas-Brigham-McClure-Stryker-Taylor Branch of Michigan and Illinois

The Stryker-McClure-Pierson-Taylor Branch of Morgan County and Chicago

Henry Stryker, son of Capt. John Stryker and Lydia (Cornell) Stryker of New Jersey, married Esther Harrison. The following children were born to them: Hannah Stryker; John Stryker; Maria Stryker, who married William Corbit; Charlotte Stryker, who married Dr. Daniel Babbit; Henry Stryker, who died young; Lucetta Stryker; **Henry Stryker, who married, first, Anna Addy, second, Elizabeth Addy, and third, Sophia Amelia Dart**; and Abram Stryker.[3352] For the Chicago history of the Stryker-Pierson branch of the family, see the chapters, *Builders of the Downtown* and *Genesis of a Great Lakes Frontier*. For the Chicago history of the Stryker-Williamson branch of the family, see the chapter, *Friends of the Leatherworkers*. Henry Stryker had the following children with Anna Addy:

[3351] Brigham, W. I. Tyler. (1907). The History of the Brigham Family; a record of several thousand descendants of Thomas Brigham the emigrant, 1603-1653. Emma E. Brigham, Ed. New York, NY: The Grafton Press, Genealogical Publishers. Google Books.
[3352] Stryker, William Scudder. (1887). Genealogy of the Stryker Family. Pages not marked. Camden, NJ: Sinnickson Chew, Printer.

Henry Stryker, Jr., who married Elizabeth Henshaw McClure (see history below); Charlotte Stryker; and Elizabeth Stryker, who married lawyer James English of West Virginia and Illinois. Henry Stryker had the following children with Elizabeth Addy: Jane Ann Stryker; Louisa Stryker; and **Maria Stryker, who married Ornan Pierson of Carrollton, Illinois**. Henry Stryker had the following child with Sophia Amelia Dart: Sophia Hurd Stryker, who married Morgan County lawyer John Antonio Bellatti, Esq.[3353] Maria Stryker (1840-1920) married banker and Illinois legislator Ornan Pierson (1839-1917). Their son, Joseph Henry Pierson (1864-1931), married Mary Louise Witwer (1877-1952). Joseph Henry Pierson and Mary Louise (Witwer) Pierson had the following children: Henry Stryker Pierson of Chicago and Evanston; and Stuart Witwer Pierson (1900-1978) of St. Louis.[3354]

Henry Stryker Pierson, Esq. (1903-1970) married Harriet Raynor Chittenden of St. Louis and Kansas City, Missouri.[3355] Henry Stryker Pierson became Chicago Sales Manager for Dow Chemical in 1949, succeeding Wilson I. Doan, and was still serving as Sales Office Manager of the Chicago District of Dow Chemical Company in 1952.[3356] In addition to being a corporate executive in Chicago, Pierson was a lawyer, having graduated from the Washington University of St. Louis, and having been admitted to the Missouri Bar.[3357] Pierson was a brother of both Phi Delta Theta Fraternity and the Delta Theta Phi Law Fraternity.[3358] He retired from Dow Chemical Company in 1963.[3359] Henry and Harriet retired to White Lake, Michigan. He served as President of the White Lake Community Club and served on the board of directors of the Sylvan Beach Resort Company.[3360] The Henry Stryker Pierson family included other Chicago and metropolitan area residents. Henry Stryker Pierson was a second cousin of Henry Stryker Taylor, who is discussed below.

The McClure Family

The McClure Family emigrated from Northern Ireland to Worcester, Massachusetts, during the eighteenth century.[3361] John McClure married Elizabeth

---

[3353] Stryker family historical records; Findagrave.com.

[3354] Stryker family historical records; St. Louis Post-Dispatch. (June 10, 1925). P. 19. Newspapers.com.

[3355] St. Louis Post-Dispatch. (June 10, 1925). P. 19. Newspapers.com.

[3356] The Freeport Facts. (Freeport, Texas). (November 26, 1952). P. 1. Newspapers.com; The St. Louis Star and Times. (November 10, 1949). P. 23.

[3357] Chicago Tribune. (June 13, 1970). P. 57. Newspapers.com.

[3358] Chicago Tribune. (June 13, 1970). P. 57. Newspapers.com.

[3359] Chicago Tribune. (June 13, 1970). P. 57. Newspapers.com.

[3360] Chicago Tribune. (June 13, 1970). P. 57. Newspapers.com.

[3361] McClure DNA Project: Patriarchs. John McClure and Elizabeth (Gill) McClure Descendants. Worldfamilies.net.

Gill. John and Elizabeth (Gill) McClure had the following children: John McClure, who married Sarah Coburn; David McClure, who married Lucy Kibbe; Elizabeth McClure; Thomas McClure, who married Zilpah Leach; Mary McClure, who married Asa Coburn; Anna McClure, who married Daniel Richardson; Nicholas McClure, who married Thankful Kingsbury; James McClure; Allis McClure, who married Benjamin Richardson; and **Samuel McClure, who married Phebe Edgerton** (ancestors of the McClure-Stryker-Taylor families of Illinois).[3362]

The McClure lineage migrated from Massachusetts to the Appalachian Mountains of Vermont and New York, eventually arriving in Michigan prior to Michigan statehood. The McClures remained many generations in the Appalachian Mountains of New England and New York. Mary McClure and her husband, Asa Coburn, were among the founders of Marietta, Ohio, and of the Campus Martius settlement of Ohio, in Washington County. Asa and Mary arrived in 1778 in the region of the Northwest Territory that would later become the State of Ohio on March 1, 1803 (Illinois, Indiana, Wisconsin, Michigan, and Minnesota also were created from the Northwest Territory).[3363] Asa Coburn held title to three shares of the Ohio Company, and this property entitled Coburn to more than 33,000 acres of land in the Northwest Territory.[3364] Asa Coburn and Mary (McClure) Coburn were among the founders both of Ohio and of the settlements of the upper Ohio River Valley.

Samuel McClure (b. 1758) married Phebe Edgerton, who was the daughter of Capt. Daniel Edgerton and Mary (Douglass) Edgerton of Tinmouth, Rutland County, Vermont.[3365] The Douglass Family was the same one from which the Brighams of Chicago descended (see later in this section). The Chicago Douglas/Douglass family and the McClure family of Vermont, New York, Michigan, and Illinois, were closely related. Dr. Samuel McClure and Phebe (Edgerton) McClure had a son named **David Gill McClure**.

Dr. David Gill McClure (1783-1856) married Betsy Brigham, the daughter of Jonas Brigham and Hannah (Draper) Brigham of Bakersfield, Vermont. Dr. David G. McClure helped establish the medical profession of Michigan in the early nineteenth century.[3366] A native of Rutland County, Vermont, David McClure was

[3362] McClure DNA Project: Patriarchs. John McClure and Elizabeth (Gill) McClure Descendants. Worldfamilies.net.

[3363] Washington County (Ohio) Biographies. Asa Coburn Family. Ohgen.net. Content contributed by Debbie Noland Nitsche.

[3364] Washington County (Ohio) Biographies. Asa Coburn Family. Ohgen.net. Content contributed by Debbie Noland Nitsche.

[3365] Cutter, William Richard. (1912). Genealogical And Family History of Central New York. Vol. II. P. 1077. New York, NY: Lewis Historical Publishing Company. Google Books or Hathitrust.org.

[3366] Durant, Samuel W. (1880). History of Ingham And Eaton Counties Michigan. P. 116. Philadelphia, PA: D. W. Ensign & Company. Google Books.

the son of Samuel McClure and Phebe (Edgerton) McClure.[3367] David McClure additionally established a land development and property management company at Lansing, Michigan.[3368] The McClure Land Company constituted a central and significant land development company in Lansing.[3369] In its early years the company property included a drug store and a grocery store, as well as residential rental space.[3370] The company continued through multiple generations, with Elizabeth Henshaw (McClure) Stryker and Judge Henry Stryker, Jr., of Jacksonville, Illinois, inheriting the company.[3371] The land company continued, in total, through five generations of the McClure-Stryker-Taylor family.[3372]

In 1911, S. S. Kresge Company of Detroit entered into business with the McClure Land Company of Lansing and Illinois in order to construct a new S. S. Kresge store on a parcel of land in Lansing that was owned by the McClure Land Company.[3373] The relevant lot stood at 114 S. Washington Avenue, in Lansing.[3374] The Mills Dry Goods Company was the prior occupant of the commercial space.[3375] *The Lansing State Journal* report indicated that the Kresge store was expected to hold its grand opening sometime in the first week of September, 1911.[3376] The firm of Wilcox & Early was the contractor for the preparation of the building for occupation by the new S. S. Kresge five and dime store.[3377] Judge Henry Stryker owned the McClure-Stryker Land Company at this time.[3378] Dissolution of the company occurred sometime during the time when joint ownership was held by Henry Stryker Taylor and the multiple additional Stryker relatives of Illinois. The dissolution of the McClure-Stryker Land Company was

---

[3367] Durant, Samuel W. (1880). History of Ingham And Eaton Counties Michigan. P. 116. Philadelphia, PA: D. W. Ensign & Company. Google Books.

[3368] Durant, Samuel W. (1880). History of Ingham And Eaton Counties Michigan. P. 116. Philadelphia, PA: D. W. Ensign & Company. Google Books.

[3369] Durant, Samuel W. (1880). History of Ingham And Eaton Counties Michigan. P. 116. Philadelphia, PA: D. W. Ensign & Company. Google Books.

[3370] Durant, Samuel W. (1880). History of Ingham And Eaton Counties Michigan. P. 116. Philadelphia, PA: D. W. Ensign & Company. Google Books.

[3371] Lansing State Journal. (August 30, 1911). P. 10. Newspapers.com. Taylor v. S. S. Kresge Company. (1952). 332 Mich. 65. 50 N.W.2d 851. https://casetext.com/case/taylor-v-ss-kresge-company

[3372] Taylor v. S. S. Kresge Company. (1952). 332 Mich. 65. 50 N.W.2d 851. https://casetext.com/case/taylor-v-ss-kresge-company

[3373] Lansing State Journal. (August 30, 1911). P. 10. Newspapers.com.

[3374] Lansing State Journal. (August 30, 1911). P. 10. Newspapers.com.

[3375] Lansing State Journal. (August 30, 1911). P. 10. Newspapers.com.

[3376] Lansing State Journal. (August 30, 1911). P. 10. Newspapers.com.

[3377] Lansing State Journal. (August 30, 1911). P. 10. Newspapers.com.

[3378] Lansing State Journal. (August 30, 1911). P. 10. Newspapers.com.

effected by Henry Stryker Taylor and multiple cousins from the Stryker, Capps, Hart, family of Michigan, Illinois, California.[3379]

Judge Henry McClure was a businessman of Lansing, Michigan, and a lawyer and judge at Jacksonville, Morgan County, Illinois.[3380] Henry Brigham McClure was the son of Dr. David Gill McClure (1783-1856) and Betsy (Brigham) McClure.[3381] Betsy Brigham, a native of Bakersfield, Vermont, was a daughter of Jonas Brigham, and Hannah (Draper) Brigham.[3382] Dr. David Gill McClure served as one of the founders of Jackson, Michigan.[3383] McClure served also as one of the founders of Lansing, Michigan, and of the State of Michigan as a whole, having contributed much to the development of both the Michigan Territory and the State of Michigan. He was a founder of Jackson County and Ingham County in Michigan.

Henry Brigham McClure received academic training at the Castleton Seminary.[3384] He subsequently attended and graduated from Middlebury College, in approximately 1830.[3385] Henry's brother-in-law, Rev. Truman Marcellus Post, Esq., also was a Middlebury alumnus (See Chapter 1, *Genesis of a Great Lakes Frontier*). McClure taught school at Champlain, New York.[3386] McClure then received training in law through having read law under apprenticeship in New York, and gained admission to the State Bar of New York in 1835.[3387] He was sworn into the State Bar of New York at Albany, and practiced law in New York

---

[3379] Information regarding this company provided in interview with Elizabeth Taylor Greer.

[3380] Pioneer Society of the State of Michigan. (1906). Pioneer Collections: Report of the Pioneer Society of the State of Michigan. Vol. 4. Pp. 259-263. Lansing, MI: Wynkoop Hallenbeck Crawford Co., State Printers. Google Books.

[3381] Durant, Samuel W. (1880). History of Ingham And Eaton Counties Michigan. P. 116. Philadelphia, PA: D. W. Ensign & Company. Google Books.

[3382] Durant, Samuel W. (1880). History of Ingham And Eaton Counties Michigan. P. 116. Philadelphia, PA: D. W. Ensign & Company. Google Books. Brigham and McClure genealogical records.

[3383] Durant, Samuel W. (1880). History of Ingham And Eaton Counties Michigan. P. 116. Philadelphia, PA: D. W. Ensign & Company. Google Books.

[3384] Pioneer Society of the State of Michigan. (1906). Pioneer Collections: Report of the Pioneer Society of the State of Michigan. Vol. 4. Pp. 260-261. Lansing, MI: Wynkoop Hallenbeck Crawford Co., State Printers. Google Books.

[3385] Pioneer Society of the State of Michigan. (1906). Pioneer Collections: Report of the Pioneer Society of the State of Michigan. Vol. 4. P. 260-261. Lansing, MI: Wynkoop Hallenbeck Crawford Co., State Printers. Google Books.

[3386] Pioneer Society of the State of Michigan. (1906). Pioneer Collections: Report of the Pioneer Society of the State of Michigan. Vol. 4. P. 261. Lansing, MI: Wynkoop Hallenbeck Crawford Co., State Printers. Google Books.

[3387] Pioneer Society of the State of Michigan. (1906). Pioneer Collections: Report of the Pioneer Society of the State of Michigan. Vol. 4. P. 261. Lansing, MI: Wynkoop Hallenbeck Crawford Co., State Printers. Google Books.

for many years.[3388] Afterwards, McClure relocated to Jackson, Michigan, in the 1830s.[3389] He then moved to Jacksonville, Illinois, but retained a strong commercial interest in Michigan, where he continued the land management business of the McClure Land Company, and helped to establish the Little Traverse Bay summer resort community of Wequetonsing, located in Emmet County, Michigan.[3390] Henry Brigham McClure and his father, Dr. David G. McClure, were founders of Lansing and Ingham County, Michigan. Multiple generations of the McClure, Stryker, Capps, Hart, Taylor, and Bunn families would spend summer seasons at the Wequetonsing resort, which was known in short form as "Weque."[3391] Dr. David Gill McClure and Henry Brigham McClure were, respectively, the fourth-great-grandfather and third-great-grandfather of author Andrew Taylor Call.

Henry Brigham McClure held the office of General Counsel to the Jacksonville Branch of the Illinois State Bank.[3392] Robert Irwin of Springfield, brother of Sarah (Irwin) Ferguson and uncle-in-law of Jacob Bunn, served on the board of directors of the State Bank of Illinois, a parent company whose Chicago Branch constituted the first bank in Chicago history. Irwin served, therefore, on the board of directors of the banking company and banking system that were the first to exist at Chicago. Henry McClure also practiced law in a firm at Jacksonville, Illinois, in partnership with his son-in-law, Henry Stryker, Jr., and with Richard Yates, who served as Governor of Illinois during the Civil War.[3393] McClure practiced government law for a time, having served as City Attorney for Jacksonville.[3394] At one time, the McClure Law Firm was situated directly opposite the law office of statesman

---

[3388] Pioneer Society of the State of Michigan. (1906). Pioneer Collections: Report of the Pioneer Society of the State of Michigan. Vol. 4. P. 261. Lansing, MI: Wynkoop Hallenbeck Crawford Co., State Printers. Google Books.

[3389] Pioneer Society of the State of Michigan. (1906). Pioneer Collections: Report of the Pioneer Society of the State of Michigan. Vol. 4. P. 261. Lansing, MI: Wynkoop Hallenbeck Crawford Co., State Printers. Google Books.

[3390] Pioneer Society of the State of Michigan. (1906). Pioneer Collections: Report of the Pioneer Society of the State of Michigan. Vol. 4. P. 260. Lansing, MI: Wynkoop Hallenbeck Crawford Co., State Printers. Google Books.

[3391] McClure, Stryker, Post, Capps, Hart, Taylor, Bunn family historical records.

[3392] Pioneer Society of the State of Michigan. (1906). Pioneer Collections: Report of the Pioneer Society of the State of Michigan. Vol. 4. P. 261. Lansing, MI: Wynkoop Hallenbeck Crawford Co., State Printers. Google Books.

[3393] Pioneer Society of the State of Michigan. (1906). Pioneer Collections: Report of the Pioneer Society of the State of Michigan. Vol. 4. P. 261. Lansing, MI: Wynkoop Hallenbeck Crawford Co., State Printers. Google Books.

[3394] Pioneer Society of the State of Michigan. (1906). Pioneer Collections: Report of the Pioneer Society of the State of Michigan. Vol. 4. P. 261. Lansing, MI: Wynkoop Hallenbeck Crawford Co., State Printers. Google Books.

Stephen Arnold Douglas, Esq.[3395] Henry McClure helped with Morgan County school administration, having held on two occasions the office of Morgan County School Commissioner.[3396] He also owned an agricultural depot at Jacksonville, presumably a retail emporium company that served the regional farms and farmers.[3397] The value of the Lansing assets of the McClure Land Company were stated to be $50,000 in 1881.[3398] This land company owned additional assets in Morgan County, Illinois, and possibly elsewhere in Illinois and Michigan.[3399] McClure always remained active in the development of Lansing and Jacksonville.[3400] As a lawyer and businessman, McClure probably traveled to Chicago with some frequency. He was listed as a visitor of the Sherman Hotel at Chicago in late October, 1874.[3401]

In May, 1881, while developing a major real estate construction project in Lansing, McClure suffered a fatal heart attack while a passenger aboard a Michigan Central Railroad Company train at Chicago.[3402] McClure was developing a tall building at the corner of Allegan Street and Washington Avenue in Lansing. The construction project was to include a structure made of stone.[3403] The project furthermore was intended by McClure to constitute one of the most physically prominent buildings in Lansing, if not the most prominent one.[3404] The fate of the architectural blueprints for the McClure building of Lansing after

---

[3395] Pioneer Society of the State of Michigan. (1906). Pioneer Collections: Report of the Pioneer Society of the State of Michigan. Vol. 4. P. 261. Lansing, MI: Wynkoop Hallenbeck Crawford Co., State Printers. Google Books.

[3396] Pioneer Society of the State of Michigan. (1906). Pioneer Collections: Report of the Pioneer Society of the State of Michigan. Vol. 4. P. 261. Lansing, MI: Wynkoop Hallenbeck Crawford Co., State Printers. Google Books.

[3397] Jacksonville City Directory. Complete publication information now unknown.

[3398] Pioneer Society of the State of Michigan. (1906). Pioneer Collections: Report of the Pioneer Society of the State of Michigan. Vol. 4. P. 260. Lansing, MI: Wynkoop Hallenbeck Crawford Co., State Printers. Google Books.

[3399] Pioneer Society of the State of Michigan. (1906). Pioneer Collections: Report of the Pioneer Society of the State of Michigan. Vol. 4. P. 260. Lansing, MI: Wynkoop Hallenbeck Crawford Co., State Printers. Google Books.

[3400] Pioneer Society of the State of Michigan. (1906). Pioneer Collections: Report of the Pioneer Society of the State of Michigan. Vol. 4. P. 260. Lansing, MI: Wynkoop Hallenbeck Crawford Co., State Printers. Google Books.

[3401] The Inter-Ocean. (October 26, 1974). P. 8. Newspapers.com.

[3402] Pioneer Society of the State of Michigan. (1906). Pioneer Collections: Report of the Pioneer Society of the State of Michigan. Vol. 4. P. 260. Lansing, MI: Wynkoop Hallenbeck Crawford Co., State Printers. Google Books.

[3403] Pioneer Society of the State of Michigan. (1906). Pioneer Collections: Report of the Pioneer Society of the State of Michigan. Vol. 4. P. 260. Lansing, MI: Wynkoop Hallenbeck Crawford Co., State Printers. Google Books.

[3404] Pioneer Society of the State of Michigan. (1906). Pioneer Collections: Report of the Pioneer Society of the State of Michigan. Vol. 4. P. 260. Lansing, MI: Wynkoop Hallenbeck Crawford Co., State Printers. Google Books.

McClure's death on the train at Chicago remains entirely unknown at this time. McClure had stated the following regarding the Lansing building project: "'I am coming to Lansing to build my monument.'"[3405] McClure's remains were removed from the train and were carried to the Palmer House Hotel to await return to Jacksonville for funeral and burial services.[3406]

The McClure funeral service was held at Trinity Episcopal Church of Jacksonville.[3407] Reverend J. D. Easter officiated at the service.[3408] The hymns that were performed by the Trinity Episcopal Church choir at the McClure funeral service were, "Jesus, Savior of My Soul" and "Just as I Am."[3409] The Bible scripture that was read at the funeral service comprised, at least in part, that of 1 Corinthians 15:20, which reads as follows: "But now is Christ risen from the dead, *and* become the firstfruits of them that slept."[3410]

McClure was a devoted Christian, as were almost all of the McClures, Strykers, and other kin.[3411] Among the relatives who attended Henry Brigham McClure's funeral at Jacksonville were the Strykers and the Posts of St. Louis. Rev. Truman M. Post, Esq. of St. Louis and Chicago, whose biography and contributions to Chicago and Cook County are discussed in Chapter 1, attended the Henry McClure funeral.[3412]

[3405] Pioneer Society of the State of Michigan. (1906). Pioneer Collections: Report of the Pioneer Society of the State of Michigan. Vol. 4. P. 260. Lansing, MI: Wynkoop Hallenbeck Crawford Co., State Printers. Google Books.

[3406] Pioneer Society of the State of Michigan. (1906). Pioneer Collections: Report of the Pioneer Society of the State of Michigan. Vol. 4. P. 261. Lansing, MI: Wynkoop Hallenbeck Crawford Co., State Printers. Google Books.

[3407] Pioneer Society of the State of Michigan. (1906). Pioneer Collections: Report of the Pioneer Society of the State of Michigan. Vol. 4. P. 262. Lansing, MI: Wynkoop Hallenbeck Crawford Co., State Printers. Google Books.

[3408] Pioneer Society of the State of Michigan. (1906). Pioneer Collections: Report of the Pioneer Society of the State of Michigan. Vol. 4. P. 262. Lansing, MI: Wynkoop Hallenbeck Crawford Co., State Printers. Google Books.

[3409] Pioneer Society of the State of Michigan. (1906). Pioneer Collections: Report of the Pioneer Society of the State of Michigan. Vol. 4. P. 262. Lansing, MI: Wynkoop Hallenbeck Crawford Co., State Printers. Google Books.

[3410] Pioneer Society of the State of Michigan. (1906). Pioneer Collections: Report of the Pioneer Society of the State of Michigan. Vol. 4. P. 262. Lansing, MI: Wynkoop Hallenbeck Crawford Co., State Printers. Google Books. 1 Corinthians 15:20. King James Bible. Biblehub.com.

[3411] McClure, Stryker, Post, Taylor, *et al.* records.

[3412] Pioneer Society of the State of Michigan. (1906). Pioneer Collections: Report of the Pioneer Society of the State of Michigan. Vol. 4. P. 263. Lansing, MI: Wynkoop Hallenbeck Crawford Co., State Printers. Google Books.

Judge Henry Brigham McClure married Harriet Hillhouse Henshaw.[3413] Harriet Hillhouse Henshaw (1811-1867) was a daughter of Daniel Henshaw, a shipping merchant of Connecticut, and Sarah Esther (Prentiss) Henshaw, whose family were founders of New London.[3414] Harriet Henshaw was an alumna of the Troy Female Seminary, known subsequently as Emma Willard School.[3415] The Henshaw and Prentice/Prentiss genealogies receive treatment and discussion within the chapters concerning the Wolcott, Kinzie, Post, and Henshaw families, which families all contributed to the founding and development of Chicago.[3416] One daughter was born to Henry Brigham McClure and Harriet Hillhouse (Henshaw) McClure: Elizabeth Henshaw McClure (1838-1919).[3417] Elizabeth Henshaw McClure married Henry Stryker (1830/1832-1922).[3418] For the genealogy of the Prentice/Prentiss family and the explanations of how those families relate to the structure of this book, see Chapter 1, *Genesis of a Great Lakes Frontier*.

Elizabeth Henshaw (McClure) Stryker engaged in multiple civic organizations in Jacksonville and Morgan County. She served as one of the two elected delegates to the National Congress of the Daughters of the American Revolution, having been elected from the membership of the James Caldwell Chapter of the D.A.R., the Jacksonville chapter of the D.A.R., on January 26, 1904.[3419] The other delegate who was elected from this same conference was Mrs. S. D. Osborne.[3420] The alternates who were elected at the Jacksonville conference included Mrs. John A. Bellatti (Sophia Hurd Stryker) of Jacksonville, and Mrs. H. P. Gordon of Washington, D.C.[3421] The January Jacksonville conference consisted additionally of a lecture concerning the history of the early schools of Morgan County,

---

[3413] Binney, C. J. F. (1883). The History and Genealogy of the Prentice, or Prentiss Family, of New England, Etc. from 1631 to 1883. 2nd Ed. P. 294. Boston, MASS: C. J. F. Binney.

[3414] Binney, C. J. F. (1883). The History and Genealogy of the Prentice, or Prentiss Family, of New England, Etc. from 1631 to 1883. 2nd Ed. Pp. 293-294. Boston, MASS: C. J. F. Binney.

[3415] Sage, Margaret Olivia Slocum. (1898). Emma Willard and Her Pupils: Or Fifty Years of Troy Female Seminary: 1822-1872. P. 65. New York, NY: Mrs. Russell Sage. Google Books.

[3416] See herein especially Chapter 1: "Genesis of a Great Lakes Frontier."

[3417] Binney, C. J. F. (1883). The History and Genealogy of the Prentice, or Prentiss Family, of New England, Etc. from 1631 to 1883. 2nd Ed. P. 294. Boston, MASS: C. J. F. Binney. NOTICE: C. J. F. Binney mistakenly indicated the middle initial of Elizabeth Henshaw McClure as "P," instead of "H." See P. 294.

[3418] Sage, Margaret Olivia Slocum. (1898). Emma Willard and Her Pupils: Or Fifty Years of Troy Female Seminary: 1822-1872. P. 65. New York, NY: Mrs. Russell Sage. Google Books.

[3419] The Jacksonville Daily Journal. (January 28, 1904). P. 2. Newspapers.com.

[3420] The Jacksonville Daily Journal. (January 28, 1904). P. 2. Newspapers.com.

[3421] The Jacksonville Daily Journal. (January 28, 1904). P. 2. Newspapers.com.

Illinois.[3422] Mrs. Gates Strawn delivered the lecture on the subject of the history of the Morgan County schools.[3423] Elizabeth (McClure) Stryker also served as a member of the Board of Directors of the James Caldwell Chapter of the D.A.R.[3424]

In 1905, Elizabeth (McClure) Stryker was one of the several founders of the Monday Conversation Club, a Jacksonville women's club whose organizational purpose was the presentation and analysis of diverse subjects and issues.[3425] The initial Monday Conversation Club meeting calendar, which was scheduled at the time of establishment of the Club, included subjects ranging from immigration, labor policy, and penal systems, to municipal property ownership issues, technical schools, institutes of technology, parks and boulevards, and travels to the country of Brazil.[3426] Elizabeth was a member of the National Federation of Women's Clubs. She participated as an organizer of the ceremonial tribute to Mrs. Isabella Laning Candee of Cairo, Illinois, who was a former president of the National Federation of Women's Clubs.[3427]

Henry Stryker, Jr., Esq., the husband of Elizabeth Henshaw McClure, was a lawyer and judge in Jacksonville, Morgan County, Illinois. Stryker practiced law for a period of time with his father-in-law, Henry Brigham McClure.[3428] Henry Stryker served as a Morgan County judge, holding the office of Master in Chancery, as the immediate successor to Judge Cyrus Epler in 1870.[3429] In 1873, the State of Illinois adopted a new constitution among whose contents was a law that created the office of Master in Chancery.[3430] Judge Cyrus Eppler appointed Henry Stryker, Esq., to the office of Master in Chancery in 1873, when the judicial office was formally established within the recently adopted Illinois constitutional jurisprudence.[3431] The new constitution created the office of Master in Chancery within each county in Illinois, thus constructing and replicating the formal public office within the multiple county governments that existed across the State of Illinois.[3432] Judge Henry Stryker, Jr., furthermore, entered the banking business and owned a local private financing company at least as early as 1902, and possibly much earlier.[3433] He maintained a banking office at 24 ½ Public Square, in

[3422] The Jacksonville Daily Journal. (January 28, 1904). P. 2. Newspapers.com.
[3423] The Jacksonville Daily Journal. (January 28, 1904). P. 2. Newspapers.com.
[3424] The Jacksonville Daily Journal. (December 4, 1902). P. 3. Newspapers.com.
[3425] The Jacksonville Daily Journal. (August 24, 1905). P. 5. Newspapers.com.
[3426] The Jacksonville Daily Journal. (August 24, 1905). P. 5. Newspapers.com.
[3427] The Jacksonville Daily Journal. (December 6, 1903). P. 8. Newspapers.com.
[3428] Pioneer Society of the State of Michigan. (1906). Pioneer Collections: Report of the Pioneer Society of the State of Michigan. Vol. 4. P. 261. Lansing, MI: Wynkoop Hallenbeck Crawford Co., State Printers. Google Books.
[3429] The Jacksonville Daily Journal. (April 1, 1934). P. 9. Newspapers.com.
[3430] The Jacksonville Daily Journal. (April 1, 1934). P. 9. Newspapers.com.
[3431] The Jacksonville Daily Journal. (April 1, 1934). P. 9. Newspapers.com.
[3432] The Jacksonville Daily Journal. (April 1, 1934). P. 9. Newspapers.com.
[3433] The Jacksonville Daily Journal. (November 5, 1902). P. 2. Newspapers.com.

Jacksonville. The financial products offered by the Stryker Banking Company included loans.[3434] According to a 1902 advertisement that appeared in the *Jacksonville Daily Journal*, the company offered the following principal financial product under the following conditions: "REAL ESTATE LOANS— without commission, at current rates and with liberal prepayment privileges. Family funds only."[3435]

The McClures, Strykers, and Posts were among the founders and developers of the Michigan summer resort of Wequetonsing, located on the northern shore of Little Traverse Bay, a large bay of Lake Michigan.[3436] Wequetonsing is immediately east of Harbor Springs, west of Bay View, and across Little Traverse Bay from Petoskey and Walloon Lake. Ernest Hemingway and his family spent the summers at nearby Walloon Lake. In August of 1885, Henry Stryker, Esq. and his uncle-in-law, Rev. Truman Marcellus Post, Esq. of St. Louis and Chicago, along with approximately 200 other people, visited Mackinac Island from Petoskey, Michigan.[3437] Howard Van Doren Shaw, the renowned Chicago architect, was also among the company of visitors to Mackinac Island that week in August, 1885.[3438] Shaw designed the Quadrangle Club in the Hyde Park community of Chicago, many houses in Hyde Park and Lake Forest, and the Eleanor Robinson Countiss Mansion of Gold Coast neighborhood. The Countiss Mansion now houses the International Museum of Surgical Science, which was founded by Dr. Max Thorek and is both one of Chicago's most significant museums and one the world's most significant medical museums.[3439] Howard Van Doren Shaw also designed the Harry Capps House of Jacksonville, Illinois.[3440] Harry Capps was a cousin of William Thomas Capps. Henry Stryker participated in the leadership of the Episcopal Archdiocese of Springfield, Illinois.[3441] He was a member of the Standing Committee of the Episcopal Archdiocese of Springfield.[3442] The Diocese of Springfield was established in 1877, and Henry

---

[3434] The Jacksonville Daily Journal. (November 5, 1902). P. 2. Newspapers.com.

[3435] The Jacksonville Daily Journal. (November 5, 1902). P. 2. Newspapers.com.

[3436] Taylor, Stryker, McClure, Hart, Capps, Post family records.

[3437] The Inter-Ocean. (August 30, 1885). P. 9. Newspapers.com.

[3438] The Inter-Ocean. (August 30, 1885). P. 9. Newspapers.com.

[3439] International Museum of Surgical Science. imss.org.

[3440] List of Works by Howard Van Doren Shaw. Wikipedia.

[3441] Journal of the Twelfth Annual Synod of the Holy Catholic Church In The Diocese of Springfield. (1889). P. 3. St. Louis, MO: Woodward & Tiernan Printing Company. Google Books.

[3442] Journal of the Twelfth Annual Synod of the Holy Catholic Church In The Diocese of Springfield. (1889). P. 3. St. Louis, MO: Woodward & Tiernan Printing Company. Google Books.

Stryker served on the diocesan Standing Committee with Rev. John D. Easter, D. W. Dresser, Walter Moore, Charles E. Hay, and S. H. Treat.[3443]

The children born to Henry Stryker and Elizabeth Henshaw (McClure) Stryker included the following persons: Harriet McClure Stryker (1872-1879); Henry McClure Stryker (1873-1892); Charlotte Stryker (1875-1908); Louise McClure Stryker (1877-1968); and Elizabeth Henshaw Stryker (1880-1949).[3444] Harriet McClure Stryker died as a child.[3445] Henry McClure Stryker died at the age of nineteen from a fall in which it was supposed that he struck his head, fell to the ground in an unconscious state, and suffocated due to the physical position in which he collapsed.[3446] He was a freshman at Lafayette College in Easton, Pennsylvania, and played second base on the Lafayette College Nine Baseball Team.[3447] Charlotte Stryker married Robert Cunningham Taylor, Sr. (1868-1936), of Virginia, Cass County, Illinois.[3448] Louise McClure Stryker married William Thomas Capps, Sr. (1871-1933) of Jacksonville, Morgan County, Illinois.[3449] Elizabeth Henshaw Stryker married Dr. Joseph Hall Hart, Sr., of Cincinnati, Ohio.[3450] Joseph Hart was a graduate of Yale University and had taught at the University of Pennsylvania, the University of Chicago, and at Illinois College. He probably resided in Hyde Park when he was a member of the University of Chicago faculty.[3451] He taught Physics and Mathematics. Elizabeth Henshaw Stryker attended Smith College in Massachusetts.[3452]

Louise McClure (Stryker) Capps, William Capps, and a Great Textile Company

Louise McClure Stryker (1877-1968) married William Thomas Capps (1871-1933) of Jacksonville, Illinois.[3453] Capps was the son of William Edward Capps and Margaret (Gallaher) Capps of Jacksonville.[3454] William T. Capps attended

[3443] The Living Church Annual And Clergy List Quarterly. (November 16, 1885). Vol. I. Number II. P. 163. Milwaukee, WI. Google Books.

[3444] Stryker family genealogical records. Cemetery records from Diamond Grove Cemetery, Jacksonville, Illinois. findagrave.com.

[3445] Stryker family genealogical records. Cemetery records from Diamond Grove Cemetery, Jacksonville, Illinois. findagrave.com.

[3446] The Inter-Ocean. (May 2, 1892). P. 6. Newspapers.com.

[3447] The Inter-Ocean. (May 2, 1892). P. 6. Newspapers.com.

[3448] The Inter-Ocean. (May 8, 1904). P. 7. Newspapers.com.

[3449] The Jacksonville Daily Journal. (September 22, 1905). P. 8. Newspapers.com.

[3450] The Cincinnati Enquirer. (August 18, 1949). P. 14. Newspapers.com.

[3451] Taylor, Stryker, Hart records.

[3452] Taylor, Stryker, Hart records; The Jacksonville Daily Journal. (December 29, 1905). P. 5. Newspapers.com.

[3453] Stryker and Capps family history records.

[3454] Swayne, Noah H. (1918). Twenty-Five Year Record: Class of Ninety-Three, Yale College. P. 168. New Haven, CT: The Tuttle, Morehouse & Taylor Company. Google Books.

Illinois College, transferred to Yale, and graduated from Yale in 1893.[3455] Capps worked with different businesses in the manufacturing and mining sectors in Illinois and the Appalachian Mountains of Virginia.[3456] Capps was Vice-President and later President of the J. Capps & Sons Company of Jacksonville, which was one of the premier clothing manufacturers of the United States.[3457] Joseph Capps formed the company in 1839 in Jacksonville, produced Indian blankets, and served the Midwestern and Trans-Mississippi western clothing markets.[3458] Stephen Capps took over the company after the death of his father, Joseph, and continued the development of the firm.[3459] The company became one of the largest wool textile makers in the Midwest.[3460] The company once sold many Indian blankets to William "Buffalo Bill" Cody, who was known to be one of the star customers of the company.[3461] The company grew steadily and, by 1964, was producing 90,000 to 100,000 coats per year, as well as a great quantity of trousers and other garments.[3462] Capps employees collectively earned annual wages and benefits totaling about $2,000,000 as of 1964.[3463]

The J. Capps & Sons Company innovated defensive technology when it created multiple new forms of bulletproof clothing.[3464] The company developed and marketed several clothing lines around 1975, which contained Du Pont Kevlar bulletproof material.[3465] The different product lines included, "men's sportscoats, vests and under garments for both men and women,"[3466] and all of these could

---

[3455] Swayne, Noah H. (1918). Twenty-Five Year Record: Class of Ninety-Three, Yale College. P. 168. New Haven, CT: The Tuttle, Morehouse & Taylor Company. Google Books.

[3456] Stryker and Capps family history records; Swayne, Noah H. (1918). Twenty-Five Year Record: Class of Ninety-Three, Yale College. P. 168. New Haven, CT: The Tuttle, Morehouse & Taylor Company. Google Books.

[3457] Chicago Tribune. (January 1, 1911). P. 10. Newspapers.com; Swayne, Noah H. (1918). Twenty-Five Year Record: Class of Ninety-Three, Yale College. P. 168. New Haven, CT: The Tuttle, Morehouse & Taylor Company. Google Books; Stryker and Capps family history records.

[3458] The Dispatch (Moline, Illinois). (January 29, 1975). P. 32. Newspapers.com; Stryker and Capps family history records.

[3459] Bulletin of the National Association of Wool Manufacturers. (1914). Vol. 44. P. 372. Boston, MASS: The Rockwell and Churchill Press. Google Books.

[3460] The Dispatch (Moline, Illinois). (January 29, 1975). P. 32. Newspapers.com; Stryker and Capps family history records.

[3461] The Dispatch (Moline, Illinois). (January 29, 1975). P. 32. Newspapers.com; Stryker and Capps family history records.

[3462] The Jacksonville Daily Journal. (June 21, 1964). P. 14. Newspapers.com.

[3463] The Jacksonville Daily Journal. (June 21, 1964). P. 14. Newspapers.com.

[3464] The Dispatch (Moline, Illinois). (January 29, 1975). P. 32. Newspapers.com; Stryker and Capps family history records.

[3465] The Dispatch (Moline, Illinois). (January 29, 1975). P. 32. Newspapers.com; Stryker and Capps family history records.

[3466] The Dispatch (Moline, Illinois). (January 29, 1975). P. 32. Newspapers.com.

"withstand pistol shots from point blank range."[3467] The company marketed the bulletproof clothing products under the brand name, ProLife Apparel.[3468] The power and durability of the clothing lines were capable of withstanding, "shark bites and assaults with meat cleavers, knives and razor blades."[3469] The ProLife Apparel garment prices ranged from $80.00 to $250.00 as of the 1975 company product report from *The Moline Dispatch*, and William Thomas Capps, Jr., who was President of the company, expected to produce 1,000,000 ProLife Apparel clothing products annually.[3470] The ProLife Apparel product line would have generated an anticipatory extrapolated gross sales revenue of $80,000,000 to $250,000,000 by circa 1976.[3471] The product was described as being, "'five times stronger than steel but . . .almost as pliable as foam rubber.'"[3472] The company was receiving a high volume of interest in its ProLife Apparel product lines from diverse potential customers, including police organizations, the United States Army, and bartenders.[3473] J. Capps & Sons Company possessed a major market presence in Chicago and the metropolitan region, and would have served many clothing markets there.

William T. Capps served as a member of the board of directors of the Southern Gypsum Company.[3474] The United States Geological Survey, an instrumentality of the United States Department of the Interior, provided an encyclopedic account in 1913 of United States business economies and their relationships to geological sciences and discoveries. Waldemar Lindgren was Chief Geologist of the United States Geological Survey at the time of the production and publication of this reference work, and Otis Smith served as Director of the Survey at the same time.[3475] Lindgren and Smith, therefore, oversaw the production of the 1913 geological survey encyclopedia, and this reference work contained key information about the Southern Gypsum Company. Southern Gypsum was a

---

[3467] The Dispatch (Moline, Illinois). (January 29, 1975). P. 32. Newspapers.com.

[3468] The Dispatch (Moline, Illinois). (January 29, 1975). P. 32. Newspapers.com; Stryker and Capps family history records.

[3469] The Dispatch (Moline, Illinois). (January 29, 1975). P. 32. Newspapers.com; Stryker and Capps family history records.

[3470] The Dispatch (Moline, Illinois). (January 29, 1975). P. 32. Newspapers.com; Stryker and Capps family history records.

[3471] The Dispatch (Moline, Illinois). (January 29, 1975). P. 32. Newspapers.com; Stryker and Capps family history records.

[3472] The Dispatch (Moline, Illinois). (January 29, 1975). P. 32. Newspapers.com.

[3473] The Dispatch (Moline, Illinois). (January 29, 1975). P. 32. Newspapers.com.

[3474] Swayne, Noah H. (1918). Twenty-Five Year Record: Class of Ninety-Three, Yale College. P. 169. New Haven, CT: The Tuttle, Morehouse & Taylor Company. Google Books.

[3475] United States Department of the Interior. United States Geological Survey Bulletin 530. (1913). P. Title page. Washington, D.C.: Government Printing Office. Google Books.

gypsum mining company whose principal office was at North Holston, Smyth County, Virginia, near Saltville, also in Smyth County.[3476] The Southern Gypsum Company was an important industrial concern in southwest Virginia, and would have positively impacted the important southwest Virginia communities of North Holston, Saltville, Tazewell, Claypool Hill, Richlands, Doran, Marion, Grundy, Bishop, Bluefield, Wise, Norton, Stonega, Pound, Haysi, Hurley, Pennington Gap, Cumberland Gap, Bristol, Abingdon, and Big Stone Gap, among many others. Southern Gypsum Company would also have positively impacted the West Virginia communities of Bluefield, Welch, Premier, Matewan, Williamson, Beckley, Princeton, White Sulphur Springs, Lewisburg, Shaft Hollow, Charleston, Huntington, Wheeling, Morgantown, Marlinton, Prince, Mullins, Alderson, Hinton, Bramwell, Bluewell, Cucumber, War, Roderfield, and many others.

Southern Gypsum Company operated a gypsum mine at the Pierson planter-bank farm, which was located near the north branch of the Holston River.[3477] The company mined the gypsum resource associated with the great MacCrady Gypsum Formation and operated a bucket tram system, roasting plant, grinding plant, and a railroad that linked the minehead to Saltville.[3478] Charles Hull Ewing of Chicago and Lake Forest served as Secretary and Treasurer of the Southern Gypsum Company, and engaged heavily in Chicago real estate.[3479] Ewing also was President of the Lake Street Business Men's Association in Chicago.[3480] That William T. Capps and Charles H. Ewing were acquainted was a known fact, because while Capps served on the board of directors of Southern Gypsum Company in 1911, Ewing served as Secretary and Treasurer of the company, according to the January 1, 1911, edition of the *Chicago Tribune*.[3481] Capps served as President of J. Capps & Sons Company at the same time when he was on the board of directors of Southern Gypsum Company.[3482] Gypsum was an essential ingredient in the creation of plaster. Southern Gypsum became famous for its plaster products and particularly so for its Cherokee Cement Plaster, a brand of plaster which was specially tailored for durability in hot, moist, tropical, and subtropical climates and weathers.[3483] There was evidence that Southern Gypsum

---

[3476] United States Department of the Interior. United States Geological Survey Bulletin 530. (1913). P. 246. Washington, D.C.: Government Printing Office. Google Books.

[3477] United States Department of the Interior. United States Geological Survey Bulletin 530. (1913). P. 246. Washington, D.C.: Government Printing Office. Google Books.

[3478] United States Department of the Interior. United States Geological Survey Bulletin 529. (1913). P. 246. Washington, D.C.: Government Printing Office. Google Books.

[3479] Currey, Josiah Seymour, and Beck, Juergen. (Year not apparent at time of reference). Vol. 5. Page number not apparent at time of reference. Google Books.

[3480] Currey, Josiah Seymour, and Beck, Juergen. (Year not apparent at time of reference). Vol. 5. Page number not apparent at time of reference. Google Books.

[3481] Chicago Tribune. (January 1, 1911). P. 10. Newspapers.com.

[3482] Chicago Tribune. (January 1, 1911). P. 10. Newspapers.com.

[3483] The Tampa Tribune. (April 10, 1912). P. 3. Newspapers.com.

Company possessed a sales office at Chicago, although the relevant record has been lost. The April 2, 1921, edition of the New York City-based industry journal known as *Textile World*, reported that Southern Gypsum Company operated agencies in, "every city in the South."[3484]

William T. Capps co-founded the Midland Casualty Company of Chicago in January, 1911.[3485] Capps founded the company with Charles Hull Ewing, O. S. Edwards, A. C. Pegram, Paul F. Beich, William G. Agar, A. W. Benson, Hon. Albert E. Bergland, P. A. Peterson, Hon. McKenzie Clelland, O. S. Edwards, C. O. Frisbie, W. E. Gillespie, Charles W. Inman, E. J. Johnson, H. Lindemann, C. W. Maxon, A. H. Heureuther, George P. Hummer, Dr. Michael Leininger, Hon. W. O. Potter, C. B. Munday, Frederick H. Smith, Henry Trares, and Charles H. Voegele.[3486] *Best's Insurance Reports*, a New York City publication, reported the initial capitalization money to be $205,000, but noted that the capital was expected to grow to $1,000,000 soon after the time of the report.[3487] It is noteworthy that Capps and Charles Hull Ewing worked together both with the Southern Gypsum Company and with the Midland Casualty Company. The Midland Casualty Company operated in conjunction with the Midland Investment Company and the Midland Operating Company.[3488] The Badger Casualty Company of Green Bay, Wisconsin, absorbed the Midland Casualty Company and numerous others in a 1915 company consolidation.[3489] When William Capps died in 1933, he left his entire estate, inclusive of real and personal property, to his wife, Louise (Stryker) Capps.[3490]

William T. Capps served on the board of directors of the Midland Casualty Company of Chicago for many years.[3491] The company created policies of health and accident insurance and operated at the Insurance Exchange of Chicago.[3492] F. S. Cable was President of the company in 1914. O. S. Edwards was Vice-President, H. C. Pegram served as Secretary, E. J. Johnson was the Assistant Secretary, and

---

[3484] Textile World. (April 2, 1921). P. 80. New York, NY: Textile World. Google Books.
[3485] Best's Insurance Reports: Fire, Marine and Miscellaneous. (1911-1912). Vol. 12. P. 439. New York, NY: Alfred M. Best Company, Incorporated. Google Books.
[3486] Best's Insurance Reports: Fire, Marine and Miscellaneous. (1911-1912). Vol. 12. P. 439. New York, NY: Alfred M. Best Company, Incorporated. Google Books.
[3487] Best's Insurance Reports: Fire, Marine and Miscellaneous. (1911-1912). Vol. 12. P. 439. New York, NY: Alfred M. Best Company, Incorporated. Google Books.
[3488] Best's Insurance Reports: Fire, Marine and Miscellaneous. (1911-1912). Vol. 12. P. 439. New York, NY: Alfred M. Best Company, Incorporated. Google Books.
[3489] Green Bay Press-Gazette. (July 29, 1915). P. 1. Newspapers.com.
[3490] The Jacksonville Daily Journal. (October 27, 1933). P. 4. Newspapers.com.
[3491] The Insurance Almanac. (1914). P. 109. New York, NY: The Weekly Underwriter. Google Books.
[3492] The Insurance Almanac. (1914). P. 109. New York, NY: The Weekly Underwriter. Google Books.

McKenzie Clelland was the General Counsel for the company.[3493] The 1914 board of directors consisted of William T. Capps, Paul F. Beich, Hon. A. E. Bergland, P. A. Peterson, Hon. McKenzie Clelland, O. S. Edwards, C. O. Frisbie, W. E. Gillespie, Charles W. Inman, E. J. Johnson, H. Lindemann, C. W. Maxon, A. H. Heureuther, H. C. Pegram, Frederick H. Smith, Henry Trares, Charles H. Voegele, William Gottenstrater, and H. A. Soverhill.[3494]

William T. Capps participated in leadership in the Trinity Church of Jacksonville, serving ten years as a Vestryman of that church, and thereby continuing a long tradition of leadership within the Episcopal Archdiocese of Morgan County, which was the regional Episcopal church polity that Judge Henry Stryker, father-in-law of William T. Capps, had co-founded long before.[3495] William T. Capps was a tournament golfer at the Jacksonville Country Club, where he and his wife, Louise (Stryker) Capps, and his sisters-in-law, Charlotte (Stryker) Taylor, and Elizabeth (Stryker) Hart, had all been members and accomplished golfers.[3496] William T. Capps and Louise (Stryker) Capps had three children: William Thomas Capps, Jr.; Henry McClure Capps; and Elizabeth Stryker Capps.[3497] Louise (Stryker) Capps inherited the J. Capps & Sons Company from her husband when he died, and their son, William Thomas Capps, Jr., assumed the leadership of the company.[3498] Henry McClure Capps was a Yale alumnus, became an artist and the Art Director for Metro-Goldwyn-Mayer Studios of California, and married Ruth Goldwyn, who was the daughter of the movie producer Samuel Goldwyn.[3499] McClure Capps was Art Director for the following television shows: *The High Chaparral* from 1967 to 1968; *A Man Called Shenandoah* (1965); *The Life of Riley* from 1953 to 1957; *The Great Gildersleeve* from 1955 to 1956; *My Little Margie* from 1952 to 1955; *The Stu Erwin Show* from 1950 to 1955; *The Amos n' Andy Show* from 1951 to 1955; and many others. Capps was also Art Director for films such as *Tarzan and the Huntress* (1947), *Tarzan's Magic*

[3493] The Insurance Almanac. (1914). P. 109. New York, NY: The Weekly Underwriter. Google Books.

[3494] The Insurance Almanac. (1914). P. 109. New York, NY: The Weekly Underwriter. Google Books.

[3495] Swayne, Noah H. (1918). Twenty-Five Year Record: Class of Ninety-Three, Yale College. P. 169. New Haven, CT: The Tuttle, Morehouse & Taylor Company. Google Books; Stryker and Capps family history records.

[3496] The Jacksonville Daily Journal. (June 23, 1931). P. 7. Newspapers.com; Stryker family history records.

[3497] Swayne, Noah H. (1918). Twenty-Five Year Record: Class of Ninety-Three, Yale College. P. 169. New Haven, CT: The Tuttle, Morehouse & Taylor Company. Google Books; Stryker and Capps family history records; findagrave.com, Elizabeth Stryker Capps, Diamond Grove Cemetery in Jacksonville, Illinois.

[3498] Stryker and Capps family history records.

[3499] Stryker and Capps family history records.

Fountain (1949), *Tarzan and the Mermaids* (1948), and *The Du Pont Story* (1950), among many others.[3500]

Elizabeth Stryker Capps attended MacMurray College in Jacksonville, received a Master's Degree from Columbia University in New York City, studied American Sign Language, and became a teacher of the deaf at the Illinois School for the Deaf in Jacksonville. Elizabeth, known as "Dee Dee," was the godmother of author Andrew Taylor Call, and a close friend of the famous Chicago physician, Dr. Augusta Webster, M.D., who was a Northwestern University alumna and medical doctor of Chicago.[3501] Dee Dee Capps studied dance under the instruction of Lucille Mackness of Jacksonville, and performed dances at the Waukegan Garden Club Fete in June, 1934, where she was accompanied by singer Helen Burt from the University of Illinois, and Lucille Mackness.[3502] More than 300 people attended the event, which was held at the gardens of E. L. Ross, President of the Waukegan Garden Club.[3503] Lucille Mackness studied dance in Chicago, and both she and Dee Dee Capps attended graduate school at Columbia University for the purpose of becoming teachers of the deaf.[3504]

Four Jacksonville women, Helen Dial, Dorothy Farrell, Elizabeth Stryker Capps, and Lucille Mackness, all chose to become teachers of the deaf, and all four received scholarships to attend Columbia University to study instruction of the deaf.[3505] Dee Dee Capps became a highly esteemed teacher of the deaf in Illinois and devoted her life to the education of deaf people. She spent the summers in Wequetonsing, Emmet County, Michigan, a summer resort that had been founded partly by her grandfather, Hon. Henry Stryker, her great-grandfather, Hon. Henry Brigham McClure, and by many other relatives from the Stryker and Post families of Illinois and St. Louis.[3506] Dee Dee Capps had married William Maxwell "Max" Thompson of Jacksonville. Max owned Thompson Jewelry Company of Jacksonville.[3507] They had no children.

[3500] IMDB.com. Henry McClure Capps.
[3501] Stryker and Capps family history records.
[3502] The Jacksonville Daily Journal. (June 24, 1934). P. 11. Newspapers.com.
[3503] The Jacksonville Daily Journal. (June 24, 1934). P. 11. Newspapers.com.
[3504] The Jacksonville Daily Journal. (June 24, 1934). P. 11. Newspapers.com; The Jacksonville Daily Journal. (May 9, 1936). P. 2. Newspapers.com.
[3505] The Jacksonville Daily Journal. (May 9, 1936). P. 2. Newspapers.com.
[3506] Stryker and Capps family history records.
[3507] Stryker, Capps family historical records; findagrave.com.

The Hall and Hart Family of Cincinnati and their Contributions to Chicago

Elizabeth Henshaw Stryker (1880-1949), the youngest child of Judge Henry Stryker and Elizabeth Henshaw (McClure) Stryker, married Dr. Joseph Hall Hart of Cincinnati.[3508] Elizabeth attended the Jacksonville Academy and then Smith College in Northfield, Massachusetts. She also traveled extensively in Europe.[3509] Elizabeth was a championship golfer in Illinois and was a member of the Central Illinois Golf Association.[3510] Dr. Joseph Hall Hart was the son of John Babinger Hart and Katherine Louise (Hall) Hart of Cincinnati.[3511] Dr. Joseph Hall Hart received both a Bachelor's Degree and a Doctoral Degree in Physics from Yale, and taught Physics at the University of Chicago, at Illinois College in Jacksonville, and at the University of Pennsylvania.[3512] Dr. Joseph Hall Hart, who married Elizabeth Stryker, was the grandson of Joseph Lloyd Hall of Cincinnati, who was the founder of the Hall Safe & Lock Company of Cincinnati, and who built the company into the largest safe and lock company in the world.[3513] Many family members attended the Stryker-Hart wedding at the Judge Henry Stryker home at 919 W. College Avenue in Jacksonville. Judge Henry Stryker and Elizabeth (McClure) Stryker welcomed a large wedding party at their home, and Rev. William Mitchell of Trinity Church officiated the wedding.[3514] Clara Harrison Post of St. Louis, who was a first cousin of the Stryker sisters, was one of the bridesmaids for Elizabeth Stryker, and Henry Ridgeway Hart was a groomsman for his brother, Joseph Hall Hart.[3515] Charlotte (Stryker) Taylor also attended her sister's wedding, and a Miss Katherine Patterson of Lake Forest, possibly a relative, also attended the wedding.[3516]

Joseph L. Hall of Cincinnati manufactured safes and locks of myriad varieties and served almost the entire world's security market. Hall Safe & Lock joined with other safe and lock manufacturers to form the Herring-Hall-Marvin Safe and Lock Company of Cincinnati. The Hall's Safe and Lock Company will be discussed extensively below. Joseph Hall's daughter, Kate Hall, married John Babinger Hart, a retail shoe company owner of Cincinnati.[3517] Three sons were born to John and

---

[3508] The Jacksonville Daily Journal. (December 29, 1905). P. 5. Newspapers.com; findagrave.com.

[3509] The Jacksonville Daily Journal. (December 29, 1905). P. 5. Newspapers.com.

[3510] The Jacksonville Daily Journal. (December 29, 1905). P. 5. Newspapers.com.

[3511] Taylor, Stryker, Hart family records.

[3512] The Jacksonville Daily Journal. (December 29, 1905). P. 5. Newspapers.com.

[3513] The Cincinnati Enquirer. (May 2, 1943). P. 23. Newspapers.com; see also: Goss, Charles Frederic. (1912). Cincinnati: The Queen City, 1788-1912. Vol. IV. Pp. 172-173. Chicago, IL: S. J. Clarke Publishing Company. Archive.org.

[3514] The Jacksonville Daily Journal. (December 29, 1905). P. 5. Newspapers.com.

[3515] The Jacksonville Daily Journal. (December 29, 1905). P. 5. Newspapers.com.

[3516] The Jacksonville Daily Journal. (December 29, 1905). P. 5. Newspapers.com.

[3517] The Cincinnati Enquirer. (May 2, 1943). P. 23. Newspapers.com.

Kate (Hall) Hart: Joseph Hall Hart, John Babinger Hart, and Henry Ridgeway Hart.[3518] Henry Ridgeway Hart was a Princeton alumnus. Joseph Hall Hart, married Elizabeth Henshaw Stryker of Jacksonville.[3519] Two sons were born to Dr. Joseph Hall Hart and Elizabeth (Stryker) Hart: Joseph Hall Hart, Jr. and John Babinger Hart. These brothers were first cousins of Henry Stryker Taylor and Robert Cunningham Taylor of Cass County, Illinois, Springfield, and Chicago.[3520]

Captain Joseph Hall Hart, Jr., Flight 121, and Eugene Roddenberry

John B. Hart and Joseph Hall Hart, Jr., were both graduates of the University of Cincinnati, and both worked extensively with Pan-American World Airways.[3521] John B. Hart was, at the time of the death of his grandmother, Kate (Hall) Hart, in 1943, a superintendent of Pan-Am.[3522] Joseph Hall Hart, Jr., was one of the most celebrated Pan-Am Clipper pilots, and established several flight records for Clipper flights between South America and Africa.[3523] Joseph Hart, Jr., graduated with a degree in aerodynamics from the University of Cincinnati and received aviation training as a member of the 359th Observation Squadron at Lunken Airport at Cincinnati.[3524] He trained at Randolph Field in San Antonio, at March Field in California, and graduated from the Army Air Corps School, with additional training received at Mitchell Field on Long Island. After completion of these pilot training programs, Hart entered the service of Pan-Am.[3525]

Joseph flew President Franklin D. Roosevelt to the Yalta Conference, and handled the Pan-Am Clipper routes for South America, Africa, and Asia throughout many years of service with Pan-Am.[3526] Captain Joseph Hall hart, Jr. was piloting a Pan-Am Clipper, known as the Eclipse, from Karachi, India, to Istanbul, Turkey, in 1947, when one of the plane engines failed and caught fire midflight.[3527] Karachi was then still a city within India, as the country of Pakistan would be created two months later, on August 14, 1947, by Great Britain when Great Britain dissolved the British Imperial Raj of India and divided India into India and Pakistan.

[3518] The Cincinnati Enquirer. (May 2, 1943). P. 23. Newspapers.com.
[3519] The Cincinnati Enquirer. (August 18, 1949). P. 14. Newspapers.com.
[3520] Taylor, Stryker, Hart records.
[3521] Taylor, Stryker, Hart family records.
[3522] The Cincinnati Enquirer. (May 2, 1943). P. 23. Newspapers.com.
[3523] The Cincinnati Enquirer. (May 2, 1943). P. 23. Newspapers.com.
[3524] The Cincinnati Enquirer. (April 27, 1938). Kentucky Edition, P. 15.
[3525] The Cincinnati Enquirer. (April 27, 1938). Kentucky Edition, P. 15.
[3526] Taylor, Stryker, Hart records.
[3527] The Cincinnati Enquirer. (June 20, 1947). P. 3. Newspapers.com.

The propulsion failure aboard the Eclipse caused the plane to become incapable of flight.[3528] The burning plane engine destroyed all airworthiness of the Eclipse, rendered impossible any further viable powered flight for the plane, and forced a crash landing.[3529] Captain Hart administered a crash landing over the deserts of Syria, and crashed the plane on the banks of the Euphrates River.[3530] Captain Hart was killed along with fourteen other plane passengers, but twenty-two people survived the crash.[3531] The report from *The Cincinnati Enquirer* stated that eighteen passengers and three crew members survived the plane crash, and that thirty-six people, inclusive of crew and passengers, were aboard the Eclipse at the time of the crash.[3532]

The Eclipse crew members who were killed in the Syrian crash were Captain Joseph Hall Hart, Jr. of Cincinnati and Greenwich, Connecticut; First Officer Robert Stanley McCoy of New York City; Second Officer (Navigator) Howard Thompson of New York City; First Engineer Robert B. Donnelly of New York City; Second Engineer W. E. Morris of New York City; First Radio Officer Nelson C. Miles of Port Washington, New York; and Second Radio Officer Arthur O. Olson of New York City.[3533] Seven of the eight Eclipse passengers who were killed in the crash were H. A. Bhattia of Karachi; Mrs. Joyce E. Abbott of Bombay; Maurice A. Abbott of Bombay; Noel W. Porteous of Taunton, England; Desmond Vernon of Madras; Rukmani Goeneka of Calcutta; and a Mrs. Hughes.[3534] The surviving crew members of the crash of the Eclipse were Stewardess Jane Bray of New York City; Purser Anthony Volpe of New York City; and Third Officer Eugene W. Roddenberry of River Edge, New Jersey.[3535] Third Officer Eugene W. Roddenberry, who received some flight instruction from Capt. Joseph Hall Hart, Jr., would go on to create the science fiction series, saga, and story universe known as *Star Trek*.[3536]

John Babinger Hart of Cincinnati

John Babinger Hart, son of Dr. Joseph Hall Hart and Elizabeth (Stryker) Hart, had worked as the airport manager for Pan-Am in Brownsville, Texas, and

---

[3528] The Cincinnati Enquirer. (June 20, 1947). P. 3. Newspapers.com.
[3529] The Cincinnati Enquirer. (June 20, 1947). P. 3. Newspapers.com.
[3530] The Cincinnati Enquirer. (June 20, 1947). P. 3. Newspapers.com.
[3531] Standard-Sentinel. (Hazleton, Pennsylvania). (June 23, 1947). P. 1. Newspapers.com.
[3532] The Cincinnati Enquirer. (June 20, 1947). P. 3. Newspapers.com.
[3533] The Cincinnati Enquirer. (June 20, 1947). P. 3. Newspapers.com.
[3534] The Cincinnati Enquirer. (June 20, 1947). P. 3. Newspapers.com.
[3535] The Cincinnati Enquirer. (June 20, 1947). P. 3. Newspapers.com.
[3536] Clark, Mark. (2012). Star Trek FAQ: Everything Left To Know About The First Voyages Of The Starship Enterprise. Pages not apparent. Milwaukee, WI: Applause Theatre & Cinema Books. Google Books.

subsequently as station superintendent for the Miami Pan-Am operation.[3537] He was transferred from Miami in 1946 to Rio De Janeiro to help reorganize the Ground Operations for Pan-Am in Brazil.[3538] John B. Hart and Folger Athearn reorganized the Brazilian Ground Operations for Pan-Am.[3539] Folger Athearn was the Assistant Operations Manager for the Brazilian Operations of Pan-Am.[3540]

After leaving Pan-Am, Hart started the John B. Hart Construction Company, a construction company of Fort Lauderdale, Florida.[3541] The Hart Construction Company became a prominent Fort Lauderdale contractor. John, his wife Mildred (Hyde) Hart, and his mother, Elizabeth (Stryker) Hart, were early residents of Las Olas Boulevard.[3542] In Cincinnati, Joseph Hall Hart, Jr. was Vice-President of the Builders Credit Company, a company of which Joseph Hall Hart, Sr., was an officer.[3543] As of April, 1938, John B. Hart worked as Field Superintendent for Pan-Am at Port-of-Spain, Trinidad.[3544]

John and Joseph Hart were raised at the family home located at 3593 Alaska Avenue, in the Avondale neighborhood of Cincinnati.[3545] The Harts were neighbors of William Henry Burtner, Jr., a famous Cincinnati lawyer and industrialist who was part of the Call-Baldwin-Burtner family of Pittsburgh, Allegheny County, and Butler County, Pennsylvania.[3546] John Babinger Hart and Joseph Hall Hart, Jr., entered into business with their father, Dr. Joseph Hall Hart, Sr., at Cincinnati as young men. Joseph Hall Hart, Sr., Joseph Hall Hart, Jr., and John Babinger Hart founded the Cincinnati Builders Credit Company in 1929, while both brothers were in their early twenties.[3547] The association with the Cincinnati Builders Credit Company suggests that John B. Hart had gained early connection to the construction industry, which would possibly explain why John entered the construction industry at Fort Lauderdale after leaving Pan-Am.[3548]

Cincinnati helped to build Chicago in multiple significant ways, and Joseph Hall was one of the vanguards of connecting Cincinnati and Chicago industries.[3549] Hall established the Hall Safe and Lock Company in 1845 in Pittsburgh, but relocated

---

[3537] The Brownsville Herald. (October 1, 1946). P. 8. Newspapers.com.

[3538] The Brownsville Herald. (October 1, 1946). P. 8. Newspapers.com.

[3539] The Brownsville Herald. (October 1, 1946). P. 8. Newspapers.com.

[3540] The Brownsville Herald. (October 1, 1946). P. 8. Newspapers.com.

[3541] Fort Lauderdale News. (February 10, 1951). P. 8. Newspapers.com.

[3542] Taylor, Stryker, Hart records.

[3543] The Cincinnati Enquirer. (April 27, 1938). Kentucky Edition, P. 15.

[3544] The Cincinnati Enquirer. (April 27, 1938). Kentucky Edition, P. 15.

[3545] The Cincinnati Enquirer. (April 27, 1938). Kentucky Edition, P. 15.

[3546] Call, Baldwin, Burtner family records.

[3547] The Cincinnati Enquirer. (July 6, 1929). P. 13.

[3548] The Cincinnati Enquirer. (April 27, 1938). Kentucky Edition, P. 15; The Cincinnati Enquirer. (July 6, 1929). P. 13.

[3549] Records and Briefs of the United States Supreme Court. (1906). P. 513. Washington, D.C.: Supreme Court of the United States. Google Books.

the company to Cincinnati, where it remained from that point and forward.[3550] The company expanded with great speed and global scope.[3551] By 1884, Hall's Safe And Lock had achieved annual sales revenues of $2,000,000 and employed around 1,000 people.[3552] The Cincinnati headquarters was located at 183 W. Pearl Street, and the company owned offices at Chicago, Cleveland, New York City, San Francisco, and Omaha, as of 1884.[3553] The authors of the S. B. Nelson's 1894 history of Cincinnati and Hamilton County reported the extraordinary production power, quality, and market credibility of Hall's Safe and Lock Company, noting that the company possessed 1,200,000 square feet of factory space at Cincinnati, and manufactured 10,000 safes per year.[3554] The company possessed an extremely powerful presence in Europe, and owned branches at London and Berlin as of 1894.[3555] The company owned over twenty branches in the United States in 1894, in addition to the European branch offices. The S. B. Nelson Company authors reported that the company represented a capital structure of $3,300,000. The corporate money was apparently produced by equity financing, and was fully paid in.[3556] The capital safety and soundness of the company were discernible from the 1894 description of the company financing.[3557] The 1894 report stated that the company continually employed more than 2,000 persons.[3558] Edward C. Hall served as President of the company at the time of the 1894 report; William F. Hall served as Treasurer, and Richard F. Pullen served as Secretary.[3559]

[3550] History of Cincinnati and Hamilton County, Ohio: Their Past And Present. Vol 1. P. 318. Cincinnati, OH: S. B. Nelson & Co., Publishers. Google Books.

[3551] History of Cincinnati and Hamilton County, Ohio: Their Past And Present. Vol 1. P. 318. Cincinnati, OH: S. B. Nelson & Co., Publishers. Google Books.

[3552] The Industries of San Francisco, California. (1884). P. 79. San Francisco, CA: Payot, Upham & Co. Google Books.

[3553] The Industries of San Francisco, California. (1884). P. 79. San Francisco, CA: Payot, Upham & Co. Google Books; Garwood, D. A. (1900). The Railway Purchasing Agent's Directory. P. 365. Indianapolis, IN: The Railway Equipment & Finance Company. Google Books.

[3554] History of Cincinnati and Hamilton County, Ohio: Their Past And Present. Vol 1. P. 318. Cincinnati, OH: S. B. Nelson & Co., Publishers. Google Books.

[3555] History of Cincinnati and Hamilton County, Ohio: Their Past And Present. Vol 1. P. 318. Cincinnati, OH: S. B. Nelson & Co., Publishers. Google Books.

[3556] History of Cincinnati and Hamilton County, Ohio: Their Past And Present. Vol 1. P. 318. Cincinnati, OH: S. B. Nelson & Co., Publishers. Google Books.

[3557] History of Cincinnati and Hamilton County, Ohio: Their Past And Present. Vol 1. P. 318. Cincinnati, OH: S. B. Nelson & Co., Publishers. Google Books.

[3558] History of Cincinnati and Hamilton County, Ohio: Their Past And Present. Vol 1. P. 318. Cincinnati, OH: S. B. Nelson & Co., Publishers. Google Books.

[3559] History of Cincinnati and Hamilton County, Ohio: Their Past And Present. Vol 1. P. 318. Cincinnati, OH: S. B. Nelson & Co., Publishers. Google Books.

Hall's Safe And Lock Company was probably the most important source of security technology during the Great Chicago Fire of 1871.[3560] Testimony to support this fact appeared within a Hall's Catalogue from 1906, which accompanied a United States Supreme Court report.[3561] The catalogue specifically was joined to the 1906 *Records and Briefs of the United States Supreme Court*.[3562] The report clearly and dramatically stated the absolute significance of Hall's Safe and Lock Company as a force for good in Chicago.[3563] To be discovered among the smoldering embers of the Great Fire of 1871 were myriads of Hall's Safe And Lock Company safes.[3564] The safes lay strewn about the immense landscape of ruin, and safeguarded their contents without yielding in the slightest measure to the destructive powers of the fires.[3565] These safes were among the only non-combustible relics that survived the urban incineration, and provided total safety to the goods stored within them through the many days of lingering burning and property destruction, according to multiple Chicago businessmen who used the safes.[3566] The Chicago testimony of the security that Hall's contributed during the Great Fire was extensive, and included the following descriptions:

> "THE BURNING OF CHICAGO. Hall's Safes in the Great Conflagration from 40 to 240 Hours. Below will be found a partial list of Prominent Business Houses who had our Safes in use during the fire, and have given voluntary testimony as to their reliability.
> Chicago, October 18, 1871.
>
> HALL'S SAFE AND LOCK CO.
>
> Gentlemen:— We, the undersigned, having had your Safes in use during the terrible fire of October 8th and 9th, wish to add our testimony to the already high reputation of your work. In the fire so unprecedented for long continued and intense heat, it is a sufficiently high compliment to your

[3560] Records and Briefs of the United States Supreme Court. (1906). P. 513. Washington, D.C.: Supreme Court of the United States. Google Books.
[3561] Records and Briefs of the United States Supreme Court. (1906). P. 513. Washington, D.C.: Supreme Court of the United States. Google Books.
[3562] Records and Briefs of the United States Supreme Court. (1906). P. 513. Washington, D.C.: Supreme Court of the United States. Google Books.
[3563] Records and Briefs of the United States Supreme Court. (1906). P. 513. Washington, D.C.: Supreme Court of the United States. Google Books.
[3564] Records and Briefs of the United States Supreme Court. (1906). P. 513. Washington, D.C.: Supreme Court of the United States. Google Books.
[3565] Records and Briefs of the United States Supreme Court. (1906). P. 513. Washington, D.C.: Supreme Court of the United States. Google Books.
[3566] Records and Briefs of the United States Supreme Court. (1906). P. 513. Washington, D.C.: Supreme Court of the United States. Google Books.

Safes to say they brought their contents out in good condition, notwithstanding the fact that in many cases they lay roasting in the burning debris for over a week. As they have been 'tried and not found wanting,' we take pleasure in recommending them to all who may be in want of Fire-Proof Safes. Keith Brothers, J. W. Stearns & Sons, Wells, French & Co., Massachusetts Life Ins. Co., Global Mutual Life Ins. Co., S. N. Wilcox."[3567]

The November 9, 1871, edition of *The Lawrence Daily Journal*, a Kansas newspaper, contained a short comment about the Hall's Safe and Lock Company and its importance to Chicago.

"HALL'S SAFE AND LOCK CO. have established an office at 66 West Madison street. Hall's safes, like those of Herring's, have passed through the fiery ordeal unharmed. Hundreds of their celebrated safes, when opened after the fire, have saved their contents of valuables, books, &c., without a leaf being scorched."[3568]

Thus, a magnificent friendship between Chicago and Cincinnati was forged and framed through the melting elements of the Great Chicago Fire.[3569] Halls' Safe And Lock Company not only was the largest safe and lock manufacturer in the world, but also probably possessed the most significant share of the Chicago market.[3570] As of at least July, 1888, Hall's had achieved market supremacy in the safe and lock industry and operated offices and distributorships globally.[3571] Cincinnati was the headquarters of Hall's Safe and Lock Company. Chicago, Cleveland, St. Louis, San Francisco, Louisville, and New York City were other branch locations for the company.[3572] The company reported in a full-page advertisement in the July, 1888, *Bankers' Directory*, that they had provided the following Chicago banking organizations with their security technologies: the Commercial Safety Deposit Company, Royal Insurance Safety Deposit Vaults, Home Insurance Safety Deposit Vaults, Prairie State Safety Deposit Company, and

---

[3567] Records and Briefs of the United States Supreme Court. (1906). P. 513. Washington, D.C.: Supreme Court of the United States. Google Books.

[3568] The Lawrence Daily Journal. (November 9, 1871). P. 2. Newspapers.com.

[3569] Records and Briefs of the United States Supreme Court. (1906). P. 513. Washington, D.C.: Supreme Court of the United States. Google Books.

[3570] The Bankers' Directory and List of Bank Attorneys. (July, 1888). P. 9. Chicago, IL: Rand, McNally & Company. Google Books.

[3571] The Bankers' Directory and List of Bank Attorneys. (July, 1888). P. 9. Chicago, IL: Rand, McNally & Company. Google Books.

[3572] The Bankers' Directory and List of Bank Attorneys. (July, 1888). P. 9. Chicago, IL: Rand, McNally & Company. Google Books.

the Dime Savings Safety Deposit Company.[3573] Having been well-established at the time when Jacob Bunn, Potter Palmer, George Pullman, Robert Todd Lincoln, and others started the Chicago Secure Depository Company, Hall's Safe And Lock Company was probably the company that manufactured the security technology for that Chicago company.[3574] It is merely historically sound probability and not proof, however, that supports this theory. The times, places, markets, and companies all match up. Hall's Safe And Lock Company appears to have either relocated their Chicago office to, or to have added to the 66 West Madison Street office, an office located at 77 Dearborn.[3575] A. L. Deane & Company, consisting of A. L. Deane and J. W. Donnell, were the western agents for Hall's Safe And Lock, and were based at 77 Dearborn.[3576] Cincinnati has contributed much to the technological, economic, and industrial development of Chicago and Cook County. The Hall's Safe and Lock Company, Lodge & Davis Machine Tool Company, and the Davis & Egan Machine Tool Company were Cincinnati companies that possessed major branches and market shares at Chicago, and all three firms were vital elements of the growth of Cook County economic power, soundness, and stability. Joseph L. Hall, William Henry Burtner, William Lodge, Henry Luers, Charles Davis, Thomas Egan, and others were corporate and industrial men of both Cincinnati and Chicago and demonstrated the strength and excellence of interurban community and alliance that existed so brilliantly within the Gilded Age United States.

The Strykers and Taylors of Jacksonville, Morgan County, Illinois:

Charlotte Stryker (1875-1908) and Elizabeth Henshaw Stryker (1880-1949), daughters of Judge Henry Stryker and Elizabeth (McClure) Stryker, both were champion golfers in Illinois. Both sisters were members of the Jacksonville Country Club and the Central Illinois Golf Association.[3577] Charlotte was a member of the Wednesday Musical Club of Jacksonville.[3578] Charlotte was also an alumna of the Mary A. Burnham School, now the Stoneleigh-Burnham School, of Greenfield, Massachusetts.[3579] One *Book of Common Prayer* that Charlotte Stryker

---

[3573] The Bankers' Directory and List of Bank Attorneys. (July, 1888). P. 9. Chicago, IL: Rand, McNally & Company. Google Books.

[3574] The Bankers' Directory and List of Bank Attorneys. (July, 1888). P. 9. Chicago, IL: Rand, McNally & Company. Google Books.

[3575] The Lakeside Annual Directory of the City of Chicago. (1887). P. 2007. Chicago, IL: The Chicago Directory Company. Google Books; The Lawrence Daily Journal. (November 9, 1871). P. 2. Newspapers.com.

[3576] The Lakeside Annual Directory of the City of Chicago. (1887). P. 427. Chicago, IL: The Chicago Directory Company. Google Books.

[3577] The Inter-Ocean. (March 13, 1904). P. 13. Newspapers.com.

[3578] The Jacksonville Daily Journal. (December 19, 1902). P. 3. Newspapers.com.

[3579] Stryker family records.

owned was given to her by her husband, Robert "Bert" Cunningham Taylor, Sr., who was himself a Presbyterian, but who appreciated the Episcopalian tradition and its prayer book. Bert gave Charlotte this *Book of Common Prayer* on the occasion of their wedding on April 25, 1905. This particular *Book of Common Prayer* has been handed down through multiple generations of the Stryker-Taylor family, and to the author, Andrew Taylor Call.[3580] Elizabeth "Ibby" Taylor, mother of Andrew Taylor Call, carried this heirloom copy of the *Book of Common Prayer* to her 1974 wedding to Matthew Baldwin Call, father of Andrew Taylor Call.[3581]

Charlotte Stryker traveled in Europe, was a student of German culture and civilization, and sang German Lieder (art songs). She sang at the choir at the Trinity Episcopal Church in Jacksonville, which had been founded by her father, Judge Henry Stryker and others. Charlotte died in late January, 1908, a week after giving birth to her second child, Henry Stryker Taylor (1908-1994), who is discussed below. Charlotte suffered many physical complications as a result of giving birth to her second son and she bled to death as a result of these complications. Her two sons, Robert Cunningham Taylor, Jr. and Henry Stryker Taylor grew up with no mother. Their father's Taylor cousin, Rebecca MacEachran of Ontario, Canada, was brought in to help care for the two boys in the absence of their mother. Aunt Becky MacEachran was sixty years old at the time when she came to care for the Taylor boys.[3582]

The children of Charlotte Stryker and Robert Cunningham Taylor were the following: Robert "Bob" Cunningham Taylor, Jr. (1906-1944), a banker of Chicago and Springfield; and Henry Stryker Taylor (1908-1994), a banker, farmland and commercial property company owner, and capitalist of Springfield and Chicago, and someone who participated heavily in the Chicago railroad and banking industries. We next will address the Chicago history of the Douglas-Brigham-McClure-Stryker-Taylor family of Cass County, Sangamon County, and Chicago.

The Taylor and Cunningham Families of Chicago, Cass County, and Springfield

The Taylor family and the Cunningham family of Illinois include several people who were among the earliest settlers at Chicago and Cook County. The people who are discussed in this chapter include the following individuals: Robert Taylor, Robert Cunningham Taylor, James Cunningham, Charles Cunningham, Andrew Cunningham, John Cunningham, Ellen (Taylor) Cunningham, Henry Stryker

---

[3580] Interview with Elizabeth Taylor Greer. (May 30, 2017). Memoir concerning the Stryker and Taylor families.

[3581] Interview with Elizabeth Taylor Greer. (May 30, 2017). Memoir concerning the Stryker and Taylor families.

[3582] Interview with Elizabeth Taylor Greer. (May 30, 2017). Memoir concerning the Stryker and Taylor families.

Taylor, Robert Cunningham Taylor, Jr., and Elizabeth (Bunn) Taylor, among others.

The first of the family to arrive at Chicago was Andrew Cunningham, in approximately the year 1834. The second to arrive there was Robert Taylor, in the year 1840.[3583] Robert Taylor (1816-1902), the father of Robert Cunningham Taylor, and grandfather of Henry Stryker Taylor and Robert Cunningham Taylor, Jr., was a native of Scotland.[3584] Robert Taylor had immigrated first to Ohio, and then to Chicago, in 1840, where he remained for an unknown period of time. After some time at Chicago, Robert Taylor settled in Cass County, a western geographical neighbor of Springfield and Sangamon County.[3585] Robert Taylor engaged in farming and cattle raising, in addition to the grain business.[3586] He served as Vice-President of the Farmers National Bank of Virginia, Illinois, a bank which he also served as a member of the board of directors. Robert's Ohio cousin, Samuel McIntire Taylor (1856-1916), was Secretary of State of Ohio, a member of the Ohio General Assembly (from Champaign County), a lawyer, and was both United States Consul General for Callao, Peru, and U.S. Consul to Glasgow, Scotland (appointed by President William McKinley of Ohio).[3587]

The Taylors were Scottish Highlanders, tenant farmers, and natives of the Campbelltown region of Argyleshire, on the Mull of Kintyre peninsula of southwestern Scotland.[3588] The Taylor family is a Sept of Clan Cameron. Robert Taylor and Angus Taylor, two sons of Angus Taylor and Florence (MacTavish) Taylor, emigrated to the United States in 1835.[3589] They set sail from Greenock, Scotland, on May 16, 1835, aboard the *John Hale*, and arrived in New York City on July 4, 1835.[3590] From there the brothers traveled up the Hudson River to the Erie Canal, and then west to Urbana, Champaign County, Ohio, where their uncles, Alexander Taylor and John S. Taylor, resided. On May 3, 1837, Archibald Taylor, Duncan Taylor, Alexander Taylor, John Taylor, William Taylor, Flora Taylor, and their mother emigrated to Illinois from Scotland.[3591] At Urbana, Ohio, Robert Taylor (1816-1902) learned the trades of tanner and butcher from Douglas

---

[3583] Cox, Marcia. History of the Taylor Family and the Cunningham Family.

[3584] Cox, Marcia. History of the Taylor Family and the Cunningham Family.

[3585] Cox, Marcia. History of the Taylor Family and the Cunningham Family.

[3586] Cox, Marcia. History of the Taylor Family and the Cunningham Family.

[3587] Bulletin of the Internaitonal Bureau of the American Republics. (July-December, 1909). Vol. XXIX. Pp. 996-997. Washington, D.C. Google Books.

[3588] Taylor, Flora E. (Undated). A Sketch Of The Taylor Family. Taylor family history records.

[3589] Taylor, Flora E. (Undated). A Sketch Of The Taylor Family. Taylor family history records.

[3590] Taylor, Flora E. (Undated). A Sketch Of The Taylor Family. Taylor family history records.

[3591] Taylor, Flora E. (Undated). A Sketch Of The Taylor Family. Taylor family history records.

Luce.[3592] Robert Taylor came to Chicago in 1840, and remained there for a time before settling in Cass County, Illinois.[3593] The Taylors had planned to move from Ohio to Iowa, but decided to settle in Illinois when a tremendous snowstorm prevented the family from traveling any farther west at the time. The Taylors then discovered that they could buy a farm in the Sangamon Valley that was every bit as excellent as any in Iowa.[3594] Multiple Taylor families have contributed much to the civic and industrial life of Chicago.[3595]

The Robert Cunningham Taylor branch of the family included members who were residents of Hyde Park and Beverly, and who were owners and co-owners of large and important industrial companies in Chicago, Springfield, and Cass County. The Lachlan McNeil-Florey Taylor branch of the family included lawyers and businessmen who have developed business and industry in Chicago. Henry Stryker Taylor (1908-1994) was President of the Taylor Land and Investment Company, which was a major diversified land company of Illinois and Michigan. Henry S. Taylor also became one of the two largest individual (non-institutional) stockholders of the Pennsylvania Railroad Company, which was one of the largest corporations in the world. The Pennsylvania Railroad Company was one of the most important corporations of Philadelphia, New York City, and Chicago, as will be discussed below. Robert Cunningham Taylor, Jr. (1906-1944) was a banker, owner of a land and investment company, and a resident of the Hyde Park and Beverly communities of the South side of Chicago. Oswell Laurie McNeil was a Chicago lawyer, Northwestern University law alumnus, and founder of multiple Chicago corporations, including the National Sunday School Publishing Company, the Railway and Supplymen's Mutual Catalogue Company, Delmar's Candy and Ice Cream Company of Edgewater and Uptown, and a land company. Oswell was a resident of Chicago and Blue Island. Let us proceed to the Taylor genealogy, which forms the framework for this portion of the present chapter.

Angus Taylor (1735-1796) married Florence MacTavish (surname anglicized to Thompson, the English form of MacTavish). Their son, Robert Taylor (circa 1768-1819), married Mary "Miza" McCoig (1780-1845). Miza McCoig was the daughter of Neil McCoig (1735-1828) and Catherine (McKinven) McCoig (1745-1834) of Argyllshire, Scotland, and resided about ten miles from Campbelltown. The children born to Robert Taylor and Miza (McCoig) Taylor were the following: Angus Taylor; Neil Taylor, who married Margaret McMillian; Alexander Taylor; Archibald Taylor; **Florence "Florey" Taylor, who married Lachlan McNeil**; Duncan Taylor; John Taylor; **Robert Taylor, who married Jeanette**

[3592] Taylor, Flora E. (Undated). A Sketch Of The Taylor Family. Taylor family history records.
[3593] Taylor family history records.
[3594] Taylor, Flora E. (Undated). A Sketch Of The Taylor Family. Taylor family history records.
[3595] Taylor family history records.

Cunningham; and William MacDonald Taylor, who married Mary Ellen Horrom.[3596]

Florence "Florey" Taylor married Lachlan McNeil. Their children were Robert McNeil, who married Amanda Mavina Moore; Elizabeth McNeil; Mizey McNeil; Florence McNeil; Margaret McNeil, who married David Carr; and Charles McNeil, who married Mary Paschal.[3597]

Robert Lachlan McNeil married Amanda Mavina Moore. Robert and Amanda (Moore) McNeil had the following children: Florence McNeil; William L. McNeil; Archibald Lachlan McNeil; Anna Keziah McNeil; **Robert Lincoln McNeil**; **Oswell Laurie McNeil**; and Amanda McNeil.[3598] Florence (Taylor) McNeil was the sister of Robert Taylor (1816-1902), who was the father of Robert Cunningham Taylor, and the grandfather of Robert Cunningham Taylor, Jr., and Henry Stryker Taylor of Cass County, Springfield, and Chicago (see below).[3599]

Robert Taylor (1816-1902) married Jeanette Cunningham (1824-1910). Jeanette was the daughter of John Cunningham and Ellen (Taylor) Cunningham. John Cunningham was a native of Bonnington, Scotland, in metropolitan Edinburgh, and was a mill owner in Buffalo, New York, before relocating finally to Cass County, Illinois.[3600] The children born to Robert Taylor and Jeanette (Cunningham) Taylor were the following: Ellen Taylor; Angus Taylor, who married Mary Robertson; John Taylor; Flora Taylor; Margaret Taylor, who married Henry Campbell; Miza Taylor; Alice Taylor; Archibald Taylor, who married Margaret Reid; Duncan Taylor, who married Lillian Kendall; Katie Taylor; Janet Taylor, who married Will Sudbrink; and **Robert Cunningham Taylor, who married Charlotte Stryker**.[3601] The Taylor-McNeil family and the Taylor-Cunningham family both gave to the civic and industrial development of Chicago and Cook County. We will discuss the Chicago history of the Taylor-McNeil family first, and the Chicago history of the Taylor-Cunningham family second. The Cunninghams of Edinburgh and Bonnington were wealthy lairds and owned many industries of metropolitan Edinburgh for multiple generations.[3602]

[3596] Taylor, Flora E. (Undated). A Sketch Of The Taylor Family. Taylor family history records.

[3597] Taylor, Flora E. (Undated). A Sketch Of The Taylor Family. Taylor family history records.

[3598] Moore, Diana. McNeil family genealogy. Ancestry.com.

[3599] Taylor, Flora E. (Undated). A Sketch Of The Taylor Family. Taylor family history records.

[3600] Cox, Marcia. Taylor and Cunningham Family History; Taylor and Cunningham family history records.

[3601] Taylor, Flora E. (Undated). A Sketch Of The Taylor Family. Taylor family history records.

[3602] Cox, Marcia. Taylor and Cunningham Family History; Taylor and Cunningham family history records.

The Taylor and McNeil Branch of Chicago

This section of the chapter concerns the Chicago history of the McNeil and Taylor branches of my mother's family. The principal persons that appear in this chapter are Oswell Laurie McNeil and Robert Lincoln McNeil. The Taylor Family has been importantly connected to Chicago and Cook County since the early settlement period of the village and city.[3603] Oswell Laurie McNeil, who was a second cousin through the family of my grandfather, Henry Stryker Taylor, was one of many Taylors to spend considerable time in The Windy City.[3604] Oswell L. McNeil graduated from Northwestern University School of Law.[3605] McNeil also graduated from Illinois College in Jacksonville, Illinois.[3606] After graduation from Northwestern University in 1906, McNeil commenced the practice of law at Chicago. He was a member of the Delta Theta Phi Law Fraternity (Wigmore Chapter) at Northwestern University. McNeil combined law practice with engagement in different forms of business in Chicago.[3607] McNeil passed the Illinois bar examination on October 8, 1907, the notice of his success on the bar exam having been posted in 1908.[3608]

At the time of the announcement that McNeil had passed the Illinois bar examination, McNeil resided at 2645 Paulina Street, in Chicago.[3609] The 2645 Paulina address was probably the one located in the Lincoln Park Community of Chicago, and not the one located in the Lower West Side Community of Chicago. The Illinois bar examination was administered at Springfield, and under the authority of the Illinois State Board of Law Examiners.[3610] James Thomas Jarrell, Jr., of Delaware, and a graduate of Dickinson College, was a classmate and friend of Oswell McNeil's at Northwestern University.[3611]

[3603] See sources and references contained herein generally.

[3604] Taylor family records.

[3605] Northwestern University: Bulletin of the School of Law. (May-July, 1906). Series 5, Number 1. P. 35. Chicago, Illinois: Northwestern University Office of Publication. Google Books.

[3606] Northwestern University: Bulletin of the School of Law. (May-July, 1906). Series 5, Number 1. P. 35. Chicago, Illinois: Northwestern University Office of Publication. Google Books.

[3607] See sources and references herein, *infra*.

[3608] Bradwell, James B., Helmer, B. Bradwell (Editors). The Chicago Legal News: A Journal of Legal Intelligence. Vol. XL. (August 17, 1907-August 8, 1908). P. 71. Chicago, Illinois: Chicago Legal News Company. Google Books.

[3609] Bradwell, James B., Helmer, B. Bradwell (Editors). The Chicago Legal News: A Journal of Legal Intelligence. Vol. XL. (August 17, 1907-August 8, 1908). P. 71. Chicago, Illinois: Chicago Legal News Company. Google Books.

[3610] Bradwell, James B., Helmer, B. Bradwell (Editors). The Chicago Legal News: A Journal of Legal Intelligence. Vol. XL. (August 17, 1907-August 8, 1908). P. 71. Chicago, Illinois: Chicago Legal News Company. Google Books.

[3611] Northwestern University: Bulletin of the School of Law. (May-July, 1906). Series 5, Number 1. P. 35. Chicago, Illinois: Northwestern University Office of Publication. Google Books.

Jarrell and McNeil would remain friends and business colleagues in Chicago for many years after their graduation from Northwestern University.[3612] McNeil entered the publishing business in Chicago at least as early as 1908.[3613] The "New Incorporations" report contained in the *Chicago Tribune* edition of April 11, 1908, listed the incorporation of the National Sunday School Publishing society of Chicago.[3614] The report stated that $50,000 constituted the capitalization money at the time of incorporation. The report contained no further facts regarding the financing of the company.[3615] No description of the classes of financing, stock moneys, or debt moneys, accompanied the notice. The corporate purpose was described as, "general publishing and merchandising."[3616] Neal Chickering, Oswell McNeil, and E. M. Bumphrey were the three founders and incorporators of the National Sunday School Publishing Company.[3617] Searches for more information relevant to this company have failed to produce additional discoveries of information as of the time of authorship of this book.

On June 7, 1909, McNeil served as an incorporator of the Delmar's Candy & Ice Cream Company of Chicago. The company was small, having been incorporated with a capital of $2,500.[3618] The company incorporators were Oswell L. McNeil, James T. Jarrell, and W. R. Wiley.[3619] The corporate purpose of the company was the manufacture of candy and ice cream, and the operation of a restaurant.[3620] Delmar's Candy and Ice Cream Company owned a factory located at 1114 Bryn Mawr Avenue, located in the Edgewater neighborhood, and in what would technically be recognized in 1980 as the Edgewater community.[3621] The President/Manager of the company was William F. Neuert, who resided at 3732

[3612] See sources and references, *infra*.

[3613] Chicago Tribune. (April 11, 1908). P. 17. Newspapers.com.

[3614] Chicago Tribune. (April 11, 1908). P. 17. Newspapers.com.

[3615] Chicago Tribune. (April 11, 1908). P. 17. Newspapers.com.

[3616] Chicago Tribune. (April 11, 1908). P. 17. Newspapers.com.

[3617] Chicago Tribune. (April 11, 1908). P. 17. Newspapers.com.

[3618] The National Corporation Reporter: Devoted to the Interests of Business and Municipal Corporations, Law, Finance and Commerce. (February 18, 1909-August 12, 1909). Vol. 38. P. 523. Chicago, Illinois: The United States Corporation Bureau. Google Books.

[3619] The National Corporation Reporter: Devoted to the Interests of Business and Municipal Corporations, Law, Finance and Commerce. (February 18, 1909-August 12, 1909). Vol. 38. P. 523. Chicago, Illinois: The United States Corporation Bureau. Google Books.

[3620] The National Corporation Reporter: Devoted to the Interests of Business and Municipal Corporations, Law, Finance and Commerce. (February 18, 1909-August 12, 1909). Vol. 38. P. 523. Chicago, Illinois: The United States Corporation Bureau. Google Books.

[3621] Certified List of Illinois Corporations And Supplemental List of Foreign Corporations. (1911). P. 105. Danville, Illinois: Illinois Printing Company. Google Books.

Ward Street.[3622] The Secretary of the company was O. F. Paisley, who resided at 5801 Winthrop Avenue.[3623] The *1910 United States Census* indicated that McNeil was a lawyer and that he resided at 2036 W. Harrison Street.[3624] The McNeil residence was located in Ward 20, and in Census Enumeration District 864.[3625] The cartographic orientation of Census Enumeration District 864 placed the McNeil residence west of Robey Avenue (Damen), east of Leavitt Street, and near to Hoyne Avenue.[3626] This point is within or near the East Garfield Park community, the Near West Side community, and the Tri-Taylor Neighborhood.

Delmar's Candy Company (this was the abbreviated company name that appeared in this and in other advertisements in the *Chicago Daily Tribune*) advertised, "FRESH PEACH ICE CREAM," on July 26, 1912, in the *Chicago Daily Tribune*.[3627] Delmar's Candy Company manufactured its own candy.[3628] The ice cream retailed for sixty cents per quart.[3629] The company also advertised that it delivered to customers from the location of 1114 Bryn Mawr Avenue, in Edgewater.[3630] The telephone number provided for the company in the advertisement was Edgewater 1541.[3631] Only days later, Delmar's Candy Company advertised again in the *Chicago Daily Tribune* that they sold, "FRESH SALTED JUMBO PEANUTS."[3632] The peanuts were roasted daily and were sold for forty cents per pound.[3633] This advertisement appeared in the bargain section of the *Chicago Daily Tribune* from August 3, 1912.[3634] The location of the

---

[3622] Certified List of Illinois Corporations And Supplemental List of Foreign Corporations. (1911). P. 105. Danville, Illinois: Illinois Printing Company. Google Books.

[3623] Certified List of Illinois Corporations And Supplemental List of Foreign Corporations. (1911). P. 105. Danville, Illinois: Illinois Printing Company. Google Books.

[3624] 1910 United States Census.

[3625] 1910 United States Census.

[3626] 1910 Census Ward 20 Enumeration Districts of Chicago, Illinois. Alookatcook.com

[3627] Chicago Daily Tribune. (July 26, 1912). P. 7. Retrieved from ProQuest Newspapers: Chicago Tribune. Database at Northwestern University.

[3628] Chicago Daily Tribune. (July 26, 1912). P. 7. Retrieved from ProQuest Newspapers: Chicago Tribune. Database at Northwestern University.

[3629] Chicago Daily Tribune. (July 26, 1912). P. 7. Retrieved from ProQuest Newspapers: Chicago Tribune. Database at Northwestern University.

[3630] Chicago Daily Tribune. (July 26, 1912). P. 7. Retrieved from ProQuest Newspapers: Chicago Tribune. Database at Northwestern University.

[3631] Chicago Daily Tribune. (July 26, 1912). P. 7. Retrieved from ProQuest Newspapers: Chicago Tribune. Database at Northwestern University.

[3632] Chicago Daily Tribune. (August 3, 1912). P. 7. Retrieved from ProQuest Newspapers: Chicago Tribune. Database at Northwestern University.

[3633] Chicago Daily Tribune. (August 3, 1912). P. 7. Retrieved from ProQuest Newspapers: Chicago Tribune. Database at Northwestern University.

[3634] Chicago Daily Tribune. (August 3, 1912). P. 7. Retrieved from ProQuest Newspapers: Chicago Tribune. Database at Northwestern University.

company was 1114 Bryn Mawr, located in the Edgewater neighborhood.[3635] The Delmar's advertisement from the *Chicago Daily Tribune* of April 13, 1913, contained the following representation: "Many of our goodies are exclusive mixtures."[3636] The April 13, 1913, advertisement also represented the candy as "delicious and pure."[3637] This advertisement also showed that the company operated two separate stores at the time of the advertisement.[3638] One store was located at 1114 Bryn Mawr Avenue in Edgewater.[3639] The second store was located at 1068 Argyle Street.[3640] The latter place would be part of the Uptown community of the North Side of Chicago.

The Delmar's Candy Company advertisement in the *Chicago Tribune* from June 21, 1913, indicated that the company operated two stores.[3641] Again, the one store remained at the 1114 Bryn Mawr Avenue location in Edgewater.[3642] Likewise, the second store was located at 1068 Argyle Street.[3643] The company telephone number remained Edgewater 1541.[3644] The 1913 advertisement represented that the candies were manufactured in a "sanitary kitchen."[3645] The representation concerning the safety and quality of the candy factory echoed the social and sanitary concerns prevalent at the time, during the Progressive Era. Upton Sinclair had published his book, *The Jungle*, an exposition of the severe health issues that arose from the industrial processes associated with the Chicago meatpacking industry, in 1906, approximately one year prior to the establishment of Delmar's Candy and Ice Cream Company of Chicago. Though only an educated guess, the theory that Delmar's Candy and Ice Cream Company would wish to craft advertisements in a manner compatible with the safety and welfare concerns of the

---

[3635] Chicago Daily Tribune. (August 3, 1912). P. 7. Retrieved from ProQuest Newspapers: Chicago Tribune. Database at Northwestern University.

[3636] Chicago Daily Tribune. (April 13, 1913). P. H10. Retrieved from ProQuest Newspapers: Chicago Tribune. Database at Northwestern University.

[3637] Chicago Daily Tribune. (April 13, 1913). P. H10. Retrieved from ProQuest Newspapers: Chicago Tribune. Database at Northwestern University.

[3638] Chicago Daily Tribune. (April 13, 1913). P. H10. Retrieved from ProQuest Newspapers: Chicago Tribune. Database at Northwestern University.

[3639] Chicago Daily Tribune. (April 13, 1913). P. H10. Retrieved from ProQuest Newspapers: Chicago Tribune. Database at Northwestern University.

[3640] Chicago Daily Tribune. (April 13, 1913). P. H10. Retrieved from ProQuest Newspapers: Chicago Tribune. Database at Northwestern University.

[3641] Chicago Daily Tribune. (June 21, 1913). P. 11. Retrieved from ProQuest Newspapers: Chicago Tribune. Database at Northwestern University.

[3642] Chicago Daily Tribune. (June 21, 1913). P. 11. Retrieved from ProQuest Newspapers: Chicago Tribune. Database at Northwestern University.

[3643] Chicago Daily Tribune. (June 21, 1913). P. 11. Retrieved from ProQuest Newspapers: Chicago Tribune. Database at Northwestern University.

[3644] Chicago Daily Tribune. (June 21, 1913). P. 11. Retrieved from ProQuest Newspapers: Chicago Tribune. Database at Northwestern University.

[3645] Chicago Daily Tribune. (June 21, 1913). P. 11. Retrieved from ProQuest Newspapers: Chicago Tribune. Database at Northwestern University.

day, particularly being a Chicago manufacturing organization, remains most probable, credible, and convincing.

Delmar's Candy and Ice Cream Company advertised in the July 5, 1913, *Chicago Daily Tribune*.[3646] The company sought to employ immediately a, "SODA DISPENSER—FIRST CLASS, AT ONCE."[3647] The July 5, 1913, advertisement listed only one address for the company, the address of 1114 Bryn Mawr Avenue.[3648] The August 5, 1913, *Chicago Daily Tribune* advertisement for Delmar's Candy Company listed both the 1114 Bryn Mawr Avenue address, and the 1068 Argyle Street address.[3649] Records discovered thus far have not disclosed whether soda fountains were located at both of the company stores, or only at the 1114 Bryn Mawr Avenue store location.

In addition to having organized the McNeil Law Firm, Oswell McNeil entered the railway supply industry in Chicago.[3650] In approximately January, 1911, or perhaps slightly prior to that time, McNeil served as an incorporator of the Railway and Supply Men's Mutual Catalogue Company, a Chicago corporation whose purpose was the manufacture and publication of a catalogue of railroad supplies.[3651] The company was incorporated with a capital of $10,000.[3652] The incorporators of the catalogue production company were Oswell L. McNeil, Fred D. Jackson and G. K. Armstrong.[3653] The Railway and Supply Men's Mutual Catalogue Company participated in the Fourth Annual Exhibit of the Railway Appliances Association in Chicago.[3654] The exhibit was described prospectively in detail under the, "With the Manufacturers" segment of the *Railway Engineering and Maintenance of Way* journal, from the winter of 1912.[3655] The exhibit took place at the Coliseum in Chicago, and lasted from March 18 until March 23,

[3646] Chicago Daily Tribune. (July 5, 1913). P. 16. Retrieved from ProQuest Newspapers: Chicago Tribune. Database at Northwestern University.
[3647] Chicago Daily Tribune. (July 5, 1913). P. 16. Retrieved from ProQuest Newspapers: Chicago Tribune. Database at Northwestern University.
[3648] Chicago Daily Tribune. (July 5, 1913). P. 16. Retrieved from ProQuest Newspapers: Chicago Tribune. Database at Northwestern University.
[3649] Chicago Daily Tribune. (August 5, 1913). P. 16. Retrieved from ProQuest Newspapers: Chicago Tribune. Database at Northwestern University.
[3650] Printing Trade News. Vol. 40. Number 2. (January 14, 1911). P. 81. New York, NY. Google Books.
[3651] Printing Trade News. Vol. 40. Number 2. (January 14, 1911). P. 81. New York, NY. Google Books.
[3652] Printing Trade News. Vol. 40. Number 2. (January 14, 1911). P. 81. New York, NY. Google Books.
[3653] Printing Trade News. Vol. 40. Number 2. (January 14, 1911). P. 81. New York, NY. Google Books.
[3654] Railway Engineering and Maintenance of Way. (January, 1912). Vol. 8. Pp. 80-81. Chicago, Illinois: Railway Engineering and Maintenance of Way Office of Publication. Google Books.
[3655] Railway Engineering and Maintenance of Way. (January, 1912). Vol. 8. P. 80. Chicago, Illinois: Railway Engineering and Maintenance of Way Office of Publication. Google Books.

1912.[3656] The exhibit took place concurrently with the conference of the American Railway Engineering Association.[3657] The entire exhibit occupied more than 54,000 square feet of space, and included the Coliseum main floor space, annex, and balcony.[3658] The exhibit essentially overflowed the Coliseum space, and also occupied the First Regiment Armory located at Michigan Avenue and Sixteenth Street.[3659] Both the conference and the exhibit occupied the bulk of that week in 1912.[3660]

In February of 1913, McNeil was appointed a Notary Public at Chicago. Also in 1913, McNeil co-founded a company known as the Chicago Adjustment Agency.[3661] The business organization was incorporated with Oswell L. McNeil, James T. Jarrell, and S. Graff serving as the incorporators.[3662] The corporate capitalization money was $2,500.[3663] The report contained no description of the financing, but the small size of the investment money suggests that a simple equity financing was used for capitalization.[3664] Additional information concerning the Chicago Adjustment Agency has proved unavailable at this juncture.

[3656] Railway Engineering and Maintenance of Way. (January, 1912). Vol. 8. Pp. 80-81. Chicago, Illinois: Railway Engineering and Maintenance of Way Office of Publication. Google Books.

[3657] Railway Engineering and Maintenance of Way. (January, 1912). Vol. 8. Pp. 80-81. Chicago, Illinois: Railway Engineering and Maintenance of Way Office of Publication. Google Books.

[3658] Railway Engineering and Maintenance of Way. (January, 1912). Vol. 8. P. 80. Chicago, Illinois: Railway Engineering and Maintenance of Way Office of Publication. Google Books.

[3659] Railway Engineering and Maintenance of Way. (January, 1912). Vol. 8. P. 80. Chicago, Illinois: Railway Engineering and Maintenance of Way Office of Publication. Retrieved from

[3660] Railway Engineering and Maintenance of Way. (January, 1912). Vol. 8. P. 80. Chicago, Illinois: Railway Engineering and Maintenance of Way Office of Publication. Google Books.

[3661] The National Corporation Reporter: Devoted to the Interests of Business and Municipal Corporations, Law, Finance and Commerce. (February 13-August 7, 1913). Frederick A. Rowe, Editor. Vol. 46. P. 671. Chicago, Illinois: The United States Corporation Bureau. Google Books.

[3662] The National Corporation Reporter: Devoted to the Interests of Business and Municipal Corporations, Law, Finance and Commerce. (February 13-August 7, 1913). Frederick A. Rowe, Editor. Vol. 46. P. 671. Chicago, Illinois: United States Corporation Bureau. Google Books.

[3663] The National Corporation Reporter: Devoted to the Interests of Business and Municipal Corporations, Law, Finance and Commerce. (February 13-August 7, 1913). Frederick A. Rowe, Editor. Vol. 46. P. 671. Chicago, Illinois: United States Corporation Bureau. Google Books.

[3664] The National Corporation Reporter: Devoted to the Interests of Business and Municipal Corporations, Law, Finance and Commerce. (February 13-August 7, 1913). Frederick A. Rowe, Editor. Vol. 46. P. 671. Chicago, Illinois: United States Corporation Bureau. Google Books.

Oswell McNeil practiced corporate litigation at Chicago.[3665] He represented his fellow Northwestern University alumnus, colleague, and manufacturing business partner, James T. Jarrell, in the case of *James T. Jarrell v. Northwestern Elevated Railway Company* (Case number 3923).[3666] The State Public Utilities Commission of Illinois possessed jurisdiction over the case.[3667] The law case contained facts and issues that occurred within the Rogers Park community of Chicago.[3668] James T. Jarrell was at the time of the case a resident of Rogers Park.[3669] Central among the history and facts that composed the factual situation of the case was the improvement of passenger railroad transportation service in Rogers Park.[3670] The issues of the case involved these factors.[3671]

James T. Jarrell, who held the party status of *petitioner* in the case, brought suit against the Chicago utility organization known as the Northwestern Elevated Railway Company, which held the party status of *respondent*.[3672] The principal issue of the case involved the dispute over whether the Northwestern Elevated Railway Company would construct an elevated railway station at the place of North Shore Avenue in Rogers Park.[3673] Oswell McNeil, serving as counsel for petitioner James T. Jarrell, filed pleadings that were accompanied by the following prayer: that the utility company known as the Northwestern Elevated Railway Company would construct a railway station at the place of North Shore Avenue,

---

[3665] State Public Utilities Commission of Illinois. (1916). Opinions and Orders For the Year Ending November 30, 1915. Vol. 2. Pp. 285, 286. Springfield, Illinois: Illinois State Journal Co., State Printers. Google Books.

[3666] State Public Utilities Commission of Illinois. (1916). Opinions and Orders For the Year Ending November 30, 1915. Vol. 2. Pp. 285, 286. Springfield, Illinois: Illinois State Journal Co., State Printers. Google Books.

[3667] State Public Utilities Commission of Illinois. (1916). Opinions and Orders For the Year Ending November 30, 1915. Vol. 2. Pp. 285, 286. Springfield, Illinois: Illinois State Journal Co., State Printers. Google Books.

[3668] State Public Utilities Commission of Illinois. (1916). Opinions and Orders For the Year Ending November 30, 1915. Vol. 2. Pp. 285, 286. Springfield, Illinois: Illinois State Journal Co., State Printers. Google Books.

[3669] State Public Utilities Commission of Illinois. (1916). Opinions and Orders For the Year Ending November 30, 1915. Vol. 2. P. 285. Springfield, Illinois: Illinois State Journal Co., State Printers. Google Books.

[3670] State Public Utilities Commission of Illinois. (1916). Opinions and Orders For the Year Ending November 30, 1915. Vol. 2. Pp. 285, 286. Springfield, Illinois: Illinois State Journal Co., State Printers. Google Books.

[3671] State Public Utilities Commission of Illinois. (1916). Opinions and Orders For the Year Ending November 30, 1915. Vol. 2. Pp. 285, 286. Springfield, Illinois: Illinois State Journal Co., State Printers. Google Books.

[3672] State Public Utilities Commission of Illinois. (1916). Opinions and Orders For the Year Ending November 30, 1915. Vol. 2. Pp. 285, 286. Springfield, Illinois: Illinois State Journal Co., State Printers. Google Books.

[3673] State Public Utilities Commission of Illinois. (1916). Opinions and Orders For the Year Ending November 30, 1915. Vol. 2. Pp. 285, 286. Springfield, Illinois: Illinois State Journal Co., State Printers. Google Books.

located in Rogers Park.[3674] Petitioner Jarrell filed complaint upon the grounds that the distance that existed between the Loyola Station and the Morse Station exceeded the average distance that existed between the railway stations located at other places within the Edgewater and Rogers Parks route systems of the respondent's railway system.[3675] Petitioner Jarrell, through Oswell McNeil, relied upon a theory in which recovery was formulated through the lessening of station interval distance by means of construction of the North Shore Avenue station at a point between the respondent's railway stations in Rogers Park.[3676] Grounds for the suit implicitly hinged on the need for transit development in Rogers Park through improvements to access to transportation service.[3677] These constituted the petitioner's pleadings, complaint, prayer, theory of recovery, reasons, and grounds for filing of the suit with the Illinois Public Utilities Commission.[3678]

McNeil filed the aforementioned pleadings, testimonies, prayer, complaint, grounds, reasons, and theory of recovery to obtain from the Illinois Public Utilities Commission a judgment that would obligate the respondent's construction of the station at North Shore Avenue in Rogers Park.[3679] McNeil filed testimony to support the pleadings and prayer that were filed for petitioner Jarrell.[3680] The petitioner's testimony included statements from residents of Rogers Park that indicated the residents' preference and potential market for the railway station at North Shore Avenue.[3681] Respondent company filed an answer to Jarrell's

[3674] State Public Utilities Commission of Illinois. (1916). Opinions and Orders For the Year Ending November 30, 1915. Vol. 2. Pp. 285, 286. Springfield, Illinois: Illinois State Journal Co., State Printers. Google Books.

[3675] State Public Utilities Commission of Illinois. (1916). Opinions and Orders For the Year Ending November 30, 1915. Vol. 2. Pp. 285, 286. Springfield, Illinois: Illinois State Journal Co., State Printers. Google Books.

[3676] State Public Utilities Commission of Illinois. (1916). Opinions and Orders For the Year Ending November 30, 1915. Vol. 2. Pp. 285, 286. Springfield, Illinois: Illinois State Journal Co., State Printers. Google Books.

[3677] State Public Utilities Commission of Illinois. (1916). Opinions and Orders For the Year Ending November 30, 1915. Vol. 2. Pp. 285, 286. Springfield, Illinois: Illinois State Journal Co., State Printers. Google Books.

[3678] State Public Utilities Commission of Illinois. (1916). Opinions and Orders For the Year Ending November 30, 1915. Vol. 2. Pp. 285, 286. Springfield, Illinois: Illinois State Journal Co., State Printers. Google Books.

[3679] State Public Utilities Commission of Illinois. (1916). Opinions and Orders For the Year Ending November 30, 1915. Vol. 2. Pp. 285, 286. Springfield, Illinois: Illinois State Journal Co., State Printers. Google Books.

[3680] State Public Utilities Commission of Illinois. (1916). Opinions and Orders For the Year Ending November 30, 1915. Vol. 2. Pp. 285, 286. Springfield, Illinois: Illinois State Journal Co., State Printers. Google Books.

[3681] State Public Utilities Commission of Illinois. (1916). Opinions and Orders For the Year Ending November 30, 1915. Vol. 2. Pp. 285, 286. Springfield, Illinois: Illinois State Journal Co., State Printers. Google Books.

complaint.[3682] Here follows analysis of the relevant places and distances that constituted the physical element of the issue in the case.

<u>Distances Between the Relevant Railway Stations of Respondent Northwestern Elevated Railway Company</u>

1. Loyola Avenue Station to Morse Avenue Station: 3,028 feet.[3683]
2. Loyola Avenue Station to proposed North Shore Avenue Station: 1,320 feet.[3684]
3. Average distance between respondent's railway stations from North Edgewater Station to the northern terminus of the respondent's railway line: 2,500 feet.[3685]

One will notice that the first listed distance of 3,028 feet, between Loyola Avenue Station and Morse Avenue Station, is significantly greater than the average distances between the relevant railway stations operated by the respondent company.[3686] One will also notice that the distance between Loyola Avenue Station and Morse Avenue Station is even more dramatically great than the distance between the Loyola Avenue Station and the proposed North Shore Avenue Station.[3687] Oswell McNeil formulated a remedy and theory of recovery that was derived from the differences among these comparative distances, and this would have plausibly served not only as an improvement to access, but as an aid to the development of Rogers Park and Edgewater.[3688]

[3682] State Public Utilities Commission of Illinois. (1916). Opinions and Orders For the Year Ending November 30, 1915. Vol. 2. Pp. 285, 286. Springfield, Illinois: Illinois State Journal Co., State Printers. Google Books.
[3683] State Public Utilities Commission of Illinois. (1916). Opinions and Orders For the Year Ending November 30, 1915. Vol. 2. P. 286. Springfield, Illinois: Illinois State Journal Co., State Printers. Google Books.
[3684] State Public Utilities Commission of Illinois. (1916). Opinions and Orders For the Year Ending November 30, 1915. Vol. 2. P. 286. Springfield, Illinois: Illinois State Journal Co., State Printers. Google Books.
[3685] State Public Utilities Commission of Illinois. (1916). Opinions and Orders For the Year Ending November 30, 1915. Vol. 2. P. 286. Springfield, Illinois: Illinois State Journal Co., State Printers. Google Books.
[3686] State Public Utilities Commission of Illinois. (1916). Opinions and Orders For the Year Ending November 30, 1915. Vol. 2. P. 286. Springfield, Illinois: Illinois State Journal Co., State Printers. Google Books.
[3687] State Public Utilities Commission of Illinois. (1916). Opinions and Orders For the Year Ending November 30, 1915. Vol. 2. P. 286. Springfield, Illinois: Illinois State Journal Co., State Printers. Google Books.
[3688] State Public Utilities Commission of Illinois. (1916). Opinions and Orders For the Year Ending November 30, 1915. Vol. 2. Pp. 285, 286. Springfield, Illinois: Illinois State Journal Co., State Printers. Google Books.

The State Public Utilities Commission of Illinois granted hearing of the case on July 15, 1915.[3689] The hearing took place at Chicago.[3690] The Commission's deliberation produced a judgment for respondent company that resulted in a denial of petitioner Jarrell's prayer, and a quashal of petitioner Jarrell's complaint.[3691] The reasons and grounds supplied by the Commission, and upon which the Commission based its judgment of the issue, its denial of the petitioner's prayer, and its quashal of the petitioner's complaint, included the fact that despite the comparatively longer distance that existed between respondent's Loyola Station and Morse Station, the place of service at issue in Rogers Park still received transit service to and from downtown Chicago by means of the Chicago and Northwestern Railway Company and by means of surface car services that operated within several blocks of the North Shore Avenue location.[3692] Consequently, multiple alternatives existed for passenger transportation service near the eastern segment of North Shore Avenue in Rogers Park. These service alternatives obviated the urgency of any additional station construction in that neighborhood.

Oswell McNeil and James Jarrell both held real estate interests in Edgewater.[3693] McNeil sold an amount of real estate to Jarrell in 1915.[3694] The real estate was located on Foster Avenue, 120 feet east of Winthrop Avenue.[3695] Attached to the land was an unspecified encumbrance valued at $10,000.[3696] The undescribed encumbrance was probably a mortgage. McNeil was a resident also of Blue Island in southern Cook County. McNeil possibly suggested to his cousin, Robert Cunningham Taylor, Jr., that Taylor move to the Beverly community of Chicago, which adjoins Blue Island to the north. We will next discuss the Chicago history of the Taylor-Cunningham family.

<u>The Taylor and Cunningham Branch of Chicago, Cass County, and Springfield</u>

Robert Taylor married Jeannette Cunningham, the daughter of John Cunningham and Ellen (Taylor) Cunningham, all of whom were natives of Argyle, Scotland, or

[3689] State Public Utilities Commission of Illinois. (1916). Opinions and Orders For the Year Ending November 30, 1915. Vol. 2. P. 285. Springfield, Illinois: Illinois State Journal Co., State Printers. Google Books.

[3690] State Public Utilities Commission of Illinois. (1916). Opinions and Orders For the Year Ending November 30, 1915. Vol. 2. P. 285. Springfield, Illinois: Illinois State Journal Co., State Printers. Google Books.

[3691] State Public Utilities Commission of Illinois. (1916). Opinions and Orders For the Year Ending November 30, 1915. Vol. 2. Pp. 285, 286. Springfield, Illinois: Illinois State Journal Co., State Printers. Google Books.

[3692] State Public Utilities Commission of Illinois. (1916). Opinions and Orders For the Year Ending November 30, 1915. Vol. 2. Pp. 285, 286. Springfield, Illinois: Illinois State Journal Co., State Printers. Google Books.

[3693] The Economist. (July 3, 1915). P. 44. Chicago, Illinois. Google Books.

[3694] The Economist. (July 3, 1915). P. 44. Chicago, Illinois. Google Books.

[3695] The Economist. (July 3, 1915). P. 44. Chicago, Illinois. Google Books.

[3696] The Economist. (July 3, 1915). P. 44. Chicago, Illinois. Google Books.

suburban Edinburgh. The Cunninghams, like the Taylors, immigrated to and settled in Cass County, Illinois, during the nineteenth century.[3697] Andrew Cunningham, son of James Cunningham and Marion (Wright) Cunningham of Bonnington, Scotland, an important industrial suburb of Edinburgh, was the uncle of Jeannette Cunningham. James Cunningham of Bonnington and Edinburgh owned extensive manufacturing companies, including a grist mill and a carding mill.[3698] Edinburgh-native Andrew Cunningham immigrated to Chicago in approximately 1834-1835.[3699] Andrew Cunningham traveled extensively throughout the frontier Midwest, having spent considerable amounts of time at Chicago and at Detroit, Michigan. Eventually, Andrew Cunningham settled in Cass County, Illinois.[3700] Cunningham relocated to Chicago for a time to attend a business college there.[3701] The author has not yet been able to identify and confirm the name of the Chicago business college that he attended. Cunningham walked several thousand miles throughout the Midwest and Great Lakes region in the early nineteenth century, collecting experiences and notes, and killing rattlesnakes with his walking stick at night on the trails.[3702] He was a consummate explorer and documenter of the Great Lakes and general Midwest, and was very familiar with Chicago and Detroit, having spent a lot of time in both settlements.[3703]

Charles Cunningham, son of James Cunningham and Marion (Wright) Cunningham, and brother of John Cunningham of Cass County, Illinois, and Andrew Cunningham of Chicago and Cass County, Illinois, remained in Europe.[3704] Charles Cunningham served the British Empire as Her Royal Majesty Queen Victoria's Consul to Galatz in Romania.[3705] Cunningham also served as

---

[3697] Cox, Marcia Ferguson. History of the Taylor and Cunningham Families of Cass County, Illinois; Cass County, Illinois Genealogy and History (Genealogy Trails History Group). Genealogytrails.com.

[3698] Cox, Marcia Ferguson. History of the Taylor and Cunningham Families of Cass County, Illinois; see also: Bell, Thomas. (Date not known). Master's Thesis about Andrew Cunningham. University of Illinois; Cass County, Illinois Genealogy and History (Genealogy Trails History Group). Genealogytrails.com.

[3699] Cox, Marcia Ferguson. History of the Taylor and Cunningham Families of Cass County, Illinois; see also: Bell, Thomas. (Date not known). Master's Thesis about Andrew Cunningham. University of Illinois.

[3700] Memoirs of Andrew Cunningham; Cox, Marcia Ferguson. History of the Taylor and Cunningham Families of Cass County, Illinois; see also: Bell, Thomas. (Date not known). Master's Thesis about Andrew Cunningham. University of Illinois.

[3701] Cox, Marcia Ferguson. History of the Taylor and Cunningham Families of Cass County, Illinois.

[3702] Bell, Thomas. (Date not known). Master's Thesis about Andrew Cunningham. University of Illinois.

[3703] Bell, Thomas. (Date not known). Master's Thesis about Andrew Cunningham. University of Illinois.

[3704] Cox, Marcia Ferguson. History of the Taylor and Cunningham Families of Cass County, Illinois.

[3705] Blair's Executors, et al. v. Taylor, et al. (January 18, 1876). Cases Decided In The Court Of Session, Court Of Justiciary, And House Of Lords, From July 20, 1875, To

British Consul to Turkey.[3706] Charles Cunningham engaged as a merchant at Smyrna (now Izmir), located in western Turkey along the Anatolian coast of the Aegean Sea.[3707] While stationed at Galatz, in Romania, Charles Cunningham contributed centrally to the establishment of the Danube River Commission, an organization that sought to regulate European economies and taxation laws along the Danube River.[3708] Galatz, also spelled Galati, is a major port city along the Danube River and is located northwest of the point of debouchment of the Danube at the Black Sea. Historian Edward Krehbiel stated in his 1918 study of the multinational public administration of the Danube River and the commerce and laws pertinent to it that Charles Cunningham was the originator of the Danube River Commission, a multilateral European organization whose jurisdiction encompassed the laws and policies relevant to Danube River commerce.[3709] Krehbiel stated:

> "The suggestion to establish an international commission to free the river from impediments seems to have originated with Charles Cunningham, British vice-consul at Galatz, who in a report of September 30, 1850, proposed as one of several methods 'that the different nations interested in the navigation of the Danube should name Commissioners (as seems to be done on the Rhine), and the Commission to attend to the duties of clearing the Sulina,' a branch of the Danube delta."[3710]

Robert "Bert" Cunningham Taylor (1868-1936) was the youngest of the thirteen children of Robert Taylor and Jeanette (Cunningham) Taylor, and the grand-nephew of British Imperial Consul Charles Cunningham of Great Britain, Romania, Turkey, and Russia (discussed immediately above). Bert Taylor was a graduate of Knox College in Galesburg, Illinois, where he had been a member of the Drama Club. Robert engaged in banking, retail, agribusiness, and land

---

August 15, 1876. Fourth Series, Vol. III. P. 362. Edinburgh, Scotland: T. & T. Clark, Law Booksellers. Google Books.

[3706] Blair's Executors, et al. v. Taylor, et al. (January 18, 1876). Cases Decided In The Court Of Session, Court Of Justiciary, And House Of Lords, From July 20, 1875, To August 15, 1876. Fourth Series, Vol. III. P. 362. Edinburgh, Scotland: T. & T. Clark, Law Booksellers. Google Books.

[3707] Blair's Executors, et al. v. Taylor, et al. (January 18, 1876). Cases Decided In The Court Of Session, Court Of Justiciary, And House Of Lords, From July 20, 1875, To August 15, 1876. Fourth Series, Vol. III. P. 362. Edinburgh, Scotland: T. & T. Clark, Law Booksellers. Google Books.

[3708] Krehbiel, Edward. (March, 1918). The European Commission of the Danube: An Experiment in International Administration. *Political Science Quarterly*. Pp. 38-55. Jstor.org.

[3709] Krehbiel, Edward. (March, 1918). The European Commission of the Danube: An Experiment in International Administration. *Political Science Quarterly*. Pp. 38-55. Jstor.org.

[3710] Krehbiel, Edward. (March, 1918). The European Commission of the Danube: An Experiment in International Administration. *Political Science Quarterly*. P. 39. Jstor.org.

businesses in Cass County and in the surrounding counties. The People's Bank of Virginia, located in Virginia, Cass County, Illinois, had been co-founded in 1918 by Robert Cunningham Taylor, father of Henry Taylor. Bert Taylor served as President of the People's Bank of Virginia. Additionally, he served as co-founder of the Cass County Title & Trust Company, and as a partner in the furniture and funeral service company known as King & Taylor, in the Town of Virginia.

Bert Taylor also operated a large land and farm company that possessed extensive property throughout Illinois. Bert married Charlotte Stryker in April, 1905. Charlotte was thirty. Charlotte Stryker of Jacksonville, Morgan County, Illinois, was the daughter of Judge Henry Stryker, Jr., and Elizabeth Henshaw (McClure) Stryker. The Stryker family and the McClure family both included multiple founders of Chicago, Cook County, and Chicago industry. The extended Stryker-McClure-Henshaw family included direct and collateral ancestors who were instrumental in the founding of both the State of Illinois and Chicago. Robert Cunningham Taylor and Charlotte Stryker both, therefore, descended from founding families or early settling families of Chicago and Cook County.

Robert Cunningham Taylor and Charlotte (Stryker) Taylor had two sons: Robert Cunningham Taylor, Jr. (1906-1944), and the aforementioned Henry Stryker Taylor (1908-1994). Robert Cunningham Taylor, Jr., known as "Bob," graduated from Virginia High School (Cass County, Illinois) as Valedictorian. He graduated from Knox College in 1929.[3711] After moving to Chicago and working at a bank as a clerk for a time, Bob completed a Master of Business Administration degree at Harvard University, having graduated in the Class of 1931.[3712] Bob Taylor moved to Chicago at least as early as 1930.[3713] Bob worked as a bank clerk as of April, 1930, when Donald Weaver collected and recorded the Census information from Ward 5 in Chicago.[3714] Discovery of the name of the bank at which Taylor was employed has not yet occurred. Bob also operated an investment company, and at the time of his death in 1944, he controlled thousands of shares of stock in the United States Steel Corporation, as well as other properties.[3715] The form of the investment business appears from both the legal record and the historical record to have been a sole proprietorship company.[3716]

The *1930 United States Census* listed Robert C. Taylor, Jr., as a resident of 5124 Harper Avenue in Chicago.[3717] He was a roomer at this address. The Taylor residence was within Ward 5 and within Census Enumeration District 16-164.[3718]

[3711] Galesburg Register-Mail. (November 17, 1953). P. 21. Newspapers.com; Harvard Alumni Bulletin. (1945). Vol. 47, Issue 14. Page number unavailable. Google Books.

[3712] Galesburg Register-Mail. (November 17, 1953). P. 21. Newspapers.com; Harvard Alumni Bulletin. (1945). Vol. 47, Issue 14. Page number unavailable. Google Books; 1930 United States census. Ancestry.com.

[3713] 1930 United States census. Ancestry.com.

[3714] 1930 United States census. Ancestry.com.

[3715] Will and Estate of Robert Cunningham Taylor, Jr. (1944). Cass County, Illinois.

[3716] Will and Estate of Robert Cunningham Taylor, Jr. (1944). Cass County, Illinois.

[3717] 1930 United States census. Ancestry.com.

[3718] 1930 United States census. Ancestry.com.

The Taylor residence was located within the Hyde Park Community, close to the boundary of the Kenwood Community and the Hyde Park Community.[3719] Two important landmark buildings and organizations that were located very close to the Robert C. Taylor, Jr., residence, in 1930, included the Hyde Park-Kenwood National Bank and the Timothy Beach Blackstone Memorial Library.

Although it is only a theory, it was possible, even probable, that Bob Taylor worked at the newly-established Hyde Park-Kenwood National Bank, which was located only two blocks from the Taylor residence in Hyde Park.[3720] The Hyde Park-Kenwood National Bank entered existence in 1929, and was the outcome of the combination of the Hyde Park Bank and the Kenwood Bank.[3721] The consolidated capital resource money of the new Hyde Park-Kenwood National Bank consisted of $12,000,000 at the time of the merger.[3722] The bank celebrated a grand opening on April 20, 1929, and the opening celebration and party occupied most of the day, having taken place from 8:00 A.M. until 9:00 P.M.[3723] The new 10-story office building contained the banking space, as well as club space, and office space.[3724] The founding leadership structure and membership for the Hyde Park-Kenwood National bank included the following persons and jobs.

Person	**Job**
John A. Carroll	Chairman of the Board of Directors
Eugene E. Ford	President
Matthew A. Harmon	Vice-President
Edwin S. Ford	Vice-President
E. Abegg	Vice-President
John J. O'Connell	Secretary
Frank L. Johnson	Cashier
Irene M. Reynolds	Assistant Cashier
H. H. Potter	Assistant Cashier
Frederick A. Helmholz	Assistant Cashier
Ernest F. Smelter	Assistant Cashier
W. H. Willis	Assistant Cashier[3725]

Board of Directors

A. K. Brown
Leonard J. Burke
John A. Carroll

[3719] 1930 Census Ward 5 Enumeration Districts of Chicago, Illinois. Alookatcook.com.
[3720] 1930 United States census. Ancestry.com; Chicago Tribune. (April 20, 1929). P. 25. Newspapers.com.
[3721] Chicago Tribune. (April 20, 1929). P. 25. Newspapers.com.
[3722] Chicago Tribune. (April 20, 1929). P. 25. Newspapers.com.
[3723] Chicago Tribune. (April 20, 1929). P. 25. Newspapers.com.
[3724] Chicago Tribune. (April 20, 1929). P. 25. Newspapers.com.
[3725] Chicago Tribune. (April 20, 1929). P. 25. Newspapers.com.

Thomas A. Collins
Eugene E. Ford
Edwin S. Ford
Matthew A. Harmon
Frank W. Howes
Charles E. Fox
Frederic J. Greenebaum
Robert R. Levy
Willis O. Nance
Mark J. Oliver
William J. Pringle
W. W. Sherman[3726]

Civic vision, coupled with municipal and community-based patriotism, accompanied the grand opening of the bank. The *Chicago Tribune* edition of April 20, 1929, included a large notice of the creation of the Hyde Park-Kenwood National Bank, and an equally large enthusiasm for the civic ramifications of the new South Side organization.[3727] The words of the report and notice stated that the bank would cause, "the permanent establishment of the corner of 53rd Street and Lake Park Avenue as Hyde Park's center of gravity."[3728] Chicago historian, author, banker, and civic leader, Janice A. Knox, has stated that this particular neighborhood of Hyde Park community was known as Hyde Park Center, because of its commercial centrality within the community.[3729]

The promotional report and notice exuded a sense of the bank as the center of Hyde Park and as the anchor of the downtown of the Hyde Park community.[3730] Civic loyalty to Kenwood and Hyde Park also manifested through the *Chicago Tribune*'s journalistic language, and indicated that the bank was a triumph for the public interests and the private interests of, "Outlying Banking. . .[and] general outlying *business development*."[3731] While no proofs or evidences have been discovered to confirm the theory that Bob Taylor worked for the new Hyde Park-Kenwood National Bank in 1929 or 1930, the theory nevertheless possesses probability and credibility, both because of the proximity of the Taylor residence to the newly-formed bank in April of 1930, and because no proofs or evidences have yet been discovered to challenge the theory.[3732] Also, the prominence of the new financial organization would have created its own set of opportunities desirable for young bankers, such as the 23-year-old Taylor, who was just starting out in the Chicago banking profession at that time.[3733]

[3726] Chicago Tribune. (April 20, 1929). P. 25. Newspapers.com.

[3727] Chicago Tribune. (April 20, 1929). P. 25. Newspapers.com.

[3728] Chicago Tribune. (April 20, 1929). P. 25. Newspapers.com.

[3729] Knox, Janice A. Multiple historical discussions with Andrew Taylor Call.

[3730] Chicago Tribune. (April 20, 1929). P. 25. Newspapers.com.

[3731] Chicago Tribune. (April 20, 1929). P. 25. Newspapers.com.

[3732] 1930 United States census. Ancestry.com

[3733] 1930 United States census. Ancestry.com

Bob Taylor returned to Chicago after graduation from the school of business of Harvard University, and resided at approximately 105th Street and Campbell Avenue in the Beverly community.[3734] The precise house number was partially obscured by an imperfection in the paper and ink within the original document and report.[3735] The Beverly community is located at the far southwestern corner of the City of Chicago, and adjoins the other City of Chicago communities of Morgan Park, Washington Heights, and Mt. Greenwood. The independent Cook County municipalities of Blue Island, Harvey, and South Holland are close to Beverly. Bob Taylor's cousin, Oswell L. McNeil, Esq., resided at Blue Island, a suburb located close to the Beverly, Morgan Park, and Mt. Greenwood communities. It is possible that McNeil had suggested the Beverly community to Taylor as a place of residence. John Stryker, as a founder and owner of the Chicago & Rock Island Railroad Company, contributed much to the creation of Beverly, Morgan Park, Mt. Greenwood, and Washington Heights, among other places.

Robert "Bert" Cunningham Taylor, Sr. died in 1936, having suffered a heart attack the day he retired from banking, which was the day that President Franklin Delano Roosevelt ordered the banks to close during the Great Depression. Bert collapsed on the floor of the People's Bank of Virginia (in Cass County, Illinois), and his son Henry had to carry him home.[3736] Bert died the day he retired as president of the People's Bank of Virginia, Illinois, the bank he had co-founded eighteen years prior.[3737] Bob Taylor served in World War II, and was killed in action during Operation Market Garden. Bob was interred at Margraaten Cemetery in The Netherlands.

Henry Stryker Taylor, known often as "Hanko," inherited the large business interests held by both his father and brother. Henry managed the extensive farm land holdings and remained in banking, but at Springfield.[3738] At some point in time near 1937, Henry met Elizabeth "Biz" Bunn at a party at The Drake Hotel in Chicago.[3739] Elizabeth Bunn, daughter of Willard Bunn and Ruth (Regan) Bunn, attended Northwestern University, where she was a Voice Major.[3740] At Northwestern, Elizabeth served as Co-Chair of the Social Committee for the Willard Hall Annex, and then pledged Kappa Alpha Theta Sorority. She resided at Willard Hall in her freshman year at Northwestern and resided at Kappa Alpha Theta Sorority in her sophomore year there. Henry Taylor and Elizabeth Bunn married in 1938, at Springfield, Illinois. Henry was raised in a Presbyterian home, and Elizabeth was a Roman Catholic.[3741] Biz and Henry were both accomplished golfers in Illinois, Michigan, and Florida, and were members of the Illini Country

---

[3734] Chicago Telephone Directories. (September, 1936-June, 1937).
[3735] Chicago Telephone Directories. (September, 1936-June, 1937).
[3736] Taylor family records.
[3737] Taylor family historical records.
[3738] Taylor family records.
[3739] Taylor family records.
[3740] Taylor and Bunn family records.
[3741] Taylor and Bunn family records.

Club in Springfield, the Wequetonsing Golf Club and Little Harbor Club in Michigan, and the Gulf Stream Golf Club, the Little Club, the Delray Beach Club, and the Everglades Club, all in Palm Beach County, Florida. Henry and Biz Taylor were also founding members of the Delray Yacht Club of Delray Beach, Florida, and were founding members of the Little Club in Gulf Stream, Florida.

Track Lanes and Railroad Tracks

After graduation from Virginia High School in Virginia, Illinois, Henry Stryker Taylor attended Knox College, from which he graduated in 1930. Robert "Bert" Cunningham Taylor, Sr., and Robert "Bob" Cunningham Taylor, Jr., both graduated from Knox College, and Henry followed them there. A champion sprinter, Henry S. Taylor earned four letters in track, was Captain of the Knox College Track Team during his senior year and set a Knox College record for performance in the 100-Yard Dash event.[3742] Taylor ran the 100-Yard Dash in 9.6 seconds and won championships in both the 100-Yard Dash and the 220-Yard Dash events during his junior and senior years at Knox. His achievements in track earned him the moniker, "The Knox Flash."[3743] He served as Treasurer of the Knox College Senior Class.[3744] He also was a member of the Glee Club, the K-Council, and the Phi Delta Gamma fraternity at Knox.[3745]

After graduation from Knox in 1930, Taylor entered the Olympic Games trials for Track and Field for the 1932 Olympic Games in Los Angeles. He joined the Los Angeles Athletic Club and trained under Coach Boyd Comstock for the Games.[3746] The trials would prove dramatic for Taylor, because he defeated every contestant at the Los Angeles Olympic trials but one other man, whom he tied for first place.[3747] The Olympic Games officials elected the coin toss as the means by which to judge which of the two sprinters would enter the Olympic Games. Taylor received the downside of the coin toss and was consequently eliminated from the Olympic Games by the randomness of chance.[3748] He returned to Illinois, where he worked for his father's bank, the Peoples Bank of Virginia, located on the southwest corner of the Virginia Town Square.[3749] Taylor would always be remembered by his family and friends as the champion sprinter from Cass County. Henry Taylor's three daughters donated, in 1993, the Henry Stryker Taylor Sprint

---

[3742] Taylor family records.

[3743] The Knox-Lombard Athletic Hall of Fame. *Henry S. Taylor*. Knox College Prairie Fire. Prairiefire.knox.edu; Taylor family records.

[3744] The Knox-Lombard Athletic Hall of Fame. *Henry S. Taylor*. Knox College Prairie Fire. Prairiefire.knox.edu; Taylor family records.

[3745] The Knox-Lombard Athletic Hall of Fame. *Henry S. Taylor*. Knox College Prairie Fire. Prairiefire.knox.edu; Taylor family records.

[3746] The Knox-Lombard Athletic Hall of Fame. *Henry S. Taylor*. Knox College Prairie Fire. Prairiefire.knox.edu; Taylor family records.

[3747] Taylor family records.

[3748] Taylor family records.

[3749] Taylor family records.

Lanes to the T. Fleming Fieldhouse at Knox College, in honor of their father and his outstanding record in track.

Henry Taylor would remain connected to Chicago business in different ways for multiple years. He was said to have been a major depositor at the Northern Trust Company of Chicago and was said to have served on the board of directors of the Northern Trust Company.[3750] The fact of this membership on the board of directors of the Northern Trust Company has not been confirmed but was related in a memoir by a deceased family member, Margot McKay, who knew Henry and Elizabeth very well as a close friend and Regan family first cousin in Chicago.[3751]

Henry was a member of both the Chicago Athletic Association and the Racquet Club of Chicago.[3752] Henry Taylor's largest connection to Chicago and Cook County would have been his ownership and leadership association with the Pennsylvania Railroad Company. This was so not only because of the immense presence of the Pennsylvania Railroad Company as a Chicago company, but also through the diverse and voluminous array of subsidiary companies in Chicago that the Pennsylvania Railroad Company owned at the time when Henry Taylor and Howard Butcher were the two largest individual (non-institutional) stockholders of the railroad.[3753] During the decade of the 1960s, Henry Taylor and Howard Butcher were the two largest individual (natural person) shareholders of the Pennsylvania Railroad Company.[3754] The fact of Taylor's majority stockholder position in the Pennsylvania Railroad had been attested multiple times over multiple years by multiple people who knew Taylor, but the truth of the fact was finally confirmed by official testimony found within the records of railroad merger policy analysis hearings before the United States Senate.[3755]

Allow us now to discuss the specific facts concerning the Pennsylvania Railroad Company and its profound presence in Chicago and Cook County, as well as in the surrounding geographical region. The Pennsylvania Railroad Company was incorporated on April 13, 1846, under the authority of the corporation laws of the Commonwealth of Pennsylvania.[3756] A new line was added from Harrisburg to

---

[3750] McKay, Margot. (Undated). Oral Family History Memoir conducted telephonically by Andrew Taylor Call.

[3751] McKay, Margot. (Undated). Oral Family History Memoir conducted telephonically by Andrew Taylor Call with Margot McKay.

[3752] Taylor family oral memoirs (undated).

[3753] Railway Carmen's Journal. (1962). Vols. 67-68. Brotherhood Railway Carmen of the United States and Canada.

[3754] Hearings Before The Subcommittee On Antitrust and Monopoly Of The Committee On The Judiciary, United States Senate. (1962). Eighty-Seventh Congress, Second Session. Part 2. Pp. 1305-1306.

[3755] Hearings Before The Subcommittee On Antitrust and Monopoly Of The Committee On The Judiciary, United States Senate. (1962). Eighty-Seventh Congress, Second Session. Part 2. Pp. 1305-1306.

[3756] St. Clair, Frank J. (Editor-in-Chief) (1962). Moody's Transportation Manual: Railroads-Airlines-Shipping-Traction, Bus And Truck Lines American and Foreign. Pp. 1080, 1093, 1116-1117, 1125-1126, 1135-1136. New York, NY: Moody's Investors Service, Inc.

Altoona, Pennsylvania, in 1850.[3757] Additional rail line was constructed from Altoona to Pittsburgh, in the year 1852.[3758] The Pennsylvania Railroad Company connected to Chicago and Cook County at a relatively early time in the company's organizational history.[3759] Newton Bateman, Paul Selby, and Alexander Strange reported the history of certain principal elements of the Pennsylvania Railroad Company presence at Chicago in their *1918 Historical Encyclopedia of Illinois*.[3760]

The Pennsylvania Railroad Company contracted to lease of the Pittsburgh, Fort Wayne & Chicago Railway Company.[3761] The time of the corporate lease began on July 1, 1869, and was contracted for a time of 999 years.[3762] The Pittsburgh, Fort Wayne & Chicago Railway Company was established from the joinder and union of three prior railroad companies: the Ohio & Pennsylvania, the Fort Wayne & Chicago, and the Ohio & Indiana.[3763] The consolidation took place on August 1, 1856.[3764] The new company opened for full transportational service in 1859.[3765] The company was subsequently sold under terms of foreclosure in 1861.[3766] The

---

[3757] St. Clair, Frank J. (Editor-in-Chief) (1962). Moody's Transportation Manual: Railroads-Airlines-Shipping-Traction, Bus And Truck Lines American and Foreign. P. 1080. New York, NY: Moody's Investors Service, Inc.

[3758] St. Clair, Frank J. (Editor-in-Chief) (1962). Moody's Transportation Manual: Railroads-Airlines-Shipping-Traction, Bus And Truck Lines American and Foreign. P. 1080. New York, NY: Moody's Investors Service, Inc.

[3759] Bateman, Newton, Selby, Paul, Strange, Alexander T. (1918). Historical Encyclopedia Of Illinois And History Of Montgomery County. Vol. 1. Pp. 425-426. Chicago, IL: Munsell Publishing Company. Google Books.

[3760] Bateman, Newton, Selby, Paul, Strange, Alexander T. (1918). Historical Encyclopedia Of Illinois And History Of Montgomery County. Vol. 1. Pp. 74, 425-426. Chicago, IL: Munsell Publishing Company. Google Books.

[3761] Bateman, Newton, Selby, Paul, Strange, Alexander T. (1918). Historical Encyclopedia Of Illinois And History Of Montgomery County. Vol. 1. P. 426. Chicago, IL: Munsell Publishing Company. Google Books.

[3762] Bateman, Newton, Selby, Paul, Strange, Alexander T. (1918). Historical Encyclopedia Of Illinois And History Of Montgomery County. Vol. 1. P. 426. Chicago, IL: Munsell Publishing Company. Google Books.

[3763] Bateman, Newton, Selby, Paul, Strange, Alexander T. (1918). Historical Encyclopedia Of Illinois And History Of Montgomery County. Vol. 1. P. 426. Chicago, IL: Munsell Publishing Company. Google Books.

[3764] Bateman, Newton, Selby, Paul, Strange, Alexander T. (1918). Historical Encyclopedia Of Illinois And History Of Montgomery County. Vol. 1. P. 426. Chicago, IL: Munsell Publishing Company. Google Books.

[3765] Bateman, Newton, Selby, Paul, Strange, Alexander T. (1918). Historical Encyclopedia Of Illinois And History Of Montgomery County. Vol. 1. P. 426. Chicago, IL: Munsell Publishing Company. Google Books.

[3766] Bateman, Newton, Selby, Paul, Strange, Alexander T. (1918). Historical Encyclopedia Of Illinois And History Of Montgomery County. Vol. 1. P. 426. Chicago, IL: Munsell Publishing Company. Google Books.

company underwent reorganization in 1862.[3767] Seven years later, the Pennsylvania Railroad Company would acquire the Pittsburgh, Fort Wayne & Chicago.[3768] As of 1898, the capital value of the Pittsburgh, Fort Wayne & Chicago Railway was $52,549,990.[3769]

Bateman, Selby, and Strange furthermore reported that the Pennsylvania Railroad Company controlled the Pittsburgh, Cincinnati, Chicago & St. Louis Railroad Company as of 1918.[3770] Representing capital assets of $47,791,601 in 1898, the subsidiary company was established by the joinder and union of the Pittsburg, Cincinnati & St. Louis Railway Company; the Chicago, St. Louis & Pittsburg Railway Company; the Cincinnati & Richmond; and the Jeffersonville, Madison & Indianapolis Railroad companies.[3771]

Historian William B. Sipes commented in his 1875 work, *THE PENNSYLVANIA RAILROAD: ITS ORIGIN, CONSTRUCTION, CONDITION AND CONNECTIONS*, upon the history of the Pennsylvania Railroad Company's connection to Chicago and Cook County.[3772] Sipes reported the significance, competition, and urgency that accompanied the Pennsylvania Railroad's development of a route to Chicago from the East Coast and the Appalachian Mountains.[3773] Sipes stated:

> "The Pittsburg, Fort Wayne & Chicago Railroad was one of the first to receive encouragement and assistance. This road, running from the western terminus of the Pennsylvania Railroad to Chicago, the great metropolis of the North-west, was an essential link in the chain which was to bind together the Atlantic seaboard with the Mississippi valley, and every assistance possible was extended to secure its completion. . .Being

---

[3767] Bateman, Newton, Selby, Paul, Strange, Alexander T. (1918). Historical Encyclopedia Of Illinois And History Of Montgomery County. Vol. 1. P. 426. Chicago, IL: Munsell Publishing Company. Google Books.

[3768] Bateman, Newton, Selby, Paul, Strange, Alexander T. (1918). Historical Encyclopedia Of Illinois And History Of Montgomery County. Vol. 1. P. 426. Chicago, IL: Munsell Publishing Company. Google Books.

[3769] Bateman, Newton, Selby, Paul, Strange, Alexander T. (1918). Historical Encyclopedia Of Illinois And History Of Montgomery County. Vol. 1. P. 426. Chicago, IL: Munsell Publishing Company. Google Books.

[3770] Bateman, Newton, Selby, Paul, Strange, Alexander T. (1918). Historical Encyclopedia Of Illinois And History Of Montgomery County. Vol. 1. P. 425. Chicago, IL: Munsell Publishing Company. Google Books.

[3771] Bateman, Newton, Selby, Paul, Strange, Alexander T. (1918). Historical Encyclopedia Of Illinois And History Of Montgomery County. Vol. 1. P. 425. Chicago, IL: Munsell Publishing Company. Google Books.

[3772] Sipes, William B. (1875). THE PENNSYLVANIA RAILROAD: ITS ORIGIN, CONSTRUCTION, CONDITION AND CONNECTIONS. Pp. 17-18. Philadelphia, PA: The Passenger Department. Google Books.

[3773] Sipes, William B. (1875). THE PENNSYLVANIA RAILROAD: ITS ORIGIN, CONSTRUCTION, CONDITION AND CONNECTIONS. Pp. 17-18. Philadelphia, PA: The Passenger Department. Google Books.

four hundred and sixty-eight miles in length, (with its branches nearly six hundred,) running through a new country comparatively undeveloped, and having, above all, the rivalry of the Lake Shore lines, controlled by New York interests, to contend with, its construction was attended with many difficulties."[3774]

Sipes' reference to the Lake Shore railroad companies that were controlled by New York interests referred to the John Stryker railroad interests that connected Chicago to Cleveland, Detroit, and New York, and that represented one of the principal foundations of Chicago's earliest railroad industry. The Stryker Empire, as it was called by historian William Norman Stryker, controlled many of the lake shore lines from Chicago to New York.[3775] The Pennsylvania Railroad, therefore, met its most challenging competition from the Stryker Empire system, with which it would merge in 1968 to form the Penn Central Transportation Company.

The Pennsylvania Railroad Company developed a route from Philadelphia to Chicago through acquisition of the Pittsburg, Fort Wayne & Chicago Railroad Company.[3776] The Pittsburg-Chicago route was 468.3 miles in length, according to Sipes.[3777] The construction attached a new railroad party to the growing Great Lakes-Atlantic Plain transportation market and network.[3778] It is of historical interest that two members of the Stryker family were prominently connected to Chicago railroading. John Stryker served as founder, financier, and owner of the Michigan Southern Railroad Company of Chicago, Cleveland, and New York, as well as of the New York Central Railroad Company, in addition to multiple other Chicago, Ohio, and New York railroad companies.[3779]

Henry Stryker Taylor, a later member of the family, would be one of the two largest individual stockholders of the Pennsylvania Railroad Company, which was the greatest historical competitor of the old Stryker Empire railroad system of Chicago-New York railroad companies.[3780] The Stryker family founded, financed,

---

[3774] Sipes, William B. (1875). THE PENNSYLVANIA RAILROAD: ITS ORIGIN, CONSTRUCTION, CONDITION AND CONNECTIONS. P. 17. Philadelphia, PA: The Passenger Department. Google Books.

[3775] Stryker, William Norman. (1979). The Stryker Family in America. Vol. 1. P. 550. W. N. Stryker, Publisher. Google Books

[3776] Sipes, William B. (1875). THE PENNSYLVANIA RAILROAD: ITS ORIGIN, CONSTRUCTION, CONDITION AND CONNECTIONS. Pp. 17-18. Philadelphia, PA: The Passenger Department. Google Books.

[3777] Sipes, William B. (1875). THE PENNSYLVANIA RAILROAD: ITS ORIGIN, CONSTRUCTION, CONDITION AND CONNECTIONS. P. 252. Philadelphia, PA: The Passenger Department. Google Books.

[3778] Sipes, William B. (1875). THE PENNSYLVANIA RAILROAD: ITS ORIGIN, CONSTRUCTION, CONDITION AND CONNECTIONS. Pp. 17-18. Philadelphia, PA: The Passenger Department. Google Books.

[3779] Stryker, William Norman. (1979). The Stryker Family in America. Vol. 1. P. 550. W. N. Stryker, Publisher. Google Books

[3780] Stryker, William Norman. (1979). The Stryker Family in America. Vol. 1. P. 550. W. N. Stryker, Publisher. Google Books; Hearings Before The Subcommittee On Antitrust

administered, and co-owned many Chicago, Cleveland, Michigan, and New York railroad companies.[3781]

The Pennsylvania Railroad Company acquired controlling property in the Calumet River Railroad Company at least as early as 1898, according to Bateman, Selby, and Strange.[3782] The Calumet River Railroad was established in 1883, and operated a route from 100th Street in Chicago to Hegewisch.[3783] At the time of the incorporation of the Calumet River Railroad Company, the place of its operation would have been largely included within Hyde Park Township, which remained an independent suburb of Chicago until its municipal incorporation into Chicago in 1889. Therefore, the Pennsylvania Railroad Company impacted Chicago and the suburbs of Cook County in the time of its earlier years of presence and operation in Illinois.[3784]

The Pennsylvania Railroad Company, in 1962, constituted an immense parent and compound company, and was a corporation that contained an entire economy of subsidiary corporations. It was a parent organization richly and thickly composed of subsidiary organizations, many of which possessed significant presence in, and connection to, Chicago and Cook County.[3785] The Pennsylvania Railroad Company initially operated a line that ran from Harrisburg, Pennsylvania, to Pittsburgh, Pennsylvania.[3786] As of the close of the year 1961, the Pennsylvania Railroad Company possessed corporate assets valued at $2,330,170,083.[3787] The total value of corporate assets had experienced a consistent and steady decline since the year 1956, when the entirety of corporate assets equaled

---

and Monopoly Of The Committee On The Judiciary, United States Senate. (1962). Eighty-Seventh Congress, Second Session. Part 2. Pp. 1305-1306.

[3781] Stryker, William Norman. (1979). The Stryker Family in America. Vol. 1. P. 550. W. N. Stryker, Publisher. Google Books; Hearings Before The Subcommittee On Antitrust and Monopoly Of The Committee On The Judiciary, United States Senate. (1962). Eighty-Seventh Congress, Second Session. Part 2. Pp. 1305-1306.

[3782] Bateman, Newton, Selby, Paul, Strange, Alexander T. (1918). Historical Encyclopedia Of Illinois And History Of Montgomery County. Vol. 1. P. 74. Chicago, IL: Munsell Publishing Company. Google Books.

[3783] Bateman, Newton, Selby, Paul, Strange, Alexander T. (1918). Historical Encyclopedia Of Illinois And History Of Montgomery County. Vol. 1. P. 74. Chicago, IL: Munsell Publishing Company. Google Books.

[3784] Bateman, Newton, Selby, Paul, Strange, Alexander T. (1918). Historical Encyclopedia Of Illinois And History Of Montgomery County. Vol. 1. Pp. 74, 425-426. Chicago, IL: Munsell Publishing Company. Google Books.

[3785] St. Clair, Frank J. (Editor-in-Chief) (1962). Moody's Transportation Manual: Railroads-Airlines-Shipping-Traction, Bus And Truck Lines American and Foreign. P. 1080. New York, NY: Moody's Investors Service, Inc.

[3786] St. Clair, Frank J. (Editor-in-Chief) (1962). Moody's Transportation Manual: Railroads-Airlines-Shipping-Traction, Bus And Truck Lines American and Foreign. P. 1080. New York, NY: Moody's Investors Service, Inc.

[3787] St. Clair, Frank J. (Editor-in-Chief) (1962). Moody's Transportation Manual: Railroads-Airlines-Shipping-Traction, Bus And Truck Lines American and Foreign. P. 1093. New York, NY: Moody's Investors Service, Inc.

$2,468,593,408.[3788] In 1957 the Pennsylvania Railroad Company corporate assets stood at $2,427,610,382.[3789] The corporate assets were $2,403,641,998 in 1958.[3790] In 1959 corporate assets equaled $2,385,394,862.[3791] The year 1960 witnessed the Pennsylvania Railroad Company assets fall to $2,334,368,779.[3792]

The Pennsylvania Railroad Company possessed a prominent and complex commercial, industrial, and infrastructural connection to Chicago and Cook County.[3793] What follows here is a list of the subsidiary companies of the Pennsylvania Railroad Company as of December 31, 1961.[3794] The Pennsylvania Railroad Company possessed a major and powerful presence in Chicago and Cook County not only as the parent corporation itself, but also through a complex portfolio of subsidiary companies.[3795]

1. American Contract & Trust Company
2. Baltimore & Eastern Railroad Company
3. Central Indiana Railway Company
4. Cherry Tree & Dixonville Railroad Company
5. Chicago Union Station Company
6. Cleveland & Pittsburgh Railroad Company
7. Connecting Railway Company
   a. Akron Union Passenger Depot Company

[3788] St. Clair, Frank J. (Editor-in-Chief) (1962). Moody's Transportation Manual: Railroads-Airlines-Shipping-Traction, Bus And Truck Lines American and Foreign. P. 1093. New York, NY: Moody's Investors Service, Inc.

[3789] St. Clair, Frank J. (Editor-in-Chief) (1962). Moody's Transportation Manual: Railroads-Airlines-Shipping-Traction, Bus And Truck Lines American and Foreign. P. 1093. New York, NY: Moody's Investors Service, Inc.

[3790] St. Clair, Frank J. (Editor-in-Chief) (1962). Moody's Transportation Manual: Railroads-Airlines-Shipping-Traction, Bus And Truck Lines American and Foreign. P. 1093. New York, NY: Moody's Investors Service, Inc.

[3791] St. Clair, Frank J. (Editor-in-Chief) (1962). Moody's Transportation Manual: Railroads-Airlines-Shipping-Traction, Bus And Truck Lines American and Foreign. P. 1093. New York, NY: Moody's Investors Service, Inc.

[3792] St. Clair, Frank J. (Editor-in-Chief) (1962). Moody's Transportation Manual: Railroads-Airlines-Shipping-Traction, Bus And Truck Lines American and Foreign. P. 1093. New York, NY: Moody's Investors Service, Inc.

[3793] St. Clair, Frank J. (Editor-in-Chief) (1962). Moody's Transportation Manual: Railroads-Airlines-Shipping-Traction, Bus And Truck Lines American and Foreign. Pp. 1080, 1093, 1116-1117, 1125-1126, 1135-1136. New York, NY: Moody's Investors Service, Inc.

[3794] St. Clair, Frank J. (Editor-in-Chief) (1962). Moody's Transportation Manual: Railroads-Airlines-Shipping-Traction, Bus And Truck Lines American and Foreign. P. 1080. New York, NY: Moody's Investors Service, Inc.

[3795] St. Clair, Frank J. (Editor-in-Chief) (1962). Moody's Transportation Manual: Railroads-Airlines-Shipping-Traction, Bus And Truck Lines American and Foreign. Pp. 1080, 1116-1117, 1125-1126, 1135-1136. New York, NY: Moody's Investors Service, Inc.

8. Delaware Railroad Company
9. Elmira & Williamsport Railroad Company
10. Erie & Pittsburgh Railroad Company
11. Green Real Estate Company
12. Lake Erie & Pittsburgh Railway Company
13. Little Miami Railroad Company
14. Long Island Railroad Company
15. Manor Real Estate Company
    a. Cambria Land Company
    b. Pennsylvania Car Leasing Company
    c. C. I. West Virginia Corporation
    d. Delaware Car Leasing Company
    e. D. F. S. Corporation
    f. DTB Corporation
    g. General Car Leasing Corporation
    h. Greencar Corporation
    i. G. S. C. Leasing Corporation
    j. Western Allegheny Railroad Company
16. New York and Long Branch Railroad Company
17. New York Connecting Railroad Company
18. Northern Central Railway Company
    a. Union Railroad of Baltimore
    b. Shamokin Valley & Pottsville Railroad Company
19. Penndel Company
    a. Mackinac Transportation Company
    b. Norfolk & Portsmouth Belt Line Railroad Company
20. Penndiana Improvement Corporation
21. Pennsylvania & Atlantic Railroad Company
22. Pennsylvania Company
    a. Detroit, Toledo & Ironton Railroad Company
    b. Wabash Railroad Company
    c. Illinois Northern Railway Company
    d. Montour Railroad Company
23. Pennsylvania-Reading Seashore Lines
24. Pennsylvania Tunnel & Terminal Railroad Company
25. Pennsylvania Truck Lines, Inc.
26. Philadelphia & Trenton Railroad Company
27. Philadelphia, Baltimore & Washington Railroad Company
    a. Rosslyn Connecting Railroad Company
    b. Washington Terminal Company
    c. Indianapolis Union Railway Company
    d. Pittsburgh, Chartiers & Youghiogheny Railway
    e. Tylerdale Connecting Railroad Company
    f. Union Depot Company (Columbus, Ohio)
    g. Waynesburg & Washington Railroad Company

28. Pittsburgh, Fort Wayne & Chicago Railway Company
29. Pittsburgh Joint Stock Yards Company
30. Pittsburgh, Youngstown & Ashland Railway Company
31. Potomac Public Service Company
32. United New Jersey Railroad & Canal Company
33. West Jersey & Seashore Railroad Company
34. Western Warehousing Company
35. Wilkes-Barre Connecting Railroad Company[3796]

The Pennsylvania Railroad Company subsidiary known as the Penndel Company owned multiple short railroad track lines both in Chicago and Cook County.[3797] The Penndel Company was a subsidiary of the Pennsylvania Railroad Company.[3798] Penndel was incorporated on November 20, 1953, in the State of Delaware.[3799] The Penndel Company served as the means by which the Pennsylvania Railroad Company purchased multiple railroad companies.[3800] Among the Penndel Company railroad lines that existed in Chicago, and within the extended metropolitan region of Cook County, was a line that was a 4.4-mile line that connected South Chicago to Hegewisch.[3801] Additionally, there existed a Pennsylvania Railroad Company line located at Hammond, Indiana, that was .94 miles in length.[3802] A Pennsylvania Railroad Company-owned rail line that was 1.87-miles in length ran from the state line of Illinois and Indiana to Hammond.[3803] There existed, furthermore, a Pennsylvania Railroad Company line that was 2.39

[3796] St. Clair, Frank J. (Editor-in-Chief) (1962). Moody's Transportation Manual: Railroads-Airlines-Shipping-Traction, Bus And Truck Lines American and Foreign. P. 1080. New York, NY: Moody's Investors Service, Inc.

[3797] St. Clair, Frank J. (Editor-in-Chief) (1962). Moody's Transportation Manual: Railroads-Airlines-Shipping-Traction, Bus And Truck Lines American and Foreign. P. 1116. New York, NY: Moody's Investors Service, Inc.

[3798] St. Clair, Frank J. (editor-In-Chief). (1963). Moody's Transportation Manual. P. 1036. New York, NY: Moody's Investors Service, Inc. Robert H. Messner, Publisher.

[3799] St. Clair, Frank J. (editor-In-Chief). (1963). Moody's Transportation Manual. P. 1036. New York, NY: Moody's Investors Service, Inc. Robert H. Messner, Publisher.

[3800] St. Clair, Frank J. (editor-In-Chief). (1963). Moody's Transportation Manual. P. 1036. New York, NY: Moody's Investors Service, Inc. Robert H. Messner, Publisher.

[3801] St. Clair, Frank J. (Editor-in-Chief) (1962). Moody's Transportation Manual: Railroads-Airlines-Shipping-Traction, Bus And Truck Lines American and Foreign. P. 1116. New York, NY: Moody's Investors Service, Inc.

[3802] St. Clair, Frank J. (Editor-in-Chief) (1962). Moody's Transportation Manual: Railroads-Airlines-Shipping-Traction, Bus And Truck Lines American and Foreign. P. 1116. New York, NY: Moody's Investors Service, Inc.

[3803] St. Clair, Frank J. (Editor-in-Chief) (1962). Moody's Transportation Manual: Railroads-Airlines-Shipping-Traction, Bus And Truck Lines American and Foreign. P. 1116. New York, NY: Moody's Investors Service, Inc.

miles in length within Chicago.[3804] The board of directors of the Penndel Company consisted of the following persons in 1963: D. C. Bevan, P. D. Fox, B. H. Roberts, H. J. Ward, and J. B. Jones.[3805] The total value of property owned by the Penndel Company in 1962, as reported in 1963, was $315,923,059.[3806] The Penndel Company executive leadership consisted of the following persons and jobs in 1963:

1. D. C. Bevan
   a. President
2. J. B. Jones
   a. Vice President
3. P. D. Fox
   a. Vice President
4. B. H. Roberts
   a. Secretary
5. W. R. Gerstnecker
   a. Treasurer
6. W. S. Cook
   a. Comptroller
7. J. B. Prizer
   a. General Counsel[3807]

The Penndel Company was not the only Pennsylvania Railroad Company subsidiary corporation that possessed an important presence at Chicago. The Pennsylvania Company, another subsidiary of the Pennsylvania Railroad Company, also possessed a prominent presence at Chicago and Cook County.[3808] The Pennsylvania Company entered corporate existence on December 12, 1958, with the place of incorporation at Delaware.[3809] The purpose of the Pennsylvania Company within the structure of the Pennsylvania Railroad Company system was the purchase and administration of multiple railroad companies that operated west

---

[3804] St. Clair, Frank J. (Editor-in-Chief) (1962). Moody's Transportation Manual: Railroads-Airlines-Shipping-Traction, Bus And Truck Lines American and Foreign. P. 1116. New York, NY: Moody's Investors Service, Inc.

[3805] St. Clair, Frank J. (editor-In-Chief). (1963). Moody's Transportation Manual. P. 1036. New York, NY: Moody's Investors Service, Inc. Robert H. Messner, Publisher.

[3806] St. Clair, Frank J. (editor-In-Chief). (1963). Moody's Transportation Manual. P. 1036. New York, NY: Moody's Investors Service, Inc. Robert H. Messner, Publisher.

[3807] St. Clair, Frank J. (editor-In-Chief). (1963). Moody's Transportation Manual. P. 1036. New York, NY: Moody's Investors Service, Inc. Robert H. Messner, Publisher.

[3808] St. Clair, Frank J. (Editor-in-Chief) (1962). Moody's Transportation Manual: Railroads-Airlines-Shipping-Traction, Bus And Truck Lines American and Foreign. P. 1116. New York, NY: Moody's Investors Service, Inc.

[3809] St. Clair, Frank J. (editor-In-Chief). (1963). Moody's Transportation Manual. P. 1036. New York, NY: Moody's Investors Service, Inc. Robert H. Messner, Publisher.

of Pittsburgh and west of Erie, Pennsylvania.[3810] On April 8, 1959, the Pennsylvania Company purchased the assets and liabilities of another corporation known as the Pennsylvania Company, which had entered organizational existence as a Pennsylvania-based company on April 7, 1870.[3811] In 1963, the Board of Directors of the Pennsylvania Company included the following persons: Fred Carpi, G. P. Harnwell, C. J. Ingersoll, J. E. Gowen, J. M. Symes, O. N. Frenzel, R. K. Mellon, D. C. Bevan, J. P. Newell, P. R. Clarke, J. B. Hollister, J. H. Thompson, R. G. Rincliffe, W. L. Day, T. L. Perkins, E. J. Hanley, A. J. Greenough, and Howard Butcher, III.[3812]

The Pennsylvania Company owned the Pittsburgh, Fort Wayne & Chicago Railway Company.[3813] Additionally, the Pennsylvania Company owned the South Chicago & Southern Railroad Company.[3814] The Pittsburgh, Cincinnati, Chicago & St. Louis Railroad Company was owned by the Pennsylvania Company subsidiary of the Pennsylvania Railroad Company.[3815] The Pennsylvania Railroad Company, moreover, owned the Englewood Connecting Railway Company of Chicago.[3816] Henry S. Taylor and Howard Butcher were the two largest individual (non-institutional) stockholders of the Pennsylvania Railroad Company at the time when the Pennsylvania Railroad Company owned the Penndel Company, the Pennsylvania Company, the Wabash Railroad Company, the Pittsburgh, Fort Wayne & Chicago Railroad Company, and all of the other Chicago subsidiaries named here.

The 1963 Moody's corporate and financial report stated that Pennsylvania Company assets possessed a value of $321,543,803.[3817] In addition to these Chicago-connected railroad companies, the Pennsylvania Railroad Company owned, through its subsidiary, the Pennsylvania Company, the Wabash Railroad

---

[3810] St. Clair, Frank J. (editor-In-Chief). (1963). Moody's Transportation Manual. P. 1036. New York, NY: Moody's Investors Service, Inc. Robert H. Messner, Publisher.

[3811] St. Clair, Frank J. (editor-In-Chief). (1963). Moody's Transportation Manual. P. 1036. New York, NY: Moody's Investors Service, Inc. Robert H. Messner, Publisher.

[3812] St. Clair, Frank J. (editor-In-Chief). (1963). Moody's Transportation Manual. P. 1037. New York, NY: Moody's Investors Service, Inc. Robert H. Messner, Publisher.

[3813] St. Clair, Frank J. (Editor-in-Chief) (1962). Moody's Transportation Manual: Railroads-Airlines-Shipping-Traction, Bus And Truck Lines American and Foreign. P. 1116. New York, NY: Moody's Investors Service, Inc.

[3814] St. Clair, Frank J. (Editor-in-Chief) (1962). Moody's Transportation Manual: Railroads-Airlines-Shipping-Traction, Bus And Truck Lines American and Foreign. P. 1116. New York, NY: Moody's Investors Service, Inc.

[3815] St. Clair, Frank J. (Editor-in-Chief) (1962). Moody's Transportation Manual: Railroads-Airlines-Shipping-Traction, Bus And Truck Lines American and Foreign. P. 1116. New York, NY: Moody's Investors Service, Inc.

[3816] St. Clair, Frank J. (Editor-in-Chief) (1962). Moody's Transportation Manual: Railroads-Airlines-Shipping-Traction, Bus And Truck Lines American and Foreign. P. 1116. New York, NY: Moody's Investors Service, Inc.

[3817] St. Clair, Frank J. (editor-In-Chief). (1963). Moody's Transportation Manual. P. 1037. New York, NY: Moody's Investors Service, Inc. Robert H. Messner, Publisher.

Company.[3818] The equity interest that the Pennsylvania Railroad Company held in the Wabash Railroad Company, through the means of corporate ownership of the Pennsylvania Company, equaled 788,099 shares.[3819] Within this equity amount, the entirety of the Wabash Railroad Company preferred stock shares equaled 192,904, and the entirety of the Wabash Railroad Company common stock shares totaled 595,158.[3820] John Whitfield Bunn was one of the founders of the Wabash Railroad Company, as is discussed in Chapter 2, *Builders of the Downtown*.

The Pennsylvania Railroad Company controlled the Pittsburgh, Fort Wayne and Chicago Railway Company.[3821] The nature of the Pennsylvania Railroad Company property in the Pittsburgh, Fort Wayne and Chicago Railway Company was dual, existing partly in the nature of a lease and partly in the nature of equity property, and largely so through the ownership of 88.4 percent of the Pittsburgh, Fort Wayne and Chicago Railway Company.[3822] The line of the Pittsburgh, Fort Wayne and Chicago Railway Company ran 467.57 miles from Pittsburgh to Chicago.[3823] The total value of the assets of the Pittsburgh, Fort Wayne and Chicago Railway Company equaled $144,945,762 as of the close of the year 1961.[3824]

During the period from 1960 until 1970, the Pennsylvania Railroad Company undertook an important diversification plan that entailed multiple construction projects and leasing projects in Philadelphia, New York City, and Chicago.[3825] The company contributed to the development of commercial space at Madison Square Garden in Manhattan as well as commercial space at Penn Station in Philadelphia.[3826] In Chicago, the Pennsylvania Railroad Company contributed to the further physical development of Union Station and significantly to the air space

---

[3818] St. Clair, Frank J. (Editor-in-Chief) (1962). Moody's Transportation Manual: Railroads-Airlines-Shipping-Traction, Bus And Truck Lines American and Foreign. P. 1135. New York, NY: Moody's Investors Service, Inc.

[3819] St. Clair, Frank J. (Editor-in-Chief) (1962). Moody's Transportation Manual: Railroads-Airlines-Shipping-Traction, Bus And Truck Lines American and Foreign. P. 1135. New York, NY: Moody's Investors Service, Inc.

[3820] St. Clair, Frank J. (Editor-in-Chief) (1962). Moody's Transportation Manual: Railroads-Airlines-Shipping-Traction, Bus And Truck Lines American and Foreign. P. 1135. New York, NY: Moody's Investors Service, Inc.

[3821] St. Clair, Frank J. (Editor-in-Chief) (1962). Moody's Transportation Manual: Railroads-Airlines-Shipping-Traction, Bus And Truck Lines American and Foreign. Pp. 1125-1126. New York, NY: Moody's Investors Service, Inc.

[3822] St. Clair, Frank J. (Editor-in-Chief) (1962). Moody's Transportation Manual: Railroads-Airlines-Shipping-Traction, Bus And Truck Lines American and Foreign. Pp. 1125-1126. New York, NY: Moody's Investors Service, Inc.

[3823] St. Clair, Frank J. (Editor-in-Chief) (1962). Moody's Transportation Manual: Railroads-Airlines-Shipping-Traction, Bus And Truck Lines American and Foreign. P. 1126. New York, NY: Moody's Investors Service, Inc.

[3824] St. Clair, Frank J. (Editor-in-Chief) (1962). Moody's Transportation Manual: Railroads-Airlines-Shipping-Traction, Bus And Truck Lines American and Foreign. P. 1126. New York, NY: Moody's Investors Service, Inc.

[3825] The Pennsylvania Railroad Company. Annual Report. (1966). P. 15.

[3826] The Pennsylvania Railroad Company. Annual Report. (1966). P. 15.

that was vertically appurtenant to that building complex.[3827] These three development projects involved investment creativity on the part of the company, because the company converted property rights into different species of civic and economic benefits. The Pennsylvania Railroad did this through contractually administered opportunities: opportunities for property and land development for urban development parties; and opportunities for the creation of lease contract revenue for the railroad company.[3828] Additionally, a third benefit attached to the company's diversification plan in that the lease contract opportunities described herein fostered a mutual participation in the urban development in Chicago, New York City, and Philadelphia, of all parties to the contracts that were produced by the company's diversification plan.[3829]

The Pennsylvania Railroad Company's diversification plan produced contracts either for lease, or for sale, of the company's rights to various classes of urban air space properties.[3830] The contracts produced by the diversification plan bore multiple benefits for all parties to the contracts.[3831] The *117th Annual Report of The Pennsylvania Railroad Company*, which accounted for the company year that ended on December 31, 1963, provided information about the development plan for three 20-story buildings that would occupy air space over Chicago Union Station; Chicago Union Station was a key real estate asset in which the Pennsylvania Railroad Company held a fifty-percent interest.[3832] The real estate segment of the annual report provided description as well as photographic representation of the planned buildings. The report stated the following in the prospectus: "Gateway Center at Chicago is expected to cost the developers another $100 million. Work has begun on the first of three 20-story office buildings that will utilize air space over tracks at Chicago Union Station."[3833] The *1964 Annual Report of the Pennsylvania Railroad Company* contained additional facts about the Gateway Center development project at Chicago Union Station that reflected the project's continued development.

> "During the year, work by a developer proceeded rapidly on the $100 million Gateway Center in Chicago. The first of three 20-story office buildings is nearing completion. They will utilize air space over tracks of Union Station, in which the Pennsylvania has 50 per cent ownership."[3834]

The *1965 Annual Report of the Pennsylvania Railroad Company* enumerated the multiple property interests and projects that composed the company's

---

[3827] The Pennsylvania Railroad Company. Annual Report. (1966). P. 15.

[3828] The Pennsylvania Railroad Company. Annual Report. (1966). P. 15.

[3829] The Pennsylvania Railroad Company. Annual Report. (1966). P. 15.

[3830] The Pennsylvania Railroad Company. Annual Report. (1966). P. 15.

[3831] The Pennsylvania Railroad Company. Annual Report. (1966). P. 15.

[3832] The Pennsylvania Railroad. Annual Report. (1964). P. 19.

[3833] The Pennsylvania Railroad. Annual Report. (1963). Pp. 16-17; The Pennsylvania Railroad. Annual Report. (1963). Pp. 16-17.

[3834] The Pennsylvania Railroad. Annual Report. (1964). Pp. 18-19.

diversification plan.[3835] Within the air space diversification plan, development continued with respect to the Gateway Center at Chicago Union Station. "In Chicago, developers completed one office building occupying air rights on lease over Union Station property and started construction on another."[3836] The *1966 Annual Report* for the company showed the continuity of development for the Gateway Center construction project. The report stated the following with respect to the project: "In Chicago's Gateway Center, developers are nearing completion of a second office building occupying leased air rights over Union Station, in which we hold a 50 per cent interest. Negotiations to erect a third building are under way."[3837] In 1964, Herbert M. Phillips served as Vice-President and General Manager of the Western Region, headquartered in Chicago.[3838] George C. Vaughan served as General Manager of the Eastern Region, based in Philadelphia.[3839] George M. Smith served as General Manager of the Central Region, based in Pittsburgh.[3840]

Henry Stryker Taylor and Howard Butcher, because of their controlling (non-institutional) ownership of the Pennsylvania Railroad Company, were also among the most important people in the coal and coal transportation sectors of the United States economy. This was so because the Pennsylvania Railroad Company was one of the world's largest coal hauling railroads. Taylor and Butcher also were the controlling stockholders of the Pennsylvania Railroad Company when the Pennsylvania owned the Norfolk & Western Railway Company of Roanoke, Virginia. The Norfolk & Western was one of the largest coal-hauling railroad companies in America. The Norfolk & Western connected the important coal and steel city of Roanoke, Virginia, to Cincinnati, Ohio, to southwest Virginia, to southern West Virginia, to Kentucky, and to Norfolk, Virginia. Like the Chesapeake & Ohio Railway Company of Cleveland, the Norfolk & Western Railway Company hauled coal from the great Appalachian coalfields of Virginia, West Virginia, and Ohio, to the coal markets of the Great Lakes, the Ohio Valley, and the East Coast.

Both Springfield and Chicago were major centers of the North American coal industry, and both cities were heavily connected to the Appalachian Mountains commercially, industrially, socially, civically, and historically. The Coal Miner Memorial, designed by sculptor John Szaton and lyrically inscribed by the poet and coal miner Vachel Davis, stands on the east lawn of the Illinois State Capitol grounds.[3841] Jacob Bunn, John W. Bunn, William Douglas Richardson, Willard Bunn, Sr., Henry Stryker Taylor, and others were among the most important Illinois coal entrepreneurs and industrialists, and these men contributed much to coal exploration, coal discovery, coal development, and coal transportation

---

[3835] The Pennsylvania Railroad. Annual Report. (1965). P. 12.

[3836] The Pennsylvania Railroad. Annual Report. (1965). P. 12.

[3837] The Pennsylvania Railroad Company. Annual Report. (1966). P. 15.

[3838] The Pennsylvania Railroad. Annual Report. (1964). P. 2.

[3839] The Pennsylvania Railroad. Annual Report. (1964). P. 2.

[3840] The Pennsylvania Railroad. Annual Report. (1964). P. 2.

[3841] The Illinois State Capitol. Exterior Statues. Ilstatehouse.com.

throughout the Midwest, Great Lakes, and Appalachia.[3842] Richardson and the Bunn brothers were founders of the great Bunn Coal Company, Springfield Iron Company, Springfield Coal Trust Company, Wabash Railroad Company, and Chicago & Alton Railroad Company, all of which produced or shipped coal.[3843] And, Henry S. Taylor was one of the most important business leaders of railroad-based coal transportation.[3844] John Llewellyn Lewis (1880-1969), who founded the Congress of Industrial Organizations (CIO) and who was President of the United Mine Workers of America (UMWA), is buried in Oak Ridge Cemetery in Springfield.[3845] Sangamon County and Cook County, therefore, were two of the greatest centers of the coal industry.

Henry Stryker Taylor and Howard Butcher, III, helped to govern and direct the Pennsylvania Railroad Company and its complex portfolio of subsidiary companies, and by doing so Taylor and Butcher held great influence over Chicago industry, New York City industry, Pittsburgh industry, Philadelphia industry, and national industry. Taylor and Butcher were prominently associated with the founding of the Pennsylvania Central Transportation Company in 1968. This was the largest transportation company in the history of the world. Taylor, Butcher, and so many other members of the top leadership of the company were genuinely invested in the long-term growth and prosperity of the company and the American railroad industry. The failure of the company was due to multiple factors including the poor federal railroad policy that failed to protect the industry, the fact of growing competition from developing highway freight transit and changing American economic culture. The Penn Central failed in catastrophic financial disaster after 1968 and declared bankruptcy. The Penn Central bankruptcy was the largest bankruptcy in history at that time, and Taylor, Butcher, and scores of thousands of shareholders lost their investments in the Penn Central Transportation Company.[3846] The United States created the National Railroad Passenger Corporation (AMTRAK) because of the failure of the Penn Central, in order to accommodate the passenger railroad market that could no longer be served by the Penn Central Transportation Company system.

The Brigham and Douglas Branches of Chicago:

Railroads, Refrigeration, and Urban Reform

The genealogy of the Brigham family contained herein was derived from the 1907 published work of Willard Irving Tyler Brigham, Esq., who was a distant cousin of Andrew Taylor Call, and a Chicago lawyer and historian. Brigham's work, *The History of the Brigham Family: A Record of Several Thousand*

[3842] Taylor and Bunn family history records.
[3843] Bunn and Richardson family history records.
[3844] Taylor and Bunn family history records.
[3845] John Llewellyn Lewis. Findagrave.com.
[3846] Taylor family history records.

Descendants of Thomas Brigham the Emigrant (1603-1653), possesses central and perennial significance as a reference resource relevant to the Brigham family in America.[3847] The herculean historical work and achievement undertaken by W. I. Tyler Brigham has proved invaluable to the research and assembly of the immediate chapter of the present book.

The original American ancestors of the Brigham family were the Puritan immigrant Thomas Brigham (1603-1653), and his wife Mercy Hurd (d. 1693), both originally of England.[3848] Thomas and Mercy Brigham settled in Cambridge, Massachusetts. Among the children of Thomas Brigham and Mercy (Hurd) Brigham was Thomas Brigham, who married Mary Rice.[3849] Mary was the daughter of Henry Rice and Elizabeth (Moore) Rice.[3850] Among the children of Thomas Brigham and Mary (Rice) Brigham was David Brigham (1678-1750).[3851]

David Brigham first married Deborah (whose surname is unknown).[3852] Two children were born to this marriage: John Brigham and David Brigham.[3853] David Brigham, son of Thomas Brigham and Mary (Rice) Brigham, married a second time.[3854] The second wife of David Brigham was Mary (Leonard) Newton.[3855] Mary Leonard (Newton) Brigham was a descendant of James Chilton, a passenger

[3847] Brigham, W. I. Tyler. (1907). The History of the Brigham Family; a record of several thousand descendants of Thomas Brigham the emigrant, 1603-1653. Emma E. Brigham, Ed. New York, NY: The Grafton Press, Genealogical Publishers. Google Books.

[3848] Brigham, W. I. Tyler. (1907). The History of the Brigham Family; a record of several thousand descendants of Thomas Brigham the emigrant, 1603-1653. Emma E. Brigham, Ed. New York, NY: The Grafton Press, Genealogical Publishers. Google Books.

[3849] Brigham, W. I. Tyler. (1907). The History of the Brigham Family; a record of several thousand descendants of Thomas Brigham the emigrant, 1603-1653. Emma E. Brigham, Ed. New York, NY: The Grafton Press, Genealogical Publishers. Google Books.

[3850] Brigham, W. I. Tyler. (1907). The History of the Brigham Family; a record of several thousand descendants of Thomas Brigham the emigrant, 1603-1653. Emma E. Brigham, Ed. New York, NY: The Grafton Press, Genealogical Publishers. Google Books.

[3851] Brigham, W. I. Tyler. (1907). The History of the Brigham Family; a record of several thousand descendants of Thomas Brigham the emigrant, 1603-1653. Emma E. Brigham, Ed. New York, NY: The Grafton Press, Genealogical Publishers. Google Books.

[3852] Brigham, W. I. Tyler. (1907). The History of the Brigham Family; a record of several thousand descendants of Thomas Brigham the emigrant, 1603-1653. Emma E. Brigham, Ed. New York, NY: The Grafton Press, Genealogical Publishers. Google Books.

[3853] Brigham, W. I. Tyler. (1907). The History of the Brigham Family; a record of several thousand descendants of Thomas Brigham the emigrant, 1603-1653. Emma E. Brigham, Ed. New York, NY: The Grafton Press, Genealogical Publishers. Google Books.

[3854] Brigham, W. I. Tyler. (1907). The History of the Brigham Family; a record of several thousand descendants of Thomas Brigham the emigrant, 1603-1653. Emma E. Brigham, Ed. New York, NY: The Grafton Press, Genealogical Publishers. Google Books.

[3855] Brigham, W. I. Tyler. (1907). The History of the Brigham Family; a record of several thousand descendants of Thomas Brigham the emigrant, 1603-1653. Emma E. Brigham, Ed. New York, NY: The Grafton Press, Genealogical Publishers. Google Books.

of the Mayflower in 1620 and Plymouth Colony founder.[3856] The children of David Brigham and Mary (Leonard) Newton Brigham were as follows: Silas Brigham, Jemima Brigham, Deborah Brigham, Levi Brigham, **Jonas Brigham**, and Asa Brigham.[3857]

Captain Jonas Brigham, son of David Brigham and Mary (Leonard Newton Brigham, married Persis Baker.[3858] The children of Jonas and Persis (Baker) Brigham included the following persons: Martha Brigham; **Jonas Brigham, Jr.**; Edward Brigham; Barnabas Brigham; Hannah Brigham; Antipas Brigham; Eli Brigham; Persis Brigham; William Brigham; Daniel Brigham; David Brigham; Antipas Brigham; and Joseph Brigham.[3859]

Jonas Brigham, Jr., married Hannah Draper.[3860] The children born to this marriage included the following persons: Michael Brigham; Eli Brigham; Jonas Brigham; Hannah Brigham; Sally Brigham; Patty Brigham; **Luther Brigham**; Asa Brigham; **Cheney Brigham**; and **Betsy Brigham**.[3861] **Betsy Brigham, daughter of Jonas Brigham and Hannah (Draper) Brigham, married Dr. David Gill McClure**, a founder of Lansing, Michigan, and the patriarch of the McClure-Stryker-Taylor families that are discussed previously in this chapter.[3862]

The Brigham-Cogan Branch of Chicago

Cheney Brigham (1793-1865), son of Jonas Brigham and Hannah (Draper) Brigham, a native of Bakersfield, Vermont, married his cousin, Elizabeth

[3856] McClure, Brigham, Douglas, Leonard family history records.

[3857] Brigham, W. I. Tyler. (1907). The History of the Brigham Family; a record of several thousand descendants of Thomas Brigham the emigrant, 1603-1653. Emma E. Brigham, Ed. New York, NY: The Grafton Press, Genealogical Publishers. Google Books.

[3858] Brigham, W. I. Tyler. (1907). The History of the Brigham Family; a record of several thousand descendants of Thomas Brigham the emigrant, 1603-1653. Emma E. Brigham, Ed. New York, NY: The Grafton Press, Genealogical Publishers. Google Books.

[3859] Brigham, W. I. Tyler. (1907). The History of the Brigham Family; a record of several thousand descendants of Thomas Brigham the emigrant, 1603-1653. Emma E. Brigham, Ed. New York, NY: The Grafton Press, Genealogical Publishers. Google Books.

[3860] Brigham, W. I. Tyler. (1907). The History of the Brigham Family; a record of several thousand descendants of Thomas Brigham the emigrant, 1603-1653. Emma E. Brigham, Ed. New York, NY: The Grafton Press, Genealogical Publishers. Google Books.

[3861] Brigham, W. I. Tyler. (1907). The History of the Brigham Family; a record of several thousand descendants of Thomas Brigham the emigrant, 1603-1653. Emma E. Brigham, Ed. New York, NY: The Grafton Press, Genealogical Publishers. Google Books.

[3862] Durant, Samuel W. (1880). History of Ingham And Eaton Counties Michigan. P. 116. Philadelphia, PA: D. W. Ensign & Company. Google Books. McClure genealogical records.

Brigham.[3863] Elizabeth was the daughter of Uriah Brigham and Elizabeth (Fay) Brigham.[3864] The children born to Cheney Brigham and Elizabeth (Brigham) Brigham included the following persons: Augustus Kendall Brigham (1821-1870), who married Maria Shaw Lathrop; Elizabeth Fay Brigham; and Robert Breck Brigham. One line of the Chicago Brighams included Susie Augusta Brigham, the daughter of Augustus Kendall Brigham.[3865]

Susie Augusta Brigham (b. 1871) married Bernard Joseph Cogan (b. 1873), a native of Liverpool, England, who had immigrated to Chicago.[3866] Bernard and Susie Cogan resided at 5722 S. Indiana Avenue, located within the Washington Park community of Chicago.[3867] Washington Park community is located within what was once the independent Hyde Park Township and includes the large and architecturally significant Washington Park. Bernard J. Cogan was a wholesale liquor merchant.[3868] The children born to Bernard J. Cogan and Susie Augusta (Brigham) Cogan were Bernard Brigham Cogan (b. 1903), and Elizabeth Genevieve Cogan (b. 1904), both of Chicago.[3869]

Elizabeth Genevieve Cogan, known in her adult years as Genevieve, graduated from Radcliffe College,[3870] and subsequently received a Master's Degree from the University of Chicago in 1950.[3871] She was a resident of Lombard, a Cook County suburb, at the time of her graduation from the University of Chicago.[3872] Genevieve worked in Chicago for the merchandising department of the Fred Harvey Company.[3873] She was employed at Chicago Union Station and was responsible for having selected the name, "Isle of Gifts," for the Fred Harvey Company gift

[3863] Brigham, W. I. Tyler. (1907). The History of the Brigham Family; a record of several thousand descendants of Thomas Brigham the emigrant, 1603-1653. Emma E. Brigham, Ed. New York, NY: The Grafton Press, Genealogical Publishers. Google Books.

[3864] Brigham, W. I. Tyler. (1907). The History of the Brigham Family; a record of several thousand descendants of Thomas Brigham the emigrant, 1603-1653. Emma E. Brigham, Ed. New York, NY: The Grafton Press, Genealogical Publishers. Google Books.

[3865] Brigham, W. I. Tyler. (1907). The History of the Brigham Family; a record of several thousand descendants of Thomas Brigham the emigrant, 1603-1653. Emma E. Brigham, Ed. New York, NY: The Grafton Press, Genealogical Publishers. Google Books.

[3866] Brigham, W. I. Tyler. (1907). The History of the Brigham Family; a record of several thousand descendants of Thomas Brigham the emigrant, 1603-1653. Emma E. Brigham, Ed. New York, NY: The Grafton Press, Genealogical Publishers. Google Books.

[3867] The Chicago Tribune. (May 4, 1909). P. 3. Newspapers.com.

[3868] The Chicago Tribune. (May 4, 1909). P. 3. Newspapers.com.

[3869] Brigham, W. I. Tyler. (1907). The History of the Brigham Family; a record of several thousand descendants of Thomas Brigham the emigrant, 1603-1653. Emma E. Brigham, Ed. New York, NY: The Grafton Press, Genealogical Publishers. Google Books.

[3870] The Chicago Tribune. (July 24, 1957). Part 1, P. 19. Newspapers.com.

[3871] The Chicago Tribune. (July 9, 1950). Part 3, P. 5. Newspapers.com.

[3872] The Chicago Tribune. (July 9, 1950). Part 3, P. 5. Newspapers.com.

[3873] The Chicago Tribune. (April 14, 1957). Part 3, P. 11. Newspapers.com.

shop at Chicago Union Station.[3874] She received an award of $100 for having won the naming contest for the new Union Station gift store name.[3875] Charles P. Hunter delivered the award to Cogan.[3876] Hunter served as the Vice-President of the Fred Harvey Company at that time.[3877]

Robert Breck Brigham (1826-1900) was a multimillionaire Boston merchant and hotelier, and the son of Cheney Brigham and Elizabeth (Brigham) Brigham.[3878] In 1900 Robert Breck Brigham left an immense estate.[3879] The Brigham will contained words that provided for the creation of a Boston hospital.[3880] The new hospital created by the Brigham will was known by the name, "Robert B. Brigham Hospital for Incurables."[3881] This hospital joined another Boston hospital that was founded by a cousin, Peter Brigham, and became Brigham and Women's Hospital in Boston. Robert's wife, Elizabeth (Brigham) Brigham, survived him. Robert Breck Brigham was a first cousin of Judge Henry Brigham McClure of Lansing and Jacksonville, Illinois (discussed earlier in this chapter).

The Brigham-Holt Branch of Chicago

Dr. Luther Brigham (1785-1856) married Eunice Hawley.[3882] The children born to this marriage, and to a second marriage (Betsey Ayers), included the following persons: Lucretia Brigham; Jonas C. Brigham, prominent founding industrialist of Detroit, Michigan; Lemuel Hawley Brigham; Martha Eliza Brigham; **Hannah Brigham**; Eunice Brigham; George Homer Brigham; Elizabeth Ann Brigham; Luther Ayers Brigham; Charlotte Rice Brigham; William Henry Brigham; and Emma Francis Brigham.[3883] **Hannah Brigham (b. 1821), daughter of Dr. Luther Brigham and Eunice (Hawley) Brigham, married George Holt**.[3884]

[3874] The Chicago Tribune. (April 14, 1957). Part 3, P. 11. Newspapers.com.
[3875] The Chicago Tribune. (April 14, 1957). Part 3, P. 11. Newspapers.com.
[3876] The Chicago Tribune. (April 14, 1957). Part 3, P. 11. Newspapers.com.
[3877] The Chicago Tribune. (April 14, 1957). Part 3, P. 11. Newspapers.com.
[3878] Brigham, W. I. Tyler. (1907). The History of the Brigham Family; a record of several thousand descendants of Thomas Brigham the emigrant, 1603-1653. Emma E. Brigham, Ed. Pp. 249, 556. New York, NY: The Grafton Press, Genealogical Publishers. Google Books; Reading Times. (January 11, 1900). P. 1. Newspapers.com.
[3879] Reading Times. (January 11, 1900). P. 1. Newspapers.com.
[3880] Reading Times. (January 11, 1900). P. 1. Newspapers.com.
[3881] Reading Times. (January 11, 1900). P. 1. Newspapers.com.
[3882] Brigham, W. I. Tyler. (1907). The History of the Brigham Family; a record of several thousand descendants of Thomas Brigham the emigrant, 1603-1653. Emma E. Brigham, Ed. New York, NY: The Grafton Press, Genealogical Publishers. Google Books.
[3883] Brigham, W. I. Tyler. (1907). The History of the Brigham Family; a record of several thousand descendants of Thomas Brigham the emigrant, 1603-1653. Emma E. Brigham, Ed. New York, NY: The Grafton Press, Genealogical Publishers. Google Books.
[3884] Ramsdell, George Allen, and Colburn, William P. (1901). The History of Milford. P. 747. Concord, NH: The Rumford Press. Google Books.

George Holt (1818-1898) was the son of Abiel Holt and Betsey (Holt) Holt.[3885] George and Hannah (Brigham) Holt relocated from Milford, New Hampshire, to Minnesota, and then subsequently to Chicago.[3886] The *1880 United States Census* indicated that George and Hannah Holt resided at 314 Walnut Street, in Chicago.[3887] The *1880 Census* also indicated that George was employed as a cabinetmaker at that time.[3888] The *1880 Census* enumerated Hannah's occupation as that of housewife.[3889] George Holt died on December 3, 1898.[3890] He and Hannah resided at 16 N. Francisco Avenue at the time of his death.[3891] George Holt was interred at Forest Home Cemetery in Cook County.[3892] The address of 16 N. Francisco Avenue is located within the East Garfield Park community of Chicago. George and Hannah (Brigham) Holt had two children, a son and a daughter: George F. Holt (b. 1862) and Emma Holt (1848-1877).[3893] Emma Holt married Charles C. Carson, and they resided in Chicago.[3894] The *1900 United States Census* enumerated George F. Holt, and his widowed mother, Hannah (Brigham) Holt, both as residents of a rented house located at 618 Walnut Street, in Chicago.[3895] The *1900 United States Census* identified George F. Holt's occupation as machinist.[3896] The Walnut Street address was located in what is now the West Loop community, at a point that that is close to Wolf Point and to the Fulton House. Fulton House is a building that was designed by Frank Abbott and was constructed two years previous to the *1900 United States Census*, in 1898.[3897] The Holts would have known the building well.

The Douglas Family of New England

The next segment of this chapter concerns the Douglas-Brigham family of Chicago. The individuals discussed within this segment include George French

[3885] Ramsdell, George Allen, and Colburn, William P. (1901). The History of Milford. P. 747. Concord, NH: The Rumford Press. Google Books.
[3886] Ramsdell, George Allen, and Colburn, William P. (1901). The History of Milford. P. 747. Concord, NH: The Rumford Press. Google Books.
[3887] 1880 United States Census. Ancestry.com.
[3888] 1880 United States Census. Ancestry.com.
[3889] 1880 United States Census. Ancestry.com.
[3890] The Chicago Tribune. (December 4, 1898). P. 7. Newspapers.com.
[3891] The Chicago Tribune. (December 4, 1898). P. 7. Newspapers.com.
[3892] The Chicago Tribune. (December 4, 1898). P. 7. Newspapers.com.
[3893] Ramsdell, George Allen, and Colburn, William P. (1901). The History of Milford. P. 747. Concord, NH: The Rumford Press. Google Books.
[3894] Ramsdell, George Allen, and Colburn, William P. (1901). The History of Milford. P. 747. Concord, NH: The Rumford Press. Google Books.
[3895] 1900 United States Census. Ancestry.com.
[3896] 1900 United States Census. Ancestry.com.
[3897] Koziarz, Jay. (March 14, 2016). River Views Define This One-Bedroom Unit In Former Cold Storage Building. *Curbed Chicago*. Chicago.curbed.com.

Brigham, Sr., Aurilla (Douglas) Brigham, Henry Hanson Brigham, Edmund Douglas Brigham, and George French Brigham, Jr., all of Chicago and Wisconsin. Dr. David Gill McClure, whose biographical information is discussed previously in this chapter, was a member of the Douglas family, the Edgerton family, and the Edgecomb family, as well as a member of the McClure family discussed extensively above.

Deacon William Douglas was almost certainly a native of Scotland. He married Ann Mattle. William and Ann (Mattle) Douglas had the following children: Ann Douglas, who married Nathaniel Geary of Lynn, Massachusetts; **Robert Douglas, who married Mary Hempstead**, who was the daughter of Robert Hempstead; Elizabeth Douglas, who married Deacon John Chandler; Sarah Douglas, who married John Keeney; and William Douglas, who married, first, Abiah Hough, and second, Mrs. Mary Bushnell.[3898] Robert Hempstead founded New London with the Winthrop family.[3899]

Robert Douglas was born in 1639, and probably in Scotland. He was the son of William Douglas and Ann (Mattle) Douglas, who emigrated to New London, Connecticut, in 1640.[3900] Robert Douglas married Mary Hempstead. The following children were born to them: William Douglas, who married Hannah (surname not indicated); Mary Douglas, who married George Chappell; Ann Douglas, who married Jacob Waterhouse; John Douglas, who died as an infant; Hannah Douglas, who married Stephen Hurlbut; Sarah Douglas, who married Samuel Comstock; Elizabeth Douglas, who married Henry Rowland; **Thomas Douglas, who married Hannah Sperry**; Phebe Douglas, who married John Baker; Susannah Douglas, who married Edward DeWolf; and Ruth Douglas, who married Isaac Woodworth.[3901]

Thomas Douglas of New London married Hannah Sperry of New Haven, Connecticut. Thomas was a leader in the New London Church and in the New

[3898] Douglas, Charles Henry James. (1879). A Collection Of Family Records, With Biographical Sketches, And Other Memoranda Of Various Families And Individuals Bearing The Name DOUGLAS. Pp. 54-61. Providence, RI: E. L. Freeman & Co., Publishers. Google Books.

[3899] Douglas, Charles Henry James. (1879). A Collection Of Family Records, With Biographical Sketches, And Other Memoranda Of Various Families And Individuals Bearing The Name DOUGLAS. P. 62. Providence, RI: E. L. Freeman & Co., Publishers. Google Books.

[3900] Douglas, Charles Henry James. (1879). A Collection Of Family Records, With Biographical Sketches, And Other Memoranda Of Various Families And Individuals Bearing The Name DOUGLAS. Pp. 54-55, 62. Providence, RI: E. L. Freeman & Co., Publishers. Google Books.

[3901] Douglas, Charles Henry James. (1879). A Collection Of Family Records, With Biographical Sketches, And Other Memoranda Of Various Families And Individuals Bearing The Name DOUGLAS. Pp. 62-63. Providence, RI: E. L. Freeman & Co., Publishers. Google Books.

London government. The children born to Thomas and Hannah (Sperry) Douglas were the following: John Douglas, who died young; **Robert Douglas, who married Sarah Edgecomb**; Thomas Douglas; James Douglas, who married Sarah Gee; Daniel Douglas, who married Lois Caulkins; Mary Douglas, who married Daniel Sexton; Stephen Douglas, who married Patience Atwell; Nathan Douglas, who married Anne Dennis; and John Douglas, who married Esther Leach.[3902]

Robert Douglas was a native of New London and married Sarah Edgecomb.[3903] Robert Douglass and Sarah (Edgecomb) Douglas had the following children, all of whom were born in New London: Hannah Douglas, who married Nicholas Bishop; Thomas Douglas, who married Grace Richards; Sarah Douglas, who married Edward Raymond; Robert Douglas, who married Hannah Gardiner; **Mary Douglas, who married Daniel Edgerton (ancestors of the McClure family of Morgan County, Chicago, and Michigan)**; Samuel Douglas, who married Rebecca Avery; Mehitabel Douglas, who married Benjamin Gorton; Joseph Douglas, who married Mary Thompson; and **Daniel Douglas, who married Lydia Douglas (ancestors of the Brigham family of Chicago and Wisconsin)**.[3904] It is important at this point to note that two children of Robert Douglas and Sarah (Edgecomb) Douglas were patriarchs of two significant industrial families in Chicago history: the **Daniel Edgerton-Mary Douglas branch**, which would include the Stryker and Taylor branches of Chicago, Morgan County, and Michigan (all discussed above); and the **Daniel Douglas-Lydia Douglas branch**, which would include the Brigham branch of Chicago and Walworth County, Wisconsin (discussed below).

Two Douglas Lines of Chicago: The Daniel Edgerton and Mary (Douglas) Edgerton Line; and the Daniel Douglas and Lydia (Douglas) Douglas Line

The Douglas-Edgerton Branch

Mary Douglas was the daughter of Robert Douglas and Sarah (Edgecomb) Douglas. Mary Douglas married Capt. Daniel Edgerton. They had a daughter,

---

[3902] Douglas, Charles Henry James. (1879). A Collection Of Family Records, With Biographical Sketches, And Other Memoranda Of Various Families And Individuals Bearing The Name DOUGLAS. P. 67. Providence, RI: E. L. Freeman & Co., Publishers. Google Books.

[3903] Douglas, Charles Henry James. (1879). A Collection Of Family Records, With Biographical Sketches, And Other Memoranda Of Various Families And Individuals Bearing The Name DOUGLAS. P. 71. Providence, RI: E. L. Freeman & Co., Publishers. Google Books.

[3904] Douglas, Charles Henry James. (1879). A Collection Of Family Records, With Biographical Sketches, And Other Memoranda Of Various Families And Individuals Bearing The Name DOUGLAS. P. 72. Providence, RI: E. L. Freeman & Co., Publishers. Google Books.

Phebe Edgerton, who married Dr. Samuel McClure of Rutland, Vermont. Samuel McClure and Phebe (Edgerton) McClure had a son, David Gill McClure, who would later become a founder of Lansing, Michigan, and Ingham County, Michigan, as well as one of the fathers of the State of Michigan. Dr. David Gill McClure married Betsey Brigham. To them was born a son, Henry Brigham McClure, who married Harriet Hillhouse Henshaw. Henry McClure and Harriet (Henshaw) McClure were the parents of Elizabeth Henshaw McClure. Elizabeth Henshaw McClure married Henry Stryker, Jr., of Jacksonville, Illinois. The McClure and Stryker families participated significantly in the civic, industrial, and financial development and leadership of Chicago, Springfield, Sangamon County, Morgan County, Greene County, and St. Louis. The Douglas-Edgerton branch and its McClure family, Stryker family, and Taylor family branches are all discussed previously in this chapter (see above).

The Douglas-Brigham Branch

   Capt. Daniel Douglas was a son of Robert Douglas and Sarah (Edgecomb) Douglas. Capt. Daniel Douglas married his cousin, Lydia Douglas of New London, Connecticut. Capt. Daniel Douglas and Lydia (Douglas) Douglas had a son, Edmund Douglas, who first married Orilla Hyde, and second, married Elizabeth Rowley. Edmund Douglas' daughter, Aurilla Douglas, married George French Brigham. George F. Brigham and Aurilla (Douglas) Brigham had three sons who would become major developers of industry in Chicago, St. Louis, and Tulsa, Oklahoma. Those three sons were Henry Hanson Brigham, George French Brigham, Jr., and Edmund Douglas Brigham. The full list of children born to Daniel Douglas and Lydia (Douglas) Douglas follows here: **Edmund Douglas, who married first, Orilla Hyde, and second, Elizabeth Rowley**; Lydia Douglas, who married The Hon. Jacob Houghton; Gilbert Denison Douglas, who married Elizabeth Hamilton; Benjamin Douglas, who married Lucy Townshend; Christopher Douglas, who married Phebe Douglas; William Douglas, who married Anna Eddy; Sarah Douglas; and Daniel Wetherel Douglas, who married Hannah Fenner.[3905]

   Edmund D. Douglas, son of Capt. Daniel Douglas and Lydia (Douglas) Douglas, married first, Orilla Hyde, and second, Elizabeth Rowley.[3906] The

[3905] Douglas, Charles Henry James. (1879). A Collection Of Family Records, With Biographical Sketches, And Other Memoranda Of Various Families And Individuals Bearing The Name DOUGLAS. Pp. 90-91. Providence, RI: E. L. Freeman & Co., Publishers. Google Books.
[3906] Douglas, Charles Henry James. (1879). A Collection Of Family Records, With Biographical Sketches, And Other Memoranda Of Various Families And Individuals Bearing The Name DOUGLAS. P. 163. Providence, RI: E. L. Freeman & Co., Publishers. Google Books.

children born to Edmund Douglas included the following persons, in addition to others whose names are unknown: Daniel Douglas of St. Louis, Missouri; Gilbert Douglas of California; Caroline Douglas of Madison, Iowa; **Aurilla Douglas, who married George French Brigham, Sr.**; Marian Douglas of Michigan; Edmund Douglas of Byron, New York; Henry Douglas of Byron, New York; and Rowley Douglas of Byron, New York.[3907]

George French Brigham, Sr., married Aurilla Douglass.[3908] George F. Brigham held the historical distinction and honor of being one of the founders of telegraphy in Chicago.[3909] The Chicago *Inter-Ocean* newspaper indicated in its 1914 obituary for Brigham that when Brigham had arrived in Chicago during the 1860s, the United States Telegraph Company was the only telegraph service company in existence at Chicago.[3910] As an employee of the United States Telegraph Company at this time, Brigham held the distinction of being the sole telegraph operator in Chicago.[3911] The *Inter-Ocean* stated not only that Brigham was the sole telegrapher in Chicago at that time in the 1860s, but also that he was the manager of the entire Chicago telegraph office of the United States Telegraph Company.[3912] This office was located at the Sherman House Hotel.[3913] The *Inter-Ocean* identified the elements of the telegraph job as follows: "He solicited business, waited on the counter, received messages from other cities, and sent them out."[3914]

After working for numerous years as a founding technologist and promoter of the Chicago telegraphy industry, Brigham entered the employ of the Chicago & Northwestern Railway Company at the age of 35.[3915] Subsequently, at approximately the age of 46, Brigham was called by God to enter Christian ministry.[3916] He thereafter combined the railroad industry work with that of Christian ministry, having taken Deacon's orders within the Episcopal Church.[3917] Brigham maintained the work of Christian ministry and railroad work until the age

---

[3907] Douglas, Charles Henry James. (1879). A Collection Of Family Records, With Biographical Sketches, And Other Memoranda Of Various Families And Individuals Bearing The Name DOUGLAS. P. 163. Providence, RI: E. L. Freeman & Co., Publishers. Google Books.

[3908] The Minute Man. (February, 1930). The Sons of the Revolution in the State of Illinois. Vol. XX, Number 1. P. 7. Chicago, IL: Illinois Society of Sons of the Revolution. Google Books.

[3909] The Inter-Ocean. (March 18, 1914). P. 3. Newspapers.com.

[3910] The Inter-Ocean. (March 18, 1914). P. 3. Newspapers.com.

[3911] The Inter-Ocean. (March 18, 1914). P. 3. Newspapers.com.

[3912] The Inter-Ocean. (March 18, 1914). P. 3. Newspapers.com.

[3913] The Inter-Ocean. (March 18, 1914). P. 3. Newspapers.com.

[3914] The Inter-Ocean. (March 18, 1914). P. 3. Newspapers.com.

[3915] The Inter-Ocean. (March 18, 1914). P. 3. Newspapers.com.

[3916] The Inter-Ocean. (March 18, 1914). P. 3. Newspapers.com.

[3917] The Inter-Ocean. (March 18, 1914). P. 3. Newspapers.com.

of 70, when he relinquished the railroad work and concentrated exclusively on Christian ministry.[3918] Apparently, it was upon retirement from the Chicago railroad industry when George Brigham relocated to Sharon, Wisconsin, to pastor a church congregation there.[3919] Being counted among the earliest generation of United States telegraphers caused Brigham to be among the so-called "Forty-Niners," an honored class of telegraphy pioneers who were members of the Old Time Telegraphers' Association.[3920] Also among the Forty-Niners was Scottish-American Pittsburgh industrialist Andrew Carnegie.[3921]

Henry Hanson Brigham (1868-1930) was a son of George French Brigham, Sr., and Aurilla (Douglas) Brigham.[3922] Henry H. Brigham was born in Sharon, Wisconsin.[3923] He entered the railroad industry by beginning employment with the Chicago & Northwestern Railway Company.[3924] The Chicago & Northwestern Railway Company provided jobs for all three of the Brigham brothers: Henry Hanson Brigham, Edmund Douglas Brigham, and George French Brigham, Jr.[3925] The jobs and experiences with this railroad company must have contributed to all three brothers deciding to move to Chicago. Henry Hanson Brigham began as a telegraph worker for the Chicago & Northwestern Railway Company.[3926] At some point prior to March, 1898, the Chicago & Northwestern Railway Company assigned Brigham to work at their office at Ashland, Wisconsin, which is a city located on Chequamegon Bay of Lake Superior.[3927] Brigham furthermore worked for the Nickel Plate Road (New York, Chicago & St. Louis Railroad Company) at an unspecified time.[3928] In approximately March of 1898, Henry Brigham changed jobs and accepted the office of General Manager of the Traffic Department of Armour & Company in Chicago.[3929]

[3918] The Inter-Ocean. (March 18, 1914). P. 3. Newspapers.com.

[3919] The Inter-Ocean. (March 18, 1914). P. 3. Newspapers.com.

[3920] The Inter-Ocean. (March 18, 1914). P. 3. Newspapers.com.

[3921] The Inter-Ocean. (March 18, 1914). P. 3. Newspapers.com.

[3922] The Minute Man. (February, 1930). The Sons of the Revolution in the State of Illinois. Vol. XX, Number 1. P. 7. Chicago, IL: Illinois Society of Sons of the Revolution. Google Books.

[3923] The Minute Man. (February, 1930). The Sons of the Revolution in the State of Illinois. Vol. XX, Number 1. P. 7. Chicago, IL: Illinois Society of Sons of the Revolution. Google Books.

[3924] The Minute Man. (February, 1930). The Sons of the Revolution in the State of Illinois. Vol. XX, Number 1. P. 7. Chicago, IL: Illinois Society of Sons of the Revolution. Google Books.

[3925] The Inter-Ocean. (March 18, 1914). P. 3. Newspapers.com.

[3926] The Minute Man. (February, 1930). The Sons of the Revolution in the State of Illinois. Vol. XX, Number 1. P. 7. Chicago, IL: Illinois Society of Sons of the Revolution. Google Books.

[3927] The Ironwood Times. (March 5, 1898). P. 5. Newspapers.com.

[3928] Stevens Point Journal. (February 28, 1898). P. 4. Newspapers.com.

[3929] The Ironwood Times. (March 5, 1898). P. 5. Newspapers.com.

Brigham accepted the position of Traffic Manager with A. Booth & Company of Chicago.[3930] As of 1919, Brigham served as President of the North American Car Company of Chicago, as well as President of the Atlantic Seaboard Despatch Company, also of Chicago.[3931] Brigham held memberships in the following Chicago and Cook County clubs: Union League Club, Chicago Yacht Club, Skokie Golf Club, Traffic Club, and the Petroleum Club.[3932] Brigham participated prominently in the civic life of Glencoe, a northern Chicago suburb.[3933] He served as Warden of St. Elizabeth's Episcopal Church in Glencoe and as Chairman of the Glencoe War Emergency Union.[3934] He was a member of the Glencoe Lodge Number 983, Associated Free and Accepted Masons.[3935] Brigham also held membership in the Sons of the American Revolution and in the Brigham Family Association, a genealogical organization of Boston.[3936] Henry Brigham, Edmund Douglas Brigham, and their wives, were also members of the Ravenswood Club of Chicago.[3937] They were listed in attendance at the February, 1900, celebration and memorial of the birthday of President George Washington, an event produced and hosted by the Ravenswood Club.[3938]

Henry Hanson Brigham cooperated with multiple additional persons in the establishment of the Calumet Insurance Company of Chicago at some point in either the summer or fall of 1904, or the winter of 1905.[3939] The issue of *The National Corporation Reporter* that accounted for the time period from August,

---

[3930] Hoffman, Roy, Bixby, Edson K., Steenrod, F. L., Harrison, W. M. (Eds.). (1919). P. 87. Oklahomans and Their State.: A Newspaper Reference Work. Oklahoma City, OK: The Oklahoma Biographical Association. Google Books.

[3931] Hoffman, Roy, Bixby, Edson K., Steenrod, F. L., Harrison, W. M. (Eds.). (1919). P. 87. Oklahomans and Their State.: A Newspaper Reference Work. Oklahoma City, OK: The Oklahoma Biographical Association. Google Books.

[3932] Hoffman, Roy, Bixby, Edson K., Steenrod, F. L., Harrison, W. M. (Eds.). (1919). P. 87. Oklahomans and Their State.: A Newspaper Reference Work. Oklahoma City, OK: The Oklahoma Biographical Association. Google Books.

[3933] Hoffman, Roy, Bixby, Edson K., Steenrod, F. L., Harrison, W. M. (Eds.). (1919). P. 87. Oklahomans and Their State.: A Newspaper Reference Work. Oklahoma City, OK: The Oklahoma Biographical Association. Google Books.

[3934] Hoffman, Roy, Bixby, Edson K., Steenrod, F. L., Harrison, W. M. (Eds.). (1919). P. 87. Oklahomans and Their State.: A Newspaper Reference Work. Oklahoma City, OK: The Oklahoma Biographical Association. Google Books.

[3935] Hoffman, Roy, Bixby, Edson K., Steenrod, F. L., Harrison, W. M. (Eds.). (1919). P. 87. Oklahomans and Their State.: A Newspaper Reference Work. Oklahoma City, OK: The Oklahoma Biographical Association. Google Books.

[3936] Hoffman, Roy, Bixby, Edson K., Steenrod, F. L., Harrison, W. M. (Eds.). (1919). P. 87. Oklahomans and Their State.: A Newspaper Reference Work. Oklahoma City, OK: The Oklahoma Biographical Association. Google Books.

[3937] The Inter-Ocean. (February 25, 1900). P. 18. Newspapers.com.

[3938] The Inter-Ocean. (February 25, 1900). P. 18. Newspapers.com.

[3939] The National Corporation Reporter. (1904-1905). Vol. 29. P. 376. The United States Corporation Bureau. Google Books.

1904, until February, 1905, provided extensive reportage on the subject of the establishment of the Calumet Insurance Company of Chicago.[3940] The declaration of proposal for charter of the new insurance company appeared within *The National Corporation Reporter*.[3941] The law firm that represented the promoters and establishers of the company was Gann, Peaks & Haffenberg.[3942] This law firm had offices at 1301 Ashland Block.[3943] The declaration presented to the Honorable William R. Vredenburgh, who was then the Superintendent of the Illinois Insurance Department, statements of name, purpose, description, capitalization, powers, and leadership staff of the new company.[3944]

The commercial purpose of the company included the creation of policies of insurance upon a complex class of risks.[3945] The classes of insurable risk upon which the corporation proposed to create policies of insurance included the risks to dwelling houses, buildings, stores, and the furniture contents of houses, caused by fires, lightning, and tornadoes.[3946] The intended class of insurable risks also included, "vessels, boats, cargoes, goods, merchandise, freights and other property against loss or damage by all or any of the risks of lake, river, canal and island navigation and transportation. . ."[3947] These policies of insurance, by their very nature and operation, would have probably often implicated admiralty jurisprudence. The corporate purpose encompassed, therefore, the creation of insurance policies upon risks that attached to properties of residential, commercial, maritime, and industrial character.[3948] The Illinois law that regulated, in cooperation with all relevant amendments, the creation of such companies was the Act of March 11, 1869, whose preamble stated the following with respect to the

---

[3940] The National Corporation Reporter. (1904-1905). Vol. 29. P. 376. The United States Corporation Bureau. Google Books.
[3941] The National Corporation Reporter. (1904-1905). Vol. 29. P. 376. The United States Corporation Bureau. Google Books.
[3942] The National Corporation Reporter. (1904-1905). Vol. 29. P. 376. The United States Corporation Bureau. Google Books.
[3943] The National Corporation Reporter. (1904-1905). Vol. 29. P. 376. The United States Corporation Bureau. Google Books.
[3944] The National Corporation Reporter. (1904-1905). Vol. 29. P. 376. The United States Corporation Bureau. Google Books.
[3945] The National Corporation Reporter. (1904-1905). Vol. 29. P. 376. The United States Corporation Bureau. Google Books.
[3946] The National Corporation Reporter. (1904-1905). Vol. 29. P. 376. The United States Corporation Bureau. Google Books.
[3947] The National Corporation Reporter. (1904-1905). Vol. 29. P. 376. The United States Corporation Bureau. Google Books.
[3948] The National Corporation Reporter. (1904-1905). Vol. 29. P. 376. The United States Corporation Bureau. Google Books.

statutory purpose: "An Act to Incorporate and to Govern Fire, Marine and Inland Navigation Insurance Companies doing business in the State of Illinois."[3949]

The capital structure of the Calumet Insurance Company consisted of capital stock money of $200,000.[3950] This quantity was divided into 20,000 shares, each of which possessed a par value of $10.00.[3951] The organizational life time of the company was established to be 30 years.[3952] The charter of the company established a leadership structure in which a board of directors of 25 persons was to govern the policy and operation of the corporation.[3953] The stockholders possessed voting powers with respect to the members of the board of directors, and elections were to occur annually.[3954] The charter commissioned the board of directors to elect a president, vice-president, treasurer, and secretary of the company.[3955] The board of directors possessed the power to establish additional executive leadership offices, according to their judgments of the need for such additional offices within the leadership structure of the company.[3956]

The articles of incorporation attached duties of production and maintenance of records of the corporate accounts, such that all elements of the commerce of the company were accounted for in proper and relevant records.[3957] The charter also attached to the board of directors a duty of annual report (for the benefit of the stockholders) with respect to the business of the company.[3958] The board of directors possessed the power of removal with respect to any officer whose removal was to be judged proper for the company.[3959] The incorporators included the following persons: Henry Hanson Brigham, George Koster, James W. Nye, W.

[3949] The National Corporation Reporter. (1904-1905). Vol. 29. P. 376. The United States Corporation Bureau. Google Books.

[3950] The National Corporation Reporter. (1904-1905). Vol. 29. P. 376. The United States Corporation Bureau. Google Books.

[3951] The National Corporation Reporter. (1904-1905). Vol. 29. P. 376. The United States Corporation Bureau. Google Books.

[3952] The National Corporation Reporter. (1904-1905). Vol. 29. P. 376. The United States Corporation Bureau. Google Books.

[3953] The National Corporation Reporter. (1904-1905). Vol. 29. P. 376. The United States Corporation Bureau. Google Books.

[3954] The National Corporation Reporter. (1904-1905). Vol. 29. P. 376. The United States Corporation Bureau. Google Books.

[3955] The National Corporation Reporter. (1904-1905). Vol. 29. P. 376. The United States Corporation Bureau. Google Books.

[3956] The National Corporation Reporter. (1904-1905). Vol. 29. P. 376. The United States Corporation Bureau. Google Books.

[3957] The National Corporation Reporter. (1904-1905). Vol. 29. P. 376. The United States Corporation Bureau. Google Books.

[3958] The National Corporation Reporter. (1904-1905). Vol. 29. P. 376. The United States Corporation Bureau. Google Books.

[3959] The National Corporation Reporter. (1904-1905). Vol. 29. P. 376. The United States Corporation Bureau. Google Books.

G. Walling, Bernard F. Rogers, and Nathan Kice, all of Chicago; A. W. Haight, Henry Fowler, and William Cowle, all of Syracuse, New York; William H. Kinns of New York City; Stuart Morgan and Frank J. Macklin of Columbus, Ohio; Alexander L. Metzel of Elgin, Illinois; Lake W. Sanborn of Galesburg, Illinois; Stephen D. Sexton of East St. Louis, Illinois; John L. Beeler of Hamilton, Ohio; H. N. Leighton of Minneapolis, Minnesota; G. H. Hale of Malone, New York; Jonas B. Wise and Joseph M. Yates of Sharon, Wisconsin; Charles L. Gurney of Buffalo, New York.[3960]

George French Brigham, Jr., entered the railroad industry in Wisconsin and Michigan, working at Sharon, Wisconsin, at Ishpeming, Michigan, and Escanaba, Michigan.[3961] He also worked in Chicago and in Kansas City.[3962] George F. Brigham additionally worked in St. Louis as General Agent of the Chicago & North Western Railroad Company.[3963] After the United States Railway Administration takeover of the Chicago & North Western Railroad Company assets at St. Louis, Brigham entered the petroleum industry.[3964] He served as President of the Commerce Petroleum Company, a corporation based both in Chicago and in Tulsa, Oklahoma.[3965] George F. Brigham belonged to multiple Chicago clubs and industry organizations, including the Traffic Club, the Petroleum Club, the American Petroleum League, and the Independent Oil Men's Association.[3966]

The Brigham brothers founded the Commerce Petroleum Company in 1922. The Commerce Petroleum Company was incorporated in 1922, probably in

---

[3960] The National Corporation Reporter. (1904-1905). Vol. 29. P. 376. The United States Corporation Bureau. Google Books.

[3961] Hoffman, Roy, Bixby, Edson K., Steenrod, F. L., Harrison, W. M. (Eds.). (1919). P. 87. Oklahomans and Their State.: A Newspaper Reference Work. Oklahoma City, OK: The Oklahoma Biographical Association. Google Books.

[3962] Hoffman, Roy, Bixby, Edson K., Steenrod, F. L., Harrison, W. M. (Eds.). (1919). P. 87. Oklahomans and Their State.: A Newspaper Reference Work. Oklahoma City, OK: The Oklahoma Biographical Association. Google Books.

[3963] Hoffman, Roy, Bixby, Edson K., Steenrod, F. L., Harrison, W. M. (Eds.). (1919). P. 87. Oklahomans and Their State.: A Newspaper Reference Work. Oklahoma City, OK: The Oklahoma Biographical Association. Google Books.

[3964] Hoffman, Roy, Bixby, Edson K., Steenrod, F. L., Harrison, W. M. (Eds.). (1919). P. 87. Oklahomans and Their State.: A Newspaper Reference Work. Oklahoma City, OK: The Oklahoma Biographical Association. Google Books.

[3965] Hoffman, Roy, Bixby, Edson K., Steenrod, F. L., Harrison, W. M. (Eds.). (1919). P. 87. Oklahomans and Their State.: A Newspaper Reference Work. Oklahoma City, OK: The Oklahoma Biographical Association. Google Books.

[3966] Hoffman, Roy, Bixby, Edson K., Steenrod, F. L., Harrison, W. M. (Eds.). (1919). P. 87. Oklahomans and Their State.: A Newspaper Reference Work. Oklahoma City, OK: The Oklahoma Biographical Association. Google Books.

September.[3967] The new company shared a headquarters location and address with the North American Car Company at 327 La Salle Street, Chicago.[3968] The Commerce Petroleum Company incorporation capital totaled $227,155.[3969] At the time of formation, George French Brigham, Jr., served as President of the company, and A. W. Peterson served as Secretary of the company.[3970] The Commerce Petroleum Company occupied premises located in the Clearing community of southwest Chicago.[3971] The company shared the Clearing community with the following other companies in 1940: Continental Can Company, Educator Biscuit Company, Pepsodent Company, Lock-Joint Pipe Company, Arkell Safety Bag Company, Inland Glass Works, National Aluminate Corporation, General Printing Ink Corporation, Chicago Steel Tank Company, Rapinwax Paper Company, Bethlehem Steel Company, A-1 Union Furnace Fittings Company, Buick Motor Company, McGraw Electrical Company, Western Electric Company, American Brake Shoe and Foundry Company, Borg and Beck Company, Howard Aircraft, and the Lloyd and Fry Roofing Company.[3972] The 1940 article reported that 126 companies were located in the Clearing community in 1940.[3973]

The January 26, 1921, issue of the *National Petroleum News*, a weekly oil industry journal of Cleveland, Ohio, announced that Henry Brigham was in Tulsa visiting his brother, George F. Brigham Jr. George Brigham was President of the Commerce Petroleum Corporation at this time. The reporter alluded to Henry Brigham's service on the Cook County Grand Jury in connection with the 1919 Chicago Black Sox Scandal: "The brothers are making a tour of Oklahoma, Texas and Louisiana to check up on prospective oil business. As foreman of the Chicago grand jury that indicted the baseball gamblers and crooks Henry H. Brigham may be somewhat disappointed because of the bad finish of a good start."[3974]

The Commerce Petroleum Company developed a significant industrial connection for Chicago and Tulsa, as was reported in the November, 1918, issue

---

[3967] Petroleum Age. (1922). Vol. 10, Number 7. P. 106. Chicago, IL: Graffis-Sutton Publishing Company. Google Books.

[3968] Petroleum Age. (1922). Vol. 10, Number 7. P. 106. Chicago, IL: Graffis-Sutton Publishing Company. Google Books. Petroleum Register: An International Annual Directory and Statistical Record of the World's Petroleum Industry. (1922). P. 463. New York, NY: Oil Trade Journal, Inc. Google Books.

[3969] Petroleum Age. (1922). Vol. 10, Number 7. P. 106. Chicago, IL: Graffis-Sutton Publishing Company. Google Books.

[3970] Petroleum Age. (1922). Vol. 10, Number 7. P. 106. Chicago, IL: Graffis-Sutton Publishing Company. Google Books.

[3971] Chicago Tribune. (July 28, 1940). P. 125. Newspapers.com.

[3972] Chicago Tribune. (July 28, 1940). P. 125. Newspapers.com.

[3973] Chicago Tribune. (July 28, 1940). P. 125. Newspapers.com.

[3974] National Petroleum News. (1921). Vol. 13, Number 66. P. 53. Cleveland, OH: National Petroleum News. Google Books.

of *Petroleum Age*. George F. Brigham, Jr., who was President of the Commerce Petroleum Company, hired W. K. Evans as Sales Manager for the Chicago office of the Commerce Petroleum Company.[3975] Evans would work from the office located at Number 930 at the Webster Building, which was located at 327 S. LaSalle Street.[3976] Brigham also hired D. A. Curry as Sales Manager for the Tulsa branch of the company, where Curry would work from the corporate office at office number 1003 at the Daniel Building.[3977]

The railroad technology industry proliferated both in answers to market needs, and in opportunities for commercial development and growth. Refrigeration technology evolved quickly in railroading. That technical evolution generated opportunities for novel technologies and accompanying visionary entrepreneurship. In 1907 and 1908, Henry Brigham co-founded the North American Car Company, a Chicago railroad manufacturing and leasing company.[3978] This would become one of the most significant railroad companies in Chicago history.

The Morning Tulsa Daily World contained a report on the recently constructed North American Car Company terminal at Blue Island, a Chicago suburb located in Cook County.[3979] The report attested the commercial and transportational innovation that North American Car Company had exhibited; namely, a change in the mode of management of oil tanker cars for independent refining companies.[3980] The news report apparently indicated that the Brigham brothers chose to offer the service of storage to independent petroleum refiners who would not otherwise have received the benefit.[3981] The Brigham method attached a novel benefit to the class of independent petroleum refiners by supplying this service.[3982] *The Morning Tulsa Daily World* stated that the new benefit improved the commercial competitiveness of the independent refiners in that the refiners, who had previously not possessed their own railroad tracks and storage spaces, now could rely upon the North American Car Company to offer such space.[3983] This logistical service constituted

[3975] Petroleum Age. (November, 1918). Vol. 5, Number 10. P. 362. Chicago, IL: The Oil Publishing Company. Google Books.
[3976] Petroleum Age. (November, 1918). Vol. 5, Number 10. P. 362. Chicago, IL: The Oil Publishing Company. Google Books.
[3977] Petroleum Age. (November, 1918). Vol. 5, Number 10. P. 362. Chicago, IL: The Oil Publishing Company. Google Books.
[3978] The Minute Man. (February, 1930). The Sons of the Revolution in the State of Illinois. Vol. XX, Number 1. P. 7. Chicago, IL: Illinois Society of Sons of the Revolution. Google Books. Pittsburgh Post-Gazette. (August 28, 1924). P. 19. Newspapers.com.
[3979] The Morning Tulsa Daily World. (March 2, 1921). P. 11. Newspapers.com.
[3980] The Morning Tulsa Daily World. (March 2, 1921). P. 11. Newspapers.com.
[3981] The Morning Tulsa Daily World. (March 2, 1921). P. 11. Newspapers.com.
[3982] The Morning Tulsa Daily World. (March 2, 1921). P. 11. Newspapers.com.
[3983] The Morning Tulsa Daily World. (March 2, 1921). P. 11. Newspapers.com.

a notable improvement for the independent refiners of the United States.[3984] The service created a logistical benefit for the smaller refiners.[3985] Henry H. Brigham, Edmund Douglas Brigham, and George French Brigham, Jr., all practiced the moral principle that defined the "Wheelbarrow Dialogue," a case in which one who possesses the benefits of power, leadership, and opportunity offers to share those benefits with those who do not possess them.[3986] Jacob Bunn (1814-1897), already well-established in Illinois commerce and industry, offered his younger brother, John Whitfield Bunn (1831-1920), opportunity to join him in Illinois as an entry-level employee with the J. Bunn Grocery Company of Springfield, Illinois.[3987] John accepted the opportunity and rose from the position of collecting stones in a wheelbarrow in Hunterdon County, New Jersey, the original and multi-generational home of the Bunns, to being the co-founder of multiple immense railroad companies, banks, manufacturing companies, and civic organizations of Chicago, Springfield, Urbana-Champaign, and elsewhere.[3988] The Brigham brothers extrapolated the principle of the Wheelbarrow Dialogue to a collective level of operation when they offered an opportunity and benefit to an entire class of industrial entrepreneurs.[3989]

Henry Brigham bought 23 acres of land in Blue Island in March, 1919, to build a new railroad car construction factory.[3990] Brigham bought the land from A. Heitmann, and the space was located at 135th Street at a point where four railroad companies shared rights of way; the Indiana Harbor Belt, the Baltimore & Ohio, the Rock Island, and the Chicago Terminal shared rights of way and routes at the place of the planned Brigham factory.[3991] Proximity to the multi-company crossings and access probably constituted the key benefit that motivated Brigham's choice of this place for the car factory.[3992]

The Morning Tulsa Daily World, a newspaper of Tulsa, Oklahoma, contained an advertisement for the North American Car Company.[3993] The advertisement noted

---

[3984] The Morning Tulsa Daily World. (March 2, 1921). P. 11. Newspapers.com.

[3985] The Morning Tulsa Daily World. (March 2, 1921). P. 11. Newspapers.com.

[3986] Call, Andrew Taylor. (2005). Jacob Bunn: Legacy of an Illinois Industrial Pioneer. Lawrenceville, VA: Brunswick Publishing Corporation.

[3987] Call, Andrew Taylor. (2005). Jacob Bunn: Legacy of an Illinois Industrial Pioneer. Lawrenceville, VA: Brunswick Publishing Corporation.

[3988] Call, Andrew Taylor. (2005). Jacob Bunn: Legacy of an Illinois Industrial Pioneer. Lawrenceville, VA: Brunswick Publishing Corporation.

[3989] The Morning Tulsa Daily World. (March 2, 1921). P. 11. Newspapers.com.

[3990] The Chicago Economist. (March 8, 1919). Vol. 61. P. 426. Chicago, IL. Google Books.

[3991] The Chicago Economist. (March 8, 1919). Vol. 61. P. 426. Chicago, IL. Google Books.

[3992] The Chicago Economist. (March 8, 1919). Vol. 61. P. 426. Chicago, IL. Google Books.

[3993] The Morning Tulsa Daily World. (December 29, 1921). P. 10. Newspapers.com.

that the company constructed, leased, and repaired railroad tank cars.[3994] At this time, George French Brigham, Jr., served as District Manager for the company, with offices at the Daniel Building in Tulsa.[3995]

In 1922, North American Car Company added new equipment to its corporate facility at Coffeeville, Kansas.[3996] The purpose of the equipment was the repair and maintenance of the company railroad cars.[3997] Edmund Douglas Brigham, then Superintendent of the Coffeeville works of North American Car Company, indicated that the new equipment, valued at $25,000, would constitute an improvement of the plant, and would enable the hire of 200 to 300 plant employees.[3998] Edmund D. Brigham noted that at the time of the construction of the new equipment the Coffeeville works employed nobody, presumably because the works had yet to attain full functionality.[3999] The operations of the Coffeeville works apparently remained, at that time, anticipatory.

North American Car Company occupied the Webster Building in 1923.[4000] Heralded as one of the leading buildings of Chicago, the Webster Building was located on LaSalle Street and Van Buren Street.[4001] Albert A. McCaslin, the President of the Webster Building Corporation, provided detailed information to the *Chicago Tribune* regarding the Webster Building in an advertisement designed to promote the sale of financing instruments for the Webster Building Corporation during the winter of 1923.[4002] The fact that McCaslin considered it an honor to count the North American Car Company among the tenants of the Webster Building was manifest in his statement in support of a debt financing plan that was advertised in the *Chicago Tribune* of January 18, 1923.[4003] The building's tenants in 1923 included the following companies, in addition to North American Car Company: Nickel Plate Road (New York, Chicago & St. Louis Railroad Company), the National Railways of Mexico, Baltimore Steamship Company, United American Lines, Gulf Coast Lines, the Fleischmann Company, the Boston & Maine Railroad Company, and the Pere Marquette Railroad system.[4004] The Utilities Power & Light Company also occupied the Webster Building at that time.[4005]

[3994] The Morning Tulsa Daily World. (December 29, 1921). P. 10. Newspapers.com.
[3995] The Morning Tulsa Daily World. (December 29, 1921). P. 10. Newspapers.com.
[3996] The Coffeeville Daily Journal. (January 4, 1922). P. 1. Newspapers.com.
[3997] The Coffeeville Daily Journal. (January 4, 1922). P. 1. Newspapers.com.
[3998] The Coffeeville Daily Journal. (January 4, 1922). P. 1. Newspapers.com.
[3999] The Coffeeville Daily Journal. (January 4, 1922). P. 1. Newspapers.com.
[4000] The Chicago Tribune. (January 18, 1923). P. 22. Newspapers.com.
[4001] The Chicago Tribune. (January 18, 1923). P. 22. Newspapers.com.
[4002] The Chicago Tribune. (January 18, 1923). P. 22. Newspapers.com.
[4003] The Chicago Tribune. (January 18, 1923). P. 22. Newspapers.com.
[4004] The Chicago Tribune. (January 18, 1923). P. 22. Newspapers.com.
[4005] The Chicago Tribune. (January 18, 1923). P. 22. Newspapers.com.

In the summer of 1924, the North American Car Company Equipment Trust advertised in the *Pittsburgh Post-Gazette* a growth-purposed financing plan that supplied investment opportunity to potential investors.[4006] The offer would raise $700,000 for the company.[4007] The financing and investment plan included the offer of gold certificates that possessed a return rate of five percent.[4008] The North America Car Company communicated an assumption of the risks that attached to both the principal and to the yield of the newly offered money instruments.[4009] No conditions attached to the underwriting promise stated by the company in regard to the offered gold certificates.[4010] The certificates encompassed the following operational elements: yield payments were to be made upon a semiannual calendar basis in quantities of $35,000, from March 15, 1925, until March 15, 1934.[4011] The North American Car Company retained a right of redemption over the certificates.[4012] The advertisement pegged the redemption rate at 102.5 percent of the principal value and accrued interest value of the certificates at the time of the exercise of the redemption right.[4013] Certificate holders were to present certificates and yield warrants to the Office of the Trustee.[4014] The yield warrants were marked as registrable on either March 15 or September 15, in accordance with the contemplated payment and yield plan that attached to the certificates.[4015]

Summary of a letter of support and comfort from Henry Hanson Brigham accompanied the advertisement in the *Pittsburgh Post-Gazette*. The summary stated the following: "The North American Car Company, with general offices in Chicago, was organized in 1908 and owns and operates 832 refrigerator cars and 944 tank cars. The Company also owns well-equipped car building and repair shops located at convenient points."[4016] The purpose of this element of the letter was to describe the company, the purpose of the company, and the size of the company.[4017]

The company constructed a security interest plan to ensure the economic safety and soundness of the offered certificate instruments.[4018] The contemplated security interest plan bolstered the investment desirability of the issued certificate instruments. This, in turn, communicated safety and soundness to potential

---

[4006] Pittsburgh Post-Gazette. (August 28, 1924). P. 19. Newspapers.com.

[4007] Pittsburgh Post-Gazette. (August 28, 1924). P. 19. Newspapers.com.

[4008] Pittsburgh Post-Gazette. (August 28, 1924). P. 19. Newspapers.com.

[4009] Pittsburgh Post-Gazette. (August 28, 1924). P. 19. Newspapers.com.

[4010] Pittsburgh Post-Gazette. (August 28, 1924). P. 19. Newspapers.com.

[4011] Pittsburgh Post-Gazette. (August 28, 1924). P. 19. Newspapers.com.

[4012] Pittsburgh Post-Gazette. (August 28, 1924). P. 19. Newspapers.com.

[4013] Pittsburgh Post-Gazette. (August 28, 1924). P. 19. Newspapers.com.

[4014] Pittsburgh Post-Gazette. (August 28, 1924). P. 19. Newspapers.com.

[4015] Pittsburgh Post-Gazette. (August 28, 1924). P. 19. Newspapers.com.

[4016] Pittsburgh Post-Gazette. (August 28, 1924). P. 19. Newspapers.com.

[4017] Pittsburgh Post-Gazette. (August 28, 1924). P. 19. Newspapers.com.

[4018] Pittsburgh Post-Gazette. (August 28, 1924). P. 19. Newspapers.com.

investors while corroborating the viability of the financing plan for North American Car Company.[4019] The security interest plan contemplated a program of collateralization in which the value of 500 refrigerator cars would constitute the source of support for the value of the offered certificate instruments.[4020] The relevant financial report indicated that the depreciated value of the collateral, which was comprised of the 500 railroad refrigerator cars, stood at $1,174,194.40, at approximately the time of the corporate financing opportunity offer.[4021] The collateral value, therefore, exceeded the certificate issue value by 67.74 percent, thereby constituting a sound foundation of support for the promised security interest.[4022] This collateral value surplus meant that the relevant security interests were rooted in a foundation of capital surplus, and not merely a foundation of minimal capital adequacy.[4023] More than enough collateralized security money, therefore, was available to cover the liabilities that stemmed from the debt financing plan.

Investors could derive testimony of the viability of both the company and the relevant corporate equipment collateral from the fact that the refrigerated railcar collateral elements were in use at the time of issuance of the certificates.[4024] Their use proved their viability. Their viability proved their value for producing security interests. The refrigerator cars were under lease by the New York, Chicago, & St. Louis Railway Company (Nickel Plate Road), as well as by the Nashville, Chattanooga & St. Louis Railway Company, and the Jacob Dold Packing Company.[4025] The rates of rent payable under the leases of the assets that supported the certificate payments were stated to possess capital adequacy with respect to payment of the certificate moneys, which consisted of the yield moneys, matured principal moneys, and relevant costs.[4026] The lease rents payable for use of the railcars produced, therefore, revenues that were capable of amortizing any liabilities that derived from the relevant debt financing plan.

The Henry H. Brigham letter also proved the continued growth of the company, thus thickening the proof of the soundness and viability of the advertised investment opportunity for the audience of potential investors.[4027] The Brigham letter stated: "The Company has never had an unprofitable year since its organization in 1908."[4028] The letter then proceeded to report the annualized

---

[4019] Pittsburgh Post-Gazette. (August 28, 1924). P. 19. Newspapers.com.
[4020] Pittsburgh Post-Gazette. (August 28, 1924). P. 19. Newspapers.com.
[4021] Pittsburgh Post-Gazette. (August 28, 1924). P. 19. Newspapers.com.
[4022] Pittsburgh Post-Gazette. (August 28, 1924). P. 19. Newspapers.com.
[4023] Pittsburgh Post-Gazette. (August 28, 1924). P. 19. Newspapers.com.
[4024] Pittsburgh Post-Gazette. (August 28, 1924). P. 19. Newspapers.com.
[4025] Pittsburgh Post-Gazette. (August 28, 1924). P. 19. Newspapers.com.
[4026] Pittsburgh Post-Gazette. (August 28, 1924). P. 19. Newspapers.com.
[4027] Pittsburgh Post-Gazette. (August 28, 1924). P. 19. Newspapers.com.
[4028] Pittsburgh Post-Gazette. (August 28, 1924). P. 19. Newspapers.com.

earnings.[4029] McLaughlin, MacAfee & Company of Pittsburgh, as well as Freeman & Company of New York City, provided the brokerage services for the offer of the debt financing instruments for the North American Car Company.[4030]

As of March, 1914, Henry H. Brigham served as President of the Atlantic Seaboard Dispatch Company.[4031] This organization was a Chicago company.[4032] At this time, Edmund Douglas Brigham served as Assistant Freight Manager of the Chicago & Northwestern Railway Company.[4033] Also at this time, George French Brigham, Jr., served as General Agent of the Chicago & Northwestern Railway Company.[4034]

In the winter of 1907, multiple people who were engaged in the transportation industry decided to establish a transportation club in Chicago.[4035] The people recognized the potential benefits that such an organization would cause to accrue to their commercial work.[4036] *The Philadelphia Inquirer* reported on February 24, 1907, the establishment of the new Chicago commercial organization.[4037] "Plans for the formation of a traffic club where shippers and railroad representatives may meet to discuss matters of interest on the subject of transportation were formulated recently at a meeting held in the Union League Club."[4038] The company of founders included Chicago shipping entrepreneurs as well as traffic and freight managers employed in different railroad companies.[4039] The founders gave the new organization the name, "Chicago Traffic Club."[4040] Thomas C. Moore, who represented the National Piano Association, served as Chairman of the formative conference of the Traffic Club.[4041] The co-founders of the Traffic Club included Henry Hanson Brigham, O. Bell, G. A. Wightman, Thomas C. Moore, J. Ilse, C. A. Hayes, and F. Spink, all of whom collectively constituted the Membership Committee of the Traffic Club.[4042] The 1907 news report identified T. Stockton, F. T. Bentley, C. W. Clark, and D. W. Cooke as co-founders of the Traffic Club, and as members of the Constitution and Bylaws Committee of the Club.[4043] F. T. Bentley, who represented the Illinois Steel Company, stated the purpose of the

[4029] Pittsburgh Post-Gazette. (August 28, 1924). P. 19. Newspapers.com.
[4030] Pittsburgh Post-Gazette. (August 28, 1924). P. 19. Newspapers.com.
[4031] The Inter-Ocean. (March 18, 1914). P. 3. Newspapers.com.
[4032] The Inter-Ocean. (March 18, 1914). P. 3. Newspapers.com.
[4033] The Inter-Ocean. (March 18, 1914). P. 3. Newspapers.com.
[4034] The Inter-Ocean. (March 18, 1914). P. 3. Newspapers.com.
[4035] The Philadelphia Inquirer. (February 24, 1907). P. 5. Newspapers.com.
[4036] The Philadelphia Inquirer. (February 24, 1907). P. 5. Newspapers.com.
[4037] The Philadelphia Inquirer. (February 24, 1907). P. 5. Newspapers.com.
[4038] The Philadelphia Inquirer. (February 24, 1907). P. 5. Newspapers.com.
[4039] The Philadelphia Inquirer. (February 24, 1907). P. 5. Newspapers.com.
[4040] The Philadelphia Inquirer. (February 24, 1907). P. 5. Newspapers.com.
[4041] The Philadelphia Inquirer. (February 24, 1907). P. 5. Newspapers.com.
[4042] The Philadelphia Inquirer. (February 24, 1907). P. 5. Newspapers.com.
[4043] The Philadelphia Inquirer. (February 24, 1907). P. 5. Newspapers.com.

Traffic Club to be one of community, alliance, and cooperation among people working in the transportation industry.[4044] Bentley stated the organizational purpose as follows: "'The club is to be formed primarily to bring together these men interested in traffic matters for social intercourse and pleasure. Banquets and other forms of entertainment will be given, at which general matters of interest in the transportation of freight will be discussed.'"[4045]

The *Petroleum Register* reported in its 1922 annual edition several significant facts about the North American Car Company.[4046] The North American Car Company headquarters stood at 327 LaSalle Street, within the Loop community of Chicago.[4047] North American Car owned branch offices at Tulsa, Oklahoma, and Coffeeville, Kansas. Henry Hanson Brigham was President of the company at that time.[4048] Erwin R. Brigham served as Vice President of the company at that time.[4049] Mead F. Russell served as Secretary of the company in 1922.[4050] The corporate purpose included the manufacture of railroad tank cars, the lease of these cars, and the manufacture of petroleum refining machinery.[4051] Via the subsidiary organizational instrumentality of the North American Oil Terminal, the North American Car Company offered oil storage services at the company facilities located at Stoney Island, Illinois (in Chicago), and in Blue Island, a Cook County suburb of Chicago.[4052]

The United States Federal Trade Commission published a report in 1919 that contained a tremendous quantity of information relevant to the United States

---

[4044] The Philadelphia Inquirer. (February 24, 1907). P. 5. Newspapers.com.
[4045] The Philadelphia Inquirer. (February 24, 1907). P. 5. Newspapers.com.
[4046] Petroleum Register: An International Annual Directory and Statistical Record of the World's Petroleum Industry. (1922). P. 463. New York, NY: Oil Trade Journal, Inc. Google Books.
[4047] Petroleum Register: An International Annual Directory and Statistical Record of the World's Petroleum Industry. (1922). P. 463. New York, NY: Oil Trade Journal, Inc. Google Books.
[4048] Petroleum Register: An International Annual Directory and Statistical Record of the World's Petroleum Industry. (1922). P. 463. New York, NY: Oil Trade Journal, Inc. Google Books.
[4049] Petroleum Register: An International Annual Directory and Statistical Record of the World's Petroleum Industry. (1922). P. 463. New York, NY: Oil Trade Journal, Inc. Google Books.
[4050] Petroleum Register: An International Annual Directory and Statistical Record of the World's Petroleum Industry. (1922). P. 463. New York, NY: Oil Trade Journal, Inc. Google Books.
[4051] Petroleum Register: An International Annual Directory and Statistical Record of the World's Petroleum Industry. (1922). P. 463. New York, NY: Oil Trade Journal, Inc. Google Books.
[4052] Petroleum Register: An International Annual Directory and Statistical Record of the World's Petroleum Industry. (1922). P. 463. New York, NY: Oil Trade Journal, Inc. Google Books.

private railcar industry.[4053] The 1919 report has proven useful as a resource for corporate information about the Chicago Brigham refrigeration and transportation companies.[4054] The Atlantic Seaboard Despatch Company was incorporated in 1908.[4055] This Chicago company owned 310 rail cars in 1919, according to the report.[4056] The fleet included 46 beef refrigerator rail cars, which contained brine tanks and utility rails for the movement of the beef cargo.[4057] The fleet also included 185 refrigerator cars that contained ice tanks, as well as 79 ventilator refrigerator cars without ice tanks.[4058] The Atlantic Seaboard Despatch Company leased 200 refrigerator cars to the New York Central & St. Louis Railway Company, as well as to the Delaware, Lackawanna & Western Railroad Company.[4059] The two identified lessees jointly operated the leased Atlantic Despatch refrigerator cars in the dairy product transportation service called the Nickel Plate-Lackawanna Dairy Line.[4060] The Federal Trade Commission indicated that the Atlantic Seaboard Despatch Company operated within a state of mutual organizational connection with the Mid-West Despatch Car Company.[4061]

[4053] United States Federal Trade Commission. (June 27, 1919). Report Of The Federal Trade Commission On Private Car Lines. P. 213. Washington, D.C.: Government Printing Office. Google Books.

[4054] United States Federal Trade Commission. (June 27, 1919). Report Of The Federal Trade Commission On Private Car Lines. P. 213. Washington, D.C.: Government Printing Office. Google Books.

[4055] United States Federal Trade Commission. (June 27, 1919). Report Of The Federal Trade Commission On Private Car Lines. P. 213. Washington, D.C.: Government Printing Office. Google Books.

[4056] United States Federal Trade Commission. (June 27, 1919). Report Of The Federal Trade Commission On Private Car Lines. P. 213. Washington, D.C.: Government Printing Office. Google Books.

[4057] United States Federal Trade Commission. (June 27, 1919). Report Of The Federal Trade Commission On Private Car Lines. P. 213. Washington, D.C.: Government Printing Office. Google Books.

[4058] United States Federal Trade Commission. (June 27, 1919). Report Of The Federal Trade Commission On Private Car Lines. P. 213. Washington, D.C.: Government Printing Office. Google Books.

[4059] United States Federal Trade Commission. (June 27, 1919). Report Of The Federal Trade Commission On Private Car Lines. P. 213. Washington, D.C.: Government Printing Office. Google Books.

[4060] United States Federal Trade Commission. (June 27, 1919). Report Of The Federal Trade Commission On Private Car Lines. P. 213. Washington, D.C.: Government Printing Office. Google Books.

[4061] United States Federal Trade Commission. (June 27, 1919). Report Of The Federal Trade Commission On Private Car Lines. P. 213. Washington, D.C.: Government Printing Office. Google Books.

The report stated that the two companies shared the same executive leadership.[4062] Henry Hanson Brigham was founder and co-owner of these companies, in addition to North American Car Company, Commerce Petroleum Company, and others, all of Chicago, Tulsa, and Kansas.

The 1908 Pocket List of Railroad Officials disclosed the existence of another Brigham refrigerator company: the Overland Refrigerator Despatch Company.[4063] Henry Hanson Brigham served as President of the Overland Refrigerator Despatch Company in 1908.[4064] This Chicago company owned 250 rail cars in 1908.[4065] G. A. Bennis served as Secretary of the company that same year.[4066] The company headquarters were located at 438 1st National Bank Building.[4067] The 1910 Pocket List of Railroad Officials listed Henry H. Brigham as President and General Manager of the Atlantic Seaboard Despatch Company, and stated the company address to be 253 La Salle Street, in the Loop community of Chicago.[4068] The 1910 directory also named G. A. Bennis as Secretary and Treasurer of the company.[4069] Brigham and Bennis contributed jointly, therefore, to the leadership and administration of at least two different Chicago refrigeration and railroad companies by the year 1910.[4070]

Edmund Douglass Brigham served as a member of the board of directors of the Metropolitan Trust and Savings Bank in 1906.[4071] The bank was located at the corner of LaSalle Street and Washington Street in the Loop community.[4072] The

---

[4062] United States Federal Trade Commission. (June 27, 1919). Report Of The Federal Trade Commission On Private Car Lines. P. 213. Washington, D.C.: Government Printing Office. Google Books.

[4063] The Pocket List of Railroad Officials. (1908). P. 560. New York, NY: The Railway Equipment and Publication Company. Google Books.

[4064] The Pocket List of Railroad Officials. (1908). P. 560. New York, NY: The Railway Equipment and Publication Company. Google Books.

[4065] The Pocket List of Railroad Officials. (1908). P. 560. New York, NY: The Railway Equipment and Publication Company. Google Books.

[4066] The Pocket List of Railroad Officials. (1908). P. 560. New York, NY: The Railway Equipment and Publication Company. Google Books.

[4067] The Pocket List of Railroad Officials. (1908). P. 560. New York, NY: The Railway Equipment and Publication Company. Google Books.

[4068] The Pocket List of Railroad Officials. (1910). P. 603. New York, NY: The Railway Equipment and Publication Company. Google Books.

[4069] The Pocket List of Railroad Officials. (1910). P. 603. New York, NY: The Railway Equipment and Publication Company. Google Books.

[4070] The Pocket List of Railroad Officials. (1908). P. 560. New York, NY: The Railway Equipment and Publication Company. Google Books. The Pocket List of Railroad Officials. (1910). P. 603. New York, NY: The Railway Equipment and Publication Company. Google Books.

[4071] Directory of Directors In The City Of Chicago. (1906). P. 518. Chicago, IL: The Audit Company of New York.

[4072] Directory of Directors In The City Of Chicago. (1906). P. 518. Chicago, IL: The Audit Company of New York. Archives.org.

1906 leadership of the bank included the following persons.[4073] James H. Gilbert was President of the bank.[4074] S. E. Bliss was Vice-President.[4075] Fritz Goetz served as Second Vice-President.[4076] John A. Schmidt was the Cashier.[4077] Calvin F. Craig was Assistant Cashier.[4078] Robert T. Nelson served as Trust Officer.[4079]

1922 marked the time of reincorporation of North American Car Company as a Delaware corporation.[4080] The company was still a Chicago company in practically every regard, but the place of technical incorporation was Delaware, as of April 17, 1922.[4081] The *1924 Moody's* analysis and investment report contained invaluable historical, statistical, and managerial data for this company.[4082] The 1924 executive leadership structure and staff of the North American Car Company consisted of the following persons and jobs:

Person	Job
Henry Hanson Brigham	President
Erwin R. Brigham	Vice-President and Secretary
Herbert Nicholson	Vice-President
G. A. Johnson	Treasurer

Board of Directors
Henry H. Brigham
Erwin R. Brigham

[4073] Directory of Directors In The City Of Chicago. (1906). P 518. Chicago, IL: The Audit Company of New York.

[4074] Directory of Directors In The City Of Chicago. (1906). P. 518. Chicago, IL: The Audit Company of New York.

[4075] Directory of Directors In The City Of Chicago. (1906). P. 518. Chicago, IL: The Audit Company of New York.

[4076] Directory of Directors In The City Of Chicago. (1906). P. 518. Chicago, IL: The Audit Company of New York.

[4077] Directory of Directors In The City Of Chicago. (1906). P. 518. Chicago, IL: The Audit Company of New York.

[4078] Directory of Directors In The City Of Chicago. (1906). P. 518. Chicago, IL: The Audit Company of New York.

[4079] Directory of Directors In The City Of Chicago. (1906). P. 518. Chicago, IL: The Audit Company of New York.

[4080] Moody's Analyses Of Investments And Security Rating Books: Industrial Securities. Maurice N. Blakemore (Ed.). (1924). P. 1457. New York, NY: Moody's Investors Service.

[4081] Moody's Analyses Of Investments And Security Rating Books: Industrial Securities. Maurice N. Blakemore (Ed.). (1924). P. 1457. New York, NY: Moody's Investors Service.

[4082] Moody's Analyses Of Investments And Security Rating Books: Industrial Securities. Maurice N. Blakemore (Ed.). (1924). P. 1457. New York, NY: Moody's Investors Service.

Herbert Nicholson

G. A. Johnson

F. Brigham[4083]

The office of the corporation was located at 327 S. La Salle Street.[4084] The company consolidated balance sheet enumerated total assets and liabilities of $3,780,062.[4085] North American Car Company had entered into three equipment trusts as a beneficiary party, according to the 1924 report and analysis.[4086] Henry Brigham also controlled the Marsh Refrigerator Service Company. The three North American Car Company refrigerator equipment trusts represented the Marsh Refrigerator Service Company car mortgage 5s series A, the North American Car Company six percent car trust note, and the North American Car Company seven percent equipment note.[4087] The North American Car Company undertook financing by means of the Marsh Refrigerator Service Company.[4088] The financing plan of the North American Car Company consisted of debt financing as well as equity financing.[4089] In 1929, W. E. Strohmeyer of the North American Car Company represented the company at the annual banquet of the Traffic Club of Franklin, Pennsylvania.[4090] The facts reported by *The News-Herald*, a newspaper of Franklin, appeared to indicate that W. E. Strohmeyer was the sole representative from Chicago at this banquet event.[4091]

[4083] Moody's Analyses Of Investments And Security Rating Books: Industrial Securities. Maurice N. Blakemore (Ed.). (1924). P. 1457. New York, NY: Moody's Investors Service.

[4084] Moody's Analyses Of Investments And Security Rating Books: Industrial Securities. Maurice N. Blakemore (Ed.). (1924). P. 1457. New York, NY: Moody's Investors Service.

[4085] Moody's Analyses Of Investments And Security Rating Books: Industrial Securities. Maurice N. Blakemore (Ed.). (1924). P. 1457. New York, NY: Moody's Investors Service.

[4086] Moody's Analyses Of Investments And Security Rating Books: Industrial Securities. Maurice N. Blakemore (Ed.). (1924). P. 1457. New York, NY: Moody's Investors Service.

[4087] Moody's Analyses Of Investments And Security Rating Books: Industrial Securities. Maurice N. Blakemore (Ed.). (1924). P. 1457. New York, NY: Moody's Investors Service.

[4088] Moody's Analyses Of Investments And Security Rating Books: Industrial Securities. Maurice N. Blakemore (Ed.). (1924). P. 1457. New York, NY: Moody's Investors Service.

[4089] Moody's Analyses Of Investments And Security Rating Books: Industrial Securities. Maurice N. Blakemore (Ed.). (1924). P. 1457. New York, NY: Moody's Investors Service.

[4090] The News-Herald. (March 28, 1929). P. 7. Newspapers.com.

[4091] The News-Herald. (March 28, 1929). P. 7. Newspapers.com.

The *Moody's Manual of Investments* for the year 1930 noted that the North American Car Company history had grown more complex from an organizational standpoint.[4092] The new North American Car Company was incorporated February 1, 1926, in Illinois. The new company encompassed the prior North American Car Company, which had been established in 1908, and reincorporated in 1922.[4093] The corporate purpose remained continuous and compound, comprising transportation and refrigeration services, lease and ownership of railroad refrigerator cars, as well as the repair of refrigerator cars.[4094] The company owned 8,040 railroad cars as of March 31, 1930.[4095] 3,671 tank cars, 1,960 refrigerator cars, and 2,409 poultry cars constituted the total fleet of North American Car Company as of March, 1930.[4096] The total assets and liabilities equaled $14,915,378 as of December 31, 1929.[4097] The corporate office was located at 327 S. LaSalle Street, in Chicago.[4098] General Robert E. Wood served on the board of directors of the North American Car Company at this time.[4099] Wood served as Chairman of Sears, Roebuck Corporation.

Multiple Chicago banks of central significance to the financial and industrial economies of the city, Cook County, and the Midwest, represented financing issuances of the North American Car Company. Financial representation through such key Chicago organizations communicated the qualities of strength and soundness with respect to the North American Car Company. The Northern Trust Company of Chicago acted as the transfer agent for the preferred stock of the North American Car Company.[4100] The First Union Trust & Savings Bank of Chicago acted as transfer agent for the common stock issued by North American Car

---

[4092] Moody's Manual Of Investments American And Foreign. John Sherman Porter (Ed.). (1930). P. 1709. New York, NY: Moody's Investors Service.

[4093] Moody's Manual Of Investments American And Foreign. John Sherman Porter (Ed.). (1930). P. 1709. New York, NY: Moody's Investors Service. Moody's Analyses Of Investments And Security Rating Books: Industrial Securities. Maurice N. Blakemore (Ed.). (1924). P. 1457. New York, NY: Moody's Investors Service.

[4094] Moody's Manual Of Investments American And Foreign. John Sherman Porter (Ed.). (1930). P. 1709. New York, NY: Moody's Investors Service.

[4095] Moody's Manual Of Investments American And Foreign. John Sherman Porter (Ed.). (1930). P. 1709. New York, NY: Moody's Investors Service.

[4096] Moody's Manual Of Investments American And Foreign. John Sherman Porter (Ed.). (1930). P. 1709. New York, NY: Moody's Investors Service.

[4097] Moody's Manual Of Investments American And Foreign. John Sherman Porter (Ed.). (1930). P. 1709. New York, NY: Moody's Investors Service.

[4098] Moody's Manual Of Investments American And Foreign. John Sherman Porter (Ed.). (1930). P. 1709. New York, NY: Moody's Investors Service.

[4099] Moody's Manual Of Investments American And Foreign. John Sherman Porter (Ed.). (1930). P. 1709. New York, NY: Moody's Investors Service.

[4100] Moody's Manual Of Investments American And Foreign. John Sherman Porter (Ed.). (1930). P. 1712. New York, NY: Moody's Investors Service.

Company.[4101] Continental Illinois Bank & Trust Company served as registrar for the preferred stock issued by the North American Car Company.[4102] Frank Hatch Jones, Esq., who was the son-in-law of Jacob Bunn, was junior executive, Secretary, and co-founder of the Continental Illinois Bank & Trust Company, in 1910.[4103] Central Trust Company of Illinois, also a Chicago organization, was registrar for the common stock of the North American Car Company.[4104]

The April, 1911, edition of *The Official Railway Equipment Register* contained an advertisement for the Atlantic Seaboard Despatch Company of Chicago.[4105] Such advertisements prove their research utility robustly by supplying abundant data.[4106] This class of advertisement often contains the names of the people who staff the leadership structure of organizations, as well as the places of operation of the organizations that are advertising.[4107] *The Official Railway Equipment Register*, a New York City-based industrial journal of invaluable significance to research and information collection, provided a detailed report of the leadership and administrative staff of Atlantic Seaboard Despatch, as well as of certain commercial rates of service offered by the company.[4108] The advertisement listed Henry H. Brigham as President and General Manager of the company, with offices at Chicago.[4109] George A. Bennis served as Secretary and Treasurer of the company, with offices at Chicago.[4110] D. J. McGillivray held the office of General Eastern Agent, with offices at New York City.[4111] F. W. Sharp served as Agent for

---

[4101] Moody's Manual Of Investments American And Foreign. John Sherman Porter (Ed.). (1930). P. 1712. New York, NY: Moody's Investors Service.

[4102] Moody's Manual Of Investments American And Foreign. John Sherman Porter (Ed.). (1930). P. 1712. New York, NY: Moody's Investors Service.

[4103] The Commercial & Financial Chronicle. (July 2, 1910). Vol. 91. P. 17. New York, NY: William B. Dana Company, Publishers. Google Books.

[4104] Moody's Manual Of Investments American And Foreign. John Sherman Porter (Ed.). (1930). P. 1712. New York, NY: Moody's Investors Service.

[4105] The Official Railway Equipment Register. (1911). P. 505. Vol. XXVII, Number 11. New York, NY: The Railway Equipment And Publication Company. Google Books.

[4106] The Official Railway Equipment Register. (1911). P. 505. Vol. XXVII, Number 11. New York, NY: The Railway Equipment And Publication Company. Google Books.

[4107] The Official Railway Equipment Register. (1911). P. 505. Vol. XXVII, Number 11. New York, NY: The Railway Equipment And Publication Company. Google Books.

[4108] The Official Railway Equipment Register. (1911). P. 505. Vol. XXVII, Number 11. New York, NY: The Railway Equipment And Publication Company. Google Books.

[4109] The Official Railway Equipment Register. (1911). P. 505. Vol. XXVII, Number 11. New York, NY: The Railway Equipment And Publication Company. Google Books.

[4110] The Official Railway Equipment Register. (1911). P. 505. Vol. XXVII, Number 11. New York, NY: The Railway Equipment And Publication Company. Google Books.

[4111] The Official Railway Equipment Register. (1911). P. 505. Vol. XXVII, Number 11. New York, NY: The Railway Equipment And Publication Company. Google Books.

a more western market, with offices at Des Moines, Iowa.[4112] James Powell was the General Foreman for the company, with offices at Chicago.[4113] The company headquarters occupied an office at 253 La Salle Street, in Chicago.[4114] The New York City office was located at a place identified as Pier 23, North River.[4115] The company operated with two different telephone numbers at this time: Harrison 1672; and Harrison 7003.[4116] The New York City telephone number for the company was Franklin 1863.[4117]

The 1911 advertisement that appeared in *The Official Railway Equipment Register* described the commercial purpose of the company, as well as the service rates, that the company offered at the time. The principal business purpose was conducted through the formation of service contracts.[4118] The company offered contracts of lease for the use of railroad tanker cars and railroad refrigerator cars.[4119] Railroad companies and shippers constituted the two principal classes of consumer of the company's services.[4120] The reports of Atlantic Seaboard Despatch Company railcar movement, mileage reports, and repair bills, were to be filed with the main office at 253 S. La Salle Street, in Chicago.[4121]

The North American Car Company, with a fleet of 7,502 railcars in operation in 1929, had unquestionably established a powerful presence within the railroad refrigerator and tank car markets of the United States.[4122] North American Car undertook a market diversification plan when it established the North American Fruit & Steamship Company as a subsidiary at some point 1929 to serve as an expansion of transportation service into maritime and Caribbean markets.[4123] The

[4112] The Official Railway Equipment Register. (1911). P. 505. Vol. XXVII, Number 11. New York, NY: The Railway Equipment And Publication Company. Google Books.
[4113] The Official Railway Equipment Register. (1911). P. 505. Vol. XXVII, Number 11. New York, NY: The Railway Equipment And Publication Company. Google Books.
[4114] The Official Railway Equipment Register. (1911). P. 505. Vol. XXVII, Number 11. New York, NY: The Railway Equipment And Publication Company. Google Books.
[4115] The Official Railway Equipment Register. (1911). P. 505. Vol. XXVII, Number 11. New York, NY: The Railway Equipment And Publication Company. Google Books.
[4116] The Official Railway Equipment Register. (1911). P. 505. Vol. XXVII, Number 11. New York, NY: The Railway Equipment And Publication Company. Google Books.
[4117] The Official Railway Equipment Register. (1911). P. 505. Vol. XXVII, Number 11. New York, NY: The Railway Equipment And Publication Company. Google Books.
[4118] The Official Railway Equipment Register. (1911). P. 505. Vol. XXVII, Number 11. New York, NY: The Railway Equipment And Publication Company. Google Books.
[4119] The Official Railway Equipment Register. (1911). P. 505. Vol. XXVII, Number 11. New York, NY: The Railway Equipment And Publication Company. Google Books.
[4120] The Official Railway Equipment Register. (1911). P. 505. Vol. XXVII, Number 11. New York, NY: The Railway Equipment And Publication Company. Google Books.
[4121] The Official Railway Equipment Register. (1911). P. 505. Vol. XXVII, Number 11. New York, NY: The Railway Equipment And Publication Company. Google Books.
[4122] Detroit Free Press. (August 22, 1929). P. 18. Newspapers.com.
[4123] Detroit Free Press. (August 22, 1929). P. 18. Newspapers.com.

transportation market diversification plan revealed the faith that the North American Car leadership placed in the continuity of the company's economic growth and stability.[4124] Henry Hanson Brigham stated: "Our general business in all lines is showing a steady and permanent growth."[4125] Brigham noted the importance of exploring new markets:

> "The heavy movement of perishables continues and the refrigerator car division has been taxed beyond its capacity. Organization recently of the North American Fruit and Steamship corporation for handling tropical fruits has brought a substantial increase in business from southern ports."[4126]

The new steamship company, the North American Fruit & Steamship Company, acquired a third ship in 1929 to provide service in the refrigerator vessel line of the company.[4127]

The North American Car Company acquired the National Tank Car Company in 1920.[4128] The National Tank Car Company was a Chicago company whose purpose included the lease and operation of tank cars.[4129] The financial structure of National Tank Car appeared from the 1923 report in *Moody's Analysis of Investments And Security Rating Books* to have consisted exclusively of equity financing, because the report produced no evidence to prove the existence of any species of debt financing at that time within the capital structure.[4130] The equity financing created two classes of stock moneys: common stock money, and preferred stock money.[4131]

North American Car undertook a series of acquisitions during the 1920s and 1930s which broadened the range of commercial activity of the company.[4132] The

---

[4124] Detroit Free Press. (August 22, 1929). P. 18. Newspapers.com.

[4125] Detroit Free Press. (August 22, 1929). P. 18. Newspapers.com.

[4126] Detroit Free Press. (August 22, 1929). P. 18. Newspapers.com.

[4127] Salt Lake Telegram. (August 19, 1929). P. 8. Newspapers.com.

[4128] Moody's Analyses Of Investments And Security Rating Books: Industrial Investments. Maurice N. Blakemore (Ed.). (1923). P. 1274. New York, NY: Moody's Investors Service.

[4129] Moody's Analyses Of Investments And Security Rating Books: Industrial Investments. Maurice N. Blakemore (Ed.). (1923). P. 1274. New York, NY: Moody's Investors Service.

[4130] Moody's Analyses Of Investments And Security Rating Books: Industrial Investments. Maurice N. Blakemore (Ed.). (1923). P. 1274. New York, NY: Moody's Investors Service.

[4131] Moody's Analyses Of Investments And Security Rating Books: Industrial Investments. Maurice N. Blakemore (Ed.). (1923). P. 1274. New York, NY: Moody's Investors Service.

[4132] Porter, John Sherman. (1946). Moody's Manual of Investments American And Foreign: Industrial Securities. P. 1086. New York, NY: Moody's Investors Service.

acquisition of Palace Poultry Car Company took place in 1926.[4133] The acquisition of Premier Poultry Manure Company took place probably near the time when the company acquired Palace Poultry Car Company.[4134] North American Car purchased the Live Poultry Transit Company through a bifurcated equity financing plan in which two series of stock moneys were issued to enable purchase of the target company.[4135] National Tank Car Company became part of the North American Car Company in April, 1939.[4136] This purchase and acquisition comported with the terms of a 1937 reorganization plan that governed the target company.[4137]

North American Car Company assets totaled $13,703,725 in 1938, continuing a pattern of annual asset growth over multiple years.[4138] Rental service revenue also followed a trend of growth over multiple years, totaling $3,293,553 in 1938, representing growth of $223,659 over the 1937 revenue of $3,069,894, and $407,953 over 1936 revenue of $2,885,600.[4139]

The period of years from 1936 to 1944 constituted a time of reduction in the subsidiary company portfolio of North American Car Company.[4140] North American Car dissolved multiple subsidiaries during this time.[4141] 1936 witnessed the dissolution of two subsidiaries of North American Car Company: the dissolution of the Palace Live Poultry Car Company took place on December 31, 1936; the dissolution of the Premier Poultry Manure Company took place also on December 31, 1936.[4142] North American Car undertook dissolution of yet another subsidiary company, the North American Fruit & Steamship Company, on May

---

[4133] Porter, John Sherman. (1946). Moody's Manual of Investments American And Foreign: Industrial Securities. P. 1086. New York, NY: Moody's Investors Service.
[4134] Porter, John Sherman. (1946). Moody's Manual of Investments American And Foreign: Industrial Securities. P. 1086. New York, NY: Moody's Investors Service.
[4135] Porter, John Sherman. (1946). Moody's Manual of Investments American And Foreign: Industrial Securities. P. 1086. New York, NY: Moody's Investors Service.
[4136] Porter, John Sherman. (1946). Moody's Manual of Investments American And Foreign: Industrial Securities. P. 1086. New York, NY: Moody's Investors Service.
[4137] Porter, John Sherman. (1946). Moody's Manual of Investments American And Foreign: Industrial Securities. P. 1086. New York, NY: Moody's Investors Service.
[4138] Porter, John Sherman (Ed.). (1939). Moody's Manual of Investments American And Foreign: Industrial Securities. P. 1341. New York, NY: Moody's Investors Service.
[4139] Porter, John Sherman (Ed.). (1939). Moody's Manual of Investments American And Foreign: Industrial Securities. P. 1341. New York, NY: Moody's Investors Service.
[4140] Porter, John Sherman. (1946). Moody's Manual of Investments American And Foreign: Industrial Securities. P. 1086. New York, NY: Moody's Investors Service.
[4141] Porter, John Sherman. (1946). Moody's Manual of Investments American And Foreign: Industrial Securities. P. 1086. New York, NY: Moody's Investors Service.
[4142] Porter, John Sherman. (1946). Moody's Manual of Investments American And Foreign: Industrial Securities. P. 1086. New York, NY: Moody's Investors Service.

28, 1939.[4143] On July 12, 1939, North American Car dissolved the subsidiary known as North American Transit Refrigeration, Inc.[4144] The dissolutions of Central State Equipment Company, Centorp Corporation, and Palace Poultry Car Company occurred on December 31, 1943, May 30, 1944, and October 6, 1944, respectively.[4145] In 1946, L. H. S. Roblee, who had served as Secretary of North American Car in 1930, served as President.[4146] Henry Hanson Brigham, Jr., served as Vice-President of the company in 1946.[4147] W. M. Spencer served as Chairman of the company in 1946.[4148] Gen. Robert E. Wood of Sears, Roebuck & Company continued as a member of the Board of Directors in 1946.[4149]

The graph provided below indicates the following data for the North American Car Company, where available: quantity of refrigerator cars and tank cars that the company operated in service at time of annual financial report. The company also owned a large quantity of poultry cars and possessed the oil storage capacity of 20,000,000 gallons, with oil storage facilities both in and near Chicago.

Year	Refrigerator Cars	Tank Cars
1922:	833	880[4150]
1923:	841	863[4151]

[4143] Porter, John Sherman. (1946). Moody's Manual of Investments American And Foreign: Industrial Securities. P. 1086. New York, NY: Moody's Investors Service.
[4144] Porter, John Sherman. (1946). Moody's Manual of Investments American And Foreign: Industrial Securities. P. 1086. New York, NY: Moody's Investors Service.
[4145] Porter, John Sherman. (1946). Moody's Manual of Investments American And Foreign: Industrial Securities. P. 1086. New York, NY: Moody's Investors Service.
[4146] Porter, John Sherman. (1946). Moody's Manual of Investments American And Foreign: Industrial Securities. P. 1086. New York, NY: Moody's Investors Service. See: Moody's Manual of Investments American And Foreign. John Sherman Porter (Ed.). (1930). P. 1709. New York, NY: Moody's Investors Service.
[4147] Porter, John Sherman. (1946). Moody's Manual of Investments American And Foreign: Industrial Securities. P. 1086. New York, NY: Moody's Investors Service.
[4148] Porter, John Sherman. (1946). Moody's Manual of Investments American And Foreign: Industrial Securities. P. 1086. New York, NY: Moody's Investors Service.
[4149] Porter, John Sherman. (1946). Moody's Manual of Investments American And Foreign: Industrial Securities. P. 1086. New York, NY: Moody's Investors Service.
[4150] Moody's Analyses Of Investments And Security Rating Books: Industrial Investments. Maurice N. Blakemore (Ed.). (1923). P. 1274. New York, NY: Moody's Investors Service.
[4151] Moody's Analyses Of Investments And Security Rating Books: Industrial Investments. Maurice N. Blakemore (Ed.). (1924). P. 1457. New York, NY: Moody's Investors Service.

1924:	834	933[4152]
1925:	1,000	1,400[4153]
1926:	1,168	2,280[4154]
1930:	1,960	3,671[4155]
1935:	1,756	2,414[4156]
1939:	2,254	4,709[4157]
1944:	4,357	4,357[4158]

The table proves the steady growth of the company's fleets of refrigerator cars and tanker cars. By 1944 the company owned 8,714 refrigerator and tank railcars.

We will close this portion of the present chapter with the history of the 1919 Black Sox Scandal, which remains one of the most devastating, iconic, and memorable catastrophes in the history of Chicago and United States sports. Joseph Jefferson Jackson (1888-1951) was a native of Greenville, South Carolina.[4159] He experienced poverty as a youth and suffered sicknesses due to working in cotton mills.[4160] Jackson demonstrated prodigious athletic talent and played for the baseball team of the cotton mill when he was 13 years old.[4161] Jackson eventually played for the Greenville Spinners, a local South Carolina baseball team.[4162] He

---

[4152] Moody's Analyses Of Investments And Security Rating Service: Industrial Investments. John Sherman Porter (Ed.). (1925). P. 1656. New York, NY: Moody's Investors Service.

[4153] Moody's Analyses Of Investments And Security Rating Service: Industrial Investments. John Sherman Porter (Ed.). (1926). P. 1711. New York, NY: Moody's Investors Service.

[4154] Moody's Analyses Of Investments And Security Rating Service: Industrial Investments. John Sherman Porter (Ed.). (1927). P. 2047. New York, NY: Moody's Investors Service.

[4155] Moody's Manual Of Investments American And Foreign: Industrial Securities. John Sherman Porter (Ed.). (1930). P. 1709. New York, NY: Moody's Investors Service.

[4156] Moody's Analyses Of Investments American And Foreign: Industrial Securities. John Sherman Porter (Ed.). (1935). P. 703. New York, NY: Moody's Investors Service.

[4157] Moody's Analyses Of Investments And Security Rating Service: Industrial Investments. John Sherman Porter (Ed.). (1940). P. 650. New York, NY: Moody's Investors Service.

[4158] Moody's Analyses Of Investments And Security Rating Service: Industrial Investments. John Sherman Porter (Ed.). (1945). P. 1057. New York, NY: Moody's Investors Service.

[4159] Asinof, Eliot. (2017). *Shoeless Joe Jackson*. Britannica Academic. http://academic.eb.com/levels/collegiate/article/Shoeless-Joe-Jackson/342942.

[4160] Asinof, Eliot. (2017). *Shoeless Joe Jackson*. Britannica Academic. http://academic.eb.com/levels/collegiate/article/Shoeless-Joe-Jackson/342942.

[4161] Asinof, Eliot. (2017). *Shoeless Joe Jackson*. Britannica Academic. http://academic.eb.com/levels/collegiate/article/Shoeless-Joe-Jackson/342942.

[4162] Asinof, Eliot. (2017). *Shoeless Joe Jackson*. Britannica Academic. http://academic.eb.com/levels/collegiate/article/Shoeless-Joe-Jackson/342942.

then transferred to the Philadelphia Athletics when Connie Mack purchased his contract from the Greenville Spinners in 1908.[4163] Jackson was deterred from his new Philadelphia team membership due to a self-consciousness and embarrassment over what he perceived to be, "hayseed illiteracy,"[4164] and the fact of deeply missing his wife.[4165] After returning to South Carolina, Jackson eventually played baseball for the Philadelphia Athletics when Connie Mack was owner of that team.[4166] Jackson was traded to the Cleveland Naps in 1910.[4167] This team would later become the Cleveland Indians.[4168] Charles Comiskey brought Jackson to play for the Chicago White Sox in 1915.[4169] Comiskey paid $65,000 for Jackson, and Jackson performed with great success for the Chicago White Sox.[4170] The White Sox won the 1919 Pennant and faced the Cincinnati Reds at the 1919 World Series.[4171] Historian Eliot Asinof analyzed the culture of the 1919 Chicago White Sox organization and diagnosed numerous issues that negatively affected the players' values, loyalty, and attitudes.[4172] Asinof stated the following:

> "The United States was different after the war, tainted by a growing cynicism. In baseball, gamblers and fixers openly operated in big league cities with impunity, while club owners swept all rumours of corrupted games under the rug, lest the public lose faith in the national pastime. The White Sox, though runaway pennant winners in 1919, were a team of disgruntled underpaid players who were embittered by Comiskey's penuriousness, his failure to pay promised bonuses, and his high-handed refusal to discuss their grievances. It was also a team riddled with hostile cliques and dissension. The outcome was that eight of its ballplayers

---

[4163] Asinof, Eliot. (2017). *Shoeless Joe Jackson*. Britannica Academic. http://academic.eb.com/levels/collegiate/article/Shoeless-Joe-Jackson/342942.
[4164] Asinof, Eliot. (2017). *Shoeless Joe Jackson*. Britannica Academic. http://academic.eb.com/levels/collegiate/article/Shoeless-Joe-Jackson/342942.
[4165] Asinof, Eliot. (2017). *Shoeless Joe Jackson*. Britannica Academic. http://academic.eb.com/levels/collegiate/article/Shoeless-Joe-Jackson/342942.
[4166] Asinof, Eliot. (2017). *Shoeless Joe Jackson*. Britannica Academic. http://academic.eb.com/levels/collegiate/article/Shoeless-Joe-Jackson/342942.
[4167] Asinof, Eliot. (2017). *Shoeless Joe Jackson*. Britannica Academic. http://academic.eb.com/levels/collegiate/article/Shoeless-Joe-Jackson/342942.
[4168] Asinof, Eliot. (2017). *Shoeless Joe Jackson*. Britannica Academic. http://academic.eb.com/levels/collegiate/article/Shoeless-Joe-Jackson/342942.
[4169] Asinof, Eliot. (2017). *Shoeless Joe Jackson*. Britannica Academic. http://academic.eb.com/levels/collegiate/article/Shoeless-Joe-Jackson/342942.
[4170] Asinof, Eliot. (2017). *Shoeless Joe Jackson*. Britannica Academic. http://academic.eb.com/levels/collegiate/article/Shoeless-Joe-Jackson/342942.
[4171] Asinof, Eliot. (2017). *Shoeless Joe Jackson*. Britannica Academic. http://academic.eb.com/levels/collegiate/article/Shoeless-Joe-Jackson/342942.
[4172] Asinof, Eliot. (2017). *Shoeless Joe Jackson*. Britannica Academic. http://academic.eb.com/levels/collegiate/article/Shoeless-Joe-Jackson/342942.

conspired with gamblers—including former boxer <u>Abe Attell</u>—to throw the World Series to the Cincinnati Reds."[4173]

Shoeless Joe Jackson was one of eight Chicago White Sox team members who was a party to the conspiracy to throw the 1919 World Series.[4174] Jackson was to receive $20,000 for his performance in the conspiracy.[4175] Asinof noted that the consideration money that Jackson bargained for as a party to the conspiratorial contract significantly exceeded his annual White Sox player wage of $6,000.[4176] This fact would have supported an inference that Jackson would have been potentially induced to join the conspiracy, and, thereby, to become a party to the fraud. The illegal money that was due Jackson, however, never occurred, and Jackson received only $5,000 for his part in throwing the World Series.[4177] Asinof explained that the precise character of Shoeless Joe Jackson's participation in the 1919 conspiracy is not completely understood, and specified that Jackson, "never returned the bribe, [but] he went on to hit an outstanding .375 for the series while playing errorless ball in the field."[4178] Jackson's subsequent attempts to explain the conspiracy to Charles Comiskey failed, because Comiskey refused to meet with him.[4179] The facts, evidences, and proofs of the baseball conspiracy emerged quite violently in 1920, however, when a grand jury was convened at which Joe Jackson confessed his complicity in the conspiracy.[4180]

The Cook County Grand Jury convened to investigate the allegations that corruption, fraud, and gambling among major league ball players had infiltrated the 1919 World Series competition between the Chicago White Sox and the Cincinnati Reds.[4181] *The Palladium-Item*, a newspaper of Richmond, Indiana, reported that the Cook County Grand Jury collected the facts and evidences relevant to the charges, complaints, and allegations. *The Palladium-Item* reported that the grand jury deliberated upon the facts and evidence and judged the evidence

[4173] Asinof, Eliot. (2017). *Shoeless Joe Jackson*. Britannica Academic. http://academic.eb.com/levels/collegiate/article/Shoeless-Joe-Jackson/342942.
[4174] Asinof, Eliot. (2017). *Shoeless Joe Jackson*. Britannica Academic. http://academic.eb.com/levels/collegiate/article/Shoeless-Joe-Jackson/342942.
[4175] Asinof, Eliot. (2017). *Shoeless Joe Jackson*. Britannica Academic. http://academic.eb.com/levels/collegiate/article/Shoeless-Joe-Jackson/342942.
[4176] Asinof, Eliot. (2017). *Shoeless Joe Jackson*. Britannica Academic. http://academic.eb.com/levels/collegiate/article/Shoeless-Joe-Jackson/342942.
[4177] Asinof, Eliot. (2017). *Shoeless Joe Jackson*. Britannica Academic. http://academic.eb.com/levels/collegiate/article/Shoeless-Joe-Jackson/342942.
[4178] Asinof, Eliot. (2017). *Shoeless Joe Jackson*. Britannica Academic. http://academic.eb.com/levels/collegiate/article/Shoeless-Joe-Jackson/342942.
[4179] Asinof, Eliot. (2017). *Shoeless Joe Jackson*. Britannica Academic. http://academic.eb.com/levels/collegiate/article/Shoeless-Joe-Jackson/342942.
[4180] Asinof, Eliot. (2017). *Shoeless Joe Jackson*. Britannica Academic. http://academic.eb.com/levels/collegiate/article/Shoeless-Joe-Jackson/342942.
[4181] Palladium-Item. (September 25, 1920). P. 7. Newspapers.com.

to be not only adequate, but so convincing with respect to the alleged corruption that the grand jury would extend its term beyond the September 30, 1925 termination time.[4182] The grand jury would continue its evidentiary collection and deliberation in special session.[4183]

Henry Hanson Brigham served as Foreman of the Cook County grand jury that investigated the 1919 Black Sox Scandal.[4184] The *Palladium-Item* newspaper summarized what Brigham stated to their reporters as follows: "The ramifications of the alleged gambling were so widespread that it would be impossible to complete a thorough investigation during the regular session."[4185] Brigham offered the following opinion regarding the searches and discoveries that he and his fellow Cook County grand jurors were undertaking: "The jury has received evidence which indicated an attempt by nationwide ring of gamblers to pollute baseball and ruin the great national game in the same way boxing was killed and horse racing crucified."[4186]

The 1919 conspiracy caused severe division within the baseball community.[4187] Charles Comiskey, who at that time served as President of baseball's Chicago American League Club, complained of the weak support that he received from B. B. Johnson, who was President of the American League at the time, in Comiskey's work to investigate the corruption of the White Sox.[4188] Comiskey's complaint and allegation of B. B. Johnson's meager support of Comiskey's investigative work incited August Herrmann, who was President of the Cincinnati Baseball Club, to allege defensively that Johnson had indeed undertaken an investigation with diligence.[4189]

A concluding comment from Henry H. Brigham suffixed the *Palladium-Item* newspaper article, and indicated the judgment that the Cook County grand jury would soon deliver indictments, on grounds of conspiracy, against the ball players at issue.[4190] "Indictments based on charges of conspiracy to defraud may be the result of the Cook County grand jury's investigation of alleged crookedness by the players in last fall's world's series, it was indicated by Henry H. Brigham, foreman of the jury."[4191] Henry H. Brigham, as grand jury foreman, commented that charge, and not ignoramus (this word means refusal to charge), would be the probable outcome of the grand jury deliberation and verdict. Brigham stated: "There seems

[4182] Palladium-Item. (September 25, 1920). P. 7. Newspapers.com.
[4183] Palladium-Item. (September 25, 1920). P. 7. Newspapers.com.
[4184] Palladium-Item. (September 25, 1920). P. 7. Newspapers.com.
[4185] Palladium-Item. (September 25, 1920). P. 7. Newspapers.com.
[4186] Palladium-Item. (September 25, 1920). P. 7. Newspapers.com.
[4187] Palladium-Item. (September 25, 1920). P. 7. Newspapers.com.
[4188] Palladium-Item. (September 25, 1920). P. 7. Newspapers.com.
[4189] Palladium-Item. (September 25, 1920). P. 7. Newspapers.com.
[4190] Palladium-Item. (September 25, 1920). P. 7. Newspapers.com.
[4191] Palladium-Item. (September 25, 1920). P. 7. Newspapers.com.

to be more than sufficient evidence to support such charges."[4192] Henry Brigham announced that a subpoena had been issued to Arnold Rothstein of New York, owner of the Havre De Grace Race Track.[4193] Brigham reported also that he and the other grand jurors would issue subpoenas for William Burns, who was a former pitcher for the Chicago American League teams and the Cincinnati National League teams. Brigham also noted that subpoenas would be issued to featherweight champion Abe Attell, as well as sportsmen suspected of complicity in the 1919 World Series conspiracy.[4194]

The *1900 United States Census* listed the Henry H. Brigham family as residents of the Town of Lake View in the City of Chicago and County of Cook.[4195] The 1900 Lake View residential address for the Brighams was 2756 N. Winchester Street.[4196] The 1900 address was in Ward 26, and in Census Enumeration District 811.[4197] The *1910 United States Census* listed the Henry Hanson Brigham family as residents of Glencoe, located in New Trier Township, in Cook County.[4198] The family were civically active in Glencoe.

The Burtners and Criswells of Pennsylvania and Ohio:

Builders of Pittsburgh, Allegheny County, Butler County, the State of Ohio, and

Chicago

Philip Jacob Bortner (circa 1735-1786) married Maria Elizabetha Velt (1741 to circa 1800).[4199] Philip Jacob Bortner, a son of Balthasar Porterner (Bortner) and Maria Elizabetha Bortner, served as a member of the Pennsylvania Militia in the Revolutionary War.[4200] The children born to Philip and Maria were Henry Bordner; George Bordner; **John Burtner**; **Philip Burtner**; Elizabeth Burtner; Hannah Burtner; Juliana Burtner; Balser Burtner; Magdalena Burtner; and Christina

[4192] Palladium-Item. (September 25, 1920). P. 7. Newspapers.com.
[4193] Palladium-Item. (September 25, 1920). P. 7. Newspapers.com.
[4194] Palladium-Item. (September 25, 1920). P. 7. Newspapers.com.
[4195] 1900 United States Census. Ancestry.com.
[4196] 1900 United States Census. Ancestry.com
[4197] 1900 United States Census. Ancestry.com
[4198] 1910 United States Census. Ancestry.com
[4199] Bordner, Howard W. (1967). The Bordner And Burtner Families And Their Bortner Ancestors in America. P. 96. Washington, D.C.
[4200] Bordner, Howard W. (1967). The Bordner And Burtner Families And Their Bortner Ancestors in America. P. 96. Washington, D.C.

Burtner.[4201] Brothers John Burtner and Philip Burtner were founders of Pittsburgh, Allegheny County, and Butler County, Pennsylvania.

John Burtner (1765-1833) married Christina Emerich (circa 1770-circa 1820).[4202] The children born to John and Christina (Emerich) Burtner were: **Philip Burtner, who married Elenora Gallagher**; Jacob Burtner; **Barbara Burtner, who married Isaac Haws**; Elizabeth Burtner; William Burtner; Catharine Burtner; Mary Burtner; Christina Burtner; Daniel Burtner; and Andrew Burtner.[4203] John Burtner was a farmer, a manufacturer of plows, and a founder of Pittsburgh and Allegheny County. Many of John and Christina's descendants were important Pittsburgh and Butler farmers, businessmen, civic leaders, church promoters, and industrialists.

Philip Burtner (circa 1794-1827) married Ellen (Elenora) Gallagher (circa 1800-unknown death date).[4204] Philip was a War of 1812 veteran.[4205] The children born to Philip and Ellen (Gallagher) Burtner were John Burtner; **Peter Burtner**; **Philip Burtner, who married Rebecca Shobert**; **William Burtner**; and Veronica Burtner.[4206]

Capt. Philip Burtner (1820-1912) married Rebecca Shobert (1825-1907).[4207] The children born to Philip and Rebecca (Shobert) Burtner were the following: William Henry Harrison Burtner; **John Edward Burtner, who married Susannah Belle Criswell**; Mary Burtner; Catherine Helen Burtner; Henrietta Burtner; Eliza Burtner; Rebecca Burtner; Fannie Burtner; Annie Burtner; and Edward Burtner.[4208]

John Edward Burtner (1845-1917) married Susannah (Susan) Belle Criswell (1849-1930).[4209] John was a Union Army soldier, and served in Company

[4201] Bordner, Howard W. (1967). The Bordner And Burtner Families And Their Bortner Ancestors in America. P. 96. Washington, D.C.

[4202] Bordner, Howard W. (1967). The Bordner And Burtner Families And Their Bortner Ancestors in America. P. 236. Washington, D.C.

[4203] Bordner, Howard W. (1967). The Bordner And Burtner Families And Their Bortner Ancestors in America. P. 236. Washington, D.C.

[4204] Bordner, Howard W. (1967). The Bordner And Burtner Families And Their Bortner Ancestors in America. P. 247. Washington, D.C.

[4205] Bordner, Howard W. (1967). The Bordner And Burtner Families And Their Bortner Ancestors in America. P. 247. Washington, D.C.

[4206] Bordner, Howard W. (1967). The Bordner And Burtner Families And Their Bortner Ancestors in America. P. 247. Washington, D.C.

[4207] Bordner, Howard W. (1967). The Bordner And Burtner Families And Their Bortner Ancestors in America. P. 247. Washington, D.C.

[4208] Bordner, Howard W. (1967). The Bordner And Burtner Families And Their Bortner Ancestors in America. P. 247. Washington, D.C.

[4209] Bordner, Howard W. (1967). The Bordner And Burtner Families And Their Bortner Ancestors in America. P. 238. Washington, D.C.

C of the One-Hundredth Pennsylvania Infantry during the Civil War.[4210] The children born to John Edward Burtner and Susannah (Criswell) Burtner were the following: **James Criswell Burtner, who married Carrie Block**; Rebecca Burtner; Jonathan Edmund Burtner; Norman Philip Burtner; William Henry (Harry William) Burtner; George Wirt Burtner; Katherine May Burtner; Eliza Lydia Jane Burtner, who married Edgar Chandler Huselton; Letitia Vernell Burtner, who married George Hill; Zella Mable Burtner, who married Paul Stampfle; and **Theresa May Burtner, who married Stanley Ward Baldwin**.[4211] Many of these children resided in Pittsburgh, Allegheny County, Butler County, Cleveland, Ohio, Barberton, Ohio, and Detroit, Michigan.

<u>Three Sons of Philip Burtner and Ellen (Gallagher) Burtner</u>

<u>Help to Develop Pittsburgh and Cincinnati</u>

Captain Philip Burtner (1820-1912), son of Philip Burtner and Ellen (Gallagher) Burtner, was a pioneer businessman, farmer, and civic leader of Pittsburgh, Allegheny County, and the Pittsburgh suburbs of Saxonburg and Clinton Township, which both are located in neighboring Butler County.[4212] Philip Burtner founded a packet boat company at Pittsburgh and became a noted river captain and businessman of the Pittsburgh Canal and Pennsylvania Canal.[4213] The Pennsylvania and Pittsburgh Canals were a statewide waterway system of which Philip Burtner's granduncle, Philip Burtner, of Pittsburgh and the suburb of Harrison Township in Allegheny County, had been a founder and promoter.[4214] Captain Philip Burtner established a construction company at Saxonburg and formed a land investment company in metropolitan Pittsburgh.[4215] He also was a founding committeeman of the Butler County Centennial Exposition and served as a member of the Relics Committee for the Centennial Association and Exposition.[4216] The purposes of the Relics Committee were the collection, preservation, and curatorship of artifacts associated with the settlements and histories of the suburban Pittsburgh county of Butler.[4217] In 1887, Burtner served as a member of the Butler County Republican Committee for the Republican

---

[4210] Bordner, Howard W. (1967). The Bordner And Burtner Families And Their Bortner Ancestors in America. P. 238. Washington, D.C.
[4211] Bordner, Howard W. (1967). The Bordner And Burtner Families And Their Bortner Ancestors in America. P. 238. Washington, D.C.
[4212] Call, Baldwin, and Burtner family records.
[4213] Pittsburgh Daily Post. (November 7, 1912). P. 2. Newspapers.com.
[4214] Cooper, Grace. (May 10, 2017). This Old Pittsburgh House: Beautifying the Burtner House. Pittsburgh Magazine. Pittsburghmagazine.com.
[4215] Call, Baldwin, Burtner family records.
[4216] Butler Citizen. (February 22, 1900). P. 3. Newspapers.com.
[4217] Butler Citizen. (February 22, 1900). P. 3. Newspapers.com.

Convention being held at the time.[4218] In addition to these responsibilities, he served as Constable of Saxonburg Borough.[4219] He married Rebecca Shobert, and many children were born to them. Rebecca Shobert was the daughter of John Shobert of Luzerne County, Pennsylvania. The family was German-American.

William Burtner, a son of Philip Burtner and Ellen (Gallagher) Burtner, was a founder of St. Luke's Lutheran Church in Butler County and was a farmer and an oil explorer in suburban Pittsburgh.[4220] William participated in the oil industry as a company director and a possible founder of the Thorn Creek Oil Company, which was formed on February 2, 1870.[4221] Burtner served on the board of directors of Thorn Creek Oil Company with H. F. Aderhold, E. A. Helmbold, Robert Douthett, H. Osborn, Francis Laube, John Wareham, H. T. Tolley, John Bulford, J. Q. A. Kennedy, James Gribben, and Alex Welsh.[4222] The company operated for approximately eight years within the Thorn Creek District of the great Pittsburgh-Butler oilfields.[4223]

Peter Burtner, another son of Philip Burtner and Ellen (Gallagher) Burtner, was one of the few members of the Burtner family to leave the Pittsburgh region. He relocated to Cincinnati early in the Queen City's history, prior to 1846.[4224] There he established the Burtner & Ferree Construction Company with W. M. Ferree, which became an early and important fixture on the infrastructural development landscape of nineteenth century Cincinnati.[4225] Burtner was a founder, developer, and promoter of Cincinnati's Lincoln Park. He served as a member of the Lincoln Park Society and of the meeting committee of the Society.[4226] He additionally served as a Delegate to the 1878 Ohio Republican Convention at Cincinnati, representing the Second Precinct of the Twenty-Second Ward of Cincinnati.[4227] Peter was the father of Cincinnati and Chicago industrialist William Henry Burtner, who co-founded what was both the largest machine tool company of Chicago and possibly the largest in Cincinnati. William Henry Burtner is discussed herein, *infra*. Peter Burtner was the grandfather of Cincinnati lawyer and industrialist William Henry Burtner, Jr., who is discussed in the chapter titled *Builders of the Downtown*. William Henry Burtner, Jr., served on the board of directors of the American Automobile Association, which was based in Chicago.

[4218] Butler Citizen. (June 10, 1887). P. 3. Newspapers.com.

[4219] Butler Citizen. (June 5, 1891). P. 3. Newspapers.com.

[4220] History of Butler County, Pennsylvania. (1883). Rootsweb.

[4221] History of Butler County, Pennsylvania. (1883). Rootsweb.

[4222] History of Butler County, Pennsylvania. (1883). Rootsweb.

[4223] Reed, George Edward. Editor. Pennsylvania Archives. Fourth Series. Papers of the Governors. (1902). Vol. X. P. 88. Harrisburg, PA: State of Pennsylvania. Google Books.

[4224] The Cincinnati Enquirer. (October 25, 1896). P. 24. Newspapers.com.

[4225] Williams Cincinnati Directory. (1867). Pp. 185. Cincinnatilibrary.org.

[4226] The Cincinnati Enquirer. (March 25, 1883). P. 2. Newspapers.com.

[4227] The Cincinnati Daily Star. (June 10, 1878). P. 4. Newspapers.com.

William Henry Burtner, Sr., and William Henry Burtner, Jr., were, respectively, first and second cousins of John Edward Burtner (1845-1917) of Pittsburgh, Saxonburg, and Barberton, Ohio. The Burtners and Emerichs were friends and business associates of John Augustus Roebling of Butler County. Both Roebling and Peter Burtner relocated to Cincinnati from Butler County, and probably knew each other. Roebling designed and constructed the Roebling Bridge of Cincinnati and later designed and constructed the Brooklyn Bridge of New York City.[4228]

Cincinnati Helps to Build Chicago

William Henry Burtner, the son of Peter Burtner of Pittsburgh and Cincinnati, was a founder of two globally significant companies which were based in Cincinnati and Chicago. These companies helped to centralize and develop the American machine tool industry as the international standard for machinery. The two companies were the Lodge & Davis Machine Tool Company and the Davis & Egan Machine Tool Company. Both corporations were headquartered in Cincinnati and possessed major Chicago branches and factories.

Charles Davis, William Henry Burtner, Sr., Thomas P. Egan, and Thomas McDougal, all of Cincinnati, founded the Davis & Egan Machine Tool Company of Cincinnati and Chicago.[4229] This corporation was a multi-city firm and was the largest machine tool manufacturer in Chicago.[4230] The Lodge & Davis Machine Tool Company, predecessor of the Davis & Egan Machine Tool Company, was formed in 1880, reorganized in 1888, and produced locomotive engines, railroad cars, street railcars, typewriters, sewing machines, dynamos, electric motors, and weapon-making machinery, among other forms of machine tool.[4231] The corporation provided the United States government with a vast quantity of its arms-making technologies and rifles.[4232] By 1894 the company possessed a global presence and distributed its product in North America, South America, Europe, and Asia. By 1894 the annual sales revenue of the company reached approximately $2,000,000.[4233] Charles Davis served as President of the company; William Henry

---

[4228] Burtner and Emerich/Emerick/Emrick family history records.
[4229] History of Cincinnati And Hamilton County, Ohio; Their Past And Present. (1894). P. 318. Cincinnati, OH: S. B. Nelson & Co., Publishers. Google Books.
[4230] French, Lester Gray. (February, 1896). *Machinery*. Vol. 2. P. 187. Google Books.
[4231] History of Cincinnati And Hamilton County, Ohio; Their Past And Present. (1894). P. 318. Cincinnati, OH: S. B. Nelson & Co., Publishers. Google Books.
[4232] History of Cincinnati And Hamilton County, Ohio; Their Past And Present. (1894). P. 318. Cincinnati, OH: S. B. Nelson & Co., Publishers. Google Books.
[4233] History of Cincinnati And Hamilton County, Ohio; Their Past And Present. (1894). P. 318. Cincinnati, OH: S. B. Nelson & Co., Publishers. Google Books.

Burtner served as Vice-President of the company; and Henry Luers served as the Secretary-Treasurer of the company.[4234]

Thomas P. Egan of Cincinnati served as one of the Ohio members of the National Advisory Committee of the National Business League at the same time when Jacob Bunn, Jr. served as one of the Illinois members of the National Advisory Committee of the National Business League.[4235] The National Business League was a Chicago-based national public policy and legislative advocacy organization that was centrally responsible for establishing the United States Department of Commerce and Labor in 1903.[4236] Both Jacob Bunn, Jr., of Chicago and Springfield, and Thomas P. Egan of Cincinnati, among many other people from every one of the U.S. States, were prominently associated with the creation and establishment of the U.S. Department of Commerce and Labor.[4237] For more about the role of Chicago and Cincinnati in the establishment of the Department of Commerce and Labor, see Chapter 8, *Ode to Pylons and Cannery Windows.*

Daniel J. Kenny commented on the importance of Cincinnati's contributions to Chicago and Cook County in his 1895 historical encyclopedia of the Ohio city's work at the 1893 Chicago Columbian Exposition. At the time of the Exposition, Charles Davis served as President of Lodge & Davis and William Henry Burtner served as Vice-President of the firm.[4238] Henry Luers served as Secretary and Treasurer of the company.[4239] The Lodge & Davis Machine Tool Company held the distinction of being one of the largest and most significant exhibitors at the 1893 World's Columbian Exposition.[4240] The company spent more than $25,000 on the creation and construction of its Chicago exhibit. At the time of the Exposition the company was renowned for its market preeminence in South America, Mexico, and Cuba.[4241] The company employed a staff of Spanish speakers who profitably represented the company in Latin America. These representatives efficiently solicited extensive and profitable contracts for Lodge &

[4234] History of Cincinnati And Hamilton County, Ohio; Their Past And Present. (1894). P. 318. Cincinnati, OH: S. B. Nelson & Co., Publishers. Google Books.

[4235] Constitution and Official Directory of the National Business League. (1903). Pp. 38, 45. Chicago, IL. Google Books.

[4236] Constitution and Official Directory of the National Business League. (1903). Pp. 1-12, 38, 45. Chicago, IL. Google Books.

[4237] Constitution and Official Directory of the National Business League. (1903). Pp. 1-12, 38, 45. Chicago, IL. Google Books.

[4238] Kenny, Daniel J. (1895). Illustrated Guide to Cincinnati and the World's Columbian Exposition. Pp. 349-351. Cincinnati, OH: R. Clarke.

[4239] Kenny, Daniel J. (1895). Illustrated Guide to Cincinnati and the World's Columbian Exposition. Pp. 349-351. Cincinnati, OH: R. Clarke.

[4240] Kenny, Daniel J. (1895). Illustrated Guide to Cincinnati and the World's Columbian Exposition. Pp. 349-351. Cincinnati, OH: R. Clarke.

[4241] Kenny, Daniel J. (1895). Illustrated Guide to Cincinnati and the World's Columbian Exposition. Pp. 349-351. Cincinnati, OH: R. Clarke

Davis throughout South America, Mexico, and Cuba.[4242] The company earned annual sales revenues of $2,000,000 during approximately the fiscal years of 1890, 1891, 1892, and 1893, according to Kenny.[4243] The multiannual stability of the $2,000,000 sales earnings and revenues was demonstrated jointly by the Lester Gray French report on the Davis & Egan Machine Tool Company of Chicago and Cincinnati in 1896, and in the Daniel J. Kenny report of Cincinnati contributions to Chicago at the Exposition, in 1893.[4244]

William Burtner played a key role in the centralization and combination of the machine tool economies of Cincinnati and Chicago.[4245] Lester Gray French reported in the February, 1896, edition of the machine tool journal, *Machinery*, that the Lodge & Davis Machine Tool Company had been reorganized, with immediately consequent changes to the corporate name and leadership.[4246] William Lodge sold his interest in the Lodge & Davis Machine Tool Company of Cincinnati, and Charles Davis, Thomas Egan, Robert Laidlaw, Thomas McDougal, and William Burtner established the Davis & Egan Machine Tool Company as a successor to the Lodge & Davis Company.[4247] Charles Davis had served as President of the former Lodge & Davis Company; Thomas Egan served as President of the J. A. Fay & Egan Company; and Robert Laidlaw was President of the Laidlaw-Dunn-Gordon Company.[4248] William Burtner was Vice-President of the Lodge & Davis Company.[4249] Lester French did not report the specific corporate associations of Thomas McDougal other than that McDougal was a founder of the Davis & Egan Company along with executive officers Davis, Burtner, and Egan.[4250]

Charles Davis served as President of the new Davis & Egan Machine Tool Company.[4251] William Henry Burtner served as Vice-President of the company, and B. B. Quillen was Secretary of the firm.[4252] The new Cincinnati-Chicago corporation was the largest machine tool company in Chicago. It was probably the

---

[4242] Kenny, Daniel J. (1895). Illustrated Guide to Cincinnati and the World's Columbian Exposition. Pp. 349-351. Cincinnati, OH: R. Clarke

[4243] Kenny, Daniel J. (1895). Illustrated Guide to Cincinnati and the World's Columbian Exposition. Pp. 349-351. Cincinnati, OH: R. Clarke

[4244] Kenny, Daniel J. (1895). Illustrated Guide to Cincinnati and the World's Columbian Exposition. Pp. 349-351. Cincinnati, OH: R. Clarke; Hathi Trust Digital Library; French, Lester Gray. (February, 1896). *Machinery*. Vol. 2. P. 187. Google Books.

[4245] French, Lester Gray. (February, 1896). *Machinery*. Vol. 2. P. 187. Google Books.

[4246] French, Lester Gray. (February, 1896). *Machinery*. Vol. 2. P. 187. Google Books.

[4247] French, Lester Gray. (February, 1896). *Machinery*. Vol. 2. P. 187. Google Books.

[4248] French, Lester Gray. (February, 1896). *Machinery*. Vol. 2. P. 187. Google Books.

[4249] French, Lester Gray. (February, 1896). *Machinery*. Vol. 2. P. 187. Google Books.

[4250] French, Lester Gray. (February, 1896). *Machinery*. Vol. 2. P. 187. Google Books.

[4251] French, Lester Gray. (February, 1896). *Machinery*. Vol. 2. P. 187. Google Books.

[4252] French, Lester Gray. (February, 1896). *Machinery*. Vol. 2. P. 187. Google Books.

largest in Cincinnati, as well.[4253] French reported that, "Mr. Charles Davis and Mr. Thomas P. Egan are now in Chicago for the purpose of combining the large interests operated by each company in that city."[4254] Burtner worked with Davis and Egan in the consolidation of the Chicago and Cincinnati corporations.[4255] French noted that Davis and Egan had, "been strong competitors, and operated the two largest machinery houses at Chicago."[4256] French referred to the practical market supremacy of the new company in the global machine tool market when he stated that, "the consolidation of these three companies form one of the strongest concerns in the world."[4257] The Davis & Egan Machine Tool Company employed over 2,000 men at the time of the 1896 corporate consolidation and manufactured a broad class of machines, ranging from locomotive engines, electric motors, dynamos, and sewing machines, to steam pumps, mining machineries, agricultural machineries, and woodworking tools.[4258]

The new company adopted a strategic production plan to maximize the range of production so as to include every machine tool technology from the smallest to the largest in scope and function.[4259] The plan contemplated a comprehensive scope of production whose purpose was to serve as exhaustively as possible the full range of technological demand diversity within the machine tool economy.[4260] Chicago and Cincinnati were the centers of the company's plans of consolidation, strategy, and expansion. French provided a positive report that the capital structure of the Davis & Egan Machine Tool Company consisted of a simple equity financing that was comprised of common stock money, devoid of preferred stock money, and without debt money.[4261] French furthermore alleged that the capital resource of the new company was practically limitless, was without debt-based responsibility at the time of the 1896 consolidation, and was thus comparatively free from various risks that would typically attach to corporate financial structures.[4262] French essentially described the company as not only one of safety and soundness, but one of great strength, power, and growth probability.[4263] In addition to the more than 2,000 employees of the company at consolidation, seventy-five more were expected to be added to the workforce.[4264] The February, 1896, edition of *The Iron Age*, stated that the Davis & Egan Machine Tool Company had yielded a dividend

---

[4253] French, Lester Gray. (February, 1896). *Machinery*. Vol. 2. P. 187. Google Books.
[4254] French, Lester Gray. (February, 1896). *Machinery*. Vol. 2. P. 187. Google Books.
[4255] French, Lester Gray. (February, 1896). *Machinery*. Vol. 2. P. 187. Google Books.
[4256] French, Lester Gray. (February, 1896). *Machinery*. Vol. 2. P. 187. Google Books.
[4257] French, Lester Gray. (February, 1896). *Machinery*. Vol. 2. P. 187. Google Books.
[4258] French, Lester Gray. (February, 1896). *Machinery*. Vol. 2. P. 187. Google Books.
[4259] French, Lester Gray. (February, 1896). *Machinery*. Vol. 2. P. 187. Google Books.
[4260] French, Lester Gray. (February, 1896). *Machinery*. Vol. 2. P. 187. Google Books.
[4261] French, Lester Gray. (February, 1896). *Machinery*. Vol. 2. P. 187. Google Books.
[4262] French, Lester Gray. (February, 1896). *Machinery*. Vol. 2. P. 187. Google Books.
[4263] French, Lester Gray. (February, 1896). *Machinery*. Vol. 2. P. 187. Google Books.
[4264] French, Lester Gray. (February, 1896). *Machinery*. Vol. 2. P. 187. Google Books.

of six percent on the company stock money since approximately August, 1895, a time of six months prior to the 1896 report.[4265] This report of the semiannual equity yield stability showed the early soundness and strength of the new company.[4266]

William Burtner served as Vice-President and Treasurer of the company at this time, having replaced Henry Luers as Treasurer.[4267] Charles Davis was the President and B. B. Quillen had replaced Henry Luers as Secretary at this point, Luers having occupied both the positions of Secretary and Treasurer prior.[4268] Davis & Egan was located at 68 and 70 S. Canal Street in the Near West Side community of the Chicago downtown.[4269] The Cincinnati and Chicago-based firm gave considerable technological support to Germany, through the firm's branches at Berlin, and supplied machinery to German markets at Munich and Dusseldorf.[4270] The Lodge & Davis Machine Tool Company office, moreover, had also been located at 68 and 70 S. Canal Street within the Near West Side community in 1895.[4271] J. B. Doan was the Chicago Manager and Agent of the Lodge & Davis Machine Tool Company at this time.[4272] The proximity of the company to the Barnum & Richardson Company may have been intentional, because both companies possessed possibly complementary market supremacies: the Barnum & Richardson Company was the largest railroad parts manufacturer in Chicago and in the world; the Lodge & Davis Machine Tool Company was the largest machine tool manufacturer in Chicago and in Cincinnati. The two companies probably contracted with each other many times over many years.

John Edward Burtner and Susannah (Criswell) Burtner

John Edward Burtner (1845-1917), a son of Capt. Philip Burtner and Rebecca (Shobert) Burtner, served during the Civil War as a member of Company C, 100th Pennsylvania Infantry.[4273] He returned from the war and worked as a store clerk, as a janitor for the Columbia Chemical Company of Barberton, Ohio, and later as

[4265] The Iron Age. (February 13, 1896). Vol. 57. P. 430. Google Books.

[4266] The Iron Age. (February 13, 1896). Vol. 57. P. 430. Google Books.

[4267] The Iron Age. (February 13, 1896). Vol. 57. P. 430. Google Books.

[4268] The Iron Age. (February 13, 1896). Vol. 57. P. 430. Google Books.

[4269] The Lakeside Annual Business Directory of the City of Chicago. (1896). P. 388. Chicago, IL: Reuben H. Donnelly, Compiler; The Chicago Directory Company. Google Books.

[4270] Modern Machinery. (January-June, 1898). Vol. III. P. 570. Google Books.

[4271] Chicago Directory. (1895).

[4272] Chicago Directory. (1895).

[4273] Border, Howard W. (1967). The Bordner And Burtner Families And Their Bortner Ancestors In America. P. 238. Washington, D.C. archive.org.

a farmer of Saxonburg.[4274] John owned the Burtner family farm, known as Home View, in the northern Pittsburgh suburb of Saxonburg, and there engaged in general farming until his death.[4275] John was one of the many founders of Harvey Post, Number 514, Grand Army of the Republic on March 25, 1886.[4276] He and Susannah were members of the Westminster Presbyterian Church of Saxonburg and of the Presbyterian Church of Barberton, Ohio.[4277] In addition to having been residents of Saxonburg and Barberton, John and Susannah were residents of Etna, a northeastern Pittsburgh suburb located in Allegheny County and in the direction of Saxonburg along the Allegheny River.[4278] After John Edward Burtner died in 1917, Home View farm passed to his widow, Susannah, and to their son, Norman Philip Burtner, who continued the farming operations there.[4279]

Susannah Belle (Criswell) Burtner (1849-1930) married John Edward Burtner, and was the daughter of Judge James Criswell (1791-1870) and Jane (Brownlow) Criswell.[4280] James Criswell was the Justice of the Peace of Clinton Township from 1865 to 1870, and was a financial manager for the township.[4281] Susannah was active in church and civic affairs in Barberton and Saxonburg. At Barberton she was a member of the Women's Missionary Society of the First Presbyterian Church.[4282] She belonged to the Barberton Women's Christian Temperance Union and the Barberton Eastern Star and was also a member of the board of directors of the Eastern Star of Barberton, an organization which she served as Warden.[4283]

The Children of John Edward Burtner and Susannah (Criswell) Burtner

Jonathan Edward Burtner and the Texas Oilfields

Jonathan Edward (sometimes Edmund) Burtner started an oil drilling company, probably in the form of a partnership with a man named Flanagan, near the Spindletop Oilfield of Texas, prior to 1903.[4284] Burtner was also associated with

---

[4274] Border, Howard W. (1967). The Bordner And Burtner Families And Their Bortner Ancestors In America. P. 238. Washington, D.C. archive.org;

[4275] Call, Baldwin, Burtner family records.

[4276] History of Butler County, Pennsylvania. (1895). P. 481. R. C. Brown & Co., Publishers. Archive.org.

[4277] Call, Baldwin, Burtner family records.

[4278] Border, Howard W. (1967). The Bordner And Burtner Families And Their Bortner Ancestors In America. P. 238. Washington, D.C. archive.org.

[4279] Call, Baldwin, Burtner family history records.

[4280] History of Butler County, Pennsylvania. (1895). P. 898. R. C. Brown & Co., Publishers. Archive.org.

[4281] History of Butler County, Pennsylvania. (1895). P. 478. R. C. Brown & Co., Publishers. Archive.org; Criswell family historical records.

[4282] Call, Baldwin, Burtner family records.

[4283] Call, Baldwin, Burtner family records.

[4284] Butler Citizen. (October 8, 1903). P. 2. Newspapers.com; Pittsburgh Daily Post. (October 4, 1903). P. 18. Newspapers.com.

his best friend, J. W. Dyon of San Antonio, presumably within the Texas oil business.[4285] At the time of Burtner's death, a journal was discovered that recorded the evidence of the Burtner-Flanagan oil company in Texas. The Spindletop Oilfield would be developed by Andrew William Mellon (1855-1937) of Pittsburgh. Andrew Mellon's grandaunt, Margaret Negley (1776-1857), married Philip Burtner (1762-1848). Philip Burtner was the great-granduncle of John Edward Burtner. The Burtners and Negleys were both founding families of Pittsburgh, Allegheny County, and Butler County, Pennsylvania.[4286] Andrew Mellon was founder of Gulf Oil, Aluminum Company of America, and the Mellon Bank, all of Pittsburgh. Mellon also served as United States Secretary of the Treasury under Presidents Warren G. Harding, Calvin Coolidge, and Herbert Hoover. Mellon was a noted philanthropist.

James Criswell Burtner and the Ohio Oil and Gas Industries

James Criswell Burtner (1870-1932), son of John Edward Burtner and Susannah (Criswell) Burtner, was one of the most important developers of the oilfields and gas fields of Ohio and was a major force in the development of the Cuyahoga County oilfield and the Columbus natural gas economy. Burtner founded the Burtner & Murphy Company probably prior to 1915.[4287] The Burtner & Murphy Company produced natural gas, operated one gas well on the Royalton-Wooster Road, and probably owned additional wells elsewhere in northern Ohio.[4288] Burtner also founded the Burtner & Odenkirk Company, with partner H. B. Odenkirk.[4289] This firm was an oil and gas drilling company in Wayne County, Ohio, with probable operations at other counties in Ohio.[4290]

James C. Burtner established the Burtner, Morgan & Stephens Company, a drilling contracting company, with James C. Morgan, and J. O. Stephens.[4291] The company was reported to have been the oldest of all oil drilling companies in Ohio

---

[4285] Butler Citizen. (October 8, 1903). P. 2. Newspapers.com; Pittsburgh Daily Post. (October 4, 1903). P. 18. Newspapers.com.

[4286] Burtner family history records.

[4287] The Natural Gas Journal. (1915). Vol. 9. Page number uncertain. Natural Gas Association of America. Google Books.

[4288] The Natural Gas Journal. (1915). Vol. 9. Page number uncertain. Natural Gas Association of America. Google Books.

[4289] 1932 obituary for James Criswell Burtner at Wooster, Ohio. The newspaper record has been lost, but the relevant facts cited herein are certain.

[4290] 1932 obituary for James Criswell Burtner at Wooster, Ohio. The newspaper record has been lost, but the relevant facts cited herein are certain.

[4291] 1932 obituary for James Criswell Burtner at Wooster, Ohio. The newspaper record has been lost, but the relevant facts cited herein are certain; Wooster Directory (Ohio) (1930). P. 86. Ancestry.com.

as of 1970.[4292] James Morgan was President of the Ohio Oil & Gas Association,[4293] an organization which Burtner had served as a member of the board of directors. The Burtner, Morgan & Stephens Company also established a West Virginia office, and probably operated in the great Pittsburgh-Butler oilfield of Pennsylvania at some point, because Burtner himself was a native of the Butler County part of the Pittsburgh metropolitan area, and often traveled there to visit family and compete in trap shooting tournaments.[4294]

Burtner founded the Tuber Manufacturing Company in 1911 with Frank Brotsman, Jerome Snyder, L. E. Snyder, and John H. Swisher.[4295] The company was based in Barberton, Summit County, Ohio, and its purpose was the manufacture of farm implements.[4296] Burtner joined the Wooster Tool & Supply Company as Vice-President at least as early as 1925, and at the same time maintained active executive leadership participation in multiple other Ohio companies.[4297] John J. Klise served as President of Wooster Tool & Supply Company, Burtner was Vice-President, and B. L. Peterson was Treasurer and General Manager.[4298] Curt Hudson served as Secretary.[4299] The company was formed in 1924.[4300]

James Burtner served on the boards of directors of both the Columbus Natural Gas Company and the Medina Gas & Fuel Company.[4301] The Columbus Natural Gas Company owned and operated fuel production facilities at Perry County, Licking County, and Fairfield County, all of which are located within the Columbus metropolitan area.[4302] The company owned distribution networks that included Granville, Pataskala, Shepard, East Columbia, Alexandria, Outville, Kirkersville, Union Station, Etna, and Reynoldsburg, all of which are Columbus

[4292] Obituary for James Criswell Burtner at Wooster, Ohio.

[4293] The Logan Daily News. (February 28, 1967). P. 8. Newspapers.com.

[4294] Beckley Post-Herald. (August 17, 1973). P. 19. Newspapers.com.

[4295] The Implement Age. (1911). Vol. 38. P. 26. Springfield, OH: The Implement Age. Google Books.

[4296] The Implement Age. (1911). Vol. 38. No. 19. P. 28. Springfield, OH: The Implement Age. Google Books.

[4297] National Petroleum News. (1925). Vol. 17. Page number uncertain. National Petroleum Publishing Company. Google Books.

[4298] National Petroleum News. (1925). Vol. 17. Page number uncertain. National Petroleum Publishing Company. Google Books.

[4299] National Petroleum News. (1925). Vol. 17. Page number uncertain. National Petroleum Publishing Company. Google Books.

[4300] The Cincinnati Enquirer. (March 20, 1924). P. 14. Newspapers.com.

[4301] Moody's Manual of Railroads and Corporation Securities. (1921). Vol. 1. Pp. 1532-1533. New York, NY: Moody's. Google Books.

[4302] Moody's Manual of Railroads and Corporation Securities. (1921). Vol. 1. P. 1532. New York, NY: Moody's. Google Books.

suburbs.[4303] As of 1920, the Columbus Natural Gas Company owned and operated 138 active gas wells and 183.006 miles of pipeline for the distribution of fuel for the Columbus metropolitan area.[4304] The company leased 20,125.01 acres of land for the gas production.[4305] The company natural gas production amount for 1920 totaled 683,236,000 cubic feet, and the sales amount for 1920 totaled 659,779,000 cubic feet.[4306] Frank W. Frueauff served as the company President, and Fenwick Ewing was Vice-President.[4307] Ira L. Neely was Vice-President and General Manager; N. E. Shupe was Secretary and Treasurer.[4308] The board of directors included James C. Burtner, Frank W. Frueauff, Ira L. Neely, N. E. Shupe, Fenwick Ewing, H. L. Doherty, and H. H. Scott.[4309]

The Medina Gas & Fuel Company owned and operated production facilities in the Ohio counties of Wayne, Medina, Holmes, and Ashland, and leased 242,505.58 acres of gas lands in these four counties for production.[4310] The company owned 115 active gas wells and served communities within the Cleveland metropolitan area, the Wooster and Akron metropolitan areas, and the Mansfield area.[4311] Medina Gas & Fuel gas production for the year 1920 totaled 2,266,502,000 cubic feet, and was distributed through a 321.875-mile pipeline network.[4312] The company's distribution and service included the communities of Pleasant Home, Creston, Harpster, Chippewa Lake, Medina, Brunswick, Burbank, Lafayette, Leroy, Lodi, Morral, Mt. Victory, Nevada, Rittman, Seville, Rowsburg, Sterling, West Salem, and Wyandotte.[4313] The production, distribution, geographical scope, and service of the Medina Gas & Fuel Company established the company firmly

---

[4303] Moody's Manual of Railroads and Corporation Securities. (1921). Vol. 1. P. 1532. New York, NY: Moody's. Google Books.

[4304] Moody's Manual of Railroads and Corporation Securities. (1921). Vol. 1. P. 1532. New York, NY: Moody's. Google Books.

[4305] Moody's Manual of Railroads and Corporation Securities. (1921). Vol. 1. P. 1532. New York, NY: Moody's. Google Books.

[4306] Moody's Manual of Railroads and Corporation Securities. (1921). Vol. 1. P. 1532. New York, NY: Moody's. Google Books.

[4307] Moody's Manual of Railroads and Corporation Securities. (1921). Vol. 1. P. 1532. New York, NY: Moody's. Google Books.

[4308] Moody's Manual of Railroads and Corporation Securities. (1921). Vol. 1. P. 1532. New York, NY: Moody's. Google Books.

[4309] Moody's Manual of Railroads and Corporation Securities. (1921). Vol. 1. P. 1532. New York, NY: Moody's. Google Books.

[4310] Moody's Manual of Railroads and Corporation Securities. (1921). Vol. 1. P. 1532. New York, NY: Moody's. Google Books.

[4311] Moody's Manual of Railroads and Corporation Securities. (1921). Vol. 1. P. 1532. New York, NY: Moody's. Google Books.

[4312] Moody's Manual of Railroads and Corporation Securities. (1921). Vol. 1. P. 1532. New York, NY: Moody's. Google Books.

[4313] Moody's Manual of Railroads and Corporation Securities. (1921). Vol. 1. P. 1532. New York, NY: Moody's. Google Books.

as a geopolitical element of the Cleveland-Columbus industrial corridor during the early twentieth century.[4314] The leadership structure and staff paralleled those of the Columbus Natural Gas Company: Frank W. Frueauff served as the Medina Gas & Fuel President; Fenwick Ewing served as Vice-President; Ira L. Neely served as Vice-President and General Manager; and N. E. Shupe served as Secretary and Treasurer. The board of directors consisted of James C. Burtner, Fenwick Ewing, Ira L. Neely, Frank Frueauff, H. L. Doherty, N. E. Shupe, and H. H. Scott.[4315]

Burtner was a member and agent of the Doherty Organization, a New York City company which exerted tremendous political and economic powers over the United States oil industry and oil industry policies in the Midwest and the East.[4316] Burtner served many years as a member of the board of directors of the Ohio Gas and Oil Men's Association, a Columbus organization.[4317] Burtner was elected to the board of directors of the Ohio Gas and Oil Men's Association at least as early as 1922, the fourth year of the Association's existence.[4318] The 1922 board of directors consisted of Burtner, Ira L. Neely, J. W. McMahon, J. M. Garard, George W. Trimble of Lancaster, T. J. Jones, Martin B. Daly, John J. Klise, and Warren E. Burns.[4319] It is highly probable that Burtner, Klise, Neely, and Frueauff were all founding members of the Ohio Gas and Oil Men's Association in 1917. As has been demonstrated, Burtner, Klise, and Neely were mutually associated as executives and directors of multiple other organizations in Ohio. In addition to holding membership and board of directors membership within the Ohio Gas and Oil Men's Association, Burtner was a member of the Natural Gas Association of America, and was an active participant therein, having been among the Ohio representatives at the great 1922 Natural Gas Association of America Gas Convention and Gas Show at Kansas City, Missouri.[4320]

James Criswell Burtner was an accomplished sportsman and marksman, as were many of the Burtners and Criswells. James Burtner was a nationally ranked and respected trap shooter.[4321] He was a member of both the Columbia Gun Club of

---

[4314] Moody's Manual of Railroads and Corporation Securities. (1921). Vol. 1. P. 1532. New York, NY: Moody's. Google Books.
[4315] Moody's Manual of Railroads and Corporation Securities. (1921). Vol. 1. P. 1533. New York, NY: Moody's. Google Books.
[4316] Record has been lost, but the facts cited are certain and reliable.
[4317] Natural Gas. (October, 1922). Vol. III. No. 10. P. 3. Natural Gas Association of America. Google Books.
[4318] Natural Gas. (October, 1922). Vol. III. No. 10. P. 3. Natural Gas Association of America. Google Books.
[4319] Natural Gas. (October, 1922). Vol. III. No. 10. P. 3. Natural Gas Association of America. Google Books.
[4320] Natural Gas. (June, 1922). Vol. III. No. 10. P. 22. Natural Gas Association of America. Google Books.
[4321] The Cincinnati Enquirer. (August 4, 1918). P. 22. Newspapers.com.

Barberton, Ohio, and the Western Pennsylvania Trap Shooters' League.[4322] He also was prominently associated with the Butler Rod and Gun Club of Butler, Pennsylvania.[4323] Burtner competed in the Grand American Handicap trap shooting tournament in Chicago in 1918.[4324] This tournament was probably hosted by the Lincoln Park Gun Club, which was located at Diversey and Lake Michigan, in Lincoln Park, and at the border of the Lincoln Park community and the Lake View community.

Burtner won the Columbia Gun Club trap shoot tournament at Barberton, Ohio, in March, 1905, winning both the championship cup and the championship pin, and defeating H. A. Galt, who had held the Columbia Gun Cub championship solidly for six months.[4325] Burtner was ranked and classified as a professional marksman and trap shooter at least as early as 1916, and probably far earlier than that.[4326] He remained active in shooting tournaments both in the Pittsburgh-Butler gun clubs and in the Columbia Gun Club of Barberton.[4327] Cousin Roy Irving Burtner of Butler had held a world rifle competition record for more than one decade straight and was reputed to have been able to strike a target perfectly at a distance of 1,000 yards.[4328] Roy, who had served in the Spanish-American War, also held pistol shooting records.[4329]

Having worked for decades to build the Ohio oil and gas industries, James C. Burtner helped to produce and administer nearly 3 billion cubic feet of natural gas per year for the Cleveland-Columbus Corridor during the 1920s.[4330] Much of this resource fueled the power and utility needs of Columbus, a fact that placed Burtner, Frank Frueauff, Fenwick Ewing, Ira Neely, and other associates at the forefront of Ohio metropolitan energy production and distribution.[4331] Burtner contributed significantly to the industrial development of Columbus, Cleveland, Wooster, Barberton, Akron, Canton, and the multiple neighboring towns and counties. Burtner married Carrie Block of Ohio.

[4322] Akron Beacon Journal. (March 6, 1905). P. 4. Newspapers.com; Pittsburgh Daily Post. (June 18, 1916). P. 23. Newspapers.com.

[4323] Pittsburgh Daily Post. (June 18, 1916). P. 23. Newspapers.com.

[4324] The Cincinnati Enquirer. (August 4, 1918). P. 22. Newspapers.com.

[4325] The Cincinnati Enquirer. (August 4, 1918). P. 22. Newspapers.com; Akron Beacon Journal. (March 6, 1905). P. 4. Newspapers.com.

[4326] Pittsburgh Daily Post. (June 18, 1916). P. 23. Newspapers.com.

[4327] Pittsburgh Daily Post. (June 18, 1916). P. 23. Newspapers.com; Akron Beacon Journal. (March 6, 1905). P. 4. Newspapers.com.

[4328] Call, Baldwin, Burtner family history and records.

[4329] Call, Baldwin, Burtner family history and records.

[4330] Moody's Manual of Railroads and Corporation Securities. (1921). Vol. 1. Pp. 1532-1533. New York, NY: Moody's. Google Books.

[4331] Moody's Manual of Railroads and Corporation Securities. (1921). Vol. 1. Pp. 1532-1533. New York, NY: Moody's. Google Books.

Stanley Ward Baldwin and Theresa May (Burtner) Baldwin

Of Cleveland, Barberton, and Metropolitan Pittsburgh

Theresa May Burtner (1894-1926) was the youngest daughter of John Edward Burtner and Susannah Belle (Criswell) Burtner. Known often as "Tress," she was a younger sister of Ohio oil industrialist James Criswell Burtner. Theresa graduated from the Cleveland Emergency Hospital school of nursing.[4332] In September of 1915, Theresa Burtner served as one of the founding nurses of the Barberton Citizens' Hospital of Barberton, Ohio.[4333] Cora Page and Hulda Gram were, respectively, the founding Hospital Administrator and founding Nursing Administrator of the Barberton Citizens' Hospital. Theresa Burtner, Helen Thesing, and a Miss Justice were the founding nurses of the Barberton Citizen's Hospital.[4334] Theresa first married Daniel Ayrault Huling, who was a chemical engineer of Cleveland.[4335] After divorcing Huling, she married Stanley Ward Baldwin (1893-1923), an oil-driller, chiropractor, and building contractor of Cleveland, Pittsburgh, and Butler, Pennsylvania.[4336] Stanley was the only child of La Drew Baldwin (1858-1935) and Elizabeth (Haire) Baldwin (1865-1909) of Cleveland, and was the grandson of Henry Baldwin and Sarah Phillips, who were respectively from Tompkins County, New York, and Crawford County, Pennsylvania.[4337] The Baldwins and Haires were large families that had resided in Cleveland and Cuyahoga County for multiple generations.[4338] Five generations of the Baldwin and Haire family have resided in Cleveland and Cuyahoga County.

La Drew Baldwin and the Baldwins of Cleveland and Akron

La Drew Baldwin owned the Baldwin Harness Company, a Cleveland harness and carriage parts manufacturing company. He also owned a sewing goods and notions store.[4339] Baldwin owned two real estate companies of Cleveland and the metropolitan area for many years in the early twentieth century.[4340] Baldwin was president of the Baldwin Brokerage Company of Lakewood and Cleveland, and

---

[4332] Akron Beacon Journal. (January 28, 1915). P. 7. Newspapers.com.
[4333] Akron Evening Times. (September 25, 1915). P. 10. Newspapers.com.
[4334] Akron Evening Times. (September 25, 1915). P. 10. Newspapers.com.
[4335] Marriage License for Daniel A. Huling and Theresa M. Burtner. (June 27, 1916). Detroit, Michigan, Marriages. Familysearch.org.
[4336] Marriage License for Stanley Ward Baldwin and Theresa M. Burtner. Detroit, Michigan Marriages. (February 23, 1917). Familysearch.org.
[4337] Baldwin family records. Cuyahoga County Death Certificate for LaDrew Baldwin. (February 1, 1935). Familysearch.org; Call, Baldwin, Burtner family history records.
[4338] Baldwin family records.
[4339] Call, Baldwin, Burtner family history records.
[4340] Cleveland City Directories. Baldwin family records.

had been a partner in the Baldwin & Holcomb Company, a realty firm of Cleveland and Lakewood.[4341] Stanley Ward Baldwin, who had served as a U.S. Army sergeant in World War I, owned a chiropractic company in Cleveland and a small Cleveland construction company, but died in 1923 after a serious fall.[4342] Theresa (Burtner) Baldwin died in 1926 of an illness contracted while she was working at a Pittsburgh hospital.[4343] La Drew Baldwin's sister, Alma Permelia Baldwin, married Elton Crane, and both resided in Cleveland.[4344] Another Baldwin sister, Hattie Baldwin, was a resident of Cleveland and Detroit.[4345]

Dr. Homer Aaron Baldwin, first cousin of La Drew Baldwin, was a dentist and civic leader in metropolitan Cleveland and in Summit County, Ohio. Dr. Baldwin was a graduate of the Western Reserve University Dental College in 1899. He co-founded the Methodist Church at Wadsworth, Summit County, Ohio, in 1902, and served as Secretary of the Church Building Committee. Homer Baldwin also served as Vice-President of the Summit County Dental Association. Baldwin was elected as a Delegate to the 1903 Ohio Republican Convention, representing Wadsworth. He also was President of the Wadsworth Automobile Club and was prominently associated with the construction, development, and administration of the Benjamin Franklin Memorial Highway of Ohio. Homer Baldwin co-founded the Wadsworth Rotary Club in 1925. Baldwin co-founded the Wadsworth Chamber of Commerce with Charles Seiberling. Seiberling was a founder of the Goodyear Tire & Rubber Company of Akron. Stanley Ward Baldwin and Theresa (Burtner) Baldwin had one child, a daughter named Mary Elizabeth Baldwin.[4346]

William Frederic Call and Mary Elizabeth (Baldwin) Call of Ohio

Mary Elizabeth "Betty" Baldwin (1917-2001) was the daughter of Stanley Ward Baldwin (1893-1923) and Theresa May (Burtner) Baldwin (1894-1926). Betty was the niece of Ohio oil industrialist James Criswell Burtner, Texas oil entrepreneur Jonathan Edward Burtner, Saxonburg farmer Norman Philip Burtner, Letitia Vernell (Burtner) Hill, Lydia Jane (Burtner) Huselton, Zella Mable (Burtner) Stampfle, Katherine May Burtner, Rebecca Burtner, Harry Burtner, and George Wirt Burtner, who all were residents of the metropolitan Pittsburgh towns of Saxonburg and Butler, and Ohio and Detroit. Betty Baldwin first attended the Butler County Public Schools in Pennsylvania. She then became a student at The Andrews School for Girls, a leading historic private boarding school for girls in

---

[4341] Cleveland City Directories. Baldwin family records.

[4342] Cuyahoga County Death Certificate for Stanley Ward Baldwin. (March 5, 1923). Familysearch.org.

[4343] Call, Baldwin, Burtner family history records.

[4344] Call, Baldwin, Burtner family history records.

[4345] Call, Baldwin, Burtner family history records.

[4346] Call, Baldwin, Burtner family history records.

Willoughby, Ohio.[4347] Betty Baldwin's roommate was Daisy Neely, who may have been a relative of Ohio oilman Ira L. Neely, the close friend and business partner of Betty Baldwin's uncle, James Criswell Burtner. Betty Baldwin served as Class Treasurer in her Eighth Grade year at The Andrews School, and declared a Foods Major while a student there.[4348] Betty later would study the harp and become an amateur concert harpist in Los Angeles and Denver, Colorado, when she and William Frederic Call moved to those places later.

Betty married William Frederic Call of Martin's Ferry and Cleveland, Ohio, on March 23, 1935, in Cleveland.[4349] Rev. W. W. T. Duncan, a Methodist minister of Cleveland, married them. Betty had been raised as a Presbyterian, and William was raised a Methodist. They were active in Cleveland civic life. Betty Call, Gay Andrews, and many other friends of hers were members of the Cleveland Junior Federation, which was a women's civic board of Cleveland.[4350] Both Betty and William were active with the Cleveland Orchestra Guild during the 1930s and were supporters of the Cleveland Symphony Orchestra at University Circle.[4351] Elizabeth (Bunn) Taylor, the maternal grandmother of Andrew Taylor Call, was a cousin of the Holdens of Cleveland and Bratenahl, Ohio, who were also supporters of the Cleveland Orchestra.

William F. Call would serve as a personnel officer, public relations officer, sales officer, and company newsletter editor for Hankins Container Company of Cleveland and Chicago.[4352] Call was a graduate of Lakewood High School in Lakewood, Ohio, located in west suburban Cleveland, and had attended Martin's Ferry High School for Ninth and Tenth grades.[4353] He excelled in Latin and was a member of the Track Team, Swimming Team, and the Drama Club while in high school.[4354] He was one of the first employees in the history of Hankins Container Company.[4355] This company was a large multi-state manufacturer of corrugated shipping containers. Call began there as a laborer, entered the company's sales force, rose to officer status, and became Assistant to Edward R. Hankins (1882-1954), who was the President and founder of the company.[4356] As a protégé of Edward R. Hankins, William F. Call helped to build Hankins Container Company into a large Great Lakes corporation that possessed not only a headquarters and

---

[4347] Call, Baldwin, Burtner family history and records.
[4348] Call, Baldwin, Burtner family history and records.
[4349] Call, Baldwin, Burtner family history and records.
[4350] Call, Baldwin, Burtner family history and records.
[4351] Call, Baldwin, Burtner family history and records.
[4352] Call, Baldwin, Burtner family history and records.
[4353] Call, Baldwin, Burtner family history and records.
[4354] Call, Baldwin, Burtner family history and records.
[4355] Call, Baldwin, Burtner family history and records.
[4356] Call, Baldwin, Burtner family history and records.

main factory in Cleveland, but also a major factory in Chicago.[4357] Hankins Container owned a factory in the southwest side of Chicago near the Clearing, West Lawn, and Chicago Lawn communities.[4358] Call also worked with Stone Publishing Company of Cleveland while he was employed by Hankins Container Company.[4359] The Chicago branch of Hankins Container Company was located at 6935 W. 65th Street in 1947.[4360] Call served for twenty years as a personnel and public relations officer for Hankins Container Company.[4361] The Cleveland factory of Hankins Container Company was located at 3044 W. 106th Street.[4362]

William Call took business courses through the University of Michigan and Toledo University, and Betty Call took courses through Toledo University.[4363] Betty Call co-founded the Symphony Harp Quartet in metropolitan Los Angeles with Mary Jane Barton and two other harpists. The Symphony Harp Quartet performed harp music at various events throughout metropolitan Los Angeles.[4364] Betty taught harp to many students, remained a devoted student of classical music, and played as a guest harpist with the San Gabriel Symphony Orchestra of California. She later performed as a guest harpist with the Denver Businessmen's Orchestra, where she performed under the baton of orchestra conductor Antonia Brico (1902-1989).[4365] Betty Call co-founded the Colorado Chapter of the American Harp Society in Denver.[4366] She was also a friend of the Denver native and Pulitzer Prize-winning playwright Mary Chase, who was the author of the play, *Harvey*. Interestingly, both Thomas Stephen Hogan, Esq., and Dr. Frank Richardson (See Chapter 7 and Chapter 5) were residents of Denver. Dr. Frank Richardson retired to Denver and died there. Thomas Hogan served as Chairman of the Denver Coal Board and was one of the founders of the Denver and Colorado coal industries. Multiple members of the Call and Hogan families attended the University of Colorado-Boulder.

William and Betty Call relocated from Ohio to California in 1949, where William continued working in the corrugated shipping container industry. William Call co-founded the Santa Ana Container Company in 1956 with E. E. Jacobson and Charles W. Kyle. Jacobson served as President of the company; Kyle served as Vice-President of the company; and Call served as Secretary and Treasurer of

---

[4357] Dayton Daily News. (August 19, 1958). P. 20; Call, Baldwin, Burtner family history and records.
[4358] Call, Baldwin, Burtner family history and records.
[4359] Call, Baldwin, Burtner family history and records.
[4360] Chicago Tribune. (September 29, 1947). P. 43. Newspapers.com.
[4361] The Tustin News. (May 31, 1956). P. 5. Newspapers.com.
[4362] Rose, William Ganson. (1950 and reprinted 1990). Cleveland: The Making of a City. P. 907. Kent, OH: The Kent State University Press. Google Books.
[4363] Call, Baldwin, Burtner family history and records.
[4364] Call, Baldwin, Burtner family history and records.
[4365] Call, Baldwin, Burtner family history and records.
[4366] Call, Baldwin, Burtner family historical records.

the company.[4367] The company was the first shipping container company in Santa Ana, and manufactured crates and kraft containers for California produce and other cargo. The Santa Ana Container Company operated a 12,500-square-foot factory at 1024 Fuller Street in Santa Ana.[4368] E. E. Jacobson was a prominent building contractor; Charles W. Kyle was an officer within the Corrugated Container and Folding Carton Sales Division of Fibreboard Corporation; William F. Call was also an officer with the Fibreboard Corporation in Los Angeles after having been many years an officer of Hankins Container Company of Cleveland and Chicago.[4369] Call also served as Sales Manager of the Industrial Packaging Division of Fibreboard Corporation in Los Angeles. Call and Kyle, therefore, would have almost certainly known each other through Fibreboard. Fibreboard was headquartered in the Russ Building on Montgomery Street in the Financial District of San Francisco and shared the Russ Building with the great Miller & Lux Company (see Chapter 4, *Friends of the Leatherworkers*). For a time, William F. Call and Thomas Keister Greer, Esq., who were, respectively, the paternal grandfather and the stepfather of author Andrew Taylor Call, commuted often to the Russ Building for corporate meetings during the same years. The two men probably passed each other in the hallways and elevators of the Russ Building.

Fibreboard transferred Call to Denver, Colorado, and gave him the job of establishing the Intermountain Packaging Division of Fibreboard. The Intermountain Division was headquartered in Denver and encompassed all company territory from the Mississippi River to the Rocky Mountains. In the position of General Manager of the Intermountain Packaging Division, Call managed a workforce of 800 people. He successfully managed the Division and earned the respect and favor of the board of directors in San Francisco. The board wished to promote Call to the position of Vice-President of Sales. His promotion to the job of Vice-President of Sales, which would have been based in San Francisco, never materialized, however. Concurrently, the affairs of the company turned downward fast for all levels of the company leadership. When Fibreboard Corporation began to suffer economic losses, they terminated the Intermountain Division. The closure ended the employment of the 800 workers. Call personally searched for, procured, and confirmed employment for every single one of his 800 employees, and in so doing guaranteed each employee a job. When the time came for Call to seek a new position for himself, however, he was confronted with a rapidly changing business culture, one in which the Master of Business Administration degree was gaining ascendancy in upper management and executive leadership. Call had attended university classes but had been unable to finish a college degree due to the economic circumstances of the Great Depression.

[4367] The Tustin News. (May 31, 1956). P. 5. Newspapers.com.
[4368] The Tustin News. (May 31, 1956). P. 5. Newspapers.com.
[4369] The Tustin News. (May 31, 1956). P. 5. Newspapers.com.

Consequently, Call was unable to locate a new job for himself. The tragedy, combined with the economic pressure and stresses of the situation, caused him to suffer a stroke. He died in 1973. One of Call's employees commented that Call was responsible for making possible all of the success that the employee had experienced in business.

Call was held in the highest esteem by his community, his employees, superior company officers, and peers. Outside of his work at Fibreboard Corporation, William Call co-founded a gold mining partnership company in Denver with several other partners. The company owned gold mine properties and other precious metal mine properties in the Rocky Mountains of southwestern Colorado. Call served as Chairman of the Board of Directors of First Church of Christ, Scientist, Denver, and managed the trust and investment money for the church for a period of time. He and Betty also were founders of First Church of Christ, Scientist, Tustin, California, and were co-founders of First Church of Christ, Scientist, Berea, Ohio. William Call served also as a consultant to the shipping container industry and was instrumental in the design and planning for American corrugated shipping container factories. William Frederic Call and his first cousin, Loren Ralph Dodson (1897-1972), who helped reorganize and build the Continental Can Company of Chicago, New York City, and Pittsburgh, into the largest container company in the world, both served the United States shipping container industry. Dodson was one of the most important corporate and industrial executives of Chicago and New York City, and it is possible, through not proven, that Dodson was the one who had counseled Call to enter the shipping container industry in Ohio.[4370]

The Criswells of Pittsburgh, Allegheny County, and Butler County

William Criswell and the Building of Industrial Pittsburgh

William Criswell (1829-1910), son of Judge James Criswell (1791-1870) and Jane (Brownlow) Criswell, was a Pittsburgh building contractor and carpenter who worked as an apprentice in construction during the period of industrialization of Pittsburgh and Allegheny County. William was the uncle of Theresa (Burtner) Baldwin and the granduncle of Mary Elizabeth (Baldwin) Call. He apprenticed with the Smith & Bungey Company, one of Pittsburgh's most important construction firms, and after two years working in the timber industry of

---

[4370] Call, Baldwin, Burtner family history records.

Minnesota, returned to Pittsburgh to take charge of the company where he had learned construction. He became a partner of the Smith & Bungey Company. Mr. Bungey retired, and the name of the business then changed to Smith & Criswell. William Criswell specialized in industrial construction. He built grain elevators, steel mills, and railroads, among many other forms of property. Particularly famous for railroad bridge and tressel construction, Criswell was called upon to rebuild the railroad bridges of Pennsylvania that had been damaged by the Confederate military during the Civil War. He also built the Pittsburgh & Connellsville Railroad Company bridges from Pittsburgh to Cumberland, Maryland, and much of the Allegheny Valley Railroad. He served as President of Criswell & Burgoyne Company, which was a subsequent iteration of the Smith & Criswell Company. He was a Trustee of First Presbyterian Church of Allegheny City, located on the Pittsburgh North Side. Additionally, he was a founder, stockholder, and officer of the Masonic Hall Association Company of Allegheny City. Criswell was a partner, owner, and possibly a founder of two Allegheny-Pittsburgh banking companies: the Allegheny Savings Bank Company and the Franklin Savings Bank Company. He built the support framework for the Swamp Angel, a noted canon used by the United States military in the bombardment of Confederate forces at Charleston, South Carolina.

Criswell was connected to multiple Pittsburgh and Allegheny City companies and civic organizations, including McKinley Post 318, Free and Accepted Masons, of which he was a board member, and the Odd Fellows Endowment Association of Western Pennsylvania, the latter of which he served both as Treasurer and member of the board of directors. He worked closely with George C. Johnstone, a close friend and another Pittsburgh building contractor, in administering the money of the Odd Fellows Endowment Association and helped distribute some $800,000 of its charitable moneys by 1898. Criswell and the other corporate directors sent the charitable moneys to Pittsburgh regional recipients, including the widows of Odd Fellows members. Criswell built the Old Allegheny Conservatory and many bridges across the rivers of Pittsburgh and Allegheny County. Criswell was one of the most significant and large-scale building contractors in the history of both Pittsburgh and Pennsylvania.[4371]

Robert Ross Criswell and the Pittsburgh-Butler Oilfields

Robert Ross Criswell (1845-1912), son of Judge James Criswell and Jane (Brownlow) Criswell, was an oil explorer, developer of petroleum technology, and a corporate executive of Pittsburgh. He worked in the Pittsburgh-Butler oilfields as a torpedo man. Torpedo men were oil technologists whose specialization was the construction and subterannean deployment of nitroglycerin rockets for the purpose of the subterranean liquefaction of the geological elements that

---

[4371] Criswell, Burtner, and Baldwin family history records.

interlocked with liquid petroleum resources. This process and machinery enabled easier extraction of oil from the ground. Ross Criswell became President and owner of the Washington Torpedo Company of Washington, Pennsylvania, a western Pittsburgh suburb. The company operated a headquarters at Washington, in the Pittsburgh-Butler oilfield, and maintained offices at Wheeling, West Virginia, and Cleveland, Ohio, possibly in addition to other places. Criswell earned a legendary reputation as an oil executive and torpedo man who never suffered death as a result of the work, death being a common occurrence of petroleum workers who worked with nitroglycerin rockets. Ross's daughters, Cora Criswell and Eleanor Criswell, inherited the Washington Torpedo Company from their father, and carried on the Criswell reputation and mystique for their apparent invincibility in working constantly with nitroglycerin technologies. Atypical for women of the Gilded Age, Cora and Eleanor assumed leadership and ownership of the company and its operations. The Criswell sisters drove the company nitroglycerin trucks all through the Appalachian Mountains and Great Lakes oil districts in order to bring the company machinery to market. Thomas Criswell, son of Judge James Criswell and Jane (Brownlow) Criswell, worked in the lumber industry of Pittsburgh, and resided at McKeesport. Robert Ross Criswell and Thomas Criswell were uncles of Theresa (Burtner) Baldwin, and granduncles of Mary Elizabeth (Baldwin) Call.[4372]

Judge Joseph Criswell:

Judge, Oil and Gas Entrepreneur, and Land Developer of Metropolitan Pittsburgh

The Honorable Joseph Criswell (1840-1916), son of Judge James Criswell and Jane (Brownlow) Criswell, was a judge, oil and gas producer, banker, real estate investor, bibliophile, and political figure in Pittsburgh and Butler. He was the uncle of Theresa (Burtner) Baldwin, and granduncle of Mary Elizabeth (Baldwin) Call. He served as Clerk of Courts for Butler County, and later became a Justice of the Peace at Lyndora, in Butler County. He was Mayor of Lyndora, a municipality of 5,000, and one inhabited largely by Eastern European immigrant families. Criswell married Rebecca Richardson Burkhart, whose ancestors had come to America with William Penn and were founders of Pennsylvania. Joseph and Rebecca Criswell owned a farm in Butler County. They developed a large natural gas production works from the Criswell farm and once supplied all or much of the gas resource for the City of Butler in metropolitan Pittsburgh.

Joseph was a member of the board of directors of the Lyndora National Bank and served as founder and President of the million-dollar Lyndora Building and Loan Association Company at around the beginning of the twentieth century. He also started a real estate investment company and owned many properties in

---

[4372] Criswell, Burtner, and Baldwin family history records.

Pittsburgh. Judge Criswell handled cases of all varieties, including murder cases, battery cases, railroad property cases, and many other forms. It is estimated that he adjudicated some 800 cases a year.[4373]

James Criswell, Jr. and James Criswell, III.:

Brickworkers and Furnace Manufacturers of Pittsburgh and the Nation

James Criswell, Jr. (1831-1904), son of James Criswell and Jane (Brownlow) Criswell, worked as a brick mason at Sharpsburg, a Pittsburgh suburb. He also owned a masonry company in and around Sharpsburg and Pittsburgh, according to one record that was discovered many years ago. James married Hannah Ann Harvey (1837-1902).[4374] James Criswell, III (1859-1940), son of James and Hannah (Harvey) Criswell, was a Pittsburgh manufacturer of steelworking and furnace technologies, furnaces, and factory components. He worked for the S. R. Smythe Company of Pittsburgh and served as Samuel R. Smythe's company Superintendent, eventually becoming Vice-President of the S. R. Smythe Company. This company was one of Pittsburgh's most significant steelworking machinery companies. Criswell left the employ of Smythe to establish the James Criswell Company in 1931. Headquartered at the Kenan Building in downtown Pittsburgh, the James Criswell Company rapidly acquired a national scope and portfolio of business. James Criswell, III, manufactured steelworking furnaces for the Ford Motor Company, and was a personal friend of Henry Ford. The company was a manufacturer of factory technologies for large industries and helped to build much of the technology for the Michigan automotive industry in addition, of course, to a tremendous amount of Pittsburgh infrastructure. James married Jennie Riddle (1857-1935), and the couple resided in and around Pittsburgh.

James Homer Criswell, son of James Criswell, III, and Jennie (Riddle) Criswell, was an engineer, and established the Criswell Brothers Company of Pittsburgh with his brother, John Russell Criswell. Homer and John worked for their father at the James Criswell Company, as had their brother, William Harvey Criswell. All three men had held executive leadership positions in the James Criswell Company. James Homer Criswell served as President of the Overbrook Chamber of Commerce in Pittsburgh and was an active community leader. John Russell Criswell served on the Pittsburgh Borough Council and was a Bucknell University alumnus.[4375]

James Burkhart Criswell of Pittsburgh and Knoxville, Tennessee

---

[4373] Criswell, Burtner, and Baldwin family history records.
[4374] Criswell, Burtner, and Baldwin family history records; Findagrave.com.
[4375] Criswell, Burtner, and Baldwin family history records.

James Burkhart Criswell, son of Judge Joseph Criswell and Rebecca Richardson (Burkhart) Criswell, relocated from Pittsburgh to Knoxville, Tennessee, where he began employment as a salesman for the Haynes-Henson Company, a shoe and boot manufacturer. Criswell worked for company founders Jonathan Paris Haynes and James Alexander Henson, rose to the vice-presidency of the company, and was elected to membership on the Haynes-Henson Company board of directors. Known as, "Knoxville's Million Dollar Shoe Company," Haynes-Henson was allegedly the largest footwear manufacturer in the entire South. The firm employed a staff of representatives from the Atlantic seaboard to Mexico and became a multimillion dollar company by at least the early twentieth century, and possibly before. James was a founding executive of the Appalachian Exposition of Knoxville in 1910 and was Chairman of the Publicity Committee for the Exposition. The Appalachian Exposition was a very large regional fair, essentially a smaller version of a Worlds Fair. Politically active as a Republican, Criswell was Delegate to the 1924 Republican National Convention at Kansas City, a Tennessee elector, and a leader in the Knoxville Chamber of Commerce. He never married. When he died, his sisters from Pittsburgh came to Knoxville to bring their brother back home to Pittsburgh to be interred there.[4376]

It is quite possible that James B. Criswell overlapped with Harry Earl Richardson in Knoxville, because both Criswell and Richardson were Knoxville residents and worked in the clothing manufacturing industry there. Harry Earl Richardson was a son of Charles Richardson of Springfield, a nephew of William Douglas Richardson of Chicago, and a first cousin of Ada Willard (Richardson) Bunn (See Chapter 5, *The Foundations of Jackson Park*). Harry was Sales Manager of the Southeast Division of the Patent Button Company, a button manufacturer.

Jean Rebecca (Criswell) Littlewood and Rev. W. Clifton Littlewood:

Civic and Business Developers of Pittsburgh and Miami

Jean Rebecca Criswell, daughter of Judge Joseph Criswell and Rebecca Richardson (Burkhart) Criswell, was one of the most significant civic leaders of Pittsburgh and Miami, Florida, during the Gilded Age. Jean held multiple degrees in music, and was an alumna of the University of Pittsburgh, the Western Conservatory of Music in Chicago, and the St. Louis Music Institute of St. Louis. After returning to Pittsburgh, Jean married lawyer John P. Wilson, Esq. To them

---

[4376] Criswell, Burtner, and Baldwin family history records.

one son was born, Joseph Criswell Wilson. Joseph died young. Joseph had been a noted member of the Boys' Choir at St. Paul's Episcopal Church of Pittsburgh. Jean and John divorced, and Jean subsequently married Rev. William Clifton Littlewood, a minister of Pittsburgh. Jean (Criswell) Littlewood combined multiple forms of philanthropy and leadership in Pittsburgh and Allegheny County. She was President of the Western Conservatory of Music, a Pittsburgh conservatory, and helped develop musical education not only in Allegheny County, but also in Miami during the 1920s Florida Land Boom. Jean was a first cousin of Theresa (Burtner) Baldwin and a first cousin once removed of Mary Elizabeth (Baldwin) Call.

Jean (Criswell) Littlewood co-founded and developed the Congress of Women's Clubs of Western Pennsylvania, which was a Pittsburgh organization. The Congress constituted one of Pittsburgh's most important social and political institutions, and was the central organization for all planning, administration, and government of the women's clubs of Western Pennsylvania. Jean was a member of the Congress of Women's Clubs, which she helped establish, and was a member of the Women's Club of Pittsburgh. She directed the musical programs for the Women's Club of Pittsburgh. For a time, Jean resided in California and served as a member of the California State Board of Education.

After returning to Pittsburgh, she and Clifton joined a large coterie of Pittsburghers who became heavily interested in the commercial development of south Florida during what is referred to as the Florida Land Boom of the 1920s.[4377] Jean and Clifton were prominently associated with the Pittsburgh-Miami Corporation and held executive and advisory positions with the company.[4378] Clifton served as Secretary of the corporation, a position in which he oversaw the development of the Sweetwater community of Dade County.[4379] Jean was an advisor to the corporation, and it is possible that Jean and Clifton were co-founders of the company with the company's president. Jean and Clifton both were founders of the Everglades Development Association company, a development company that sought to extend the Tamiami Trail into Miami and western Dade County.[4380] James F. Jaudon, originally of Texas, was a principal force in the founding and leadership of the Everglades Development Association, and many others participated as officers and members.[4381] The development company was successful to a point, and employed the immense Bay City Dredges, manufactured

[4377] Call, Criswell family records.
[4378] The Miami News. (October 7, 1924). P. 11. Newspapers.com.
[4379] The Miami News. (October 7, 1924). P. 11. Newspapers.com; Miami News. (December 11, 1923). P. 24. Newspapers.com.
[4380] Miami News. (August 5, 1924). P. 5. Newspapers.com; Miami News. (January 1, 1924). P. 26. Newspapers.com.
[4381] Miami News. (August 5, 1924). P. 5. Newspapers.com; Miami News. (January 1, 1924). P. 26. Newspapers.com.

at Bay City, Michigan, for the construction of the highway across the Everglades to Miami. Jean was the first Vice-President of the Everglades Development Association. Clifton also held executive office within the company. The Tamiami Trail remains one of the most important highways of south Florida, of Miami, and of Miami-Dade County.

Jean founded the Miami School of Applied Art and served as its Director.[4382] She also formed the New York-Miami Gallery for the promotion of a multi-city arts community in Miami. Jean became a member of the Miami Women's Club and remained active with the club. She was a founder of the Miami Women's Athletic Club and served on the board of directors of the Athletic Club, working with other Pittsburghers and Chicagoans in the club's leadership. Rev. Clifton Littlewood became Associate Pastor of the Congregational Church of Coconut Grove and Jean taught Sunday School there. Jean was a member of at least two political clubs in Florida, which were the Women's Better Government Club of Miami and the Howie For Governor Club. Jean was also a founding supporter of the Riverside Women's Club of Miami and donated much or all of the reference library of her late father, Judge Joseph Criswell, to the Riverside Women's Club, a club whose philanthropic purpose included the improvement of library resources for Miami and Dade County. Jean helped with the establishment of the Miami-Dade Public Library system, and the large reference work collection of Judge Joseph Criswell contributed to its earliest collection and body. Jean died in 1951 and was brought home to Pittsburgh for interment.[4383]

Kathryn Criswell and Thomas Charles Stephens of Pittsburgh

The Criswell and Burtner family members were founders of many Pittsburgh and Miami social and civic clubs and were members of no fewer than twenty clubs of Pittsburgh and the Pittsburgh metropolitan region, including the Duquesne Club, the Oakmont Country Club, and the Women's Club of Pittsburgh.[4384] The family also held memberships in clubs in Ohio and Miami. Kathryn (Criswell) Stephens, sister of Jean (Criswell) Littlewood, and niece of Susannah (Criswell) Burtner, was, like all her sisters, very active in Pittsburgh civic and club life. Kathryn's husband, Thomas Charles Stephens was the Treasurer of the Colonial Trust Company of Pittsburgh, which was at that time the fourth-largest bank in the United States. Thomas was a major builder of Colonial Trust Company, having been an officer of the company almost since its inception. Thomas also was a railroad founder and investor in western Pennsylvania. Joseph Thomas Stephens, son of Thomas Charles Stephens and Kathryn (Criswell) Stephens, and a

---

[4382] Miami News. (September 16, 1945). P. 28. Newspapers.com.
[4383] Criswell, Burtner, and Baldwin family history records.
[4384] Criswell, Burtner, and Baldwin family history records.

grandnephew of Susannah (Criswell) Burtner, was President of the both the American Institute of Banking and the Pittsburgh Chapter of the American Institute of Banking. Joseph also was an executive with the Mellon Bank of Pittsburgh.[4385] Henry Barrell House of Chicago, a member of the Bunn-Irwin-Stockdale family, was a prominent member of the Chicago Chapter of the American Institute of Banking (See Chapter 2, *Builders of the Downtown*).

<u>William Clifford Criswell of Pittsburgh</u>

William Clifford Criswell, son of Judge Joseph Criswell and Rebecca Richardson (Burkhart) Criswell, and brother of Jean (Criswell) Littlewood, Kathryn (Criswell) Stephens, Josephine (Criswell) Henninger, and James Burkhart Criswell, co-founded the Butler & Chicora Street Railway Company in 1907, which served a population of at least 25,000 in northern metropolitan Pittsburgh. Criswell served as Secretary and Treasurer of the company.[4386] Criswell was one of the owners of the Allegheny Valley Lumber & Manufacturing Company and was possibly also a co-founder of that company. Criswell was the nephew of Susannah (Criswell) Burtner.[4387]

<u>Philip Edgar Henninger and Josephine (Criswell) Henninger of Pittsburgh</u>

Josephine Criswell, daughter of Judge Joseph Criswell and Rebecca Richardson (Burkhart) Criswell, married Philip Edgar Henninger, a Pittsburgh and Butler County electrical engineer. Philip worked for Westinghouse Electric Company at Pittsburgh and engineered multiple projects of colossal scale throughout the United States. He co-engineered and supervised the construction of the Kingsbridge Power Station and generators of New York City and co-engineered the electrification of both the subway system and the elevated railway system of New York City.[4388] He also oversaw the electrification of the Sarnia-Port Huron Tunnel of Michigan and Ontario, Canada.[4389] He was President of the Westinghouse Veterans' Association of Pittsburgh.[4390] Josephine (Criswell) Henninger was a member of the Forum Club of Pittsburgh, and the Rockledge Garden Club of the suburbs.[4391] The Criswells and Burtners were also connected as co-founders, owners, and operators to many more companies and civic institutions of Pittsburgh, Allegheny County, and Butler County, Pennsylvania.

[4385] Criswell, Burtner, and Baldwin family history records.
[4386] Pittsburgh Daily Post. (October 16, 1907). P. 11. Newspapers.com.
[4387] Criswell, Burtner, and Baldwin family history records.
[4388] Pittsburgh Press. (June 22, 1958). P. 47. Newspapers.com.
[4389] Pittsburgh Press. (June 22, 1958). P. 47. Newspapers.com.
[4390] Pittsburgh Post-Gazette. (January 28, 1923). P. 13. Newspapers.com.
[4391] Criswell, Burtner, and Baldwin family history records.

Philip Criswell Henninger, who was the son of Philip Edgar Henninger and Josephine (Criswell) Henninger, was a University of Michigan alumnus and a Pittsburgh lawyer. Philip Criswell Henninger, F. B. Doane, and Alfred V. DeForest co-founded the Magnaflux Corporation of Chicago and Pittsburgh in 1934. This company developed, invented, patented, and manufactured testing machinery.[4392] The company was located on the northwest side of Chicago at 5916-5946 Northwest Highway, having purchased 50,000 square feet of factory space and adjacent real estate in 1940.[4393] J. F. Seifried was the architect for the property. Henry G. Zander & Company brokered the sale of land for the seller, and H. E. Schuett of Lang, Weise & Cella brokered the sale for Magnaflux.[4394] At this time Magnaflux was well-known for its scientific process for the search and discovery of physical defects in steel structures. The U.S. Army, U.S. Navy, commercial airlines, and aircraft manufacturers were all large customers of the Magnaflux Corporation, and used Magnaflux metal strength trial processes on aircraft engines and other aircraft components.[4395]

Andrew Jackson Haws:

Brickmaker for Pittsburgh, Johnstown, Chicago, and America

This portion of the chapter concerns the Burtner family of my paternal grandmother, Mary Elizabeth (Baldwin) Call. Andrew Jackson Haws (1825-1899) was a native of Allegheny County, Pennsylvania, and an industrialist of Johnstown, Cambria County, and Pittsburgh. He was the son of Isaac Haws and Barbara (Burtner) Haws of Allegheny County and was a first cousin of the Burtners of Pittsburgh, Allegheny County, and Butler County, who are discussed above.[4396] Andrew J. Haws worked for the Cambria Iron Company, where he helped manufacture the earliest iron rails ever produced west of the Allegheny Mountains.[4397] He experimented with forms of silicon and clay, and discovered that a mixture of clay with silica could create a form of brick that possessed high heat strength and durability. Haws is considered the inventor of the silica fire brick and the father of the industrial brick manufacturing industry.[4398] He established the A. J. Haws Company at Johnstown, Pennsylvania, and redefined industrial construction and construction technologies with the invention of the silica fire

---

[4392] The Pittsburgh Press. (May 31, 1934). P. 69. Newpapers.com.
[4393] Chicago Tribune. (August 4, 1940). P. 19. Newspapers.com.
[4394] Chicago Tribune. (August 4, 1940). P. 19. Newspapers.com.
[4395] Chicago Tribune. (August 4, 1940). P. 19. Newspapers.com.
[4396] Biographical And Portrait Cyclopedia of Cambria County, Pennsylvania. (1896). P. 70. Philadelphia, PA: The Union Publishing Company. Google Books.
[4397] Biographical And Portrait Cyclopedia of Cambria County, Pennsylvania. (1896). P. 71. Philadelphia, PA: The Union Publishing Company. Google Books.
[4398] Biographical And Portrait Cyclopedia of Cambria County, Pennsylvania. (1896). P. 71. Philadelphia, PA: The Union Publishing Company. Google Books.

brick.[4399] Haws contributed to Chicago and Cook County with powerful impact. In 1895, the A. J. Haws & Son Company occupied an office at Number 647, The Rookery Building, in the Loop community.[4400] L. S. Boomer was employed as the Chicago Manager and Agent of the A. J. Haws & Son Company at the same time.[4401]

The A. J. Haws & Son Company employed about 500 men, produced 22,000,000 bricks annually as of the late 1890s, and owned additional offices in Pittsburgh and Philadelphia.[4402] The company made many classes of brick, tuyers, brick converter bottoms, bottom cast elements, nozzles, stopper rod sleeves, and blast furnace linings, and operated a distribution network from Portland, Maine, to Pueblo, Colorado.[4403] Haws was a multimillionaire during the nineteenth century, and was president, director, and owner of many Johnstown and Pittsburgh companies.[4404] *The Inter Ocean* edition of November 12, 1891, reported that the A. J. Haws & Son Company did a very heavy business in Chicago and provided brickwork and furnace construction technologies to almost every iron company and every glass company in the United States.[4405] Andrew married Louise Brinker, and several children were born to them. One son, Henry Yeagley Haws, assumed leadership of the Haws companies when Andrew died in 1899, and was also a business partner of Thomas Coleman Du Pont.[4406]

A daughter, Sarah Haws, married Charles S. Price, who, after many years in the service of Cambria Steel Company, became the president and a reorganizing founder of the $78,000,000 Cambria Steel Company in about 1900.[4407] Andrew J. Haws founded the Cambria National Bank in 1897 and was its Vice-President until his death in 1899, at which time he was succeeded in that post by son Henry Y. Haws.[4408] The Haws companies owned subsidiary coal companies, clay companies, other brick companies, and at least one railroad company.[4409] The Great Lakes freighter *S.S. Charles S. Price*, owned by the Mahoning Steamship Company of Cleveland, was one of the largest of the Great Lakes freighters.[4410] The *Charles S. Price* sank in Lake Huron in the Great Storm of 1913, a hurricane-

---

[4399] Biographical And Portrait Cyclopedia of Cambria County, Pennsylvania. (1896). P. 71. Philadelphia, PA: The Union Publishing Company. Google Books.
[4400] Chicago Directory. (1895).
[4401] Chicago Directory. (1895).
[4402] The Times (Philadelphia, Pennsylvania). (June 4, 1899). P. 19. Newspapers.com.
[4403] The Times (Philadelphia, Pennsylvania). (June 4, 1899). P. 19. Newspapers.com.
[4404] Call, Baldwin, Burtner family history records.
[4405] The Inter Ocean. (November 12, 1891). P. 10. Newspapers.com.
[4406] Call, Baldwin, Burtner family history records.
[4407] Call, Baldwin, Burtner family history records.
[4408] The Times. (Philadelphia, Pennsylvania). (June 4, 1899). P. 20. Newspapers.com.
[4409] Call, Baldwin, Burtner family history records.
[4410] Charles S. Price Shipwreck. Waymarking.com.

like blizzard storm on Lake Huron.[4411] For a time, the tip of one end of the 504-foot-long steamship remained slightly above the surface of the water .[4412]

Brownell Car Company of St. Louis

This company was co-founded by Milo Barnum Richardson, who was the son of Leonard Richardson and Lucy (Barnum) Richardson of Lime Rock, Connecticut, and Chicago. Milo Barnum Richardson was a first cousin of William Douglas Richardson of Chicago, who was the founder and president of the Richardson Construction Company of Chicago. James Cox, who was Secretary of the Bureau of Information for the St. Louis Autumnal Festivities Association, edited and compiled an encyclopedic book concerning the significance of the State of Missouri as a participant at the 1893 Chicago World's Fair.[4413] Cox provided numerous facts of relevance to the contributions of St. Louis to Chicago's transportational development.[4414] Milo Barnum Richardson helped to develop St. Louis as one of the global centers of railcar manufacturing.[4415] Richardson was a founder of the Brownell Car Company of St. Louis.[4416] This company not only constituted a significant component of the railroad infrastructure economy of St. Louis, but also constituted a key factor in the development and supply of the Chicago urban railroad market.[4417] Missouri led the world in the manufacture of streetcars and Brownell Car Company was celebrated as the leader of the entire streetcar production industry.[4418]

Andrew Wight established in 1858 a streetcar manufacturing company at St. Louis.[4419] In 1875 Wight formed the Andrew Wight Company.[4420] Wight served as President of the 1875 company and F. B. Brownell served as Vice-President of the

---

[4411] Charles S. Price Shipwreck. Waymarking.com.

[4412] Charles S. Price Shipwreck. Waymarking.com.

[4413] Cox, James. Editor. Missouri at the World's Fair. (1893). P. 109. World's Fair Commission of Missouri. Woodward & Tiernan Printing Company. Google Books.

[4414] Cox, James. Editor. Missouri at the World's Fair. (1893). P. 109. World's Fair Commission of Missouri. Woodward & Tiernan Printing Company. Google Books.

[4415] Cox, James. Editor. Missouri at the World's Fair. (1893). P. 109. World's Fair Commission of Missouri. Woodward & Tiernan Printing Company. Google Books.

[4416] Cox, James. Editor. Missouri at the World's Fair. (1893). P. 109. World's Fair Commission of Missouri. Woodward & Tiernan Printing Company. Google Books.

[4417] Cox, James. Editor. Missouri at the World's Fair. (1893). P. 109. World's Fair Commission of Missouri. Woodward & Tiernan Printing Company. Google Books.

[4418] Cox, James. Editor. Missouri at the World's Fair. (1893). P. 109. World's Fair Commission of Missouri. Woodward & Tiernan Printing Company. Google Books.

[4419] Cox, James. Editor. Missouri at the World's Fair. (1893). P. 109. World's Fair Commission of Missouri. Woodward & Tiernan Printing Company. Google Books.

[4420] Cox, James. Editor. Missouri at the World's Fair. (1893). P. 109. World's Fair Commission of Missouri. Woodward & Tiernan Printing Company. Google Books.

firm.[4421] Company reorganizations occurred both in 1881 and in 1891.[4422] The 1891 restructuring produced the Brownell Car Company of St. Louis, with F. B. Brownell as President, and Milo Barnum Richardson of Connecticut and Chicago as Secretary and Treasurer.[4423] The Brownell Car Company achieved international status at least as early as 1893, having contracted with Canada and Mexico for the production and exportation of streetcars.[4424] Domestically, Brownell Car gained a tremendous market share at Chicago, Cincinnati, Detroit, Brooklyn, St. Louis, and Baltimore, and Cox reported that Brownell Car had manufactured streetcars for every major United States city as of 1893.[4425]

President F. B. Brownell invented the Accelerator Car, a form of streetcar which bore mechanical benefits and improvements regarding passenger embarkation and disembarkation.[4426] The Accelerator Car furthermore provided the benefits of improved safety, physically expanded vehicular boarding platforms for passengers, and increased boarding efficiencies.[4427] Charles Tyson Yerkes of Chicago acknowledged the engineering novelty that derived from the technical improvements of the Accelerator Car in the following words: "'[The Accelerator Car is] a decided improvement on the usual style, and it is a wonder to me that in the many years of business experience none of us have struck on the plan before.'"[4428] Yerkes also noted the improvements to performance efficiencies that F. B. Brownell had introduced: "'We can save eight minutes on a trip of one hour and twelve minutes by using the car made with your patent doors.'"[4429] Milo Richardson exerted a positive influence on the economies of Connecticut, Chicago, and St. Louis, in addition to New York City, Rochester, and other places. Through his leadership of the Barnum & Richardson Company, he turned Chicago into what was the world's foremost railroad parts production center. Through his leadership of Brownell Car Company, he and F. B. Brownell developed St. Louis into the

[4421] Cox, James. Editor. Missouri at the World's Fair. (1893). P. 109. World's Fair Commission of Missouri. Woodward & Tiernan Printing Company. Google Books.
[4422] Cox, James. Editor. Missouri at the World's Fair. (1893). P. 109. World's Fair Commission of Missouri. Woodward & Tiernan Printing Company. Google Books.
[4423] Cox, James. Editor. Missouri at the World's Fair. (1893). P. 109. World's Fair Commission of Missouri. Woodward & Tiernan Printing Company. Google Books.
[4424] Cox, James. Editor. Missouri at the World's Fair. (1893). P. 109. World's Fair Commission of Missouri. Woodward & Tiernan Printing Company. Google Books.
[4425] Cox, James. Editor. Missouri at the World's Fair. (1893). P. 109. World's Fair Commission of Missouri. Woodward & Tiernan Printing Company. Google Books.
[4426] Cox, James. Editor. Missouri at the World's Fair. (1893). P. 109. World's Fair Commission of Missouri. Woodward & Tiernan Printing Company. Google Books.
[4427] Cox, James. Editor. Missouri at the World's Fair. (1893). P. 109. World's Fair Commission of Missouri. Woodward & Tiernan Printing Company. Google Books.
[4428] Cox, James. Editor. Missouri at the World's Fair. (1893). P. 109. World's Fair Commission of Missouri. Woodward & Tiernan Printing Company. Google Books.
[4429] Cox, James. Editor. Missouri at the World's Fair. (1893). P. 109. World's Fair Commission of Missouri. Woodward & Tiernan Printing Company. Google Books.

world's foremost streetcar producer, and by extension of this fact, both men built much of the Chicago streetcar and urban railway industry.[4430]

Volume 10 of *The Street Railway Journal* expressed in 1894 the demand for Brownell Accelerator Cars in Chicago and stated that the North Chicago Street Railway Company and the Chicago Electric Transit Company both executed contracts with Brownell Car Company for the production of cars for their transit routes.[4431] The journalist commented that these orders collectively constituted the fifth order that Chicago had executed with Brownell Car Company of St. Louis for production of street railcars.[4432] These proofs additionally show the importance of St. Louis as a technological builder of Chicago and Cook County.[4433]

The Ensign Manufacturing Company of West Virginia

Milo Barnum Richardson was a son of Leonard Richardson and Lucy Ann (Barnum) Richardson of Lime Rock, Connecticut, and Chicago. Milo was the first cousin of William Douglas Richardson of Chicago, and a nephew of Henry Earle Richardson of Lime Rock. Milo served as a founder of the Ensign Manufacturing Company of Huntington, West Virginia, in May, 1872.[4434] The other Ensign Manufacturing Company founders were William Henry Barnum of Salisbury, Connecticut, Charles W. Barnum of Salisbury, Collis Potter Huntington of New York City, John Ketchum of Dover Plains, New York, Virgil F. McNeil of Cornwall Bridge, Connecticut, James H. Storrs of Brooklyn, Effingham B. Sutton of New York City, Delos W. Emmons of Huntington, West Virginia, William A. Wheeler of Malone, New York, Ely Ensign of Lime Rock, Connecticut, Sydney P. Ensign of Lime Rock, Nathaniel C. Ward of North Canaan, Connecticut, and Richard Franchote of Schenectady.[4435] The headquarters of the company was located at Huntington, and the purpose of the corporation was the production of railroad wheels, cars, railroad castings, and multiple additional forms of machinery.[4436] John M. Phelps, Secretary of State of West Virginia, signed the

---

[4430] Cox, James. Editor. Missouri at the World's Fair. (1893). P. 109. World's Fair Commission of Missouri. Woodward & Tiernan Printing Company. Google Books.

[4431] The Street Railway Journal. (June, 1894). Vol. 10. P. 405. New York, NY: Street Railway Publishing Company. Google Books.

[4432] The Street Railway Journal. (June, 1894). Vol. 10. P. 405. New York, NY: Street Railway Publishing Company. Google Books.

[4433] The Street Railway Journal. (June, 1894). Vol. 10. P. 405. New York, NY: Street Railway Publishing Company. Google Books.

[4434] Acts Of The Legislature Of West Virginia At Its Eleventh Session, 1872-3. (1873). Pp. 811-812. Charleston, WV: Henry S. Walker, Public Printer. Google Books.

[4435] Acts Of The Legislature Of West Virginia At Its Eleventh Session, 1872-3. (1873). Pp. 811-812. Charleston, WV: Henry S. Walker, Public Printer. Google Books.

[4436] Acts Of The Legislature Of West Virginia At Its Eleventh Session, 1872-3. (1873). Pp. 811-812. Charleston, WV: Henry S. Walker, Public Printer. Google Books.

articles of incorporation for Ensign Manufacturing Company.[4437] This company would have significantly supplied the Chicago and Cook County railroad markets.

The George Whitfield Bunn Branch

George Whitfield Bunn, Sr. (1820-1894), a brother of Jacob Bunn and John Whitfield Bunn of Illinois, relocated to California from New Jersey, unsuccessfully sought work at a quartz mill, settled first at Sonoma County, and settled finally at Tomales, in Marin County.[4438] He was associated with Cornelius Vanderbilt in some business activity whose specific facts have, unfortunately, been lost to the family record.[4439] Bunn co-founded the Bank of Tomales and a California warehouse company.[4440] The Bank of Tomales provided discounts, deposits and loans, and was incorporated on June 30, 1875 by Bunn, E. H. Kowalsky, Warren Dutton, Thomas J. Abels, and John Griffin.[4441] Bunn served as an owner and director of the bank, owned a large ranch in Marin County, and helped with multiple civic organizations there, including the public library and the public school system.[4442] George Bunn additionally entered the Texas land market in about 1882 and accumulated a large property company there.[4443] The Bunn land holdings included a 10,880-acre ranch in Crockett County, in the vicinity of the Pecos River.[4444] The Bunn Ranch operated in both cattle and horses, and possessed a large petroleum resource that was discovered in the twentieth century.[4445] Bunn purchased the ranchland from a railroad company. The identity of the grantor

---

[4437] Acts Of The Legislature Of West Virginia At Its Eleventh Session, 1872-3. (1873). Pp. 811-812. Charleston, WV: Henry S. Walker, Public Printer. Google Books.

[4438] Munro-Fraser, J. P..(1880). History of Marin County, California. P. 488. San Francisco, CA: Alley, Bowen & Co., Publishers. Google Books.

[4439] Bunn family history records; Multiple historical memoirs related by Wendy Overom Paymard to Andrew Taylor Call.

[4440] Munro-Fraser, J. P. (1880). History of Marin County, California. P. 488. San Francisco, CA: Alley, Bowen & Co., Publishers. Google Books; the warehouse company reference source has been lost.

[4441] Munro-Fraser, J. P. (1880). History of Marin County, California. Pp. 409-410. San Francisco, CA: Alley, Bowen & Co., Publishers. Google Books.

[4442] Munro-Fraser, J. P. (1880). History of Marin County, California. Pp. 409-410, 488. San Francisco, CA: Alley, Bowen & Co., Publishers. Google Books; Multiple historical memoirs related by Wendy Overom Paymard to Andrew Taylor Call.

[4443] Bunn family history records; Multiple historical memoirs related by Wendy Overom Paymard to Andrew Taylor Call.

[4444] Bunn family history records; Multiple historical memoirs related by Wendy Overom Paymard to Andrew Taylor Call.

[4445] Bunn family history records; Multiple historical memoirs related by Wendy Overom Paymard to Andrew Taylor Call.

railroad company has been lost to the family record.[4446] George married Mahala Ann Bloom.

George Whitfield Bunn, Jr., son of George Whitfield Bunn, Sr., and Mahala Ann (Bloom) Bunn, remained in Texas, and worked many years in Dallas.[4447] He married Alice Fishbough of New Jersey, and later of Ohio.[4448] George and Alice had two children: Chester Selden Bunn and Emily Mae Bunn.[4449] George W. Bunn worked as warehouse and storage manager for the Dallas Storage & Warehouse Company, and became President of the company in about 1911.[4450] Chester Selden Bunn served as Secretary of the Dallas Storage & Warehouse Company in 1911, when George Bunn served as the President of the company.[4451] G. A. Sprague served as Treasurer of the company at the same time.[4452] The Dallas Storage & Warehouse Company was a transfer agent and provided transfer, receiving, and forwarding services.[4453] The company was headquartered at 1007-1009 Camp Street in Dallas and operated two warehouses, one located at 1007-1009 Camp Street, and one located at the Powhatan & Santa Fe Railway Company.[4454] During the presidency of George W. Bunn, the company administered a nationwide portfolio of clients and transfer services, which included the following companies in 1912: Advance Concrete Mixer Company of Jackson, Michigan; American Steel & Wire Company of Chicago; Champion Potato Machinery Company of Hammond, Indiana; Christensen Engineering Company of Milwaukee; Fish Brothers Manufacturing Company of Clinton, Iowa; Ford Manufacturing Company of Rockford, Illinois; Gas Traction Company of Minneapolis; Geiser Manufacturing Company of Waynesboro, Pennsylvania; George D. Pohl of Vernon, New York; Haring Cotton Picker Company of Goliad, Texas; Hubble, Slack & Company of Houston; J. D. Adams & Company of Indianapolis; J. Peyton Hunter of Dallas; Kentucky Wagon Manufacturing Company of Louisville; Manson Campbell Company, Ltd., of Detroit; Naylor Manufacturing Company of Plano, Illinois; Peden Iron & Steel Company of Houston; South Bend Chilled Plow

---

[4446] Multiple historical memoirs related by Wendy Overom Paymard to Andrew Taylor Call.
[4447] United States Census records for 1910, 1920; Dallas, Texas, City Directory for multiple years. Ancestry.com and Fold3.com.
[4448] Multiple historical memoirs related by Wendy Overom Paymard to Andrew Taylor Call.
[4449] Multiple historical memoirs related by Wendy Overom Paymard to Andrew Taylor Call.
[4450] Dallas, Texas, City Directory. (1911). P. 358. Ancestry.com.
[4451] Dallas, Texas, City Directory. (1911). P. 358. Ancestry.com.
[4452] Dallas, Texas, City Directory. (1911). P. 358. Ancestry.com.
[4453] Dallas, Texas, City Directory. (1911). P. 359. Ancestry.com.
[4454] Dallas, Texas, City Directory. (1911). P. 359. Ancestry.com.

Company of South Bend, Indiana; Swenson Grubber Company of Cresco, Iowa; and the Wabash Manufacturing Company of Wabash, Indiana.[4455]

George and Alice (Fishbough) Bunn eventually moved to Duluth, Minnesota, where George served as Vice-President of the H. Miscampbell Body Corporation. This company was stated to have been the largest maker of truck cabs and truck bodies in the Northwest.[4456] The June 4, 1921, edition of *The Duluth Herald* included a detailed advertisement and picture of the H. Miscampbell Body Corporation, and listed H. Miscampbell as President, George W. Bunn as Vice-President, H. L. Palmer as Treasurer, E. T. Harris as Secretary, and W. E. Wessinger as General Manager.[4457] H. L. Palmer was Horace Lucius Palmer, husband of Emily Mae Bunn, and son-in-law of George Whitfield Bunn, Jr.[4458] H. Miscampbell was Hugh Miscampbell. The advertisement noted that the capital stock of the company was $350,000 and expressed an optimistic prediction about the coming motor vehicle technologies.[4459] The advertisement described the new technologies as follows: "Trucks are here to stay. Every truck needs a cab and some description of a body. Bus bodies are in great demand. Have you thought of the auto bus? It's the coming mode of transportation. We build real bus bodies."[4460] The Greyhound Bus Company, which had been founded in nearby Hibbing, Minnesota, probably contracted with H. Miscampbell Body Corporation for construction of motor buses. Chester S. Bunn worked as an accountant for the American Steel & Wire Company in Duluth and served as Assistant Chief Accountant for the Morgan Park factory of this company in Duluth.[4461] The American Steel & Wire Company at that time was a subsidiary of the United States Steel Corporation of Pittsburgh.[4462]

Chester Bunn married Ina Belle Johnson of Wisconsin, and later of Minnesota.[4463] They resided in Duluth for many years.[4464] Chester invested in

[4455] 1912 Implement Blue Book. (1912). P. 522. St. Louis, MO: Midland Publishing Company. Google Books.

[4456] The Duluth Herald. (June 1, 1921-June 30, 1921). Minnesota Historical Society. Archive.org.

[4457] The Duluth Herald. (June 4, 1921). P. 5. Archive.org.

[4458] Historical memoir related by Jamie (Overom) Pyzik.

[4459] The Duluth Herald. (June 4, 1921). P. 5. Archive.org.

[4460] The Duluth Herald. (June 4, 1921). P. 5. Archive.org.

[4461] Skillings' Mining Review. (1945). Vol. 34. Page number not discernible at time of reference. Google Books; Multiple historical memoirs related by Wendy Overom Paymard to Andrew Taylor Call.

[4462] Skillings' Mining Review. (1945). Vol. 34. Page number not discernible at time of reference. Google Books.

[4463] Multiple historical memoirs related by Wendy Overom Paymard to Andrew Taylor Call.

[4464] Multiple historical memoirs related by Wendy Overom Paymard to Andrew Taylor Call.

California silver mining property and held the claim to at least one silver mine in Kern County.[4465] Chester and Ina (Johnson) Bunn retired to California.[4466] Emily Bunn, daughter of George and Alice (Fishbough) Bunn, married Horace Lucius Palmer, and resided in Duluth, Minnesota.[4467] Horace and Emily (Bunn) Palmer had a daughter, Dorothy Palmer, who married Walter Jager of Chicago. In their later years, Horace and Emily moved to Illinois, and resided in Elmhurst with their daughter and son-in-law, Dorothy (Palmer) Jager and Walter Jager.[4468] Walter Jager started the Jager & Associates Company of Chicago, which was a company that brokered metal products contracts for multiple industries.[4469] He later acquired the Pattee Pattern Works Company of Chicago, which made metal products, brokered metalwork contracts, and was located in the Near West Side community.[4470] The Pattee Pattern Works Company was located at 2332 W. Walnut Street.[4471]

[4465] Bunn family history records; Bakersfield, Kern County, California land records.

[4466] Multiple historical memoirs related by Wendy Overom Paymard to Andrew Taylor Call.

[4467] Multiple historical memoirs related by Wendy Overom Paymard to Andrew Taylor Call.

[4468] Multiple historical memoirs related by Wendy Overom Paymard to Andrew Taylor Call.

[4469] Multiple historical memoirs related by Wendy Overom Paymard to Andrew Taylor Call.

[4470] Multiple historical memoirs related by Wendy Overom Paymard to Andrew Taylor Call.

[4471] Multiple historical memoirs related by Wendy Overom Paymard to Andrew Taylor Call. Many thanks also to Jamie (Overom) Pyzik, sister of Wendy (Overom) Paymard, for historical input in this section of the book.

Chapter 7

Chicago Irish and Old Brickwork

"God bless the corners of this house
And be the lintel blessed.
Bless the hearth, the table too
And bless each place of rest.
Bless each door that opens wide
To stranger, kith and kin;
Bless each shining window-pane
That lets the sunshine in.
Bless the roof-tree up above
Bless every solid wall.
The peace of Man, the peace of love,
The peace of God on all."

—Traditional Irish Christian Prayer and Blessing[4472]

<u>Introduction</u>

The present chapter concerns the Chicago and Cook County history of the Regan, McKay, Powers, Hogan, Trudelle, Sugars, and Driscoll branches of my mother's family. These families were Irish-American, and immigrated to the United States during the middle nineteenth century.[4473] The various ancestors journeyed to Wisconsin and resided in Milwaukee, Chippewa Falls, Wisconsin Rapids, Superior, Cadott, and Hurley, among other places.[4474] The children of Charles Timothy Regan and Margaret (Hanrahan) Regan were Ruth Regan, Mary Regan, Charles Regan, Robert Giles Regan, John Hanrahan Regan, Jean Regan, and Frank Regan.[4475] All of these children either lived in, or were connected to, Chicago and Cook County in some manner.[4476]

The histories in this chapter are Irish-American histories, and they contain the times, places, and experiences of Irish people in Wisconsin and Chicago during the nineteenth and twentieth centuries. These are histories of devout Christian faith, loyalty to the Roman Catholic Church, loyalty to community, civic development and improvement, and societal welfare. The people discussed in this chapter represent a broad and diverse class of work and experience in America. This range of experience includes development of large Chicago construction and housing development companies, the building of some of the largest and most important architectural structures of Chicago and Joliet, and multiple services in

---

[4472] Traditional Irish Christian Prayer. appleseeds.org.
[4473] Regan family history records.
[4474] Regan family history records.
[4475] Regan family history records.
[4476] See sources and references herein.

public office around the United States. The works discussed here also include the establishment of the International Bar Association, the creation of the New York Museum of Costume Art, contributions to the legal profession, and development of the cities and petroleum industries of the Permian Oil Basin of Texas and the Kevin-Sunburst Oil Field of Montana.

The genealogy of our Irish-American families is provided below with separate sections for the different branches. These families contributed significantly to the industrial development of Chicago, Cook County, and Will County, as well as to the communities and industrial economies of multiple places in Wisconsin, California, New York City, Texas, Montana, and Colorado. Multiple members of the family participated in the search, discovery, development, and technological standardization of the petroleum, gold mining, lumber manufacturing, and coal mining industries of the Trans-Mississippi West. Summaries of these histories will follow below. This chapter discusses the importance of the contributions of Wisconsin people to the development of Chicago and the metropolitan region.

The O'Keefe, Hogan, Hanrahan, and Regan Families of Wisconsin and Chicago

Patrick Hogan married Johannah O'Keefe (sometimes O'Keeffe) in Ireland. Multiple family branches and descendants of Patrick and Johanna resided in Chicago and the metropolitan region over multiple generations. The following children were born to Patrick and Johanna (O'Keefe) Hogan: Hannah Hogan, who married John Long; Michael Hogan, who married Mary Jane Gallagher; **John Hogan, who married Bridget Ahern**; **Mary Rose Hogan, who married Michael Hanrahan**; **Johannah Hogan, who married Michael Powers**; and Margaret Hogan, who married James B. Sullivan.[4477] We will now proceed to the Chicago histories of each branch of the O'Keefe, Hogan, Hanrahan, and Regan families.

The Michael Hogan and Mary (Gallagher) Hogan Branch

of Wisconsin and Chicago

Michael Hogan (1828/1829-1908) was the son of Patrick Hogan and Johannah (O'Keefe) Hogan of Clonmel, Ireland, and later of Wisconsin. Michael married Mary Jane Gallagher (1833-1901), who was from Grenville, Quebec, Canada.[4478] Michael was one of the founders of the Notre Dame Church of Chippewa Falls. He served as City Assessor of Chippewa Falls for eleven years and was an Alderman on the Chippewa Falls City Council.[4479] After working on the Hudson

---

[4477] Hogan family historical records. Kathleenmanuel.com.

[4478] Daily Independent. (January 24, 1908). Page not given. Findagrave.com and Kathleenmanuel.com.

[4479] Daily Independent. (Chippewa Falls, Wisconsin). (January 24, 1908). Page not given. Kathleenmanuel.com; Daily Independent. (Chippewa Falls, Wisconsin). (January 26, 1908). Page not given. Kathleenmanuel.com.

River Railroad stone wall construction and on the construction of the State Capitol of Ohio in Columbus, he settled at Chippewa Falls.[4480] Hogan worked at the Marrineau Sawmill with Charles Marrineau. When Marrineau became sick, Hogan was forced to conduct the operations of the sawmill alone. The challenge presented an opportunity, and, as a result of the problem presented, Hogan, "invented and planned the first semi-automatic sawmill successfully operated."[4481] Hogan helped establish the City Waterworks of Chippewa Falls and insisted that water be provided for free to the local parochial schools. Hogan believed that the schools deserved free water service in exchange for the educational service they provided to the community.[4482] Michael Hogan, Mary Jane (Gallagher) Hogan, and Reverend Sister Rose founded St. Joseph's Hospital of Chippewa Falls.[4483] Michael negotiated the necessary real estate contracts for the hospital and its location.[4484] Michael never charged churches, schools, or hospitals for his construction and real estate services and believed that such organizations merited gratuitous infrastructural services.[4485] He served as Treasurer of the Irish League, which was an Irish-American social, civic, and support club.[4486] Michael and Mary Jane had two sons: Patrick Gallagher Hogan (1861-1862), and **John Joseph Hogan** (1876-1934), who moved to Chicago.

John Joseph Hogan (1876-1934) was the son of Michael Hogan and Mary Jane (Gallagher) Hogan of Chippewa Falls.[4487] He was an electrician and inventor with Western Electric Company in the West Side Chicago, near Cicero. He received a degree in Electrical Engineering from the University of Wisconsin-Madison and was a consulting engineer on many large construction and engineering projects.[4488] John also worked as a designing engineer for Western Electric Company in Chicago.[4489] He was said to have been a genius, but perhaps a bit crazy, too. Characterization of John Joseph Hogan is found in the following family memoir:

[4480] Daily Independent. (January 24, 1908). Page not given. Findagrave.com and Kathleenmanuel.com.

[4481] Daily Independent. (January 24, 1908). Page not given. Findagrave.com and Kathleenmanuel.com.

[4482] Daily Independent. (January 24, 1908). Page not given. Findagrave.com and Kathleenmanuel.com.

[4483] Daily Independent. (January 24, 1908). Page not given. Findagrave.com and Kathleenmanuel.com.

[4484] Daily Independent. (January 24, 1908). Page not given. Findagrave.com and Kathleenmanuel.com.

[4485] Daily Independent. (January 24, 1908). Page not given. Findagrave.com and Kathleenmanuel.com.

[4486] Daily Independent. (January 24, 1908). Page not given. Findagrave.com and Kathleenmanuel.com.

[4487] Hogan family history records. Kathleenmanuel.com.

[4488] Eau Claire Leader. (February 4, 1934). P. 11. Newspapers.com.

[4489] Eau Claire Leader. (April 12, 1912). P. 5. Newspapers.com.

"Michael's surviving son, John Joseph, was born in 1876 and later married his wife Elizabeth E. and became an engineer. By the age of 43 and 44, John and Elizabeth had no children. Family tradition says that John Joseph was an inventor who worked for Western Electric on the border between Chicago and Cicero, Illinois, That plant has since been torn down. A descendent [Ruth Regan, who married Willard Bunn] from the Hanrahan branch who studied music in Chicago in 1904 and stayed with John Joseph's family there described him as 'brilliant but nuts' and found him over-protective."[4490]

John Joseph married Elizabeth (b. 1878). Unfortunately, very little additional information has been rediscovered about John Joseph Hogan at the time of the writing of this book.

The John Hogan and Bridget Ahern Branch of Wisconsin and Chicago

John Hogan (circa 1828-1904), son of Patrick Hogan and Johannah (O'Keefe) Hogan, married Bridget Ahern (circa 1828-1919). They had the following children: Mary Theresa Hogan, who married James Patrick Sheehy; **Johanna Hogan (1856-1883), who married Thomas Sugars**; Patrick Robert Hogan, who married Etta Nauman; Michael Emmet Hogan, who married Catherine Burke; John Carol Hogan, who married Lily Miles; **William David Hogan, who married Luella Alice Deborde**; Amelia Bridget Hogan, who married David Jackson Manning; James Hogan; and **Thomas Stephen Hogan (1869-1957), who married Kathryn Agnes Donovan**.[4491]

Thomas Sugars married Johanna Hogan. Thomas worked for the Wisconsin Central Railway Company of Chicago up until 1893, when he relocated to Chippewa Falls and became active in Chippewa County Republican politics and town leadership.[4492] Dr. Roy T. Sugars, son of Thomas and another wife, Elizabeth (Daly) Sugars, moved to Chicago and was active in the Rogers Park community. Dr. Roy T. Sugars was a medical doctor who practiced medicine at 809 Madison in the District 40 section of Chicago.[4493] Dr. Roy Sugars was Commander and member of the Rogers Park American Legion post.[4494] Sugars and multiple other Rogers Park American Legion officers officiated at the induction of new members in February, 1944, at 6424 N. Western Avenue, at which fifty new members were

---

[4490] Hogan family history records. Kathleenmanuel.com.
[4491] Hogan family historical records. Kathleenmanuel.com.
[4492] Chippewa Herald Telegram (Chippewa Falls, Wisconsin). (November 25, 1929). Kathleenmanuel.com.
[4493] Suburbanite Economist. (January 6, 1965). P. 39. Newspapers.com.
[4494] Chicago Tribune. (February 20, 1944). P. 43. Newspapers.com.

inducted into membership.[4495] The place of the induction ceremony was the 50th Ward Democratic Hall. The leadership structure of the Rogers Park post included the following persons and jobs: Harvey Holm was Chairman and Chaplain; Conrad A. Suerth, Henry C. Hitzeman, Les Leibson, Joseph A. McCarthy, and Emil L. Petry were all Past Commanders; Dr. Roy T. Sugars was present Commander; Carl W. Stuke was Senior Vice Commander; R. O. Schneider was Adjutant; Lionel Brenner was Sergeant at Arms; Hugh Shannon, John C. Miller, Dewey Phillips, and Ben Beeler were all Comrades.[4496] Other distinguished guests present at the induction ceremony included Walter Swanwick, Al Roth, and Edward Roberts, all of whom had held leadership offices within the American Legion.[4497]

Dr. Roy Sugars served in 1952 as Medical Officer of the Rogers Park American Legion, when Albert B. Mullenix served as Commander and when Joseph K. Kissane and Walter C. Bauman were the Vice Commanders.[4498] Dr. Roy Sugars also served as Child Welfare Chairman for the Seventh District of Chicago.[4499] Roy and his wife resided at 7424 N. Winchester Avenue in the Rogers Park community of Chicago.[4500] Roy and his wife were active members of the Chicago Medical Society, and Mrs. Sugars was an officer of the Chicago Medical Society.[4501] Maude Sugars, the sister of Roy T. Sugars, married Frank Hopper, and was a resident of Joliet, Illinois, for around thirty years.[4502]

Thomas Stephen Hogan (1869-1957), son of John Hogan and Bridget (Ahern) Hogan, was a lawyer, civic activist, industrialist, entrepreneur, and developer of oil, coal, and metal mining properties in Texas, Mexico, Colorado, Montana, and other places. Hogan founded the National Farm Loan Bank, a St. Louis-based federal banking system designed to help United States farmers and agriculture during the Great Depression. He also founded the Hogan Oil Company of Texas, was a principal developer of the Permian Oil Basin of Texas and the City of Midland, Texas, and built a continental network of petroleum and coal resources. Much of Hogan's biography is captured autobiographically in his Letter to the Young Democrats, as follows:

> "With deep regret I must admit that my invitation to speak to you is predicated on the fact that I am no longer young. That is their idea, not

[4495] Chicago Tribune. (February 20, 1944). P. 43. Newspapers.com.

[4496] Chicago Tribune. (February 20, 1944). P. 43. Newspapers.com.

[4497] Chicago Tribune. (February 20, 1944). P. 43. Newspapers.com.

[4498] Chicago Tribune. (August 21, 1952). P. 34. Newspapers.com.

[4499] Chicago Tribune. (December 22, 1940). P. 35. Newspapers.com.

[4500] The Bulletin of the Chicago Medical Society. (1959). Vol. 62. Page number not visible at time of reference. Chicago, IL. Google Books.

[4501] The Bulletin of the Chicago Medical Society. (1959). Vol. 62. Page number not visible at time of reference. Chicago, IL. Google Books.

[4502] The Daily Telegram (Eau Claire, Wisconsin). (December 13, 1969). P. 12. Newspapers.com.

mine, as I refuse to accept the computation of passing years as the true measure of the youthfulness and virility of the mind.

The Law of Evidence requires counsel to qualify the witness before he is permitted to give testimony, so I must waste a few of the brief moments at my disposal with a skeleton sketch of my experience. My experience in the public service bagan [sic] in 1896 as Secretary of State of Montana; later served as a member of the Senate for four years; served in the initial organization of the Federal Farm Loan Bank System; was Assistant Solicitor in the Department of the Interior; and from 1933 to 1935 was Chairman of the National Coal Labor Board.

As a private citizen, I taught school when 16 and 17 years old; left the farm shortly thereafter and worked on railroad construction on the pacific Coast and in Montana; worked 3 1/2 years in the copper smelters of Anaconda on a strictly 12-hour day and seven-day week basis; practiced law for 16 years; at various times in the last 44 years operated mines in Montana, Idaho, and Old Mexico; been active in the oil business for more than 55 years including well-drilling or other explorations in Montana, Wyoming, Colorado, New Mexico, Texas, Illinois, Indiana, Oklahoma and Old Mexico and during this made a rather extensive study of the oil reserves of the world; owned and operated a fairly large farm and cattle ranch in Montana. When 22 years old I was elected head of what was then the largest labor organization in Montana and many years later was president of the Beet Growers Association of the United States. Many other activities need not be mentioned here. I respectfully submit to this Court of Public Opinion that the evidence submitted should qualify me as one who knows America and its people and on their behalf I wish to speak.

Old timers may thrill you with stories of the 'good old days' and sometimes the younger generation is induced to turn back to a wholly mythical past. We are prone to look back and attribute to the then existing laws and customs the joys of existence that were really due to our abounding youth and limitless optimism which painted the distant horizons of the future with all the glorious colors of a western sunrise. Except to the fortunate few, they were not always the 'good old days' but the 'bad old days'.

Poverty, degradation and illiteracy was the permanent status of a considerable percentage of the people. Every step upward in the social and economic status of a great majority of the people has been won through the efforts of the limited few who devoted their time and efforts to the progressive cause. Through all these years these men and women have been victims of the bitter and disparaging attacks of practically all those in high places in industry, finance, banking, and generally even in the government itself.

Just forty years ago we succeeded in enacting into the laws of Montana the eight-hour day for miners and smeltermen. It took years of work, effort and sacrifice on the part of the progressive few to put that law on the statute books and we were denounced as dangerous radicals seeking to destroy the prosperity of the whole nation. Even after all these years I can still name over a hundred of Dewey's principal supporters and scores of the leading newspapers who charged that this nefarious eight-hour day law would wreck the whole business structure of the United States. And these people and these newspapers still presume to speak with authority on politics and government.

We had no collective bargaining in those days and thousands of workers were summarily fired for even being suspected of favoring the eight-hour day. These men and newspapers could prove -- to their own satisfaction -- that anything less than a twelve-hour day and seven-day week in the smelters meant national ruin. Among them and typical of these opponents of progress was a certain great engineer -- in fact, 'The Great Engineer' -- who never recommended a mining or other property to his employers and investors unless he could finish his report with the stereotyped commendation, 'This property is located in an area where there is a great abundance of cheap, docile and unorganized labor.' In their philosophy, that is the acme of all perfect conditions.

Let me hasten to say that such an attitude no longer reflects the opinion of intelligent industrial employers. Gradually and definitely they have learned that their prosperity is dependent on the purchasing power of well-paid labor working reasonable hours which permits them to purchase and enjoy the production of our great industrial machine. In simple justice it should not be forgotten that years ago the biggest of them all established a minimum $5 per day pay and eight-hour day at a time when the head of the United States Steel Company was vehemently defending a $2.50 pay and a 12-hour day as the only hope for a prosperous America. In a nation disposed to idolatry of wealth and power, it took the great prestige of this liberal employer to convince the American people of the soundness of the philosophy of good wages and a short work day. We can well afford to forgive him for his subsequent aberrations in matters of national and international affairs.

But wages and hours are by themselves only part of the picture and cannot alone supply the fundamental basis of prosperity and human well-being. My time limit forbids even passing reference to the great battles of the past for social, economic and legislative progress in establishing and protecting the rights of the submerged masses. From personal experience I can tell you that the battles have been long and bitter and that when we finally won any appreciable progress our enemies were the first to claim it

646

as their accomplishment. Of this we have a glaring example in this political campaign.

It is the grave responsibility of the youth of today to meet simultaneously two tremendous problems; one is to readjust our great industrial machine and agricultural system in a manner that will make abundance a blessing rather than a curse to all the people; the other is to establish sound and friendly relations with the rest of the world in a manner that will make future wars not only improbable but also impossible. These jobs can be done and you are the people who must do them. In this election you will perform the first and foremost task by the election of Roosevelt and a Congress favorable to his policies.

As one who has witnessed as an observing and interested spectator the passing parade of our way of life and government, I can certify that the present national Administration, with all of its minor faults, has crystallized into law and established accomplishments more of the progressive programs and aspirations of the common people than all of its predecessors. What matter if occasionally it gets credit for the work and sacrifices of previous and unknown workers in the vineyard?

Surely you will not turn your back on progress and support the ossified and reactionary forces of the opposition."[4503]

Thomas Stephen Hogan and the American Coal Industry

Thomas Stephen Hogan was Chairman of the Denver Coal District Board of Colorado and was a Christian counselor to United States business, industry, law, and public policy.[4504] He helped establish the coal industry of Colorado. Hogan worked with President Franklin Delano Roosevelt in the founding of the National Coal Labor Board in 1933. Hogan then served as the founding Chairman of the National Coal Labor Board from 1933 to 1935.[4505] In this capacity Hogan served in one of the most powerful and important positions relevant to the public administration of the United States coal industry and its labor issues and organizations.[4506] Hogan helped Roosevelt administer the National Industrial Recovery Act (NIRA) regime of 1933 by serving as Chairman of the National Coal

---

[4503] Hogan, Thomas Stephen. (Circa 1940). Letter to the Young Democrats of the United States. Kathleenmanuel.com.

[4504] Hogan, Regan, Hanrahan family history records.

[4505] Hogan, Thomas Stephen. (Circa 1940). Letter to the Young Democrats of the United States. Kathleenmanuel.com.

[4506] Hogan, Thomas Stephen. (Circa 1940). Letter to the Young Democrats of the United States. Kathleenmanuel.com; Pittsburgh-Post gazette. (October 3, 1933). P. 2. Newspapers.com.

Labor Board, which operated within the original National Labor Board of 1933.[4507] The National Coal Labor Board possessed the powers of negotiation, bargain, and contract with coal labor organizations, possessed the powers of hearing, deliberation, and judgment with respect to coal labor cases, and worked extensively with the United Mine Workers of America (UMWA).[4508] The National Coal Labor Board consisted of executive members who were appointed by the President of the United States.[4509] The National Coal Labor Board affected the policies and laws of the United States coal industry on a national level. Thomas Hogan was also an extensive coal mine developer and owner.

Thomas Hogan, William Hogan, Patrick Hogan, John Hogan, Charles Regan,

and the Rocky Mountain Oil and Metal Industries

Thomas Stephen Hogan co-founded, with his brother Patrick Robert Hogan, the Hogan Oil Company of the Kevin-Sunburst Oil Field of Montana in 1922.[4510] William David Hogan, another brother of Thomas Stephen Hogan and Patrick Robert Hogan, was a gold mine industrialist of the Rocky Mountains. William D. Hogan founded the Butte and Oro Grande Gold Mining Company, the Hogan Mining Company, the Crooked River Mining and Milling Company, and the Cleopatra Mining Company, all within the Rocky Mountains. Charles Timothy Regan of Chippewa Falls, Wisconsin (see below), who married Margaret Hanrahan, who was a first cousin of brothers William David Hogan, Thomas Stephen Hogan, Patrick Robert Hogan, and John Carroll Hogan, worked with the Hogans as an executive and founder in the mining and railroad companies.

Patrick R. Hogan, brother of Thomas Stephen Hogan and William David Hogan, established the Hogan Lumber Company of Aberdeen, Washington, which was one of the largest lumber companies of the Pacific Northwest.[4511] Patrick R. Hogan also co-founded the $2,500,000 Hogan Oil Company of the Kevin-Sunburst Oil

[4507] Hogan, Thomas Stephen. (Circa 1940). Letter to the Young Democrats of the United States. Kathleenmanuel.com; Pittsburgh-Post gazette. (October 3, 1933). P. 2. Newspapers.com.

[4508] Hogan, Thomas Stephen. (Circa 1940). Letter to the Young Democrats of the United States. Kathleenmanuel.com; Pittsburgh-Post gazette. (October 3, 1933). P. 2. Newspapers.com.

[4509] Hogan, Thomas Stephen. (Circa 1940). Letter to the Young Democrats of the United States. Kathleenmanuel.com; Pittsburgh-Post gazette. (October 3, 1933). P. 2. Newspapers.com.

[4510] Great Falls Tribune. (Great Falls, Montana). (December 19, 1922). P. 1. Newspapers.com.

[4511] Great Falls Tribune. (Great Falls, Montana). (December 19, 1922). P. 1. Newspapers.com.

Field of Montana in 1922.[4512] Patrick Hogan co-founded the company with Thomas Stephen Hogan and R. M. Hart of the Albin-Hart Stores Company of Great Falls, Montana.[4513] By the 1920s, Patrick was a millionaire lumber manufacturer and Thomas was a multimillionaire petroleum producer.[4514] William David Hogan, Thomas Stephen Hogan, Patrick R. Hogan, John C. Hogan, and Charles Timothy Regan founded, owned, and developed many multimillion-dollar oil, mining, and railroad companies in the Rocky Mountains prior to 1930.

John Carroll Hogan, a lawyer and University of Wisconsin-Madison alumnus, was one of the foremost lumber industry lawyers of Washington State and helped establish the first logging and lumber companies of the Gray's Harbor region of Washington.[4515] John C. Hogan also served in the Washington State Legislature.[4516] John C. Hogan held the long-distance running championship at the University of Wisconsin when he was a student there.[4517] He helped to shape the lumber industry of the Pacific Northwest.

William David Hogan established the Oro Grande Gold Mining Company of Elk City, Idaho.[4518] The headquarters was in Spokane, Washington, at 210 Columbia Building. The incorporators were William Hogan, J. N. Pickrell, J. E. Pickrell, and H. W. Hewitt.[4519] The company was capitalized at $1,500,000 and owned a 560-hoursepower hydroelectric power plant and compressor, as well as a 300-ton cyanide plant. Fifty men were employed.[4520] As with every subject in this book, much more could be written here about the Hogan brothers but for the limits of space.

[4512] Great Falls Tribune. (Great Falls, Montana). (December 19, 1922). P. 1. Newspapers.com.

[4513] Great Falls Tribune. (Great Falls, Montana). (December 19, 1922). P. 1. Newspapers.com.

[4514] Great Falls Tribune. (Great Falls, Montana). (December 19, 1922). P. 1. Newspapers.com; Hogan, Regan, Hanrahan family historical records.

[4515] Aberdeen Daily World (Aberdeen, Washington). (November 24, 1947). Page number not given. Kathleenmanuel.com.

[4516] Aberdeen Daily World (Aberdeen, Washington). (November 24, 1947). Page number not given. Kathleenmanuel.com.

[4517] Aberdeen Daily World (Aberdeen, Washington). (November 24, 1947). Page number not given. Kathleenmanuel.com.

[4518] American Mining Manual. (1920). Vol. 28. P. 187. Chicago, IL: The Mining Manual Company. Google Books.

[4519] American Mining Manual. (1920). Vol. 28. P. 187. Chicago, IL: The Mining Manual Company. Google Books.

[4520] American Mining Manual. (1920). Vol. 28. P. 187. Chicago, IL: The Mining Manual Company. Google Books.

<u>The Michael Powers and Johannah Hogan Branch of Wisconsin and Chicago</u>

Michael Powers (1842-1905) married Johannah Hogan (1842-1891). The following children were born to them: **Margaret Powers, who married John R. Trudelle**; Mary Powers, who married James Lavelle; Katherine Powers; Esther Powers, who married Dennis Quinlan; Anna Powers, who married Thomas Morris; John P. Powers, who married Maud Lynch; Joseph Powers, who married Elizabeth; and Agnes Powers.[4521] Catherine Trudelle (1902-1970), daughter of Margaret (Powers) Trudelle and John R. Trudelle, resided at 2842 N. Sheridan Road, which is located in the Lake View community and near to Lincoln Park and Diversey Harbor.[4522] Catherine attended the Notre Dame-McDonell School of Chippewa Falls and the Mercy School of Nursing at Loyola University in Chicago.[4523] She worked as a nurse at Columbus Hospital of Chicago.[4524] Joseph Benedict Trudelle (1899-1971), son of John R. Trudelle and Margaret (Powers) Trudelle, was a Chicago resident along with his wife, Mildred (Fosdick) Trudelle.[4525] Joseph and Mildred (Fosdick) Trudelle also resided at 4925 W. Columbus Drive in Oak Lawn. Joseph was a businessman with the Chicago North Division General Service Department at 3500 N. California Avenue for many years.[4526] John Trudelle (1905-1990), son of John R. Trudelle and Margaret (Powers) Trudelle, was also Chicago resident. Other Hogan-Powers-Trudelle cousins resided in and around Chicago, as well.

<u>The Michael Hanrahan and Mary Rose Hogan Branch of Wisconsin and Chicago</u>

Michael Hanrahan (1823-1898) married Mary Rose Hogan (1825-1883), who was the daughter of Patrick Hogan and Johannah (O'Keefe) Hogan. Michael was the son of John Hanrahan and Mary (possibly Callahan) Hanrahan, both natives of Ireland. The following children were born to them: Joanna Hanrahan, who married Edward Patten; **Margaret Hanrahan, who married Charles Timothy Regan**; and John Hanrahan.[4527] Charles Timothy Regan and Margaret (Hanrahan) Regan had the following children: Charles E. Regan; John Hanrahan Regan, who married Inez (surname unknown); Mary Regan; Jean Regan, who married Paul W. McKay; Ruth Regan, who married Willard Bunn; Frank Regan, who married Alma

[4521] Hogan family historical records. Kathleenmanuel.com.
[4522] Leader-Telegram (Eau Claire, Wisconsin). November 17, 1970. P. 21. Newspapers.com.
[4523] Leader-Telegram (Eau Claire, Wisconsin). November 17, 1970. P. 21. Newspapers.com.
[4524] Leader-Telegram (Eau Claire, Wisconsin). November 17, 1970. P. 21. Newspapers.com.
[4525] Chicago Tribune. (September 21, 1971). P. 23. Kathleenmanuel.com.
[4526] Leader-Telegram (Eau Claire, Wisconsin). November 17, 1970. P. 21. Newspapers.com; Chicago Tribune. (January 24, 1965). Page not clear. Newspapers.com.
[4527] Hogan family historical records. Kathleenmanuel.com.

(surname not known); and Robert Giles Regan, who married Frances Lockwood.[4528] Many members of this branch of the Hogan-Regan family settled in Chicago, Cook County, and Will County. We proceed to discuss this branch of the family now.

The Regans / Ragans of Wisconsin and Chicago

Timothy Regan (circa 1832-1882)[4529] of Ireland married Margaret Dacey (1827-1898), who was a native of Cork.[4530] They married in Ireland, emigrated to New York City, settled for a time in New York State, and came to Iowa afterward. They then moved to Wisconsin, where they would remain permanently.[4531] These were the immigrant ancestors of the family in the United States.[4532] The family resided in County Cork, Ireland, and emigrated to the United States in 1849.[4533] The six-week journey across the Atlantic was one rife with disease, and Timothy and Margaret Regan were said to have hidden their son, Patrick Regan, then an infant and one of only two children yet born to Margaret and Timothy, in a trunk aboard the ship.[4534] It was customary practice at the time for diseased infants to be thrown overboard into the ocean and to their deaths.[4535] Fearing that this would be the fate of their infant son Patrick, Margaret and Timothy kept Patrick hidden throughout the entire journey to New York City.[4536] The Regans were counted among the immigrant population associated with the Irish Potato Famine. Timothy and Margaret (Dacey) Regan arrived first at New York City, and then proceeded to Syracuse, New York.[4537] From Syracuse, the family relocated to Farley, Iowa.[4538] After remaining in Iowa for a time, the Regans relocated to the region near Lake

---

[4528] Hogan family historical records. Kathleenmanuel.com.

[4529] The Chippewa Herald. (March 24, 1882). P. 1. Newspapers.com

[4530] The Daily Tribune of Wisconsin Rapids, Wisconsin (March 4, 1922). P. 5. Newspapers.com; Montreal River Miner and Iron County Republican. (March 10, 1898). P. 1. Newspapers.com.

[4531] Montreal River Miner and Iron County Republican. (March 10, 1898). P. 1. Newspapers.com.

[4532] The Daily Tribune of Wisconsin Rapids, Wisconsin (March 4, 1922). P. 5. Newspapers.com.

[4533] The Daily Tribune of Wisconsin Rapids, Wisconsin (March 4, 1922). P. 5. Newspapers.com.

[4534] The Daily Tribune of Wisconsin Rapids, Wisconsin (March 4, 1922). P. 5. Newspapers.com.

[4535] The Daily Tribune of Wisconsin Rapids, Wisconsin (March 4, 1922). P. 5. Newspapers.com.

[4536] The Daily Tribune of Wisconsin Rapids, Wisconsin (March 4, 1922). P. 5. Newspapers.com.

[4537] The Daily Tribune of Wisconsin Rapids, Wisconsin (March 4, 1922). P. 5. Newspapers.com.

[4538] The Daily Tribune of Wisconsin Rapids, Wisconsin (March 4, 1922). P. 5. Newspapers.com.

Chetek, which is located in far northwestern Wisconsin.[4539] The northward migration to Wisconsin from Iowa comprised multiple different relocations for the different members of the Regan family, according to available historical reference sources.[4540] Timothy Regan, the patriarch of the family in America, entered a homestead claim at Moose Ear Creek, Wisconsin.[4541] This place is located in what would subsequently become Barron County. The journey from Iowa to Lake Chetek took nine days by lumber wagon.[4542]

Timothy Regan and his son, John Richard Regan (1862-1934), also resided at the Wisconsin home of Timothy and Margaret Regan's daughter, Mrs. Henry J. Dixon.[4543] Timothy and John Richard Regan resided at the Dixon-Regan residence during the three-year time when the father and son were establishing the Moose Ear Creek homestead.[4544] This meant that Timothy and John Richard divided residence between Moose Ear Creek and Lake Chetek for approximately three years.[4545] The historical record appears to prove that during this three-year time in Wisconsin Margaret (Dacey) Regan and the nine Regan children remained in Farley, Iowa.[4546] The family was reunited when Timothy and Margaret established a permanent residence at Chippewa Falls, which was a place located to the southeast of Lake Chetek and Moose Ear Creek.[4547] Chippewa Falls was emerging as an important commercial and industrial place in northern Wisconsin. The Chippewa River, a tributary of the Eau Claire River, connected the town of Chippewa Falls to its larger municipal neighbor, Eau Claire, and by extension thereof, to the Mississippi River.

The children known to have been born to Timothy Regan and Margaret (Dacey) Regan included the following persons: Ellen Ragan, who married John D. Coleman of Minneapolis; **Charles Timothy Ragan, who married Margaret Hanrahan**; Marguerite Ragan, who married Charles Woelflen of Lewiston, Idaho; Patrick

[4539] The Daily Tribune of Wisconsin Rapids, Wisconsin (March 4, 1922). P. 5. Newspapers.com.

[4540] The Daily Tribune of Wisconsin Rapids, Wisconsin (March 4, 1922). P. 5. Newspapers.com.

[4541] The Daily Tribune of Wisconsin Rapids, Wisconsin (March 4, 1922). P. 5. Newspapers.com.

[4542] The Daily Tribune of Wisconsin Rapids, Wisconsin (January 22, 1934). P. 2. Newspapers.com.

[4543] The Daily Tribune of Wisconsin Rapids, Wisconsin (March 4, 1922). P. 5. Newspapers.com.

[4544] The Daily Tribune of Wisconsin Rapids, Wisconsin (January 22, 1934). P. 2. Newspapers.com.

[4545] The Daily Tribune of Wisconsin Rapids, Wisconsin (March 4, 1922). P. 5. Newspapers.com.

[4546] The Daily Tribune of Wisconsin Rapids, Wisconsin (March 4, 1922). P. 5. Newspapers.com.

[4547] The Daily Tribune of Wisconsin Rapids, Wisconsin (March 4, 1922). P. 5. Newspapers.com.

Ragan; Michael Ragan; John Richard Ragan, who married Annie Hinterthuer; James Ragan; Mary Ragan; and Anna Ragan.[4548] The family surname was spelled variously and simultaneously as "Ragan," and as "Regan." There appears to have been no comprehensive standardization of the spelling of the Regan/Ragan surname by the family. Proof of this fact is that the different siblings and the different lines of cousins spelled the surname in both forms for multiple generations. Both forms of the surname appear within this book, according to how the name was spelled by the individual person, or by the writers of the various historical reports that contained the surname. We will next discuss the children of Timothy Ragan and Margaret (Dacey) Ragan.

Patrick Regan, who had been hidden by his parents as an infant in the trunk aboard the ship from Ireland to New York City, resided at Cadott, which is located in Chippewa County, Wisconsin. Marguerite Regan married Charles Woelflen and they resided in Lewiston, Idaho.[4549] Ellen Regan married Henry D. Dixon and resided at various times at Superior, Wisconsin, at Poplar, Wisconsin, at Chippewa Falls, Wisconsin, and at Minneapolis.[4550] Another daughter of Timothy and Margaret (Dacey) Regan married Robert Ballentine and both resided in Pendleton, Oregon.[4551] Margaret (Dacey) Ragan died in 1898, at her home in Hurley, Iron County, Wisconsin.[4552] She was 70 years old, and had suffered a very severe fall from which she did not recover.[4553] Margaret (Dacey) Regan, after her husband's death, resided in Hurley, Iron County, Wisconsin, among the great Wisconsin-Michigan Iron Belt Mountains, which includes the Gogebic Mountains, the Marquette Mountains, the Whitecap Mountains, and the Porcupine Mountains.

Michael Ragan and the North Woods Winter Stoves

Michael Ragan (1862-1895), son of Timothy Ragan and Margaret (Dacey) Ragan, resided at Cadott, in Chippewa County, and engaged in the stove manufacturing and heating business.[4554] *The Chippewa Herald*, a newspaper of Chippewa Falls, reported that Michael Ragan, John Cirkel, and August Cirkel co-founded and incorporated the Cadott Stove and Heating Company in July, 1893.[4555]

[4548] Regan/Ragan family historical records.

[4549] Regan/Ragan family historical records.

[4550] Regan/Ragan family historical records.

[4551] Montreal River Miner and Iron County Republican. (March 10, 1898). P. 1. Newspapers.com.

[4552] Montreal River Miner and Iron County Republican. (March 10, 1898). P. 1. Newspapers.com.

[4553] Montreal River Miner and Iron County Republican. (March 10, 1898). P. 1. Newspapers.com.

[4554] The Star Tribune of Minneapolis, Minnesota. (February 14, 1895). P. 10. Newspapers.com.

[4555] The Chippewa Herald. (July 21, 1893). P. 1. Newspapers.com.

The articles of incorporation for the stove company were filed with the Secretary of State of Wisconsin at Madison on Tuesday, July 18, 1893.[4556] Michael served as Manager of the stove and heating company at Cadott and served as Secretary of the Northwestern Heating and Stove Association.[4557] The article report did not specify the facts of the company financing, but stated that the incorporation money was $25,000.[4558] Michael died young, before the age of 35.

Mary Regan and John D. Coleman of Minneapolis

Mary Regan married John D. Coleman. The Colemans resided in Minneapolis, where John worked for the Crane Company of Chicago and was Credit Manager for the Minneapolis Division of the company.[4559] John and Mary's daughter, Helen Coleman, attended the University of Minnesota, the University of Chicago, and the University of Paris (Sorbonne), and was civically active in Minneapolis.[4560]

John Richard Ragan of Wisconsin Rapids

John Richard Regan (1862-1934) married Annie Hinterthuer. *The Chippewa Herald* reported that John Richard and brother Michael established the M. W. Ragan & Brothers Company at Cadott.[4561] John was nineteen years old when he entered the partnership with Michael, who was two years older than John.[4562] The dry goods company originated as M. W. Ragan's Store, but when John turned 21 years old, the company became known as M. W. Ragan & Brother, the name change being reflective of the new partnership status that then defined the enterprise.[4563] John Richard purchased the interest of Michael Ragan in the company in June of 1893, as Michael was then changing his business interests and focus to the manufacture of stoves.[4564] Michael sold his interest in the Ragan Brothers Company, a general mercantile firm, and appears to have entered the stove and heating manufacturing business at that time.[4565] *The Daily Tribune*, a newspaper of Wisconsin Rapids, reported in an interview with John Richard Ragan the following words and memory about the M. W. Ragan & Brother Company.

[4556] The Chippewa Herald. (July 21, 1893). P. 1. Newspapers.com.
[4557] The Star Tribune of Minneapolis, Minnesota. (February 14, 1895). P. 10. Newspapers.com.
[4558] The Chippewa Herald. (July 21, 1893). P. 1. Newspapers.com.
[4559] Star Tribune. (Minneapolis, Minnesota). November 26, 1942. P. 6. Newspapers.com.
[4560] Regan family historical records.
[4561] The Chippewa Herald. (June 16, 1893). P. 1. Newspapers.com.
[4562] The Daily Tribune of Wisconsin Rapids, Wisconsin. (November 16, 1931). P. 2. Newspapers.com.
[4563] The Daily Tribune of Wisconsin Rapids, Wisconsin. (November 16, 1931). P. 2. Newspapers.com.
[4564] The Chippewa Herald. (June 16, 1893). P. 1. Newspapers.com.
[4565] The Chippewa Herald. (June 16, 1893). P. 1. Newspapers.com.

"'We sold everything there was to sell in those days,' says John, 'groceries, dry goods, clothing and everything. We were so young and inexperienced that our competitors dubbed our establishment the 'Kids' Store' but we stayed on and were in business after the others were gone.'"[4566]

The Weekly Leader, a newspaper of nearby Eau Claire, Wisconsin, contained multiple advertisements for M. W. Ragan & Brother, in the autumn of 1889.[4567] On October 6, 1889, *The Weekly Leader* advertised several forms of wood product: 16-inch hardwood, 2-foot maple and oak, and 4-foot in wood of all kinds, with all of the advertised wood products being dry stock.[4568] The advertisement contained the following words: "Every household should secure one or more car loads of hard wood for the winter. Apply to M. W. Ragan & Bro Cadott, Wis."[4569] The identical advertisement appeared in the October 20, 1889, edition of *The Weekly Leader*.[4570] M. W. Ragan & Brother shipped wood products from the store at Cadott to the market at Eau Claire.[4571] The year 1889 marked a high-volume sales year for M. W. Ragan & Brother, as was noted by the, "50 Years Ago in Eau Claire" memorial column that appeared in the October 3, 1939, edition of *The Eau Claire Leader*.

"'Mr. M. W. Ragan, the wood man of Cadott, is in town at the Galloway. He is delivering large quantities of dry hard wood in all lengths to our dealers here and to people buying in car lots. He shipped fifty cars during the last month.'"[4572]

John Richard Ragan started the J. R. Ragan Furniture Company of Wisconsin Rapids, in Wood County.[4573] He and his son, Fred Ragan, built the business into the largest furniture company in central Wisconsin.[4574] John was elected President of the Wisconsin Rapids Retailers' Association, and served on the Association board of directors with August Gottshalk, T. P. Peerenboom, W. F. Kellogg, Leonard Reinhart, I. E. Wilcox, Peter Reiland, Walter Zeaman, F. J. Daly, and

---

[4566] The Daily Tribune of Wisconsin Rapids, Wisconsin. (November 16, 1931). P. 2. Newspapers.com.

[4567] The Weekly Leader. (October 6, 1889). P. 3. Newspapers.com; The Weekly Leader. (October 13, 1889). P. 2. Newspapers.com; The Weekly Leader. (October 20, 1889). P. 2. Newspapers.com.

[4568] The Weekly Leader. (October 6, 1889). P. 3. Newspapers.com.

[4569] The Weekly Leader. (October 13, 1889). P. 2. Newspapers.com.

[4570] The Weekly Leader. (October 20, 1889). P. 2. Newspapers.com.

[4571] The Weekly Leader. (October 6, 1889). P. 3. Newspapers.com.

[4572] The Eau Claire Leader. (October 3, 1939). P. 4. Newspapers.com.

[4573] The Daily Tribune. (Wisconsin Rapids). (May 7, 1925). P. 1. Newspapers.com.

[4574] The Daily Tribune. (Wisconsin Rapids). (May 7, 1925). P. 1. Newspapers.com.

Ernest Anderson.[4575] John R. Ragan co-founded the Wisconsin Rapids Baseball Club, served as President of the Wisconsin Funeral Directors' Association, served on the Wisconsin State Embalmers Examining Board, was a member of the National Funeral Directors' Association, the Catholic Order of Foresters, the Catholic Knights of Wisconsin, Modern Woodmen of America, and many other organizations.[4576] John was President of the Wisconsin Valley Furniture Dealers' Association and was a member of the board of directors of the Wisconsin Retailers' Association.[4577] He was a member of the board of directors of the Wisconsin Rapids Chamber of Commerce.[4578]

John and Anna (Hinterthuer) Ragan were members of the Saints Peter and Paul Catholic Church of Wisconsin Rapids. Their son, Fred Ragan, ran the J. R. Ragan Furniture Company after his father's death. John and Anna's daughter, Marguerite Ragan, graduated from Northwestern University with a degree in Oratory/Rhetoric and taught drama and speech at public schools in Ironwood, Michigan, and Eveleth, Minnesota.[4579] Marguerite was beloved and highly respected by her many students over the years.[4580]

Charles Timothy Regan and Margaret (Hanrahan) Regan of

Chippewa Falls and Chicago

Charles Timothy Regan (1856-1922), son of Timothy Ragan and Margaret (Dacey) Ragan, married Margaret Hanrahan (1858-1940). Margaret was born in Milwaukee and was the daughter of Michael Hanrahan (1823-1898) and Mary Rose (Hogan) Hanrahan (circa 1823-1883).[4581] Michael Hanrahan owned Wisconsin lumber interests and was a farmer. Mary Rose Hanrahan helped manage the family farm.[4582] The Hanrahans moved to Chippewa Falls in about 1860.[4583] The Regan and Hanrahan families were members of Notre Dame Church at Chippewa Falls. Michael Hanrahan, who emigrated from Ireland to Wisconsin, was an alumnus of Trinity College in Dublin.

Charles T. Regan and Margaret (Hanrahan) Regan had the following children: Charles E. Regan; Mary Regan (who changed her surname to Rehan); Ruth Regan, who married Willard Bunn; John Hanrahan Regan, who married Inez (surname

---

[4575] The Daily Tribune. (Wisconsin Rapids). (January 26, 1927). P. 1. Newspapers.com.
[4576] The Daily Tribune. (March 4, 1922). P. 5. Newspapers.com; Regan family historical records.
[4577] The Daily Tribune. (Wisconsin Rapids). (January 22, 1934). P. 2. Newspapers.com.
[4578] The Daily Tribune. (Wisconsin Rapids). (January 22, 1934). P. 2. Newspapers.com.
[4579] Regan family historical records; The Daily Tribune. (Wisconsin Rapids). (January 22, 1934). P. 2. Newspapers.com.
[4580] Regan family historical records.
[4581] Eau Claire Leader. (December 3, 1940). P. 7. Newspapers.com.
[4582] Regan, Hanrahan family history records.
[4583] Eau Claire Leader. (December 3, 1940). P. 7. Newspapers.com.

unknown); Jean Regan, who married Paul W. McKay; Robert Giles Regan, who married Frances Lockwood; and Francis Regan (known as "Cy" and as "Frank"), who married Alma (surname unknown).

Charles T. Regan was a salesman with the Chippewa Valley Mercantile Company of Wisconsin and held multiple civic offices in Chippewa Falls.[4584] Charles was Secretary of the Butte and Oro Grande Mining Company of Idaho in 1908, and commented on the revenue of the company in a report from *The Mining Review* of Salt Lake City: "'The mine and mill under present operation, and treating our low-grade ore, is paying the company a net profit of about $200 a day.'"[4585] Regan in 1908 was reported to be the head of a grocery company in Chippewa Falls; this was the Chippewa Valley Mercantile Company.[4586] The leadership of the Butte and Oro Grande Mining Company consisted of the following persons and jobs: George McCall of Chippewa Falls was President; O. G. Kinny of Colfax, Wisconsin, was Vice-President; Charles T. Ragan of Chippewa Falls; and N. C. Gilstad of Barron, Wisconsin, was Treasurer. The board of directors consisted of McCall, Ragan, Kinny, Gilstad, Ernest Horan of Eau Claire; Peter Elmon of Superior, Wisconsin; C. C. Coe of Barron; P. E. Stookey of Lewiston, Idaho; and John Finn of Two Harbors, Minnesota.[4587] The company employed twenty miners at the time of the Salt Lake City report and expected to employ a total of about fifty men shortly after the time of the report.[4588] The company processed 125 tons of ore every twenty-four hours.[4589] Charles T. Regan, O. G. Kinney, George McCall, C. C. Coe, Peter Elmon, P. E. Stookey, Ernest Horan, and N. C. Gilstad co-founded the Elk City, Lewiston & Spokane Electric Railway Company, and the men invested $100,000 in the new railway company in 1908.[4590]

Charles T. Regan was Vice-President of the Crooked River Mining and Milling Company, which acquired the old Hogan Mining Company gold mine at Oro

---

[4584] Regan family historical records; The Mining Review. (Salt Lake City, Utah). (August 15, 1908). P. 23. Newspapers.com.

[4585] The Mining Review. (Salt Lake City, Utah). (August 15, 1908). P. 23. Newspapers.com.

[4586] The Mining Review. (Salt Lake City, Utah). (August 15, 1908). P. 23. Newspapers.com.

[4587] The Mining Review. (Salt Lake City, Utah). (August 15, 1908). P. 23. Newspapers.com.

[4588] The Mining Review. (Salt Lake City, Utah). (August 15, 1908). P. 23. Newspapers.com.

[4589] The Mining Review. (Salt Lake City, Utah). (August 15, 1908). P. 23. Newspapers.com.

[4590] The Mining Review. (Salt Lake City, Utah). (August 15, 1908). P. 23. Newspapers.com.

Grande, Idaho.[4591] *The Mining World*, a mining industry news journal based at The Monadnock Building of Chicago, reported the facts relevant to the company in 1905. The company shipped metal ore via the freight service of the Northern Pacific Railroad Company from the station at Stiles, located 63 miles from the minehead and ore factory.[4592] The company owned approximately 1,000 acres of metal mining lands in the Oro Grande vicinity, and, for the operation of the Oro Grande gold vein formation, constructed a dyke that was 7,000 feet in length, 600 feet in breadth, and 600 feet in depth.[4593] The leadership structure of the firm consisted of the following persons and jobs: William Hogan was President and General Manager; Charles T. Ragan was Vice-President; Peter Elmon was Treasurer; W. W. Strickland was Secretary; and J. H. McCormick was Superintendent.[4594] Ragan and Hogan were from Chippewa Falls; Elmon and Strickland were from Superior, Wisconsin.[4595]

Charles T. Ragan, George McCall, T. J. Connor, William Bowe, and Emmett Horan started a large land company in Chippewa Falls around May, 1902, for the purpose of developing 9,000 acres of Sawyer County, Wisconsin.[4596] The company appears to have been profitable, because Regan sold a large piece of real estate in Sawyer County in July, 1902.[4597] The transaction was probably derivative of the land company. We will next discuss the Chicago history of the children of Charles T. Regan and Margaret (Hanrahan) Regan. Charles was Clerk for Chippewa Falls at the same time when Michael Hogan, who was Margaret (Hanrahan) Regan's relative, served as Assessor of Chippewa Falls.[4598] Charles was elected President of the Ancient Order of Hibernians in 1896, at the conference in La Crosse.[4599] The Order provided social and financial support to Irish-American families in Wisconsin.[4600] Margaret (Hanrahan) Regan was Vice-President and board member of the Chippewa Falls League of Women Voters.[4601] Margaret was a founding

---

[4591] The Mining World. (July 8-December 30, 1905). Vol. 23. P. 395. Chicago, IL. Google Books.

[4592] The Mining World. (July 8-December 30, 1905). Vol. 23. P. 395. Chicago, IL. Google Books.

[4593] The Mining World. (July 8-December 30, 1905). Vol. 23. P. 395. Chicago, IL. Google Books.

[4594] The Mining World. (July 8-December 30, 1905). Vol. 23. P. 395. Chicago, IL. Google Books.

[4595] The Mining World. (July 8-December 30, 1905). Vol. 23. P. 395. Chicago, IL. Google Books.

[4596] The Weekly Telegram. (Eau Claire, Wisconsin). (May 22, 1902). P. 6. Newspapers.com.

[4597] Eau Claire Leader. (July 10, 1902). P. 3. Newspapers.com.

[4598] Eau Claire Leader. (April 9, 1885). P. 3. Newspapers.com.

[4599] The Weekly Wisconsin. (July 4, 1896). P. 7. Newspapers.com.

[4600] The Weekly Wisconsin. (July 4, 1896). P. 7. Newspapers.com.

[4601] Eau Claire Leader. (July 13, 1922). P. 8. Newspapers.com.

member of the Faber Reading Circle, a book club of Chippewa Falls, in 1895.[4602] The Regan home was located at 922 Superior Street in Chippewa Falls. Margaret was a member of the Wisconsin State Federation of Women's Clubs and helped organize the Eleventh Convention of the Federation in 1911.[4603] She was also a member of the Chippewa Falls Women's Club.[4604]

Ruth Regan and Willard Bunn of Chicago and Springfield

Ruth Regan, daughter of Charles Timothy Regan and Margaret (Hanrahan) Regan, won a free scholarship to the Chicago Musical College around 1905.[4605] The Chicago Musical College was owned by Florenz Ziegfeld. Ruth also was an alumna of the Bush Temple of Music in Chicago.[4606] Ruth married Willard Bunn (1888-1959) on January 9, 1913, at the home of Rev. A. B. C. Dunne in Eau Claire. Rev. Father Murphy officiated the ceremony.[4607] Charlotte Starrs of Chicago was the bridesmaid for Ruth Regan and was possibly a cousin of the Regan family. Jacob Bunn, Jr., of Springfield and Chicago, was the best man for Willard Bunn.[4608] The wedding reception took place at the Eau Claire Club, and others in attendance included George Wallace Bunn and Ada Willard (Richardson) Bunn, who were the parents of the groom, Alice Bunn, Jacob Bunn, Jr., Henry Barrell House of Chicago and Springfield, and many others.[4609] Willard and Ruth honeymooned in Chicago and the South, before returning to Springfield.[4610] While in Chicago, prior to her marriage to Bunn, Ruth resided part of the time with her cousin, John Joseph Hogan. Ruth (Regan) Bunn was President of the Springfield Musical Society, co-founder of Blessed Sacrament Church and School of Springfield, and was a supporter of church, music, and education.

Robert Giles Regan and the Chicago Construction Industry

Robert Giles Regan (1895-1948), son of Charles Timothy Regan and Margaret (Hanrahan) Regan, established the two Chicago construction companies known as the Robert G. Regan Company and the Regan Contracting Company.[4611] He served as 1st Sergeant in the 103rd Field Artillery, 26th Division, in World War I.[4612] In

---

[4602] Eau Claire Leader. (February 18, 1922). P. 5. Newspapers.com.

[4603] Eau Claire Leader. (May 18, 1911). P. 5. Newspapers.com.

[4604] Eau Claire Leader. (January 18, 1921). P. 7. Newspapers.com.

[4605] Eau Claire Leader. (January 6, 1905). P. 2. Newspapers.com.

[4606] Eau Claire Leader. (January 9, 1913). P. 6. Newspapers.com.

[4607] Eau Claire Leader. (January 9, 1913). P. 6. Newspapers.com.

[4608] Eau Claire Leader. (January 9, 1913). P. 6. Newspapers.com.

[4609] Eau Claire Leader. (January 9, 1913). P. 6. Newspapers.com.

[4610] Eau Claire Leader. (January 9, 1913). P. 6. Newspapers.com.

[4611] Chicago Daily Tribune. (October 1, 1939). P. 20. Retrieved from ProQuest Newspapers: Chicago Tribune. Database at Northwestern University; Regan family history records.

[4612] Robert Giles Regan tombstone. Hope Cemetery. Chippewa Falls, Wisconsin.

1939, Robert Regan co-founded and co-owned the Chicago development company known as Chatham Park, Inc.[4613] The Robert G. Regan Company was awarded the general contract for the construction of the Chatham Park Housing development.[4614] Designed by the architectural firm of Shaw, Knaess & Murphy, the Chatham Park development was planned to comprise 554 housing units.[4615] Chatham Park was reported by the *Chicago Tribune* to have been the largest privately financed housing development in Chicago history.[4616] Regan oversaw and/or employed approximately 2,200 employees who were connected with the construction of the Chatham Park housing project.[4617] The cost of the development project was $3,443,000.[4618] The Chatham Park development was located at the southwest corner of Cottage Grove Avenue and E. 83rd Street.[4619]

As of October 1, 1939, the Robert G. Regan Company had completed sixteen of the house foundations within the development.[4620] Regan stated the following with regard to the necessary infrastructure of the Chatham Park development: "Five miles of sewers must be installed throughout the grounds and thirteen main street connections must be built to handle them."[4621] Additionally, Regan described the electrical infrastructure as follows: "An even larger amount of wiring for the electric utilities will be required, as well as sufficient concrete to build private roadways totaling more than a mile."[4622] Regan stated that the contractual prices for the construction materials were agreed upon prior to the market price increases caused by World War II.[4623] Regan commented on the economic consequences and benefits of having negotiated the contract prices for the building materials prior to

[4613] Chicago Daily Tribune. (August 6, 1939). P. C16. Retrieved from ProQuest Newspapers: Chicago Tribune. Database at Northwestern University

[4614] Chicago Daily Tribune. (October 1, 1939). P. 20. Retrieved from ProQuest Newspapers: Chicago Tribune. Database at Northwestern University.

[4615] Chicago Daily Tribune. (October 1, 1939). P. 20. Retrieved from ProQuest Newspapers: Chicago Tribune. Database at Northwestern University.

[4616] Chicago Daily Tribune. (January 3, 1940). P. 27. Retrieved from ProQuest Newspapers: Chicago Tribune. Database at Northwestern University

[4617] Chicago Daily Tribune. (October 1, 1939). P. 20. Retrieved from ProQuest Newspapers: Chicago Tribune. Database at Northwestern University.

[4618] Chicago Daily Tribune. (October 1, 1939). P. 20. Retrieved from ProQuest Newspapers: Chicago Tribune. Database at Northwestern University.

[4619] Chicago Daily Tribune. (October 1, 1939). P. 20. Retrieved from ProQuest Newspapers: Chicago Tribune. Database at Northwestern University.

[4620] Chicago Daily Tribune. (October 1, 1939). P. 20. Retrieved from ProQuest Newspapers: Chicago Tribune. Database at Northwestern University.

[4621] Chicago Daily Tribune. (October 1, 1939). P. 20. Retrieved from ProQuest Newspapers: Chicago Tribune. Database at Northwestern University.

[4622] Chicago Daily Tribune. (October 1, 1939). P. 20. Retrieved from ProQuest Newspapers: Chicago Tribune. Database at Northwestern University.

[4623] Chicago Daily Tribune. (October 1, 1939). P. 20. Retrieved from ProQuest Newspapers: Chicago Tribune. Database at Northwestern University.

the time when wartime market forces drove up the construction costs.[4624] "This means that it will be possible for us to erect the buildings as originally planned and yet rent them at a figure which it may be impossible to duplicate for years to come."[4625] Regan stated that the Chatham Park development construction project necessitated the consumption of more than 2,500,000 feet of lumber and 1,200 tons of steel.[4626] He said that construction of the brickwork for the stories above the first stories of the Chatham Park development buildings would occur by approximately October 7, 1939.[4627]

Robert G. Regan served as a member of the Board of Directors of Chatham Park, Inc., the development corporation responsible for the Chatham Park development.[4628] Other members of the Board of Directors of Chatham Park, Inc., included George H. Dovenmuehle, Henry Crown, Preston Boyden, and Gael Sullivan.[4629] Henry Crown served also as Chairman of the Material Service Corporation.[4630] The executive leadership structure of Chatham Park, Inc., in 1939, included the following persons and offices:

1. George H. Dovenmuehle
    a. President of Chatham Park, Inc.
    b. Vice President of Dovenmuehle, Inc.
2. Preston Boyden
    a. Vice President of Chatham Park, Inc.
    b. Attorney at law with the firm of Taylor, Miller, Busch & Boyden.
3. Theodore A. Buenger
    a. Treasurer of Chatham Park, Inc.
    b. Buenger served as President of Dovenmuehle, Inc.
4. Harry C. Eigelberner
    a. Secretary of Chatham Park, Inc.
    b. Eigelberner served as Secretary of Dovenmuehle, Inc.[4631]

[4624] Chicago Daily Tribune. (October 1, 1939). P. 20. Retrieved from ProQuest Newspapers: Chicago Tribune. Database at Northwestern University.

[4625] Chicago Daily Tribune. (October 1, 1939). P. 20. Retrieved from ProQuest Newspapers: Chicago Tribune. Database at Northwestern University.

[4626] Chicago Daily Tribune. (October 1, 1939). P. 20. Retrieved from ProQuest Newspapers: Chicago Tribune. Database at Northwestern University.

[4627] Chicago Daily Tribune. (October 1, 1939). P. 20. Retrieved from ProQuest Newspapers: Chicago Tribune. Database at Northwestern University.

[4628] Chicago Daily Tribune. (August 21, 1941). P. 22. Retrieved from ProQuest Newspapers: Chicago Tribune. Database at Northwestern University.

[4629] Chicago Daily Tribune. (August 21, 1941). P. 22. Retrieved from ProQuest Newspapers: Chicago Tribune. Database at Northwestern University.

[4630] Chicago Daily Tribune. (August 21, 1941). P. 22. Retrieved from ProQuest Newspapers: Chicago Tribune. Database at Northwestern University.

[4631] Chicago Daily Tribune. (August 6, 1939). P. C16. Retrieved from ProQuest Newspapers: Chicago Tribune. Database at Northwestern University.

Robert G. Regan was a stockholder in Chatham Park, Inc., as well.[4632] Alfred Shaw, the senior partner of the architectural firm that designed Chatham Park, was a stockholder in Chatham Park, Inc.[4633] Chicago Mayor Edward Joseph Kelly broke ground, with many other people, for the Chatham Park development in August, 1939.[4634] The Chatham Park development, when completed, encompassed twenty-two acres and seventy-two buildings.[4635] Eugene L. Duval was the District Supervisor of the Federal Housing Administration at the time of the Chatham Park development.[4636] Duval laid the final brick in what was a celebratory ceremony of the completed construction of the development.[4637] Duval laid the five-millionth brick, which was symbolically the final brick in the project.[4638] The firm of C. Wallace Johnson, Inc., acted as the rental agent for Chatham Park, Inc., and had rented 187 of the Chatham Park apartments as of June 23, 1940.[4639] It was reported that 1,500 prospective lessees every weekend were visiting the two model apartments on display at Chatham Park.[4640]

The property management company of C. Wallace Johnson, Inc., administered a portfolio of 231 buildings as of November, 1939.[4641] The occupancy rate for the C. Wallace Johnson properties was reported to average 98.3 percent.[4642] C. Wallace Johnson, who oversaw the leasing of the Chatham Park development residential units, stated the rates of rent for the various classes of apartment available at Chatham Park.[4643] The schedule of rents contained the following information:

[4632] Chicago Daily Tribune. (August 6, 1939). P. C16. Retrieved from ProQuest Newspapers: Chicago Tribune. Database at Northwestern University.
[4633] Chicago Daily Tribune. (August 6, 1939). P. C16. Retrieved from ProQuest Newspapers: Chicago Tribune. Database at Northwestern University.
[4634] Chicago Daily Tribune. (August 6, 1939). P. C16. Retrieved from ProQuest Newspapers: Chicago Tribune. Database at Northwestern University.
[4635] Chicago Daily Tribune. (June 23, 1940). P. B10. Retrieved from ProQuest Newspapers: Chicago Tribune. Database at Northwestern University.
[4636] Chicago Daily Tribune. (June 23, 1940). P. B10. Retrieved from ProQuest Newspapers: Chicago Tribune. Database at Northwestern University.
[4637] Chicago Daily Tribune. (June 23, 1940). P. B10. Retrieved from ProQuest Newspapers: Chicago Tribune. Database at Northwestern University.
[4638] Chicago Daily Tribune. (June 23, 1940). P. B10. Retrieved from ProQuest Newspapers: Chicago Tribune. Database at Northwestern University.
[4639] Chicago Daily Tribune. (June 23, 1940). P. B10. Retrieved from ProQuest Newspapers: Chicago Tribune. Database at Northwestern University.
[4640] Chicago Daily Tribune. (June 23, 1940). P. B10. Retrieved from ProQuest Newspapers: Chicago Tribune. Database at Northwestern University.
[4641] Chicago Daily Tribune. (November 26, 1939). P. 22. Retrieved from ProQuest Newspapers: Chicago Tribune. Database at Northwestern University.
[4642] Chicago Daily Tribune. (November 26, 1939). P. 22. Retrieved from ProQuest Newspapers: Chicago Tribune. Database at Northwestern University.
[4643] Chicago Daily Tribune. (November 26, 1939). P. 22. Retrieved from ProQuest Newspapers: Chicago Tribune. Database at Northwestern University.

1. The average monthly rent per room would stand at $16.00.[4644]

2. Chatham Park contained 105 three-room suites available at a range of rents from $47.50 per month, to $50 per month.[4645]

3. Chatham Park contained 123 four-room suites available at a range of rents from $62.50 per month, to $67.50 per month.[4646]

4. Chatham Park contained 78 additional four-room suites available at a range of rents from $62.50 per month, to $65 per month.[4647]

5. Chatham Park contained 12 five-room suites available at a rent of $75 per month.[4648]

6. Chatham Park contained 160 duplex houses available at a range of rents from $72.50 per month, to $77.50 per month.[4649]

In 1934 the Chromium Corporation of America granted a contract to the Robert G. Regan Company for the expansion and improvement of the Chromium Corporation of America's factory located at 4645 W. Chicago Avenue.[4650] The architectural firm of Olsen & Urbain designed the new structure.[4651] The *Chicago Tribune* reported that once the Olsen & Urbain structural addition was built by Robert R. Regan, the factory of the Chromium Corporation of America would be the largest factory in the world whose purpose was the manufacture of industrial chromium plating products.[4652] The location of the Chromium Corporation of America was approximately at the boundaries of the Chicago communities of West Garfield Park, Humboldt Park, and Austin.[4653] The reconstructed and improved factory was reported to have been able to process the following product: "It will

---

[4644] Chicago Daily Tribune. (November 26, 1939). P. 22. Retrieved from ProQuest Newspapers: Chicago Tribune. Database at Northwestern University.
[4645] Chicago Daily Tribune. (November 26, 1939). P. 22. Retrieved from ProQuest Newspapers: Chicago Tribune. Database at Northwestern University.
[4646] Chicago Daily Tribune. (November 26, 1939). P. 22. Retrieved from ProQuest Newspapers: Chicago Tribune. Database at Northwestern University.
[4647] Chicago Daily Tribune. (November 26, 1939). P. 22. Retrieved from ProQuest Newspapers: Chicago Tribune. Database at Northwestern University.
[4648] Chicago Daily Tribune. (November 26, 1939). P. 22. Retrieved from ProQuest Newspapers: Chicago Tribune. Database at Northwestern University.
[4649] Chicago Daily Tribune. (November 26, 1939). P. 22. Retrieved from ProQuest Newspapers: Chicago Tribune. Database at Northwestern University.
[4650] Chicago Daily Tribune. (October 28, 1934). P. B12. Retrieved from Proquest Newspapers: Chicago Tribune. Database at Northwestern University.
[4651] Chicago Daily Tribune. (October 28, 1934). P. B12. Retrieved from Proquest Newspapers: Chicago Tribune. Database at Northwestern University.
[4652] Chicago Daily Tribune. (October 28, 1934). P. B12. Retrieved from Proquest Newspapers: Chicago Tribune. Database at Northwestern University.
[4653] Map of Humboldt Park. Zipmap.net.

be equipped to handle articles weighing up to forty or fifty tons and as long as 22 feet and up to 14 feet in diameter."[4654]

Robert G. Regan was a close personal friend of Paul V. Galvin, who founded Motorola.[4655] Regan and Galvin collaborated on industrial projects in Chicago.[4656] In 1936, the *Chicago Tribune* reported that the Galvin Manufacturing Corporation granted the general contract to Robert Regan for the construction of a $250,000 factory to be located at 4545 W. Augusta Boulevard.[4657] The factory would contain 85,000 square feet of space.[4658] The factory purpose was the manufacture of radios for households and automobiles.[4659] The architect for the new factory was Victor L. Charn, who designed the factory with blue and white terra cotta exteriors and abundant window lighting.[4660] The plant was to contain sections of one story, and two stories, with the executive offices to be located within the second story section of the plant.[4661] The realty company of Preston and Cook brokered the acquisition of the place of the factory's construction.[4662]

Also in 1936 the Robert G. Regan Company received the contract for the demolition, construction, and improvement of the site that was located at the northeast corner of Clark Street and Division Street.[4663] This corner is located in the Gold Coast Neighborhood. Andrew Spohrer originally held, and his heirs later held, title to the building that was to be demolished and rebuilt with significant physical improvements and additions.[4664] Andrew Spohrer, who came to Chicago in 1836, and the Spohrer family descendants had owned this land for close to 100 years at the time of the Regan construction improvement contract.[4665] The corner portion of the building possessed 45 feet of frontage on Clark Street and 62 feet on

---

[4654] Chicago Daily Tribune. (October 21, 1934). P. A10. Retrieved from ProQuest Newspapers: Chicago Tribune. Database at Northwestern University.
[4655] Telephone interview with Margot McKay regarding Regan family history.
[4656] Telephone interview with Margot McKay regarding Regan family history.
[4657] Chicago Daily Tribune. (December 27, 1936). P. 16. Retrieved from ProQuest Newspapers: Chicago Tribune. Database at Northwestern University.
[4658] Chicago Daily Tribune. (December 27, 1936). P. 16. Retrieved from ProQuest Newspapers: Chicago Tribune. Database at Northwestern University.
[4659] Chicago Daily Tribune. (December 27, 1936). P. 16. Retrieved from ProQuest Newspapers: Chicago Tribune. Database at Northwestern University.
[4660] Chicago Daily Tribune. (December 27, 1936). P. 16. Retrieved from ProQuest Newspapers: Chicago Tribune. Database at Northwestern University.
[4661] Chicago Daily Tribune. (December 27, 1936). P. 16. Retrieved from ProQuest Newspapers: Chicago Tribune. Database at Northwestern University.
[4662] Chicago Daily Tribune. (December 27, 1936). P. 16. Retrieved from ProQuest Newspapers: Chicago Tribune. Database at Northwestern University.
[4663] Chicago Daily Tribune. (May 17, 1936). P. B14. Retrieved from ProQuest Newspapers: Chicago Tribune. Database at Northwestern University.
[4664] Chicago Daily Tribune. (May 17, 1936). P. B14. Retrieved from ProQuest Newspapers: Chicago Tribune. Database at Northwestern University.
[4665] Chicago Daily Tribune. (May 17, 1936). P. B14. Retrieved from ProQuest Newspapers: Chicago Tribune. Database at Northwestern University.

Division Street.[4666] The company known as the Liggett Drug store occupied the corner portion.[4667] The article reported that the corner portion would be built to two stories in height after the tenant leases that existed in the building expired.[4668] The architectural firm of Olsen & Urbain designed the plans for the new buildings to be constructed by the Robert G. Regan Company.[4669]

Regan participated in realization of an architecturally innovative design for a freight transportation depot located at 18th Street and Canal Street.[4670] The *Chicago Tribune* described in the article entitled, *Motor Freight Line to Build Big Terminal*, the structural novelty and uniqueness of the depot.[4671] "What is claimed to be the first use of the cantilever type of reinforced concrete for heavy duty and warehousing is at the new terminal warehouse of the Interstate Motor Freight system, being erected at 18th and Canal streets."[4672] The article identified the depot terminal architect somewhat ambiguously as the "MacMillan system."[4673] The construction contract was given to the Robert G. Regan Company.[4674] Construction cost would total $175,000.[4675] The depot structure consisted of a building, "200 feet long, forty feet wide, and two stories high."[4676] The article identified the "Interstate system"[4677] as the organization that commissioned the construction of the depot and that would operate the depot.[4678] The Interstate system was described as a transportation network that operated in the Midwest and Atlantic seaboard

---

[4666] Chicago Daily Tribune. (May 17, 1936). P. B14. Retrieved from ProQuest Newspapers: Chicago Tribune. Database at Northwestern University.

[4667] Chicago Daily Tribune. (May 17, 1936). P. B14. Retrieved from ProQuest Newspapers: Chicago Tribune. Database at Northwestern University.

[4668] Chicago Daily Tribune. (May 17, 1936). P. B14. Retrieved from ProQuest Newspapers: Chicago Tribune. Database at Northwestern University.

[4669] Chicago Daily Tribune. (May 17, 1936). P. B14. Retrieved from ProQuest Newspapers: Chicago Tribune. Database at Northwestern University.

[4670] Chicago Daily Tribune. (July 19, 1936). P.A14. Retrieved from ProQuest Newspapers: Chicago Tribune. Database at Northwestern University.

[4671] Chicago Daily Tribune. (July 19, 1936). P.A14. Retrieved from ProQuest Newspapers: Chicago Tribune. Database at Northwestern University.

[4672] Chicago Daily Tribune. (July 19, 1936). P.A14. Retrieved from ProQuest Newspapers: Chicago Tribune. Database at Northwestern University.

[4673] Chicago Daily Tribune. (July 19, 1936). P.A14. Retrieved from ProQuest Newspapers: Chicago Tribune. Database at Northwestern University.

[4674] Chicago Daily Tribune. (July 19, 1936). P.A14. Retrieved from ProQuest Newspapers: Chicago Tribune. Database at Northwestern University.

[4675] Chicago Daily Tribune. (July 19, 1936). P.A14. Retrieved from ProQuest Newspapers: Chicago Tribune. Database at Northwestern University.

[4676] Chicago Daily Tribune. (July 19, 1936). P.A14. Retrieved from ProQuest Newspapers: Chicago Tribune. Database at Northwestern University.

[4677] Chicago Daily Tribune. (July 19, 1936). P.A14. Retrieved from ProQuest Newspapers: Chicago Tribune. Database at Northwestern University.

[4678] Chicago Daily Tribune. (July 19, 1936). P.A14. Retrieved from ProQuest Newspapers: Chicago Tribune. Database at Northwestern University.

regions.[4679] Harry Bylenga served as President of the Interstate system organization at the time of the construction of the new Chicago freight and transportation depot.[4680]

The *Chicago Tribune* reported on April 3, 1938, plans for the construction of another major Chicago freight trucking depot.[4681] The depot would serve interstate truck freights and transfers.[4682] The depot would occupy land located at 34th Street and Iron Street.[4683] This place is located within the Chicago community of McKinley Park.[4684] The architect Frederick Dolke designed a freight depot whose structure would comprise 516 feet by 75 feet and which could serve the loading and unloading of 112 freight trucks, simultaneously.[4685] The American Terminal Company was the company that operated the depot and terminal, and operated from offices located at Harrison Street and Michigan Avenue in the Loop.[4686] The building that the American Terminal Company occupied was the Fairbanks Morse Building.[4687] The industrial space acquired for the construction of the depot and terminal of the American Terminal Company was leased from the estate of Levi Leiter for a time of 25 years.[4688] The contract for lease contained as a term of consideration the option for the tenant, American Terminal Company, to renew the lease for an additional 25 years.[4689] The corporation and depot served to accommodate the long-haul interstate trucking market and the commercial needs that attached to that particular transportation market.[4690] The company and depot, moreover, helped establish Chicago as a continental center for trucking

---

[4679] Chicago Daily Tribune. (July 19, 1936). P.A14. Retrieved from ProQuest Newspapers: Chicago Tribune. Database at Northwestern University.

[4680] Chicago Daily Tribune. (July 19, 1936). P.A14. Retrieved from ProQuest Newspapers: Chicago Tribune. Database at Northwestern University.

[4681] Chicago Daily Tribune. (April 3, 1938). P.B10. Retrieved from ProQuest Newspapers: Chicago Tribune. Database at Northwestern University.

[4682] Chicago Daily Tribune. (April 3, 1938). P.B10. Retrieved from ProQuest Newspapers: Chicago Tribune. Database at Northwestern University.

[4683] Chicago Daily Tribune. (April 3, 1938). P.B10. Retrieved from ProQuest Newspapers: Chicago Tribune. Database at Northwestern University.

[4684] Map of Chicago. Google Maps.

[4685] Chicago Daily Tribune. (April 3, 1938). P.B10. Retrieved from ProQuest Newspapers: Chicago Tribune. Database at Northwestern University.

[4686] Chicago Daily Tribune. (April 3, 1938). P.B10. Retrieved from ProQuest Newspapers: Chicago Tribune. Database at Northwestern University.

[4687] Chicago Daily Tribune. (April 3, 1938). P.B10. Retrieved from ProQuest Newspapers: Chicago Tribune. Database at Northwestern University.

[4688] Chicago Daily Tribune. (April 3, 1938). P.B10. Retrieved from ProQuest Newspapers: Chicago Tribune. Database at Northwestern University.

[4689] Chicago Daily Tribune. (April 3, 1938). P.B10. Retrieved from ProQuest Newspapers: Chicago Tribune. Database at Northwestern University.

[4690] Chicago Daily Tribune. (April 3, 1938). P.B10. Retrieved from ProQuest Newspapers: Chicago Tribune. Database at Northwestern University.

transportation. The executive leadership structure of the American Terminal Company included the following persons and jobs.

1. Louis C. Seaverns
   a. President
   b. Board of Directors
2. Charles H. Morse, Jr.
   a. Vice-President
   b. Board of Directors
3. Jefferson D. Currier
   a. Secretary and Treasurer
   b. Board of Directors
4. J. M. Bruce
   a. General Manager
   b. Board of Directors
5. S. M. Rinaker
   a. Board of Directors
6. W. W. Witwer
   a. Board of Directors[4691]

Frances "Frodie" (Lockwood) Regan, widow of Robert Giles Regan, resided in an apartment at The Drake Hotel and was a longtime resident of Gold Coast neighborhood.[4692] Frances was a longstanding member of St. Chrysostom Episcopal Church located on North Dearborn Parkway.[4693] She was a member of the Women's Guild of St. Chrysostom's.[4694] A native of Eau Claire, Wisconsin, Frances was an alumna both of Rosemary Hall Finishing School and of Smith College.[4695] Frodie Regan was famous in the Gold Coast neighborhood of Chicago for her mustard sauce recipe.[4696] Frodie was a beloved resident of The Drake Hotel, where the hotel staff held her in very high esteem.

[4691] Chicago Daily Tribune. (April 3, 1938). P.B10. Retrieved from ProQuest Newspapers: Chicago Tribune. Database at Northwestern University.

[4692] Telephone interview with Margot McKay about the Regan family history.

[4693] Obituary for Frances (Lockwood) Regan. Chicago Tribune (January 2, 1988). P. 8. Retrieved from ProQuest Newspapers: Chicago Tribune. Database at Northwestern University.

[4694] Obituary for Frances (Lockwood) Regan. Chicago Tribune (January 2, 1988). P. 8. Retrieved from ProQuest Newspapers: Chicago Tribune. Database at Northwestern University.

[4695] Obituary for Frances (Lockwood) Regan. Chicago Tribune (January 2, 1988). P. 8. Retrieved from ProQuest Newspapers: Chicago Tribune. Database at Northwestern University.

[4696] Anecdote shared with Andrew Taylor Call by friends of Frances Lockwood Regan at St. Chrysostom Episcopal Church, Chicago.

In 1934, the Robert G. Regan Company was awarded the contract for a $100,000 construction project in Evanston.[4697] The place of the project was the southwest corner of Hinman Avenue and Davis Street.[4698] The construction project consisted of a garage, a store, and a gas station.[4699] Olsen & Urbain were the architects for the planned building.[4700] The building walls were projected to contain Lannon stone from Wisconsin.[4701] The garage was to be constructed underground and would possess a capacity capable of holding 110 cars at a time.[4702] Matson B. Hill held title to the land where the project was planned, and the Georgian Hotel stood across the street from the place of construction.[4703] Northwestern University and the Evanston downtown were both located nearby. The building was designed by Olsen & Urbain to contain multiple stores as well as the service station.[4704] Pure Oil Company leased the space to operate a service station at the location.[4705]

In 1935, Regan collaborated again with the architecture firm of Olsen & Urbain, this time in the construction of a one-story addition to the Tabin & Picker Company building located at 4119 W. Belmont Avenue.[4706] Tabin & Picker was a clothing manufacturer, and produced in excess of four million garments annually by 1935.[4707] Regan was the contractor for the construction of the original clothing factory located at 4119-4127 W. Belmont Avenue, and Olsen & Urbain was the architect for the original factory, which was being improved with the new added space.[4708] The new factory space was said to be able to accommodate 350 new

---

[4697] Chicago Daily Tribune. (March 13, 1934) P. 24. Retrieved from ProQuest Newspapers at Northwestern University.
[4698] Chicago Daily Tribune. (March 13, 1934) P. 24. Retrieved from ProQuest Newspapers at Northwestern University.
[4699] Chicago Daily Tribune. (March 13, 1934) P. 24. Retrieved from ProQuest Newspapers at Northwestern University.
[4700] Chicago Daily Tribune. (March 13, 1934) P. 24. Retrieved from ProQuest Newspapers at Northwestern University.
[4701] Chicago Daily Tribune. (March 13, 1934) P. 24. Retrieved from ProQuest Newspapers at Northwestern University.
[4702] Chicago Daily Tribune. (March 13, 1934) P. 24. Retrieved from ProQuest Newspapers at Northwestern University.
[4703] Chicago Daily Tribune. (March 13, 1934) P. 24. Retrieved from ProQuest Newspapers at Northwestern University.
[4704] Chicago Daily Tribune. (March 13, 1934) P. 24. Retrieved from ProQuest Newspapers at Northwestern University.
[4705] Chicago Daily Tribune. (March 13, 1934) P. 24. Retrieved from ProQuest Newspapers at Northwestern University.
[4706] Chicago Daily Tribune. (October 13, 1935) P. B8. Retrieved from ProQuest Newspapers at Northwestern University.
[4707] Chicago Daily Tribune. (October 13, 1935) P. B8. Retrieved from ProQuest Newspapers at Northwestern University.
[4708] Chicago Daily Tribune. (October 13, 1935) P. B8. Retrieved from ProQuest Newspapers at Northwestern University.

employees. The estimated construction project cost was reported to have been $90,000.[4709]

At the time of Robert Regan's death, he and Frances resided at a farm in Mokena, Illinois, located in Will County.[4710] Robert died of a heart attack while at Silver Cross Hospital in Joliet, Will County, Illinois.[4711] *The Joliet Herald-News* edition of August 17, 1948, ran an extensive and detailed obituary for Robert Regan.[4712] The obituary is reproduced here in part, and provides the names of additional important construction contracts that Regan received in Chicago, Cook County, Joliet, and in Grundy County, Illinois:

> "Mr. Regan was in charge of several current building projects. He was the contractor in charge of the remodeling of the Higinbotham building purchased by the Joliet Federal Savings and Loan and also of the Coca Cola Bottling company plant on the Plainfield road. He was contractor for one of the additions to Silver Cross hospital; for the Munroe Hatchery; the Public Service garage and offices; the Atlas Wallpaper company at Coal City; the Public Service substation at Bradley; the Tractor-Motive corporation building at Deerfield; the Kennedy Cochran corporation plant at Hillside. Chicago buildings which he constructed included the Motorola corporation plant, the Tropic-Aire plant, and the Petralager building. He also was in charge of the Chatham Housing project. A son of the late Mr. and Mrs. Charles Regan, he was born in Chippewa Falls, Wis. He was educated there. As a young man, he joined the army during World War I at Connecticut and with the 26th division was sent overseas. He remained on overseas duty for almost four years before returning to the states. With his return to civilian life, he began in the contracting business, first for a brief time in Wisconsin and then moving to Chicago."[4713]

Robert G. Regan also started the Regan Contracting Company of Chicago. He operated both this company and the Robert G. Regan Construction Company in Chicago and the metropolitan region.[4714] Robert became one of the most important

---

[4709] Chicago Daily Tribune. (October 13, 1935) P. B8. Retrieved from ProQuest Newspapers at Northwestern University.

[4710] Obituary for Robert Giles Regan. Chicago Tribune (August 18, 1948). P. A2. Retrieved from ProQuest Newspapers: Chicago Tribune. Database at Northwestern University.

[4711] Obituary for Robert Giles Regan. Chicago Tribune (August 18, 1948). P. A2. Retrieved from ProQuest Newspapers: Chicago Tribune. Database at Northwestern University.

[4712] ROBERT G. REGAN, CONTRACTOR, SUCCUMBS at 52. Obituary for Robert G. Regan. The Joliet Herald-News. (August 17, 1948). P. 1. Kathleenmanuel.com.

[4713] ROBERT G. REGAN, CONTRACTOR, SUCCUMBS at 52. Obituary for Robert G. Regan. The Joliet Herald-News. (August 17, 1948). P. 1. Kathleenmanuel.com.

[4714] Regan family historical records.

building contractors of the Chicago region, built many of the most architecturally and industrially significant corporate, commercial, and residential properties there, and was a leader of the Irish-American business community in Chicago. Many of the most important construction companies in Chicago were founded and owned by Irish-American businessmen. As Irish people emigrated to Chicago, and after the time when the Richardson Construction Company, which is discussed in Chapter 5, *The Foundations of Jackson Park*, dissolved, many Irish construction companies grew to immense importance. Both the Robert G. Regan Construction Company and the Regan Contracting Company exemplified this socioeconomic trend. Robert Giles Regan helped to build the manufacturing and transportational infrastructure of Chicago and the metropolitan region and contributed centrally to establishing the prominence of Chicago as a national and continental center for trucking and highways.

John Hanrahan Regan and Inez Regan of Chicago

John "Jack" Hanrahan Regan (1886-1955) was another son of Charles Timothy Regan and Margaret (Hanrahan) Regan. John served in World War I as a Private in the 2nd Company, Casual Detachment, from Minnesota.[4715] John Regan and wife Inez L. Regan (1891-1978), both of Chicago, resided at 1100 N. Dearborn Parkway, in the Gold Coast neighborhood during the 1950s and possibly earlier.[4716] John attended the Law School of the University of Michigan, in Ann Arbor, Michigan. Relocating to Chicago, John entered the lumber brokerage business. In 1930, John and wife Inez resided at 1263 Pratt Boulevard, located in Rogers Park.[4717] The Regan apartment was in Ward 49.[4718] John was listed as a salesman of excavating equipment at this time.[4719] Inez, a native of the State of Washington, and the daughter of a Norwegian mother and a Massachusetts-native father, worked as a stationer of bonds.[4720] The Pratt Boulevard residence was a rented apartment.[4721] The Regans owned a radio and paid a rent of $110 per month.[4722] As of 1940, John and Inez Regan resided at 420 Wrightwood Avenue in Lincoln Park.[4723] John and Inez had resided at the Wrightwood address since at least as early as 1935.[4724] In 1940, John was listed as a wholesale lumber broker.[4725] Inez

---

[4715] John Hanrahan Regan tombstone. Hope Cemetery. Chippewa Falls, Wisconsin.

[4716] John H. Regan Obituary. Chicago Daily Tribune. (August 10, 1955). P. B6. Retrieved from ProQuest Newspapers: Chicago Tribune. Database at Northwestern University.

[4717] 1930 United States Census. John H. Regan. Chicago. Retrieved from Ancestry.com.

[4718] 1930 United States Census. John H. Regan. Chicago. Retrieved from Ancestry.com.

[4719] 1930 United States Census. John H. Regan. Chicago. Retrieved from Ancestry.com.

[4720] 1930 United States Census. John H. Regan. Chicago. Retrieved from Ancestry.com.

[4721] 1930 United States Census. John H. Regan. Chicago. Retrieved from Ancestry.com.

[4722] 1930 United States Census. John H. Regan. Chicago. Retrieved from Ancestry.com.

[4723] 1940 United States Census. John H. Regan. Chicago. Retrieved from Ancestry.com.

[4724] 1940 United States Census. John H. Regan. Chicago. Retrieved from Ancestry.com.

[4725] 1940 United States Census. John H. Regan. Chicago. Retrieved from Ancestry.com.

worked as a saleslady at an unspecified department store.[4726] John and Inez resided at various times in the Rogers Park community, the Lincoln Park community, and the Gold Coast neighborhood of the Near North Community.[4727] Jack and Inez retired to Boynton Beach, in Palm Beach County, Florida. Jack died at Boynton Beach in August of 1955, and was interred at Chippewa Falls, Wisconsin.[4728] He was buried at Hope Cemetery, where his wife and siblings all were interred over the years.[4729] After her husband's death, Inez Regan became the housemother of Elizabeth Hall at Rollins College in Winter Park, Florida, at the same time when her grandniece, Charlotte Taylor, was a student at Rollins College and resident of Elizabeth Hall. By entering the lumber business, John Hanrahan Regan continued a multigenerational Regan family tradition of working in the lumber business. His father, Charles Timothy Regan, his uncles, Michael Regan and John Richard Regan, his grandfather, Michael Hanrahan, his granduncle, Michael Hogan, and his cousins, Patrick R. Hogan and Fred T. Ragan, all owned lumber companies, furniture companies, or wood-product companies in Wisconsin and Washington.

Frank Regan and Charles Regan of Chicago

Francis (Frank) "Cy" Regan (b. 1890), a Chicago resident and a son of Charles Timothy Regan and Margaret (Hanrahan) Regan, worked as a laborer in the steel mills of Gary, Indiana. Frank later resided in Indianapolis and retired to Shreveport, Louisiana. Cy Regan was reported to have been a Chicago street fighter, and possibly a prize fighter for a time in Chicago and St. Louis.[4730] His brother, Charles E. Regan (1884-1955), was a graduate of St. Thomas College in St. Paul, Minnesota. Charles resided in Chicago for forty years and went deaf as a young man. Charles' sister, Ruth (Regan) Bunn, his nephew, Robert Regan McKay, and his niece, Elizabeth (Bunn) Taylor, all went deaf at various points in their llives, as well. Cousin Margot McKay reported that Charles worked for a Chicago hardware store. It is possible that he worked also as a janitor in Chicago.[4731] Charles resided for a long time at the Victor Fremont Lawson Y.M.C.A. at the corner of Chicago Avenue and Dearborn Street at the southwest boundary of the Gold Coast neighborhood in the Near North Side community. Charles may have worked for his brothers, Robert Giles Regan and John Hanrahan Regan, who both owned Chicago companies (discussed above). Charles often wore

---

[4726] John H. Regan Obituary. Chicago Daily Tribune. (August 10, 1955). P. B6. Retrieved from ProQuest Newspapers: Chicago Tribune. Database at Northwestern University; 1930 United States Census. John H. Regan. Chicago. Retrieved from Ancestry.com; 1940 United States Census. John H. Regan. Chicago. Retrieved from Ancestry.com.
[4727] 1940 United States Census. John H. Regan. Chicago. Retrieved from Ancestry.com.
[4728] John H. Regan Obituary. Chicago Daily Tribune. (August 10, 1955). P. B6. Retrieved from ProQuest Newspapers: Chicago Tribune. Database at Northwestern University.
[4729] Hope Cemetery Records. Chippewa Falls, Wisconsin.
[4730] Memoir and anecdote given to Andrew Taylor Call by Robert Hatcher Bunn.
[4731] McKay, Margot. (Undated). Memoir of Regan, Hanrahan, McKay, Hogan family history. Telephone interview recorded by Andrew Taylor Call.

a trench coat, walked the streets of the city alone, and was isolated socially because of deafness, according to his late niece, Margot McKay.

Paul W. McKay and Jean (Regan) McKay of Chicago

Paul W. McKay (1884-1959), who was a son of Rev. William John McKay (1847-1921) and Arabella Abergale (Roberts) McKay (1846-1926), married Jean Regan (1892-1970), who was the daughter of Charles Timothy Regan and Margaret (Hanrahan) Regan.[4732] Rev. William John McKay of Madison, Wisconsin, walked from Madison to Evanston in order to attend Northwestern University. William John McKay graduated from Northwestern and became a famous Methodist minister in Illinois and Wisconsin. He also owned real estate interests. Northwestern University was a Methodist university. Many members of the Regan-McKay family have attended Northwestern University over many generations. William married Arabella Roberts, whose family, orignally from Raleigh Courthouse, West Virginia, had moved from Raleigh Courthouse to Chicago.[4733] Raleigh Courthouse became Beckley, West Virginia.

Paul W. McKay and Jean Regan were married at Holy Name Cathedral in Chicago on June 19, 1917.[4734] Paul W. McKay was a real estate broker in Chicago. In 1924, McKay operated an office at 77 W. Washington Street, located in the Loop.[4735] The firm went by the business name of P. W. McKay & Company.[4736] The company telephone number in December, 1924, was listed as Dearborn 9795.[4737] In 1936, Paul was appointed chief officer of the Industrial Real Estate section of a company known as Bills Realty, Inc.[4738] Paul McKay also worked for Hogan & Farwell.[4739] In 1912, McKay, employed by H. O. Stone & Company, brokered the $35,000 sublease of two floors of space on North Morgan Street to the E. W. Bredemeier Company.[4740] McKay and John W. Cameron were the brokers for the sale of 609 N. La Salle to La Salle Laboratories, Inc.[4741] The seller

---

[4732] Regan, Hanrahan, McKay family historical records; findagrave.com. Forest Hill Cemetery, Madison Wisconsin.
[4733] Regan, McKay family historical records.
[4734] Eau Claire Leader. (June 19, 1917). P. 7. Newspapers.com.
[4735] Chicago Daily Tribune. (December 10, 1924). P. 41. Retrieved from ProQuest Newspapers: Chicago Tribune. Database at Northwestern University.
[4736] Chicago Daily Tribune. (December 10, 1924). P. 41. Retrieved from ProQuest Newspapers: Chicago Tribune. Database at Northwestern University.
[4737] Chicago Daily Tribune. (December 10, 1924). P. 41. Retrieved from ProQuest Newspapers: Chicago Tribune. Database at Northwestern University.
[4738] Chicago Daily Tribune. (August 30, 1936). P. 23. Retrieved from ProQuest Newspapers: Chicago Tribune. Database at Northwestern University.
[4739] Chicago Daily Tribune. (January 28, 1945). P. A6. Retrieved from ProQuest Newspapers: Chicago Tribune. Database at Northwestern University.
[4740] Chicago Daily Tribune. (October 6, 1912). P. A3. Retrieved from ProQuest Newspapers: Chicago Tribune. Database at Northwestern University.
[4741] Chicago Daily Tribune. (January 28, 1945). P. A6. Retrieved from ProQuest Newspapers: Chicago Tribune. Database at Northwestern University.

party to the land sale contract was the Lake Shore National Bank.[4742] The five-story building was redesigned by Frank O. De Money.[4743] The new occupant was stated to be a manufacturer of bathroom accessories.[4744] Paul also engaged in Chicago land investment, having sold a single-story, 6,000-square foot building at the northeast corner of Palmer and Knox, to Charles F. Glaeser.[4745] The real estate was located in or near the Hermosa community of Chicago.[4746] The sale price of the McKay property was reported to be $26,000.[4747] Glaeser planned to use the building for the production of laundry machines.[4748] Paul McKay brokered the lease contract of a building located at 4711 W. Lake Street, in which the landlord, Solomon G. Robbins, leased the building to the Chicago Machine Products Company for the contextually presumed purpose of making automobile locks.[4749] The building was designed by the architecture firm of Olsen & Urbain, and contained 10,000 square feet of floor space.[4750] In 1944, as an employee of Hogan & Farwell, McKay brokered the lease of 822 S. Michigan Avenue to the General Controls Company of Glendale, California.[4751] The contract of lease stipulated a rent of $18,000.[4752] The listed lessors were American Radiator and the Standard Sanitary corporation.[4753]

Robert Regan McKay (1921-2016), son of Paul W. McKay and Jean (Regan) McKay, also worked for the Hogan & Farwell Company of Chicago.[4754] In 1956, McKay brokered the contract for the lease of land located at 333 W. Lake Street

[4742] Chicago Daily Tribune. (January 28, 1945). P. A6. Retrieved from ProQuest Newspapers: Chicago Tribune. Database at Northwestern University.

[4743] Chicago Daily Tribune. (January 28, 1945). P. A6. Retrieved from ProQuest Newspapers: Chicago Tribune. Database at Northwestern University.

[4744] Chicago Daily Tribune. (January 28, 1945). P. A6. Retrieved from ProQuest Newspapers: Chicago Tribune. Database at Northwestern University.

[4745] Chicago Daily Tribune. (December 6, 1925). P. B2. Retrieved from ProQuest Newspapers: Chicago Tribune. Database at Northwestern University.

[4746] Perry, Marilyn Elizabeth. (2005). Hermosa. The Encyclopedia of Chicago. encyclopedia.chicagohistory.org.

[4747] Chicago Daily Tribune. (December 6, 1925). P. B2. Retrieved from ProQuest Newspapers: Chicago Tribune. Database at Northwestern University.

[4748] Chicago Daily Tribune. (December 6, 1925). P. B2. Retrieved from ProQuest Newspapers: Chicago Tribune. Database at Northwestern University.

[4749] Chicago Daily Tribune. (September 29, 1922). P. 24. Retrieved from ProQuest Newspapers: Chicago Tribune. Database at Northwestern University.

[4750] Chicago Daily Tribune. (September 29, 1922). P. 24. Retrieved from ProQuest Newspapers: Chicago Tribune. Database at Northwestern University.

[4751] Chicago Daily Tribune. (December 24, 1944). P. A4. Retrieved from ProQuest Newspapers: Chicago Tribune. Database at Northwestern University.

[4752] Chicago Daily Tribune. (December 24, 1944). P. A4. Retrieved from ProQuest Newspapers: Chicago Tribune. Database at Northwestern University.

[4753] Chicago Daily Tribune. (December 24, 1944). P. A4. Retrieved from ProQuest Newspapers: Chicago Tribune. Database at Northwestern University.

[4754] Chicago Daily Tribune. (February 22, 1969). P. A5. Retrieved from ProQuest Newspapers: Chicago Tribune. Database at Northwestern University.

to Marquette Cement Manufacturing Company.[4755] Marquette Cement planned to use its portion of the 250,000-square foot space for a laboratory.[4756] The building contained ten stories.[4757] Robert White served as Vice-President of Hogan & Farwell, Inc. at the time of the report of this contract for lease.[4758] In 1961, McKay acted as broker for the contract for sale of the 6,000-square foot building located at Elston-Central.[4759] McKay was employed by Hogan & Farwell at this time.[4760] In 1963, Robert McKay and Robert McKenna, both employed by the Hogan & Farwell Company, brokered the contract for the sale of the Hotpoint Company building located at 1961 S. Laramie, in Cicero, located in Cook County.[4761] The buyer of the real estate was Aldens, Inc., a mail order business.[4762] The seller was Hotpoint, Inc., which was a subsidiary company of General Electric.[4763] In 1961, McKay served as broker of the Hotpoint Company contract for lease of land from the Commonwealth Edison Company.[4764] The land property element of the consideration of the Hotpoint lease contract included space located at the Edison building.[4765] McKay worked for Hogan & Farwell, Inc., at the time of this lease brokerage, as well.[4766] In 1962, the *Chicago Tribune* reported that Chicago contained approximately 35,000,000 square feet of office space.[4767] The article reported multiple plans for construction of new buildings.[4768] The time period from 1958 until 1962 was reported as a time of corporate movement and relocation to

[4755] Chicago Daily Tribune. (June 30, 1956). P. B5. Retrieved from ProQuest Newspapers: Chicago Tribune. Database at Northwestern University.
[4756] Chicago Daily Tribune. (June 30, 1956). P. B5. Retrieved from ProQuest Newspapers: Chicago Tribune. Database at Northwestern University.
[4757] Chicago Daily Tribune. (June 30, 1956). P. B5. Retrieved from ProQuest Newspapers: Chicago Tribune. Database at Northwestern University.
[4758] Chicago Daily Tribune. (June 30, 1956). P. B5. Retrieved from ProQuest Newspapers: Chicago Tribune. Database at Northwestern University.
[4759] Chicago Daily Tribune. (June 18, 1961). P. A9. Retrieved from ProQuest Newspapers: Chicago Tribune. Database at Northwestern University.
[4760] Chicago Daily Tribune. (June 18, 1961). P. A9. Retrieved from ProQuest Newspapers: Chicago Tribune. Database at Northwestern University.
[4761] Chicago Daily Tribune. (July 6, 1963). P. 5. Retrieved from ProQuest Newspapers: Chicago Tribune. Database at Northwestern University.
[4762] Chicago Daily Tribune. (July 6, 1963). P. 5. Retrieved from ProQuest Newspapers: Chicago Tribune. Database at Northwestern University.
[4763] Chicago Daily Tribune. (July 6, 1963). P. 5. Retrieved from ProQuest Newspapers: Chicago Tribune. Database at Northwestern University.
[4764] Chicago Daily Tribune. (July 7, 1961). P. C7. Retrieved from ProQuest Newspapers: Chicago Tribune. Database at Northwestern University.
[4765] Chicago Daily Tribune. (July 7, 1961). P. C7. Retrieved from ProQuest Newspapers: Chicago Tribune. Database at Northwestern University.
[4766] Chicago Daily Tribune. (July 7, 1961). P. C7. Retrieved from ProQuest Newspapers: Chicago Tribune. Database at Northwestern University.
[4767] Chicago Daily Tribune. (June 22, 1962). P. C8. Retrieved from ProQuest Newspapers: Chicago Tribune. Database at Northwestern University.
[4768] Chicago Daily Tribune. (June 22, 1962). P. C8. Retrieved from ProQuest Newspapers: Chicago Tribune. Database at Northwestern University.

the downtown of Chicago.[4769] Leo J. Sheridan, who was Chairman of the Leo J. Sheridan Company, had assembled a list of companies that relocated to downtown Chicago, and reported that there was a "return-to-the city movement"[4770] among companies located within the Chicago vicinity.[4771] Sheridan indicated that the company migration, "accounted for 500,000 square feet of space. . ."[4772] This time was one defined by rapid and vibrant commercial growth and change for the Chicago downtown.[4773]

Robert Regan McKay and myriad other industrial brokers participated in this time and phenomenon of commercial movement, corporate migration, and commercial geographical renaissance in Chicago.[4774] In 1962, McKay brokered the sale, effected by the seller party St. Regis Paper Company, of 61,000 square feet of real estate located at 1440 W. 21st Place, to the purchaser party Flexi-Mat Corporation.[4775] Howard E. Kaplan collaborated with McKay as broker of this sale.[4776] The sale price of the land at W. 21st Place was reported to be $180,000.[4777] In 1969 McKay and Carl Tritchsler brokered the $650,000 sale of the Air Lines Pilot Association International building located at 6440 S. Cicero Avenue.[4778] The purchaser party was the Central States Motor Freight Bureau, Inc.[4779] McKay and Tritchsler brokered the sale of the building along with the 97,000 square feet of space attached to the building site.[4780]

Paul W. McKay was a Voice Major at Northwestern University, and was said to have been a Glee Club member while at Northwestern.[4781] It was Paul McKay who

---

[4769] Chicago Daily Tribune. (June 22, 1962). P. C8. Retrieved from ProQuest Newspapers: Chicago Tribune. Database at Northwestern University.
[4770] Chicago Daily Tribune. (June 22, 1962). P. C8. Retrieved from ProQuest Newspapers: Chicago Tribune. Database at Northwestern University.
[4771] Chicago Daily Tribune. (June 22, 1962). P. C8. Retrieved from ProQuest Newspapers: Chicago Tribune. Database at Northwestern University.
[4772] Chicago Daily Tribune. (June 22, 1962). P. C8. Retrieved from ProQuest Newspapers: Chicago Tribune. Database at Northwestern University.
[4773] Chicago Daily Tribune. (June 22, 1962). P. C8. Retrieved from ProQuest Newspapers: Chicago Tribune. Database at Northwestern University.
[4774] Chicago Daily Tribune. (June 22, 1962). P. C8. Retrieved from ProQuest Newspapers: Chicago Tribune. Database at Northwestern University.
[4775] Chicago Daily Tribune. (June 22, 1962). P. C8. Retrieved from ProQuest Newspapers: Chicago Tribune. Database at Northwestern University.
[4776] Chicago Daily Tribune. (June 22, 1962). P. C8. Retrieved from ProQuest Newspapers: Chicago Tribune. Database at Northwestern University.
[4777] Chicago Daily Tribune. (June 22, 1962). P. C8. Retrieved from ProQuest Newspapers: Chicago Tribune. Database at Northwestern University.
[4778] Chicago Daily Tribune. (February 22, 1969). P. A5. Retrieved from ProQuest Newspapers: Chicago Tribune. Database at Northwestern University.
[4779] Chicago Daily Tribune. (February 22, 1969). P. A5. Retrieved from ProQuest Newspapers: Chicago Tribune. Database at Northwestern University.
[4780] Chicago Daily Tribune. (February 22, 1969). P. A5. Retrieved from ProQuest Newspapers: Chicago Tribune. Database at Northwestern University.
[4781] Bunn, Regan, and McKay family history.

had been a major source of encouragement for my grandmother, Elizabeth "Biz" Bunn (later, Mrs. Henry Stryker Taylor), to attend Northwestern University.[4782] Elizabeth Bunn matriculated at Northwestern as a member of the Class of 1939.[4783] Paul McKay was a member of the City Club of Chicago, a public policy discussion and analysis club that had been established in Chicago in 1903.[4784] Paul W. McKay was listed as a new member of the City Club of Chicago as of January 6, 1919, along with eighty-two other people.[4785] Of significant interest is the fact that another one of the eighty-three new members of the City Club of Chicago, as of January 6, 1919, was, "Robert A. Millikan, Professor of Physics, University of Chicago."[4786] Due to the alphabetical order within the City Club's 1919 membership announcement, Professor Robert A. Millikan's name appeared immediately after Paul W. McKay's name in the list of new members.[4787] The eighty-three members of the City Club of Chicago included many notable people with diverse occupations and backgrounds.[4788] Frank Hatch Jones, Esq., son-in-law of Jacob Bunn and Elizabeth (Ferguson) Bunn, was one of the founders of the City Club of Chicago in 1903. For more about this history, see Chapter 2, *Builders of the Downtown*.

Mary Regan/Rehan of Wisconsin and New York City

Mary Regan (1887-1963) was the eldest daughter of Charles Timothy Regan and Margaret (Hanrahan) Regan. Mary moved to New York City, where she studied theater, became an actress on Broadway, and performed in many important plays. She performed with the Ben Greet Players of New York City and was the first actress to portray "Jo" in the Broadway production of *Little Women*.[4789] She also performed the role of "Night" in Maeterlinck's *Blue Bird*, and acted under the theater direction of Jessie Bonstelle.[4790] During World War I Mary managed the Stage Women's War Relief in France.[4791] Due to having her name billed erroneously as "Mary Rehan" in the cast of one of her theater performances, Mary

---

[4782] Bunn, Regan, and McKay family history.

[4783] Bunn, Regan, and McKay family history.

[4784] The City Club Bulletin: A Journal of Active Citizenship. (January 6, 1919). Vol. 12, Number 1. P. 7. Google Books.

[4785] The City Club Bulletin: A Journal of Active Citizenship. (January 6, 1919). Vol. 12, Number 1. P. 7. Google Books.

[4786] The City Club Bulletin: A Journal of Active Citizenship. (January 6, 1919). Vol. 12, Number 1. P. 7. Google Books.

[4787] The City Club Bulletin: A Journal of Active Citizenship. (January 6, 1919). Vol. 12, Number 1. P. 7. Google Books.

[4788] The City Club Bulletin: A Journal of Active Citizenship. (January 6, 1919). Vol. 12, Number 1. P. 7. Google Books.

[4789] New York Times. (August 20, 1963). Page not given. Kathleenmanuel.com; Regan family history records.

[4790] New York Times. (August 20, 1963). Page not given. Kathleenmanuel.com.

[4791] New York Times. (August 20, 1963). Page not given. Kathleenmanuel.com.

assumed the incorrect name and used it as her professional name from that point onward.

After a career in acting, Mary attended night law school at the Brooklyn Law School. Upon graduation, she passed the New York Bar and worked for the Barnes, Chilvers & Halstead Law Firm of New York City, where she developed practice specializations in international trade law and tax law.[4792] She subsequently started the Rehan Law Firm of New York City and Washington, D.C., and earned an international reputation for excellence in trade jurisprudence.[4793] She participated in New York City civic life. She founded the Museum of Costume Art in New York City with Irene Lewisohn and Nelson Rockefeller.[4794] Mary served as Secretary and Treasurer of the Museum of Costume Art.[4795] The Metropolitan Museum of Art acquired the Museum of Costume Art, and Mary served both as Director of the Costume Institute of the Metropolitan Museum of Art, and as an Honorary Life Fellow of the Metropolitan Museum of Art.[4796] Mary also co-founded the International Bar Association and supported and developed this organization.[4797]

Mary Rehan was a member of the Women's National Republican Club, a friend and supporter of Franklin Delano Roosevelt, and a friend of Eleanor Roosevelt.[4798] She was co-founder and Treasurer of the Independent Coalition of American Women.[4799] Another co-founder of the Independent Coalition of American Women was Mrs. Kellogg Fairbank of Chicago.[4800] Margot McKay of Chicago, niece of Mary Rehan, stated that Mary had been friends with the Everleigh Sisters of Chicago. No further information has been discovered regarding that friendship and association, but Mary Rehan and the Everleigh Sisters may have known each other through Chicago Vaudevillian and Burlesque circles.

Multiple other members of the Ragan/Regan-Hogan-Powers family resided in and around Chicago at some time or another. Mary Driscoll, a cousin of the Regans of Chippewa Falls and Chicago, resided in Woodstock, Illinois.[4801] The Regans visited their cousin Mary Driscoll, were good friends of hers, and were very much in touch with her, according to newspapers records. This concludes the history of our Irish-American families from Wisconsin and Chicago.

[4792] New York Times. (August 20, 1963). Page not given. Kathleenmanuel.com.
[4793] New York Times. (August 20, 1963). Page not given. Kathleenmanuel.com.
[4794] New York Times. (August 20, 1963). Page not given. Kathleenmanuel.com.
[4795] New York Times. (August 20, 1963). Page not given. Kathleenmanuel.com.
[4796] New York Times. (August 20, 1963). Page not given. Kathleenmanuel.com.
[4797] New York Times. (August 20, 1963). Page not given. Kathleenmanuel.com.
[4798] New York Times. (August 20, 1963). Page not given. Kathleenmanuel.com; Regan family historical records.
[4799] New York Times. (August 20, 1963). Page not given. Kathleenmanuel.com.
[4800] Pittsburgh Post-Gazette. (July 1, 1936). P. 2. Newspapers.com.
[4801] Regan/Ragan, Driscoll family historical records.

Willard Bunn. Of Springfield. Member of Board of Directors of the Chicago-based Illinois Chamber of Commerce. President of Springfield Chamber of Commerce. Coal entrepreneur. Land entrepreneur. Restauranteur. Director of Sangamo Electric Company of Springfield and Chicago. Vice-President and Director of Illinois Watch Company of Springfield and Chicago. Director of Central Illinois Public Service Company, a company of Springfield and Chicago which owned the Joliet Electric Railway, the Dellwood Park Company, and the Joliet Traction Company, located within Will County and Cook County. President of Bunn Capitol Grocery Company of Springfield. Co-financier of Heath Bar and of the Steak n' Shake Company. Member of Illini Country Club and Sangamo Club of Springfield. Son of George Wallace Bunn, Sr., and Ada Willard (Richardson) Bunn. Husband of Ruth (Regan) Bunn. Brother of George Wallace Bunn, Jr. Great-grandfather of Andrew Taylor Call. (Image courtesy of author's personal collection).

Willard Bunn, Sr., in later years. (Image courtesy of author's personal collection).

George Wallace Bunn, Jr. Of Springfield and New York City. President of Springfield Marine Bank. Director of Sangamo Electric Company of Springfield and Chicago. Member of the University Club of Chicago. Member of the Chicago and Springfield-based Illinois Frozen Asset Board. Trustee of Blackburn College. Author and woodworker. Son of George Wallace Bunn, Sr., and Ada Willard (Richardson) Bunn. Brother of Willard Bunn. Husband of Melinda (Jones) Bunn. Graduate of Princeton University. Publishing partner of Sinclair Lewis in the Lewis & Bunn Company. (Image courtesy of author's personal collection).

Brothers Willard Bunn, Sr. (right), and George Wallace Bunn, Jr. (left), as young men. Sons of George Wallace Bunn, Sr. and Ada Willard (Richardson) Bunn. Grandsons of Jacob Bunn and Elizabeth (Ferguson) Bunn. Grandsons of William Douglas Richardson of Chicago. Grand-nephews of James Henry Richardson of Chicago. Cousins of Col. Charles Richardson of Chicago, Charles Richardson, Esq., and Hiram Adsit Richardson of Chicago, and multiple other family members from Chicago. Great-grandnephews of James Moore Willard of Chicago. (Image courtesy of author's personal collection).

Ruth Regan as a young woman. Of Wisconsin, Chicago, and Springfield. Native of Chippewa Falls, Wisconsin. Graduate of the Chicago Musical College. Resident of Evanston and Chicago. Married Willard Bunn of Springfield. Great-grandmother of author Andrew Taylor Call. (Image courtesy of author's personal collection).

Ruth (Regan) Bunn. Pianist. President of the Springfield Music Club. Co-founder of Blessed Sacrament Church and School. Member of Blessed Sacrament Church, Springfield. (Image courtesy of author's personal collection).

Col. Charles Richardson, Jr. Of Chicago and Springfield. Commander of the Illinois Civil Air Patrol. Founder of the Chicago Headquarters of the Illinois Civil Air Patrol. Co-founder and reorganizer of the Illinois Civil Air Patrol. Prominently associated with the founding of the United States Civil Air Patrol. Executive at a Chicago heating company. Developer of Chicago aviation infrastructure and technology. Developer of Chicago airborne search, surveillance, rescue, and security systems. Resident of Rogers Park community of Chicago and later of Glenview, a Cook County suburb. Nephew of William Douglas Richardson. Husband of Hazel Howard. Father of Willard Harding Richardson and Howard Chandler Richardson. Cousin of Ada Willard (Richardson) Bunn. (Images courtesy of Ruth Solomon).

Robert Giles Regan and sister Mary Regan. Of Chicago and New Lenox. Robert was the founder and President of R. G. Regan Construction Company of Chicago. Founder and President of Regan Contracting Company of Chicago. Co-founder and Director of Chatham Park, Inc., the Chicago real estate and development company that developed the immense Chatham Park housing neighborhood on S. Cottage Grove Avenue. Chatham Park was, at the time of its construction, the largest housing complex in Chicago. Building contractor for Chatham Park neighborhood in South Side of Chicago. Building contractor for multiple industrial buildings and spaces throughout Chicago, Joliet, Evanston, and much of the metropolitan region. Builder of many large industrial buildings of Cook County and Will County. Headquarters of R. G. Regan Construction Company was located at the Builders' Building on Wacker Drive, in the Loop. Son of Charles and Margaret (Hanrahan) Regan of Wisconsin. (Image courtesy of author's personal collection).

Charles Regan. Of Chicago. Laborer and employee of a dry goods store in Chicago. Resident of the Victor Fremont Lawson Y.M.C.A., located in the Near North Side community. Alumnus of St. Thomas College in Minnesota. Became deaf. Resident of Chicago for at least forty years. Son of Charles T. Regan and Margaret (Hanrahan) Regan of Wisconsin. (Image courtesy of author's personal collection).

John Hanrahan Regan. Of Chicago. Founder and President of Regan Lumber Company, a Chicago lumber brokerage company. Alumnus of the University of Michigan, where he studied law. Resident of Rogers Park, Lincoln Park, and Gold Coast. Retired to Boynton Beach, Florida. Son of Charles T. Regan and Margaret (Hanrahan) Regan of Wisconsin. (Image courtesy of author's personal collection).

Jean (Regan) McKay. Of Wisconsin, Chicago, Evanston, and Wilmette. Saleslady at Marshall Field & Company. Organist at a Catholic church in Evanston. Wife of Paul W. McKay. Resident of Chicago and Evanston. Daughter of Charles T. Regan and Margaret (Hanrahan) Regan. (Image courtesy of author's personal collection).

Paul W. McKay as Child with Mother. Of Chicago, Evanston, and Wilmette. Real estate broker with Hogan & Farwell Company of Chicago. Founder and President of McKay Realty Company of Chicago. Land investor. Member of the City Club of Chicago. Specialist in urban commercial and industrial real estate brokerage. Husband of Jean Regan of Wisconsin and Chicago. Son of Rev. William John McKay of Chicago, Evanston, and Madison, Wisconsin, and Arabella (Roberts) McKay. (Image courtesy of author's personal collection).

Mary Regan. Of Wisconsin and New York City. Actress on Broadway with Ben Greet Players. First to portray Jo in *Little Women* on Broadway. Became an international and domestic trade lawyer. Actress in New York City. Said to have been friends with the Everleigh Sisters of Chicago. Co-founder of the Museum of Costume Art in New York City. Honorary Fellow of the Metropolitan Museum of Art in New York City. Co-founder and supporter of the International Bar Association. Founder of international law firm of New York City and Washington, D.C. National political activist and reformer. She changed her surname to Rehan after she was accidentally billed under that name for a theater performance. (Image courtesy of author's personal collection).

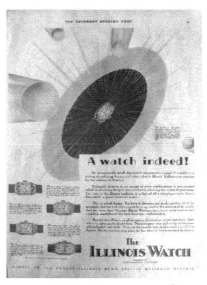

Illinois Watch Company Advertisements. The Illinois Watch Company was based in Springfield and possessed a preeminent commercial and technological presence in Chicago and Cook County. (Image courtesy of author's personal collection).

Sangamo Electric Company Advertisement. The Sangamo Electric Company was based in Springfield and possessed a preeminent commercial and technological presence in Chicago and Cook County. (Image courtesy of author's personal collection).

Illinois Watch Company railroad pocket watches (left).
Sangamo Electric Company tachograph (top right).
Sangamo Electric Company electric mantle clock (bottom right).
(Images and objects courtesy of author's personal collection).

Illinois Watch Company wallet and memorial wooden box.
(Images and objects courtesy of author's personal collection).

Robert Carr Lanphier. Of Springfield. Engineer and inventor. Graduate of Yale University. Co-founder of Sangamo Electric Company, which possessed a major industrial presence in Chicago. Developer of electric meter technologies for the whole world. Protégé of Jacob Bunn, Jr., Henry Bunn, and John W. Bunn of Chicago and Springfield. Cousin of Annie Richardson (Lanphier) Lynn of Springfield and Toronto. (Image courtesy of *Sangamo: A History of Fifty Years*, by Robert Carr Lanphier and Benjamin P. Thomas, 1949).

Part of the Taylor family of Cass County, Illinois. Henry Stryker Taylor standing second from left. Robert Cunningham Taylor, Jr. standing at right. The Taylor brothers both were connected to business in Chicago, Springfield, and Cass County. Robert was a resident of Hyde Park and Beverly. Robert owned an investment company. Henry was President of the McClure-Stryker-Taylor Land Company. Lady second from right is Rebecca MacEachran, who was a Taylor cousin from Ontario, Canada. Rebecca was brought in to help care for Henry and Robert after the boys' mother, Charlotte (Stryker) Taylor, died one week after Henry's birth in 1908. (Image courtesy of author's personal collection).

Carle Cotter Conway. Of Oak Park, Chicago, and New York City. One of the most important industrial leaders and builders of Chicago and Cook County, as well as of New York City and the Pittsburgh region. Principal builder and leader of the Continental Can Company of Chicago, New York City, and Pennsylvania. Business mentor and teacher to Loren Ralph Dodson of Columbus, Ohio, New York City, and Chicago. (Image courtesy of Heather and Barton Pembroke).

Carle Cotter Conway. Of Oak Park and Chicago. Pictured here as a young boy. Son of Edwin Stapleton Conway and Sarah Judson (Rogers) Conway. (Image courtesy of Heather and Barton Pembroke).

Loren Ralph Dodson. Of Columbus, Ohio, New York City, and Chicago. Member of the Van Duyn-Peterson-Ramsey-Call Family of Ohio, Indiana, and Illinois. Secretary and Treasurer of Continental Can Company, one of the largest Chicago corporations of all time. Secretary of Continental Can Company of Chicago, Inc. Vice-President of White Cap Company of Chicago. Secretary-Treasurer of Cameron Can Machine Company of Chicago. Secretary-Treasurer of the Conway Company of Massachusetts and Chicago. Secretary-Treasurer of the Elmer Mills Plastics Company, another Chicago division of Continental Can Company. As a protégé of Carle Cotter Conway, Dodson served as one of the co-founders of the reorganized Continental Can Company in the 1920s. As a major builder and executive of Continental Can Company (the parent corporation), as well as of multiple Continental Can Company subsidiaries, Dodson was prominently connected with at least 24 major Chicago companies and industrial organizations as executive officer, consultant, and in certain cases, co-founder. Member of Board of Directors of the Firemen's Mutual Insurance Company of Providence, Rhode Island. (Images courtesy of The Ohio State University and its Archives).

Robert Grogan Call. Of Ohio and West Virginia. First chemist in the history of the American Gas and Electric Company (American Electric Power Company) of Ohio and New York City. Founder of the chemistry and chemical engineering sections of American Gas and Electric Co. Early builder of the American Gas and Electric Co. Co-founder and co-reorganizer of the American Gas & Electric Company/American Electric Power Company in 1937. Founder of the American Gas and Electric Service Corporation Laboratory. Co-founder and founding chemist of the American Gas & Electric Service Corporation. Chief Chemist and Senior Engineer, American Electric Power Company. The American Electric Power Company contributed prominently to Chicago and Cook County through cooperation with the Comed Company of Chicago in construction of a two-company power line cooperation and alliance system that connected Cook County to St. Joseph County, Indiana, via powerlines and pylons. Early member and builder of the American Society of Lubrication Engineers, a national organization of Chicago and Pittsburgh. Inventor of industrial soaps. Inventor of power station washing technologies that have long since been employed throughout the world. Inventor of the world's first process and chemical for the caustic washing of power station turbines. Member of the Van Duyn-Peterson-Ramsey-Call Family of Ohio, Indiana, and Illinois, and the Nixon-Humphreys-McCullough-Call Family of Ohio. (Image courtesy of author's personal collection).

Robert Grogan Call in the American Gas and Electric Service Corporation General Laboratory. Call founded the General Laboratory and served with Philip Sporn as co-founder of the American Gas & Electric Service Corporation of New York City. While Philip Sporn was President of the Service Corporation and while Robert G. Call served as the Chief Chemist and Senior Engineer of the Service Corporation, the company exerted tremendous impact on Chicago and the metropolitan region through the promotion of nuclear energy technologies. (Image courtesy of author's personal collection).

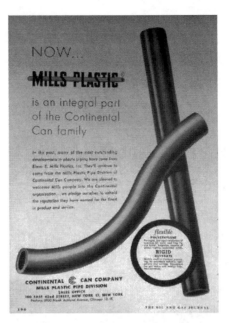

Continental Can Company advertisement for the Elmer Mills Plastics Division of Chicago. Under the leadership of Carle C. Conway, Loren R. Dodson served as a co-founder, builder, and leader of Continental Can Company. He also was Secretary-Treasurer of Elmer Mills Plastics Company of Chicago, when it was a subsidiary of the Continental Can Company. (Image courtesy of author's personal collection).

Frank Regan. Of Chicago and Gary, Indiana. Son of Charles Timothy Regan and Margaret (Hanrahan) Regan of Wisconsin. Laborer in the steel mills of Gary, Indiana. Later moved to Indianapolis. Retired to Shreveport, Louisiana. (Image courtesy of author's personal collection).

Henry Stryker Taylor. Of Springfield and Delray Beach, Florida. Banker, bank director, farm manager, and capitalist. Husband of Elizabeth Bunn. Father of three. Grandfather of author Andrew Taylor Call. Taylor was one of the two controlling individual (non-institutional) stockholders of the Pennsylvania Railroad Company, a corporation that possessed immense presence in Chicago. Associated, as a controlling stockholder of the Pennsylvania Railroad Company, with multiple subsidiary Chicago railroad companies and properties including the Pittsburgh, Fort Wayne & Chicago Railroad Company, the Wabash Railroad Company (which had been founded largely by John Whitfield Bunn), the Englewood Connecting Railway Company, and multiple short line railroads of Chicago and the metropolitan region. Director of Springfield Marine Bank. President of the McClure-Stryker-Taylor land company of Illinois and Michigan. Graduate of Knox College. Reported to have been prominently associated with Northern Trust Company of Chicago, perhaps as investor, depositor, and possibly as a Director. Member of the Racquet Club of Chicago and the Chicago Athletic Association. (Image courtesy of Fabian Bachrach, 1960s, and author's personal collection).

693

Robert Cunningham Taylor, Jr. Of Chicago, Cass County, and Springfield. Brother of Henry Stryker Taylor. Graduate of Knox College. Received an M.B.A. from Harvard University. Banker and capitalist at Chicago. Resident of the Hyde Park and Beverly communities. Formed a large sole proprietorship investment company that controlled thousands of shares of the United States Steel Corporation, as well as large quantities of Illinois real estate. Died in service in U.S. Army in 1944, in Operation Market Garden, in WWII. (Image courtesy of author's personal collection).

Robert Cunningham Taylor, Jr. (Man at center, in suit). 1930s photograph. (Image courtesy of author's personal collection).

William Frederic Call. Of Ohio, California, and Denver. Executive Assistant to the President and founder of Hankins Container Company, a major shipping container manufacturing company of Cleveland, Ohio, and Chicago. Editor of the company newsletter of Hankins Container Company. A protégé of company founder Edward Hankins, Call was a builder of the Hankins Container Company of Cleveland and Chicago over many years, having been among the very first employees in the history of the company. Sales and personnel executive within the company. Co-founder, Secretary, and Treasurer of the Santa Ana Container Company of Southern California, a manufacturer of cargo shipping containers for produce and other cargo. Founding General Manager of the Inter-Mountain Packaging Division of Fibreboard Corporation of San Francisco. Co-founder of a gold mining partnership company in the Rocky Mountains of Colorado. Consultant to the United States shipping container industry. Member of the Van Duyn-Peterson-Ramsey-Call Family of Ohio, Indiana, and Illinois. Member of the Nixon-Humphreys-McCullough-Call Family of Ohio. Attended Martin's Ferry High School in Martin's Ferry, Ohio. Graduated from Lakewood High School in Lakewood, Cuyahoga County, Ohio. Married Mary Elizabeth Baldwin of Butler County, Pennsylvania, Cleveland, and Lakewood, Ohio. Grandfather of author Andrew Taylor Call. (Image courtesy of author's personal collection).

Henry Stryker Pierson, Esq. Of Chicago and Evanston. Lawyer. Sales Manager of the Chicago District of Dow Chemical Company. Graduate of Washington University of St. Louis. Cousin of Henry Stryker Taylor (below). Member of the Stryker family of Chicago, St. Louis, and Jacksonville, Illinois. (Image courtesy of the *St. Louis Star and Times*, November 10, 1949, and courtesy of the *St. Louis Post-Dispatch*).

Henry Stryker Taylor. Cousin of Henry Stryker Pierson (above). President of the McClure-Stryker-Taylor Land Company. Vice-President and Director of the Springfield Marine Bank. One of the two largest individual stockholders of the Pennsylvania Railroad Co., which was one of the largest corporations in Chicago, New York City, and Philadelphia. Taylor was one of the leading people in North American coal transportation. Track and Field contestant in the 1932 Olympic Trials in Los Angeles. Grandfather of Andrew Taylor Call. (Image courtesy of author's personal collection).

Henry Stryker Taylor. Captain of the Knox College Track Team. Taylor ran the 100 Yard Dash in 9.6 seconds. He tried out for the 1932 Olympics in Los Angeles and was associated with the Los Angeles Athletic Club. (Image courtesy of author's personal collection).

Henry Stryker Taylor and Robert Cunningham Taylor, Jr. Photograph believed to have been taken in Jacksonville, Illinois, near the Stryker house. (Image courtesy of author's personal collection).

Henry Stryker Taylor and Robert Cunningham Taylor, Jr. Location probably the Robert Cunningham Taylor, Sr., house in Virginia, Cass County, Illinois. Winter season discernible from the snow outside the window. (Image courtesy of author's personal collection).

Robert Cunningham Taylor, Jr. Resident of Hyde Park community of Chicago and the Beverly community of Chicago. Banker. Owner of a large sole proprietorship land and investment company. Granduncle of Andrew Taylor Call. (Image courtesy of author's personal collection).

Exterior view of Union Station, Chicago, Illinois, 1925. The Pennsylvania Railroad Company at one time owned fifty-percent of Union Station. Henry Stryker Taylor was one of the two controlling individual (non-institutional) shareholders of the Pennsylvania Railroad Company at the time when the railroad company jointly owned Union Station. (Image courtesy of the Chicago History Museum; CHM-Digital Obj ID: ICHi-038858; Kaufman & Fabry Co., photographer).

Exterior view of Union Station from the northeast corner of the Jackson Boulevard Bridge, Chicago, Illinois, June 19, 1959. (Image courtesy of the Chicago History Museum; CHM-Digital Obj ID: ICHi-065062; J. Sherwin Murphy, photographer).

Interior view of Chicago Union Station. (Image courtesy of the Chicago History Museum; CHM-Digital Obj ID: ICHi-69655).

699

Joseph Hall Hart, Jr. Of Cincinnati and Greenwich, Connecticut. Son of Dr. Joseph Hall Hart, Sr., and Elizabeth (Stryker) Hart. Joe was a University of Cincinnati alumnus, and studied Civil Engineering. He founded the Cincinnati Builders Credit Company in cooperation with his father and brother. Joe became one of the most renowned pilots for Pan American World Airways, specializing in the piloting of Pan Am Clippers. He set multiple aviation records. (Image courtesy of the Archives and Rare Books Library at the University of Cincinnati in Cincinnati, Ohio).

John Babinger Hart. Of Cincinnati and Fort Lauderdale, Florida. Son of Dr. Joseph Hall Hart. Sr., and Elizabeth (Stryker) Hart. John was a University of Cincinnati alumnus. He founded the Cincinnati Builders Credit Company in cooperation with his father and brother. He worked as an airport manager and airport developer for Pan American World Airways. John Hart helped manage airports in Texas, Miami, Brazil, Port of Spain, Trinidad, Haiti, and Jamaica. John founded the John B. Hart Construction Company of Fort Lauderdale. (Image courtesy of ancestry.com).

Walter Jager. Of Chicago. Manufacturer and broker of metal products. Founder of the Jager & Associates Company of Chicago, broker of metal products. Owner of Pattee Pattern Works Company of Chicago, manufacturer and broker of metal castings. Husband of Dorothy (Palmer) Jager. Member, by marriage, of the Bunn Family of Chicago and Springfield. (Image courtesy of Jamie Overom Pyzik and Wendy Overom Paymard).

Chester Selden Bunn. Of Dallas, Texas, and Duluth, Minnesota. Member of the Bunn Family of New Jersey, Illinois, Texas, and California. Secretary of the Dallas Storage and Warehouse Company of Texas. This company engaged in a transfer and storage trade that spanned the United States and included multiple counterparties in and around Chicago. Assistant Chief Accountant of American Steel and Wire Company of Duluth. Son of George Whitfield Bunn, Jr., and Alice (Fishbough) Bunn of Dallas, Texas, and Duluth, Minnesota. Husband of Ina Belle Johnson of Wisconsin. Brother of Emily May Bunn, who married Horace Lucius Palmer. (Image courtesy of Jamie Overom Pyzik and Wendy Overom Paymard).

Horace Lucius Palmer. Of Duluth, and later of Elmhurst, Illinois. Treasurer of the H. Miscampbell Body Corporation of Duluth. Husband of Emily May Bunn. Son-in-law of George Whitfield Bunn, Jr. Father of Dorothy Palmer, who married Walter Jager of Chicago. (Image courtesy of Jamie Overom Pyzik and Wendy Overom Paymard).

Henry Stryker Taylor. Circa 1961. Picture taken at a party celebrating Taylor's twenty years on the Board of Directors of Springfield Marine Bank of Illinois, which was the bank where Abraham Lincoln had an account. This bank was founded by Jacob Bunn, Robert Irwin, and others, in 1851, and was the oldest extant bank in Illinois in the 1990s when it was acquired. (Image courtesy of author's personal collection).

MRS. HENRY S. TAYLOR, *Springfield, Ill.*
by Fritz Werner

Elizabeth (Bunn) Taylor. Of Springfield and Delray Beach, Florida. Northwestern University alumna (Class of 1939). Majored in Voice and Music. Member of Kappa Alpha Theta Sorority. Social Chairman of the Willard Hall Annex at Northwestern during Freshman year at the university. Philanthropist. Wife of Henry Stryker Taylor. Daughter of Willard Bunn and Ruth (Regan) Bunn. Sister of Willard Bunn, Jr. Mother of three daughters. Maternal grandmother of author Andrew Taylor Call. Alumna of Villa Duchesne School of St. Louis and graduate of Miss Porter's School in Farmington, Connecticut. Member and supporter of Catholic churches in Springfield and in Florida. This portrait of Elizabeth "Biz" Taylor was commissioned in 1949, and painted by Fritz Werner, a noted portraitist. (Portrait and image courtesy of author's personal collection).

Willard Bunn, Jr. Of Springfield. Chairman of Springfield Marine Bank. Director of Sangamo Electric Company of Springfield and Chicago. Was one of the longest serving members of the Board of Directors of Illinois Bell Telephone Company of Chicago. Member of the Council for Branch Banking, based in Chicago and Springfield. Advocate for Illinois branch banking policy and law. Civic leader of Illinois. Member of the Union League Club. Great-grandson of Jacob Bunn. Son of Willard Bunn and Ruth (Regan Bunn). Father of three. Granduncle of author Andrew Taylor Call. (Image courtesy of author's personal collection).

Dr. Charles Kane Zelle, M.D. Of Springfield and Chicago. One of the leading obstetricians and gynecologists of Illinois. Graduate of Lake Forest Academy, Dartmouth College, and Northwestern University Medical School. Professor of Medicine at Northwestern University. Medical Director and Vice-President of Medical Affairs for Arnar-Stone Laboratories, Inc., of Mt. Prospect, in metropolitan Chicago. Founder of a large real estate investment company in Chicago. Dr. Zelle was a member of the Irwin-Stockdale-Brittin Family of Springfield and Chicago and was a cousin of the Bunns and Irwins of Springfield and Chicago. He was a close friend of Henry Stryker Taylor and Elizabeth (Bunn) Taylor. (Image courtesy of author's personal collection).

Willard Harding Richardson (on right) and Howard Chandler Richardson (on left) as young boys. Sons of Charles Richardson, Jr. of Chicago. Grandsons of Charles Richardson, Sr., of Springfield. Grand-nephews of William Douglas Richardson, Dr. Frank Richardson, James Henry Richardson, and others. Cousins of Myron Richardson and Charles Richardson, Esq. of Chicago. Cousins of Ada Willard (Richardson) Bunn. Howard died as a young man. Willard worked for many decades for Marshall Field & Company in Chicago where he worked as a cargo loader and in other cargo management capacities. Willard was a resident of Rogers Park, and a graduate of Sullivan High School. (Image courtesy of Ruth Solomon).

Lydia Morton Lee. Of Chicago. Member of the Ferguson family of Chicago, Springfield, and Pennsylvania. Graduate of the University of Chicago. Daughter of William Lee and Florence (Ferguson) Lee. Graduate of Hyde Park High School. Cousin of Elizabeth Jane (Ferguson) Bunn and Benjamin Hamilton Ferguson. Resident of Hyde Park community. (Image courtesy of Susan Alland and her family).

Margot McKay. Of Chicago, Evanston, and Wilmette. Graduate of New Trier High School. Saleslady at Marshall Field & Company for many decades. Helped open the branch stores of Marshall Field & Company at Milwaukee, Wisconsin, and at Park Forest, Illinois. Daughter of Paul W. McKay and Jean (Regan) McKay. (Image courtesy of author's personal collection).

Robert Regan McKay. Of Chicago, Evanston, and Wilmette. Brother of Margot McKay. U.S. Army veteran of World War II. Real estate broker with Hogan & Farwell Company of Chicago. Founder and President of Robert R. McKay Realty Company of Chicago. Specialist in urban commercial and industrial real estate brokerage. Resident of Gold Coast neighborhood. Son of Paul W. McKay and Jean (Regan) McKay. (Image courtesy of author's personal collection).

Chapter 8

Ode to Pylons and Cannery Windows

A Chemist's Prayer

"O God, come into the laboratory
Of my soul and take the catalysts of perspective
And maturity of mind that control
And activate me and my reactions
And its effect on others. . . Please neutralize
The irritating acids of my selfishness
With the basic elements of your love
To yield kindness and thoughtfulness. . . Lord, Crystallize in me some of the
beauty of Jesus. . .
Now before you leave, Lord,
Remember the corrosive fumes
Diffusing through the laboratory air
And the constant change wrought by
The worldly variables, and that without you
I am amenable to their effects.
So please it you, O God,
To give me enough of yourself and your essence
To effectively buffer me against these subtle forces.
I thank you for yourself and for hearing me, heavenly Father,
Omniscient and understanding Chemist
Of the laboratory of my soul. Amen."[4802]

—H. Orville Heisey

Introduction

This chapter presents the histories of the Call, Dodson, Peterson, and Bunn families of Chicago. For the other histories of the Bunn family, consult the following chapters: Chapter 2, *Builders of the Downtown* (for the Wabash Railroad Company history, the Chicago & Alton Railroad Company history, the Chicago Republican Company/Inter Ocean Company history, the Springfield Iron Company history); and Chapter 5, *The Foundations of Jackson Park* (for the 1893 World's Columbian Exposition history). The surnames from my paternal family that are included within this chapter are Call, Dodson, Ramsey, McCullough, Peterson, and Van Duyn. Throughout multiple generations, the Calls have served United States industry in myriad capacities through the founding and leadership of multiple industrial corporations and related organizations in Ohio, Illinois, and

---

[4802] Heisey, H. Orville. (1957). A Chemist's Prayer. Journal of the American Scientific Affiliation. Asa3.org.

California.[4803] Several members of this family have exerted an exceedingly important impact on the growth and development of industry and civic organizations in Chicago and Cook County.[4804] Robert Grogan Call,[4805] Loren Ralph Dodson,[4806] and John Abel Peterson[4807] all were principal builders of major Chicago and Cook County organizations.[4808] These organizations include the Continental Can Company,[4809] the American Society of Lubrication Engineers,[4810] the Farmers' National Life Insurance Company of America,[4811] the Chicago Union Stockyards canning factories,[4812] and many others.

The Illinois Watch Company

The Illinois Watch Company of Springfield developed a key industrial presence in Chicago over a period of time and must be considered both a Springfield company and a Chicago company for multiple reasons. The company was established as the Springfield Watch Company in Springfield, in 1870, by John C. Adams, John Whitfield Bunn, John Todd Stuart, Dr. George Pasfield, George N. Black, John Williams, and William B. Miller.[4813] The corporation financing produced $100,000 in original capital.[4814] John Stuart, who was a law partner of Abraham Lincoln, became the first president of the company. William Miller was the first Secretary, and the first board of directors consisted of Stuart, Bunn,

---

[4803] See generally: references sources and support herein.

[4804] See generally: references sources and support herein.

[4805] See generally: references sources and support herein.

[4806] See generally: references sources and support herein.

[4807] See generally: references sources and support herein.

[4808] See generally: references sources and support herein.

[4809] Porter, John Sherman. (Editor-in-Chief). (1959). Moody's Industrial Manual: American and Foreign. P. 2754. New York, NY: Moody's Investors Service.

[4810] Call, Ramsey, Peterson, Van Duyn, and Pittenger family records.

[4811] Whitson, Rolland Lewis. (General Editor). (1914). Centennial History of Grant County, Indiana: 1812-1912. Vol. 2. P. 1293. Chicago, IL: The Lewis Publishing Company. Google Books.

[4812] Murphy, James Francis. (1958). The Pre-Supervisory Training Program (Continental Can Company) at Plant # 51 (Stockyards): A Case Study. Loyola University Chicago Master's Theses. Paper 1660. Ecommons.luc.edu.

[4813] Call, Andrew Taylor. (2005). Jacob Bunn: Legacy of an Illinois Industrial Pioneer. Pp. 180-181. Lawrenceville, VA: Brunswick Publishing Corporation; Anonymous. (Circa 1913). Illinois Watch Company, Springfield, Illinois, U.S.A. pp. 1-4. (In possession of the Sangamon Valley Collection of the Lincoln Library (The Public Library of Springfield)).

[4814] Call, Andrew Taylor. (2005). Jacob Bunn: Legacy of an Illinois Industrial Pioneer. Pp. 180-181. Lawrenceville, VA: Brunswick Publishing Corporation; Anonymous. (Circa 1913). Illinois Watch Company, Springfield, Illinois, U.S.A. Pp. 1-4. (In possession of the Sangamon Valley Collection of the Lincoln Library (The Public Library of Springfield)).

Pasfield, Williams, Black, and Miller.[4815] The company formation plan, inclusive of financing, incorporation, factory construction, and the watch-making machinery installations, occupied about two years, from 1869 until 1871.[4816] The company constructed a factory complex on North Grand Avenue, between Ninth Street and Eleventh Street, in Springfield. The Springfield Watch Company awarded the $18,025 factory construction contract to John T. Rhodes, who completed the construction by approximately January of 1871. Watch production commenced circa May, 1871, and the first batch of completed timepieces was presented in January, 1872.[4817] Watch production reached a rate of 100 watches per month by March, 1872.[4818]

The Panic of 1873, which destabilized the United States economy and resultantly, much of the world economy, forced the company to the edge of insolvency and dissolution, and caused the J. Bunn Bank of Springfield to fail in 1878.[4819] The Panic of 1873 caused the market for the Springfield Watch Company timepieces to disappear; this market failure left the company with a large stock of watches, little capital with which to dissolve costs, and little market from which to create revenues and profits.[4820] The Panic of 1873 caused, therefore, the activation

---

[4815] Call, Andrew Taylor. (2005). Jacob Bunn: Legacy of an Illinois Industrial Pioneer. Pp. 180-181. Lawrenceville, VA: Brunswick Publishing Corporation; Anonymous. (Circa 1913). Illinois Watch Company, Springfield, Illinois, U.S.A. Pp. 1-4. (In possession of the Sangamon Valley Collection of the Lincoln Library (The Public Library of Springfield)).

[4816] Call, Andrew Taylor. (2005). Jacob Bunn: Legacy of an Illinois Industrial Pioneer. Pp. 180-182. Lawrenceville, VA: Brunswick Publishing Corporation; Anonymous. (Circa 1913). Illinois Watch Company, Springfield, Illinois, U.S.A. pp. 1-4. (In possession of the Sangamon Valley Collection of the Lincoln Library (The Public Library of Springfield)); Meggers, William, and Ehrhardt, Roy. (1985). American Pocket Watches: Illinois Watch Company. Vol. 2. P. 21. Heart of America Press.

[4817] Call, Andrew Taylor. (2005). Jacob Bunn: Legacy of an Illinois Industrial Pioneer. Pp. 180-182. Lawrenceville, VA: Brunswick Publishing Corporation; Anonymous. (Circa 1913). Illinois Watch Company, Springfield, Illinois, U.S.A. Pp. 1-4. (In possession of the Sangamon Valley Collection of the Lincoln Library (The Public Library of Springfield)); Meggers, William, and Ehrhardt, Roy. (1985). American Pocket Watches: Illinois Watch Company. Vol. 2. P. 21. Heart of America Press.

[4818] Call, Andrew Taylor. (2005). Jacob Bunn: Legacy of an Illinois Industrial Pioneer. Pp. 180-182. Lawrenceville, VA: Brunswick Publishing Corporation; Anonymous. (Circa 1913). Illinois Watch Company, Springfield, Illinois, U.S.A. Pp. 1-4. (In possession of the Sangamon Valley Collection of the Lincoln Library (The Public Library of Springfield)); Meggers, William, and Ehrhardt, Roy. (1985). American Pocket Watches: Illinois Watch Company. Vol. 2. P. 21. Heart of America Press.

[4819] Weekly Davenport Democrat (Iowa). (January 10, 1878). P. 1. Newspapers.com.

[4820] Call, Andrew Taylor. (2005). Jacob Bunn: Legacy of an Illinois Industrial Pioneer. Pp. 183-184. Lawrenceville, VA: Brunswick Publishing Corporation; Anonymous. (Circa 1913). Illinois Watch Company, Springfield, Illinois, U.S.A. Pp. 1-4. (In possession of the Sangamon Valley Collection of the Lincoln Library (The Public Library of

of the most severe market risk that could have faced the new company. The resultant market failure forced the company leadership to undertake an emergency-driven financing, which produced $50,000 in emergency equity money.[4821] The new equity sum, however, was too small to allay the financial disaster that faced the company, and despite the sales of more than 10,000 watches by circa December, 1872, the Springfield Watch Company stood on the brink of failure and probable consequent dissolution.[4822] The competition risk that Elgin Watch Company and Waltham Watch Company brought about for the Springfield Watch Company combined with the Panic of 1873-derived market risk to form a perfect storm of blended risk and economic failure for the Springfield corporation.[4823] Subsequent failed financing endeavors took place during the years 1874 through 1877, and the ultimate failure of the company provided a crucial opportunity for corporate reorganization.[4824] As of January, 1877, one year prior to the closure of the J. Bunn Bank, Springfield Watch Company generated sales revenue that was gravely inadequate in light of the company operational costs, the market risk caused by the ongoing fallout of the Panic of 1873, and the continual competition risk stemming from the Elgin and Waltham companies.[4825]

Springfield)); Meggers, William, and Ehrhardt, Roy. (1985). American Pocket Watches: Illinois Watch Company. Vol. 2. P. 21. Heart of America Press.

[4821] Call, Andrew Taylor. (2005). Jacob Bunn: Legacy of an Illinois Industrial Pioneer. Pp. 183-184. Lawrenceville, VA: Brunswick Publishing Corporation; Anonymous. (Circa 1913). Illinois Watch Company, Springfield, Illinois, U.S.A. Pp. 1-4. (In possession of the Sangamon Valley Collection of the Lincoln Library (The Public Library of Springfield)); Meggers, William, and Ehrhardt, Roy. (1985). American Pocket Watches: Illinois Watch Company. Vol. 2. P. 21. Heart of America Press.

[4822] Call, Andrew Taylor. (2005). Jacob Bunn: Legacy of an Illinois Industrial Pioneer. Pp. 183-184. Lawrenceville, VA: Brunswick Publishing Corporation; Anonymous. (Circa 1913). Illinois Watch Company, Springfield, Illinois, U.S.A. Pp. 1-4. (In possession of the Sangamon Valley Collection of the Lincoln Library (The Public Library of Springfield)); Meggers, William, and Ehrhardt, Roy. (1985). American Pocket Watches: Illinois Watch Company. Vol. 2. P. 21. Heart of America Press.

[4823] Call, Andrew Taylor. (2005). Jacob Bunn: Legacy of an Illinois Industrial Pioneer. Pp. 183-184. Lawrenceville, VA: Brunswick Publishing Corporation; Anonymous. (Circa 1913). Illinois Watch Company, Springfield, Illinois, U.S.A. Pp. 1-4. (In possession of the Sangamon Valley Collection of the Lincoln Library (The Public Library of Springfield)); Meggers, William, and Ehrhardt, Roy. (1985). American Pocket Watches: Illinois Watch Company. Vol. 2. Pp. 21-22. Heart of America Press.

[4824] Call, Andrew Taylor. (2005). Jacob Bunn: Legacy of an Illinois Industrial Pioneer. Pp. 183-184. Lawrenceville, VA: Brunswick Publishing Corporation; Anonymous. (Circa 1913). Illinois Watch Company, Springfield, Illinois, U.S.A. Pp. 1-4. (In possession of the Sangamon Valley Collection of the Lincoln Library (The Public Library of Springfield)); Meggers, William, and Ehrhardt, Roy. (1985). American Pocket Watches: Illinois Watch Company. Vol. 2. Pp. 21-22. Heart of America Press.

[4825] Call, Andrew Taylor. (2005). Jacob Bunn: Legacy of an Illinois Industrial Pioneer. Pp. 183-184. Lawrenceville, VA: Brunswick Publishing Corporation; Anonymous. (Circa

The corporate failure provided an excellent opportunity for immediate and exigent reorganization that John W. Bunn, Jacob Bunn, Otis Hoyt, and W. J. Konkling seized, thereby capturing an economically dramatic victory from an apparently inevitable defeat.[4826] On January 3, 1877, John W. Bunn, Hoyt, and Konkling formed an emergency reorganization board. Deliberation by the board produced a plan whose terms contemplated the sale of the company with the condition that the buyer would assume all corporate debt and absolve the existing stockholders of all corporate liability.[4827] The plan thus called for the purchase of the company, but not dissolution, and called for the removal of the residual stockholder liabilities and assumption of company debts.

The company was never sold, however, and the plan of January 3, 1877, was never realized. An alternative plan superseded the January, 1877, plan on March 22, 1877, when Illinois Secretary of State George N. Harlew approved the pleading for incorporation of the Illinois Springfield Watch Company, which was the organizational successor to the Springfield Watch Company.[4828] The new company was capitalized with $100,000. The new name reflected the desire to distinguish the company from the New York Watch Company, which possessed a location in Springfield, Massachusetts, and which manufactured a line of watches under the name "Springfield."[4829] The reorganization plan which began in March, 1877, was

1913). Illinois Watch Company, Springfield, Illinois, U.S.A. Pp. 1-4. (In possession of the Sangamon Valley Collection of the Lincoln Library (The Public Library of Springfield)); Meggers, William, and Ehrhardt, Roy. (1985). American Pocket Watches: Illinois Watch Company. Vol. 2. Pp. 21-23. Heart of America Press.

[4826] Call, Andrew Taylor. (2005). Jacob Bunn: Legacy of an Illinois Industrial Pioneer. Pp. 183-187. Lawrenceville, VA: Brunswick Publishing Corporation; Anonymous. (Circa 1913). Illinois Watch Company, Springfield, Illinois, U.S.A. Pp. 1-4. (In possession of the Sangamon Valley Collection of the Lincoln Library (The Public Library of Springfield)); Meggers, William, and Ehrhardt, Roy. (1985). American Pocket Watches: Illinois Watch Company. Vol. 2. Pp. 21-25. Heart of America Press.

[4827] Call, Andrew Taylor. (2005). Jacob Bunn: Legacy of an Illinois Industrial Pioneer. Pp. 183-186. Lawrenceville, VA: Brunswick Publishing Corporation; Anonymous. (Circa 1913). Illinois Watch Company, Springfield, Illinois, U.S.A. Pp. 1-4. (In possession of the Sangamon Valley Collection of the Lincoln Library (The Public Library of Springfield)); Meggers, William, and Ehrhardt, Roy. (1985). American Pocket Watches: Illinois Watch Company. Vol. 2. Pp. 21-25. Heart of America Press.

[4828] Call, Andrew Taylor. (2005). Jacob Bunn: Legacy of an Illinois Industrial Pioneer. Pp. 183-186. Lawrenceville, VA: Brunswick Publishing Corporation; Anonymous. (Circa 1913). Illinois Watch Company, Springfield, Illinois, U.S.A. Pp. 1-4. (In possession of the Sangamon Valley Collection of the Lincoln Library (The Public Library of Springfield)); Meggers, William, and Ehrhardt, Roy. (1985). American Pocket Watches: Illinois Watch Company. Vol. 2. Pp. 21-25. Heart of America Press.

[4829] Call, Andrew Taylor. (2005). Jacob Bunn: Legacy of an Illinois Industrial Pioneer. Pp. 183-185. Lawrenceville, VA: Brunswick Publishing Corporation; Anonymous. (Circa 1913). Illinois Watch Company, Springfield, Illinois, U.S.A. Pp. 1-4. (In possession of the Sangamon Valley Collection of the Lincoln Library (The Public Library of

completed in July, 1877, and included, among other points of law, the cancellation of much of the debt that remained from the Springfield Watch Company.[4830] Sales revenue remained deficient and incapable of covering operational costs as of December, 1877, and Erastus Newton Bates, who was the second president of the company after John Todd Stuart, resigned from office with the belief that the company was fiscally futile and hopeless.[4831]

The Bates resignation in July, 1878, led to the final reorganization of the watch company and the process that would transform the company into a center of global market power. The board of directors of the Illinois Springfield Watch Company published a notice on November 18, 1878, which contained a summons of a stockholders' meeting.[4832] The purpose of the first meeting was the deliberation regarding the issue of change in the corporation name from Illinois Springfield Watch Company to Illinois Watch Company. The stockholders supported the name change and the name changed to Illinois Watch Company in November or December, 1878. The change in names appeared in a public notice and report of December 31, 1878.[4833] Jacob Bunn performed a central function in the change of the name to Illinois Watch Company and he soon became the third president of the company, in December, 1878. The Jacob Bunn years revolutionized the company and the entire watchmaking industry of the world. Contemporary reports stated

Springfield)); Meggers, William, and Ehrhardt, Roy. (1985). American Pocket Watches: Illinois Watch Company. Vol. 2. Pp. 21-25. Heart of America Press.

[4830] Call, Andrew Taylor. (2005). Jacob Bunn: Legacy of an Illinois Industrial Pioneer. Pp. 183-186. Lawrenceville, VA: Brunswick Publishing Corporation; Anonymous. (Circa 1913). Illinois Watch Company, Springfield, Illinois, U.S.A. Pp. 1-4. (In possession of the Sangamon Valley Collection of the Lincoln Library (The Public Library of Springfield)); Meggers, William, and Ehrhardt, Roy. (1985). American Pocket Watches: Illinois Watch Company. Vol. 2. Pp. 21-25. Heart of America Press.

[4831] Call, Andrew Taylor. (2005). Jacob Bunn: Legacy of an Illinois Industrial Pioneer. Pp. 183-186. Lawrenceville, VA: Brunswick Publishing Corporation; Anonymous. (Circa 1913). Illinois Watch Company, Springfield, Illinois, U.S.A. Pp. 1-4. (In possession of the Sangamon Valley Collection of the Lincoln Library (The Public Library of Springfield)); Meggers, William, and Ehrhardt, Roy. (1985). American Pocket Watches: Illinois Watch Company. Vol. 2. Pp. 21-25. Heart of America Press.

[4832] Call, Andrew Taylor. (2005). Jacob Bunn: Legacy of an Illinois Industrial Pioneer. Pp. 183-187. Lawrenceville, VA: Brunswick Publishing Corporation; Anonymous. (Circa 1913). Illinois Watch Company, Springfield, Illinois, U.S.A. Pp. 1-4. (In possession of the Sangamon Valley Collection of the Lincoln Library (The Public Library of Springfield)); Meggers, William, and Ehrhardt, Roy. (1985). American Pocket Watches: Illinois Watch Company. Vol. 2. Pp. 21-25. Heart of America Press.

[4833] Call, Andrew Taylor. (2005). Jacob Bunn: Legacy of an Illinois Industrial Pioneer. Pp. 183-187. Lawrenceville, VA: Brunswick Publishing Corporation; Anonymous. (Circa 1913). Illinois Watch Company, Springfield, Illinois, U.S.A. Pp. 1-4. (In possession of the Sangamon Valley Collection of the Lincoln Library (The Public Library of Springfield)); Meggers, William, and Ehrhardt, Roy. (1985). American Pocket Watches: Illinois Watch Company. Vol. 2. Pp. 21-25. Heart of America Press.

that Jacob Bunn had lost approximately $1,000,000 in the two watch companies as of January, 1879, in addition to the approximately $1,000,000 which he had lost in the failure of the J. Bunn Bank, and the hundreds of thousands which he had lost in the Chicago Republican Company.[4834]

Jacob Bunn served as president and co-founder of the new Illinois Watch Company, and Charles Smorowski served as secretary of the firm.[4835] The 1881 *History of Sangamon County, Illinois*, contains a detailed report of the post-reorganization growth of the Illinois Watch Company, and this report detailed the prosperity of the first four years of the Jacob Bunn presidency of the company. The company employed 160 people in 1877, 180 people in 1878, 260 people in 1879, and 400 people in 1880.[4836] The annualized production output of the company grew constantly during the Jacob Bunn years and totaled 18,040 watches in 1877, 19,035 watches in 1878, 33,285 watches in 1879, and 47,065 watches in 1880.[4837] The total annualized employee wages also concurrently increased at a constant rate, with $84,000 in 1877, $96,000 in 1878, $125,000 in 1879, and $207,000 in 1880.[4838] Growth continued and, as of about 1911, the Illinois Watch Company had cumulatively paid around $20,000,000 in worker wages from about 1870 until about 1911, according to one historical source.

The Bunn family and the Illinois Watch Company promoted worker safety, worker rights, and fair work schedules, having instituted an eight-hour workday for the approximately 600 company employees in January, 1885.[4839] The company also paid for the vaccination of its entire workforce against smallpox on November 5, 1901.[4840] The Illinois Watch Company became a key party to much of the Chicago watch market and manufactured multiple brands of watch for many of the largest Chicago dry goods companies.[4841] United States lawyer and corporate historian Frederic J. Friedberg, Esq., who is the author of a multivolume series of books about the Illinois Watch Company, discussed the multiple famous and important Chicago production contracts that the Illinois Watch Company

---

[4834] Call, Andrew Taylor. (2005). Jacob Bunn: Legacy of an Illinois Industrial Pioneer. P. Lawrenceville, VA: Brunswick Publishing Corporation.

[4835] History Of Sangamon County, Illinois. (1881). P. 574. Chicago, IL: Inter-State Publishing Company. Google Books.

[4836] History Of Sangamon County, Illinois. (1881). P. 574. Chicago, IL: Inter-State Publishing Company. Google Books.

[4837] History Of Sangamon County, Illinois. (1881). P. 574. Chicago, IL: Inter-State Publishing Company. Google Books.

[4838] History Of Sangamon County, Illinois. (1881). P. 574. Chicago, IL: Inter-State Publishing Company. Google Books.

[4839] St. Louis Post-Dispatch. (January 3, 1885). P. 12. Newspapers.com.

[4840] The St. Louis Republic. (November 6, 1901). P. 12. Newspapers.com.

[4841] Friedberg, Frederic J. (2018). The Illinois Watch & Its Hamilton Years: The Finale Of A Great American Watch Company. Vol. 2. Altglen, PA: Schiffer Publishing, Ltd.

performed.[4842] Montgomery Ward and Company contracted with Illinois Watch Company to manufacture the entire "Washington Watch Company" brand of watches, which was a private label merchandise line that Montgomery Ward and Company carried exclusively.[4843] Illinois Watch Company, therefore, produced and supplied an entire brand of merchandise for Montgomery Ward and Company of Chicago.[4844] Friedberg described the elements of the contracted-for process as having included the formation of the production contract between the Illinois Watch Company and Montgomery Ward and Company, the manufacture of the watches by Illinois Watch Company, the stamping of the watches by Illinois Watch, and the subsequent supply of the watches to Montgomery Ward and Company by Illinois Watch.[4845] Upon receipt of the watches under the Washington Watch Company brand name, Montgomery Ward and Company would attach watch cases to the Illinois watch movements and provide the timepieces for sale through its company stores and sales catalogues.[4846]

The Illinois Watch Company produced two separate lines of watches for Sears, Roebuck and Company: one line under the private label called Plymouth Watch Company, which was owned and sold exclusively by Sears, Roebuck and Company; and the other line under the label called Interstate Chronometer.[4847] Some measure of irony can be discovered in the fact that Sears, Roebuck and Company would encase the Illinois Watch Company movements for the Interstate Chronometer label in Dueber Watch Case Company cases.[4848] The Illinois Watch Company co-founded and helped administer the largely Chicago-based monopoly known as the American Watch Trust Company (known also as the American Jewelers' Trust), which had commercially opposed and subdued the Dueber Watch Case Company when Dueber failed to obey American Watch Trust Company price

---

[4842] Friedberg, Frederic J. (2018). The Illinois Watch & Its Hamilton Years: The Finale Of A Great American Watch Company. Vol. 2. Altglen, PA: Schiffer Publishing, Ltd.
[4843] Friedberg, Frederic J. (2018). The Illinois Watch & Its Hamilton Years: The Finale Of A Great American Watch Company. Vol. 2. P. 354-355. Altglen, PA: Schiffer Publishing, Ltd.
[4844] Friedberg, Frederic J. (2018). The Illinois Watch & Its Hamilton Years: The Finale Of A Great American Watch Company. Vol. 2. P. 354-355. Altglen, PA: Schiffer Publishing, Ltd.
[4845] Friedberg, Frederic J. (2018). The Illinois Watch & Its Hamilton Years: The Finale Of A Great American Watch Company. Vol. 2. P. 354-355. Altglen, PA: Schiffer Publishing, Ltd.
[4846] Friedberg, Frederic J. (2018). The Illinois Watch & Its Hamilton Years: The Finale Of A Great American Watch Company. Vol. 2. P. 354-355. Altglen, PA: Schiffer Publishing, Ltd.
[4847] Friedberg, Frederic J. (2018). The Illinois Watch & Its Hamilton Years: The Finale Of A Great American Watch Company. Vol. 2. Pp. 355-357. Altglen, PA: Schiffer Publishing, Ltd.
[4848] Chicago Tribune. (April 10, 1895). P. 7. Newspapers.com.

and sales policies.[4849] The Sears Roebuck Interstate Chronometer brand line consisted of multiple forms of watch from the Illinois Watch Company, including the 15-jewel watch movement in zero size, the 17-jewel watch movement in zero size, the 17-jewel watch movement in 12 size, 21-jewel watch movement in 12 size, and both the 17-jewel watch movement and the 23-jewel watch movement in both the 16 size and the 18 size.[4850] The watches were signed with the brand name, Interstate Chronometer.[4851]

The Illinois Watch Company produced a line of watches for Marshall Field and Company and did so under the label of Ariston U.S.A. Illinois manufactured the watch movements (the actual watch machinery) and dials (watch faces), but Marshall Field and Company produced the watch cases.[4852] The Ariston U.S.A. product line of Marshall Field and Company included the Ariston U.S.A., Ariston, Jr., Ariste, and Ariston Rated brands as subsidiary product labels within the same overall product family.[4853] Friedberg reported that the Ariste brand watches were, "among the very first 6/0 size, grade 903 movements produced by Illinois."[4854] In addition, the Illinois Watch Company was the principal producer of watches for the Burlington Watch Company of Chicago, and this was a commercial relationship which would only have strengthened the already immense Chicago market and sales presence of the Illinois Watch Company.[4855]

Willard Bunn, Sr. (1888-1959), who was Vice-President and a director of the Illinois Watch Company, negotiated the sale of the company to Hamilton Watch Company of Lancaster, Pennsylvania, in 1927. The acquisition contract that Bunn negotiated stipulated that Hamilton would purchase the Illinois Watch factory, goodwill, and intellectual property for between $5,000,000 and $6,000,000.[4856]

[4849] Chicago Tribune. (April 10, 1895). P. 7. Newspapers.com.

[4850] Friedberg, Frederic J. (2018). The Illinois Watch & Its Hamilton Years: The Finale Of A Great American Watch Company. Vol. 2. Pp. 355-357. Altglen, PA: Schiffer Publishing, Ltd.

[4851] Friedberg, Frederic J. (2018). The Illinois Watch & Its Hamilton Years: The Finale Of A Great American Watch Company. Vol. 2. Pp. 355-357. Altglen, PA: Schiffer Publishing, Ltd.

[4852] Friedberg, Frederic J. (2018). The Illinois Watch & Its Hamilton Years: The Finale Of A Great American Watch Company. Vol. 2. Pp. 357-359. Altglen, PA: Schiffer Publishing, Ltd.

[4853] Friedberg, Frederic J. (2018). The Illinois Watch & Its Hamilton Years: The Finale Of A Great American Watch Company. Vol. 2. Pp. 357-359. Altglen, PA: Schiffer Publishing, Ltd.

[4854] Friedberg, Frederic J. (2018). The Illinois Watch & Its Hamilton Years: The Finale Of A Great American Watch Company. Vol. 2. Pp. 357-359. Altglen, PA: Schiffer Publishing, Ltd.

[4855] Friedberg, Frederic J. (2018). The Illinois Watch & Its Hamilton Years: The Finale Of A Great American Watch Company. Vol. 2. Pp. 357-359. Altglen, PA: Schiffer Publishing, Ltd.

[4856] The Star Press. (Muncie, Indiana). (January 1, 1928). P. 1. Newspapers.com.

John Whitfield Bunn owned eleven twelfths of the Illinois Watch Company at the time of his death only a few years before the sale.[4857] The sale and transfer of ownership were successful.[4858] It should be noted that the Illinois Watch Company was only one of many companies owned and co-owned by the Bunns and the many interconnected families. The Great Depression took place soon after the sale. People would often ask Willard Bunn, Sr., if he was happy about his decision to sell Illinois Watch Company, and Bunn would answer, "every time I wind my watch."[4859]

Willard Bunn served on the board of directors of the Chicago-based Illinois Chamber of Commerce and served nearly three decades on the board of directors of the Central Illinois Public Service Company, which controlled several Chicago metropolitan regional companies. Bunn was President of the Springfield Chamber of Commerce and was a member of the boards of directors of the Sangamo Electric Company, Bunn Capitol Company (formerly J. W. Bunn & Company), and Springfield Marine Bank, in addition to being a restauranteur and the head of a large and diversified midwestern land company. Bunn was thus connected to Chicago, Cook County, and Will County through many diverse directorships and investments. The Illinois Watch Company created such technologically precise instrumentation that their watches became the standard for the world, the new standard for all railroad timekeeping, and the horological foundation for the railroad industry and its scheduling and logistics.[4860] The company manufactured around 6,000,000 watches in total, and probably generated cumulative gross revenues of close to $100,000,000 from about 1870 to about 1930.[4861]

The American Watch Trust Company (American Jewelers' Trust Company)

Jacob Bunn and John Whitfield Bunn were founders of the American Jewelers' Trust Company, also known both as the American Watch Trust Company and as the Jewelers' Trust.[4862] The Trust was a multimillion-dollar monopolistic company that consisted of the Illinois Watch Company, Elgin Watch Company, and Waltham Watch Company, among many others firms.[4863] Elgin, Waltham, and Illinois were the three largest and most powerful members of the Trust. The Trust

---

[4857] Decatur Herald. (January 3, 1928). P. 8. Newspapers.com.

[4858] The Star Press. (Muncie, Indiana). (January 1, 1928). P. 1. Newspapers.com.

[4859] Bunn family history records.

[4860] Call, Andrew Taylor. (2005). Jacob Bunn: Legacy of an Illinois Industrial Pioneer. Lawrenceville, VA: Brunswick Publishing Corporation.

[4861] Call, Andrew Taylor. (2005). Jacob Bunn: Legacy of an Illinois Industrial Pioneer. Lawrenceville, VA: Brunswick Publishing Corporation.

[4862] Chicago Tribune. (September 26, 1889). Page not apparent. ProQuest Historical Newspapers.

[4863] Chicago Tribune. (September 26, 1889). Page not apparent. ProQuest Historical Newspapers.

possessed a capital value of $11,000,000 in 1889.[4864] The Jewelers' Trust money was probably measured in terms of the collective total of the member company asset moneys. The Trust presence in Chicago was powerful because Elgin Watch was headquartered in the western suburb of Elgin, because Illinois Watch had such a strong Chicago presence, and because of the M. Eppenstein & Company of Chicago, also a Trust member.[4865] Illinois Watch, though headquartered in Springfield, possessed a tremendous presence in Chicago and sold watches in the Chicago market through M. Eppenstein & Company and many other firms, as has been discussed.[4866]

The American Jewelers' Trust controlled the watch jobbers of the United States and essentially acquired continental control over the industry.[4867] Jacob Bunn, who served as President of the Illinois Watch Company, worked closely with the Elgin Watch Company, as was noted by the Canton, Ohio, news report that was syndicated in the *Chicago Tribune* edition of September 26, 1889.[4868]

> "Then again the Illinois Watch company is closely allied with the Elgin Watch company through its president, Jacob Bunn, who came into unenviable notoriety some months ago in relation to certain legislation on the subject of trusts before the Springfield legislature."[4869]

The Canton, Ohio, and Chicago reports furnished facts that partially elucidated the jurisprudence of the American Jewelers' Trust.[4870] The Trust was a compound company, an organization of multiple companies within the American timepiece production and distribution industry.[4871] The Trust comprised a system of membership and alliance in which the member companies executed contracts that governed the prices and distributions of product.[4872] The Trust was built from the

---

[4864] Chicago Tribune. (September 26, 1889). Page not apparent. ProQuest Historical Newspapers.
[4865] Chicago Tribune. (September 26, 1889). Page not apparent. ProQuest Historical Newspapers.
[4866] Chicago Tribune. (September 26, 1889). Page not apparent. ProQuest Historical Newspapers.
[4867] Chicago Tribune. (September 26, 1889). Page not apparent. ProQuest Historical Newspapers.
[4868] Chicago Tribune. (September 26, 1889). Page not apparent. ProQuest Historical Newspapers.
[4869] Chicago Tribune. (September 26, 1889). Page not apparent. ProQuest Historical Newspapers.
[4870] Chicago Tribune. (September 26, 1889). Page not apparent. ProQuest Historical Newspapers.
[4871] Chicago Tribune. (September 26, 1889). Page not apparent. ProQuest Historical Newspapers.
[4872] Chicago Tribune. (September 26, 1889). Page not apparent. ProQuest Historical Newspapers.

jurisprudential fibers of contract, alliance, loyalty, and monopoly.[4873] The alliance that constituted the substance of the Trust company possessed, however, an arguably inevitable vulnerability to dissolution.[4874] The factors that constituted the organizational vulnerability derived from the fact that other commercial alliances and loyalties existed among the various Trust members.[4875] The non-trust loyalties and alliances among the Trust members could supersede the loyalties and alliances of those members to the Trust itself at any time.[4876] Breach of the price contracts and price policy by several Trust members led to gradual erosion of the Trust and the gradual dissolution of the watch and jewel monopoly.[4877]

M. Eppenstein & Company of Chicago was a member of the Trust, but was expelled from the organization when it reduced the prices of its products below the contracted price limit, thus breaching Trust price policy.[4878] The Illinois Watch Company of Springfield and Chicago, and M. Eppenstein & Company of Chicago, apparently possessed mutual loyalty, and this loyalty and alliance superseded the loyalties and alliances of both companies to the Trust organization itself.[4879] The expulsion of M. Eppenstein & Company was expected to precipitate the Illinois Watch Company's abandonment of the Trust, because of the alliance and loyalty that existed between the two firms independently of the Trust.[4880] The Herzog Company of New York City was similarly expelled for breach of Trust price policy for the act, like that of Eppenstein, of having reduced prices below the contracted Trust price limit.[4881] The Trust governance attached the less severe punishment of a $500 fine to both the Floyd, Pratt & Rounds Company of Boston and to the King & Eisle Company of Buffalo, which both were convicted of violations of the contracted Trust price policy.[4882] The Canton-Chicago report contained the

---

[4873] Chicago Tribune. (September 26, 1889). Page not apparent. ProQuest Historical Newspapers.

[4874] Chicago Tribune. (September 26, 1889). Page not apparent. ProQuest Historical Newspapers.

[4875] Chicago Tribune. (September 26, 1889). Page not apparent. ProQuest Historical Newspapers.

[4876] Chicago Tribune. (September 26, 1889). Page not apparent. ProQuest Historical Newspapers.

[4877] Chicago Tribune. (September 26, 1889). Page not apparent. ProQuest Historical Newspapers.

[4878] Chicago Tribune. (September 26, 1889). Page not apparent. ProQuest Historical Newspapers.

[4879] Chicago Tribune. (September 26, 1889). Page not apparent. ProQuest Historical Newspapers.

[4880] Chicago Tribune. (September 26, 1889). Page not apparent. ProQuest Historical Newspapers.

[4881] Chicago Tribune. (September 26, 1889). Page not apparent. ProQuest Historical Newspapers.

[4882] Chicago Tribune. (September 26, 1889). Page not apparent. ProQuest Historical Newspapers.

journalistic opinion that dissolution of the Trust was immanent simultaneously because of the expulsion of the Chicago and New York City companies, the alliance-destructive pecuniary punishments levied against the Boston and Buffalo companies, and the expected abandonment of the Trust by the Illinois Watch Company, the Trust's most important member.[4883] The following comment proved the well-known alliance between the Illinois Watch Company and the M. Eppenstein & Company, and predicated the contemporary journalistic forecast for the termination of the Trust upon the fact and opinion that follow here: "Eppenstein & Co. are large customers of the Illinois [Watch] company, and it has long been asserted that if the trust managers carried out their threat of expelling this firm the Illinois company would withdraw from the trust."[4884]

The Canton-Chicago forecast was realized when the Illinois Watch Company left the Trust on January 20, 1890, as reported by the *Chicago Daily Tribune* of January 21, 1890, which received the report from New York City.[4885] After the Trust expelled M. Eppenstein & Company from membership for the breach of Trust price policy, the Illinois Watch Company demonstrated the priorities of its corporate alliances by continuing its contractual relationship with Eppenstein of Chicago.[4886] The Illinois Watch Company executed a contract with Eppenstein in 1888, and apparently preserved the contract in violation of the Trust policy that banned contractual relationships between Trust member companies and non-Trust companies.[4887] Dispersion of the rumor that the Illinois Watch Company, which along with Elgin Watch Company and Waltham Watch Company was one of the three leaders of the Trust, would exit the Trust caused a confrontation among the three leader-member companies.[4888] John Cutler of the Elgin company, and a Mr. Fitch of the Waltham company confronted A. E. Bentley of the Illinois Watch Company, and demanded an explanation of the Illinois Watch Company's plan for Trust membership.[4889] Elgin and Waltham proposed the punishment of Illinois

---

[4883] Chicago Tribune. (September 26, 1889). Page not apparent. ProQuest Historical Newspapers.

[4884] Chicago Tribune. (September 26, 1889). Page not apparent. ProQuest Historical Newspapers.

[4885] Chicago Daily Tribune. (January 21, 1890). Page not apparent. ProQuest Historical Newspapers.

[4886] Chicago Daily Tribune. (January 21, 1890). Page not apparent. ProQuest Historical Newspapers.

[4887] Chicago Daily Tribune. (January 21, 1890). Page not apparent. ProQuest Historical Newspapers.

[4888] Chicago Daily Tribune. (January 21, 1890). Page not apparent. ProQuest Historical Newspapers.

[4889] Chicago Daily Tribune. (January 21, 1890). Page not apparent. ProQuest Historical Newspapers.

Watch for its continued contract with Eppenstein.[4890] The Illinois Watch Company surrendered its membership in the Trust on January 20, and the resignation was accepted by the Trust.[4891]

The fact that Illinois Watch Company withdrew from the American Jewelers' Trust in 1890 provided no immunity from subsequent monopoly charges and monopoly-based litigation risk for Illinois Watch, however. Illinois Watch Company was joined as a co-defendant party to a multi-defendant antitrust lawsuit instituted by plaintiff Deuber Watch Case Manufacturing Company in 1895.[4892] Deuber Watch Case Manufacturing Company filed a complex suit and complaint whose claims and allegations stemmed from an antitrust theory.[4893] The defendant parties included Illinois Watch Company, Elgin Watch Company, Waltham Watch Company, Bay State Watch Case Company, Brooklyn Watch Case Company, Keystone Watch Case Company, Seth Thomas Clock Company, Joseph Fahys & Company, R. Muir's Sons Company, Duhme & Company, and Joseph M. Bates and George M. Bacon, who had previously constituted the Bates & Bacon Company.[4894]

The plaintiff party's complaint contained multiple allegations, chief among which was that the defendant parties contracted on or around November 16, 1887, to boycott the products of Deuber through a contractually-enforced trade ban.[4895] The boycott contract and ban were thus contractually executed, enforced, and mediated through the Jewelers' Trust Company and consisted of the ban on all sales of Trust member products to any person, company, or association that purchased or sold products from Deuber.[4896] The Deuber complaint furthermore alleged that the defendant Jewelers' Trust parties sent notices and warnings to the purchasers of Dueber product telling them to stop purchasing from Deuber; these notices and warnings caused those purchasers of Dueber product to terminate their contracts with Deuber.[4897] The New York report, appearing in the April 10, 1895, edition of the *Chicago Daily Tribune*, contained relatively sparse description of the theory that underlay the Deuber complaint against the Jewelers' Trust Company members.[4898] Nevertheless, the description was substantial enough to reveal that the plaintiff's theory relied primarily upon antitrust policy, which was

---

[4890] Chicago Daily Tribune. (January 21, 1890). Page not apparent. ProQuest Historical Newspapers.
[4891] Chicago Daily Tribune. (January 21, 1890). Page not apparent. ProQuest Historical Newspapers.
[4892] Chicago Daily Tribune. (April 10, 1895). P. 7. Newspapers.com.
[4893] Chicago Daily Tribune. (April 10, 1895). P. 7. Newspapers.com.
[4894] Chicago Daily Tribune. (April 10, 1895). P. 7. Newspapers.com.
[4895] Chicago Daily Tribune. (April 10, 1895). P. 7. Newspapers.com.
[4896] Chicago Daily Tribune. (April 10, 1895). P. 7. Newspapers.com.
[4897] Chicago Daily Tribune. (April 10, 1895). P. 7. Newspapers.com.
[4898] Chicago Daily Tribune. (April 10, 1895). P. 7. Newspapers.com.

a policy that was then still inchoate at the federal level of United States jurisprudence and public administration.[4899] Deuber joined to its complaint a prayer for recovery which sought remedy in the form of $500,000 against the defendant Jewelers' Trust Company parties.[4900]

At the time of the New York-Chicago report, the Deuber case had advanced to trial and remained *lis pendens* before Judge McClennon and a jury in New York City.[4901] The Deuber case was a window into the public policy culture of the United States Gilded Age. The Deuber civil case contained complaints, pleadings, prayers, policies, and theories that collectively illuminated the developing antitrust law and public policy landscape of the time, because federal legislative policy had only culminated in the enactment of the Sherman Antitrust Act on July 2, 1890, roughly four years and nine months before the New York-Chicago report of the Deuber case against the American Jewelers' Trust Company.[4902] Chicago was central to the American Jewelers' Trust Company because the Trust contained the Elgin Watch Company, the Illinois Watch Company, and M. Eppenstein & Company, all three of which dominated Chicago and Cook County timepiece technology and manufacturing.[4903]

John and Jacob Bunn, among multiple others, were founders and builders of the $11,000,000 Jewelers' Trust Company, which governed the timepiece industry of the United States.[4904] Significantly, the Bunn brothers took the Illinois Watch Company out of the Jewelers' Trust Company when the brothers judged the Trust to be unethical.[4905] The original purpose of the Jewelers' Trust Company was to protect, "manufacturers from ruinous competition."[4906] Max Eppenstein was President of the Illinois Watch Case Company of Chicago, and Solomon C. Eppenstein was also an executive officer in that firm.

[4899] Chicago Daily Tribune. (April 10, 1895). P. 7. Newspapers.com.

[4900] Chicago Daily Tribune. (April 10, 1895). P. 7. Newspapers.com.

[4901] Chicago Daily Tribune. (April 10, 1895). P. 7. Newspapers.com.

[4902] Chicago Daily Tribune. (April 10, 1895). P. 7. Newspapers.com.

[4903] Chicago Daily Tribune. (April 10, 1895). P. 7. Newspapers.com; Chicago Tribune. (September 26, 1889). Page not apparent. ProQuest Historical Newspapers.

[4904] Chicago Daily Tribune. (April 10, 1895). Page not apparent. ProQuest Historical Newspapers; Chicago Tribune. (September 26, 1889). Page not apparent. ProQuest Historical Newspapers.

[4905] Chicago Daily Tribune. (January 21, 1890). Page not apparent. ProQuest Historical Newspapers.

[4906] Chicago Tribune. (September 26, 1889). Page not apparent. ProQuest Historical Newspapers.

The Call, Ramsey, and Peterson Family of Ohio:

The Building of Ohio, Chicago, New York City, and West Virginia Industry

The Call family were centrally involved in the establishment and/or reorganization, leadership, and development of multiple industries and corporations of Ohio, Chicago, Pittsburgh, and New York City, including the Continental Can Company, the American Gas & Electric Company (American Electric Power Company/AEP), the American Gas & Electric Service Corporation, the Farmers National Life Insurance Company of America, and the Washington Brewing Company. All of these companies are discussed extensively herein, along with their relevance to Chicago, to Cook County, and to other regions. A family history and genealogy will precede the civic and industrial history here for the purpose of explaining the culture, history, and foundation from which the Call family contributed to United States industry and, specifically, the industrial development of Chicago, Ohio, Pittsburgh, West Virginia, and New York City. Much of the industrial work performed by the Call family centered on the Midwest, Chicago, Cook County, and the adjoining regions, in addition to New York City.

The Call-Ramsey-Peterson Family, in addition to its many interrelated families, has resided in Ohio since before the creation of Ohio statehood on March 1, 1803, and came to the region during the time when the territory was administered as the Northwest Territory.[4907] These families were among the founding families of Ohio. The earliest ancestors of the Call Family in Ohio were the Peterson family, the Pittenger family, and the Van Duyn family.[4908] Peter Peterson was a farmer and milling entrepreneur from New Jersey who journeyed, in at least 1787, to Ohio County, Virginia (now West Virginia), in the upper Ohio River Valley.[4909] Peter Peterson married Maria Pittenger in or about 1752.[4910] Maria Pittenger was the daughter of Hendrick Pittenger and Maria Louw (the family subsequently changed the spelling of the surname, which means "lion" in Dutch, to Lowe).[4911] Peter Peterson and Maria (Pittenger) Peterson were descendants of multiple founding Dutch and Scottish families of New York City and New Jersey.[4912] Among these

---

[4907] Call, Ramsey, Peterson, Van Duyn, and Pittenger family records. See generally: Peterson, William L. (1987). Ancestors and Descendants of Garrett Peterson and Nancy Smock. Pp. 1-100. Baltimore, MD: Gateway Press, Inc. Lds.org.

[4908] See generally: Peterson, William L. (1987). Ancestors and Descendants of Garrett Peterson and Nancy Smock. Pp. 1-100. Baltimore, MD: Gateway Press, Inc. Lds.org.

[4909] Peterson, William L. (1987). Ancestors and Descendants of Garrett Peterson and Nancy Smock. P. 92. Baltimore, MD: Gateway Press, Inc. Lds.org.

[4910] Peterson, William L. (1987). Ancestors and Descendants of Garrett Peterson and Nancy Smock. P. 55. Baltimore, MD: Gateway Press, Inc. Lds.org.

[4911] Peterson, William L. (1987). Ancestors and Descendants of Garrett Peterson and Nancy Smock. P. 55. Baltimore, MD: Gateway Press, Inc. Lds.org.

[4912] See generally: Peterson, William L. (1987). Ancestors and Descendants of Garrett Peterson and Nancy Smock. Pp. 1-100. Baltimore, MD: Gateway Press, Inc. Lds.org; See generally: Call, Ramsey, Peterson, Van Duyn, and Pittenger family records.

ancestral and interconnected families were Peterson, Pittenger, Waldron, Delamater, Swart, Lowe, and Van Duyn, among others.[4913]

The historical records prove that at Ohio County, Virginia, Peter Peterson formed a grist manufacturing partnership company with Dr. Benjamin Johnston.[4914] Peter Peterson and Dr. Benjamin Johnston shared the profits of the partnership company from approximately 1787 until 1805.[4915] Peter Peterson and Dr. Benjamin Johnston were co-founders of what was one of the earliest manufacturing industries in the upper Ohio River Valley.[4916] One of the Peterson and Van Duyn cousins, Dennis Cassatt (son of David Cossart/Cassatt and Sarah Van Duyn), was a land developer and land agent of the upper Ohio River Valley during the original development of the Northwest Territory and western Pennsylvania. Robert Simpson Cassatt, son of Dennis Cassatt and Lydia (Simpson) Cassatt, and member of the Call-Ramsey-Peterson-Van Duyn family of New York City, New Jersey, Pennsylvania, and Ohio, served as Mayor of Allegheny City, a municipality that became a major part of Pittsburgh, Pennsylvania.[4917] Robert Simpson Cassatt married Katherine Kelso Johnston. Robert and Katherine (Johnston) Cassatt's son, Alexander Johnston Cassatt of Pittsburgh, was President of the Pennsylvania Railroad Company. Robert and Katherine's daughter, Mary Stevenson Cassatt of Pittsburgh, was the renowned American painter.[4918] Alexander J. Cassatt was a cousin of Henry Stryker Taylor through the Van Duyn family; Taylor later held the controlling individual equity ownership of the Pennsylvania Railroad Company. Both the Calls and the Strykers are descendants of the Van Duyn family of New York City and New Jersey; therefore, Henry Stryker Taylor and William Frederic Call, the grandfathers of author Andrew Taylor Call, were cousins.[4919]

Ralph Peterson, son of Peter Peterson and Maria (Pittenger) Peterson, married Susannah Van Duyn, in the year 1790.[4920] Ralph was a carpenter, farmer, and businessman in Adams County, Ohio. Ralph Peterson and Susannah (Van Duyn) Peterson's daughter, Eliza Peterson (1810-1878), married John Albert Ramsey, Sr. (1806-1878).[4921] Among the many children of John Ramsey and Eliza (Peterson) Ramsey was Nancy Jane Ramsey (1841-1923), who married William Call (1837-

[4913] See generally: Peterson, William L. (1987). Ancestors and Descendants of Garrett Peterson and Nancy Smock. Pp. 1-100. Baltimore, MD: Gateway Press, Inc. Lds.org; See generally: Call, Ramsey, Peterson, Van Duyn, and Pittenger family records.

[4914] Peterson, William L. Ancestors and Descendants of Garrett Peterson and Nancy Smock. P. 92. Baltimore, MD: Gateway Press, Inc. Lds.org.

[4915] Peterson, William L. (1987). Ancestors and Descendants of Garrett Peterson and Nancy Smock. P. 92. Baltimore, MD: Gateway Press, Inc. Lds.org.

[4916] Peterson, William L. (1987). Ancestors and Descendants of Garrett Peterson and Nancy Smock. P. 92. Baltimore, MD: Gateway Press, Inc. Lds.org.

[4917] Call, Ramsey, Peterson, Van Duyn family history records.

[4918] Call, Ramsey, Peterson, Van Duyn family history records.

[4919] Call, Ramsey, Peterson, Van Duyn family history rcords.

[4920] Peterson, William L. (1987). Ancestors and Descendants of Garrett Peterson and Nancy Smock. Pp. 95-96. Baltimore, MD: Gateway Press, Inc. Lds.org.

[4921] Call, Ramsey, Peterson, Van Duyn, and Pittenger family records.

1903).[4922] John Albert Ramsey, a native of the Eagle Creek region of Adams County, Ohio, owned a farm and apple orchard in Jackson County, Ohio.[4923] William Call, son of Pennsylvania natives Peter Call (b. 1796) and Margaret Call (b. circa 1796), was also a native of Pennsylvania.[4924] William Call and his brother Joseph Call both worked in the coal mines of Jackson County, Ohio.[4925] William Call worked as a firewatcher at an iron blast furnace in Jackson County. During the Civil War, William Call served in the Union Army in West Virginia as a wagon driver. Call received a federal military pension for his Civil War service.[4926]

The children born to William Call and Nancy Jane (Ramsey) Call included the following people: Peter A. J. Call, Eliza Catherine "Katie" Call, Alice Call, **John McClelland Call**, **James Custer Call**, **Nellie Call**, Ralph Edward "Teddy" Call, Charles (Carl) Wallace Call, Edna Call, William Call, Teresa Call, and Hattie Call.[4927] Most of the Calls and many of the Ramseys relocated to Columbus, Ohio; the Call and Ramsey family has resided in Columbus continuously for at least five generations.[4928] A few of the Calls remained in Jackson County, Ohio, along with certain members of the Ramsey family.[4929] Other members of the Call and Ramsey family relocated to Youngstown, Ohio, Martin's Ferry, Ohio, and to Cleveland and the surrounding metropolitan region of Cleveland and Cuyahoga County.[4930] Peter A. J. Call married Mary Stiffler Price of Ohio.[4931] Eliza "Katie" Catherine Call married Daniel Titus of Ohio.[4932] John McClelland Call married first, Mary Harley of Glasgow, Scotland, and Columbus, and second, Nettie Baxter of Ohio.[4933] Alice Call married Dennis Sweet of Illinois, and they both resided in Jackson County, Ohio, and then in Columbus.[4934] Edna Call married William J. Andres of Ohio. Theresa Call married William Norton Darby of Ohio, who was both Chief Warden of the Ohio Penitentiary in Columbus, and co-founder of the Baldwin Forging & Tool Company of Columbus and Parkersburg, West Virginia, which was the world's largest manufacturer of shovels.[4935] William Call married Gayle Kessinger

---

[4922] Marriage Certificate for William Call and Nancy Jane Ramsey (Jackson County, Ohio, February, 1857). See also: Call, Ramsey, Peterson, Van Duyn, and Pittenger family records.

[4923] Call, Ramsey, Peterson, Van Duyn, and Pittenger family records.

[4924] 1850 United States Census. Call, Ramsey, Peterson, Van Duyn, and Pittenger family records.

[4925] Call family history records.

[4926] United States Civil War service pension Record for William Call. Call, Ramsey, Peterson, Van Duyn, and Pittenger family records.

[4927] Call family history records.

[4928] Call family history records.

[4929] Call family history records.

[4930] Call family history records.

[4931] Call family history records.

[4932] Call family history records.

[4933] Call family history records.

[4934] Call family history records.

[4935] Call family history records.

of Ohio. Hattie Call did not marry.[4936] Nellie Call married Frank Steel Dodson of Columbus, Ohio.[4937] James Custer Call first married Collie Brandt of Ohio, and had one son with her, who was Charles Harmon Call, who was a resident of Columbus and Youngstown.[4938] After Collie (Brandt) Call died, James Custer Call married Mahalia "Mattie" McCullough of Ohio in 1893, and they had five children together, who were: **Robert Grogan Call** (see below), who married Freda Plantz of Ohio; Theresa Lucille Call, who married Paul Kuckuk of Cleveland; Elizabeth Gertrude Call, who married Glenn Oscar Covey of Ohio; Richard Call, who died young; and **William Frederic Call** (see below), who married Mary Elizabeth Baldwin of Butler County, Pennsylvania, and of Cleveland.[4939]

Nancy Jane (Ramsey) Call moved to Columbus to be with her children after the death of her husband, William Call, in 1903.[4940] Ralph Edward Call worked as a railroad engineer at Columbus.[4941] Charles Wallace Call worked as a railroad car inspector at Jackson, Ohio, and was killed in a railroad car accident in 1914.[4942] James Custer Call resided in Columbus at least as early as 1890 and worked at the Ohio Pipe Company of Columbus and as a coal miner, stationary engineer, water tender, and fireman at an iron blast furnace in Jackson and Martin's Ferry, Ohio.[4943] James Custer Call and Mattie (McCullough) Call moved among Jackson, Ohio, Martin's Ferry, Columbus, and Tiltonsville. James Custer Call was a member of both the Sons of Union Army Veterans and the Knights of Pythias, and he and Mattie (McCullough) Call were active in the Methodist Church, as were many of the other Calls and McCulloughs.[4944] Peter A. J. Call established the Call Coal Company in Jackson, Ohio, and worked as a coal operator in that county for multiple years. Peter was President and owner of the Call Coal Company when he died in 1922.[4945]

The Washington Brewing Company and The Joyce Products Company:

A Prominent Ohio-Chicago Connection

John McClelland Call, who was often known by the abbreviated names of "Clelland" Call, and "J. C." Call, served as a prison guard in the Ohio Penitentiary at Columbus.[4946] It was during his time of service as a prison guard at the Ohio

---

[4936] Call family history records.

[4937] Call family history records.

[4938] Call family history records.

[4939] Call family history records.

[4940] Call family history records.

[4941] Call family history records.

[4942] Call family history records.

[4943] Death Certificate for James Custer Call. (1920). Belmont County, Ohio.

[4944] Call family history records.

[4945] Death Certificate for Peter Call. (1922). Jackson County, Ohio.

[4946] Executive Documents. Annual Reports for 1902 Made to the Seventy-Sixth General Assembly of the State of Ohio. (1903). Part 1. P. 639. Springfield, OH: The Springfield Publishing Company, State Printers. Google Books.

Penitentiary that Call became the acquaintance of William Sydney Porter.[4947] William Sydney Porter, known by the *nom de plume* "O. Henry," had been sentenced to incarceration at Columbus due to conviction on charges of financial misconduct in Texas.[4948] The judicial process contained a trial that resulted in the conviction of Porter.[4949] The court consequently ordered his punishment and sentence of incarceration in Columbus, Ohio.[4950] Porter began his time of incarceration on April 25, 1898, at Columbus, and was released on July 24, 1901.[4951] Charles Alphonso Smith, biographer of O. Henry, wrote that it was at the prison in Columbus that Porter experienced his early development as a writer. "It was here that he wrote his first twelve stories and assumed the now famous pseudonym, O. Henry."[4952] Smith stated that Porter took the name "O. Henry" from the United States Dispensatory while working as a drug clerk in North Carolina, Texas, and Ohio.[4953] Smith noted that the pseudonym that Porter chose was based on the initials of the name of the famous French pharmacist, Etienne-Ossian Henry.[4954]

John McClelland Call left employment with the prison service in the very early twentieth century, and entered the liquor business at Columbus.[4955] He established J. C. Call & Company, a well-known and longstanding liquor and saloon company located at 218 N. High Street, located in the downtown of Columbus.[4956] John McClelland Call also promoted the beer manufacturing and brewing industry of Ohio when, in 1905, he co-founded the Washington Brewing Company of Columbus.[4957] Volume XIX of the *American Brewers' Review* contained reports and notices of new brewing companies and gave certain details regarding the new firms.[4958] The report contained the information on the Washington Brewing

---

[4947] Call, Ramsey, Peterson, Van Duyn, and Pittenger family records.

[4948] Smith, Charles Alphonso. (1921). O. Henry (William Sidney Porter). P. 2354-C. Atlanta, GA: The Martin & Hoyt Company. Google Books.

[4949] Smith, Charles Alphonso. (1921). O. Henry (William Sidney Porter). P. 2354-C. Atlanta, GA: The Martin & Hoyt Company. Google Books.

[4950] Smith, Charles Alphonso. (1921). O. Henry (William Sidney Porter). P. 2354-C. Atlanta, GA: The Martin & Hoyt Company. Google Books.

[4951] Smith, Charles Alphonso. (1921). O. Henry (William Sidney Porter). P. 2354-C. Atlanta, GA: The Martin & Hoyt Company. Google Books.

[4952] Smith, Charles Alphonso. (1921). O. Henry (William Sidney Porter). P. 2354-C. Atlanta, GA: The Martin & Hoyt Company. Google Books.

[4953] Smith, Charles Alphonso. (1921). O. Henry (William Sidney Porter). P. 2354-C. Atlanta, GA: The Martin & Hoyt Company. Google Books.

[4954] Smith, Charles Alphonso. (1921). O. Henry (William Sidney Porter). P. 2354-C. Atlanta, GA: The Martin & Hoyt Company. Google Books.

[4955] Death Certificate for John McClelland Call. (1919). Franklin County, Ohio.

[4956] Columbus City Directory. (1909-1910). Vol. XXXIV. P. 203. Columbus, OH: R. L. Polk & Company, and J. Wiggins. Google Books.

[4957] American Brewers' Review. (January-December, 1905). Vol. XIX. P. 497. Chicago, IL: American Brewers' Review. Google Books.

[4958] American Brewers' Review. (January-December, 1905). Vol. XIX. P. 497. Chicago, IL: American Brewers' Review. Google Books.

Company. The report stated that the financing of the Washington Brewing Company consisted of an initial stock money of $200,000.[4959] The report made no mention of corporate financing by means of debt money and confirmed that the subscriptions had produced adequate stock money for commencement of business as of the time of the report.[4960] No additional facts about the financing of the company appeared in the report.[4961] Omission of reference to debt money allows for reasonable inference that stock money was the sole means of corporate financing in the case of Washington Brewing Company, at least at the time of incorporation.[4962] The founders of the Washington Brewing Company were Clement T. Hoy; William Henry Joyce; John McClelland Call; John Bauermeister; Charles Engel; George F. Mooney; Edward Trautman; Jacob Becker; John Wall; D. J. Minton; and Adam Dunkle.[4963] The original corporate leadership structure for the firm consisted of the following persons and jobs:

Person	Job (Including Board of Directors Service)
Clement T. Hoy	President, Director
John Bauermeister	Vice-President, Director
Charles Engel	Treasurer, Director
George F. Mooney	Secretary and Manager, Director

Board of Directors
William Henry Joyce
John McClelland Call
Edward Trautman
Jacob Becker
John Wall
D. J. Minton
Adam Dunkle[4964]

The company operated a large factory and industrial site, two city blocks in size, that was bounded by Perry Street, Percy Street, Second Avenue, and the Olentangy

---

[4959] American Brewers' Review. (January-December, 1905). Vol. XIX. P. 497. Chicago, IL: American Brewers' Review. Google Books.

[4960] American Brewers' Review. (January-December, 1905). Vol. XIX. P. 497. Chicago, IL: American Brewers' Review. Google Books.

[4961] American Brewers' Review. (January-December, 1905). Vol. XIX. P. 497. Chicago, IL: American Brewers' Review. Google Books.

[4962] American Brewers' Review. (January-December, 1905). Vol. XIX. P. 497. Chicago, IL: American Brewers' Review. Google Books.

[4963] American Brewers' Review. (January-December, 1905). Vol. XIX. P. 497. Chicago, IL: American Brewers' Review. Google Books.

[4964] American Brewers' Review. (January-December, 1905). Vol. XIX. P. 497. Chicago, IL: American Brewers' Review. Google Books.

River.[4965] The original production power was 50,000 barrels per year.[4966] The corporation received transportation service from four railroad lines at the place of the factory and was well-furnished with sources of water and gas.[4967] The Washington Brewing Company rapidly grew to become one of the largest brewing companies in Ohio, producing 200,000 to 300,000 barrels of beer annually by approximately 1907; this growth represented a six-hundred to seven-hundred percent increase in output power and output in the span of two years.[4968] At one time, Washington Brewing Company was second only to the Louis Hoster Company of Columbus as the city's largest brewer.

Volume 33 of the *The Western Brewer* reported that, "Washington Brewing Co., Columbus, is greatly increasing the capacity of its bottling house."[4969] Clement T. Hoy, President of the company, died in October, 1908.[4970] As of December, 1905, Washington Brewing Company had contracted with the Chicago architecture firm of Bernard Barthel, which was famous for its design portfolio of American breweries.[4971] The company worked with Barthel to construct an addition to the Columbus factory for the purpose of creating an annual production output power of 150,000 barrels.[4972] The architecture firm also designed a new storehouse for the company capable of holding 60,000 barrels in storage.[4973] At the time of the two physical improvements and expansions, C. T. Hoy served as President of the company and George F. Mooney remained Secretary and Manager.[4974]

Several Chicago companies played central and essential roles in the construction of the factory and infrastructure of the Washington Brewing Company.[4975] Volume XX of the *American Brewers' Review* noted that Bernard Barthel of Chicago had chosen the "[feudal] castle" design for the Washington Brewing Company

---

[4965] American Brewers' Review. (January-December, 1905). Vol. XIX. P. 497. Chicago, IL: American Brewers' Review. Google Books.

[4966] American Brewers' Review. (January-December, 1905). Vol. XIX. P. 497. Chicago, IL: American Brewers' Review. Google Books.

[4967] American Brewers' Review. (January-December, 1905). Vol. XIX. P. 497. Chicago, IL: American Brewers' Review. Google Books.

[4968] The relevant record has been lost, but recollection of its contents is certain.

[4969] The Western Brewer: And Journal of the Barley, Malt and Hop Trades. (May, 1908). Vol. 33. P. 245. Chicago, IL: H. S. Rich & Co. Google Books.

[4970] The Western Brewer: And Journal of the Barley, Matl and Hop Trades. (November, 1908). Vol. 33. P. 592. Google Books.

[4971] Ice And Refrigeration Illustrated. (July to December, 1905). Vol. 29. P. 303. Chicago, IL: Nickerson & Collins Co., Publishers. Google Books.

[4972] Ice And Refrigeration Illustrated. (July to December, 1905). Vol. 29. P. 303. Chicago, IL: Nickerson & Collins Co., Publishers. Google Books.

[4973] Ice And Refrigeration Illustrated. (July to December, 1905). Vol. 29. P. 303. Chicago, IL: Nickerson & Collins Co., Publishers. Google Books.

[4974] Ice And Refrigeration Illustrated. (July to December, 1905). Vol. 29. P. 303. Chicago, IL: Nickerson & Collins Co., Publishers. Google Books.

[4975] American Brewers' Review. (July to December, 1906). Vol. XX. P. 297. Chicago, IL: American Brewers' Review. Google Books.

industrial campus.[4976] Washington Brewing had created an architectural challenge event in which different architects submitted their designs to the company leadership for choice and approval for use in the design of the Columbus factory complex.[4977] Bernard Barthel of Chicago won the event and he designed the entire company architecture.[4978] The Chicago company known as the Herman Stier Manufacturing Company contributed to the Washington Brewing Company through its construction of the copper and tank work for the Ohio company.[4979] A third Chicago organization gave essential service to the Washington Brewing Company when the firm of Wendnagel & Company constructed the cooperage works.[4980] The firm of Kaestner & Company, also of Chicago, provided the construction of milling and machinery works for the Columbus company.[4981] Finally, the Weinman Machine Works Company of Columbus, Ohio, provided the construction of the pump machinery for Washington Brewing Company.[4982] Four Chicago companies played vital roles in the construction of the Washington Brewing Company.[4983] Chicago, through these four companies, contributed architecture, construction, engineering, and manufacturing to the development of the Columbus brewing industry.[4984]

Labor issues arose in 1907 when the International Brewery Workers' Union and the American Federation of Labor competed for contracts, labor jurisdiction, and recognition from the Washington Brewing Company leadership.[4985] The April 9, 1907, edition of *The Marion Star*, a newspaper of Marion, Ohio, reported the facts. The American Federation of Labor sought contractual jurisdiction over the firemen and engineers of the Washington Brewing Company and the Hoster-Columbus Company, the latter of which controlled the Schlee Company, the Born Company, the Louis Hoster Company, and the Columbus Brewing Company, all of Columbus.[4986] The companies frustrated the jurisdictional ambition of the

---

[4976] American Brewers' Review. (July to December, 1906). Vol. XX. P. 297. Chicago, IL: American Brewers' Review. Google Books.

[4977] American Brewers' Review. (July to December, 1906). Vol. XX. P. 297. Chicago, IL: American Brewers' Review. Google Books.

[4978] American Brewers' Review. (July to December, 1906). Vol. XX. P. 297. Chicago, IL: American Brewers' Review. Google Books.

[4979] American Brewers' Review. (July to December, 1906). Vol. XX. P. 297. Chicago, IL: American Brewers' Review. Google Books.

[4980] American Brewers' Review. (July to December, 1906). Vol. XX. P. 297. Chicago, IL: American Brewers' Review. Google Books.

[4981] American Brewers' Review. (July to December, 1906). Vol. XX. P. 297. Chicago, IL: American Brewers' Review. Google Books.

[4982] American Brewers' Review. (July to December, 1906). Vol. XX. P. 297. Chicago, IL: American Brewers' Review. Google Books.

[4983] American Brewers' Review. (July to December, 1906). Vol. XX. P. 297. Chicago, IL: American Brewers' Review. Google Books.

[4984] American Brewers' Review. (July to December, 1906). Vol. XX. P. 297. Chicago, IL: American Brewers' Review. Google Books.

[4985] The Marion Star. (April 9, 1907). P. 1. Newspapers.com.

[4986] The Marion Star. (April 9, 1907). P. 1. Newspapers.com.

American Federation of Labor when they instead executed the labor contracts with the International Brewery Workers Union on April 8, 1907.[4987] Factory expansion and improvement continued over the years. Volume 50 of the New York City and Chicago-based industrial journal known as *The National Provisioner* contained a report of refrigeration technology sales.[4988] The Triumph Ice Machine Company of Cincinnati had executed multiple sales of refrigeration machines to multiple companies.[4989] Washington Brewing Company continued operational improvement when it purchased a, "55-ton complete refrigerating plant" from Triumph.[4990]

William H. Joyce co-founded the Washington Brewing Company in 1905 with John McClelland Call and the other men named above.[4991] Joyce consolidated governance of several companies over time, and presided jointly over the Washington Brewing Company and the Joyce Products Company of Ohio at the time of his death.[4992] The Joyce Products Company was incorporated on March 10, 1927, as an Ohio corporation.[4993] John R. Downey, Warren N. Boyd, John M. Riley, and L. A. Stanton co-founded the company with William Joyce.[4994] The original capitalization money of the Joyce Products Company consisted of $60,000, apparently in the form of stock money.[4995] The news report contained no more facts relevant to the financing of the company.[4996] The Washington Brewing Company constituted a major part of what would become the compound Joyce Products Company, as described below.[4997] Joyce died in 1933, having built a network of beverage manufacturing companies.[4998] Volume 34 of the journal called *Industrial Refrigeration* reported in its obituary for Joyce his dual management

---

[4987] The Marion Star. (April 9, 1907). P. 1. Newspapers.com.

[4988] The National Provisioner. (May 9, 1914). Vol. 50. P. 21. Chicago, IL: The National Provisioner. Google Books.

[4989] The National Provisioner. (May 9, 1914). Vol. 50. P. 21. Chicago, IL: The National Provisioner. Google Books.

[4990] The National Provisioner. (May 9, 1914). Vol. 50. P. 21. Chicago, IL: The National Provisioner. Google Books.

[4991] American Brewers' Review. (January-December, 1905). Vol. XIX. P. 497. Chicago, IL: American Brewers' Review. Google Books.

[4992] Industrial Refrigeration. (1934). Page number not available at time of reference. Chicago, IL: Nickerson & Collins. Google Books.

[4993] The Cincinnati Enquirer. (March 11, 1927). P. 21. Newspapers.com.

[4994] The Cincinnati Enquirer. (March 11, 1927). P. 21. Newspapers.com.

[4995] The Cincinnati Enquirer. (March 11, 1927). P. 21. Newspapers.com.

[4996] The Cincinnati Enquirer. (March 11, 1927). P. 21. Newspapers.com.

[4997] American Brewers' Review. (January-December, 1905). Vol. XIX. P. 497. Chicago, IL: American Brewers' Review. Google Books; The Cincinnati Enquirer. (March 11, 1927). P. 21. Newspapers.com; The Cincinnati Enquirer. (November 9, 1933). P. 12. Newspapers.com; The Marion Star. (January 16, 1953). P. 18. Newspapers.com; Joyce Products Company-Washington Breweries, Inc. matchbook advertisement cover. Author's personal collection.

[4998] The Cincinnati Enquirer. (November 9, 1933). P. 12. Newspapers.com.

roles with Washington Brewing Company and with Joyce Products Company.[4999] *The Cincinnati Enquirer* edition of November 9, 1933, reported the obituary from November 8: "William H. Joyce, President and General Manager of the Washington Breweries, Inc., and the Joyce Products, Inc., died today."[5000] Joyce Products Company of Ohio became a manufacturer of the soda known as Seven-Up.[5001] The Joyce Products Company joined multiple other Joyce companies to develop a network of Seven-Up soda manufacturing firms across the Great Lakes region.[5002] William H. Joyce laid the foundation for the Great Lakes expansion of the Joyce-Washington company combination.[5003] After William H. Joyce's death, John R. Downey carried on leadership of the company.[5004] Downey served as President of the Joyce Products Company, as President of the Washington Breweries, Inc. (the renamed Washington Brewing Company of Columbus), and as President of the company known as Beverage Management, Inc.[5005] At the time of Downey's death in 1953, the Joyce network of companies owned Seven-Up factories in seven Ohio cities, and in Detroit.[5006]

The overarching Joyce company, which existed at least as a *de facto* company made of multiple subsidiary companies, if not as a juristically official holding corporation, contained the companies known as Washington Breweries, Inc., the Joyce Products Company, and multiple Great Lakes region Seven-Up manufacturing companies.[5007] The union of companies and products within the parent Joyce Company was expressed within the advertisement media of the company.[5008] The compound Joyce Company produced many matchbooks that bore twin advertisements for the Washington Breweries Company and for the

[4999] Industrial Refrigeration. (1934). Page number not available at time of reference. Chicago, IL: Nickerson & Collins. Google Books.

[5000] The Cincinnati Enquirer. (November 9, 1933). P. 12. Newspapers.com.

[5001] The Marion Star. (January 16, 1953). P. 18. Newspapers.com; The Cincinnati Enquirer. (November 9, 1933). P. 12. Newspapers.com; Joyce Products Company-Washington Breweries, Inc. matchbook advertisement cover. Author's personal collection.

[5002] The Marion Star. (January 16, 1953). P. 18. Newspapers.com; The Cincinnati Enquirer. (November 9, 1933). P. 12. Newspapers.com; Joyce Products Company-Washington Breweries, Inc. matchbook advertisement cover. Author's personal collection.

[5003] The Marion Star. (January 16, 1953). P. 18. Newspapers.com; The Cincinnati Enquirer. (November 9, 1933). P. 12. Newspapers.com.

[5004] The Marion Star. (January 16, 1953). P. 18. Newspapers.com; The Cincinnati Enquirer. (November 9, 1933). P. 12. Newspapers.com.

[5005] The Marion Star. (January 16, 1953). P. 18. Newspapers.com.

[5006] The Marion Star. (January 16, 1953). P. 18. Newspapers.com.

[5007] Joyce Products Company-Washington Breweries, Inc. matchbook advertisement cover. Author's personal collection.

[5008] Joyce Products Company-Washington Breweries, Inc. matchbook advertisement cover. Author's personal collection.

Joyce Products Company and its Seven-Up soda product.[5009] The physical form of the promotional matchbook cover consisted of a two-faced folded paper, on the one face of which appeared the advertisement bearing the name, logo, and artistic illustration of the Joyce Products Company Seven-Up beverage, and on the opposite face of which appeared the name, logo, and artistic illustration of the Washington Breweries Company products.[5010] The reader of the promotional media from the Joyce matchbooks could easily discern the compound quality and union of the Joyce Company and its products.[5011]

The Joyce companies would include Chicago in their scope.[5012] John Michael Joyce, brother of William H. Joyce, became senior partner of Joyce Seven-Up of Joliet, Illinois, in 1935.[5013] John M. Joyce served as Chairman of the Boards of Directors of the Chicago Seven-Up Bottling Company, the Joliet Seven-Up Bottling Company, the Madison, Wisconsin, Seven-Up Bottling Company, and the New York City Seven-Up Bottling Company.[5014] He was a member of the Board of Trustees of De Paul University in Chicago and served as Chairman of the Board of Directors of the First National Bank of Joliet.[5015] Joyce held membership on the Board of Directors of the Union National Bank & Trust Company of Joliet and was Chairman of the Joliet-Will County Community Chest.[5016] He served the emergency public financing efforts during wartime by presiding as State Chairman of the Illinois State War Fund.[5017] John Michael Joyce was a friend of Willard Bunn and Ruth (Regan) Bunn. The Joyces and Bunns were summer season neighbors and homeowners in the historic summer resort of Minocqua, Wisconsin.[5018] Joyce was a member of the Minocqua Country Club, the South Shore Country Club of Chicago, the Chicago Athletic Association, and the Lake Shore Club of

---

[5009] Joyce Products Company-Washington Breweries, Inc. matchbook advertisement cover. Author's personal collection.
[5010] Joyce Products Company-Washington Breweries, Inc. matchbook advertisement cover. Author's personal collection.
[5011] Joyce Products Company-Washington Breweries, Inc. matchbook advertisement cover. Author's personal collection.
[5012] The American Catholic Who's Who. (1960, 1961). Vol. 14. P. 226. Grosse Pointe, MI: Walter Romig, Publisher. Google Books.
[5013] The American Catholic Who's Who. (1960, 1961). Vol. 14. P. 226. Grosse Pointe, MI: Walter Romig, Publisher. Google Books.
[5014] The American Catholic Who's Who. (1960, 1961). Vol. 14. P. 226. Grosse Pointe, MI: Walter Romig, Publisher. Google Books.
[5015] The American Catholic Who's Who. (1960, 1961). Vol. 14. P. 226. Grosse Pointe, MI: Walter Romig, Publisher. Google Books.
[5016] The American Catholic Who's Who. (1960, 1961). Vol. 14. P. 226. Grosse Pointe, MI: Walter Romig, Publisher. Google Books.
[5017] The American Catholic Who's Who. (1960, 1961). Vol. 14. P. 226. Grosse Pointe, MI: Walter Romig, Publisher. Google Books.
[5018] Family history memoir and interview with Margot McKay. Conducted via telephone by Andrew Taylor Call. (Undated).

Chicago.[5019] Jacob Bunn, Jr., and Henry Stryker Taylor, who was a son-in-law of Willard and Ruth (Regan) Bunn, were also members of the Chicago Athletic Association. Bunn was a member of the club at an earlier time, but Taylor probably knew John Michael Joyce, and was his contemporary.

By 1907, Washington Brewing Company was the second largest brewing company in Columbus, second only to the Lewis Hoster Company. John McClelland Call remained many years on the board of directors of the Washington Brewing Company.[5020] Joseph Bernhard had been elected to the Board of Directors of the company as of May, 1908.[5021] John McClelland Call died in 1917. He also owned the Call Grocery Company of Columbus, in addition to the J. C. Call & Company liquor and saloon business and part of the Washington Brewing Company.[5022] John McClelland Call's son, John Edward Call, owned a cigar store in Columbus and was for a time the owner of the Jai Lai Restaurant of Columbus, one of the largest and most famous restaurant companies in Ohio, and one which possessed an exotic American Empire theme.[5023] John McClelland Call's daughters, Katherine Call and Nellie Call, married, respectively, Leo Kremer, an Ohio beer manufacturer and designer and architect of breweries, and Alexander Washington Krumm, Jr., who served as Vice-President of the Ohio National Bank in Columbus.[5024] Alexander Washington Krumm was the son of the senior Alexander Washington Krumm, a renowned Ohio lawyer and the City Attorney for the City of Columbus.[5025] Martin Krumm, the grandfather of Alexander Washington Krumm, Jr., was a manufacturer of fire escape technology at Columbus.[5026] Julius Kremer, father of Leo Kremer and father-in-law of Katherine (Call) Kremer, was a brewer and a developer of the German Village neighborhood of Columbus.[5027]

James Custer Call, son of William Call and Nancy Jane (Ramsey) Call, was born in Marietta, Ohio, on March 19, 1865, and thus shared Marietta as a birthplace with Charles Gates Dawes of Chicago and Evanston, who served as United States Vice President under President Calvin Coolidge.[5028] Dawes was born August 27, 1865, in Marietta, Ohio, thus sharing both a birth year and a birthplace with James Custer Call. James Custer Call was a younger brother of John McClelland Call. James Custer Call first married Collie Brandt, in 1886. One child was born to them:

[5019] The American Catholic Who's Who. (1960, 1961). Vol. 14. P. 226. Grosse Pointe, MI: Walter Romig, Publisher. Google Books.

[5020] The Western Brewer: And Journal of the Barley, Malt and Hop Trades. (1908). Vol. 33. P. 223. Chicago, IL: H. S. Rich & Co. Google Books.

[5021] The Western Brewer: And Journal of the Barley, Malt and Hop Trades. (1908). Vol. 33. P. 223. Chicago, IL: H. S. Rich & Co. Google Books.

[5022] Call family history records.

[5023] City Directory of Columbus, Ohio. (1945). Ancestry.com.

[5024] Call family history records.

[5025] Call family history records.

[5026] Call family history records.

[5027] Call family history records.

[5028] Call family history records.

Charles Harmon Call, who was born in September of 1888. Charles was a resident of Columbus and Youngstown. Charles Harmon Call served as the informant on the State of Ohio Death Certificate for his father, James Custer Call, in March of 1920.[5029] After Collie (Brandt) Call died, James Custer Call married Mahalia "Mattie" McCullough, in 1893, at Jackson, Ohio.[5030] Mattie McCullough (1874-1957) was the younger daughter of Rev. Richard McCullough and Martha Jane (Humphreys) McCullough.[5031] Rev. Richard McCullough, born in 1845, was a son of Rev. John McCullough (1814-1890) and Sarah (Nixon) McCullough (1815-1902).[5032] The elder daughter of Rev. Richard McCullough and Martha J. (Humphreys) McCullough was Anna McCullough, who married Henry Baesman.[5033] Fred Baesman, son of Henry Baesman and Anna (McCullough) Baesman, co-owned Jackson Battery & Electric Company, a machine supply company with offices throughout southern Ohio. The children born to James Custer Call and Mattie (McCullough) Call were Robert Grogan Call (1897-1974), Elizabeth Gertrude Call, Theresa Call, Richard Call (1910-1912), and William Frederic Call (1912-1973).[5034] Two of these children, Robert Grogan Call and William Frederic Call, would possess significant connections to Chicago and Cook County.[5035] The Calls and McCulloughs were Methodist, Scottish, and Republican.

Rev. John McCullough was a Scotsman, and was the son of Capt. William McCullough and Anne (Johnston) McCullough, both of whom were natives of Edinburgh, Scotland, and later residents of Whitehaven, England.[5036] John McCullough trained as a Methodist minister and immigrated to Ohio from Whitehaven in about 1845 with his family.[5037] One of the McCulloughs completed a Theology Degree at Oxford University in England.[5038] This was most probably Rev. John McCullough.[5039] Rev. John married Sarah Nixon, who was a native of Bildershaw, Durham, England, and who was the daughter of Richard Nixon and Mary (Swinbanke) Nixon.[5040] Please note, however, that there is absolutely no known family relationship between the Nixon-McCullough-Call family and the family of the deceased former United States President, Richard Milhous Nixon. It is possible, however, that the prominent Cincinnati and Chicago businessman, Wilson Nixon, whose family had also emigrated to Ohio from Whitehaven, England, was a cousin of Sarah (Nixon) McCullough, whose full maiden name has

---

[5029] Call family history records.
[5030] Call family history records.
[5031] McCullough family history records.
[5032] McCullough family history records.
[5033] McCullough family history records.
[5034] Call family history records.
[5035] Call family history records.
[5036] McCullough family history records.
[5037] McCullough family history records.
[5038] McCullough family history records.
[5039] McCullough family history records.
[5040] McCullough family history records.

been recorded as Sarah Wilson Nixon.[5041] Wilson Nixon, if related, would probably have been a close cousin of the Ohio McCulloughs and Nixons.

Among the children born to Rev. John McCullough and Sarah (Nixon) McCullough were: William Henry McCullough; John Bainbridge McCullough; Miriam McCullough, who married Robert Grogan; Sarah J. McCullough, who married John Grogan; and Richard McCullough, who married Martha Jane Humphreys.[5042] Rev. John McCullough helped to bring the Gospel of Jesus Christ to nineteenth century Ohio and the Ohio River Valley, and also served as a developer of early heavy industry in Ohio.[5043] John was a coal explorer in the Ohio River Valley.[5044] The Call and McCullough family history recorded that Rev. John McCullough was the first to discover coal at Middleport, in Meigs County, Ohio, during the middle nineteenth century, thus helping to establish the coal industry of southern Ohio.[5045] Having become aware of the growing transportation economy of the Ohio River, Rev. John McCullough established and operated a shipping business on the Ohio River, presumably based in either Middleport, or Coalport, in Meigs County, Ohio.[5046] Additionally, Rev. McCullough established a coal mining company in Athens County, located in the western Appalachian Mountain coalfields of southern Ohio.[5047] Rev. Richard McCullough joined his father, Rev. John McCullough, in the McCullough Coal Company in Athens County, and the father and son operated coal production contracts.[5048] Rev. John McCullough also served as a founder and Chairman of the Board of Directors of the Coalport Wesleyan Methodist Church of Coalport, located in Meigs County, Ohio.[5049] Family reports indicate that many of the McCullough men served as Methodist ministers in Ohio.[5050] Following the call of God to Christian ministry in the Ohio River Valley, Richard McCullough became a Methodist minister, as his father John had done before him.[5051] Family reports stated that another McCullough family member, Sir Henry McCullough, served as a Captain in Queen Victoria's Royal Guard, before immigrating to Ohio, as his other relatives had done long before.[5052]

Robert Grogan Call of Ohio

Robert Grogan Call was born December 21, 1897, in Jackson, Ohio.[5053] Robert "Bob" Call was the first son and eldest child of James Custer Call (1865-1920) and

[5041] McCullough family history records.
[5042] McCullough family history records.
[5043] McCullough family history records.
[5044] McCullough family history records.
[5045] Call and McCullough family records. Author's personal collection.
[5046] Call and McCullough family records. Author's personal collection.
[5047] 1870 United States Census.
[5048] 1870 United States Census.
[5049] McCullough family history records.
[5050] Recollections of multiple McCullough and Call family members.
[5051] Recollections of multiple McCullough and Call family members.
[5052] Recollections of multiple McCullough and Call family members.
[5053] Call, Ramsey, Peterson, Van Duyn, and Pittenger family records.

Mattie (McCullough) Call (1874-1957), who both were natives of Ohio, and who both were descendants of founding and pioneering families of Ohio, as discussed previously.[5054] James Custer Call worked as a coal miner, water tender, and an industrial manager in Columbus, Jackson, and the Wheeling-Martin's Ferry region, all in Ohio and West Virginia.[5055] Mattie McCullough was the daughter of Rev. Richard McCullough and Martha J. (Humphreys) McCullough, both of Meigs County, Ohio.[5056] The McCulloughs, Humphreys, and Grogan families of the Call-Ramsey-Peterson-McCullough-Nixon family of Ohio, Indiana, and Illinois were residents of the same part of the Ohio Valley where our McClure and English families had resided some years prior. Eliza Stryker, who was a daughter of Henry Stryker of Jacksonville, Illinois, married attorney James English, whose family had relocated to Illinois from Mason County, Virginia (now West Virginia).[5057] Mary McClure, who married Asa Coburn, was a founder of Marietta and the Campus Martius settlement of Ohio in 1788. For the histories of the McClure and Stryker families, see Chapter 6, *Sprinters of the Steel Track*. The McClures, Strykers, and Englishes were maternal ancestors of Andrew Taylor Call.

Robert Grogan Call studied chemistry and chemical engineering through correspondence courses and at West Virginia University.[5058] Already a chemist during World War I, Call served in the United States Army during World War I.[5059] After service in the Great War, he entered employment with the American Gas & Electric Company of New York City.[5060] Robert G. Call served as the first chemist in the history of the American Gas & Electric Company (later known as the American Electric Power Company), and was the founder of the chemical research division of the American Gas & Electric Company.[5061] Call, as a West Virginia University alumnus, was once invited to be the commencement speaker for the university in Morgantown, West Virginia.[5062]

Robert G. Call invented numerous chemicals and chemical engineering processes that were relevant to the industrial cleaning of power stations, power turbines, industrial plumbing, and related power utility machineries.[5063] He was a developer of patented caustic industrial soaps by which power station turbines, industrial plumbing, and other machinery could be washed clean of different forms

---

[5054] Call, Ramsey, Peterson, Van Duyn, and Pittenger family records.
[5055] Death Certificate for James Custer Call. (1920). Belmont County, Ohio.
[5056] Call, McCullough, Humphreys, and Nixon family history records.
[5057] Palmer, John M. (1899). The Bend And Bar Of Illinois. Vol. II. Pp. 1101-1102. Chicago, IL: The Lewis Publishing Company. Google Books.
[5058] Glover, Beverly (Call). (Undated). Oral Family History Memoir conducted telephonically by Andrew Taylor Call.
[5059] World War I Draft Card for Robert Grogan Call. Ancestry.com
[5060] American Electric Power (AEP) Retirement Memorial for Robert Grogan Call.
[5061] American Electric Power (AEP) Retirement Memorial for Robert Grogan Call.
[5062] Glover, Beverly (Call). (Undated). Oral Family History Memoir conducted telephonically by Andrew Taylor Call.
[5063] American Electric Power (AEP) Retirement Memorial for Robert Grogan Call.

of sludges and rusts.[5064] The industrial soap chemicals and caustic washing technologies developed by Call contributed to the increase in efficiencies of power generation plants and factories throughout the world.[5065] Call also conducted extensive collaborative research in the sciences of industrial chemistry and tribology (lubrication engineering), having been published extensively along with W. L. Webb and other industrial chemists and corporate officers.[5066] Call was one of the early members and committeemen of the Ohio River Valley Water Sanitation Commission (ORSANCO) of Cincinnati, which was and remains an environmental policy and water protection organization.[5067] Call was Chairman of the Water Users Committee of ORSANCO.

Robert G. Call was Chairman of the Prime Movers Committee of the Edison Electric Institute of New York City. As an Edison Electric Institute officer, R. G. Call worked with a fellow Edison Electric Institute member named C. K. Poarch in studying and developing specifications, tests, methods, trials, standards, and scientific judgments for electrical insulating materials.[5068] Call also served as Chairman of the Steam Pollution Committee of the Edison Electric Institute, and served on one of the Edison Electric Institute steering committees with F. W. Argue, V. F. Estcourt, W. L. Jackson, and S. T. Powell.[5069] In 1951 Call served as Vice-Chairman of the Power Station Chemistry Subcommittee of the Prime Movers Committee of the Edison Electric Institute.[5070] T. J. Finnegan served as Chairman of the Power Station Subcommittee at the time when R. G. Call served as Vice-Chairman of the Subcommittee.[5071] Call wrote, co-wrote, and published many chemical and industrial research papers which spread throughout the world and which helped standardize and improve electric power creation and administration around the world.[5072] Robert G. Call and his wife, Freda (Plantz) Call, were both championship golfers at the Wheeling Country Club and the Oblebay Country Club in West Virginia. Bob and Freda had one child, a daughter named Beverly Ann Call, who married Richard Glover.

Robert Grogan Call helped to build the American Gas & Electric Company into one of the largest public utility corporations in the world, and the largest utility

---

[5064] Call family history records.

[5065] Call family history records.

[5066] Call family history records.

[5067] Ohio River Valley Water Sanitation Commission. (1948). Google Books.

[5068] The Edison Electric Institute. (1958). Vols. 56-57. Page numbers not apparent at time of reference. Google Books.

[5069] The Edison Electric Institute Bulletin. (1957). Vols. 25-26. Page numbers not apparent at time of reference. Google Books.

[5070] Power Station Chemistry. (1951). The Edison Electric Institute. Page numbers not apparent at time of reference. Google Books.

[5071] Power Station Chemistry. (1951). The Edison Electric Institute. Page numbers not apparent at time of reference. Google Books.

[5072] Multiple telephone interviews with Beverly (Call) Glover. (Undated). Recorded by Andrew Taylor Call.

company in the United States.[5073] The American Gas and Electric Company service territory ranged from the State of New York to the Lake Michigan shores of the State of Michigan, and to northwestern Indiana, including Ohio, West Virginia, Virginia, and Kentucky. The company would also have a positive impact on Chicago, Cook County, and the other nearby counties of Illinois and Indiana, as will be discussed subsequently herein. The enactment of the Wheeler-Rayburn Public Utility Holding Company Act (PUHCA) of 1935 created a new federal regime of law and policy under which public utility companies were to be governed.[5074] The Wheeler-Rayburn Act specifically placed a burden of obligatory organizational change and restructuring upon public utility companies.[5075] The 1935 Act constituted, as one element of the new regime of law and policy, a duty under which public utility holding companies were required to divest themselves organizationally of their research, development, and engineering company subsidiaries.[5076] Company compliance with the divestiture duty under the new Wheeler-Rayburn Act policy regime led to complete reorganization of the American Gas & Electric Company.[5077]

This case of new federal policy and law necessitated the restructuring of the organizational economies of public utility corporations in the United States. Pursuant to compliance with the new obligatory divestiture law of the Wheeler-Rayburn Act, the American Gas & Electric Company divested itself of its chemistry, research, and engineering subsidiary. Consequent to the policy and law regime established by the Wheeler-Rayburn Act, Robert G. Call served as one of the founders of the new American Gas & Electric Service Corporation of New York City, in 1937.[5078] Call co-founded the new company with his friend and

---

[5073] American Electric Power (AEP) Retirement Memorial for Robert Grogan Call. See also: Chicago Daily Tribune. (May 20, 1958) P. B5. Retrieved from ProQuest Newspapers at Northwestern University.

[5074] Public Utility Holding Company Act of 1935. SEC.gov. See also: United States Securities Exchange Commission. (1943). Judicial Decisions: Comprising All Court Decisions, Reported and Unreported, in Civil and Criminal Cases Involving Statutes Administered by the Securities and Exchange Commission, Volume 3. Page number not discernible at time of reference. Google Books.

[5075] Public Utility Holding Company Act of 1935. SEC.gov. See also: United States Securities Exchange Commission. (1943). Judicial Decisions: Comprising All Court Decisions, Reported and Unreported, in Civil and Criminal Cases Involving Statutes Administered by the Securities and Exchange Commission, Volume 3. Page number not discernible at time of reference. Google Books.

[5076] United States Securities Exchange Commission. (1943). Judicial Decisions: Comprising All Court Decisions, Reported and Unreported, in Civil and Criminal Cases Involving Statutes Administered by the Securities and Exchange Commission, Volume 3. Page number not discernible at time of reference. Google Books.

[5077] United States Securities Exchange Commission. (1943). Judicial Decisions: Comprising All Court Decisions, Reported and Unreported, in Civil and Criminal Cases Involving Statutes Administered by the Securities and Exchange Commission, Volume 3. Page number not discernible at time of reference. Google Books.

[5078] Call family history records.

fellow American Gas & Electric Company engineer and executive, Philip Sporn, who had begun employment with the American Gas & Electric Company in 1920, one year after Call had entered employment with the American Gas & Electric Company system.[5079] Call and Sporn were close friends and worked together for many decades.[5080] Philip Sporn spent much time with the Call family at the Call home in West Virginia.[5081] Robert Call and Freda (Plantz) Call would often entertain President Philip Sporn at their home in Power, West Virginia, located near Wheeling. Philip Sporn served as President of the American Gas & Electric Service Corporation, and Robert G. Call served as Chief Chemist, Senior Engineer, and Director of Research of the American Gas and Electric Service Ccorporation.[5082] Sporn, known as the "Henry Ford" of the electric power industry, also served as President of the entire American Gas & Electric Company system. Philip Sporn and Robert Grogan Call, having begun employment, respectively, with the American Gas & Electric Company in 1920, and 1919, both served as principal builders of the entire American Gas & Electric Company (now known as AEP). Sporn and Call were co-founders of the American Gas & Electric Service Corporation, whose research, chemistry, engineering, and consultative jurisdiction encompassed the entire American Gas & Electric Company.[5083]

The American Gas & Electric Company changed its name to American Electric Power Company in approximately May of 1958.[5084] Also in May, 1958, the American Electric Power Company and the Commonwealth Edison Company of Chicago created an electric utility alliance in which the two companies joined their respective power generation and distribution networks within Chicago and the Cook County region.[5085] Philip Sporn served as President of American Electric Power at the time of the creation of the alliance between the two colossal utility company networks in the Calumet Corridor of Chicago, Cook County, and northwestern Indiana.[5086] Willis Gale served as President of Commonwealth Edison Company at the time of the said Chicago-Indiana electric power network and alliance between the American Gas and Electric Company and Commonwealth Edison.[5087] The plan of the two-company Calumet Corridor power system joinder and union entailed the construction of a ninety-mile long power line

---

[5079] Call family history records.

[5080] Call family history records.

[5081] Call family history records.

[5082] Call family history records.

[5083] Call family history records.

[5084] Chicago Daily Tribune. (May 20, 1958) P. B5. ProQuest Newspapers at Northwestern University.

[5085] Chicago Daily Tribune. (May 20, 1958) P. B5. ProQuest Newspapers at Northwestern University.

[5086] Chicago Daily Tribune. (May 20, 1958) P. B5. ProQuest Newspapers at Northwestern University.

[5087] Chicago Daily Tribune. (May 20, 1958) P. B5. ProQuest Newspapers at Northwestern University.

system that linked the networks and systems of the two utility corporations.[5088] The cost of the construction project was $28,000,000.[5089] The power line ran from Orland Park, located in Cook County, Illinois, to New Carlisle, located in St. Joseph County, Indiana.[5090] The power line possessed a capacity of 345,000 volts, and constituted at that time the largest system for bulk electricity supply between two power company systems in the United States.[5091] The Commonwealth Edison—American Electric Power network in the Calumet Corridor represented, therefore, a twentieth century layer of technology and industry which had been built upon the earlier foundations of the Calumet Corridor: the Wabash Railroad Company, the Michigan Southern Railroad Company, the Lake Shore & Northern Indiana Railroad Company, the Northern Indiana & Chicago Railroad Company, and the New York Central Railroad Company. These railroads had all been co-founded and co-managed by John Whitfield Bunn and John Stryker (see Chapter 1, *Genesis of a Great Lakes Frontier*; Chapter 2, *Builders of the Downtown*).

One purpose of the Calumet Corridor power line cooperation plan was the mutual enablement and supply of emergency infrastructural aid.[5092] Among the benefits that attached to the new and immense Illinois-Indiana power line was the mutual facilitation of emergency utility aid for both companies, should an emergency occur in which either or both of the companies should suffer damage of some sort.[5093] Connectivity and cooperation were mutually deemed key by the two utility companies for the purpose of utility-relevant and infrastructural benefits.[5094] The Calumet Corridor powerline alliance, moreover, constituted an excellent system of systemic risk assessment and risk prevention. American Electric Power Company and Commonwealth Edison Company received benefits from the immense Illinois-Indiana powerline connectivity system.[5095] The powerline infrastructure comprised 498 steel pylon towers.[5096] The pylons averaged 145 feet in height. American Electric Power Company and Commonwealth Edison Company both possessed power generation capacity in excess of 4,000,000 kilowatts at the time of their

---

[5088] Chicago Daily Tribune. (May 20, 1958) P. B5. ProQuest Newspapers at Northwestern University.
[5089] Chicago Daily Tribune. (May 20, 1958) P. B5. ProQuest Newspapers at Northwestern University.
[5090] Chicago Daily Tribune. (May 20, 1958) P. B5. ProQuest Newspapers at Northwestern University.
[5091] Chicago Daily Tribune. (May 20, 1958) P. B5. ProQuest Newspapers at Northwestern University.
[5092] Chicago Daily Tribune. (May 20, 1958) P. B5. ProQuest Newspapers at Northwestern University.
[5093] Chicago Daily Tribune. (May 20, 1958) P. B5. ProQuest Newspapers at Northwestern University.
[5094] Chicago Daily Tribune. (May 20, 1958) P. B5. ProQuest Newspapers at Northwestern University.
[5095] Chicago Daily Tribune. (May 20, 1958) P. B5. ProQuest Newspapers at Northwestern University.
[5096] Chicago Daily Tribune. (May 20, 1958) P. B5. ProQuest Newspapers at Northwestern University.

construction of the new integrative Calumet Corridor powerline.[5097] American Electric Power Company held the status of largest seller of kilowatt hours in the United States.[5098] At the same time, Commonwealth Edison Company held the status of second largest seller of kilowatt hours.[5099]

Robert Grogan Call served as a negotiator between American Electric Power Company laborers and the relevant labor organizations connected to these workers.[5100] As a committed Republican technologist and corporate leader, Call won both the respect of the laborers and labor unions with which he worked and the respect of his fellow company executives, and brought management and labor together in peace.[5101] From 1919 until his retirement many decades later, Robert Grogan Call served constantly as a major builder and developer of the American Gas & Electric Company (American Electric Power Company). Call and Philip Sporn were fathers both of the corporate growth and strength of the American Electric Power Company, and of the technological advancement, achievement, and innovation within this great American company.[5102] The American Electric Power Company impacted Chicago and Cook County infrastructure in important ways, having been the partner of the Commonwealth Edison Company in the great Cook County—St. Joseph County / Calumet Corridor powerline, and having contributed much to the development of the first nuclear power system for the Chicago metropolitan area, which we discuss next.

The Chicago Metropolitan Nuclear Power System

Robert G. Call was the Chief Chemist, Senior Engineer, and Director of Research of the American Gas & Electric Service Corporation through the years when the company played a central role in the creation of the first nuclear power systems for Chicago and the metropolitan region.[5103] Call would almost certainly have been prominently associated, at least indirectly, with the creation of the Nuclear Power Group of Chicago, the Nuclear Power Group, Inc., of Chicago, and the Chicago metropolitan nuclear power system.[5104] This conjecture is strongly supported by

---

[5097] Chicago Daily Tribune. (May 20, 1958) P. B5. Retrieved from ProQuest Newspapers at Northwestern University.

[5098] Chicago Daily Tribune. (May 20, 1958) P. B5. Retrieved from ProQuest Newspapers at Northwestern University.

[5099] Chicago Daily Tribune. (May 20, 1958) P. B5. Retrieved from ProQuest Newspapers at Northwestern University.

[5100] Call family history records.

[5101] Call family history records.

[5102] Call family history records.

[5103] Mauk, James F. (1956). Industrial Research Laboratories of the United States. 10th Ed. Publication 379. P. 21. Washington, D.C.: National Academy of Sciences—National Research Council. Google Books; The McHenry Plain Dealer. (August 18, 1955). P. 11. Newspapers.com. The DeKalb Daily Chronicle. (April 1, 1955). P. 9. Newspapers.com; Robert G. Call Retirement Memorial from American Electric Power Company.

[5104] Mauk, James F. (1956). Industrial Research Laboratories of the United States. 10th Ed. Publication 379. P. 21. Washington, D.C.: National Academy of Sciences—National

the following facts: Call was one of the founders of the American Gas and Electric Service Corporation of New York City; he founded the American Gas and Electric Service Corporation Laboratory in West Virginia, which formed both the operational heart of the Service Corporation, and the research, operational, and technological management heart of the American Gas and Electric Company; Call held top engineering executive positions with the American Gas and Electric Service Corporation and with the American Gas and Electric Company; he was an internationally recognized chemist, engineer, tribologist, and inventor; and he was a close friend, colleague, and collaborator with Philip Sporn, who was President of both the American Gas and Electric Service Corporation and the American Gas and Electric Company both of New York City.[5105]

Philip Sporn, President of the American Gas & Electric Service Corporation, was one of the pioneers of nuclear technology for utilities and was a key force in the development of the Chicago and Cook County nuclear power infrastructure.[5106] The April 1, 1955, edition of *The DeKalb Daily Chronicle* of DeKalb, Illinois, reported that the United States Atomic Energy Commission had received the pleading and proposal from the Commonwealth Edison Company of Chicago for the establishment of nuclear power facilities for the metropolitan region.[5107] The proposal was filed almost at the deadline for the time that had, on January 10, 1955, been set by the Atomic Energy Commission for the submission of such proposals.[5108] General Electric Corporation would construct the nuclear plant and Commonwealth Edison would own the plant.[5109] Willis Gale served as Chairman of Commonwealth Edison at the time of the nuclear power utility proposal and was the one who filed the proposal with the Commission.[5110] Gale and Commonwealth Edison were members of the Nuclear Power Group, an organization whose compound purpose was the preparation, pleading, argument, and advocacy in support of a nuclear power utilities system for Chicago and the metropolitan region.[5111] The Nuclear Power Group was formed in 1953 and was headquartered

Research Council. Google Books; The McHenry Plain Dealer. (August 18, 1955). P. 11. Newspapers.com. The DeKalb Daily Chronicle. (April 1, 1955). P. 9. Newspapers.com; Robert G. Call Retirement Memorial from American Electric Power Company.

[5105] Mauk, James F. (1956). Industrial Research Laboratories of the United States. 10th Ed. Publication 379. P. 21. Washington, D.C.: National Academy of Sciences—National Research Council. Google Books; The McHenry Plain Dealer. (August 18, 1955). P. 11. Newspapers.com. The DeKalb Daily Chronicle. (April 1, 1955). P. 9. Newspapers.com; Robert G. Call Retirement Memorial from American Electric Power Company.

[5106] Mauk, James F. (1956). Industrial Research Laboratories of the United States. 10th Ed. Publication 379. P. 21. Washington, D.C.: National Academy of Sciences—National Research Council. Google Books; The McHenry Plain Dealer. (August 18, 1955). P. 11. Newspapers.com. The DeKalb Daily Chronicle. (April 1, 1955). P. 9. Newspapers.com; Robert G. Call Retirement Memorial from American Electric Power Company.

[5107] The DeKalb Daily Chronicle. (April 1, 1955). P. 9. Newspapers.com.

[5108] The DeKalb Daily Chronicle. (April 1, 1955). P. 9. Newspapers.com.

[5109] The DeKalb Daily Chronicle. (April 1, 1955). P. 9. Newspapers.com.

[5110] The DeKalb Daily Chronicle. (April 1, 1955). P. 9. Newspapers.com.

[5111] The DeKalb Daily Chronicle. (April 1, 1955). P. 9. Newspapers.com.

at Chicago.[5112] The Nuclear Power Group was a company that comprised a continental and nationally-sourced corporate membership.[5113] The founders of the Nuclear Power Group were the American Gas and Electric Service Corporation of New York City, the Commonwealth Edison Co. of Chicago, the Pacific Gas & Electric Co. of San Francisco, the Union Electric Company of St. Louis, and the Bechtel Corporation of San Francisco.[5114]

The McHenry Plain Dealer of McHenry, Illinois, a northwest suburb of Chicago, reported the details of the federal approval processes and developments. The Atomic Energy Commission approved the proposal submitted by Willis Gale and Commonwealth Edison on behalf of the Nuclear Power Group of Chicago.[5115] Pursuant to the federal approval, Commonwealth Edison Co. executed a construction contract with General Electric Co. in which Commonwealth Edison would pay $45,000,000 to General Electric to build a 180,000-kilowatt boiling reactor nuclear plant for Chicago and the metropolitan region.[5116] The site of the new plant was to be located 47 miles southwest of Chicago and located along the Illinois Waterway system.[5117] Eight companies were founders and sponsors of the Chicago and metropolitan region nuclear plant, which was at the time the largest wholly nuclear power facility in the world.[5118]

The same eight companies founded, as co-incorporators, the Chicago company known as Nuclear Power Group, Inc.[5119] This company was the formalized incorporated successor to the prior Nuclear Power Group that the same eight power companies had started in 1953.[5120] Philip Sporn served not only as the President of American Gas and Electric Service Corporation, but also as President of Nuclear Power Group, Inc.[5121] It was Sporn who announced the corporate formation of Nuclear Power Group, Inc., and who helped make American Gas and Electric Service Corporation of New York City a prime actor and influence in Chicago and Cook County nuclear development.[5122] The eight companies divided the $45,000,000 nuclear construction cost, with Commonwealth Edison paying $30,000,000 of the cost, and the remaining seven companies collectively paying the remaining $15,000,000 construction cost.[5123] *The McHenry Plain Dealer*

[5112] The DeKalb Daily Chronicle. (April 1, 1955). P. 9. Newspapers.com.
[5113] The DeKalb Daily Chronicle. (April 1, 1955). P. 9. Newspapers.com.
[5114] The DeKalb Daily Chronicle. (April 1, 1955). P. 9. Newspapers.com.
[5115] The McHenry Plain Dealer. (August 18, 1955). P. 11. Newspapers.com.
[5116] The McHenry Plain Dealer. (August 18, 1955). P. 11. Newspapers.com.
[5117] The McHenry Plain Dealer. (August 18, 1955). P. 11. Newspapers.com.
[5118] The McHenry Plain Dealer. (August 18, 1955). P. 11. Newspapers.com.
[5119] The McHenry Plain Dealer. (August 18, 1955). P. 11. Newspapers.com.
[5120] The McHenry Plain Dealer. (August 18, 1955). P. 11. Newspapers.com. See: The DeKalb Daily Chronicle. (April 1, 1955). P. 9. Newspapers.com.
[5121] The McHenry Plain Dealer. (August 18, 1955). P. 11. Newspapers.com.
[5122] The McHenry Plain Dealer. (August 18, 1955). P. 11. Newspapers.com.
[5123] The McHenry Plain Dealer. (August 18, 1955). P. 11. Newspapers.com.

journalist reported that a large body of engineering work would be done to prepare for the construction: "The plant is scheduled for completion by 1960. The actual construction work at the plant site will be preceded by extensive engineering and developmental work."[5124]

When Philip Sporn and American Gas and Electric Service Corporation founded the Nuclear Power Group and the Nuclear Power Group, Inc., both of Chicago, Robert G. Call was Director of Research, Senior Chemist, and Senior Engineer for American Gas and Electric Service Corporation, whose headquarters was located at 30 Church Street, New York City.[5125] Call thus helped manage and oversee the engineering staff for the American Gas and Electric Service Corporation and, resultantly, for the whole American Gas and Electric Company.[5126] The fact that Call held these offices within American Gas and Electric Service Corporation, and that he was also a key technological executive within the American Gas and Electric Company, meant that Call would almost certainly have played an essential role in the technological and engineering counsel, preparation, and research that were essential to the founding of Nuclear Power Group of Chicago, its corporate successor, Nuclear Power Group, Inc., and the first Chicago nuclear power system itself.[5127] The Chief Chemist, Senior Engineer, and Director of Research would have played significant roles in the scientific, technological, and consultative leadership associated with the Nuclear Power Group, Nuclear Power Group, Inc., and the Chicago nuclear plant system.[5128] The American Gas and Electric Service Corporation, Union Electric Company, Bechtel Corporation, and Pacific Gas and Electric Company all helped to build the Chicago and Cook County nuclear power utilities system.[5129] Viewed from the perspective of intermunicipal cooperation and

---

[5124] The McHenry Plain Dealer. (August 18, 1955). P. 11. Newspapers.com.

[5125] Mauk, James F. (1956). Industrial Research Laboratories of the United States. 10th Ed. Publication 379. P. 21. Washington, D.C.: National Academy of Sciences—National Research Council. Google Books.

[5126] Mauk, James F. (1956). Industrial Research Laboratories of the United States. 10th Ed. Publication 379. P. 21. Washington, D.C.: National Academy of Sciences—National Research Council. Google Books.

[5127] Mauk, James F. (1956). Industrial Research Laboratories of the United States. 10th Ed. Publication 379. P. 21. Washington, D.C.: National Academy of Sciences—National Research Council. Google Books; The McHenry Plain Dealer. (August 18, 1955). P. 11. Newspapers.com. The DeKalb Daily Chronicle. (April 1, 1955). P. 9. Newspapers.com; Robert G. Call Retirement Memorial from American Electric Power Company.

[5128] Mauk, James F. (1956). Industrial Research Laboratories of the United States. 10th Ed. Publication 379. P. 21. Washington, D.C.: National Academy of Sciences—National Research Council. Google Books; The McHenry Plain Dealer. (August 18, 1955). P. 11. Newspapers.com. The DeKalb Daily Chronicle. (April 1, 1955). P. 9. Newspapers.com; Robert G. Call Retirement Memorial from American Electric Power Company.

[5129] Mauk, James F. (1956). Industrial Research Laboratories of the United States. 10th Ed. Publication 379. P. 21. Washington, D.C.: National Academy of Sciences—National Research Council. Google Books; The McHenry Plain Dealer. (August 18, 1955). P. 11.

alliance, New York City, Huntington, West Virginia, St. Louis, and San Francisco joined with Commonwealth Edison Company of Chicago to build the first nuclear power system for Chicago and Cook County.[5130] Viewed from the standpoint of multiregional cooperation, the Midwest, East Coast, and West Coast joined together in technological alliance, and in so doing expressed an ethical policy of national entrepreneurial union, aid, and alliance.[5131]

Call served as an early member of the American Society of Lubrication Engineers, a scientific research organization that was founded in Chicago in 1944. Call was a builder of the organization and served in at least two executive posts with the organization.[5132] He held the Presidency of the Wheeling, West Virginia, chapter of the organization.[5133] Additionally, Call served as the co-founder and Vice-President of the Huntington, West Virginia, chapter of the organization.[5134] It is probable that Call was one of the founders of the whole organization and that he attended the initial organizational conference in Pittsburgh. Let us next turn to the container manufacturing industry of Chicago, which constituted one of the most colossal industries in Chicago history and, indeed, in United States history. Let us next address the history of the involvement of another member of the Call family, Loren Ralph Dodson of Columbus, Ohio, who made immense contributions to the industrial development of Chicago, Cook County, and the surrounding geographical and economic region.

Loren Ralph Dodson

and the Continental Can Company of New York City and Chicago

Loren Ralph Dodson was born on December 21, 1897.[5135] Both Loren Ralph Dodson and Robert Grogan Call, who were first cousins, were born on December 21, 1897, in Ohio.[5136] Born in Columbus, Ohio, Loren Ralph Dodson was the son

---

Newspapers.com. The DeKalb Daily Chronicle. (April 1, 1955). P. 9. Newspapers.com; Robert G. Call Retirement Memorial from American Electric Power Company.

[5130] Mauk, James F. (1956). Industrial Research Laboratories of the United States. 10th Ed. Publication 379. P. 21. Washington, D.C.: National Academy of Sciences—National Research Council. Google Books; The McHenry Plain Dealer. (August 18, 1955). P. 11. Newspapers.com. The DeKalb Daily Chronicle. (April 1, 1955). P. 9. Newspapers.com; Robert G. Call Retirement Memorial from American Electric Power Company.

[5131] Mauk, James F. (1956). Industrial Research Laboratories of the United States. 10th Ed. Publication 379. P. 21. Washington, D.C.: National Academy of Sciences—National Research Council. Google Books; The McHenry Plain Dealer. (August 18, 1955). P. 11. Newspapers.com. The DeKalb Daily Chronicle. (April 1, 1955). P. 9. Newspapers.com; Robert G. Call Retirement Memorial from American Electric Power Company.

[5132] Organizational history of the American Society of Lubrication Engineers.

[5133] Organizational history of the American Society of Lubrication Engineers.

[5134] Organizational history of the American Society of Lubrication Engineers.

[5135] Call family history records.

[5136] Call family history records.

of Nellie (Call) Dodson and Frank Steel Dodson.[5137] Loren Dodson was the grandson of William Call (1837-1903) and Nancy Jane (Ramsey) Call (1841-1923), both of Jackson County, Ohio.[5138] After the death of William Call, widow Nancy Jane (Ramsey) Call relocated to Columbus, Ohio, where many of her children and grandchildren resided.[5139] Loren Ralph Dodson's mother, Nellie Call, was a younger sister of James Custer Call, and was one of the youngest children of William Call and Nancy Jane (Ramsey) Call.[5140] Loren Ralph Dodson, therefore, was the nephew of James Custer Call, John McClelland Call, Peter Call, Ralph Edward Call, Charles Wallace Call, William Call, Jr., Edna Call, Eliza Catherine "Katie" Call, Alice Call, and Teresa Call, all of Ohio.[5141] Many of these people resided in Columbus.[5142]

Frank Steel Dodson and Nellie (Call) Dodson also had an older son named Robert Call Dodson, born November 7, 1895, in Columbus, Ohio.[5143] Robert Call Dodson later resided at Tuckahoe, Westchester County, New York, near his brother and sister-in-law, Loren Ralph Dodson and Margaret (Anderson) Dodson, who were residents of Larchmont.[5144] Nellie (Call) Dodson moved to Larchmont to reside with her son, Loren, after the death of her husband, Frank Steel Dodson, in 1941 in Columbus.[5145] Frank Steel Dodson and his brother, R. Clifford Dodson, owned Dodson Hardware Company of Columbus, which was a large and well-known Columbus hardware dealer.[5146] Robert Call Dodson later relocated to Decatur, Macon County, Illinois, with his wife Gertrude (Waterman) Dodson.[5147] Robert Call Dodson worked for the Johnson Asphalt Company.[5148] Robert Call Dodson also co-founded in 1950, with Guy N. Phillips, the Dodson & Phillips Company of Decatur, which was a wallpaper company.[5149] The Dodson & Phillips Company was located at 915 East Wood Street in Decatur.[5150] Robert and Gertrude were members of Westminster Presbyterian Church in Decatur. Both Robert Call Dodson and his first cousin, Robert Grogan Call, were World War I veterans and members of the Elks Club.[5151] Robert and Gertrude (Waterman) Dodson were

---

[5137] Call family history records.

[5138] Call family history records.

[5139] Death Certificate for Nancy Jane (Ramsey) Call. April, 1923. Columbus, Franklin County, Ohio.

[5140] Call, Ramsey, Peterson, Van Duyn, and Pittenger family records.

[5141] Call family history records.

[5142] Call, Ramsey, Peterson, Van Duyn, and Pittenger family records.

[5143] Robert C. Dodson, 62, Here 12 Years, Dies. Obituary for Robert Call Dodson.

[5144] Call family history records.

[5145] Call family history records.

[5146] Call family history records.

[5147] Obituary for Robert Call Dodson.

[5148] Obituary for Robert Call Dodson.

[5149] The Decatur Review. (May 24, 1950). P. 10. Newspapers.com.

[5150] The Decatur Review. (May 24, 1950). P. 10. Newspapers.com.

[5151] The Decatur Herald. (December 21, 1957). P. 2. Newspapers.com.

members of the South Side Country Club of Decatur, where they both were golfers, and where Gertrude was an active member of the Women's Bridge Association.[5152]

Loren Ralph Dodson was given the middle name of Ralph most probably in honor of his uncle, Ralph Edward "Teddy" Call of Columbus, who worked as a railroad engineer. The given name Ralph, within the Call family, has been established prominently for multiple generations as an ancestral name.[5153] Among the Call ancestors who possessed the name Ralph were the following people: Ralph (Roelof) Van Duyn, who was an early Ohio pioneer; Ralph Peterson, an early Ohio carpenter and builder; Ralph Peterson, Jr., also a carpenter and builder in Ohio; Ralph Van Dine Peterson, a businessman from Ohio and later of Grant County, Indiana; and Ralph Humphreys Wilson Peterson, a judge and member of the Ohio House of Representatives, representing Adams County.[5154] All of these men are ancestors of the Call-Ramsey-Peterson family of Ohio, Indiana, and Illinois.[5155]

Loren Ralph Dodson attended The Ohio State University, and graduated with a degree in Accountancy in 1919.[5156] Dodson married Margaret Anderson in 1923.[5157] Loren and Margaret Dodson were accomplished golfers in New York and Florida, and Margaret Dodson was a noted garden club officer, member, and flower expert in New York, Florida, and Illinois.[5158] At some point in the early 1920's, Loren Dodson became acquainted with Carle Cotter Conway of Oak Park, Illinois, and Chicago, and gained employment with Conway's companies. Carle Cotter Conway became perhaps the most important business mentor for Loren Dodson. Dodson served early on as an executive assistant to Carle Conway. After several years of employment with Battelle & Battelle in Dayton, Ohio, Dodson was hired by the Conway Company, a corporation of Boston and New Jersey.[5159] Loren and Margaret resided in Larchmont, New York, and in Naples, Florida, but were closely connected to Chicago in many ways. Loren would become a major builder and executive of Chicago industry. Loren and Margaret's daughter, Bettie Louise (Dodson) Borton, and their son-in-law, J. Kenneth Borton, were Chicago residents.[5160]

Dodson worked as a statistician for the Conway Company and quickly rose in positions of increasing responsibility within the manufacturing corporation. The Conway Company had originated as a manufacturer of pianos, but diversified into the can manufacturing industry when, in 1908, Conway Company purchased an interest in the Continental Can Company, which had been incorporated in 1904 by

[5152] The Decatur Daily Review. (November 30, 1952). P. 32. Newspapers.com.
[5153] Call, Ramsey, Peterson, Van Duyn, and Pittenger family records. See also: Peterson, William L. (1987). Ancestors and Descendants of Garrett Peterson and Nancy Smock. Pp. 95-96. Baltimore, MD: Gateway Press, Inc. dcms.lds.org.
[5154] Call, Ramsey, Peterson, Van Duyn, and Pittenger family records.
[5155] Call, Ramsey, Peterson, Van Duyn, and Pittenger family records.
[5156] Marquis Who's Who. Article entry on Loren Ralph Dodson.
[5157] Marquis Who's Who. Article entry on Loren Ralph Dodson.
[5158] Call, Ramsey, Peterson, Dodson family history reocrds.
[5159] Marquis Who's Who. Article entry on Loren Ralph Dodson.
[5160] Call, Ramsey, Peterson, Dodson family history records.

Edwin Norton, Thomas Cranwell, and Frederick Assman.[5161] Conway Company owned the Hallett & Davis Piano Company, and, through the instrumentality of this ownership, owned the Simplex Player Action Company of Worcester, Massachusetts.[5162] The board of directors of the Conway Company in 1922 consisted of E. E. Conway, who was Chairman, Carle C. Conway, who was President, T. P. Brown, who was Vice-President, J. L. Cotter, who was Secretary and Treasurer, P. A. Munro, R. O. Ainslie, E. W. Gray, H. E. Benedict, and J. R. Turner.[5163] Loren R. Dodson served as one of the Trustees in Dissolution for the Conway Company when the company came to an end.[5164] Dodson also was a member of the board of trustees of one of the Conway Family memorial trusts.[5165]

The Cameron Can Machinery Company was one of the most significant Chicago subsidiaries of the parent Continental Can Company, which was itself a corporation of Chicago, New York City, Canonsburg, and Syracuse. Loren R. Dodson served as Secretary and Treasurer of the Cameron Can Machine Company.[5166] He held this position in 1954 and probably for multiple years. The company was based in the Near West Side community and was located at 240 N. Ashland Avenue.[5167] The Green Line route of the Chicago Transit Authority, headed to and from the Loop, Oak Park, Forest Park, and River Forest, passes immediately to the south of the old Cameron Can Machinery Company at Ashland Avenue and Lake Street, where the factory, windows, and old clock tower of the company remain clearly visible to this day.

The Continental Can Company of 1904, which was a corporate ancestor of the Continental Can Company of 1913, began as a New Jersey corporation.[5168] The first board of directors of the 1904 corporation included T. G. Cranwell, F. P. Assman, A. W. Norton, J. C. Taliferro, and B. H. Larkin.[5169] Cranwell was elected

---

[5161] Ingham, John N. (1983). Biographical Dictionary of American Business Leaders (A-G). P. 188. Westport, CT: Greenwood Press. Google Books.

[5162] Moody's Analyses of Investments and Security Rating Book: Industrial Investments. (1922). Vol. 13. P. 441. New York, NY: Moody's Investors Service. Google Books.

[5163] Moody's Analyses of Investments and Security Rating Book: Industrial Investments. (1922). Vol. 13. P. 441. New York, NY: Moody's Investors Service. Google Books.

[5164] The original record has been lost, but the information has been preserved in the Call, Ramsey, Peterson family historical record.

[5165] Call, Ramsey, Peterson family historical record.

[5166] Certified List of Domestic and Foreign Corporations for the Year 1953. (1953-1954). P. 470. Office of the Secretary of State of Illinois. P. Google Books.

[5167] Certified List of Domestic and Foreign Corporations for the Year 1953. (1953-1954). P. 470. Office of the Secretary of State of Illinois. P. Google Books.

[5168] The Metal Worker, Plumber, and Steam Fitter. (December 10, 1904). Vol. LXII. No. 24. P. 54. New York, NY. Google Books.

[5169] The Metal Worker, Plumber, and Steam Fitter. (December 10, 1904). Vol. LXII. No. 24. P. 54. New York, NY. Google Books.

President of the 1904 corporation.[5170] Norton was elected Vice-President of the corporation, and Assman was elected Secretary and Treasurer.[5171] Chicago was an early part of the original Continental Can Company, and A. W. Norton worked with his father, Edwin Norton, at the Automatic Vacuum Can Company of Chicago.[5172] Edwin Norton also was a founder of the Continental Can Company. A. W. Norton graduated from the University of Michigan as an engineer.[5173] The 1904 Continental Can Company acquired land at Syracuse, New York, and in Chicago, for the manufacture of containers.[5174] Chicago and Cook County were, therefore, elemental places in the history of the Continental Can Company.[5175] It appears that A. Suydam was retained as the original sales agent for the packers' can department products of Continental Can Company.[5176]

Continental Can Company built a can production factory at Grand Avenue and Kilpatrick Street, located approximately within the Hermosa community of the West Side of Chicago. The factory output power exceeded 2.5 million cans per day. The extrapolated hypothetical annualized output of the Hermosa factory would have stood, therefore, at approximately one billion cans in about 1915.[5177] Loren Ralph Dodson would become connected to Continental Can Company about one decade after publication of this 1914 news report.

Carle Cotter Conway (1877-1959), was a native of Oak Park, Illinois.[5178] Conway's father was Edwin Stapleton Conway and his mother was Sarah Judson (Rogers) Conway.[5179] A graduate of Yale University in 1899, Conway was employed by the W. W. Kimball Company of Chicago.[5180] The W. W. Kimball

---

[5170] The Metal Worker, Plumber, and Steam Fitter. (December 10, 1904). Vol. LXII. No. 24. P. 54. New York, NY. Google Books.

[5171] The Metal Worker, Plumber, and Steam Fitter. (December 10, 1904). Vol. LXII. No. 24. P. 54. New York, NY. Google Books.

[5172] The Metal Worker, Plumber, and Steam Fitter. (December 10, 1904). Vol. LXII. No. 24. P. 54. New York, NY. Google Books.

[5173] The Metal Worker, Plumber, and Steam Fitter. (December 10, 1904). Vol. LXII. No. 24. P. 54. New York, NY. Google Books.

[5174] The Metal Worker, Plumber, and Steam Fitter. (December 10, 1904). Vol. LXII. No. 24. P. 54. New York, NY. Google Books.

[5175] The Metal Worker, Plumber, and Steam Fitter. (December 10, 1904). Vol. LXII. No. 24. P. 54. New York, NY. Google Books.

[5176] The Metal Worker, Plumber, and Steam Fitter. (December 10, 1904). Vol. LXII. No. 24. P. 54. New York, NY. Google Books.

[5177] The International Confectioner. (January, 1914). Vol. 23. P. 86. New York, NY. Google Books.

[5178] Ingham, John N. (1983). Biographical Dictionary of American Business Leaders (A-G). P. 188. Westport, CT: Greenwood Press. Google Books.

[5179] Ingham, John N. (1983). Biographical Dictionary of American Business Leaders (A-G). P. 188. Westport, CT: Greenwood Press. Google Books.

[5180] Ingham, John N. (1983). Biographical Dictionary of American Business Leaders (A-G). P. 188. Westport, CT: Greenwood Press. Google Books.

Company was a manufacturer of pianos.[5181] Edwin Stapleton Conway served the W. W. Kimball Company as Vice-President.[5182] Carle Cotter Conway had been a principal organizer of the Conway Company, along with his brother, in the year 1905.[5183] The Conway Company, which had originally manufactured pianos and owned both the Hallett and Davis Piano Company and the Simplix Player Piano Company, drastically shifted and remolded its commercial and corporate purposes in 1908, when the company acquired the Continental Can Company.[5184] When the Continental Can Company was incorporated on January 17, 1913, Carle Conway assumed the office of Vice-President of the new corporation.[5185] Conway also served as a member of the Executive Committee of the newly-formed Continental Can Company.[5186]

Loren Ralph Dodson began employment with the Conway Company and Continental Can Company in 1924.[5187] The Conway Company reorganized in 1927, at which time the company acquired nine can manufacturing corporations throughout the United States. In the year 1927, at approximately the same time when the Conway Company of New Jersey had changed its corporate purpose to that of an investment company, Loren Ralph Dodson became a top executive officer within the corporation.[5188] "In 1927 the Conway Company became an investment corporation, having disposed of the piano business."[5189] Dodson served the Conway Company as Secretary-Treasurer from 1928 until 1934.[5190] Dodson assumed the offices of Secretary and Treasurer of the Conway Company immediately subsequent to, and quite possibly simultaneously with, the alteration of the Conway Company from a piano manufacturer to an investment corporation interested primarily in can manufacturing.[5191] In either case, however, Loren

---

[5181] Ingham, John N. (1983). Biographical Dictionary of American Business Leaders (A-G). P. 188. Westport, CT: Greenwood Press. Google Books.

[5182] Ingham, John N. (1983). Biographical Dictionary of American Business Leaders (A-G). P. 188. Westport, CT: Greenwood Press. Google Books.

[5183] Ingham, John N. (1983). Biographical Dictionary of American Business Leaders (A-G). P. 188. Westport, CT: Greenwood Press. Google Books.

[5184] Ingham, John N. (1983). Biographical Dictionary of American Business Leaders (A-G). P. 188. Westport, CT: Greenwood Press. Google Books.

[5185] Ingham, John N. (1983). Biographical Dictionary of American Business Leaders (A-G). P. 188. Westport, CT: Greenwood Press. Google Books.

[5186] Ingham, John N. (1983). Biographical Dictionary of American Business Leaders (A-G). P. 188. Westport, CT: Greenwood Press. Google Books.

[5187] Marquis Who's Who. Loren Ralph Dodson.

[5188] Marquis Who's Who. Loren Ralph Dodson.
See also: Ingham, John N. (1983). Biographical Dictionary of American Business Leaders (A-G). P. 188. Westport, CT: Greenwood Press. Google Books.

[5189] Ingham, John N. (1983). Biographical Dictionary of American Business Leaders (A-G). P. 188. Westport, CT: Greenwood Press. Google Books.

[5190] Marquis Who's Who. Loren Ralph Dodson.

[5191] Marquis Who's Who. Loren Ralph Dodson.
See also: Ingham, John N. (1983). Biographical Dictionary of American Business Leaders (A-G). P. 188. Westport, CT: Greenwood Press. Google Books.

Dodson served as one of the founding executive leaders, and initial restructuring agents, behind the reconstituted Conway Company.[5192] Carle Cotter Conway was the principal founder and organizer of the new Continental Can Company in 1927, and Loren Ralph Dodson was one of the co-founders of the new Continental Can Company, having worked under the leadership of his mentor, Carle Conway.[5193] Conway, Dodson, and multiple others would lead and build the newly reorganized Continental Can Company into the largest container technology manufacturer in the world, and one of the largest corporations ever to exist in Chicago, in Cook County, and indeed, in the entire world.[5194]

It will be necessary for the reader to bear in mind, henceforth, that the name "Continental Can Company," as used herein, refers strictly to the parent corporation which owned multiple subsidiary companies. This chapter will identify and describe the relevant subsidiaries of Continental Can Company by their individual corporate names. Carle Cotter Conway, Loren Ralph Dodson, and many others identified herein, were the builders of the parent company, known as the Continental Can Company. These people also helped build multiple subsidiaries of the parent corporation. In addition to his service as a co-founder, reorganizer, Assistant Secretary, Assistant Treasurer, Secretary, and Treasurer of the parent Continental Can Company, Loren Dodson served as an executive and board of directors member of multiple subsidiaries of the parent Continental Can Company. Dodson maintained close and active executive leadership and management relationships with the Continental Can Company and its many subsidiaries, for nearly forty years. Carle Cotter Conway, Sydney J. Steele, Lucius Clay, Thomas C. Fogarty, Hans Eggerss, Jacob Egenolf, William Mackie Cameron, Allen Marshall Cameron, Sherlock McEwen, Philip O'Connell White, and Loren Ralph Dodson, among others, all helped to build the Continental Can Company into a billion-dollar company by 1956, and a corporation that employed scores of thousands of employees. These people all contributed immensely to the industrial economy of Chicago and Cook County.[5195]

In my previous book, *Jacob Bunn: Legacy of an Illinois Industrial Pioneer*, (Brunswick Publishing Corporation, 2005), I described a concept that I identified as the "principle of visionary succession."[5196] The essence of the concept was this: one who gains positions of stewardship, leadership, and responsibility has a moral obligation to share the blessings of stewardship, leadership, and responsibility with people in subsequent generations, so as not only to train successors, but also to

---

[5192] Marquis Who's Who. Loren Ralph Dodson.
See also: Ingham, John N. (1983). Biographical Dictionary of American Business
Leaders (A-G). P. 188. Westport, CT: Greenwood Press. Google Books.
[5193] Call family history records.
[5194] Call family history records.
[5195] See references herein, infra.
[5196] Call, Andrew Taylor. (2005). Jacob Bunn: Legacy of an Illinois Industrial Pioneer.
Pp. 37-38, 243. Lawrenceville, VA: Brunswick Publishing Corporation; Journal of the
Illinois State Historical Society. Vol. XIII, Number 1. (1920). Pp. 273-274. Springfield,
IL: Illinois State Historical Society.

perpetuate the culture, ethics, and concepts of good moral stewardship, leadership, and responsibility.[5197] Jacob Bunn practiced the principle of visionary succession when he offered his younger brother, John Whitfield Bunn, who was seventeen years his junior, opportunities to work in multiple companies in Springfield, Illinois.[5198] Jacob and John Whitfield Bunn were two of the most important founders and leaders of Chicago and Cook County industry.[5199] Similarly, Jacob Bunn, Jr., served as a mentor to Robert Carr Lanphier when Bunn offered the significantly younger Lanphier an opportunity to help establish Sangamo Electric Company in 1899 in Springfield, Illinois. Jacob Bunn, Jr., and Robert Carr Lanphier also contributed immensely to Chicago industry. The principle of visionary succession manifests again in the case of Carle Cotter Conway of Illinois, and his protégé, Loren Ralph Dodson of Ohio.[5200] Conway hired Dodson when Dodson was a young man. Conway offered multiple stewardship, leadership, and responsibility opportunities to Loren Dodson. Carle Cotter Conway must be recognized, therefore, not only as a grand industrial visionary, and one of the most important builders of Chicago industry and American industry, but also as a brilliant and generous mentor to younger businessmen, such as Loren Ralph Dodson. It is crucial that the ethics of honorable leadership, as exhibited by Conway, Dodson, and the many other people mentioned herein, govern the world of commerce, or else the world of commerce will become wholly unfit for mankind.

In the year 1936, Continental Can Company owned two facilities that were located at the Chicago Union Stockyards.[5201] At this point in time, the corporation owned forty-one factories that were located in the United States and in Canada. The corporation occupied a major corporate and industrial presence in Chicago and in Cook County.[5202] "The Chicago district is one of its principal manufacturing

---

[5197] Call, Andrew Taylor. (2005). Jacob Bunn: Legacy of an Illinois Industrial Pioneer. Pp. 37-38, 243. Lawrenceville, VA: Brunswick Publishing Corporation; Journal of the Illinois State Historical Society. Vol. XIII, Number 1. (1920). Pp. 273-274. Springfield, IL: Illinois State Historical Society.

[5198] Call, Andrew Taylor. (2005). Jacob Bunn: Legacy of an Illinois Industrial Pioneer. Pp. 37-38, 243. Lawrenceville, VA: Brunswick Publishing Corporation; Journal of the Illinois State Historical Society. Vol. XIII, Number 1. (1920). Pp. 273-274. Springfield, IL: Illinois State Historical Society.

[5199] Call, Andrew Taylor. (2005). Jacob Bunn: Legacy of an Illinois Industrial Pioneer. Pp. 37-38, 243. Lawrenceville, VA: Brunswick Publishing Corporation; Journal of the Illinois State Historical Society. Vol. XIII, Number 1. (1920). Pp. 273-274. Springfield, IL: Illinois State Historical Society.

[5200] Call, Andrew Taylor. (2005). Jacob Bunn: Legacy of an Illinois Industrial Pioneer. Pp. 37-38, 243. Lawrenceville, VA: Brunswick Publishing Corporation; Journal of the Illinois State Historical Society. Vol. XIII, Number 1. (1920). Pp. 273-274. Springfield, IL: Illinois State Historical Society.

[5201] Continental Can To Sell 10 Million Stock. (May 6, 1936). *Chicago Tribune*. P.35. Chicago Tribune Archives.

[5202] Continental Can To Sell 10 Million Stock. (May 6, 1936). *Chicago Tribune*. P.35. Chicago Tribune Archives.

centers."[5203] In the year 1949, the Continental Can Company employed 23,491 workers, and by 1950 the company possessed sixty-three physical plants in total, many of which were located in Chicago and Cook County.[5204] These various industrial units collectively constituted a diverse class of manufacturing purposes, and capitalized upon diverse industrial markets.[5205] The gross revenue generated by the parent corporation for the year 1949 totaled $335,832,363.[5206] The Cameron Can Machinery Company of Chicago constituted one subsidiary of the Continental Can Company and produced can-making machinery.[5207] Continental Can owned four separate metal can manufacturing units in Chicago among its forty-two metal can plants that were referenced in the 1950 *Moody's Manual of Investments*.[5208] The executive leadership structure and staff membership of the parent corporation for the year 1950 included the following persons and jobs:

Name and Job

1. Gen. Lucius D. Clay
   a. Chairman of the Board of Directors
2. Hans A. Eggerss
   a. President
3. J. S. Snelham
   a. Vice-President and Comptroller
4. P. E. Pearson
   a. Vice-President of Research and Engineering
5. A. M. Cameron
   a. Vice-President of Equipment Design and Development
6. T. C. Fogarty
   a. Vice-President of Sales
7. J. E. Niederhauser
   a. Vice-President

[5203] Continental Can To Sell 10 Million Stock. (May 6, 1936). *Chicago Tribune*. P.35. Chicago Tribune Archives.

[5204] Porter, John Sherman. (Editor-In-Chief). (1950). Moody's Manual Of Investments American And Foreign: Industrial Securities. P. 1877. New York, NY: Moody's Investors Service.

[5205] Porter, John Sherman. (Editor-In-Chief). (1950). Moody's Manual Of Investments American And Foreign: Industrial Securities. P. 1877. New York, NY: Moody's Investors Service.

[5206] Porter, John Sherman. (Editor-In-Chief). (1950). Moody's Manual Of Investments American And Foreign: Industrial Securities. P. 1877. New York, NY: Moody's Investors Service.

[5207] Porter, John Sherman. (Editor-In-Chief). (1950). Moody's Manual Of Investments American And Foreign: Industrial Securities. P. 1877. New York, NY: Moody's Investors Service.

[5208] Porter, John Sherman. (Editor-In-Chief). (1950). Moody's Manual Of Investments American And Foreign: Industrial Securities. P. 1877. New York, NY: Moody's Investors Service.

8. Sherlock McKewen
   a. Secretary and Treasurer
9. Loren Ralph Dodson
   a. Assistant Secretary and Assistant Treasurer
10. G. J. Barry
    a. Assistant Treasurer
11. J. J. Kennedy, Jr.
    a. Assistant Treasurer[5209]

The Board of Directors of Continental Can Company consisted of the following persons in 1950, at least two of whom were from Chicago and Cook County (Carle Cotter Conway and S. J. Steele):

<u>Names and Places of Residence</u>

1. A. G. Chase
   a. Syracuse, New York
2. L. D. Clay
   a. New York
3. Carle Cotter Conway
   a. New York (but a native of Oak Park, Illinois, a major Chicago suburb and village of Cook County)
4. G. P. Edmonds
   a. Wilmington, Delaware
5. H. A. Eggerss
   a. New York
6. F. L. Elmendorf
   a. Cleveland, Ohio
7. H. B. Farr
   a. New York
8. E. M. Hopkins
   a. Montpelier, Vermont
9. J. L. Johnston
   a. New York
10. J. S. Morgan
    a. New York
11. Dr. W. I. Myers
    a. Ithaca, New York
12. S. J. Steele
    a. River Forest, Illinois (also a major village in Cook County and an important suburb of Chicago)
13. S. J. Weinberg

[5209] Porter, John Sherman. (Editor-In-Chief). (1950). Moody's Manual Of Investments American And Foreign: Industrial Securities. P. 1877. New York, NY: Moody's Investors Service.

a. New York[5210]

The 1951 fiscal and business year witnessed multi-faceted growth for the Continental Can Company.[5211] By 1951, Loren Dodson was fully established as Secretary and Treasurer of the Continental Can Company.[5212] The corporation generated gross revenue of $397,863,767 in the year 1950.[5213] The workforce increased to 27,761, representing an increase of more than 4,000 employees from the year 1950.[5214] S. J. Steele of River Forest, Illinois, remained a member of the Board of Directors in 1951, as did Carle Cotter Conway.[5215] Four Continental Can Company metal can plants operated at Chicago in 1951.[5216] Allen Cameron served as an unspecified executive officer of the corporation in 1951.[5217] William M. Cameron served as Vice-President of the Central Metal Division in 1951.[5218]

The year 1951 witnessed gross corporate revenue of $460,595,487.[5219] This represented an increase of more than $60,000,000 from the gross revenue total that

---

[5210] Porter, John Sherman. (Editor-In-Chief). (1950). Moody's Manual Of Investments American And Foreign: Industrial Securities. P. 1877. New York, NY: Moody's Investors Service.

[5211] Porter, John Sherman. (Editor-In-Chief). (1951). Moody's Manual Of Investments American And Foreign: Industrial Securities. P. 2653. New York, NY: Moody's Investors Service.

[5212] Porter, John Sherman. (Editor-In-Chief). (1951). Moody's Manual Of Investments American And Foreign: Industrial Securities. P. 2653. New York, NY: Moody's Investors Service.

[5213] Porter, John Sherman. (Editor-In-Chief). (1951). Moody's Manual Of Investments American And Foreign: Industrial Securities. P. 2653. New York, NY: Moody's Investors Service.

[5214] Porter, John Sherman. (Editor-In-Chief). (1951). Moody's Manual Of Investments American And Foreign: Industrial Securities. P. 2653. New York, NY: Moody's Investors Service. See: Porter, John Sherman. (Editor-In-Chief). (1950). Moody's Manual Of Investments American And Foreign: Industrial Securities. P. 1877. New York, NY: Moody's Investors Service.

[5215] Porter, John Sherman. (Editor-In-Chief). (1951). Moody's Manual Of Investments American And Foreign: Industrial Securities. P. 2653. New York, NY: Moody's Investors Service.

[5216] Porter, John Sherman. (Editor-In-Chief). (1951). Moody's Manual Of Investments American And Foreign: Industrial Securities. P. 2653. New York, NY: Moody's Investors Service.

[5217] Porter, John Sherman. (Editor-In-Chief). (1951). Moody's Manual Of Investments American And Foreign: Industrial Securities. P. 2653. New York, NY: Moody's Investors Service.

[5218] Porter, John Sherman. (Editor-In-Chief). (1951). Moody's Manual Of Investments American And Foreign: Industrial Securities. P. 2653. New York, NY: Moody's Investors Service.

[5219] Porter, John Sherman. (Editor-In-Chief). (1952). Moody's Manual Of Investments American And Foreign: Industrial Securities. P. 1491. New York, NY: Moody's Investors Service.

was reported for the year 1950.[5220] In 1952, Carle C. Conway remained a member of the Board of Directors of the Continental Can Company, as did S. J. Steele of River Forest, Illinois.[5221] Principal metal can factories located at Chicago remained at four.[5222] In 1952, William M. Cameron of Chicago served as Vice-President of the Central Metal Division of the corporation and Allen M. Cameron served as Vice-President of the corporation.[5223] Loren R. Dodson served as Secretary and Treasurer of the corporation in 1952.[5224]

In 1953, Loren Dodson served as Secretary and Treasurer of the Continental Can Company.[5225] Allen Cameron continued as Vice-President.[5226] William Cameron served as Vice-President of the Central Metal Division of the corporation.[5227] The roster of the Board of Directors for 1953 showed the absence of S. J. Steele of River Forest.[5228] Carle Conway continued as a Director of the corporation.[5229] The 1953 corporate report indicated a 1952 net sales and operations revenue of

---

[5220] Porter, John Sherman. (Editor-In-Chief). (1952). Moody's Manual Of Investments American And Foreign: Industrial Securities. P. 1491. New York, NY: Moody's Investors Service. See: Porter, John Sherman. (Editor-In-Chief). (1951). Moody's Manual Of Investments American And Foreign: Industrial Securities. P. 2653. New York, NY: Moody's Investors Service.

[5221] Porter, John Sherman. (Editor-In-Chief). (1952). Moody's Manual Of Investments American And Foreign: Industrial Securities. P. 1491. New York, NY: Moody's Investors Service.

[5222] Porter, John Sherman. (Editor-In-Chief). (1952). Moody's Manual Of Investments American And Foreign: Industrial Securities. P. 1491. New York, NY: Moody's Investors Service.

[5223] Porter, John Sherman. (Editor-In-Chief). (1952). Moody's Manual Of Investments American And Foreign: Industrial Securities. P. 1491. New York, NY: Moody's Investors Service.

[5224] Porter, John Sherman. (Editor-In-Chief). (1952). Moody's Manual Of Investments American And Foreign: Industrial Securities. P. 1491. New York, NY: Moody's Investors Service.

[5225] Porter, John Sherman. (Editor-In-Chief). (1953). Moody's Manual Of Investments American And Foreign: Industrial Securities. P. 1231. New York, NY: Moody's Investors Service.

[5226] Porter, John Sherman. (Editor-In-Chief). (1953). Moody's Manual Of Investments American And Foreign: Industrial Securities. P. 1231. New York, NY: Moody's Investors Service.

[5227] Porter, John Sherman. (Editor-In-Chief). (1953). Moody's Manual Of Investments American And Foreign: Industrial Securities. P. 1231. New York, NY: Moody's Investors Service.

[5228] Porter, John Sherman. (Editor-In-Chief). (1953). Moody's Manual Of Investments American And Foreign: Industrial Securities. P. 1231. New York, NY: Moody's Investors Service.

[5229] Porter, John Sherman. (Editor-In-Chief). (1953). Moody's Manual Of Investments American And Foreign: Industrial Securities. P. 1231. New York, NY: Moody's Investors Service.

$476,884,615.[5230] The company continued to operate four metal can factories at Chicago in 1953.[5231] The corporation operated one can factory at Milwaukee in 1953.[5232] Continental Can Company operated many other can factories throughout the United States.[5233]

In the year 1954, Loren Dodson continued as Secretary and Treasurer of the Continental Can Company.[5234] Allen M. Cameron served as Vice-President of Equipment and Engineering for the company.[5235] William M. Cameron served as Vice-President of the Central Metal Division of the company.[5236] Four metal can plants continued in operation at Chicago, and the 1954 company financial report indicated 1953 net sales and operational revenue of $554,436,932, representing an increase of nearly $80,000,000 over the gross company revenue of $476,884,615 that was generated in the year 1952.[5237] One metal can plant also operated at Milwaukee.[5238] Many other Continental Can Company factories existed in other places.[5239]

The 1955 Continental Can Company corporate and financial report indicated an increase in the number of primary metal can factories located at Chicago from four to five.[5240] The 1955 corporate report indicated that there was also one metal can plant operating at Gary, Indiana, at that time.[5241] Gary, located in Lake County, Indiana, is both an important industrial city in and of itself, and a major suburb of

[5230] Porter, John Sherman. (Editor-In-Chief). (1953). Moody's Manual Of Investments American And Foreign: Industrial Securities. P. 1231. New York, NY: Moody's Investors Service.

[5231] Porter, John Sherman. (Editor-In-Chief). (1953). Moody's Manual Of Investments American And Foreign: Industrial Securities. P. 1231. New York, NY: Moody's Investors Service.

[5232] Porter, John Sherman. (Editor-In-Chief). (1953). Moody's Manual Of Investments American And Foreign: Industrial Securities. P. 1231. New York, NY: Moody's Investors Service.

[5233] Porter, John Sherman. (Editor-In-Chief). (1953). Moody's Manual Of Investments American And Foreign: Industrial Securities. P. 1231. New York, NY: Moody's Investors Service.

[5234] Porter, John Sherman. (Editor-In-Chief). (1954). Moody's Industrial Manual American And Foreign. P. 2159. New York, NY: Moody's Investors Service.

[5235] Porter, John Sherman. (Editor-In-Chief). (1954). Moody's Industrial Manual American And Foreign. P. 2159. New York, NY: Moody's Investors Service.

[5236] Porter, John Sherman. (Editor-In-Chief). (1954). Moody's Industrial Manual American And Foreign. P. 2159. New York, NY: Moody's Investors Service.

[5237] Porter, John Sherman. (Editor-In-Chief). (1954). Moody's Industrial Manual American And Foreign. Pp. 2159-2160. New York, NY: Moody's Investors Service.

[5238] Porter, John Sherman. (Editor-In-Chief). (1954). Moody's Industrial Manual American And Foreign. P. 2159. New York, NY: Moody's Investors Service.

[5239] Porter, John Sherman. (Editor-In-Chief). (1954). Moody's Industrial Manual American And Foreign. P. 2159. New York, NY: Moody's Investors Service.

[5240] Porter, John Sherman. (Editor-In-Chief). (1955). Moody's Industrial Manual American And Foreign. P. 2534. New York, NY: Moody's Investors Service.

[5241] Porter, John Sherman. (Editor-In-Chief). (1955). Moody's Industrial Manual American And Foreign. P. 2534. New York, NY: Moody's Investors Service.

Chicago and Cook County. Continental Can Company also owned a metal can factory at Milwaukee.[5242] The 1955 report indicated a 1954 net sales and operating revenue of $616,163,898.[5243] This revenue amount represented an increase of more than $60,000,000 over the 1953 reported gross corporate revenue amount.[5244] The Board of Directors included Carle C. Conway.[5245] The executive leadership of the company included Loren Ralph Dodson as Secretary and Treasurer, and William M. Cameron as Vice-President of the Central Metal Division.[5246] Allen M. Cameron was no longer listed as an executive officer of the corporation in 1955.[5247] The Continental Can Company workforce totaled 31,775 persons in 1955.[5248]

The year 1956 witnessed growth in both gross revenue for the Continental Can Company and organizational growth for the corporation.[5249] The firm's industrial and corporate presence in Chicago increased significantly in 1956 with the acquisition of a major container technology manufacturing company: the White Cap Company.[5250] Continental Can Company acquired the White Cap Company of Chicago on January 4, 1956.[5251] The acquisitive growth was effected through the purchase of the entirety of the common stock money of the White Cap Company.[5252] The consideration of the purchase contract included the exchange of 210,000 shares of common stock.[5253] Loren Dodson continued as Secretary and

---

[5242] Porter, John Sherman. (Editor-In-Chief). (1955). Moody's Industrial Manual American And Foreign. P. 2534. New York, NY: Moody's Investors Service.

[5243] Porter, John Sherman. (Editor-In-Chief). (1955). Moody's Industrial Manual American And Foreign. P. 2534. New York, NY: Moody's Investors Service.

[5244] Porter, John Sherman. (Editor-In-Chief). (1955). Moody's Industrial Manual American And Foreign. P. 2534. New York, NY: Moody's Investors Service.

[5245] Porter, John Sherman. (Editor-In-Chief). (1955). Moody's Industrial Manual American And Foreign. P. 2534. New York, NY: Moody's Investors Service.

[5246] Porter, John Sherman. (Editor-In-Chief). (1955). Moody's Industrial Manual American And Foreign. P. 2534. New York, NY: Moody's Investors Service.

[5247] Porter, John Sherman. (Editor-In-Chief). (1955). Moody's Industrial Manual American And Foreign. P. 2534. New York, NY: Moody's Investors Service.

[5248] Porter, John Sherman. (Editor-In-Chief). (1955). Moody's Industrial Manual American And Foreign. P. 2534. New York, NY: Moody's Investors Service.

[5249] Porter, John Sherman. (Editor-In-Chief). (1956). Moody's Industrial Manual American And Foreign. P. 2862. New York, NY: Moody's Investors Service. D. B. McCruden, Publisher.

[5250] Porter, John Sherman. (Editor-In-Chief). (1956). Moody's Industrial Manual American And Foreign. P. 2862. New York, NY: Moody's Investors Service. D. B. McCruden, Publisher.

[5251] Porter, John Sherman. (Editor-In-Chief). (1956). Moody's Industrial Manual American And Foreign. P. 2862. New York, NY: Moody's Investors Service. D. B. McCruden, Publisher.

[5252] Porter, John Sherman. (Editor-In-Chief). (1956). Moody's Industrial Manual American And Foreign. P. 2862. New York, NY: Moody's Investors Service. D. B. McCruden, Publisher.

[5253] Porter, John Sherman. (Editor-In-Chief). (1956). Moody's Industrial Manual American And Foreign. P. 2862. New York, NY: Moody's Investors Service. D. B. McCruden, Publisher.

Treasurer of the parent corporation.[5254] William M. Cameron continued as Vice-President of the Central Metal Division of the corporation.[5255] Philip O'Connell White was added to the executive staff, occupying the position of Vice-President and General Manager of the White Cap Company subsidiary of the Continental Can Company.[5256] Continental Can continued to operate five metal can plants at Chicago, one metal can plant at Milwaukee and one such plant in Gary.[5257] By 1956, the parent company owned eighty-six factories throughout the United States and Canada.[5258]

The year 1957 witnessed continuity of the major physical and commercial growth of Continental Can Company in Chicago and Cook County.[5259] The 1957 corporate report stated that Continental Can Company owned 138 factories with eight metal manufacturing plants located in Chicago.[5260] Additionally, the company acquired the Hazel-Atlas Glass Company, and now owned one factory for the manufacture of glass containers at Plainfield, located in Cook County, Illinois.[5261] The Crown and Cork products divisions of the Continental Can Company included the White Cap Company of Chicago and possibly one other Chicago container top and cap technology factory.[5262] The Boxboard and Folding Carton Division of the Continental Can Company also operated a factory in

---

[5254] Porter, John Sherman. (Editor-In-Chief). (1956). Moody's Industrial Manual American And Foreign. P. 2862. New York, NY: Moody's Investors Service. D. B. McCruden, Publisher.

[5255] Porter, John Sherman. (Editor-In-Chief). (1956). Moody's Industrial Manual American And Foreign. P. 2862. New York, NY: Moody's Investors Service. D. B. McCruden, Publisher.

[5256] Porter, John Sherman. (Editor-In-Chief). (1956). Moody's Industrial Manual American And Foreign. P. 2862. New York, NY: Moody's Investors Service. D. B. McCruden, Publisher.

[5257] Porter, John Sherman. (Editor-In-Chief). (1956). Moody's Industrial Manual American And Foreign. P. 2862. New York, NY: Moody's Investors Service. D. B. McCruden, Publisher.

[5258] Porter, John Sherman. (Editor-In-Chief). (1956). Moody's Industrial Manual American And Foreign. P. 2862. New York, NY: Moody's Investors Service. D. B. McCruden, Publisher.

[5259] Porter, John Sherman. (Editor-In-Chief). (1957). Moody's Industrial Manual American And Foreign. P. 2927. New York, NY: Moody's Investors Service. D. F. Shea, Publisher.

[5260] Porter, John Sherman. (Editor-In-Chief). (1957). Moody's Industrial Manual American And Foreign. P. 2927. New York, NY: Moody's Investors Service. D. F. Shea, Publisher.

[5261] Porter, John Sherman. (Editor-In-Chief). (1957). Moody's Industrial Manual American And Foreign. P. 2928. New York, NY: Moody's Investors Service. D. F. Shea, Publisher.

[5262] Porter, John Sherman. (Editor-In-Chief). (1957). Moody's Industrial Manual American And Foreign. P. 2928. New York, NY: Moody's Investors Service. D. F. Shea, Publisher.

Chicago.[5263] Finally, the Continental Can Company Paper Container Division and the Equipment Manufacturing Division collectively operated at least three Chicago factories in 1957.[5264] The workforce amount totaled 53,000 persons as of the winter of 1957.[5265] The 1957 financial report indicated a 1956 net sales and operating revenue of more than one billion dollars: $1,010,268,000.[5266] Carle Cotter Conway continued as a member of the Board of Directors of the corporation and Loren Ralph Dodson continued as Secretary and Treasurer of the corporation.[5267] William M. Cameron continued as Vice-President of Metal Operations.[5268] Philip O. White continued as Vice-President of the Continental Can Company and as President of the White Cap Company subsidiary of Continental Can Company in Chicago.[5269] The timber resource assets of the Continental Can Company included approximately 1,000,000 acres of timberland that were controlled either through means of ownership or through means of lease.[5270] Loren R. Dodson served on the boards of directors of the Southern Paperboard Corporation, the Gair Woodlands Corporation, and the North Louisiana & Gulf Railroad Company, all of which were Continental Can Company subsidiaries.[5271]

In 1958, Loren Ralph Dodson continued to serve as Secretary and Treasurer of the Continental Can Company.[5272] Carle Cotter Conway continued to serve as a member of the Board of Directors of the company, and Philip O. White continued

---

[5263] Porter, John Sherman. (Editor-In-Chief). (1957). Moody's Industrial Manual American And Foreign. P. 2928. New York, NY: Moody's Investors Service. D. F. Shea, Publisher.
[5264] Porter, John Sherman. (Editor-In-Chief). (1957). Moody's Industrial Manual American And Foreign. P. 2928. New York, NY: Moody's Investors Service. D. F. Shea, Publisher.
[5265] Porter, John Sherman. (Editor-In-Chief). (1957). Moody's Industrial Manual American And Foreign. P. 2928. New York, NY: Moody's Investors Service. D. F. Shea, Publisher.
[5266] Porter, John Sherman. (Editor-In-Chief). (1957). Moody's Industrial Manual American And Foreign. P. 2928. New York, NY: Moody's Investors Service. D. F. Shea, Publisher.
[5267] Porter, John Sherman. (Editor-In-Chief). (1957). Moody's Industrial Manual American And Foreign. P. 2928. New York, NY: Moody's Investors Service. D. F. Shea, Publisher.
[5268] Porter, John Sherman. (Editor-In-Chief). (1957). Moody's Industrial Manual American And Foreign. P. 2928. New York, NY: Moody's Investors Service. D. F. Shea, Publisher.
[5269] Porter, John Sherman. (Editor-In-Chief). (1957). Moody's Industrial Manual American And Foreign. P. 2928. New York, NY: Moody's Investors Service. D. F. Shea, Publisher.
[5270] Porter, John Sherman. (Editor-In-Chief). (1957). Moody's Industrial Manual American And Foreign. P. 2928. New York, NY: Moody's Investors Service. D. F. Shea, Publisher.
[5271] Call, Ramsey, Peterson, Dodson family history records.
[5272] Porter, John Sherman. (Editor-In-Chief). (1958). Moody's Industrial Manual American And Foreign. P. 2350. New York, NY: Moody's Investors Service. D. F. Shea, Publisher.

to serve both as Vice-President of Continental Can Company and as President of White Cap Company of Chicago, a subsidiary of Continental Can Company.[5273] Philip O. White now also served as President of the Bond Crown Division of Continental Can Company, which also possessed a presence in Chicago.[5274] William M. Cameron served as Vice-President of the Metal Operations of the Central Division.[5275] The 1958 financial report stated 1957 net sales and operating revenue of $1,046,267,000, representing an increase of approximately $36,000,000 over the 1956 gross revenue reported of the parent corporation.[5276] The Continental Can Company possessed an increasingly immense corporate, commercial, physical, and infrastructural presence in Chicago and Cook County.[5277] Of the 139 Continental Can Company factories, the many plants in Chicago and Cook County represented many manufacturing purposes.[5278]

There existed in 1958 nine Chicago-based metal operations factories, in addition to at least one factory operated under the umbrella of the Bond Crown and White Cap Company divisions.[5279] The Paper Container Division operated at least one factory in Chicago, and the Equipment Manufacturing Division operated two factories in Chicago.[5280] The Hazel-Atlas Glass Division operated a factory in Plainfield, in Cook County.[5281]

[5273] Porter, John Sherman. (Editor-In-Chief). (1958). Moody's Industrial Manual American And Foreign. P. 2350. New York, NY: Moody's Investors Service. D. F. Shea, Publisher.

[5274] Porter, John Sherman. (Editor-In-Chief). (1958). Moody's Industrial Manual American And Foreign. P. 2350. New York, NY: Moody's Investors Service. D. F. Shea, Publisher.

[5275] Porter, John Sherman. (Editor-In-Chief). (1958). Moody's Industrial Manual American And Foreign. P. 2350. New York, NY: Moody's Investors Service. D. F. Shea, Publisher.

[5276] Porter, John Sherman. (Editor-In-Chief). (1958). Moody's Industrial Manual American And Foreign. P. 2350. New York, NY: Moody's Investors Service. D. F. Shea, Publisher.

[5277] Porter, John Sherman. (Editor-In-Chief). (1958). Moody's Industrial Manual American And Foreign. P. 2350. New York, NY: Moody's Investors Service. D. F. Shea, Publisher.

[5278] Porter, John Sherman. (Editor-In-Chief). (1958). Moody's Industrial Manual American And Foreign. Pp. 2349-2350. New York, NY: Moody's Investors Service. D. F. Shea, Publisher.

[5279] Porter, John Sherman. (Editor-In-Chief). (1958). Moody's Industrial Manual American And Foreign. P. 2350. New York, NY: Moody's Investors Service. D. F. Shea, Publisher.

[5280] Porter, John Sherman. (Editor-In-Chief). (1958). Moody's Industrial Manual American And Foreign. P. 2350. New York, NY: Moody's Investors Service. D. F. Shea, Publisher.

[5281] Porter, John Sherman. (Editor-In-Chief). (1958). Moody's Industrial Manual American And Foreign. P. 2350. New York, NY: Moody's Investors Service. D. F. Shea, Publisher.

In 1959, Continental Can Company owned 142 factories.[5282] The Metal Operations Group operated nine plants in Chicago, and the White Cap and Bond Crown Division operated one plant in Chicago.[5283] The Hazel-Atlas Glass Division operated one plant in Plainfield.[5284] The Paper Container Division operated two plants in Chicago, and the Robert Gair Products Group operated at least one plant in Chicago.[5285] The Equipment Manufacturing Division operated two factories in Chicago in 1959.[5286] In 1959, Loren Ralph Dodson continued as Secretary and Treasurer of Continental Can Company and Philip O'Connell White continued as Vice-President of the White Cap and Bond Crown Divisions of the parent company.[5287] In 1959, Carle Cotter Conway was no longer listed as a member of the Board of Directors of the Continental Can Company.[5288] William M. Cameron served as the Executive Vice-President of the Glass and Plastics Operations Group of the company.[5289] The 1959 financial report stated a 1958 net sales and operating revenue of $1,080,393,000, an amount which represented an approximately $34,000,000 revenue increase over the gross corporate revenue reported of the parent company for the year 1957.[5290]

The year 1959 was an important year for Continental Can Company not only because of the remarkable success and revenue that year, but also for the following two momentous historical reasons: the first reason was that Carle Cotter Conway

[5282] Porter, John Sherman. (Editor-In-Chief). (1959). Moody's Industrial Manual American And Foreign. Pp. 2754-2755. New York, NY: Moody's Investors Service. D. F. Shea, Publisher.

[5283] Porter, John Sherman. (Editor-In-Chief). (1959). Moody's Industrial Manual American And Foreign. P. 2754. New York, NY: Moody's Investors Service. D. F. Shea, Publisher.

[5284] Porter, John Sherman. (Editor-In-Chief). (1959). Moody's Industrial Manual American And Foreign. P. 2754. New York, NY: Moody's Investors Service. D. F. Shea, Publisher.

[5285] Porter, John Sherman. (Editor-In-Chief). (1959). Moody's Industrial Manual American And Foreign. P. 2754. New York, NY: Moody's Investors Service. D. F. Shea, Publisher.

[5286] Porter, John Sherman. (Editor-In-Chief). (1959). Moody's Industrial Manual American And Foreign. P. 2755. New York, NY: Moody's Investors Service. D. F. Shea, Publisher.

[5287] Porter, John Sherman. (Editor-In-Chief). (1959). Moody's Industrial Manual American And Foreign. P. 2755. New York, NY: Moody's Investors Service. D. F. Shea, Publisher.

[5288] Porter, John Sherman. (Editor-In-Chief). (1959). Moody's Industrial Manual American And Foreign. P. 2755. New York, NY: Moody's Investors Service. D. F. Shea, Publisher.

[5289] Porter, John Sherman. (Editor-In-Chief). (1959). Moody's Industrial Manual American And Foreign. P. 2755. New York, NY: Moody's Investors Service. D. F. Shea, Publisher.

[5290] Porter, John Sherman. (Editor-In-Chief). (1959). Moody's Industrial Manual American And Foreign. P. 2755. New York, NY: Moody's Investors Service. D. F. Shea, Publisher.

passed away in 1959.[5291] The second reason was that Loren Ralph Dodson retired from the corporate offices of Secretary and Treasurer of the company in 1959.[5292] The Continental Can Company possessed 142 factories and plant facilities as of the year 1959.[5293] At this time, Loren Ralph Dodson held the corporate executive offices of both Secretary and Treasurer of the entire parent corporation, the Continental Can Company.[5294] Continental Can Company owned no fewer than fifteen factories in Chicago, and one in Plainfield, Illinois, by the year 1959.[5295] As a parent corporation comprised of multiple and diverse subsidiary industrial companies, the Continental Can Company owned a variegated portfolio of manufacturing corporations.[5296] The executive officer staff of Continental Can Company during the year 1959 continued to represent a complex structure of duties, jobs, and executive leadership.[5297] The company employed a workforce of 51,000 persons by February, 1959.[5298] The equity capital of the corporation was owned, in 1959, by more than 54,000 shareholders.[5299]

Having achieved the remarkable economic status of a billion-dollar corporation by the year 1956, the Continental Can Company generated gross sales revenues in excess of $1,100,000,000 by 1957. The company surpassed in sales volume its longstanding industrial competitor, the American Can Company, to become the largest container manufacturer in the world.[5300] Continental Can Company generated annual revenues of $2 billion by the early 1970s and employed 6,000 people in and around Chicago by that time.[5301] Given the organizational complexity and colossal magnitude of the Continental Can Company and its numerous subsidiary companies and units, a table has been provided below that will enumerate the principal known companies within the Continental Can Company that existed and operated in Chicago or in Cook County.

[5291] Ingham, John N. (1983). Biographical Dictionary of American Business Leaders (A-G). P. 188. Westport, CT: Greenwood Press. Google Books.

[5292] Loren D. (sic) Dodson. (May 28, 1972). *The New York Times*. Nytimes.com.

[5293] Porter, John Sherman. (Editor-in-Chief). (1959). Moody's Industrial Manual: American and Foreign. P. 2754. New York, NY: Moody's Investors Service.

[5294] Porter, John Sherman. (Editor-in-Chief). (1959). Moody's Industrial Manual: American and Foreign. P. 2755. New York, NY: Moody's Investors Service.

[5295] Porter, John Sherman. (Editor-in-Chief). (1959). Moody's Industrial Manual: American and Foreign. Pp. 2754-2755. New York, NY: Moody's Investors Service.

[5296] Porter, John Sherman. (Editor-in-Chief). (1959). Moody's Industrial Manual: American and Foreign. P. 2754. New York, NY: Moody's Investors Service.

[5297] Porter, John Sherman. (Editor-in-Chief). (1959). Moody's Industrial Manual: American and Foreign. P. 2755. New York, NY: Moody's Investors Service.

[5298] Porter, John Sherman. (Editor-in-Chief). (1959). Moody's Industrial Manual: American and Foreign. P. 2755. New York, NY: Moody's Investors Service.

[5299] Porter, John Sherman. (Editor-in-Chief). (1959). Moody's Industrial Manual: American and Foreign. P. 2755. New York, NY: Moody's Investors Service.

[5300] Encyclopedia of Chicago. (2005). Continental Can Co. encyclopedia.chicagohistory.org.

[5301] Encyclopedia of Chicago. (2005). Continental Can Co. encyclopedia.chicagohistory.org.

<u>Table of Key Continental Can Company Subsidiary Companies in Chicago</u>

1. **Continental Can Company (the parent corporation)**[5302]
2. Conway Company (probaby connected to Chicago)
3. Continental Can Company of Chicago, Inc. (this is a subsidiary company, not the parent company)
4. Continental Can Company Chicago Union Stockyards Plant 1
5. Continental Can Company Chicago Union Stockyards Plant 2
6. Central Research Division and Laboratory
7. White Cap Company
8. Cameron Can Machinery Company
9. Elmer Mills Plastics Company and Division
10. Carl Leigh Associates Company
11. TEE-PAK Corporation
12. MacDonald Machinery Company[5303]
13. American Paper Goods Company
14. Bond Manufacturing Company (Bond Crown & Cork Company)[5304]
15. Fort Wayne Corrugated Container Company
16. Robert Gair Company
17. Hazel-Atlas Glass Company
18. Owens-Illinois Can Company[5305]
19. Shellmar Products, Inc.
20. Shellmar-Betner, Inc.
21. Bowes Industries, Inc.

Explanation of Several Key Chicago Subsidiary Companies of

the Continental Can Company

<u>Continental Can Company of Chicago, Inc.</u>

[5302] See sources and references herein.

[5303] Porter, John Sherman (Editor-In-Chief). (1949). Moody's Manual Of Investments American And Foreign: Industrial Securities. P. 2045. New York, New York: Moody's Investors Service.

[5304] Porter, John Sherman (Editor-In-Chief). (1949). Moody's Manual Of Investments American And Foreign: Industrial Securities. P. 2045. New York, New York: Moody's Investors Service.

[5305] Porter, John Sherman (Editor-In-Chief). (1949). Moody's Manual Of Investments American And Foreign: Industrial Securities. P. 2045. New York, New York: Moody's Investors Service.

In addition to serving as Secretary and Treasurer of the parent Continental Can Company of New York City and Chicago, Loren R. Dodson served as Secretary of Continental Can Company of Chicago, Inc., which was a separate and subsidiary company within the parent Continental Can Company.[5306] Continental Can Company of Chicago, Inc., owned a headquarters at the Field Building, 135 S. La Salle, within the Loop community, and this subsidiary company administered the Chicago presence of the parent company, which was based in New York City and Chicago. Dodson, therefore, held key executive leadership positions in both the parent corporation and the principal Chicago subsidiary corporation, in addition to many other Continental Can Company subsidiary companies in Chicago and elsewhere in the United States.

White Cap Company

Loren Dodson was Vice-President of the White Cap Company of Chicago, which was a major cap and sealing machinery subsidiary of Continental Can Company. Philip White, George White, and William P. White started the White Cap Company in Chicago in 1926.[5307] The purpose of the business was to manufacture closing and sealing technologies for glass containers.[5308] White Cap grew to become the largest maker of food container closures in the world.[5309] Continental Can Company bought the White Cap Company in 1956, and in doing so acquired supremacy in the food container closing machinery industry.[5310] Continental Can operated the White Cap Company as the White Cap Division after 1956, and maintained the White Cap Research and Development center in Chicago.[5311] Loren R. Dodson was Secretary and Treasurer of Continental Can Company when the company acquired White Cap Company.[5312] After the acquisition, and in addition to holding the positions of Secretary and Treasurer of Continental Can Company, Dodson served as Vice-President of White Cap Company.[5313] The White Cap Company factory was located at 1819 N. Major Avenue in the Austin community on the west side of Chicago, and near Galewood Park and the Galewood neighborhood of Austin.[5314] The Belmont-Cragin community is located only a short distance to the north of the old White Cap factory. White Cap Company

---

[5306] Call family historical records; Cook County Industrial Directories from the 1960s.

[5307] Standard-Speaker. (Hazleton, Pennsylvania). (April 5, 1976). P. 25. Newspapers.com.

[5308] Standard-Speaker. (Hazleton, Pennsylvania). (April 5, 1976). P. 25. Newspapers.com.

[5309] Standard-Speaker. (Hazleton, Pennsylvania). (April 5, 1976). P. 25. Newspapers.com.

[5310] Standard-Speaker. (Hazleton, Pennsylvania). (April 5, 1976). P. 25. Newspapers.com.

[5311] Standard-Speaker. (Hazleton, Pennsylvania). (April 5, 1976). P. 25. Newspapers.com.

[5312] Call family history records.

[5313] Poor's Register of Directors and Executives: United States and Canada. (1957). Part 1. Page number not visible at time of reference. New York, NY: Standard & Poor's Corporation. Google Books.

[5314] Chicago Tribune. (December 17, 1950). P. 8. Newspapers.com.

employed 1,000 people when it was acquired by the Continental Can Company.[5315] The 1957 White Cap executive leadership staff consisted of George P. White as Chairman, Philip O'Connell White as President, William P. White, Jr., as Vice-President of Manufacturing, Robert P. White as Vice-President and Secretary, Loren Ralph Dodson as Vice-President, E. H. Farrell as Treasurer, Louis L. Green as Comptroller, John C. Swift as Sales Manager, Charles S. Roberts as Advertising Manager, Fred Boedekker as Personnel Manager, Herbert Renner and Nick Arvis as Purchasing Agents, Charles B. Hayes as Engineering Director, and George Chaplin as Product Engineer.[5316] The White Cap Company was both a leader in technology development and one of the most significant Chicago container machinery manufacturers, having been one of the commercial pillars of the global industrial standing of the city in the world at that time.

Elmer Mills Plastics, Inc.

Loren Dodson served as Secretary and Treasurer of the Elmer Mills Plastics Company subsidiary of Continental Can Company. The company of Elmer E. Mills Plastics, Inc., was a pacesetter in plastic pipe technologies, and was a major party to that market.[5317] *The Oil And Gas Journal* from 1953 or 1954 contained an advertisement for Continental Can Company in which Continental publicized its recent acquisition of Mills Plastics.[5318] Continental Can welcomed the Mills workforce into the Continental community.[5319] The absorbed plastics company became the Mills Plastic Pipe Division of Continental Can, and owned a factory that was located at 2930 North Ashland Avenue, in Chicago.[5320] The Sales Office for Mills Plastic Pipe Division was based at the Continental Can Company parent headquarters in New York City, located at 100 East 42nd Street.[5321] Mills manufactured both flexible and rigid pipe products, including the flexible

---

[5315] Poor's Register of Directors and Executives: United States and Canada. (1957). Part 1. Page number not visible at time of reference. New York, NY: Standard & Poor's Corporation. Google Books.

[5316] Poor's Register of Directors and Executives: United States and Canada. (1957). Part 1. Page number not visible at time of reference. New York, NY: Standard & Poor's Corporation. Google Books.

[5317] The Oil And Gas Journal. (1954). Continental Can Company advertisement. P. 100. No further bibliodata or publication information discernible.

[5318] The Oil And Gas Journal. (1954). Continental Can Company advertisement. P. 100. No further bibliodata or publication information discernible.

[5319] The Oil And Gas Journal. (1954). Continental Can Company advertisement. P. 100. No further bibliodata or publication information discernible.

[5320] The Oil And Gas Journal. (1954). Continental Can Company advertisement. P. 100. No further bibliodata or publication information discernible.

[5321] The Oil And Gas Journal. (1954). Continental Can Company advertisement. P. 100. No further bibliodata or publication information discernible.

polyethylene pipe and the rigid butyrate pipe.[5322] The polyethylene pipe was manufactured for two-pipe jet wells, municipal water systems, irrigation plumbing systems, various and diverse water transfer systems, gas and vapor plumbing, and suspended solid transfer plumbing.[5323] The rigid butyrate pipe, contrastively, was manufactured for purposes of fossil fuel transfers and uses, and was useful to petroleum work, agricultural work, and utilities work.[5324] The Mills Plastic Pipe Division consisted of its own executive leadership structure, which was staffed as follows in 1956. Hans Eggerss was President of the Mills Division of Continental Can Company; Loren Ralph Dodson was Secretary and Treasurer; J. G. Murray was Vice-President; J. C. Jennings was Sales Manager; and G. C. Heidrich was the Plant Manager.[5325]

Hazel-Atlas Glass Company of Plainfield in Cook County

Continental Can Company acquired the Hazel-Atlas Glass Company of Plainfield, in Cook County, in 1956.[5326] Hazel-Atlas was headquartered in Wheeling, West Virginia, and possessed a large presence in Chicago.[5327] Hazel-Atlas built the Plainfield glass factory, one of fourteen Hazel-Atlas factories, in 1955-1956, at a cost of about $4,000,000, and planned to employ as many as 1,000 people there.[5328] J. H. McNash was President of Hazel-Atlas in 1955, and the company produced annual gross revenue of $78,000,000 by 1955.[5329]

Robert Gair Company

Continental Can Company bought the Robert Gair Company in 1956, adding another layer to its corporate presence in Chicago.[5330] The Continental purchase of Robert Gair Company perfected the Continental Can integration and diversification plan, because with the 1956 addition of Robert Gair, Continental possessed manufacturing power in absolutely every sector of the container industry.[5331] Gen. Lucius Clay was Chairman of Continental at the time of the purchase of Robert Gair, and George E. Dyke was Chairman of Gair at the same

---

[5322] The Oil And Gas Journal. (1954). Continental Can Company advertisement. P. 100. No further bibliodata or publication information discernible.

[5323] The Oil And Gas Journal. (1954). Continental Can Company advertisement. P. 100. No further bibliodata or publication information discernible.

[5324] The Oil And Gas Journal. (1954). Continental Can Company advertisement. P. 100. No further bibliodata or publication information discernible.

[5325] Modern Plastics encyclopedia. (1955). Plastics Catalogue Corporation. Google Books.

[5326] Chicago Tribune. (August 25, 1955). P. 25. Newspapers.com.

[5327] Chicago Tribune. (August 25, 1955). P. 25. Newspapers.com.

[5328] Chicago Tribune. (August 25, 1955). P. 25. Newspapers.com.

[5329] Chicago Tribune. (August 25, 1955). P. 25. Newspapers.com.

[5330] The Cincinnati Enquirer. (June 29, 1956). P. 27. Newspapers.com.

[5331] The Cincinnati Enquirer. (June 29, 1956). P. 27. Newspapers.com.

time.[5332] Gair Company owned twenty-eight factories throughout the United States and Canada in 1956 and was a leading producer of paper products, including paperboard, folding cartons, and boxes.[5333] Loren Ralph Dodson was Secretary and Treasurer of Continental Can at the time of the purchase of Robert Gair Company.[5334] The Robert Gair Company owned a Chicago office at the Hearst Building.[5335] Arthur B. Crowell of Park Ridge served as the Illinois agent for the Gair Company in 1913.[5336]

Owens Illinois Can Company

Continental Can Company acquired the Owens Illinois Can Company in 1944, adding a major factory in the Clearing community, near Midway Airport, to the Continental Can Company portfolio of subsidiary companies.[5337] The Clearing community factory of Owens Illinois contained 400,000 square feet of space, and employed about 650 people in 1944.[5338] Established in 1935, Owens Illinois Can made food containers, forms of metal pails, and multiple forms of can.[5339] Carle Cotter Conway served as Chairman of Continental at this time, and Loren R. Dodson served as Assistant Secretary and Assistant Treasurer of Continental.[5340] Interestingly, William Frederic Call, who was a first cousin of Loren Ralph Dodson, was an officer of Hankins Container Company of Cleveland and Chicago at the same time when Dodson was an executive officer of Continental Can.[5341] Both the Continental Can Company and the Hankins Container Company owned large factories and offices in or near the Clearing community of Chicago at about the same time. Edward R. Hankins, William F. Call, Carle Cotter Conway, Gen. Lucius Clay, and Loren Ralph Dodson were all prominently connected to the industrial development of the Clearing community and its vicinity.[5342]

Shellmar Products Company and Shellmar Products International Company

---

[5332] The Cincinnati Enquirer. (June 29, 1956). P. 27. Newspapers.com.
[5333] The Cincinnati Enquirer. (June 29, 1956). P. 27. Newspapers.com.
[5334] Call family historical records.
[5335] Certified List Of Illinois Corporations Filed With The Recorder. (1913). P. 569. Danville, IL: Illinois Printing Company. Google Books.
[5336] Certified List Of Illinois Corporations Filed With The Recorder. (1913). P. 569. Danville, IL: Illinois Printing Company. Google Books.
[5337] Chicago Tribune. (October 11, 1944). P. 33. Newspapers.com.
[5338] Chicago Tribune. (October 11, 1944). P. 33. Newspapers.com.
[5339] Chicago Tribune. (October 11, 1944). P. 33. Newspapers.com.
[5340] Chicago Tribune. (October 11, 1944). P. 33. Newspapers.com; Call family historical records.
[5341] Call family historical records.
[5342] Chicago Tribune. (October 11, 1944). P. 33. Newspapers.com; Call family historical records.

Loren R. Dodson was Secretary and Treasurer of both Shellmar Products Company and the Shellmar Products International Company, which both were partly Chicago companies.[5343] Shellmar Products Company owned a large presence in Chicago at least as early as 1949 and produced annual revenue of $12,000,000 by 1949.[5344] Shellmar made containers and container machineries.[5345] Continental Can Company bought Shellmar Products Company in 1953 and added further to its Chicago corporate presence by doing so.[5346] Dodson was Secretary and Treasurer of Continental Can at the time of the purchase of Shellmar Products. In August, 1948, the United States granted Shellmar a patent, patent 501,917, for the invention of a novel form of sterilized disposable nursing bottle.[5347] The patent report stated Shellmar as a Chicago corporation at the time of the patent pleading and grant.[5348] The United States also granted patent 2,446,264 to Shellmar in 1948 for a novel form of molded pulp carton.[5349] The Shellmar International Company, another subsidiary of Continental Can Company, also operated a Chicago office, and Dodson held the position of Secretary and Treasurer of the Shellmar International Company, as well.

Cameron Can Machinery Company

Loren Dodson was Secretary and Treasurer of the Cameron Can Machinery Company, and as such participated as a major figure in the industrial economy of the Near West Side community of Chicago.[5350] William Mackie Cameron graduated from the University of Illinois and then joined the staff of the Cameron Can Machinery Company of Chicago.[5351] Cameron Can Machinery was located at 240 N. Ashland Avenue, in the Near West Side community, and directly north of Lake Street and the present Green Line train route (formerly the Lake Street Line). Continental Can Company purchased Cameron Can Machinery Company in

---

[5343] Poor's Register of Directors and Executives: United States and Canada. (1957). Part 2. Page number not visible at time of reference. New York, NY: Standard & Poor's Corporation. Google Books.

[5344] Portland Press Herald. (Maine). (May 26, 1949). P. 1. Newspapers.com.

[5345] Portland Press Herald. (Maine). (May 26, 1949). P. 1. Newspapers.com.

[5346] Coffee and Tea Industries: The Flavor Field. (1953). Vol. 76. Page not visible at time of reference. Spice Mill Publishing Company. Google Books.

[5347] Official Gazette of the United States Patent Office. (August, 1948). United States Patent Office. P. XV. Google Books.

[5348] Official Gazette of the United States Patent Office. (August, 1948). United States Patent Office. P. XV. Google Books.

[5349] Official Gazette of the United States Patent Office. (August, 1948). United States Patent Office. P. XXXII. Google Books.

[5350] Call family historical records.

[5351] The Times Recorder. (Zanesville, Ohio). (September 29, 1958). P. 20. Newspapers.com.

1944.[5352] William M. Cameron became a Vice-President within the Continental Can Company system at the time of the acquisition, and co-founded the Continental Overseas Corporation in 1944.[5353] Loren Ralph Dodson also co-founded the Continental Overseas Corporation in 1944, with Chairman Carle Cotter Conway, William M. Cameron, and others.[5354] Cameron served as Vice-President of Continental Overseas Corporation in 1944.[5355] Cameron was chosen to be the Sales Manager of the Central Metal Division of Continental Can Company in 1949, and in 1950 Cameron became the Vice-President of the Central Metal Division.[5356] Cameron became Vice-President of the Glass and Plastics Division of Continental Can in 1958, and E. L. Hazard succeeded Cameron as Vice-President of the Central Metal Division.[5357] Hazard previously served as Director of Staff for the Vice-President of the Continental Metal Operations Division.[5358] Cameron was a resident of Gold Coast neighborhood.[5359] At the time of the Cameron and Hazard promotions, Gen. Lucius Clay served as Chairman and Chief Executive Officer of the entire Continental Can Company, and Loren Ralph Dodson served as Secretary and Treasurer of the entire Continental Can Company.[5360] Charles B. Stauffacher, previously Vice-President for Finance, succeeded Norman Greenway as Vice-President of the Continental Robert Gair Division in 1958, and Lawrence Wilkinson, previously Vice-President of the Glass and Plastics Division, succeeded Charles B. Stauffacher as Vice-President of Finance and Administration for Continental Can in 1958.[5361] Reuben L. Perin served as Vice-President of the Continental Can Company Metal Operations Group in 1958, a job whose scope included the management of the Eastern Metal Division, Central Metal Division, and the Pacific Metal Division, and whose jurisdiction encompassed the factory works and output for over half of the total

[5352] The Times Recorder. (Zanesville, Ohio). (September 29, 1958). P. 20. Newspapers.com.
[5353] The Times Recorder. (Zanesville, Ohio). (September 29, 1958). P. 20. Newspapers.com.
[5354] Call family historical records.
[5355] The Times Recorder. (Zanesville, Ohio). (September 29, 1958). P. 20. Newspapers.com.
[5356] The Times Recorder. (Zanesville, Ohio). (September 29, 1958). P. 20. Newspapers.com.
[5357] The Times Recorder. (Zanesville, Ohio). (September 29, 1958). P. 20. Newspapers.com.
[5358] The Times Recorder. (Zanesville, Ohio). (September 29, 1958). P. 20. Newspapers.com.
[5359] The Times Recorder. (Zanesville, Ohio). (September 29, 1958). P. 20. Newspapers.com.
[5360] The Times Recorder. (Zanesville, Ohio). (September 29, 1958). P. 20. Newspapers.com; Call family historical records.
[5361] The Times Recorder. (Zanesville, Ohio). (September 29, 1958). P. 20. Newspapers.com.

Continental Can Company revenue of more than $1,000,000,000.[5362] The Metal Operations Group, therefore, encompassed approximately $500,000,000 in annual sales revenue by 1958.[5363] The Chicago factories of Continental Can Company produced much of this portion of the total company revenue.

Continental Can Company Union Stockyards Factory 1 and Factory 2

Continental Can Company owned two factories at the Chicago Union Stockyards, and both factories were situated in the vicinity of the Morgan District.[5364] One factory was located at the intersection of 39th Street and Ashland Avenue; the other factory was located at the intersection of 41st Street and Racine Avenue, and adjacent north-wise to the great Donovan Industrial Park.[5365] The *Chicago Tribune* edition of September 16, 1935, announced that Continental would build a $1,000,000, 160,000-square-foot factory at the Union Stockyards for the purpose of serving the meatpacking industry there with sixteen different lines of can production.[5366] Loren R. Dodson was a key executive with Continental Can Company at this time.[5367]

Bowes Industries Company

Continental Can Company also owned Bowes Industries, Inc., which was a Chicago company that manufactured plates and plasticware. Bowes Industries was located at 5545 N. Clark Street in the neighborhood that would become the Edgewater community.[5368] The company was located near the crossroads of Clark, Ashland, and Bryn Mawr. General Lucius DuBignon Clay (1897-1978), who served as United States Military Governor of Germany, led the acquisition of Bowes Industries in 1953.[5369] Loren R. Dodson was Secretary and Treasurer of Continental Can Company at the time of the acquisition of Bowes Industries. Bowes also owned factories in Three Rivers, Michigan, Cayuga, Indiana, and Watertown, New York.[5370]

[5362] The Times Recorder. (Zanesville, Ohio). (September 29, 1958). P. 20. Newspapers.com.
[5363] The Times Recorder. (Zanesville, Ohio). (September 29, 1958). P. 20. Newspapers.com.
[5364] Chicago Tribune. (July 23, 1972). P. 73. Newspapers.com.
[5365] Chicago Tribune. (July 23, 1972). P. 73. Newspapers.com.
[5366] Chicago Tribune. (September 16, 1935). P. 21. Newspapers.com.
[5367] Call family historical records.
[5368] Chicago Tribune. (January 10, 1950). P. 34. Newspapers.com; Chicago Tribune. (February 21, 1953). P. 23. Newspapers.com.
[5369] The Herald-Palladium. (Saint Joseph, Michigan). (October 19, 1953). P. 3. Newspapers.com.
[5370] The Herald-Palladium. (Saint Joseph, Michigan). (October 19, 1953). P. 3. Newspapers.com.

McDonald Machine Company

Continental Can also acquired the McDonald Machine Company of Chicago in about April of 1929. The McDonald Machine Company manufactured can-making machinery.[5371] This acquisition took place in the early years of the reorganization of Continental Can Company from a piano manufacturer to a container manufacturer. Loren R. Dodson was a new executive with Continental Can Company at this time and helped reorganize Continental Can Company as a container technology company.

Chicago Central Research and Engineering Division and Laboratory

The Continental Can Company established the Central Research and Engineering Division and Laboratory in Chicago. The Central Research and Engineering Division was located at 7622 S. Racine Avenue.[5372] The Central Research Division employed scientists and researchers for technological and product development. The Central Research Division employed twenty-six chemists; one chemical engineer; fifteen materials engineers to study designs, costs, and machines; two food engineers; one mathematician; sixteen metallurgists; eleven physicists; two toxicologists; fourteen technicians; and thirty-four auxiliary employees.[5373] Loren Ralph Dodson was Assistant Secretary, Assistant Treasurer, or Secretary and Treasurer, with the Continental Can Company at this time, and was involved heavily in the Chicago expansion of the parent company and its subsidiary portfolio.[5374] As of 1960, the Central Research and Engineering Division employed at least 122 people in research and development jobs in Chicago.

Partial List of Chicago Locations of Continental Can Company

Chicago factories and offices of Continental Can Company included 135 S. La Salle (Chicago headquarters), 4711 W. Foster Avenue, 4645 W. Grand Avenue, 7600 S. Racine Avenue, 5535 W. 65th Street, 5343 W. 65th Street, 1645 W. Grand Avenue, 5401 W. 65th Street, 6501 W. 65th Street, 7622 S. Racine Avenue, 4533 W. Roscoe, 4345 Roscoe, 240 N. Ashland Avenue, 2930 N. Ashland Avenue, 111 W. Washington, 7800 S. Racine Avenue, 2201 S. Halsted, and 2727 Higgins Road

---

[5371] The Cincinnati Enquirer. (April 23, 1929). P. 4. Newspapers.com.

[5372] Gribbin, John H., and Krogfus, Sue Singer. (1960). Industrial Research Laboratories of the United States. Publication 844. P. 123. National Academy of Sciences and National Research Council. Washington, D.C. Google Books.

[5373] Gribbin, John H., and Krogfus, Sue Singer. (1960). Industrial Research Laboratories of the United States. Publication 844. P. 123. National Academy of Sciences and National Research Council. Washington, D.C. Google Books.

[5374] Call, Ramsey, Peterson family historical records.

in Elk Grove Village, among many other local locations.[5375] As with all the subjects discussed in this book, much more could be said regarding the Continental Can Company and its presence in, significance to, and contributions to Chicago. The limits of space require us to conclude our discussion of Continental Can Company at this point. In summary, Continental Can Company helped to develop Chicago and Cook County industries in multiple diverse ways. The parent company and its many Chicago subsidiaries collectively constituted one of the largest, most powerful, and most important corporate conglomerates ever to exist in Chicago. Carle Cotter Conway, Gen. Lucius D. Clay, Loren Ralph Dodson, William M. Cameron, Allen M. Cameron, Sherlock McKewen, Hans Eggerss, Jacob Egenolf, Thomas Fogarty, Philip O'Connell White, and many others built Continental Can Company into one of the largest and most important companies in Chicago and in the world.

The Peterson Brothers of Indiana and Chicago

This chapter concerns the history of the Chicago contributions of the Peterson family from Ohio and Indiana. The Peterson family are among my paternal ancestors from Ohio. One branch of the Peterson family relocated in 1860 to Grant County, Indiana, from Adams County, Ohio.[5376] John Abel Peterson (1862-1935) of Grant County, Indiana, was the son of Ralph Van Dyne Peterson and Viannah (Jones) Peterson, both natives of Ohio.[5377] In the specific case of the ancestrally-derivative middle name of Van Dyne, for Ralph Van Dyne Peterson, the surname Van Duyn had undergone change from its original form of "Van Duyn," to the forms of "Van Dyne" and "Van Dine," as Ralph Peterson's middle name.[5378] The Petersons were members of the Disciples of Christ denomination and Ralph Van Dyne Peterson served as an officer within this church.[5379] Ralph Van Dyne Peterson was also a farmer and businessman in Grant County, Indiana.[5380] Two of the sons of Ralph Van Dyne Peterson contributed to Chicago and Cook County, as well as to neighboring Lake County, Indiana. One son contributed to the Illinois medical profession in Chicago, and the other son contributed to the Chicago and

---

[5375] Various collected notes on Continental Can Company locations in Chicago.

[5376] Whitson, Rolland Lewis. (Editor). (1914). Centennial History of Grant County, Indiana: 1812-1912. Vol. 2. Pp. 1292-1293. Chicago, Illinois: The Lewis Publishing Company. Google Books.

[5377] Whitson, Rolland Lewis. (Editor). (1914). Centennial History of Grant County, Indiana: 1812-1912. Vol. 2. Pp. 1292-1293. Chicago, Illinois: The Lewis Publishing Company. Google Books.

[5378] Peterson family historical records.

[5379] Whitson, Rolland Lewis. (Editor). (1914). Centennial History of Grant County, Indiana: 1812-1912. Vol. 2. Pp. 1292-1293. Chicago, Illinois: The Lewis Publishing Company. Google Books.

[5380] Whitson, Rolland Lewis. (Editor). (1914). Centennial History of Grant County, Indiana: 1812-1912. Vol. 2. Pp. 1292-1293. Chicago, Illinois: The Lewis Publishing Company. Google Books.

Great Lakes insurance industries. These two sons were John Abel Peterson and Dr. Mahlon Bluford Peterson (1884-1953).

John Abel Peterson co-founded and helped to build two large life insurance companies, one company located in Chicago, and one organizationally-related life insurance company located in East Chicago, in Lake County, Indiana, within the Chicago vicinity.[5381] John Peterson co-founded the Farmers National Life Insurance Company of America in 1912.[5382] This life insurance company was one of the large insurance companies of Chicago.[5383]

In 1913, John Abel Peterson served as a member of the boards of directors of two organizationally connected, yet organizationally distinct, life insurance companies.[5384] The first company was the Farmers National Life Insurance Company. This company was located in Chicago.[5385] The second company was the Farmers National Life of America, and was located in East Chicago, Indiana.[5386] The 1913 edition of the life and health insurance industry journal called *The Insurance Yearbook* enumerated the officers, directors, and places of licensed operation of the two interconnected insurance companies. The Farmers National Life of America possessed the rights to create policies of insurance in Illinois, Indiana, and Michigan, as of 1913.[5387] *The Insurance Yearbook* also indicated that the Farmers National Life of America was waiting to receive the rights to operate in unspecified agrarian states.[5388] The executive leadership structure and membership of the Farmers National Life Insurance Company (the Chicago company) for the year 1913 included the following offices and named persons:

1. John M. Stahl
   a. President
2. C. F. Sanford
   a. First Vice-President
3. The Honorable J. W. Williams
   a. Second Vice-President
4. E. W. Wickey

[5381] The Insurance Yearbook: 1913-1914. (1913). P. 231. New York, NY: The Spectator Company. Google Books.

[5382] The Insurance Yearbook: 1913-1914. (1913). P. 231. New York, NY: The Spectator Company. Google Books.

[5383] The Insurance Almanac and Encyclopedia. (1922). P. 218. New York, NY: The Underwriter Printing And Publishing Company. Google Books.

[5384] The Insurance Yearbook: 1913-1914. (1913). P. 231. New York, NY: The Spectator Company. Google Books.

[5385] The Insurance Yearbook: 1913-1914. (1913). P. 231. New York, NY: The Spectator Company. Google Books.

[5386] The Insurance Yearbook: 1913-1914. (1913). P. 231. New York, NY: The Spectator Company. Google Books.

[5387] The Insurance Yearbook: 1913-1914. (1913). P. 231. New York, NY: The Spectator Company. Google Books.

[5388] The Insurance Yearbook: 1913-1914. (1913). P. 231. New York, NY: The Spectator Company. Google Books.

a. Third Vice-President
b. Secretary
5. C. E. Fowler
a. Treasurer
6. C. S. Stanton, M.D.
a. Medical Director[5389]

The Board of Directors of the Farmers National Life Insurance Company included the following persons in 1913: J. M. Stahl, the Honorable C. F. Sanford, the Honorable I. E. Switzer, the Honorable J. C. Billheimer, H. Schrage, the Honorable W. L. Ames, H. P. Swindeman, J. T. Johnston, the Honorable S. C. Spohn, E. S. Jones, the Honorable J. W. Williams, J. M. Ashby, the Honorable J. H. Kimble, W. S. Baugh, A. J. Dawson, R. H. Kirby, J. A. Peterson (John Abel Peterson), the Honorable E. M. Wasmuth, B. F. Biliter, C. E. Fowler, the Honorable L. Morrison, L. L. Newton, and E. W. Wickey.[5390] The executive leadership structure and membership of the Farmers National Life of America (the company in East Chicago, Indiana) consisted in 1913 of the following persons and jobs:
1. J. M. Stahl
a. President
2. C. F. Sanford
a. Vice-President
3. E. W. Wickey
a. Secretary
4. C. E. Fowler
a. Treasurer[5391]

The Board of Directors of the Farmers National Life of America consisted of the following persons in 1913: J. M. Stahl, the Honorable C. F. Sanford, the Honorable I. E. Switzer, the Honorable J. C. Billheimer, H. Schrage, the Hon. W. L. Ames, H. P. Swindeman, J. T. Johnston, the Honorable S. C. Spohn, E. S. Jones, the Honorable J. W. Williams, J. M. Ashby, the Honorable J. H. Kimble, W. S. Baugh, A. J. Dawson, R. H. Kirby, John Abel Peterson, the Honorable E. M. Wasmuth, B. F. Biliter, C. E. Fowler, the Honorable L. Morrison, L. L. Newton, and E. W. Wickey.[5392] The corporate office of Farmers National Life Insurance Company of America was located at 3401 S. Michigan Avenue, near what is now U.S. Cellular

---

[5389] The Insurance Yearbook: 1913-1914. (1913). P. 231. New York, NY: The Spectator Company. Google Books.
[5390] The Insurance Yearbook: 1913-1914. (1913). P. 231. New York, NY: The Spectator Company. Google Books.
[5391] The Insurance Yearbook: 1913-1914. (1913). P. 231. New York, NY: The Spectator Company. Google Books.
[5392] The Insurance Yearbook: 1913-1914. (1913). P. 231. New York, NY: The Spectator Company. Google Books.

Field (formerly Comisky Park), within the Douglas community of Chicago.[5393] The company possessed offices in Illinois, Indiana, Iowa, Ohio, New Mexico, and Missouri, by 1922.[5394] The first decade of commercial existence of the company saw financial growth and diversity among the classes of insurance policies created.[5395] Life insurance, accident insurance, total disability insurance, and income insurance constituted the four classes of insurance that the company created upon corresponding classes of risk.[5396] John Abel Peterson remained a member of the board of directors of the company ten years after he helped establish the company in 1912.[5397] John M. Stahl was a Northwestern University alumnus.[5398]

The Farmers National Life Insurance Company of America possessed a culture in which the values of organizational independence, organizational development, internal workforce community, loyalty, skill, and knowledge, predominated. [5399] *The Insurance Almanac and Encyclopedia* for the year 1922 presented a company report for Farmers National Life of America in which the authors indicated that the commercial culture of Farmers National Life varied significantly from the common merger-based corporate culture that was prevalent at the time. The report contained the following comparison and distinguishment: "This company has taken no part in the mergers or consolidations which have marked the course of some of the newer Western companies. . ."[5400]

The 1922 summary and report contained additional testimony of the company's conservative culture by stating that the company leadership carefully and diligently chose the risks upon which to create policies of insurance. The report communicated notice of the fact that farmers as a class of insured persons possessed a lower risk of insurable events, because of the generally common quality of healthiness among farmers.[5401] The report contained a comment that noted that the values of care, diligence, and informed administration constituted a cultural foundation upon which the company engaged in the business of insurance of risk. "A feature of the company's management is the presence of the agency

---

[5393] The Insurance Almanac and Encyclopedia. (1922). New York, NY: The Underwriter Printing And Publishing Company. Google Books.

[5394] The Insurance Almanac and Encyclopedia. (1922). New York, NY: The Underwriter Printing And Publishing Company. Google Books.

[5395] The Insurance Almanac and Encyclopedia. (1922). New York, NY: The Underwriter Printing And Publishing Company. Google Books.

[5396] The Insurance Almanac and Encyclopedia. (1922). New York, NY: The Underwriter Printing And Publishing Company. Google Books.

[5397] The Insurance Almanac and Encyclopedia. (1922). New York, NY: The Underwriter Printing And Publishing Company. Google Books.

[5398] The relevant reference work has been lost, but its contents are recollected correctly.

[5399] The Insurance Almanac and Encyclopedia. (1922). New York, NY: The Underwriter Printing And Publishing Company. Google Books.

[5400] The Insurance Almanac and Encyclopedia. (1922). P. 218. New York, NY: The Underwriter Printing And Publishing Company. Google Books.

[5401] The Insurance Almanac and Encyclopedia. (1922). P. 218. New York, NY: The Underwriter Printing And Publishing Company. Google Books.

director and the three leading agents on the executive committee of the company, thus establishing a close and most helpful cooperation between the home office and the field."[5402] The company possessed more than $22,000,000 of life insurance in force in 1922, and the company assets were reported to be $1,392,136 in 1922.[5403] The leadership structure and membership of the Farmers National Life Insurance Company included the following persons in 1922. One should take notice of the continuity of leadership and participation from persons who were connected with the establishment of the company in 1912.

1. John M. Stahl
   a. President
2. John W. Williams
   a. Vice-President
3. C. F. Sanford
   a. Vice-President
4. W. L. Ames
   a. Vice-President
5. B. F. Biliter
   a. Secretary
6. W. R. Presnall
   a. Assistant Secretary
7. William E. Swift
   a. Assistant Secretary
8. John R. Pearce
   a. Acting Treasurer
9. S. C. Stanton, M.D.
   a. Medical Director
10. R. L. Otwell
    a. General Counsel
11. Marcus Gunn
    a. Actuary[5404]

The Board of Directors of the Farmers National Life Insurance Company in 1922 consisted of the following persons: John M. Stahl, C. F. Sanford, Isaac E. Switzer, W. L. Ames, H. P. Swindeman, J. W. Williams, A. J. Dawson, John A. Peterson, A. F. Ackerman, B. F. Biliter, Charles Bartlett, H. J. Smith, Dr. S. C. Stanton, J. E.

[5402] The Insurance Almanac and Encyclopedia. (1922). P. 218. New York, NY: The Underwriter Printing And Publishing Company. Google Books.
[5403] The Insurance Almanac and Encyclopedia. (1922). P. 218. New York, NY: The Underwriter Printing And Publishing Company. Google Books.
[5404] The Insurance Almanac and Encyclopedia. (1922). P. 218. New York, NY: The Underwriter Printing And Publishing Company. Google Books.

Kenney, J. E. Stephens, W. C. Ivins, James I. Leach, Jackson R. Pearce, Levi J. Orr, F. C. Amsbury, Frank J. Penick, W. R. Presnall, and A. O. Schipfer.[5405]

John Peterson was a founder and director of multiple Indiana companies. He and his wife were also engaged in Christian philanthropy. In 1915 John Peterson and his wife donated $10,000 to the Bloomington Bible Chair at Indiana University in Bloomington.[5406] Peterson gifted the capital with the condition that $10,000 more be gifted by other donors, so that a fund of $20,000 could be used for the financing of a Chair in Biblical Studies at Indiana University. The philanthropic report indicated that $2,000 of the conditional additional amount had been contributed as of August, 1915, so that the entire capital fund equaled $12,000 as of August, 1915. Joseph C. Todd served as Dean of the Bloomington Bible Chair at the time of Peterson's donation. The report contained the comment, prediction, and opinion that the entire $20,000 would be donated, thus meeting the condition attached to the Peterson gift and consequently causing the original gift capital to vest in the Bloomington Bible Chair at Indiana University.[5407] John Abel Peterson also co-founded the Indiana Farmers' Institute, which served as an organizational forerunner of the National Farmers' Institute, which was organized in Chicago. John A. Peterson, M. M. Alexander, and J. W. Thomson founded the Marion Fence Machinery Company in 1921 for the purpose of manufacturing special machinery and components for fencing.[5408] The company operated from a headquarters in Marion, Grant County, Indiana.[5409]

John A. Peterson was one of the founders and builders of the Indiana Farm Grain Dealers Association.[5410] He served many years on the board of directors of the organization and helped to standardize the grain industry of Indiana and the Midwest.[5411] The Indiana Farm Grain Dealers Association, which organized and coordinated many, if not most, of the grain elevators and grain elevator companies of Indiana, operated a large printing press and agricultural news journal in

---

[5405] The Insurance Almanac and Encyclopedia. (1922). P. 218. New York, NY: The Underwriter Printing And Publishing Company. Google Books.

[5406] Morrison, Charles Clayton (Editor). The Christian Century. (August 12, 1915). Vol. 32, Number 32. P. 14. Chicago, IL: Disciples of Christ in the Interest of the Kingdom of God. Google Books.

[5407] Morrison, Charles Clayton (Editor). The Christian Century. (August 12, 1915). Vol. 32, Number 32. P. 14. Chicago, IL: Disciples of Christ in the Interest of the Kingdom of God. Google Books.

[5408] The Iron Age. (January 27, 1921). P. 299. New York, NY: The Iron Age. Google Books.

[5409] The Iron Age. (January 27, 1921). P. 299. New York, NY: The Iron Age. Google Books.

[5410] Call, Ramsey, Peterson family history records.

[5411] The Huntington Herald. (Huntington, Indiana). (March 12, 2921). P. 12. Newspapers.com.

Chicago, and owned the Steinhart Grain Company of Indianapolis.[5412] By 1920 more than 100 Indiana grain elevator companies had joined the Indiana Farm Grain Dealers Association.[5413] J. S. Minch, who was president of the Farm Grain Dealers Association in 1920, predicted that every Indiana grain elevator company would join the Association by 1921.[5414] John A. Peterson was a member of the Farmers National Congress as early as 1915.[5415] The National Farm Bureau was founded in Chicago and it is probable that John Peterson was one of the founders of the National Farm Bureau, because of its close connection to the Indiana men who started the Indiana farm organizations discussed here.[5416] John Abel Peterson married Gertrude Alice Leisure of Indiana.[5417]

Dr. Mahlon Bluford Peterson of Indiana and Chicago

Dr. Mahlon Bluford Peterson (1884-1953) was a younger brother of John Abel Peterson (1862-1935).[5418] Mahlon Peterson moved to Chicago from Grant County, Indiana, to pursue a medical education.[5419] At Chicago, Mahlon Peterson attended the Chicago College of Medicine and Surgery, from which he graduated with the degree of Doctor of Medicine in 1916.[5420] At the time when Mahlon Peterson received the Illinois State Board of Health certificate granting the right to practice medicine in Illinois, he resided at 3433 W. Congress Street.[5421] This address is located in the East Garfield Park community of Chicago. The Garfield Park Conservatory and the Garfield Park Fieldhouse are both located nearby. Mahlon Peterson was thirty-one years old when he graduated from the Chicago College of Medicine and Surgery.[5422] Peterson completed his medical internship at St. Luke's

[5412] The Huntington Herald. (Huntington, Indiana). (March 12, 2921). P. 12. Newspapers.com.
[5413] The Richmond Palladium and Sun-Telegram. (Richmond, Indiana). (February 27, 1920). P. 4. Newspapers.com.
[5414] The Richmond Palladium and Sun-Telegram. (Richmond, Indiana). (February 27, 1920). P. 4. Newspapers.com.
[5415] The Waterloo Press. (August 12, 1915). Newspapers.com.
[5416] The Fairmount News. (January 19, 1923). P. 1. Newspapers.com.
[5417] John Abel Peterson and Gertrude Alice (Leisure) Peterson Memorial. Findagrave.com.
[5418] Whitson, Rolland Lewis. (Editor). (1914). Centennial History of Grant County, Indiana: 1812-1912. Vol. 2. Pp. 1292-1293. Chicago, Illinois: The Lewis Publishing Company. Google Books.
[5419] Whitson, Rolland Lewis. (Editor). (1914). Centennial History of Grant County, Indiana: 1812-1912. Vol. 2. Pp. 1292-1293. Chicago, Illinois: The Lewis Publishing Company. Google Books.
[5420] Illinois Health News. (1916). Vol. 2, Number 1. P. 202. Springfield, IL: Illinois State Board of Health. Google Books.
[5421] Illinois Health News. (1916). Vol. 2, Number 1. P. 202. Springfield, IL: Illinois State Board of Health. Google Books.
[5422] Illinois Health News. (1916). Vol. 2, Number 1. P. 202. Springfield, IL: Illinois State Board of Health. Google Books.

Hospital in Chicago[5423] and afterwards practiced medicine in Chicago.[5424] St. Luke's Hospital had been established partly by Juliette Magill Kinzie, a cousin of the Taylors and Strykers of Chicago through the Stryker-Henshaw ancestors of Charlotte Stryker Taylor. Mahlon was a medical doctor and surgeon in Houston, Texas, after his time in Chicago. Mahlon married Anna Leona Clark of Ohio.[5425]

The Sangamo Electric Company

The Sangamo Electric Company possessed a powerful and multifaceted presence in Chicago for many generations. Robert Carr Lanphier (1875-1939) wrote *Forty Years of Sangamo*, which chronicled the history and development of the Sangamo Electric Company of Springfield.[5426] The opening paragraph of the work showed the importance of Chicago to the formation of the Sangamo Electric Company. The company was an organizational descendant of the Illinois Watch Company.[5427] The Waltham Watch Company of Massachusetts filed a suit against the Illinois Watch Company in which plaintiff Waltham alleged that Illinois had breached an intellectual property right to a specific form of watch mechanism.[5428] The Master Mechanic for Illinois Watch Company was a man named Tom Sheridan, and it was Sheridan who provided the technological representation of the rights of Illinois Watch Company in the Waltham-Illinois lawsuit.[5429] The lawsuit motivated Sheridan to study law, particularly patent law, and Sheridan consequently became a lawyer at Chicago.[5430] As a patent lawyer, Sheridan met a client named Ludwig Gutmann, a German-American inventor who was seeking financing and protective

[5423] Nu Sigma Nu Bulletin. (1923). Vol. 13. (Page number not visible). Google Books.

[5424] Whitson, Rolland Lewis. (Editor). (1914). Centennial History of Grant County, Indiana: 1812-1912. Vol. 2. P. 1293. Chicago, Illinois: The Lewis Publishing Company. Google Books.

[5425] Dr. Mahlon Bluford Peterson and Anna Leona (Clark) Peterson Memorial. Findagrave.com.

[5426] Lanphier, Robert Carr. (1936). Forty Years of Sangamo. Appearing in Sangamo: A History of Fifty Years. (1949). P. Chicago, IL: Sangamo Electric Company. Archive.org.

[5427] Lanphier, Robert Carr. (1936). Forty Years of Sangamo. Appearing in Sangamo: A History of Fifty Years. (1949). Pp. 3-13. Chicago, IL: Sangamo Electric Company. Archive.org.

[5428] Lanphier, Robert Carr. (1936). Forty Years of Sangamo. Appearing in Sangamo: A History of Fifty Years. (1949). P. 3. Chicago, IL: Sangamo Electric Company. Archive.org.

[5429] Lanphier, Robert Carr. (1936). Forty Years of Sangamo. Appearing in Sangamo: A History of Fifty Years. (1949). P. 3. Chicago, IL: Sangamo Electric Company. Archive.org.

[5430] Lanphier, Robert Carr. (1936). Forty Years of Sangamo. Appearing in Sangamo: A History of Fifty Years. (1949). P. 3. Chicago, IL: Sangamo Electric Company. Archive.org.

property rights for an electrical device that Gutmann had been developing.[5431] Gutmann had studied with Ernst Werner von Siemens in Germany, with Lucien Gaulard and John Dixon Gibbs in France, and with Otto Blathy of Budapest. Gutmann afterwards emigrated to the United States in 1887, where he found employment with the Westinghouse Electric Company.[5432] Gutmann worked with street railway motor development, relocated to Chicago, and afterwards moved to Peoria.[5433] Gutmann and Otto Blathy had both developed concepts and plans for the construction of a metering machine that could measure the wattage amounts of electrical current.[5434]

Gutmann brought this concept to the United States and sought financing and support in Illinois when he retained Tom Sheridan of Chicago for representation and counsel regarding the Gutmann prototype concepts for electrical metering.[5435] Sheridan relied on his experience with the Illinois Watch Company in giving counsel to Gutmann.[5436] Sheridan counseled Gutmann to present his electrical meter concepts and plans to the Illinois Watch Company of Springfield, and to seek their counsel, support, and financing for the Gutmann prototype proposals.[5437] Sheridan recognized that the proposed electric meter would require an element called a recording train, and that the Illinois Watch Company possessed the manufacturing skills and powers necessary for the construction of the recording train element of the prototype meters.[5438] Sheridan of Chicago brokered a happy

---

[5431] Lanphier, Robert Carr. (1936). Forty Years of Sangamo. Appearing in Sangamo: A History of Fifty Years. (1949). P. 3. Chicago, IL: Sangamo Electric Company. Archive.org.

[5432] Lanphier, Robert Carr. (1936). Forty Years of Sangamo. Appearing in Sangamo: A History of Fifty Years. (1949). P. 3. Chicago, IL: Sangamo Electric Company. Archive.org.

[5433] Lanphier, Robert Carr. (1936). Forty Years of Sangamo. Appearing in Sangamo: A History of Fifty Years. (1949). P. 3. Chicago, IL: Sangamo Electric Company. Archive.org.

[5434] Lanphier, Robert Carr. (1936). Forty Years of Sangamo. Appearing in Sangamo: A History of Fifty Years. (1949). P. 4. Chicago, IL: Sangamo Electric Company. Archive.org.

[5435] Lanphier, Robert Carr. (1936). Forty Years of Sangamo. Appearing in Sangamo: A History of Fifty Years. (1949). P. 4. Chicago, IL: Sangamo Electric Company. Archive.org.

[5436] Lanphier, Robert Carr. (1936). Forty Years of Sangamo. Appearing in Sangamo: A History of Fifty Years. (1949). P. 4. Chicago, IL: Sangamo Electric Company. Archive.org.

[5437] Lanphier, Robert Carr. (1936). Forty Years of Sangamo. Appearing in Sangamo: A History of Fifty Years. (1949). P. 4. Chicago, IL: Sangamo Electric Company. Archive.org.

[5438] Lanphier, Robert Carr. (1936). Forty Years of Sangamo. Appearing in Sangamo: A History of Fifty Years. (1949). P. 4. Chicago, IL: Sangamo Electric Company. Archive.org.

match between Gutmann and the Illinois Watch Company, because of two mutual factors.[5439] Gutmann required financing, support, and productive means, and the Illinois Watch Company, which had recovered from an economic downturn, required business opportunity and market in order to regain financial stability and soundness.[5440] The watch company possessed abundant manufacturing space that was suitable for re-adaptation to meter manufacture, and Sheridan's brokerage of the opportunity led to a meeting with Jacob Bunn, Jr. (1864-1926), who was Vice-President of the Illinois Watch Company.[5441] Jacob Bunn, Jr., consulted with his father, Jacob Bunn, Sr., about Sheridan's proposal, but received a negative answer from the senior Bunn, most probably because the elder Bunn had suffered much economic failure in the Panic of 1873, had prioritized the return of the moneys belonging to his former bank clients from the J. Bunn Bank, and was averse to the additional market risk that attached to the electric meter opportunity.[5442]

Despite the understandable rejection from his father, Jacob Bunn, Jr., assumed the market risk of Sheridan's proposal and contracted to support, finance, and manage production of the Gutmann invention.[5443] Robert Carr Lanphier indicated that Jacob Bunn, Jr., classified the Gutmann venture as a business trial which would lead quickly to judgment of approval or rejection based on the results of the meter trials and experiences conducted by the Illinois Watch Company.[5444] The agreement stipulated that Illinois Watch Company would manufacture the components for the Gutmann meters, and that Gutmann, at Peoria, would assemble the necessary means and data, run trials, and report the results to Bunn, concerning

[5439] Lanphier, Robert Carr. (1936). Forty Years of Sangamo. Appearing in Sangamo: A History of Fifty Years. (1949). P. 4. Chicago, IL: Sangamo Electric Company. Archive.org.

[5440] Lanphier, Robert Carr. (1936). Forty Years of Sangamo. Appearing in Sangamo: A History of Fifty Years. (1949). P. 4. Chicago, IL: Sangamo Electric Company. Archive.org.

[5441] Lanphier, Robert Carr. (1936). Forty Years of Sangamo. Appearing in Sangamo: A History of Fifty Years. (1949). P. 4. Chicago, IL: Sangamo Electric Company. Archive.org.

[5442] Lanphier, Robert Carr. (1936). Forty Years of Sangamo. Appearing in Sangamo: A History of Fifty Years. (1949). P. 4. Chicago, IL: Sangamo Electric Company. Archive.org; Call, Andrew Taylor. (2005). Jacob Bunn: Legacy of an Illinois Industrial Pioneer. Pp. Lawrenceville, VA: Brunswick Publishing Company.

[5443] Lanphier, Robert Carr. (1936). Forty Years of Sangamo. Appearing in Sangamo: A History of Fifty Years. (1949). P. 4. Chicago, IL: Sangamo Electric Company. Archive.org.

[5444] Lanphier, Robert Carr. (1936). Forty Years of Sangamo. Appearing in Sangamo: A History of Fifty Years. (1949). Pp. 4-5. Chicago, IL: Sangamo Electric Company. Archive.org.

the Peoria meter trials.[5445] The Springfield-Peoria meter trials ended in 1896, and Gutmann reported the findings to Bunn.[5446] Gutmann had consulted with Professor R. B. Owen of the University of Nebraska to obtain comments, opinions, and judgment concerning the viability of the meters.[5447] The meters that were in operation in the United States at the time of the Springfield-Peoria meter trials were amperehour meters, and operated on direct current circuits, but not on alternating current circuits.[5448] The novelties that defined the Gutmann meters, according to Lanphier, inhered in the fact that the new meters would provide metrics upon alternating current circuits, upon the wattage of electrical current, and not merely upon the amperage element of the current.[5449]

Electric metering technology was inchoate at the time of the Springfield-Peoria meter trials, and the existing contemporary forms of electrical meters were largely imperfect in the production of metrics.[5450] The Thomson meters of 1895 produced metrics apparently upon both the wattage (metric of the power of current) and the amperage (metric of the flow of current) of both alternating current and direct current circuits.[5451] The Diamond Meter Company had produced a wattage meter to measure electrical current power, but the meter produced deficient metrics for inductive loads.[5452] The Westinghouse Electric Company produced a superior watthour meter which incorporated the Shallenberger adjustment concept and machine, which enabled more precise metrics for inductive loads through a form

---

[5445] Lanphier, Robert Carr. (1936). Forty Years of Sangamo. Appearing in Sangamo: A History of Fifty Years. (1949). P. 5. Chicago, IL: Sangamo Electric Company. Archive.org.

[5446] Lanphier, Robert Carr. (1936). Forty Years of Sangamo. Appearing in Sangamo: A History of Fifty Years. (1949). P. 5. Chicago, IL: Sangamo Electric Company. Archive.org.

[5447] Lanphier, Robert Carr. (1936). Forty Years of Sangamo. Appearing in Sangamo: A History of Fifty Years. (1949). P. 5. Chicago, IL: Sangamo Electric Company. Archive.org.

[5448] Lanphier, Robert Carr. (1936). Forty Years of Sangamo. Appearing in Sangamo: A History of Fifty Years. (1949). P. 5. Chicago, IL: Sangamo Electric Company. Archive.org.

[5449] Lanphier, Robert Carr. (1936). Forty Years of Sangamo. Appearing in Sangamo: A History of Fifty Years. (1949). P. 5. Chicago, IL: Sangamo Electric Company. Archive.org.

[5450] Lanphier, Robert Carr. (1936). Forty Years of Sangamo. Appearing in Sangamo: A History of Fifty Years. (1949). P. 5. Chicago, IL: Sangamo Electric Company. Archive.org.

[5451] Lanphier, Robert Carr. (1936). Forty Years of Sangamo. Appearing in Sangamo: A History of Fifty Years. (1949). P. 5. Chicago, IL: Sangamo Electric Company. Archive.org.

[5452] Lanphier, Robert Carr. (1936). Forty Years of Sangamo. Appearing in Sangamo: A History of Fifty Years. (1949). P. 5. Chicago, IL: Sangamo Electric Company. Archive.org.

of justification of the inaccurate inductive load metrics produced by the amperage meters up to that time.[5453] The Westinghouse meters, incorporative of the Shallenberger justification machine, could produce accurate metrics upon inductive loads.[5454] Nevertheless, metering technologies remained largely imperfect and nascent at the time of the Springfield-Peoria trials, and much market for improvement existed for those who would dare to challenge the technology.[5455] Professor Owen recommended development and improvement of the Gutmann meters, thus delivering an expert opinion of approval.[5456] Because of the sparseness of contemporary electrical metering performance standards and metrics, Professor Owen's comments, opinions, and judgments relevant to the technical and commercial viabilities of the Gutmann meters were positive and approbative, but were tempered with caution and warning.[5457] Gutmann decided that he could not afford to make the improvements at that time, and, consequently, Jacob Bunn, Jr. retired the plans for the development and production of the Gutmann meters.[5458] Bunn temporarily retired the plans, but did not dismiss them.[5459]

A young graduate of Yale University, Robert Carr Lanphier, had recently returned to Springfield from New Haven at about the time of the Springfield-Peoria meter trials.[5460] On July 4, 1897, Lanphier met Jacob Bunn, Jr., at a summer

[5453] Lanphier, Robert Carr. (1936). Forty Years of Sangamo. Appearing in Sangamo: A History of Fifty Years. (1949). P. 5. Chicago, IL: Sangamo Electric Company. Archive.org.

[5454] Lanphier, Robert Carr. (1936). Forty Years of Sangamo. Appearing in Sangamo: A History of Fifty Years. (1949). P. 5. Chicago, IL: Sangamo Electric Company. Archive.org.

[5455] Lanphier, Robert Carr. (1936). Forty Years of Sangamo. Appearing in Sangamo: A History of Fifty Years. (1949). P. 5. Chicago, IL: Sangamo Electric Company. Archive.org.

[5456] Lanphier, Robert Carr. (1936). Forty Years of Sangamo. Appearing in Sangamo: A History of Fifty Years. (1949). P. 5. Chicago, IL: Sangamo Electric Company. Archive.org.

[5457] Lanphier, Robert Carr. (1936). Forty Years of Sangamo. Appearing in Sangamo: A History of Fifty Years. (1949). P. 5. Chicago, IL: Sangamo Electric Company. Archive.org.

[5458] Lanphier, Robert Carr. (1936). Forty Years of Sangamo. Appearing in Sangamo: A History of Fifty Years. (1949). P. 6. Chicago, IL: Sangamo Electric Company. Archive.org.

[5459] Lanphier, Robert Carr. (1936). Forty Years of Sangamo. Appearing in Sangamo: A History of Fifty Years. (1949). P. 6. Chicago, IL: Sangamo Electric Company. Archive.org.

[5460] Lanphier, Robert Carr. (1936). Forty Years of Sangamo. Appearing in Sangamo: A History of Fifty Years. (1949). P. 6. Chicago, IL: Sangamo Electric Company. Archive.org.

evening event.[5461] Bunn asked Lanphier about his electrical engineering studies at Yale and invited the young engineer to examine the Gutmann meters that Bunn had stored in a drawer at the watch factory.[5462] Lanphier recollected what Bunn said to him as follows:

> "'Oh, by the way, I got interested last year, through Tom Sheridan, in some kind of electric meter invention of a man named Gutmann, who lives over in Peoria, and had a couple of models made, which are in a box out at the factory. I don't know anything about these electrical devices, so maybe, if you've learned anything at Yale, you could tell me whether there's anything to this meter.'"[5463]

Lanphier told Bunn that he would gladly examine the meter parts and the Owen report accompanying the meter parts. Bunn and Lanphier went to the watch company on July 5 and located the box of Gutmann meter components.[5464] Lanphier was able to understand certain parts of the meter, but noted in his memoir that the Yale electrical engineering curriculum contained little information on watthour metering.[5465] Lanphier stated: "Even with my very slight acquaintance with watthour meters, for little was then taught about them to electrical students, I recognized the purpose of some of the parts, and tried my best to make Mr. Bunn feel I knew 'what it was all about.'"[5466]

Bunn encouraged Lanphier to think about the subject of the watthour meter prototype and this led Lanphier to consult with Professor Henry Bumstead of Yale as to how to proceed with the study of watthour metrics and meters.[5467] Lanphier

---

[5461] Lanphier, Robert Carr. (1936). Forty Years of Sangamo. Appearing in Sangamo: A History of Fifty Years. (1949). P. 6. Chicago, IL: Sangamo Electric Company. Archive.org.

[5462] Lanphier, Robert Carr. (1936). Forty Years of Sangamo. Appearing in Sangamo: A History of Fifty Years. (1949). P. 6. Chicago, IL: Sangamo Electric Company. Archive.org.

[5463] Lanphier, Robert Carr. (1936). Forty Years of Sangamo. Appearing in Sangamo: A History of Fifty Years. (1949). P. 6-7. Chicago, IL: Sangamo Electric Company. Archive.org.

[5464] Lanphier, Robert Carr. (1936). Forty Years of Sangamo. Appearing in Sangamo: A History of Fifty Years. (1949). P. 7. Chicago, IL: Sangamo Electric Company. Archive.org.

[5465] Lanphier, Robert Carr. (1936). Forty Years of Sangamo. Appearing in Sangamo: A History of Fifty Years. (1949). P. 7. Chicago, IL: Sangamo Electric Company. Archive.org.

[5466] Lanphier, Robert Carr. (1936). Forty Years of Sangamo. Appearing in Sangamo: A History of Fifty Years. (1949). P. 7. Chicago, IL: Sangamo Electric Company. Archive.org.

[5467] Lanphier, Robert Carr. (1936). Forty Years of Sangamo. Appearing in Sangamo: A History of Fifty Years. (1949). P. 7. Chicago, IL: Sangamo Electric Company. Archive.org.

noted that Bumstead had indicated the shallowness of the watthour metering technological data pool that existed at the time.[5468] In August, 1897, Lanphier met with Bunn and Gutmann in Springfield.[5469] Gutmann approved of Lanphier, and Bunn and Gutmann gave Lanphier authority to run trials and tests on the meters, with Lanphier reporting his results to both men.[5470] Bunn arranged for Otis White, one of the leading technologists of the Illinois Watch Company, to work with Lanphier in the Springfield meter trials.[5471] The problem of the only source of light at the watch factory being that of gaslight caused Lanphier to have to relocate the laboratory to the Springfield Electric Light Company.[5472] Robert Carr Lanphier carried out the Springfield meter trials with the support of Otis White over a time of several months, and delivered regular reports to Bunn and Gutmann about the trial process.[5473]

Lanphier made multiple changes to the Gutmann meter, including the addition of spiral slots to the cylindrical element of the meter for the purpose of avoiding the vertical slot form of the contemporary Nikola Tesla patent.[5474] The diversity in the meter slot form, therefore, prevented an infringement of the Tesla patent rights. Lanphier recommended the Gutmann meter for a pre-commercial (not for regular mass production) trial production by the Illinois Watch Company in November, 1897.[5475] Bunn granted approvals of the Lanphier models of the Gutmann meter and charged Lanphier with the production of a series of model Gutmann meters

---

[5468] Lanphier, Robert Carr. (1936). Forty Years of Sangamo. Appearing in Sangamo: A History of Fifty Years. (1949). P. 7. Chicago, IL: Sangamo Electric Company. Archive.org.
[5469] Lanphier, Robert Carr. (1936). Forty Years of Sangamo. Appearing in Sangamo: A History of Fifty Years. (1949). P. 7. Chicago, IL: Sangamo Electric Company. Archive.org.
[5470] Lanphier, Robert Carr. (1936). Forty Years of Sangamo. Appearing in Sangamo: A History of Fifty Years. (1949). Pp. 7-8. Chicago, IL: Sangamo Electric Company. Archive.org.
[5471] Lanphier, Robert Carr. (1936). Forty Years of Sangamo. Appearing in Sangamo: A History of Fifty Years. (1949). P. 8. Chicago, IL: Sangamo Electric Company. Archive.org.
[5472] Lanphier, Robert Carr. (1936). Forty Years of Sangamo. Appearing in Sangamo: A History of Fifty Years. (1949). P. 7. Chicago, IL: Sangamo Electric Company. Archive.org.
[5473] Lanphier, Robert Carr. (1936). Forty Years of Sangamo. Appearing in Sangamo: A History of Fifty Years. (1949). Pp. 7-8. Chicago, IL: Sangamo Electric Company. Archive.org.
[5474] Lanphier, Robert Carr. (1936). Forty Years of Sangamo. Appearing in Sangamo: A History of Fifty Years. (1949). P. 9. Chicago, IL: Sangamo Electric Company. Archive.org.
[5475] Lanphier, Robert Carr. (1936). Forty Years of Sangamo. Appearing in Sangamo: A History of Fifty Years. (1949). P. 9. Chicago, IL: Sangamo Electric Company. Archive.org.

for additional trial and judgment. Production of the models took place from December, 1897, until March, 1898.[5476] The Springfield production facilities were inadequate for the proper trials needed for the meter models, and this led Lanphier to seek help from John Whitfield Bunn, the Treasurer and a founder of the University of Illinois, to locate proper trial space.[5477] John W. Bunn arranged for Lanphier to have use of the electrical engineering laboratory of the University of Illinois for the Urbana meter trials.[5478] Professor Albert P. Carman of the University of Illinois Department of Physics aided Lanphier in the Urbana meter trials. Lanphier completed the Urbana meter trials and reported the viabilities and vulnerabilities of the Gutmann meter to Bunn and Gutmann.[5479] Jacob Bunn decided to proceed with a plan to manufacture the meters on a commercial basis.[5480]

The Illinois Watch Company commenced the retooling of the factory for meter production from September, 1898, to, December, 1898, creating a metering subdivision of the company.[5481] Lanphier prepared the main spring building of the watch company to be the new meter house, and Otis White, "looked after the tools and machinery."[5482] Levi Millard represented the Electric Appliance Company of Chicago and visited Lanphier, Bunn, and White to ask if Electric Appliance Company might be able to serve as the Sales Agent for the new Illinois Watch Company meter product.[5483] A happy alliance was immediately formed with the

---

[5476] Lanphier, Robert Carr. (1936). Forty Years of Sangamo. Appearing in Sangamo: A History of Fifty Years. (1949). Pp. 9-10. Chicago, IL: Sangamo Electric Company. Archive.org.

[5477] Lanphier, Robert Carr. (1936). Forty Years of Sangamo. Appearing in Sangamo: A History of Fifty Years. (1949). P. 10. Chicago, IL: Sangamo Electric Company. Archive.org.

[5478] Lanphier, Robert Carr. (1936). Forty Years of Sangamo. Appearing in Sangamo: A History of Fifty Years. (1949). P. 10. Chicago, IL: Sangamo Electric Company. Archive.org.

[5479] Lanphier, Robert Carr. (1936). Forty Years of Sangamo. Appearing in Sangamo: A History of Fifty Years. (1949). Pp. 10-11. Chicago, IL: Sangamo Electric Company. Archive.org.

[5480] Lanphier, Robert Carr. (1936). Forty Years of Sangamo. Appearing in Sangamo: A History of Fifty Years. (1949). P. 11. Chicago, IL: Sangamo Electric Company. Archive.org.

[5481] Lanphier, Robert Carr. (1936). Forty Years of Sangamo. Appearing in Sangamo: A History of Fifty Years. (1949). P. 11. Chicago, IL: Sangamo Electric Company. Archive.org.

[5482] Lanphier, Robert Carr. (1936). Forty Years of Sangamo. Appearing in Sangamo: A History of Fifty Years. (1949). P. 11. Chicago, IL: Sangamo Electric Company. Archive.org.

[5483] Lanphier, Robert Carr. (1936). Forty Years of Sangamo. Appearing in Sangamo: A History of Fifty Years. (1949). P. 12. Chicago, IL: Sangamo Electric Company. Archive.org.

Chicago company. Jacob Bunn, Jr., contracted with Electric Appliance Company, and the sales agency between the Chicago company and the Springfield company remained in place for about thirty years, until the Chicago company ceased to exist.[5484] In December, 1898, Jacob Bunn, Jr., decided that a new corporation would be beneficial for the business administration of the metering division of Illinois Watch Company.[5485]

In January, 1899, a new Illinois corporation was formed with the name of Sangamo Electric Company.[5486] The Sangamo Electric Company property consisted of the money contributed by Bunn, the patents held by Gutmann, and the labor contributed by Lanphier, the Bunns, Gutmann, White, and Jim Edwards, who was the Senior Foreman of the company.[5487] Jacob Bunn chose the name "Sangamo," to pay honor to local history and heritage, and to Sangamo himself, who was the Chief of the Illini Native Americans of central Illinois during the early nineteenth century.[5488] Henry Bunn served as President of the Sangamo Electric Company; Ludwig Gutmann served as Vice-President; Jacob Bunn, Jr., served as Secretary and Treasurer.[5489] Gutmann and Lanphier, of course, were the founding engineers of the company. The historical record appears to show that the Electric Appliance Company of Chicago was the first contracted sales representative for Sangamo Electric Company, thus again prominently bringing Chicago into the development of the new Springfield company.[5490] W. W. Low of Chicago, President of the Electric Appliance Company, signed the contract with the Bunns

---

[5484] Lanphier, Robert Carr. (1936). Forty Years of Sangamo. Appearing in Sangamo: A History of Fifty Years. (1949). P. 12. Chicago, IL: Sangamo Electric Company. Archive.org.

[5485] Lanphier, Robert Carr. (1936). Forty Years of Sangamo. Appearing in Sangamo: A History of Fifty Years. (1949). P. 12. Chicago, IL: Sangamo Electric Company. Archive.org.

[5486] Lanphier, Robert Carr. (1936). Forty Years of Sangamo. Appearing in Sangamo: A History of Fifty Years. (1949). P. 12. Chicago, IL: Sangamo Electric Company. Archive.org.

[5487] Lanphier, Robert Carr. (1936). Forty Years of Sangamo. Appearing in Sangamo: A History of Fifty Years. (1949). P. 12. Chicago, IL: Sangamo Electric Company. Archive.org.

[5488] Lanphier, Robert Carr. (1936). Forty Years of Sangamo. Appearing in Sangamo: A History of Fifty Years. (1949). Pp. 12-13. Chicago, IL: Sangamo Electric Company. Archive.org.

[5489] Lanphier, Robert Carr. (1936). Forty Years of Sangamo. Appearing in Sangamo: A History of Fifty Years. (1949). P. 12. Chicago, IL: Sangamo Electric Company. Archive.org.

[5490] Lanphier, Robert Carr. (1936). Forty Years of Sangamo. Appearing in Sangamo: A History of Fifty Years. (1949). P. 12. Chicago, IL: Sangamo Electric Company. Archive.org.

in January, 1899.[5491] The agency contract brought Sangamo Electric to Chicago through product representation and distribution.[5492] From its inception, through Tom Sheridan, Levi Millard, and W. W. Low, therefore, Sangamo Electric Company possessed a Chicago presence. The Cook County presence of Sangamo would increase through establishment of a sales branch and two Chicago subsidiary companies.

When intellectual property litigation confronted Sangamo Electric Company in the company's second year of corporate existence, Charles A. Brown, Esq., patent attorney of the firm of Barton & Brown, a Chicago law firm, defended Sangamo against the complaints and allegations that had been filed against the company, in 1901.[5493] Brown had been General Manager of Western Electric when Enos Barton was President of that company.[5494] Enos Barton helped support Brown's legal education and Brown entered law practice partnership with attorney George Barton, who was the brother of Enos Barton.[5495] Charles Brown retained the expert counsel and opinion of Professor Dugald C. Jackson in the defense of Sangamo Electric in the intellectual property litigation.[5496] Jackson was at the time of the lawsuit the chief of the University of Wisconsin Department of Electrical Engineering and later became chief of the Electrical Department of the Massachusetts Institute of Technology.[5497] Charles Brown of Chicago represented Sangamo for many years.[5498]

[5491] Lanphier, Robert Carr. (1936). Forty Years of Sangamo. Appearing in Sangamo: A History of Fifty Years. (1949). Pp. 12-13. Chicago, IL: Sangamo Electric Company. Archive.org.

[5492] Lanphier, Robert Carr. (1936). Forty Years of Sangamo. Appearing in Sangamo: A History of Fifty Years. (1949). Pp. 12-13. Chicago, IL: Sangamo Electric Company. Archive.org.

[5493] Lanphier, Robert Carr. (1936). Forty Years of Sangamo. Appearing in Sangamo: A History of Fifty Years. (1949). P. 20. Chicago, IL: Sangamo Electric Company. Archive.org.

[5494] Lanphier, Robert Carr. (1936). Forty Years of Sangamo. Appearing in Sangamo: A History of Fifty Years. (1949). P. 20. Chicago, IL: Sangamo Electric Company. Archive.org.

[5495] Lanphier, Robert Carr. (1936). Forty Years of Sangamo. Appearing in Sangamo: A History of Fifty Years. (1949). P. 20. Chicago, IL: Sangamo Electric Company. Archive.org.

[5496] Lanphier, Robert Carr. (1936). Forty Years of Sangamo. Appearing in Sangamo: A History of Fifty Years. (1949). P. 20. Chicago, IL: Sangamo Electric Company. Archive.org.

[5497] Lanphier, Robert Carr. (1936). Forty Years of Sangamo. Appearing in Sangamo: A History of Fifty Years. (1949). P. 20. Chicago, IL: Sangamo Electric Company. Archive.org.

[5498] Lanphier, Robert Carr. (1936). Forty Years of Sangamo. Appearing in Sangamo: A History of Fifty Years. (1949). Pp. 20-25. Chicago, IL: Sangamo Electric Company. Archive.org.

Robert Carr Lanphier and Jacob Bunn, Jr., narrowly missed being victims of the horrendous tragedy that was the Iroquois Theater Fire of December 30, 1903.[5499] Bunn and Lanphier were stopping over at Chicago while traveling to Detroit and Windsor, Ontario, Canada, for the purpose of determining a place for the construction of the new Canadian factory of Sangamo Electric Company.[5500] While in Chicago on December 30, 1903, Bunn and Lanphier attempted to purchase tickets to the show that was being performed at the Iroquois Theater that same day.[5501] They discovered that the show was sold out entirely and that no tickets would be available whatsoever.[5502] After learning that they could not attend the Iroquois Theater performance, Bunn and Lanphier left by train that same afternoon for Detroit.[5503] When they reached Kalamazoo, Michigan, they heard the news of the Iroquois Theater Fire that took place that same afternoon, and which killed around 600 people.[5504]

It is important for us to take a moment here to describe briefly the occurrence of the Iroquois Theater Fire, a disaster which cost so many lives, and which indicated such grave failures in construction, design, and safety infrastructure. The Iroquois Theater Fire was one of the worst tragedies in Chicago history and in American history.[5505] The factors of the disaster included multiple design, construction, and infrastructure deficiencies within the Iroquois Theater itself.[5506] *The Weekly Gazette* of Colorado Springs, Colorado, reported a Chicago news transcript of multiple testimonies that were collected in connection to the fire.[5507] To honor those who had been killed or injured in the fire, Mayor Carter Henry Harrison, Jr., declared that there would be no New Year's holiday celebration for Chicago that

[5499] Lanphier, Robert Carr. (1936). Forty Years of Sangamo. Appearing in Sangamo: A History of Fifty Years. (1949). P. 26. Chicago, IL: Sangamo Electric Company. Archive.org.

[5500] Lanphier, Robert Carr. (1936). Forty Years of Sangamo. Appearing in Sangamo: A History of Fifty Years. (1949). P. 26. Chicago, IL: Sangamo Electric Company. Archive.org.

[5501] Lanphier, Robert Carr. (1936). Forty Years of Sangamo. Appearing in Sangamo: A History of Fifty Years. (1949). P. 26. Chicago, IL: Sangamo Electric Company. Archive.org.

[5502] Lanphier, Robert Carr. (1936). Forty Years of Sangamo. Appearing in Sangamo: A History of Fifty Years. (1949). P. 26. Chicago, IL: Sangamo Electric Company. Archive.org.

[5503] Lanphier, Robert Carr. (1936). Forty Years of Sangamo. Appearing in Sangamo: A History of Fifty Years. (1949). P. 26. Chicago, IL: Sangamo Electric Company. Archive.org.

[5504] Lanphier, Robert Carr. (1936). Forty Years of Sangamo. Appearing in Sangamo: A History of Fifty Years. (1949). P. 26. Chicago, IL: Sangamo Electric Company. Archive.org.

[5505] The (Colorado Springs) Weekly Gazette. (January 7, 1904). P. 5. Newspapers.com.

[5506] The (Colorado Springs) Weekly Gazette. (January 7, 1904). P. 5. Newspapers.com.

[5507] The (Colorado Springs) Weekly Gazette. (January 7, 1904). P. 5. Newspapers.com.

year, and that a time of mourning would take place in its stead. The mayor's decision met with public approval.[5508] The testimony of Miss Anna Ward provided haunting and detailed descriptions of the occurrences leading to, and constituting, the lethal conflagration and its ensuing chaos.[5509] Anna Ward's testimony follows here:

> "'I plainly saw the fire. I am a large woman, weighing close to 180 pounds, and I made up my mind that if there was to be a panic it would be wise for me to beat it to the street. I left my seat in the balcony, went down stairs to the first balcony and from there started to pass out through the very door in which so many people were killed a few minutes later. The door was closed and a man standing on the outside refused to open it for me. Whether he was an employe of the theater I do not know; but he had evidently determined that no one should leave the theater, and in doing so started a panic. I was leaving quietly up to this time but when he refused to allow me to pass out peacefully, I determined to get out if I had to make all sorts of noise. I went along the balcony about ten feet to a glass partition and smashed it with the point of my umbrella. I went out and down the stairs. When I was about half way down I heard the roar of the crowd as it came after me and I hurried with all the speed I had. They overtook me, however, knocked me down, and, but for the fact that I was close to the door, I think my chances of life would have been almost nothing. As it was, I think I must have walked the last ten feet of my passage to the exit on the bodies of those who had fallen.'"[5510]

The Chicago journalist, as reported in *The Weekly Gazette*, discussed the then uncertain causation of the Iroquois fire, noting that several theories of causation had been reported.[5511] The journalist's comment follows here, and exhibits the high level of confusion that surrounded the issue of the causation of the fire:

> "The best evidence at present obtainable is that the fire was started by sparks from an arc light striking the edge of the drop curtain, but this has not been proved. There are so many statements as to the cause at present and they differ so widely that it is impossible to ascertain the exact truth of the matter."[5512]

[5508] The (Colorado Springs) Weekly Gazette. (January 7, 1904). P. 5. Newspapers.com.
[5509] The (Colorado Springs) Weekly Gazette. (January 7, 1904). P. 5. Newspapers.com.
[5510] The (Colorado Springs) Weekly Gazette. (January 7, 1904). P. 5. Newspapers.com.
[5511] The (Colorado Springs) Weekly Gazette. (January 7, 1904). P. 5. Newspapers.com.
[5512] The (Colorado Springs) Weekly Gazette. (January 7, 1904). P. 5. Newspapers.com.

Terrible negligence in the building and code inspections of the Iroquois Theater contributed to the catastrophe.[5513] William Curran inspected the theater only moments before the fire broke out and had reported that the building was safe for occupancy.[5514] Curran gave his report to Chicago Deputy Building Commissioner Stanhope on the morning of January 7, 1904.[5515] Also on January 7, 1904, Deputy Building Commissioner Stanhope went to the Iroquois Theater to inspect the ruins in the company of Inspector Lense, Inspector Laughlin, and Inspector Dalton.[5516] Prior to completing the inspection of the theater ruins, Stanhope said the building had satisfied the applicable legal standards for safety.[5517] The theater building was, in fact, in direct violation of multiple Chicago building code laws, according to the Colorado Springs report.[5518]

Section 185 of the Chicago City Code required that buildings belonging to the class of buildings to which the Iroquois Theater belonged must possess automatic sprinkler systems.[5519] The Iroquois possessed no such sprinkler system.[5520] When questioned about this building failure and vulnerability, Inspector Stanhope answered that, "There was no sprinkler system in the theater, but the provision about the iron doors made it unnecessary for the theater to have them."[5521] Section 189 of the City Code also required all Chicago theaters to possess fire alarm systems connected to the city fire alarm warning system.[5522] Stanhope's testimony as to the failure of the theater to possess the legally required fire alarm and warning system, and the connection thereof to the central city fire alarm and warning system, conflicted with the testimony of Chicago City Electrician Hyland.[5523] Stanhope claimed that the Iroquois Theater possessed fire alarm connections to the city fire alarm system, but that he did not actually see the box that contained the connection and warning machinery.[5524] City Electrician Hyland contradicted Stanhope, and stated that, "The Iroquois had no fire alarm connection with the city alarm system. No application is on file for any such connection."[5525]

The fire alarm warning for the Iroquois Theater fire was, in fact, delivered to the central city alarm system from a fire connection box located, "more than half a

[5513] The (Colorado Springs) Weekly Gazette. (January 7, 1904). P. 5. Newspapers.com.
[5514] The (Colorado Springs) Weekly Gazette. (January 7, 1904). P. 5. Newspapers.com.
[5515] The (Colorado Springs) Weekly Gazette. (January 7, 1904). P. 5. Newspapers.com.
[5516] The (Colorado Springs) Weekly Gazette. (January 7, 1904). P. 5. Newspapers.com.
[5517] The (Colorado Springs) Weekly Gazette. (January 7, 1904). P. 5. Newspapers.com.
[5518] The (Colorado Springs) Weekly Gazette. (January 7, 1904). P. 5. Newspapers.com.
[5519] The (Colorado Springs) Weekly Gazette. (January 7, 1904). P. 5. Newspapers.com.
[5520] The (Colorado Springs) Weekly Gazette. (January 7, 1904). P. 5. Newspapers.com.
[5521] The (Colorado Springs) Weekly Gazette. (January 7, 1904). P. 5. Newspapers.com.
[5522] The (Colorado Springs) Weekly Gazette. (January 7, 1904). P. 5. Newspapers.com.
[5523] The (Colorado Springs) Weekly Gazette. (January 7, 1904). P. 5. Newspapers.com.
[5524] The (Colorado Springs) Weekly Gazette. (January 7, 1904). P. 5. Newspapers.com.
[5525] The (Colorado Springs) Weekly Gazette. (January 7, 1904). P. 5. Newspapers.com.

block from the theater."[5526] What was more, the city law required that theaters possess a ventilation shaft at the back of the stage for removal of flames and smoke, but the theater possessed no such shaft.[5527] Twelve Chicago Aldermen formed an investigation commission and examined the theater ruins on January 7, 1904.[5528] The aldermanic committee confronted Deputy Building Commissioner Stanhope at the Building Department and demanded to see the architectural plan for the theater.[5529] When Alderman Jones asked Deputy Stanhope, "'How about sprinklers?'"[5530] Stanhope answered that, "'The way the theater is built, they can be left out. . .And, anyhow, the flames spread so rapidly no sprinkler system would have availed anything.'"[5531] Alderman Jones reminded Stanhope that city law required all exit routes to be marked as exit routes.[5532] Stanhope acknowledged the law on that point and assured Jones that the issue of the building's failure of that legal duty would be investigated.[5533] Alderman Herman challenged Stanhope with the fact that the theater had been so dark that nobody inside could have readily discerned the exit routes.[5534] Herman used the theater design diagram to argue and prove the facts of deficient exit routes and deficient exit sign notices.[5535] Herman stated:

> "'Here is a passageway on the south side of the first balcony which looks as thought it led to a stairway. But in the darkness people scrambling through it were caught like rats in a trap. They could not get either way. The confusion of exits was such that no one could find his way in the dark. If those things are regarded as exits, I do not know what constitutes an exit that would be of any use.'"[5536]

Stanhope insisted that he had judged that the theater possessed no structural vulnerability or deficiency.[5537] Mayor Carter Harrison inspected the building ruins on January 7, 1904, in the company of Building Commissioner Williams, Alderman Mayer, and multiple architects.[5538] Architect T. P. Marshall, who had designed the Iroquois, went with Harrison, Williams, and Mayer to investigate.[5539]

[5526] The (Colorado Springs) Weekly Gazette. (January 7, 1904). P. 5. Newspapers.com.
[5527] The (Colorado Springs) Weekly Gazette. (January 7, 1904). P. 5. Newspapers.com.
[5528] The (Colorado Springs) Weekly Gazette. (January 7, 1904). P. 5. Newspapers.com.
[5529] The (Colorado Springs) Weekly Gazette. (January 7, 1904). P. 5. Newspapers.com.
[5530] The (Colorado Springs) Weekly Gazette. (January 7, 1904). P. 5. Newspapers.com.
[5531] The (Colorado Springs) Weekly Gazette. (January 7, 1904). P. 5. Newspapers.com.
[5532] The (Colorado Springs) Weekly Gazette. (January 7, 1904). P. 5. Newspapers.com.
[5533] The (Colorado Springs) Weekly Gazette. (January 7, 1904). P. 5. Newspapers.com.
[5534] The (Colorado Springs) Weekly Gazette. (January 7, 1904). P. 5. Newspapers.com.
[5535] The (Colorado Springs) Weekly Gazette. (January 7, 1904). P. 5. Newspapers.com.
[5536] The (Colorado Springs) Weekly Gazette. (January 7, 1904). P. 5. Newspapers.com.
[5537] The (Colorado Springs) Weekly Gazette. (January 7, 1904). P. 5. Newspapers.com.
[5538] The (Colorado Springs) Weekly Gazette. (January 7, 1904). P. 5. Newspapers.com.
[5539] The (Colorado Springs) Weekly Gazette. (January 7, 1904). P. 5. Newspapers.com.

Mayor Harrison tried the doors and at one point stepped accidentally upon a lock of hair that had been torn from the head of one of the victims.[5540] Mayor Harrison took notice of the fact that the theater possessed no clear signs marking exit routes and questioned architect Marshall about why curtains had been placed over the exit doors.[5541] Marshall responded that the curtains had been placed over the doors to enhance the cosmetic value of the theater.[5542] *The Weekly Gazette* article contained the names of the people known to have died in the fire.[5543]

William McMullen was the arc light operator of the arc lamp that started the fire.[5544] Chicago police officers arrested McMullen and Wilson Kerr, who worked as a fly man at the theater.[5545] Both men were incarcerated and interrogated with questions about the cause of the fire.[5546] McMullen provided testimony that was reported in Chicago and in the Colorado Springs newspaper.[5547] McMullen described how the arc lamp, also known as a shot light, caught fire when McMullen was transitioning the lamp from a white light to a blue light in the second act of the performance.[5548] As McMullen tried to change the lights the light sparked and ignited the nearby curtain.[5549] McMullen tried to extinguish the flame with his hands, but failed.[5550] He called the theater fireman, who came with a fire extinguisher, but the extinguisher failed to extinguish the flames.[5551] The fire quickly moved out to the theater audience.[5552] McMullen jumped to the stage and carried a young girl to safety who had already been severely burned.[5553] After getting the girl to safety, McMullen returned to the exit doors and helped as many people as possible to escape, until, "'it was useless to stay any longer.'"[5554] The Iroquois Theater remains one of the most devastating tragedies to have befallen Chicago and Cook County. If Jacob Bunn, Jr., and Robert Carr Lanphier had managed to purchase tickets to the show at The Iroquois that day, the two would most probably have perished, and the world of electrical technology would have been quite different. Sangamo Electric Company and the inventions developed by

[5540] The (Colorado Springs) Weekly Gazette. (January 7, 1904). P. 5. Newspapers.com.
[5541] The (Colorado Springs) Weekly Gazette. (January 7, 1904). P. 5. Newspapers.com.
[5542] The (Colorado Springs) Weekly Gazette. (January 7, 1904). P. 5. Newspapers.com.
[5543] The (Colorado Springs) Weekly Gazette. (January 7, 1904). P. 5. Newspapers.com.
[5544] The (Colorado Springs) Weekly Gazette. (January 7, 1904). P. 5. Newspapers.com.
[5545] The (Colorado Springs) Weekly Gazette. (January 7, 1904). P. 5. Newspapers.com.
[5546] The (Colorado Springs) Weekly Gazette. (January 7, 1904). P. 5. Newspapers.com.
[5547] The (Colorado Springs) Weekly Gazette. (January 7, 1904). P. 5. Newspapers.com.
[5548] The (Colorado Springs) Weekly Gazette. (January 7, 1904). P. 5. Newspapers.com.
[5549] The (Colorado Springs) Weekly Gazette. (January 7, 1904). P. 5. Newspapers.com.
[5550] The (Colorado Springs) Weekly Gazette. (January 7, 1904). P. 5. Newspapers.com.
[5551] The (Colorado Springs) Weekly Gazette. (January 7, 1904). P. 5. Newspapers.com.
[5552] The (Colorado Springs) Weekly Gazette. (January 7, 1904). P. 5. Newspapers.com.
[5553] The (Colorado Springs) Weekly Gazette. (January 7, 1904). P. 5. Newspapers.com.
[5554] The (Colorado Springs) Weekly Gazette. (January 7, 1904). P. 5. Newspapers.com.

this company would change the world of electrical engineering, electrical manufacturing, and national defense many times over.

When Sangamo Electric faced severe financial trouble during the years of 1904 through 1911, John Whitfield Bunn came to the rescue of the company and loaned money to Sangamo to preserve the company during that decade of thin sales revenues.[5555] In 1913, business improved and Jacob Bunn, Jr., Robert C. Lanphier, and the other Sangamo men reimbursed John W. Bunn in full for his generous support.[5556] E. A. Bennett of Chicago worked with Sangamo Electric to promote and represent the Sangamo Electric mercury meters from 1909 until 1910.[5557] Sangamo Electric Company acquired another Chicago representative in 1911, when Robert C. Lanphier convinced Herbert W. Young to contract with Sangamo to represent them in the Chicago market.[5558] Young had worked as a salesman for Westinghouse Electric Company prior to establishing the Delta-Star Electric Company of Chicago.[5559] The Sangamo offer was a good idea for Young, who, as Lanphier noted, had only just begun with a new company.[5560] Sangamo Electric constructed an exhibit at the 1915 Panama-Pacific Exposition of San Francisco and received highest marks for its category of electrical technologies.[5561] In 1917, Sangamo developed a form of watthour meter for street railway cars, which led to another corporate presence in Chicago for Sangamo.[5562]

[5555] Lanphier, Robert Carr. (1936). Forty Years of Sangamo. Appearing in Sangamo: A History of Fifty Years. (1949). P. 59. Chicago, IL: Sangamo Electric Company. Archive.org.

[5556] Lanphier, Robert Carr. (1936). Forty Years of Sangamo. Appearing in Sangamo: A History of Fifty Years. (1949). P. 59. Chicago, IL: Sangamo Electric Company. Archive.org.

[5557] Lanphier, Robert Carr. (1936). Forty Years of Sangamo. Appearing in Sangamo: A History of Fifty Years. (1949). Pp. 44-45. Chicago, IL: Sangamo Electric Company. Archive.org.

[5558] Lanphier, Robert Carr. (1936). Forty Years of Sangamo. Appearing in Sangamo: A History of Fifty Years. (1949). P. 45. Chicago, IL: Sangamo Electric Company. Archive.org.

[5559] Lanphier, Robert Carr. (1936). Forty Years of Sangamo. Appearing in Sangamo: A History of Fifty Years. (1949). P. 45. Chicago, IL: Sangamo Electric Company. Archive.org.

[5560] Lanphier, Robert Carr. (1936). Forty Years of Sangamo. Appearing in Sangamo: A History of Fifty Years. (1949). P. 45. Chicago, IL: Sangamo Electric Company. Archive.org.

[5561] Lanphier, Robert Carr. (1936). Forty Years of Sangamo. Appearing in Sangamo: A History of Fifty Years. (1949). P. 62. Chicago, IL: Sangamo Electric Company. Archive.org.

[5562] Lanphier, Robert Carr. (1936). Forty Years of Sangamo. Appearing in Sangamo: A History of Fifty Years. (1949). Pp. 62-63. Chicago, IL: Sangamo Electric Company. Archive.org; The Iron Trade Review. (August 30, 1917). Vol. LXI. P. 467. Cleveland, OH: The Penton Publishing Company. Google Books.

Jacob Bunn, Jr., Robert C. Lanphier, Larry E. Gould, and Alonzo Hoff founded the Economy Electric Devices Company of Chicago in 1917.[5563] Larry Gould of Chicago was a respected authority on street car technologies, and, therefore, possessed the skill to represent Sangamo Electric watthour meters efficiently for the Chicago street railway market.[5564] Lanphier reported that Larry Gould enabled Sangamo to enter the street railway car meter market with strength and power and that Gould's representation of Sangamo in the street railway meter market led to the distribution of Sangamo meters across a broad geography.[5565] Volume 61 of *The Iron Trade Review*, an industrial journal of Cleveland, Ohio, noted the incorporation of the Economy Electric Devices Company of Chicago in its August 30, 1917, edition. The 1917 report mentioned that the company possessed an original capitalization of $20,000, but omitted details pertinent to the corporate financing, and was silent as to the specific functions of stock money and debt money in the original capitalization plan.[5566] Larry Gould represented Sangamo Electric so efficiently that contracts for Sangamo meters firmly established Sangamo Electric's market reputation across the globe.[5567] Robert C. Lanphier noted that Sangamo meters had been used on, "most of the important systems in this country [United States], and many in foreign cities, Paris, Rio de Janeiro, Amsterdam, Yokohama, etc. . ."[5568] After Sangamo had plumbed nearly the entire street railcar meter market, Bunn turned over ownership of Economy Electric Devices Company to Larry Gould, who continued the company with success in Chicago.[5569]

[5563] Lanphier, Robert Carr. (1936). Forty Years of Sangamo. Appearing in Sangamo: A History of Fifty Years. (1949). Pp. 62-63. Chicago, IL: Sangamo Electric Company. Archive.org; The Iron Trade Review. (August 30, 1917). Vol. LXI. P. 467. Cleveland, OH: The Penton Publishing Company. Google Books.
[5564] Lanphier, Robert Carr. (1936). Forty Years of Sangamo. Appearing in Sangamo: A History of Fifty Years. (1949). Pp. 62-63. Chicago, IL: Sangamo Electric Company. Archive.org.
[5565] Lanphier, Robert Carr. (1936). Forty Years of Sangamo. Appearing in Sangamo: A History of Fifty Years. (1949). Pp. 62-63. Chicago, IL: Sangamo Electric Company. Archive.org.
[5566] The Iron Trade Review. (August 30, 1917). Vol. LXI. P. 467. Cleveland, OH: The Penton Publishing Company. Google Books.
[5567] Lanphier, Robert Carr. (1936). Forty Years of Sangamo. Appearing in Sangamo: A History of Fifty Years. (1949). Pp. 62-63. Chicago, IL: Sangamo Electric Company. Archive.org.
[5568] Lanphier, Robert Carr. (1936). Forty Years of Sangamo. Appearing in Sangamo: A History of Fifty Years. (1949). Pp. 62-63. Chicago, IL: Sangamo Electric Company. Archive.org.
[5569] Lanphier, Robert Carr. (1936). Forty Years of Sangamo. Appearing in Sangamo: A History of Fifty Years. (1949). Pp. 62-63. Chicago, IL: Sangamo Electric Company. Archive.org.

The February, 1920, issue of *Electric Traction*, a Chicago-based street railway industry journal, contained an advertisement for Economy Electric Devices Company, and specified several key facts about the concern. The company was headquartered at the Old Colony Building located on Van Buren Street in the Loop.[5570] Economy Electric possessed branch offices in Pittsburgh through the agency of Ludwig Hommel & Company, at Los Angeles through the agency of Jerry G. Monahan, at San Francisco through the agency of L. A. Nott, and at Seattle through the agency of the Burton R. Stare Company.[5571] The historical record demonstrates that Sangamo possessed not only a powerful Chicago presence but also a powerful Pacific Coast presence as early as 1920.[5572] Jacob Bunn and Robert C. Lanphier met Jerry G. Monahan at the Panama-Pacific Exposition of San Francisco in 1915, and a friendship fast formed among them.[5573] Bunn hired Jerry Monahan to represent Sangamo Electric at Los Angeles.[5574] Jerry Monahan's sales agency for Sangamo lasted at least through 1920, as was indicated by the advertisement that appeared in the February, 1920, issue of *Electric Traction*.[5575]

Jacob Bunn, Jr., established the manufacturing presence of Sangamo Electric Company at Toronto, Ontario, in 1916, when he built a factory at Adelaide Street, West.[5576] Prior to that time, the Sangamo presence in Canada was mediated through Sangamo Electric product importation from Illinois but not through a factory presence in Canada.[5577] Bunn corroborated the Sangamo presence in Toronto in 1918 when he bought a factory at 183 George Street, pursuant to the business

---

[5570] Electric Traction. (February, 1920). Vol. 16. Number 2. P. 145. Chicago, IL. Google Books.

[5571] Electric Traction. (February, 1920). Vol. 16. Number 2. P. 145. Chicago, IL. Google Books.

[5572] Electric Traction. (February, 1920). Vol. 16. Number 2. P. 145. Chicago, IL. Google Books.

[5573] Lanphier, Robert Carr. (1936). Forty Years of Sangamo. Appearing in Sangamo: A History of Fifty Years. (1949). P. 62. Chicago, IL: Sangamo Electric Company. Archive.org.

[5574] Lanphier, Robert Carr. (1936). Forty Years of Sangamo. Appearing in Sangamo: A History of Fifty Years. (1949). P. 62. Chicago, IL: Sangamo Electric Company. Archive.org.

[5575] Electric Traction. (February, 1920). Vol. 16. Number 2. P. 145. Chicago, IL. Google Books.

[5576] Lanphier, Robert Carr. (1936). Forty Years of Sangamo. Appearing in Sangamo: A History of Fifty Years. (1949). P. 64. Chicago, IL: Sangamo Electric Company. Archive.org.

[5577] Who's Who In Canada: An Illustrated Biographical Record Of Men And women Of The Time. (1922). B. M. Greene, Editor. P. 1534. Toronto, Ontario, Canada: International Press Limited, Toronto. Google Books.

counsel of Alfred Collyer and Scott Lynn.[5578] The Toronto branch of Sangamo performed with great success and represented the Illinois company to the Canadian markets with great profitability.[5579] Scott Lynn served as General Manager, and as Secretary and Treasurer, of Sangamo Electric Company of Canada, Limited.[5580] Lynn was a graduate of the United States Naval Academy and was the son of William Penn Lynn and Lily Lynn, natives, respectively, of Mercer County, Pennsylvania, and Salt Lake City, Utah.[5581] Scott Lynn married Anne Richardson Lanphier, who was the daughter of Charles Henry Lanphier and Emma Louise (Richardson) Lanphier of Springfield.[5582] Anne Richardson Lanphier was a niece of Ada Willard (Richardson) Bunn of Springfield and a granddaughter of William Douglas Richardson of Chicago.[5583] Anne Richardson Lanphier was also a cousin of Robert Carr Lanphier of Springfield, who was the co-founder of Sangamo Electric Company in 1899.[5584] Scott and Anne Richardson (Lanphier) Lynn were members of the Mississauga Golf and Country Club, and Scott belonged to the Engineers' Club of Toronto.[5585] Scott and Anne (Lanphier) Lynn had two children.[5586]

William Douglas Richardson of Chicago and the elder members of the Studebaker family of South Bend, Indiana, partnered in the original United States-influenced industrialization of Argentina prior to 1923.[5587] Jacob Bunn, Jr., Robert Carr Lanphier, Henry Bunn, and the other Sangamo Electric Company men would

---

[5578] Lanphier, Robert Carr. (1936). Forty Years of Sangamo. Appearing in Sangamo: A History of Fifty Years. (1949). P. 64. Chicago, IL: Sangamo Electric Company. Archive.org.

[5579] Lanphier, Robert Carr. (1936). Forty Years of Sangamo. Appearing in Sangamo: A History of Fifty Years. (1949). P. 64. Chicago, IL: Sangamo Electric Company. Archive.org.

[5580] Who's Who In Canada: An Illustrated Biographical Record Of Men And women Of The Time. (1922). B. M. Greene, Editor. P. 1534. Toronto, Ontario, Canada: International Press Limited, Toronto. Google Books.

[5581] Who's Who In Canada: An Illustrated Biographical Record Of Men And women Of The Time. (1922). B. M. Greene, Editor. P. 1534. Toronto, Ontario, Canada: International Press Limited, Toronto. Google Books.

[5582] Who's Who In Canada: An Illustrated Biographical Record Of Men And women Of The Time. (1922). B. M. Greene, Editor. P. 1534. Toronto, Ontario, Canada: International Press Limited, Toronto. Google Books.

[5583] Solomon, Ruth. Richardson family history and genealogy records.

[5584] Solomon, Ruth. Richardson family history and genealogy records.

[5585] Who's Who In Canada: An Illustrated Biographical Record Of Men And Women Of The Time. (1922). B. M. Greene, Editor. P. 1534. Toronto, Ontario, Canada: International Press Limited, Toronto. Google Books.

[5586] Who's Who In Canada: An Illustrated Biographical Record Of Men And Women Of The Time. (1922). B. M. Greene, Editor. P. 1534. Toronto, Ontario, Canada: International Press Limited, Toronto. Google Books.

[5587] The Foley Onlooker. (December 13, 1923). P. 1. Newspapers.com.

have built further upon that foundation of initial United States-influenced industrial economy in Argentina when they established Sangamo Electric Company as a multinational corporate presence in South America.[5588] Jacob Bunn, Jr., worked with William B. Hale, Caxton Brown, and Edward Weston to design a plan for Sangamo Electric Company's promotion and market entry in the Latin American electrical technologies markets.[5589] William Hale undertook a market representation circuit for Sangamo throughout every South American country in 1917, and produced robust market presence for Sangamo at Rio de Janeiro, Brazil, Lima, Peru, and at Buenos Aires, Argentina.[5590] Hale eventually managed the Rio de Janeiro branch of Sangamo Electric, before managing the Buenos Aires branch of the company.[5591] Sangamo also contracted with the Argentine company of Newbery & Rodriguez for representation in the Argentine markets, and this relationship bore many benefits.[5592]

Sangamo Electric Company became a publicly traded company in June, 1927, when it received a listing on the Chicago Stock Exchange.[5593] Paul H. Davis & Company of Chicago and Kissel, Kinnicutt Company of New York City approached Sangamo with the proposal for an initial public offering and a listing on the city's exchange.[5594] The company worked with both investment banks to engineer the public offering after a capital restructuring in which 125,000 shares of common stock and 10,000 shares of preferred stock were authorized.[5595] Public

---

[5588] Lanphier, Robert Carr. (1936). Forty Years of Sangamo. Appearing in Sangamo: A History of Fifty Years. (1949). P. 65. Chicago, IL: Sangamo Electric Company. Archive.org.

[5589] Lanphier, Robert Carr. (1936). Forty Years of Sangamo. Appearing in Sangamo: A History of Fifty Years. (1949). P. 65. Chicago, IL: Sangamo Electric Company. Archive.org.

[5590] Lanphier, Robert Carr. (1936). Forty Years of Sangamo. Appearing in Sangamo: A History of Fifty Years. (1949). P. 65. Chicago, IL: Sangamo Electric Company. Archive.org.

[5591] Lanphier, Robert Carr. (1936). Forty Years of Sangamo. Appearing in Sangamo: A History of Fifty Years. (1949). P. 65. Chicago, IL: Sangamo Electric Company. Archive.org.

[5592] Lanphier, Robert Carr. (1936). Forty Years of Sangamo. Appearing in Sangamo: A History of Fifty Years. (1949). P. 65. Chicago, IL: Sangamo Electric Company. Archive.org.

[5593] Lanphier, Robert Carr. (1936). Forty Years of Sangamo. Appearing in Sangamo: A History of Fifty Years. (1949). P. 84. Chicago, IL: Sangamo Electric Company. Archive.org.

[5594] Lanphier, Robert Carr. (1936). Forty Years of Sangamo. Appearing in Sangamo: A History of Fifty Years. (1949). P. 84. Chicago, IL: Sangamo Electric Company. Archive.org.

[5595] Lanphier, Robert Carr. (1936). Forty Years of Sangamo. Appearing in Sangamo: A History of Fifty Years. (1949). P. 84. Chicago, IL: Sangamo Electric Company. Archive.org.

offers of much of both of these equity money classes brought Sangamo Electric to the public stock market.[5596] The Sangamo public offering brought both Chicago and New York City into the company leadership, with Herbert I. Markham from Paul Davis & Company assuming a position on the Sangamo Electric board of directors, and Walter Robbins of Kissel, Kinnicutt and Company doing the same.[5597] Lanphier commented that Markham and Robbins provided excellent leadership and counsel to Sangamo as directors.[5598]

Sangamo Electric built an exhibit for the 1933 Century of Progress Exposition at Chicago, which was a second world's fair for the city, and one that commemorated the first century of Chicago history since the settlement's establishment in 1833.[5599] The company exhibit was located in the Electricity Building of the 1933 Exposition and contained an HC meter, as well as, "three large dioramas showing Faraday, Ferraris and Edison. . ."[5600] Sangamo Electric Company was one of the founding donors of the Julius Rosenwald Museum of Science and Industry in 1933.[5601] Sangamo Electric donated its Century of Progress Exposition exhibits to the Rosenwald Museum in 1933, and so contributed one of the founding collections to the museum.[5602] Julius Rosenwald (1862-1932) was the son of Samuel Rosenwald and Augusta (Hammerslough) Rosenwald of Springfield and later of Chicago.[5603] Illinois historian Bruce A. Campbell stated that Jacob Bunn, Sr., was a business partner of Samuel Rosenwald of Springfield, and that both men worked with Benjamin Hamilton Ferguson and Clinton

---

[5596] Lanphier, Robert Carr. (1936). Forty Years of Sangamo. Appearing in Sangamo: A History of Fifty Years. (1949). P. 84. Chicago, IL: Sangamo Electric Company. Archive.org.

[5597] Lanphier, Robert Carr. (1936). Forty Years of Sangamo. Appearing in Sangamo: A History of Fifty Years. (1949). P. 84. Chicago, IL: Sangamo Electric Company. Archive.org.

[5598] Lanphier, Robert Carr. (1936). Forty Years of Sangamo. Appearing in Sangamo: A History of Fifty Years. (1949). P. 84. Chicago, IL: Sangamo Electric Company. Archive.org.

[5599] Lanphier, Robert Carr. (1936). Forty Years of Sangamo. Appearing in Sangamo: A History of Fifty Years. (1949). Pp. 97-98. Chicago, IL: Sangamo Electric Company. Archive.org.

[5600] Lanphier, Robert Carr. (1936). Forty Years of Sangamo. Appearing in Sangamo: A History of Fifty Years. (1949). Pp. 97-98. Chicago, IL: Sangamo Electric Company. Archive.org.

[5601] Lanphier, Robert Carr. (1936). Forty Years of Sangamo. Appearing in Sangamo: A History of Fifty Years. (1949). Pp. 97-98. Chicago, IL: Sangamo Electric Company. Archive.org.

[5602] Lanphier, Robert Carr. (1936). Forty Years of Sangamo. Appearing in Sangamo: A History of Fifty Years. (1949). Pp. 97-98. Chicago, IL: Sangamo Electric Company. Archive.org.

[5603] Julius Rosenwald cemetery marker at Rosehill Cemetery, Chicago. Findagrave.com.

Conkling to establish the Springfield Board of Trade in 1869.[5604] Ferguson was a brother-in-law of Jacob Bunn, and was also heavily connected to Illinois industry and finance both in Springfield and Chicago. Ferguson's cousins were founders of the Pullman community and neighborhood on the Chicago south side (see chapter 3: *The Horizons of Hyde Park*). The Rosenwalds knew the Bunns, Fergusons, and other Bunn-connected family members, and it was highly probable that the Bunns wished specifically to contribute to the formation of Julius Rosenwald's Museum of Science and Industry after the 1933 Fair, both from a position of personal friendship with the Rosenwalds, and from a position of wishing to promote Illinois civic development.[5605]

The Ogden Standard-Examiner of Ogden, Utah, described the Museum of Science and Industry in a report of January 4, 1931. Rosenwald donated $4,000,000 for the purpose of creating a science and technology museum in Chicago to be located in the Palace of Fine Arts Building of Jackson Park, a building which remained from the 1893 World's Columbian Exposition.[5606] The Utah report stated that the Rosenwald museum would contain over nine miles of exhibits and about 60,000 specimens of industrial technologies.[5607] The museum curatorial staff aimed to produce as many life-sized industrial specimens as possible, but would resort to the construction of smaller models when space limits barred the construction of life-size exhibits.[5608] Rosenwald, who owned Sears, Roebuck & Company, was one of the founding fathers of American retail business, a leader in large-scale philanthropy, and a father of museum organization and development.

Another major Cook County connection for Sangamo Electric Company occurred in 1942, when Sangamo purchased the Allied Tool and Machine Company of Chicago.[5609] Allied manufactured tools and dies, both of which were necessary components for the Sangamo product output.[5610] The *1942 Annual Report for Sangamo Electric Company* described the purchase and the purpose

---

[5604] Campbell, Bruce A. (1979). The Sangamon Saga. P. 109. Springfield, IL: Phillips; Call, Andrew Taylor. (2005). Jacob Bunn: Legacy of an Illinois Industrial Pioneer. Pp. 40-41. Lawrenceville, VA: Brunswick Publishing Corporation.

[5605] Campbell, Bruce A. (1979). The Sangamon Saga. P. 109. Springfield, IL: Phillips; Call, Andrew Taylor. (2005). Jacob Bunn: Legacy of an Illinois Industrial Pioneer. Pp. 40-41. Lawrenceville, VA: Brunswick Publishing Corporation.

[5606] The Ogden Standard-Examiner. (January 4, 1931). P. 11. Newspapers.com.

[5607] The Ogden Standard-Examiner. (January 4, 1931). P. 11. Newspapers.com.

[5608] The Ogden Standard-Examiner. (January 4, 1931). P. 11. Newspapers.com.

[5609] Thomas, Benjamin P. (1949). Sangamo In Peace And War. P. 131. Appearing in Sangamo: A History of Fifty Years. (1949). Chicago, IL: Sangamo Electric Company. Archives.org.

[5610] Thomas, Benjamin P. (1949). Sangamo In Peace And War. P. 131. Appearing in Sangamo: A History of Fifty Years. (1949). Chicago, IL: Sangamo Electric Company. Archives.org.

thereof.[5611] Benjamin P. Thomas wrote *Sangamo In Peace And War*, which joined Robert Carr Lanphier's *Forty Years of Sangamo* to constitute the two-book (single book in two parts) volume, *Sangamo: A History of Fifty Years*. Thomas mentioned the purchase of Allied Tool and Machine Company and stated that when Sangamo had constructed and added adequate machine tools for its production processes, Sangamo sold Allied back to its original owners.[5612]

Sangamo Electric Company invented many forms of SONAR technology for the United States and the United Kingdom and was considered both the foremost electric meter manufacturer of the world and the foremost SONAR technology manufacturer of the Western Hemisphere, and possibly in the world.[5613] The company grew to immense size and possessed a market presence in every country of the world by 1939.[5614] The list that follows includes some of the most significant technologies that Sangamo Electric Company invented: type C meter; mercury motor-watthour meter; type E condenser alternating current mercury meter; permanent magnet for carburetor manufacturing uses; type F mercury meter for alternating current measurement; type D-5 mercury meter for direct current measurement; type H meter; Delco ampere-hour meter for Cadillac Car Company of Michigan; distant dial ampere-hour meter; molded mercury meter; variable resistor for ampere-hour meters; ampere-hour meter for Pullman Company railroad cars; H-2 meter; MS ampere-hour meter; various forms of refrigeration machines; street railway meter; LC ampere-hour meter; type N ampere-hour meter; S-2 meter for export trade; Pressley kit; type E non-self-starting synchronous

---

[5611] 1942 Annual Report. Sangamo Electric Company. Springfield, IL: Sangamo Electric Company; Call, Andrew Taylor. (2005). Jacob Bunn: Legacy of an Illinois Industrial Pioneer. P. 254. Lawrenceville, VA: Brunswick Publishing Corporation; Thomas, Benjamin P. (1949). Sangamo In Peace And War. P. 131. Appearing in Sangamo: A History of Fifty Years. (1949). Chicago, IL: Sangamo Electric Company. Archives.org.
[5612] Thomas, Benjamin P. (1949). Sangamo In Peace And War. P. 131. Appearing in Sangamo: A History of Fifty Years. (1949). Chicago, IL: Sangamo Electric Company. Archives.org.
[5613] Lanphier, Robert Carr. (1936). Forty Years of Sangamo. Appearing in Sangamo: A History of Fifty Years. (1949). Pp. 97-98. Chicago, IL: Sangamo Electric Company. Archive.org; Thomas, Benjamin P. (1949). Sangamo In Peace And War. P. 131. Appearing in Sangamo: A History of Fifty Years. (1949). Chicago, IL: Sangamo Electric Company. Archives.org; Call, Andrew Taylor. (2005). Jacob Bunn: Legacy of an Illinois Industrial Pioneer. Pp. 249-252. Lawrenceville, VA: Brunswick Publishing Corporation; Bunn family history records and memoirs.
[5614] Lanphier, Robert Carr. (1936). Forty Years of Sangamo. Appearing in Sangamo: A History of Fifty Years. (1949). Pp. 97-98. Chicago, IL: Sangamo Electric Company. Archive.org; Thomas, Benjamin P. (1949). Sangamo In Peace And War. P. 131. Appearing in Sangamo: A History of Fifty Years. (1949). Chicago, IL: Sangamo Electric Company. Archives.org; Call, Andrew Taylor. (2005). Jacob Bunn: Legacy of an Illinois Industrial Pioneer. Pp. 249-252. Lawrenceville, VA: Brunswick Publishing Corporation; Bunn family history records and memoirs.

motor; type F synchronous motor; various forms of electric clock; type A condenser; the Illini condenser; forms of electric switch technology; forms of flashing electric sign technology; three-coin prepayment meter; tachograph; type J meter; various forms of mechanical time fuse technologies; the BC-608 contactor; the range recorder for SONAR technology; the attack teacher for submarine warfare; mica capacitor; paper capacitor; radio compass tuning loop motors; transmitter and receiver radio compass indicators; electrical instrumentation for Link trainers; the portable anemometer; timing mechanisms; relay mechanisms; indicating instrumentation technologies; type H motor; and the type S time switch.[5615]

The Sangamo Electric Company entered the railcar lighting electricity measurement market in 1912-1913, when the company officials negotiated a contract with the Pullman Company of Chicago.[5616] Lanphier stated that Ernest Lunn, to whom he gave the title, "father of the amperehour meter," had left Commonwealth Edison to work for the Pullman Company.[5617] Lunn spoke highly of the Sangamo meters and recommended them to the Pullman Company to be used as the Pullman railcar electricity meters.[5618] Pullman agreed with Lunn, executed meter contracts with Sangamo Electric, and the positive result of the relationship was that by approximately 1916, nearly every Pullman railcar that existed possessed a Sangamo meter.[5619] Lanphier stated that Sangamo meters were attached to about 6,000 Pullman cars by about 1916.[5620] Once again, Sangamo had established another technologically central presence in Chicago, and one that enabled the electrification of almost all of the Pullman Company railcars.

[5615] Lanphier, Robert Carr. (1936). Forty Years of Sangamo. Appearing in Sangamo: A History of Fifty Years. (1949). Pp. 97-98. Chicago, IL: Sangamo Electric Company. Archive.org; Call, Andrew Taylor. (2005). Jacob Bunn: Legacy of an Illinois Industrial Pioneer. Pp. 249-252. Lawrenceville, VA: Brunswick Publishing Corporation.
[5616] Lanphier, Robert Carr. (1936). Forty Years of Sangamo. Appearing in Sangamo: A History of Fifty Years. (1949). Pp. 58-59. Chicago, IL: Sangamo Electric Company. Archive.org.
[5617] Lanphier, Robert Carr. (1936). Forty Years of Sangamo. Appearing in Sangamo: A History of Fifty Years. (1949). Pp. 58-59. Chicago, IL: Sangamo Electric Company. Archive.org.
[5618] Lanphier, Robert Carr. (1936). Forty Years of Sangamo. Appearing in Sangamo: A History of Fifty Years. (1949). Pp. 58-59. Chicago, IL: Sangamo Electric Company. Archive.org.
[5619] Lanphier, Robert Carr. (1936). Forty Years of Sangamo. Appearing in Sangamo: A History of Fifty Years. (1949). Pp. 58-59. Chicago, IL: Sangamo Electric Company. Archive.org.
[5620] Lanphier, Robert Carr. (1936). Forty Years of Sangamo. Appearing in Sangamo: A History of Fifty Years. (1949). Pp. 58-59. Chicago, IL: Sangamo Electric Company. Archive.org.

Jacob Bunn, Jr., and the National Business League of Chicago

Jacob Bunn, Jr., was an early and long-term member and guiding force of the National Advisory Committee of the National Business League, a Chicago organization.[5621] The National Business League was organized on January 26, 1897, and was a nonpartisan public policy organization based at the Chicago Stock Exchange Building, at the corner of LaSalle Street and Washington Street in the Loop community.[5622] Bunn was possibly, even probably, one of the founders of the National Business League itself, the National Advisory Committee of the League, and the International Advisory Committee. The purpose of the organization was to promote and develop commercial and industrial activity in the United States and to protect United States commercial and industrial interests.[5623] The constitution of the League stated, *inter alia*, the following:

> "To enlarge the field of commercial and industrial activity by promoting such national legislation as promises to further that result, and combating such measures as threaten to be injurious, is the special province of the National Business League. The organization is non-partisan, and directs its efforts solely to the forwarding of great movements for the general good. Its particular function is to concentrate the business sentiment of the country on any important question, and bring all business interests to act thereon, simultaneously and with harmony. Prominent manufacturers, merchants, bankers, and railway officials in more than one hundred and fifty cities, covering every state in the Union, are connected with the League and participate in its activities."[5624]

The most significant achievement of the National Business League was the League's powerful, central, instrumental, and successful effort to convince the government of the United States to create a Department of Commerce and Labor.[5625] The National Business League reported in its *1903 Annual Report* the success of the League's national public policy undertaking as follows:

> "DEPARTMENT OF COMMERCE AND LABOR. This measure, on which the League took the initiative in systematic, organized effort,

---

[5621] Constitution and Official Directory of the National Business League. (1903). P. 38. Chicago, IL. Google Books.

[5622] Constitution and Official Directory of the National Business League. (1903). P. 1. Chicago, IL. Google Books.

[5623] Constitution and Official Directory of the National Business League. (1903). P. 3. Chicago, IL. Google Books.

[5624] Constitution and Official Directory of the National Business League. (1903). P. 3. Chicago, IL. Google Books.

[5625] Constitution and Official Directory of the National Business League. (1903). P. 3. Chicago, IL. Google Books.

continuing the work uninterruptedly for six years, was enacted during the last regular session of Congress. Nearly every commercial organization, national, state, and municipal, joined in the movement for the creation of the new Department. Men of both political parties favored the measure. Great credit is due President [Theodore] Roosevelt for his potent efforts to secure enactment, without which success would have been doubtful; also to Senator Knute Nelson of Minnesota, who had charge of the bill in the Senate; the Committee on Commerce of the Senate, the Committee on Interstate and Foreign Commerce of the House, and to the Fifty-seventh Congress of the United States. The Department is now being carefully and thoroughly organized under the able direction of Hon. George B. Cortelyou, whose appointment as Secretary by President Roosevelt gave general satisfaction to the manufacturing and commercial interests of the country."[5626]

Jacob Bunn, Jr., served on the National Advisory Committee of the National Business League when the League was actively and devotedly promoting the creation of the Department of Commerce and Labor. Bunn and the many other members of the League collectively played a preeminent and central role in the creation of the Department of Commerce and Labor. Serving with Bunn on the National Advisory Committee were Dr. Edmund J. James, who was President of Northwestern University, Dr. William Rainey Harper, who was the founding President of the University of Chicago, Dr. Andrew S. Draper, who was President of the University of Illinois, Dr. Edgar M. Smith, who was President of Illinois Wesleyan University in Bloomington, Frank W. Tracy, who was President of the First National Bank of Springfield, R. F. Herndon, who was President of R. F. Herndon Company of Springfield, M. W. Jack, who was President of Streator Bottle and Glass Company in metropolitan Chicago, and O. D. Powell, who was President of the National Bank of Aurora, also in metropolitan Chicago.[5627] Significantly, Thomas P. Egan of Cincinnati served as one of the Ohio members of the National Advisory Committee at the same time when Jacob Bunn, Jr., served as one of the Illinois members of the Committee.[5628] Egan was associated with Charles Davis and William Henry Burtner of Cincinnati in the formation of the Davis & Egan Machine Tool Company, which was the largest machine tool manufacturer in Chicago, one of the largest in Cincinnati, and one of the largest in

---

[5626] Constitution and Official Directory of the National Business League. (1903). Pp. 3-4. Chicago, IL. Google Books.
[5627] Constitution and Official Directory of the National Business League. (1903). P. 38. Chicago, IL. Google Books.
[5628] Constitution and Official Directory of the National Business League. (1903). P. 45. Chicago, IL. Google Books.

the entire world.[5629] Bunn, Egan, James, Smith, Harper, Draper, and the other National Business League members supported and helped enact the Nelson Act of 1903, which was the federal organic statute for the Department of Commerce and Labor.[5630] For extensive history of the Lodge & Davis Machine Tool Company of Cincinnati and Chicago, and the Davis & Egan Machine Tool Company of Cincinnati and Chicago, see Chapter 6, *Sprinters of the Steel Track.*

The Central Illinois Public Service Company

The present segment concerns the Chicago history of the Bunn branch of my mother's family. Willard Bunn was born July 14, 1888, in Springfield, Illinois.[5631] He was the son of George Wallace Bunn, Sr., (1861-1938), and Ada Willard (Richardson) Bunn (1861-1945).[5632] Willard was the grandson of Jacob Bunn and Elizabeth Jane (Ferguson) Bunn.[5633] Willard Bunn attended The Lawrenceville School and served in the United States Marine Corps during World War I. He returned to Springfield to begin employment with the J. W. Bunn Grocery Company. Willard was known as "Toy" by his family and friends. His wife, Ruth (Regan) Bunn, was known as "Tute" (pronounced "Toot") by her family and friends.

Willard Bunn served as President of the Springfield Chamber of Commerce.[5634] Bunn also served as a member of the Board of Directors of the Illinois Chamber of Commerce, a Chicago-based organization discussed *infra.*[5635] Having held the positions of President and Treasurer of the Bunn Capitol Grocery Company, Bunn contributed leadership and development to the food production and distribution sectors of the Illinois economy. He contributed to the establishment of the Steak n Shake Company of Illinois. He also helped to finance the Heath Bar Company, another Illinois company, that developed and manufactured the Heath Bar. Bunn was proprietor of the Colonial Restaurant in Springfield.[5636] It was stated by a late family member that Bunn possibly also was either owner, or co-owner, of Maldaner's, the renowned downtown Springfield restaurant that had been

---

[5629] History of Cincinnati And Hamilton County, Ohio; Their Past And Present. (1894). P. 318. Cincinnati, OH: S. B. Nelson & Co., Publishers. Google Books; French, Lester Gray. (February, 1896). *Machinery.* Vol. 2. P. 187. Google Books.

[5630] Constitution and Official Directory of the National Business League. (1903). Pp. 1-12, 38, 45. Chicago, IL. Google Books.

[5631] Willard Bunn, Sr., 71, Dies Suddenly. Obituary for Willard Bunn, Sr. October 4, 1959. Illinois State Journal. P. 1. Kathleenmanuel.com.

[5632] Willard Bunn, Sr., 71, Dies Suddenly. Obituary for Willard Bunn, Sr. October 4, 1959. Illinois State Journal. P. 1. Kathleenmanuel.com.

[5633] Bunn Family Records.

[5634] Willard Bunn, Sr., 71, Dies Suddenly. Obituary for Willard Bunn, Sr. October 4, 1959. Illinois State Journal. P. 1. Kathleenmanuel.com.

[5635] Willard Bunn, Sr., 71, Dies Suddenly. Obituary for Willard Bunn, Sr. October 4, 1959. Illinois State Journal. P. 1. Kathleenmanuel.com.

[5636] Telephone interviews with Margot McKay. (Undated). Conducted and recorded by Andrew Taylor Call.

established by John Maldaner of Wisconsin. Bunn's ownership interest in Maldaner's has not been confirmed, however, and remains speculative and uncertain.

Central Illinois Public Service Company was present in Chicago for many decades, and even operated a headquarters there in 1920. The three offices of the company in 1920 were located at 72 West Adams Street in the Loop, at the Farmers Bank Building of Springfield, and in Mattoon.[5637] The company registrar at this time was the Illinois Trust and Savings Bank Company of Chicago, and Samuel Insull was Chairman of the company at this time.[5638]

Service on the Board of Directors of the Central Illinois Public Service Company not only connected Bunn and the other dirctors to the construction and development of the public utilities of central Illinois and southern Illinois, but also connected the entire Board of Directors to Chicago, Cook County, Joliet, and Will County.[5639] Bunn held a position on the Board of Directors of the Central Illinois Public Service Company for twenty years, from 1939 until 1959.[5640] The Central Illinois Public Service Company entered existence through incorporation on September 1, 1923.[5641] The organization was chartered under Illinois incorporation law.[5642] The corporation represented a joinder of the Middle West Power Company and a prior corporation that also possessed the name Central Illinois Public Service Company.[5643] The prior corporation of the name Central Illinois Public Service Company was an organizational derivative of the Mattoon City Railway Company.[5644] The Mattoon City Railway Company entered corporate existence on May 26, 1902, under Illinois incorporation law.[5645] The corporate name, Mattoon City Railway Company, was changed to Central Illinois Public Service Company

---

[5637] The Economist: Investors' Section. (July, 1920). P. 29. Chicago, IL. Google Books.

[5638] The Economist: Investors' Section. (July, 1920). P. 29. Chicago, IL. Google Books.

[5639] See: Porter, John Sherman. (Editor in Chief). 1939. Moody's Manual of Investments American and Foreign: Public Utility Securities. Pp. 1404-1405. New York, NY: Moody's Investors Service.

[5640] See references sources that follow, *infra*.

[5641] Porter, John Sherman. (Editor in Chief). 1939. Moody's Manual of Investments American and Foreign: Public Utility Securities. P. 1404. New York, NY: Moody's Investors Service.

[5642] Porter, John Sherman. (Editor in Chief). 1939. Moody's Manual of Investments American and Foreign: Public Utility Securities. P. 1404. New York, NY: Moody's Investors Service.

[5643] Porter, John Sherman. (Editor in Chief). 1939. Moody's Manual of Investments American and Foreign: Public Utility Securities. P. 1404. New York, NY: Moody's Investors Service.

[5644] Porter, John Sherman. (Editor in Chief). 1939. Moody's Manual of Investments American and Foreign: Public Utility Securities. P. 1404. New York, NY: Moody's Investors Service.

[5645] Porter, John Sherman. (Editor in Chief). 1939. Moody's Manual of Investments American and Foreign: Public Utility Securities. P. 1404. New York, NY: Moody's Investors Service.

on August 23, 1910.[5646] In the early years of its corporate existence the company started a plan of commercial growth, industrial growth, and infrastructural growth through extensive combination with other utilities.[5647] The utility company acquired multiple individual and additional utility companies in Illinois.[5648]

The Central Illinois Public Service Company acquired multiple physical properties of multiple corporations during the years 1925, 1927, 1928, 1929, 1930, and 1931.[5649] The principal connection and relevance of the Central Illinois Public Service Company to Chicago, Cook County, and the metropolitan region stemmed from the fact that the parent company had acquired at least three subsidiary companies located in and near to Chicago and Cook County.[5650] These three subsidiary companies, the Chicago & Joliet Electric Railway Company, the Chicago & Joliet Transportation Company, and the Dellwood Park Company, constituted a major connection between the Springfield utility company that was Central Illinois Public Service Company and the geography and economy of Chicago, Cook County, Joliet, Will County, Lemont, and the metropolitan vicinity.[5651]

The Dellwood Park Company entered corporate existence on February 13, 1906, and represented a capitalization of $150,000 as of the year 1939.[5652] The company possessed sixty-three acres of land located three miles from Joliet in a place called Dellwood.[5653] The Dellwood Park Company was a dormant company as of the year

[5646] Porter, John Sherman. (Editor in Chief). 1939. Moody's Manual of Investments American and Foreign: Public Utility Securities. P. 1404. New York, NY: Moody's Investors Service.

[5647] Porter, John Sherman. (Editor in Chief). 1939. Moody's Manual of Investments American and Foreign: Public Utility Securities. P. 1404. New York, NY: Moody's Investors Service.

[5648] Porter, John Sherman. (Editor in Chief). 1939. Moody's Manual of Investments American and Foreign: Public Utility Securities. P. 1404. New York, NY: Moody's Investors Service.

[5649] Porter, John Sherman. (Editor in Chief). 1939. Moody's Manual of Investments American and Foreign: Public Utility Securities. Pp. 1405-1406. New York, NY: Moody's Investors Service.

[5650] Porter, John Sherman. (Editor in Chief). 1939. Moody's Manual of Investments American and Foreign: Public Utility Securities. P. 1404. New York, NY: Moody's Investors Service.

[5651] Porter, John Sherman. (Editor in Chief). 1939. Moody's Manual of Investments American and Foreign: Public Utility Securities. P. 1404. New York, NY: Moody's Investors Service.

[5652] Porter, John Sherman. (Editor in Chief). 1939. Moody's Manual of Investments American and Foreign: Public Utility Securities. P. 1406. New York, NY: Moody's Investors Service.

[5653] Porter, John Sherman. (Editor in Chief). 1939. Moody's Manual of Investments American and Foreign: Public Utility Securities. P. 1406. New York, NY: Moody's Investors Service.

1939, however.[5654] In 1940, the Central Illinois Public Service Company possessed the Dellwood Park Company and the Chicago & Joliet Electric Railway Company, as subsidiary corporations.[5655] In 1941, the Central Illinois Public Service Company employed 1,423 people and continued its possession of the Chicago & Joliet Electric Railway Company and the Dellwood Park Company.[5656]

During much of Willard Bunn's time of service on the board of directors of Central Illinois Public Service Company, the company possessed the Chicago & Joliet Electric Railway Company and the Dellwood Park Company.[5657] One should take notice of the fact that other people who were connected to Chicago and Cook County served as members of the board of directors of the Central Illinois Public Service Company contemporaneously with Willard Bunn, who himself also held leadership positions in several other Chicago organizations.[5658]

The American Railways Company of Philadelphia caused the Chicago & Joliet Rapid Transit Company, the Chicago and Desplaines Valley Electric Railway Company, and the Desplaines Valley Electric Railway Company to undergo organizational joinder.[5659] The resultant organization was the Chicago & Joliet Electric Railway Company.[5660] The rail line opened in September, 1901, and the route paralleled the line of the Chicago and Alton Railroad Company,[5661] a corporation that Jacob Bunn had co-founded and co-owned many years prior.[5662] The Chicago & Joliet Electric Railway Company line connected to Lemont, located in southwestern Cook County, and connected also to, "some of the largest

---

[5654] Porter, John Sherman. (Editor in Chief). 1939. Moody's Manual of Investments American and Foreign: Public Utility Securities. P. 1406. New York, NY: Moody's Investors Service.

[5655] Porter, John Sherman. (Editor in Chief). 1940. Moody's Manual of Investments American and Foreign: Public Utility Securities. P. 717. New York, NY: Moody's Investors Service.

[5656] Porter, John Sherman. (Editor in Chief). 1941. Moody's Manual of Investments American and Foreign: Public Utility Securities. Pp. 573-574. New York, NY: Moody's Investors Service.

[5657] See reference sources that follow, *infra*

[5658] See relevant reference sources herein.

[5659] Western Electrician. (July 6-December 28, 1901). Vol. XXIX, Nos. 1-26. P. 218. Chicago, IL: Electrician Publishing Company. Google Books.

[5660] Western Electrician. (July 6-December 28, 1901). Vol. XXIX, Nos. 1-26. P. 218. Chicago, IL: Electrician Publishing Company. Google Books.

[5661] Western Electrician. (July 6-December 28, 1901). Vol. XXIX, Nos. 1-26. P. 218. Chicago, IL: Electrician Publishing Company. Google Books.

[5662] See: AN ACT to incorporate the Chicago and Alton Railroad Company. Private Laws of the State of Illinois Passed By The Twenty-Second General Assembly, Convened January 7, 1861. (1861). P. 489. Springfield: Bailhache & Baker, Printers. Google Books; See: Snodgrass, Mary Ellen. (2015). The Civil War Era and Reconstruction: An Encyclopedia of Social, Political, Cultural, and economic History. Vols. 1-2. P. 515. New York City, NY: Routledge. Google Books.

stone quarries in the state,"[5663] where Nathaniel Jennison Brown, Lemuel Brown, and multiple other members of the Brown family cousins of Ada Willard (Richardson) Bunn had developed communities and industry. It is interesting that Willard Bunn, a cousin of the Browns of Chicago and Lemont, would serve for two decades as a member of the board of directors of a company that connected prominently to southwestern Cook County, where the Browns were founders of Lemont and the stone quarry industries.[5664] For the Chicago history of the Brown family, see Chapter 5, *The Foundations of Jackson Park*. Willard Bunn was a cousin of the Browns of Chicago and Cook County.

The Chicago & Joliet Electric Railway Company connected Joliet, in Will County, to Chicago and Cook County.[5665] The railway line terminated at Archer Avenue and Cicero Avenue in Chicago.[5666] The transportation service was available typically at hourly intervals, and the rail line used arched-roof train cars.[5667] The Great Depression caused financial destruction to overtake the company, and the firm eventually was acquired by the Central Illinois Public Service Company,[5668] after a period of time as a subsidiary of American Gas & Electric Company. The Chicago & Joliet Electric Railway Company also served Lockport, Illinois.[5669]

The company contributed to urban development and recreational development when the firm developed Dellwood Park.[5670] The Chicago & Joliet Electric Railway Company undertook an integrated construction and development project when, in 1905 and 1906, the company developed Dellwood Park, located in Lockport, a suburb of Joliet, and part of the greater Chicago metropolitan region.[5671] Dellwood Park consisted of recreational park grounds with a dam.[5672] The Chicago & Joliet Electric Railway Company's purpose for the development

---

[5663] Western Electrician. (July 6-December 28, 1901). Vol. XXIX, Nos. 1-26. P. 218. Chicago, IL: Electrician Publishing Company. Google Books.

[5664] Western Electrician. (July 6-December 28, 1901). Vol. XXIX, Nos. 1-26. P. 218. Chicago, IL: Electrician Publishing Company. Google Books; Bunn and Brown family history records.

[5665] Hilton, George W., Due, John F. (1960). The Electric Interurban Railways in America. P. 339. Stanford, CA: Stanford University Press. Google Books.

[5666] Hilton, George W., Due, John F. (1960). The Electric Interurban Railways in America. P. 339. Stanford, CA: Stanford University Press. Google Books.

[5667] Hilton, George W., Due, John F. (1960). The Electric Interurban Railways in America. P. 339. Stanford, CA: Stanford University Press. Google Books.

[5668] Hilton, George W., Due, John F. (1960). The Electric Interurban Railways in America. P. 339. Stanford, CA: Stanford University Press. Google Books.

[5669] Lamb, John. (1999). Lockport, Illinois: The Old Canal Town. Pages not indicated numerically. Charleston, SC: Arcadia Publishing. Google Books.

[5670] Belden, David A. (2009). Will County. Pages not indicated numerically. Charleston, SC: Arcadia Publishing. Google Books.

[5671] Belden, David A. (2009). Will County. Pages not indicated numerically. Charleston, SC: Arcadia Publishing. Google Books.

[5672] Belden, David A. (2009). Will County. Pages not indicated numerically. Charleston, SC: Arcadia Publishing. Google Books.

of Dellwood Park was to foster the growth of a customer market for the transportation services offered by the company.[5673]

Willard Bunn served as a member of the Board of Directors of the Illinois Chamber of Commerce, an organization that possessed headquarters in Chicago.[5674] The Illinois Chamber of Commerce was located at 10 South LaSalle Street within the Business District neighborhood of the Loop community of Chicago.[5675] Bunn served also as President of the Springfield Chamber of Commerce.[5676] Willard Bunn died in October, 1959. He and Ruth (Regan) Bunn had five children: Willard Bunn, Jr. (1913-2002); George Regan Bunn (1915-2002); Elizabeth Bunn (1917-2007); Ruth Margaret Bunn (1925-1992); and John Michael Bunn (1929-1997). Elizabeth Bunn married Henry Stryker Taylor (1908-1994), and these are the maternal grandparents of author Andrew Taylor Call. For the Chicago history of the Taylors and Strykers, see Chapter 6, *Sprinters of the Steel Track*; Chapter 1, *Genesis of a Great Lakes Frontier*; Chapter 3, *The Horizons of Hyde Park*; and Chapter 4, *Friends of the Leatherworkers*. Willard Bunn, Sr., is the great-grandfather of Andrew Taylor Call. Other chapters herein contain additional biographical information about Willard Bunn and his work in Illinois business.

George Wallace Bunn, Jr. and the Illinois Frozen Asset Board of Chicago

George Wallace Bunn, Jr. (1890-1973) was the son of George Wallace Bunn (1861-1938) and Ada Willard (Richardson) Bunn (1861-1945) of Springfield. He was the brother of Willard Bunn, the grandson of Jacob and Elizabeth (Ferguson) Bunn, and the grandson of William Douglas Richardson and Lucy (Willard) Richardson. George and Willard were, therefore, both descendants of the Willard and Richardson families of Chicago (See Chapter 5, *The Foundations of Jackson Park*).[5677] George W. Bunn, Jr., known as "Gib" (pronounced "Jib") by family and friends, was a graduate of Princeton University.[5678] At Princeton, Bunn was an English Major, a member of the Tiger Inn, and a member of the Triangle Club.[5679]

[5673] Belden, David A. (2009). Will County. Pages not indicated numerically. Charleston, SC: Arcadia Publishing. Google Books.

[5674] Willard Bunn, Sr., 71, Dies Suddenly. Obituary for Willard Bunn, Sr. October 4, 1959. Illinois State Journal. P. 1. Kathleenmanuel.com; Illinois Chamber of Commerce. (1921). Illinois Facts. Pp. 0-1. Chicago, IL: Illinois Chamber of Commerce. Google Books.

[5675] Illinois Chamber of Commerce. (1921). Illinois Facts. Pp. 0-1. Chicago, IL: Illinois Chamber of Commerce. Google Books.

[5676] Willard Bunn, Sr., 71, Dies Suddenly. Obituary for Willard Bunn, Sr. October 4, 1959. Illinois State Journal. P. 1. Kathleenmanuel.com.

[5677] Bunn family historical records.

[5678] Bunn, George W. (1972). Oral Memoir. Interview by Sally Schanbacher. Pp. 12-13. University of Illinois at Springfield. Library.uis.edu

[5679] Bunn, George W. (1972). Oral Memoir. Interview by Sally Schanbacher. Pp. 12-13. University of Illinois at Springfield. Library.uis.edu

As a member of Triangle Club, Bunn co-wrote a play with friend and fellow Princetonian Cyrus Hall McCormick, III, of Chicago.[5680]

After graduation from Princeton, Bunn moved to New York City and worked as an editor for the *New York Morning Sun*.[5681] At the *Sun* Bunn worked as the Night Police Editor, and was given the job of collecting the facts and story for the 1912 New York City murder of the famous gambler, Herman "Rosy" Rosenthal.[5682] Rosenthal was murdered outside the Metropole Hotel.[5683] Bunn noted in an oral memoir that the investigation into the Rosenthal murder led to the discovery that Charles E. Becker of the Detective Bureau had arranged Rosenthal's death.[5684] Bunn stated that Lefty Louie, Gyp the Blood, and Big Jack Zelig were three of the main leaders of organized crime at that time.[5685] While Bunn did not write any of the major stories about the Rosenthal murder, he certainly collected and assembled the lion's share of the facts that went into the major reports about the crime.[5686]

Frank Ward O'Malley and Will Irwin were the two most important reporters at the *New York Sun* when Bunn was a beginning reporter and editor for the paper.[5687] Bunn recalled how O'Malley and Irwin had been generous supporters of Bunn and the other new young *Sun* editors and staffers.[5688] It is of literary significance that author F. Scott Fitzgerald referred to the murder of Herman Rosenthal in his 1925 novel, *The Great Gatsby*. Fitzgerald introduces the historical facts of Rosenthal's death through the medium of the dialogue between the novel's protagonist, Nick Carraway, and the bootlegger boss and gambler named Meyer Wolfsheim. Wolfsheim tells Carraway that he remembers Rosenthal's death, and describes the event to Carraway with a tone of sentimental reminiscence.[5689]

[5680] Bunn, George W. (1972). Oral Memoir. Interview by Sally Schanbacher. P. 15. University of Illinois at Springfield. Library.uis.edu

[5681] Bunn, George W. (1972). Oral Memoir. Interview by Sally Schanbacher. Pp. 15-16. University of Illinois at Springfield. Library.uis.edu

[5682] Bunn, George W. (1972). Oral Memoir. Interview by Sally Schanbacher. Pp. 15-16. University of Illinois at Springfield. Library.uis.edu

[5683] Bunn, George W. (1972). Oral Memoir. Interview by Sally Schanbacher. Pp. 15-16. University of Illinois at Springfield. Library.uis.edu

[5684] Bunn, George W. (1972). Oral Memoir. Interview by Sally Schanbacher. Pp. 15-16. University of Illinois at Springfield. Library.uis.edu

[5685] Bunn, George W. (1972). Oral Memoir. Interview by Sally Schanbacher. Pp. 15-16. University of Illinois at Springfield. Library.uis.edu

[5686] Bunn, George W. (1972). Oral Memoir. Interview by Sally Schanbacher. Pp. 15-16. University of Illinois at Springfield. Library.uis.edu

[5687] Bunn, George W. (1972). Oral Memoir. Interview by Sally Schanbacher. Pp. 15-16. University of Illinois at Springfield. Library.uis.edu

[5688] Bunn, George W. (1972). Oral Memoir. Interview by Sally Schanbacher. Pp. 15-16. University of Illinois at Springfield. Library.uis.edu

[5689] Fitzgerald, F. Scott. (1925). The Great Gatsby.

Gib Bunn was a member of the Princeton Club of New York City.[5690] He also was a member of the University Club of Chicago.[5691] Bunn worked as an assistant to author Sinclair Lewis in a literary review company that provided book reviews for United States newspapers.[5692] Lewis was the editor of the book review company, and, at some point, Bunn and Lewis formed the Lewis and Bunn Publishing Company.[5693]

One organization that arose during the Great Depression in the Midwest was the Illinois Frozen Asset Board. The purpose of the Board was to liquidate, and consequently free up, frozen bank deposits in the Midwest.[5694] The Frozen Asset Board was largely a Chicago organization, and possessed public administrative jurisdiction that was coextensive with that of the Seventh Federal Reserve District, which was the district in which the Board sat.[5695] James R. Leavell was President of the Continental Illinois National Bank and Trust Company of Chicago. Leavell held appointment power over the Frozen Asset Board in 1933. The *Alton Evening Telegraph* edition of October 27, 1933, reported the acts of the Board. Leavell appointed George Wallace Bunn, Jr., of Springfield, William L. O'Connell of Chicago, Melvin Traylor of Chicago, Gen. Robert E. Wood of Chicago, and Abner J. Stillwell of Chicago to membership on the Frozen Asset Board.[5696] Bunn, at that time, was Executive Vice-President of the Springfield Marine Bank; William L. O'Connell was Receiver of Closed Banks for the State of Illinois; Melvin A. Traylor was President of First National Bank of Chicago; Gen. Robert E. Wood was President of Sears Roebuck and Company of Chicago; and Abner J. Stilwell was Vice-President of Continental Illinois National Bank and Trust Company.[5697]

Edward J. Barrett was State Auditor of Illinois at this time, and it was Barrett who appointed O'Connell to the job of Receiver of Closed Banks for the State of Illinois.[5698] Leavell also appointed two people to the Frozen Asset Board from each of the five states within the Seventh Federal Reserve District.[5699] Bunn was active in civic leadership in many organizations and served as President of the Abraham Lincoln Association, an organization which had been founded by his granduncle, John Whitfield Bunn, by Melville Weston Fuller of Chicago, and by others.[5700] Gib

[5690] Bunn, George W. (1972). Oral Memoir. Interview by Sally Schanbacher. Pp. 15-16. University of Illinois at Springfield. Library.uis.edu
[5691] Bunn family historical records.
[5692] Bunn, George W. (1972). Oral Memoir. Interview by Sally Schanbacher. Pp. 16-17. University of Illinois at Springfield. Library.uis.edu
[5693] Bunn family historical records. See Special Collections of the University of Virginia for certain publications of George Wallace Bunn, Jr., and certain biographical facts about Bunn.
[5694] Alton Evening Telegraph. (October 27, 1933). P. 1. Newspapers.com.
[5695] Alton Evening Telegraph. (October 27, 1933). P. 1. Newspapers.com.
[5696] Alton Evening Telegraph. (October 27, 1933). P. 1. Newspapers.com.
[5697] Alton Evening Telegraph. (October 27, 1933). P. 1. Newspapers.com.
[5698] Alton Evening Telegraph. (October 27, 1933). P. 1. Newspapers.com.
[5699] Alton Evening Telegraph. (October 27, 1933). P. 1. Newspapers.com.
[5700] The Ithaca Journal. (February 12, 1953). P. 1. Newspapers.com.

Bunn served as Chairman of Springfield Marine Bank, served on the board of directors of Sangamo Electric Company, and was prominently connected to many other companies.[5701]

When Sinclair Lewis asked Gib Bunn for suggestions for a name for Lewis' new novel, Bunn suggested the name, "Main Street," because that had been the name of a musical that Bunn had written while a student at Princeton. Lewis liked the name and used it. This work by Sinclair Lewis is the famous novel, *Main Street*.[5702] Gib Bunn was a noted golfer in Illinois, and competed, along with his brother, Willard Bunn, Charles "Chick" Evans of Chicago, and others from around the United States, in the Barnes Decatur Invitational Golf Tournament held in August of 1911.[5703] Dr. William Barnes of Decatur hosted the tournament at the Decatur Country Club.[5704] Chick Evans had held the Western Amateur Golf Championship prior to 1911.[5705] Bunn defeated Evans in the Barnes Invitational at the Decatur Country Club.[5706] Gib Bunn also won the Individual Golf Championship of the Central Illinois Country Clubs Association in 1909, which was held in Decatur.[5707]

Willard Bunn, Jr.

Willard Bunn, Jr. of Springfield (1913-2002), the eldest son of Willard Bunn and Ruth (Regan) Bunn, served as one of the longest-serving members of the board of directors of the Illinois Bell Telephone Company.[5708] Willard was known as "Bunch" by family and friends. He was a member of the Union League Club of Chicago and held leadership positions in multiple civic organizations. Bunn was President, and later Chairman, of Springfield Marine Bank, which had been established by Jacob Bunn and others in January, 1851.[5709] Willard was Treasurer of the Abraham Lincoln Association, a member of the board of directors of the St. John's Hospital Foundation in Springfield, an accomplished golfer, and a regional affairs director of the United States Golf Association.[5710]

Willard Bunn, Jr., was a key proponent of the creation of the law and policy that would create branch banking in the State of Illinois.[5711] The Illinois Council for Branch Banking, of which Bunn was a founding member, was a policy board that was based in Chicago and Springfield. This policy board sought to introduce and institute branch banking in Illinois through public policy and legislative advocacy.

[5701] Bunn family historical records.

[5702] Memoir from Elizabeth Taylor Greer.

[5703] The Daily Review. (Decatur, Illinois). (August 19, 1911). P. 8. Newspapers.com.

[5704] The Daily Review. (Decatur, Illinois). (August 19, 1911). P. 8. Newspapers.com.

[5705] The Daily Review. (Decatur, Illinois). (August 19, 1911). P. 8. Newspapers.com.

[5706] The Decatur Herald. (August 21, 1911). P. 3. Newspapers.com.

[5707] The Decatur Daily Review. (July 24, 1939). P. 4. Newspapers.com.

[5708] Bunn family history records.

[5709] Obituary for Willard Bunn, Jr. (July 10, 2002). Illinois State Journal-Register. (July 11, 2002). P. 32. Kathleenmanuel.com.

[5710] Obituary for Willard Bunn, Jr. (July 10, 2002). Illinois State Journal-Register. (July 11, 2002). P. 32. Kathleenmanuel.com.

[5711] Chicago Tribune. (April 29, 1965). P. 62. Newspapers.com.

Bunn gave testimony in support of a bill to legalize branch banking in 1965.[5712] Paul J. Randolph, an Illinois Republican legislator of Chicago, sponsored the branch banking bill.[5713] The bill called for referendum on the subjects and issues of branch banking in Illinois.[5714] At this time, Illinois was one of the only states not to permit branch banking.[5715] On April 28, 1965, the House Banking Committee of the Illinois legislature recommended for passage a bill to introduce branch banking to Illinois.[5716]

John McCarthy, President of the Illinois Bankers' Association, reported that the bill was opposed by 845 of the 1,043 banks that existed in Illinois.[5717] This represented a heavy majority rejection of the policy within the Illinois banking community.[5718] The branch banking policy would permit banks to organize branches within the home counties of the principal banks (home banks).[5719] Willard Bunn, Jr., testified that the potential law, "would strengthen the state's economy and give better service to depositors."[5720] Additional financial executives provided testimony in support of the branch banking policy and bill.[5721] One Chicago bank executive wanted to establish banks in nine different Chicago wards that possessed no banking services at all.[5722]

Willard Bunn, Jr., served as Chairman of the Executive Board of the Illinois Council for Branch Banking at least as early as February, 1967.[5723] Bunn specifically diagnosed one twenty-five-year-long Illinois capital market crisis as an excellent and urgent reason for the enactment of the branch banking authorization law in Illinois.[5724] Bunn specifically identified that the slow growth of deposit moneys in Illinois banks had severely diminished the lending powers of those banks, and had thus prevented the banks from participating efficiently in the multiple loan markets of Illinois.[5725] Stated alternatively, the torpor in the growth of statewide deposit moneys caused deficits both in the statewide powers of loan among Illinois banks and in the statewide adequacy of capital within Illinois banks.[5726] Bunn described the multiannual and multilateral disequilibrium that existed among deposit money growth, capital market growth, and financial institutional loan power, in the February 15, 1967, edition of *The Decatur Herald*

[5712] Chicago Tribune. (April 29, 1965). P. 62. Newspapers.com.
[5713] Chicago Tribune. (April 29, 1965). P. 62. Newspapers.com.
[5714] Chicago Tribune. (April 29, 1965). P. 62. Newspapers.com.
[5715] Chicago Tribune. (April 29, 1965). P. 62. Newspapers.com.
[5716] Chicago Tribune. (April 29, 1965). P. 62. Newspapers.com.
[5717] Chicago Tribune. (April 29, 1965). P. 62. Newspapers.com.
[5718] Chicago Tribune. (April 29, 1965). P. 62. Newspapers.com.
[5719] Chicago Tribune. (April 29, 1965). P. 62. Newspapers.com.
[5720] Chicago Tribune. (April 29, 1965). P. 62. Newspapers.com.
[5721] Chicago Tribune. (April 29, 1965). P. 62. Newspapers.com.
[5722] Chicago Tribune. (April 29, 1965). P. 62. Newspapers.com.
[5723] The Decatur Herald. (February 15, 1967). P. 5. Newspapers.com.
[5724] The Decatur Herald. (February 15, 1967). P. 5. Newspapers.com.
[5725] The Decatur Herald. (February 15, 1967). P. 5. Newspapers.com.
[5726] The Decatur Herald. (February 15, 1967). P. 5. Newspapers.com.

of Illinois. Bunn's exact words were as follows: "'[slow deposit growth] has seriously handicapped banking's ability to meet the personal, commercial, industrial and agricultural needs of the state.'"[5727] The Decatur report noted that, outside of Illinois, only Kansas and West Virginia had policies that banned branch banking.[5728] The State of Illinois enacted a law in 1923 that created a ban on branch banking throughout the state.[5729] Bunn and the other Council members believed the ban to be lethal to the Illinois economy.

The Chicago Tribune contained a report in its February 15, 1967, edition, of the Illinois Council for Branch Banking's formal proposal of the referendum-based branch banking bill before the Seventy-Fifth Illinois General Assembly. Bunn and the other Council members collaborated with Rep. Paul J. Randolph of Chicago to introduce the bill.[5730] The article stated that Rep. Randolph had introduced the branch banking bill on four previous occasions, each prior bill having ended in failure during the legislative process.[5731] The fourth attempt met with defeat on June 17, 1965.[5732] Bunn described the policy of the 1967 proposed law as follows: "'The permissive legislation we advocate would enable banks to establish one or more branches in the county in which the principal office is located, subject to the approval of the state and federal regulatory agencies.'"[5733]

The particular structure of the legislation surrounding the 1967 bill would consist of either legislative approval, or legislative rejection, with approval granting the right of Illinois voters to vote on the bill at a consequent referendum.[5734] Bunn and the other Council members supported their pleading for the branch banking law with the argument that the 1923 statute, which banned Illinois branch banking, was causing severe and dangerous deficits in financial services throughout Illinois.[5735] The *Mt. Vernon Register-News* of Illinois quoted Bunn as follows: "'The State of Illinois is the most underbanked populous state in the nation on a per capita basis.'"[5736] Tragically, the approval of Illinois branch banking would occur only incrementally and over multiple years, as was recorded by the Illinois Department of Financial & Professional Regulation in its, "Illinois Bank Branching History" section.[5737] The Illinois ban on branch banking sprang from a deep wellspring of Illinois public policy that was traceable to the 1870 State Constitution.[5738] Illinois statutory laws from 1976, 1988, 1989, and 1990, however, contained approval policies that gradually eroded the old anti-branch banking policy and the ban on

---

[5727] The Decatur Herald. (February 15, 1967). P. 5. Newspapers.com.
[5728] The Decatur Herald. (February 15, 1967). P. 5. Newspapers.com.
[5729] The Decatur Herald. (February 15, 1967). P. 5. Newspapers.com.
[5730] Chicago Tribune. (February 15, 1967). P. 53. Newspapers.com.
[5731] Chicago Tribune. (February 15, 1967). P. 53. Newspapers.com.
[5732] Chicago Tribune. (February 15, 1967). P. 53. Newspapers.com.
[5733] Chicago Tribune. (February 15, 1967). P. 53. Newspapers.com.
[5734] Mt. Vernon Register-News. (February 14, 1967). P. 5. Newspapers.com.
[5735] Mt. Vernon Register-News. (February 14, 1967). P. 5. Newspapers.com.
[5736] Mt. Vernon Register-News. (February 14, 1967). P. 5. Newspapers.com.
[5737] Illinois Department of Financial & Professional Regulation. Idfpr.com.
[5738] Illinois Department of Financial & Professional Regulation. Idfpr.com.

branch-banking that derived from that policy.[5739] Willard Bunn, Jr., the other members of the Council, Rep. Paul J. Randolph, and the others who worked with them, must be viewed as founding fathers of branch banking in Illinois, and as vanguards of necessary policy change, economic modernization, financial institutional improvement, and financial service improvement for the State of Illinois and the economy thereof. Willard Bunn, Jr., brilliantly continued the longstanding Bunn, Regan, Richardson, Ferguson, Willard, and Hogan family traditions of banking, finance, and civic leadership.

George Regan Bunn of Springfield

George Regan Bunn (1915-2002) was the second son of Willard Bunn and Ruth (Regan) Bunn of Springfield. George was an alumnus of both The Lawrenceville School of New Jersey and Princeton University. George was a member of the Cap and Gown Club at Princeton. He served in the United States Marine Corps in World War II and served in the Pacific Theater of the war.[5740] George worked for the Bunn Capitol Grocery Company, the wholesale grocery company of Springfield that had been established in 1840 by his great-grandfather, Jacob Bunn.[5741] George served as Chairman of Bunn Capitol Grocery Company and was an important civic leader in Illinois.[5742] George served as Springfield District Vice-President of the Illinois Chamber of Commerce, having been elected in 1966 to that position.[5743] He invented multiple forms of coffee equipment and was the founder and Chairman of the Bunn-O-Matic Corporation of Springfield, which remains one of the foremost beverage equipment and beverage technology developers and manufacturers of the world.[5744] George was one of the founders of Sangamon State University, which is now the University of Illinois at Springfield.[5745] He also was a founder of the Southern Illinois University Medical School, which is also located in Springfield.[5746] He was an accomplished farmer and horseman.[5747] George Regan Bunn, Sr., brilliantly continued the longstanding Bunn, Regan, Richardson, Ferguson, Willard, and Hogan family traditions of agriculture, agribusiness, invention, groceries, manufacturing, and civic leadership.

[5739] Illinois Department of Financial & Professional Regulation. Idfpr.com.

[5740] Memorial to George Regan Bunn. (Princeton, Class of 1938). Princeton University. Paw.princeton.edu.

[5741] Journal Gazette. (Mattoon, Illinois). (October 22, 1966). P. 3. Newspapers.com.

[5742] Memorial to George Regan Bunn. (Princeton, Class of 1938). Princeton University. Paw.princeton.edu.

[5743] Journal Gazette. (Mattoon, Illinois). (October 22, 1966). P. 3. Newspapers.com.

[5744] Memorial to George Regan Bunn. (Princeton, Class of 1938). Princeton University. Paw.princeton.edu.

[5745] The Bunn Family. Sangamoncountyhistory.org.

[5746] The Bunn Family. Sangamoncountyhistory.org.

[5747] Memorial to George Regan Bunn. (Princeton, Class of 1938). Princeton University. Paw.princeton.edu.

Epilogue:

Return to the Place of the Wild Onions

"For inquire, I pray thee, of the former age, and prepare thyself to the search of their fathers . . ."

Job 8:8[5748]

My hope is that this book will inspire people to come to know the Chicago that has been largely lost and forgotten, to know how this city, county, and region have connected to other places, and to know how business, civic organizations, family, and industry built the city and the region. Many of the historical persons who appear in this book are well-known, but many are obscure and practically unknown. It is time that we restore these histories, retrieve them from the historiographical oblivion into which they have fallen, and use these histories to help show the world why Chicago was, and remains still, one of the greatest cities of the world.

My hope also is that this book will teach people the moral excellence and goodness that characterize this city and its history. All too often Chicago has been cast and condemned as a city of crime and violence. It is crucially necessary to concentrate on the morality, excellence, civic vision, and patriotic citizenship demonstrated by the people contained in this work and by the countless others like them, both past and present, who have defined and shaped the city and region. Correct knowledge and personal stewardship of history are necessary for this to occur. Chicago, like all the Midwestern cities discussed herein, was built by railroads, manufacturing, mining, industrial banking, and the culture that supported and protected these social, political, and economic phenomena. One cannot know the history of Chicago, or any of the other places named herein, without careful study of these good forces and the men and women, from the laborers, teachers, farmers, activists, and social and civic leaders, to the corporate executive officers and statesmen, who made these achievements possible.

The Midwest has been largely neglected in the present age, an age when a gravely disproportionate degree of attention is paid to the East Coast and West Coast. Midwestern histories have been largely overlooked and forgotten. The Midwest built America. This book should inspire and invite members of generations young and old to claim their unique stewardships of the people, times, places, histories, and experiences that collectively made Chicago and the metropolitan region uniquely great in world history. My favorite cities are Chicago, Cleveland, Ohio, Pittsburgh, Pennsylvania, Cincinnati, Ohio, and St. Louis, Missouri. I possess very

---

[5748] Job 8:8.

deep heritage in each of these cities. These and the other Midwestern cities are sister cities in the civic and industrial leadership and legacy of the United States. The Midwest is connected to the entire history of the United States. I perceive the glorious sounds and reflections of the Great Lakes and Midwest in the Appalachian Mountains where I grew up. I perceive the glorious sounds and reflections of the Appalachian Mountains in the Great Lakes and Midwest where I now reside. These places are not separate but are merely different, intricately interwoven, aspects of American history and heritage.

Carl Sandburg, the ingenious Illinois poet, wrote a poem called, *Chicago*. In it he praised many singular achievements of the city and called the city the, "city of big shoulders."[5749] The qualities and achievements of the city that he specifically glorified are the very same ones that are praised, honored, and chronicled in the present book. Sandburg, in his poem, honored and described the City of Chicago as, "Hog Butcher, Tool Maker, Stacker of Wheat, Player with Railroads and Freight Handler to the Nation."[5750] My intention for the present book is that it will provide a familial, industrial, and civic history of the City of Big Shoulders, a city whose shoulders have singularly and selflessly given incomprehensible power and force for the building up of the United States of America and the world. Let us always retain, therefore, a stewardful and protective proudness that we are, "Hog Butcher, Tool Maker, Stacker of Wheat, Player with Railroads and Freight Handler to the Nation."[5751] It is imperative that everyone claims his or her own personal, unique, sincere, and relentless stewardship over the people, histories, experiences, achievements, and heritages that are contained in this book and in others like it, because these histories and heritages belong to everyone and to everyone uniquely.

This is the conclusion of the history presented in this book. Now, therefore, we have returned to our starting concept of *the place of the wild onions*. The word, *Chicago*, means "place of the wild onions." The history of one place reflects the histories of many places. The wild onions of the nineteenth century prairie where Chicago was born are reflected in the wild onions that grew along the old decommissioned Floyd-Franklin Turnpike in my old home of Franklin County, Virginia. The Floyd-Franklin Turnpike, which began next to my old house in the Town of Rocky Mount, Virginia, connected many different people, times, and places over many generations. The history of Chicago, like an old mountain turnpike, connects the people and histories of many other places, states, counties, cities, towns, and foreign countries. The States of Ohio, Wisconsin, Pennsylvania, Virginia, West Virginia, Michigan, Indiana, New York, Connecticut, Massachusetts, Louisiana, Mississippi, Arkansas, Kentucky, and the many people, cities, towns, and counties of these states and others, have helped to build Chicago

[5749] Sandburg, Carl. Chicago. (1914). Carl-sandburg.com.
[5750] Sandburg, Carl. Chicago. (1914). Carl-sandburg.com.
[5751] Sandburg, Carl. Chicago. (1914). Carl-sandburg.com.

and Cook County in diverse and remarkable ways. Chicago, moreover, helped to build these same places, the United States of America, and the world, in immeasurably great ways. Let us invite the United States and the world, therefore, to know now as they have never known before, the singular greatness of Chicago, the city of the wild onions, and its people, both past and present.

THE END

General Subject Index by Chapter

Notice: The subjects are organized by chapter and appeared on too many different pages to allow for convenient pagination-based indexing.

About the Author

Andrew Taylor Call was born in south Florida, raised in Virginia, and educated in Virginia and Chicago. Call holds a Bachelor of Arts degree in History from the University of Virginia, a Juris Doctor from the Appalachian School of Law, two LL.M. (Master of Laws) degrees from The John Marshall Law School of Chicago, and will soon receive a Master of Arts degree in Public Policy and Administration from Northwestern University. He is a member of the State Bar of Wisconsin and several federal court bars in Wisconsin and Illinois. He has owned several small businesses over many years in both Chicago and Virginia. Call has published five books prior to the present book.

Since 2006, Call has held membership in more than 100 civic organizations of Chicago and Cook County, ranging from general memberships to memberships on civic boards of directors, advisory boards, auxiliary boards, and various forms of committees. Some of the boards of directors that Call has served on include the American National Business Hall of Fame of Columbus, Ohio, and Chicago, the Illinois Business Hall of Fame, the Hyde Park Historical Society of Chicago, and the International Museum of Surgical Science of Chicago. He also has held many memberships in civic and professional organizations in Wisconsin, Ohio, Pittsburgh, Pennsylvania, Virginia, and Florida. Call's maternal families were among the founders of Chicago and the States of Illinois, Wisconsin, Ohio, and Michigan. Call's paternal families were among the founders of Pittsburgh, Pennsylvania, and the State of Ohio. Through the different branches of his family, Call is an eighth-generation Illinoisan, a seventh-generation Wisconsinite, an eighth-generation Ohioan, and a tenth-generation Pennsylvanian. Call is a Christian.   AUTHOR WEBSITE: www.chicagoillinoisrediscovered.com